# DATE DUE

| | | | |
|---|---|---|---|
| | | | |
| | | | |
| | | | |
| | | | |
| | | | |
| | | | |
| | | | |
| | | | |
| | | | |
| | | | |
| | | | |
| | | | |
| | | | |
| | | | |
| | | | |
| | | | |
| | | | |
| | | | |

DEMCO 38-296

# METHODS AND TECHNIQUES IN HUMAN GEOGRAPHY

# METHODS AND TECHNIQUES IN HUMAN GEOGRAPHY

## Guy M. Robinson

Professor of Geography, Kingston University, Surrey

John Wiley & Sons

Chichester · New York · Weinheim · Brisbane · Toronto · Singapore

Copyright © 1998 by John Wiley & Sons Ltd,
~~Baffins Lane, Chichester,~~
D, England

7
43 779777
customer service enquiries): cs-books@wiley.co.uk
n http://www.wiley.co.uk
r http://www.wiley.com

*Other Wiley Editorial Offices*

John Wiley & Sons, Inc., 605 Third Avenue,
New York, NY 10158-0012, USA

VCH Verlagsgesellschaft mbH, Pappelallee 3,
D-69469 Weinheim, Germany

Jacaranda Wiley Ltd, 33 Park Road, Milton,
Queensland 4064, Australia

John Wiley & Sons (Asia) Pte Ltd, 2 Clementi Loop #02-01,
Jin Xing Distripark, Singapore 129809

John Wiley & Sons (Canada) Ltd, 22 Worcester Road,
Rexdale, Ontario M9W 1LI, Canada

**British Library Cataloguing in Publication Data**
A catalogue record for this book is available from the British Library

ISBN 0-471-96231-7 (hardback)
     0-471-96232-5 (paperback)
Typeset in 10/12pt Times from the author's disks by Keytec Typesetting Ltd
Printed and bound in Great Britain by Bookcraft (Bath) Ltd. Midsomer Norton
This book is printed on acid-free paper responsibly manufactured from sustainable forestry for which at least two trees are planted
for each one used for paper production.

# CONTENTS

# ACKNOWLEDGEMENTS

The largest vote of thanks should go to students in a number of universities (notably Oxford, Regina, Edinburgh, Canterbury and Kingston) who have been subjected to the contents of this book in earlier forms. Their input has greatly affected my thinking, challenging many of my own views and modifying long-held beliefs. Unsettling challenges have also come from various colleagues, of whom Liz Bondi, Eric Pawson and Hilary Winchester deserve special mention.

Various people have read drafts of individual chapters, including Alan Alexander, Lyn Collins, Bob Hodgart, Annie Hughes, Kenny Lynch, Susan Robinson, David Sugden, Michael Summerfield and Peter Sunley. I am greatly in their debt. Alan Alexander also analysed some of the data used in examples quoted, notably by employing the computing packages GLIM and SPSS when I ingloriously failed to correctly translate the instructions in the respective manuals.

My own crude cartography has been rendered beautiful by Anona Lyons and Nicola Exley at Edinburgh and by Debbie Millard at Kingston. Other technical assistance was provided by Ray Harris, Ed Parsons and Matt Toon.

Some of the writing for this book was done whilst I was on sabbatical at the Universities of Queensland and Newcastle, New South Wales. I am grateful to these two institutions for their support, to Terry Coppock and the Carnegie Trust for the Universities of Scotland who funded research work during these sabbaticals, and to my colleagues at Edinburgh for being so keen that I should reside in the Antipodes for extended periods rather than in Scotland.

I owe a great debt to my strongest critic, my wife Susan, a philosopher still unconvinced as to the academic merits of geography. She has provided unfailing support through change of job, move of house, a wildly fluctuating golf handicap, the demise of West Bromwich Albion and the England cricket team, and recurrent back trouble preventing full participation in gardening duties but permitting frequent retreat to the nearest golf course.

Finally, I am very grateful to Iain Stevenson, who encouraged me to start this book, and to various unknown referees who had the unmitigated pleasure of reading my prose in uncensored form.

Epsom Downs
September 1997

## ACKNOWLEDGEMENTS TO PUBLISHERS

I am grateful to the following publishers for their kind permission to reproduce the figures listed below:

- Longman for Figure 11.11; R.J. Johnston for Figure 1.1; N. Wrigley for Figure 6.8;
- Holt, Rinehart and Winston for Figure 5.3 from Child (1970);
- P.H. Rees for Figure 5.4 from Rees (1970) and R. Abler for Figures 10.2, 10.3, 10.6d and 10.7 from Abler et al (1971);
- Cambridge University Press for Figure 5.6 from

Robson (1969), Figure 8.6 from Batty (1976a) and Figure 10.16 from Cliff et al (1975c);

- John Wiley & Sons Ltd for Figures 5.10 and 5.12 from Davis (1986);
- David & Charles for Figure 5.11 from Smith (1975);
- Association of American Geographers for Figure 6.3 from Berry (1964) and Figure 10.9 from Loytonen (1991);
- HarperCollins Publishers for Figure 7.1 from Thomas and Huggett (1980);
- North British Publishing for Figure 7.2 from Robinson (1988);
- *Midwest Journal of Political Science* for Figure 7.7 from Kaiser (1966);
- Taylor & Francis for Figure 7.8 from Macmillan and Pierce (1994);
- Ohio State University Press for Figure 8.1 from Taylor (1971) and Figure 11.1 from Mabogunje (1970);
- D. Reidel for Figure 8.2 from Sheppard (1986);
- Pion for Figure 8.3 from Berechman and Small (1988), Figure 14.2 from O'Neill (1989) and Figure 14.3 from Barnes (1990);

- Routledge and Kegan Paul for Figure 8.4 from Batty (1981b);
- Edward Arnold for Figure 9.1 from Forer (1978) and Figure 10.17 from Haggett et al (1977);
- Department of Geography, University of Salford, for Figure 9.6 from Gatrell (1977);
- Institute of British Geographers for Figures 9.13, 9.14 and 9.15 from Gatrell et al (1996); Figure 10.18 from Cliff and Ord (1995);
- University of Chicago Press for Figure 10.4 from Hagerstrand (1967a);
- Houghton Mifflin Co. for Figure 10.6a–c from Lowe and Moryadas (1975);
- Croom Helm for Figure 11.2 from Bertuglia et al (1987);
- University of Michigan Press for Figure 11.7 from Kiel and Elliott (1996b);
- IPC Magazines for Figure 11.9 from Mandelbrot (1990);
- Pergamon for Figures 11.12 and 11.13 from Robinson et al (1989);
- Methuen for Figure 12.4 from Rushton (1981); and
- Hutchinson for Figure 14.1 from Gregory (1978b).

# PREFACE

In over 20 years of teaching statistical and quantitative methods to geography students, I have been conscious of a growing reluctance of undergraduates to engage in the comprehension of even the simplest techniques. The appearance of any formulae containing Greek symbols causes eyes to glaze and brains to enter "shut down" mode. The non-mathematical background of many geography students must be one reason for this suspicion of formulae. It is a background frequently associated with distrust of numbers and an inability to perform the simplest of numerical tasks. The current vogue for qualitative methods in human geography has much sound philosophical and methodological support, but I think it also partly echoes the same suspicions harboured amongst some of the undergraduate community. Sadly, students soon translate the oft-voiced criticism of positivism into a more wide-ranging excuse for ignoring statistical techniques and quantification altogether. Given this scenario, it has become harder than ever to preach the virtues of a balanced geographical education that teaches wise use of numerical information combined with appropriate application of qualitative approaches, not to mention the honing of the geographer's traditional skills with maps and diagrams.

There have been many texts dealing with statistical techniques in human geography, the majority of which have aimed at covering introductory techniques, generally in the form of a "how to use" guide. A succession of these texts has been produced since the early 1960s, often making little reference to theoretical underpinning of the techniques and actually covering a relatively limited range of material. Some of the texts have made attempts to illustrate how statistical techniques have been employed by geographers, but with little reference to the changing role of the use of such techniques within the discipline. This role has changed greatly since the rush to adopt quantitative techniques in the late 1950s and 1960s. Not only has the range of techniques been extended to cover methods well beyond introductory statistics, but developments in mathematical modelling, computing and information systems have also had profound effects upon geography. Equally as important, though, the use of quantification, and especially its association with positivism, has been attacked strongly by proponents of different philosophical approaches to geographical problems. In conjunction with these different approaches, a new set of techniques and methods has been utilised with an emphasis upon qualitative, interpretive and introductory data exploration methods.

There is great scope therefore for a text that not only deals with the nature of the wide range of quantitative and qualitative techniques utilised within human geography but also is representative of how their utilisation has changed during the past three decades. Furthermore, there is a need to add some consideration of the evolving relationship between philosophical approach, the types of problem to which the techniques have been applied, and the techniques themselves.

This text covers a wide range of techniques used in the discipline, examining their operation, their application to geographical problems and their changing relationship to the ideas underlying geographical research. Amongst the material covered are introductory and advanced statistical techniques, mathematical models, qualitative and interpretive methods, and (very briefly) the rapid development of geographical information systems. Examples are drawn from a wide range of geographical literature and with consideration of the arguments for and against particular approaches, thereby making reference to the extensive debates on geographical methodology during recent decades.

Overall, it aims to provide an introduction to the variety of techniques employed in the discipline during the last three decades. Emphasis is placed upon two sharply differing foci – one technically orientated, the other focused on individuals – the former typified by statistical analysis and, more recently, geographical information systems (GIS), the latter by interpretive and contextual approaches.

Despite the current vogue for mistrusting quantitative techniques, in terms of constructing this book I have followed the practice of most of my "techniques" teaching at Edinburgh, by starting with the numbers first! I feel strongly that human geographers should be encouraged at the outset to be numerate and to engage with the basis of the scientific method and its critique before they move on to alternative approaches. Here this takes the form of first dealing with exploratory data analysis and stressing the need for data exploration to be a thorough and inquisitive process preceding any confirmatory analysis that involves the testing of hypotheses. There follows coverage of the statistical techniques that dominate many of the introductory statistics texts for geographers, including correlation and regression. However, rather than stopping at the same point as these texts, which is usually where mention is made of multivariate methods, I have extended the coverage of statistics to include these methods and also a more detailed treatment of correlation and regression. This introduces the possibilities of following approaches to regression once popularised by sociologists and includes the methods of categorical data analysis championed by some geographers in the 1980s and whose potential, I believe, has not been fully appreciated.

I have deliberately tried to avoid writing a "cookbook" or to be overly reliant on lengthy screeds of statistical formulae. Wherever possible I have minimised the use of formulae in the text and have attempted to describe techniques succinctly in words. Formulae are used, where appropriate, to indicate the basis of certain methods, but the emphasis is upon the use of techniques and their relationship to the evolving nature of geographical research. This means that techniques are viewed in the broader context of the changing nature of human geography, and so consideration has been given to the concept of geography as a spatial science, the critique of this concept, and the adoption of new approaches including the incorporation of critical social theory within the geographer's domain. Therefore the wider role of techniques is considered, and the book examines statistical, mathematical and qualitative methods from the perspectives of their use within human geography and their relationship to philosophical changes therein. Techniques such as factorial ecology, linear programming, Monte Carlo methods and Fourier analysis are considered in context as well as more recently popularised methods such as participant observation and depth interviewing.

To a degree the book also attempts to highlight different views of human geography and of the changing role of various techniques within it. Finally, there is an attempt at an evaluation of four decades of change in human geography by way of a review of the current research agenda and prospects for further disciplinary evolution in the 1990s.

# 1

# INTRODUCTION

## NEW GEOGRAPHIES

From the early days of geography's "*Quantitative Revolution*" in the 1950s and 1960s the discipline has had an ample number of texts covering the basic forms of *statistical analysis*. The most well known amongst the first of these were those by Duncan et al (1961) and Gregory (1963), which set the tone for a series of similar publications that followed during succeeding decades, including those by Ebdon (1977), Hammond and McCullagh (1974), King (1969), Norcliffe (1977), Silk (1979) and Yeates (1968, 1974). These concentrated on a "how to use" approach, with worked examples employing geographical data.

It was these texts that sustained many of the first tertiary courses on statistics taught within geography departments, and the texts' popularity has been attested by revised editions appearing over a period of time, the most popular being those by Ebdon, Gregory, Hammond and McCullagh, and Norcliffe. Although there was some consideration of problems that might be encountered in the application of statistical analysis to geographical data, these books were largely of the form that Johnston (1978:xv) describes as "the cookbook". They contained recipes for performing certain types of analysis upon quantitative geographical data, but they made little or no reference to the philosophical underpinnings accompanying this form of analysis and, implicitly, were part of a broader spatial science development of the discipline in the 1960s as typified in books by Abler et al (1971), Berry and Marble

(1968), Bunge (1962), Chorley and Haggett (1967), Haggett and Chorley (1969), and Haggett (1965).

Strong critiques of the *positivist philosophy* underlying the application of this statistical work did little to diminish the teaching of statistics within tertiary courses in geography. Nor did they reduce the flow of books covering "introductory" statistics. However, they assuredly brought a greater awareness of the limitations of some of the statistical techniques. In addition, there was a deeper consideration of the philosophical foundations of geographical work (see Gregory, 1978b; Johnston, 1979, 1983, 1997) and also the development of a wider range of quantitative methods. The latter included mathematical techniques, spatial statistics and the extension of statistical analysis beyond an introductory suite of methods (e.g. Haggett et al, 1977). Literature covering the broader range of techniques also increased, with texts by Cole and King (1968), Johnston (1978), Smith (1975), Taylor (1977) and Wilson (1974), all advancing beyond the introductory level. Some of these contained more than just "how to use" accounts of techniques, and considered their application by geographers so that a clearer impression could be gained of the impact of quantitative methods upon geographical research. Perhaps the best of the earlier accounts of this impact was that by Abler et al (1971) which gave particular attention to the application of the techniques they were describing. At the same time, Harvey's (1969) *Explanation in geography* gave a detailed account of the positivist route to explanation, drawing heavily upon Braithwaite's (1960) *Scientific explanation*. However, just four years later, the same author's *Social justice and the city* (Harvey, 1973) signified the growing strength of reaction to the positivist approach and the emerging support for alternatives. This support was not always quite so dismissive of quantitative techniques as Harvey, but during the 1970s and 1980s much more attention was devoted by geographers to ideological, theoretical and philosophical concerns than had previously been the case (see Johnston, 1983).

Although it is an over-simplification to portray the critics of positivist approaches as being either *Marxists* or *humanists*, undoubtedly these were the two "camps" in the 1980s that produced the most sustained and effective alternatives to the discipline's previous paradigm. They presented strong arguments for reducing the empirical content of geographical studies, significantly shifting the focus onto theoretical concerns and, in some cases, use of a new set of techniques. Hence, *qualitative methods* came more to the fore, following their greater use by sociologists and anthropologists – as described by Antaki (1988), Fielding (1988) and Yin (1984) amongst others. In some quarters the use of quantitative methods was strongly criticised, partly because of their close association with positivism (e.g. Harvey, 1974a). However, other geographers working within a broad realist epistemology maintained that quantitative methods are a perfectly appropriate set of techniques to employ for the investigation of certain problems involving particular types of information, and provided adequate attention is paid to the contextual setting and the theory upon which the research draws (see Johnston, 1986a; Sayer, 1984). Meanwhile, other geographers, most notably physical geographers and those concerned with mathematical modelling and/or geographical information systems (GIS), have forged ahead with the use of quantitative techniques. Thus both the use and development of these techniques have by no means been entirely halted by over two decades of critical examination (Haining, 1990a; Macmillan, 1989a), though their presence is almost completely ignored in readers in human geography published in the mid-1990s (e.g. Agnew et al, 1996; Daniels and Lee, 1995).

The result of four decades of substantial change within human geography has been the establishment of two sharply contrasting "new" geographies, one belonging essentially to the early and mid-1960s, and the other crystallising in the mid- and late 1980s. The contrast between these two "new" geographies is great: the first representing the widespread adoption of statistical and mathematical techniques and the use of a methodology that owed much to the philosophy of logical positivism; and the second bringing human geography much closer to other social sciences via the use of *critical social theory*, the injection of spatial considerations into that theory and, recently, an engagement with *postmodernist thinking* that has been part of a so-called "cultural turn".

The "new geography" of the 1980s spawned a number of important books covering the changing methodologies and growing awareness of critical social theory, perhaps those by Gregory (1978b), Johnston (1983), Massey (1984), Sayer (1984), N. Smith (1990), and Smith and Jackson (1984) being the most influential initially. Furthermore, the closer links between human geography and other social sciences have been symbolised by geographers' contributions to new trends within the social sciences, including the powerful statements on postmodernism by Harvey (1989a) and Soja (1989). Yet, some links with the earlier "new" geography have been maintained. Quantitative methods, used both within new methodological contexts and as part of positivistic work, have not been abandoned and a number of good introductory texts on statistical techniques in geography have continued to appear (e.g. Barber, 1988; Burt and Barber, 1996; Matthews, 1981; Walford, 1995), some covering multivariate techniques (e.g. Shaw and Wheeler, 1985, 1994).

## GEOGRAPHY'S QUANTITATIVE REVOLUTION

In March 1963 at the Royal Geographical Society (RGS), in London, which, in some ways, represented the "old school" of geography with an emphasis upon exploration and discovery, a young Cambridge geographer called Peter Haggett presented a paper on forested areas in Brazil. In this he made use of a variety of statistical techniques, including probability sampling, analysis of variance and trend surface analysis (Haggett, 1964). At the time these were still a novelty within British geography and they occasioned wide interest. In the discussion following the paper the then President of the RGS, Dudley Stamp, commented that (Stamp, 1964:380):

> Our lecturer this afternoon ... has introduced some of us to the modern quantitative approach. Some of us may not like the look of it. We may even feel that here is an enormous steam hammer! How is it working in the cracking of nuts? One does hear that said facetiously, but I can remember on one occasion seeing an enormous steam hammer so deliciously adjusted that it did the best cracking of nuts I have ever seen. With new statistical techniques we geographers are being given a new weapon.
> ... This afternoon we may [have seen] important advances in our subject.

Over the following 10–15 years in British geography a large array of analytical tools was absorbed into the subject, about seven or eight years after their introduction to American geography (Morrill, 1984). Thus, it was possible for an observer of this "Quantitative Revolution" to claim in North America in 1963 that the revolution was over (Burton, 1963) whereas the assimilation of new methods in British, European and Australasian geography was only just beginning then (Haggett, 1964).

For many different reasons, both during the Revolution and subsequently, geographers have expressed reservations about the influx of the new techniques. Initially there was a widespread lack of understanding of quantitative methods, partly assisted by their poor presentation in geographical literature. But added to this there was often an echo of Stamp's "sledgehammer feeling", a concern about the incorrect application of the techniques and widespread dissatisfaction with the results of their use (Gregory, 1976). However, despite a range of initial criticisms and a growing search for alternatives, three seductively persuasive "beliefs" encouraged the propagation of quantitatively based work broadly related to an attempt to make human geography more scientific and emphasising the basic ideals of a philosophy known as *logical positivism* (see below) (Mercer, 1984):

- there exists only one true scientific method;
- knowledge is neutral;
- the standards of precision and accuracy operating in the physical sciences offer the only genuinely explanatory framework for the generation of scientific knowledge.

These beliefs represent part of what Taylor (1976) described as the "triumph" of the Quantitative Revolution over the previously prevailing paradigm within the discipline, the "regional approach" (see James, 1972). He referred to four stratagems that effectively destroyed the old order: (i) attacks on the prevailing orthodoxy, (ii) retention of some aspects of the old (e.g. areal differentiation) but introducing new terminology, (iii) introducing unfamiliar techniques some of which could not be easily assimilated, and (iv) incorporation of a new methodology to replace existing approaches. This new methodology was the so-called *scientific method*, the adoption of which was fitted by some into Kuhn's (1970) concept of revolutionary change in academic disciplines via distinctive paradigm shifts (Stoddart, 1981).

Positivism is a philosophy originally proposed by Auguste Comte in the 1820s and 1830s, initially as a means of distinguishing science from metaphysics and religion (Andreski, 1974). The philosophy can be expressed in various forms, but essentially determined the scientific status of statements by the following steps (as summarised by Gregory, 1994a:455):

1. Scientific statements were to be grounded in a direct, immediate and empirically accessible experience of the world. Therefore observation statements were privileged over theoretical ones.
2. Scientific observations had to be repeatable, and their generality was to be ensured by a unitary scientific method that was accepted and drawn upon routinely by the scientific community as a whole.
3. Science could then advance through the formal construction of theories which, if verified empirically, would assume the status of scientific laws.
4. These scientific laws would have a strictly technical function, in that they would reveal the effectiveness

or the necessity of specific conjunctions of events (such as "if A, then B").

5. Scientific laws would be progressively unified and integrated into a single and incontrovertible system of knowledge and truth.

These ideas were generally adopted by geographers during the Quantitative Revolution as the basis for a scientific approach, though usually via the implicit acceptance of a modified Comtean view produced in the work of the Vienna Circle. This was a group of philosophers, mathematicians and natural scientists in the 1920s and 1930s who formalised logical positivism in which there was a distinction between analytic statements and empirical or synthetic statements. The former were judged to be true by definition (by virtue of an internal logic) whilst the former had to be verified (Guelke, 1978). Hence geographers adopted procedures whereby hypotheses could be tested and law-like statements produced, though not necessarily by verifying statements. Instead Popper's *principle of falsification* was widely adopted and for most geographers it was this that constituted "the scientific method" (see below and Chapter 3; for further discussion see Bowen, 1979; Bryant, 1985; Hay, 1979a).

Whilst the extent of this dominance of the scientific method within the discipline in the 1960s can be disputed (see Billinge et al, 1984), the growth of geographical work using statistical techniques certainly cannot. For example, for articles in the principal American geographical journals, a sharp increase in the use of quantitative methods between 1956 and 1966 can be observed (Slocum, 1990). Over the 30 year period from 1956 to 1986, correlation and regression analyses were the most popular techniques, followed by multiple regression, testing hypotheses using the chi-squared test, and factor analysis.

After the first wave of adoption of these quantitative techniques, the most popular of which initially were correlation, regression and hypothesis testing, there were a series of important developments in their use:

- extending the use of statistical hypothesis testing to the full range of tests found in inferential statistics, especially the non-parametric tests;

- extending the study of relationships from the measurement of the strength of bivariate relationships (via correlation and linear regression analysis) to multivariate situations, e.g. multiple regression and factor analysis;
- generating specifically spatial statistics, from simple applications such as the nearest-neighbour statistic through to more complex spatial autocorrelation;
- linking the temporal and spatial realms through time series analysis, analysing the spatial form of temporal change through forecasting and predictive methods, and examining diffusion processes through the use of stochastic processes;
- using new techniques both to analyse and to generate maps, e.g. trend surface analysis.

Therefore, from the late 1960s the use of quantitative methods was extended to deal with new problems. One aspect of this is worth emphasising. Quantitative methods were used in a wide variety of studies under the umbrella term "applied" geography, i.e. geography that is intended to impinge upon public policy and possessing a practical problem-oriented basis rather than fulfilling a purely academic role (Johnston, 1981). The quantitative methods were used to examine different aspects of public policy (Bennett, 1981): in the construction of theories of how policy should be formulated; in analysing the workings of policy in terms of economic, social and political impacts; and in assessing the direct and indirect impacts of policies against criteria of economic efficiency, referring to considerations of price, economic stability and economic growth, social equity and political effect.

These developments were accompanied by the use of a range of models (including statistical and mathematical models), spatial economic analysis and systems analysis. Spatial economic analysis was closely related to work on location theory and led to the growth of regional science in which closer links were developed between geography and economics, though this work was often highly abstracted from reality. This and the development of systems analysis was part of an attempt by some geographers to produce a comprehensive *spatial science*, an attempt that was subsequently largely submerged beneath a welter of criticism and re-evaluation of quantitative methods. Indeed, during the 1970s, "spatial science" became akin to a term of abuse as a series of alternative approaches were adopted by geographers who objected to the abstract relations emphasised by spatial science and its claim to being value-free (Harvey, 1973). Even the developments in spatial science that have been produced more recently have frequently been dismissed on the grounds that they fail to consider the nature of the human beings who create the patterns, flows and hierarchies being examined.

Burton (1963) identified five types of critic of quantitative methods:

- those who felt geography was being led in the wrong direction;
- those who felt geographers should adhere to their proven tool – the map;
- those who felt that quantification was suitable for certain tasks only;
- those who felt that means were being advanced ahead of ends, and that there was too much research on methods for methods' sake;
- those who objected not to quantification itself but to the attitudes of quantifiers!

This developing concern over the misuse and mystique associated with quantitative methods was accompanied by arguments over their philosophical underpinnings. It must be stressed, though, that a concern with the philosophy behind the quantitative methods was not really much of a consideration for many of the initial practitioners of these methods, even if many have argued that the philosophical and theoretical developments were the most significant aspects of the new geography (e.g. Wilson, 1984). Only with hindsight have the philosophical implications of the new methods been incorporated in the term "Quantitative Revolution". For example, one definition of the quantitative revolution is (Gregory, 1994b:494):

> the radical transformation of spirit and purpose which Anglo-American geography underwent in the 1950s and 1960s, replacing an earlier ideographic concern with areal differentiation by a nomothetic search for models of spatial structure . . . its chief characteristics were . . . that it was not confined to the application of statistical and mathematical methods but also involved the conjoint construction of formal theories of spatial organisation.

Yet, a recognition that statistical techniques could form part of a clearly stated philosophy, the positivist scientific method (e.g. Abler et al, 1971), was not widespread amongst geographers in the 1950s and early 1960s, notwithstanding the critique of Hartshorne's (1939) statement of the regional paradigm by Schaefer, who argued that "geography has to be conceived as the science concerned with the formulation of the laws governing the spatial distribution of certain features on the surface of the earth" (Schaefer, 1953:227).

It is important to recognise that much of the Quantitative Revolution was only loosely tied to the scientific method and that many practitioners of the "new" geography were only dimly aware of the philosophical underpinnings behind their use of quantitative techniques (Johnston, 1984a). Thus Gregory's interpretation seems a rather grandiose view of what for many geographers was more of a thankful opportunity simply to use new techniques and break away from the perceived inconsequentiality of much of the "old-style" regional geography. It is ironic then that the quantifiers' own work has also been dismissed subsequently as "inconsequential" on the grounds that its own philosophical roots and explanations were deeply flawed (e.g. Slater, 1975).

In its fullest form the quantitative–scientific mode of analysis involved six significant features (Gregory, 1994b:494), though these were often only partially discernible in the 1960s' "new geography":

1. the use of theory to indicate data needs;
2. controlled experimentation;
3. sensible and appropriate use of analytical techniques;
4. the quest for explanation as well as prediction;
5. a logical problem-solving approach;
6. ability to feed back information to established theory.

Although the scientific method can be set out systematically as a series of distinct stages of data analysis (see Figure 1.1), much geographical analysis of the 1950s and 1960s could be best described as *speculative empiricism* in which work was tied neither to well defined theory nor to a clearly defined analytical sequence. Frequently, data were collected in order to see if a relationship existed between selected variables, and from this some more general statement may or may not have been formulated. This is what Cattell (1966) has termed the *inductive–hypothetico–deductive (IHD) spiral*, in which research asks only very vague questions about relationships and differences between places. Well thought-out theory, formulation of hypotheses and testing of these hypotheses did not play a significant role in most of the early quantitative work by human geographers. This meant that human geographers were distanced from the more systematic workings of experimental science and have largely remained so.

Yet, even if much use of quantitative methods by geographers has been divorced from the scientific method, it has been part of what Giddens (1984a:3–4)

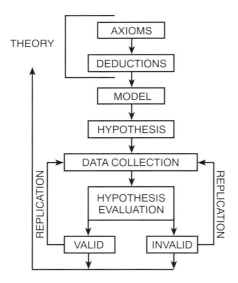

*Figure 1.1*   The Set of Procedures Comprising the Positivist Scientific Method. (*Source:* Johnston, 1978:16)

has termed the "positivistic attitude". This contains three propositions (Johnston, 1986a:83–4):

1. The methodological procedures of natural science can be adapted directly to the social sciences. That is, phenomena associated with human values and actions are treated as objects to be studied in the same way as those investigated in the natural sciences.
2. The outcomes of such applications are statements of law-like character.
3. The law-like statements can be used as instruments in the conduct of practical policy.

Of these, the last has often been used by geographers to argue that positivistic work merely supports the status quo (e.g. Gregory, 1980). Again, this is a slightly misleading view that ignores the character of the researcher involved (Coppock, 1974). It can be argued that positivistic work does not explicitly support any particular given position *a priori*. In contrast, much of the work of geographers in the 1980s and 1990s, based on social theory, has an in-built preconception of the nature of society that differentiates it from positivistic work. In Eastern Europe and the former USSR the application of geography from the 1940s to the late 1980s was based upon particular forms of non-positivist social theory that can equally well be charged with supporting the status quo, that is being used for *instrumentalist ends* by or for the State. Unfortunately the debate about the nature of positivism's instrumentalism and its "objectivity" versus the "subjectivity" within certain other approaches has been a confused one suffering from a surfeit of entrenched philosophical positions. Johnston (1986a:85) illustrates some of the problems arising from this:

> ... the critique and the defence of positivism are being argued on different grounds. In particular, this has led to a widespread belief that quantification and hypothesis testing are invalid methods because they have been used for the development of instrumentalist ends. To confuse means with ends is to do an injustice to the means in many cases ...

## FROM ONE "NEW" GEOGRAPHY TO ANOTHER

During the 1970s significant changes within human geography brought a series of pressures to bear upon the utilisation of quantitative techniques in the discipline. Initially, there were changes in the application of the techniques themselves:

- a movement away from the use of spatial geometry via a greater concentration upon process rather than form;
- a general reappraisal of the nature and appropriateness of statistical inference;
- the growing stimulus of "applied" forms of geographical research which directed it into new areas, generating a need for both different types of approach and different forms of analysis;
- increased criticism of the use of quantitative methods as part of a widespread critique of positivist approaches.

Some of the criticisms of quantitative methods, which were made in a rush to adopt new philosophical stances in the 1970s, were misdirected in that the real target was positivism not quantification. Given that many uses of quantification were only loosely based upon positivism, it was perhaps unfair to equate the two so closely. For example, Bennett (1981) criticised this "oversimplification" in *Explanation in geography* in which Harvey (1969) saw geography as a primarily inductive, objective science seeking universal laws. The association of quantification with such a simple but all-embracing purpose led to widespread criticism of quantitative techniques, instead of directing critical attention explicitly at positivism and at the specific situations to which the techniques were applied.

What the critique of both quantitative methods and positivism did yield was the introduction of exciting new approaches in the discipline. Mercer (1984:162) describes the development of these new approaches as representing a cleavage between contrasting perspectives: on the one hand, a technocratic orientation towards geography, focusing upon computation and quantification, and, on the other, a prescriptive orienta-

tion with a number of roots, the most notable being in humanistic and Marxist traditions. Yet, whilst the technocratic focus received a concerted series of attacks in the 1970s, the continuing growth of computer-related developments in the handling of spatial data has enabled a significant technical approach to persist and, judging from the trend in academic appointments on both sides of the Atlantic, to be revived from the mid-1980s through the flowering of *geographical information systems* (GIS).

From the "prescriptive orientation" the two critiques with the most lasting influences upon the discipline have been the *humanistic* and *Marxist/structuralist* approaches. A number of articles appeared in the 1970s outlining the basic premises of humanism and their potential application to geography (e.g. Ley and Samuels, 1978; Meinig, 1979; Tuan, 1979) and similarly for Marxism (incorporating both historical materialism and structuralism) (e.g. Harvey, 1974a, 1975a; N. Smith, 1979; Gregory, 1978a,b). Some of the initial apparent reluctance to move outside theoretical considerations relating to humanism and historical materialism was replaced by work utilising new methods as part of analysis and, in some cases, even building upon those techniques introduced to the discipline in the 1960s (e.g. Ley, 1984).

Some of the outright rejection of positivistic studies in human geography, with quantitative techniques as a central component, has now given way to a degree of reappraisal. For example, in her review of geographers' use of statistical inference and quantification, Pratt (1989:110) argues that:

> the use of statistical inference does not necessarily imply the reduction of theory to empirical regularities or the ontological assumption of atomistic monism [i.e. that all of reality can be reduced to a single constituent entity]. It need not necessarily lead to impoverished theoretical categories or a reductive, mechanistic view of human nature.

This does appear to accept that statistical inference can be used without destroying the "purity" of non-positivist approaches. That is, there is quantitative research that can be performed outside a positivist explanatory framework. In this case the argument is that humanistic and/or historical materialist theories may form the basis for qualitative and quantitative work that can help to explain social processes, whereas the positivistic work of the 1960s could not do this. Effectively, this viewpoint contains two fundamental criticisms of work carried out as part of the Quantitative Revolution: firstly, that much of it was speculative empiricism which was "theoretically uninformed" and so could not possibly feed into any cumulative understanding of processes underlying spatial pattern; secondly, that the positivist philosophy which formed the springboard for the use of quantitative methods was actually unsuitable for the subject matter that was of the greatest importance in helping to understand economic and social change. Therefore quantitative methods have to be viewed as techniques for dealing with just one type of information, and they are complemented by qualitative methods supported by theories helping to give a more relational, contextual understanding.

In extending Pratt's arguments, it is clear that both humanists and structuralists (and, more recently, postmodernists and feminists) have had difficulties in embracing quantification because of the association between quantitative techniques and positivism. The underlying difficulty is summarised by Sayer (1992:53), contending that "the methodological principles of statistical inference presuppose the fatally-flawed empiricist situations of atomism and regularity generalisation". This stresses a fundamental discontinuity existing between the use of statistical inference and the philosophical tenets of certain "realist ideas" underlying structuralist and humanistic approaches (see Chapters 13–16). For example, humanistic approaches have emphasised the development of "logical inferences" based on detailed case studies, often involving the generation of qualitative data, whereas statistical inference is based on the notion of generating representative random samples and then analysing them (S. J. Smith, 1984).

Pratt (1989) further summarises the criticisms of quantitative research associated with positivist approaches under four headings:

1. the critique of theory as empirical regularity;
2. the rejection of an atomistic (reductionist) ontology;
3. the realisation that facts are interpreted;
4. the rejection of the reduction of humanity to physical properties and, with it, a neglect of meaning, human intentionality and choice.

For Marxists the first two of these are possibly the most significant. The first refers to the view that the *falsification model* associated with Popper (1968), and used in testing hypotheses, is not acceptable (this is detailed in Chapter 3). Therefore the model of data analysis depicted as the scientific method in Figure 1.1 is not accepted and neither are generalisations on the basis of observed regularities. This is largely because these critics subscribe to a view of the world which prefers the construction of abstract models, sometimes referred to as a *Baconian view* (Hacking, 1975). This abstraction may seem out of step with the Marxists' abiding concern for the "real" social well-being of humanity. However, their analysis is based upon strong theoretical considerations. Some, though, have now accepted that statistical techniques may be used to aid explanation, but in a different fashion to that employed in the scientific method (for example, in the form of *exploratory analysis* rather than through the *confirmatory analysis* associated with statistical hypothesis testing).

An important criticism of the scientific method has been that it can divorce empirical "facts" from their context and therefore produces interpretations of statistical descriptions and even inferences that should be subject to considerable questioning. Thus "contextual understanding" over and above the "findings" of any statistical analysis is a prerequisite for any work utilising such analysis. Humanists have argued that a vital element of context is a concern for "meaning, human intentionality and choice" (Jarrie, 1983). They argue that by relegating *human agency* to an unimportant position, much work involving quantitative techniques tended to focus too much upon generalities and empirical regularities at the expense of deeper considerations of the "actors" effecting social change (Samuels, 1979).

The outcome of these critiques has been a greater

recognition that quantitative techniques have definite limitations, and that certain properties and aspects of problems investigated by geographers are not amenable to numerical measurement. Therefore quantitative techniques have to be used in conjunction with others or, depending on one's viewpoint, must be replaced by others to enable greater understanding of social processes. Hence, alternative, qualitative methods have assumed a greater importance within human geography, though it is possible to see quantitative and qualitative analysis as being complementary (e.g. Samuels, 1978; Giddens, 1979).

The distinction between quantitative and qualitative techniques is certainly important, but their use, both separately and in tandem, can be made most effective with due thought and care. This is not to deny, though, that there have been some trenchant criticisms of eclecticism (e.g. Harvey, 1987a), namely the combination of various types of analysis and methodology, and there is certainly continued distrust and/or rejection of the usage of quantitative techniques based on an essentially positivist framework. A consensus view is that statistical analysis cannot subsume theoretical development and must be accompanied by substantive (non-positivist) theory, as speculative empiricism is not of value in helping to explain social processes. Therefore quantitative techniques are seen as ones for "organising one type of information, information that needs necessarily to be complemented by a more relational, contextual understanding, as well as more abstract theoretical development" (Pratt, 1989:114). However, how this theory is constructed and tested has also proved highly problematic (e.g. Foot et al, 1989; Couclelis and Golledge, 1983; Chouinard et al, 1984), as will be considered in Chapters 13–16.

In effect then, quantitative methods must be seen as just a subset of all possible methods. They may be highly appropriate for certain kinds of investigation, but not for others. Unfortunately, during the Quantitative Revolution many geographers tended to hold quantitative methods in such high esteem that they deified them and failed to be aware of their defects. Subsequently, other geographers have vilified these methods and some seem to have developed a paranoia about anything numerical, seeking instead to elevate the status of theory at the expense of a concern with how actual people behave in the economic, social and political realms of actual places (though most recognise that theory is the basis from which understanding of "reality" is derived).

Despite criticism and much re-evaluation, quantitative methods have continued to be an important element of geographical studies. In part this reflects the continuing presence of two of the main catalysts of the Quantitative Revolution, the computer and the generation of large amounts of quantitative information. Undoubtedly, one of the main stimuli towards the greater adoption of statistical and mathematical forms of analysis post-1945 has been the generation of an increased amount of numerical data from central government departments, international organisations and local authorities. In addition, this growing supply of data has been handled more readily through the development of electronic data-handling devices: calculators and computers. Especially from the mid-1960s, these devices completely revolutionised the amount of data storage, retrieval, manipulation and analysis that was possible and thereby reinforced the movement towards further collection and analysis of numerical information. Subsequently, advances such as the development of personal computers and the WorldWideWeb have extended this computing revolution into new areas.

It can be argued that much of the antipathy towards quantitative methods still rests upon criticisms based on consideration of quantitative work carried out in the 1950s and 1960s rather than upon attempts to examine the more complete range of quantitative work performed during the last two decades. This more recent work, together with relevant criticism, is presented here in the form of an account of the quantitative techniques employed by human geographers, their application and the problems associated with their usage. This account is presented in conjunction with the particular limitations imposed by the nature of geographical information. This also recognises the philosophical and methodological consequences of the critiques of quantitative methods and so considers the emergence of qualitative techniques and the nature of new philosophies within the discipline. Therefore humanistic, Marxist, feminist and postmodernist perspectives are introduced to reflect the growing extension of human geography into "mainstream" social science theory and method.

Initially, this examination begins with quantitative techniques and differences between exploratory and confirmatory techniques (Chapter 2). The basis of the latter is discussed through a brief introduction to probability theory and probability distributions before a more detailed review of statistical hypothesis testing (Chapter 3). This precedes examination of the two techniques that were at the heart of the Quantitative Revolution, correlation and linear regression (Chapter 4). At the end of Chapter 4 more complex regression techniques are considered as a prelude to wide-ranging coverage of multivariate methods in Chapter 5. This deals both with techniques such as factor analysis, which were popular in the Quantitative Revolution, and with more general techniques, such as cluster analysis, which have a practical utility exploited today. That part of the book dealing exclusively with statistical techniques closes with Chapter 6, in which the statistical analysis of categorical data is discussed. Here methods popularised from the early 1980s are examined, their assumptions and statistical roots contrasting with those of the techniques discussed in previous chapters.

The role of statistics and mathematics in geographical models is discussed in Chapter 7 (allocation models), Chapter 8 (interaction models) and Chapter 9 (spatial models), the latter encompassing a range of spatial statistics from the descriptive to the analytical. The companion set of temporal measures and forms of analysis are covered in Chapter 10. This part of the book is concluded in Chapter 11, which deals with geographers' formal analysis of social and economic systems. The latter part of the chapter introduces the computerised analysis of information systems via geographical information systems (GIS). Although this branch of geography has only been a significant component of the discipline for just over a decade, its scope is large and extends well beyond the ability of this book to cover. However, some basic principles and problems are aired.

The final part of the book deals with techniques that were introduced to geography largely in response to criticisms of either the usage of or the underlying assumptions made by techniques discussed in earlier chapters. In Chapter 12 the behavioural geographers' contribution is reviewed as is the use of questionnaires as a generator of behavioural and other information. The strong critique of behaviourism is also covered as a precursor to discussion of a wide range of qualitative measures in Chapter 13.

In contrast to the numerous books on statistics in human geography, far less attention has been given by textbooks to the geographical application of qualitative techniques. In part this reflects a different attitude to qualitative work by its proponents compared with that shown towards statistics applied within a broad positivist framework. This different approach is typified by one of the best geographical texts on qualitative methods, by Eyles and Smith (1988), in which a series of studies utilising qualitative and interpretive approaches is the subject material. Quite deliberately this is not a book on how to use qualitative techniques or even a systematic account of various such techniques. Instead it details and evaluates the qualitative as part of a series of specific geographical investigations. In this way the "technique" is not divorced from its context and it is not seen as a separate entity somehow distanced from the rest of the research process. This difference of approach reflects a contrasting philosophical underpinning for much of the qualitative work in human geography which, in many ways, is antithetical to that accompanying the quantitative. This underpinning is considered in more detail in Chapter 13, but the approach adopted by Eyles and Smith is deliberately avoided. Although it is certainly possible to understand how qualitative techniques can be used by geographers through examples of their application, the lack of more rigorous considerations of pros and cons has tended to perpetuate certain myths about qualitative methods that need to be overcome – notably that they are somehow less demanding and simpler to apply than statistical and mathematical techniques. In attempting to dispel these notions, this book follows the same approach to qualification as it follows for quantification – coverage of a range of techniques, with examples of their application, and reference to their role within the development of thinking within human geography.

In recognising the breadth of the "new geography" of the 1990s, the coverage of qualitative techniques here extends to consideration of the *dialectic* as applied by Marxists (Chapter 14), methods employed by feminist geographers (Chapter 15) and some of the ramifications of the postmodernist turn in human geography (Chapter 16). Particular attention is given to ways in which ethnographic and interpretive approaches have been applied by geographers, whereby the standard application of questionnaire surveys has been replaced by methods emphasising observation and participation, and enabling the views of the human subject to be heard in their own language rather than the quasi-objective interpretation by a researcher. This recognition that the role of an individual researcher needs to be questioned and its character recognised symbolises the degree of difference between the current "new" geography and that of the 1960s when research was held to be an unbiased search for objectivity.

# 2

# EXPLORING GEOGRAPHICAL DATA

## CONSTRUCTING GEOGRAPHICAL DATA

Geographical data may take many forms, being obtained from a number of different sources and generated in a variety of ways. Perhaps, conventionally, geographers have thought of their basic information as data existing in numerical form and obtainable either from official sources or generated by survey research using questionnaires. But whilst numerical information, official statistics and questionnaire surveys certainly do play significant roles in geographical investigations, the broader range of material utilised by human geographers must not be overlooked. It is a range that encompasses maps, landscapes, the spoken word, films, photographs, books and art as well as, occasionally, the rock, plant and soil samples more commonly associated with research in the earth sciences.

It has been common to differentiate between quantitative and qualitative information and also between the pre-constructed data from official sources and the researcher-constructed data from interviews and participant observation. Such distinctions are convenient and necessary when detailing particular techniques that make use of specific types of data, but good research can combine the quantitative and the qualitative. It can also use data from different origins, provided the research has a sound theoretical basis and acknowledges the data's limitations. These limitations may take many forms, related both to the inherent characteristics of the data themselves and to

their relationship with the researcher. The latter refers to the fact that both qualitative and quantitative information is "constructed" by researchers, insofar as research by human geographers is an interactive and creative process that is never entirely neutral nor objective. Steps may be taken to make research as objective as possible, but researchers bring their own preconceptions and predilections to any investigation, and these affect both data construction and interpretation.

The process of construction is perhaps most transparent when researchers generate data via surveys and interviews. Depending upon the technique used to produce such data, there is a degree of social interaction between the researcher and the "object" being researched. This interaction may be kept to a minimum in the taking of a questionnaire survey or it may form a prominent role in an investigation requiring the researcher to become an integral part of the community or social group being studied. Also, data produced by "official" sources are not entirely value-free. They are a reflection of the particular circumstances affecting data collection, the presentation of data in a form deemed suitable for public consumption and the priorities of the official agency itself. In any analysis of data the process of construction and the nature of the relationship between the researcher and the object(s) of research need to be understood for the analysis to achieve its potential. The extent to which the individual researcher intrudes particular prejudices and preconceptions must not be overlooked and neither must the fact that all data are socially constructed. This applies particularly to work involving researcher-constructed data, but pre-constructed data from official sources also come with particular social conditions of production that need to be recognised. This need may be more apparent and necessary for data from non- and semi-official sources.

Geographical data analysis has commonly been associated with a process of applying particular analytic techniques to data assembled by a researcher. This is a conceptualisation in which the link between data and technique is a central element in a broader process of investigation involving both theoretical underpinnings of research and interpretation of results (Figure 2.1). However, the linkages between theory, data construction, analysis and interpretation are not simple and static. The need to apply a sampling technique in the process of data gathering can mean that there is a technical component to data construction. Similarly, there can be a considerable amount of interpretation within the process of data construction, as may occur when a researcher is both a participant in and an observer of a social group. It is important to recognise ways in which interpretation both draws upon and, in turn, modifies theoretical and philosophical positions within a research programme.

In practice, then, the different stages of research, from theory to presentation of results, are rarely so clearly distinguishable, separate or sequential as may appear at first sight. "Analysis" in its broadest sense can include initial evaluation of data, the generation or construction of data and the application of particular analytical techniques that interrogate data. It is on the latter that this book concentrates, but with an attempt to show how geographers' use of techniques has been interwoven with the adoption of particular theoretical and philosophical stances. The convenient approach of treating qualitative and quantitative techniques separately is adopted here. However, this book tries not to associate these techniques with the traditional view of, respectively, "soft" and "hard" forms of analysis. Instead, their complementarity is stressed, as is the need for the utilisation of techniques appropriate to any given research context.

## EXPLORATORY DATA ANALYSIS AND GRAPHICAL SUMMARIES OF DATA

Although geographers utilised graphical methods and simple descriptive statistics well before the Quantitative Revolution, only recently have they made extensive use of these methods in the form now referred to as *exploratory data analysis* (EDA) (see Bartels and Ketallapper, 1979). In this, "attempts are made to identify the major features of a data set of interest and to generate ideas for further investigation" (Cox and Jones, 1981:135). In the Quantitative Revolution geographers tended to focus much more upon the *confirmatory data analysis* of model specification, parameter estimation and hypothesis testing. However, following innovatory work by the statistician John Tukey (Tukey, 1972, 1977; Tukey and Mosteller, 1977), a number of the social sciences, including human geography, have given more attention to EDA (e.g. Erickson and Nosanchuck, 1992; Open University, 1983). Indeed, it has been argued that social scientists should devote more attention to exploratory

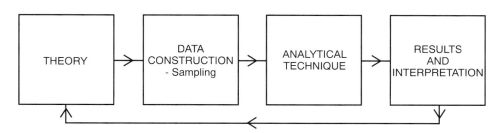

*Figure 2.1*    Linkages in Analytical Research

techniques rather than subjecting poorly understood data to complex forms of analysis (Besag and McNeil, 1976). Whilst Tukey developed some new methods, EDA includes both these and a range of other, more familiar methods in what can be an holistic, coherent approach to the initial stages of research using quantitative information (Burn and Fox, 1986). The methods incorporate both graphical and simple statistical techniques, such as those described below.

EDA emphasises the importance of examining available data very carefully using simple numerical description, such as measures of dispersion and centrality (see below), in conjunction with imaginative graphical representation, like stem-and-leaf displays. Such analysis is intended to give the researcher an intimate knowledge of the data before embarking upon further investigation. Therefore a simple three-stage process of graphical analysis, numerical description and relevant statistical testing can help to avoid many of the mistakes made in the past by those who rushed into complex analysis of spatial data, ignoring many of the problems associated with such an approach.

EDA may be used both to help formulate hypotheses and for evaluating models (Good, 1983). However, its most common use is in attempting to identify the major features of a dataset so as to generate ideas for further investigation (Cox and Jones, 1981:135). This can then lead to the generation of hypotheses and the use of some confirmatory data analysis in which hypotheses are tested. So, "the data explorer works like a numerical detective, sifting and sorting through the data so as to produce evidence for the judicial procedures of confirmatory analysis" (K. Jones, 1984:216). Moreover, EDA may also be employed with data that are not very accurate or are of unknown reliability (e.g. Hoaglin et al, 1983, 1985).

Sibley (1990:4) argues that EDA encourages and facilitates repeated references to data and a more cautious, even sceptical, attitude to theory than that implied in most work using confirmatory analysis. EDA precedes and may preclude inferential (confirmatory) statistics by suggesting further research which might require a different approach. At the heart of EDA is the emphasis on the display of numerical data

and the use of graphical summaries so that there can be repeated reference to the original data and to patterns therein. This enables individual cases to remain in focus. EDA can also be extended to correlation and regression analysis as indicated in Chapter 4. Most importantly, the careful use of both graphical and numerical summaries can reveal more information about any given dataset than reliance on just one of these summaries.

Once numerical data have been collected, a common first step in interpretation and analysis is to search for patterns within them. For geographers this might mean investigating spatial distribution by mapping the data, but preliminary investigation can also involve representing the data pictorially. The origin of systematic display and analysis of data is generally attributed to William Playfair (1759–1823) who utilised bar charts, time series plots, proportional symbol displays and pie charts. Further use of graphical display was made by Minard and Marey in the nineteenth century, but this form of analysis was then eclipsed by the development of mathematical statistics in the twentieth century. Graphics became "devices for showing the obvious to the ignorant" until interest was resuscitated in the 1970s by Tukey, who developed new forms of graphical presentation of data, and by computer technology, which permitted greater ease of such displays (Chambers et al, 1983; Dunn, 1987). Amongst the new forms were *boxplots* and *stem-and-leaf diagrams*, discussed below with other graphical data summaries.

## Stem-and-Leaf Diagrams (Stemplots)

In this pictorial representation, data such as those shown in Table 2.1a are treated as consisting of two parts: that to the left of the decimal point and that to the right. The former can be portrayed as the *stem* and the latter as the *leaf* in an arrangement that orders the data (Table 2.1b). Different parts of one dataset may be compared in a *back-to-back stemplot*, as shown in Table 2.1c, which provides an illustration that, in the area under study, farms on which cereals are the main enterprise are generally larger than those on which cattle are the main enterprise. Back-to-back stemplots

*Table 2.1*    Stemplots

(a) Data collected on the size of farms (ha) in Lothian Region, Scotland

98.0, 67.7, 74.6, 16.6, 39.9, 80.8, 18.2, 15.4, 89.6, 125.6, 41.2, 56.6, 21.5, 166.1, 13.4, 33.1, 83.6, 41.3, 31.8, 70.6

$n = 20$, where $n =$ the size of the sample (in this case the number of farms for which farm size is given above).

(b) Data ordered in the form of a stemplot

| Stem:Leaf | |
|---|---|
| 13\|4 | |
| 15\|4 | |
| 16\|6 | |
| 18\|2 | |
| 21\|5 | |
| 31\|8 | |
| 33\|1 | |
| 39\|9 | |
| 41\|23 | i.e. one farm is 41.2 ha and |
| 56\|6 | one is 41.3 ha |
| 67\|7 | |
| 70\|6 | |
| 74\|6 | |
| 80\|8 | |
| 83\|6 | |
| 89\|6 | |
| 98\|0 | |
| 125\|6 | |
| 166\|1 | |

Nb: 41 is said to have a depth of 2, i.e. two farms are represented at this level.

may also be useful when comparing two different datasets, for example one containing information on men and one containing information on women. Stemplots can also highlight *outliers*, which are individual values lying well below or above the main body of data (e.g. the value 166.1 in Table 2.1b). The individual values in a dataset are usually termed *observations*. The number of leaves associated with each element of the stem is known as the depth of the stem or the number of observations for each element of the stem (see Table 2.1d).

*Table 2.1*    (continued)

(c) Data ordered as a back-to-back stemplot

| Cereals as Main Enterprise | | Cattle as Main Enterprise |
|---|---|---|
| | \| | 13\|4 |
| | \| | 15\|4 |
| | \| | 16\|6 |
| | \| | 18\|2 |
| 5\| | 21\| | |
| | \| | 31\|8 |
| | \| | 33\|1 |
| | \| | 39\|9 |
| 3\| | 41\|2 | |
| | \| | 56\|6 |
| 7\| | 67\| | |
| 6\| | 70\| | |
| | \| | 74\|6 |
| 8\| | 80\| | |
| | \| | 83\|6 |
| 6\| | 89\| | |
| 0\| | 98\| | |
| 6\| | 125\| | |
| 1\| | 166\| | |

| $n = 9$ | | $n = 11$ |
|---|---|---|

(d) Stemplot of the populations of the West German states (millions)

| Stem:Leaf | Depth |
|---|---|
| 0\|7 | 1 |
| 1\|169 | 3 |
| 2\|6 | 1 |
| 3\|6 | 1 |
| 4\| | 0 |
| 5\|6 | 1 |
| 6\| | 0 |
| 7\|2 | 1 |
| 8\| | 0 |
| 9\|3 | 1 |
| 10\| | 0 |
| 11\|0 | 1 |
| 12\|8 | 1 |
| 13\| | 0 |
| 14\| | 0 |
| 15\| | 0 |
| 16\| | 0 |
| 17\|0 | 1 |

$n = 12$

## Lineplots

Small datasets may be easily portrayed by representing each observation as a dot or a mark on a scale (Table 2.2). Again, this can be a useful way of examining two or more sets of data if they are compared along the same scale.

## Bar Graphs and Histograms

Examinations of the spread (dispersion) of values in a dataset often begin with a graphical plot of the distribution of the data. As indicated in Figure 2.2, this usually takes one of four forms: bar graphs, histograms, frequency curves and ogives. For data that only have values in the form of whole numbers (0, 1, 2, 3, ..., *n*), that is *discrete data*, a *bar graph* can be constructed to illustrate the frequency of occurrence of a particular value. For example, Figure 2.2a is a bar graph depicting the data given in Table 2.3. The values in the right-hand column of Table 2.3 are said to form a *frequency distribution* as they indicate the frequencies with which a particular value or event occurs. Therefore the bar graph is a graphical representation of a frequency distribution.

*Histograms* can be used to display continuous data, that is data which can take any value in a specified interval on a continuous scale, e.g. heights, ages, crop yields, rainfall amounts. In plotting a histogram the data must be divided into a series of *classes* as indicated in Table 2.4. The difference between the upper and lower limits of a class, known as the *class interval*, may be varied to reflect the detail of the distribution. Also, the number of class intervals must

be selected with this notion of reflecting detail in mind.

In plotting a histogram, the rectangles constructed for each class have areas proportional to the frequency of each class (Figure 2.2b).

## Frequency Curves

*Frequency curves* are produced by plotting continuous data on the *x*-axis (horizontal) against the frequency of occurrence on the *y*-axis (vertical). So a histogram can be transformed into a frequency curve, with the latter being a smooth curve drawn through the tops of each rectangle of the histogram (Figure 2.2c).

## Cumulative Frequency Curves or Ogives

In the case of a *cumulative frequency curve* or *ogive* the *y*-axis becomes cumulative frequencies so that the slope of the curve now becomes proportional to the frequency density in a particular range (Figure 2.2d). These graphs have been used for descriptive purposes in many geographical studies (see Gardiner and Gardiner, 1980:6–8).

## Quartiles

The nature of the spread of observations in a dataset may be clarified by depicting their *range* and *interquartile range*. The range is the difference between the highest ($E_U$) and lowest ($E_L$) observations in a dataset, i.e. ($E_U - E_L$), so it is very sensitive to extreme values (Table 2.5). Of more utility may be the

*Table 2.2*   Lineplot of Farm Size Data

Plot of data used in Table 2.1c

Cattle Enterprises ($n = 11$)

Cereal Enterprises ($n = 9$)

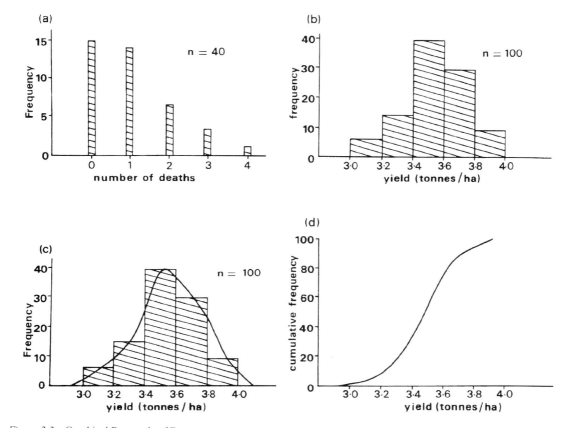

*Figure 2.2*  Graphical Portrayals of Data
(a) Bar graph of Table 2.3; (b) histogram of Table 2.4; (c) frequency curve of Table 2.4; (d) cumulative frequency curve or ogive of Table 2.4

removal of any extremes by eliminating observations that fall within the top and bottom quarters of a dataset. This may be done by ranking the data from the highest value to the lowest and then dividing the data into *quartiles*, each containing 25 per cent of the observations. As shown in Table 2.5, the *quartile values* are:

- $Q_L$ = the lower quartile, the value below which one-quarter of observations occur;
- $M$ = the value below which half the observations occur, known as the *median*;
- $Q_U$ = the upper quartile, the value below which three-quarters of the observations occur.

The *interquartile range* is the difference between the upper and lower quartile values, i.e. $(Q_U - Q_L)$. Sometimes division of a large set of observations into tenths or *deciles* can also be useful as an indicator of the spread of values within a dataset.

If the number of observations in a dataset is even, the median is halfway between the two middle observations when all observations are placed in ascending or descending order. If the number of observations in the dataset is $n$, then if $n$ is exactly divisible by 4, the lower quartile is halfway between the two neighbouring observations at $n/4$ and $n/4 + 1$, and the upper quartile is halfway between the two neighbouring observations at $3n/4$ and $3n/4 + 1$. If $n/4$ is not a

*Table 2.3*  Frequency Distribution of the Number of Deaths by Misadventure per Month in the Construction Industry (sample size $n = 40$ months)

| Number of Deaths | Frequency |
|---|---|
| 0 | 15 |
| 1 | 14 |
| 2 | 7 |
| 3 | 3 |
| 4 | 1 |
| 5 | 0 |
| Total $n = 40$ | |

*Table 2.4*  Frequency Distribution of Average Crop Yields (sample size $n = 100$)

| Crop Yield (tonnes/ha) | Frequency | Cumulative Frequency |
|---|---|---|
| 3.0–3.19 | 6 | 6 |
| 3.2–3.39 | 15 | 21 |
| 3.4–3.59 | 40 | 61 |
| 3.6–3.79 | 30 | 91 |
| 3.8–3.99 | 9 | 100 |
| $n = 100$ | | |

*Table 2.5*  Median and Quartiles for Two Samples

Data on daily commuting times

| Travel Time (minutes) from A to B | Travel Time (minutes) from A to C |
|---|---|
| 28.4\| $E_U = 28.4$ | 49.3  $E_U = 49.3$ |
| 27.9 | 41.1 |
| 27.8 | 38.4 |
| 27.5\| $Q_U = 27.5$ | 37.9\| $Q_U = 37.85$ |
| 27.4 | 37.8 |
| 27.4 | 35.5 |
| 27.2\|   $M = 27.15$ | 35.4 |
| 27.1\| | 33.4 |
| 27.0 | 32.2\|   $M = 31.15$ |
| 26.9 | 30.1 |
| 26.8\| $Q_L = 26.8$ | 30.0 |
| 26.8 | 28.9\| $Q_L = 28.85$ |
| 26.7 | 28.8\| |
| 26.3\| $E_L = 26.3$ | 26.8 |
| | 26.7 |
| | 23.3\| $E_L = 23.3$ |
| $(E_U - E_L) = 28.4 - 26.3$ $= 2.1$ | $(E_U - E_L) = 49.3 - 23.3$ $= 26.0$ |
| $(Q_U - Q_L) = 27.5 - 26.8$ $= 0.7$ | $(Q_U - Q_L) = 37.85 - 28.85$ $= 9.0$ |

whole number then the quartiles occur at the observation which is the next whole number larger than $n/4$ and $3n/4$ respectively. This is illustrated in Table 2.5.

## Boxplots

*Summary statistics* can be used to provide more specific information on the characteristics of datasets. Summary statistics are termed *letter values*, which are a collection of observations drawn systematically from a dataset, more densely from the tails than from the middle (Hoaglin, 1983:33). The values are termed "resistant" in that they themselves are not affected by extreme or anomalous values. For example, as the middle value in a dataset, the *median* can be described as a resistant summary statistic, in contrast to the

arithmetic mean (or average) which is not resistant because it can be affected by extreme values. For example, in the dataset 16, 23, 42, 43, 47, the median is 42 and the average is 34.2. However, in the dataset 16, 23, 42, 50, 121, the median is still 42 whilst the average is 50.4 (greater than all but one of the individual observations). The principal letter values are the median and the upper and lower quartiles.

Letter values are described in terms of their *depth* or position from the lowest value in a dataset to the highest value. So the median or middle value has a depth of $(n + 1)/2$, where $n$ is the number of observations (individual values) in the dataset. Letter values can be used in a graphical display known as a *boxplot* which acts as a summary of a frequency distribution. The salient features of boxplots are shown in Figure 2.3a and b. The chief value of boxplots is in comparing a number of related samples. In the example shown in Figure 2.3b the characteristics of two com-

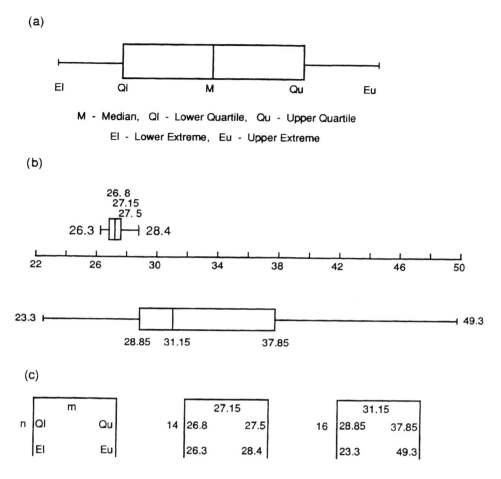

*Figure 2.3*   Boxplots and Five-Figure Summaries
(a) The letter values in a boxplot; (b) boxplots of data in Table 2.5; (c) five-figure summary

muter journeys are compared. The comparison is between the times of travel of a number of individuals travelling on different days between A and B and between A and C. Figure 2.3b shows that there is a much greater spread of times involved in travel from A to C. The median time of travel from A to C is much closer to the lower quartile than to the upper quartile, and the upper extreme time for the journey is a clear outlier.

The data in a boxplot can be summarised in a *five-figure summary* as shown in Figure 2.3c. This form of

representation can be a useful way of comparing the characteristics of different datasets. Another form of comparison is used by Sibley (1990:19–20) in which all boxplots are centred on their median, treating each median as being equal to zero, i.e. by subtracting the median from each member of the dataset. This is known as *removing a level*. If the members of the dataset, with the median subtracted, are now divided by the value of the interquartile range, the dataset is said to have been standardised. The resulting value is termed the *standard score*:

$$\text{standard score} = (x_i - x_\mathrm{m})/(Q_\mathrm{U} - Q_\mathrm{L})$$

where $x_i$ = any individual value (or observation) in the dataset and $x_\mathrm{m}$ = the median.

The usefulness of this standardisation for comparative purposes is shown in Figure 2.4. This takes data used by Emerson and Stresio (1983) in a comparison of city-size distributions for various European countries (minus the largest city which would give a bias towards the upper extreme value). Figure 2.4a shows the effect of centring each sample on a zero-valued median: England clearly has a greater spread of city sizes than Sweden. The symmetry of this spread for England is more apparent in the standardised boxplots

(Figure 2.4b), with a "tail" towards the bigger cities for the other three countries.

## MEASUREMENT AND NOTATION

### Scales of Measurement

Just as geographical data may take various forms, so the types or scales of measurement associated with those data can vary. The differences between the scales are very important because they play a crucial role in determining what types of analysis can be performed on the data. Four common scales of numer-

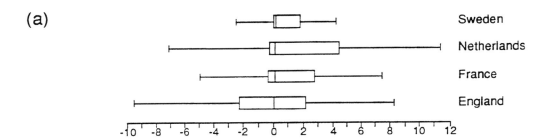

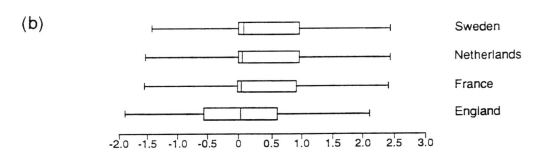

*Figure 2.4*    The Use of Boxplots to Portray Data
(a) Boxplots of city-size distributions (with medians removed); (b) standardised boxplots of city-size distributions. (After Sibley, 1990:20)

ical measurement are usually recognised: nominal, ordinal, interval and ratio (Amedeo and Golledge, 1975:95–134; Stevens, 1946). Proceeding through this list of scales, from nominal to ratio, data must satisfy more rigorous requirements.

(a) *Nominal scale*. Data take the form of categories, e.g. male:female, arable:pasture, with observations allocated to the particular categories.

(b) *Ordinal scale*. This involves ranking one observation against another as in a rank-ordered list (1st, 2nd, 3rd, ..., nth) or in a system of broadly defined classes. Such data might be produced from a questionnaire survey asking for preferences to be placed in rank order (e.g. Harris and O'Brien, 1988). The fact that one category may be ranked 'first', another 'second' and another 'third' does not provide information on the relative 'distance' between first, second and third. For example, in a horse race the second horse may come two lengths behind the first horse but be 10 lengths ahead of the third horse. On an ordinal scale the positions of the horses would simply be recorded as first, second and third.

(c) *Interval scale*. This enables observations to be sorted and ranked as for the previous two scales, but it also gives the magnitude of the differences separating each observation. This scale provides data in the form of both *integers* (whole numbers) and *fractions* (decimals), e.g. 63.31, 27.24, 51.1, 16, −12.987, 37, 29.578, −46. However, the data need not possess an absolute zero, as in the case of temperature readings where a temperature of 30 °C is not twice as warm as 15 °C because 0 °C is an arbitrary baseline and not absolute zero.

(d) *Ratio scale*. This has a known and absolute origin. It is the highest level of measurement and many data used by geographers are measured on this scale. Both interval and ratio scale data can usually be treated in the same way when performing standard statistical procedures. With ratio and interval measurements, observations can occupy any position along the measurement continuum, and so they are termed *continuous scales*. In contrast, the nominal and ordinal scales are *discrete* in that observations can be placed only at certain points – into a particular category or rank.

## Statistical Notation

When geographers utilise statistical analysis of numerical data they encounter different forms of notation to those associated with standard arithmetical methods. So not only has a range of statistical techniques become a required part of the geographer's canon of knowledge, but so too has statistical notation, with its subscripts and Greek symbols.

The most commonly used statistical symbols are listed in Table 2.6. In addition to these, the notation $\{x_{ij}\}$ is used to refer to data arranged in a *matrix* of rows and columns. The notation associated with a typical matrix is depicted in Figure 2.5. From this it can be seen that the observation for row 5 and column 2 is $x_{5,2}$, which has a value of 106, so $x_{5,2} = 106$. For data in this form, double summation signs must be used when addition is to take place for all rows and all columns, i.e.

$$\sum_{i=1}^{n} \sum_{j=1}^{m} x_{ij}$$

This indicates that all values in the matrix are to be added, for a matrix of numbers composed of $n$ rows and $m$ columns.

## Logarithms

In formulae frequently employed by geographers the use of *logarithms* (from the Greek *logos* = arithmetic) is amongst the least familiar to many students, as the logarithmic tables well known by previous generations of secondary school students have now been replaced by electronic calculators. The use of the logarithmic scale acknowledges that any arithmetic number greater than 0 has a counterpart on this logarithmic scale. The expression $\log x$, where $x$ is an integer value, refers to the *common logarithm* of the number $x$ and is sometimes written as $\log_{10} x$ indicating that it is a logarithm to the base 10. The meaning of this reference "to the base 10" can be seen from the following two examples:

$$100 = 10^2 \quad \text{so} \quad \log_{10} 100 = 2.0$$

$$30 = 10^{1.4771} \quad \text{so} \quad \log_{10} 30 = 1.4771$$

*Table 2.6*    Standard Statistical Symbols

A *population* is the entire aggregate of individuals or items (sometimes called *observations*) from which samples are drawn.

A *sample* is a set of individuals or items (sometimes called *observations*) selected from a *population* so that properties or parameters of the population may be estimated.

A *variable* may be any set of numerical values being investigated, such as values of temperature, prices, earnings, distances. The term "variable" denotes that it possesses a number of different values. To indicate these different values a special notation is used: $x_i$

| Sequence (i) | Number ($x_i$) | Numerical Value |
|:---:|:---:|:---:|
| 1 | $x_1$ | 16.2 |
| 2 | $x_2$ | 5.3 |
| 3 | $x_3$ | 10.1 |
| 4 | $x_4$ | −0.4 |
| 5 | $x_5$ | 1.7 |

| For a Population | | For a Sample | |
|:---|:---|:---|:---|
| Number of observations | $= N$ | Number of observations | $= n$ |
| Mean | $= \mu$ | Mean | $= \overline{x}$ |
| Variance | $= \sigma^2$ | Variance | $= s^2$ |
| Standard deviation | $= \sigma$ | Standard deviation | $= s$ |

$\sum$ = sum all scores or quantities that follow, e.g. the notation $\sum x$ means that all values of a variable $x$ should be added $\sum_{i=1}^{n} x_i$ = sum all quantities from $x_1$ to $x_n$ in the series,

$$x_1 + x_2 + x_3 + \ldots + x_n$$

So, in the series above, $\sum_{i=1}^{n} x_i$ = sum the sequence from $x_1$ to $x_5 = 32.9$

Note that $\sum_{i=5}^{15} x_i$ means, starting at $x_5$ sum the sequence to $x_{15}$

$H_1$ = the research or alternative hypothesis
$H_0$ = the null hypothesis
$\alpha$ = the level of significance of a hypothesis test, i.e. the degree of certainty concerning the likelihood of a particular event being due to chance or due to a consistently operating factor (usually $= 0.05$ or 5%; or 0.01 or 1%)

$>$ more than; $<$ less than
$\geqslant$ equal to or more than; $\leqslant$ equal to or less than

e.g. $x > y$ means $x$ is greater than $y$;
      $x \leqslant y$ means $x$ is equal to or less than $y$

| | columns | | | | |
|---|---|---|---|---|---|
| | $j=1$ | 2 | 3 | 4 | 5 |
| $i=1$ | $\times_{11}$ | $\times_{12}$ | $\times_{13}$ | $\times_{14}$ | $\times_{15}$ |
| 2 | $\times_{21}$ | $\times_{22}$ | $\times_{23}$ | $\times_{24}$ | $\times_{25}$ |
| rows 3 | $\times_{31}$ | $\times_{32}$ | $\times_{33}$ | $\times_{34}$ | $\times_{35}$ |
| 4 | $\times_{41}$ | $\times_{42}$ | $\times_{43}$ | $\times_{44}$ | $\times_{45}$ |
| 5 | $\times_{51}$ | $\times_{52}$ | $\times_{53}$ | $\times_{54}$ | $\times_{55}$ |

*Figure 2.5*    Matrix Notation

variables (indices)

| Location in City | Wealth | Age of Buildings | No. of Children | Car Ownership | Public Services |
|---|---|---|---|---|---|
| city centre | 84 | 69 | 61 | 77 | 96 |
| northern suburbs | 102 | 79 | 88 | 91 | 94 |
| southern suburbs | 137 | 126 | 101 | 140 | 127 |
| eastern suburbs | 126 | 109 | 121 | 119 | 109 |
| western suburbs | 86 | 106 | 130 | 99 | 92 |

Logarithms of fractions less than 1.0 have negative values, e.g. $0.1 = 10^{-1}$, so $\log_{10} 0.1 = -1.0$.

The conversion of a logarithmic value to an arithmetic number can be performed by consulting specially prepared tables (e.g. Godfrey and Siddons, 1970). The tables enable substitution of addition and subtraction for multiplication and division respectively, and multiplication and division for *involution* (raising a number by a power) and *evolution* (extracting a root from a given power, e.g. the square root) respectively. Thus, the sum of the logarithms of any two or more numbers is the logarithm of their product, e.g. $120 \times 40$ can be translated into logarithms as $2.0792 + 1.6021 (= 3.6813)$. The sum can be translated into the correct arithmetic number by referring to tables of antilogarithms. In this case the antilogarithm of 3.6813 is 4800 (so $120 \times 40 = 4800$).

Common logarithms were invented in the early seventeenth century by Henry Briggs whilst *natural logarithms* were developed at this time by the Scottish mathematician John Napier. Natural logarithms are based on the incommensurable number $2.718\,28 \ldots$, which is designated by the symbol e, i.e. $\log_e x$. The natural log of 2.7183 is 1.0, i.e. $\log_e e = \log_e 2.7193 = 1$. Also

$$\log_e e^2 = 2 \qquad \log_e e^3 = 3 \qquad \ldots \qquad \log_e e^n = n$$

$$\log x = 0.4343 \log_e x$$

$$\log_e x = 2.303 \log x$$

An alternative notation for $\log_e x$ is $\ln x$.

## STATISTICAL DESCRIPTION

The eminent statistician Sir Maurice Kendall (1970, 1977) identified the seventeenth century as the time when "genuine" statistical inquiries were first instituted in Britain. In many countries this was when greater emphasis began to be placed upon the exchange value of commodities and so upon the quantifiable aspects of people, events and objects. There was a growing demand for more precise measurements and accounting procedures, and a development of statistical analysis of the labour force and particular elements within the population. From this work, several statistical techniques were developed for analysing experimental data, for creating effective designs in gathering data and for controlling the quality of manufactured products. However, these developments, spanning over two centuries of the evolution of statistics as a clearly recognisable subset of mathematics, impinged little upon the work of geographers prior to the 1940s. Even then it was only relatively simple descriptions of geographical data that were employed (e.g. Bracey, 1953; Davies, 1948; Trewartha, 1943), so that averages, percentages and graphical descriptions of data were geographers' main contact with statistics: the art and science of gathering, analysing and making inferences from data.

The basis of the elementary statistical description employed by geographers from the 1930s onwards has been the four statistical "moments": the arithmetic mean, the standard deviation, the skewness and the kurtosis.

## The Arithmetic Mean $\bar{x}$

This is defined as

$$\text{arithmetic mean } \bar{x} = \frac{\sum x_i}{n}$$

where $\sum x_i$ = the sum of all values (observations) of variable $x$, and $n$ = number of observations.

The arithmetic mean is a *measure of central tendency*, in addition to which there are two other commonly used measures, the mode and the median, and two less frequently used, the geometric and harmonic means.

(a) *The mode*. This is the most frequently occurring value in a set of observations. If observations are portrayed graphically as shown in Figure 2.2a, the mode is the value at which the graph reaches its maximum height – in this case the modal value is 0. If a set of observations has two equally dominant values, it is said to be *bimodal* (the data depicted in Figure 2.2a are close to being bimodal). If no one or two values dominate then the distribution is *multimodal*. The mode is perhaps most useful as a measure of central tendency for describing observations which readily form frequency distributions, that is counts of particular phenomena (see Tables 2.3 and 2.4). If the counts (frequencies) can be grouped into classes as shown in Table 2.4, the modal class, containing the most frequencies, may be a useful description.

(b) *The median*. This is the mid-point of a set of observations, so that half the values lie above the median and half below once the values have been placed in rank order. If $n$ is an odd number, say 59, then the median is the 30th in the series (i.e. 29 observations both above and below this). If $n$ is even, say 60, then the median is the average of the 30th and 31st observations in the series.

(c) *The geometric mean*. This is used to calculate the mean in a set of observations increasing in value geometrically, e.g. 3, 9, 27, 81. Thus

$$\text{geometric mean } \bar{x} = \frac{\sum \log x_i}{n}$$

(expressed as an antilog)

(d) *The harmonic mean*. This may be used for observations concerned with rates of movement in which these rates are variable. Thus

$$\text{harmonic mean } \bar{x} = \frac{n}{\sum (1/x_i)}$$

These measures of central tendency may be used to indicate certain characteristics of a set of observations. Examples of this use are shown in Figure 2.6. In particular, the positioning of the mean, median and mode within a frequency distribution indicate the *degree of skewness* (or the extent to which observations occur on one particular side of the mean) and the nature of the way in which the observations are spread or dispersed around the measures of central tendency. The mode occurs under the peak of the curve whilst the median divides the area under the curve into two equal parts. The mean marks the centre of gravity of the area under the curve. The *skewness* is said to be a *measure of dispersion* and is one of several such measures that add to the set of descriptive statistical measures for numerical observations.

## The Standard Deviation ($s$ or $\sigma$)

This is defined as

$$s \text{ (or } \sigma) = \sqrt{\left( \frac{(x_i - \bar{x})^2}{n - 1} \right)}$$

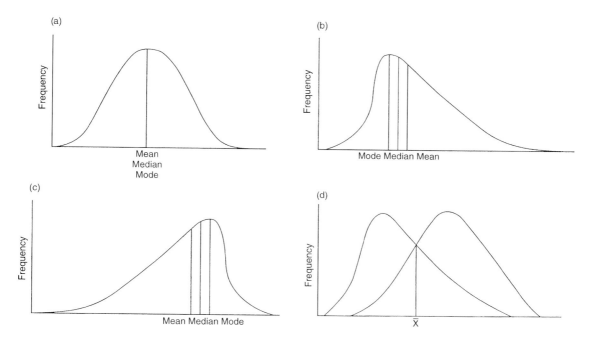

*Figure 2.6* Frequency Distributions, (a) Symmetrical (normal) distribution; (b) right-skewed distribution; (c) left-skewed distribution; (d) distributions giving the same mean

The *standard deviation*, which is the square root of the *variance* ($s^2$), measures the average deviation of a set of observations about the mean. The variance expresses this variation of observations about the mean in terms of units of squared deviations. So to obtain a measure of dispersion in terms of the units of the original data, the square root of the variance, i.e. the standard deviation, is frequently preferred as it is an absolute measure of dispersion. Geographers have often used the standard deviation as class intervals when mapping a set of observations (see Figure 2.7).

The use of ($n - 1$) instead of $n$ as the denominator may seem puzzling, but it is used in situations involving a sample dataset. In dealing with a sample, it is unlikely that the value of the population mean ($\mu$) will be known. If it is, then $n$ can be employed as the denominator, otherwise use of $n - 1$ is found to give a better estimate of the true population standard deviation ($\sigma$) and variance ($\sigma^2$) than $n$.

Consider the comparison of output from textile factories in two different regions in which the average production per factory per annum is similar (Table 2.7). If the standard deviation of the output in region X is smaller than that for region Y, this means that there is a larger variation in the output of factories in region Y compared with those in region X. This suggests that factories in X may be more similar in size, with similar production capacities, whereas those in Y have different capacities and perhaps have more variable production regimes.

When two sets of observations are compared, the standard deviation is often replaced by a relative measure, especially if the two datasets being compared are of different orders of magnitude or are measured in different units. For example, a standard deviation of 10 may be insignificant if the average observation is around 20 000 but it may be substantial if the average observation is around 20. In such cases the *coefficient of variation (CV)* may be used:

$$CV = \frac{s}{\bar{x}} \times 100\%$$

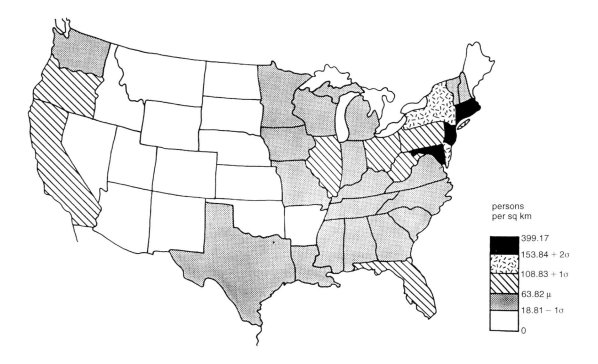

persons
per sq km

399.17
153.84 + 2σ
108.83 + 1σ
63.82 μ
18.81 − 1σ
0

*Figure 2.7*    Using Standard Deviations in the Mapping of Spatial Distributions: Population Density in the USA

## Skewness and Kurtosis

The first is defined as

$$\text{skewness} = \frac{\bar{x} - \text{mode}}{s}$$

This can also be expressed as

$$\frac{3(\bar{x} - \text{median})}{s} = \frac{(x_i - \bar{x})^3}{ns_x^3}$$

The second is defined as

$$\text{kurtosis} = \frac{(x_i - \bar{x})^4}{ns_x^4}$$

With its formula involving the quadrupling of $(x_i - \bar{x})$, the kurtosis is known as the *fourth moment measure*. Thus the skewness is the *third moment measure*, the variance the *second moment measure* and the mean the *first moment measure*. Both the skewness and the kurtosis are measurements of the shape of a frequency distribution. For a perfectly symmetrical distribution the skewness is zero; positive values show *positive (or right) skewness* (Figure 2.6b); negative values indicate *negative (or left) skewness* (Figure 2.6c). The skewness has proved a useful statistic in testing to see if a distribution conforms to a particular form, and also in comparisons of different frequency distributions.

The kurtosis represents the degree of peakedness of a frequency distribution, a value of 3 indicating a symmetrical (or normal) distribution (see end of this chapter). A distribution with a high peak is said to be *leptokurtic* and has a kurtosis greater than 3 (Figure 2.8a); a distribution with only moderate peakedness is *mesokurtic* (Figure 2.8b); and a distribution with limited or no peakedness is *platykurtic* and has a

*Table 2.7*  Calculation of the Standard Deviation (s) for Textile Production in Two Regions (expressed as an index of gross output for sample factories)

| Region X | $(x_i - \bar{x})$ | $(x_i - \bar{x})^2$ | Region Y | $(y_i - \bar{y})$ | $(y_i - \bar{y})^2$ |
|---|---|---|---|---|---|
| 675 | −18.3 | 334.9 | 456 | −257.6 | 66357.8 |
| 789 | 95.7 | 9158.5 | 908 | 194.4 | 37791.4 |
| 564 | −129.3 | 16718.5 | 1020 | 306.4 | 93881.0 |
| 549 | −144.3 | 20822.5 | 747 | 33.4 | 1115.6 |
| 892 | 198.7 | 39481.7 | 505 | −208.6 | 43513.0 |
| 679 | −14.3 | 204.5 | 619 | −94.6 | 8949.2 |
| 741 | 47.7 | 2275.3 | 872 | 158.4 | 25090.6 |
| 520 | −173.3 | 30032.9 | 1001 | 287.4 | 82598.8 |
| 589 | −104.3 | 10878.5 | 334 | −379.6 | 144096.2 |
| 663 | 30.3 | 918.1 | 559 | −154.6 | 23901.2 |
| 901 | −207.7 | 43139.3 | 829 | 115.4 | 13317.2 |
| 698 | 4.7 | 22.1 | | | |
| 753 | 59.7 | 3564.1 | | | |

$$\Sigma = 9013 \qquad \Sigma = 177550.9 \qquad \Sigma = 7850 \qquad \Sigma = 540612.0$$

$$\bar{x} = \frac{9013}{13} \qquad s_x = \sqrt{\frac{177550.9}{12}} = \sqrt{14795.9} \qquad \bar{y} = \frac{7850}{11} \qquad s_y = \sqrt{\frac{540612.0}{10}} = \sqrt{54061.2}$$

$$= 693.3 \qquad\qquad\qquad = 121.6 \qquad\qquad\qquad = 713.6 \qquad\qquad\qquad = 232.5$$

kurtosis of less than 3 (Figure 2.8c). As with the skewness, kurtosis is a useful measure when comparing frequency distributions and may be used to show how far a particular distribution deviates from a predetermined form.

## SAMPLING

### The Sampling Process

In the 1950s and 1960s the construction of geographical data by researchers increasingly drew upon *sam-*

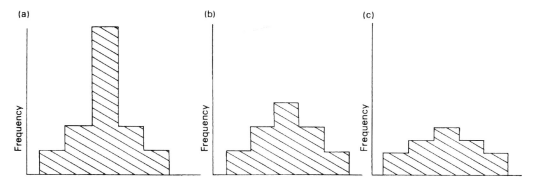

*Figure 2.8*  Frequency Distributions with Different Types of Kurtosis
(a) Leptokurtic, (b) mesokurtic, and (c) platykurtic

*pling procedures* and the use of sample data to represent the characteristics of larger *statistical populations*. A statistical population is a dataset comprising all possible measurements or observations; that is a complete set of counts or measurements derived from all objects possessing one or more common characteristics. These objects can be discrete, e.g. people sampled using a questionnaire, or they can be continuous, e.g. slope angles measured on a hillside.

Initially, geographers failed to appreciate the full range of considerations represented in the sampling process, though subsequently Harvey (1969:274–86) drew attention to these, listing a number of areas of difficulty experienced by geographers in both sampling and using data derived from sampling in the testing of hypotheses (see Chapter 3). He also discussed the six basic stages of the sampling process, listed in Table 2.8.

Different sampling plans are adopted according to different requirements, the chief aim usually being for the sample to act as a reliable substitute for the whole statistical population from which the sample is being drawn. This is because, in inferential statistics, sample data are used to infer to the population. Therefore the sample should avoid bias or the inclusion of unrepresentative proportions of data from different parts of the population. As the sample is used as a substitute

for the population, it should represent the characteristics of that population as closely as possible. So the first step in a sampling exercise is to identify the population from which the sample is to be drawn.

This identification is not nearly so straightforward as it might first appear. For example, if a sample is taken of farmers in Maine, is the population all the farmers in Maine, or really all the farmers in New England, or even North-East USA as a whole? Recognition of this type of problem is crucial because the sample will usually form the basis upon which inferences are made about the population. Therefore both the population and individual elements within it need to be defined carefully at the start of a research project. This involves considerations relating to the population's spatial and temporal extent, and the individual units or entities to be sampled. Possible units include individual people, households, cooperatives or operational groups, villages or social groups, plots of land, farm holdings, mapped areas, places where specific activities occur and areas administered as single entities.

Having resolved these preliminary problems a suitable *sampling frame* is selected which lists all the entities (e.g. persons, places) from which a sample is to be drawn. Electoral registers and telephone directories are commonly used sampling frames (Dixon

*Table 2.8*  Stages in the Sampling Process

| Stages | Processes |
|---|---|
| 1. Define the population | Defined in terms of: (a) units, (b) elements, (c) area, (d) time period |
| 2. Define sampling frame | How the elements of the population can be described |
| 3. Specify sampling unit | Identify units for sampling, e.g. city streets, households |
| 4. Determine sampling method | Method by which units are to be sampled, e.g. probability versus non-probability schemes |
| 5. Determine size of sample | The number of units to be selected |
| 6. Specify sampling plan and method of collecting data | The operational procedures necessary for selecting data |

*Source*: Shaw and Wheeler (1994:49)

and Leach, 1978:27–9). Sampling frames can be aspatial, as in these two examples, or they can be spatial if locations on a map constitute the individual elements in a sample. Such spatial sampling frames have been common in physical geography, examples including work on slope angles, soil horizons and drainage basins.

When they have employed maps as their sampling frame, geographers have used three different ways to ensure that all parts of the map stand a chance of being selected in the sample:

- Use of *point samples* – these are generally based on grid intersections or map coordinates (Figure 2.9a and b).
- Use of *line samples* (*transects*) (Figure 2.9c).
- Use of *area samples* (*quadrats*) (Figure 2.9d) – these are frequently used in botanical sampling exercises.

Haggett's (1963) well known comparison of these three types of sample selection in the estimation of woodland cover from a land use map found that transects gave the most accurate result. The key factors in the degree of accuracy of a sample are the particular statistical sampling procedure followed and the size of sample selected (Moser and Kalton, 1971). The importance of sample size is considered further below.

## Sampling Procedures

If a study of an entire population is not possible or is not desirable, perhaps on grounds of time and cost, there are both *non-probability* and *probability sampling schemes* that can be followed. The former do not permit formal development of inferences because of their lack of generality. They are represented by *convenience*, *purposive* and *quota sampling*. The first often typifies consumer surveys in which the first *n* customers entering a shop might be interviewed. A quota sample of these customers might be made on the basis of age and sex, e.g. interviewing the same numbers of young, middle-aged and elderly of both sexes. In contrast, a purposive sample represents the

selection of "typical individuals", more usually known as the *case study approach* in which, for example, a "typical" place is selected for study because it is believed to possess particular characteristics.

The two basic probability sampling designs are *random* and *systematic sampling*. In the former an individual element in the population is as likely to be included in the sample as any other. This is achieved by the use of a *random number table* (Appendix A) or a *tombola system*. For example, the individuals in a population of, say, 100 could be numbered from 00 to 99; and then, if the aim was to select 10 individuals at random from this list, using the first random numbers encountered in Appendix A, the individuals numbered 91, 41, 34, 75, 78, 07, 32, 44, 47 and 01 would be selected. In contrast, systematic sampling involves selection from the population at regular intervals, say every fifth person, perhaps after selecting the first observation at random. This has the advantage over random sampling of achieving a more uniform coverage of the population. It is possible for a random sample to overlook some parts of a population and provide over-representation of others (Figure 2.10a). For systematic sampling a problem may be that it could replicate underlying regularities in the population by virtue of its selection interval.

The chief refinement to these two basic types of sampling is the introduction of some degree of *stratification* in which the population is divided into subsets, with separate samples drawn from each (Figure 2.10b), as in dividing people into different age groups and drawing separate samples from each group. Such stratification may be very important if there are "natural" strata in the population, such as female/male, socio-economic groups, age groups, soil horizons, geological strata, altitude bands. The use of purposive or "non-natural" strata may be employed as a means of ensuring adequate coverage of all parts of the population.

A combination of random, systematic and stratified sampling for use with a spatial sampling frame and allocation of point samples was developed by Berry (1962) as *stratified systematic unaligned sampling*. As shown in Figure 2.11, this involves the use of a spatial

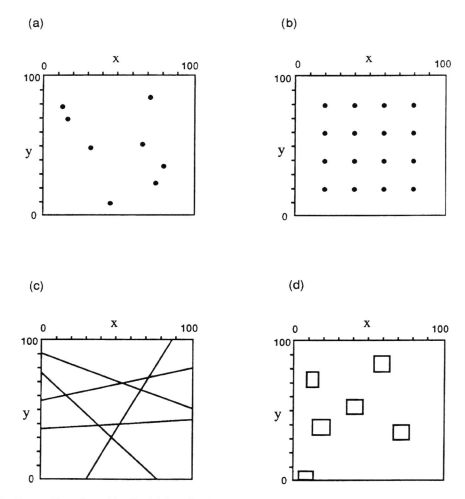

*Figure 2.9* Types of Sampling with a Spatial Sampling Frame
(a) Point sample: simple random sampling; (b) point sample: systematic sampling; (c) line sample: random coordinates; (d) quadrat sample: random squares

grid. Within the first grid square the $x$ coordinate is selected from a random number table but is then kept constant across the first row of grid squares whilst the $y$ coordinate is varied in each cell, again through random selection (Figure 2.11a). For the first column of the grid the $y$ coordinate is kept constant in each cell whilst the $x$ coordinate is varied. This procedure is then repeated for each successive row and column until a point location has been selected in each cell. A comparison of sampling designs by Keyes et al (1976), using land use maps of southwestern Wisconsin as the sampling frame, found this type of sampling design to be superior to random, stratified random and systematic designs.

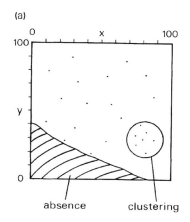

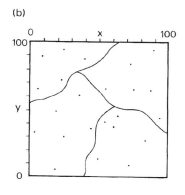

*Figure 2.10*   Random Sampling with a Spatial Sampling Frame
(a) Random point sample; (b) random point sample with stratification

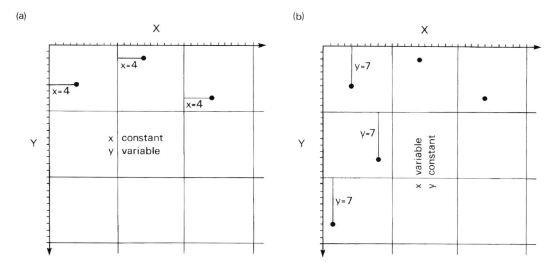

*Figure 2.11*   Stratified Systematic Unaligned Sampling
(a) *x* constant, *y* variable; (b) *x* variable, *y* constant. (After Berry, 1962)

## Multi-Stage Designs and Cluster Sampling

Although for much geographical research the sampling plan utilised has been fairly simple, some work has approximated the more complex *multi-stage designs* employed in national surveys. In these large-scale examples the number sampled is usually determined by considerations of time and the number of interviewers available. Refinement of the sampling technique has also contributed to the general use of very small sample sizes (e.g. $< 3000$ people in the United Kingdom) to represent the national population. This has become a part of national life in much of the

Developed World via political opinion polls from organisations such as Gallup and Mori.

The use of small samples to represent the opinions of a large population was pioneered in the 1930s by the American opinion-pollster George Gallup. He established his polling organisation in the USA in 1935 and its British counterpart one year later. In the UK the Gallup organisation is perhaps best known for using a sample of around 1000 people to reflect the voting intentions of the whole population. Average error per party has been no more than 1.4 per cent in the 14 general elections in the UK since Gallup began such surveys in 1945. This degree of accuracy was achieved in the two general elections held in the 1980s by taking a sample of 1000 individuals from the 43 million electors. The sample was produced by sorting the parliamentary constituencies into regions. Within each region, the constituencies were listed in descending order of the Conservative Party's majority, continuing to constituencies held by the Labour Party in ascending order of their majority. The regional lists were then consolidated, with the cumulative total of electors provided against each constituency. When this cumulative total reached 430 000, or one-hundredth of the total number of voters, that particular constituency was selected. This process proceeded until 100 constituencies had been chosen. Individuals within each of these selected constituencies were then chosen for interview on the basis of a stratified design using interviewers who were given a quota of men and women in different age and social class groups. The relatively poor predictions made for the 1992 general election suggest that it was the basis of this selection of individuals by age, sex and social class that could produce slight but vital distortions to the survey results. For example, interviewers filling their quota by interviewing people in the street tended to produce an over-estimation of the vote for the Labour Party.

The geographical coverage of sample polls is an important element in minimising bias, with geographical stratification accompanying stratification on the basis of socio-economic groups. This is illustrated by the UK National Market Research Survey (NMRS). This survey of the adult civilian population aged 16 years and over interviewed 3600 individuals to obtain a minimum of 3000 responses. Starting from a register of electors as the sampling frame, the multi-stage stratified design made selections from administrative districts, polling districts, households and finally individuals, as follows:

1. Selection of administrative districts as sampling units, with a selection of 90 from a possible 1765 districts and stratification into the 12 Standard Regions, and then urban/rural districts on a proportional basis, ensuring a selection of a range of functional types of urban district.
2. Random selection of polling districts to give a total of 320, using socio-economic stratification.
3. Selection of every $n$th household in the chosen polling districts, to give a total of 3600 households.
4. Selection of one individual per household.

A commonly used procedure to select individuals from chosen households is that designed by Kish (1965). This numbers the selected households systematically from 1 to 12. Then lists are made of all people in each household who fit the requirements of the investigation (e.g. all eligible to vote). Males are listed first from eldest to youngest, then females in the same way. A special grid is then used (see Table 2.9) to select a particular person based on the number assigned to that household and the number of eligible people in the household. For example, in a household assigned the number 6 and containing four eligible persons, the first person (most likely to be the eldest man or eldest woman) would be interviewed.

The NMRS and similar multi-stage designs make use of *cluster sampling*, the selection of clusters of units of observation, which can reduce the time and cost of a sampling exercise by restricting a sample to a limited number of geographical areas, i.e. by combining subsamples from the populations of selected areas. For example, this is the practice adopted in the Family Expenditure Survey (FES) performed annually on 7000 households in the UK. Table 2.10 compares the characteristics of stratified and cluster sampling.

Appropriate methodology for cluster sampling is considered by Fingleton (1988) who recommends it as potentially being more cost-effective than simple ran-

*Table 2.9*    Grid for Selecting Individuals in Multi-stage Sampling

| Assigned Number of address | Total Number of Eligible Persons | | | | | |
|---|---|---|---|---|---|---|
| | 1 | 2 | 3 | 4 | 5 | 6 or more |
| 1 or 2 | 1 | 1 | 2 | 2 | 3 | 3 |
| 3 | 1 | 2 | 3 | 3 | 3 | 5 |
| 4 or 5 | 1 | 2 | 3 | 4 | 5 | 6 |
| 6 | 1 | 1 | 1 | 1 | 2 | 2 |
| 7 or 8 | 1 | 1 | 1 | 1 | 1 | 1 |
| 9 | 1 | 2 | 3 | 4 | 5 | 5 |
| 10 or 11 | 1 | 2 | 2 | 3 | 4 | 4 |
| 12 | 1 | 1 | 1 | 2 | 2 | 2 |

*Source*: Hoinville et al (1985:82); de Vaus (1991:69).

*Table 2.10*    Comparison of Stratified and Cluster Sampling

| Stratified Sample | Cluster Sample |
|---|---|
| Strata should be parts of the population which are internally similar | Clusters should be parts of the population which are internally representative of the whole population |
| Every member of the population must be in exactly one stratum | A member of the population need not be in any one cluster |
| A stratified sample includes members of every stratum | A cluster sample usually excludes all the members of some of the clusters |
| Stratified sampling decreases sampling error (i.e. it is more efficient) but slightly increases costs | Cluster sampling often decreases costs but usually increases sample error (i.e. it is less efficient) |

*Source*: Open University (1983, Unit A4:24).

dom sampling. For example, if there are $k$ clusters each of size $C$, the gathering of a sample of size $kC$ is likely to involve travelling to $k$ separate destinations rather than $kC$ destinations. Clusters could be a random selection from among enumeration districts in a city, perhaps comprising all households in these chosen districts. In another context, separate cells of a grid may be regarded as clusters and sampling could take place within each of these clusters. Errington (1985), in an analysis of sampling frames for farm surveys, employed a variant of cluster sampling by grouping contiguous farms within a specified areal unit. This reduced the sampling bias towards larger holdings, which is a problem for purely random sampling. The clusters must maximise the diversity of farm characteristics being examined. This can be achieved by using a pilot or control run first to identify components of variability within the sampling frame (see also Clark and Gordon, 1980; Emerson and Macfarlane, 1995).

Many published sources of data used by geographers are based on the use of sample surveys such as the

NMRS and the FES. In using such data it is important to be aware of the nature of this sampling component as it is such a key part of data construction.

A key issue in multi-stage sampling is how many clusters (i.e. areal units, blocks of streets, households) to select at each stage of the process. If there is a desired final sample size then there is a trade-off between the number of clusters selected and the number of samples taken from them. Usually a relatively large number of initial clusters are chosen followed by selection of much fewer individuals from each cluster. This maximises variation in the types of areas that form the sample. Therefore if variety is increased in the initial stages, this helps maintain representativeness at later stages (de Vaus, 1991:69). A constraint on this attractive scenario is that, as the number of clusters chosen initially increases, so too may the travelling costs involved in interviewing individuals in the final sample. An important refinement in multi-stage sampling is the use of stratification of the areal units. Stratification is a useful way of ensuring that different types of city block or enumeration district are properly represented. An added refinement may be to base block selection on the number of households a block contains. Thus a block with three times as many households as an adjacent block has a three times greater chance of being selected. This is referred to as *probability proportionate to size (PPS) sampling* (Kish, 1965:217–46). It ensures proper representation of densely populated blocks. However, whilst blocks with large numbers of households are more likely to be selected, there is actually a lower probability of a particular household in that block being chosen. For further details see Kalton's (1983) *Introduction to survey sampling.*

Before choosing a sampling procedure in a research project, it is useful to consider a range of alternatives:

1. What is the appropriate sampling frame to employ?
2. Is there other, more aggregate, information about the population and its distribution available that might be used?
3. If random sampling is not possible, what type of sampling should be employed to best minimise bias?

4. Which design will spread the sample as widely as possible, given available resources and time?
5. If non-random methods are used, what will be the limitations and dangers involved in drawing inferences from the sample?

With reference to point 1, bias can also be created by *non-response*. This encompasses a variety of reasons for non-inclusion of selected individuals in the final provision of data. For example, some people in a sample may refuse to answer questions and some may be uncontactable. Allowance may be made for some non-response by drawing a sample larger than needed. However, non-response usually affects particular segments of the population more than others, especially the elderly, those with less education and recent immigrants, so that increasing the sample size may not produce correct proportions of those parts of the population that do not respond. To adjust for non-response from certain segments of the population, the following may be possible:

- Use what observable information can be gathered about non-responders, e.g. observations can be made regarding age, sex, ethnicity and housing conditions of non-respondents.
- Additional information may be obtained from some sampling frames if these take the form of official records.
- Comparison can be made about information for the entire population and that obtained from a sample. Some differences may be inferred as being due to omission of non-respondents.

In addition, one crucial consideration when taking a sample is to determine its most appropriate size. This depends upon the accuracy required from the sample given the limitations of the resources available. The accuracy of a sample increases with sample size, but the relationship between accuracy and size is not a simple linear one. To understand the nature of this relationship, and so gain more understanding of appropriate sample size, some knowledge of probability and probability distributions is required. Similarly, such knowledge is essential before the use of statistical testing of hypotheses can be performed.

# PROBABILITY DISTRIBUTIONS

## Probability Theory

Once sample data have been collected and examined using graphical techniques and/or the calculation of summary statistics, it is possible to use the data to infer characteristics of the population from which the sample was taken. Such a use of sample data is part of *inferential statistics* in which *statistical theory* is employed to estimate particular characteristics of the population. The basis for inferential statistics is *probability theory*, and the products of any inferential analysis are statements of a probabilistic nature. Therefore to understand and solve many statistical (inferential) problems some knowledge of probability is required (see Chatfield, 1983:37–55).

Fortunately, there are occasions when simple illustrations of basic probability theory occur in daily life, and these can provide a useful introduction to how the theory operates. For example, if we are playing a game like *Monopoly* which involves throwing a die, each score on the die has an equal chance of occurring in every single throw. So there is a one in six chance of, say, throwing a 3, or a probability ($P$) of $1/6$: $P(3) = 1/6$. The probability of throwing a number less than 4 is $P(1, 2, 3) = 1/6 + 1/6 + 1/6 = 1/2$ (or a one in two chance). This is a very simple example of a variable quantity (i.e. the scores on a die) whose values (or *realisations*) occur according to a law of chance. The values are said to have a *probability distribution*; in this case a distribution in which each probability is $1/6$. If $P = 0$, this indicates absolute impossibility; if $P = 1$, this indicates absolute certainty. The variable quantity (in this example the score on the die) is known as a *random variable* because it has not been determined by a definite algebraic formula. Random variables may be *discrete* or *continuous*, the former only being able to take certain values, as with the scores on a die. A continuous random variable can take any value over its possible range, as

with the times of arrival of trains at a station. In the example of the die, if the random variable $E$ is the score on the die and the probability of $E = 1$ is $1/6$, this can be denoted as $P(E = 1) = 1/6$. If two dice are thrown there are 36 equally likely realisations, so the probability of obtaining two "1"s, $P(E = 1 \cap 1)$, is $1/36$ (i.e. $1/6 \times 1/6$), where $\cap$ is the symbol representing the intersection of two events: in this case the two events are "throwing a 1 with each die". (Frequently $E$ is omitted, so the expression would be $P(1 \cap 1) = 1/36$.) The distribution of the random variable $T$ ($=$ total score on the dice) is a discrete probability distribution. This means that $T$ can take values $t_1$, $t_2$, ... $t_n$, with probabilities $p_1$, $p_2$, ..., $p_n$, where $p_1 + p_2 + \ldots + p_n = 1$ and $p_i > 0$ for all $i$.

The calculation of the probability of obtaining a particular score when throwing two dice illustrates the *general product law* for independent events. Two events, such as throwing two dice, are said to be independent if the knowledge that one of them (say, throwing a 3 with one of the dice) has occurred and has no effect on the probability of the second event (say, throwing a 5 with the other die). If two events are independent then the probability of their conjunctive occurrence (or intersection) can be calculated by applying the formula.

$$P(E_1 \cap E_2) = P(E_1)P(E_2)$$

For example, if households in a town are sampled and it is known that $E_1 = P$ (household with no children) $= 0.21$, and $E_2 = P$ (household with no car) $= 0.29$, and we assume that the two events are independent but not mutually exclusive, then

$$P(E_1 \cap E_2) = 0.21 \times 0.29 = 0.061$$

i.e. there is a probability of 0.061 that a household in the town will have no car and will also have no children.

If the two events are not independent then the general product law becomes

$$P(E_1 \cap E_2) = P(E_2)P(E_1/E_2)$$

where $P(E_1/E_2)$ is the conditional probability of $E_1$, given that $E_2$ has occurred, which is

$$P(E_1/E_2) = \frac{P(E_1 \cap E_2)}{P(E_2)}$$

Similarly,

$$P(E_1 \cap E_2) = P(E_1)P(E_2/E_1)$$

For example, if there are two dice and at least one 3 has been obtained, it is possible to calculate the probability that the sum of the two dice will be 7:

$$P(E_1 = \Sigma = 7/E_2 = 3) = \frac{P(E_1 \cap E_2)}{P(E_2)} = \frac{2/36}{11/36}$$

$$= 2/11$$

A second probability law is the *general addition law*. This applies when the union (or disjunction) of two events is being considered. This is denoted as $P(E_1 \cup E_2)$ and represents the probability of either $E_1$ or $E_2$ occurring. It is calculated by summing the probabilities of $E_1$ and $E_2$ and subtracting any intersection that may occur between them:

$$P(E_1 \cup E_2) = P(E_1) + P(E_2) - P(E_1 \cap E_2)$$

$$= P(E_1) + P(E_2) - P(E_1)P(E_2/E_1)$$

So if $E_1 = P$(household with no children) $= 0.21$, and $E_2 = P$(household with no car) $= 0.29$, and we assume that the two events are independent but not mutually exclusive, then

$$P(E_1 \cup E_2) = 0.21 + 0.29 - P(E_1)P(E_2)$$

$$= 0.50 - 0.061$$

$$= 0.439$$

Therefore the probability of a household having either no children or no car is 0.439. This situation can be summarised in a *Venn (or Euler) diagram* (Figure 2.12). A Venn diagram represents sets of events by areas whose relative positions give the relationships between the sets. The probabilities associated with the sets can either be omitted in the diagram (Figure 2.12a) or they can be indicated (Figure 2.12b). In Figure 2.12a the entire set, as depicted by the outer rectangle, represents countries of the world. The three smaller sets are A = African countries, B = OPEC (Organisation of Petroleum Exporting Countries) countries and C = NATO (North Atlantic Treaty Organisation) countries. The overlap between A and B indicates that some, but not all, OPEC members are African countries, such as Nigeria (N). The lack of overlap between B and C shows that no country is both an OPEC member and a member of NATO.

Using the probabilities for households with children and cars referred to above, Figure 2.12b depicts two different situations:

(i) if $E_1$ and $E_2$ are mutually exclusive then $P(E_1) + P(E_2) = 0.21 + 0.29 = 0.5$;
(ii) if $E_1$ and $E_2$ are not mutually exclusive, they can be represented in this fashion. This includes both $P(E_1 \cup E_2)$ and $P(E_1 \cap E_2)$, where $P(E_1 \cup E_2) =$ probability of a household having either no car or no children, and $P(E_1 \cap E_2) =$ probability of a household having both no child and no car. These different situations are also summarised in Table 2.11.

Probability theory has been utilised in many ways by geographers. In particular, it has been used in inferential statistics which makes use of our ability to model the behaviour of unpredictable events in real life by using *theoretical probability distributions* whose properties are well known. In other words, real events can be approximated by *models* which utilise different types of probability distributions to replicate or represent those events. Three of the most common distributions utilised are the binomial, the normal and the Poisson, each of which is introduced below.

## The Binomial Distribution

In a binomial distribution there are a number of independent similar trials, the outcome of each trial

(a)

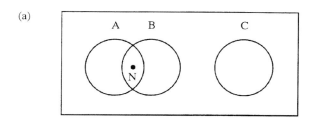

(b)

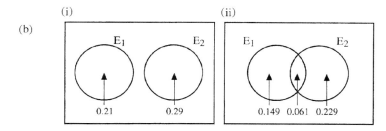

*Figure 2.12*   Venn Diagrams
(a) Without probabilities; (b) showing probabilities; (i) $E_1$ and $E_2$ mutually exclusive, (ii) $E_1$ and $E_2$ not mutually exclusive

*Table 2.11*   Types of Events

1. Mutually exclusive
$$P(E_1 \cap E_2) = 0$$
$$P(E_1 \cup E_2) = P(E_1) + P(E_2)$$

2. Not mutually exclusive
$$P(E_1 \cup E_2) = P(E_1) + P(E_2) - P(E_1 \cap E_2)$$
   • Dependent
$$P(E_1 \cap E_2) = P(E_1)P(E_2/E_1)$$
   • Independent
$$P(E_1 \cap E_2) = P(E_1)P(E_2)$$

For notation, see text.

• There are only two possible, mutually exclusive, outcomes, e.g. heads and tails when tossing a coin, or wet and dry to describe weather conditions.
• Probabilities associated with the two outcomes are constant.
• The outcomes of successive trials (e.g. as in the tossing of a coin) are mutually independent.

The commonest occurrence of such a distribution is in a series of repeated trials, such as the random selection of items from a population to see if they possess a given characteristic. Under these conditions,

$$P(x) = {}^nC_x p^x (1 - p)^{n-x}$$

where $x = 0, 1, \ldots, n$ and ${}^nC_x$ = the number of ways in which $x$ items can be selected from $n$ distinct items, disregarding the order of the selection. It represents

having just one of two possibilities. If the outcomes have probabilities $p$ and $q$, then $P(p + q) = 1$.

The binomial distribution is applicable under the following conditions:

the number of combinations of $n$ items taken $x$ at a time, and can also be denoted as:

$$^nC_x = \frac{^nP_x}{x!} = \frac{n!}{(n-x)!x!} = {^nC_{n-x}}$$

where $^nP_x$ = the number of permutations of $n$ items taken $x$ at a time, i.e. the number of ways in which $x$ items can be selected from $n$ distinct items, taking notice of the order of selection. This is

$$^nP_x = P(n, x)$$
$$= n(n-1)\ldots(n-x+1)$$
$$= \frac{n!}{(n-x)!}$$

where ! is the factorial sign and carries the instruction to multiply all whole numbers up to and including that indicated, e.g. $3! = 3 \times 2 \times 1 = 6$. Thus if $n = 6$ and $x = 4$,

$$^nC_x = {^6C_4} = \frac{^6P_4}{4!} = \frac{6!}{(6-4)!4!} = \frac{720}{2(24)} = 15$$

The number of combinations of the letters a, b, c taken two at a time is:

$$^3C_2 = \frac{^3P_2}{2!} = \frac{3!}{(3-2)!2!} = \frac{6}{2!} = 3$$

i.e. ab, bc, ac. The number of permutations of the letters a, b, c taken two at a time is:

$$^3P_2 = \frac{3!}{(3-2)!} = \frac{3 \times 2}{1} = 6$$

i.e. ab, bc, ac, ba, cb, ca.

If $P(x) = 0.5$ then the binomial distribution obtained is a symmetrical one as shown in Figure 2.13d. As the value of $P(x)$ moves away from 0.5, so a skewed distribution will ensue.

Summary statistics for the binomial distribution can be calculated as follows:

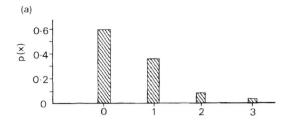
(a)

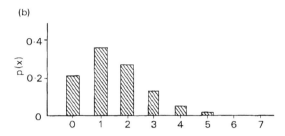
(b)

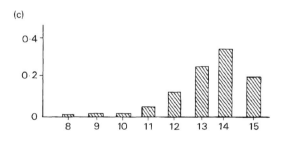
(c)

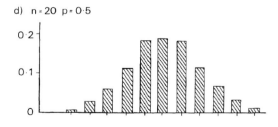
d)  n = 20  p = 0.5

*Figure 2.13*   The Binomial Distribution
(a) $n = 3$, $p = 1/6$; (b) $n = 15$, $p = 0.1$; (c) $n = 15$, $p = 0.9$; (d) $n = 20$, $p = 0.5$

- Binomial mean, $\mu = nx$
- Binomial variance, $\sigma^2 = nx(1 - x)$
- Binomial standard deviation, $\sigma = nx(1 - x)$
- Binomial skewness, $\alpha = \dfrac{x - (1 - x)}{nx(1 - x)}$

The binomial distribution applies to dichotomous variables, such as male:female, urban:rural, but can also be produced from interval and ratio data. For example, people can be divided on the basis of whether they are under or over a given age. As shown in Figure 2.13, the shape of the distribution varies according to the values of $n$ and $p$ (see also Ashcroft and Love, 1989).

## The Normal Distribution

Figure 2.2b showed how observations on a continuous variable $x$ could be plotted as a histogram. As further observations are taken and class intervals are made smaller, the histogram tends towards a smooth frequency curve. If the height of the curve is standardised so that the area underneath is equal to unity, then the graph is called a probability curve, and $P$(any value of $x$ underneath the curve) $= 1$. Because the curve now indicates the relative density of probability, it is called a *probability density function* (pdf).

The distribution portrayed in Figure 2.14a, which represents a sample of men's heights, is sometimes described as a bell-shaped distribution. It is symmetrical and is usually termed the *normal or Gaussian distribution* (or curve), after the German mathematician, Carl Gauss, who calculated its complex formula. It is the most important of all the probability distributions as it has a very wide range of practical applications.

The curve is symmetric about the point $x = \mu$, where $\mu$ is the mean of the distribution (Figure 2.14b). The variance of the normal distribution is equal to $\sigma^2$, and so the standard deviation is equal to $\sigma$. The bigger the value of $\sigma$, the more spread out the normal distribution will be (see Figure 2.14c). However, whatever the values of $\mu$ and $\sigma$, the distribution is such that around one observation in three lies more than one standard deviation from the mean, and about one observation in 20 lies more than two standard deviations from the mean.

If values of a normally distributed variate, $x$, are expressed in terms of deviations from the mean, the newly created values are standardised ones, and hence the process is termed *standardisation*. The units of expression are proportions of the standard deviation

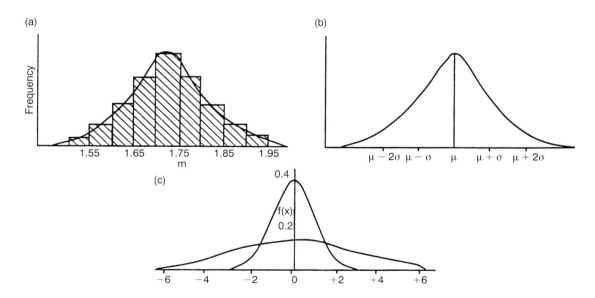

*Figure 2.14*   The Normal Distribution
(a) The distribution of a sample of men's heights; (b) the normal distribution centred on $\mu$; (c) comparison of two normal distributions

and are termed *z values*. Positive *z* values represent observations greater than the mean, and negative *z* values represent observations less than the mean, i.e.

$$z = \frac{x - \mu}{\sigma}$$

where $z$ = the number of standard deviations by which $x$ departs from $\mu$.

The process of standardisation leads to the term *standardised normal curve*, which possesses the same detailed form irrespective of the nature of the raw data. Its mathematical regularities have proved extremely useful and have formed an important role in inferential statistics. In particular, probabilities of particular events can be easily estimated using the curve, by employing pre-prepared tables, known as *z* tables (see Appendix B), which provide the relative area or probability between any two *z* values. For example, if we wish to know the relative area beneath the normal curve between the mean, where $z = 0.0$, and $z = +0.5$, this value may be read directly from the table. The value is given as $P = 0.191\,46$, indicating that the probability of obtaining a value of $z$ between 0.0 and $+0.5$ is $0.191\,46$. There is a probability of $(0.5 - 0.191\,46)$ of a value greater than $+0.5$ (Figure 2.15a). Figure 2.15b shows $z$ values associated with one, two and three standard deviations on either side of the mean. Frequently, for convenience, the limits at $P = 0.95$ are used in preference to $P = 0.9545$. From the $z$ tables it can be seen that a value of $P = 0.95$ corresponds with $z = 1.96$, and so there is a probability of 0.05 (or a one in 20 chance) that values will lie outside $z = +1.96$.

For normally distributed data the $z$ values of $+1.96$ may be easily converted into the equivalent raw data

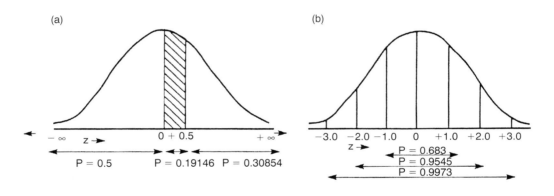

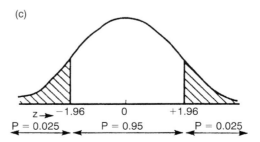

*Figure 2.15* The Normal Distribution
(a) $P(z = 0$ to $0.5)$; (b) probabilities and $z$ values; (c) regions of rejection ($P = 0.05$)

by using $z = (x - \mu)/\sigma$. Therefore $x = z\sigma + \mu$. So if $\mu = 1.725$ and $\sigma = 0.075$ (from Figure 2.14), at $z = 1.96$,

$$x = 1.96 \times 0.075 + 1.725$$

$$= 0.147 + 1.725 = 1.972$$

Figure 2.15 depicts the standardised normal curve as continuing to infinity in both positive and negative directions. This implies that events of any magnitude are possible theoretically, if highly improbable. The very low levels of probability associated with such extreme values are utilised in statistical testing of hypotheses as discussed in the following chapter.

## Uses of the Normal Distribution

There are five principal uses of the normal distribution.

(a) Many physical measurements closely approximate to this distribution: (i) data containing random errors, and (ii) data in the form of measurements in which there are natural variations, such as heights of people. It should be noted, though, that behavioural, attitudinal and socio-economic data gathered in geographical surveys or from official sources may not be normally distributed (Ilbery, 1977a).

(b) Even if physical phenomena are not normally distributed, they can be transformed to normality using a mathematical transformation. Several such transformations have been commonly used in geographical research, depending on the character of the data. The commonest transformations employed have been: (i) *logarithmic* – for data with a marked positive skew (Figure 2.16a); (ii) *square root* – for data with a mild positive skew (Figure 2.16b); (iii) *power* – for data with negative skew (Figure 2.16c). Angular transforms are sometimes employed for percentage data (Freeman and Tukey, 1950).

(c) The normal distribution is a good approximation to the binomial distribution if $n$ is large and if $p$ is not close to 0 or 1. For example, if $n > 20$, the approximation is valid for $0.3 < p < 0.7$. The larger the value of $n$, the wider the range for $p$ that is permissible. For any given binomial distribution, the corresponding normal distribution can be found by putting $\mu = np$ and $\sigma^2 = np(1 - p)$. This is most useful for large values of $n$ when the binomial distribution can be difficult to evaluate.

(d) Any random variable formed by taking a linear combination of independent normally distributed random variables will itself be normally distributed. This situation commonly arises in certain manufacturing processes, for example those in which components have normally distributed dimensions.

(e) If a random sample is taken from a statistical population and the mean value, $\bar{x}$, is calculated, it is unlikely that this sample mean will correspond exactly with the population mean ($\mu$). Indeed, if the process is repeated several times, using the same size of sample each time, a series of values of $\bar{x}$ will be generated. This series is termed the *sampling distribution* of $\bar{x}$,

(a)

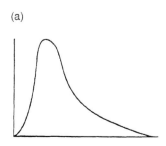

(b)

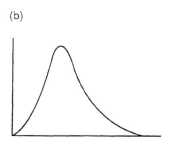

(c)

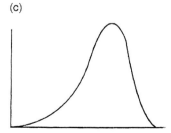

*Figure 2.16* Transformations
(a) Logarithmic, (b) square root, and (c) power

and, provided it is repeated at least 30 times, when plotted in graphical form it will give a normal distribution centred on the population mean ($\mu$). This is known as the *central limit theorem*, and it applies even if the population itself is not normally distributed. The mean is the particular population characteristic being investigated in this case, so the sample mean ($\bar{x}$) is an estimate of the population mean ($\mu$). Furthermore, the sample mean can be treated as a normally distributed random variable, so that the equation $z = (x - \mu)/\sigma$ can be rewritten as $z = (\bar{x} - \mu)/\sigma_{\bar{x}}$. The standard deviation of the sampling distribution generated is known as the *standard error*: in this example it is the *standard error of the mean* ($SE_{\bar{x}}$), where $SE_{\bar{x}} = s/\sqrt{n}$, $s$ = the standard deviation of the sample, and $n$ = sample size. Thus, even if it is not possible to take a large number of samples from a population, it is still possible to calculate the standard error. This has a number of uses, one being to assist in determining required sample sizes.

Referring to the description of the standardised normal curve above and to Figure 2.15b, there is a 68.3 per cent probability that the population mean ($\mu$) will lie within $\pm 1$ standard error of $\bar{x}$. There is a 95.45 per cent probability that the population mean ($\mu$) will lie within $\pm 2$ standard errors of $\bar{x}$, and a 99.7 per cent probability that $\mu$ lies within $\pm 3$ standard errors of $\bar{x}$.

The number of standard errors can be denoted as $z$ values. The two $z$ values utilised most frequently are 1.96 and 2.58, as these correspond to the 95 per cent (0.95) and 99 per cent (0.99) *confidence limits* respectively (Figure 2.15c). Thus higher confidence limits are achieved only at the expense of a wider interval (the *confidence interval*) between the limits. So, using sample data, a confidence interval is "that interval within which a parameter [such as the mean] of a parent population is calculated ... to have a stated probability of lying. The larger the sample size, the smaller is the confidence interval; in other words, the more accurate is the estimate of the parent mean" (Porkess, 1988:44). Confidence limits are the lower and upper boundaries of a confidence interval.

The discussion of sampling distributions indicates that, while measures of central tendency and dispersion are usually referred to as descriptive statistics, in

that they represent descriptive summaries of a dataset, it is also possible for them to be used inferentially. If they are measures derived from a sample then those sample measures may be treated as estimates of population parameters, and so an inference can be made about the value of those parameters.

A simple demonstration of this inferential use is a sampling exercise such as the selection of 200 farmers in a region, revealing a mean age ($\bar{x}$) of 50 years and a standard deviation ($s$) of 20 years. This information enables an estimate to be made of the standard error of the population mean, $SE$, where

$$SE_{\mu} = \widehat{SE}_{\mu} = SE_{\bar{x}} = \frac{\sigma}{\sqrt{n}} = \frac{\hat{\sigma}}{\sqrt{n}} = \frac{s}{\sqrt{n}} = \frac{20}{\sqrt{200}}$$

$$= 1.41$$

Thus, if a series of samples of 200 farmers had been taken and $\bar{x}$ calculated each time, a sampling distribution of $\bar{x}$ would have been generated, centred on $\mu$ and with a standard deviation of about 1.41.

Therefore there is a probability of 0.68 (or 68 per cent) that $\mu$ lies between $50 \pm 1.41$ years, i.e. 48.59 to 51.41 years (Figure 2.17a). If the size of sample was increased then this range would decrease (Figure 2.17b), as the larger the sample size, the smaller is the confidence interval. Such an increase in sample size may be deemed desirable so that a minimum size of sample will be sought in order to ensure that $\mu$ can be estimated within specified limits. Therefore, for sampling in small-scale geographical surveys, one way of determining the desired size of sample is to make use of the standard error (i.e. the standard deviation of the sampling distribution). For example, if the specified value of $SE_{\bar{x}}$ is $d$, then

$$SE_{\bar{x}} = d = \frac{\sigma}{\sqrt{n}} = \frac{\hat{\sigma}}{\sqrt{n}} = \frac{s}{\sqrt{n}}$$

i.e.

$$\sqrt{n} = \frac{s}{d}$$

or

(a)

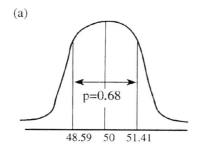

(b)

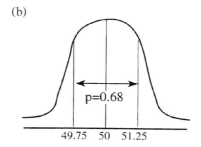

*Figure 2.17*   The Normal Distribution
(a) 68% confidence intervals for farmers' average age, $n = 200$; (b) 68% confidence intervals for farmers' average age, $n = 256$

$$n = \left(\frac{s}{d}\right)^2$$

In the present example, if the required value of $d$ is 1.25 rather than 1.41, then

$$n = \left(\frac{20}{1.25}\right)^2 = 16^2 = 256$$

Casley and Lury (1982:75–9) used another method of defining the required sample size, defining this size as a function of the variability of the characteristic measured, and of the degree of precision required. The variability can be expressed as the *coefficient of variation* ($V$) of the characteristic concerned, i.e. $V = \sigma / \bar{x}$ (where $\sigma$ = the standard deviation of the characteristic). The degree of precision has two components, $D$ and $K$, where $D$ = the largest acceptable difference between the value estimated from the sample and the true population value; and $K$ = the measure of confidence with which it can be stated that the result lies within the range represented by ±D. If $K$ is high, then the greater the degree of confidence. A value of $K = 2$ is often used as this represents the 95 per cent confidence interval or odds of 19:1. In contrast, a value of $K = 1$ gives odds of 2:1. The variables $n$, $K$, $V$ and $D$ are related in the formula

$$n = \frac{K^2 V^2}{D^2}$$

Thus as the desired precision ($D$) is increased, so the value of $n$ will be increased too. For example, if it is desirable to obtain an estimate of a given characteristic to within 8 per cent of the true population value, with 95 per cent confidence, and with a coefficient of variation of 0.5, then $K = 2$, $V = 0.5$, $D = 0.08$ and

$$n = \frac{2^2(0.5)^2}{(0.08)^2} = \frac{1}{0.0064} \simeq 156$$

(where the sign $\simeq$ means "approximately equal to"). If a higher level of precision is required, say with $D = 5$ per cent, then

$$n = \frac{2^2(0.5)^2}{(0.05)^2} = \frac{4(0.25)}{0.0025} = 400$$

As a general rule, for a sampling design to be more appropriate than a simple random sample, for the same sample size, it should yield estimates of population parameters with smaller standard errors. Alternatively, it should yield the same level of accuracy, but using a smaller sample size.

Samples should be accurate, that is they should avoid bias by providing unbiased estimates of the population mean, and they should be precise or efficient in that the sampling procedure should generate sampling distributions with small variances. A sample design that demonstrates a smaller variance of the sampling distribution of means, as compared with another sample design, is a superior one. Ultimately, though, the final sample size utilised in any research project is a compromise between cost, desired accuracy, time and ensuring sufficient numbers for realistic analysis of subgroups in a population.

## The Poisson Distribution

Like the binomial distribution, the *Poisson distribution* is applicable to discrete data. Named after its discoverer, a French mathematician, the Poisson distribution applies to situations in which there are rare events which occur as "points" within long periods of time or space. For example, earthquakes, tsunamis and catastrophic floods are events for which the probability of them not occurring at a particular time is very high and the probability of their actual occurrence is very low (Gumbel, 1958). Similarly, if we are dealing with the location of factories, shopping malls or robberies, there are an almost infinite number of locations where such phenomena could occur, even within a single city, compared with the limited number of locations where they actually do occur. In such situations, the probability distribution for the variable concerned was demonstrated by Poisson to be given by

$$P(x) = \frac{e^{-\mu}\mu^x}{x!} \qquad (2.1)$$

where $x = 0, 1, 2, \ldots, \mu > 0$, and e = the constant 2.7183. This can also be expressed as

$$P(x) = \frac{\lambda^x e^{-\lambda}}{x!}$$

where $\lambda$ = the average density or average occurrence of $x$ in a given space or time.

For the Poisson distribution the mean, $\mu = \lambda t$, where $\lambda$ = the average number of occurrences in time $t$ or in a given area $t$. Also, the variance of the distribution is equal to $\mu$.

The appearance of the distribution varies considerably according to the value of $\mu$, as shown in Figure 2.18. It approximates the binomial distribution if the binomial parameter $p$ is small.

Two typical situations to which the Poisson distribution is applicable are the occurrence of hazards, such as accidental deaths, and the location of points in space, e.g. shopping malls in an urban area. For example, Table 2.12 records the number of farm equipment-related deaths of farmworkers in an area over a 50-year period. The total number of deaths is 28, so that the average number of deaths per year from this cause is $28/50 = 0.56$, i.e. although each event (each accidental death) is a discrete single entity, the average per year can still be a fractional value less than one. This actual distribution can be compared with the one predicted by the Poisson probabilities, using equation (2.1) above, e.g.

$$P(x = 2) = \frac{0.56^2}{2!}(2.7183)^{-0.56}$$

$$= \frac{0.31}{2}(0.57) = 0.088$$

As the value of $\lambda$ increases, so the Poisson distribution becomes more symmetrical and approximates to the normal distribution. When this occurs, deviations about the Poisson mean may be expressed by $z$ values, i.e.

$$z = \frac{x - \mu}{\sigma} = \frac{x - \lambda}{\sqrt{\lambda}}$$

where $\mu$ = normal distribution mean, $\sigma$ = normal distribution standard deviation, $\lambda$ = Poisson distribution mean, $\sqrt{\lambda}$ = Poisson distribution standard deviation, and $x$ = an individual observation.

These differences between the values predicted by a theoretical probability distribution and those associated with actual events reflect the presence of non-random forces occurring in "real life". The binomial, normal and Poisson distributions all assume that there are random variables consisting of independent observations scattered randomly about the mean, with no non-random forces that could concentrate events into specific ranges or exclude them from others. In reality such non-random forces do occur and hence concentrations can be produced. However, the significance of differences between actual and theoretical distribu-

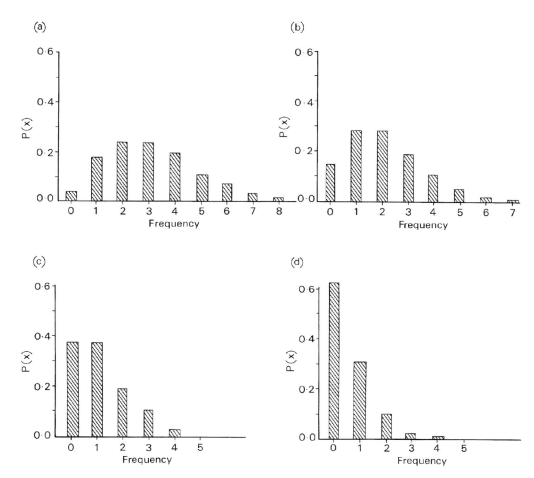

*Figure 2.18*   The Poisson Distribution
(a) $\lambda = 3.0$, (b) $\lambda = 2.0$, (c) $\lambda = 1.0$, and (d) $\lambda = 0.5$

*Table 2.12*   Accidental Deaths of Workers on Farms in a Rural Area

| Deaths | Number of Years This Number of Deaths Reported |
|:---:|:---:|
| 0 | 33 |
| 1 | 9 |
| 2 | 6 |
| 3 | 1 |
| 4 | 1 |
| 5 | 0 |
|  | $n = 50$ |

tions can be tested statistically as demonstrated in both the following chapter and, using the Poisson distribution, in Chapter 9. It is such statistical testing that enables a wide variety of hypotheses to be investigated.

# 3

# TESTING HYPOTHESES

## HYPOTHESES AND THE TESTING OF HYPOTHESES

Geographers have utilised the word "hypothesis" in cavalier fashion. Some have used it to postulate specific, directional relationships between phenomena; others to state more general relationships; and others "equate it with question, explanation, conclusion, contention, assumption and model" (Newman, 1973:22). These different uses have posed problems regarding the notion of *hypothesis testing* in geography. However, in terms of using statistical techniques to test a hypothesis, the following definition is generally accepted as a valid starting point: "A scientific hypothesis is a general proposition about all the things of a certain sort. It is an empirical proposition in the sense that it is testable by experience; experience is relevant to the question as to whether or not the hypothesis is true, i.e. as to whether or not it is a scientific law" (Braithwaite, 1953:2). In other words, a hypothesis is a statement in the form of an unproven theory.

There are many examples of geographers using hypothesis testing to advance their understanding of the relationships between phenomena. However, before considering the nature of the statistical testing of hypotheses, it should be recognised that it is an approach that has been problematic, partly through deficiencies in the formulation of hypotheses and in their testing. For example, tests have frequently been unconnected to a substantial body of theory, so that, even when allied to statistical methods, relatively little has been gained.

Geographers have often made speculative investigations using hypothesis testing, but have weakened the effectiveness of such work by ignoring basic characteristics of their enquiries. For example, hypothesis testing has been used extensively to focus upon the relationship between two particular variables, but often to the exclusion of other variables, placing too much onus on simple bivariate relationships. Other criticisms include a failure to appreciate the full range of tests at the disposal of the analyst and the broader charge that geographers have used hypothesis testing to investigate the trivial (Harvey, 1984).

Testing of hypotheses lies at the heart of the scientific method described in Chapter 1, and it has played a major part in research based on this method. Its role is summarised as follows (Salmon, 1986:273):

> From a general hypothesis and particular statements of initial conditions, a particular predictive statement is deduced. The statements of initial conditions, at least for the time, are accepted as true; the hypothesis is the statement whose truth is at issue. By observation we determine whether the predictive statement turned out to be true. If the predictive consequence is false, the hypothesis is disconfirmed. If observation reveals that the predictive statement is true, we say that the hypothesis is confirmed to some extent. A hypothesis is not, of course, conclusively proved by any one or more positively confirming instances, but it may become highly confirmed. A hypothesis that is sufficiently confirmed is accepted, at least tentatively.

In applying this method a statement must be capable of verification, if it is to be accepted as correct, or falsification to determine that it is incorrect (see Amedeo and Golledge, 1975:22–74; Hanfling, 1981). Statistical testing of hypotheses produces probabilistic statements about given situations, based on the *principle of induction*, that is the derivation of general statements from accumulated observation of specific instances and the projection of a regularity in future instances (see Table 3.1). This principle can be described as follows (Chalmers, 1976:5):

> If a large number of A's have been observed under a wide variety of conditions, and if all those observed A's without exception possessed the property B, then all A's have the property B.

Both this type of *inductive reasoning* (inferring a general law or principle from the observation of particular instances) and also *deductive reasoning* (from the general to the particular) are incorporated within the scientific method: the inductive procedure from facts to laws and theories is followed by a process of deduction to predictions and explanations, from which laws and theories may be proven (see Figure 1.1). However, the reliance upon induction can present certain problems.

In simple operational terms, for the statistical testing of hypotheses, the number of observations forming the basis of a generalisation must be large, the observations should be repeated under a variety of conditions and no observation should contradict the derived universal law. Both human and physical geographers face the problem that the laboratory in which hypotheses are tested is usually the "uncontrolled" laboratory of the real world. Therefore it is frequently

*Table 3.1*   Deductive and Inductive Logic

**Deduction**

An argument is deductively valid if and only if it is impossible that its conclusion is false while its premises are true.

Deduction can be sound or unsound. An argument is either deductively valid or it is not.

**Induction**

An argument is inductively strong if and only if it is improbable that its conclusion is false while its premises are true, and it is not deductively valid. The degree of inductive strength depends on how improbable it is that the conclusion is false while the premises are true.

There are degrees of inductive strength. Inductive logic must measure the inductive strength of arguments.

There are no universally accepted rules for constructing inductively strong arguments; no general agreement on a way of measuring the inductive strength of arguments; no precise, uncontroversial definition of inductive probability.

Deductive and inductive logic are not distinguished by the different types of arguments with which they deal but by the different standards against which they evaluate arguments.

Arguments deductively valid

Degrees of inductive strength

Worthless

**Hume's problem**

If we attempt to rationally justify scientific induction by use of an inductively strong argument, we are in the position of having to assume that scientific induction is reliable in order to prove that scientific induction is reliable.

*Source*: Skyrms (1966).

impossible to control contingent conditions sufficiently to be in a position to perform a hypothesis test with any hope that its results will not be equivocal (Minnery, 1981). In effect, a myriad of outside influences may impinge upon the variables being examined in a hypothesis test, thereby both affecting the nature of the relationship between these variables and complicating the interpretation of empirical results.

The process of induction occurs without a guarantee that the sample being examined is a representative one, as the nature of geographical problems may limit the number of observations available and the "real world" may not easily replicate laboratories in which observations are readily repeated. For example, the "untrue" statement that "all swans are white" could be accepted on the basis of millions of observations of swans in Europe, but it would still be an incorrect hypothesis as black swans *do* exist in other parts of the world (Popper, 1972:27–39). Similarly, observations of cities in the Developed World could lead to general "laws" that could then be disproven in the Developing World (Berry, 1973). This is a problem concerning the quality and representative nature of the sample.

There is even an implication that induction itself is problematic as "induction cannot provide proof of statements induced" (Hume, 1965). This is sometimes referred to as *Hume's problem* (Magee, 1973:21–2). Deductive reasoning cannot be used to substantiate an inductive argument, but using an inductive argument presupposes that induction is sound! Popper's (1968) answer to Hume's problem has been adopted in the use of hypothesis testing which incorporates the *principle of falsification*: "If a statement is logically capable of being disproved but has not yet been shown to be wrong then, in simple terms, it can be considered scientific" (Minnery, 1981:36). So, for a hypothesis to be capable of falsification (and therefore suitable for scientific testing), it must be clearly stated, unambiguous and precise (containing a high information content), and the conditions under which it could be rendered as false must be established.

The chief benefit of this method is that a standard procedure is available to test observable "facts", no matter how these facts may have been filtered through human prejudice, theory, ideology and beliefs. Therefore speculative conjectures and theories built upon detailed observation can be accommodated and subjected to a process of testing under the principle of falsification. In practice this has been translated into the application of statistical testing of hypotheses to generate probabilistic statements about the theories being tested.

This method is known as *critical rationalism*, in which refutation or falsification, rather than validation, of a hypothesis is sought (Haines-Young and Petch, 1980; Marshall, 1985). A single refutation means that a hypothesis must be rejected in its present form. The classical test methodology utilised for this purpose does have certain shortcomings (as described below). Nevertheless, for proponents, its attraction is its perceived embodiment of a set of logically consistent, universal and unchanging procedures used to discover "the truth". It is a method that assumes that order can be derived from the apparent complexity of the world, but, and this is often ignored by its critics, the order is not absolute but is expressed only in degrees of certainty and probabilities. Even so, it is an approach that has often been referred to as *absolutism* (e.g. Curry, 1985) and contrasts with the relativism that places emphasis upon human decision-making and the context of human actions.

Two types of hypothesis may be identified:

1. An unrestricted hypothesis in which the actual hypothesis being tested represents a large number of similar situations (e.g. "all birds have wings").
2. A restricted hypothesis which is only relevant to the context within which it is being tested (e.g. "visitors to the Edinburgh Festival and Fringe have a better appreciation of the location of famous buildings in the city than other tourists").

Most of the testing of hypotheses by geographers has been of the latter form so that, usually, the notion of particular events being accounted for as examples of a general law has been avoided (Johnston, 1986a:88). In practice, the testing of restricted hypotheses has enabled geographers to gain greater understanding of certain events, generally producing results that can then feed into evaluations of particular limited theorising. This type of testing therefore yields a restricted result that deals with outcomes of particular sets of conditions, known as contingently related conditions, rather than focusing upon generalities. Yet, statistical hypothesis testing by geographers has been criticised for its implicit support for general laws underlying human behaviour: that is, regarding people as objects acting according to predetermined rules and with replicability of actions and outcomes accepted (Cloke et al, 1991:13–20).

The "limited" approach of statistical hypothesis testing can be contrasted with many of the arguments made during the Quantitative Revolution that there are general laws of spatial behaviour from which come general patterns of spatial behaviour (e.g. Haggett, 1965; Morrill, 1970a). This notion of general laws underlies many of the models adopted by geographers in the 1960s, such as those by von Thunen, Christaller and Burgess, but can be criticised on a number of grounds. The main critique charges that the general laws ignore the character of human behaviour, overlook the existence of certain vital underlying structures (e.g. government controls) and treat the world as an unchanging laboratory in which laws are always obeyed. In practice, much of the statistical hypothesis testing performed by geographers has focused on "laws" of a far more limited form, emphasising contingently related conditions, especially referring to the relationship between phenomena in a given location or under particular circumstances. Furthermore, it has been spatial irregularities in the "real world", as opposed to the world of models and general laws, that have usually been the subject of hypothesis testing by geographers. Indeed, much of geographers' statistical testing of hypotheses has involved hypotheses only loosely connected with well-articulated theories or models .

Statistical tests of hypotheses have taken the form of determining whether an observed outcome, from a sample in which the chance of selection of each individual is known, is or is not the result of chance. If the test then rules out "chance", for a given level of statistical significance, this advances empirical knowledge about the population from which the sample was drawn, but only for the particular situation at hand. Therefore, if the situation under scrutiny is limited, then knowledge may have been advanced only slightly by this form of analysis. Furthermore, little may have been gained by way of explaining the outcome of the test, especially as most geographical uses of formalised hypothesis testing have only made what Johnston (1983:15), drawing upon Ayer (1964:11), refers to as "weakly-verified statements" expressed in terms of probabilities. These statements have expressed the likelihood of particular outcomes being due or not due to chance. This and the other limitations described above have led to a number of very strong criticisms of statistical hypothesis testing. Harvey (1989b:212), for example, argues that "it proved . . . very difficult to evolve any real theoretical augmentation with . . . mathematical languages and even more difficult to apply positivist standards of verification and falsification under conditions where the phenomena being studied looked more like a continuous stream of historical–geographical evolution". Nevertheless, statistical testing of hypotheses, embedded firmly in the replicable and easily recognised framework of scientific methodology, remains a powerful analytical tool with a number of advantages over other approaches to the "testing" of theoretic formulations. The chief advantages are replicability, the use of probabilistic conclusions, and avoidance of certain individual prejudices and dogmas through reliance on a repeatable and transferable method.

## STATISTICAL TESTING OF HYPOTHESES

### Basic Procedures

It was only after a series of studies in the USA in the 1950s, which concentrated on the use of correlation and regression (see Chapter 4), that geographers began to give greater attention to more formalised statistical hypothesis testing and to the use of such testing as a means of generating "geographical laws". This was accompanied by a closer approximation to the systematic application of positivist methods, with a clearer sequence of analytical stages followed:

1. Statement of the problem, which could include formulation of theory and hypotheses, and use of operational definitions (e.g. the social class of a household was frequently translated into the occupation of the male "head of household", so that terms such as professional and semi-skilled would be used).
2. Collection of data, using a range of sampling techniques.
3. Description of data, using tables, graphs and descriptive statistics.
4. Analysis of data, including testing of hypotheses.

With respect to the latter, it often proved relatively easy to formulate a hypothesis as a statement of anticipated conclusions or an unproven theory, but the mechanics of its statistical testing could be quite problematic. Undoubtedly, some of the complexities were overlooked by geographers until the "watershed" publication of Harvey's (1969) *Explanation in geography* which highlighted several areas of difficulty. This has not eliminated all violation of underlying assumptions of either hypothesis testing in general or of a specific test. However, there has been a growing awareness of the limitations of statistical hypothesis testing, accompanied by arguments about the consequences of violating particular requirements.

Statistical testing of hypotheses makes use of probabilistic language and probability theory, usually utilising the language developed by Neyman and Pearson (Neyman, 1950; Neyman and Pearson, 1967) in which a set of rules are defined by which a hypothesis may be accepted or rejected. So the events under examination, such as shopping behaviour, migration, income disposal, are conceptualised in terms of basic probability language. These events are investigated by sampling from a statistical population to which inferences are then made in terms of probabilistic statements.

As summarised by Harvey (1969:276–83), the logical sequence of statistical hypothesis testing provides several areas of difficulty when geographical data are utilised:

1. Specification of the *geographical hypothesis*: it may be difficult to use probabilistic language if the situation being examined is a purely deterministic one, for example in the case of von Thunen's agricultural location theory.
2. Specification of the *sampling procedures*: samples must be selected so as to avoid bias (see "Sampling" in Chapter 2).
3. Specification of the *appropriate test procedure*: see "Non-parametric tests" below.
4. Specification of the *target (geographical) population*: this is crucial as researchers must be able to give a clear answer to the question "to what does the inference apply once the hypothesis test is completed?" – in most cases this is clear, but, as the following section shows, it is a question that has caused controversy.
5. Specification of *inferences*: this should be fairly straightforward once a particular test has been selected, but it is important at the conclusion of a test to review the original hypothesis and the procedures followed so that the researcher is clear about the nature of the inferences being drawn from the test.

## Inferences from Samples and Populations

There are two basic situations to consider:

1. In examining if a relationship exists between $x$ and $y$ (e.g. annual income of head of household, and distance of journey to work of head of household in a particular city), sample values of $x$ and $y$ could be obtained from larger populations of "$x$"s and "$y$"s. The relationship indicated in the sample would be obtained and subjected to a test of significance in order to assess the likelihood of that relationship existing in the population as a whole. In this situation the population needs to be strictly defined, and the inference that is drawn from the hypothesis test is then applied only to that population.

2. In examining if a relationship exists between $x$ and $y$, information for the entire statistical population might be obtained (for all the households in the city). In this case one argument is that it is not possible to draw an inference from this situation because the relationship established is factual; it applies to the population and therefore there is no larger population to which an inference can be made (Galtung, 1967:361–70). In commenting on this situation, Gould (1970) totally rejected the notion of applying significance tests "to see if the result could have occurred by chance".

Summerfield (1983) summarises the arguments pertaining to these situations by citing seven ways in which it may be possible to make a probabilistic statement from consideration of a statistical population:

(a) *Temporal-sample argument*. The population is regarded as a sample in time, and therefore conclusions drawn from it may be inferred to past and future states of that population (Court, 1972). However, there is still the problem of the length of time over which such inferences may be valid.

(b) *Spatial-sample argument*. The findings from one population are inferred to apply to other areas for which no observations are available. This ignores lack of an *a priori* definition of the population and has no basis in the theory of statistical inference.

(c) *Measurement-error argument*. This assumes that population data contain random and independent measurement errors which may be modelled by standard probability distributions, and hence significance tests can be applied to such data. In reality, though, this supposition of randomness and independence is hard to substantiate.

(d) *Arbitrary-measure-of-target-phenomena argument*. This proposes that the population data actually only represent one way of measuring a broader "target population". This implies that several other types of measurement of the population may be possible, but statistical inference provides no basis for assessing the significance of such measures as compared with all other forms of measurement.

(e) *Modifiable-areal-unit argument*. This focuses upon the fact that the particular spatial categorisation of data encountered in the population may be only one amongst an almost infinite number that are actually or conceptually possible. A particular arrangement of areal units might be considered to be a random arrangement, and therefore probabilistic statements could be attached to data pertaining to such an arrangement. In practice, though, this randomness is illusory as many boundaries of areal units have a systematic relationship to the phenomena being studied, simply through a myriad of economic, social and political factors linking both the phenomena and the zoning system used for aggregating the data (e.g. states, counties, parishes). Other problems associated with the concept of modifiable areal units are considered in Chapter 4.

(f) *Vetting argument*. When applied to data for a population, statistical inference is often intended as a "vetting procedure" to distinguish between relationships which, on the basis of a random model, would be likely to occur and those which would be unlikely. This has the implied assumption that the population is at least a potentially randomly generated phenomenon. Furthermore, use of significance testing in this fashion is a dubious method for judging the importance of relationships, especially given that the size of large populations will have a major effect upon the calculation of a statistic (see the penultimate subsection "Uses of the normal distribution" in Chapter 2).

(g) *Stochastic-process argument*. The population is regarded as just one outcome of some stochastic (random) process. Therefore the population can be equated with stochastically generated data or a theoretical sampling distribution. This argument has been used by some sociologists and economists (e.g. Blalock, 1979:242), but it has also been argued that such use of significance tests is "at best completely unassessable, since the extent to which the assumption of randomness is met is unknown" (Morrison and Henkel, 1970:306).

Therefore, at the outset of the hypothesis test, it is very important to specify the limits of the population and also what constitutes an individual or element in that population. Without this, confusing and inaccurate inferences may be drawn at the conclusion of the test. Furthermore, fundamental consideration should be given to the relevance of any test to the situation at hand.

Summerfield (1983:148) cautions that "statistical inference in geography should be confined to those contexts which are known to satisfy the requirements of statistical theory", but Hay (1985a) is willing to consider the use of statistical hypothesis testing in a wider range of cases, specifically in three instances:

1. The *classical sample case*, where data are sample data and inferences are being made about a finite and definite population from which the sample was drawn.
2. The *errors case*, where data are not sample data but in which the test allows inferences to be made about the chance that observed effects have arisen purely from the cumulative effect of errors. In this case the inference is confined to the set of individuals studied, and the conclusion takes the form that the effect observed is unlikely to have arisen merely from some chance arrangement of errors.
3. The *probabilistic hypothesis case*, in which statements investigated attribute probabilities as properties of the phenomena under study, and in which the researcher tests the agreement between the statements and reality. The inference is confined to the set of individuals studied.

## The Null Hypothesis

Statistical hypothesis testing begins with a formal statement of the hypothesis itself. In fact, there are three types of hypothesis that can be stated. First, there is a general statement of the *research hypothesis*, which geographers have tended to apply in a relatively restricted form and which may or may not be directly associated with a well-defined body of theory. A typical example is, "there is a reason to believe that productivity varies between one group of businesses (*A*) and another group (*B*)", perhaps based on the knowledge of production conditions in the two groups. This can be translated into the so-called *alternative hypothesis* ($H_1$), in this example taking the form: "productivity in *A* is not the same as productivity in

*B*". But the hypothesis that is effectively employed in statistical testing is the *null hypothesis* ($H_0$) which frequently takes the form "there is no difference ...￼"; in this example, "there is no difference between productivity per business in group *A* and productivity per business in group *B*", i.e. $H_0$: $A = B$. The object of the hypothesis test then becomes to accept or reject this null hypothesis for a specific level of statistical significance.

Therefore the hypothesis test is asking whether any apparent difference between two sets of sample data on productivity is a statistically significant difference or the result of mere chance related to the particular sample of businesses for which data were obtained. Statistical significance in this type of situation can be regarded as an extreme improbability that any difference between the two sets of data could have occurred by chance. In other words, if we had access to information on data for the whole population of firms then the difference between the two groups would still be apparent. The determination of "statistical significance" can be described with reference to the following account of the selection of different types of hypothesis test.

## Selecting Non-Parametric and Parametric Tests

Once $H_0$ has been formulated there are various tests that might be utilised, the selection of the most appropriate one to use being partly determined by the type of data in the samples. A *parametric hypothesis test* requires data on the interval or ratio scales whilst *non-parametric tests* operate on ordinal-scale (ranked) or nominal-scale (categorised) data. Given that the majority of geographical data are on the interval or ratio scales, the foremost reason for converting this into ranks or categories, and thereby permitting the use of a non-parametric test, is because the original interval- or ratio-scale data fail to conform to three crucial requirements made by the parametric tests:

- The population from which the sample(s) is (are) drawn is (are) normally distributed.
- The population is *homoscedastic*, i.e. samples

drawn from the population should have equal variances. Violation of this assumption would be produced by samples that are heteroscedastic, i.e. having different variances.

- Observations are independent of one another, i.e. it should not be possible to order individual observations or elements in the population in space and time and have a better than random chance of predicting values of some when the values of others are known.

For some time geographers generally assumed that the third of these requirements was fulfilled automatically, and so problems associated with independence of observations and *spatial autocorrelation* were either unknown or were ignored (see Chapter 9). There has tended to be a greater recognition that non-normality and heteroscedasticity in the population can lead to incorrect results being obtained when applying parametric tests to interval- or ratio-scale data drawn from such populations. Yet, this has not always deterred geographers from using parametric tests. This may be because these tests are felt to be "more powerful" than their non-parametric counterparts or because violations of the tests' assumptions are not felt to be very important.

The view that parametric tests are preferable to non-parametric ones is reflected in the use of *transformations* to convert into a suitable form those samples not conforming to the assumptions of the parametric tests. In particular, these transformations have been utilised frequently for normalisation, i.e. to convert non-normally distributed data into a normal form (e.g. Robinson, 1976). The commonly used transformations are described in the penultimate subsection in Chapter 2, "Uses of the normal distribution". However, these procedures can be questioned on the grounds that they alter fundamental characteristics of the data, and can make it extremely difficult to interpret tests and other statistical procedures using such transformations. Norcliffe (1977:68) argues that if it is possible to convert a non-normal distribution to an approximately normal form without too much effort then the effort is probably warranted. However, if it is difficult to remove skewness or other irregularities then it is better to use

the appropriate non-parametric test. Over time, normalisation has been appreciated as a less important prerequisite for statistical testing, and the non-parametric tests have assumed a greater popularity.

Non-parametric tests have five advantages over their parametric counterparts (Siegal, 1956):

- Probability statements obtained from most non-parametric tests are exact probabilities, regardless of the shape of the probability distribution.
- Non-parametric tests can deal with very small samples.
- Non-parametric statistics can utilise data on a variety of measurement scales.
- There are suitable non-parametric tests for analysing samples taken from several different populations.
- Non-parametric tests are usually easier to apply than parametric ones because they involve more limited calculations (though the use of computers and electronic calculators has restricted this advantage), and they do not make assumptions about the background population from which samples are drawn.

Despite these advantages, the loss of information involved in using ordinal- or nominal-scale data means that occasionally non-parametric tests will give a different result to that from a parametric test performed on the same data. This gives rise to the term *power efficiency* which provides a means of comparing the effectiveness of different tests. The power efficiency examines the amount of increase in sample size that is necessary to make test $B$ as powerful as test $A$, where the term "powerful" refers to the ability of the test to evaluate $H_0$ (Siegal, 1956:20−1). The power efficiency can be measured using,

$$\text{power efficiency of test } (B) = \frac{n_a}{n_b} \times 100\%$$

where test $A$ is the most powerful known test of its type, and test $B$ is another test that can be used on the same research design and which is just as powerful with a sample size of $n_b$ cases as is test $A$ with a sample size of $n_a$. So if test $B$ has a power efficiency of 80 per cent when compared with test $A$, then test $B$ would require a sample size of 40 to give it the same power efficiency of test $A$ operating on a sample size of 32. Therefore it is possible to avoid having to make some of the assumptions made by the most powerful tests, the parametric, and yet not lose power by just using a non-parametric test with a larger sample size. The power efficiencies of the principal non-parametric tests when compared with their most powerful equivalent tests are given in Table 3.2. Hence the non-parametric Mann–Whitney $U$ test has a power efficiency of 95.5 per cent compared with the parametric Student's $t$ test. In effect, 4.5 times out of 100 Mann–Whitney will accept or reject the null hypothesis when Student's $t$ does the opposite while operating on the same size of sample.

So the power of a test refers to its ability to state correctly whether a hypothesis is true or false. This ability can be influenced by the size of samples under consideration, and hence a test's efficiency can be considered in terms of the increase in sample size that is required to increase the power of a test. Therefore non-parametric tests of low power efficiency require a larger sample to reach the same degree of accuracy as a parametric test.

## Applying The Test

When performing a hypothesis test, a *test statistic* is calculated based upon the sampling distribution associated with the particular statistic, where a sampling distribution is the distribution that would be obtained by drawing all possible samples of a given size from a specified population. The character of these distributions varies from test to test as illustrated in Figure 3.1, though some, for example Student's $t$ test, resemble the normal curve. When performing a hypothesis test the sampling distribution of a test statistic is examined, e.g. $\chi^2$, $t$, $F$. For each of the tests the actual procedure employed is very simple:

1. State $H_0$.
2. Specify the desired *significance level* $\alpha$.
3. Perform calculations to generate the test statistic.
4. Compare the test statistic with the critical value in the sampling distribution.

*Table 3.2*    The Power Efficiency of Statistical Hypothesis Tests

| Statistical Tests | Efficiency (%) |
|---|---|
| Binomial (dichotomised continuous data) | 63 to 95% ($n = 6$) for any test using equivalent data |
| Fisher's | the most powerful of the one-tailed tests |
| Kendall's | 91% compared with Pearson's product-moment coefficient and Spearman's rank coefficient |
| Kolmogorov–Smirnov, one sample | superior to $\chi^2$ for relatively small samples |
| Kolmogorov–Smirnov, two sample | 96% compared with Student's $t$ |
| Kruskal–Wallis | 95.5% compared with Snedecor's $F$ |
| Mann–Whitney | 95.5% compared with Student's $t$ |
| Wilcoxon | 95.5% compared with Student's $t$ |

Based on Siegal (1956).

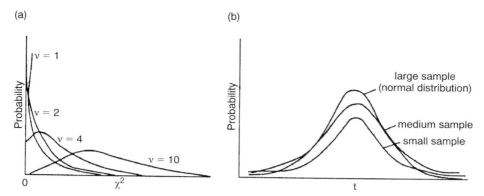

*Figure 3.1*  Sampling Distributions of Test Statistics
(a) $\chi^2$ and (b) Student's $t$

As shown in Figure 3.2, the specification of $\alpha$ is vital, and should be stated at the start of any hypothesis test. The value of $\alpha$ determines the extent of the *region of rejection*, shown by the shaded areas in Figure 3.2. If the calculated value of the test statistic falls within this region of rejection, $H_0$ is rejected. The critical value is the value of the statistical distribution at the point at which the region of rejection begins.

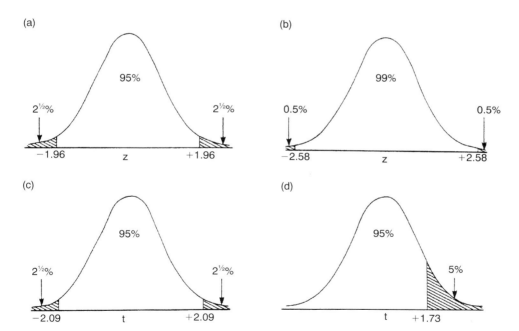

*Figure 3.2*  Confidence Limits, Regions of Rejection, and One- and Two-Tailed Hypothesis Tests
(a) Normal distribution, two-tailed test with significance level = 95%; (b) normal distribution, two-tailed test with significance level = 99%; (c) Student's $t$ test, two-tailed test with significance level = 95%; (d) Student's $t$ test, one-tailed test with significance level = 95%

For example, in the normal distribution portrayed in Figure 3.2a, the critical values of $z$ are $\pm 1.96$. If the calculated value of $z$ (the test statistic) exceeds these critical values then the null hypothesis being tested must be rejected.

If a null hypothesis takes the form "no difference ..." ($A = B$), the region of rejection is divided between the two ends of the sampling distribution, and hence the term *two-tailed test* (Figure 3.2a, b and c). If a null hypothesis takes the form "$A$ is not greater than/less than B" ($A \ngtr B$, $A \nless B$), the hypothesis is said to be directional, and a *one-tailed test* is performed in which only one end of the sampling distribution is considered (Figure 3.2d). The convention established by Fisher (1956) is for $\alpha = 0.05$ (5 per cent) or 0.01 (1 per cent), so that the statement made at the conclusion of the hypothesis test is of the form "at the 0.01 significance level $H_0$ can be rejected". In this case the calculated value exceeds the critical value at the 0.01 (99 per cent) confidence limit. This critical value is determined from statistical tables and varies according to the size of sample being studied.

The importance of the specification of $\alpha$ is illustrated in Figure 3.2c and d. In the two-tailed Student's $t$ test shown in Figure 3.2c, if the calculated value of $t$ is 1.7, this is clearly less than the critical value 2.09 at the 0.025 level: there are no grounds for rejecting $H_0$. However, if the value is 2.35, this is greater than the critical value 2.09, and it can be argued that there are fewer than five chances in every 100 (i.e. $P < 0.05$) that this result could have occurred by chance. It is still possible, though, to reject $H_0$ at the 0.01 level as the calculated value of 2.35 is less than the critical value of 2.86 for the 0.01 level. If the null hypothesis had taken the form "$A$ is not greater than $B$" then a one-tailed test would apply, as shown in Figure 3.2d. In this example a calculated value of $t > 1.73$ falls into the region of rejection and therefore would indicate rejection of $H_0$ at the 0.05 level of significance.

For most purposes in social science research the statement that "there is less than one chance 100 that $A$ is different from $B$" ($P < 0.01$) is an acceptable one. This might not be the case, though, in medical experimentation where probabilities of less than one in 1000

might be more desirable, as in testing the side-effects of a new drug. In such cases $\alpha$ would be reduced below 0.01. As $\alpha$ is reduced so the probability of being wrong when rejecting the null hypothesis is reduced. This error is referred to as a *type-one error*, but conversely, as a type-one error is reduced then so *type-two errors* are increased, in which the null hypothesis is wrongly accepted. Thus the specification of $\alpha$ should really be determined by the consequences of incurring a type-one or type-two error. In medical testing the type-two error needs to be avoided at all costs and therefore is made very small. For most geographical work the adoption of Fisher's criterion suffices.

The power function ($p$) of a test is defined as the probability that a test statistic rejects the null hypothesis conditional to some real value $p$, where $p$ is the probability of occurrence of an event (Brouwer and Nijkamp, 1984):

$$p = 1 - B$$

where $B$ = probability of a type-two error, i.e. accepting $H_0$ when it is incorrect. So if $B$ is small ($< 0.001$) then $p$ will approximate to 1.

Box (1953) introduced the term *robustness* to describe the ability of a statistical test to avoid a type-one error despite violation of basic assumptions when performing the test, as in using non-normal data in a parametric test. He favoured the use of parametric tests rather than non-parametric ones on the grounds that parametric tests were robust, especially when sample sizes were equal (Box and Anderson, 1955). However, investigations of the effects of non-normality using computer simulations have shown that certain parametric tests are quite sensitive to non-normality (Mitchell, 1974). This is evidence supporting either the use of normalisation procedures on non-normal data prior to the application of parametric tests or the use of non-parametric tests.

## NON-PARAMETRIC TESTS

As shown in Table 3.3 there are several different types of non-parametric hypothesis test, their utility being

*Table 3.3*    Statistical Hypothesis Tests

| No. of Samples | Non-Parametric | | Parametric |
| --- | --- | --- | --- |
| | Nominal Data | Ordinal Data | Interval Data |
| 1 | $\chi^2$<br>Sign test<br>Kolmogorov–Smirnov test<br>Runs test | Wilcoxon signed-rank test | z test<br>t test |
| 2 | $\chi^2$<br>Kolmogorov–Smirnov test | Mann–Whitney $U$ test<br>Wilcoxon rank-sum test | t test |
| > 2 | $\chi^2$ | Kruskal–Wallis $H$ test | Snedecor's $F$ test |

dependent upon the particular situation under investigation. The ones employed most frequently by geographers have been the chi-squared test, the Kolmogorov–Smirnov test, the Mann–Whitney $U$ test and the Wilcoxon signed-rank and rank-sum tests. The characteristics of the tests listed in Table 3.3 are now outlined.

## The Sign Test

The oldest of the formal statistical tests is the *sign test*, for which there is evidence of its use in the early eighteenth century (Arbuthnott, 1710). The test is aptly named for it operates on data that are in the form of "+" and "−" signs. Table 3.4 illustrates a common example of such data in the form of information on measurement error. The sign test provides a formal test of the hypothesis that there is an approximately equal number of "+"s and "−"s. The test statistic, $S$ = whichever of the "+"s and the "−"s has the smaller number. In Table 3.4, $S = 12$, as there are 12 "−"s and 34 "+"s.

H$_0$ takes the form: the number of "+"s = the number of "−"s, i.e. "there is no difference between the number of '+'s and the number of '−'s". If H$_0$ is true then every one of the $n$ observations in the sample data gives rise to a "+" or a "−" sign, each with a probability of 0.5. Given a random sample then the distribution of the "+" and "−" signs follows the

binomial distribution as described towards the end of Chapter 2. Therefore all probabilities associated with values of $S$ can be calculated directly from

$$P(X = S) = \binom{n}{x} p^x q^{n-1}$$

For the data in Table 3.4,

$$P(12) = \binom{46}{12}\left(\tfrac{1}{2}\right)^{12}\left(\tfrac{1}{2}\right)^{34}$$

This is an extremely small probability, making $P(12)$ effectively equal to zero. Therefore, H$_0$ can be very confidently rejected: there is a clear bias towards +ve errors in the observations on the map, and this could not have occurred by chance.

It is usually impossible to find critical values corresponding exactly with $\alpha = 0.05$ or 0.01. However, as shown in Table 3.5, when tabulating critical values for the test, the table indicates the largest critical value whose significance level is no greater than the nominal figure. For the above example, where $S = 12$ for $n = 46$, the value of $S$ is below the critical value at the 0.01 level.

If $n > 50$ the distribution of $S$ approximates to the normal distribution and so

$$S = \mu - z\sigma - 1/2$$

where

*Table 3.4*   Sample Data on the Errors in Edward's Map of Angus, Scotland, 1678

| Observation Number | Degrees of Error | Rank | Observation Number | Degrees of Error | Rank |
|---|---|---|---|---|---|
| 1 | +8.13 | 42 | 24 | +1.13 | 9 |
| 2 | +8.13 | 42 | 25 | +1.13 | 9 |
| 3 | +0.13 | 2.5 | 26 | +7.13 | 39 |
| 4 | +9.13 | 44.5 | 27 | −3.87 | 22.5 |
| 5 | −0.87 | 6 | 28 | −3.87 | 22.5 |
| 6 | −6.87 | 38 | 29 | +4.37 | 26.5 |
| 7 | +2.87 | 17.5 | 30 | +4.37 | 26.5 |
| 8 | +0.13 | 2.5 | 31 | +1.63 | 12 |
| 9 | +17.23 | 46 | 32 | +4.13 | 24.5 |
| 10 | +9.13 | 44.5 | 33 | +4.13 | 24.5 |
| 11 | −4.87 | 29.5 | 34 | +4.63 | 28 |
| 12 | +8.13 | 42 | 35 | +2.63 | 16 |
| 13 | +6.13 | 35.5 | 36 | −0.87 | 6 |
| 14 | +3.13 | 19.5 | 37 | +6.63 | 37 |
| 15 | +5.13 | 31 | 38 | −0.37 | 4 |
| 16 | +2.13 | 14.5 | 39 | +0.01 | 1 |
| 17 | −0.87 | 6 | 40 | +2.13 | 14.5 |
| 18 | +1.13 | 9 | 41 | +5.63 | 32 |
| 19 | −2.87 | 17.5 | 42 | +7.37 | 40 |
| 20 | +3.37 | 21 | 43 | −5.87 | 33.5 |
| 21 | −4.87 | 29.5 | 44 | +3.13 | 19.5 |
| 22 | +1.87 | 13 | 45 | +6.13 | 35.5 |
| 23 | −5.87 | 33.5 | 46 | +1.37 | 11 |

"+"s = 34; "−"s = 12

Sum of ranks for + ve errors = 832.5

Sum of ranks for − ve errors = 248.5

$H_0$ = there is no difference between the number of positive errors and the number of negative errors

$$\alpha = 0.05$$

Refer to Appendix C for critical values (S) of the sign test. The 46 signs include only 12 minuses, and so $S = 12$. Tabulated value of S for $n = 46$, $\alpha = 0.5$ in a two-tailed test is 15. This is more than the calculated value and so therefore reject $H_0$: there is a difference between the number of positive errors and the number of negative errors at the 0.05 level.

$\mu = np = n/2$ and $\sigma = (\sqrt{n})/2 = \sqrt{[np(1 - p)]}$.

For a two-tailed test with $\alpha = 0.05$, $n = 50$, $z = 1.96$ (see Table 2.11),

$$S = \frac{n}{2} - \frac{z\sqrt{n}}{2} - \frac{1}{2} \quad \text{(in integer form)}$$

$$= \frac{50}{2} - \frac{1.96\sqrt{50}}{2} - \frac{1}{2}$$

$= 25 - 1.96 \times 3.54 - 0.5$

$= 17.56$

$= 17$    (which is the corresponding value given in Appendix C)

For an "advanced" application of the sign test see the work of Cliff (1970) in which the test was used for evaluating the goodness of fit between maps of area-based data.

*Table 3.5* Data for One-Sample (Goodness-of-Fit) $\chi^2$ Test

| Country of Birth | Nos. in Lothian Region | Percentage of All Foreign-Born in Scotland |
|---|---|---|
| England | 52796 | 61.20 |
| Wales | 2292 | 2.62 |
| Northern Ireland | 4915 | 7.22 |
| Irish Republic | 3790 | 5.56 |
| Old Commonwealth | 2650 | 3.14 |
| New Commonwealth (plus Pakistan) | 7496 | 8.15 |
| Other EC countries | 4293 | 4.28 |
| Other European countries | 2124 | 2.02 |
| Other foreign-born | 5395 | 5.81 |
| | 85751 | 100 |

$H_0$ = there is no difference between the proportions of foreign-born residents in Lothian Region and those in Scotland as a whole (data from Population Census)

$$\alpha = 0.05$$

$$\text{Degrees of freedom } (v) = (\text{rows} - 1) = 8$$

To calculate expected values (e) in this case, we have to calculate the distribution of the total frequency (85751) as if it were distributed according to the percentages for each country of birth, e.g.

$$\text{for } o = 52796, \quad e = 85751 \times 61.20\% = 52480$$

For each observed value (o) this gives:

| o | e | (o − e) | (o − e)² | (o − e)²/e |
|---|---|---|---|---|
| 52796 | 52480 | 316 | 99856 | 1.90 |
| 2292 | 2247 | 45 | 2025 | 0.90 |
| 4915 | 6191 | −1276 | 1628176 | 263.00 |
| 3790 | 4768 | −978 | 956484 | 200.60 |
| 2650 | 2693 | −43 | 1849 | 0.69 |
| 7496 | 6989 | −507 | 257049 | 36.78 |
| 4293 | 3670 | 623 | 388129 | 105.76 |
| 2124 | 1732 | 392 | 153664 | 88.72 |
| 5395 | 4982 | 413 | 170569 | 34.24 |
| | | | $\sum = \chi^2 =$ | 732.59 |

From Appendix D, $\chi^2_{8,0.05} = 15.51$

Calculated value of $\chi^2$ is more than this, so therefore reject $H_0$: at the 0.05 level there is a difference between the proportions of foreign-born citizens in Lothian and in all of Scotland.

## The Chi-Squared ($\chi^2$) Test

Of all the non-parametric tests the one with the greatest utility is the *chi-squared ($\chi^2$) test*, and this is reflected in its popularity within geographical research. It can be applied to one, two or more independent samples, so that it can be used to see if one set of data corresponds to a particular type of distribution, as well as comparing two or more samples. Partly offsetting this flexibility, because of its very simple requirements, it is less powerful than some other non-parametric tests.

The chi-squared distribution was formulated in 1876 by Friedrich Robert Helmert and "rediscovered" in 1900 by Karl Pearson (1900). The critical values they calculated for the $\chi^2$ test are shown in Appendix D. The test operates on data on the nominal scale, in the form of frequencies of observations in discrete categories or classes. So it can be suitable for comparing a sample set of observed categorical frequencies with a predetermined set, known as the expected frequencies. Such a test is referred to as a one-sample test or a test of goodness of fit, as the distribution of an observed set of frequencies is compared with an expected set based on a predetermined distribution. A typical example is shown in Table 3.5. Frequently the predetermined or hypothesised set refers to the notion of data conforming to a particular probability distribution such as the Poisson (Table 3.6) or normal (Table 3.7) distributions.

The chi-squared test can also operate on two samples arranged in a *contingency table* (Tables 3.8 and 3.9) in which two samples of observations are compared with each other rather than with a particular statistical distribution. The null hypothesis ($H_0$) takes the form "there is no difference between the two samples", inferring that they were drawn from the same statistical population. The difference between this type of application and that of the one-sample case is in the method by which the expected frequencies and degrees of freedom (see below) are derived.

In a two-sample case, as shown in Table 3.8, the expected frequencies ($e_{ij}$) are calculated from:

$$e_{ij} = \frac{\text{row total} \times \text{column total}}{\text{grand total}}$$

The test statistic, $\chi^2$, is calculated from

$$\chi^2 = \sum \frac{(o_{ij} - e_{ij})^2}{e_{ij}}$$

where $o_{ij}$ = the observed frequencies in a category, and $e_{ij}$ = the expected frequencies in a category.

The form of the $\chi^2$ distribution does not depend precisely upon the number of rows ($r$) and columns ($c$) in the contingency table, but on the value ($r - 1$)($c - 1$). This value is known as the *number of degrees of freedom ($v$)*: or the number of expected frequencies that have to be inserted in the table before being able to calculate the remaining expected frequencies by subtraction from the row and column totals, as illustrated in Figure 3.3. If the expected frequencies for each of the shaded cells are known, then it is possible to calculate the remaining expected frequencies by subtraction from the appropriate row and column totals. So the degrees of freedom represent the number of cells we are "free" to fill given the marginal totals. In Figure 3.3 the number of degrees of freedom

$$v = (c - 1)(r - 1)$$
$$= (6 - 1)(5 - 1)$$
$$= 5 \times 4 = 20$$

If $v = 1$, as in the simple $2 \times 2$ contingency table shown in Table 3.8, then *Yates's correction* must be applied. This is the subtraction of 0.5 from the absolute value of ($o - e$), usually signified by the notation $|o - e|$. The absolute value means that the sign of the result of the calculation of ($o - e$) is ignored when 0.5 is subtracted.

For the $\chi^2$ distribution to be applicable, the total number of observations should exceed 20 and the expected frequency in any one category should be greater than five. Also, if the degrees of freedom are $v > 1$, then $\chi^2$ should only be used if less than one-fifth of the cells in the frequency table have expected

*Table 3.6* Data for a One-Sample (Goodness-of-Fit) $\chi^2$ Test to See Whether Data Conform to the Poisson Distribution

| No. of Floods $n$ | Frequency $o$ |
|---|---|
| 0 | 4 |
| 1 | 7 |
| 2 | 11 |
| 3 | 15 |
| 4 | 8 |
| 5 | 5 |
| 6 or more | 7 |
| | $\sum = 57$ |

$H_0$ = the observed distribution of episodes of flooding is not different from the Poisson distribution

$$\alpha = 0.05$$

Degrees of freedom $(v) = (\text{rows} - 1) = 6 - 1 = 5$
(no. of rows condensed to conform to requirement of $e > 5$ per cell)

$p$ = Poisson probabilities

| $n$ | $o$ | $p$ | $e = p(o_i)$ | $(o - e)$ | $(o - e)^2$ | $(o - e)^2/e$ |
|---|---|---|---|---|---|---|
| 0/1 | 11 | 0.185 | 10.55 | 0.45 | 0.20 | 0.02 |
| 2 | 11 | 0.217 | 12.37 | −1.37 | 1.88 | 0.15 |
| 3 | 15 | 0.223 | 12.71 | 2.29 | 5.24 | 0.41 |
| 4 | 8 | 0.173 | 9.86 | −1.86 | 3.46 | 0.35 |
| 5 | 5 | 0.107 | 6.10 | −1.10 | 1.21 | 0.19 |
| 6/6+ | 7 | 0.0942 | 5.37 | 1.63 | 2.66 | 0.50 |
| | $\sum = 57$ | | $\sum = 57$ | | | $\sum = \chi^2 = 1.62$ |

From Appendix D, $\chi^2_{5,0.05} = 11.07$

Calculated value of $\chi^2$ is less than this, so therefore accept $H_0$: at the 0.05 level there is no difference between the observed distribution of episodes of flooding and that predicted by the Poisson distribution.

frequencies $< 5$ and if no cell has an expected frequency of $< 1$. To meet this requirement, cells can be aggregated, though this means the analysis loses a certain amount of detail. However, if an arbitrary selection of categories is used, this can produce misleading results (Ballantyne and Cornish, 1979).

The commonest use of a two-sample $\chi^2$ test is when two samples are measured on a dichotomous variable, such as male:female, yes:no, arable:pasture, under 50 years:above 50 years (e.g. Robinson, 1986). This generates a table of frequencies such as that shown in Table 3.9.

For a situation in which there are more than two samples, known as a *k*-sample case and a multiple

*Table 3.7*   Data for a One-Sample (Goodness-of-Fit) $\chi^2$ Test to See Whether Data Conform to the Normal Distribution

| Long Axis (cm) | Frequency |
|---|---|
| < 6.50 | 8 |
| 6.50–8.49 | 7 |
| 8.50–10.49 | 12 |
| 10.50–12.49 | 3 |
| 12.50–14.49 | 4 |
| 14.50–16.49 | 4 |
| 16.50–18.49 | 4 |
| > 18.50 | 8 |
| | $\sum = n = 50$ |

$$\bar{x} = 12.24, \; s = 6.37$$

$H_0 =$ the observed distribution of the long axes of stones in a sample is not different from the normal distribution

$$\alpha = 0.05$$

Degrees of freedom $(v) = (\text{rows} - 1) = 4 - 1 = 3$
Nb: no. of rows condensed to conform to requirement of $e > 5$ per cell

To calculate expected frequencies $(e_i)$ we need to use $z$ tables:

$$z = \frac{\text{class boundary} - \bar{x}}{s}$$

For the first cell,

$$z = \frac{6.5 - 12.24}{6.37} = -0.903$$

From $z$ tables (Appendix B), this equals a probability of 0.316. The area outside this $= 0.5 - 0.32 = 0.184$

*Table 3.7*   (*Continued*)

Therefore $e = (0.184)\,n = 9.2$

| o | e | $(o - e)$ | $(o - e)^2$ | $(o - e)^2/e$ |
|---|---|---|---|---|
| 8 | 9.2 | −1.2 | 1.44 | 0.16 |
| 7 | 4.8 | 2.2 | 4.84 | 1.01 |
| 12 | 5.7 | 6.3 | 39.69 | 6.97 |
| 7 | 12.3 | −5.3 | 28.09 | 2.29 |
| 8 | 10.0 | −2.0 | 4.00 | 0.40 |
| 8 | 8.1 | −0.1 | 0.01 | 0.001 |
| | | | | $\sum = \chi^2 = 10.831$ |

From Appendix D, $\chi^2_{3,0.05} = 7.82$

Calculated value of $\chi^2$ is less than this, so therefore accept $H_0$: at the 0.05 level there is no difference between the observed distribution of the long axes of stones and that predicted by the normal distribution.

contingency table, the $\chi^2$ test operates as described above for two samples, but the number of columns $(k)$ is increased. For a multiple contingency table, $\chi^2$ does not provide estimates of the "effects" of the table variables on each other, and, for three or more variables (i.e. a multivariate situation), the mathematics becomes complex. If $\chi^2$ is still deemed appropriate for analysis of multivariate contingency tables, a *log-linear model* can be incorporated in the analysis. This converts the frequencies of the contingency table to probabilities, takes the logarithm of each probability and expresses it as the sum of a number of effects, as described in "Logistic, logit and probit models" in Chapter 6. Then hypotheses specifying that the effects of certain variables, or combinations of variables, are zero can be tested.

## The Kolmogorov–Smirnov Test

An alternative test to $\chi^2$ in one- and two-sample situations is the *Kolmogorov–Smirnov test*, devised by A.N. Kolmogorov (1933) as a goodness-of-fit test and by N.V. Smirnov (1939) as a two-sample application. Essentially it was designed as a quick-and-easy graphical test ideally suited to testing in a relatively rough-and-ready manner in the field. In its simplest form it compares sample $A$ with either sample $B$ or with a particular distribution by portraying them as cumulative frequency distributions, using the same intervals or classifications for both distributions, and examining the maximum difference between the two (Table 3.10 and Figure 3.4). A large difference $D$ indicates that the two distributions do not belong to the same statistical population:

$$D = \max (x_o - x_e)$$

Table 3.8 A 2 × 2 Contingency Table for a $\chi^2$ Test

| Origin | Under 30s | Over 30s | Row Total |
|---|---|---|---|
| Urban | 5 | 12 | 17 |
| Rural | 20 | 13 | 33 |
| Column total | 25 | 25 | 50 |

$H_0$ = there is no difference in the origins of the two age groups

$$\alpha = 0.05$$

Degrees of freedom $(v) = (\text{rows} - 1)(\text{columns} - 1) = (2 - 1)(2 - 1) = 1$

$$\text{Expected frequency}(e) = \frac{\text{row total} \times \text{column total}}{\text{grand total}}$$

For top left and top right cells,

$$e = \frac{17 \times 25}{50} = 8.5$$

For bottom left and bottom right cells,

$$e = \frac{33 \times 25}{50} = 16.5$$

Tabulate, applying Yates's correction:

| o | e | $|(o - e)|$ | $|(o - e)|^2$ | $(o - e)|2/e$ |
|---|---|---|---|---|
| 5 | 8.5 | 3 | 9 | 1.06 |
| 12 | 8.5 | 3 | 9 | 1.06 |
| 20 | 16.5 | 3 | 9 | 0.55 |
| 13 | 16.5 | 3 | 9 | 0.55 |
| | | | $\sum = \chi^2 =$ | 3.22 |

From Appendix D, $\chi^2_{1, 0.05} = 3.84$

Calculated value of $\chi^2$ is less than this, so therefore accept $H_0$: at the 0.05 level there is no difference between the origins of migrants of different age groups.

where $x_o$ = the observed relative cumulative frequency, and $x_e$ = the expected relative cumulative frequency.

$D$ can be subjected to a significance test and therefore the test is comparable with others. Critical values for $D$ are given in Appendix E. According to Goodman (1954), for large samples ($n > 50$),

Table 3.9 A 10 × 2 Contingency Table for a $\chi^2$ Test

| Age Category | Nos. Economically Active | | Row Totals |
|---|---|---|---|
| | East Lothian | Edinburgh City | |
| 21–24 | 81 | 80 | 161 |
| 25–29 | 75 | 81 | 156 |
| 30–34 | 76 | 79 | 155 |
| 35–39 | 81 | 83 | 164 |
| 40–44 | 85 | 86 | 171 |
| 45–49 | 84 | 87 | 171 |
| 50–54 | 81 | 84 | 165 |
| 55–59 | 73 | 77 | 150 |
| 60–64 | 45 | 53 | 98 |
| 65–69 | 12 | 14 | 26 |
| Totals | 693 | 724 | 1417 |

$H_0$ = there is no difference between the proportions of the population who are economically active in Edinburgh and in East Lothian (data from sample of 100 people in each location for each age category)

$$\alpha = 0.05$$

Degrees of freedom $(v) = (\text{rows} - 1)(\text{columns} - 1) = 10 \times 1 = 10$

$$\text{Expected frequency}(e) = \frac{\text{row total} \times \text{column total}}{\text{grand total}}$$

e.g. for the first value of $o(= 81)$,

$$e = \frac{161 \times 693}{1417} = 78.7$$

*continued overleaf*

$$\chi^2 = 4D^2[(n_1 n_2)/(n_1 + n_2)]$$

where $\chi^2$ has a sampling distribution with the number of degrees of freedom $(v) = 2$ if $n_1$ and $n_2 > 30$. Therefore $\chi^2$ tables can be used to ascertain the significance of $D$ for large samples. Tables designed by Lilliefors (1967) can be used when employing a Kolmogorov–Smirnov test for normality when $\mu$ and $\sigma$ are unknown.

Comparisons between the $\chi^2$ and Kolmogorov–Smirnov tests, made by Mitchell (1971) and by Ilbery (1977a), showed that the latter test was a useful alternative to $\chi^2$ when the assumptions of $\chi^2$ were not

Table 3.9    (Continued)

For each observed value (o) this gives:

| o | e | (o − e) | (o − e)² | (o − e)²/e |
|---|---|---|---|---|
| 81 | 78.7 | 2.3 | 5.29 | 0.067 |
| 80 | 82.3 | −2.3 | 5.29 | 0.064 |
| 75 | 76.3 | −1.3 | 1.69 | 0.022 |
| 81 | 79.7 | 1.3 | 1.69 | 0.021 |
| 76 | 75.8 | 0.2 | 0.04 | 0.001 |
| 79 | 79.2 | −0.2 | 0.04 | 0.001 |
| 81 | 80.2 | 0.8 | 0.64 | 0.008 |
| 83 | 83.8 | −0.8 | 0.64 | 0.008 |
| 85 | 83.6 | 1.4 | 1.96 | 0.023 |
| 86 | 87.4 | −1.4 | 1.96 | 0.022 |
| 84 | 83.6 | 0.4 | 0.16 | 0.002 |
| 87 | 87.4 | −0.4 | 0.16 | 0.002 |
| 81 | 80.7 | 0.3 | 0.09 | 0.001 |
| 84 | 84.3 | −0.3 | 0.09 | 0.001 |
| 73 | 73.4 | −0.4 | 0.16 | 0.002 |
| 77 | 76.6 | 0.4 | 0.16 | 0.002 |
| 45 | 47.9 | −2.9 | 8.41 | 0.176 |
| 53 | 50.1 | 2.9 | 8.41 | 0.169 |
| 12 | 12.7 | −0.7 | 0.49 | 0.039 |
| 14 | 13.3 | 0.7 | 0.49 | 0.037 |

$$\sum = \chi^2 = 0.668$$

From Appendix D, $\chi^2_{10,0.05} = 18.31$

Calculated value of $\chi^2$ is less than this, so therefore accept $H_0$: at the 0.05 level there is no difference between the proportions of the population who are economically active in Edinburgh and in East Lothian.

met. For example, Kolmogorov–Smirnov does not have an expected frequency requirement and this is a significant advantage when the sample size is small or is scattered through a relatively large number of discrete categories (and therefore does not meet the $\chi^2$ requirement of > 5 expected frequencies per cell).

There may be cases where the cells of a contingency table contain values that are very small, some that are equal to 0, and where the variables studied are not divided into the same interval classifications. If so neither the $\chi^2$ nor the Kolmogorov–Smirnov test is appropriate as their requirements are not fulfilled. However, it is possible to employ the *Goodman and Kruskal tau test* (Goodman and Kruskal, 1954),

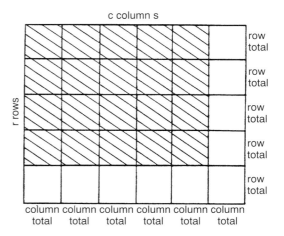

*Figure 3.3*    Illustration of Degrees of Freedom for the 6 × 5 Contingency Table

though it has been little used by geographers; it is a measure of the predictability of one variable in a cross-tabulation when the second variable is known (Mitchell, 1974:64; Ilbery, 1977a).

## The Mann–Whitney *U* Test

This test, published in the 1940s by H.B. Mann and D.R. Whitney (1947), operates on ordinal data, comparing two samples which do not have to be of equal size. It can be used for small samples ($n < 30$) and is the most powerful non-parametric equivalent to the parametric Student's $t$ test. For sample sizes between 8 and 20 the test statistic is calculated from:

$$U_1 = n_1 n_2 + \frac{n_1(n_1 + 1)}{2} - R_1$$

where $n_1$ = size of first sample, $n_2$ = size of second sample, $R_1$ = sum of ranks in the first sample,

$$U_2 = n_1 n_2 + \frac{n_2(n_2 + 1)}{2} - R_2$$

where $R_2$ = sum of ranks of the second sample and,

$$U = U_1 \text{ if } U_1 < U_2$$

*Table 3.10*   Sample Fenland Farm Sizes for a Kolmogorov–Smirnov One-Sample Test

|  | Farm Size (ha) | | | |
| --- | --- | --- | --- | --- |
|  | 0–19.9 | 20–39.9 | 40–59.9 | 60–79.9 |
| No. of holdings ($n = 25$) | 16 | 5 | 3 | 1 |
| Cumulative frequency | 16 | 21 | 24 | 25 |
| Cumulative proportion | 0.64 | 0.84 | 0.96 | 1.00 |
| Percentage of holdings in E. Anglia | 50 | 29 | 14 | 7 |
| Cumulative proportion | 0.5 | 0.79 | 0.93 | 1.00 |
| Difference between cumulative proportions | 0.14 | 0.05 | 0.03 | 0 |

Maximum difference, $D = 0.14$

$H_0 =$ there is no difference between the distribution of farm sizes in the Fens and the distribution of farm sizes in East Anglia

$$\alpha = 0.05$$

From Appendix E, $D_{25, 0.05} = 0.27$

Calculated value of $D$ is less than this, so therefore accept $H_0$: at the 0.05 level there is no difference between the distribution of farm sizes in the Fens and the distribution of farm sizes in East Anglia.

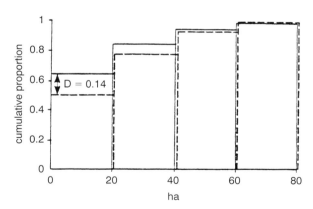

*Figure 3.4*   The Kolmogorov–Smirnov Test

$$U = U_2 \text{ if } U_2 < U_1$$

For larger samples the distribution of $U$ approximates to the normal and a $z$ score can be calculated (Shaw and Wheeler, 1994:159–60). Two examples of the test are given in Tables 3.11 and 3.12, in which it is applied to small samples. Critical values of $U$ are given in Appendix F.

*Table 3.11*  Infant Mortality Rates in a Sample of Major Cities in the USA, for Use in a Mann–Whitney $U$ Test

Infant deaths per 1000 live births

| Caucasians ($n_1 = 9$) | Rank | Non-Caucasians ($n_2 = 7$) | Rank |
|---|---|---|---|
| 16.6 | 8 | 13.6 | 15 |
| 21.5 | 6 | 14.9 | 12 |
| 25.5 | 4 | 14.8 | 13 |
| 27.7 | 2 | 15.1 | 11 |
| 24.6 | 5 | 16.1 | 8 |
| 28.1 | 1 | 15.9 | 9.5 |
| 26.0 | 3 | 14.3 | 14 |
| 21.4 | 7 | | |
| 15.9 | 9.5 | $\sum = R_2 = 82.5$ | |
| $\sum = R_1 = 45.5$ | | | |

$H_0$ = there is no difference in the frequency of infant mortality between Caucasians and non-Caucasians in major cities in the USA

$$\alpha = 0.05$$

$$U_1 = n_1 n_2 + \frac{n_1(n_1 + 1)}{2} - R_1 = 9 \times 7 + \frac{9(9 + 1)}{2} - 45.5$$

$$= 63 + \frac{90}{2} - 45.5 = 62.5$$

$$U_2 = n_1 n_2 + \frac{n_2(n_2 + 1)}{2} - R_2 = 9 \times 7 + \frac{7(7 + 1)}{2} - 82.5$$

$$= 63 + \frac{56}{2} - 82.5 = 8.5$$

$U$ = (the smaller of $U_1$ and $U_2$) = 8.5

From Appendix F, $U_{9,7,0.05} = 12$

The calculated value of $U$ is less than this. However, as $U$ is defined to be whichever count would be expected to be small when $H_1$ is true, then small values of $U$ are significant. Therefore at the 0.05 level reject $H_0$: there is a difference between the infant mortality rates of Caucasians and non-Caucasians.

## The Wilcoxon Tests

There are several variants of a test designed by F. Wilcoxon (1945, 1949). One, known as the *Wilcoxon signed-rank test*, extends the basic sign test

*Table 3.12*  Income Data for the Medical Profession for a Sample of UK Towns, for a Mann–Whitney $U$ Test

Sample annual earnings (£000) (general practitioners and dentists)

| Town A ($n_1 = 11$) | Rank | Town B ($n_2 = 12$) | Rank |
|---|---|---|---|
| 32.5 | 6 | 34.9 | 12 |
| 48.5 | 23 | 25.8 | 1 |
| 45.6 | 22 | 33.5 | 7 |
| 43.8 | 20 | 31.7 | 4 |
| 45.5 | 21 | 31.0 | 3 |
| 33.8 | 8 | 30.4 | 2 |
| 36.9 | 16 | 37.1 | 17 |
| 38.9 | 18 | 34.0 | 9 |
| 36.5 | 15 | 34.4 | 10 |
| 35.1 | 14 | 34.5 | 11 |
| 35.0 | 13 | 40.5 | 19 |
| | | 32.5 | 5 |
| $\sum = R_1 = 176$ | | $\sum = R_2 = 100$ | |

$H_0$ = there is no difference in the annual earnings of the medical profession in towns A and B

$$\alpha = 0.05$$

$$U_1 = n_1 n_2 + \frac{n_1(n_1 + 1)}{2} - $$

$$R_1 = 11 \times 12 + \frac{11(11 + 1)}{2} - 176$$

$$= 132 + \frac{132}{2} - 176 = 22$$

$$U_2 = n_1 n_2 + \frac{n_2(n_2 + 1)}{2} - $$

$$R_2 = 11 \times 12 + \frac{12(12 + 1)}{2} - 100$$

$$= 132 + \frac{156}{2} - 100 = 110$$

$U$ = (the smaller of $U_1$ and $U_2$) = 22

From Appendix F, $U_{11,12,0.05} = 33$

The calculated value of $U$ is less than this. However, as $U$ is defined to be whichever count would be expected to be small when $H_1$ is true, then small values of $U$ are significant. Therefore at the 0.05 level reject $H_0$: there are differences between earnings in the medical profession in town A and town B.

described just above. Provided the data are approximately symmetric, the test operates on ranked data and so is not such a drastic reduction of data as its representation as "+"s and "−"s. As shown in Table 3.4, the data are ranked, ignoring whether they are positive or negative, from 1 for the smallest to $n$ for the largest, where $n$ = the number of observations (note how tied ranks are dealt with). The *Wilcoxon signed-rank statistic* ($T$) is then calculated as the sum of the ranks of either the positive differences or the negative differences, depending on which a one-tailed hypothesis test suggests should be the smaller.

In the example given in Table 3.4, $H_0$ takes the form "the number of positive errors is not greater than the number of negative errors", for $\alpha = 0.05$. Therefore it is the sum of the ranks of the negative errors that is calculated, i.e. $T = 248.5$. As with Table 3.5 for the sign test, the critical values for the Wilcoxon test in Appendix G are given in terms of small values of the signed-rank statistic. So for $\alpha = 0.05$, $n = 46$, and $T = 248.5$: this value of $T$ is well below the tabulated value of $T = 389$. So the null hypothesis can be confidently rejected: there is a bias towards positive errors in the measurements for the map of Angus.

Wilcoxon's test involving two samples is known as the *Wilcoxon rank-sum test* and proceeds in identical fashion to the signed-rank test described above. There is also a version of the test designed for matched pairs, known as the *Wilcoxon signed-rank test for matched pairs*. An example of this is given in Table 3.13.

As with the Mann–Whitney test, the sampling distribution of the Wilcoxon test statistic approaches the normal distribution as the sample sizes become large. However, both Mann–Whitney and Wilcoxon tend to be used most often when dealing with small samples. The main differences between the two tests are that, for matched pairs, firstly, Wilcoxon only operates on samples of equal size, and, secondly, Wilcoxon does not consider the actual ranks of the samples but examines a ranking of the differences between the values of the paired samples.

Table 3.13  Employment Data for a Wilcoxon Test for Paired Samples

Employment index for twinned towns

| Scottish Group A | French Group B | A − B | Rank A − B |
|---|---|---|---|
| 310 | 300 | 10 | 2 |
| 340 | 320 | 20 | 1 |
| 290 | 360 | −70 | 5 |
| 270 | 320 | −50 | 4 |
| 370 | 540 | −170 | 6 |
| 330 | 360 | −30 | 3 |
| 320 | 680 | −360 | 7 |
| 320 | 1120 | −800 | 8 |

High index = tends to full employment and high income
Low index = tends towards rising unemployment and low income

Sum of ranks for +ve values of A − B = 3
Sum of ranks for −ve values of A − B = 33

$$n = 8$$

$H_0$ = there is no difference in the employment indices of the twinned towns

$$\alpha = 0.05$$

The test statistic $T$ is the smaller of the sums of ranks. In this case this is the sum for +ve values of A − B = 3

From Appendix G, $T_{8,0.05} = 3$. Therefore at the 0.05 level reject $H_0$: there are differences in the employment indices of the twinned towns.

## The Kruskal–Wallis Test

The non-parametric version of Snedecor's $F$ test (see below) is the *Kruskal–Wallis one-way analysis of variance by ranks*, which operates on ordinal data. It uses the formula:

$$H_a = \left[ \frac{12}{N(N+1)} \sum^{k} \frac{R^2}{n} \right] - 3(N+1)$$

where $R$ = sum of ranks in each sample, $N$ = total number of observations (i.e. for all samples), $n$ = number of observations per sample, and $k$ = number of samples.

One of the assumptions of this test is that the samples are taken from continuous populations, so as to avoid the problem of tied observations. However, ties can occur, perhaps via rounding errors when recording observations or because the data were actually taken from discrete distributions. If there are only a small number of ties, a correction factor can be utilised. Once $H_a$ has been calculated the correction factor for tied ranks can be performed by dividing $H_a$ by $1 - \sum T/(N^3 - N)$, where, if $t$ = number of tied ranks, $T = \sum t^3 - t$. In this case, the Kruskal-Wallis statistic is calculated using,

$$H = \frac{H_a}{1 - \sum T/(N^3 - N)}$$

For this test, the data are ranked over all the observations irrespective of which sample they are in. If all the samples have $> 5$ individual observations then the distribution of $H$ approximates the $\chi^2$ statistic with $k - 1$ degrees of freedom. Alternatively, for very small sample sizes, and including unequal sizes of sample, special $H$ tables may be used (e.g. Neave and Worthington, 1988:392–4).

A typical example, using data on burglary rates in 30 randomly selected villages, is shown in Table 3.14. This example also shows the use of the correction factor for tied ranks.

## The Fisher Exact Probability Test

This is used for analysing either nominal or ordinal data with two small independent samples, when the observed frequencies from the two samples all fall into one or the other of two mutually exclusive classes (see Siegal, 1956:96–104). The observed frequencies can be represented in a $2 \times 2$ contingency table, a typical example of which is shown in Table 3.15. The test determines whether two groups (in this case Democrats and Republicans) differ in the proportion with which they fall into the two classifications (male and female). So, for this dataset, it is possible to determine if the Democratic and Republican votes differ significantly in terms of the gender basis of the vote.

*Table 3.14* Data on Burglary Rates in Villages, for a Kruskal–Wallis One-Way Analysis of Variance by Ranks

| | Location | | | | | | |
| North | | South | | East | | West | |
| Rate | Rank | Rate | Rank | Rate | Rank | Rate | Rank |
|------|------|------|------|------|------|------|------|
| 4.5 | 12 | 6.2 | 21.5 | 4.5 | 12 | 3.9 | 4 |
| 4.5 | 12 | 5.2 | 18.5 | 3.7 | 1 | 4.1 | 5 |
| 6.2 | 21.5 | 7.1 | 29.5 | 4.3 | 9 | 5.2 | 18.5 |
| 4.8 | 15.5 | 6.8 | 24.5 | 5.2 | 18.5 | 4.5 | 12 |
| 6.8 | 24.5 | 4.8 | 15.5 | 3.8 | 2.5 | 7.0 | 27 |
| 4.2 | 7 | 7.0 | 27 | 4.5 | 12 | 4.2 | 7 |
| | | 6.3 | 23 | 4.2 | 18.5 | 3.8 | 2.5 |
| | | 7.0 | 27 | 7.1 | 29.5 | 4.2 | 7 |

| $R_1 = 92.5$ | $R_2 = 186.5$ | $R_3 = 103$ | $R_4 = 83$ |
|---|---|---|---|
| $N_1 = 6$ | $N_2 = 8$ | $N_3 = 8$ | $N_4 = 8$ |

$$N = 30$$

$$k = 4$$

$H_0$ = there is no difference between burglary rates in villages in four selected regions of France

$$\alpha = 0.05$$

Degrees of freedom, $v = k - 1 = 4 - 1 = 3$

$$H_a = \frac{12K}{N(N+1)} - 3(N+1) \qquad K = \sum_{}^{k} \frac{R^2}{n}$$

First calculate $K$,

$$K = \frac{R_1^2}{N_1} + \frac{R_2^2}{N_2} + \frac{R_3^2}{N_3} + \frac{R_4^2}{N_4}$$

$$= \frac{(92.5)^2}{6} + \frac{(186.5)^2}{8} + \frac{(103)^2}{8} + \frac{(83)^2}{8}$$

$$= 7961.07$$

Substitute this value of $K$ into the formula for $H_a$

$$H_a = \frac{12(7961.87)}{30(30+1)} - 3(30+1) = 102.723 - 93 = 9.723$$

In effect this test assumes that, from a finite dataset, a specified overall frequency will occur by chance. The exact probability ($P$) of observing a particular set of frequencies in a $2 \times 2$ contingency table, when the marginal totals (i.e. the sums of the rows and columns) are fixed, is given by

*Table 3.14   (Continued)*

Then correct for tied ranks: first calculate $T$, $T = (t^3 - t)$

| | |
|---|---|
| $t$ for 12 has 5 observations, | $(t^3 - t) = 120$ |
| $t$ for 21.5 has 2 observations, | $(t^3 - t) = 6$ |
| $t$ for 15.5 has 2 observations, | $(t^3 - t) = 6$ |
| $t$ for 24.5 has 2 observations, | $(t^3 - t) = 6$ |
| $t$ for 7 has 3 observations, | $(t^3 - t) = 24$ |
| $t$ for 18.5 has 4 observations, | $(t^3 - t) = 60$ |
| $t$ for 29.5 has 2 observations, | $(t^3 - t) = 6$ |
| $t$ for 27 has 3 observations, | $(t^3 - t) = 24$ |
| $t$ for 2.5 has 2 observations, | $(t^3 - t) = 6$ |
| | $\sum = 258$ |

Use this value of $T$ in

$$H = \frac{H_a}{1 - \sum T/(N^3 - N)} = 1 - \frac{9.723}{258/[(30)^3 - 30]}$$

$$= \frac{9.723}{1 - 0.0096} = \frac{9.723}{0.99} = 9.82$$

From Appendix D, $\chi^2_{3,0.05} = 7.82$. This is less than the calculated value and therefore reject $H_0$: there is a difference between burglary rates in villages in the four selected regions of France.

*Table 3.15*   Data on Voting Preferences Amongst a Small Sample of People ($n < 30$) for a Fisher Exact Probability Test

| | Males | Females | Totals |
|---|---|---|---|
| Democrats | 7 A | 12 B | 19 |
| Republicans | 5 C | 4 D | 9 |
| | 12 | 16 | 28 |

$H_0 =$ there is no difference between Democratic and Republican voting preference with respect to the gender basis of the preference

$$\alpha = 0.05$$

For calculations, see text.

$$P = \frac{(A + B)!(C + D)!(A + C)!(B + D)!}{n!A!B!C!D!}$$

where $n =$ the total number of independent observations, and $A$, $B$, $C$ and $D$ are the values in the contingency table, as shown in Table 3.15. In this example,

$$P = \frac{19!9!12!16!}{28!7!12!5!4!} = \frac{24}{115} = 0.21$$

Therefore the probability of such a distribution of frequencies as appears in Table 3.15 is 0.21. This indicates that at the 0.05 level $H_0$ must be accepted, and there is no significant difference between the two groups.

In the above example a clear-cut answer is provided just on the basis of calculating the value of $P$ for one set of observed frequencies. However, for a full evaluation of $H_0$ the probability of this occurrence should be summed with the probability of all the more extreme possibilities by which $A$ and $B$ can sum to 19 and $C$ and $D$ can sum to 9. Such calculations would be extremely tedious, but statistical tables can be consulted as an easier alternative (e.g. Siegal, 1956:256–70). This test was used by Gregory (1976) on precipitation data for Wigan waterworks, Lancashire, to reveal certain periods of 10, 20 and 30 years as having significantly non-random patterns of precipitation.

As part of this work Gregory (1976) championed the use of statistical hypothesis tests on the grounds that they provide practical methods of testing theories and models. He also compared the use of hypothesis tests within human and physical geography, concluding that it had been human geography that had made greater use of hypothesis testing to test and question existing ideas and theories. Therefore he argued that the often-voiced view, that physical geography had less need of change in the light of the Quantitative Revolution because it was already more "scientific", was something of a myth. His own use of the Fisher test pointed to the growing awareness by the mid-1970s that parametric tests are not necessarily always the most appropriate to apply. Nevertheless, parametric statistics remain important, whether applied directly or to data that have been normalised through application of transforms such as the square root, logarithms or raising by a power.

## PARAMETRIC TESTS

### Student's *t* Test

This test was named after W.C. Gosset, an employee of the brewers Guinness, who developed it at a time when he was writing under the pen-name 'Student'. The test makes a comparison between sample means of two samples or compares the mean of one sample with that of a set distribution. The test statistic is $t = $ difference between sample means/standard error of the differences between sample means:

$$t = \frac{\bar{x} - \bar{y}}{SE_{(\bar{x} - \bar{y})}}$$

$$= \frac{\bar{x} - \bar{y}}{\hat{\sigma}_x^2 / n_x + \hat{\sigma}_y^2 / n_y}$$

$$= \frac{\bar{x} - \bar{y}}{\hat{\sigma}\sqrt{(1/n_x + 1/n_y)}}$$

To provide the estimates $\hat{\sigma}_x^2$ and $\hat{\sigma}_y^2$, $s_x$ and $s_y$ can be used to give a pooled best estimate $(\hat{\sigma})$ of the population standard deviation, which is usually unknown in most geographical applications:

$$\hat{\sigma} = \frac{s_x^2(n_x - 1) + s_y^2(n_y - 1)}{n_x + n_y - 2}$$

The number of degrees of freedom $= n_x + n_y - 2$.

The distribution of $t$, like $\chi^2$, is dependent upon the sample size. In the case of $t$, as the sample size (and the number of degrees of freedom) increases, then the distribution approximates more closely to the normal curve. If $n_x + n_y \geq 60$, the $t$ distribution approximates to the normal, and $z$ tables can be used (see Appendix H). Because it compares two sets of data, Student's $t$ test is commonly used for testing the significance of correlation coefficients (see Chapter 4). A typical example of Student's $t$, comparing the means of two independent samples, is shown in Table 3.16.

*Table 3.16*   Educational Data for a Student's *t* Test

Examination results (mean %)

| Schools in Town X | Schools in Town Y |
|---|---|
| 80 | 68 |
| 79 | 71 |
| 78 | 58 |
| 69 | 62 |
| 68 | 52 |
| 78 | 67 |
| 75 | 63 |
| 74 | 70 |
| 73 | 59 |
| 81 | 61 |
| $\bar{x} = 75.5$ | $\bar{y} = 63.1$ |
| $s_x = 4.50$ | $s_y = 5.97$ |
| $s_x^2 = 20.28$ | $s_y^2 = 35.66$ |

$n_x =$ number of observations in town X $= 10$
$n_y =$ number of observations in town Y $= 10$

$H_0 =$ there is no difference in the examination results obtained by schools in towns X and Y

$$\alpha = 0.05$$

Calculating $t$ involves two steps:

(a) Calculate $\hat{\sigma}$, the pooled best estimate of $\hat{\sigma}$:

$$\hat{\sigma} = \sqrt{\frac{s_x^2(n_x - 1) + s_y^2(n_y - 1)}{n_x + n_y - 2}}$$

$$= \sqrt{\frac{(20.28)9 + (35.66)9}{10 + 10 - 2}} = \sqrt{\frac{182.52 + 320.94}{18}}$$

$$= \sqrt{\frac{503.46}{18}} = \sqrt{27.97} = 5.29$$

(b) Insert value of $\hat{\sigma}$ into equation for $t$:

$$t = \frac{\bar{x} - \bar{y}}{\hat{\sigma}\sqrt{(1/n_x + 1/n_y)}} = \frac{75.5 - 63.1}{5.29\sqrt{(1/10 + 1/10)}}$$

$$= \frac{12.4}{5.29(\sqrt{0.2})} = \frac{12.4}{5.29 \times 0.45} = \frac{12.4}{2.38} = 5.21$$

From Appendix H, $t_{0.05, 18} = 2.10$.

Calculated value of $t$ is more than this, so therefore reject $H_0$: at the 0.05 level there is a difference between the examination performances of schools in town X and town Y.

## Analysis of Variance

Whilst Student's $t$ test and most of the non-parametric tests operate on one or two samples, *analysis of variance (anova)* operates on more than two samples. An anova is assessing whether the difference between several samples (usually referred to as groups) of data is significant or not. Such an assessment may often be essential before any consideration is given to what is causing any difference between the groups. As it is examining variance, as opposed to means (as in the case of Student's $t$), the calculations in an anova tend to be more complex for both parametric and non-parametric versions.

The parametric test statistic, *Snedecor's F*, is the ratio of the between-groups' variance to the within-groups' variance. Its critical values are shown in Appendix I. Essentially the test is determining whether differences between the groups are large when compared with the variation of values within the groups (see Figure 3.5). The analysis initially involves calculating three *sums of squares*:

1. The *total sum of squares* ($SS_t$). All the observations ($x_{ij}$) are treated as if they belong to one large sample (group) in order to obtain the total variance:

$$SS_t = \sum x_{ij}^2 - GT$$

where $SS_t$ = the total variance of all observations; $x_{ij}$ = the $i$th observation (or *replicate*) in the $j$th sample (group); $GT$ = the grand total,

$$GT = \frac{(\sum x)^2}{N} = \frac{(x_1 + x_2 + \ldots + x_m)^2}{N}$$

$m$ = the number of samples (groups) $n$ = the number of observations (replicates) in a sample (group); and $N$ = the number of observations (or the number of replicates per sample times the number of samples, i.e. $N = nm$).

2. The *between-groups' sum of squares* ($SS_a$). This is

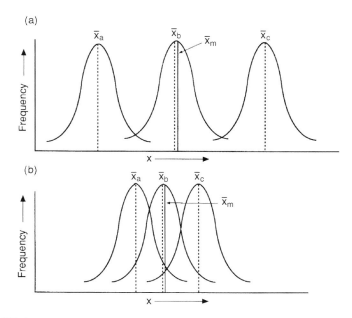

*Figure 3.5* Snedecor's $F$ Test
(a) Three distinct groups; (b) three overlapping groups, $x_a$, $x_b$ and $x_c$ = group means; $x_m$ = mean of all observations

the variance between the two or more groups being compared:

$$SS_a = \frac{(\sum x_{ij}^2)}{n} - GT$$

3. The *within-groups' sum of squares* ($SS_w$). This represents the difference between the total variation and the between-groups' variance:

$$SS_w = SS_t - SS_a$$

The relationships between these three are shown in Table 3.17. The hypothesis test assumes that

$$\bar{x}_j = \bar{x}_{ij} + y_i + e_j$$

where $\bar{x}_j =$ the mean value in sample $j$; $\bar{x}_{ij} = GT =$ the grand mean (i.e. of all the observations); $y_j =$ the variable "explaining" the variance; and $e_j =$ an error term, corresponding to the within-samples' variance.

Anovas may be of greater complexity than this basic form, which is the simplest type and is referred to as a *one-way anova* in which variance is attributed to one chosen explanatory variable. A one-way anova is asking whether the explanatory variable accounts for a significant proportion of the total variance. In the example given in Table 3.18, the explanatory variable is variation in migration rates. As for other tests, the test statistic is compared with a probability distribution, in this case the $F$ distribution (Appendix I).

Typically, one-way anovas have been used in assessments of whether any apparent difference between the results of a succession of similar experiments is due to real differences of a substantive nature or merely through measurement imperfections (and hence the number of groups is often referred to as the number of replications or treatments). Because of their applicability to experimental research, one-way anovas have been used extensively in the physical and biological sciences.

Greater complexity can be introduced by increasing the number of explanatory variables to two in a *two-way anova* in which the structure of the data being analysed is often referred to as a *factorial design*. This type of anova is commonly used in quality control, product development and the testing of biological specimens. In a two-way anova, for every level of the initial explanatory variable (or factor) there are now observations for every level of the second variable (or factor) and vice versa. Thus a two-way anova is used to estimate the effect of two explanatory variables upon another variable which is termed the dependent variable as it is dependent upon the explanatory variables. For instance, Silk (1981) gives the example of a survey of shoppers' perceived knowledge of the location of grocery stores in Oxford, in which both position in the life-cycle and access to a motor car were hypothesised as the two explanatory factors accounting for variations in perception (see Table 3.19). Respondents were placed in one of three categories on the basis of car availability, and in one of three life-cycle categories.

As shown in Table 3.19b, a two-way anova showed that differences due to life-cycle were significant at the 0.05 level, but that those due to car availability

*Table 3.17*   The Standard One-Way Anova Table

| Source of Variation | Sum of Squares $(x_i - x)^2$ | Degrees of Freedom | Mean Squares | F Test |
|---|---|---|---|---|
| Between groups | $SS_a$ | $m - 1$ | $\frac{SS_a}{m - 1} = MS_a$ | $\frac{MS_a}{MS_w}$ |
| Within groups | $SS_w$ | $N - m$ | $\frac{SS_w}{N - m} = MS_w$ | |
| Total variation | $SS_t$ | $N - 1$ | | $\frac{MS_w}{MS_a}$ |

*Table 3.18*  Migration Data for a One-Way Analysis of Variance

In-migrants as a percentage of population $(x_i)$

| Blaby RD | Meriden RD | Lutterworth RD |
|----------|------------|----------------|
| 25.6 | 29.9 | 8.0 |
| 32.8 | 54.0 | 9.3 |
| 24.1 | 18.6 | 17.6 |
| 29.7 | 22.2 | 14.6 |
| 48.6 | 13.0 | 22.2 |
| 15.8 | 22.7 | 19.6 |
| 24.3 | 14.2 | 11.7 |
| 15.5 | 10.2 | 5.5 |
| 53.3 | 18.7 | 12.0 |
| 29.3 | 30.0 | 17.4 |

$H_0 =$ there is no difference in the percentages of population moving into sample parishes in three rural districts over the same time period (data from Population Census)

$$\alpha = 0.05$$

$m = 3; N = 30$

| $x_B$ | $x_B^2$ | $x_M$ | $x_M^2$ | $x_L$ | $x_L^2$ |
|-------|---------|-------|---------|-------|---------|
| 25.6 | 655.4 | 29.9 | 894.0 | 8.0 | 64.0 |
| 32.8 | 1075.8 | 54.0 | 2916.0 | 9.3 | 86.5 |
| 24.1 | 580.8 | 18.6 | 346.0 | 17.6 | 309.8 |
| 29.7 | 882.1 | 22.2 | 492.8 | 14.6 | 213.2 |
| 48.6 | 2362.0 | 13.0 | 169.0 | 22.2 | 492.8 |
| 15.8 | 249.6 | 22.7 | 515.3 | 19.6 | 384.2 |
| 24.3 | 590.5 | 14.2 | 201.6 | 11.7 | 136.9 |
| 15.5 | 240.3 | 10.2 | 104.0 | 5.5 | 30.3 |
| 53.3 | 2840.9 | 18.7 | 349.7 | 12.0 | 144.0 |
| 29.3 | 858.5 | 30.0 | 900.0 | 17.4 | 302.8 |

$\sum x_B = 299.0$  $\sum x_B^2 = 10\,335.9$  $\sum x_M = 233.5$  $\sum x_M^2 = 6888.4$  $\sum x_L = 137.9$  $\sum x_L^2 = 2164.5$

Calculate grand total (*GT*):

$$GT = \frac{(\sum x)^2}{N} = \frac{(\sum x_B + \sum x_M + \sum x_L)^2}{N}$$

$$= \frac{(299.0 + 233.5 + 137.9)^2}{30}$$

$$= \frac{(670.4)^2}{30} = \frac{449\,436.18}{30} = 14\,981.2$$

*continued overleaf*

*Table 3.18*    (*Continued*)

Calculate

$$SS_t = \sum x^2 - GT = \left(\sum x_B^2 + \sum x_M^2 + \sum x_L^2\right) - GT$$
$$= (10\,335.9 + 6888.4 + 2164.5) - 14\,981.2$$
$$= 19\,388.8 - 14\,981.2 = 4407.6$$

Calculate

$$SS_a = \frac{\left(\sum x_B\right)^2}{n_B} + \frac{\left(\sum x_M\right)^2}{n_M} + \frac{\left(\sum x_L\right)^2}{n_L} - GT$$
$$= \frac{(299.0)^2}{10} + \frac{(233.5)^2}{10} + \frac{(137.9)^2}{10} - 14\,981.2$$
$$= 8940.1 + 5452.2 + 1901.6 - 14\,981.2$$
$$= 1312.7$$

Calculate

$$SS_w = SS_{wB} + SS_{wM} + SS_{wL}$$
$$SS_{wB} = \sum x_B^2 - \frac{\left(\sum x_B\right)^2}{n_B} = 10\,335.9 - \frac{(299)^2}{10}$$
$$= 10\,335.9 - 8940.1 = 1395.8$$
$$SS_{wM} = \sum x_M^2 - \frac{\left(\sum x_M\right)^2}{n_M} = 6888.4 - \frac{(233.5)^2}{10}$$
$$= 6888.4 - 5452.2 = 1436.2$$
$$SS_{wL} = \sum x_L^2 - \frac{\left(\sum x_L\right)^2}{n_L} = 2164.5 - \frac{(137.9)^2}{10}$$
$$= 2164.5 - 1901.6 = 262.9$$
$$SS_w = 1395.8 + 1436.2 + 262.9 = 3094.9$$

Alternatively,

$$SS_w = SS_t - SS_a = 4407.6 - 1312.7 = 3094.9$$

Calculate $MS_a$

$$MS_a = \frac{SS_a}{m-1} = \frac{1312.7}{3-1} = 656.4$$

Calculate $MS_w$

$$MS_w = \frac{SS_w}{N-m} = \frac{3094.9}{30-3} = 114.6$$

Calculate $F$

$$F = \frac{\text{greater variance estimate}}{\text{lesser variance estimate}} = \frac{656.4}{114.6} = 5.73$$

From Appendix I, $F_{0.05,2,27} = 3.35$. This is less than the calculated value. Therefore, at the 0.05 level reject $H_0$: there is a difference in the percentages of population moving into sample parishes in three rural districts.

*Table 3.19*  Shopping Behaviour Data for a Two-Way Analysis of Variance

(a) Cell means and variances

|  |  | Factor B = Life-Cycle | | |
|---|---|---|---|---|
|  |  | Middle-Aged | Young, No Children | Young, With Children |
| Factor A = Car Availability | No car | 59.34<br>17.77 | 61.06<br>13.16 | 48.67 mean<br>87.24 var. |
|  | Some car | 55.89<br>75.19 | 57.62<br>39.23 | 55.10 mean<br>84.57 var. |
|  | Full car | 53.98<br>75.38 | 59.35<br>29.70 | 59.72 mean<br>22.39 var. |

(b) Two-way anova table (data logarithmically transformed)

| Source of Variation | Sum of Squares | Degrees of Freedom | Mean Squares | F Ratio |
|---|---|---|---|---|
| A Car availability | 0.751 | 2 | 0.376 | 1.510 |
| B Life-cycle | 3.933 | 2 | 1.966 | 7.896 |
| Interaction | 6.664 | 4 | 1.666 | 6.691 |
| Within groups | 44.853 | 180 | 0.249 |  |
| Totals | 46.200 | 188 |  |  |

*Source*: Silk (1981:36).

$$\alpha = 0.05$$

$H_0$ = there are no differences in shopping behaviour due to car availability.

$$F = 1.510$$

From Appendix I, $F_{0.05,2,180} = 2.99$. This is more than the calculated value. Therefore, at the 0.05 level accept $H_0$: there is no difference in shopping behaviour due to car availability.

$H_0$ = there are no differences in shopping behaviour due to life-cycle

$$F = 7.896$$

From Appendix I, $F_{0.05,2,180} = 2.99$. This is less than the calculated value. Therefore, at the 0.05 level reject $H_0$: there is a difference in shopping behaviour due to life-cycle.

$H_0$ = there is no interaction between the effects of life-cycle and car availability

$$F = 6.691$$

From Appendix I, $F_{0.05,4,180} = 2.37$. This is less than the calculated value. Therefore, at the 0.05 level reject $H_0$: there is an interaction between the effects of life-cycle and car availability.

were not significant at this level. These two findings confirm the situation depicted in Figure 3.6b. This shows that ignorance of the location of stores decreases consistently with increase in car availability for young households with no children, but that there is an opposite trend for middle-aged households. A different pattern is shown by young households with no children: those having only some access to a car show a greater knowledge than those with either no car or high car accessibility. These patterns obviously require information on other characteristics of the respondents if they are to be interpreted adequately.

The example shown in Table 3.20 compares attitudes to landscape (measuring attitude on a continuous numerical scale) by a small sample of tourists divided into groups: of resident nationals and non-nationals on the one hand, and city-dwellers and ruralites on the other. This type of problem enables a number of hypotheses to be tested: Do nationals differ significantly from non-nationals in their attitudes to landscape? Does urban or rural residence have a relationship with attitudes? Is there an interaction effect between nationality and residence?

In this two-way anova, the variance can be apportioned between:

- factor $A$ – the effect of residence on the variance;
- factor $B$ – the effect of nationality on the variance;
- interaction between $A$ and $B$ – the combined

effects of residence and nationality on the variance;
- error effects or the within-groups' variance due to uncontrolled factors.

Given the lengthy calculations involved, a computer program is usually used to perform them. A comparison of Tables 3.18 and 3.21 shows the greater complexity of the two-way anova compared with the one-way anova. This complexity is increased if the effects of interaction are included. In the example given in Table 3.20, the two-way anova revealed that:

- Non-nationals have different attitudes to landscape from nationals.
- Rural-dwellers give a higher rating to landscape than city-dwellers.
- There is no interaction effect in the results, that is the combined effect of nationality and location of residence does not affect the results.

The two-way anova can be expressed as

$$y_{ijk} = \tau + A_i + B_j + e_{ijk}$$

where $A_i$ = effects due to factor $A$; $B_j$ = effects due to factor $B$; $\tau$ = the grand mean; $i$ = number of rows; $j$ = number of columns; and $k$ = the position within

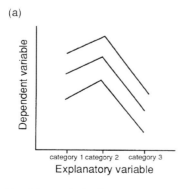

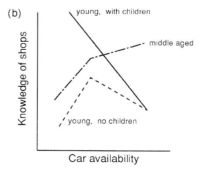

*Figure 3.6*   Two-Way Analysis of Variance (anova)
(a) Plot of cell means with no interaction effects (a perfectly additive model); (b) plot of cell means indicating presence of interaction. (Based on Silk, 1981:31–2)

*Table 3.20* Data on Attitudes to Landscape for a Two-Way Analysis of Variance

(a) Contingencies

|  |  | Variable (Factor) B | |
|---|---|---|---|
|  |  | Nationals | Non-Nationals |
| Variable (Factor) A | Rural-dwellers | 9.2<br>9.5<br>9.7<br>9.9 | 8.4<br>9.0<br>8.5<br>8.8 |
|  | City-dwellers | 7.9<br>7.5<br>7.2<br>8.1 | 7.3<br>6.9<br>7.5<br>7.0 |

(b) Two-way anova table

| Source of Variation | Sum of Squares | Degrees of Freedom | Mean Squares | F Ratio |
|---|---|---|---|---|
| A Location | 11.56 | 1 | 11.56 | 114.46 |
| B Ethnicity | 1.96 | 1 | 1.96 | 19.41 |
| Interaction | 0.16 | 1 | 0.16 | 1.58 |
| Within groups | 1.21 | 12 | 0.101 | |
| Totals | 14.89 | 15 | | |

$$\alpha = 0.05$$

$H_0 =$ there are no differences in attitude due to location

$$F = 114.46$$

From Appendix I, $F_{0.05,1,12} = 4.75$. This is less than the calculated value. Therefore, at the 0.05 level reject $H_0$: there is a difference in attitude due to location.

$H_0 =$ there are no differences in attitude due to ethnicity

$$F = 19.41$$

From Appendix I, $F_{0.05,1,12} = 4.75$. This is less than the calculated value. Therefore, at the 0.05 level reject $H_0$: there is a difference in attitude due to ethnicity.

$H_0 =$ there is no interaction between the effects of location and ethnicity

$$F = 1.58$$

From Appendix I, $F_{0.05,1,12} = 4.75$. This is more than the calculated value. Therefore, at the 0.05 level accept $H_0$: there is no interaction between the effects of location and ethnicity.

*Table 3.21*    The Standard Two-Way Anova Table (Without Interaction)

| Source of Variation | Sum of Squares $(x_i - x)^2$ | Degrees of Freedom | Mean Squares | F Tests |
|---|---|---|---|---|
| Between groups Factor A | $SS_a$ | $m - 1$ | $\dfrac{SS_a}{m-1} = MS_a$ | $\dfrac{MS_{a*}}{MS_e}$ |
| Factor B | $SS_b$ | $n - 1$ | $\dfrac{SS_b}{n-1} = MS_b$ | $\dfrac{MS_{b\dagger}}{MS_e}$ |
| Error/within groups | $SS_e$ | $(m-1)(n-1)$ | $\dfrac{SS_e}{(m-1)(n-1)}$ | |
| Total variation | $SS_t$ | $N - 1$ | | |

*Test of significance of differences between samples.
†Test of significance of difference between treatments.

the *ij*th cell (e.g. in Table 3.20, the second observation in cell (2,1) is $y_{2,1,2} = 7.5$).

The two-way anova equation assumes that the row and column effects are additive in their influence on values of the dependent variable. Norcliffe (1977:161) explains this with the following example:

> Suppose turnips are being grown, and two sources of variation are considered, namely the treatment of plots with phosphates and with nitrates. The model states that the mean yield of turnips in plots treated with both fertilisers is the grand average yield plus the effect due to phosphate treatment, plus the effect due to nitrate treatment, plus a random error term.

One of the problems with two-way anovas, such as the one described above, is that it is possible that the two factors are not additive, in which case they are said to interact, and the effect of such behaviour is described as *interaction*. This interaction refers to the interrelations between the two sources of variation being investigated. If interaction is present it reflects intercorrelation between the two sources or their joint effect. If the amount of interaction is statistically insignificant its occurrence is usually deemed to be due to sampling error and it is added to the within-classes effect, known as the *error* or *residual effect*. If the interaction effect is statistically significant then different denominators must be used to measure *F*. These denominators are usually:

1. *The within-classes estimate*. If only random, error variance remains as a possible contributor to the dependent variable then this variance estimate is the best denominator and is the within-classes estimate.
2. *The interaction estimate*. If other, unidentified variables are thought to be influencing the dependent variable then their effect may be absorbed in the interaction. If this is the case then the interaction estimate is used as the denominator. This contrasts the selected explanatory variables with those that have not been selected.

For example, in the case of the two factors cited in Table 3.19, position in the life-cycle and access to a motor car, there is a clear interaction. This is shown in Figure 3.6 where the graphical plots behave differently in particular categories of each factor, showing no steady increase or decrease. If this occurs, one or more of the cells must be considered individually rather than in terms of the "additive" anova model. This involves averaging over all cells in a given row or column (Silk, 1981:30). The two-way anova enables determination of whether this interaction is statistically significant.

Interaction can be investigated by means of another hypothesis test, the *Tukey test*, which identifies which of the cell means are significantly different. This uses the formula

$$T = q \frac{(\text{within-group variance})(\text{error variance})}{N}$$

where $N$ = number of observations from which each mean is calculated; and $T$ = the test statistic. The value of $q$ can be found from specially prepared tables (e.g. Cohen and Holliday, 1982:332–3). For the data in Table 3.20 the Tukey test confirms that,

- Rural nationals give higher landscape values than rural non-nationals.
- Rural nationals give higher landscape values than city-dwelling nationals.
- Rural non-nationals give higher landscape values than city-dwelling nationals.
- City-dwelling nationals do not give higher landscape values than city-dwelling non-nationals.

It is possible for differences in group size to bias results in a one-way analysis of variance, but this bias can be of greater importance in two-way analyses. Each cell should contain the same number of observations, so that a clear distinction can be made between the row factor ($A$) and the column factor ($B$). Differences in the number of observations in the various cells of the analysis can also accentuate the interaction effect (Johnston, 1978:108–10) and produce results that may be interpreted in different ways. If it is impossible to avoid unequal sizes of sample then any induced interaction effect may be avoided by ignoring the within-classes effect and treating each cell as a single observation. The limitation of this approach is that it ignores the possibility that the within-classes variation is substantial. So, whilst avoiding one problem, it creates another which may lead to a type-two error through acceptance of a false hypothesis. Johnston (1978:110) notes that therefore it is more desirable to perform a two-way analysis using equal cell sizes. However, this is most readily feasible in experimental work and is not always applicable within human geography.

One example is Murdie's (1976) work on Toronto, in which the city was divided into six concentric zones radiating around the central business district (CBD) and into six sectors or wedges, each one narrow at the CBD but widening out into the suburbs. This arrangement was then used to test two hypotheses:

1. that certain characteristics of local populations vary zonally around the CBD, with the richer people living further away from the CBD;
2. that the variation in some population characteristics is sectoral in form, with the sectors focusing on the CBD.

Data on housing and population characteristics were used for the 36 cells created by the arrangement of concentric zones and wedge-shaped sectors, the data for enumeration districts being matched to the cells. Six indices were investigated: economic status, Italian ethnic status, Jewish ethnic status, household and employment characteristics, family status, and recent population growth. The zonal hypothesis was strongly supported for the latter three indices, and the sectoral hypothesis for the first three. However, for all except recent population growth, interaction effects were significant at the 0.05 level, implying that there were some strong spatial trends amongst the cells, such as strong concentrations or absences of the relevant indices. Johnston (1978:108) concluded that, as these interaction effects were small compared with both the error variance estimate and the $F$ ratios themselves between sectors and/or between zones, they only represented minor deviations from general trends.

Bearing in mind the limitations imposed by the need for even numbers per individual cell, the number of independent variables in an analysis of variance may be higher than two. In such cases the main sources of variation comprise individual variables rather than rows and columns. The sources of interaction are increased and comprise each possible combination of the $n$ independent (explanatory) variables. However, more complicated $n$-way anovas ($n > 2$) involve complex calculations to generate the test statistic.

The use of $n$-way anovas can be an effective way of isolating the influences of a number of independent variables, both separately and in combination. However, they are best applied in situations in which close control can be exerted over sampling so that equal cell sizes can be produced. Therefore their potential for use in human geography is relatively limited as the discipline so rarely generates strictly controlled experimental research. The greater poten-tial within physical geography, though, was recog-nised in early applications of statistical analysis to geographical data (Haggett, 1961). Alternative tech-niques for analysing problems involving a number of independent variables are considered in Chapter 4, and for problems with a large number of interrelated variables see Chapter 5.

# 4

# MEASURING ASSOCIATIONS

## CORRELATION COEFFICIENTS

It was not until the 1950s that geographers began to pay concerted attention to forms of statistical analysis more elaborate than simple statistical description. This changing emphasis coincided with a growing awareness of alternatives to the prevailing regional paradigm, which were represented by the growth of systematic studies and a gradual move towards more analytic geography. The latter was initially most pronounced in the USA where there was a direct challenge by Schaefer (1953) upon regional geography as interpreted by Hartshorne (1939).

Although Schaefer's article on scientific method was published in 1953, most work around this time by those human geographers who employed a substantial empirical component in their research made no reference to it. Much human geography in the 1950s did not employ any clearly recognisable scientific method, but there was some pioneering of statistical techniques. For example, Schaefer's colleagues at the University of Iowa were led by Harold McCarty who employed *correlation analysis* in his research. He focused on the ideas of the logical positivist Gustav Bergmann, and concentrated on "establishing the degree of correspondence between two or more geographical patterns" (McCarty, 1954:97). This was similar to Schaefer's "laws of accordance" (Bunge, 1979), and in McCarty's work represented an attempt to explain the location of phenomena by looking at spatial distributions of different variables. Amongst the phenomena investigated were the distribution of

manufacturing industry in the USA and Japan, rural population densities in the American Mid-West, intra-urban land value patterns and the spacing of urban settlements (McCarty, 1953; McCarty et al, 1956). Interrelationships were investigated using correlation analysis as the principal statistical tool, thereby replicating procedures used earlier in work by a few geographers who had contacts with agricultural economists, for example Rose (1936) and Weaver (1943) who related agricultural production to physical variables. McCarty's focus upon correlation was repeated in work by A.H. Robinson (Robinson and Bryson, 1957; Robinson et al, 1961) who also stressed the need to concentrate upon investigation of relationships between variables.

### Pearson's Product-Moment Coefficient

The initial work by geographers on the measurement of the strength of a relationship between two variables relied primarily upon the *Pearson product-moment correlation coefficient* ($r_{xy}$), with its values lying in the range from $+1.0$ to $-1.0$. A value of $+1.0$ represents a perfect positive relationship between the two variables, i.e. as $y$ increases so does $x$ to an equal degree (Figure 4.1a), and $-1.0$ is a perfect inverse relationship, i.e. as $y$ increases so $x$ decreases to an equal degree (Figure 4.1b). A value of $r_{xy} = 0.0$ indicates the absence of any statistical relationship between $x$ and $y$ (Figure 4.1c). A value of $r_{xy}$ tending towards $\pm 1.00$ indicates high positive or high negative

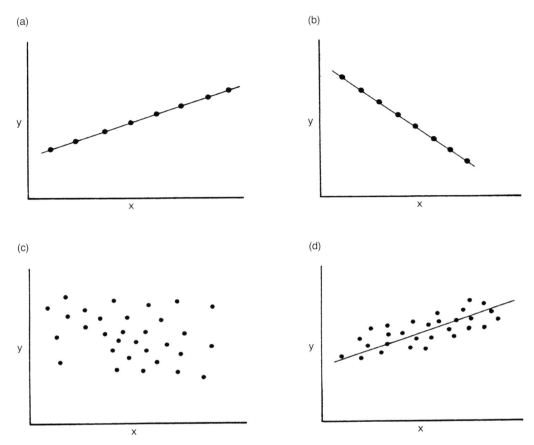

*Figure 4.1*    Correlation Coefficients
(a) Perfect postive correlation; (b) perfect negative correlation; (c) no correlation; (d) high positive correlation

correlation (Figure 4.1d). The representation of these relationships on *scattergraphs*, as shown in Figure 4.1, provides an opportunity to incorporate a visual display of statistical relationships as an integral part of analysis together with the calculation of the correlation coefficient. The relationship's strength can be expressed further by calculating the *coefficient of determination* ($100r_{xy}^2$). This measures the proportion of the variance in the two variables "explained" by their correlation. Hence a correlation coefficient of +0.90 produces a coefficient of determination of 81 per cent, leaving 19 per cent of the variance of the two variables that is not coincident.

The use of the Pearson product-moment correlation coefficient means that the measurement of bivariate relationships is based upon *covariance* ($s_{xy}$), or the correspondence of two variables together:

$$s_{xy} = \frac{1}{n-1}\sum(x_i - \bar{x})(y_i - \bar{y})$$

This is an extension of the use of the variance in which a measure is obtained of the variation of one set of observations about their mean value (see subsection on "Sampling procedures" in Chapter 2). Like the variance, covariance is an absolute measure and so its value varies according to the units in which $x$ and $y$ are measured. To transform this absolute measure into one constrained to the range $+1.0$ to $-1.0$, the covariance of $x$ and $y$ is divided by the product of the standard deviations of $x$ and $y$ to give the correlation coefficient ($r_{xy}$):

$$r_{xy} = \frac{\sum(x_i - \bar{x})(y_i - \bar{y})}{\sqrt{\sum(x_i - \bar{x})^2(y_i - \bar{y})^2}}$$

This can also be expressed as

$$r_{xy} = \frac{1}{n-1} \frac{(x_i - \bar{x})(y_i - \bar{y})}{s_x s_y}$$

and as

$$r_{xy} = \frac{x_i y_i - (\sum x_i)(\sum y_i)/n}{[x_i^2 - (\sum x_i)^2/n][y_i^2 - (\sum y_i)^2/n]}$$

A worked example is shown in Table 4.1, using this last formula, which provides greatest ease of computation.

Although graphical representation of the relationship between two variables supplemented by a correlation coefficient can act as a powerful descriptive summary, a major attraction of correlation analysis is the ability to assess the coefficient's statistical significance. The significance testing of correlation coefficients draws upon ideas embodied in the central limit theorem, relating to the outcome of drawing samples from a statistical population, as described in the penultimate subsection "Uses of the normal distribution" in Chapter 2. Therefore the assessment of significance takes a probabilistic form, indicating to what extent the coefficient has arisen by chance rather than reflecting a genuine and non-random association. So a correlation analysis can produce not only a correlation coefficient giving the strength of a relationship between two variables but also an indication of how significant this relationship is. For example, a correlation of $+0.90$ suggests a high positive association between two variables and this may be reinforced by an assessment of the relationship's statistical significance, which may state that such a value could only occur by chance once in 100 samples.

A significance test can be carried out to see if the observed correlation coefficient ($r_{xy}$) is significantly different from zero. If a difference can be ascertained at a given level of significance, this indicates that the derived coefficient reflects a genuine non-random association. When $r_{xy} = 0$, $r_{xy}\sqrt{(n-2)}/\sqrt{(1 - r_{xy}^2)}$ has a $t$ distribution with $(n-2)$ degrees of freedom, provided that the variables are bivariate normal. Therefore, a correlation coefficient is significantly different from zero at the level of significance if

$$\frac{r_{xy}\sqrt{(n-2)}}{\sqrt{(1 - r_{xy}^2)}} > t/_{2,n-2}$$

Special tables have been prepared to short-cut this calculation (Appendix J). They show the importance of sample size in establishing the critical value of $r_{xy}$. Shaw and Wheeler (1985:154−5) demonstrate that values of $r_{xy}$ may also be converted to $z$ values for significance testing.

Although a correlation coefficient measures the degree of association between just two variables, it has been common for geographers to investigate the characteristics of such bivariate relationships for multiple variables. In so doing the complexity of the world is acknowledged and multiple relationships of complex economic and social systems have become the focus of attention. Given the ready availability of census data on a tremendous range of population characteristics, it is not surprising that there should be a focus upon interrelationships between large numbers of census variables. However, Pearson's product-moment coefficient has played a central part in multivariate investigations of such data, as much multivariate research is based on a *correlation matrix* portraying several bivariate relationships.

A typical correlation matrix is shown in Table 4.2, summarising Smith's (1975) correlation analysis of social indicators for the states of the USA. Each individual bivariate relationship is represented in the matrix which can be interpreted by focusing upon the highest and most significant correlations. For example, all correlations in the matrix with $r_{xy} > +0.36$ are significant at the 0.01 level (see Table 4.2). Thus the social indicator "income, wealth and employment" has high positive correlations with indicators for hous-

*Table 4.1* Agricultural Data for the Calculation of $r_{xy}$

Densities per 100 ha of agricultural land

| County | Dairy Cattle x | Pigs y |
|---|---|---|
| A | 15.68 | 11.93 |
| B | 9.62 | 6.34 |
| C | 13.28 | 8.37 |
| D | 10.95 | 7.03 |
| E | 15.70 | 15.15 |
| F | 12.75 | 10.91 |
| G | 9.96 | 9.15 |
| H | 13.08 | 14.04 |

$$H_0 = r_{xy} = 0.0$$

$$\alpha = 0.05$$

Calculate $xy$, $x^2$, $y^2$:

| County | x | y | xy | $x^2$ | $y^2$ |
|---|---|---|---|---|---|
| A | 15.68 | 11.93 | 187.06 | 245.86 | 142.32 |
| B | 9.62 | 6.34 | 60.99 | 92.54 | 40.20 |
| C | 13.28 | 8.37 | 111.15 | 176.36 | 70.06 |
| D | 10.95 | 7.03 | 76.98 | 119.90 | 49.42 |
| E | 15.70 | 15.15 | 237.86 | 246.49 | 229.52 |
| F | 12.75 | 10.91 | 139.10 | 162.56 | 119.03 |
| G | 9.96 | 9.15 | 91.13 | 99.20 | 83.72 |
| H | 13.08 | 14.04 | 183.64 | 171.09 | 197.12 |
| $(n = 8)$ | $\sum = 101.02$ | $\sum = 82.92$ | $\sum = 1087.91$ | $\sum = 1314.00$ | $\sum = 931.39$ |

$$\overline{x} = 12.67, \overline{y} = 10.37$$

$$
\begin{aligned}
r_{xy} &= \frac{\sum x_i y_i - (\sum x_i)(\sum y_i)/n}{[x_i^2 - (\sum x_i)^2/n][y_i^2 - (\sum y_i)^2/n]} \\[2mm]
&= \frac{1087.91 - (101.02)(82.92)/8}{[1314.00 - (101.02)^2/8][931.39 - (82.92)^2/8]} \\[2mm]
&= \frac{1087.91 - 8376.58/8}{(1314.00 - 10\,205.04/8)(931.39 - 6875.73/8)} \\[2mm]
&= \frac{1087.91 - 1047.07}{(1314.00 - 1275.63)(931.39 - 859.47)} \\[2mm]
&= \frac{40.84}{(38.37)(71.92)} = \frac{40.84}{2759.57} = \frac{40.84}{52.53} = 0.78
\end{aligned}
$$

*Table 4.1    (Continued)*

Test the significance of this value using Appendix J or using $t$ tables for degrees of freedom, $v = n - 2$
$H_0$ = there is no significant difference between the correlation coefficient and a value obtained by chance

$$\alpha = 0.05$$

$$v = n - 2 = 8 - 2 = 6$$

$$t = \frac{r_{xy}\sqrt{(n-2)}}{\sqrt{(1 - r_{xy}^2)}} = \frac{(0.78)\sqrt{6}}{0.626} = \frac{1.91}{0.626} = 3.05$$

From Appendix H, $t_{0.05,6} = 2.45$. The calculated value of the test statistic is greater than this, therefore reject $H_0$. The correlation coefficient ($r_{xy} = +0.78$) is significant at the 0.05 level (i.e. has not occurred by chance).
In Appendix J, the critical value for $n = 8$ and $\alpha = 0.05$ is 0.707. The calculated value is greater than this, therefore the calculated value is significant at the 0.05 level.

*Table 4.2*    Correlation Matrix of Social Indicators in the USA (for the 50 States)

$r_{xy}$

| Variables | Variables | | | | | | |
|---|---|---|---|---|---|---|---|
| | 1 | 2 | 3 | 4 | 5 | 6 | 7 |
| 1. Income, wealth and employment | 1.00 | 0.91 | 0.76 | 0.82 | −0.30 | 0.67 | 0.88 |
| 2. Housing | 0.91 | 1.00 | 0.85 | 0.85 | −0.24 | 0.67 | 0.90 |
| 3. Health | 0.76 | 0.85 | 1.00 | 0.85 | −0.20 | 0.75 | 0.88 |
| 4. Education | 0.82 | 0.85 | 0.85 | 1.00 | −0.12 | 0.79 | 0.92 |
| 5. Social disorganisation | −0.30 | −0.24 | −0.20 | −0.12 | 1.00 | 0.11 | 0.05 |
| 6. Participation | 0.67 | 0.67 | 0.75 | 0.79 | 0.11 | 1.00 | 0.87 |
| 7. General social well-being | 0.88 | 0.90 | 0.88 | 0.92 | 0.05 | 0.87 | 1.00 |

*Source:* Smith (1975:271).

ing, health, education, participation and general social well-being. Therefore states with high values on this indicator will tend to have high values on these five social indicators. There is a negative correlation (−0.30) with social disorganisation, but this is not significant at the 0.01 level. Indeed, there are no negative correlations in the matrix that are significant at this level. This suggests that the seven chosen social indicators are closely intercorrelated. Even social disorganisation has no high negative correlations, perhaps suggesting that the data for the 50 states represent broad aggregates that are average pictures tending to mask any concentrations of social disorganisation that occur. Indeed, juxtapositions of great

wealth and great poverty within states such as New York or California will appear as "average" state figures. It is most important that this degree of aggregation is considered when interpreting correlation coefficients.

Another way of examining interrelationships between correlated variables is shown in the *linkage diagram* based on this correlation matrix (Figure 4.2). In this the arrows indicate the direction and strength of the highest correlation exhibited by each variable. This shows the close interrelationship between general social well-being and education, and between income and housing. The strength of the links between these two pairs is shown by the dotted lines. Social dis-

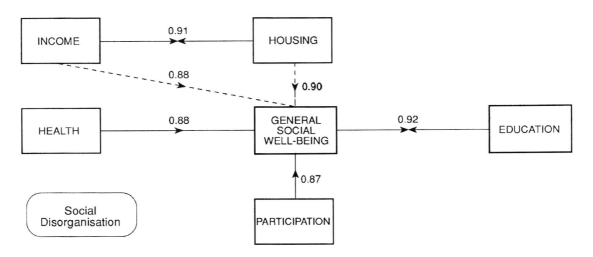

*Figure 4.2*    Correlation Linkage Diagram

organisation, with no significant positive correlations, stands apart from the other six indicators.

Further analysis of the correlation matrix can form the basis for statistical examination of multivariate relationships (as discussed in Chapter 5), thereby emphasising the importance of Pearson's product-moment coefficient.

## Spearman's Rank Coefficient

Given that most of the initial geographical studies utilising correlation were analysing data on the interval or ratio scale, the Pearson product-moment coefficient was the measure commonly employed. Some consideration was given to problems associated with underlying assumptions about the data being analysed, but, initially, there was relatively little work utilising alternative measures of correlation. The chief of these alternatives is *Spearman's rank correlation coefficient* ($\rho_{xy}$), which is used for ordinal or ranked data. In this case the correlation coefficient represents a measure of the differences in rank between two variables:

$$\rho_{xy} = 1 - \frac{6\sum D^2}{n(n^2 - 1)}$$

where $D$ = differences between ranks of corresponding values of $x$ and $y$; and $n$ = number of pairs of $x$, $y$ values.

In addition to avoiding some of the assumptions of Pearson's coefficient (see below), Spearman's coefficient also has the advantage of ease of computation (Table 4.3). However, its use of ordinal data means it is operating on information one step removed from the interval- or ratio-scale data so commonly available in information generated both by researchers and by official sources. This can pose problems when using ranked data containing several observations with the same rank value, but may be preferable if the accuracy of interval or ratio data is in doubt. In addition, there are numerous occasions when geographical data are in ordinal form, especially in behavioural studies where interviewees are asked to place preferences in ranked order.

In testing the significance of $\rho_{xy}$, a $t$ value may be calculated from

$$t = \rho_{xy} \frac{(n - 2)}{(1 - \rho_{xy}^2)}$$

with degrees of freedom $v = (n - 2)$. A table of critical values for $\rho_{xy}$ is given in Appendix K.

*Table 4.3*  A Spearman's Rank Correlation Applied to Data on Skins Shipped from the Eastern Rockies, Canada, in 1856

| Skin Type | Number x | Rank | Price/Skin y (pence) | Rank | d | $d^2$ |
|-----------|----------|------|----------------------|------|---|-------|
| Beaver | 58 899 | 3 | 9 | 3.5 | 0.5 | 0.25 |
| Marten | 139 154 | 2 | 15 | 2 | 0 | 0 |
| Mink | 39 223 | 4 | 9 | 3.5 | 0.5 | 0.25 |
| Muskrat | 269 100 | 1 | 0.5 | 6 | 5 | 25 |
| Buffalo tongue | 4 629 | 6 | 2.17 | 5 | 1 | 1 |
| Buffalo robes | 18 000 | 5 | 20 | 1 | 4 | 16 |
| $(n = 6)$ | | | | | | $\sum = 42.5$ |

$$\alpha = 0.05$$

$$H_0: \rho = 0.0$$

$$\rho = 1 - \frac{6(42.5)}{(6)^3 - 6} = 1 - \frac{255}{216 - 6} = 1 - \frac{255}{210} = 1 - 1.21 = -0.21$$

Critical value of $\rho$ for $n = 6$ and $\alpha = 0.05$ is $\pm 0.829$ (see Appendix K). This is more than the calculated value, and therefore $H_0$ can be accepted: there is no significant correlation between $x$ and $y$.

An alternative correlation coefficient to Spearman's, also operating on ordinal data, is *Kendall's tau* ($\tau$). This is sometimes preferred for use with small samples and a special form of correlation, known as *partial correlation* (see below):

$$\tau = \frac{S}{0.5\, n(n - 1)}$$

where $n$ = number of ranks being paired, and $S$ = sum of ranks for one variable.

## The Point Biserial Coefficient

Measures of correlation for nominal data involve examination of the relationship between two variables measured on the nominal scale. Two such measures that have been employed are the *point biserial coefficient* ($r_{pb}$) and the *phi coefficient* ($\phi$). Though they have not been widely used, the classic study of central places by Berry and Garrison (1958) in Snohomish County, Washington State, employed the point biserial coefficient to examine the relationship between the size of central places and other functional character-

istics (Table 4.4). Fifteen attributes were correlated with the populations of centres in which they appeared. This revealed that higher correlations were associated with the occurrence of functions such as public libraries, sewage systems and bakeries in larger

*Table 4.4*  Point Biserial Correlation Coefficients ($r_{pb}$) Between Functions and Population Size for Snohomish County, Washington

|  | $r_{pb}$ |
|---|-----|
| General store | −0.347 |
| Feed mill | 0.265 |
| Post office | 0.290 |
| Weekly newspaper | 0.458 |
| Telephone exchange | 0.584 |
| Incorporated city | 0.615 |
| Movie theatre (cinema) | 0.616 |
| Bakery | 0.619 |
| Electricity distribution | 0.646 |
| Water supply system | 0.646 |
| Sewage system | 0.691 |
| State liquor store | 0.691 |
| Public library | 0.758 |
| Printing press | 0.759 |

*Source*: Berry and Garrison (1958).

centres. The point biserial coefficient requires a continuous variable, such as size of settlement, to be correlated with a dichotomous (or binary) variable, such as presence or absence of a quality, i.e. only taking the values of 0 or 1:

$$r_{pb} = \frac{\overline{Y}_1 - \overline{Y}_0}{\hat{s}_y} \sqrt{\left[\frac{N_1 N_0}{N(N-1)}\right]}$$

where $r_{pb}$ = the point biserial coefficient; $N_0$ = number of observations with an $X$ value of 0; $N_1$ = number of observations with an $X$ value of 1;

$$\overline{Y}_0 = \sum Y_{0i}/N_0 \qquad \overline{Y}_1 = \sum Y_{1i}/N_1$$

$$\sum Y_2 = \sum Y_0^2 + Y_1^2 \qquad s_y = \frac{NY^2 - (Y)^2}{N(N-1)}$$

and

$$Y = Y_0 + Y_1$$

The continuous variable must be normally distributed and the two subsamples of the dichotomous variable should be fairly similar in terms of the number of observations in each subset.

A Student's $t$ test may be used to test the significance of the coefficient obtained, with

$$t = r_{pb} \frac{(N-2)}{(1 - r_{pb}^2)}$$

## The Phi ($\phi$) Coefficient

This represents an extension of the $\chi^2$ test, using a $2 \times 2$ contingency table for two dichotomous variables. Unlike $\chi^2$, $\phi$ only has values between $-1$ and $+1$:

$$\phi = \sqrt{(\chi^2/n)}$$

where $\chi^2$ = the chi-squared statistic calculated for the $2 \times 2$ contingency table, and $n$ = the total number of observations.

The significance of $\phi$ can only be determined by referring to the significance of the $\chi^2$ value. However, using the above equation for $\phi$ will always yield a positive value which is only a realistic result if the contingency table is constructed so that $A$ and $D$ represent the frequencies of individuals who possess both traits or neither trait, and $B$ and $C$ represent frequencies of individuals who possess one trait but not the other (see Table 4.5). In testing the significance of $\phi$, a $\chi^2$ test may be used, with $\chi^2 = \phi^2 n$.

Table 4.5  The Phi Coefficient ($\phi$) Applied to Sample Data on School Selection

| Religious Affiliation | Private Schools | | State-Sector Schools | | Total |
|---|---|---|---|---|---|
| Catholic | A | 220 | B | 145 | 365 |
| Non-Catholic | C | 175 | D | 235 | 410 |
| | | 395 | | 380 | 775 |

$$H_0: \phi = 0.0$$

$$\alpha = 0.05$$

$$\phi = \frac{AD - BC}{[(A+B)(C+D)(A+C)(B+D)]}$$

$$= \frac{(220 \times 235) - (145 \times 175)}{[(220 + 145)(175 + 235)(220 + 175)(145 + 235)]}$$

$$= \frac{51700 - 25375}{365 \times 410 \times 395 \times 380} = \frac{26325}{149875} = +0.176$$

This would seem to indicate only a relatively weak association between school selection and religious affiliation (though note the large number of observations used). There is no method for finding confidence limits for $\phi$, but $\phi$ can be converted into a $\chi^2$ value by using $\chi^2 = \phi^2 N$, where $N$ = total number of observations, in this case $N = 775$. Therefore

$$\chi^2 = (0.176)^2 \times 775 = 24.01$$

This value is above the critical value of $\chi^2_{1,0.05} = 3.84$ given in Appendix D. Therefore the correlation coefficient is significant at the 0.05 level. Religious affiliation and school selection are related.

## LIMITATIONS IMPOSED BY THE NATURE OF GEOGRAPHIC DATA

During A.H. Robinson's pioneering work on correlation within human geography, several critical problems were exposed, not least of which was the need for careful interpretation of correlation coefficients. In most cases bivariate relationships are only indirect or casual, with correlations generally dependent on intermediate factors. For example, high correlations may often be found between crop yields and the amount of rainfall received, but intermediate factors, such as the amounts of fertiliser, pesticide, irrigation and labour

used, will be crucial in determining the actual nature of the correlation. In addition to this general problem of interpretation, there are four key difficulties that have been shown to affect the results of correlation analysis of geographical data: the unequal size and shape of areal units, the ecological fallacy, closed number sets, and spatial autocorrelation.

### The Unequal Size and Shape of Areal Units

For the spatial configuration of counties in Nebraska, as shown in Figure 4.3a(i), Robinson (1956) calcu-

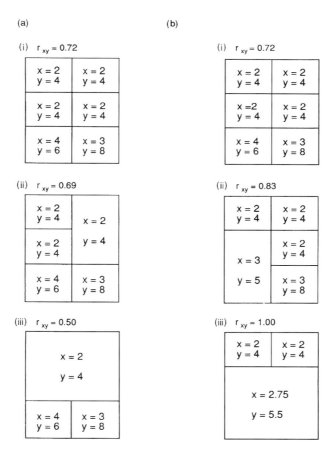

*Figure 4.3*  Modifiable Areal Units
(a) After Robinson (1956); (b) after Thomas and Anderson (1965)

lated the correlation coefficient between annual rainfall ($x$) and the number of farmsteads per square mile ($y$). By amalgamating some of the counties to obtain different spatial arrangements, with units now of unequal sizes, he discovered that different correlation coefficients were obtained (Figure 4.3a(ii) and (iii)). He attributed this to the fact that the smaller areal units were being given the same weighting as larger ones, and argued that this could be countered prior to the calculation of $r_{xy}$ by multiplying all values of $x$ and $y$ by the area of the county to which they referred.

Subsequently, Thomas and Anderson (1965) showed that Robinson's solution applied only in the particular case in which all the counties he was amalgamating had the same values for $x$ and $y$. They presented two alternative county systems for which the correlation coefficients differed from those of the original system both before and after weighting the data to take account of areal variations (Figure 4.3b). They were demonstrating that the boundaries of any system of areal units can be combined to alter radically the value of correlations between variables measured for those areal units.

Thomas and Anderson's study added to similar findings by the statisticians Yule and Kendall (1950). Working with English counties as their areal units, the latter found that the correlations between wheat and potato yields increased when the counties were grouped into larger regional units. They found their results to "measure . . . not only the variation of the quantities under consideration, but the properties of the unit mesh which we have imposed on the system in order to measure it" (Yule and Kendall, 1950:312). As the nature of most "unit meshes" is arbitrary, then work relating to them has an element of arbitrariness within it. Most geographers have tended to ignore this, accepting aggregate data for government-determined administrative boundaries as the best available or most meaningful form of aggregation. However, it is a problem that is essentially unpredictable in its intensity, especially in its effects in multivariate statistical analysis (Perle, 1977) (see Chapter 5). Openshaw (1978) too has demonstrated that different aggregations of areal units produce very different results in a correlation analysis. He argued that the problem could

be dealt with in a number of ways, though few of these have achieved great popularity (Openshaw and Taylor, 1979, 1981).

This problem is now generally referred to as the *modifiable-areal-units problem* (see Fotheringham and Wong, 1991; Openshaw, 1983; Wrigley, 1995). It is related to the recognition of a second critical problem associated with calculating correlation coefficients, namely *ecological correlation*.

## Ecological Correlation

This refers to the difficulties encountered when inferring individual characteristics from group data. In such cases the so-called *ecological fallacy* can occur. The fallacy was demonstrated in a classic paper by W.S. Robinson (1950), examining the correlation between "the percentage of the American population over ten years of age who were negroes . . . and . . . the percentage who were illiterate (in 1930)". Using data for the nine principal census divisions of the USA, he obtained a correlation coefficient of $+0.95$ between these two variables. However, when the same two variables were correlated for the 48 states, a value of only $+0.77$ was recorded. And when the correlation was performed for the entire 97 million Americans over ten years of age, the correlation was reduced to $+0.20$. Therefore, on an individual basis, there was a relatively low probability that an African-American was also illiterate despite the fact that they tended to be spatially concentrated in the same states and regions as illiterates.

Robinson also utilised an even more extreme case to demonstrate the ecological fallacy, showing that the correlation between the percentage of the population which was illiterate and that which had been foreign-born changed from $-0.69$, for the nine principal census divisions, to $+0.118$ when individuals were considered.

Growing awareness of the problems of interpretation of ecological correlation, and the distortions introduced by unevenly sized spatial units, produced some re-evaluation by geographers and other social scientists of their use of correlation. In particular, it is clear that statements concerning relationships between variables must be made within the context of the areal units being used. For example, a conclusion from a correlation analysis using aggregate data for a number of countries could make a statement such as "small farms in the thirty counties were found in conjunction with a high incidence of labour input". Such a conclusion does not necessarily mean that, if every farm in the 30 counties had been examined separately, a high positive correlation would have been established between small farms and high labour input. Instead, the conclusion is drawing attention to the similarity of the distribution of the two variables amongst the 30 counties rather than to the likely relationship between the variables in the case of individual observations.

The need to make this crucial nuance of interpretation has led to some rejection of correlation as a suitable technique to employ in certain types of geographical investigation. In particular, this has been the case within social geography which has developed a greater focus upon the individual, though there are occasions in this part of the discipline when ecological analysis can be pursued successfully. Elsewhere, though, if the focus has been upon the characteristics of areal units, such as administrative units or political constituencies, the difference between ecological correlation and individual correlation has not always been a crucial consideration. However, the variations in the size of areal units can affect statistical inferences made and therefore care has to be taken when interpreting correlations based on data for unevenly sized areal units.

Further consideration of the complex interactions between the modifiable-areal-unit problem and the ecological fallacy has been made recently by Wrigley (1995). He refers to the development of rules for aggregation of data and the partitioning of space by Amrhein (1994) and champions the urgent need for progress in two areas: formulating an adequate statistical framework for treating these problems, and developing a practical method for using areal data to draw meaningful inferences about individual/household-level relationships. He feels there is the possibility that collaboration between geographers and statisticians may shed new light on a seemingly intractable problem.

## Closed Number Sets

Geographers frequently utilise *closed number sets* such as proportions or percentages. These are number sets in which all the data sum to one (e.g. proportions) or to 100 (e.g. percentages). To counter the problem of dealing with areas of different shapes or sizes, it is common to use densities, percentages and proportions in order to bring each observation to a common scale. For example, in a correlation analysis between the numbers of cereal farms per county and the numbers of tractors per county, the two variables could be simply different measures of a county's size. Contrast this with a correlation between the percentage of farms per county which are cereal farms and the density of tractors per county. However, the use of closed number systems can pose certain problems in the calculation of correlation coefficients. In particular it biases correlation structures by recording the same thing more than once.

This problem is demonstrated in Table 4.6, repre-

*Table 4.6* Data Illustrating the Problem of Closed Ratios

(a) An Open Number System

| Region | Land Type (100 km²) | | | |
|--------|--------|--------|--------|--------|
| | Arable $x$ | Pasture $y$ | Scrub $z$ | |
| A | 5 | 2 | 1 | |
| B | 7 | 4 | 2 | $r_{xy} = 0.99$ |
| C | 8 | 6 | 4 | $r_{yz} = 0.96$ |
| D | 10 | 8 | 5 | $r_{yz} = 0.89$ |

(b) A Closed Number System

| Region | Land Type (%) | | | |
|--------|--------|--------|--------|--------|
| | Arable $x$ | Pasture $y$ | Scrub $z$ | |
| A | 63 | 25 | 12 | |
| B | 54 | 31 | 15 | $r_{xy} = -0.97$ |
| C | 44 | 33 | 23 | $r_{yz} = -0.98$ |
| D | 43 | 35 | 22 | $r_{yz} = 0.89$ |

senting the common situation in which a population is divided into groups, with membership of each group expressed as a percentage of the population. *Closure* is represented by the fact that once the values in any two land-use classes in the table are known then the percentage in the remaining one is effectively predetermined. The larger the number of classes in a closed number system, the less the degree to which any correlation between any two of them is fixed. However, with a large number of variables it is difficult to identify such fixed correlations.

Evans and Jones (1981), commenting on an earlier correlation analysis of cropland in Ohio, noted quite strong closure effects which they felt reduced the degree of positive correlations and made interpretation difficult. They recommended the adoption of a *null model* to give expected correlations due solely to the closure constraint. Several such models are available, though rarely applied by geographers because of their complexity (see e.g. Mosimann, 1962; Chayes and Kruskal, 1966).

There are four alternatives to correlating closed ratios:

1. Some of the problems of closure with respect to correlation and regression analysis were discussed by Wrigley (1973) who recommended the transformation of percentage values into an infinite ratio scale, using a *logistic transformation* (often abbreviated to logit):

$$L_j = \log_e \left[ \frac{P_{ij}}{(100 - P_{ij})} \right]$$

where $P_{ij}$ = percentage value at observation $j$, and $L_j$ = logit value for observation $j$. In a regression analysis (see below) this transformation modifies the dependent variable so that it conforms with the assumptions of linear regression. However, this may not entirely eliminate closure. The logit transformation is considered in greater detail in Chapter 6.

2. Use of partial correlations between counts or measurements, though this could lose any benefit gained from using ratios. Partial correlation is considered later in this chapter in the section on "Multiple regression".

3. Correlate chi-squared values (see "Non-parametric tests" in Chapter 3).

4. Use the index of dissimilarity based on absolute numbers (see "Spatial indices" in Chapter 9).

## Spatial Autocorrelation

> It is common for many variables (economic, social and physical) to be characterised by correlations between adjacent values in space or in time.
> (Clark and Hosking, 1986:378)

This occurrence is known as *autocorrelation* or *serial correlation*, which has long been of considerable interest to economists who have produced a number of tests for the analysis of autocorrelated time series data (see Chapter 10). However, geographers were slower to appreciate the significance of the presence of autocorrelation in spatially distributed variables. They also found it harder to test for *spatial autocorrelation* because of the greater complexity of spatial distributions when compared with time series. Yet, the presence of autocorrelation in spatial data is common and it violates some of the key assumptions made in statistical analysis. The two principal violations are of the assumption of independence of observations and of lack of bias in the error terms and residuals in regression analysis (see below). Such violations highlight the fact that the original development of correlation and regression was for the purposes of identifying significant relationships in conditions where sampling can be performed on a population lacking both spatial and temporal parameters (Whitley and Clark, 1985). Therefore application of such methods to situations in which samples carry locational characteristics can conflict with essential assumptions of the statistical techniques. Logical problems are raised by this situation, though frequently geographers have ignored them. Hence geographers' use of standard inferential statistics has often overlooked the presence of spatial autocorrelation. However, geographers have also designed spatial models incorporating autocorrelation, and they have developed a number of ways of testing for the presence of spatial autocorrelation (e.g. Cliff and Ord, 1973).

The problems posed by spatial autocorrelation are examined in more detail in Chapter 9, in which both practical measures of the phenomenon are outlined and further discussion is made of associated philosophical arguments.

# REGRESSION ANALYSIS

## Simple Linear Regression

In two particular circumstances geographers have found it profitable to extend the investigation of the strength of bivariate relationships to a consideration of its form by means of conducting a regression analysis. The prime situation for this is when one variable is deemed to be dependent upon another. For example, crop yield might be dependent upon labour input. In this case crop yield is the dependent variable ($y$) and labour input is the independent variable ($x$). As well as calculating $r_{xy}$, the scattergraph of $y$ versus $x$ can be used to investigate the form of the relationship (Figure 4.4). The line of best fit through the scatter of points in the scattergraph is the linear regression line whose equation $y = a + bx$ (where $a$ is the intercept on the $y$-axis and $b$ is the slope of the line) can be utilised in various ways. One of these refers to the second principal situation in which regression can be applied profitably: when there is a need to predict the value of the dependent variable for given values of the independent variable. In this case the regression equation can be employed predictively. For example, in Figure 4.4 it could be predicted that a labour input of $Z$ is likely to produce a crop yield of $P$.

The level of explanation of the dependent variable by the independent variable, known as the *coefficient of determination* ($C$), is equal to $r_{xy}^2 \times 100\%$:

$$C = \frac{\text{regression variance}}{\text{overall variance}}$$

where regression variance = variability of the values

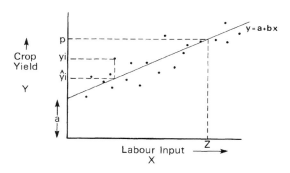

*Figure 4.4* Regression Line and Scattergraph ($y$ = crop yield, $x$ = labour input)

of $y$ around the regression line, and overall variance = variability of values of $y$ around $\bar{y}$, i.e.

$$C = \frac{\sum(y_i - \bar{y})^2 - \sum(y_i - \hat{y}_i)}{\sum(y_i - \bar{y})^2} \times 100\%$$

where $\hat{y}_i$ = the corresponding values of $y_i$ shown on the regression line for any chosen $x_i$ (see Figure 4.4).

The coefficient $C = 100\%$ if all observations lie directly on the regression line. However, this is rarely the case and so the regression line is the line of best fit through the scatter of points on a scattergraph. The distance from an individual point to the regression line is known as the *residual*. Therefore, if an observation lies on the line, its residual is zero. The residuals represent unexplained or residual variation after the fitting of a regression model.

If residuals are too big to have reasonably occurred by chance, then the model chosen is inadequate. The value of the coefficient of determination gives one indication of a model's suitability. Another is to depict confidence limits which occur on either side of the regression line, thereby using confidence limits by way of examining the reliability of estimates of $y$ made using the regression equation. Thus 95 per cent of the observations in a regression analysis can be said to lie within two standard errors of the regression line. The standard error of the residuals ($SE^2$) is calculated from

$$SE^2 = \frac{\sum(\hat{y}_i - y_i)^2}{n - k - 1}$$

where $\hat{y}_i$ = estimated values of $y_i$, and $k$ = number of independent variables (always 1 in simple linear regression). Alternatively,

$$SE^2 = S_y^2(1 - c^2)$$

where $S_y^2$ = the variance of $y$, and $c$ = the coefficient of determination.

For small samples ($< 30$ observations) a correction factor can be used to counteract the underestimation of variances that can occur in such cases, i.e.

$$\hat{\sigma}_e = SE\sqrt{\left(\frac{n}{n - k - 1}\right)}$$

where $\hat{\sigma}_e$ = the best estimate of the population standard error.

It must be noted, though, that if the regression line is recognised as just representing one sampling outcome, and will therefore vary from sample to sample, then $SE$ on its own cannot be used to establish the reliability of predicted values of $y$. In addition, as the coefficients $a$ and $b$ are based on samples taken from an unknown population, they are subject to sampling error. The sampling error of $a$ means that the true value of the regression line will lie in the shaded area depicted in Figure 4.5a. The effect of the sampling error of $b$ is shown in Figure 4.5b, that is a rotational effect about the intersection of $\bar{y}$ and $\bar{x}$, through which all lines will pass but with differing slopes. The sampling errors of $a$ and $b$ produce curved confidence limits as indicated in Figure 4.5c, showing that the margins of error increase away from the means of $x$ and $y$.

The standard error of the estimate of $y$ ($SE_{\hat{y}}$) at any point $x_k$ is calculated as follows:

$$SE_{\hat{y}} = \hat{\sigma}_e\sqrt{\left(\frac{1 + (x_k - \bar{x})^2}{n\sum(x_i - \bar{x})}\right)}$$

where $\hat{\sigma}_e$ = standard error of residuals, and $x_k$ = selected value of $x_i$.

The standard errors can be converted into confidence limits by use of an appropriate hypothesis test.

## The Analysis of Residuals

Any prediction based on linear regression will be imperfect unless there is a perfect correlation between the dependent and independent variables (i.e. $r_{xy} = \pm1.00$). If this is not the case then some of the individual $x$, $y$ values will not lie on a line of best fit drawn through those values. In such cases the line of best fit has to be drawn in such a way that the sum of the squares of the distances from each $x$, $y$ value to the line is minimised – and hence the references to *ordinary least-squares (OLS) regression* (e.g. Mark and Peucker, 1978). This means that the positive and negative deviations (or residuals) from each $x$, $y$ value to the line must sum to zero, and that the sum of the squared deviations must be smaller than those from any other line.

The vertical distance between an individual observation and the regression line is that part of the value of $y$ for that observation which is unaccounted for by the independent variable $x$. This distance is known as the residual of $y$, that is the difference between the actual and estimated values of $y$, or $(y_i - \hat{y}_i)$, as predicted by the regression equation. Residuals may be positive or negative as shown in Figure 4.6. As the size of the residuals increases so the utility of the regression line decreases in terms of its practical predictive value or in its ability to "explain" the relationship between the dependent and independent variables. Hence if $y$ explains less than, say, 70 per cent of the variation in $x$, simple linear regression analysis is likely to be deemed superfluous. As predictive uses for the regression analysis have been relatively few in human geography, it would seem that regression analysis offers little scope for understanding bivariate relationships. However, several geographers have demonstrated the value of closer investigation of the residuals in regression analysis, making this one of the main reasons for adopting this procedure (Thomas, 1968).

One problem with residuals is that a single exceptional value can influence the slope of the regression line to the extent that it becomes a fairly meaningless

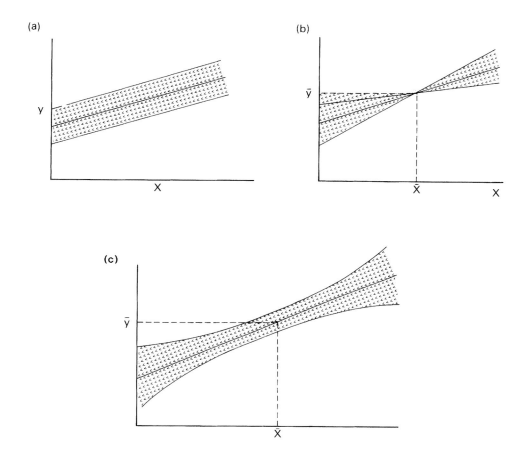

*Figure 4.5*    Sampling Error and the Regression Line

summary of the relationship between $x$ and $y$. This problem can be overcome by comparing the equations obtained from both a full dataset and from one with any extreme data points removed. Such a comparison indicates the influence of the exceptional values on the overall pattern. Alternatively, extreme observations can be weighted to reduce their influence on the regression equation. More straightforward, though, is an exploratory approach based on the use of medians of three groups of observations of both $x$ and $y$. So the paired values $(x, y)$ are divided into three equal-sized groups once the $x$ values have been ranked in the order that they occur from left to right on a scattergraph. The calculation of the medians of $x$ and $y$ for each of

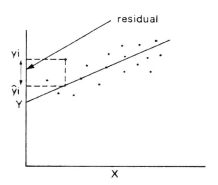

*Figure 4.6*    Regression Line and Scattergraph with Residuals

the three groups then produces three "summary" points $(x_L, y_L)$, $(x_M, y_M)$ and $(x_R, y_R)$. The slope and intercept of the regression line can then be estimated from:

$$a = \tfrac{1}{3}[(y_L - bx_L) + (y_M - bx_M) + (y_R - bx_R)]$$

and

$$b = \frac{y_R - y_L}{x_R - x_L}$$

This gives a good estimate of the relationship between $x$ and $y$. Furthermore, residuals can be placed in a stem-and-leaf display to extend data exploration.

Whereas the regression equation is quantifying a relationship between two variables, a focus upon residuals returns the investigator's attention to the original observations (the original $x$, $y$ values). In many examples of geographical research these observations are for particular places, and so an examination of residuals represents a spatial dimension in the analysis. This was the case in initial work on the use of regression analysis by geographers – for example in Clark's (1967) research on dairy farming in New Zealand and McCarty's on voting patterns in Wisconsin (Thomas, 1968). They both made use of *standardised residuals* in which the size of each residual is expressed in terms of standard error units from the regression line, i.e.

$$\text{standardised residual} = \frac{x_i - \hat{x}}{\hat{\sigma}_e}$$

A detailed consideration of how mapped residuals can be examined was made by Thomas (1960, 1968) in which he identified three main types of use:

- the formation and modification of hypotheses relating to the existence of spatial associations between variables, and searching for new variables to help "explain" the dependent variable;
- the establishment and modification of regional boundaries, so that, in using economic variables in regression analysis, economic regions may be de-

fined on the basis of groupings of residuals;
- the identification and selection of specific study areas for intensive fieldwork, e.g. farming in areas with high or low residuals which are representative of a regression model's poor prediction of values of a dependent agricultural variable.

An early example of geographical research focusing upon residuals from linear regression analysis was work by Robinson and Bryson (1957) in which the rural farm population density in Nebraska was regressed on mean annual precipitation (see Figure 4.7). Positive residuals were recorded in the north-east and west of the state, where the density of the rural farm population was greater than that predicted by the regression equation. But in the central part of the state there were negative residuals, where the density of the rural farm population was less than predicted by the equation. Where they occurred these residuals implied that factors other than mean annual precipitation needed to be considered as an explanation of the population density. So, in situations like this, the research focus may become directed at these "deviant" areas with high residuals. Alternatively, the use of the chosen independent variable may be reconsidered if the residuals are large. For example, in Robinson et al's (1961) regression analysis using population density on the Great Plains as the dependent variable and annual precipitation as the independent variable, consideration of residuals led to the proposal of two additional independent variables affecting population density: distance to centres of over 10 000 population and percentage cropland. When incorporated in a more complex multiple regression equation (see below), these two variables increased the value of the coefficient of determination ($100r^2$) whilst reducing the residuals. Scrutiny of remaining residuals suggested that an additional independent variable might be a measure of farm labour per unit area of cropland.

## The Assumptions of Regression Analysis

The linear regression model makes six basic assumptions (Poole and O'Farrell, 1971):

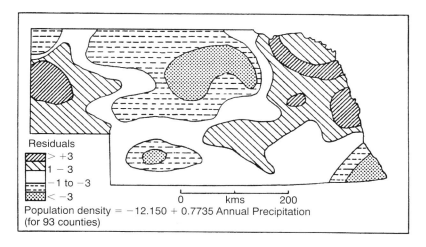

*Figure 4.7*   Map of Residuals for Linear Regression Analysis, Nebraska, USA
$y$ = population density (dependent variable); $x$ = mean annual precipitation (independent variable). (After Robinson and Bryson, 1957)

(a) *Linearity*. Too frequently geographers have paid insufficient attention to basic characteristics of their data and have assumed that linear relationships are the norm rather than considering curvilinear or other forms of relationship. Greater use of exploratory analysis prior to calculation of the regression equation could emphasise the fact that linearity is not always an appropriate assumption. More commonly, though, if a non-linear relationship has been suspected, geographers have employed *mathematical transformations* to "restore" linearity, e.g. exponential, power and Pareto functions (Figure 4.8).

Although much use of correlation and regression in human geography has relied on the linear model, there are a suite of curvilinear methods that can be applied if theory postulates non-linear relationships. For example, different but frequently occurring trends can be described by the following curves:

- the *simple power curve*, $Y = aX^b$
- the *simple exponential curve*, $Y = a/e^{bX}$
- the *simple logarithmic curve*, $Y = a + b \log X$

All three curves can be converted into linear form by transforming either or both variables.

(b) *Residuals* (i.e. the values of $(y_i - \hat{y}_i)$ for every value of $x$) are normally distributed. The values of $(y_i - \hat{y}_i)$ are known as the *conditional distributions* of the residuals.

(c) For every value of $x$ the mean of the $y$ residuals must be zero, i.e. the mean of $(y_i - \hat{y}_i) = 0$. This means that observations must have a constant variance about the regression line as shown in Figure 4.9.

(d) *Homoscedasticity*. There must be equal variances in the conditional distributions of the values of $(y_i - \hat{y}_i)$ for every value of $x$. This assumption is often violated in geographical datasets containing large numbers of observations with small values of $x$ relative to those with large values, e.g. town sizes, streams of various orders in a river basin. In such cases a logarithmic transformation may be appropriate.

*Heteroscedasticity* may be produced by data that contain some internal hierarchical structure, giving rise to within-group correlation or non-independence of observations as manifest in a clustering of residuals. For example, this clustering effect may be produced by the influence of different schools if educational attainment of individual children is regressed on social class (Aitken and Longford, 1986).

One way of overcoming the presence of a hierarch-

(a)

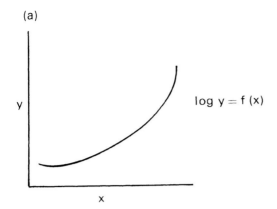

$\log y = f(x)$

(b)

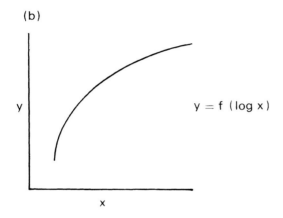

$y = f(\log x)$

(c)

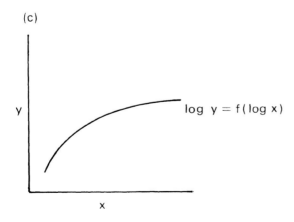

$\log y = f(\log x)$

*Figure 4.8*   Transformations for Linearity
(a) Exponential, (b) power, and (c) Pareto

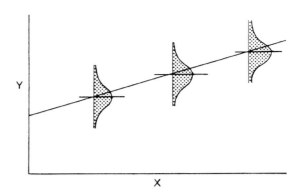

*Figure 4.9*   Observations with Constant Variance About the Regression Line

ical structure within a sample is to adopt a *multi-level approach*, as demonstrated by several statisticians dealing with educational data (e.g. Goldstein, 1987). This method is described below ("Multiple regression" in Chapter 4).

(e) *Autocorrelation*. The value of each observation on the independent variable should be independent of all the values of all other observations, i.e. given one value of $x$ another value is not predetermined. This is a complex issue which is considered in further detail in Chapter 9.

(f) *Lack of measurement error*. The variables should be measured without error. If a measurement error of unknown magnitude occurs then regression coefficients may be biased. Furthermore, error terms in the regression model must be independent. For instance, if data used in the analysis have normally distributed error terms, the independence of these error terms may be tested using the *Durbin–Watson test* (Durbin and Watson, 1950/51). In this the test statistic ($D$) is calculated from

$$D = \frac{(E_t - E_{t-1})^2}{E_t^2}$$

where $E_t$ and $E_{t-1}$ are successive residuals. If error terms are positively correlated, the difference between successive residuals is small; whilst if errors are negatively correlated, the difference between successive residuals is large. Therefore small values of $D$ indicate that positive correlation exists while large values of $D$ indicate that negative correlation exists. The significance of a calculated value of $D$ can be determined using the appropriate tables (see Neter and Wasserman, 1974). Cliff and Ord (1972) present a simple case in which the data have a geographic ordering which requires a modification of this test for independence of error terms. They use an alternative statistic which can test for correlation among geographically located error terms arising from least-squares regression.

In addition to these six assumptions, problems may occur in linear regression if the dependent variable is a closed ratio, in which case use of ordinary least-squares regression may yield nonsensical predictions of the dependent variable. Hence a transformation of the dependent variable is required. Commonly used ones are the logistic and probit transforms (see above subsection on "Closed number sets"), the latter being based on the cumulative normal distribution.

## MULTIPLE REGRESSION

In pioneering work on the application of regression to a geographical problem, the close investigation of residuals led McCarty to extend his analysis from simple linear regression to produce a more complex explanation of the dependent variable (Thomas, 1968:341–4). In his investigation of the distribution of votes for Senator Joe McCarthy in the 1952 election in Wisconsin, the correlation coefficient between percentage vote for McCarthy ($y$) and percentage of the population living in rural areas ($x$) was $r_{xy} = 0.58$ and $100r_{xy}^2 = 33.64$ per cent. So only one-third of the variation in the vote for McCarthy was explained by the percentage of population that was rural. The map of residuals (Figure 4.10) shows that a much greater vote than predicted by the regression equation had occurred around McCarthy's home town of Appleton. Indeed, there was a *distance-decay effect* for the residuals: under-prediction around Appleton and over-prediction further away from the town. This indicated that the percentage vote for McCarthy was dependent

upon not just one independent variable, but at least two, distance from Appleton being the second. Therefore $y$ was a function of two dependent variables ($x_1$ and $x_2$). This illustrates the clear distinction between simple linear regression in which $y = f(x)$ and multiple regression in which $y = f(x_1, x_2, \ldots, x_n)$.

In this example, using just two independent variables, the *multiple regression* equation took the form

$$y = a + b_1 x_1 + b_2 x_2 \pm e$$

where $a$ = the intercept on the $y$-axis, $b_1$ and $b_2$ = partial regression coefficients, and $e$ = an error term.

In this case a least-squares regression plane can be fitted in three-dimensional space, but for more than two independent variables the concept of least-squares applies only to a notional "surface" fitted in multi-dimensional space. Hence, the calculations involved in determining multiple regression equations of the form $y = a + b_1 x_1 + b_2 x_2 + \ldots + b_i x_i \pm e$ usually utilise computers.

Initially the use of multiple regression arose from insufficient explanation of a dependent variable by a single independent variable. A good example is provided by Robinson et al's (1961) work on farming in the Mid-West of the USA, attempting to account for variations in rural farm population density. Using the level of annual precipitation ($x_1$) as the only independent variable, the level of explanation obtained was 64 per cent. However, inclusion of two further independent variables ($x_2$ and $x_3$) raised the level of explanation to 81 per cent:

$$y = -4.854 + 0.304x_1 - 0.012x_2 + 0.80x_3$$

where $y$ = rural farm population density, $x_1$ = level of annual precipitation, $x_2$ = distance to urban centres of $> 10\,000$ population, and $x_3$ = percentage of area in cropland.

In the multiple regression equation the slope coefficients $b_1, b_2, \ldots, b_n$ are termed *partial regression coefficients* and have values in the same units used to measure the respective independent variables (in this case millimetres, miles and per cent respectively). This means that they cannot be compared directly with

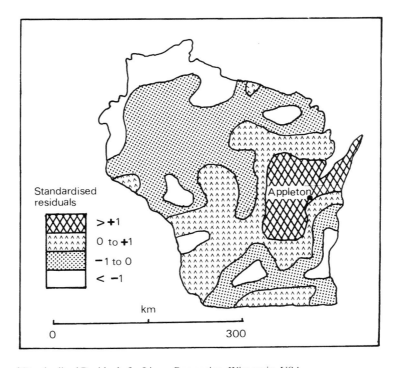

*Figure 4.10*   Map of Standardised Residuals for Linear Regression, Wisconsin, USA
$y = \%$ vote for McCarthy in 1952 election (dependent variable); $x = \%$ population in rural areas (independent variable). (After Thomas, 1968)

one another unless they are transformed into *beta weights* $(\beta_i)$:

$$\beta_i = b_i(s_{xi}/s_y)$$

where $b_i =$ slope coefficient of independent variable $x_i$, $s_{xi} =$ standard deviation of the independent variable under consideration, and $s_y =$ standard deviation of the dependent variable.

Beta weights show how much change in the dependent variable is produced by a standardised change in one of the independent variables, with the influence of the other independent variables controlled. Therefore beta weights enable assessment of the effects of the individual independent variables in the regression equation: the higher the beta weight, the greater the

rate at which the dependent variable increases with an increase in the particular independent variable (see Taylor, 1980).

This is demonstrated in work on the factors influencing industrial employment in Scotland between 1945 and 1970 (Henderson, 1980a,b). The level of employment provided by in-migrant industry in a number of zones was the dependent variable $(y)$, for which a series of multiple regression equations were generated for four different time periods. Six independent variables measured on the interval scale were examined: $x_1 =$ female unemployment; $x_2 =$ total unemployment; $x_3 =$ percentage female unemployment; $x_4 =$ percentage total unemployment; $x_5 =$ sites/premises; $x_6 =$ new advance factories; $x_7 =$ image. The results were as follows:

- 1945–51

$$y = -459.41 + 0.17x_2 + 258.94x_4 + 979.52x_5$$

beta weights $x_2 = 0.35$, $x_4 = 0.18$, $x_5 = 0.59$ (i.e. $x_5$ was given about 65 per cent more weight in the location decision than $x_2$); $r_2 = 0.86$.

- 1952–59

$$y = 220.51 + 0.28x_2 + 232.26x_5$$

beta weights $x_2 = 0.71$, $x_5 = 0.37$; $r_2 = 0.84$.

- 1960–65

$$y = -631.63 + 0.37x_1 + 204.19x_3$$
$$+ 40.66x_5 + 137.81x_6$$

beta weights $x_1 = 0.30$, $x_3 = 0.21$, $x_5 = 0.48$, $x_6 = 0.30$; $r^2 = 0.89$.

- 1966–70

$$y = 223.97 + 1.26x_1 + 17.81x_5$$
$$+ 74.58x_6 - 233.98x_7$$

beta weights $x_1 = 0.86$, $x_5 = 0.24$, $x_6 = 0.36$, $x_7 = -0.32$; $r^2 = 0.83$.

These equations show that, in the immediate post-war period, site factors and availability of premises were the most important variables in determining employment growth through attraction of in-migrant industry. This was also the case in the early 1960s, but by the late 1960s the level of female unemployment had become the most important variable. The availability of labour and factory space stand out as the only variables important to immigrant establishments in every period. However, as shown by the beta weights, their relative importance varied through time, with the availability of unskilled and semi-skilled female labour becoming particularly important to incoming industry in the 1960s.

A more recent exemplification of the use of beta weights is in work by Hoggart (1995), in which a series of multiple regressions are used to investigate relationships between political parties and the implementation of homeless legislation by non-metropolitan districts in England and Wales.

## Multiple and Partial Correlation

One of the main aims of multiple regression is to increase the level of explanation of the dependent variable. This level of explanation is measured by calculating the coefficient of determination which is based on the *multiple correlation coefficient*. The multiple correlation coefficient measures the correlation between $y$ and all the independent variables, i.e. $r_{y.x_1 x_2 ... x_n}$. The coefficient is derived in the same way as the product-moment correlation coefficient, though now incorporating sums of squares for several variables. Therefore,

$$r_{y.x_1 x_2 ... x_n} = \text{variation explained by all independent}$$
$$\text{variables divided by variation of } y_i.$$

This calculation is not entirely straightforward because the independent variables are unlikely to be completely unrelated to one another. This situation is conceptualised in Figure 4.11. In Figure 4.11a simple linear regression is illustrated, in which a proportion of the variation in $y$ is "explained" by $x_1$; in Figure 4.11b a second independent variable, $x_2$, has been added, thereby increasing the explanation of $y$ – no correlation is suggested between $x_1$ and $x_2$. However, in Figure 4.11c some correlation between $x_1$ and $x_2$ is implied, where some of the covariation between $y$ and $x_1$ is also covariation between $y$ and $x_2$. So to measure the additional explanation of a series of independent variables in a multiple regression, it is the partial correlations that have to be calculated, where the partial correlation is the correlation between two variables with the effects of correlations with other specified variables removed or held constant. For example, if there are three independent variables, the following three partial correlations would have to be calculated:

$$r_{yx_1 . x_2 x_3} = \text{correlation between } y \text{ and } x_1 \text{ with}$$
$$\text{effects of } x_2 \text{ and } x_3 \text{ held constant}$$

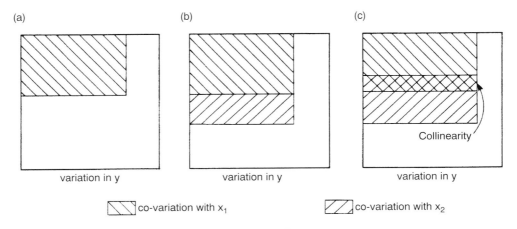

*Figure 4.11*   Conceptualisation of Collinearity in Regression Analysis

$r_{yx_2.x_1x_3}$ = correlation between $y$ and $x_2$ with the effects of $x_1$ and $x_3$ held constant

$r_{yx_3.x_1x_2}$ = correlation between $y$ and $x_3$ with the effects of $x_1$ and $x_2$ held constant

The number of variables held constant or controlled gives rise to the term *nth-order correlation coefficient*. In the above example, *second-order correlations* are being described because two variables are being held constant. For simple linear regression based on $r_{xy}$, the correlation is said to be *zero-order* because no additional variable is held constant. First-order partial correlation coefficients can be calculated from:

$$r_{yx_1.x_2} = \frac{r_{yx_1} - r_{yx_2}\, r_{x_1x_2}}{\sqrt{(1 - r_{yx_2}^2)}\sqrt{(1 - r_{x_1x_2}^2)}}$$

For second-order coefficients the formula is:

$$r_{yx_1.x_2x_3} = \frac{r_{yx_1.x_3} - r_{yx_2.x_3}\, r_{x_1x_2.x_3}}{\sqrt{(1 - r_{yx_2.x_3}^2)}\sqrt{(1 - r_{x_1x_2.x_3}^2)}}$$

Partial correlation can help to identify variables in a chain such as "A leads to B which leads to C". If A is related to C only through intervening variable B, then a partial correlation coefficient between A and C controlling for B should be close to 0. For example, there may be a link between wealth and educational attainment which is only expressed through an intervening variable referring to type of school or quality of teaching. However, partial correlations require careful interpretation, with emphasis being placed upon the formulation of a conceptual model specifying relationships between variables.

Partial correlation coefficients provide one method of measuring the separate influences of independent variables upon the dependent variable, and beta coefficients provide an alternative method. Partial correlation coefficients measure the proportion of variance in the dependent variable that is accounted for by each independent variable. Beta coefficients indicate how much change in the dependent variable is produced by a standardised change in an independent variable, with the others held constant. As partial correlation coefficients relate only to that part of the variance not associated with joint variance between independent variables, partial correlations are used as a means of selecting those independent variables adding the most explanation to the multiple regression model.

This process, illustrated in Table 4.7, is often referred to as *stepwise entry* of variables because the multiple regression equation is built up one variable at a time. Variables are added to the equation in their order of importance in reducing the variance of $y$, starting with the most important first as determined by

*Table 4.7*    Stepwise (Forward) Entry of Independent Variables to a Multiple Regression Equation

*Step 1*: Correlation matrix between the variables

|       | $x_1$   | $x_2$   | $x_3$  | $x_4$   | $x_5$   | $x_6$   | $y$     |
|-------|---------|---------|--------|---------|---------|---------|---------|
| $x_1$ | 1.000   | 0.905   | 0.913  | 0.644   | 0.951   | −0.517  | −0.780  |
| $x_2$ | 0.905   | 1.000   | 0.847  | 0.603   | 0.849   | −0.544  | −0.761  |
| $x_3$ | 0.913   | 0.847   | 1.000  | 0.778   | 0.874   | −0.494  | −0.735  |
| $x_4$ | 0.644   | 0.603   | 0.778  | 1.000   | 0.611   | −0.211  | −0.354  |
| $x_5$ | 0.951   | 0.849   | 0.874  | 0.611   | 1.000   | −0.514  | −0.744  |
| $x_6$ | −0.517  | −0.544  | −0.494 | −0.211  | −0.514  | 1.000   | 0.734   |
| $y$   | −0.780  | −0.761  | −0.735 | −0.354  | −0.744  | 0.734   | 1.000   |

$y$ = rate of population increase in rural districts
$x_1$ = % population aged > 65 years
$x_2$ = distance to towns with > 250 000 population
$x_3$ = % housing stock under local authority control
$x_4$ = % population living in rented accommodation
$x_5$ = % employed population engaged in primary activities
$x_6$ = new business start-ups

*Step 2*: Enter independent variable most highly correlated with $y$: this is $x_1$ (% population aged > 65 years)

$$r_{yx_1} = -0.780 \quad r^2_{yx_1} = 0.608$$

*Step 3*: Once one independent variable has been selected, refer to the partial correlations between the dependent variable and each of the independent variables not in the equation, controlled for the independent variable(s) in the equation. The variable with the largest partial correlation is the next candidate for inclusion. In this case the partial correlations are:

$$y_{x_2 \cdot x_1} = -0.208$$

$$y_{x_3 \cdot x_1} = -0.090$$

$$y_{x_4 \cdot x_1} = 0.310$$

$$y_{x_5 \cdot x_1} = -0.007$$

$$y_{x_6 \cdot x_1} = 0.618$$

Therefore $x_6$ is the next variable added to the equation:

$$r_{yx_1 x_6} = 0.871 \quad r^2_{yx_1 x_6} = 0.759$$

*Step 4*: Repeat step 3 until all variables have been added. This yields an equation including all independent variables:

$$y = 30.098 - 0.024x_1 + 6.597x_6 + 2.231x_4 + 0.388x_5 - 0.118x_2 - 0.070x_3$$

$$r_{yx_1 x_6 x_4 x_5 x_2 x_3} = 0.8933$$

$$r^2_{yx_1 x_6 x_4 x_5 x_2 x_3} = 0.798$$

This shows that only a limited increase in the overall explanation of the dependent variable ($y$) is achieved by adding the last four independent variables (probably because these last four are highly inter-correlated).

*continued overleaf*

*Table 4.7   (Continued)*

Therefore some criteria need to be established regarding the entry of variables to the equation. A common criterion is to specify the $F$ statistic that a variable must achieve in order to be entered. The $F$ statistic can be generated by testing a hypothesis that: $B_1 = B_2 = B_3 = B_4 = B_5 = B_6 = 0$ (i.e. that there is a linear relationship between $y$ and the independent variables). Usually the critical value specified is $F = 0.05$.

In the example given, after $x_1$ and $x_6$ have been added, the $F$ values for the remaining variables are:

| | $F$ | |
|---|---|---|
| $x_2$ | 0.318 | These are all $>0.05$, and so none of |
| $x_3$ | 0.129 | these variables should be added to the equation. |
| $x_4$ | 2.110 | Therefore the stepwise inclusion of |
| $x_5$ | 0.108 | variables should stop once $x_1$ and $x_6$ have been added |

*Conclusion*: The rate of population increase in rural districts depends primarily on new business start-ups (+ve association) and percentage of population aged $>65$ years (−ve association).

the partial correlation coefficients. Variants of this approach are described by King (1969:145–8). As Table 4.7 shows, once the first independent variable has been used in the equation, then the first-order partial correlation coefficients between $y$ and the remaining independent variables should be calculated, holding constant the one already in the equation. The largest of these partial correlations is then selected and added to the equation. The next step is to calculate second-order partial correlation coefficients, holding constant the independent variables already in the regression equation. The largest of these coefficients is selected and the relevant independent variable is included in the equation.

The stepwise process reflects the fact that a variety of regression models can be constructed from a single set of variables. For example, if there are three independent variables then seven different equations could be developed: three containing only one independent variable, three containing two independent variables, and one with all three independent variables. With 10

independent variables, 1023 models could be examined!

In Table 4.7, six independent variables are used to explain or predict rates of rural population growth. The small amount of additional explanation brought about by $x_2$, $x_3$, $x_4$ and $x_5$ may be due to multicollinearity or a high degree of intercorrelation between the independent variables. This means that two independent variables may be explaining very nearly the same variation in the dependent variable. Such intercorrelation can usually be identified by reference to zero-order correlation coefficients between the independent variables, high coefficients suggesting intercorrelation.

The decision on how many variables to include, and therefore on the nature of the multiple regression equation, can be based on the effect upon the multiple correlation coefficient of each variable entered. Small increases can be regarded as indicating the inclusion of a variable that is adding little to the overall explanation of the dependent variable.

One of the basic assumptions of the multiple regression model is that the effects of the independent variables are additive, that is each independent variable accounts for a proportion of the variance in $y$. If there is collinearity then joint variance effects must be included. However, in some cases the effects of independent variables may be multiplicative, showing a joint influence beyond that induced by collinearity. Johnston (1978:81–2) provides an example of this:

$$y = 2.43 + 0.68x_1 \qquad r_{yx_1} = 0.79$$

$$y = 4.92 + 0.30x_2 \qquad r_{yx_2} = 0.25$$

$$y = -1.01 + 0.82x_1 + 0.64x_2 \qquad r_{y.x_1x_2} = 0.94$$

Therefore, in this additive equation, $x_1$ and $x_2$ account for 88 per cent or $(0.94)^2$ of the variance in $y$. However, if $x_1$ and $x_2$ are multiplicative then

$$y = 1.19 + 0.25x_1x_2 \qquad r = 0.99$$

This type of multiplication of variables is found in geographers' use of gravity models (see Chapter 8) in which population values for different places are multiplied. Multiplication terms are usually incorporated in regression equations using a logarithmic transformation, i.e.

$$x_1x_2 = \log_{10} x_1 + \log_{10} x_2$$

Further work on multiple regression by geographers includes *staged regression analysis* (SRA) as used by Earle and Young (1992) and a three-dimensional version known as *trend surface analysis*. The latter has been popular within geology and physical geography but has been little used by human geographers since the days of the Quantitative Revolution (see Haggett, 1981; Unwin and Wrigley, 1987).

## Added Variable Plots

Graphical techniques are frequently an integral part of regression analysis, for example as a summary of the relationship between the dependent variable ($y$) and an independent variable ($x_p$) adjusted for other independent variables in a selected set. Such a plot will show whether there is a relationship between $x_p$ and $y$, and, if so, whether it is linear. If it is suspected that an additional variable ($x_{k+1}$) should be added to a regression model, a graph known as an *added variable plot* can be constructed. The plot is additional graphical information that can help to illustrate the complex interrelationships between variables under consideration (Haining, 1990a). As suggested by Anselin (1988), this may be more preferable for spatial data, with its problems of autocorrelation, than the more complex methods described above.

An added variable plot can be constructed as follows: calculate the regression equation minus $x_{k+1}$ and obtain the residuals ($\hat{e}$). Then regress $x_{k+1}$ on the initial set of independent variables ($x_1, \ldots, x_k$) and obtain the residuals ($\overset{*}{e}$). The added variable plot is a plot of the elements of $\hat{e}$ against $\overset{*}{e}$. A strong linear trend implies $x_{k+1}$ should be added to the initial regression equation (Figure 4.12a). Lack of such a trend implies that it can be omitted. The plot itself can be interpreted in the same way as a scattergraph in a regression (Haining, 1990b; Johnson and McCulloch, 1987).

For spatial data, Haining (1990b) suggests that there are other relationships that can be identified graphically and supplies examples of further reading on the topic:

- Whether the value of $y$ at location $i$ is a linear function of values of $y$ at nearby locations (see Haining, 1983a, 1987).
- Whether the value of $y$ at location $i$ is a linear function of values of an independent variable ($x_p$) both at location $i$ and at nearby locations (see Anas and Eum, 1984).
- Whether the value of $y$ at location $i$ is a linear function of values of both $y$ at nearby locations and an independent variable at both location $i$ and neighbouring locations (see Anselin, 1988; Anselin and Can, 1986).
- Whether the errors are not spatially independent and the error for location $i$ is a linear function of the errors at nearby locations (see Loftin and Ward, 1983).

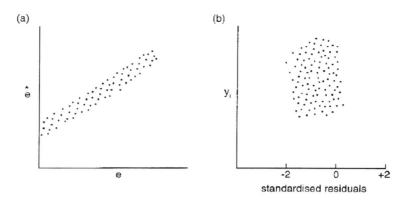

*Figure 4.12*    Exploratory Data Analysis and Regression Analysis

Haining (1990b:338–9) suggests various ways of investigating these relationships, but recommends added variable plots for exploratory investigation or for situations where formal testing procedures are not appropriate. Two related graphical procedures are as follows.

(a) *Catch-all plots.* Standardised residuals from linear regression are plotted versus the $y_i$ values. If the linear regression is appropriate then the standardised residuals should fall between $\pm2$ and will be randomly distributed about zero (Figure 4.12b). If this is not the case then the regression has not fully accounted for the variation in the dependent variable and should be respecified, perhaps with additional independent variables, or the data should be checked for errors. Other diagnostic types of results from a plot can indicate the presence of particular problems, including heteroscedasticity (so that a transformation is required), a nonlinear relationship or the combined effects of nonlinearity and heteroscedasticity, and outliers (possibly suggesting data error or mis-specification such as an omitted variable or a non-linear relationship).

(b) *Partial-residual plots.* If catch-all plots reveal problems with a regression analysis, a partial-residual plot may then be used to gain a better understanding of the problem. This involves calculating partial residuals ($\hat{E}_p$) for each explanatory variable in a multiple regression, i.e.

$$\hat{E}_p = \hat{E} + \hat{b}_j x_j$$

where $\hat{E}$ = the least squares regression residual vector, and $\hat{b}_j$ = the estimated regression coefficient associated with the explanatory variable $x_j$. These partial residuals may then be plotted against the corresponding explanatory variables to produce a plot for each explanatory variable after the effects of the other explanatory variables have been removed. If the plot is linear then the regression model has been specified correctly, but if it is curved, this implies an incorrect functional form.

## Multi-level Models

Whilst correlation coefficients at different levels of data aggregation can show distinctly different patterns, similarly in multiple regression sharply varying results may be obtained at different spatial scales. Therefore interpretations must be scale-dependent. It is this dependence, or, in other words, the "context" of an analysis that is crucial to any interpretation of the results of correlation and regression. Relationships between individuals and groups must be considered very carefully, perhaps with extra steps inserted in analysis to distinguish between them, as in so-called *multi-level approaches* (Jones, 1991; Jones et al, 1992). These approaches offer a way of overcoming the presence of a hierarchical structure within a sample, as demonstrated by several statisticians dealing with educational data (e.g. Goldstein, 1987).

*Multi-level models* combine individual and ecological modelling to allow a separation of effects associated with each level of a hierarchy within a population. The basic approach is an extension of ordinary least-squares regression and, at its simplest, is identical to an analysis of variance in which the total variance in a population is partitioned into within-group and between-group components. The operation of such models may be represented as follows, using the notation employed by Bondi and Bradford (1990):

The partitioning of variance may be considered as

$$y_{ij} = B_{0j} + e_{ij} \quad \text{(for the within-group component)}$$

$$B_{0j} = \gamma_{00} + \mu_{0j} \quad \text{(for the between-group component)}$$
$$(4.1)$$

where $y_{ij}$ = the value of the dependent variable for the $i$th case in the $j$th group, $B_{0j}$ = the value of the intercept for the $j$th group, $e_{ij}$ = error terms (residuals) for the $i$th case in the $j$th group, which are assumed to be normally distributed, with a mean of zero and a variance of $\sigma^2$, $\gamma_{00}$ = the grand mean of all cases, and $\mu_{0j}$ = the residuals associated with the $j$th group, which are assumed to be normally distributed, with a mean of zero and a variance of $\tau$.

Usually, an explanatory or control variable would be introduced to the within-group model, i.e.

$$y_{ij} = B_{0j} + B_{ij}(x_{ij}) + e_{ij}$$

where $x_{ij}$ = the value of the explanatory variable for the $i$th case in the $j$th group, and $B_{ij}$ = the regression coefficient for the explanatory variable in the $j$th group.

Variations between groups with respect to the relationship between the dependent variable and explanatory variables (as illustrated in Figure 4.13) may be investigated using

$$B_{ij} = \gamma_{10} + \mu_{1j} \qquad (4.2)$$

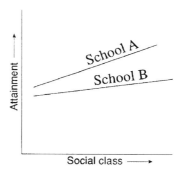

*Figure 4.13*  A Multi-Level Model

Whilst in (4.1) above the intercepts vary for different groups, in (4.2) the slopes vary. Thus the equations contain variable or "random" elements as well as "fixed" elements. The equations may be utilised so that group-level explanatory variables are introduced to the between-group equations. Bondi and Bradford (1990: 260) give the example of an investigation of educational attainment in which equation (4.1) above becomes:

$$B_{0j} = \gamma_{00} + \gamma_{01}(\bar{x})_j + \gamma_{02}(z)_j + \mu_{01}$$

where $(\bar{x})_j$ = the mean value of $x$ (an attribute associated with members of a group, e.g. social class) for the $j$th group, $(z)_j$ = the value of attribute $z$ (e.g. school status) for the $j$th group, and $\gamma_{01}$, $\gamma_{02}$ = regression coefficients for the group-level variables.

Multi-level models do not require large within-group samples and can be applied to a range of hierarchical data structures, reflecting the number of institutions or organisations with hierarchies, e.g. schools, hospitals (Jones and Duncan, 1995; Jones and Moon, 1990), retailing and manufacturing plants. They may be used to study the effects of different places upon particular relationships associated with institutions, and there are several ways in which the effects of place may be examined (Jones, 1991). Recently, further work on the application of multi-level modelling to the geography of chronic illness has demonstrated how observations for individuals "may be accounted for by factors operating both at the same level and at different levels (such as that of the neighbourhood or region)" (Richards and Wrigley, 1996:57). Furthermore, the models can be extended to multivariate situations or may incorporate a temporal element. So they present a considerable potential for geographical investigation on "the effects of social and economic institutions, locality effects and the partitioning of space" (Bondi and Bradford, 1990:262). For a debate on the merits of multi-level modelling as applied to data on crime see Herbert (1993, 1994) and Jones (1994).

## CAUSAL MODELLING

Geographers have tended to focus upon the classical least-squares regression model as described above, although growing use has been made of other variants, including polynomial regressions, regression using categorised (dummy) variables (see last section in Chapter 6), simultaneous-equation regression models, and path analysis (see subsections that follow). Most of these approaches consider more complex relationships than those specified by multiple regression. They can be regarded as variants of *causal modelling*, in which a system of causes and effects is analysed rather than examining the effects of a number of variables upon just one (dependent) variable as in multiple regression (see Cadwallader, 1985b:70–3). Some forms of causal modelling test whether a hypothesised model is consistent with empirical data rather than assuming a particular model and then estimating the values of its parameters as in multiple regression.

The basic multiple regression situation is summarised in Figure 4.14a. A one-way functional linkage exists between a dependent variable ($y$) and a number of independent variables (or regressors) ($x_1$, $x_2$, ..., $x_n$). Unexplained variance in $y$ is accounted for by "unidentified regressors" absent from the model. Two significant weaknesses in this arrangement are:

1. The independent variables may not be truly independent of one another. Linkages may exist between them, as described above, and so collinearity is present.

2. There may not be a simple one-way linkage between the dependent and independent variables. Variables may be interrelated and cannot be explained in isolation from one another as demanded in a multiple regression analysis.

So there may well be far more complex relationships between variables, such as that indicated in Figure 4.14b, dealing with unemployment in Belfast, Northern Ireland. In this example a number of variables can be found that "explain" unemployment, but they are intercorrelated and one hypothesised regressor, percentage of population that are Catholics, is associated with unemployment indirectly via family size and a measure of overcrowding (Boal et al, 1978). It is often important to identify the role played by intervening variables, such as that occupied by family size in this example.

Similarly, two variables ($x$ and $y$) may be correlated by virtue of their common dependence upon a third variable ($z$). If this association with the third variable is ignored, incorrect statements could be made regarding causality between $x$ and $y$. Therefore a range of possible causal variables needs to be considered for any given situation, and various links between variables established. However, once several variables are considered, the complexity of possible associations and interrelationships is increased considerably. There are several ways in which complex linkages can be investigated. Three are outlined below.

### The Simon–Blalock Technique

One way of examining linkages between a system of variables under investigation is to use a method known as the *Simon–Blalock technique*. This is based on a *causal diagram*, such as that depicted in Figure 4.14b, and employs partial correlation coefficients to test a hypothesised model. It is closely related to regression techniques, but considers a number of causes and effects rather than the effects of a number of variables upon one dependent variable.

A causal model is hypothesised via a causal diagram and then tested by applying a series of rules to multiple regression equations based on the diagram,

(a)

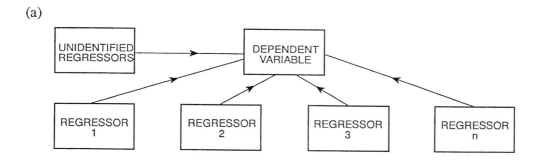

(b)

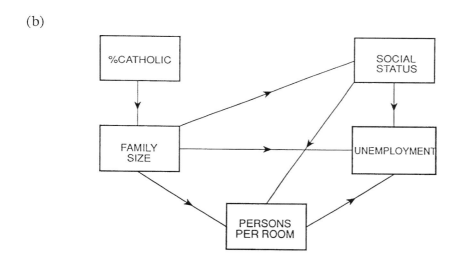

*Figure 4.14* Causal Models
(a) Causal model for a standard multiple regression model (b) causal model for unemployment in Belfast, Northern Ireland. Arrows portray direction of causality. (Based on Boal et al, 1978)

as devised by the sociologists Hubert Blalock (1960, 1962, 1964) and Herbert Simon (1957). This can be a complex procedure if there are a number of variables in a causal chain, but it is relatively simple for a small number of variables.

For example, consider a possible three-variable causal chain from Figure 4.15a, linking percentage Catholic ($x_1$) family size ($x_2$) and unemployment ($x_3$), and assuming no reciprocal relations and three possible hypotheses. Starting with the most favoured hypothesis (Figure 4.14b) that religious affiliation (percentage Catholic) has no independent influence on unemployment, this implies that $r_{x_3x_1.x_2} = 0$. This is because in the causal chain any correlation between $x_1$ and $x_3$ should represent the two correlations $r_{x_3x_2}$ and $r_{x_1x_2}$ – none of the variance of $x_3$ is explained by $x_1$ without the intervening effect of $x_2$.

Therefore the value of $r_{x_3x_1}$ can be predicted if $r_{x_1x_2}$ and $r_{x_3x_2}$ are calculated. So, if $r_{x_1x_2} = 0.627$ and $r_{x_3x_2} = 0.788$, $r_{x_1x_3} = (0.627)(0.788) = 0.494$. This

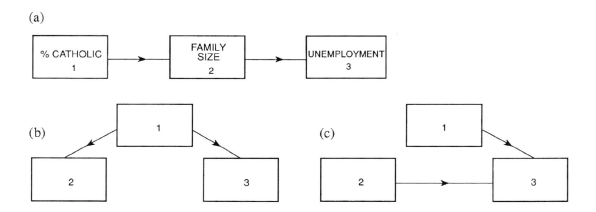

*Figure 4.15*   Alternative Three-Variable Causal Models
Arrows portray direction of causality

predicted value can then be compared with the actual value of $r_{x_1 x_3}$, which is 0.504. This similarity between predicted and actual values is a strong indication that the causal chain depicted is an appropriate one. However, no test of significance is appropriate for this "best" model, and the decision as to whether a particular model is appropriate is essentially intuitive. Usually, by following a similar procedure for other causal arrangements, such as those suggested in Figure 4.15b and c, the discrepancies between predicted and actual correlations make the selection of the most appropriate model obvious. In the example shown in Figure 4.15b, the predicted value of $r_{x_2 x_3 . x_1} = 0.0$, and in Figure 4.15c the predicted value of $r_{x_1 x_2} = 0.0$. These predictions compare with actual values of 0.70 and 0.63 respectively, strengthening the argument in support of the arrangement shown in Figure 4.15a. The analysis of more complex situations using the Simon–Blalock approach is discussed by Pringle (1980).

The basis of most work in causal modelling is the so-called *three-variable recursive model* shown in Figure 4.16a. In this the arrows indicate one-way causality: $x_2$ and $x_3$ are *endogenous variables*, that is variables within the "system" under investigation, and they have values at least partly determined by other variables within this system; $x_1$ is an *exogenous variable*, determined by forces outside the system. Assum-

ing that each variable is measured in standardised form so that the least-squares regression line passes through the origin and therefore the intercepts ($a$) are zero, the causal structure may be represented as:

$$x_1 = e_1$$

$$x_2 = b_{21}x_1 + e_2$$

$$x_3 = b_{31.2}x_1 + b_{32.1}x_2 + e_3$$

An example of a four-variable recursive model is shown in Figure 4.16b. This model can be expressed as:

$$x_1 = e_1$$

$$x_2 = b_{21}x_1 + e_2$$

$$x_3 = b_{31.2}x_1 + b_{32.1}x_2 + e_3$$

$$x_4 = b_{41.23}x_1 + b_{42.13}x_2 + b_{43.12}x_3 + e_4$$

## Path Analysis

Cadwallader (1986) criticises human geographers' continuing reliance upon single equation regression models rather than exploring reciprocal causation and the role of indirect effects on situations. Two further

(a)

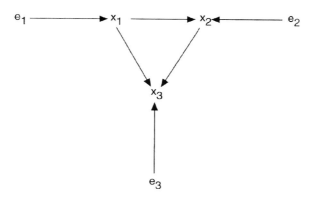

(b)

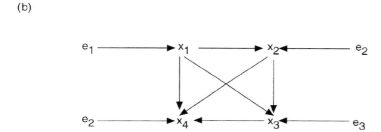

*Figure 4.16*   Recursive Models
(a) Three-variable recursive model; (b) Four-variable recursive model

possibilities for performing such exploration are the use of *path analysis*, widely used by sociologists to distinguish direct and indirect links between variables, and, in addition to the Simon–Blalock method, the use of systems of *simultaneous equations* described in the following subsection.

First developed in the 1920s and 1930s by the geneticist Sewall Wright (1934, 1960), and then as *dependence analysis* by Boudon (1965), *path analysis* estimates the magnitude of the linkages between variables whilst distinguishing the direct and indirect effects between them, and separating the correlation between any two variables into a sum of simple and

compound paths, where a compound path is the product of the simple paths comprising it. The correlation between any pair of variables can be written in terms of the paths leading from common antecedent variables. Sociologists in particular have made use of path analysis as part of work involving causal modelling and structural equation models (e.g. Winship and Mare, 1983), but geographers' use of this technique has been relatively limited. Examples include work on migration (Cadwallader, 1985a; Todd, 1980, 1983), voting behaviour (Cox, 1968), attitudes to mental health facilities (Hall and Taylor, 1983) and cognitive mapping (Golledge and Spector, 1978).

Path analysis can only be performed if variables are dependent on others as linear functions. The dependent variables are completely determined by some combination of variables in the system or else a residual variable outside the system must be introduced. The analysis relies on the depiction of a variable system in a causal diagram showing dependence. The Simon–Blalock method described above is a special form of path analysis.

Path analysis calculates standardised partial regression coefficients, known as *path coefficients*, instead of partial correlation coefficients. A path coefficient gives a quantitative measure of the relative strength of the causal link to which it refers (see Cadwallader, 1981). Therefore path analysis is often used to calibrate an accepted causal model rather than to test a hypothesised model, though the Simon–Blalock technique may be a simpler method for the latter purpose. One main value of path analysis is in making explicit the rationale for a set of regression calculations by focusing attention upon the causal scheme and upon the importance of indirect effects.

In simple recursive situations (as depicted in Figure 4.17), path coefficients can be estimated from OLS regression analysis. For example $p_{32} = b_{32.1}$, $p_{31} = b_{31.2}$, $p_{42} = b_{42.13}$, $p_{43} = b_{43.12}$. That is, unlike partial regression and correlation coeffficients, the notation for path coefficients does not identify the other variables influencing the particular endogenous variable under consideration. The path coefficient associated with the residual term is the square root of any unexplained variation in the dependent variable.

The correlation coefficients between the variables in the system under consideration can be decomposed using

$$r_{ij} = \sum p_{iq} r_{jq}$$

where $i$ and $j$ = two variables in the system, and $q =$ the index running over those variables having a direct impact on $x_i$. Thus, following Cadwallader (1986:30),

$$r_{53} = p_{53} + p_{51} p_{31} + p_{51} r_{12} p_{32} + p_{52} p_{32}$$
$$+ p_{52} r_{12} p_{31} + p_{54} p_{41} p_{31} + p_{54} p_{41} r_{12} p_{32}$$
$$+ p_{54} p_{42} p_{32} + p_{54} p_{42} r_{12} p_{31} + p_{54} p_{43}$$

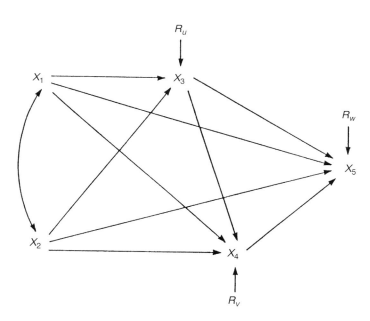

*Figure 4.17*    A Recursive Model Based on Duncan (1966)

In producing this equation, based on Figure 4.17, it must be observed that:

- no path may pass through the same variable more than once;
- no path may go back along an arrow having started forward on a different arrow;
- a path may go in either direction along a two-headed arrow, but only one such two-headed arrow can be used in any single path.

Figure 4.17 shows causal links depicted as straight lines between variables, with arrows pointing to each dependent variable from each determining variable. The curved two-headed arrow from $x_1$ to $x_2$ indicates possible correlation between the two variables which are not causally dependent on other variables in the system. Curved arrows have simple correlation coefficients and not path coefficients. In more complex models residual variables may be correlated. The equations for the three dependent variables, $x_3$, $x_4$ and $x_5$, are:

$$x_3 = p_{31}x_1 + p_{32}x_2 + p_{3u}R_u$$

$$x_4 = p_{41}x_1 + p_{42}x_2 + p_{43}x_3 + p_{4v}R_v$$

$$x_5 = p_{51}x_1 + p_{52}x_2 + p_{53}x_3 + p_{54}x_4 + p_{5w}R_w$$

where $R_u$, $R_v$ and $R_w$ refer to residual terms uncorrelated with any of the intermediate determinants of the variable to which they pertain. They are also uncorrelated with each other. The $p$ terms are path coefficients.

With no unmeasured variables except residual factors, uncorrelated residuals, and each dependent variable related directly to all the variables preceding it in the assumed causal sequence, then the basic theorem is merely a compact statement of the normal equations of regression theory for variables in standard form.

Path analysis is often applicable in situations in which the variables under investigation are composite ones that can be subdivided into component parts. For example, population growth comprises natural increase plus net migration; in turn natural increase is births minus deaths whilst net migration is the difference between in-migration and out-migration. In situations where there are composite variables like this, it is possible to use path analysis as a means of investigating:

- the relative contributions of the components to variation in the composite variable;
- how causes affecting the composite variable are transmitted via the respective component parts.

For example, in an analysis of 74 community areas in Chicago the relationship between population density ($x_0$) and two independent variables, distance ($w$) from the central business district (CBD) and the recency of growth ($z$), was investigated by subdividing population density into three component variables: persons per dwelling unit ($x_1$), dwelling units per structure ($x_2$) and the number of structures per acre ($x_3$) (see Winsborough, 1962). The correlation matrix generated is shown in Table 4.8. The path coefficients for the relationships between each variable and the two independent variables are shown in Figure 4.18a:

$$p_{01} = \sigma_1/\sigma_2 = 0.132$$

$$p_{02} = \sigma_2/\sigma_0 = 0.468$$

$$p_{03} = \sigma_3/\sigma_0 = 0.821$$

Path coefficients were then calculated for the relationships between each variable and the two independent variables: e.g. $r_{1w} = p_{1w} + p_{1z}r_{zw}$ (i.e. the multiple regression of $x_1$ on $w$ and $z$).

The full set of relationships and calculated path coefficients are shown in Figure 4.18b. This shows that $w$ has greater effects on each variable than $z$, and with different signs too. Also, $z$ and $w$ do not account for all the variation in the other variables. Therefore a profitable line of enquiry might be to examine inter-correlations of the variables via correlations between the residuals ($R_a$, $R_b$, $R_c$): e.g.

$$r_{23} = p_{2w}r_{3w} + p_{2z}r_{32} + p_{2b}p_{3c}r_{bc}$$

*Table 4.8*   Correlation Matrix Generated in an Analysis of Population Densities in Chicago

|       | $x_0$  | $x_1$  | $x_2$  | $x_3$  | $W$    | $Z$    |
|-------|--------|--------|--------|--------|--------|--------|
| $x_0$ | 1.000  | −0.419 | 0.636  | 0.923  | −0.663 | −0.390 |
| $x_1$ |        | 1.000  | −0.625 | −0.315 | 0.296  | 0.099  |
| $x_2$ |        |        | 1.000  | 0.305  | −0.594 | −0.466 |
| $x_3$ |        |        |        | 1.000  | −0.517 | −0.226 |
| $W$   |        |        |        |        | 1.000  | 0.549  |
| $Z$   |        |        |        |        |        | 1.000  |

$x_0$ = log population density
$x_1$ = log persons per dwelling unit
$x_2$ = log dwelling units per structure
$x_3$ = log structures per acre
$W$ = distance from CBD
$Z$ = recency of growth

*Source*: Winsborough (1962).

Thus correlations between residuals are second-order partial correlations, e.g. $r_{ab} = r_{12.wz}$. In this case, as shown in Figure 4.18b, $r_{23} = 0.305$ and $r_{bc} = r_{23.wz} = 0.014$. Therefore the correlation of $x_2$ and $x_3$ is satisfactorily explained by the respective relationships of these two variables to distance from the CBD and recency of growth, but this is not true of correlations involving $x_1$:

$$r_{0w} = p_{01} r_{1w} + p_{02} r_{2w} + p_{03} r_{3w}$$

$$= 0.039 - 0.278 - 0.424 = -0.663$$

and

$$r_{02} = p_{01} r_{12} + p_{02} r_{2z} + p_{03} r_{32}$$

$$= 0.013 - 0.218 - 0.185 = -0.391$$

So population density is negatively related to distance from the CBD and recency of growth, but the effects are transmitted via the first component of density and they are positive. Distance diminishes density primarily via its intermediate effect on structures per acre ($x_3$), and secondarily via dwelling units per structure ($x_2$). This comparison is reversed for recency of growth.

## Simultaneous-Equations Regression

Independent variables as portrayed in regression equations may be inadequate estimators of the dependent variable because the equation ignores certain information about the independent variables. This information may be specified in other relationships. This situation can be analysed, though, by the use of *simultaneous equations* in which the effects of variables contained in one equation are related to variables contained in other equations. In such circumstances a more rigorous definition of the nature of variables is required than that represented in the simple terminology of "dependent" and "independent" variables.

Econometricians distinguish between exogenous variables, those which are truly independent and therefore cannot be determined by a particular model, and endogenous variables, those which can be explained by a particular model and its constituent equations. Endogenous variables are deemed to be "jointly dependent": they can each have a series of exogenous variables upon which they depend, whilst exogenous variables can appear in a number of equations linking a series of variables. For example, the situation portrayed in Figure 4.19 contains two endogenous variables, population change ($P$) and change in service employment ($S$), which are related to a series of six exogenous variables: employment accessibility ($E$),

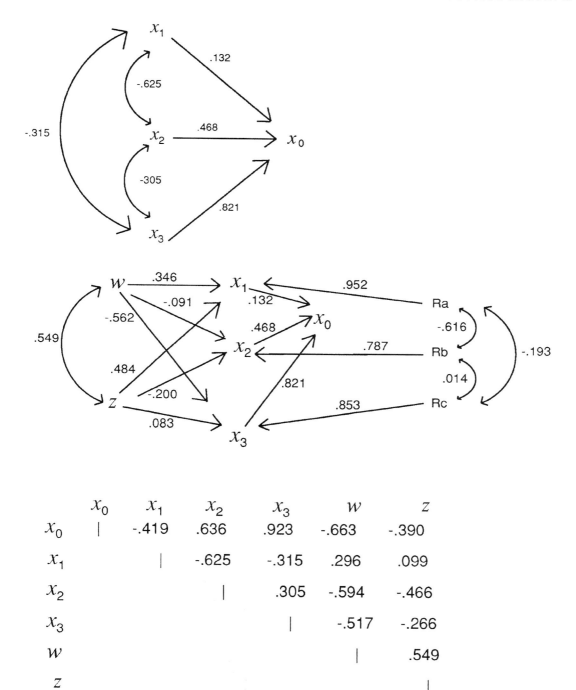

*Figure 4.18*    Path Analysis Based on Winsborough (1962)

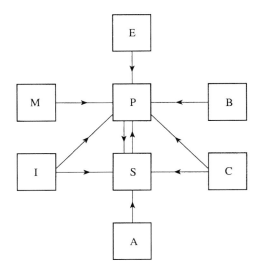

*Figure 4.19* Causal Model for Population Growth and Growth in Service Employment in the Reading Region Arrows portray direction of causality. (Based on Foot, 1974)

initial basic employment ($B$), change in basic employment ($C$), population accessibility ($A$), initial service employment ($I$) and initial population ($M$). Therefore the two equations that may be produced from these relationships are:

$$P = a_1 + a_2 C + a_3 B + a_4 M + a_5 S + a_6 I + a_7 E + e_1$$

$$S = b_1 + b_2 P + b_3 M + b_4 I + b_5 C + b_6 B + b_7 A + e_2$$

So *simultaneous-equations regression* involves "the establishment of several equations encompassing a wide spectrum of phenomena which are believed to influence, in varying degrees, the target (dependent) variables of the model" (Todd, 1979:15). The two main difficulties in the formulation of such equations are identifying the "best" equation from the multiplicity of possibilities and ensuring consistent results by recognising the different assumptions made by least-squares and simultaneous-equations regression. Further details are provided by Cadwallader (1982).

Perhaps the key difference between multiple regression and simultaneous-equations regression concerns the error or random disturbance term. In least-squares regression independent variables are not only independent of each other but are also independent from the disturbance (error) term. This is not the case in models utilising endogenous variables within a linear system of simultaneous equations. Thus endogenous variables should be expressed as functions of exogenous variables and disturbances only, perhaps by utilising a *two-stage least-squares regression* (TSLS) which is a sort of "half-way house" between least-squares regression and simultaneous-equations regression.

There are five steps in a TSLS – for a fuller description plus a worked example see Todd (1979:23–32):

1. Select an endogenous variable to act as the "target" dependent variable.
2. Determine the least-squares regression of the reduced-form equations (RFEs) for the remaining endogenous variables in the equation, where the RFE represents the endogenous variables in terms of the exogenous variables alone.
3. Replace the observed values for those remaining endogenous variables by their estimated values from step 2.
4. Perform least-squares regression of the target dependent variable on a set of variables comprising the reduced-form parameter estimates for the remaining endogenous variables and the original observed values for those variables in the equation of interest.
5. Repeat the first four steps for each target dependent variable in the model.

Clearly this is a complex procedure requiring an appropriate computer program to perform. It is also a procedure that has often been by-passed by geographers because, with a large number of explanatory variables (i.e. > 10), TSLS becomes very cumbersome. Consequently, either factor analytic techniques have been used to reduce the number of explanatory variables (see Chapter 5) or a *three-stage least-squares regression* (3SLS) has been employed. 3SLS is more complex mathematically but has the advantage over TSLS of performing the regression simultaneously on all equations in the model rather than on one at a time. It applies *generalised least-squares (GLS) estimation* to equations that have already been subjected to TSLS estimation, where GLS is like OLS but without the assumptions of homoscedasticity and zero autocorrelation for the error (or disturbance) term. The absence of these assumptions means that certain common situations can be handled by this technique – notably those involving time series data and autocorrelated data. However, the technique's complexity has limited its use by geographers (see Greenwood, 1978).

# 5

# MULTIVARIATE ANALYSIS

## SOCIAL AREA ANALYSIS

In the late 1940s the first multivariate analyses of the spatial structure of social differentiation within cities were performed in the USA. This work built on ideas contained in urban models first developed in the 1920s by *human ecologists* at the University of Chicago. The models had not been subjected to rigorous testing in the "laboratory" of real-world cities prior to the Second World War. But, after the War, testing was performed using both multivariate methods and simple indices (Duncan and Duncan, 1955; Tauber and Tauber, 1965).

The human ecologists were concerned primarily with the location of residential land use and residential differentiation. Pioneers such as Park, Burgess and McKenzie (Park et al, 1925) utilised concepts and ideas taken from plant and animal ecology. There was much use of Darwinian biological analogies and the inclusion of some economic determinism based on considerations of economic rent (Park and Burgess, 1921). Amongst the results were the formulation of three well-known models of urban social structure: Burgess's (1925) concentric zones, Hoyt's (1939) sectors, and Harris and Ullman's (1945) multiple nuclei.

Yet, despite this focus upon urban internal structure, in the 1930s and 1940s there was relatively limited study of the models' applicability to specific situations or of their general validity. However, they did act as a starting point for further study in that they implied that residential areas of cities and their populations conformed to certain patterns of behaviour, and prin-

cipally that people were segregated by social class. This was then translated into *residential segregation* in spatial terms.

In the early post-war years this concept of social and spatial segregation was examined in a multiplicity of ways (Watson, 1951) and, subsequently, concern for a myriad of social problems has played a dominant role in the development of human geography. One initial strand of work in this area was the use of very simple statistical investigations of urban social structure. This employed spatial indices (described in Chapter 9) which were based on the measurement of just one variable, such as occupation or ethnicity.

More complex multivariate investigations by geographers can be traced to the examination of "community areas" in Los Angeles by the sociologists Shevky and Williams (1949). Their work focused upon the classification of census tracts into distinctive social areas, and hence their study was termed a *social area analysis*, which was also the title of a subsequent book by Shevky and Bell (1955), also analysing social areas in Los Angeles. They argued that there were three main dimensions to social differentiation within cities: social rank or economic status; urbanisation or family status; and segregation or ethnic status.

They concluded that residential areas were distinguished with respect to these three dimensions, and they used the decennial population census to measure into which category a particular census tract fell. This was based on the tract's "performance" with respect to the three dimensions. Indicator variables from the census were used to distinguish the dimensions: for social status they were occupation, education and rental value; for family status they were fertility, female participation in the labour force and proportion of single-family dwelling units; and for ethnic status the proportion of a particular ethnic group within the overall population was used as a measure of ethnicity. Each of these variables was standardised and converted to a ratio measured along a scale running from 0 to 100.

The use of census variables in this fashion produced a classification of census tracts that could be mapped to depict social segregation. However, their procedure contained a number of flaws (see W.K.D. Davies, 1984:23; Johnston, 1971:314–15, 1976c). Perhaps the chief one was the way in which the indicator variables were interrelated across the three dimensions. For example, fertility is closely associated with occupation and education, and therefore fertility is an influence upon both economic status and family status. There is no indication that the three dimensions are discrete, but rather they are overlapping measures of social and economic character.

The social area analyses highlighted the need for research in urban social structure in which the numerous socio-economic variables of population censuses could be reduced statistically into a more manageable, smaller range of significantly associated variables denoting the underlying dimensions of social differentiation. Although Shevky and co-workers had attempted this in their initial work, they had not utilised the set of standard statistical procedures that had already been adopted for similar purposes in other disciplines. So geographers "borrowed" these procedures, first developed within psychology, and they applied a suite of multivariate techniques to the question of urban social differentiation. The techniques were part of a body of multivariate methods known as *factor analysis*, and hence their application to the testing of ecological models was termed *factorial ecology*. Factor analysis was applied to socio-economic variables from the population census, and during the 1960s a succession of factorial ecologies were performed for North American cities. Applications spread to other parts of the Developed World, to cities in the Developing World and also to other multivariate datasets. Consequently,

a large body of literature was produced, generating a wide-ranging debate on the method and philosophy of factorial ecology, and contributing to a subsequent reappraisal of the underlying logic of this type of approach. The development of this body of work will be considered in four stages here. Firstly, this chapter examines the techniques themselves, and, secondly, the results of the factorial ecologies. Thirdly, other multivariate techniques are outlined, and, fourthly, the subsequent critiques of multivariate analysis and formulation of alternative approaches are referred to both in this chapter and in others towards the end of the book.

## FACTOR ANALYTIC TECHNIQUES

> Factor analysis is a simple and appropriate tool for uncovering fewer common patterns of variation within a set of inter-correlated variables.
>
> (Morrill, 1990:42)

Factor analysis is a method for isolating the main differentiating "dimensions" of a group of related variables. It is possible to use it to explore relationships between variables, and it is a source of both hypothesis generation and testing (Chojnicki and Czyz, 1976).

Although factor analysis was widely used by geographers in the 1960s (see Johnston, 1971), and has remained as one of the techniques still used in many branches of the discipline, its complexity has often not been fully appreciated by researchers who can employ it by courtesy of readily available computing packages. Indeed, the complexity of factor analytic techniques means that their application rests largely upon the use of such packages, many of them not designed to meet the specific needs of geographical problems and datasets. Recognising this, Brian Berry (1971a) referred to the notion of GIGO (garbage in, garbage out) to typify much of the input of data and output of results from factor analysis. Nevertheless, the flexibility permitted by the packages has been utilised to the full, and all the 16 different factorial designs recognised by Berry (1971b) were exploited by geographers during the 1960s. The standard factor analytic model shown in Figure 5.1 can be applied to most designs:

- Factor analysis is often referred to as *R-mode analysis* as it is based on a Pearson product-moment correlation matrix formed from a geographical matrix of *m* columns (for *m* variables) and *n* rows (*n* observations).

It should be noted, though, that there are also a number of other possible modes of analysis for this matrix, reflecting the multiplicity of multivariate techniques.

- In *Q-mode analysis*, often referred to as *cluster analysis*, the *n* observations form the columns and the *m* variables the rows.

If a temporal dimension is introduced in the form of a series of time slices for each matrix, set at a time interval (*t*) apart, then a number of other modes of analysis are possible as follows:

- In *O-mode analysis*, the *t* time slices are the columns and the *m* variables are the rows.
- In *P-mode analysis*, the *m* variables are the columns and the *t* time slices are the rows.

These two modes deal with a single place, examining inter-time-period correlations (O-mode) or inter-variable correlations over time periods (P-mode).

- In *S-mode analysis*, the *n* observations are the columns and the *t* time slices are the rows.
- In *T-mode analysis*, the *t* time slices are the rows and the *n* observations are the columns.

In these last two modes only one variable is being analysed, with the S-mode analysis examining inter-place correlation of that variable over time, and the T-mode analysis examining inter-time-period correlations.

It is also possible to construct other matrices based on rates of change through time. For example, the $\Delta$R-mode or *incremental R-mode* examines change in each variable at each observation between time $t_1$ and time $t_2$. This mode examines groups of variables with similar patterns of change over the *n* observations during a particular time period. Matrices may be analysed for a number of time periods using *three-mode factor analysis* which examines inter-variable relationships over time and space simultaneously (Cant, 1975).

Factor analysis is based on the application of the Pearson product-moment correlation coefficient ($r_{xy}$) to the standard *geographical matrix* of observations versus places (see Berry, 1964). This produces a correlation matrix (see Table 4.2). However, once a correlation matrix has been generated the factor analyst is confronted by a wide choice as to the particular type of factor analytic technique to employ. The basic choice is between two applications: *principal components analysis* (PCA) and, confusingly, factor analysis, signifying that factor analysis is both a generic term and a term representing various subclasses of the genera. Geographers have used PCA to effect a linear transformation of *m* original variables to *m* new variables, termed *components*, so that each new variable or component successively accounts for as much of the total variance as possible in the original set of variables (Daultrey, 1976). The components are the *eigenvectors* of a correlation (variance–covariance) matrix.

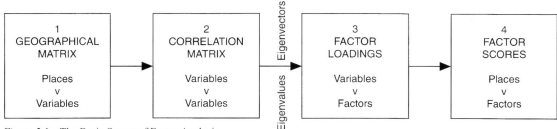

*Figure 5.1*   The Basic Stages of Factor Analysis

Although similar calculations are employed by the other factor analytic techniques, in their original form (as devised by psychologists) these techniques are based on more rigid underlying assumptions about the data being analysed than PCA. This often renders their demands inapplicable to geographical problems. Of these other techniques the most commonly used has been *principal axis factor analysis* (PAFA), sometimes termed *common factor analysis*.

For both PCA and PAFA, eigenvectors are extracted from a correlation matrix. The mathematics of this are quite complex. Therefore the explanation of the procedures involved that is provided below is given in geometrical terms, thereby minimising the use of complex statistical formulae. This account is based largely on descriptions from the psychological literature by Cattell (1965, 1978), Child (1970), Harman (1976), Morrison (1976) and Rummel (1970). For a concise statistical account see Manly (1986).

## Principal Components Analysis (PCA)

Each variable in a correlation matrix may be represented as a *vector*, that is a quantity having a magnitude and a direction denoted by a line drawn from its origin to its final position. This representation is made so that the cosine of the angle between each of the variable vectors is equal to the correlation coefficient between each pair of vectors. In this way all the vectors can be related to each other, as suggested in the example shown in Figure 5.2 based on the data in Table 5.1. By resolving these vectors the *first resultant or principal component* can be extracted. This resolution takes the form of the resultant of the different vectors, or the direction in which the join (0) of all the variable vectors would move, if free to, when experiencing the pull exerted by all the vectors. This resultant of the variable vectors is an eigenvector known as the reference vector or the first principal component (or the first factor if a factor analysis is being performed). The angles between each of the individual variable vectors and the reference vector are different, and so a new series of "correlations" have been generated: "the angle subtended between a vector and the principal component is termed a loading" (Child, 1970:24). Hence the new "correlations" generated are known as *component loadings* (or *factor loadings*), and each variable has a different loading on the first principal component, expressed as the value of the cosine of the angle between the particular

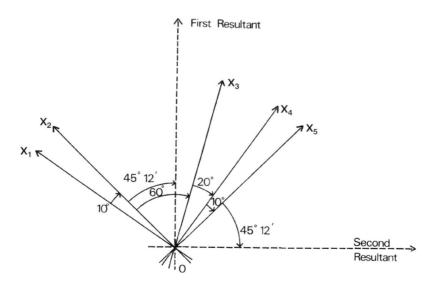

*Figure 5.2*    The Relationship Between Variable Vectors in a PCA

*Table 5.1* Correlation Matrix for Five Socio-Economic Variables

|       | $x_1$  | $x_2$ | $x_3$ | $x_4$ | $x_5$ |
|-------|--------|-------|-------|-------|-------|
| $x_1$ | 1.0    | 10    | 70    | 90    | 100   |
| $x_2$ | 0.98   | 1.0   | 60    | 80    | 90    |
| $x_3$ | 0.34   | 0.50  | 1.0   | 20    | 30    |
| $x_4$ | 0.00   | 0.17  | 0.94  | 1.0   | 10    |
| $x_5$ | −0.17  | 0.00  | 0.86  | 0.98  | 1.0   |

$x_1$ = number of cars per household
$x_2$ = % families with incomes in top decile
$x_3$ = % adults with degrees
$x_4$ = % adults with clerical jobs
$x_5$ = % foreign-born

Nb: Upper triangle gives angles between variables (vectors); lower triangle gives corresponding correlations.

variable vector and the component. Another component is then erected at right angles to the first, and so a different set of loadings is obtained for this second resultant. The *m* variables can be arranged as an *m*-dimensional ellipse so that the process of erecting components at right angles can be continued until there are as many components as there are variables. The obvious complexity of this arrangement is a good indicator of the need to use computer programs to perform the requisite calculations.

The first component identifies the largest axis of the ellipse, the second component the next largest and so on until the *m*th component. Therefore the resolution operates in such a way that the first component always accounts for the greatest variance amongst the variables, the second component the next highest variance and the *m*th component the *m*th highest (see Table 5.2). The variance amongst the variables accounted for by each component is equal to the sum of the squares of the loadings, known as the *eigenvalue* or *latent root* (Gould, 1967). This value is usually expressed as a percentage of the maximum possible variance, that is the percentage variance of a component is equal to 100 times the eigenvalue divided by the number of variables. This gives a measure of the importance of each component.

This third stage of the analytical process (see Figure 5.1) produces a matrix in which the chosen variables are replaced by a much smaller set of components. So, whilst it is possible to extract as many components as variables, the first few can account for sufficient of the overall variance (e.g. > 70 per cent) to be regarded as an effective replacement. This replacement represents the basic differentiating features of the chosen variables, with the individual component loadings enabling the character of the component to be discerned. To assist with interpretation, as component loadings represent the correlations between the variables and the component, they can be subjected to a significance test to determine the probability of a particular loading having occurred by chance. A Student's *t* test may be used for this purpose or a special test devised by Burt and Banks (1947), taking into account the number of variables used in the analysis and the number of components being tested (see Appendix L). This calculates the standard error of a loading by multiplying the standard error of a correlation by

$$\frac{n}{\sqrt{(n + 1 - F)}}$$

where $n$ = number of variables in the analysis, and $F$ = the component (factor) number or the position of the component (factor) during extraction.

When components are extracted from a correlation matrix, two types can be distinguished: *common components*, with high loadings on many of the variables, and *unique components*, with only one or two high loadings. It is the common or general components that are of interest as these represent composites of the original variables. Frequently, these common components are distinguished as being those which have an eigenvalue > 1 (point B in Figure 5.3). This is known as *Kaiser's criterion* and was recommended by Cattell (1966). Another way is to employ the *scree-slope method* shown in Figure 5.3, in which components are plotted against their eigenvalues. The break of slope in such a graph denotes the division between common and unique components (point A in Figure 5.3, giving 11 common components).

For geographers one of the main attractions of this particular technique has been the final stage of the analysis in which a set of *component scores* is com-

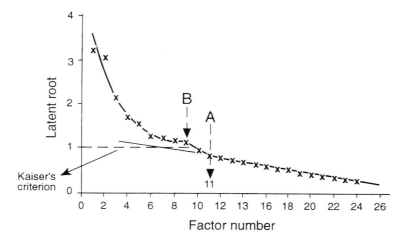

*Figure 5.3*    The Scree-Slope Method
(Here for 24 variables.) (*Source*: Child, 1970)

puted. This produces a matrix of the original observations (usually places) versus components. Hence the final product of any PCA can be a map portraying the distribution of the components extracted from the correlation matrix (Figure 5.4). The matrix of component scores is a measure of the importance of each component in the various places being examined (frequently enumeration districts in urban areas), expressed in standard deviation units from the average score. So this final result is a map of a combination of variables which replaces a series of maps of the individual variables. For the factorial ecologists this meant that, rather than mapping a series of individual socio-economic variables for the city, maps of three or four components could be used instead to portray the spatial configurations of the main differentiating features of the city's socio-economic structure. For PCA this final step of the analysis is produced by calculating the standard score of every variable in each area and multiplying it by the appropriate component loading. Thus the component score ($c_{ab}$) for area $a$ on component $b$ is:

$$c_{ab} = \sum_{i=1}^{m} (s_{ai})(l_{ib})$$

where $m$ = the number of variables; $s$ = the standard score in area $a$ of variable $i$ on component $b$, with $s_{ai} = (i - \hat{i})/\sigma_i$; and $l_{ib}$ = the component loading of variable $i$ on component $b$.

There are important distinctions between PCA and other factor analytic techniques, differences that have generally favoured the greater use of PCA by geographers. In particular, PCA makes no prior assumptions concerning the structure of the correlation matrix. It simply replaces $m$ variables with $m$ components representing amalgams of these variables. No prior hypothesis is stated about the number of components to be extracted, so that Kaiser's criterion is used to determine which components may be regarded as general. The components generated are uncorrelated and from them component scores can be calculated directly as shown above. PCA, whilst not without criticism, has generally been viewed more favourably than other factor analytic techniques, Davis (1986:501) for example concluding that "PCA belongs to that category of techniques, including cluster analysis, in which utility is judged by performance and not by theoretical considerations".

PCA is essentially a descriptive simplifying device whose main functional weakness is the interpretation of the component loading matrix. This interpretation

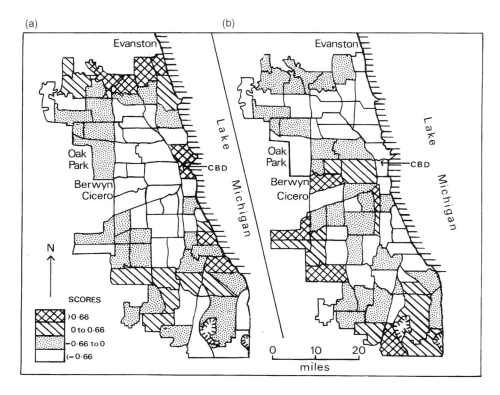

*Figure 5.4*    Map of Component Scores from a PCA of Socio-Economic Variables in Chicago
(a) Component 1; (b) component 2. (*Source*: Rees, 1970)

is usually highly subjective, generally being based on screening of the significant loadings to derive labels for the components (Palm and Caruso, 1972). Two different interpretations of the components extracted can be made (Chojnicki and Czyz, 1976):

1. *Descriptive*. This names the subset of dependent variables with the highest component loadings, and so components are classificatory terms with descriptive meaning.
2. *Theoretical*. This treats components as if they were theoretical terms, that is as conceptual constructs with several meanings.

The labelling of components and factors usually "involves summarising the context of the factor by reference to the highest loadings, preferably by a one or two word title" (W.K.D. Davies, 1984:186). An alternative might be to use some theoretically suggestive title linked to the cause of the pattern of loadings or one likely to stimulate future work. Reference to the distribution of component (factor) scores has also been used in the process of component (factor) labelling. Overall, there is generally a high degree of subjectivity in component (factor) labelling, and there are several examples in which close scrutiny of loading patterns reveals authors' choices of unrepresentative labels (Cattell, 1978:232). For example, W.K.D. Davies (1984:192–3) refers to a number of studies in which negative loadings in factors were largely ignored when factor labels were assigned (e.g. King, 1969:179).

Labelling should recognise differences amongst situations with *bi-polar loadings*, that is factors with both high positive and high negative loadings (e.g. component 2 in Table 5.2). Bi-polarity may highlight variables representing opposite extremes of a particular indicator, such as "life-cycle", in which variables referring to old age/maturity may have high positive loadings, and variables referring to youth/young families may have high negative loadings. Alternatively, bi-polar axes may contrast variables in which there is no obvious causal link, e.g. variables with ethnic associations contrasted with ones referring to income or education. In such cases labelling of both poles of the component (factor) is important to convey meaning.

An example of a PCA applied to socio-economic variables for areal units within a major American city is shown in Table 5.2. This is Rees's (1970) PCA of 57 normalised variables for 222 community areas of the City of Chicago and 147 municipalities in the suburbs of the city. Only loadings for the five most important components are shown. Also, only loadings greater than +0.4 or less than −0.4 are included in the table in order to help interpretation. There are six variables which have no loadings within this range for the first five components. These components can be interpreted as follows:

(a) *Component 1 – Socio-economic status*. This has high loadings on variables for schooling, white-collar occupations, professional and clerical employees, high incomes, high rents and sound housing. On the opposite pole of the component are blue-collar workers, labourers and service workers, with low incomes and low-rent housing. The majority of variables indicative of class position or social status have their highest loadings on this component.

(b) *Component 2 – Stage in the life-cycle (or family status)*. This has high loadings for variables indicative of large family size, young age structure and new single-dwelling, owner-occupied housing. On the opposite pole are variables for elderly population, older housing stock, high female participation rates, pedestrian commuters, foreign-born and unemployed. This is a component distinguishing between different types of families:

young middle-class versus older residents and poorer families.

(c) *Component 3 – Race and residence*. This has a strong ethnic dimension to it, with high negative loadings on the black location quotient and the percentage of non-whites. There are also high negative loadings for percentage unemployed, low incomes and overcrowding. The opposite pole picks out native (US-born) whites, white Protestants, German and British ethnic origins, and commuting by car. Rees (1970:333–9) concludes that this association between blacks and variables suggestive of poverty indicates the systematic inequality in the allocation of resources between this ethnic group and others.

(d) *Component 4 – Immigrants and Catholic status*. This has high positive loadings for three ethnic groups (Italians, Czechs and Poles) as well as foreign-born and Catholics. The contrast is with high negative loadings for blacks, non-whites, native-born and recent in-migrants. The result is a component distinguishing between established Catholic immigrant communities and both long-term non-white residents and recent in-migrants (who, by implication, are not from the same three ethnic groups highlighted by the positive loadings). This dimension is relatively free of association with the socio-economic status or family status sets of variables.

(e) *Component 5 – Size*. The positive loadings refer to the close association between unemployment and high population densities. These are also associated with housing units in three- or more-unit structures, but contrasted with one-unit structures and housing stock built in the 1940s.

Together these first five components account for under two-thirds of the total variation amongst the variables (63.4 per cent), and hence Rees also examined the next five most important components, which highlighted the Jewish and Russian population (number 6), 1940s housing and commuting by car (7), the Irish and Swedish population (8), mobility (9) and other non-white population and Italians (10). These

*Table 5.2*  Component Loadings (×100) for a PCA of Census Tracts in the Chicago Standard Metropolitan Statistical Area

| Variables | Components | | | | |
|---|---|---|---|---|---|
| | 1 | 2 | 3 | 4 | 5 |
| Percentage professional employees | 93 | | | | |
| Percentage white-collar workers | 92 | | | | |
| Percentage families: income > $10 000 | 91 | | | | |
| Percentage craftsmen/operatives | −87 | | | | |
| Percentage four years of high school or more | 87 | | | | |
| Median school years completed | 85 | | | | |
| Median annual income | 79 | | | | |
| Percentage clerical and sales workers | 66 | | | | |
| Median rent | 56 | | | | |
| Percentage housing in two-unit structure | −44 | | | | |
| Canadian l.q.* | 43 | | | | |
| Population/household | | 92 | | | |
| Percentage population < 18 years | | 89 | | | |
| Percentage population > 65 years | | −89 | | | |
| Median age of population | | −77 | | | |
| Percentage housing built pre-1940 | | −76 | | | |
| Percentage housing built post-1950 | | 74 | | | |
| Percentage women 14+ in labour force | | −72 | | | |
| Percentage housing in one-unit structure | | 60 | | | |
| Percentage housing in three-unit structure or more | | −60 | | | |
| Percentage owner-occupied housing | | 59 | | | |
| Percentage commuting on foot | | −45 | | | |
| Black l.q. | | | −75 | −50 | |
| Percentage non-white population | | | −74 | −50 | |
| Native white l.q. | | | 73 | | |
| Percentage white Protestant population | | | 71 | | |
| Percentage families: income < $3000 | −44 | | −67 | | |
| Percentage labourers | −60 | | −65 | | |
| Percentage unemployed | | | −62 | | |
| Percentage workers in service occupations | −50 | | −56 | −41 | |
| Percentage overcrowded houses | | | −54 | | |
| German l.q. | | | 53 | | |
| Percentage sound housing units | 46 | | 51 | | |
| British l.q. | | | 49 | | |
| Percentage commuters by bus | | | −47 | | |
| Percentage population native-born of foreign or mixed parents | | | | 86 | |
| Percentage population native-born of native parents | | | | −83 | |
| Foreign stock l.q. | | | | 83 | |
| Percentage white Catholic population | | | | 76 | |
| Percentage foreign-born population | | −45 | | 66 | |
| Polish l.q. | | | | 58 | |
| Percentage commuters by rail | | | | −39 | |
| Czech l.q. | | | | 36 | |
| Total unemployment | | −45 | | | 79 |

Table 5.2   (Continued)

| Variables | Components | | | | |
|---|---|---|---|---|---|
| | 1 | 2 | 3 | 4 | 5 |
| Percentage total unemployment | | | | | 79 |
| Population | | | | | 68 |
| Population density | | | −42 | | 65 |
| Percentage housing built 1940–49 | | | | | −46 |
| Percentage commuters by car | | | 42 | | |
| Percentage families moved since 1955 | | | | −45 | |
| Italian l.q. | | | | 43 | |
| Median home value | | | | | |
| Russian l.q. | | | | | |
| Percentage Jewish population | | | | | |
| Irish l.q. | | | | | |
| Swedish l.q. | | | | | |
| Other non-white l.q. | | | | | |
| Eigenvalue | 10.2 | 8.1 | 7.4 | 6.2 | 4.3 |
| Percentage of variance | 17.8 | 14.2 | 13.1 | 10.8 | 7.5 |

*l.q. = location quotient (for formulae see Chapter 8).

Source: Rees (1970).

additional five components brought the total "explanation" to over three-quarters of total variation.

One of the most informative aspects of the PCA is the spatial distributions revealed by mapping the component scores. Two examples of this for the PCA of Chicago are shown in Figure 5.4 which portrays the distribution of components 1 (Figure 5.4a) and 2 (Figure 5.4b) in the community areas of the city (but excluding adjacent municipalities). The high status areas of component 1 are predominantly found in the suburbs beyond the community areas. Therefore much of the city itself has low status areas, especially in a broad arc around the inner city which contains areas of blue-collar residence close to the principal industrial areas of the metropolis. High status areas in the city are on the northern margin and parts of the South Side and Lake Shore.

The spatial pattern of component 2 picks out communities with above-average numbers of elderly and single people in multi-unit structures in the central city and innermost suburbs. On the southwestern fringes of the city are concentrations of young families characteristic of more outlying suburbs. The presence of young families in the inner city gives rise to positive scores there, for example in the West Side and South Side ghettoes. The highest negative scores are for inner western suburbs not depicted in Figure 5.4, such as Oak Park, Cicero and Berwyn. There is a roughly concentric pattern to the distribution of scores on this component, reflecting land values which decrease with distance from the central business district (CBD). Two deviations from this are the Lake Shore, with high land values and a resultant capital-intensive development in response to proximity to Lake Michigan, and the West Side ghetto, with low land values reflecting poverty and discrimination.

## Factor Analysis

Factor analysis (including PCA) was developed initially in psychology as a hypothesis testing device. In using the technique, psychologists made certain assumptions about the nature of the variables under consideration, and the ensuing analysis depended upon these assumptions. In particular, unlike PCA, factor analysis distinguishes between different types of variance amongst the variables, using a concept known as *communality*, and it employs rotations of the initial vector structure. The chief assumption, though, is that the *m* variables being studied can be replaced by a smaller number (*l*) of underlying factors. The number of factors should be specified beforehand, but in practice geographers have usually ignored this, again preferring to use Kaiser's criterion. In extracting these factors, factor analysis pays closer attention to the nature of the variance of the variables under examination. In particular, it splits the variance into three parts:

1. *Common variance (or communality)*. The degree to which one variable varies in conjunction with other variables.
2. *Unique (or specific) variance*. The individuality of the distribution of the variable. Unique variance becomes larger as successive factors are extracted.
3. *Error variance (or unreliability)*. Any imperfections (such as sampling bias) in the original data.

It is variables with a high common variance, or communality, that are of prime interest, and it is desirable to attach more importance to these variables when extracting factors. This is achieved by calculating the communality of each variable and weighting the variables accordingly when producing the factor structure.

The communality of a variable is the sum of the squares of the variable's common factor loadings. As PCA makes no distinction between the different types of variance and extracts as many components as there are variables, the communality of variables in a PCA is equal to 1. Therefore, for PCA, variables are equally weighted. For other factor analytic techniques, only a certain number of factors are regarded as general ones, and so only a limited number of factors are extracted. Consequently, the sum of the squares of the loadings on each variable will now be less than 1. The different weightings applied to each variable modify the factor structure, giving a new set of factor loadings as shown in Tables 5.3 and 5.4. Those variables with the highest communalities are the ones to which most importance is attached when producing the reference vectors or factors. As the values of the communalities are dependent upon the number of factors extracted, the determination of this number is critical.

Differences between the solutions derived from PCA and PAFA are rarely very large for the first few factors/components unless communalities for particular variables fall well below 1, in which case PAFA can produce different loading patterns on those variables. This can be seen by comparing Tables 5.3 and 5.4, referring to an analysis of agriculture in the parishes of Norfolk, England. Instead of the socio-economic characteristics discussed for the census tracts of Chicago in Table 5.2, different agricultural land uses form the dataset, illustrating that factor analytic techniques can be applied to a wide range of multivariate data. Table 5.3 represents part of the results of a PCA for 15 variables, showing the first four components only, which account for 58.73 per cent of the total variance amongst the variables. As these four have a number of loadings on each component that are significant at the 0.05 level, they can be considered as general components. The remaining 11 components are unique rather than general because they have few or only one significant loading (Tarrant, 1974:191). All of the first four components are bipolar. Component 1 has high negative loadings on labour input (standard man-days per parish) and on crops such as horticulture and small fruit which require a high labour input. On the opposite pole, high positive loadings pick out labour-extensive crops, cereals and grass. Therefore this first component suggests that a major underlying component of variation in Norfolk's agriculture is the intensity of labour use. The other three components distinguish between different types of farming: component 2 representing cash crops (wheat, potatoes, sugar beet and peas) versus cattle production; component 3 contrasting fruit production, vining peas and beef cattle against vegetable and barley growing; component 4 distinguishing fruit and cereal production from vegetable growing and beef cattle.

When PAFA is applied to the same data, the communality of the individual variables determines their

*Table 5.3*   Component Loadings for a PCA of Agricultural Land Use in the Parishes of Norfolk, England

| Variables | Components | | | |
|---|---|---|---|---|
| | *1* | *2* | *3* | *4* |
| Wheat | 0.40* | 0.60* | 0.23 | 0.01 |
| Barley | 0.78* | 0.11 | −0.28* | 0.19 |
| Cereals | 0.47* | 0.10 | −0.20 | 0.27* |
| Potatoes | −0.36* | 0.59* | 0.31* | −0.21 |
| Stock feeding | 0.61* | −0.15 | −0.03 | 0.26* |
| Sugar beet | 0.55* | 0.59* | −0.16 | −0.01 |
| Orchards | −0.36* | −0.07 | 0.39* | 0.47* |
| Small fruit | −0.49* | 0.15 | 0.44* | 0.41* |
| Vegetables | −0.44* | −0.09 | −0.42* | −0.55* |
| Peas for vining | −0.21 | 0.32* | 0.55* | −0.26* |
| Horticulture | −0.45* | −0.26* | −0.09 | 0.30* |
| Grass | 0.53* | −0.49* | 0.46* | −0.24 |
| Dairy cattle | 0.38* | −0.41* | 0.17 | 0.14 |
| Beef cattle | 0.48* | −0.47* | 0.46* | −0.32* |
| SMD† per acre | −0.84* | −0.24* | −0.20 | 0.08 |
| Eigenvalue | 3.97 | 1.98 | 1.61 | 1.26 |
| Percentage of total variance | 26.43 | 13.19 | 10.75 | 8.36 |

* Significant at 0.05 level
† SMD = Standard man-days

*Source*: Tarrant (1974:191).

importance in locating the factor axes. Thus the low communalities for cereals, dairy cattle, vegetables and horticulture mean that they will be less important in this respect than standard man-days per acre, grass and barley. Low communalities tend to reflect variables with only localised distributions or ones with a high degree of unique variation when compared with others in the dataset. With a greater emphasis given to variables with high communalities in PAFA, different loading patterns are generated to those from the PCA (see Table 5.4). In this case the basic outlines of factor 1 are similar to those of component 1, but factor 2 is more strongly loaded on sugar beet, wheat and barley and negatively loaded on a number of activities, especially grass and beef cattle. This second factor can now be more clearly identified as representing a contrast between sugar beet, wheat and barley on the one hand, and beef cattle on the other (Tarrant, 1974:194–5). The third factor identifies crops of con-

siderable local importance within the county, whilst the fourth distinguishes between different associations of labour-intensive crops.

One of the central characteristics of factor analysis is that, for any given matrix, a number of different factor analytic solutions can be derived. Therefore the solutions are indeterminable, or many different solutions, each mathematically accurate, may be obtained from a matrix if different assumptions are made.

As described above, the two most commonly used procedures by geographers are PCA and PAFA. The basic component model can be represented algebraically as

$$Z_j = a_{j1}F_1 + a_{j2}F_2 + a_{j3}F_3 + \ldots + a_{jm}F_m$$

where $Z_j$ = the estimate of variable $j$, and $a_{jm}F_m$ = the component loading of variable $j$ on component $m$.

In the PAFA model the equation becomes

*Table 5.4*    Factor Loadings for a PCA of Agricultural Land Use in the Parishes of Norfolk, England

| Variables | Communality | Factors | | | |
|---|---|---|---|---|---|
| | | *1* | *2* | *3* | *4* |
| Wheat | 0.351 | 0.35* | 0.31* | 0.35* | 0.11 |
| Barley | 0.774 | 0.72* | 0.38* | −0.26 | −0.19 |
| Cereals | 0.187 | 0.36* | 0.19 | −0.10 | −0.11 |
| Potatoes | 0.507 | −0.30* | 0.15 | 0.56* | 0.27* |
| Stock feeding | 0.281 | 0.49* | 0.04 | −0.15 | −0.14 |
| Sugar beet | 0.536 | 0.48* | 0.53* | 0.11 | 0.11 |
| Orchards | 0.373 | −0.28* | −0.16 | 0.23 | −0.47* |
| Small fruit | 0.623 | −0.42* | −0.08 | 0.48* | −0.47* |
| Vegetables | 0.247 | −0.39* | −0.03 | −0.18 | 0.26* |
| Peas for vining | 0.280 | −0.15 | −0.05 | 0.47* | 0.18 |
| Horticulture | 0.270 | −0.44* | −0.17 | −0.21 | −0.05 |
| Grass | 0.829 | 0.63* | −0.65* | 0.05 | 0.00 |
| Dairy cattle | 0.134 | 0.30* | −0.16 | −0.13 | −0.06 |
| Beef cattle | 0.640 | 0.55* | −0.58* | 0.02 | 0.08 |
| SMD† per acre | 0.845 | −0.86* | −0.20 | −0.25* | −0.01 |
| Eigenvalue | | 3.48 | 1.47 | 1.22 | 0.71 |
| Percentage of total variance | | 50.58 | 21.37 | 17.73 | 10.32 |

\* Significant at 0.05 level
† SMD = Standard man-days

*Source*: Tarrant (1974:195).

$$Z_j = a_{j1}F_1 + a_{j2}F_2 + a_{j3}F_3 + \ldots + d_jU_j$$

where $d_jU_j$ = residual error, usually split into two parts: $b_jS_j$ = specificity or that part of the variance associated with a set of specific factors that may be produced by the particular selection of variables or because of place-specific features, and $e_jE_j$ = error or unreliability representing the unexplained or residual variance, i.e. $d_jU_j = B_jS_j + e_iE_j$.

When factor analysis was popularised by psychologists such as Burt (1940), the number of factors extracted was dictated by current theories within the discipline. However, the limitations of the theoretical underpinnings to most geographical work using factor analysis has meant that a standard criterion (Kaiser's) has usually been adopted for establishing the number of general factors. This assumes that, with the majority of the original variables closely interrelated, just a few factors will be able to account for a very high

percentage of the variance and that all communalities will be high. Unfortunately there have been several instances of factor analysts using Kaiser's criterion, but with the first few factors accounting for less than two-thirds of the overall variance in the variables. This limits the utility of such work. In particular, lack of theory to determine the appropriate number of factors to extract means that arbitrary selections can yield different results, as might occur in Table 5.4 by selecting six factors rather than four.

Another refinement of factor analysis compared with PCA is the *rotation* of the factor axes to *simple structure* as a means of aiding interpretation. This entails rotating the resultant vectors until the factor loadings created are either near ±1 or near 0. So, after rotation, each factor will have a few significantly high loadings and many insignificant ones. Therefore this should make labelling of factors easier. Rotation has been used to give the loadings shown in Table 5.4.

Rotation can be performed with factors still at right angles (*orthogonal rotation*) or the actual position of the reference vectors themselves can be altered so that they become oblique to one another (*oblique rotation*) (see King and Jeffrey, 1972).

There are numerous methods for performing rotations (Harman, 1976:247–360); the aim of all of them, though, is the attainment of what Thurstone (1930) termed "simple structure". The basis of this is the production of loadings around either ±1 or 0. The use of just the general factors in the rotation process again illustrates the importance of determining the number of general factors. Oblique rotations are usually reserved for situations in which the factors produced are expected to show a degree of intercorrelation instead of having no correlation, though the theoretical underpinning for such a situation needs to be firmly established. The commonest form of rotation used by geographers has been an orthogonal one known as the *varimax solution* (Kaiser, 1959).

Another important difference between PCA and factor analysis is that both rotated and unrotated factors utilise a different method for calculating scores to that in PCA. As described above for PCA, scores may be obtained by projecting the original areal data onto the component axes. Therefore they represent a simple mathematical transform. In factor analysis, though, scores are estimates of the contributions of each factor to each value in the geographical matrix. There are numerous ways of performing this estimation, each giving slightly different results. So factor analytic solutions can yield a variety of different scores as well as a variety of factor loadings, depending upon the researcher's subjective choice of a particular method.

It is this subjectivity, and a lack of theoretical arguments upon which to draw in the selection of a given number of general factors, that has tended to favour PCA rather than other factor analytic methods in geographical research. However, there are examples of a bewildering range of factor analyses used within human geography, often revealing little real understanding of the differences between the two basic types or of the key assumption of normality amongst the variables analysed (Robinson, 1981). The debate

on whether or not to use *varimax rotation* in conjunction with PCA is a good example of the former (Davies, 1971; Mather, 1971). In joining this debate, King (1971) made the position clear:

> Rotations are not only irrelevant (in PCA) but also will no longer represent the maximal variance. In factor analysis, however a statistical model is set up involving both general and specific factors as well as random errors. Under these circumstances factors can be rotated.

Differences between rotated and unrotated factor loadings are shown in Table 5.5, which reproduces part of Bell's (1955) testing of the basic Shevky and Williams (1949) hypothesis that three distinct dimensions of urban social differentiation could be identified in Los Angeles. As well as being an example of factor rotation, this is also an example of factor analysis as a hypothesis testing device. Bell utilised the same seven variables as Shevky and Williams for 570 census tracts in Los Angeles, using data for 1940 and applying PAFA. The initial set of factor loadings produced a very general first factor, a second factor contrasting education against single-family dwellings, female participation in the labour force and presence of ethnic groups. The third factor contrasted the ethnic groups variable with high rental values. Using an oblique rotation, the loadings on the first factor became more readily interpreted as emphasising high occupational status, high rental values and high levels of education (economic status). On the second factor, three variables now stood out: fertility, women in the labour force and percentage of single-family dwellings (family status). Finally, the ethnic groups variable was emphasised in the third factor (ethnic status). Similar results were also obtained by Bell (1958) for census tracts in San Francisco. However, it is important to note that the oblique rotation he employed indicates that the three "dimensions" are intercorrelated, with strong negative correlations existing between economic status and family status, and between ethnic status and economic status. It is not surprising therefore that, in analyses for other cities, use of orthogonal rotations and larger numbers of variables have yielded variations in the three basic underlying dimensions obtained.

*Table 5.5*  Differences Between Rotated and Unrotated Factor Loadings: Bell's Analysis of Census Tracts in Los Angeles (1940 Data)

| Variables | Factor Loadings | | | Rotated Factor Loadings | | |
|---|---|---|---|---|---|---|
| | 1 | 2 | 3 | 1 | 2 | 3 |
| Occupation | 0.89 | 0.08 | −0.23 | 0.48 | 0.19 | −0.09 |
| Education | 0.78 | 0.51 | 0.09 | 0.32 | −0.04 | 0.28 |
| Rent | 0.96 | 0.39 | −0.36 | 0.65 | −0.19 | −0.19 |
| Fertility | 0.91 | −0.19 | −0.09 | 0.11 | 0.56 | 0.18 |
| Women in the labour force | 0.65 | −0.56 | −0.19 | 0.15 | 0.62 | −0.19 |
| Percentage of single-family dwellings | 0.49 | −0.64 | 0.07 | −0.15 | 0.73 | 0.02 |
| Ethnic groups | 0.47 | −0.45 | 0.44 | −0.11 | 0.04 | 0.58 |

*Source*: Bell (1955).

Variations on PAFA can be produced in a number of ways, the most frequently used being methods for calculating factor loadings once a decision has been made on the number of common factors to extract. Examples include the "minres" solution, the maximum likelihood technique, image analysis and the generalised least-squares (GLS) solution. These and other variations, including different types of factor rotation, are discussed by W.K.D. Davies (1984:135–68). He argues that orthogonal rotations are restrictive and that it should be assumed that the axes of differentiation are correlated with one another. In the late 1970s there were some attempts by geographers to pursue this line of argument via so-called *"higher order" factor solutions* which factor analysed the factor loading matrix (e.g. Palmer et al, 1977; Perle, 1977). From this work, Davies (1980) claimed that greater understanding of the "dimensionality" of urban and regional systems could be gained. He drew a contrast between orthogonal "first-order" factor axes, and higher-order methods which could reveal correlations between these axes and assist evaluation of theories of social area variation. However, there have been few significant advances with this type of enquiry, partly reflecting the complex theory required to substantiate higher-order approaches.

## Factor Comparison

Experimental psychologists have formulated ways of tracing the development of factors through time and of comparing factors produced from identical sets of variables but different observations. However, there have been relatively few attempts by geographers to draw upon this work. Tests for factor invariance recognise that, whilst it is unlikely for two factors in successive time periods to possess exactly the same loadings, the loadings may be very similar. In such cases the two factors can be said to be invariant or identical for all practical purposes. The five main methods of examining temporal evolution of factors are: matching the loading patterns for shape (e.g. using correlation), matching the loading patterns for absolute agreement (e.g. using pattern similarity indices), matching the patterns for effect (e.g. measures of functional equivalence), and two more complex matrix comparison methods.

Correlation coefficients can give a perfect agreement between loading patterns of the same shape, whilst a *coefficient of similarity* considers both the shape of the factor loading distribution and the levels or positioning of the individual variables. Such a coefficient was developed by Cattell and Baggaley (1960) as the *salient variable similarity index* (SVSI) for factor matching. A combination of the SVSI and rank correlation was used to investigate agricultural changes for 10 five-year periods for parishes in the Vale of Evesham, England, with a similar approach to study the evolution of agriculture for the counties of Great Britain from 1875 to 1985 (Robinson, 1976, 1981, 1988).

A variant of the SVSI, the *marker variable similarity index* (MVSI), was used in a PCA of agricultural change in the High Weald, south-east England (Short, 1975; see also Winchester, 1977). In this method, markers are chosen from the variables in the geographical matrix and are then searched-for in the suspected matching factor from a different time period (or from a different study). Once the number of coincident markers in the two factors has been determined, the probability of this coincidence can be calculated and its significance tested. Naturally, the results obtained are highly dependent on the number of markers selected subjectively beforehand. The SVSI represents a standard non-parametric test in which an index is constructed on the basis of the number of variables in common in the two factors and possessing significant loadings. A significance test for this method has also been devised (Cattell, 1978:258).

Factors from two different matrices of loadings pertaining to common sets of variables but different observations may be compared using the *coefficient of congruence* ($G_{ij}$), which incorporates the magnitude as well as the pattern of any set of factor loadings (Harman, 1967). This coefficient is the correlation of the two vectors of factor loadings, and is the cosine of the angles between the factors:

$$G_{ij} = \frac{\sum_{k=1}^{n} L_{ki} L_{kj}}{\sqrt{\left( \sum_{k=1}^{n} L_{ki}^2 \sum_{k=1}^{n} L_{kj}^2 \right)}}$$

where $L_{ki}$ and $L_{kj}$ = the loadings for variable $k$ in matrix $i$ and matrix $j$ respectively; $n$ = the number of variables; and $G_{ij}$ = the coefficient of congruence between matrices $i$ and $j$. This can be translated as the sum of the product of loadings for each pair of variables divided by the square root of the product of the sum of squared loadings on axis $i$ and the sum of squared loadings on axis $j$. A significance test for $G_{ij}$ has been developed (Korth and Tucker, 1975).

This coefficient can have high values simply because the two factors being compared have high loadings, even if the pattern of loadings is different. Similarity on "unimportant" low loadings can also produce a high value of $G_{ij}$, although it is usually high values that are important for interpretation. Its chief limitation is that it is unable to focus on similarities (or dissimilarities) for specific variables. Criticisms of both the coefficient of congruence and correlation coefficients have also been made because they consider both high and low loadings whereas interpretation and labelling of factors usually ignore insignificant low loadings.

With reference to the geometrical explanation of factor analysis given earlier, it is possible to compare solutions for matrices comprising the same variables by superimposing one set of factors on the other and then rotating one set until its factors are in the same position as the factors in the other set. The extent of this rotation is a measure of inter-factor correlation, and can be expressed as the cosine of the rotation angle. In Johnston's (1973) comparison of factor analyses of 28 variables for the enumeration districts of Melbourne in 1961 and 1966, the rotation cosines showed a high similarity between the two dates, that is very high cosines along the principal diagonal. This comparison can be taken further by examining the relationships between specific variables in the two matrices. For this, after the calculation of the rotation cosines, the new loadings for the variables in the first matrix are calculated and correlated with those of the original factor structure. This produces a series of test correlations which compare the position of each variable in the factors for the first matrix with that of the same variables for the other matrix. In Johnston's analysis this highlighted differences for variables on the ethnic composition of the city.

Finally, Davies (1975) extended comparison of factors to indicate how interpretation of similar factors can proceed. He used a simple *variance allocation method* in a comparative study of the social dimensions of the five metropolitan areas of the Canadian Prairies. This method divides the variables into *common*, *specific* and *residual* categories on the basis of the strength of the loadings on similar factors (which have already been identified using congruence coefficients or marker variables): e.g. variables with loadings $> +0.3$ or $< -0.3$ on the similar factors = common variables; variables not appearing with significant loadings on a number of factors = specific variables; variables with loadings between $-0.3$ and $+0.3$ on the similar factors = residual variables. The contribution of the three kinds of variables to the overall variance of the loadings can then be identified. In Davies's study this revealed an allocation for the family status factor as shown in Table 5.6. This factor contrasts families with children, living in owner-occupied housing and smaller households, against young adults or the elderly, with a higher proportion of women in the population. It was recognisable in the five major Prairie cities, and in Regina and Saskatoon it was a significant differentiating feature of the cities' socio-economic variation. However, in Regina the factor's character was less distinct: a number of the highly loaded variables on this same factor, which were extracted in analyses of the other four cities, did not have significant loadings in Regina.

## FACTORIAL ECOLOGIES

### Testing the Shevky–Bell Constructs

The many factorial ecologies performed by geographers in the 1960s were open to the criticisms levelled at the earlier work of Shevky and Williams (1949), in that they were highly empirical, and contained both a significant degree of subjectivity and a general lack of theoretical underpinning. Rees (1971, 1972) notes that comparison of individual studies is difficult because of variation amongst them in terms of:

- the number, selection and definition of variables used;
- the study area chosen – for example, the larger the metropolitan area, the smaller is each enumeration

district relative to the total population and therefore the greater is the likelihood that each is an exclusive residential area (Johnston, 1984d:134);
- the units of observation employed;
- the time base utilised;
- the factorial model (including type of rotation) applied.

However, one way in which factorial ecologies for North American cities did add to previous work was in terms of the repetition of basic results. Primarily this represented support for the three fundamental constructs underlying social differentiation in cities: economic status, family status and ethnic status (with different ethnic groups highlighted depending on the ethnic mix of the city in question). Variants of these three factors or components, accounting for about 60 per cent of the variation amongst the socio-economic variables under analysis, were extracted for a number of North American cities (Janson, 1969). Frequently, a fourth factor reflected characteristics of mobility, but the significance of the results lay with the first three which were often close to the constructs proposed by Shevky and Bell (1955). The clearest expression of support came from work on four southern US cities copying Bell's use of oblique factor rotation and a restricted number of variables analysed (Van Arsdol et al, 1958), though with fertility related to economic status rather than ethnic status (Johnston, 1971:316).

Studies that utilised a larger number of variables produced variations on the three basic dimensions whilst generally confirming their presence. Using PAFA, some made comparisons between different cities, reaching this same general conclusion (e.g. Salins, 1971). The extraction of other important factors tended to be features of either the nature of the variables analysed or place-specific. For example, in Boston, Sweetser (1969) identified a separate Irish middle-class dimension as well as ethnic status dimensions for Italians and non-whites.

With their calculation of component or factor scores, the factorial ecologies enabled researchers to return to the spatial patterns of the original ecological models by examining how the three main factors were distributed through the urban area. For example,

*Table 5.6*  The Variance Allocation Method Applied to the Family Status Factor in an Analysis of the Metropolitan Areas of the Canadian Prairies

(a) Variance allocation (for family status factor)

| City | Percentage Explanation of Total Variance | Variable Variance Allocation (%) | | |
|------|------------------------------------------|--------|----------|----------|
|      |                                          | Common | Specific | Residual |
| Calgary | 17.36 | 13.32 | 3.2 | 0.84 |
| Edmonton | 20.04 | 17.15 | 1.7 | 1.23 |
| Regina | 27.16 | 16.23 | 10.1 | 0.88 |
| Saskatoon | 26.67 | 21.08 | 4.33 | 1.25 |
| Winnipeg | 21.80 | 19.80 | 0.77 | 0.89 |

(b) Common variables

| Average Loading | Variable |
|-----------------|----------|
| +0.84 | Persons per household |
| +0.84 | Average number of children |
| +0.83 | Fertility |
| +0.77 | Children |
| +0.77 | Owner occupation |
| +0.72 | Single detached dwellings |
| +0.66 | Family size |
| +0.58 | Large households |
| +0.53 | Mature adults |
| +0.40 | Household income* |
| | |
| −0.46 | High inter-municipal movers |
| −0.47 | Divorced |
| −0.56 | Single adults |
| −0.69 | Young adult participation rate |
| −0.71 | Females |
| −0.72 | Female participation rate† |
| −0.73 | Old aged‡ |
| −0.75 | Small dwelling |
| −0.81 | Apartments |
| −0.83 | Small households |
| −0.83 | Female household heads |

* Has a negative value in Saskatoon
† Missing in Calgary and Regina
‡ Missing in Calgary

*Source*: Davies (1975).

Anderson and Egeland (1961), in a comparison of Akron and Dayton (Ohio), Indianapolis (Indiana) and Syracuse (New York), concluded that three main spatial patterns were clear (Figure 5.5):

1. Family status varied concentrically, i.e. with distance from the central business district (CBD).
2. Economic status varied sectorally.

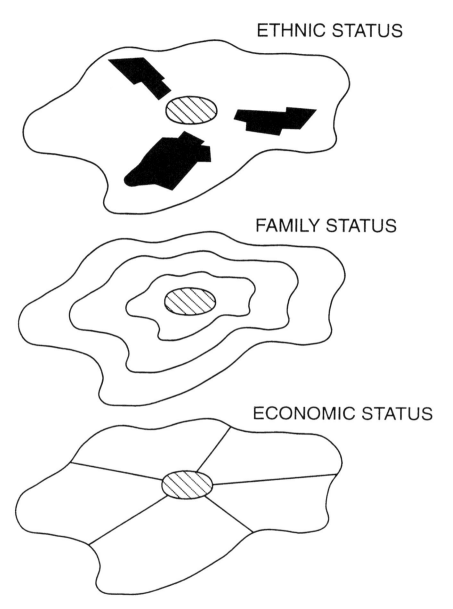

*Figure 5.5*   Schematic Portrayal of the Spatial Distribution of the General Components from PCAs of American Cities. (After Murdie, 1976)

3. Ethnic status varied in clusters, reflecting concentrations of different ethnic groups.

The more controversial of these results referred to the notion of concentric variation, given the simplicity of Burgess's original model. However, a plausible explanation was fashioned from a consideration of the nature of family status, which referred to people's propensity to change their location in a systematic fashion during their lifetime. The standard pattern described was for young adults to seek an apartment near the city centre, close to the CBD. Subsequently, after marriage, there would be a move to the suburbs where family-raising would occur. A final stage might involve a return towards the city centre once children had left the family home. In contrast, economic status tended to highlight the high-class residential areas which developed in just one or two sectors of a city rather than throughout a particular concentric zone. Ethnic concentrations reflected high degrees of black segregation in North American cities of the time.

Similar findings were reported in Murdie's (1976) work on Toronto in which he repeated the Chicago School's views that the physical space of the city was translated into social space experienced by the city's residents. This was accompanied by a clarification of the "key" variables associated with ethnic status, family status and economic status. However, this affirmation was appropriate primarily for factorial ecologies performed in North America, and different findings were obtained elsewhere.

## Factorial Ecologies Outside North America

In Britain the impress of greater planning and institutional activity was revealed in the factor and component loading patterns. The importance of Victorian bylaw housing and council housing from the 1920s onwards is indicated in many of the factorial ecologies of British cities, reflecting the fact that, in England and Wales, public (council) housing represents 30 per cent of housing stock, and in Scotland 50 per cent, compared with just 3 per cent for public (state) housing in the USA.

A typical British example was the work of Robson (1969), in a 30-variable PCA for 159 enumeration districts in Sunderland, north-east England. This produced an economic status/social class component as the first to be extracted, but with a second component that was essentially a measure of housing conditions (Table 5.7a). This was taken further in Herbert's (1967, 1970, 1977) work on both Cardiff and Swansea, which had a housing component accounting for the most variance amongst the variables analysed (Table 5.7b). These components also illustrated the different spatial patterns within British cities for, when mapped, the housing component highlighted those peripheral areas with their stocks of post-war council housing and, in some cases, the inner city redevelopment projects in which local authorities had built council houses and flats close to the city centre (Figure 5.6). The importance of housing characteristics was also revealed in factor analyses of Eastern European cities, for example Weclawowicz's (1979) factorial ecology of Warsaw, Poland.

In extending factorial ecologies to cities in Developing Countries, more divergences from the Shevky–Bell thesis were found. For example, McElrath (1968) for Accra, Ghana, identified the importance of recent migrants in the urban social structure, whilst Abu-Lughod (1969) demonstrated that family status and social rank were combined in Cairo, Egypt. This was confirmed for Indian cities (e.g. Berry and Rees, 1969), emphasising the importance of male-dominated axes linked to sex-selective migration and communal or cultural axes of differentiation.

In many cases the end-point of research utilising factor analysis was the production of factor scores and perhaps some comparison with results for other cities (Johnston, 1977). Relatively little was done to advance further understanding of the processes underlying variations in urban social structure or to use the factors extracted in additional analysis, though an exception to this was the work of Cox (1968) in an analysis of voting behaviour in London. Generally, the factorial ecologies focused upon the extraction of basic dimensions in a set of causal variables, but Cox took the notion of causation further. He investigated 21 socio-economic variables for Greater London,

*Table 5.7*   PCAs of British Cities

(a) Sunderland

| Variables | Component Loadings | | | |
|---|---|---|---|---|
| | 1 | 2 | 3 | 4 |
| **Social composition** | | | | |
| Percentage social class I | 0.78* | −0.13 | −0.36* | −0.10 |
| Percentage social class II | 0.78* | −0.08 | −0.12 | −0.01 |
| Percentage social class III | −0.51 | −0.01 | 0.38* | −0.18 |
| Percentage social class IV | −0.72* | 0.18 | −0.00 | 0.25* |
| Class (weightings I–IV) | 0.91* | 0.15 | −0.23 | −0.14 |
| Percentage terminal education at < 16 | −0.84* | 0.13 | 0.35* | −0.04 |
| Percentage females in labour force | −0.07 | −0.25 | 0.16 | 0.52* |
| Percentage females aged 20–24 married | 0.00 | 0.66* | −0.09 | −0.49* |
| Percentage qualified for jury service | 0.21 | −0.72* | −0.37* | −0.24* |
| **Age structure** | | | | |
| Percentage aged 0–14 | −0.75* | −0.32 | 0.42* | −0.33* |
| Percentage aged 20–24 | −0.01 | 0.54 | −0.12 | 0.53* |
| Percentage aged 65+ | 0.64 | 0.49 | 0.35* | 0.13 |
| Fertility ratio A | −0.14 | 0.59 | −0.12 | −0.18 |
| Fertility ratio B | −0.64 | 0.08 | −0.31 | −0.54* |
| **Household tenure** | | | | |
| Percentage owner occupiers | 0.88* | 0.05 | 0.09 | −0.24 |
| Percentage council tenants | −0.60 | −0.68* | −0.07 | 0.17 |
| Percentage renting private furnished | 0.21 | 0.58 | −0.39* | 0.29* |
| Percentage renting private unfurnished | −0.10 | 0.90* | 0.04 | −0.02 |
| **Household accommodation and composition** | | | | |
| Percentage one-person households | 0.30 | 0.76* | 0.16 | 0.12 |
| Percentage two-person households | 0.72* | 0.46 | 0.31 | −0.05 |
| Percentage six-person households | −0.65 | −0.45 | −0.19 | 0.33* |
| Average no. of persons/room | −0.92* | −0.01 | −0.13 | −0.02 |
| Percentage households > 1.5 persons/room | −0.68* | 0.40 | −0.15 | 0.04 |
| **Housing characteristics** | | | | |
| Gross rateable value | 0.60 | −0.68* | −0.28 | 0.03 |
| Percentage dwellings > 8 rooms | 0.29 | 0.37 | −0.60* | 0.33* |
| Percentage un-subdivided houses | 0.24 | −0.77* | 0.22 | −0.01 |
| Percentage one household space | 0.09 | −0.64 | 0.46* | −0.05 |
| Percentage shared dwellings | −0.05 | 0.71* | −0.46* | −0.07 |
| Percentage without bath | −0.19 | 0.87* | 0.15 | −0.19 |
| Percentage all four basic amenities | 0.08 | −0.93* | −0.08 | 0.11 |
| Eigenvalue | 9.09 | 8.60 | 2.36 | 1.85 |
| Percentage of variance | 30.3 | 28.67 | 7.87 | 6.17 |

A = persons aged 0–4 as a percentage of females aged 15–44
B = persons aged 0–9 as a percentage of females aged 15–44
* Highest 10 loadings on that component
*Source*: Robson (1969).

Table 5.7   (Continued)

(b) Cardiff and Swansea

| Variables | Component Loadings | | | | | |
| --- | --- | --- | --- | --- | --- | --- |
| | Cardiff | | | Swansea | | |
| | 1 | 2 | 3 | 1 | 2 | 3 |
| Percentage persons aged 0–4 | | | | | | 74 |
| Percentage persons aged 0–14 | 87 | | | 80 | | 34 |
| Percentage persons aged 65+ | −85 | | | −85 | | |
| Overall sex ratio | | | | | | |
| Singles as percentage of adult population | | | | | | −70 |
| Percentage women 20–24 married | | | −49 | | | 51 |
| Percentage single persons/household | −73 | | | | | |
| Percentage households sharing dwelling | | | | | −62 | |
| Percentage households without WC | | 69 | | | −75 | |
| No. of persons/room | 91 | | | 86 | | |
| Percentage households > 1.5 persons/room | | 67 | | | | |
| Percentage owner-occupier households | | | | | | |
| Percentage council tenant households | 86 | | | 79 | | |
| Percentage renting private unfurnished | | 66 | | | −74 | |
| Percentage renting furnished | | | | | | |
| Percentage born in British Caribbean | | | | | | |
| Percentage born in British Africa† | | | | | | |
| Percentage born in South Asia | | | 57 | | | |
| Percentage born in Cyprus | | | | | | |
| Percentage born in Malta | | | | | | |
| Percentage born in Ireland | | | | | | |
| Percentage born outside England/Wales | | | 55 | | | |
| Percentage males in professional occupations | | | 44 | | 52 | |
| Percentage males in manual occupations | | 66 | | 71 | | |
| Percentage terminal education at < 16 | | | −42 | | −56 | |
| Percentage recent in-migrants | | | | | | 52 |
| Percentage of variance | 27.4 | 23.5 | 10.7 | 26.8 | 14.5 | 8.7 |

† Excepting South Africa

Only highest five loadings per component shown.

Source: Herbert (1970).

which yielded four factors that were then entered into a model where they were treated as causes of variation in the number of Conservative Party votes and of variations in voter participation. This enabled testing of assumptions about spatial variations in voting, notably differences between the inner city and the suburbs.

In general, factorial ecologies performed for cities outside North America revealed the importance of cultural elements within urban socio-economic structure, highlighting the location-specific nature of the original ecological models. But, the degree to which factorial ecologies for different cities can be compared remains questionable, primarily because different

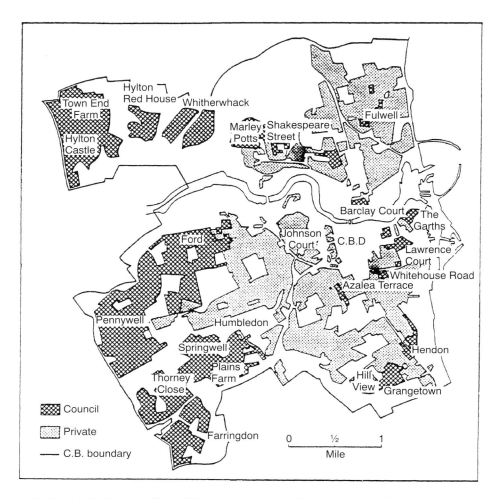

*Figure 5.6*    The Spatial Distribution of Council Housing in Sunderland. (*Source*: Robson, 1969)

ranges and numbers of variables have been employed in each study. On the one hand, it is not surprising that for North American cities similar factors were obtained more consistently because approximately the same range of socio-economic variables was used quite frequently. But, on the other hand, when a more varied range of variables was employed, then rather different factors were obtained. Hence, the factorial ecologies for British cities reflected the variables in the UK Population Census and not merely inherent socio-economic characteristics of urban differentia-

tion. This is illustrated by the range of variables represented in Table 5.7 where housing characteristics and household tenure are to the fore. The contrast between Herbert's use of ethnic status variables and the complete lack of such variables in Robson's study is noteworthy.

## Beyond Factorial Ecology

The lack of comparability between different factorial ecologies was a crucial limitation in the development of a corpus of substantive findings from this work. Theoretical weaknesses provided further limitations, but perhaps the greatest indictment is the charge that factorial ecologies became ends in themselves. They may have shed more light upon socio-economic differentiation of urban areas, but, in the social turbulence of the late 1960s, they were criticised for failing to address critical social problems. It seemed to many that strife in America's inner cities was being ignored by geographers who were still too concerned with descriptive accounts of urban internal structure. Urban problems seemed remote from academic work dealing in factor loadings, varimax rotation and communality. For many, the factorial ecologies had become as irrelevant as the original models of human ecology (Harvey, 1971). For example, instead of emphasising individual choice and locational preference as many of the factorial ecologists had, Marxist geographers interpreted residential and ethnic segregation as a product of the economic stratification of wage labour and therefore owing their material origins to the organisation of the economy and the circulation of capital (e.g. L.A. Brown, 1981).

There were various reactions to the perceived sterility of the factorial approach. One of the most influential, though, was that by Wilbur Zelinsky (1970), then President of the Association of American Geographers, who attacked the limited horizons of the factorial ecologists and called for geographical research that was more relevant to the major problems of society. He also argued that positivist-based spatial science methodology such as that employed in the factorial ecologies was not suitable for this "relevant" research. This type of argument symbolised the beginning of widespread discord within human geography. There emerged a more pronounced methodological plurality that encompassed more ideologically motivated work as well as introducing new philosophical and theoretical underpinnings to geographical research.

Whilst this dramatic set of developments cannot be attributed entirely to unfavourable reaction to factorial ecologies, undoubtedly the degree of "overkill" with this technique contributed to the strong reaction against positivist-based, statistics-dominated work. New foci and new research methods have emerged

supplanting the approach of factorial ecology, though research employing factor analysis has continued to play a role within human geography (e.g. Keys and McCracken, 1981). For example, factorial ecologies of a number of American cities were carried out in the 1980s (White, 1987) as well as for Montreal (Le Bourdais and Beaudry, 1988) and Winnipeg (Hamm et al, 1988) amongst others. In particular, though, continued work with factor analytic techniques has drawn upon their role as a classificatory device (see Beaumont and Beaumont, 1982), using classification as a starting point for further investigation rather than as an end in itself. Indeed, classification was often a key ingredient of factorial ecologies, with areas of the city classified into particular categories on the basis of factor scores. The classification both of groups of variables and of spatial units has received attention using factor analysis amongst other multivariate classificatory techniques. This particular use of factor analysis is considered below, and comparison made with alternative multivariate techniques used in classification, namely cluster analysis, discriminant analysis and canonical correlation.

## REGIONALISATION AND CLASSIFICATION

*Classification* involves the grouping of individual members of a population into groups or classes to form distinctive and mutually exclusive categories. If the individuals are areal units such as enumeration districts or counties then the process might be termed *regionalisation*, and the resultant categories would be regions, especially if the procedure had generated a group of spatially contiguous areal units. Classification can be either *deductive* or *inductive*. The former uses a previously determined set of classes and then allocates individuals to them on the basis of given criteria. This can be performed using discriminant analysis, as described in the following section. Both types of classification can be achieved using numerical methods and hence the term *numerical taxonomy*. The commonest form of inductive numerical taxonomy is *cluster analysis* (see Kaufman, 1990), though *factor analysis* can often be an appropriate alternative.

There are two basic ways in which a numerically based classification may proceed (Johnston, 1976c). The population of individuals (labelled *i* in Figure 5.7) can be treated as a single entity to be broken down into classes by a process of division (Figure 5.7b). Alternatively, each individual may be regarded as a separate class and then grouped with other individuals in a process of addition to form classes consisting of several individuals (Figure 5.7a). The latter process could continue until all the individuals belong to one single group consisting of the entire population of individuals. Figure 5.7 suggests the commonest outcome of either method is a hierarchy in which each step of the process may use a stated criterion to produce the classification. In such a process large higher-order classes can be subdivided into smaller lower-order classes. For example, a population may be divided on the basis of sex, then ethnicity, then age, then social class and, finally, by residence or location.

Although classifications generally follow a hierarchical structure, different types of classification can be recognised:

1. *Monothetic*. Classes are determined by a rigid rule which applies to one or more of the properties being classified. For example the soil classification of the US Department of Agriculture tends towards this approach as it attempts to define classes by precise limits on soil properties.
2. *Polythetic*. Classes are defined with reference to many properties of the objects being classified. The allocation is not made on the basis of rigid rules but by the overall resemblance of the object to a particular type. In the Soil Survey of England and Wales, soil profiles are allocated to that class which, overall, it most closely resembles in terms of profile properties.
3. *Natural*. These types of classification reflect underlying processes that give rise to the phenomena being classified. This is typical of biological classifications and classifications used for general purposes.

4. *Artificial*. This classification refers to a narrow subset of properties. The objective tends to ignore grouping on the basis of similar processes, but establishes groups which resemble each other in terms of particular properties. These classifications tend to be used for specialist purposes and are often monothetic in that they consider threshold values of relevant properties.

In general, classifications tend to be either artificial, specialist and monothetic, or natural, general purpose and polythetic.

## Classifying Bivariate Data

Before considering classification procedures using multiple variables, the basic principles involved can be illustrated with reference to a bivariate situation. Given the data in Table 5.8a, a simple geographical exercise is to classify the towns into types according to their values on the two variables (population size and an index measuring tourist attractions). Initially, the two variables need to be expressed on the same scale by converting them to standard normal form. They can then be plotted on a simple graph as shown in Figure 5.8a. This indicates a strong degree of correlation between population size and number of tourist attractions ($r = 0.68$). A tentative grouping of towns is suggested in the figure (the dotted line) purely on the basis of visual inspection of the graph.

The next step is to calculate the distances between each town being classified. This is usually performed using the *distance coefficient* ($d_{ij}$) which is the squared distance between observations (places) *i* and *j*:

$$d_{ij} = \sqrt{\frac{\sum_{k=1}^{m}(x_{ik} - x_{jk})^2}{m}}$$

where $x_{ik}$ = the *k*th variable measured on object (or place) *i*, $x_{jk}$ = the *k*th variable measured on object (or place) *j*, *m* = the number of variables (in this case,

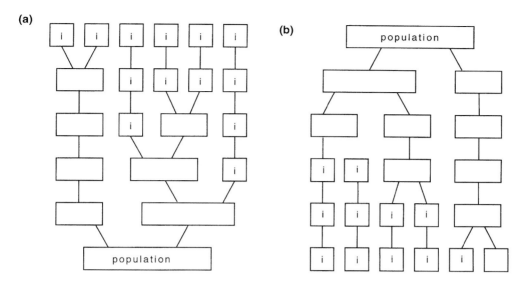

*Figure 5.7* Classification
(a) By addition of individuals to groups; (b) by division of a population into groups

*Table 5.8* Classification of Tourist Centres in South Island, New Zealand, on the Basis of (I) Population and (II) a Tourist Attractions Index

(a) Standardised values

| Location | (I)<br>Population | (II)<br>Index of<br>Tourist Attractions | Standardised | |
|---|---|---|---|---|
| | | | (I) | (II) |
| Hanmer Springs HS | 1029 | 2.67 | −0.57 | −0.62 |
| Queenstown Q | 3367 | 12.65 | 0.40 | 2.65 |
| Te Anau TA | 2610 | 2.67 | 0.08 | −0.62 |
| Wanaka W | 1155 | 4.40 | −0.52 | −0.06 |
| Kaikoura K | 2180 | 4.90 | −0.10 | 0.11 |
| Akaroa A | 694 | 4.40 | −0.71 | −0.06 |
| Murchison M | 595 | 1.80 | −0.75 | −0.91 |
| Hokitika H | 3414 | 6.90 | 0.42 | 0.76 |
| Gore G | 9185 | 4.15 | 2.81 | −0.14 |
| Takaka T | 997 | 3.00 | −0.59 | −0.52 |
| Picton P | 3220 | 6.10 | 0.34 | 0.50 |
| Omarama O | 501 | 1.20 | −0.79 | −1.11 |

*continued overleaf*

$m = 2$) and $d_{ij}$ = the distance between object $i$ and object $j$.

A small value of $d_{ij}$ indicates that two objects are similar or close together. The resulting matrix of distance coefficients is shown in Table 5.7b. From this matrix the pair of places can be selected which is more similar than any other pair by virtue of having the smallest distance coefficient. In this case the smallest

*Table 5.8  (Continued)*

(b) Distance coefficients

|     | HS   | Q    | TA   | W    | K    | A    | M    | H    | G    | T    | P    | O    |
|-----|------|------|------|------|------|------|------|------|------|------|------|------|
| HS  | 0.00 | 2.42 | 0.46 | 0.40 | 0.62 | 0.41 | 0.24 | 1.21 | 2.42 | 0.08 | 1.02 | 0.37 |
| Q   |      | 0.00 | 2.33 | 2.02 | 1.83 | 2.07 | 2.65 | 1.33 | 2.61 | 2.35 | 1.52 | 2.79 |
| TA  |      |      | 0.00 | 0.59 | 0.53 | 0.69 | 0.62 | 1.01 | 1.96 | 0.48 | 0.82 | 0.71 |
| W   |      |      |      | 0.00 | 0.32 | 0.14 | 0.63 | 0.88 | 2.36 | 0.33 | 0.72 | 0.77 |
| K   |      |      |      |      | 0.00 | 0.45 | 0.86 | 0.59 | 2.06 | 0.56 | 0.41 | 0.99 |
| A   |      |      |      |      |      | 0.00 | 0.60 | 0.99 | 2.49 | 0.34 | 0.84 | 0.74 |
| M   |      |      |      |      |      |      | 0.00 | 1.44 | 2.58 | 0.30 | 1.26 | 0.14 |
| H   |      |      |      |      |      |      |      | 0.00 | 1.81 | 1.15 | 0.19 | 1.57 |
| G   |      |      |      |      |      |      |      |      | 0.00 | 2.42 | 1.81 | 2.64 |
| T   |      |      |      |      |      |      |      |      |      | 0.00 | 0.97 | 0.44 |
| P   |      |      |      |      |      |      |      |      |      |      | 0.00 | 1.39 |
| O   |      |      |      |      |      |      |      |      |      |      |      | 0.00 |

(c) Clustering

| Towns Combined into Clusters | Similarity Level of Clusters |
|------------------------------|------------------------------|
| HS  T                        | 0.08                         |
| W   A                        | 0.14                         |
| M   O                        | 0.14                         |
| H   P                        | 0.19                         |
| HS  M                        | 0.34                         |
| W   K                        | 0.39                         |
| HS  TA                       | 0.57                         |
| HS  W                        | 0.61                         |
| HS  H                        | 0.88                         |
| HS  Q                        | 1.81                         |
| HS  G                        | 2.32                         |

coefficient is 0.08 between Hanmer Springs (HS) and Takaka (T). Their similarity can also be interpreted in terms of their contribution to the within-groups variation. Because of their similarity, when grouped, this pair makes the smallest increment to the within-groups variation:

$$C_1 = \sum_{i=1}^{n} \sum_{j=1}^{m} (x_{ij} - \bar{x}_{1j})^2 \qquad (5.1)$$

where $C_1$ = the contribution of this first group of places to the within-groups variation, $x_{ij}$ = the value for observation $i$ on variable $j$, and $\bar{x}_{1j}$ = the mean for group 1 on variable $j$.

In standardised form:

- for variable $x$, HS = $-0.57$;
- for variable $y$, HS = $-0.62$;
- for variable $x$, T = $-0.59$;
- for variable $y$, T = $-0.52$.

So, for HS, $x_j = -0.595$; and for T, $x_j = -0.555$. If these values are substituted into equation (5.1):

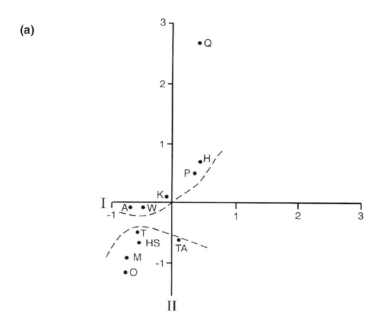

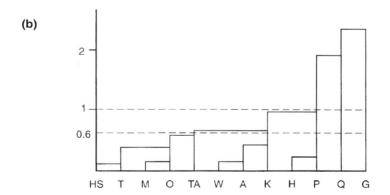

*Figure 5.8*  Classification of Small Towns in South Island, New Zealand on the Basis of Two Variables, (I) Population, (II) An Index of Tourist Attractions

(a) Tentative groupings based on graph of standardised values of (I) and (II); (b) dendrogram based on similarity coefficient

$$C_1 = [-0.57 - (-0.595)]^2 + [-0.62 - (-0.595)]^2$$

$$+ [-0.59 - (-0.555)]^2 + [-0.52 - (-0.555)]^2$$

$$= 0.0006 + 0.0006 + 0.0012 + 0.0012$$

$$= 0.0144$$

This is the contribution of the first grouping (HS and T) to the within-groups variation. The calculations can then proceed for other groupings using the general formula for $C_1$, termed the *error sum of squares*:

$$C_1 = \sum_{j=1}^{m} \sum_{i=1}^{n} x_{ij}^2 - \sum_{j=1}^{m} \left( \sum_{i=1}^{n} x_{ij} \right)^2 \Big/ n$$

where $x_{ij}$ = the value of observation $i$, which is a member of group 1, on variable $j$; $m$ = the number of variables; and $n$ = the number of observations in group 1.

When each group is formed a new group centroid is established. For example, in Figure 5.8a this would be a point mid-way between HS and T. Therefore, in calculations involving this new group, a new matrix of squared distances must be formed. Again the observation creating the smallest additional within-group variation is added. However, before new members are allocated to this first group, other groupings must be investigated by examining the matrix of distance coefficients (Table 5.8b). This reveals that the next most similar pair is Wanaka and Akaroa. Therefore these can be joined to form another group. This process can continue, establishing two-member groups until an individual observation has the closest similarity with a pre-existing pair. By grouping these together a group with three members is then created. The process can continue until all the observations have been joined together in one large single group comprising all 12 small towns. This process is termed *cluster analysis*. Figure 5.8b shows this clustering process in diagrammatic form. Interpretation of this diagram is discussed below.

## Classification Using Cluster Analysis

Geographical data generally appear as part of an existing structure of regions. Yet it is the formulation of regional boundaries that may be a desired outcome of analysis rather than such boundaries being predetermined (Dunn and Walker, 1989; Massey, 1978). However, if multivariate data are available for small enough areal units, it may be possible to use multivariate techniques to construct regions, that is grouping areal units, from such data (see Grigg, 1965). Although factor analysis (*R*-mode analysis) can be used for purposes of classifying both variables and observations in a geographical matrix, the closely related but purpose-built classificatory tool, *cluster analysis* (*Q*-mode analysis), can also be used.

Like factor analysis, cluster analysis is based on a correlation matrix, but it generally operates on one in a different form. In cluster analysis the correlation matrix depicts correlations between observations, and not between variables (as shown in Table 5.9). Therefore *Q*-mode analysis examines associations between observations, which in a geographical matrix are places.

The clustering process itself is usually based on the representation of the *Q*-mode correlation matrix in a *dendrogram*, so named because of its branching structure (Figures 5.8b and 5.9). The initial step in the dendrogram is to pick out the mutually highly correlated pairs of observations (Hanmer Springs and Takaka in Figure 5.8b and Table 5.8c). These pairs are then grouped with unattached observations until the grouping procedure has combined all the observations into one single group. There are two basic ways in which single observations may be attached to a group:

1. *Single linkage clustering*. This connects objects to clusters on the basis of the highest correlation between the object and any other object in the cluster (Figure 5.10a) (see Mather, 1976:324–7; Robinson, 1990:6–10).
2. *Weighted pair-group clustering*. The connection between an object and a cluster is based upon the average of the correlation between the object and each individual in the cluster (Figures 5.8b and 5.10b).

*Table 5.9* Correlations for Data on Canadian Provinces, 1981

| Observation | | Variables | | | | |
|---|---|---|---|---|---|---|
| | | A | B | C | D | E |
| 1 | Alberta | 77.3 | 8.7 | 20.4 | 22.6 | 12.36 |
| 2 | British Columbia | 77.9 | 2.2 | 10.0 | 15.7 | 16.58 |
| 3 | Manitoba | 70.9 | 9.5 | −0.8 | 13.2 | 21.00 |
| 4 | New Brunswick | 50.5 | 2.2 | 1.8 | 9.3 | 16.31 |
| 5 | Newfoundland | 58.4 | 0.3 | 1.0 | 8.1 | 69.03 |
| 6 | Nova Scotia | 54.9 | 2.1 | 1.4 | 9.6 | 7.12 |
| 7 | Ontario | 81.7 | 3.3 | 3.3 | 15.4 | 13.26 |
| 8 | Prince Edward Island | 36.3 | 9.8 | 3.6 | 8.1 | 0.09 |
| 9 | Quebec | 77.4 | 2.9 | 2.2 | 12.7 | 16.93 |
| 10 | Saskatchewan | 57.9 | 19.0 | 3.8 | 15.7 | 10.35 |

A = % population in urban areas
B = % population on farms
C = % population increase, 1976–81
D = GDP (Canadian $000) per capita
E = electric power generated (MWh) per capita

(a) Correlations between variables

| | A | B | C | D |
|---|---|---|---|---|
| B | −0.192 | | | |
| C | 0.373 | 0.136 | | |
| D | 0.708 | 0.352 | 0.803 | |
| E | 0.081 | −0.405 | −0.214 | −0.271 |

The highest population increases have occurred in the wealthiest provinces; provinces with higher proportions of farm population generate the least electric power per capita.

(b) Correlations between observations – cluster analysis

| | 1 | 2 | 3 | 4 | 5 | 6 | 7 | 8 | 9 |
|---|---|---|---|---|---|---|---|---|---|
| 2 | 0.98 | | | | | | | | |
| 3 | 0.92 | 0.97 | | | | | | | |
| 4 | 0.93 | 0.98 | 0.99 | | | | | | |
| 5 | 0.45 | 0.61 | 0.69 | 0.73 | | | | | |
| 6 | 0.98 | 0.99 | 0.98 | 0.98 | 0.57 | | | | |
| 7 | 0.98 | 1.00 | 0.98 | 0.98 | 0.59 | 1.00 | | | |
| 8 | 0.94 | 0.92 | 0.91 | 0.87 | 0.32 | 0.95 | 0.94 | | |
| 9 | 0.96 | 0.99 | 0.99 | 0.99 | 0.65 | 1.00 | 1.00 | 0.92 | |
| 10 | 0.92 | 0.93 | 0.96 | 0.92 | 0.46 | 0.96 | 0.96 | 0.98 | 0.95 |

Province no. 5 (Newfoundland) stands out as quite dissimilar to the others on the basis of the five variables

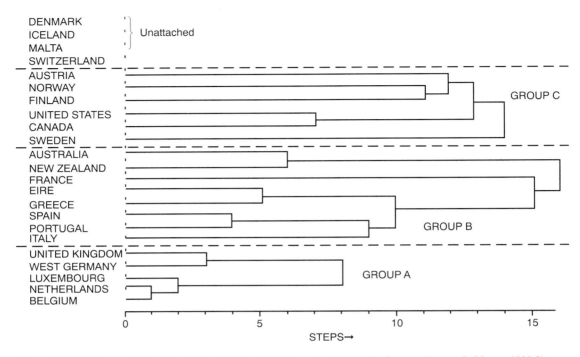

*Figure 5.9*   Dendrogram of Developed Countries Classified According to Rural Indicators. (*Source*: Robinson, 1990:8)

The two methods give slightly different results, though the latter is generally preferred as it gives a truer "group effect" than the single linkage method which relies on a single correlation between an object and one member of a cluster, and so can "group" an object at a high level of correlation to a group containing another, substantially dissimilar, object. Variations on these two basic types are discussed by Lorr (1983).

In both methods of clustering only the mutually highly correlated pairs of observations are actually entered into the dendrogram at a level of correlation depicted in the original correlation matrix between all the observations. The correlations between groups and individuals are apparent correlations only, termed *cophenetic correlations*. It is possible therefore to make comparisons between these cophenetic correlations and the original correlation matrix. The comparison reveals the degree of distortion produced by the clustering process and can assist with the decision on where to halt it. This is essentially a subjective

decision, usually made on the basis of nominating a level of correlation below which clustering will not be accepted (as shown in Figures 5.9 and 5.11). This subjectivity is a major weakness in the technique, though the decision over which clusters to reject in the clustering process can be assisted by adopting an alternative measure of similarity. Hence the distance coefficient ($d_{ij}$), which is not constrained within the range $+1$ to $-1$, is sometimes preferred to the correlation coefficient. Use of $d_{ij}$ in conjunction with the weighted pair–group method tends to create clearer distinctions between clusters.

In Figure 5.8a Queenstown and Gore stand out as being very different to the other 12 small towns. This is confirmed in Figure 5.8b where Gore is incorporated in the group containing the other 11 towns only at a value of $d_{ij} = 2.41$. Queenstown only groups with Picton at a value of $d_{ij} = 1.90$. Therefore Queenstown and Gore do remain outside any realistic grouping of the 12 towns: their population numbers and tourist

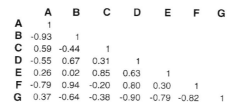

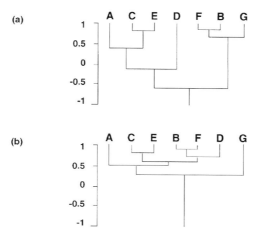

*Figure 5.10*   Classification by Clustering Based on Accompanying Correlation Matrix
(a) Simple linkage; (b) weighted pair group. (*Source*: Davis, 1986:463–5)

attractions tend to be larger than those in the other towns. If a cut-off of $d_{ij} = 1.0$ had been selected beforehand, then Queenstown and Gore would have been left as isolated individuals and the other 10 as one large group. The subdivision of this large group into two, as suggested in Figure 5.8a, could be partially achieved at $d_{ij} = 0.6$. This produces the group incorporating Takaka, Hanmer Springs, Te Anau, Murchison and Omarama, but splits the other subgroup in two by separating Akaroa, Wanaka and Kaikoura from Picton and Hokitika. Therefore the cluster analysis has both confirmed certain aspects of the grouping by eye shown in Figure 5.8a and refined the classification. Had the objects to be classified been areal units rather than towns, greater refinement could have been introduced by a more complex grouping

process that added a contiguity restriction. In this way groupings could be limited only to contiguous areal units.

## Classification Using Factor Analysis

One of the ways in which *factor analysis* can be used as a valuable tool in geographical investigation is via its output of factor or component scores. Mapping of these scores can be seen as part of a regionalising or classifying exercise which can then initiate further investigation of particular regions and of regional development through time. This method was used by D.M. Smith (1979) as part of his "welfare approach" to human geography. He employed factor analysis to map social variations in the quality of life in order to

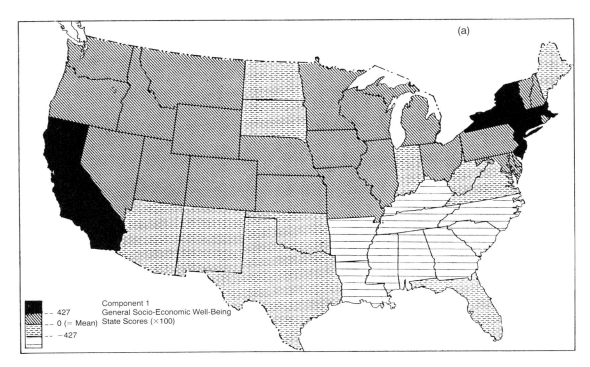

(a)

Component 1
General Socio-Economic Well-Being
State Scores (×100)

427
0 (= Mean)
−427

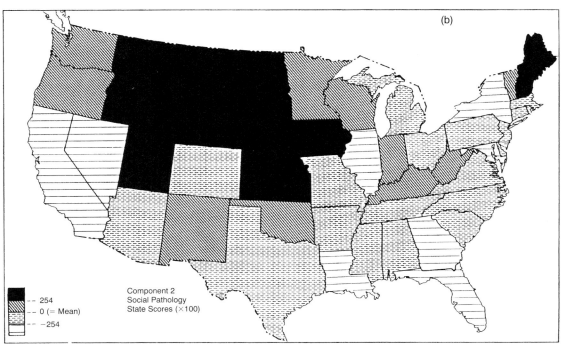

(b)

Component 2
Social Pathology
State Scores (×100)

254
0 (= Mean)
−254

highlight policy needs and enable monitoring of policy. The resulting choropleth maps shown in Figure 5.11 are a basic classification of the USA by state into different categories or regions. It has performed a task frequently seen within geography, namely splitting a population of individuals (in this case the states) into mutually exclusive categories using predetermined criteria. In Smith's example the criteria were component scores.

Factor analysis as a classificatory and regionalising technique has been employed in agricultural geography, with the simplifying role of PCA being prominent in collapsing a large number of agricultural variables into a smaller number of agricultural "systems" (Ilbery, 1981; Robinson, 1988). As in the example of the welfare approach referred to above, these classifications have the potential for further work that considers policy implications or policy evaluation rather than being simply the end-point of a data manipulation exercise.

Classification using factor analysis has also been applied to a great many other situations for which multivariate datasets are available, in both human and physical geography. Characteristics of several cities have been factor-analysed to produce classifications of cities, initially in the USA (Cadwallader, 1981), but also in the UK (Moser and Scott, 1961), Canada (King, 1966) and other parts of the world (e.g. Berry, 1969; Harris, 1970; Hirst, 1975). Other classifications based on factor analyses include perceptions of the urban system (e.g. Gould and White, 1974), inter-urban flows (e.g. Clark, 1973; Davies, 1978, 1979), historical city structures (e.g. Carter and Wheatley, 1978; Shaw, 1977), agricultural decision-making (e.g. Ilbery, 1983, 1985), and land cover using remotely sensed imagery (e.g. Chavez and Kwarteng, 1989).

A more recent variant on this classificatory work is the study of intra-urban variations in the 24 metropolitan areas of Canada by Davies and Murdie (1991). Using PCA with both varimax and direct oblimin rotations, this analysed 35 variables on 14 different categories (e.g. age, family, education, migration, ethnicity) for all 2981 census tracts in the 24 metropolitan areas. Different solutions were obtained by dividing the metropolitan areas into various size categories and applying separate PCAs to these categories. The primary intention was to examine the character of the main components derived from the analysis rather than to classify cities, though the latter was a by-product of this work. Also, variations between the different size categories were investigated, revealing a high degree of consistency, though with the largest cities displaying more complex social structures. Additional axes of differentiation to the standard three- or four-axis model of the early factorial ecologies were recognised, including an "impoverishment" dimension and several family dimensions, some featuring gender variations. The general hypothesis that post-industrial society has led to more complex cities was confirmed.

## DISCRIMINANT ANALYSIS

In a classification exercise objects are separated into groups or clusters that are both relatively homogeneous and distinct from other groups. The exercise proceeds on the basis of analysing measured variables for each observation and is internally based; that is, it is not dependent on *a priori* knowledge of existing clusters. In contrast, *discriminant analysis* usually starts with already recognised groups or clusters and then attempts to allocate individuals to these groups. It does so by establishing a linear combination of variables measured for two clearly defined groups that produces the maximum difference between the groups. If a function can be found that produces a significant difference, it can then be used to allocate samples of unknown origin to the known groups. The process therefore attempts to produce maximum discrimination between groups and also minimum probability of error in assigning new individuals or objects to one or other of the groups (see McLachan, 1992).

The function that is calculated is known as a *linear discriminant function* which transforms an original set

*Figure 5.11* Component Scores for an Analysis of American Social Characteristics (by State)
(a) First component: social well-being; (b) second component: social pathology. (*Source*: Smith, 1975:332)

of observations into a single discriminant score. It collapses a multivariate dataset into a problem of discriminating between two sets of values. The calculations involved are ones which can find a transform giving the minimum ratio of the difference between a pair of group multivariate means to the multivariate variance within the two groups. Therefore, given two clusters of points in multivariate space, discriminant analysis finds the orientation along which the two clusters have the greatest separation whilst at the same time each cluster has the least inflation. An example is shown in Figure 5.12 for a simple bivariate situation

in which A and B cannot be separated using variables $x_1$ or $x_2$, but an orientation can be found along which the two clusters are separated the most and inflated the least. The coordinates of this axis of orientation are the linear discriminant function. Regression analysis can be used to find this function, though only with the use of quite complex matrix algebra, and hence the reliance on computer programs to perform the calculations.

The distance between $R_A$ and $R_B$ along the discriminant function is termed the *Mahalanobis distance*, $D_2$. It is a measure of the separation between the two

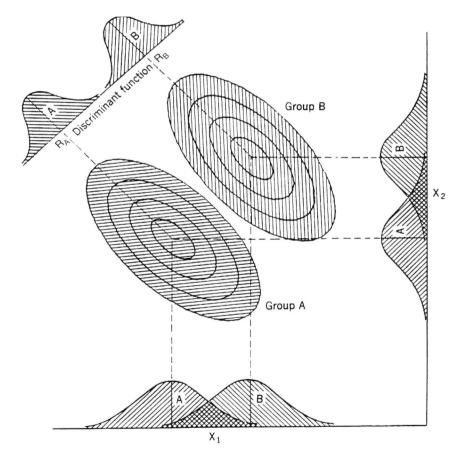

*Figure 5.12*   Plot of Two Bivariate Distributions, Showing Overlap Between Groups A and B Along Both Variables $x_1$ and $x_2$. (*Source*: Davis, 1986:444)
(Groups can be distinguished by projecting members of the two groups onto the discriminant function line)
$R_A$ = multivariate mean of Group A, $R_B$ = multivariate of Group B

multivariate means expressed in units of the pooled variance of the two groups. If more than two groups are being considered then more than one discriminant function can be calculated and the mathematics for this become more complex.

There are three principal applications of discriminant analysis:

1. In the testing of hypotheses. For example, can suburbs be distinguished from the inner city on the basis of variables relating to socio-economic characteristics? This question could be refined using discriminant analysis by investigating which variables are important and which are redundant in producing any division between the two parts of the city.
2. Evaluating a classification. Discriminant analysis can highlight incorrect attribution of boundaries to clusters or sub-optimal classification.
3. Assigning new members to pre-recognised groups.

A simple example of discriminant analysis is given in Figure 5.13 (based on work by King, 1969). This shows two "core" agricultural regions designated by the US Department of Agriculture. Between them lie 10 counties which could be classified into either of the two core regions on the basis of certain measured characteristics. The classification was based on four variables:

- $x_1 = $ density of rural farm population,
- $x_2 = $ average annual precipitation,
- $x_3 = $ percentage of county area in flat land,
- $x_4 = $ average farm size.

From this a linear discriminant function was derived:

$$y = 0.0393x_1 - 0.0811x_2 - 0.0065x_3 + 0.0922x_4$$

In this equation, $y$ is a dummy dependent variable such that for each group the mean value of $y$ is zero. New individuals (in this case, counties) can be allocated to a group on the basis of their $y$ scores, with the mean predicted $y$ score being obtained for each group by inserting in the equation the values of $x_1$, $x_2$, etc. for each group.

In King's analysis, the mean predicted score for region A was $-0.8065$ and for region B it was $-1.5284$, with a midpoint of $-1.1674$. Therefore a county with a $y$ value $> -1.1674$ was included in region A whilst counties with $y$ values $< -1.1674$ were classified into region B. The discrimination can be tested using analysis of variance (see Chapter 3). This testing operates on the assumption that the greater the proportion of variation attributable to between-class differences rather than within-group differences, the more useful the classification will be. As shown in Figure 5.13, just two counties (Buffalo and Brule) were classified into region A, with the others included in region B. One county (Faulk) in region A appeared to have been misclassified.

## CANONICAL CORRELATION

The main value of *canonical correlation* is in investigations of generalised causal hypotheses in which relationships between two groups of variables can be tested, but with the specific nature of the relations between the groups being uncertain or in need of clarification. Canonical correlation relates sets of dependent variables to sets of independent variables and may be used in situations in which a number of dependent (or independent variables) are interrelated. In this case the association between variables may be described in terms of *predictor variables* ($p$), rather than independent variables, and *criteria variables* ($q$), rather than dependent variables. These predictor and criteria variables can be calculated from a standard correlation matrix from which canonical vectors are extracted in a similar fashion to the extraction of principal components. Thus a *canonical vector* ($I$) is extracted so that the correlation between the scores on the $p$ set for that vector and the scores on the $q$ set is as high as possible. Correlations between the original variables and the canonical vectors are given by *canonical weights*, and are analogous to component loadings. Similarly, *canonical scores* are analogous to component scores and are composite indices for the

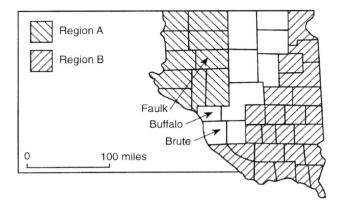

*Figure 5.13*   Discriminant Analysis for Ten Counties in Eastern South Dakota
Region A = specialised wheat farming; region B = feed grains and livestock. (Based on King, 1969:206–8)

observations on the canonical vectors (see Giffins, 1985).

The need for canonical correlation can arise if dependent variables are known to be interrelated. For example, Johnston (1978:184) quotes Gauthier's (1968) investigation of the relationships between the levels of economic development ($E$) and accessibility ($A$) for 120 locations in Brazil. Neither of these two general concepts could be adequately represented by a single variable, so composites for accessibility were obtained from a PCA of a number of variables which produced five relevant components to act as composite variables. Three indices of economic development were selected ($E_1$, $E_2$ and $E_3$; $E_1$ = value of industrial production, $E_2$ = size of urban population, $E_3$ = value of retail sales). Using the hypothesis that $E = f(A)$, it is then possible to fit three equations:

$$E_1 = f(A_1, \ldots, A_5)$$

$$E_2 = f(A_1, \ldots, A_5)$$

$$E_3 = f(A_1, \ldots, A_5)$$

However, this assumes that $E_1$, $E_2$ and $E_3$ are independent indices of the general concept, economic development. If this assumption of independence is not tenable the equation should take the form

$$(D_1, \ldots, D_m) = f(A_1, \ldots, A_5)$$

where $(D_1, \ldots, D_m)$ = components formed from the dependent variables, up to a maximum of $m$, the number of the original dependent variables. So this is an equation with composite variables on both its sides.

The differences between PCA and canonical correlation are illustrated in Figure 5.14. This depicts the extraction of two components from a set of criteria variables ($E$) (Figure 5.14a) and the extraction of two components from a set of predictor variables ($A$) (Figure 5.14b). Figure 5.14c shows that the first canonical vector extracted is located somewhere between $C_E$ and $C_A$ so that its scores on the criteria set and the predictor set are maximally correlated. From the canonical vector extracted, loadings for all variables can be calculated and, from these, two scores for each observation obtained: one on the criteria set of variables and one on the predictor set of variables.

The scores for the criteria variable set are given by:

$$C_{ik} = \sum_{i=1}^{q} D_{il} L_{lk}$$

where $C_{ik}$ = the canonical score for observation $i$ on the criteria variables associated with canonical vector $k$; $D_{il}$ = the standardised score for observation $i$ on

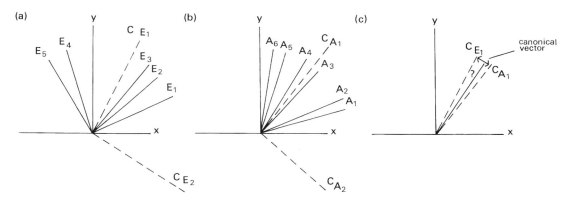

*Figure 5.14*   Comparison of PCA and Canonical Correlation
(a) Extraction of two components from a set of criteria variables ($E$); (b) extraction of two components from a set of predictor variables ($A$) for the same observations as in (a); (c) location of canonical vector for the criteria and predictor variables. (Based on Johnston 1978:186)

criteria variable $l$; and $L_{lk}$ = the canonical weight or loading for criteria variable $l$ on canonical vector $k$.

The scores for the predictor variable set are given by:

$$P_{ik} = \sum_{j=1}^{p} D_{ij} L_{jk}$$

where $P_{ik}$ = the canonical score for observation $i$ on the predictor variables associated with canonical vector $k$; $D_{ij}$ = the standardised score for observation $i$ on predictor variable $j$; and $L_{jk}$ = the canonical weight or loading for predictor variable $j$ on canonical vector $k$.

The correlation between the two sets of scores for all the observations is termed the *canonical root*. The square of this canonical root is known as the *latent root*, $\lambda$, and the canonical vector maximises this value. The significance of canonical correlations can be tested (see Manly, 1986:117–19).

Johnston (1978:190–4) identifies two ways in which canonical correlation has been applied to relationships between groups of interrelated variables. Firstly, as in the work by Corsi and Harvey (1975), specific hypotheses are tested, but without predicting the actual pattern of canonical weights. Secondly, a looser hypothesis is investigated in which the aim is to associate two different sets of variables (e.g. Cant, 1973). In the latter case, canonical correlation has a clear advantage over factor analytic techniques because it gives equal weights to each group being analysed. It emphasises correlations between groups of variables as the criterion to be maximised. In contrast, a factor analysis or PCA would give a greater emphasis to the set of variables containing the most variables.

An example of the type of results of a canonical correlation analysis is set out in Table 5.10, based on an analysis of poverty and crime in Cleveland, Ohio. In this analysis, population and housing characteristics are the predictor set of 18 variables and the criteria set of seven variables are recorded crime rates by location of offence for different crimes. The first three canonical vectors are as follows:

(a) *First canonical vector.* This is a property crime/ opportunity dimension. The highest weighting on the predictor variables is recorded for percentage of the workforce in professional occupations (−0.483). On the criteria variables the largest weights are for rates of larceny (−0.632) and auto theft (−0.743). A strong negative association is shown between these last two criteria variables and three predictor variables: percentage of census

*Table 5.10*   Canonical Correlation Analysis of Crime in Cleveland

(a) Predictor set

| Socio-economic Variables | Factor Structure | | | | Explained Variance |
|---|---|---|---|---|---|
| | I | II | III | IV | |
| Families with female head | 0.289 | −0.466 | 0.347 | 0.294 | 0.213 |
| Population under 18 | 0.737 | 0.055 | 0.064 | −0.084 | 0.336 |
| Population that lived in same house in 1965 | 0.367 | 0.291 | −0.507 | 0.049 | 0.187 |
| Male unemployment rate | 0.049 | 0.083 | 0.176 | 0.159 | 0.026 |
| Female unemployment rate | 0.039 | −0.105 | 0.071 | 0.216 | 0.061 |
| Workers in professional occupations | −0.483 | −0.046 | −0.099 | 0.376 | 0.198 |
| Workers in managerial occupations | −0.194 | 0.054 | 0.099 | 0.200 | 0.057 |
| Workers employed as labourers | 0.271 | −0.367 | 0.348 | −0.037 | 0.132 |
| Workers in service occupations | 0.219 | −0.199 | 0.412 | 0.200 | 0.128 |
| Mean family income | −0.054 | 0.333 | −0.392 | 0.203 | 0.132 |
| Families with incomes < 50% of the poverty level | 0.457 | −0.522 | 0.289 | 0.149 | 0.262 |
| Owner-occupied housing units | 0.192 | 0.775 | −0.212 | −0.002 | 0.259 |
| Vacant housing units | 0.110 | −0.731 | 0.348 | −0.187 | 0.260 |
| Housing units with > 1.5 persons per room | 0.176 | −0.416 | 0.173 | −0.117 | 0.106 |
| Housing units built between 1940–49 | 0.076 | 0.240 | −0.148 | 0.456 | 0.087 |
| Housing units built in 1939 or before | 0.029 | 0.025 | 0.255 | 0.040 | 0.029 |
| Housing units with three or more autos | 0.056 | 0.258 | 0.014 | 0.126 | 0.034 |
| Housing units with no autos | −0.114 | −0.609 | 0.322 | 0.002 | 0.194 |

(b) Criteria Set

| Crime Variables | Factor Structure | | | | Explained Variance |
|---|---|---|---|---|---|
| | I | II | III | IV | |
| Murders | −0.154 | −0.588 | −0.169 | 0.657 | 0.272 |
| Rapes and assaults to rape | 0.213 | −0.218 | −0.012 | 0.302 | 0.116 |
| Robberies and assaults to rob | −0.079 | −0.187 | 0.398 | 0.141 | 0.100 |
| Assaults | 0.121 | −0.377 | 0.178 | −0.104 | 0.087 |
| Breaking and entering | 0.099 | 0.134 | 0.236 | 0.306 | −0.074 |
| Larcenies | −0.632 | −0.093 | −0.364 | −0.070 | 0.619 |
| Auto theft | −0.743 | −0.178 | 0.114 | 0.256 | 0.500 |

tract population under 18 (0.737), percentage of census tract population aged five and over that lived in the same house in 1965 (0.367), and percentage of census tract families that have incomes below half that of the poverty level (0.457). The indication is that property crime is recorded in areas most likely to yield a high reward for the criminals.

(b) *Second canonical variable.* This is a property/ violent crimes dimension, which has its largest weightings occurring on various aspects of poverty in the predictor set, and for the violent crimes of murder and assault in the criteria set. This link between poverty and violent crime came out clearly in maps of the two sets of canonical scores on this vector, showing differences between the western (wealthier) and eastern (poorer) parts of Cleveland. This general relationship does not

*Table 5.10 (Continued)*

(c) Predictor set

| Socio-economic Variables | Explained Variance | Relative Variable Contribution |
|---|---|---|
| Families with female head | 0.213 | 0.079 |
| Population under 18 | 0.336 | 0.124 |
| Population that lived in same house in 1965 | 0.187 | 0.069 |
| Male unemployment rate | 0.026 | 0.010 |
| Female unemployment rate | 0.061 | 0.023 |
| Workers in professional occupations | 0.198 | 0.073 |
| Workers in managerial occupations | 0.057 | 0.021 |
| Workers employed as labourers | 0.132 | 0.049 |
| Workers in service occupations | 0.128 | 0.047 |
| Mean family income | 0.132 | 0.049 |
| Families with incomes < 50% of the poverty level | 0.262 | 0.097 |
| Owner-occupied housing units | 0.259 | 0.096 |
| Vacant housing units | 0.260 | 0.096 |
| Housing units with > 1.5 persons per room | 0.106 | 0.039 |
| Housing units built between 1940–49 | 0.087 | 0.032 |
| Housing units built in 1939 or before | 0.029 | 0.011 |
| Housing units with three or more autos | 0.034 | 0.013 |
| Housing units with no autos | 0.194 | 0.072 |

(d) Criteria set

| Crime Variables | Explained Variance | Relative Variable Contribution |
|---|---|---|
| Murders | 0.272 | 0.153 |
| Rapes and assaults to rape | 0.116 | 0.066 |
| Robberies and assaults to rob | 0.100 | 0.057 |
| Assaults | 0.087 | 0.049 |
| Breaking and entering | 0.074 | 0.042 |
| Larcenies | 0.619 | 0.350 |
| Auto theft | 0.500 | 0.283 |

*Source*: Corsi and Harvey (1975).

apply, though, around the downtown area where high poverty levels give negative scores on the predictor set but positive scores on the criteria set.

(c) *Third canonical vector.* Working-class areas/ robberies versus working-class areas/larceny. This vector distinguishes between the magnitude of thefts in areas with low-status occupations, by having both high positive and high negative weights on variables in the two sets.

Other uses of canonical correlation by geographers have included analysis of links between regions via flows of goods (e.g. Clark, 1973), and in investigations of the similarities between two datasets, for example comparing a simulated pattern with an actual one (e.g. Morrill, 1965) or comparing changes in matrices over time, that is a matrix at time $t_1$ could be the predictor set and a matrix for the same observations and variables at time $t_2$ the criteria set.

It should be noted that, if the input to a canonical correlation analysis comes in the form of components from a PCA, then the scope of the analysis is restricted. As component scores represent mutually orthogonal vectors, it is not possible to investigate within-group relationships within either the predictor or criteria sets. Johnston (1978:197) suggests that it is best to avoid this by running separate regression analyses using the components from the criteria set as the dependent variables and those from the predictor set as the independent variables.

## HISTORICAL NOTE

As package computing programs became more common and readily accessible in the 1960s, so the use of multivariate analysis in human geography increased. Led by the popularity of factorial ecologies, the use of multivariate methods grew to embrace the full range of techniques discussed in this chapter. However, there swiftly followed strong critiques which have subsequently contributed to a much more restricted use of multivariate methods within the discipline. Yet, these powerful statistical tools still offer great opportunities for geographers grappling with the complexities of a multivariate world. In particular, those techniques offering scope for classifying multivariate data need to be considered afresh as they have the potential to help expand geographers' understanding of regionalisation and the underlying processes behind spatial linkages between places. An even wider range of package programs is now available to help geographers utilise multivariate techniques and the greater understanding of these techniques should enable fewer errors to be made than in the pioneering work of the 1960s. However, whether there will be renewed attention upon these statistical methods will partly be determined by whether those geographers employing statistics direct their attention away from other statistical tools. They certainly did not do so in the 1980s when the "new wave" of statistics in human geography was represented by work using categorical data analysis.

# 6

# GENERALISED LINEAR MODELS AND CATEGORICAL DATA ANALYSIS

One of the major developments within quantitative geography during the past two decades has been the extension of the range of statistical techniques applied to geographical data. The evolving application of quantitative methods has brought a recognition of limitations within some of the techniques adopted in the 1950s and 1960s, and there have been attempts to utilise analytical tools more appropriate for the special demands of geographical data. One major area in which such tools have been developed is that of the *analysis of categorical data* (see Wrigley, 1979).

There are many situations in human geography when categorical data are the norm or when data exist for a collection of variables which are measured on different scales, including the nominal scale. In such cases the wide array of techniques described in this chapter are available to geographers. Furthermore "standard" regression techniques may not be appropriate for such data, as underlying statistical assumptions are violated. Therefore, categorical data analysis should be employed as it avoids many of the limitations of the standard approaches and provides robust procedures for estimating linear relationships with nominal data. It is rather surprising then that recent standard texts on statistics for geographers are still omitting to cover categorical data analysis (e.g. Shaw and Wheeler, 1994; Walford, 1995). This suggests that many human geographers interested in teaching statistical techniques and applying them in their research are still locked into the stereotypical application of a relatively limited, and sometimes inappropriate, set of statistical techniques. So Wrigley's (1979) prediction that categorical data analysis would "takeoff" in the 1980s has been only partly proved correct and there is still plenty of scope for geographers to be more aware of the potential offered by log-linear, logit, logistic and probit analysis, the use of likelihood inference and the use of dummy variables in regression analysis. Techniques for analysing categorical data have been linked to those described in the previous chapters of this book, through the formulation of a "family" of models for analysing linear relationships. This family is known as *generalised linear models* (GLMs).

## GENERALISED LINEAR MODELS (GLMs)

The value of formulating a family of models for analysing linear relationships lies in its use of a common notation and uniform procedures for apparently separate statistical models. In particular, the use of consistent notation highlights close relationships between different models. Furthermore its application has permitted a reconciliation between methods used for analysing continuous data, as detailed in the previous two chapters, and those dealing with discrete or categorical data, as discussed below.

At the heart of the use of a family of models is the suite of probability distributions referred to as the *exponential family of probability distributions* (Figure 6.1). The exponential family includes those distributions that have played important roles in geographical research, and incorporates those used in categorical data analysis, namely the Poisson, binomial and multinomial distributions. Table 6.1 summarises the main uses geographers have made of these distributions. They were combined into a family of models known as *generalised linear models* (GLMs) by two statisticians, Nelder and Wedderburn (1972), who used the common notation and unified estimation procedure referred to below. This has greatly simplified the complexities of categorical data analysis (O'Brien and Wrigley, 1984).

The exponential family can be used in a practical modelling system by applying it to the error structure or distribution of a GLM. For example, when analysing continuous data, observed predictions from a model can be compared for significance against expected values generated by the normal distribution. For categorical data other distributions can be utilised as summarised in Table 6.2.

At the heart of the GLMs is a simple equation whose form is similar to that for simple linear regression:

*Table 6.1* The Exponential Family of Probability Distributions and their Uses

| Distribution | Use |
| --- | --- |
| Normal | Regression analysis |
| Gamma, beta | Stochastic process modelling |
| Binomial, multinomial, Weibull | Analysis involving discrete choices and individual behaviour |
| Poisson, binomial, multinomial | Parametric analysis of contingency tables |

$$y_i = \mu_i + \varepsilon_i$$

where $y_i$ = an independent random variable; $\mu_i$ = the part of $y_i$ whose value is predictable – it is the mean (expected) value of $y_i$, so $\mu_i = E(y_i)$, where $E$ = the expected value; and $\varepsilon_i$ = the part of $y_i$ whose value is a random error, and $\varepsilon_i$ has values from 1 to $n$ for a random set of observations of $y_i$. Therefore this equa-

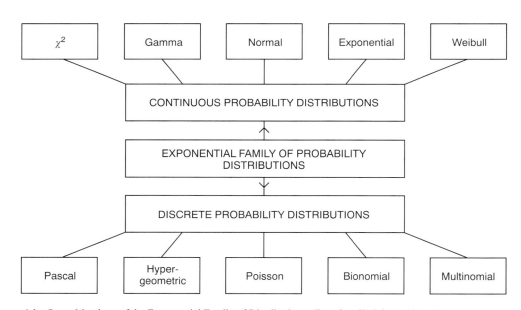

*Figure 6.1* Some Members of the Exponential Family of Distributions. (Based on Wrigley, 1985:365)

*Table 6.2* Examples of Generalised Linear Models

| Model | Link Function | Error Distribution |
|---|---|---|
| Linear regression | Identity | Normal |
| Anova | Identity | Normal |
| Anova (random effects) | Identity | Gamma |
| Log-linear model: | | |
|    symmetric | Poisson | Logarithmic |
|    asymmetric | Binomial or multinomial | Logit |
| Logit regression | Binomial or multinomial | Logit |
| Probit regression | Binomial or multinomial | Probit |

*Sources*: O'Brien (1992, 1983); O'Brien and Wrigley (1984).

tion decomposes $y$ into a predictable part and an error part, the two parts being related to each other by a mathematical function that is both linear and additive.

Any model of the variability of $y_i$ requires the following:

- information on the characteristics of other variables thought to influence the variation in $y_i$, which is expressed as a *linear predictor* ($\eta_i$), where $\eta_i = kB_k x_{ik}$ with $x_{ik} =$ known explanatory (independent) variables, $B_k =$ parameters which may either be known in advance or have to be estimated, and $k =$ the number of unknown parameters/independent variables;
- a precise definition of the theoretical probability distribution assumed for $y_i$ (Wrigley, 1985:363)
- information on the linkage which relates $\mu_i$ to these other variables, $\mu_i$ being related to the linear predictor $\eta_i$ by a *link function* (g),

$$\eta_i = g(\mu_i) \quad \text{or} \quad \mu_i = g^{-1}(\eta_i)$$

where $g^{-1}$ or $1/g$ is called the *inverse link function*.

The link function is not usually accorded a subscript because it is identical for each observation of $y_i$. There are a number of link functions that can be employed in geographical modelling. For example, in linear regression analysis, $g = 1$ so that:

$$\eta_i = \mu_i$$

This is termed an *identity link*. Other link functions are appropriate for the range of categorical models described below. Some of the more common ones are shown in Table 6.3.

Applying the linear predictor and the inverse link function to the basic equation,

$$y_i = \mu_i + \varepsilon_i$$

gives

$$y_i = g^{-1}\eta_i + \varepsilon_i$$

$$= F\left(g^{-1}\left(\sum_{k} B_k x_{ik}\right)\right)$$

$$= F(g^{-1}(B_0 + B_1 x_{i1} + B_2 x_{i2} + \ldots + B_k x_{ik}))$$

*Table 6.3* Some Common Link Functions in Generalised Linear Models

| Link | Link Function ($\eta =$) |
|---|---|
| Identity | $\mu$ |
| Logarithmic | $\log \mu$ |
| Logit | $\log (\mu/n - \mu)$ |
| Probit | $\phi^{-1}(\mu/n)$ |
| Square root | $\sqrt{\mu}$ |
| Exponent | $\mu$ raised to a power |
| Reciprocal | $1/\mu$ |

*Source*: O'Brien (1992:174).

where *F* represents the assumed exponential family of probability distributions.

Different types of model can have the same link function and the same error distribution. Basically there are two types of model (O'Brien, 1992:175):

- those such as analysis of variance and the log-linear model (described below), in which there are variables in the linear predictor representing discrete states such as the presence or absence of some phenomenon – these are termed factorial designs;
- those such as linear regression, logit regression and probit regression, in which available quantitative information can be used directly without recourse to a factorial design.

Both types of model are discussed here, following consideration of the general application of GLMs to categorical data.

## APPLYING GLMs TO THE ANALYSIS OF CATEGORICAL DATA

An integrated approach to the analysis of categorical data did not emerge until the late 1960s when a number of social scientists and statisticians in both Britain and the USA produced influential work on this topic (e.g. Goodman, 1972; Grizzle et al, 1969). This was then extended in the 1970s by Haberman (1978, 1979) and McFadden (1974) amongst others. By this time the analysis of categorical data had become one of the most rapidly developing research frontiers in statistical analysis (Wrigley, 1985:5). The use of techniques for analysing categorical data percolated into geography in the late 1970s as geographers began to make greater use of qualitative measurement. Wrigley symbolises this recognition with reference to Haggett's (1981) geographical data cube (Figure 6.2). (Compare this with Berry's geographical data matrix in Figure 6.3.) He argues that the "centre of gravity" of quanti-

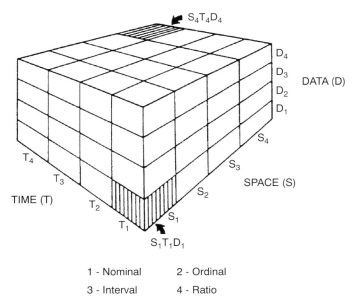

1 - Nominal      2 - Ordinal

3 - Interval      4 - Ratio

*Figure 6.2*    Haggett's Data Cube, Depicting the Interrelationships of Space, Time and Data at Each of Four Measurement Levels

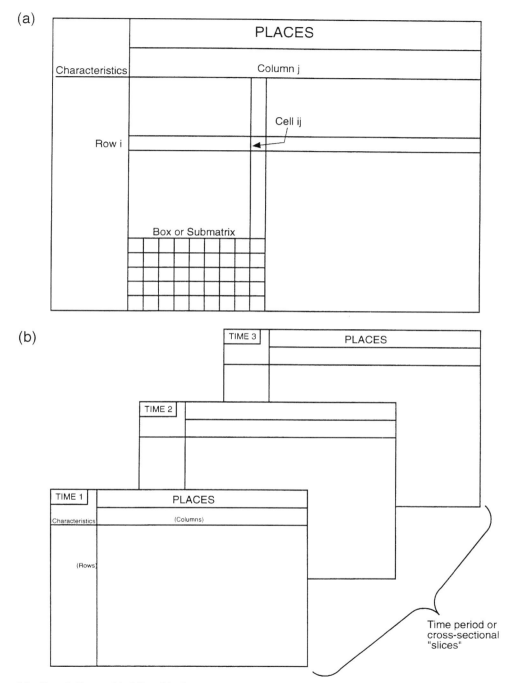

*Figure 6.3*    Berry's Geographical Data Matrix
(a) Two dimensions; (b) three dimensions. (*Source*: Berry, 1964)

tative geography in the 1980s shifted from the cell labelled $S_4T_4D_4$ towards the one labelled $S_1T_1D_1$. This represented a move from a focus upon measurement of space, time and data in continuous terms towards measurement in categorical terms at the nominal scale. This move included the use of categorical data analysis, multi-dimensional scaling (see Chapter 12), *Q*-analysis and non-parametric matrix comparison (Gatrell, 1981a; Wrigley, 1981). Two major texts by geographers on categorical data analysis have been produced by Wrigley (1985) and O'Brien (1992). The remainder of this chapter draws extensively on their work and on relevant statistical texts by Agresti (1990), Fox (1984) and Kennedy (1983).

The analysis of categorical data involves the analysis of contingency tables created by the cross-classification of categorical variables (see Upton and Fingleton, 1989:11–70). For example, the analysis of contingency tables using the $\chi^2$ test was described in the section on "Non-parametric tests" in Chapter 3. Contingency tables can be readily produced from research involving questionnaire surveys. The data in these tables consist of frequencies or counts for particular categories and hence the term *categorical data*. Sometimes this type of data is referred to as "low-level" or qualitative measurement to distinguish it from the "high-level" quantitative measurement used frequently in the physical sciences. There are different types of contingency tables and these give rise to the use of different models in their analysis. Variation in the type of contingency table depends on how the cross-classifying variables are measured and categorised. In some cases categorisation is straightforward. For example, the categories can be just two exhaustive and mutually exclusive ones, such as male: female. In other cases, categorisation can be complex and can involve a strong element of subjectivity on the researcher's part, as in the use of employment categories, where complex classifications involving multiple categories could be used. Similar examples include nationalities and land use types, whilst there are also more simple classifications (e.g. classifying employment into primary, secondary and tertiary types) (Fingleton, 1984).

If the categories are unordered then the data are measured at the nominal scale, but if some ranking of the categories is possible then data are measured at the ordinal scale. Categorical variables can be of three different types:

- *dichotomous* (e.g. presence or absence, yes or no);
- *unordered polychotomous*, meaning more than two categories (e.g. manufacturing, service, primary);
- *ordered polychotomous* (e.g. young, middle-aged, elderly).

The different forms of contingency tables can be analysed using a GLM, with appropriate linear predictors, link functions and error structures. The main models utilised are listed in Table 6.3.

The traditional type of analysis of contingency tables such as those shown in Table 6.4a would have

*Table 6.4*  The $\chi^2$ Test of a Contingency Table (Fully Nominal) Comparing Leisure Centre Usage and Travel by Public Transport

(a) The contingency table

|  |  | Leisure Centre Usage | | Total |
|---|---|---|---|---|
|  |  | Yes | No |  |
| Public Transport Usage | Yes | 33 | 64 | 97 |
|  | No | 91 | 25 | 116 |
| Total |  | 124 | 89 | 213 |

(b) Expected cell frequencies under hypothesis of independence

|  |  | Leisure Centre Usage | | Total |
|---|---|---|---|---|
|  |  | Yes | No |  |
| Public Transport Usage | Yes | 56.47 | 40.53 | 97 |
|  | No | 67.53 | 48.47 | 116 |
| Total |  | 124 | 89 | 213 |

$\chi^2 = 42.86$
$\chi^2_{0.05,1} = 3.84$

*Table 6.4  (Continued)*

(c) Some alternative relationships between values in the cells of a contingency table, the marginal totals and the grand total

(i)

|  |  | Leisure Centre Usage | | Total |
|---|---|---|---|---|
|  |  | Yes | No |  |
| Public Transport | Yes | 48 | 49 | 97 |
| Usage | No | 76 | 40 | 116 |
| Total |  | 124 | 89 | 213 |

(ii)

|  |  | Leisure Centre Usage | | Total |
|---|---|---|---|---|
|  |  | Yes | No |  |
| Public Transport | Yes | 62 | 35 | 97 |
| Usage | No | 62 | 54 | 116 |
| Total |  | 124 | 89 | 213 |

(iii)

|  |  | Leisure Centre Usage | | Total |
|---|---|---|---|---|
|  |  | Yes | No |  |
| Public Transport | Yes | 9 | 88 | 97 |
| Usage | No | 115 | 1 | 116 |
| Total |  | 124 | 89 | 213 |

been to employ a $\chi^2$ test to assess whether the two cross-classifying variables could be said to be independent of each other. In the example shown in Table 6.4a, the test would be asking if usage of public transport and patronage of a leisure centre are independent. As demonstrated in Chapter 3, this involves generating the table of cell frequencies that would be expected if the two variables were independent. These frequencies are then compared with the actual set of observations. This is shown in Table 6.4b, from which the calculated $\chi^2$ statistic reveals that the null hypothesis of independence can be rejected at the 0.05 level: the two variables, use of public transport and patronage of the leisure centre, are related in some way.

Only one set of values, the "expected" set, corresponds to the hypothesis of independence of the variables. However, as shown in Table 6.4c, other cell values can still sum to the same row and column totals (known as the *marginal totals*), suggesting that there may be other relationships besides independence that could be investigated. It is examination of these relationships that is permitted by use of a GLM.

As a number of alternative models can be fitted to the data in Table 6.4a, whilst still preserving row and column totals, this means that the alternatives can be evaluated. This evaluation can involve a number of steps (see O'Brien, 1992:243–4):

1. *Distinguishing between interdependence and dependence*. The latter is an analysis assessing how the variability in one of the categorical factors is conditionally dependent on the variability in the other. This is known as an *asymmetric problem* as the focus of attention is upon the pattern of variability in a response variable conditionally dependent on the variability in the explanatory variable, i.e. *y* depends on *x*. If the focus is interdependence, this is a symmetric problem with the pattern of association varying from row to column and vice versa.

2. *Defining a probability process for the estimation of model parameters*. For log-linear models applied to symmetric tables, as described below, this is usually the Poisson process.

3. *Applying different log-linear models to the data*. This enables residuals to be calculated by comparing the fitted model and the original observations. The total deviance of the model from the observations can be calculated and is equivalent to a total sum-of-squares measure in a linear regression model. It is frequently termed the *maximum log-likelihood statistic* ($G^2$). The different models can employ a number of parameters to reduce this deviance. If sufficient parameters are utilised the model gives the same results as the original observations. This means that every possible form of interdependence in the observed data is represented by the fitted parameters. Such a model is termed a *saturated model*, that is it has as many parameters

as there are cells and includes all main effects and all higher-order interaction effects. Therefore it is another way of describing the observed contingency table. *Unsaturated models* (sometimes called *hierarchical models*) delete those effects which fail to contribute significantly to explaining the association among the variables in the table.

These steps are now discussed in the context of various different models: log-linear, logistic, logit and probit.

## LOG-LINEAR ANALYSIS

### Log-linear Analysis of 2 × 2 Contingency Tables

*Log-linear analysis* attempts to obtain a model which is linear in the logarithms of the expected frequencies of a contingency table and which describes or fits the associations and interactions that exist in the table (Deurloo et al, 1990; Payne, 1977b; Upton and Fingleton, 1979). Thus log-linear modelling is a way of analysing contingency tables as discussed above. These tables can take a simple 2 × 2 form or they can be more complex multi-dimensional ones. The analysis is a means of specifying and quantifying patterns of association between cross-classified variables. Log-linear models are so called because they decompose a contingency table into logarithms of observed frequencies. Therefore the logarithms are another way of describing the observed contingency table.

There are two steps in the log-linear model: a table of observed frequencies, usually assumed to be produced by a particular type of frequency distribution; and a table of expected frequencies that has to be calculated. Goodness-of-fit statistics may be used to compare observed frequencies with expected frequencies and so determine the appropriateness of the model selected. If the data in a contingency table can be described perfectly by a model with as many independent parameters as there are cells in the table, then the model is called a *saturated* log-linear model. Models with fewer independent parameters than cells

in the table are said to be *unsaturated* (Scholten, 1984a:274).

The full range of models that can be fitted to a two-way contingency table is summarised in Table 6.5. The first is known as the grand mean effects model. When fitted, as shown in Table 6.6a, this maintains the same grand total as in the observed table, but the row and column totals (i.e. the marginal totals) are not the same. This is because no account has been taken of the marginal distributions (the row and column totals) of the observed table. This is the simplest log-linear model and so its explanatory power is low: its expected frequencies only reflect the sample size (i.e. the grand total) and the number of cells in the contingency table (i.e. expected cell frequencies = average of the observed total). This model will have a high deviance from the observed data.

In Table 6.5 the fifth model represents saturation, in which there is no deviance at all (see Table 6.6e). The fourth model represents independence and gives the same set of expected cell frequencies as when conducting a $\chi^2$ test (see Table 6.6d). The second and third models are ones in which only one main parameter effect is included at one time (Table 6.6b and c).

The various models that can be fitted to observed data may be tested to see which one represents the observed data most effectively (see Cadwallader, 1992). This testing can be performed by comparing a measure of goodness of fit against a value expected by chance for the same number of degrees of freedom. The effect of a given model can be examined by

*Table 6.5*   Log-Linear Models for a Two-way Contingency Table

| Model | Parameters |
|---|---|
| 1 | Grand mean |
| 2 | Grand mean + row |
| 3 | Grand mean + column |
| 4 | Grand mean + row + column |
| 5 | Grand mean + row + column + (row × column) |

Nb: (row × column) is termed a two-way interaction effect.
Based on O'Brien (1992:248).

*Table 6.6* Expected Frequencies When Performing Log-Linear Analysis of Data in Table 6.4a

(a) Expected frequencies under null model

|  |  | Leisure Centre Usage | | Total |
|---|---|---|---|---|
|  |  | Yes | No |  |
| Public Transport Usage | Yes | 53.25 | 53.25 | 106.5 |
|  | No | 53.25 | 53.25 | 106.5 |
| Total |  | 106.5 | 106.5 | 213 |

(b) Expected frequencies under non-comprehensive main effects models (preserving observed row marginals)

|  |  | Leisure Centre Usage | | Total |
|---|---|---|---|---|
|  |  | Yes | No |  |
| Public Transport Usage | Yes | 48.5 | 48.5 | 97 |
|  | No | 58 | 58 | 116 |
| Total |  | 106.5 | 106.5 | 213 |

(c) Expected frequencies under non-comprehensive main effects models (preserving observed column marginals)

|  |  | Leisure Centre Usage | | Total |
|---|---|---|---|---|
|  |  | Yes | No |  |
| Public Transport Usage | Yes | 62 | 44.5 | 106.5 |
|  | No | 62 | 44.5 | 106.5 |
| Total |  | 124 | 89 | 213 |

*Table 6.6* (*Continued*)

(d) Expected frequencies under independence model

|  |  | Leisure Centre Usage | | Total |
|---|---|---|---|---|
|  |  | Yes | No |  |
| Public Transport Usage | Yes | 56.47 | 40.53 | 97 |
|  | No | 67.53 | 48.47 | 116 |
| Total |  | 124 | 89 | 213 |

(e) Expected frequencies under saturation

|  |  | Leisure Centre Usage | | Total |
|---|---|---|---|---|
|  |  | Yes | No |  |
| Public Transport Usage | Yes | 33 | 64 | 97 |
|  | No | 91 | 25 | 116 |
| Total |  | 124 | 89 | 213 |

comparing changes in the deviance as parameter effects are added or subtracted. The deviance for given degrees of freedom has a similar distribution to $\chi^2$, and so expected values of $\chi^2$ for given degrees of freedom can be obtained and compared with observed values. "Values observed which exceed those expected indicate that the model being fitted does not correspond to the data and that its associated null hypothesis is inappropriate" (O'Brien, 1992:251).

For example, Table 6.7 shows changes in deviance and degrees of freedom for selected critical values for the data analysed in Tables 6.4 and 6.6. This suggests that the saturated model should be accepted and the grand mean, non-comprehensive main effects and independence models should be rejected.

In calculating the degrees of freedom for the basic $2 \times 2$ table, there is a maximum of four degrees of freedom. Fitting a single parameter, such as the grand effects model or each individual main effect, reduces the number of degrees of freedom by one. Therefore the independence model, with both main effects and grand mean, has one degree of freedom. In fitting the single interaction term, a model with zero degrees of freedom is produced.

As with the simple linear and multiple regressions described in Chapter 4, so the analysis of log-linear models can involve the examination of residuals, that is comparing observed data with data generated by the

*Table 6.7*   Analysis of Deviance Table for Log-Linear Analysis of Data in Table 6.6

| Model | Deviance | Degrees of Freedom | Change | |
|-------|----------|--------------------|--------|--|
| | | | Deviance | Degrees of Freedom |
| Grand mean | 51.68 | 3 | | |
| Independence* | 44.20 | 1 | 7.48 | 2 |
| Saturated† | 0.00 | 0 | 44.20 | 1 |

\* Grand mean + public transport usage + leisure centre usage
† Grand mean + interaction between public transport usage and leisure centre usage

model. Simple residuals can be calculated by subtracting the expected cell frequency from the observed cell frequency in each cell. Standardised residuals (with a mean value of 0 and a standard deviation of 1) can also be calculated as well as other more complex residuals used for special purposes (see McCullagh and Nelder, 1983):

$$residual = observed\ cell\ frequency$$
$$- expected\ cell\ frequency$$

$$\frac{standardised}{residual} = \frac{\begin{array}{c}observed\ cell\ frequency\\ -expected\ cell\ frequency\end{array}}{\begin{array}{c}square\ root\ of\ estimated\\ variances\ of\ linear\ predictors\end{array}}$$

Once the best fit for a particular log-linear model has been obtained, residuals can be scrutinised to see which individual values in the contingency table have the greatest residuals. For the data used in Table 6.4 on usage of a leisure centre, the best fit was the saturated model (grand mean plus interaction between public transport usage and leisure centre usage) and this gave no standardised residuals above ±2, suggesting that there were no extreme residuals to consider.

## Defining Parameter Effects

Log-linear models are known as *over-parametrised models* as they contain more parameters than independent pieces of information to estimate them. In order to define the various parameter effects, as listed in Table 6.5, some constraints are required upon the

models. O'Brien (1992:249–50) lists the two systems of constraints used most frequently:

1. *Corner-weighted constraints.* These set one parameter in each parameter effect to 0, and define the remaining parameters as contrasts with it:
   - for the grand mean this is the expected frequency of the top left-hand cell (cell 1,1) of the contingency table;
   - for the main effects this is the difference in the expected cell frequencies of being at level 2 of the row rather than at level 1, or at level 2 of the columns rather than at level 1;
   - for interactions this is the difference in the expected cell frequencies of being simultaneously at level 2 of the rows and columns (i.e. cell 2,2) rather than level 1.

   Corner-weighted constraints are used in calculating estimates of any over-parametrised model by GLIM, the principal computer package developed for analysing generalised linear models, and designed around the Nelder and Wedderburn approach (see O'Brien and Wrigley, 1980; Payne, 1986). The examples cited in Tables 6.4 to 6.7 and Table 6.11 are based on calculations using GLIM.

2. *Centre-weighted constraints.* This system has been referred to as the "usual constraints" (Payne, 1977b). These assume that the sum of the parameters in each parameter effect is 0. Therefore each parameter is defined as a contrast with the average for the parameter effect as a whole:
   - for the grand mean this is the average expected cell frequency in the contingency table;
   - for the main effects this is the difference in the

expected cell frequencies of being at different levels of the rows and columns rather than the average.

These constraints do not affect either calculations of expected frequencies or deviance measures as referred to above, but they do affect any estimates of individual parameters. Hence use of such estimates must be made with caution or should be avoided (see Holt, 1979).

## Log-Linear Analysis of Multi-Way Contingency Tables

Log-linear models can also be applied to multi-way contingency tables as well as two-way designs. Seven types of basic model can be fitted to the multi-way table shown in Table 6.8 (O'Brien, 1989). As summarised in Table 6.9, they are:

1. *null-effects* or *grand mean model*,
2. *non-comprehensive models*, which have nine different forms,
3. *mutual independence*,
4. *multiple independence* (which also has three different forms),
5. *conditional independence* (which has three different forms),
6. *pairwise association*,
7. *saturation*.

Models 1, 5 and 7 and some types of 2 can apply to analysis of the two-way design. The others are specific to testing interaction effects between two variables given the presence of a third. Models 2, 4 and 6 have a number of different forms reflecting the increase in the number of ways of forming two-way interactions as the number of dimensions is increased (Ofori-Amoah and Hayter, 1989). Table 6.11 shows the expected cell frequencies produced under some of these different log-linear models for a dataset (Table 6.10) referring to the distribution of stud farms and cattle grazing establishments in the Upper Hunter Valley, New South Wales, Australia.

Although any one of the 19 individual model forms

**Table 6.8** Contingency Table with a Dichotomous Dependent (Response) Variable and a Continuous Independent (Explanatory) Variable

(a) Raw data

*Question*: If offered the opportunity would you consider joining a voluntary farm conservation scheme?
Yes = 1, No = 0

$x_i$ = age of farmer (years)

| Response | $x_i$ | Response | $x_i$ | Response | $x_i$ |
|----------|-------|----------|-------|----------|-------|
| 1 | 36 | 1 | 42 | 0 | 55 |
| 1 | 28 | 0 | 47 | 0 | 67 |
| 1 | 50 | 0 | 50 | 0 | 61 |
| 0 | 49 | 1 | 33 | 1 | 44 |
| 0 | 68 | 1 | 29 | 0 | 49 |
| 1 | 41 | 1 | 41 | 0 | 50 |
| 1 | 38 | 0 | 59 | 0 | 49 |
| 1 | 37 | 0 | 61 | 1 | 43 |
| 0 | 53 | 1 | 38 | 1 | 42 |
| 0 | 54 | 0 | 57 | 0 | 60 |

(b) The contingency table

| Response Variable | Explanatory Variable $x_i$ | | | | Total |
|-------------------|------|-------|-------|------|-------|
| | < 40 | 40–49 | 50–59 | > 60 | |
| 1 | 7 | 6 | 1 | 0 | 14 |
| 0 | 0 | 4 | 7 | 5 | 16 |
| Total | 7 | 10 | 8 | 5 | 30 |

may adequately represent the general features of the observed data, the researcher is usually seeking the most parsimonious model, that is the one representing the key features of the table in as few parameters as possible. To select such a model a stepwise procedure is usually employed, adding parameter effects to a simple model or deleting parameters from a complex model such as saturation.

The most commonly used of various stepwise procedures are *Brown's screening strategy* (M.B. Brown, 1981) and *Aitkin's simultaneous testing procedure*

*Table 6.9* Log-Linear Models for a Three-way Contingency Table

| Model | Parameters |
|---|---|
| 1. Null-effects | Grand mean |
| 2. Non-comprehensive models | Grand mean $+v_1$ |
| | Grand mean $+v_2$ |
| | Grand mean $+v_3$ |
| | Grand mean $+v_1 + v_2$ |
| | Grand mean $+v_3 + v_1$ |
| | Grand mean $+v_3 + v_2$ |
| | Grand mean $+v_1 + v_2 + v_1 v_2$ |
| | Grand mean $+v_3 + v_1 + v_3 v_1$ |
| | Grand mean $+v_3 + v_2 + v_3 v_2$ |
| 3. Mutual independence | Grand mean $+v_1 + v_2 + v_3$ |
| 4. Multiple independence | Grand mean $+v_1 + v_2 + v_3 + v_3 v_1$ |
| | Grand mean $+v_1 + v_2 + v_3 + v_2 v_3$ |
| | Grand mean $+v_1 + v_2 + v_3 + v_1 v_2$ |
| 5. Conditional independence | Grand mean $+v_1 + v_2 + v_3 + v_1 v_2 + v_3 v_2$ |
| | Grand mean $+v_1 + v_2 + v_3 + v_1 v_2 + v_1 v_3$ |
| | Grand mean $+v_1 + v_2 + v_3 + v_2 v_3 + v_1 v_3$ |
| 6. Pairwise association | Grand mean $+v_1 + v_2 + v_3 + v_1 v_2 + v_1 v_3 + v_2 v_3$ |
| 7. Saturated | Grand mean $+v_1 + v_2 + v_3 + v_1 v_2 + v_1 v_3 + v_2 v_3 + v_1 v_2 v_3$ |

$v_1 =$ variable 1; $v_2 =$ variable 2; $v_3 =$ variable 3
$v_1 v_2$, $v_1 v_3$, $v_2 v_3 =$ two-way interactions
$v_1 v_2 v_3 =$ three-way interaction

Based on O'Brien (1992:256).

*Table 6.10* A Multiway Contingency Table Depicting Characteristics of Stud Farms and Cattle Enterprises in the Hunter Valley, New South Wales, Australia

| Size | | Type of Enterprise | | | | | Total |
|---|---|---|---|---|---|---|---|
| | | Studs | | | Graziers | | |
| | | 0–1 | 2 | >2 | 0–1 | 2 | >2 | |
| Location | Scone | 13 | 10 | 2 | 8 | 2 | 1 | 36 |
| | Inner | 5 | 2 | 1 | 6 | 1 | 1 | 16 |
| | Outer | 7 | 7 | 5 | 9 | 1 | 1 | 30 |
| | Total | 25 | 19 | 8 | 23 | 4 | 3 | 82 |

Nb: Size refers to hectarage: 0–1 = < 100 ha; 2 = 100–300 ha; >2 = > 300 ha
*Source*: Robinson (1996).

(STP) (Aitkin, 1980; Upton and Fingleton, 1989: 67–70).

## Screening Strategies

As in the simultaneous testing of interactions using STP (see below), this uses a baseline model in a stepwise testing of terms (see Cadwallader, 1992). However, in Brown's screening strategy, the terms are not tested simultaneously in families. Instead they are tested individually against two distinct tests of significance: a test of partial association and a test of marginal association. For example, consider an investigation examining interrelationships between gender ($S$), age ($A$) and stated preferences of individuals ($P$). If we wished to test the two-way interaction of $S$ and

*Table 6.11*    Some of the Expected Cell Frequencies Under Different Log-Linear Models

(a) Pairwise association model (grand mean + type + locn + size + type.locn + locn.size + type.size)

| Size | | Type of Enterprise (Type) | | | | | |
|---|---|---|---|---|---|---|---|
| | | Studs | | | Graziers | | |
| | | 0–1 | 2 | >2 | 0–1 | 2 | >2 |
| | Scone | 12.364 | 10.278 | 2.359 | 8.636 | 1.722 | 0.641 |
| Location | Inner | 4.494 | 2.227 | 1.279 | 6.506 | 0.773 | 0.721 |
| (Locn) | Outer | 8.142 | 6.496 | 4.362 | 7.858 | 1.504 | 1.638 |

Each pair of variables is related, but is unaffected by the presence of the third variable.

(b) Conditional independence model (grand mean + type + locn + size + locn.size + type.size)

| Size | | Type of Enterprise (Type) | | | | | |
|---|---|---|---|---|---|---|---|
| | | Studs | | | Graziers | | |
| | | 0–1 | 2 | >2 | 0–1 | 2 | >2 |
| | Scone | 10.938 | 9.913 | 2.182 | 10.063 | 2.087 | 0.818 |
| Location | Inner | 5.729 | 2.478 | 1.455 | 5.271 | 0.522 | 0.545 |
| (Locn) | Outer | 8.333 | 6.609 | 4.364 | 7.667 | 1.391 | 1.636 |

A pair of variables is independent given the presence of the third variable (Location and type, given size).

(c) Multiple independence model (grand mean + type + locn + size + locn.size)

| Size | | Type of Enterprise (Type) | | | | | |
|---|---|---|---|---|---|---|---|
| | | Studs | | | Graziers | | |
| | | 0–1 | 2 | >2 | 0–1 | 2 | >2 |
| | Scone | 13.317 | 7.610 | 1.902 | 7.683 | 4.390 | 1.098 |
| Location | Inner | 6.976 | 1.902 | 1.268 | 4.024 | 1.098 | 0.732 |
| (Locn) | Outer | 10.146 | 5.073 | 3.805 | 5.854 | 2.927 | 2.195 |

Two variables (location and size) included as a joint variable are independent of the third.

(d) Mutual independence model (grand mean + type + locn + size)

| Size | | Type of Enterprise (Type) | | | | | |
|---|---|---|---|---|---|---|---|
| | | Studs | | | Graziers | | |
| | | 0–1 | 2 | >2 | 0–1 | 2 | >2 |
| | Scone | 13.363 | 6.403 | 3.062 | 7.710 | 3.694 | 1.767 |
| Location | Inner | 5.939 | 2.846 | 1.361 | 3.427 | 1.642 | 0.785 |
| (Locn) | Outer | 11.136 | 5.336 | 2.552 | 6.425 | 3.079 | 1.472 |

All three variables are independent.

*continued overleaf*

Table 6.11    (Continued)

(e) Non-comprehensive model (grand mean + type + locn + type.locn)

| Size | | Type of Enterprise (Type) | | | | | |
|---|---|---|---|---|---|---|---|
| | | Studs | | | Graziers | | |
| | | 0–1 | 2 | >2 | 0–1 | 2 | >2 |
| Location (Locn) | Scone | 8.333 | 8.333 | 8.333 | 3.667 | 3.667 | 3.667 |
| | Inner | 2.667 | 2.667 | 2.667 | 2.667 | 2.667 | 2.667 |
| | Outer | 6.333 | 6.333 | 6.333 | 3.667 | 3.667 | 3.667 |

All size categories are equally likely given location and enterprise type.

(f) Non-comprehensive model (grand mean + locn + type)

| Size | | Type of Enterprise (Type) | | | | | |
|---|---|---|---|---|---|---|---|
| | | Studs | | | Graziers | | |
| | | 0–1 | 2 | >2 | 0–1 | 2 | >2 |
| Location (Locn) | Scone | 7.610 | 7.610 | 7.610 | 4.390 | 4.390 | 4.390 |
| | Inner | 3.382 | 3.382 | 3.382 | 1.951 | 1.951 | 1.951 |
| | Outer | 6.341 | 6.341 | 6.341 | 3.659 | 3.659 | 3.659 |

All size categories are equally likely given location and type of enterprise.

(g) Non-comprehensive model (grand mean + type + size)

| Size | | Type of Enterprise (Type) | | | | | |
|---|---|---|---|---|---|---|---|
| | | Studs | | | Graziers | | |
| | | 0–1 | 2 | >2 | 0–1 | 2 | >2 |
| Location (Locn) | Scone | 10.146 | 4.862 | 2.325 | 5.854 | 2.805 | 1.341 |
| | Inner | 10.146 | 4.862 | 2.325 | 5.854 | 2.805 | 1.341 |
| | Outer | 10.146 | 4.862 | 2.325 | 5.854 | 2.805 | 1.341 |

All categories of location are equally likely given type and size of enterprise. Type of enterprise and size of enterprise are independent.

$A$, that is $SA$, the test of partial association of $SA$ involves comparing the effects on deviance reduction of fitting the grand mean $+S+A+P+SP+AP$ rather than the grand mean $+S+A+P+SA+AP+SP$. This includes all two-way effects and comparing them with a model excluding $SA$. The test of marginal association compares the relative performances of the grand mean $+S+A+SA$ and the grand mean $+S+A$. The two tests yield terms that can be classified into one of three categories:

1. those terms significant according to both tests and which should be included in the final log-linear model;

*Table 6.11  (Continued)*

(h) Non-comprehensive model (grand mean + locn + size)

| Size | | Type of Enterprise (Type) | | | | | |
|---|---|---|---|---|---|---|---|
| | | Studs | | | Graziers | | |
| | | 0–1 | 2 | >2 | 0–1 | 2 | >2 |
| Location (Locn) | Scone | 10.537 | 5.049 | 2.415 | 10.537 | 5.049 | 2.415 |
| | Inner | 4.683 | 2.244 | 1.073 | 4.683 | 2.244 | 2.012 |
| | Outer | ? | ? | ? | ? | ? | ? |

Location and size of enterprise are independent.

(i) Non-comprehensive model (grand mean + size)

| Size | | Type of Enterprise (Type) | | | | | |
|---|---|---|---|---|---|---|---|
| | | Studs | | | Graziers | | |
| | | 0–1 | 2 | >2 | 0–1 | 2 | >2 |
| Location (Locn) | Scone | 6 | 6 | 6 | 6 | 6 | 6 |
| | Inner | 2.667 | 2.667 | 2.667 | 2.667 | 2.667 | 2.667 |
| | Outer | 5 | 5 | 5 | 5 | 5 | 5 |

Combinations of location and type of enterprise are equally likely given size of enterprise.

(j) Non-comprehensive model (grand mean + locn)

| Size | | Type of Enterprise (Type) | | | | | |
|---|---|---|---|---|---|---|---|
| | | Studs | | | Graziers | | |
| | | 0–1 | 2 | >2 | 0–1 | 2 | >2 |
| Location (Locn) | Scone | 5.778 | 5.778 | 5.778 | 3.333 | 3.333 | 3.333 |
| | Inner | 5.778 | 5.778 | 5.778 | 3.333 | 3.333 | 3.333 |
| | Outer | 5.778 | 5.778 | 5.778 | 3.333 | 3.333 | 3.333 |

Combinations of size and type of enterprise are equally likely given location.

(k) Null-effects model (grand mean)

| Size | | Type of Enterprise (Type) | | | | | |
|---|---|---|---|---|---|---|---|
| | | Studs | | | Graziers | | |
| | | 0–1 | 2 | >2 | 0–1 | 2 | >2 |
| Location (Locn) | Scone | 4.556 | 4.556 | 4.556 | 4.556 | 4.556 | 4.556 |
| | Inner | 4.556 | 4.556 | 4.556 | 4.556 | 4.556 | 4.556 |
| | Outer | 4.556 | 4.556 | 4.556 | 4.556 | 4.556 | 4.556 |

All combinations of location, type of enterprise and size of enterprise are equally likely.
*Data source*: Robinson (1996).

2. those terms insignificant according to both tests and which should be excluded from the final log-linear model;
3. those terms whose assessment differs on each test – for these, theory and/or intuition are required to determine whether or not they should be included.

An example of the selection of the most parsimonious model using screening strategies is Lakhan's analysis of resource allocation in Guyanese agriculture (Lakhan, 1990; Lakhan et al, 1995). This investigated reductions in rice yields ($Y$) due to drainage and irrigation problems in the 1980s, using two independent variables: educational attainment of farmers ($E$) and size of farm holdings ($S$). All three variables were measured on categorical scales. Nine log-linear models were evaluated, incorporating the independent variables and their interactions, eight unsaturated and one saturated as shown in Table 6.12. The models were evaluated hierarchically from the simple, with no interactions, to the more complex. As shown in Table 6.12, for each model the maximum likelihood ratio chi-squared value ($G^2$), the numbers of degrees of

*Table 6.12* Log-Linear Analysis of Guyana's Rice Industry Using Three Categorical Variables

| Model | $G^2$ | Degrees of Freedom ($v$) | Probability |
|---|---|---|---|
| 1. E  S  Y | 34.54 | 39 | 0.67 |
| 2. E  SY | 31.94 | 33 | 0.52 |
| 3. S  EY | 30.23 | 33 | 0.61 |
| 4. Y  ES | 27.65 | 30 | 0.59 |
| 5. YE  YS | 27.62 | 27 | 0.43 |
| 6. SE  SY | 25.04 | 24 | 0.40 |
| 7. ES  EY | 23.34 | 24 | 0.50 |
| 8. ES  EY  SY | 19.71 | 18 | 0.35 |
| 9. ESY | 0.01 | 0 | 1.00 |

$E$ = Educational attainment of farmers: 6.0–7.9 years; 8.0–9.9 years; 10.0–11.9 years; 12+ years
$S$ = Size of cultivated farm holdings: 0.1–1.49 ha; 1.5–2.99 ha; 3.0–4.49 ha; 4.5–5.99 ha
$Y$ = Percentage reduction in rice yields from area planted (due to drainage and irrigation problems on holdings cultivated by farm owner for the period 1981–91

*Source*: Lakhan (1990).

freedom remaining ($v$) and the probability value ($\alpha$) for $G^2$ were calculated. To determine which of the unsaturated models gives the most parsimonious description of yield changes, the values of $G^2$ for each model were considered. Model 8 has both the lowest $G^2$ and the lowest value of $v$. It also has the lowest probability level ($\alpha$). This suggests that the three two-way relationships, $ES$, $EY$ and $SY$, are the key ones affecting the dramatic decline that occurred in Guyana's rice industry in the 1980s.

A more complex investigation of the same situation considered four categorical variables based on farmers' estimates: decline in rice production ($R$), days with floods ($F$), yield reduction through flooding ($C$) and yield reduction through damage by pests and diseases ($D$). There were 166 different unsaturated models that could have been produced from the resultant four-dimensional table. Therefore the following selection procedure was adopted:

(a) Partial association tests were performed, starting with a base model including $C$, $D$, $F$ and $R$. Models were then fitted, omitting each of the main effects in sequence. For example, to test the significance of effect $R$, the model $CDF$ was fitted. The significance level was determined by finding the difference between the $G^2$ value in this case and its value for the base model. The comparison included the different degrees of freedom possessed by the two models. The resulting values of $G^2$ and $\alpha$ are shown as the first four models in Table 6.13. This suggests that $F$, $C$ and $R$ have a significant effect at the 0.05 level.

(b) To test the two-variable relationships ($CD$, $CF$, $CR$, $DF$, $DR$, $FR$) the base model including all possible pairwise associations was used, with each pair fitted in sequence. For each pair the difference between $G^2$ for that model and $G^2$ for the base model was determined as were $v$ and $\alpha$. Table 6.13 shows that this process reveals the significance of $FC$, $FR$ and $CR$.

(c) For the interaction terms, $CDF$, $CDR$, $DFR$, $CFR$, each term was tested against the base model, including all possible interactions

*Table 6.13* Log-Linear Analysis of Guyana's Rice Industry Using Four Categorical Variables

| Effect | Partial | | Marginal | |
|---|---|---|---|---|
| | $G^2$ | Probability ($\alpha$) | $G^2$ | Probability ($\alpha$) |
| 1. F | 24.51 | 0.00 | | |
| 2. C | 52.55 | 0.00 | | |
| 3. D | 1.91 | 0.10 | | |
| 4. R | 12.84 | 0.00 | | |
| 5. FC | 13.66 | 0.00 | 11.07 | 0.03 |
| 6. FD | 0.68 | 0.70 | 0.27 | 0.87 |
| 7. FR | 15.75 | 0.00 | 13.63 | 0.01 |
| 8. CD | 2.84 | 0.50 | 3.28 | 0.19 |
| 9. CR | 10.04 | 0.00 | 8.77 | 0.07 |
| 10. DR | 13.33 | 0.08 | 5.41 | 0.07 |
| 11. FCD | 0.50 | 0.97 | 0.65 | 0.96 |
| 12. FCR | 3.31 | 1.00 | 0.76 | 1.00 |
| 13. CDR | 1.40 | 0.80 | 3.65 | 0.46 |
| 14. FDR | 1.30 | 0.80 | 3.30 | 0.51 |

$R$ = Farmers' estimates for average percentage decline in rice production from their fields between 1981 and 1991: <10%; 10–25%; 25–50%; 50–75%; >75%
$F$ = Farmers' estimates of percentage number of days per annum a portion or all of one of their fields was flooded and caused crop damage: 0–10% of days; 10–25% of days; 25–50% of days; 50–75% of days; >75% of days
$C$ = Farmers' estimates of reduction in their overall rice production each year in the last ten because of crop damage due to floods: 0–10%; 10–25%; 25–50%; 50–75%; >75%
$D$ = Farmers' estimates of reduction in their overall rice production each year in the last ten because of crop damage due to pests and diseases: <10%; 10–25%; 25–50%; 50–75%; >75%

*Source*: Lakhan (1990).

among the variables. Models omitting each of the interaction terms were fitted in sequence, following the same procedure as in (b). None of these interaction terms were significant at the 0.05 level.

(d) Marginal association tests were also performed in stages following similar procedures to those described above for the partial association tests. This produced five models for which both partial and marginal tests were significant: *F*, *C*, *R*, *FC* and *FR*. One, *CR*, was significant in the partial test but not in the marginal. However, *CR* was included in the final model on the basis of a comparison between *FC*, *FR*, *CR* and *FC*, *FR* which revealed that the model including *CR* reduced $G^2$ by 11.14 for four fewer degrees of freedom (with $\alpha = 0.025$). Confirmation of this model as the best fit can be carried out using stepwise selection procedures (see below). Therefore relationships between farmers' estimates of the duration of flooding and extent of production decline through flooding, between duration of flooding and decline in rice production, and between flood damage and decline in rice production were significant ones affecting the decline of the Guyanan rice industry.

This is a result very similar to that which would have been produced by the simultaneous testing procedure.

## Simultaneous Testing of Interactions Using STP

This procedure employs the simultaneous testing of families of terms on the grounds that families of effects, such as two-way or three-way interactions, are more likely to reduce deviance than single effects. So, it is more efficient to test the family before testing specific effects. The influence of each of the families can be summarised in an analysis of deviance table, as illustrated in Table 6.7 above, each line of which shows how the value for deviance changes with the addition of specific families of effects. At saturation the deviance equals zero. Therefore, as more families are added, the value of deviation decreases until, eventually, at saturation it reaches zero. Meanwhile, the value of the number of degrees of freedom similarly decreases to reach zero when the saturation model is fitted. The basic principle is that families of effects are more likely to contribute to the reduction of deviance than single effects.

Table 6.14 represents the observed outcome of adding specific terms to the log-linear model for the data in Table 6.11. It shows that by adding the single effects, location, size and type, to the grand mean

*Table 6.14*    Analysis of Deviance Table for Log-Linear Analysis of Table 6.10

| Model | Deviance | Degrees of Freedom | Change | |
|---|---|---|---|---|
| | | | Deviance | Degrees of Freedom |
| Grand mean | 53.374 | 17 | | |
| Grand mean + L + S + T | 13.028 | 12 | 40.3460 | 5 |
| Grand mean + L + S + T + LS + LT + ST | 1.6366 | 4 | 11.3914 | 8 |
| Grand mean + L + S + T + LS + LT + ST + LST | 0 | 0 | 1.6366 | 4 |

$L$ = Location; $S$ = Size; $T$ = Type

*Data source*: Robinson (1996).

model reduces the deviance by 40.346 but also requires the addition of five extra parameters (change in degrees of freedom = 5). Similarly, the addition of eight extra parameters through incorporating the two-way effects reduces deviance by 11.3914. The addition of the three-way effects to the previous model reduces deviance by 1.6366 for the addition of four extra parameters.

To assess how many of these families of effects are reducing deviance significantly, the observed effects on deviance reduction can be compared with those amounts expected by chance from families of identical size to those employed in Table 6.14. These expected values are calculated from tables of the $\chi^2$ distribution for given degrees of freedom. The level of significance employed in making this comparison will reflect the appropriate type-one error rate for the hypothesis that all the interactions applicable to the table are insignificant. This global error rate ($y$) can be calculated from:

$$y = 1 - (1 - \alpha)^{2^r - r - 1}$$

where $\alpha$ = the significance level, and $r$ = the number of dimensions in the table, i.e. the number of categorical variables being analysed. In this case $r = 3$ as there are three categorical variables that are cross-classified. The error rate is used to test the null hypothesis that the three two-way interactions (location and size, location and type, type and size) and the single three-way interaction (location, size, type) are all insignificant. For $\alpha = 0.05$, using the formula

quoted above, the type-one error rate ($y$) = 0.185. For $\alpha = 0.10$, $y = 0.34$. Aitkin (1980) recommends that a value between 0.25 and 0.56 is generally sufficiently sensitive, and therefore in this case the value of $\alpha = 0.1$ can be used.

Once this global error rate has been established, error rates for each family of effects can be calculated. For example, for the three-way effects, if $\alpha = 0.1$,

$$y = 1 - (1 - 0.1)^2 = 0.1$$

Therefore the family error rate = 0.1 for the three-way effect. This can be used in conjunction with $\chi^2$ tables to estimate an expected level of deviance reduction of 7.78 for the three-way family, as $\chi^2_{4,0.1} = 7.78$ (where the subscript 4 refers to the number of degrees of freedom associated with the family, and the subscript 0.1 refers to the family error rate).

Once the three-way effect has been tested then the two-way effects can be tested, using the same general procedure but pooling the two-way and three-way families to form a combined family which is tested (this being a stronger test than one applied solely to the two-way effects without increasing its overall size) (O'Brien, 1992:261). In this case, $y = 0.34$. Using $\chi^2_{12,0.34}$, this gives an expected level of deviance reduction of 14.2. This compares with the observed level of deviance reduction of 11.3914, suggesting that all of the two-way effects can be eliminated from the final model. Therefore attention can be turned upon the single (one-way) effects: location, size and type, though this does not mean that every one-way effect is significant.

Once a family of effects is found that is significant there is no need to test lower-order families for significance as these families will automatically be included in the log-linear model. However, it is possible that not every interaction in a family will be significant, as the main source of the family's influence may rest with only one or two interactions. These effects can be assessed by eliminating the effects of individual interactions until the critical level of deviance reduction is exceeded (as shown in Table 6.15), the critical level being that expected by chance from the pooled test. Table 6.15 shows that the log-linear model highlighted by this is the grand mean plus size of holding. Therefore combinations of location and type of enterprise are equally likely given size of enterprise. However, all three single effects together are also nearly as significant (that is, the three variables are independent).

The main weakness with this procedure is that the order in which terms have been added to the model may have affected which terms are eliminated. This is because the observed effect on deviance associated with a particular term may be dependent on its relationships with terms already included in the model (O'Brien, 1992:262). One way of avoiding this, albeit a more complex method, involves fitting two-way effects in any order and then calculating their standardised regression coefficients (SRCs) which are the

ratios of the parameter estimates to their estimated standard errors. The individual terms can then be refitted to the main effects model in SRC order, starting with the largest first. For exemplifications of this procedure see Aitkin (1980), O'Brien (1992: 261–3) and Wrigley (1985).

O'Brien (1992:267) points out that the types of contingency tables analysed above are rather special in that they are complete and fully nominal in design. This means that there have been no observed cell frequencies restricted to a fixed value. Yet it is common for the restriction, cell frequency $= 0$, to be applicable to particular research situations. This restriction can take two forms:

1. *Sampling zeros*. There are no observations in the sample data for a particular cell. If some cells have zero values it may be possible to fit a full range of unsaturated log-linear models to the table, but problems will occur with the saturated model as the presence of the zero cells prevents calculation of the expected cell frequencies. Solutions to this problem include replacement of expected cell frequencies by the observed cell frequencies rather than relying on an estimation algorithm. Another popular alternative is to replace zero cells by a small positive value, for example 0.5. This will reduce values for deviance, but usually not by enough to produce fundamentally different inter-

Table 6.15   Revised Analysis of Deviance Table for Log-Linear Analysis of Table 6.10

| Model | Deviance | Degrees of Freedom | Change | |
|---|---|---|---|---|
| | | | Deviance | Degrees of Freedom |
| Grand mean | 53.374 | 17 | | |
| Grand mean + type | 47.398 | 16 | 5.976 | 1 |
| Grand mean + locn. | 45.095 | 15 | 2.303 | 1 |
| Grand mean + size | 27.281 | 15 | 17.814 | 0 |
| Grand mean + L + S + T | 13.028 | 12 | 14.253 | 5 |
| Main effects + LT + LS + ST | 1.637 | 4 | 11.391 | 8 |
| Eliminated terms | 0 | 0 | 1.637 | 4 |

$L$ = Location; $S$ = Size; $T$ = Type

*Data source*: Robinson (1996).

pretations. However, it is an arbitrary procedure and therefore questionable. Greater difficulties arise if a whole row or column of observations comprise zeros. If the cells containing zero values are positioned in such a way that a marginal total is also zero then additional problems arise, including difficulty in calculating degrees of freedom

2. *Structural zeros.* Cells are given a zero value by design, usually because cells can only have values of zero or a predetermined non-zero value. In this case either the table must be reformulated to eliminate zeros or modifications to the log-linear model must be made (e.g. Goodman, 1968).

## LOGISTIC, LOGIT AND PROBIT MODELS

The main five models that have been used to analyse categorical data, as listed in Table 6.3, have been incorporated in the "*didactic tableau*" used by Wrigley (Table 6.16). This conceptualises the analysis of both continuous and categorical data in terms of different types of variables involved. It considers the range of different situations in which dependent (or response) and independent (or explanatory) variables are analysed. The top row, with cells a, b and c, refers to the "traditional" models of simple linear regression, dummy variable linear regression (discussed below) and analysis of variance. Cell a has a continuous-scale explanatory variable; cell c has a categorical-scale explanatory variable; and cell b a mixture of both continuous-scale and categorical-scale variables. The bottom row, with cells d, e, f and g, refers to categorical models. A weakness of this classification is

that it relies on a clear distinction between response and explanatory variables which may be somewhat artificial or difficult to make. Also, it does not integrate the models in the way that Nelder and Wedderburn's (1972) framework does. However, useful aspects of both frameworks are employed in the following discussion of the categorical models represented by cells d to g.

The typical problems associated with cells a, b and c of Table 6.16 may be tackled by the regression models described in Chapter 4 under "Regression analysis", but cells d to g can involve the use of other forms of model known as logistic, linear logit, log-linear and probit models. The basic regression model may be extended to cater for more than two-category (polychotomous) dependent variables and for the situation in which both dependent and independent variables are categorical (see Everitt and Dunn, 1983:154–75; Fingleton, 1981; Kemper, 1984). So the model can be applied to cells d, e and f in Table 6.16. Wrigley considers models for cells d to g by describing an extension of standard linear regression for a situation in which the response variable ($y_i$) is dichotomous, for example if $y_i = 1$ for yes and $y_i = 0$ for no, whilst $x_i$ is measured on a continuous scale. Therefore this substitutes a dichotomous variable in place of the continuous response variable in cell a of Table 6.16. Given that $y_i$ can only take the values 0 and 1, this raises certain problems if a standard linear regression equation is to be used. The standard equation implies that $y_i$ may have values outside this range (see Figure 6.4a). Furthermore, the assumption of homoscedasticity is violated as the error term in the equation can have only two possible values (see Wrigley, 1985:23–4).

A number of alternative models can be specified

*Table 6.16*   Classes of Statistical Problems – a Didactic Tableau

| Response Variables (Dependent) | Explanatory Variables (Independent) | | | |
|---|---|---|---|---|
| | Continuous | Mixed | Categorical | None |
| Continuous | a | b | c | |
| Categorical | d | e | f | g |

*Source:* Wrigley (1981, 1985:7).

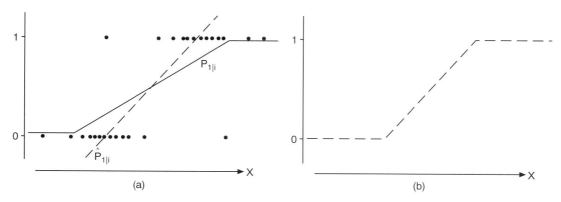

*Figure 6.4*   Regression Lines
(a) Using the ordinary least squares formula; (b) using the linear probability model

which avoid these limitations. These models may be compared with the simple linear regression equation by expressing the latter in the form of a probability model if

$$y_i = a + bx_i + \varepsilon_i$$

where $\varepsilon_i$ = an independently distributed random error term with zero mean, then $E(y_i)$, the expected value of $y_i$, is given by

$$E(y_i) = E(a + bx_i + \varepsilon_i)$$

and conventionally $E(\varepsilon_i) = 0$, so

$$E(y_i) = a + bx_i$$

$$P(y_i = 1) = 1 - P(y_i = 0)$$

$$P(y_i = 1) = E(y_i) = a + bx_i$$

where $P(y_i = 1)$ is the probability that response $y_i = 1$ is selected by respondent $i$ conditional upon $x_i$, the value of the explanatory variable relating to respondent $i$, and the values of the parameters $a$ and $b$.

The last equation can be expressed in the general form:

$$P(y_i = 1) = F(a + bx_i)$$

where $F$ = a cumulative probability function. If $F$ is a cumulative uniform probability function, this gives a linear probability model. If $F$ is a cumulative logistic probability function or a cumulative normal probability function, this gives an S-shaped curve more appropriate to the situation described above (Wrigley, 1985:27) (Figure 6.4b). Logistic and logit models are produced when $F$ is the cumulative logistic probability function.

The appropriateness of the various models depends on the type of contingency table being considered. The log-linear model can be applied to cells f and g in Table 6.16, whilst for cell f both log-linear and logit models can be used to tackle problems of asymmetric contingency tables.

## Logit Models

The logistic, logit and probit models developed out of the weaknesses encountered in applying conventional regression models to categorical data (see Aldrich and Nelson, 1984). In *logit models*, the logit (or natural logarithm of the ratio of two chances) is a linear function of an independent (explanatory) variable or a number of independent (explanatory) variables (e.g. Imrey et al, 1981).

For a two-category (dichotomous) dependent (response) variable, e.g. male:female, the *logistic model* takes the form

$$P_i = \frac{e^{f(x_i)}}{1 + e^{f(x_i)}}$$

where $P_i$ = the probability that the first category will be selected by the $i$th individual or at the $i$th location, given the values of the $k$ independent variables. This model may be rewritten to be equivalent to a linear model:

$$\log_e \left( \frac{P_i}{1 - P_i} \right) = f(x_i)$$

The left-hand side of this equation represents a transformation of $P_i$ known as the *logit transformation*, and hence the term the *linear logit model*, which can be expressed as:

$$\eta = \ln [\mu/(N - \mu)]$$

"Logit" is thus a term referring to a particular type of analytical transformation applied to a dichotomous dependent (response) variable. However, logit, log-linear and probit models can all be applied to data in contingency tables as well as for regression analysis involving categorical response variables, thereby providing a link between categorical data analysis and standard regression analysis (see Lewis, 1977: 128–46).

An example of logit analysis is Liaw's (1990) investigation of inter-provincial migration in Canada, examining the effect of personal factors and a range of economic, social and environmental variables. This work is also representative of the shift towards a focus upon individuals by migration studies rather than the macro-approach dealing with net migration volumes or rates (Foot and Milne, 1984; Shaw, 1985). The examination of individual migration decisions may involve two processes being investigated: a departure process and a destination choice process (Liaw and Ledent, 1987).

Logit models have an advantage over asymmetrical log-linear models (see below) in that they reduce the number of parameters to be estimated if the independent variables can be measured on an ordinal or a ratio level (Veldhuizen, 1984:289).

In the 1970s the lack of a behavioural content in spatial interaction models (see Chapter 7) was criticised and gave rise to the study of individual choice behaviour and discrete choice models. For example, the multinomial logit model assumes that the decision-maker's choice is known and fixed (i.e. exogenous), but this is not always so. The model can be used to analyse choice behaviour and predict choices among discrete sets of alternatives. This assumes that an individual's preferences among the available alternatives can be described with a utility function and that the individual selects the alternative with the greatest utility. The utility of an alternative is represented as the sum of two components: a systematic one accounting for systematic effects of observed factors that influence choice, and a random one that accounts for the effects of unobserved factors. The random-utility model is used to predict the probability that a randomly selected individual with given values of the observed factors will choose a particular alternative. This is equal to the probability that the utility of a particular alternative exceeds the utilities of all other alternatives (see Ben-Akiva and Lerman, 1985; Horowitz, 1991). However, the general assumption that the choice set is known and fixed is often tenuous. For example, a job-seeker cannot choose an employer who does not offer her or him a job and a high-school leaver cannot attend a university that will not admit her or him.

The *multinomial logit model* has been widely used in analyses of discrete choices. For example, when shoppers are choosing which store to patronise they are faced by "a limited and constrained set of discrete alternatives" (Wrigley, 1982). For an application using a multinomial logit model specifically designed for ordinal data see Moore's (1989) analysis of store choice in Cardiff. Another application is Fingleton's (1989) use of a similar model in the study of the movement of industrial firms in the UK between 1966 and 1978.

An alternative to the logit model, the *probit*, can be translated as the probability that the first response category selected by the $i$th individual is given by the area under the standard normal curve between $-\alpha$ and $(a + bx_i)$. The higher the value of $(a + bx_i)$ the greater is the likelihood that the $i$th individual will select the first response category. The probit model can be applied to cells d and c in Table 6.16, the choice between the logit and probit models for these two cells being largely a matter of computational convenience. The logit model has greater ease of computation, but the probit model has some advantages in its more polychotomous form. For examples see the work of Sprague (1994) using data from the Women and Employment Survey; Anim and Lyne (1994) on access to communal grazing lands in Ciskei, South Africa; and Van Lierop and Rima (1984) on residential mobility.

## LIKELIHOOD INFERENCE

One aspect of the analysis of categorical contingency tables using a GLM represents a significant departure from the type of inferential statistics described in Chapters 2 and 3. The departure is known as *likelihood inference* in which inference is based on information contained in observed data without any reliance on the probability of a hypothetical distribution or a "long run" of events. The character of likelihood inference is stated clearly by O'Brien (1992:155):

> The principal assumption underlying likelihood inference is the belief that different types of population generate different types of sample. Therefore, the information in a given sample automatically identifies its own population from among the alternatives available. By maximising the information content of the sample data, researchers are assumed to be able to describe characteristics of the population and assess hypotheses concerning it.

Therefore, this type of inference has a fundamentally different view of the role of the sample, but it can still permit similar descriptive and inferential procedures.

Just as the inferential procedures described in Chapter 3 utilised a probability function, so likelihood inference uses a likelihood function. Pickles (1986) describes the likelihood function for a binomial variable with two "outcomes", $r$ and $n - r$. In this case the likelihood function ($L$) is given by,

$$L = p^r(1 - p)^{n-r}$$

where $p =$ the probability of observing outcome $r$, $(1 - p) =$ the probability of observing outcome $n - r$, $n =$ the number of binomial trials, and $r =$ the number of trials where $r$ is the outcome.

This formula can be compared with that for the equivalent probability function ($P$) for this variable:

$$P = \frac{p^r(1 - p)^{n-r} n!}{r!(n - r)!}$$

For given values of $r$ and $n$, different values of the likelihood function can be generated by altering the value of $p$. The formula for $L$ is sometimes further simplified by expressing it as a log-likelihood function:

$$\log L = r \log p + (n - r) \log(1 - p)$$

For both the likelihood and log-likelihood functions "it is assumed that the value of the parameter which is the most likely to have generated the data is that which produces a maximum value for both functions" (O'Brien, 1992:156). Thus, the maximum likelihood method estimates the parameters of a model in which parameters are found that are the "most likely" given the observed data (Pickles, 1986). For given values of $r$ and $n$ different values may be generated for the likelihood and log-likelihood functions by altering the value of $p$. Both functions can be portrayed graphically as shown in Figure 6.5 for a random sample of 10 binary observations in which $r = 7$. The graphs are both convex, sharply sided and have a peak at $p = 0.7$. This should confirm that, given a simple random sample in which the proportion possessing a given attribute is $r/n$ then the most plausible value for the proportion possessing the attribute in the population is also $r/n$. Also, both graphs show that there are many probability values (e.g. $p = 0.2$) that could not possibly have generated the data because they are too far from the maximum, and in a more complex analysis these need to be distinguished from the maximum by use of mathematical calculus so that an exact point estimate for the maximum value can be obtained.

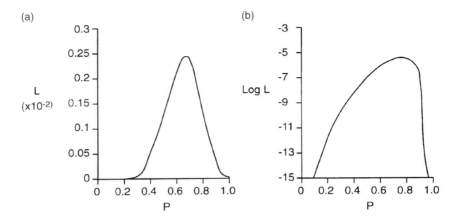

Figure 6.5    (a) Likelihood Function and (b) Log-Likelihood Function

At their maxima the values of the likelihood and log-likelihood functions depend on the observed data. To assess the most appropriate value of $p$ at the maxima, relative likelihood or relative log-likelihood functions must be calculated:

$$R = L/L_{max}$$

and

$$\log R = \log L - \log L_{max}$$

where $R$ is the relative likelihood function, and log $R$ is the relative log-likelihood function. The latter measures the departure of any value of $p$ from the most likely value. Where $p$ is greatest, log $R = 0$. These functions have standardised maxima. Log $L_{max}$ is the log-likelihood value at the maximum.

Figure 6.6 shows two different log-likelihood functions for binary observations in different sample sizes with $r = 0.7$. As the sample size increases so the curves become more peaked thereby focusing attention upon a specific value of $p$. In the figure a horizontal line has been drawn near log $R = -2$, which distinguishes between the maximum parameter estimate and parameter values which are at least 1/7 as probable (Pickles, 1986:13). This line represents a confidence interval and corresponds to the $100(1 - \alpha)$

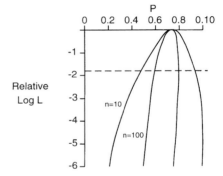

Figure 6.6    Relative Log-Likelihood Functions

per cent interval, where $\alpha$ is that value for which the relative log-likelihood value $= \chi^2_{1,\alpha}/2$.

For example, the interval defined by the line drawn at log $R = -1.92$ is the 95 per cent confidence interval, that is,

$$\chi^2_{1,\alpha}/2 = 3.84/2 = 1.92$$

This corresponds to the following values of $p$ in the two samples: for $n = 10$, the upper limit is 0.92 and the lower limit is 0.39; for $n = 100$, the upper limit is 0.61 and the lower limit is 0.78 (see Figure 6.6).

This use of the relative log-likelihood function may

be developed further (Dobson, 1983), using the expression:

$$-2\log R_a = -2(\log L_a - \log L_{\max})$$

where $\log R_a$ = the relative log-likelihood value at point $p = a$, $\log L_a$ = the log-likelihood value at point $p = a$, and $\log L_{\max}$ = the log-likelihood value at the maximum. This expression, known as the *likelihood ratio statistic*, has a chi-squared distribution for given degrees of freedom.

More complex examples of likelihood inference are discussed by Pickles (1986). However, even with more complex examples the principle of likelihood inference remains that different types of population generate different types of sample, and it is the information in the sample that identifies its particular population from the many alternatives available. The likelihood function contains all the information about $p$ possessed by the sample, and for binary data the sample size ($n$) and the number in the sample possessing a particular attribute ($r$) are the only statistics that define the likelihood function and which may be used as the basis for all further inference. Thus $n$ and $r$ are termed *sufficient statistics*, containing all the knowledge about parameter $p$. So from the likelihood and log-likelihood functions it is possible to generate sufficient statistics which contain all the information needed to produce acceptable estimates of $p$. To generate maximum likelihood parameter estimates a theoretical probability process, e.g. binomial or Poisson, must be assumed. Alternatively, the mean and variance can be used rather than a stated process. Parameters estimated on this basis are called quasi-likelihood estimators. Maximum quasi-likelihood parameter estimates are identical to those produced using least-squares methods (Godambe and Heyde, 1987).

## REGRESSION ANALYSIS WITH INDICATOR (DUMMY) VARIABLES

There are a number of instances when it is not possible to measure an independent variable on the interval scale. Different land use types, social class, housing tenure or gender are good examples as these have values on the nominal (categorical) scale. However, it is possible to incorporate qualitative (categorical) variables in a regression analysis by establishing *indicator or dummy variables*. By using an indicator or dummy variable for a qualitative variable then it is possible to analyse that qualitative variable by means of regression. The term "dummy variables" is employed to denote the use of a binary scale in conjunction with an independent variable in an OLS regression or with independent variables in a multiple regression, instead of measurement on either interval or ratio scales.

For example, in a regression analysis in which a categorical variable has values in four classes (e.g. land use divided into "arable", "pasture", "rough grazing" and "woodland"), simply recoding these four land use classes as 1, 2, 3 and 4 is meaningless. The land use coded as "1" might just as well have been assigned "3" or "2". However, dummy variables can be computed which can have just two values: 0 for a potential negative relationship with $y$ (the dependent variable, which in this case is rental value) and 1 for a potential positive relationship with $y$ (see e.g. Congdon, 1989:488–9). Although there are four land use categories, there are only three dummy variables created, $x_1$, $x_2$ and $x_3$. So the number of new (dummy) variables to be computed is one less than the number of categories in the original variable. The regression equation would be

$$y = a + b_1 x_1 + b_2 x_2 + b_3 x_3 + e$$

where

$$b_1 = b_{yx_1.x_2x_3}$$

$$b_2 = b_{yx_2.x_1x_3}$$

$$b_3 = b_{yx_3.x_1x_2}$$

The following could then apply:

$$x_1 = 1, \quad x_2 = 0, \quad x_3 = 0 \quad \text{for category 1}$$

$$x_1 = 0, \quad x_2 = 1, \quad x_3 = 0 \quad \text{for category 2}$$

$$x_1 = 0, \quad x_2 = 0, \quad x_3 = 1 \quad \text{for category 3}$$

$$x_1 = 0, \quad x_2 = 0, \quad x_3 = 0 \quad \text{for category 4}$$

This set of relationships is summarised in Table 6.17. Applying these values,

$$y_1 = b_0 + b_1$$

$$y_2 = b_0 + b_2$$

$$y_3 = b_0 + b_3$$

$$y_4 = b_0$$

Here the partial regression coefficients indicate the change in value of $y$ with an increase of 1.0 in the value of the particular independent variable. Therefore if $b_{yx_3.x_1x_2} = 2.0$, this shows an increase of 2.0 in $y$ for each increase of 1.0 in $x_3$, with independent variables $x_2$ and $x_3$ held constant. However, as $x_3$ can only take the values 0 and 1, $b_{yx_3.x_1x_2}$ represents the difference in the value of $y$ between an observation with $x_3 = 0$ and one with $x_3 = 1$. This is the same as the difference between $y$ when $x_3 = 0$ and $y$ when $x_3 = 1$.

Use of a number of dummy variables can encounter problems of collinearity. Therefore this procedure is often applied to a qualitative variable with just two or three dummy variables. A typical example is where the qualitative variable is "sex", in which case the dummy variables will be $x_1 = 1 = $ women, $x_2 = 0 = $ men. If the dependent variable ($y$) is income, and the independent variable ($x$) is weekly food expenditure, the regression equation becomes

Table 6.17 Representation of Four Categories of Land Use as Indicator (Dummy) Variables

| Land Use | x1 | x2 | x3 |
|---|---|---|---|
| 1. Arable | 1 | 0 | 0 |
| 2. Pasture | 0 | 1 | 0 |
| 3. Rough grazing | 0 | 0 | 1 |
| 4. Woodland | 0 | 0 | 0 |

1 = positive relationship with $y$ (rental value)
0 = negative relationship with $y$ (rental value)

$$y_i = b_0 + b_1 x_1 + b_2 z_i$$

where $y_i = $ the value of weekly food expenditure, $x_i = $ the value of income for case $i$, and $z_i = $ the value of the dummy variable for that case.

The use of the dummy variables enables investigation of the hypothesis that purchasing patterns of men and women are different. The regression equation can be expressed separately for each of the sexes:

$$y_i = b_0 + b_1 x_i + b_2 \quad \text{for women}$$

$$y_i = b_0 + b_1 x_i \quad \text{for men}$$

Therefore, this represents two predicted straight lines for men and women. Both lines have the same slope, $b_1$, but different intercepts: for men it is $b_0$, for women it is $b_0 + b_2$. For a fixed income, the difference between the predicted response of men and women is $b_2$. Based on sample data, the predicted arrangement is indicated in Figure 6.7a. In this case, women spend less than men.

However, the arrangement of parallel regression lines may not be appropriate if the sexes have very different spending patterns. This can be considered by examining *interaction effects*:

$$y_i = b_0 + b_1 x_i + b_2 z_i + b_3 x_i z_i$$

where $x_i z_i = $ an interaction effect between the independent variable (income) and the dummy variable (sex). For the two sexes, the corresponding models are

$$y_i = (b_0 + b_2) + (b_1 + b_3)x_i \quad \text{for women}$$

$$y_i = b_0 + b_1 x_i \quad \text{for men}$$

So $b_2$ is the difference in intercepts, with $b_3$ the difference in slopes between the two lines. If the estimate of $b_3$ is significantly different from zero, then the lines are unlikely to have the same slope.

Using the same data as shown in Figure 6.7a, the two regression lines with different slopes are shown in Figure 6.7b. This is a more appropriate arrangement, as an $F$ test for the equation with the interaction effect

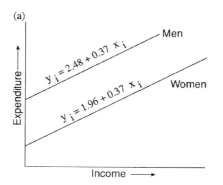
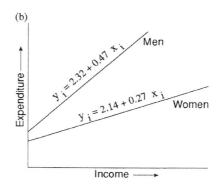

*Figure 6.7*    Regression Analysis Using Dummy Variables
(a) Regression line has same slope ($b_1$) but different intercepts for men and women; (b) regression line has similar intercept but different slopes for men and women

is significant at the 0.05 level. The equation reveals that, at all levels of income, men spend more money on food than do women, with the difference between the sexes increasing with income.

In summarising the use of categorical variables in regression equations, Wrigley (1985:92–4) recognises three ways in which categorical variables may be included. These are illustrated in Figure 6.8. The standard linear regression is portrayed in Figure 6.8a for the average number of persons per room ($y$) regressed on household income in an urban area ($x$). The average number of persons per room declines as household income rises. The first inclusion of a categorical variable (Figure 6.8b) is additive, with a dummy explanatory variable ($D$) indicating the ethnic characteristics of the household, taking the values 1 (= non-white head of household) and 0 (= white head of household). The intercepts for the two household groups differ but the slopes of the regression lines remain the same. The dummy variable parameter $B_3$ is the difference between the intercepts of the two categories of household. It is possible to test whether $B_3$ is statistically significantly different from zero in order to see if the difference between intercepts is a substantive one. The second way, shown in Figure 6.8c, is an interactive form where the original explanatory variable is multiplied by the dummy variable. This produces different slopes for the two regression lines but with the same intercept. The parameter $B_3$ now

represents the difference between the slopes of the regression lines. Again it is possible to test whether $B_3$ is statistically significantly different from zero. In Figure 6.8d both additive and interactive inclusions are incorporated. This is equivalent to fitting separate regression relationships to each household group. These three models can be applied in similar fashion for multiple-category explanatory variables. The regression equations for the four regression models portrayed in Figure 6.8 a–d are:

(a)    $y_i = B_1 + B_2 x_i + e_i$

(b)    $y_i = B_1 + B_2 x_i + B_3 D_i + e_i$

(c)    $y_i = B_1 + B_2 x_i + B_3 D_i x_i + e_i$

(d)    $y_i = B_1 + B_2 x_i + B_3 D_i + B_4 D_i x_i + e_i$

In Pattie and Johnston's (1990) analysis of unemployment in Britain in the mid-1980s, they extended their use of simple linear regression by the introduction of dummy variables. Their basic equation took the standard form,

$$y = a + b_1 x$$

where $y$ = percentage change in the number of unemployed in each political constituency, and $x$ = percentage of the economically active workforce unem-

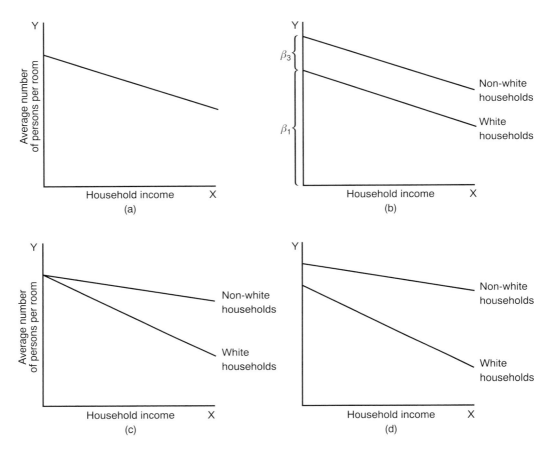

*Figure 6.8*   An Illustration of Three Different Ways of Introducing a Dummy Variable into a Simple Regression Model (a) Ordinary least squares regression; (b) simple additive manner; (c) interactive manner; (d) combination of simple additive and interactive manners. (*Source*: Wrigley, 1985:92)

ployed. The dummy variables represented additional regional variations, one set of 31 functional regions ($F$) (e.g. inner metropolitan, resort and retirement, agricultural) and one set of 22 geographical regions ($G$). They were added separately to the basic equation and then both together so that the regional geography of changing unemployment could be investigated:

$$y = a + b_1 x + b_2 F$$

$$y = a + b_1 x + b_3 G$$

$$y = a + b_1 x + b_2 F + b_3 G$$

In these two regionalisations, constituencies scored 1 on each dummy when they fell into the relevant region, and 0 when they did not.

To avoid data closure, one dummy variable was omitted from each regional set in the multiple regression equations. These were the two regions where the Conservative government had its greatest support (the agricultural functional region and the Outer South-East). These were treated as "baseline" regions so that the analysis was comparing trends in unemployment nationally with trends in the Conservative "heartland" (see Johnston et al, 1988). Regression coefficients for the remaining region dummies were interpreted as the difference between the average percentage change in unemployment in that region and the average change in the omitted region, with the impact of the initial level of unemployment ($y = a + b_1 x$) held constant. Thus the geographical dummies tested how far regions differed from the Outer South-East, and the functional dummies how far they differed from the agricultural region.

As shown in Table 6.18, the addition of the dummy variables increased the explanation of the dependent variable from 13 per cent to 59 per cent, though considering both dummies together added little to the overall explanation provided by the geographical regions. The initial unemployment rate was not a strong predictor of the percentage change in unemployment. When $F$ and $G$ were added the relationship between

**Table 6.18** Dummy Variable Regression of Unemployment in Great Britain, 1983–88

| | |
|---|---|
| Equation I | $y = a + b_1 x + b_2 F$ |
| Equation II | $y = a + b_1 x + b_3 G$ |
| Equation III | $y = a + b_1 x + b_2 F + b_3 G$ |

(a) For functional regions

| Functional Regions (F) | Regression Coefficients | |
|---|---|---|
| | Equation I | Equation III |
| Black Country | −10.63 | |
| Clydeside | 9.92 | −12.09 |
| Scottish industrial | −18.21 | |
| Scottish rural | 18.70 | −15.43 |
| Inner metropolitan | 12.62 | 10.53 |
| Very high status | 15.13 | −5.46 |
| Cities with service emp. | | 5.93 |
| Recent growth | −9.47 | |
| Stable industrial | −7.97 | −6.92 |
| Small towns | | 2.29 |
| Southern urban | −12.97 | |
| Manuf. towns + commuter zone | −8.34 | −5.65 |
| Metropolitan inner city | −10.44 | −4.39 |
| Modest affluence Scottish | | −16.70 |
| Rapid growth | −17.55 | −6.98 |
| Prosperous non-industrial | −7.99 | |
| $r^2$ | 0.36 | 0.59 |

**Table 6.18** (continued)

(b) Geographical Regions

| Geographical Regions (G) | Regression Coefficients | |
|---|---|---|
| | Equation II | Equation III |
| Strathclyde | 17.82 | 34.76 |
| East Central Scotland | 21.92 | 36.73 |
| Rural Scotland | 34.16 | 47.00 |
| Rural North | 15.00 | 15.73 |
| Industrial North-East | 12.66 | 16.91 |
| Merseyside | 12.60 | 16.22 |
| Greater Manchester | 9.02 | 13.04 |
| Rest of North-West | 8.82 | 12.03 |
| West Yorkshire | 12.40 | 15.60 |
| South Yorkshire | 22.58 | 24.94 |
| Rural Wales | 17.43 | 18.21 |
| Industrial South Wales | 7.43 | 8.95 |
| West Midlands conurbation | | 7.29 |
| East Midlands | 14.26 | 16.25 |
| Devon | 19.54 | 18.97 |
| Rest of South-West | | 4.54 |
| Inner London | 20.42 | 14.95 |
| Outer London | 10.20 | 10.24 |
| Outer Metropolitan | −8.37 | −5.68 |
| $r^2$ | 0.56 | 0.59 |

Only coefficients significant at the 0.05 level are included. The more depressed function regions are towards the top of part (a), and the more affluent are towards the bottom; the more northerly geographical regions are towards the top of part (b), and the more southerly are towards the bottom.

*Source*: Pattie and Johnston (1990).

unemployment and the various regions can be examined by considering the regression coefficients that are significantly different from zero (Table 6.18). For example, when $F$ is added, the analysis shows that constituencies in relatively affluent functional regions experienced higher percentage falls in unemployment than did the control dummy (agricultural constituencies). Unemployment fell most rapidly in some industrial parts of Scotland, areas of "rapid growth", "high status" and "southern urban" areas (high negative regression coefficients). Three functional regions performed poorly (high positive regression coefficients):

Scottish rural, inner metropolitan and Clydeside. Overall, the benefits of economic recovery in the 1980s were felt in the areas which suffered less from the preceding recession.

More of the geographical regions had significant regression coefficients, but only the Outer Metropolitan region had a fall in unemployment less than the control dummy (the Outer South-East). The highest regression coefficients (regions faring most badly) were found for Rural Scotland, South Yorkshire, East-Central Scotland and Inner London. When both $F$ and $G$ were added to the equation there was confirmation that affluent constituencies in the Midlands, south and east (excluding London) had done better during the economic recovery than depressed regions in the north and west. This is a reconfirmation of the north–south divide (Lewis and Townsend, 1989; Martin, 1988). For another example, using dummy variables to estimate economic base multipliers, see Fik and Mulligan (1994).

# 7

# SPATIAL ALLOCATION

## MODELS IN GEOGRAPHY

### Models and Quantitative Theories

As human geographers made greater use of quantitative methods in the 1950s and 1960s they also extended their use of *models* to represent the world, building upon relatively simple schemas of the internal structure of the city and the arrangement of central places. Quantification was frequently employed by geographers through the construction of statistical and mathematical models, often with the aim of comparing reality with the models. Models therefore became one of the key elements in the "new" geography, closely linked to the Quantitative Revolution and associated with geographers who have subsequently become major figures in the discipline. One of these, Peter Haggett, gives three main reasons why *model-building* has proved attractive (Haggett et al, 1977:18–19):

1. *Its inevitability.* Models are theories, laws, equations or hunches which state our beliefs about the universe we think we see and so we cannot avoid them.
2. *Its efficiency.* Model-building is economical because it enables the development of generalised information in a highly compressed form, and hence the utility of models in teaching (Chorley and Haggett, 1965:360–4).
3. *Its stimulus.* Models may "over-generalise" but in so doing they highlight areas where "improvement" is necessary and therefore should promote further research.

The terms "model" and "modelling" were often given very broad interpretations in the 1960s, incorporating those more mathematical and quantitative aspects of modelling (which are the focus of attention here) within a broader grouping of work that reflected the new systematisation of geography. So, as employed in *Models in geography*, edited by Chorley and Haggett (1967), a model could be a theory, a law, a hypothesis, a structured idea, a role, a relation, an equation, a synthesis of data, a word (e.g. "peasant"), a map, a graph and some type of computer or laboratory hardware arranged for experimental purposes. This extraordinarily catholic view reflects the general lack of work in geography at the time that could clearly be recognised as modelling in the more restricted sense in which the term is used elsewhere in science (Crowe, 1968; Unwin, 1989:53). However, since then, whilst modelling by geographers has consistently broken new ground, a narrower and more readily accepted definition of the term "model" has emerged. Furthermore, the roles of mathematics, statistics and computing within geographical modelling have become critical.

Scientific enquiry makes use of a number of definitions of the term "model". A succinct one by Haines-Young and Petch (1986:145) is "any rule that generates outputs from inputs", or, in a different form, "any device or mechanism which generates a prediction" (ibid:144). This means that models are not theories, laws or hypotheses, but are devices or mechanisms constructed on the basis of theory and which generate new information that may be used to test whether or not the theories embedded in them are adequate. They can also be used to make useful predictions about the future states of the systems which they describe (Unwin, 1989:53–4). This view of modelling, widely applied within physical geography, places it within the hypothetico-deductive framework of explanation referred to in Chapter 1. It views modelling as an activity which enables theories to be examined critically (Haines-Young, 1989:22–3). However, modelling has tended to be used in a broader sense by human geographers, extending its use beyond the hypothetico-deductive view of science, so that Wilson (1989:64) asserts "it is not necessarily positivist and functionalist simply because it is [often] a mathematical approach".

This broader range of views is recognised by Macmillan (1989b), who refers to four main interrelated uses:

1. Models as prototypes for a theory in which reasoning by analogy occurs, e.g. using the theory of gravitation as a model for a theory of migration by separating the form and content of the theories. In this sense a model is a set of propositions.
2. Models as realisations of theories, in which the model is a system of the type to which the theory refers. So a theory could be a "real" system that is a model of that theory or, if there are no real models, then the theory refers only to ideal types.
3. Models as representations, in which one entity can be said to represent another. For example, Peter Cobbold and Philip England at Oxford University have used layers of acacia honey, silicone putty and sand to represent the Earth's surface and, with a motor-driven perspex plunger to represent the Indian Sub-Continent, the effect of driving the Sub-Continent into the Eurasian landmass has been simulated. The resulting creation of "the Himalayas" has also been modelled mathematically.
4. Models as quantitative theories, in which it is hard to distinguish between the theory and the realisation of that theory.

Although models as prototypes and representations do appear in geographical literature, they do not necessarily meet the definition given by Haines-Young and Petch referred to above, because they generally lack predictive capacity. So it is the fourth usage that has been most common within human geography. Yet this use is somewhat problematic as this type of model only approximates to a quantitative theory because "their form is not explicitly deductive" (Macmillan, 1989b:97). In fact many examples of modelling in human geography, for example in work on spatial interaction, land use and location, interpret a problem's variables and parameters in mathematical form, but with constituent propositions and interrelationships often being somewhat ambiguous. This is one reason why the term "model" tends to be applied to such work rather than "quantitative theory". Another is the fact that such models are rarely tested in the sense of examining their possible falsification; but they act as descriptive devices and predict behaviour under given conditions. Nevertheless, their predictive capacity is based upon the theory in which they are grounded, and hence the better the theory, the better are the predictions.

Models are simplified representations of reality in which a complex state of affairs is reduced to something more simple but containing key characteristics. Those characteristics usually summarise a class of phenomena and so are part of a generalisation as opposed to dealing with one particularity. The generalisation of characteristics involves *mathematisation*, in which a set of deterministic relations is established in mathematical form or statistical calibration is involved (Flowerdew, 1989:245). These facets of generalisation and mathematisation are apparent in several of the models discussed in this and the following three chapters, each of which deals with models having a mathematical and statistical basis.

## Mathematical Models

The degree of simplification and abstraction in a model can vary enormously depending upon the object of enquiry (Figure 7.1). The simplest level of abstraction occurs when reality is altered only in terms of scale, as in the case of a scale model such as that employed by architects for buildings they are design-

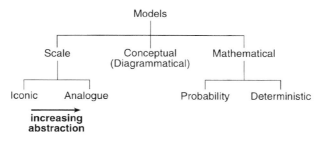

*Figure 7.1*   Types of Model. (*Source*: Thomas and Huggett, 1980:4)

ing. These are sometimes called *iconic models* as they are miniature copies of reality. If miniaturisation is accompanied by transformation of certain properties then the term *analogue model* is used. For geographers, the most commonly used analogue model is the map, in which surface features are reduced in scale and are represented in symbolic form.

At a greater level of abstraction are conceptual models in which the focus is upon relationships between different component elements of reality. *Linkage diagrams*, such as that illustrated in Figure 7.2, are frequently used examples of conceptualisation, and may precede the formulation of more abstract mathematical models which translate concepts into a formal, symbolic logic. This logic is usually expressed in the form of an equation possessing a predictive capacity. It is this capacity that extends the ability of mathematical models beyond that of the conceptual or diagrammatic stage. Mathematical models can be part of the hypothetico-deductive mode of enquiry, and so can play a role in the formulation, testing and development of theory towards generation of better explanations of reality.

Good examples of mathematical models can be found

in analyses of population structure and change (see Woods, 1979:197–225). For instance, the Malthusian idea that population grows in a geometrical series (i.e. 1, 2, 4, 8, 16, etc.) can be translated into a mathematical equation representing exponential growth:

$$P_T = P_0 e^{RT}$$

where $P_T$ = the final population size, $P_0$ = the initial population size, $R$ = the rate of growth, $T$ = the number of time units between $P_0$ and $P_T$, and e = the base of natural logarithms (2.718 28 ...). There are various other mathematical models applicable to demographic structures (see Woods and Rees, 1986).

## Deterministic and Probabilistic Models

There are two main subtypes of mathematical models: deterministic and probabilistic models. The former, *deterministic models*, are based on the notion of exact prediction, which is produced by natural, physical laws. This type of modelling has been widely applied

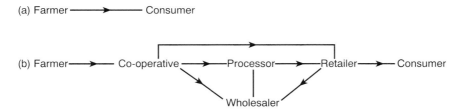

*Figure 7.2*   Linkage Diagram Portraying the Movement of Produce from Farmer to Consumer. (*Source*: Robinson, 1988:229)

by physical geographers in constructing models that predict the behaviour of physical systems (Thomas, 1989). However, simple models of population change are also examples of this type, when they deal with aggregates rather than individuals. The focus on aggregates and groups is also used in the context of *spatial interaction models* (see below) which convert observed behaviour trends displayed by groups of people into the law-like statements required for the construction of models. Deterministic modelling by human geographers has taken place through the construction of models that are *normative* in character, that is models based on assumptions of how people would or ought to behave under certain conditions. This procedure generally compares predicted optimum spatial arrangements with an observed pattern to assess the rationality of the latter against the simplifying assumptions of the normative model.

The second type of mathematical model used by geographers is *probability models*, with the construction of equations in these models involving the use of probabilities and probability theory. Usually some random element is injected so that the models can produce a range of possible outcomes rather than a single prediction (see Chapter 9). These outcomes are generally expressed in terms of a known degree of error. However, the objectives of both probability and deterministic modelling are the same: to develop a greater understanding of the mathematical structure of events in order to facilitate a more cogent knowledge of issues studied by geographers. Mathematical modelling can also combine deterministic and probabilistic elements (Thomas and Huggett, 1980:9–10). For ease of understanding, though, the treatment here is to deal with them separately.

## LINEAR PROGRAMMING

### Allocating Goods to Markets and People to Services

The development of deterministic normative models by geographers has been associated with the use of mathematical techniques for optimising stated objectives subject to the application of given constraints. The mathematics involved are generally referred to as *linear programming methods*. A linear programme is a mathematical technique used to find the optimum combination of several variables or processes. A linear programming solution to a problem involves the optimisation of an *objective function* subject to a series of constraints. Linear programming defines the quality to be maximised, states the relevant constraints and then identifies a procedure by which the optimal solution can be obtained. For example, for noxious facilities, such as garbage incinerators, the objective may be to minimise accessibility to population subject to site constraints. Most optimising problems are only soluble mathematically (Senior and Wilson, 1974), though some simple ones can be solved graphically (Found, 1971).

Geographers have used linear programming to analyse flows of goods and services, seeking to ascertain the optimal pattern of trade in a good, given a certain number of suppliers of that good and a number of markets or demand points. In such cases "optimal" has often been defined as the flow minimising the total transport costs involved in transporting the good from suppliers to markets. Many of the geographical applications of linear programming in the 1950s and 1960s focused upon economic goods such as coal, iron ore and other industrial supplies. Other applications have substituted social services for economic goods, focusing on the allocation of people to services, such as schools and hospitals, and using goals like total cost minimisation or maximising accessibility, but with constraints such as a limit upon the total number of facilities that can be located or upon the money available to construct facilities. The goals involved may also be conflicting, especially those of maximising accessibility but within a restricted budget. Because the applications are concerned with allocating goods and people to particular locations, the problems are sometimes referred to as *spatial allocation problems*.

An additional factor to consider is the capacity of the facilities: should a few large ones be located, thereby offering potential for economies of scale, or would a larger number of smaller facilities be more desirable? This variety of problems to which linear programming can be applied is further increased if the range of optimisation problems in urban planning is added, for example the design of traffic flow systems to facilitate journey-to-work trips from residential suburbs to city centres.

As a simple illustration, the optimal allocation of school-children to schools can be performed in four stages:

1. Map the location of every pupil.
2. Superimpose a grid of *n* regions for the *n* schools. The destinations for individual trips of school-children are the *n* schools. This grid of *n* regions can ensure that every location in a region is nearer to that region's centre than to any other centre. The set of regions satisfying this criterion is known as the *proximal solution*, and can be obtained geometrically using a solution proposed in the early years of the twentieth century by the climatologist A.H. Thiessen. The regions produced are known as *Thiessen polygons* (Boyle and Dunn, 1991).
3. Establish the constraints: volume of goods < number of pupils; demand < number of places in the schools.
4. Use linear programming to find the minimum cost pattern and convert this optimal pattern into a system of catchment areas around each school.

Thiessen polygons are constructed as follows. Each facility (school) (Figure 7.3a) is joined to its neighbours and these lines are then bisected vertically (Figure 7.3b). The meeting points of these bisectors define a set of regions giving a proximal solution in which consumers (school-children) are allocated to a fixed set of facilities whilst total travel distance is minimised (Figure 7.3c). If the facilities form a regular triangular pattern then Thiessen polygons form hexagons, as used in Christaller's central place theory. The construction of Thiessen polygons assumes that the facilities can cope with any allocation of consumers. Modifications must be made to accommodate different sizes of facility, though this destroys the simplicity of the Thiessen arrangement (Boots and Getis, 1988).

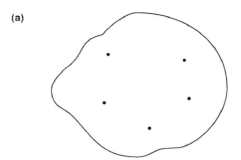

(a)

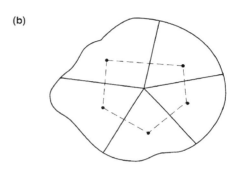

(b)

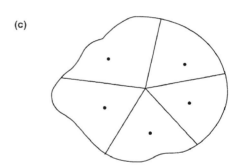

(c)

*Figure 7.3* Thiessen Polygons

There are usually three basic variables involved in the general problem of allocating goods or people to markets or facilities:

- the number of people and facilities to be assigned,
- the size or capacity of the facilities,
- the locations to which the facilities must be allocated.

Furthermore, there are three basic spatial forms that the problem may take (Hodgart, 1978:20; see also Bach, 1980):

- a general problem in which it is assumed that there are no facilities in an area so that *m* facilities may be freely assigned;
- an additional facility problem in which *k* additional facilities are located, taking existing locations of facilities into account;
- a reorganisational problem in which *m* existing centres are reorganised through closures, relocations and openings of new facilities.

One of the main difficulties in dealing with these problems is that there are a number of solutions that might be regarded as giving a series of "best" locations for the facilities. For example, it might be possible to locate three hospitals in a city in several different ways whilst each time minimising the effort required by patients to reach those hospitals. Usually, though, two different types of optimal solution can be recognised:

1. *A global solution*. This is the ultimate solution that truly maximises the accessibility of people to facilities.
2. *A local solution*. This approximates to the global solution, but if the researcher proceeds on a trial-and-error basis a shift of one facility could raise the overall cost of movement. Therefore the analysis should continue searching for another arrangement of the locations that will lower the cost of servicing the population even more.

There are a number of ways in which the global solution can be ascertained, involving degrees of simplification of the three basic variables involved (number of facilities, their capacity and their location). The most sweeping simplification is to decide both the number of the facilities and their locations before allocating the people to them. In this case only the capacities of the facilities can vary. If people are then merely allocated to their nearest facility, a *proximal solution* is created. This may happen in reality in the assigning of children to schools and patients to doctors' surgeries, though its practicality may be compromised if unequal capacities are generated or the quality of the facilities varies. Fortunately, various optimising methods can be used to deal with situations of greater complexity, the most commonly employed mathematical solution being the use of linear programming.

## The Transportation Problem

The transportation problem can be expressed in the form of a simple question: "For a given commodity what pattern of flows from suppliers to markets will minimise the total transport costs over the system?" (see Hay, 1979b). This problem has received wide attention and elaboration from planners, largely because it is subject to efficient solution. It exhibits *unimodularity* (a single optimal solution) and may frequently serve as a template for more complicated models of travel choice (e.g. Gordon and Moore, 1989).

As the solution obtained to the transportation problem is an optimal configuration, the linear programming model is a normative one. Hence differences between this normative model and the reality of real-world patterns of flows provide a measure of the level of economic efficiency reached by the system under study. But there is an implication that it is only appropriate to make such comparisons between reality and the model in situations in which it is reasonable to expect something approaching the optimal to be achieved in the real world. There are two situations that approximate to this:

1. Economies where there is a system of complete centralisation of decision-making, for example the Soviet Union between 1950 and 1980. Also, in a capitalist country, if a public agency is involved in decision-making rather than the private sector, then the absence of competition makes it possible for the agency to locate so that the total transport costs of users are minimised (Hotelling, 1929).
2. An economy where there is complete decentralisation tending towards perfect competition, for exam-

ple capitalist economies with limited governmental regulation.

In both cases the economic systems should tend to promote cost-minimising solutions and therefore make them suitable for investigation using linear programming techniques.

## The Simplex Method

Linear programming was developed by the American mathematician Dantzig (1963). In 1947 he published a procedure for solving a problem (an *algorithm*) known as the *simplex method* which could be applied to any problem in which an objective could be specified, such as maximum profit, minimum cost or minimum production time, but subject to certain constraints (Killen, 1979). Dantzig's own research was conducted on the problem of finding a combination of foods that provided an acceptable nutritional diet for the least possible cost. Hence the specified objective was that of least cost, but with the constraint that an acceptable nutritional level be attained.

The simplex method involves the specification of an objective as a *linear objective function* (Z) containing those variables whose value it is wished to minimise or maximise (see French et al, 1986). Constraints on these variables are also specified as a set of linear equations. For the typical transportation problem these equations are expressed as follows:

$$Z = \sum_{i=1}^{n} \sum_{j=1}^{m} c_{ij} x_{ij}$$

where $n =$ the number of suppliers of a good; $m =$ the number of markets or destinations for that good; $x_{ij} =$ the volume of a given commodity shipped from supplier $i$ to market $j$ at per unit transport cost $c_{ij}$; $c_{ij}x_{ij} =$ cost of shipment of the commodity from $i$ to $j$; and $Z =$ total transport costs over an entire network of $n$ suppliers and $m$ markets.

It is desired to minimise costs in this system subject to the following constraints:

1. The volume of goods $x_{ij} \leqslant$ the total volume of goods that the $i$th supplier is capable of supplying, $S_i$ (supply capacity), i.e. $\sum_{j=1}^{m} x_{ij} \leqslant S_i$ (goods from production point $i \leqslant$ production capacity of the source). Hence the total shipments from factory $i$ to all $j$ markets must not exceed the supply capacity of that supplier.

2. The volume of goods $x_{ij} \geqslant$ the demand of the $j$th market, $D_j$, i.e. $\sum_{i=1}^{n} x_{ij} \geqslant D_j$ (shipments to $j \geqslant$ demand). Hence the sum of the shipments from all $i$ suppliers into the $j$th market at least satisfies the demands of the $j$th market.

The objective function subject to constraints can be solved to produce the pattern of flows that minimises transport costs. To obtain the solution a set of values which satisfies the constraints is calculated, though initially these may not necessarily minimise the value of the objective function. This set of values is then modified until the optimum solution is reached whilst still meeting the constraints. This is known as an *iterative procedure* and, as it is a transportation problem that is being solved, an iterative transportation algorithm is employed. This is a typical linear programming routine in which a set of feasible values $\{T_{ij}\}$ are found that satisfy a given set of constraints. These values are then successively modified so that they converge gradually upon the optimum solution that minimises the value of the objective function; that is the total cost of transportation is minimised (see French et al, 1986).

The method for solving the basic transportation equation is set out in Thomas and Huggett (1980:171–4) and is generally translated into a computer program for any practical research. The computations involve calculation of both a particular type of price and a cost:

1. *Shadow prices.* These represent the relative price of the particular commodity at each factory ($U_i$) and each market ($V_j$). So, $V_j = U_i + c_{ij}$ for any market $j$ which has received a positive shipment from factory $i$. And therefore, $U_i = V_j - c_{ij}$ for any factory $i$ which has made a positive shipment to market $j$.

2. *Opportunity costs,* $\bar{c}_{ij} = V_j - U_i$. These represent

the costs for each cell assigned a zero shipment in the initial matrix.

If the main objective is to find the minimum total transportation cost subject to origin and destination constraints, there also exists a *dual problem* that involves the maximisation or minimisation of a linear relationship between the variables that constrain the main objective (or *primal problem*). If the primal problem involves minimisation of the objective function then the dual involves maximisation and vice versa.

When the value of $Z$, the primal objective function, is at a minimum, the value of the corresponding dual function ($Z'$) is at a maximum, with

$$Z' = \sum_{j}^{m} D_j V_j - \sum_{i}^{n} O_i U_i$$

where $\sum_{j}^{m} D_j V_j$ = a measure of the total revenue obtained from the sale of goods in all $m$ markets, and $\sum_{i}^{n} O_i U_i$ = a measure of the value of all goods before transportation. This is subject to the constraint

$$V_j - U_i \leq c_{ij} \qquad \text{or} \qquad \overline{c}_{ij} \leq c_{ij}$$

This is known as the *optimality criterion*, with $V_j \geq 0$ and $U_i \geq 0$. $U_i$ can be interpreted as the *location rent* accruing to each factory and $V_j$ as the *equilibrium market price* of the commodity at each destination. In an optimal solution the minimum value of $Z$ is equal to the maximum value of $Z'$.

In effect, the dual represents the set of shadow prices that maximise the value that is added to the goods during transportation. Its value is constrained so that the difference between any market price ($V_j$) and factory price ($U_i$) must be smaller than or equal to the cost of transportation between the two. These dual variables describe how the system of rents and prices reaches a condition of market equilibrium. So they help measure the locational competitiveness of production points and markets.

If shadow prices and opportunity costs are treated as location rent and equilibrium market price respectively then a spatial price equilibrium model may be

constructed. In this, $m$ buyers compete in the markets for the cheapest source of supply, and the outcome is a set of $V_j$ equilibrium prices which reflect the competitiveness of the various markets with respect to the sources of supply. This competitiveness is related to the geographical position of the market with respect to the sources of supply, and hence the use of the term location rents for $V_j$. As summarised by Thomas and Huggett (1980:184), "the optimal set of shadow prices describes a market equilibrium where no seller can increase his [her] location rent by selling to an alternative market because he [she] would be undercut by a more competitive seller; similarly, no buyer can reduce the equilibrium price by switching supplies to an alternative production point because he [she] would be undercut by a more competitive market". The assertion that equilibrium shadow prices are dependent on transportation costs depends on the assumption that the production capacities ($O_i$) and market demands ($D_j$) are fixed.

The calculations involved in applications of linear programming to transportation problems can be lengthy and are usually handled by computer. However, the calculations for a simple application are given in Table 7.1 and Figure 7.4. The existing situation is given in the form of a matrix (Table 7.1a) showing flows of goods between origins (suppliers, $O_i$) and destinations (markets, $D_j$). Table 7.1 gives the costs ($c_{ij}$) of transporting a unit of the goods from

*Table 7.1*  Solution to a Simple Transportation Problem (Based on Thomas and Huggett (1980) and Taylor (1978))

(a) Matrix of flows from suppliers ($O_i$) to markets ($D_j$) (unit transport costs $c_{ij}$)

| Suppliers ($O_i$) | Markets ($D_j$) | | | Production |
|---|---|---|---|---|
| | D | E | F | |
| A | 25 | 15 | 10 | 60 |
| B | 20 | 10 | 5 | 50 |
| C | 10 | 2.5 | 2.5 | 40 |
| Demand | 60 | 55 | 35 | 150 |

Table 7.1 (Continued)

(b) Analysis by north-west corner rule

(i) $T_{11}$ = the smaller of the first origin constraints ($O_1 = 60$) and the first destination constraint ($D_1 = 60$). Therefore 60 is the maximum possible assignment. Both constraint values are now reduced by the new value of $T_{11}$.

|  | D | E | F | Surplus Production |
|---|---|---|---|---|
| A | 60 |  |  | 0 |
| B |  |  |  | 50 |
| C |  |  |  | 40 |
| Unsatisfied Demand | 0 | 55 | 35 |  |

(ii) Repeat (i) using the north-west element of the matrix obtained by deleting the row or column whose constraint has been fully satisfied, i.e. $T_{22}$ is the new north-west element.

|  | D | E | F | Surplus Production |
|---|---|---|---|---|
| A | 60 |  |  | 0 |
| B |  | 50 |  | 0 |
| C |  |  |  | 40 |
| Unsatisfied Demand | 0 | 5 | 35 |  |

Table 7.1 (Continued)

(iii) Continue until all production ($O_i$) is used and demand is satisfied.

|  | D | E | F | Surplus Production |
|---|---|---|---|---|
| A | 60 |  |  | 0 |
| B |  | 50 |  | 0 |
| C |  | 5 |  | 35 |
| Unsatisfied Demand | 0 | 0 | 35 |  |

|  | D | E | F | Surplus Production |
|---|---|---|---|---|
| A | 60 |  |  | 0 |
| B |  | 50 |  | 0 |
| C |  | 5 | 35 | 0 |
| Unsatisfied Demand | 0 | 0 | 0 |  |

(iv) Calculate cost of initial feasible solution:

$$Z^1 = [(T_{11}^1 c_{11}) + (T_{12}^1 c_{12}) + (T_{13}^1 c_{13})$$
$$+ \ldots + (T_{33}^1 c_{33})]$$
$$= 60 \times 25 + 0 \times 15 + 0 \times 10 + 0$$
$$\times 20 + 50 \times 10 + \ldots + 35 \times 2.5$$
$$= 2100$$

continued overleaf

each supplier $i$ to each market $j$. The problem is to find the flow matrix $\{T_{ij}\}$ that minimises the total cost of transporting the 150 units of goods from the suppliers to the markets.

To calculate $\{T_{ij}\}$ an initial feasible matrix $\{T_{ij}^1\}$ is calculated by employing a procedure known as the *north-west corner rule*. This assigns shipments of the goods in the north-west corner of the flow matrix (cell 1,1) on the basis of origin and destination constraints, and then works towards the south-east corner (cell 3,3). At each stage the largest possible assignment permitted by the constraints is made. It is highly unlikely that this initial feasible solution is optimal because it ignores transport costs in assigning flows to

cells. However, this solution can now be successively modified until the optimum solution is attained.

This iterative procedure utilises shadow prices ($U_i$ and $V_j$) and opportunity costs ($\bar{c}_{ij}$), referred to above. It proceeds by finding an unused cell in the feasible flow matrix, where allocation of goods to that cell reduces total transportation costs. The maximum flow possible is assigned to this cell and the iteration continued until there is no cell in which an improvement to costs can be made (steps (v) and (vi)). As the opportunity cost ($\bar{c}_{ij}$) for any cell is bigger than the corresponding transportation cost ($c_{ij}$), then commod-

*Table 7.1*    *(Continued)*

(v) Calculate initial shadow prices ($U_i$) and ($V_j$):

$$V_j = U_i + c_{ij} \quad \text{or} \quad U_i = V_j - c_{ij} \quad (1)$$

for all markets receiving goods from supplier $i$ in the initial feasible solution. For suppliers, set $U_1 = 0$:

$$V_1 = U_1 + c_{11} = 0 + 25 = 25$$

Apply equation (1) to calculate $U_2$, $U_3$, $V_1$, $V_2$, $V_3$ (but only for markets receiving goods from supplier $i$ in the initial feasible solution).

| | | $V_j$ | |
|---|---|---|---|
| | 25 | 10 | 10 |
| | 0 | | |
| $U_i$ | 0 | | |
| | 7.5 | | |

(vi) Use shadow prices to calculate opportunity costs ($\bar{c}_{ij}$):

$$\bar{c}_{ij} = V_j - U_i$$

Calculated for all cells assigned a zero in the initial feasible matrix:

$$\bar{C}_{21} = 25 - 0 = 25 \qquad \bar{C}_{31} = 25 - 7.5 = 17.5$$

$$\bar{C}_{12} = 10 - 0 = 10$$

$$\bar{C}_{13} = 10 - 0 = 10 \qquad \bar{C}_{23} = 10 - 0 = 10$$

| | | | $c_{ij}$ | |
|---|---|---|---|---|
| | | | $V_j$ | |
| | | 25 | 10 | 10 |
| | | 0 | 10 | 10 |
| $U_i$ | | 0 | 25 | 10 |
| | | 7.5 | 17.5 | |

ity flows to that cell reduce the total transportation cost ($Z^1$) of the initial feasible solution. Differences for individual cells can be calculated between opportunity costs and transportation costs for the initial matrix. This reveals the cell with the greatest difference (in this case cell 3,1), and this cell is now used as

*Table 7.1*    *(Continued)*

(vii) Calculate differences between opportunity costs ($\bar{c}_{ij}$) and transportation costs ($c_{ij}$) for the initial matrix.

| | $(\bar{c}_{ij}) - (c_{ij})$ | | |
|---|---|---|---|
| | D | E | F |
| A | | −5 | 0 |
| B | −5 | | −5 |
| C | +7.5 | | |

(viii) Use pivot cell (*) to adjust flows in initial solution.

| | $T^1_{ij}$ | | | |
|---|---|---|---|---|
| | D | E | F | $O_i$ |
| A | 60 | | | 60 |
| B | | 50 | | 50 |
| C | * | 5 | 35 | 40 |
| $D_j$ | 60 | 55 | 35 | 150 |

If cell 3,1 receives goods then cell 1,1 will have to be reduced as will cells 3,2 and/or 3,3. Similarly cells 1,2 and 1,3 will also be affected. Keeping the number of cells to a minimum, the following table shows the gainers and losers affected by the new allocations:

| | $T^1_{ij}$ | | | |
|---|---|---|---|---|
| | D | E | F | $O_i$ |
| A | − | | + | 60 |
| B | | | | 50 |
| C | + | | − | 40 |
| $D_j$ | 60 | 55 | 35 | 150 |

a pivot around which the flows in the initial solution are adjusted: by adding flows to the pivot cell and adjusting flows in the occupied cells to satisfy origin and destination constraints (steps (vii) and (viii)).

This process is then repeated as a series of iterations until the opportunity cost for each unoccupied cell is less than the respective transportation cost. Alternatively, one or more of the opportunity costs may be

*Table 7.1 (Continued)*

The increment of the change $(\delta_T)$ should be set at the smallest value of $T_{ij}^1$ (to avoid negative flows being produced in the adjusted matrix). Thus $\delta_T = 5$. Therefore $T_{ij}^2$ becomes:

| $T_{ij}^2$ | | | | |
|---|---|---|---|---|
| | D | E | F | $O_i$ |
| A | 55 | | 5 | 60 |
| B | | 50 | | 50 |
| C | 5 | 5 | 30 | 40 |
| $D_j$ | 60 | 55 | 35 | 150 |

This yields a total cost of shipments $(Z^2) = 2062.5$. This is a reduction of 37.5 upon costs produced by $T_{ij}^1$.

(ix) This process is then repeated as a series of iterations until the opportunity cost for each unoccupied cell is less than the respective transportation cost. Alternatively, one or more of the opportunity costs may be equal to the respective transportation costs, indicating that another matrix of flows exists which equally minimises the total cost of transportation. Preference for one of these optimal solutions cannot be made on the basis of cost minimisation.

The following table gives the optimum assignment of flows, with $Z = 1825$. Therefore $Z = 1825$ is the minimum transportation cost permitted by the constraints $O_i$ and $D_j$ and so the algorithm is terminated.

| $T_{ij}^2$ | | | | |
|---|---|---|---|---|
| | D | E | F | $O_i$ |
| A | | 55 | 5 | 60 |
| B | 20 | | 30 | 50 |
| C | 40 | | | 40 |
| $D_j$ | 60 | 55 | 35 | 150 |

equal to the respective transportation costs, indicating that another matrix of flows exists which equally minimises the total cost of transportation. Preference for one of these optimal solutions cannot be made on the basis of cost minimisation. By continuing the iterative process for the data in Table 7.1 (see step (ix)), $Z$ can be reduced from 2100 to 1825. Therefore

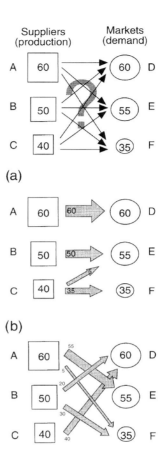

*Figure 7.4* A Basic Transportation Problem – Solutions to Problem in Table 7.2
(a) Initial feasible solution; (b) optimal solution

$Z = 1825$ is the minimum transportation cost permitted by the constraints $O_i$ and $D_j$, and so the algorithm is terminated at this stage. Figure 7.4 shows the differences between the patterns of flows that are produced in the optimal situation and those in the initial feasible solution.

Many of the geographical applications of the transportation problem in the late 1950s and early 1960s analysed flows of foodstuffs and raw materials, where transport costs were an important element in the total operating costs. For example, Henderson's (1958) analysis of coal movements in the USA divided the country into 14 regions of consumption and 11 producing regions. In this analysis $D_j$ represented the coal consumption in each of the 14 regions, and the objective was specified as the minimisation of transport costs for the flow of coal from markets to suppliers. The analysis showed that, in the traditional mining regions of West Virginia and Pennsylvania, actual production and costs of movement were 9 per cent greater than costs in the minimum-cost solution. This was attributed to sub-optimal use of shaft capacity. Both location rents and shadow prices were relatively low in the eastern USA, where levels of production and demand were high. In the less competitive and more isolated western producing regions, both location rents and equilibrium prices were high.

## Varying the Basic Assumptions of the Transportation Problem

One of the main problems of linear programming is that it assumes that economic relationships are linear in form, which may not always be the case. The basic linear programming solution also assumes that quantities of goods can be divided into an infinite number of small quantities, which may not be so for goods such as coal and bauxite. It is possible to allow for this by altering the program to take into account a fixed size of shipment. Other modifications can be introduced to bring the situation being portrayed closer to reality, such as variations in production costs, slack capacity in the system, constraints on the network's capacity, the presence of transformation centres, demand elasticity and non-linear systems (see Adrian and Watson, 1980).

(a) *Variations in production costs*. If these are introduced then the prime objective becomes to find the set of flows $\{T_{ij}\}$ that minimises the joint costs of production and transportation,

$$Z = \sum_i^n \sum_j^m T_{ij}(p_i + c_{ij})$$

where $p_i$ = the unit production cost of the $i$th factory, and $p_i + c_{ij}$ = the minimum delivered cost at market $j$ of a good from the $i$th factory, and so the cost of

delivering $T_{ij}$ units of that good is $T_{ij}(p_i + c_{ij})$. In this arrangement buyers will be attracted by factories where the joint cost of production and transportation is at a minimum.

(b) *Systems with slack capacity*. This refers to a relaxation of the assumption in the basic transportation problem that the total supply of a good is equal to the total demand for that good. The relaxation allows for more goods produced at the $n$ factories than is demanded at the $m$ markets or vice versa, i.e. $\sum_i^n O_i = \sum_j^m D_j$. In solving this type of problem, special "*slack*" *variables* are introduced into calculations (see Thomas and Huggett, 1980:186–9).

(c) *Network constraints*. These refer to the introduction of constraints on carrying capacities between markets and production points. Hence the problem under investigation now becomes a capacitated transportation problem, in which the network constraint is represented as $T_{ij} \leq N_{ij}$, where $N_{ij}$ is the route carrying capacity. The introduction of this constraint decreases the efficiency of the optimal solution. This can be demonstrated by comparing the objective function for a network without a network constraint with one to which the constraint applies. Such a comparison can reveal that part of a network requiring additional investment to increase capacity, i.e. $T_{ij} - y_{ij} \leq N_{ij}$, where $y_{ij}$ = the increased capacity of each route from $i$ to $j$ in the optimal solution. So

$$\sum_i^n \sum_j^m b_{ij} y_{ij} \leq B$$

where $b_{ij}$ = the cost of increasing the capacity of each route from $i$ to $j$ by one unit, and $B$ = the fixed budget of an entrepreneur, i.e. the total cost of the increased capacity of a system cannot exceed the fixed budget.

(d) *Introduction of a transformation centre*. In this situation production goes from a supplier, such as an iron ore mine, to a transformation centre, such as a steel mill, and then to the market. This situation gives rise to what is termed the *Beckmann–Marshack problem* in the construction of a complex algorithm. For details see Casetti's (1966) work on the coal industry of Quebec and southern Ontario in which the transformation centres represented break-of-bulk points.

Additional complexity can be introduced if the production of multiple commodities is considered (Isard, 1960:467–92).

(e) *Demand elasticity.* It is often assumed that an individual's demand for or use of a service is *inelastic*, that is demand is independent of facility location (Figure 7.5a). In reality an individual's demand or use depends on the price of obtaining the service. This is *elastic demand* (Figure 7.5b). These two types of demand have important implications for service provision as they affect costs. For example, with elastic demand, a number of small facilities should be able to supply a service with the same supply costs as a smaller number of larger facilities operating under conditions of inelastic demand. As shown in Figure 7.5a and b, if demand is elastic a distance-decay effect will show how demand falls with distance, whilst under inelastic conditions the effect shows how distance affects choice of facility. The assumption of inelasticity of demand is most likely to be correct for services such as secondary education, essential medical services, sewerage and fire services where "need" is a more appropriate term than demand (Koizumi and Inakazu, 1989; Richard et al, 1990). In contrast, recreational services have a more elastic demand. A good example of a location–allocation model incorporating elastic (price-sensitive) demand is given in the work of Wagner and Falkson (1975).

(f) *Non-linear systems.* More complex algorithms can be introduced in the form of non-linear equations, for example incorporating a non-linear production function (see below), thereby implying economies and diseconomies of scale.

## Dealing with Non-Linearities

Whilst basic location–allocation problems can be solved using linear programming methods, more complex problems contain non-linearities that effectively preclude the use of linear programming as a solution. In these cases solutions can be obtained by the following means which can involve the use of complex computer programs:

(a) *Tree-searching methods.* These represent a family of algorithms which operate by systematically evaluating all possible combinations of values for the integer variables in a given problem. This evaluation scrutinises a combinatorial "tree" representing a logical branching process. The search for an optimal combination occurs in conjunction with a branching process which eliminates from the problem large segments of the tree in which the optimal solution is inferred to be absent. For detailed examples see the pioneering work of Scott (1969a,b).

(b) *Heuristic programming.* This consists of any set of rules for the solution of a problem in which the rules define a solution process which converges in the direction of optimality but which may not produce a

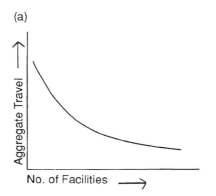

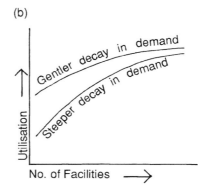

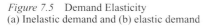

*Figure 7.5* Demand Elasticity
(a) Inelastic demand and (b) elastic demand

fully optimal result. This is an *iterative procedure*. For example, in determining the optimal location of a set of warehouses, the iterative process would be:

1. Select a finite number of sites as potential locations (for the warehouses).
2. The central facilities (warehouses) are located iteratively, one at a time. At each iteration the chosen site for a central facility is where the resulting improvement in the value of the objective function of the problem is the greatest possible.
3. Once the sequential iterations are completed, those central facilities (warehouses) which are no longer economical are deleted permanently from the problem (Kuehn and Hamburger, 1963). This approach is discussed further in the following section.

Heuristic programming can be applied to an important extension of location–allocation analysis, the problem of regionalisation or taxonomic description. This is the problem of partitioning a set of *n* data points (in Euclidean space) into *m* groups so as to optimise a specified objective function, for example to establish a set of groups in which the sum of the squares of all intra-group distances is minimally small.

This is the equivalent of what is termed the *quadratic assignment problem*, i.e.

$$\text{minimise } Z = \sum_{i=1}^{m} \sum_{j=1}^{n} \sum_{k=1}^{n} d_{jk}^2 \lambda_{ij} \lambda_{jk}$$

where $m$ = total number of groups, $n$ = total number of regions, $d_{jk}$ = Euclidean distance from point $j$ to point $k$, and $\lambda_{ij}$, $\lambda_{jk}$ = a variable having values of either 0 or 1, so that when $\lambda_{ij}$ or $\lambda_{jk} = 1$, then activity $ij$ or $jk$ is brought into existence at some positive level; and otherwise whenever $\lambda_{ij}$ or $\lambda_{jk} = 0$. This is subject to the constraints

$$\sum_{i=1}^{m} \lambda_{ij} = 1 \qquad (j = 1, 2, \ldots, n)$$

$$\lambda_{ij} = \begin{cases} 1 \\ 0 \end{cases}$$

The problem may be solved heuristically or tree-searching methods may be used to obtain an exact optimal solution (Scott, 1969b). Modifications can be introduced to permit aggregation only of contiguous regions. This is discussed further in the subsection on "Electoral districts" in the following section.

## LOCATION–ALLOCATION PROBLEMS

### Weber's Problem

The transportation problem described above is one which focuses upon the hinterlands of producers and consumers. It assumes that the capacities and locations of the facilities concerned are known prior to the analysis. However, an important question often asked in locational analysis is how to locate new facilities in an area so that the known distribution of consumers is served in the most efficient way, usually via a cost-minimising solution. This situation translates into a highly complex location–allocation problem as, in addition to finding an optimum pattern of flows, it is necessary to find optimum locations and capacities for a specified number of central facilities so as to serve best a set of demand points whose locations and demands are known (sometimes called the *central facility location problem*) (Hodgart, 1985).

This type of problem was first raised in the late nineteenth century by Alfred Weber who attempted to find the most efficient point of production between raw material sources and market locations (Friedrich, 1929). Weber argued that a firm will select a location so that the sum of the costs of transporting inputs to a processing plant at the chosen location, and from the plant to market, are minimised. This assumes fixed raw material inputs, inelastic and fixed demand, fixed prices and a goal of profit maximisation.

It is possible to solve the basic version of this problem by using a physical analogue model, known as *Varigoron's frame*, using weights and pulleys. This can be applied to the arrangement shown in Figure 7.6 in which there are two sources of materials ($M_1$ and $M_2$), a single market point (C), with P = the least-cost location for production within this locational triangle. This can be solved if information is available on the weight of commodities to be shipped from $M_1$ and $M_2$ to C, and the transport costs per unit distance. Total transport costs at alternative locations can be calculated, enabling contours of equal additional transport cost, known as *isodapanes*, to be established. Weber used isodapanes to show how the optimal location could be shifted from P by agglomeration economies or by the impact of cheap labour.

Although no suitable mathematical solution to Weber's problem was developed until the 1960s, optimal arrangements for production and consumption were proposed earlier than this in idealised patterns of spatial organisation such as those produced by Christaller (1966), Losch (1954) and Isard (1956) in the development of central place theory. Moreover, the consideration of alternative goals, variations in information and uncertainty regarding the economic environment have produced extensions to this basic theory, thereby generating much more general location theory (see Smith, 1981) and extensions including behavioural theories of location (Pred, 1967).

In the 1960s a number of independently derived solutions were formulated for Weber's problem and also for the location of multiple facilities, with simultaneous determination of optimal locations and the

allocation of demand to these locations (Ghosh and Rushton, 1987).

In the classical Weber problem the aim is to find the location for a single central facility so that the cost of all flows between the central facility and some other set of points is a minimum. This location is the median point or point of minimum aggregate travel, but with the magnitude of all flows fixed and known in advance. To solve this, the use of calculus (a particular method of calculation) is required. The problem can be expressed as the need to find spatial coordinates $U^*$ and $V^*$ of the central facility which minimise Z, i.e.

$$Z = \sum_{j=1}^{n} r_j[(U^* - U_j)^2 + (V^* - V_j)^2]^{1/2}$$

where $r_j$ = requirements of the $j$th destination point or region, and $U_j$ and $V_j$ = Cartesian coordinates of the $j$th destination point.

*Cartesian coordinates* are numbers given to a point to identify its position, being the perpendicular distances of the point from two (or three) axes. The term "Cartesian" comes from the French philosopher Rene Descartes who introduced analytic geometry in 1637, using algebraic notation and procedures for the description of geometric objects. His followers, Cartesians, developed probabilistic scientific views from observation and experiment as did empiricists, arguing that certain knowledge is derived by reason of innate ideas (Cottingham et al, 1985).

The objective function (Z) may be minimised using two simultaneous differential equations and the iterative method developed by Kuhn and Kuenne (1962).

In both the transportation problem and Weber's problem, it is assumed that distance and flow costs are directly proportional. In reality these two elements are rarely proportionally equivalent and modifying parameters can be added to the equations to allow for this. In reality,

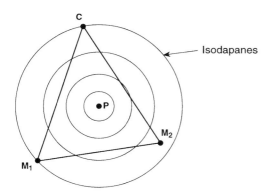

*Figure 7.6*   Varigoron's Frame

$$t = udP$$

where $t$ = cost of transportation, $d$ = distance, and $u$ and $p$ are given parameters.

## Locating New Facilities with the *p*-Median Model

The extension of the Weber problem to multiple supply points produced the *p-median location–allocation model*. This seeks the location of $p$ supply centres which minimise the aggregate distance separating them from a set of demand points (see Beaumont, 1987b). It assumes that the level of demand is independent of the centres' spatial organisation and the price of each good is constant. Therefore total revenue is known before a model is used, as all demand is satisfied. This means that the objective of profit maximisation is identical to the objective of minimising transport costs. Given a set of $p$ uncapacitated supply centres and $n$ demand locations, the objective function ($Z$) is

$$\text{minimise } Z = \sum_{i=1}^{n} \sum_{j=1}^{p} O_i \lambda_{ij} c_{ij}$$

subject to the constraints

$$\sum_{i=1}^{p} \lambda_{ij} = 1 \qquad (i = 1, \ldots, n)$$

and

$$\lambda_{ij} = \begin{cases} 1 & (i = 1, \ldots, n) \\ 0 & (j = 1, \ldots, p) \end{cases}$$

where $O_i$ = the quantity demanded at location $i$ which has the coordinates $(x_i, y_i)$; $\lambda_{ij}$ = a binary variable, equal to 1 if demand point $i$ is allocated to centre $j$, and equal to 0 if demand point $i$ is allocated elsewhere (consumers are allocated to their nearest centre).

In this arrangement, distance between the demand point ($i$) and supply point ($j$) is represented by $c_{ij}$, as generalised transport cost is assumed to be proportional to distance:

$$c_{ij} = \sqrt{[(x_i - x_j)^2 + (y_i - y_j)^2]}$$

There are a number of solutions to this problem, including heuristic procedures involving a sequence of allocating demand to centres and then relocating centres until some specified convergence criterion is achieved (Cooper, 1967, 1968). This is known as an *alternating procedure*. The model can be extended to include unit cost of a commodity at centre $j$, with the objective to minimise total transport and purchase costs:

$$\text{minimise } c = \sum_{i=1}^{n} \sum_{j=1}^{p} O_i \lambda_{ij} (r_j + c_{ij})$$

where $r_j$ = the cost of the good at centre $j$. If prices are spatially uniform, $r_j$ is a constant and the optimal pattern is identical to that produced by the previous model.

This approach can be extended by relaxing the assumptions of fixed demand and then maximising profit rather than minimising total transport costs (Beaumont, 1987b).

The *p*-median model described above applies to continuous space as opposed to a discrete network where facility locations are restricted to the vertices of a transportation network. However, applications dealing with locations on a network have also been developed (ReVelle and Swain, 1970). For locations on a network, the problem involves locating $p$ centres on a network of demand points so that the aggregate (or mean) distance of all consumers is at a minimum, with every consumer allocated to their nearest centre:

$$\text{minimise } Z = \sum_{i=1}^{n} \sum_{j=1}^{p} O_i \lambda_{ij} c_{ij}$$

subject to the constraints

$$\sum_{j=1}^{p} \lambda_{ij} = 1 \qquad (i = 1, 2, \ldots, n)$$

$$\lambda_{ij} - \lambda_{jj} \geqslant 0 \qquad (i = 1, 2, \ldots, n; j = 1, 2, \ldots, p)$$

$$\sum_{j=1}^{p} \lambda_{jj} = p$$

$$\lambda_{ij} = \begin{cases} 1 \\ 0 \end{cases}$$

where $n$ = total number of demand nodes, and $p$ = total number of centres.

From this, more complex models have been generated, relaxing the assumption that the consumers patronise the nearest centre (Beaumont, 1980), modifying the emphasis upon minimising transport cost to consider other maximising functions (such as a measure of welfare benefit to consumers) (Williams and Senior, 1978), and maximising the demand for a particular centre so that centres compete with each other rather than cooperating as in the standard $p$-median problem. Thus by developing the network formulation of the $p$-median problem, the range of situations in which location–allocation models can be applied has been extended. Linear programming can be used to solve the network $p$-median problem as well as more mathematically complex procedures.

In summarising the development of location–allocation modelling, there have been two principal phases: the initial production of the $p$-median model and applications based on this, and more recent formulation of models that can capture more complex behaviour patterns of both producers and consumers. In the initial phase, "the $p$-median problem's goal of systemwide efficiency often led to a spatial configuration in which individual accessibility to the system varied widely" (Ghosh and Rushton, 1987:4). Therefore a number of constraints and alternative objective functions were suggested:

- constraints on the maximum distance separating any individual from a facility;
- minimisation of the variance in accessibility;
- focusing on individual access rather than systemwide access, and attempts to minimise the maximum distance separating any user from the closest facility (known as the *Rawls criterion*) (Morrill and Symons, 1977).

Work dealing with the emergency services produced models well suited for the accessibility needs of such delivery systems (e.g. Daskin, 1987; Mirchandari and Reilly, 1987), with two approaches:

1. *Set covering models*. These determine the minimum number of facilities and the optimal locations that will place all individuals within a critical distance of a centre. A typical set covering model "finds the locations of the minimum number of facilities at possible sites on a network which will ensure that each point of demand can find service within a time or distance threshold" (Hudak, 1994:233).
2. *Maximal covering location models*. These restrict the number of centres to be located, but find their locations so that they cover the maximum number of people (that is, locate people within a critical distance of the facility).

These models can be solved as $p$-median problems after some amendments to the elements in the objective function (Hillsman, 1984).

More recent applications of location–allocation modelling have made greater attempts to approximate to reality and have broadened the scope of applications (Rushton, 1988). Ghosh and Rushton (1987) highlight four areas, as follows.

(a) Representation of the decision-making behaviour of the providers of services. This has involved the formulation of *multiple-objective problems* (see Chapter 8), with various methods utilised for evaluating the performance of alternative solutions according to given criteria. In some cases this has meant a move away from optimisation as a goal and, instead, use of models designed to minimise deviations from predetermined values of selected criteria (e.g. Sutcliffe et al, 1984). The key element in this approach is to identify the set of "non-inferior" solutions from which a final choice can be made. A hierarchy of such solutions has been formulated in some cases to deal with service systems, such as health care delivery, which have more than one type of facility (Church and Eaton, 1987; Eaton et al, 1982; Moore and ReVelle, 1982). For a detailed case study see Rushton's (1987,

1988) accounts of the relationship between location theory, location–allocation models and service development planning in India. Some of these ideas are pursued by Gore (1991a) who argues that planning in less developed countries needs to develop in two ways. Firstly, by analysing the assumptions about market structure made in programmes such as those supported by the World Bank; and secondly, by focusing on geographical accessibility as an integral part of the study of entitlements.

(b) More accurate representation of the process of consumer spatial choice. For example, consumers may not patronise the facility closest to them. Particular aspects of this possibility have been investigated:

- Multipurpose trips. Allocating consumers to facilities on the basis of a multipurpose trip on which they visit several types of facility (O'Kelly, 1981).
- Varying levels of service offered by a facility (Berman and Larsen, 1982).
- Consumer choice. Consumers may simply prefer facilities other than the nearest one for a wide range of reasons. This can be modelled for multiple facilities by injecting a probabilistic element (e.g. Ghosh and McLafferty, 1982; O'Kelly, 1987; Leonardi, 1983).

(c) The geography of demand and of the distances or time or transportation costs between places. The data on demand are usually aggregated according to an arbitrary spatial unit varying in size and shape, and the true centre of demand in the area is frequently unknown. This lack of information can be crucial as location–allocation algorithms are usually highly sensitive to accuracy in data representation (Gould, 1985:ch. 8).

(d) Attempts to eliminate model mis-specifications by focusing on the uncertainties in the environment in which a service is to be provided.

In addition to location–allocation models, Rushton (1989) recognises two other types of location models. These are:

1. *Spatial choice models*, in which the focus is on the locational choices made and the goal is to infer the rules of choice that decision-makers used in reaching their decisions. These are discussed in Chapter 12.
2. *Organisational decision-making models*, in which the focus is on the process of decision-making and the goal is to show who participated, what roles they played and how they decided to act at any particular stage in the decision-making process.

He laments the lack of interaction between these two types of model and location–allocation models, but until recently the former have been the subject of attention largely from researchers from a behavioural tradition (see Chapter 12) rather than from the mathematical modelling background associated with location–allocation. Links between all three types of model are now being developed and there is greater recognition of the inherent difficulties to be overcome in combining them to solve practical problems.

Key questions to be considered in this work are:

- How can locational efficiency be measured? That is, how much better are "optimal locations" selected by a location model than those locations already in existence or selected by other means?
- How can alternative rules of decision-making be best evaluated?
- How can the geographical environment be best represented? This involves representing distances, travel times, costs, service demand, the level of data aggregation and defining boundaries of study areas. Data aggregation may be especially problematic because locations identified as optimal may be sub-optimal for disaggregated data, with different objective functions obtained (Sheppard, 1986).

Development of location–allocation models in the 1980s overcame some of the limitations of earlier work on transportation problems utilising linear programming. There was also some attempt to address criticisms of the general modelling approach to the provision of services and location of facilities. Nevertheless, some of the criticisms remain valid. For example, Morrill and Symons (1977) pointed out that "contrary to the presumption of location theory, an efficient location pattern that maximises system profits or minimises system costs, including travel, may result in socially unacceptable inequality in access over space, usually owing to area variations in density and income". This weakness was noted in Sayer's (1976) critique of urban modelling in which he argued that traditional models had concealed social phenomena by failing to base their abstractions on human practice. He championed a multidisciplinary political approach based on "comprehensiveness and human practice", in which modelling played only a marginal role. However, perhaps the most damning indictment of the application of normative models to geographical problems has come from Harvey (1973:96): "It is not normative modelling which is at fault but the kind of norms built into such models." There are many geographers who would still agree with this view despite two decades of evolution of such applications!

For example, Gore (1991b) argues that modelling of service development planning in the Developing World frames the problem of such planning in too limited a way. He contends that Rushton's proposed innovations concerning the role of models in the planning process are likely to be restricted by the way in which the models are constructed. In particular the models have difficulty in interrelating the social and the spatial by virtue of the way in which they reduce complex realities to components in the model. Three important restrictions are:

1. The models reduce policy options for tackling complex geographical accessibility problems to a question of facility location.
2. The models separate the facility location decision from most other aspects of the institutionalisation of service provision.
3. The models separate the spatial impact of changes in the location of facilities from most aspects of the social and economic impact.

It is criticisms of this sort and geographers' growing concern for non-mathematical approaches to consumer and entrepreneurial behaviour that have moved modelling approaches from the geographical mainstream. However, as discussed further in Chapter 8, there have been significant advances in mathematical modelling during the past decade, including work on designing optimal electoral districts (see below), incorporating multiple criteria in models and employing game playing exercises (see last two sections in this chapter).

## Electoral Districts

Location–allocation problems also extend to the problem of designing electoral districts, with work by geographers on this topic being prompted partly by decisions in the US Supreme Court in the early 1960s which required all Congressional and State electoral districts to be equal in population (Johnston and Rossiter, 1983). After every census, each state in the USA is obliged to draw up new electoral districts with approximately equal population numbers.

Geographers' work on this topic has considered measures of the shape of areal units and optimal spatial designs to meet certain constraints (Openshaw, 1978). However, failure to consider the political implications of the optimal solutions has sometimes limited the utility of such approaches.

For a given set of $n$ sub-regions, each with a given population ($P_j$), the problem is to aggregate the sub-regions into $m$ major electoral districts or constituencies in order to render inter-regional variations of population minimally small (for example to minimise the variance of the populations of the computed electoral districts). The latter would involve finding variables $\lambda_{ij}$ having a value of either 0 or 1 to minimise

$$Z = \frac{1}{m} \sum_{i=1}^{m} \left( \sum_{j=1}^{n} P_j \lambda_{ij} - \frac{1}{m} \sum_{j=1}^{n} P_j \right)^2$$

where $i$ = the sub-regions (suppliers), $j$ = the centres of electoral districts (markets), and $(1/m)\sum P_j$ = the mean population of the set of computed districts.

The principal constraints are usually that all computed districts must be contiguous and that no region can be assigned to more than one electoral district (see Mills, 1967). If this process is expressed as a linear programme, the steps in the algorithm are as follows:

1. Choose arbitrary centres for the electoral districts.
2. Solve the transportation problem

$$\text{minimise } Z = \sum_{i=1}^{n} \sum_{j=1}^{m} c_{ij} x_{ij}$$

where $\{c_{ij}\}$ = squared distances from the geographical centres of each sub-region to the electoral district centre, and $x_{ij}$ = number of voters in each sub-region. This is subject to the constraints

$$\sum_{i=1}^{n} x_{ij} = P \qquad (j = 1, 2, \ldots, m)$$

(the assignment of sub-regions to electoral districts produces districts with equal numbers of voters)

$$\sum_{j=1}^{m} x_{ij} \leqslant p_i \qquad (i = 1, 2, \ldots, n)$$

(the assignment of voters from each sub-region to the various electoral districts does not exceed the number of voters present in that district)

$$x_{ij} \geqslant 0$$

where $x_{ij}$ = the number of voters in sub-region $i$ assigned to electoral district $j$, $P$ = the total number of voters allowed in each electoral district, and $p_i$ = the number of voters in sub-region $i$.

3. Find the new geographical centre of each electoral district as the centre of gravity of the sub-regions assigned to the district in step 2.
4. If any of the new centres differs from the old, return to step 2.

Operational definitions of equal-sized constituencies and contiguity were examined by Kaiser (1966) and by Weaver and Hess (1963) in the USA, using calculus and an index of compactness designed to eliminate geographically unwieldy areas. The same

procedure was applied by Mills (1967) to assign local polling districts to electoral wards in Bristol, England. He included an additional constraint by permanently assigning some polling districts to certain wards so that natural barriers (such as rivers) formed ward boundaries. His work showed that several solutions could be obtained to the electoral districting problem. Different solutions could have almost identical values for equality of voter numbers and compactness but still have different spatial configurations (Haggett et al, 1977:480–5). The political implications of choosing a particular configuration may be profound, as demonstrated in work on developing and evaluating school desegregation plans in the USA (Schoepfle and Church, 1991; Woodall et al, 1980). For example, use of a distance-minimisation approach in redrawing school catchment zones may produce racial integration but not socio-economic integration. Hence alternative methods, such as multi-objective programming, have been used (see following section).

Kaiser's problem was to redistrict the 12 congressional districts of Illinois outside Chicago. His algorithm had to allocate 101 counties to the 12 districts, giving equal importance to the goals of compactness and population equality. The best result from 200 computer runs is shown in Figure 7.7.

The basic *redistricting problem*, for allocating four counties to two districts, as described by Macmillan and Pierce (1994), is shown in Figure 7.8 as a *solution tree*. The bottom line of the tree contains all possible allocations. Their suitability will depend on whether or not a contiguity constraint is met. Two different spatial arrangements of counties are shown (Map 1 and Map 2). Contiguous allocations associated with each map are labelled "C" and non-contiguous ones labelled "N".

The tree illustrates two popular algorithmic strategies not employed by Weaver and Hess (who concentrated on maximising district compactness measured in terms of population distribution):

1. *A seeding procedure*. A seed county is selected for each district. The district then grows from the seed by adding counties until all counties have been assigned. In this example, the seed is county 1

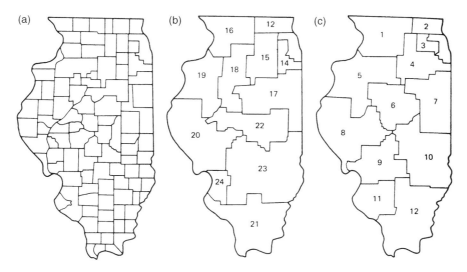

*Figure 7.7*    Proposed Reapportionment of Electoral Districts in Illinois, USA
(a) County system; (b) existing congressional districts; (c) proposed districts. (*Source*: Kaiser, 1966:210–12)

allocated to district 1 and county 2 to district 2, which is depicted as seed (1,2). All possible assignments of remaining counties are depicted by the boxes in the bottom row of the tree that are connected to (1,2) from below by the thickened lines. This is not necessarily an optimal solution as it considers only one part of the solution space, but it does generate feasible solutions (e.g. Rossiter and Johnston, 1981).

2. *Explicit optimisation and swapping.* Beginning with a box at the bottom of the tree, a county is swapped from one district to another so that the mean squared deviation is reduced at the fastest possible rate. Swapping proceeds until the "best" plan is found, in this case the dashed lines from box (1 4, 2 3). This can also give sub-optimal solutions by preventing any swaps that lead to a deterioration in the mean squared population deviation.

Another strategy for solving the redistricting problem is an optimising procedure called *simulated annealing* which incorporates the use of random elements (see Browdy, 1990; Press et al, 1986). It is based on the physical process of annealing. In this,

when a liquid metal or crystal is cooled slowly and thermal equilibrium is obtained after each temperature fall, atoms can lose energy slowly enough to permit the formation of an ordered lattice of atoms. At each temperature during cooling, the system concerned can be at any energy level. The probability of the system being at any given energy level is a function of $\exp(-E/T)$, where $E$ = energy level and $T$ = system temperature. So, as the temperature is lowered, the system always has a chance of changing to a higher energy state, though with a reducing level of probability. When the system approaches zero temperature, the atoms approach their minimum energy state. Quick cooling, known as *quenching*, in which the system is not allowed to reach thermal equilibrium, results in a higher energy state and atoms become locked into an irregular structure.

Macmillan and Pierce (1994:232) liken traditional optimisation algorithms to quenching, as they may produce only local optima. However, in simulated annealing an optimisation problem is solved slowly until the minimum state is reached. The simulation involves defining the energy level for any state of the system and a probability function to determine the chances of the system going from a given energy level

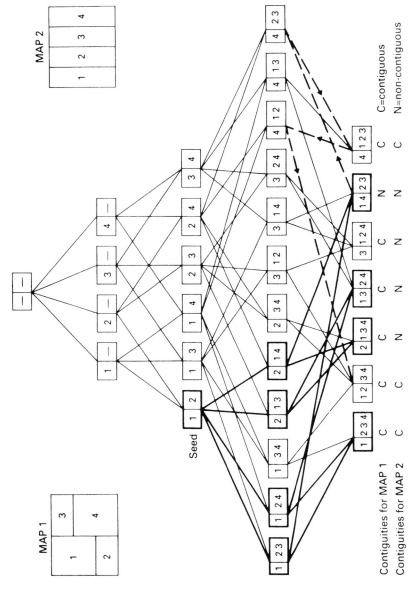

*Figure 7.8* A Solution Tree for a Simple Redistricting Problem. (*Source:* Macmillan and Pierce, 1994:225)

to a higher or lower one. As the system has the opportunity of jumping from one given energy state to a higher one then the algorithm should not become trapped at or near a local minimum. Once the energy level has been slowly lowered until it can go no further, the global minimum has been reached. This procedure also involves starting with the system in a given state with a certain energy level. Small random perturbations are introduced to produce a resulting state with a different energy level. The difference in energy levels between the new state and the previous one is determined and if a decrease in energy level is recorded then this change is accepted and the process continues with temperature steadily lowered (Kirkpatrick et al, 1983). This is a slow business requiring plenty of computer time to produce a global minimum.

When applying simulated annealing to the redistricting problem, system energy can be defined as a measure of the compactness of electoral zones or population equality. The random perturbations are moves of counties or wards between districts. This will reduce the "temperature" (energy level) towards a stopping criterion – again not necessarily the global minimum in this type of application as it is impossible to reduce "temperature" to zero in finite time. Algorithms for simulated annealing are described by Macmillan and Pierce (1994:234–45).

## MULTI-CRITERIA MODELLING

The models developed in the 1960s and 1970s tended to be incapable of dealing with conflicting and incommensurable objectives. Neither could they deal very readily with objects falling outside the realm of the traditional price and market system. For example, issues pertaining to social welfare or environmental conservation, which do not readily acquire a simple market cost, are difficult to investigate with a primary objective based on a criterion of economic efficiency. Hence the traditional models tended to have a general lack of operationality.

It has been argued that much geographic behaviour may be interpreted as optimising behaviour involving multiple objectives and subject to numerous diverse constraints (Senior, 1981), but until the 1980s there were only sporadic attempts to convert this complex behaviour into a form suitable for *multi-criteria modelling* (e.g. Nijkamp and Spronk, 1981). However, gradually, geographers have recognised that many problems of resource planning involve not a single optimisation but multiple, conflicting and possibly incommensurate objectives. This has led to dissatisfaction with the traditional objective of maximising some aggregate measure of economic efficiency. So there has been work replacing this objective with a concern for *multi-objective optimisation*, for example incorporating an environmental component.

The theory of multi-criteria decision-making and differential games deals with situations in which a single decision-maker is faced with a multiplicity of usually incompatible criteria, performance indices or *pay-offs*, or in which a number of decision-makers or game players must consider criteria each of which depends on the decisions of all the decision-makers. When there is more than one decision-maker, both cooperation and non-cooperation between players is possible. Most multiple-objective problems do not have a single optimal or supreme solution that can satisfy all of the objectives simultaneously, but various forms of optimal solution can be derived, usually by optimising linear combinations of the multiple objectives using various weightings. This involves complex mathematics which extends the application of these games well beyond the simple examples referred to below in the final section (see Leitmann, 1976). As a result of this complexity few geographers have utilised differential games in analysing decision-making. However, they have been applied in various planning contexts.

Multi-criteria decision analysis was pioneered by Dutch regional economists as a way of evaluating alternative regional planning policies. For example, van Delft and Nijkamp (1977) used this form of analysis to evaluate a set of proposed industrial development plans for the reclaimed Maasvlakte peninsula in the Rhine delta, south-west Netherlands. This work focused on a limited range of alternatives involving five plans which, together, included an integrated steelworks, a steelworks, tank storage, a trans-shipment works, a container terminal and facilities for ship and tanker cleaning. Their approach built upon *multi-attribute utility theory* developed by Lancaster (1971).

Multi-objective optimisation recognises the existence of multiple optima or a series of "non-inferior" solutions from amongst a feasible set. This implies that a decision-maker has to choose from a series of optima on the basis of preferred trade-offs between the solutions. There are several approaches towards the identification of such multiple optima, not all of which involve mathematical programming (van Delft and Nijkamp, 1977).

Another characteristic of multi-criteria models is that they consider "intangibles" that are outside the realm of the traditional price and market system. Some of the models have a finite number of feasible alternative choices. These are discrete models whilst those with an infinite number of feasibilities are continuous models, sometimes termed *multi-objective programming (MOP) models*. Both types of model can also be interval scale or ordinal scale, deterministic or stochastic, and static or dynamic.

## Multi-Objective Programming Models

MOP models replace the simplicity of a single objective to be maximised or minimised subject to stated constraints. In its place are multiple, non-commensurable objectives which characterise most decision-making in the spheres of public policy, planning and design. MOP models can also deal with situations in which different groups of people may have different priorities so that an unambiguous ranking of objectives is impossible.

MOP models can specify a number of objectives. Therefore maximisation of one of the objectives will prevent the remaining objective functions from obtaining their absolute maxima. There are choices to be made then as to which of the respective objective functions are optimal and which of the respective decision variables are optimal. There are many different solutions to these two problems so that there is a

wide variety of MOP models. A series of examples can be seen in Nijkamp (1989).

Multi-criteria evaluation is relatively simple as compared with other decision-support methodologies. It can also handle discrete decision situations where the range of possible choices can be measured and the data have either (or both) a quantitative and a qualitative character. These virtues are considered by Jankowski (1989) to be highly appropriate for applications to the public decision-making processes within regional planning. The latter has to deal with both multiple political preferences and multi-dimensionality in which the different components of the regional system, such as welfare and quality of life, compete with each other.

In applying multi-criteria evaluation methods, alternatives (the choice possibilities) are judged on the basis of multiple criteria and priority weights. The former represent various dimensions of a given problem and the latter reflect different preferences, viewpoints and opinions of the groups and individuals involved in the decision-making process. In evaluating this information an evaluation or impact matrix is employed in which the columns represent alternatives and rows represent criteria. Each element in the matrix represents a performance score of a given alternative in light of a particular criterion. Additional information is derived from a vector of priorities in which preferences regarding the evaluation criteria are expressed in terms of weights. In applying such methods to regional planning, data are usually both qualitative and quantitative and hence the method chosen must be able to deal with this.

The first step in applying the process to regional planning situations is to generate the set of alternatives to be considered. In van Delft and Nijkamp's (1977) work on alternative development plans for the reclaimed Maasvlakte area in the Dutch Rhine delta, starting from an original eight industrial activities planned for the area, they obtained $2^8 (= 256)$ alternative plan combinations. These were reduced to 151 by introducing some geographical and technological constraints. However, this combinatorial approach is just one of several ways in which a set of alternatives covering all aspects and dimensions of a given problem can be generated. Use of expert input is commonly used, but there are more complex computer-based methods too (e.g. Starr and Greenwood, 1977).

Generating evaluation criteria can be performed both deductively and inductively. Amongst a wide range of possibilities for selecting the criteria there are examination of literature sources, analytical modelling of a problem, interviews with social groups and individuals, analysis of political and social objectives, and consultation with experts.

In estimating priorities, use can be made of a *multi-attribute utility function* (see Zeleny, 1982) or, less complex and probably more appropriate to public decision-making, weightings can be derived by standardising rankings given to priorities by decision-makers and other interested parties. Various means for performing this are discussed by Voogd (1983), but they all depend on a variety of arbitrary assumptions, so it is common for several different techniques to be applied to the same problem.

## An Example of Multi-Criteria Modelling

Jankowski's (1989) work on resource development and regional planning in the Poznan-Pit area, north of Wroclaw in Poland, provides a good example of a multi-criteria evaluation using both qualitative and quantitative data. In this work the evaluation of multiple criteria was refined into a systematic and analytic procedure within the context of regional planning. The main planning issue in the study area was the conflict between plans for large-scale exploitation of brown coal (lignite) reserves and environmental and social concerns that this mining activity would be highly destructive, especially to surface- and ground-water resources. Impact studies generated a series of five equally feasible alternative plans of resource and land use development (Table 7.2a). Thirteen evaluation criteria were created (Table 7.2b), including economic, environmental and social subsets. Criterion scores were then derived for an impact matrix (Table 7.2c) (though their exact formulation is not described by Jankowski). Two sets of criterion weights were generated based on interviews with local government autho-

rities and relevant literature reflecting current public priorities. The first set ($V_1$) represent economic criteria stressed by central planning authorities and the second ($V_2$) represent environmental and social criteria which were the priority view expressed by public groups and local authorities. As shown in Table 7.3, three different techniques for measuring preferences were employed:

- a 10-point scale, from 1 = least preferred to 10 = most preferred;
- ranking, with 13 = the most important criterion to 1 = the least important;
- rating, using a constant sum approach.

There are various ways in which the criterion scores and weights can be evaluated, depending on the data types represented. In this case both ordinal and cardinal weights were used, so an evaluation method known as EVAMIX was employed (Nijkamp et al, 1985). This is based on pairwise comparison of alternatives, but using a method whereby cardinal and ordinal weights can be compared (see Jankowski, 1989:358–9; Voogd, 1983). It uses a pairwise comparison of alternatives using the criterion weights (Table 7.3a). For details of the method's operation see Voogd (1983). In Jankowski's analysis, five separate "runs" were generated with different weights employed depending on the level of measurement of the data used as evaluation criteria. Random weights ($r_i$), as used in run 4, employ a random number generator to produce a set of weights that can be used to help determine the stability of the other runs.

As shown in Table 7.3b, for $V_1$ (the economic priority view) the dominant scenario is the first alternative – "full capacity exploitation of the lignite resources." However, there is no such dominant scenario for $V_2$ (the environment–social view). Both "limited agricultural development" and "recreational and tourist development" are featured twice as the first ranking scenario under $V_2$. The comparison of the alternative rankings obtained on the randomly generated weight sets (runs 2 and 4) shows that the stable results, with respect to the ranking results, are the 10-point scale-derived set of weights representing the

*Table 7.2*   Alternative Development Scenarios, Poznan-Pit, Poland

(a) Feasible alternatives

1.   The original project: full-capacity exploitation of lignite resources, 1995–2018
2.   Partial (40% of total capacity) exploitation of lignite resources
3.   Intensive agricultural development, from 10 to 20% increase in production
4.   Limited agricultural development, from 10 to 20% increase in production
5.   Development of recreational and tourist attractions based on the region's natural amenities

(b) Variables

**Economic subset**
A   Net contribution to GMP (000 000 zlotys p.a.)
B   Household income created by the project (000 000 zlotys p.a.)
C   New jobs created by the project (000s)
D   Opportunity cost of rejecting a particular project (000 000 zlotys p.a.)

**Environmental subset**
E   Greenery and open space preserved in project-related area (%)
F   Landmarks preserved in the project-related area (number)
G   Wildlife and vegetation, native to project area, which would remain after the project realisation (%)
H   Project-generated air pollution (rank number)
I   Deterioration of water resources, measured as a percentage of the total water resources in the project-related area, either foregone or heavily polluted as a consequence of the project (%)

**Social subset**
J   Number of new apartments for people who would move into the project-related area (scalar number)
K   Number of people who would change their location (scalar number)
L   Projected intensity of social conflicts triggered as a consequence of project implementation (rank number)
M   Public support for a given project (rank number)

(c) Impact matrix

| Criterion | Alternatives | | | | |
|---|---|---|---|---|---|
| | *1* | *2* | *3* | *4* | *5* |
| A | 4400 | 1700 | 720 | 420 | 20 |
| B | 1480 | 573 | 250 | 147 | 9 |
| C | 6.6 | 2.7 | 1.6 | 1 | 0.2 |
| D | 5640.4 | 2250 | 840 | 385 | 18.2 |
| E | 80 | 92 | 96 | 98 | 99 |
| F | 1 | 4 | 7 | 10 | 10 |
| G | 15 | 32 | 76 | 95 | 90 |
| H | 3 | 5 | 9 | 9 | 9 |
| I | 0 | 0.48 | 0.87 | 0.95 | 1 |
| J | 2100 | 950 | 120 | 40 | 35 |
| K | 5500 | 3000 | 350 | 150 | 140 |
| L | 4 | 4 | 8 | 10 | 8 |
| M | 3 | 4 | 10 | 9 | 8 |

*Source*: Jankowski (1989).

*Table 7.3*   Multi-criteria Analysis of Development Projects, Poznan-Pit, Poland

(a) Criterion weights

| Criterion | 10-pt scale | | Ranking | | Rating | |
|---|---|---|---|---|---|---|
| | $V_1$ | $V_2$ | $V_1$ | $V_2$ | $V_1$ | $V_2$ |
| A | 10 | 8 | 13 | 11 | 0.13 | 0.09 |
| B | 6 | 5 | 8 | 1 | 0.09 | 0.07 |
| C | 2 | 2 | 3 | 3 | 0.04 | 0.04 |
| D | 9 | 6 | 12 | 5 | 0.12 | 0.07 |
| E | 5 | 9 | 4 | 10 | 0.06 | 0.08 |
| F | 3 | 7 | 1 | 4 | 0.06 | 0.08 |
| G | 5 | 7 | 2 | 9 | 0.07 | 0.09 |
| H | 6 | 10 | 10 | 12 | 0.08 | 0.10 |
| I | 7 | 10 | 11 | 13 | 0.10 | 0.11 |
| J | 6 | 6 | 7 | 2 | 0.07 | 0.05 |
| K | 5 | 7 | 6 | 6 | 0.06 | 0.06 |
| L | 6 | 7 | 9 | 8 | 0.07 | 0.09 |
| M | 4 | 6 | 5 | 7 | 0.05 | 0.07 |

(b) The ranking of the alternatives

| Ranking Position | Run 1 | | Run 2 | | Run 3 | | Run 4 | | Run 5 | |
|---|---|---|---|---|---|---|---|---|---|---|
| | $V_1$ | $V_2$ | $V_1$ | $V_2$ | $V_1$ | $V_2$ | $V_1$ | $V_2$ | $V_1$ | $V_2$ |
| 1 | 1 | 4 | 1 | 5 | 1 | 4 | 1 | 5 | 1 | 1 |
| 2 | 4 | 5 | 4 | 1 | 3 | 5 | 4 | 4 | 4 | 4 |
| 3 | 3 | 3 | 3 | 4 | 4 | 3 | 2 | 3 | 3 | 3 |
| 4 | 2 | 1 | 2 | 2 | 2 | 2 | 3 | 2 | 2 | 5 |
| 5 | 5 | 5 | 5 | 3 | 5 | 1 | 5 | 1 | 5 | 2 |

(c) Final rankings

The frequency of the occurrence of the *j*th alternative on the *i*th ranking position.

| Ranking Position | Alternative | | | | |
|---|---|---|---|---|---|
| | 1 | 2 | 3 | 4 | 5 |
| 1 | 3 | 0 | 0 | 1 | 0 |
| 2 | 0 | 0 | 0 | 3 | 1 |
| 3 | 0 | 0 | 4 | 0 | 0 |
| 4 | 0 | 3 | 0 | 0 | 1 |
| 5 | 1 | 1 | 0 | 0 | 2 |
| $R_j$ (final ranking) | 1 | 4 | 3 | 2 | 5 |

*Source*: Jankowski (1989).

second priority view (Jankowski, 1989:360). For these two ordinal weight sets and for the two rating-derived weight sets, the final alternative ranking is shown in Table 7.3c. This table represents elements $f_{ij}$ or the number of times alternative $j$ received the $i$th position in the final ranking. The final row of this table shows the final ranking ($R_j$) of the five choice-possibilities; $R_j = 1$ if $f_{ij}$ is maximal; $R_j = 2$ if $f_{1j} + f_{2j}$ is maximal; $R_j = n$ if $f_{1j} + f_{2j} + \ldots + f_{nj}$ is maximal. This final ranking suggests that alternative 1 is the most attractive followed by alternatives 4 and 3, conditional upon the subjective assumptions of the evaluation techniques and the alternative weighting schemes used to represent the two priority views.

The methodology of multi-criteria evaluation is relatively simple and contains the attractive feature of transforming a single "solution" plan into a process whereby several alternatives can be evaluated and compared. The evaluation can provide material for use in the political bargaining process, though the reality of most planning decisions involving resource development is that the "solution" selected by the evaluation may well be deemed undesirable on political grounds which may not be readily incorporated in the model. For further examples of the use of MOP models in a planning context see Massam (1988) and as applied to school redistricting see Diamond and Wright (1987) and November et al (1996). The latter collapsed a MOP model into a single objective of minimising the sum of a set of weighted goal deviations, with different weights for the goal deviations used to prioritise the importance of the goals to produce new school districts in Connecticut.

## GAME THEORY

The *theory of games* was formally established in the 1940s by Von Neumann and Morgenstern (1944) as a means of analysing and explaining decisions taken in situations where the outcome either depends on the choices of others or involves some form of risk. Geographers have used the theory in various ways, but especially to analyse land use decision-making. In this type of application game theory acts as a mathemati-

cal framework representing decision-making under conditions of uncertainty, usually involving a farmer or groups of farmers opposing the environment. The latter can offer a range of different conditions against which the farmers can adopt certain strategies (Gould, 1963, 1965). The theory attempts to deal with the problem of optimising decisions in the face of risk or uncertainty, with a matrix, the *pay-off matrix*, constructed to show the potential returns to the farmer under different environmental conditions (see Table 7.5a). In this situation or game, the environment's gambit could be "drought", under which conditions the farmer may select a crop which can withstand drought and so be more likely to produce favourable returns. On the other hand, the farmer may select a crop which is only partially drought-tolerant but which will produce the highest overall returns under a variety of different conditions. The "best" solution can be determined in many ways, using such devices as simple probability theory, linear programming or the adoption of specified criteria for decision-making under given conditions.

The theoretical framework for the operation of the game is essentially an extension of normative economic theory underlying both the von Thunen (1966) model and certain linear programming investigations. However, the evaluation of the pay-off matrix can take into account the "bounded rationality" of farmers rather than that of the mythical perfectly economic rational being "*Homo economicus*" (Simon, 1957; Wolpert, 1964). In other words, an optimal solution may be identified which accords with the criterion of maximum profitability. However, sub-optimal solutions may also be recognised which may be closer to the realities of life in which targets other than maximum profitability may be pursued (Agrawal and Heady, 1968; Ilbery, 1983, 1985).

### The Hotelling Model

Because of the way in which game theory enables researchers to focus on human behaviour, it has been utilised in a variety of disciplines, including biology, economics (Eichberger, 1993; Gibbons, 1992a), philosophy (Binmore, 1994), political science (Straffin,

1993) and sociology (Greenberg, 1992). Research utilising game theory has advanced from simple applications involving competition between two persons to possibilities for cooperation between individuals.

The simplest game generates a winner and a loser, as demonstrated in the classic example employed by geographers, namely the *Hotelling model*. In formulating this, Hotelling (1929) examined the highly simplified competition between two producers supplying identical goods to consumers evenly spread along a linear market. He concluded that the two producers would locate next to each other, each supplying one half of the market. Geographers have translated this into the situation of two ice-cream sellers on a beach, as an illustration of industrial agglomeration under certain demand conditions.

The Hotelling model is shown in Figure 7.9, in which production costs (*c*) are the same in all locations and the retail price (*p*) of the product reflects the transport cost to the consumer (for the sale of ice-cream on a beach, this is the effort of customers walking to the sales outlet). Conditions of infinitely inelastic demand are assumed, with everyone purchasing one unit of the product in one unit of time irrespective of price. In the arrangement of the two sales outlets (A and B) shown in Figure 7.9a, A is in the centre of the market and B is to the right. Their two sales areas split at X, half-way between the two outlets, thereby greatly favouring A. However, if B moves next to A (Figure 7.9b), B will capture some of A's sales without losing any of its own despite increasing the effort demanded of the customers to its right. Therefore the two outlets will locate at the centre of the market for maximum advantage, irrespective of their initial locations. If demand is made sensitive to price, that is discouraging more distant customers, then the arrangement shown in Figure 7.9c represents optimal positions of the two outlets. This implies that elasticity of demand stimulates industrial dispersal.

When translated into game theory, the game played is termed a *zero-sum game* as whatever one person gains the other must lose: if B moves from the middle of the beach then A gains additional business. If both vendors adopt the middle position this is termed a

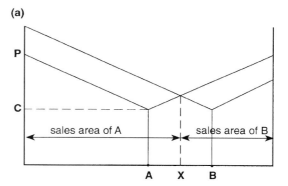

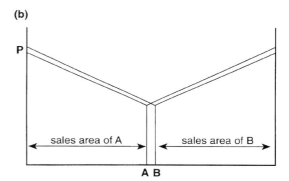

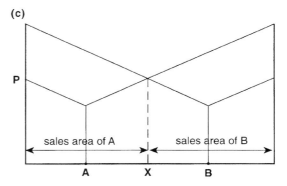

*Figure 7.9*    The Hotelling Model
(a) Sales outlet A is located in the centre of a linear market with sales outlet B to the right; (b) sales outlet B moves alongside A; (c) optimal positions

"maximin" strategy as it guarantees at least a minimum pay-off of half the market regardless of the actions of the rival vendor. If both competitors adopt this strategy, equilibrium results.

## The Prisoner's Dilemma and the Tragedy of the Commons

In more complicated games it has been demonstrated that players can cooperate to gain benefit rather than just generating a single winner (Nash, 1950). However, special circumstances are needed for the development of cooperation and collective action. This is because high individual costs can occur if collective action is taken and some individuals fail to cooperate. This is demonstrated in the so-called *prisoner's dilemma* based on *Hobbes' soldier's dilemma* (Gauthier, 1967). Two prisoners, interrogated separately, are offered a deal by their jailers. If one confesses, and as a result the other prisoner receives a substantial sentence (say 20 years), then the confession will guarantee the confessing prisoner liberty. However, if both prisoners stay silent then both will receive only a light sentence (one year). If both confess, they will both receive moderate punishments (10 years). This can be represented in the pay-off matrix shown in Table 7.4, in which prisoner A's sentences are shown by the left-hand numbers in each cell, and prisoner B's by the right-hand numbers. Given human nature, both prisoners are likely to confess as otherwise they risk a greater sentence if the other prisoner confesses and they do not! However, if the two prisoners could have cooperated, they would both have stayed silent and therefore have secured only a light sentence.

A close geographical equivalent of the prisoner's dilemma is the *tragedy of the commons* (Hardin, 1968). This is based on an understanding appreciated by the eighteenth-century philosopher, David Hume, that if citizens respond only to private incentives, then public goods will be inadequately provided and public resources over-utilised. The tragedy refers to a situation in which herders graze cattle on common land. If the herders seek to maximise returns from their cattle they will each seek to increase the number of cattle that they graze. However, the amount of return associated with each increase in numbers of cattle grazed will fall as the amount of grazing to be shared by the animals is reduced. If some herders increase their herd size and others do not, those who do not will have the returns from their herd reduced as a consequence of this depletion of the grazing resource. In contrast, those increasing their herd size will have a net gain to their returns despite sharing in the negative costs of pasture reduction (Figure 7.10). Therefore it is in the interest of every herder to increase the size of their herd.

The consequences of such increases are a fall in the value of each head of cattle and a progressive degradation of the common land, perhaps taking it beyond its carrying capacity. It is this that represents the "tragedy". Hardin (1974) argued that underlying the tragedy is the freedom of the herders to continue overstocking because, in the short term, it is in their own self-interest. So, although the long-term scenario is complete destruction of the grazing resource, its degradation is permitted by the short-term gains to be obtained from increased stocking. The obvious antidote to the tragedy is cooperation amongst the herders for mutual benefit, which could be translated into a

*Table 7.4* Pay-Off Matrix for the Prisoner's Dilemma

|  | | Prisoner B | | | |
|---|---|---|---|---|---|
|  | | No Confession | | Confession | |
| Prisoner A | No Confession | 1 | 1 | 20 | 0 |
|  | Confession | 0 | 20 | 10 | 10 |

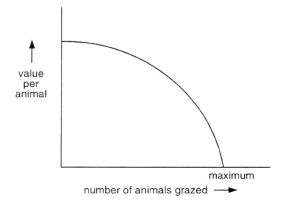

*Figure 7.10*    The Problem of the Commons

complex game (Johnston, 1989b:116–25; Ostrom, 1990; Taylor, 1988).

There has been little geographical work on co-operative game playing, though game theory has been applied by geographers to political issues. In this use the basic problem considers a committee or similar body which comprises groups of voters of varying sizes but none of which has a majority of votes. The game considers the relative bargaining strengths that the different groups possess and how they exercise them (Brams, 1975). An example of this is the investigation of the relative power of different countries within the European Community (Johnston and Hunt, 1977).

## Farmers Versus Environment

In most games the decision-maker has to make an estimate of the likelihood of a future event, but this estimate is subject to some sort of error, thereby resembling reality in which decision-making occurs under conditions of uncertainty. Typically, the games established by geographers have involved a farmer or groups of farmers opposing an environment which can offer a range of different conditions against which the farmers can adopt certain strategies. In such cases the pay-off matrix will show the potential returns to the farmers under different environmental conditions. Therefore the games may be constructed to cater for different types of decision-making by the farmers concerned (e.g. Wolpert, 1964).

In describing the use of game theory in the investigation of decision-making in agriculture, Found (1971) cited two contrasting situations in which risk is involved:

1. Risk due to a phenomenon such as a hurricane, which may be highly unlikely at any particular location (i.e. probability $< 0.1$) but may be a climatic possibility and still highly damaging. However, it is difficult to take steps to avoid crop damage under these extreme conditions.
2. Risk due to a phenomenon such as frost, which may be much more likely to be a hazard in early spring and late autumn (i.e. probability $> 0.3$). But steps could be taken to avoid crop damage from frost by planting later or harvesting earlier or by planting a different crop, less susceptible to frost.

A game can be set up to accommodate the second of these situations by establishing a contest in which the farmer as decision-maker plays the environment, with different probabilities being attached to different solutions. These probabilities are represented in a pay-off matrix from which it is possible to select various optimal solutions. For example, given the pay-off matrix shown in Table 7.5a, it is possible to obtain the following solutions:

1. If only one type of crop is to be grown and average weather conditions are assumed then soybeans would be the crop chosen.
2. Soybeans actually give a very low return if conditions are very wet or very dry. Therefore a "better" solution would be to find which crop has the highest "expected" income taking into account the probabilities of all possible weather conditions. This is calculated in Table 7.5b and gives a solution indicating that rice would be the best single crop to grow.
3. If the farmer was a complete gambler the $25 per hectare (ha) for wheat might be the main influence, leading to wheat being the chosen crop even though the probability of obtaining suitable conditions for this is only 0.1.
4. If the farmer was a pessimist then the chosen strategy may be to opt for the least damaging choice in case of poor weather. In this situation the crop selected would be the one giving the highest income under the worst possible conditions, i.e. oats, which, under very dry weather, yield $12 per ha as opposed to $11 for soybeans, $8 for wheat and $10 for rice under their respective lowest yielding weather conditions.
5. More realistically, a combination of crops could be chosen that yielded the optimum income from a number of crops given the returns indicated in the pay-off matrix. This solution could be determined by using linear programming.

In reality, farmers are unlikely to know the correct

*Table 7.5*   Average per-Hectare Income($): by Crop and Weather Type

(a) Pay-off matrix

| Crop | Weather Type | | | | |
|------|-----------|-----|---------|-----|----------|
|      | Very Dry | Dry | Average | Wet | Very Wet |
| Rice | 10 | 13 | 18 | 20 | 22 |
| Wheat | 25 | 21 | 17 | 12 | 8 |
| Soybeans | 12 | 17 | 23 | 17 | 11 |
| Oats | 12 | 13 | 17 | 19 | 21 |
| Probability of occurrence | 0.1 | 0.2 | 0.3 | 0.2 | 0.2 |

(b) Expected incomes

For rice, highest expected income
$$= 0.1(10) + 0.2(13) + 0.3(18) + 0.2(20) + 0.2(22)$$
$$= \$17\text{-}40,$$

For wheat, highest expected income
$$= 0.1(25) + 0.2(21) + 0.3(17) + 0.2(12) + 0.2(8)$$
$$= \$15\text{-}80,$$

For soybeans, highest expected income
$$= 0.1(12) + 0.2(17) + 0.3(23) + 0.2(17) + 0.2(11)$$
$$= \$17\text{-}10$$

For oats, highest expected income
$$= 0.1(12) + 0.2(13) + 0.3(17) + 0.2(19) + 0.2(21)$$
$$= \$16\text{-}90$$

probabilities of the different types of weather, and so their actual decision-making will be based on imperfect knowledge. However, comparing the optima obtained from game-playing with real-life decisions can give a good indication of what types of decisions are being made by the farmers and of how well informed they are.

One of the first geographical applications of game theory was by Gould (1963) who used it to identify optimum crop combinations for Ghanaian farmers facing uncertain weather conditions. Series of similar games between farmers and environment were used by Found (1971) to illustrate game theory in operation. Gould's work is summarised in Table 7.6 and Figure 7.11.

Despite the potential offered by games of farmer versus environment, Thomas and Huggett (1980:291) have argued that game theory should really involve a game of farmer versus farmer, as the environment cannot be regarded as a realistic "player" in a game. Their own examples, again using the farmer as decision-maker, concentrate on a decision model rather than a theoretical game and consider the strategies or plans of action that are open to the decision-maker.

The relatively restricted application of game theory in geography reflects limitations in its use as a conceptual framework for presenting the normative regulation of behaviour. Perhaps somewhat unrealistically, it usually assumes that players, besides knowing their own strategies, know all the strategies that their opponents are considering, the utilities which they themselves place on possible outcomes partly determined

*Table 7.6* Pay-Off Matrix for Farmers in Jantilla, Ghana

(a) The pay-off matrix

| Crop Choice | | Environment Moisture Choices (linear scale 0–100) | |
| | | Wet Years | Dry Years |
|---|---|---|---|
| Crop Choice | Yams | 82 | 11 |
| by | Maize | 61 | 49 |
| Farmers of | Cassava | 12 | 38 |
| Jantilla | Millet | 43 | 32 |
| | Hill rice | 30 | 71 |

(b) Mixed strategy solution

| | Wet Years | Dry Years | Difference |
|---|---|---|---|
| Maize | 61 | 49 | 12 |
| Hill rice | 30 | 71 | 41 |

Proportion under maize $= \dfrac{41}{12 + 41} = 77.4\%$

Proportion under hill rice $= \dfrac{12}{12 + 41} = 22.6\%$

*Source*: Gould (1963).

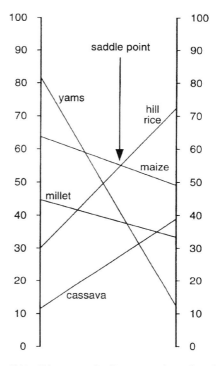

*Figure 7.11* Diagrammatic Representation of a Pay-Off Matrix (from Table 7.6a)

by their opponents' strategies, and, in some cases, the probabilities that their opponents will play their available strategies. Game theory also ignores certain parts of the decision-making process relating to goal setting, the individual's diagnosis of problems and unanticipated outcomes of decisions. These and other limitations are detailed by Prentice (1975).

Nevertheless, the potential for further applications of game theory in geography has been exposed by the award of the 1994 Nobel Prize for Economics to three of its proponents (John Nash of Princeton University, Reinhard Selten of the University of Bonn, and John Harsanyi of the University of California at Berkeley). The work of the prize-winners has highlighted three areas for possible future enquiry by geographers:

- further variants on the prisoners' dilemma in the form of games reaching an equilibrium (Nash);
- multi-stage games where the credibility of a particular player's threatened move is important (Selten);
- use of probability to work out strategies when several different ones are possible (Harsanyi).

For further details of a range of non-geographical applications, a standard introduction is provided by Gibbons (1992b). A more advanced guide is given by Rasmusen (1989), and a more philosophical approach is taken by Binmore (1994).

# 8

# SPATIAL INTERACTION

## GRAVITY MODELS

One of the foci of geography's Quantitative Revolution was the geometry of cities, with research that described and analysed the various kinds of flows that link houses, factories and retail centres. This geometry has continued to play a central role in geographical research involving predictions of flows of goods and people. Forecasting of flows is essential in making land use and transport investment decisions. Predictions can be used to reduce costs of interaction whilst maintaining diversity of choice. In the previous chapter it was the methods and models for allocating flows to locations (spatial allocation) that were examined; in this chapter the focus is upon interactions between locations (*spatial interaction*).

*Spatial interaction models* are used to predict spatial choices reflected in flows of people or goods between origins and destinations, expressing trade-offs between the accessibility of alternative destination opportunities and the perceived intrinsic "attractiveness" of these opportunities (Roy, 1990:712). These models have been shown to be of practical use in retail planning as they can be used predictively even with an input of relatively unsophisticated data (e.g. Wilson, 1976b, 1988). For example, given basic data on population, retail floorspace, travel times or distances between settlements, it is possible to establish predicted patterns of expenditure in given shopping centres. These predictions can then be compared with actual expenditures as a means of calibrating the model (by establishing the most appropriate $\beta$ value in equation

(8.1) below). Once this calibration has been established the model then describes an "equilibrium" situation at one point in time. This calibrated equilibrium model may then be used to investigate the effect of a proposed new shopping centre, assuming that the behaviour of consumers with respect to distance and the "attractiveness" of shopping centres remains constant. So it is possible to make a forecast of how much revenue the new centre will attract and how much existing centres will lose.

The application of such models has obvious attractions for both commercial concerns and planners. For investors the model can provide an indication of whether a proposed new retail complex will be viable, and eventually it could be used to suggest the ideal size of the new centre and the amount of parking space required. For planners perhaps the main role of such models is to help in the estimation of impacts upon existing retail centres, for example the effect of a new out-of-town shopping centre upon city-centre retailing. The estimated level of use of such a new shopping complex will give an indication of how much new traffic is likely to be attracted to the complex, and therefore can suggest implications for related traffic planning. In addition, at an early stage of planning, the model can be used to compare alternative plans for future retail provision.

The most commonly used basic model for examining interactions between locations has been the *gravity model*, which provides a direct analogy with *Newton's law of gravitation*, after the law formulated in 1687 by Sir Isaac Newton (1642–1727), the English scientist, mathematician and philosopher. He proposed his law to explain the observed motions of the planets and their moons, stating that any two bodies in the Universe attract each other with a force proportional to the product of their masses and inversely proportional to the square of the distance between them:

$$F = G(m_1 m_2)/R^2 = G m_1 m_2 R^{-2}$$

where $F$ = magnitude of the attractive force, $G$ = a gravitational constant, the size of which depends on the system of units used, and which is a universal constant, $m_1$ and $m_2$ = masses of the two bodies, and $R$ = the distance between them.

The first formal use of the Newtonian model in a social science context was in the 1880s by the English demographer Ravenstein (1885, 1889). From his empirical studies of migration he formulated a series of "laws" of migration, part of which can be translated into a Newtonian form (Wrigley, 1980):

$$I_{ij} = kM_iM_jd_{ij}^{-\beta} \tag{8.1}$$

where $I_{ij}$ = interaction between two locations $i$ and $j$; $M_i$ and $M_j$ = "masses" measuring the "strength" of $i$ and $j$, usually the population numbers of two settlements, $i$ and $j$, respectively $P_i$ and $P_j$; $d_{ij}$ = the distance between $i$ and $j$; and $k$ and $\beta$ = constants.

The value of $\beta$ can be altered to influence the distance decay of the interaction. It is usually varied between 0.5 and 2.5, the former giving a gradual decline with distance and the latter a sharp distance decay commonly associated with Developing Countries (see Figure 8.1). The Pareto model can be regarded as more typical of distance decay in the Developed World; distance decay in Developing Countries is more akin to the normal model and the untransformed data.

The equation is more frequently expressed as:

$$F_{ij} = kP_iP_jd_{ij}^{-\beta}$$

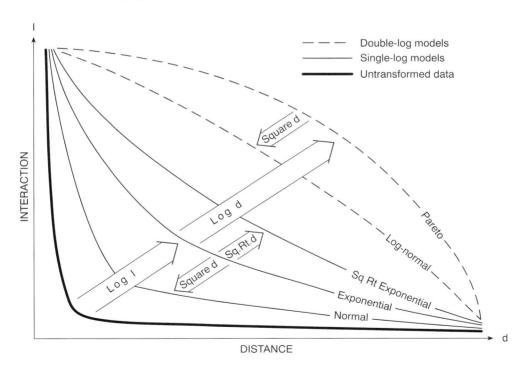

*Figure 8.1*  Distance-decay Curves. (*Source*: Taylor, 1971)

where $F_{ij}$ = the flow of migrants between two places $i$ and $j$; $P_i$ = the population of $i$; and $P_j$ = the population of $j$. This equation can be transformed into a logarithmic form so that the constants $k$ and $\beta$ can be estimated:

$$\log(I_{ij}/P_iP_j) = \log k - \beta \log d_{ij}$$

Therefore, given a knowledge of $d_{ij}$, $P_i$ and $P_j$, the *level of interaction* (or migration) between $i$ and $j$ can also be estimated. This is known as the basic gravity model of human interaction, termed the $P_1P_2/D$ *hypothesis* by Zipf (1946).

A significant limitation of the basic gravity model is that it contains no mechanism for ensuring that the predicted numbers of flows from a region are equal to the observed numbers of migrations originating in that region. Similarly, it does not ensure that the predicted number of arrivals equals the observed arrivals.

In building on the basic model, a major feature of more complex models has been to balance predicted movements with observed ones. Initially this was performed through the development of models predicting flows of retail expenditure.

## The Law of Retail Gravitation

The basic gravity model has been used in a variety of ways as a predictive tool, beginning in the 1930s with the work of W.J. Reilly (1931) who formulated a *law of retail gravitation*. This contained two rules relating to the flow of retail trade: the larger a town is, the more trade it attracts; and towns attract more trade from settlements in close proximity than they do from settlements located farther away. In other words, two cities attract retail trade from any intermediate city or town in direct proportion to the population of the two cities and in inverse proportion to the square of the distances from these two cities to the intermediate town. This translates into the following equation:

$$\frac{T_{ix}}{T_{iy}} = \frac{P_x}{P_y}\left(\frac{d_{iy}}{d_{ix}}\right)^2$$

where $T_{ix}$ and $T_{iy}$ = amount of retail trade drawn from

location $i$ to towns $x$ and $y$ respectively; $P_x$ and $P_y$ = populations of $x$ and $y$; and $d_{ix}$ and $d_{iy}$ = distances from $i$ to $x$ and $y$.

Therefore if $x$ and $y$ have the same population and are the same distance from $i$, they will receive the same amount of trade ($T_{ix}/T_{iy} = 1$). However, if the distances remain unequal but $P_x$ is twice as big as $P_y$ then $x$ will receive twice as much trade as $y$ ($T_{ix}/T_{iy} = 2$). Given the same populations but with $x$ half as far as $y$ is from $i$, then $x$ will receive four times as much trade as $y$ ($T_{ix}/T_{iy} = 4$).

When expressed in more familiar form Reilly's law becomes

$$T_{ix} = kP_xP_id_{ix}^{-2}$$

or

$$T_{iy} = kP_yP_id_{iy}^{-2}$$

The law was based on observation of the retail hinterlands of towns in Kansas and Missouri and hence the use of $\beta = 2$ as the exponent as this most closely matched the law's predictions to observed reality. One of its main uses is in delimiting retail hinterlands, by making direct use of Reilly's equation as stated by Converse (1930). For example, if the population of $x = 20\,000$, and the population of $y = 10\,000$, and $x$ and $y$ are 10 miles apart, $d_{iy}$ can be calculated as the distance along a line from $y$ to $x$ to the point where the two towns attract equal trade:

$$d_{iy} = \frac{d_{xy}}{1 + \sqrt{(P_x/P_y)}}$$

In this case,

$$d_{iy} = \frac{10}{1 + \sqrt{(20\,000/10\,000)}} = \frac{10}{1 + \sqrt{2}}$$

$$= \frac{10}{1 + 1.414} = \frac{10}{2.414} = 4.14 \text{ miles}$$

Therefore, at a distance of 4.14 miles from town $y$, the retail hinterland of town $x$ begins. Calculations involving a number of towns could be used to establish a series of such hinterlands, which may have practical application for retailers, for example coordinating advertising with markets, or in the planning of future retail provision.

There are two crucial weaknesses in the law of retail gravitation. Firstly, it lacks a solid explanatory basis. It simply makes an analogy with Newton's law without extending an adequate link between the analogy and the analogised (Luckermann, 1958). This issue is considered in more detail later in this chapter. Secondly, it ignores the reality of overlapping retail hinterlands. Each hinterland produced by Reilly's law is totally dominated by one town or retail centre. In recognising this limitation, Huff (1963) recast the law into a probabilistic framework by reformulating it as a behavioural model from the viewpoint of the consumer.

Huff argued that the probability that a consumer at point $i$ will travel to retail centre $j$ ($P_{ij}$) is a ratio of the utility of that retail centre to the consumer ($U_{ij}$) and the total utility of all retail centres considered by the consumer:

$$P_{ij} = U_{ij} \bigg/ \sum_{j=1}^{k} U_{ij}$$

where there are a set of $k$ competing centres.

The utility of a retail centre can take a gravitational form in which it increases with the size of the centre but decreases as the distance between the centre and the consumer increases:

$$U_{ij} = S_j / d_{ij}^{\beta}$$

where $S_j$ = retail floorspace in retail centre $j$; $d_{ij}$ = distance from consumer $i$ to retail centre $j$ (sometimes measured in terms of time and expressed as $t_{ij}$); and $\beta$ = an exponent to be calibrated. This could have a value of 2 as in standard gravity model formulations, but may be varied to make the outcome more realistic.

Therefore,

$$P_{ij} = \frac{S_j / d_{ij}^{\beta}}{\sum_{j=1}^{k} (S_j / d_{ij}^{\beta})}$$

If an area is divided into a number of small areal units, representing a number of "$i$"s, then maps of the probabilities of consumers patronising competing centres can be produced using this formula. $P_{ij} = 0.5$ is equivalent to the breaking point between hinterlands under Reilly's law.

In order to translate Huff's formulation into a measure of each centre's market potential, additional information is required and, in particular, the distribution of population and income for retail expenditure. For example, if consumer expenditures ($C_i$) in each area are added to Huff's formula:

$$C_{ij} = C_i \frac{S_j / d_{ij}^{\beta}}{\sum_{j=1}^{k} (S_j / d_{ij}^{\beta})}$$

where $C_{ij}$ = the amount of expenditure from consumers in area $i$ that is spent in retail centre $j$. From this the potential market ($m_j$) for retail centre $j$ can be calculated from

$$m_j = \sum_{i=1}^{n} C_{ij}$$

for $n$ consumer areas.

At around the same time as Huff's work, Lakshmanan and Hansen (1965) independently produced an equivalent model, a *singly constrained spatial interaction shopping model*, derived from the Baltimore Metropolitan Area Transportation Study. The constraint referred to is the use of knowledge of the total number of flows leaving each zone $i$ prior to making a prediction of flows. The predicted total number must equal the observed total. They developed a model that could describe the pattern of retail sales in Baltimore. Like Huff's, it can be used to predict the probability that a resident of zone $i$ in a city will shop in zone $i$, or to predict monetary flow from residents in zone $i$ to shops in zone $j$. Its basic form may be represented as:

$$T_{ij} = A_i O_i W_j C_{ij}^{-\beta} \tag{8.2}$$

where $T_{ij}$ = the flow of shopping expenditure from the residents of zone $i$ to shops in zone $j$ in a unit time period (e.g. a week or month). $O_i$ = the total shopping expenditure of residents of zone $i$ in the unit time period. In this type of application this is a composite variable comprising the population of zone $i$ ($P_i$) multiplied by the average expenditure per resident of zone $i$ on shopping goods in the unit time period (Thomas and Huggett, 1980: 166). $W_j$ = a generalised measure of the attractiveness of zone $j$ for shopping expenditure, often defined by the amount of retail floorspace in zone $j$. This replaces $M_j$ from equation (8.1). $C_{ij}$ = the cost of travel from $i$ to $j$, and $\beta$ = a distance-decay exponent. Finally,

$$A_i = 1 \left/ \sum_j^n W_j C_{ij}^{-\beta} \right.$$

where $A_i$ = the ratio between the known zonal shopping expenditure ($O_i$) and the sum of the unscaled predicted shopping expenditures leaving zone $i$ for each zone $j$, i.e.

$$A_i = O_i \left/ \left( \sum_j^n O_i W_j C_{ij}^{-\beta} \right) \right.$$

which reduces to

$$A_i = 1 \left/ \left( \sum_j^n W_j C_{ij}^{-\beta} \right) \right.$$

In effect, $A_i$ has replaced the scaling constant $k$ from the simple gravity model.

This model has been widely used for forecasting purposes and in the evaluation of a range of alternative planning policies. Its prime use has been in the prediction of monetary flows ($T_{ij}$) between zones or of retail sales ($\sum_i^n T_{ij}$) in a particular retail centre $j$, given $W_j$, the sizes of competing retail centres. Alternative sites and sizes of development may be considered on a trial-and-error basis to select optimum site and size solutions for individual retail developments (Wilson, 1974:46).

A simple example of the Lakshmanan and Hansen model is shown in Table 8.1 (for a full account see the following subsection). When the predicted sales per square metre in each zone are calculated ($T_{.j}$), these

predictions are not in direct proportion to the size of each zone because other variables are considered in the model. Thus whilst zone B has the greatest retail floorspace, it is zone A, with the highest weekly retail expenditure, that has the largest predicted sales per square metre. Also, although travel costs to zone D are greater from zones A and C, the predicted sales per square metre in D are only just below those for A and B. This may have been altered with a different distance-decay exponent (e.g. $\beta = 2$), which could have disadvantaged D.

Various modifications have improved the notion of optimal location and size of retail centres, for example by predicting the various $W_j$ together with the flows of money (Coelho and Wilson, 1976). Further extensions of the model have been made to allow for competition between the objectives of different groups: consumers, retailers and planners in the urban system, with consumers attempting to maximise welfare, retailers attempting to maximise profit, and planners attempting to influence development by giving different priorities to suburban and central shopping centres (Johnston and Wrigley, 1981:340; Wilson, 1978). This converts the retail gravitation model into a complex function to be optimised subject to the constraints set by planners, consumers and retailers. The influences of these three groups must be included in the equations as weightings, and it has been demonstrated that steady (smooth) changes in these weightings can produce discontinuous or catastrophic changes in the predicted retail structure (Poston and Wilson, 1977). Analysis of these catastrophic changes is discussed in Chapter 11.

Gravity models, and more complex models that attempt to determine how many of the trips leaving a given area or zone will terminate at a particular destination, all consider three basic elements (Sheppard, 1984):

- the number of trips generated by a place;
- the degree to which attributes of a particular destination attract trip-makers, e.g. employment, shops, entertainment – these are site characteristics of a destination;
- the inhibiting effect of distance – this refers to the attributes of a location's situation.

*Table 8.1*   The    Production-Constrained    Gravity
Model

The following data are available on a city of four
administrative regions:

| | Total weekly retail expenditure ($O_i$) (£00 000) | Retail floorspace ($W_i$) ($m^2$ 000 000) |
|---|---|---|
| A | 12 | 8 |
| B | 6 | 9 |
| C | 1 | 2 |
| D | 10 | 7 |

Costs of travel between zones $i$ and $j$ (£) $C_{ij}$:

| | | Zones | | | |
|---|---|---|---|---|---|
| | | A | B | C | D |
| | A | 1 | 2 | 2 | 4 |
| Zones | B | 2 | 1 | 2 | 2 |
| | C | 2 | 2 | 1 | 4 |
| | D | 4 | 2 | 4 | 1 |

(a)  *Step 1*: calculate $A_i$ from

$$A_i = 1 \bigg/ \left[ \sum_i^n W_i C_{ij}^{-\beta} \right]$$

assuming distance decay exponent $\beta = 1$

$A_1 = 1/[W_1/C_{11} + W_2/C_{12} + W_3/C_{13} + W_4/C_{14}]$

$= 1/[8/1 + 9/2 + 2/2 + 7/4]$

$= 1/[8 + 4.5 + 1 + 1.75]$

$= 1/15.25 = 0.066$

$A_2 = 1/[W_1/C_{21} + W_2/C_{22} + W_3/C_{23} + W_4/C_{24}]$

$= 1/[8/2 + 9/1 + 2/2 + 7/2]$

$= 1/[4 + 9 + 1 + 3.5]$

$= 1/17.5 = 0.057$

$A_3 = 1/[W_1/C_{31} + W_2/C_{32} + W_3/C_{33} + W_4/C_{34}]$

$= 1/[8/2 + 9/2 + 2/1 + 7/4]$

$= 1/[4 + 4.5 + 2 + 1.75]$

$= 1/12.25 = 0.082$

*Table 8.1*   (*Continued*)

$A_4 = 1/[W_1/C_{41} + W_2/C_{42} + W_3/C_{43} + W_4/C_{44}]$

$= 1[8/4 + 9/2 + 2/4 + 7/1]$

$= 1/[2 + 4.5 + 0.5 + 7]$

$= 1/14 = 0.071$

(b)  *Step 2*: calculate $T_{ij}$ from

$$T_{ij} = A_i O_i W_j C_{ij}^{-\beta}$$

$T_{11} = A_1 O_1 W_1/C_{11}$

$= 0.066 \times 12 \times 8/1 = 0.066 \times 12 \times 8 = 6.3$

$T_{12} = A_1 O_1 W_2/C_{12}$

$= 0.066 \times 12 \times 9/2 = 0.066 \times 12 \times 4.5 = 3.5$

(c)  *Step 3*: this series of calculations of $T_{ij}$ can be
continued to produce the following matrix of flows of
retail expenditure in the four regions of the city:

| | | A | B | C | D | $O_i$ |
|---|---|---|---|---|---|---|
| | A | 6.3 | 3.5 | 0.8 | 1.4 | 12 |
| | B | 1.4 | 3.1 | 0.3 | 1.2 | 6 |
| $T_{ij} =$ | C | 0.3 | 0.4 | 0.2 | 0.1 | 1 |
| | D | 1.4 | 3.2 | 0.4 | 5.0 | 10 |
| | $T_{.j}$ | 9.4 | 10.2 | 1.7 | 7.7 | 29 |

The sum of the individual flows of expenditure in each row
is equal to the known weekly zonal retail expenditure $O_i$,
thereby indicating the constraint imposed by the scalars
$A_i$.

$T_{.j}$ = the total amount of expenditure at each shopping
centre $j$

(d)  *Step 4*: calculate the predicted sales per square
metre in each zone

$T_{.A}/W_1 = 940\,000/8\,000\,000 = £0.1175$ per $m^2$

$T_{.B}/W_2 = 1020\,000/9\,000\,000 = £0.1133$ per $m^2$

$T_{.C}/W_3 = 170\,000/2\,000\,000 = £0.085$ per $m^2$

$T_{.D}/W_4 = 770\,000/7\,000\,000 = £0.11$ per $m^2$

In the development of gravity models from the early 1960s it has been variants on these three characteristics that have produced different types of model. In particular, three commonly used ones incorporate constraints on either or both production (i.e. number of trips generated, as described above in the Lakshmanan and Hansen model) and attraction. These are discussed below at the start of the section on "Variants of the gravity model". However, first, consideration is given to variations in the third characteristic: the inhibiting effect of distance.

## Distance-Decay Functions

*Mathematical distance-decay functions* are convenient formulations designed to reflect real behaviour or perception and response to distance (Morrill and Kelley, 1970:297). The most simple distance-decay function expresses the relative attractiveness of equivalent opportunities with increasing distance. Therefore a simple measure of attractiveness ($A$) is

$$A = 1/D^{b-1}$$

where, $D =$ distance and $b$ is the exponent. For unit distance $= \{1, 2, 3, 4, 5, 6\}$, $A = \{1, 1/2, 1/3, 1/4, 1/5, 1/6\}$, or a place three times further away than another is one-third as attractive. If

$$A = 1/D^{b-2}$$

then for the same distances $A = \{1, 1/4, 1/9, 1/16, 1/25, 1/36\}$, and so a place three times as far away as another is one-ninth as attractive. This can be contrasted with a simple exponential model, e.g.

$$A = 2/2^D$$

where, for the same distances, $A = \{1, 1/2, 1/4, 1/8, 1/16, 1/32\}$. This represents a constant degree of deterioration in attractiveness whereas the previous example had a rate of change that was greater but constant. Essentially these different functions correspond to different perceptions of distance, and it is important that this is recognised by researchers em-

ploying a model so that an adequate theoretical basis can be applied. In fact, empirical evidence suggests that people's perceptions of distance are more complex than the simple examples given above and need to be represented as combinations of the standard representations shown in Figure 8.1 (e.g. Morrill, 1963).

Figure 8.2 shows the effect of distance on trip-making behaviour in a situation where the attractiveness of destinations is the same everywhere. The vertical axis ($d_{ij}^{-\beta}$) is the size of the distance-decay effect, where $d_{ij}$ is the distance between $i$ and $j$. For larger values of $\beta$, the number of trips decays more rapidly as distance increases, e.g. if $\beta = 0.5$, then for every 100 trips of a distance of 1 mile, 58 trips will be made to destinations 3 miles away, and 33 trips will be

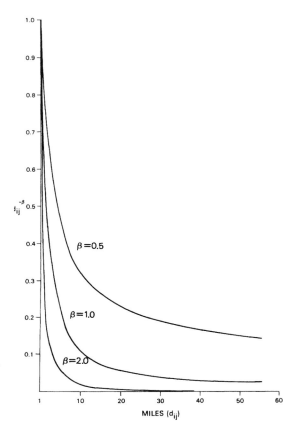

*Figure 8.2*    The Effect of Distance on Trip-Making Behaviour. (*Source*: Sheppard, 1986)

made to destinations 9 miles away (Sheppard, 1986: 102). In practice, distance decay for journey-to-work trips in a city usually looks more like Figure 5.5, as residential zones are often located at a similar distance to places of work. In fact various distance-decay functions have been used by geographers, each of which represents the effect of distance on travel in a different way (Taylor, 1975). Popular ones have been negative exponential functions, power functions and negative powers (Figure 8.1).

Distance-decay functions may be classified into six standard forms, of which the *Pareto model* has been the most common function used in spatial interaction research despite criticism of its over-estimation at shorter distances (Taylor, 1971:223–4). The spatial effects of the operation of these functions are shown in Figure 8.1. The functions are a family of exponential curves of the form:

$$I = k\,e^{-bf(d)}$$

or in linear form

$$\log I = a - bf(d)$$

where $I$ = a measure of interaction intensity over distance $d$, $f(d)$ = a monotonically decreasing function of distance, and $a = \log k$. The family includes the following:

1. the Pareto model

$$\log I = a - b \log d$$

2. the log-normal model

$$\log I = a - b(\log d)^2$$

3. the exponential model

$$\log I = a - b^d$$

4. the normal model

$$\log I = a - bd^2$$

5. the square-root exponential model

$$\log I = a - b\sqrt{d}$$

Geographers have used the concept of distance decay in many ways. They have employed it in developing an understanding of spatial processes accompanying regional economic theory. For example, processes of economic spread and backwash produce developmental change which has a general spatial form reflecting distance decay (Gaile, 1979). In another example, Mackay (1958) used the gravity model to investigate telephonic interaction between pairs of towns in the Canadian provinces of Quebec and Ontario. This clearly revealed the provincial boundary as a major constraint on communications and hence it was the major determinant of an extremely sharp distance-decay effect between the two provinces.

The distance-decay parameter can include not only a "true" friction of distance effect but also a measure of map pattern, e.g. the spatial arrangement of the boundaries of administrative districts commonly employed in gravity model formulations (Cliff et al, 1975a,c). An implication is that, while distance-decay curves may be identified empirically, it is not clear to what extent their form depends on the model structures used to replicate them. Therefore the substantive meaning of the curves' parameters is in doubt (see Sheppard, 1984). This is discussed further in Chapter 9 and in work by Fotheringham and Webber (1980) which considered complex relationships between interaction, mass (population size) and accessibility, and which leant further support to the idea that distance-decay functions are inherently complex (see also Rogerson, 1990; Johnston, 1976a).

## VARIANTS OF THE GRAVITY MODEL

The basic form of the gravity model (see Haynes and Fotheringham, 1984) may be expressed as:

$$T_{ij} = f(V_i, U_j, S_{ij})$$

where $T_{ij}$ = interaction between $i$ and $j$; $V_i$ and $U_j$ = vectors of origin and destination attributes; and $S_{ij}$ = vector of separation attributes. In applying this, modellers have focused on different terms within the equation. In some cases emphasis has been on origin attributes, $V_i$ (termed *origin-specific, production-constrained gravity models*). In others, destinations, $U_j$, are most important (termed *destination-specific, attraction-constrained models*). In *doubly constrained models* there is a balance between the two. These different types are now discussed in turn.

## Production-Constrained Gravity Models

These are used to describe types of interaction where it can be assumed that the total number of flows leaving each zone $i$ is known prior to making a prediction, and so this information can be incorporated into the model design (Table 8.1). From the basic gravity model (equation (8.1) above), the term $M_i$ (usually representing zonal population or the ability of the zone to generate trips) is replaced by the variable $O_i$ which represents the known number of flows commencing in each zone $i$. The value $O_i$ is still assumed to be proportional to a zone's ability to generate flows, but with the following constraint satisfied:

$$\sum_{j}^{n} T_{ij} = O_i$$

The sum of the flows in any row $i$ of the predicted flow matrix must be equal to the total number of flows originating in zone $i$.

The model, as used when dealing with flows of customers to retail centres, takes the form

$$T_{ij} = A_i O_i W_j C_{ij}^{-\beta}$$

This is the same formulation as equation (8.2) described above, developed by Lakshmanan and Hansen.

The main application of this model has been in the

prediction of the amount of expenditure attracted to each shopping centre ($j$) and assessing the impact of planned changes to the size of shopping centres upon the pattern of shopping expenditure.

For example, suppose it is proposed to locate an edge-of-city shopping centre with 4 000 000 m² of retail floorspace in zone D of the hypothetical city analysed in Table 8.1. The resulting predicted changes in retail expenditure are shown in Table 8.2. Comparison of Tables 8.1 and 8.2 reveals that the additional floorspace is likely to generate an extra £2.3 × 10⁵ of expenditure in zone D ((£10.0 − 7.7) × 10⁵), so that retail expenditure in D is exactly the same as total expenditure by residents of D. Expenditure in the other three regions decreases, though to a proportionally smaller extent in A. There are still net inflows of expenditure to zones B and C.

Assessment can also be made of the impact of future changes in the value of the other independent variables in the model equation: for example, considering the effects of changes in consumer expenditure on sales in retail centres or the impact of transportation improvements. The utility of such analyses de-

*Table 8.2*  The Predicted Impact of Additional Retail Floorspace Upon the Pattern of Retail Expenditure

*Problem*: To predict the pattern of retail expenditure when 4 000 000 m² of additional retail floorspace is added to zone D of the hypothetical four-zone city considered in Table 8.1.

$W_j$ now becomes   A     8
                    B     9
                    C     2
                    D    11

Calculations proceed as in Table 8.1 in order to generate a new matrix of flows of retail expenditure:

|          |   | A | B | C | D | $O_i$ |
|----------|---|---|---|---|---|-------|
|          | A | 5.9 | 3.4 | 0.7 | 2.0 | 12 |
|          | B | 1.2 | 2.8 | 0.3 | 1.7 | 6 |
| $T_{ij}=$ | C | 0.3 | 0.3 | 0.2 | 0.2 | 1 |
|          | D | 1.1 | 2.5 | 0.3 | 6.1 | 10 |
|          | $T_{.j}$ | 8.5 | 9.0 | 1.5 | 10.0 | 29 |

pends upon the close correspondence between the model's initial predictions and the observed patterns of retail expenditure flows. So calibration of the model is most important, that is finding the value of the cost exponent that minimises the difference between the observed and predicted flows. The goodness of fit may be improved by adding an exponent, $\lambda$, to $W_j$, the variable for size of shopping centre, so that:

$$T_{ij} = A_i O_i W_j^{\lambda} C_{ij}^{-\beta}$$

This additional exponent refers to the scale economies associated with the size of shopping centre. By making $\lambda$ large, it is assumed that a large shopping centre is relatively more attractive than a small one, that is $W_j^{\lambda}$ increases more rapidly than $W_j$. This may reflect the larger centre's ability to supply a bigger range of goods at lower prices than a small one. The calibration may also involve varying $\lambda$. For example, if $\lambda$ is increased then $C_{ij}^{-\beta}$ decreases more rapidly than $C_{ij}$ increases and the smaller the average trip costs. Alternative ways of dealing with solutions for production-constrained models are dealt with by Crouchley (1987b).

## The Attraction-Constrained Gravity Model

In this model the trip destinations are known and it is the allocation of flows to origins that is of interest. In its commonest form this model is used to assign workers in zone $j$ to residences in zone $i$. The predicted journey-to-work matrix is obtained from

$$T_{ij} = H_j D_j W_i C_{ij}^{-\beta}$$

with notation as for equation (8.2) above plus $D_j$ = the number of jobs available in zone $j$, and $H_j$ = a scaling constant which is calculated for each destination zone to ensure that the following constraint is satisfied:

$$\sum_{i}^{n} T_{ij} = D_j$$

Therefore the total number of journey-to-work trips arriving in zone $j$ must be equal to the number of jobs in that zone.

For any zone $j$, $H_j$ is the ratio between the known number of jobs ($D_j$) and the sum of the unscaled predicted journey-to-work flows arriving in zone $j$ from each zone $i$, i.e.

$$H_j = D_j \bigg/ \left( \sum_{i}^{n} D_j W_i C_{ij}^{-\beta} \right) = 1 \bigg/ \left( \sum_{i}^{n} W_i C_{ij}^{-\beta} \right)$$

Thus, "the attraction-constrained gravity model is a residential location model in the sense that it uses knowledge of the distribution of jobs ($D_j$), the residential attractiveness of each zone ($W_i$), and journey-to-work costs ($C_{ij}$), to assign workers to households in each zone" (Thomas and Huggett, 1980: 148). To this basic model can be added a range of variables, such as house type, income levels, house prices, income available for housing expenditure and the size of the housing stock, in order to make the equations of the residential location models more realistic (Wilson, 1974).

## The Production-Attraction-Constrained Gravity Model

If a model constrains both trip origins and trip destinations then attention can be focused upon the size of the individual flows ($T_{ij}$). This approach has been used to predict journey-to-work movements within urban areas.

In this form of gravity model, the size of flows is predicted from

$$T_{ij} = A_i O_i H_j D_j C_{ij}^{-\beta}$$

Here $A_i$ = scalars to ensure the origin constraint is satisfied, i.e.

$$\sum_{j}^{n} T_{ij} = O_i$$

or the total number of predicted flows originating in

each zone $i$ must be equal to $O_i$, the number of workers living in zone $i$. $H_j$ = scalars to ensure the destination constraint is satisfied, *i.e.*

$$\sum_i^n T_{ij} = D_j$$

or the total number of predicted trips ending in zone $j$ must be equal to $D_j$, the number of jobs in zone $j$. Thus

$$A_i = 1 \bigg/ \left( \sum_j^n H_j D_j C_{ij}^{-\beta} \right) \qquad (8.3)$$

$$H_j = 1 \bigg/ \left( \sum_i^n A_i O_i C_{ij}^{-\beta} \right) \qquad (8.4)$$

The values of $A_i$ and $H_j$ may be obtained by substituting real values of $H_j$ and $A_i$ respectively in equations (8.3) and (8.4) above. This is an iterative procedure, requiring a computer program that can be halted once a predefined level of accuracy has been obtained (see Baxter, 1976). Once determined, the values of $A_i$ and $H_j$ may be used in this model to examine how changes in the values of $O_i$ and $D_j$ affect the predicted pattern of flows, for example as with the establishment of a new industrial estate or a new housing development. A worked example is given by Thomas and Huggett (1980:146–52).

## The Garin–Lowry Model

A major reformulation by Garin (1966) extended the original Newtonian-based gravity model, by incorporating interaction submodels of the gravity type with an iterative procedure (as outlined in the preceding subsection), but distributing all activities at each iteration of the calculation. This reformulation is sometimes referred to as a *combined gravity model*. He also introduced matrix notation for the model and showed the underlying equilibrium inherent in the iterative solution procedure. This model came to be known as the *Garin–Lowry model*, as it incorporated earlier

work by Lowry (1964) which placed constraints on zonal activity densities (Foot, 1981:108–36). As shown in Figure 8.3, in a typical application "the model is first 'calibrated' by adjusting its parameters so as to reproduce as closely as possible an existing urban area; it is then used to stimulate the impact of new basic-employment forecasts or of policy changes" (Berechman and Small, 1988: 1288). It is an allocative model, used to decide where activities will be located in a region, but with links to gravity models and the concept of population potential (see below). The iterative solution has to ensure logical consistency, e.g. that total journey-to-work trips into a zone equal the number of employment opportunities in that zone, and that specified constraints on land use and population density are fulfilled. Given a gain or loss of basic employment, the model will calculate a new equilibrium pattern.

Lowry's (1964) model for the Pittsburgh region was based on the allocation of two types of activity: population and services, linking the basic gravity model with a submodel relating population and services via an economic base mechanism. The model uses economic base theory to generate overall activity levels, that is it uses theory that explains urban and regional growth in terms of a division of employment into basic and non-basic sectors. The basic sector ($B$) includes those industries meeting external or export demand and is seen as a function of national and international forces. The non-basic sector ($S$) includes locally oriented industries servicing the local population ($P$). The economic base relations can be expressed as:

$$E = S + B$$

where $E$ = total employment,

$$P = \alpha E$$

$$S = \beta P$$

where $\alpha$ and $\beta$ are coefficients that can be obtained using regression analysis on observations for a sample of cities or for one city or region over a period of

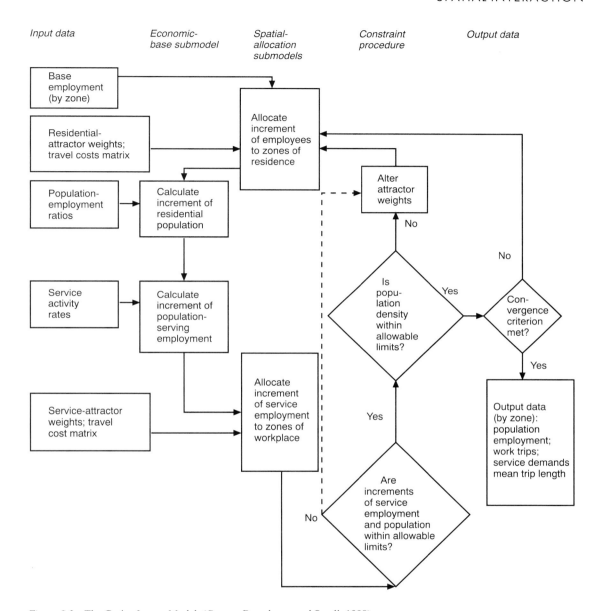

*Figure 8.3*   The Garin–Lowry Model. (*Source*: Berechman and Small, 1988)

time. In this simple theory, growth or decline of population and employment are controlled by changes in the basic sector. The impacts of changes, known as *multipliers*, can be calculated from three economic base equations,

$$E = (1 - \alpha\beta)^{-1} B$$

$$P = \alpha(1 - \alpha\beta)^{-1} B$$

$$S = \alpha\beta(1 - \alpha\beta)^{-1} B$$

A unit increase in $B$ generates $\alpha/(1 - \alpha\beta)$ units of additional local population.

In the Garin–Lowry model, urban activities are allocated to the zones of the urban region using the concepts of *population potential* and *employment potential*, calculated in a series of equations. Population potential is generally defined as a measure of accessibility of a stated number of people to a given location. The term was employed in *social physics* (see Stewart and Warntz, 1968), linking it closely to the gravity model. However, whilst the gravity model deals with separate relationships between pairs of points, population potential considers the influence of a range of points upon a single one. The potential exerted upon point $V_i$ is defined as:

$$V_i = \sum_{j=1}^{k} P_j/d_{ij}$$

where $P_j$ = the population at the $j$th point, $d_{ij}$ = the distance between points $i$ and $j$, and $k$ = the total number of points exerting a potential upon $V_i$.

Therefore the population potential is the sum of the ratios of populations at all points to the distances to those points. Distance $d_{ij}$ may be calibrated by using an exponent to reflect friction of distance. Maps of population potential can be produced to show spatial variations in general accessibility. Potential for other variables may be calculated by substituting these variables for population. The two alternatives most commonly used are purchasing power (giving a measure of market potential or accessibility to customers) and employment.

In the model, population is allocated to zones in proportion to the population potential of each zone, whilst service employment is allocated according to employment potential of the zone. The model includes constraints on maximum densities of population and minimum sizes for clusters of services.

The Garin–Lowry model may be stated in four "equations":

$$P = aE \qquad (8.5)$$

where $P$ = the total population $(P = \sum_j P_j)$, with $P_j$ = the population in region $j$, $a$ = the activity rate, and $E$ = total employment;

$$P_j \propto P \sum_i O_i f^1(C_{ij}) \qquad (8.6)$$

where $O_i$ = the activity or attraction of the origin of interaction $i$, and $f^1(C_{ij})$ = a function relating to the effect of *spatial impedance* in the population (i.e. opposition to flow);

$$S = bP \qquad (8.7)$$

where $S$ = total service employment $(S = \sum_i S_i)$, with $S_i$ = the service employment in region $i$, and $b$ = the population-serving ratio;

$$S_i \propto SD_j f^2(C_{ij}) \qquad (8.8)$$

where $D_j$ = the activity at or attraction of the destination $j$, and $f^2(C_{ij})$ = a function relating to the effect of spatial impedance in the service sector.

These four equations are usually solved using an iterative procedure, though Lowry himself used direct means, neatly summarised by Batty (1981b:183) as shown in Figure 8.4. Early modifications to this model treated location and destination as direct functions of interaction. This approach is illustrated in Figure 8.5 and can be compared with the original depicted in Figure 8.4 (see also Batty, 1976b).

Lowry (1966) applied his basic formulation to a model of labour migration, partly as a macro-adjustment model in which the wage and unemployment characteristics at origin and destination were hypothesised to be the determinants of migration. The model takes the form:

$$M_{ij} = k\left(\frac{U_i W_j L_i L_j}{U_j W_i D_{ij}}\right) = kU_i U_j^{-1} W_j W_i^{-1} L_i L_j D_{ij}^{-1}$$

where $M_{ij}$ = the number of migrants from origin $i$ to destination $j$, $U_i$, $U_j$ = the respective unemployment rates, $W_i$, $W_j$ = the respective hourly manufacturing

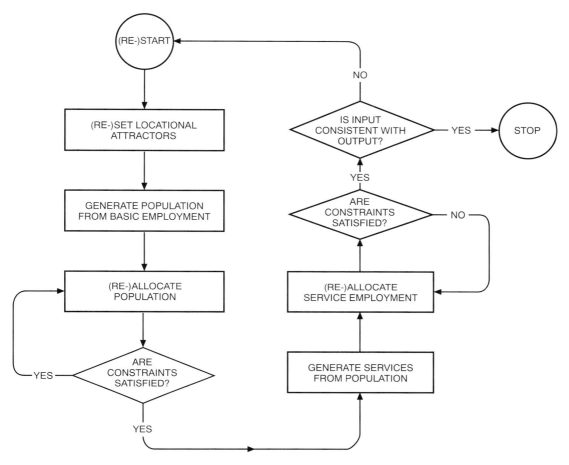

*Figure 8.4*   Solving The Garin–Lowry Model – I. (*Source*: Batty, 1981b: 183)

money wage rates, $L_i$, $L_j$ = the population components of the gravity model, and $k$ = a constant.

Two main weaknesses of this model can be identified (Clark and Ballard, 1980):

1. It is unable to explain much of the economic decision to out-migrate and its regional context (partly because its results provide only limited support for migration being based on relative wage differences).
2. It ignores certain factors crucial to individual decision-making, e.g. employment status, age and industry type.

The main direct alternative to the Lowry model, for use in modelling migration, is *human capital theory* in which individuals are the unit of observation. This has a more complex form, involving calculus, and it focuses attention upon the individual characteristics of the migrant, but it also has two crucial weaknesses:

1. Its empirical formulation is very difficult because it assumes availability of a range of data for individuals.
2. The relationship between the individual and society is not clear.

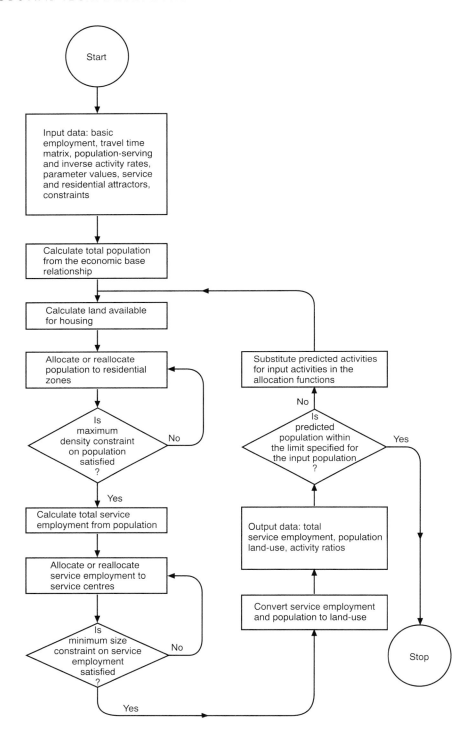

Despite significant extensions to the basic Lowry model, several problems remain. Three principal ones are:

1. Activities can be generated continuously in production as a result of economic growth, but they have to be located in areal units (zones) that have definite holding capacities.
2. The level of aggregation employed. The level chosen can have a profound effect upon the predictive accuracy of the model (e.g. Chan and Yi, 1987).
3. The development of a *general theory of bifurcation*. This refers to systems (such as journey to work in an urban area) characterised by multiple equilibria in which shifts from one equilibrium to another may involve discontinuous jumps, and in which the discontinuities reflect the properties of the system rather than the result of external influences (Yi and Chan, 1988). Analysis and interpretation of such systems are discussed in Chapter 11.

The Garin–Lowry model represented the first generation of urban and sub-regional planning and activity allocation models. Refinements replaced population potential with gravity model approaches or entropy-maximising models discussed below. For other alternatives see Smith (1991) and Fotheringham and Dignan (1984).

## Applying the Garin–Lowry Model

Various forms of model were applied widely in the USA and the UK in the 1960s and early 1970s, many of which were used for predictive purposes. One that was used in several practical applications was a version of Garin's model incorporating constraints on allocation, as described by Batty (1976a:64–79) who referred to it as an activity allocation model or, as formulated for use with retail floorspace in British cities (e.g. March et al, 1971), as a model of urban stocks and activities.

In the UK one of the most well known early

applications was that of a Garin model applied to 29 local authority areas in Central and North-East Lancashire with a total population of nearly 750 000 (Batty, 1976a:ch. 4). The 29 areas were subdivided into 51 zones of similar size in an attempt to overcome problems associated with irregularly shaped administrative areas and wide variation in population density and function. The ratio of basic to total employment in the study area was calculated as 0.5517, with a ratio of inter-zonal to intra-zonal work trips of 0.5059. Use of the model included several aspects typical of urban and regional modelling at that time.

Initially test statistics were examined to determine goodness of fit of the model to reality and then efficient methods developed for finding "best" values for the model's parameters. Trial-and-error methods were used to calibrate the model, focusing on the amount or cost of interaction via the means of the trip length or cost distributions. A fundamental issue was the values given to the intra-zonal time-distances. These were calculated by taking the average time-distance from the centre of gravity of the population distribution of an area to the periphery of the distribution. This was then modified by relating the speed of travel to the density of population. These distances were very sensitive in the model as, especially for a large town, a slight variation in this value could mean a large increase or decrease in the amount of non-basic employment or resident population located in that area (Batty, 1976a:90). Subsequently, additional modifications were made, using external "dummy" sub-areas, to account for movements across the boundaries of the study area.

Having calibrated the model and tested it for goodness of fit, it was then possible to use it predictively for successive five-year periods up to 1990. This raises the issue of whether it is legitimate to develop what is a static model in a predictive and necessarily dynamic context. Can a static model based on the spatial history of a system be expected to perform well predictively in allocating relatively marginal change? There is also the problem of how continuous change over a 30-year period can be adequately represented in a model whose purpose is to project a single locational equilibrium. These and other aspects regarding the

*Figure 8.5*   Solving the Garin–Lowry Model – II

predictive use of the model are discussed by Batty (1976a:92–6) who also lists the formulae used in developing the model as a forecasting tool. He charts the different trajectories that it is possible to project from the model's predictions, notably work-trip and service-trip distributions, changes in population and service employment and migration patterns. The latter are treated implicitly in the model, but three types of migration can be derived from it:

1. Migration that is external to the study area. Changes in basic employment result in people entering or leaving the area, and these changes can be projected independently of the model.
2. Migration that is due to the internal redistribution of basic employment in the study area.
3. Migration that is caused by the changed potential of the study area. Batty (1976a:96) supplies the formula for calculating these migration flows.

In using the model predictively, attention focused on the likely impacts of the proposed establishment of a new town in Central Lancashire. The prediction was for a migration of 30 000 to 40 000 people from North-East Lancashire to the new town, compared with 13 000 if the new town was not developed. However, this ignored likely impacts of the proposed new town upon adjacent areas outside the study area which might have competed with the study area to supply labour to the new town. Set against this was the possible under-prediction of 40 000 employees in basic industry in the new town. The most useful results from the model were the detailed forecasts regarding changes in population and employment in each of the 51 zones in the study area. It is this spatio-temporal component of the model that offered the potential for planners to assess the likely outcomes of particular planning proposals – in this case the impacts of the new town. The model revealed a likely pattern of decentralisation of population and industry from the main town, Preston, with some growth diverted to a sub-regional rival, Blackburn, which was to be more accessible to the proposed new town. In contrast, many parts of North-East Lancashire, an area formerly dominated by the textile industry, were pre-dicted to lose employment and population. This can be seen at a macro-scale, in Figure 8.6, depicting projected migration flows between Central and North-East Lancashire over four five-yearly periods. Migration on the micro-scale, for 51 zones, could also be mapped in conjunction with changing journey-to-work and population potential maps (see Batty, 1976a:106–9). This provided a good basis for further analysis of problems affecting the study area and possible planning strategies to deal with them. Key issues highlighted were new areas of urban sprawl, the scattered nature of development and substantial pockets of urban decay and industrial dereliction.

Two other examples are the application of the model to the location of the proposed third London Airport (Foot, 1981:125–8) and in evaluating impacts of alternative planning scenarios for Venice (Piasentin et al, 1978).

## INTERVENING OPPORTUNITY MODELS

Amongst the most commonly used spatial interaction models are *entropy-maximising models* and *intervening opportunity models*. The basic premise of the latter can be demonstrated with reference to the following simple example. If there are four settlements, a small village (A) and three cities (X, Y and Z), people in A may prefer to shop in city X rather than Y or Z if X is closer and therefore represents an intervening opportunity. If X, Y and Z were all located closer to A, the same preference may still apply if X is still the nearest city to A, as it is *relative* rather than *absolute* distance that is significant in the establishment of intervening opportunities.

This concept was developed by the American sociologist S.A. Stouffer (1940) to explain the pattern of human migration, but has since been applied in studies of commodity flows, shopping trips and traffic flows. His simple idea can be investigated in terms of distortions to the practice of utilising the closest service or set of services. Such distortions may be produced by cultural influences. For example, for Quebec Province, Canada, Mackay (1958) showed that its telephone

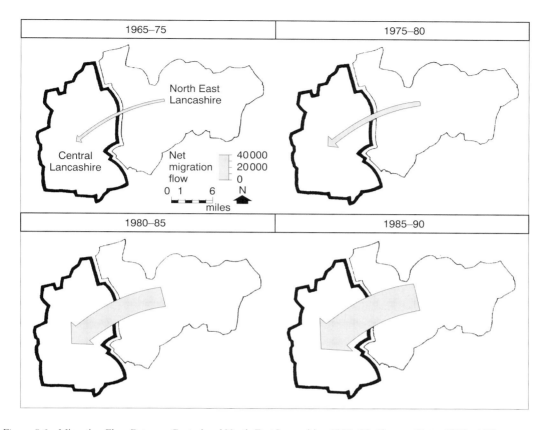

*Figure 8.6*    Migration Flow Between Central and North-East Lancashire, 1965–90. (*Source*: Batty, 1976a: 107)

traffic with the neighbouring province, Ontario, was between one-fifth and one-tenth of that predicted by the basic gravity model, and there was an even more powerful limitation on traffic from Quebec to the USA. This limitation was equivalent to the USA being located up to 50 times further away, and represented a measure of Quebec's isolation produced by cultural, and especially linguistic, barriers.

There are two basic differences between a gravity model and an intervening opportunity model:

1. In the latter the basic characteristics of a destination are measured as the number of opportunities available there.
2. Rather than distance *per se* influencing the chance

of a trip being made, the crucial factor is the number of other opportunities closer to the trip's origin than any particular destination being considered by a traveller, that is the number of intervening opportunities (Stouffer, 1940).

Stouffer's idea was taken up by Schneider (1960) in estimating trip distributions for the Chicago Area Transportation Study, but with a modification for rational choice behaviour in which the probability of a trip-maker stopping at the closest destination is proportional to the number of opportunities there. Therefore the probability of stopping at the next nearest location is dependent on the number of opportunities there and also the probability that the trip-maker did not stop at the previous location. This logic can then be applied to each destination in turn to give a model as follows:

$$P_{ij} = P(\text{trip-maker does not stop at the } (j-1)\text{th closest place})$$

$$- P(\text{trip-maker does not stop at the } j\text{th closest place})$$

$$= e^{-LV(j-1)} - e^{-LV(j)}$$

where $P_{ij}$ = probability of travelling from $i$ to $j$; $L$ = an empirical constant; and $V(j)$ = total number of opportunities to be found at all destinations up to and including the $j$th closest place.

In both the intervening opportunities model and the gravity model the number of trips from $i$ to $j$ increases as the number of opportunities at $j$ increases. The number decreases as the distance between $i$ and $j$ increases. However, both models can only be applied practically in situations where data are available on the observed distribution of trips and on attributes of the destinations. Where such data are absent then the entropy-maximising approach described below may be an alternative.

Pursuing the logic of the intervening opportunities model, the probability of any money from zone $i$ being spent at centre $j$ is:

$$\frac{F_j/d_{ij}^b}{\sum_j F_j/d_{ij}^b} = \frac{F_j d_{ij}^{-b}}{\sum_j F_j d_{ij}^{-b}} = A_i F_j d_{ij}^{-b}$$

where $F_j$ = the floorspace in shopping centre $j$; $d_{ij}$ = the distance from residential area $i$ to centre $j$; $b$ = an exponent; and $A_{ij}$ = the "balancing factor" to ensure that the expenditure leaving zone $i$ for each region $j$ sums to the known total zonal expenditure.

For the basic intervening opportunities model, assuming inelastic demand, a linear objective function can be stated,

$$Z = \sum_{i=1}^{n} p_i d_{ij}$$

where $Z$ = aggregate travel costs, $p_i$ = population of place $i$, and $d_{ij}$ = cost of travel from place $i$ to a service located in place $j$. This assumes that all demand is satisfied by $j$, the nearest service facility to $i$. In reality, though, it is more likely that this facility will satisfy most of the demand, but with small proportions of demand satisfied by more distant facilities. To cater for this, the calculation of the objective function now becomes $Z$ = minimum aggregate travel, or

$$Z = \sum_{i=1}^{n} p_i \sum_{j=1}^{m} d_{ij} \left( v_j \Big/ \sum_{j=1}^{m} v_j \right)$$

where there are $n$ sources of population (demand) and $m$ facilities, and

$$v_j = e^{-b(q-1)} - e^{-bq}$$

with $b$ = constant rate of decline of demand over distance, and $q$ = number of facilities closer to demand point $i$ than is facility $j$, inclusive of $j$. Therefore $(q-1)$ is the equivalent number at facility $(j-1)$.

This allows for overlapping catchment areas, in contrast to the $p$-median problem described in Chapter 7. The degree of overlap depends upon the value of $b$. If $b$ is large then the unsatisfied proportion of demand falls quickly with opportunities encountered. Therefore users will generally travel short distances. Small values of $b$ imply longer distances travelled and larger overlapping catchment areas as in situations where people can afford to be more selective over use of facilities or where quality of facilities varies. It may be possible to estimate the value of $b$ from data on user/consumer choice and travel distances (Hodgart, 1978:29–31). A similar model for elastic demand was developed by Abernathy and Hershey (1971), taking the total number of trips to be dependent on distance or travel time to the nearest facility. The $p$-median problem is a limiting case of this intervening opportunities formulation in which all demand is satisfied by the nearest opportunity or *b* is at a maximum and catchments are deterministic not probabilistic (Hodgart, 1978:31).

## ENTROPY-MAXIMISING MODELS

### Entropy in Thermodynamics, Information Theory and Geography

Several of the limitations in gravity model formulations have been addressed in a set of models developed initially by Alan Wilson (1967, 1970a,b) and based on earlier theoretical work by Jaynes (1957). These models represent a combination of the gravity model's deterministic assumptions and probabilistic elements. They involve maximising the *entropy* of a trip distribution (see Senior, 1979).

Georgescu-Roegen (1971), writing about the application of the entropy law to economic systems, noted that the meaning of entropy varied substantially even within the same domain of intellectual endeavour. Perhaps the main problem over the term's meaning is that it is associated both with the second law of thermodynamics and with the amount of information contained in a probability distribution. This causes confusion, especially as geographers have made use of both of these aspects of entropy, though primarily drawing upon information theory (Webber, 1979).

There are three ways in which entropy can be used by geographers (Chapman, 1977):

1. As a series of indices of variations in population distributions.
2. As an "index of redundancy" in a landscape, defining redundancy in relation to a regular sequence "so that it is possible to predict the land use at place a, for example, from knowledge of the land uses at neighbouring places" (Johnston, 1997:136).
3. As a series of measures of reactions to situations in states of uncertainty.

Essentially it has been the last of these that has been utilised by geographers in spatial interaction models,

building upon the initial work by Wilson, who described entropy as "the most likely state of a system".

The term "entropy" originated in *thermodynamics*, which is the mathematical treatment of the relation of heat to mechanical and other forms of energy. As shown in Table 8.3, there are a number of *laws of thermodynamics*. The concept of entropy is expressed in the second law, in which an increase in the entropy of a system is an increase in system uncertainty. In this sense, entropy is the name given to one of the quantitative elements which determine the thermodynamic condition of a portion of matter, as in the following passage attributed to Clausius:

> A portion of matter at uniform temperature retains its entropy unchanged so long as no heat passes to or from it, but if it receives a quantity of heat without change of temperature, the entropy is increased by an amount equal to the ratio of the mechanical equivalent of the quantity of the heat to the absolute measure of temperature on the thermodynamic scale. The entropy of a system ... is

*Table 8.3* The "Laws" of Thermodynamics

*Zeroth Law*
If two systems are each in thermal equilibrium with a third system then they are in thermal equilibrium with each other. (This statement is assumed implicitly in every measurement of temperature.)

*First Law of Thermodynamics*
The total energy of a thermodynamic system remains constant although it may be transformed from one form to another. (This is a statement of the principle of conservation of energy.)

*Second Law of Thermodynamics*
Heat can never pass spontaneously from a body at a lower temperature to one at a higher temperature (Clausius).
OR
No process is possible whose only result is the abstraction of heat from a single heat reservoir and the performance of an equivalent amount of work (Kelvin–Planck).

*Third Law of Thermodynamics*
The entropy of a substance approaches zero as its temperature approaches zero.

always increased by any transport of heat within the system; hence the entropy of the universe tends to a maximum.

As a layer of hot water is added to a body of cold water, and the hot and cold water molecules gradually mix, so the entropy increases. Therefore thermodynamic entropy is related to the most probable configuration of elements within a given system. In thermal processes, entropy is a quantity that measures the extent to which the energy of a system is available for conversion to work. For example, if a system undergoing an infinitesimal reversible change takes in a quantity of heat ($dQ$) at absolute temperature, $T$, its entropy ($S$) is increased by $dS$, where $dS = dQ/T$. For an *adiabatic process* (one without interchange of heat with the surroundings), entropy remains constant during the process.

If a thermodynamic system is considered on the micro-scale, equilibrium is associated with the distribution of molecules that has the greatest probability of occurring, that is with the greatest degree of disorder. Applying this notion, the increase in entropy in a closed system to a maximum at equilibrium is interpreted in statistical mechanics (the theoretical prediction of the behaviour of a macroscopic system by applying statistical laws to the behaviour of component particles) as the consequence of the trend from a less probable to a more probable state. A process in which no change in entropy occurs is said to be *isentropic*.

*Information theory* also utilises the concept of entropy (Shannon and Weaver, 1963), employing it to refer to the distribution of elements across a set of possible states. The distribution may vary from complete certainty, when all the elements are in the same state, to uncertainty, when the elements are equally distributed through all possible states, so that prediction of the location of any new element is most difficult.

A geographical application of this information theory concept of entropy is given by Gould (1972). He considered the probable locations of 20 individuals in an urban area. The individuals live at various distances from their workplaces in the city centre. The journey-to-work distances vary depending on availability of funds for

transportation (which can be regarded as a measure of energy). Funds (energy) vary amongst the 20 individuals and so act as a constraint on the spatial configurations of residences with respect to workplaces that they can adopt. If the total distance moved from residences to city centre is 42 miles ($\sum d_i = 42$) then Figure 8.7a and b, respectively, represent a highly unlikely configuration and a likely configuration of residences. Likelihood in this situation may be calculated from

$$W = \frac{n!}{\prod_i n_i!}$$

where $n$ = total number of individuals, $n_i$ = number of individuals who live at a given distance ($i$) from their workplace, $\prod_i$ = the product of the factorial numbers for each value of $n_i$, and $W$ = total number of distinct ways that a specified allocation of individuals to distance bands can occur.

Therefore if $n = 5$, and energy constraints dictate that three of the five must live 2 miles and the other two live 7 miles from work, then $W = 5!/(3!2!) = 10$. So there are 10 ways that the five individuals can be arranged to fulfil the energy constraints (Haggett et al, 1977:40–1). In the example shown in Figure 8.7a, $W = 7.8 \times 10^8$. This would seem to be a vast number of different arrangements, but it is several orders of magnitude smaller than the likely state depicted in Figure 8.7b, where $W = 5.9 \times 10^{12}$. So, in terms of frequency, a situation with most individuals residing near their workplace has a greater chance of occurring. This can be represented as a negative exponential function,

$$P_j = P_0 \, e^{-bj}$$

where $P_j$ = number of individuals living at distance $j$ from a focus (such as a factory or city centre), $P_0$ = number of individuals in the distance band nearest to the focus, and $b$ = a function of the energy available to each individual. If the energy decreases, so does $b$.

Shannon's (1948) general formula for measuring the amount of entropy in any set of probabilities ($H$) is:

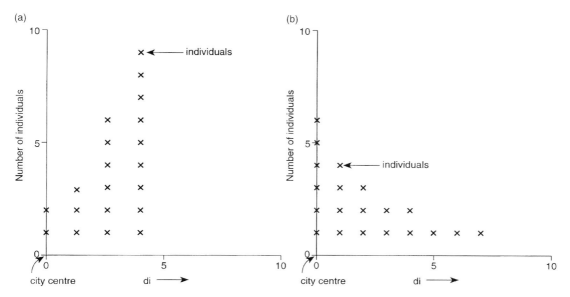

*Figure 8.7*    An Example of the Information Theory Concept of Entropy
(a) Highly unlikely configuration; (b) likely configuration. (Based on Gould, 1972)

$$H = \sum_i P_i \ln (1/P_i) = -P_i \ln (P_i)$$

where $\sum_i^n P_i = 1$, $P_i$ = the probability of event $i$ occurring, and ln is the natural logarithm. This was re-expressed by Marchand (1972) as:

$$H(i) = -P_i \log P_i$$

where $H(i)$ = the entropy, or global information, of a message $i$, and $P_i$ = the probability of the message $i$.

When $P$ tends to 0 or 1, entropy tends to 0; therefore there is no uncertainty when we are sure that an experience will have ($P = 1$) or not have ($P = 0$) a given outcome.

## Wilson's Entropy-Maximising Model

Wilson's work on flows of people and goods in cities treated movements of people and objects in the manner that particles in gases were treated in statistical mechanics "using grand canonical ensembles and distinguishing them by origin and destination as 'types' and by origin–destination pairs as 'states'" (Wilson, 1984:205). The result was the formulation of his *entropy maximising spatial interaction model*. This was a macro-geographic aggregative approach, the success of which has been the ease with which it has been possible to use it through aggregating the neoclassical models of consumers and producers. It has also been applied to the analysis of urban population density gradients.

Wilson modelled the journey to work in urban areas, dividing the city into zones of residence and employment, with interaction between zones being measured through an analysis of trip origins and trip destinations. The model examines all probabilities of trips, the trips being subject to constraints which make some journeys more likely than others. Thus Wilson's initial use of entropy was in connection with matrices depicting flows. His basic approach is illustrated in the following situation: Consider a known number of trips originating in a residential area with places of work as their destination. Given that there are a large number of possible single destinations for the trips, there is a degree of uncertainty in this flow pattern. There are three states of this system of flows:

- the *macro-state*, which comprises the number of commuters at each origin and the numbers of jobs at each destination;
- the *meso-state*, which comprises a particular flow pattern, e.g. from one "zone" to another, but with exact destinations unknown;
- the *micro-state*, in which known movements from or to a zone are known.

The relationships between macro-, meso- and micro-states are summarised in Figure 8.8.

Wilson's analysis of these flows employed what he termed entropy-maximising procedures to establish that particular meso-state with the largest number of micro-states associated with it (in which there is greatest uncertainty about the micro-state of the system). It is then possible to use this situation in model-building by testing the hypothesis that the situation of entropy maximisation conforms with reality. If this conformity does not exist it is possible to build in constraints, for example travel costs or variations in the type of commuter, with the overall aim being to describe the most likely overall system of flows from the information available. This modelling can then be utilised in planning applications, primarily for forecasting different components of complex flows within an urban or regional context, for example as applied in West Yorkshire by Wilson et al (1977). For examples of its use with other matrices see Johnston and Pattie (1993) and Wilson and Bennett (1985).

Entropy-maximising procedures share with gravity models the intention of predicting a trip matrix ($\{T_{ij}\}$):

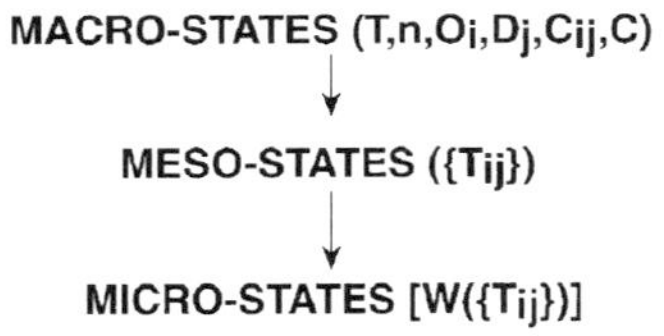

**MACRO-STATES (T,n,O$_i$,D$_j$,C$_{ij}$,C)**

↓

**MESO-STATES ($\{T_{ij}\}$)**

↓

**MICRO-STATES [W($\{T_{ij}\}$)]**

*Figure 8.8*   The Relationships Between Macro-, Meso- and Micro-States

$$\sum_i^n \sum_j^n T_{ij} = T \qquad (8.9)$$

where $T$ = the number of people travelling to work each day, and $n$ = the number of areal units (zones or regions). The values of both $T$ and $n$ are known prior to prediction, and these values may be considered to be a macro-state description of the journey-to-work system. Equation (8.9) represents the constraint that the sum over the elements, $T_{ij}$, in any predicted trip matrix, must equal the total number of trip-makers, $T$. A large number of different trip matrices may satisfy this constraint. These may be termed *meso-state descriptions* of the journey-to-work system. For example, if $n = 3$ and $T = 9$, one feasible trip matrix is

$$T_{11}(= 1) + T_{12}(= 1) + T_{13}(= 1)$$
$$+ T_{21}(= 1) + T_{22}(= 1) + T_{23}(= 1)$$
$$+ T_{31}(= 1) + T_{32}(= 1) + T_{33}(= 1) = 9$$

and another is:

$$T_{11}(= 8) + T_{12}(= 1) + T_{13}(= 0)$$
$$+ T_{21}(= 0) + T_{22}(= 0) + T_{23}(= 0)$$
$$+ T_{31}(= 0) + T_{32}(= 0) + T_{33}(= 0) = 9$$

To select a particular meso-state, the probabilistic notion of entropy can be employed, in which the entropy ($W$) of any feasible meso-state ($\{T_{ij}\}$) is determined by

$$W(\{T_{ij}\}) = \frac{T!}{\prod_i^n \prod_j^n T_{ij}!}$$

where $T!$ = the factorial number for the total number of trips (i.e. the product of all the numbers from one to the number $T$) and $\prod$ = the product of all the factorial numbers for each value $T_{ij}$. Therefore, for the first trip matrix described above,

$$W(\{T_{ij}\}) = 9!/(1! \times 1! \times \ldots \times 1!)$$

$$= (9 \times 8 \times 7 \times 6 \times 5 \times 4 \times 3 \times 2 \times 1)/1$$

$$= 362\,880$$

and for the second trip matrix (remember that 0! is *defined* as 0! = 1),

$$W(\{T_{ij}\}) = 9!/(8! \times 1! \times 0! \times \ldots \times 0!)$$

$$= 362\,880/40\,320$$

$$= 9$$

The entropy formula counts the number of micro-states that it is possible to form from a given set of meso-state trip numbers. The term "entropy maximisation" indicates that the predicted trip matrix is "the particular meso-state description for which $W$ takes on a maximum value" (Thomas and Huggett, 1980: 156), that is it is the set of trip numbers ($\{T_{ij}\}$) where the $T$ trip-makers arrange themselves among the $n^2$ journey-to-work routes in the greatest number of ways. So the entropy-maximising solution maximises the $T$ individuals' freedom to choose from those available journey-to-work routes. Therefore the entropy-maximising solution can be treated as being the most likely trip matrix.

If $T$ and $n$ are the only macro-state constraints on $W$ then the entropy-maximising trip matrix is the meso-state in which all values of $T_{ij}$ are equal, i.e. $T_{ij} = T/n^2$. However, in most analyses of journeys to work, other information is available which introduces greater complexity: for example, there may be information on macro-states in the form of the number of workers ($\{O_i\}$) living in each of the $n$ regions and the number of jobs ($\{D_j\}$) in each region. The former represents an origin constraint and the latter a destination constraint, i.e.

$$\sum_{j}^{n} T_{ij} = O_i \quad \text{and} \quad \sum_{i}^{n} T_{ij} = D_j$$

Incorporation of these two simple constraints

changes the entropy-maximising solution by limiting the number of meso-state trip matrices that satisfy the macro-state descriptions. The entropy-maximising solution can be obtained arithmetically by substituting each of the feasible trip matrices in equation (8.9) above. The inclusion of the origin and destination constraints has the effect of reducing entropy, that is reducing the number of micro-states or behavioural choices that are assumed for the $T$ trip-makers.

For example, if $n = 3$ and $T = 9$ are the only macro-state descriptions available then many thousands of meso-state trip matrices can satisfy them. However, when the constraints specified in Table 8.4

*Table 8.4* Entropy Maximisation for Feasible Trip Matrices with Origin and Destination Constraints

$n = 3$; $T = 9$

$O_i$ = distribution of workers

$D_j$ = distribution of jobs

$T_{ij}$ = feasible trip matrix

(a) $W = 7560$

|  | | *A* | *B* | *C* | $O_i$ |
|---|---|---|---|---|---|
| Zones | A | 2 | 4 | 0 | 6 |
|  | B | 0 | 0 | 1 | 1 |
|  | C | 1 | 1 | 0 | 2 |
| $D_j$ | | 3 | 5 | 1 | 9 |

(b) $W = 15120$

|  | | *A* | *B* | *C* | $O_i$ |
|---|---|---|---|---|---|
| Zones | A | 1 | 4 | 1 | 6 |
|  | B | 1 | 0 | 0 | 1 |
|  | C | 1 | 1 | 0 | 2 |
| $D_j$ | | 3 | 5 | 1 | 9 |

(c) $W = 1512$

|  | | *A* | *B* | *C* | $O_i$ |
|---|---|---|---|---|---|
| Zones | A | 0 | 5 | 1 | 6 |
|  | B | 1 | 0 | 0 | 1 |
|  | C | 2 | 0 | 0 | 2 |
| $D_j$ | | 3 | 5 | 1 | 9 |

(d) $W = 15120$

|  | | *A* | *B* | *C* | $O_i$ |
|---|---|---|---|---|---|
| Zones | A | 2 | 3 | 1 | 6 |
|  | B | 1 | 0 | 0 | 1 |
|  | C | 0 | 2 | 0 | 2 |
| $D_j$ | | 3 | 5 | 1 | 9 |

are added then $W$ is reduced significantly: by a factor of 24 in Table 8.4b and d.

A further constraint that can be introduced is one relating to cost, referring to a matrix $\{C_{ij}\}$ representing the cost of a journey to work starting in region $i$ and ending in region $j$. Furthermore, a value ($C$) may be calculated representing the amount of money available to all $T$ trip-makers for expenditure on the daily journey to work, where

$$C = \sum_i^n \sum_j^n T_{ij} C_{ij}$$

This translates the cost constraints into the form that the sum of the products of each journey multiplied by the cost of that journey must equal the total available expenditure on journey-to-work trips ($C$). Given the application of this constraint as well as the origin and destination constraints, it is possible to make a statement about the degree of confidence of the actual occurrence of the trip patterns ($\{T_{ij}\}$) contained in the entropy-maximising solution, or

$$\max L\,[\max W(\{T_{ij}\})]$$

$$= \frac{\text{number of micro-states associated with the entropy-maximising trip matrix}}{\text{total number of micro-states associated with all feasible trip matrices}}$$

where $\max L$ = the likelihood of the entropy-maximising trip matrix, $[\max W(\{T_{ij}\})]$.

The addition of constraints can be demonstrated to increase the likelihood that the entropy-maximising trip matrix actually occurs in reality (Thomas, 1977).

For example, if the matrix of trip costs shown in Table 8.5 is added to the feasible trip matrices given in Table 8.4 then the constraint can be interpreted as

$$[(T_{11} \times C_{11}) + (T_{12} \times C_{12}) + (T_{13} \times C_{13})$$
$$+ (T_{21} \times C_{21}) + (T_{22} \times C_{22}) + (T_{23} \times C_{23})$$
$$+ (T_{31} \times C_{31}) + (T_{32} \times C_{32}) + (T_{33} \times C_{33})] = C$$

When this calculation is performed for the four matrices in Table 8.4, (a) and (d) are the only two feasible solutions ($C = £9$).

The equations that predict the set of values $\{T_{ij}\}$, which maximise the value of $W$, may be found using complex Lagrangian multipliers (see Wilson and Kirkby, 1975), which are a mathematical device for finding the maximum of any function, subject to a series of constraints. For any city divided into $n$ zones, $T_{ij}$ is predicted from

$$T_{ij} = O_i A_j D_j B_j\, e^{-\beta C_{ij}} \qquad (8.10)$$

where

$$A_i = 1 \left/ \left( \sum_j^n B_j D_j\, e^{-\beta C_{ij}} \right) \right.$$

and

$$B_j = 1 \left/ \left( \sum_i^n A_i O_i\, e^{-\beta C_{ij}} \right) \right.$$

The value given to $\beta$ must maximise the entropy and satisfy known values of the constraints. Its value approximates to the reciprocal of the average cost ($\overline{C}$) of a work trip within the study area, i.e. $\hat{\beta} \simeq 1/\overline{C}$, where $\overline{C} = C/T$.

The sets of values for the scalars $\{A_i\}$ and $\{B_i\}$

Table 8.5 Entropy Maximisation for Feasible Trip Matrices with Origin, Destination and Cost Constraints

$C_{ij}$ = cost of travelling from region $i$ to region $j$
$C_{ij}$ = £10

| | | Zones | | |
|---|---|---|---|---|
| | | A | B | C |
| Zones | A | 0 | 1 | 3 |
| | B | 1 | 0 | 1 |
| | C | 3 | 1 | 0 |

play the same role as in the doubly constrained gravity model. An iterative computer program to find values for $A_i$, $B_j$ and $\beta$ which both satisfy the three constraints and maximise the value of entropy, $W$, is given by Baxter (1976). In effect therefore, entropy-maximising models may represent alternative versions of linear programming models of residential location.

Following Wilson's pioneering work, the notion of optimising entropy, subject to various spatial and locational constraints, was included in broad theories of non-linear optimisation, especially for transport problems (see Williams et al, 1990; Wilson et al, 1981). Specific applications disaggregated the urban models, providing formal links to population density, urban rent models and the micro-economic theory of housing markets. From the initial work on entropy maximisation new methods for estimating the structures of non-linear models have been incorporated into dynamic frameworks based on catastrophe, bifurcation and chaos theories (see Chapter 11).

Webber (1977) took the complex subject of entropy further in his identification of an *entropy-maximising paradigm* which is applicable to:

- location models – the probability of an individual being in a particular place at a particular time;
- interaction models – the probability of a particular trip occurring at a particular time;
- joint location and interaction models.

The paradigm essentially focuses upon aggregate social relations to give answers to "short-run operational problems" (Webber, 1977:266) by examining information provided at what Wilson (1977) described as the meso-scale. Here "answers" can clearly be equated with "planner's needs", but Webber recognised the variability of economic systems which can alter the nature of the constraints and region under consideration. Therefore he set a research task for "entropists" (Webber, 1977:266):

1. To identify constraints which operate upon urban systems, which is partly an economic problem.
2. To deduce some facets of the economic relations among the individuals within the system.

3. To construct a theory explaining the origins of the constraints.

In this way the paradigm can be used in the sense of a model for forecasting. It may also be a hypothesis, in that to understand flows the key constraints must be explained. Webber saw this explanatory role as the ultimate aim and so sought to carry studies of entropy beyond macro-geographic descriptions.

Although entropy-maximising procedures were used initially to produce maximum likelihood estimates of traffic flows, they were also used in the 1980s to study spatial variations in voting behaviour. In these applications entropy maximisation provides maximum likelihood estimates of the values for the empty cells of an $l \times m \times n$ matrix, for which the marginal totals only are known. The procedures followed in this approach are described by Johnston and Pattie (1991); see also Johnston et al, (1984) and Johnston and Hay (1983).

## Further Developments in Entropy-Maximising Models

In summarising the "Wilson family" of entropy-maximising models, Pooler (1994a:19) listed eight models, of which only the two production-constrained members are truly derivable from entropy maximisation. He also highlighted problems in estimating the total cost in these models, such as the fact that measurement and survey errors may easily yield a total cost figure ($C$) that is outside the relatively narrow range allowed by the origin/destination conditions (Haynes and Phillips, 1987).

Pooler (1994a:21; 1994b) stated that it is possible to extend the basic family of constrained spatial interaction models by considering relaxed models in which the marginals of the predicted matrix are not constrained to match exact totals in the usual way, but are constrained to lie in a specified range of values. For example, this approach replaces

$$\sum_j T_{ij} = O_i \qquad \text{where } j = 1, \ldots, n$$

and

$$\sum_i T_{ij} = D_j \qquad \text{where } i = 1, \ldots, m$$

with

$$O_i^{\text{L}} \leqslant \sum_j T_{ij} \leqslant O_i^{\text{U}} \qquad \text{where } i = 1, \ldots, m$$

and

$$D_j^{\text{L}} \leqslant \sum_i T_{ij} \leqslant D_j^{\text{U}} \qquad \text{where } j = 1, \ldots, n$$

where L and U are lower and upper bounds on the marginal totals and are specified *a priori*.

Therefore it is possible to have three different types of model:

1. *production-constrained, attraction-relaxed model*, where $O_i$ is constrained in the usual way, but $D_j$ is allowed to lie in a range $(D_j^{\text{L}}, D_j^{\text{U}})$;
2. *production-relaxed, attraction-constrained model*, where $O_i$ is allowed to lie in a range $(O_i^{\text{L}}, O_i^{\text{U}})$;
3. *doubly relaxed models*, that is *production-attraction relaxed-models*.

With these relaxed models, the researcher maintains some degree of control over the ranges of values on the origins and destinations while, in a production-attraction-unconstrained model, no consistency is maintained in the predicted inflow or outflow totals. Furthermore, the travel cost constraint can be relaxed in the calibration process:

$$C^L \leqslant \sum_i \sum_j T_{ij} C_{ij} \leqslant C^{\text{U}}$$

where $i = 1, \ldots, m$ and $j = 1, \ldots, n$.

The model travel cost is constrained to lie in a range of $C^{\text{L}}$ to $C^{\text{U}}$ rather than to match exactly an observed travel cost. The range reflects theoretical or hypothetical *a priori* estimates of the total travel cost in the system. The seven-member family of relaxed models is shown in Table 8.6. The last of these, the totally relaxed model, has the values of $O_i$, $D_j$ and $C$ unknown *a priori*. Further details, including extensions involving an information-minimising approach, are given by Pooler (1993, 1994a, b) and Roy (1987).

An alternative approach is the use of a *multinomial logit model* (see "Logistic, logit and probit models" in Chapter 6). This focuses on individual spatial choice, that is on discrete choices made by individual travellers rather than on aggregate trip data. Logit models are calibrated with disaggregate, individual-level data using maximum likelihood methods. They work best if the focus is the understanding of the spatial choice process rather than the forecasting of flows. However, logit models were not developed originally in a spatial context and hence carry certain problems that need to be addressed when they are applied to spatial data (Fotheringham and O'Kelly, 1989:74–8):

1. The logit method assumes an optimising strategy on behalf of travellers, whereas it is believed that the spatial decision-making process is hierarchical.
2. The independence from irrelevant alternatives is inherent.
3. It is not possible in logit models to increase the probability of selecting an existing destination when a new alternative is added to the choice set.
4. The nested logit approach is a viable interaction modelling strategy only when the composition of spatial choice clusters as perceived by trip-makers is identifiable by the modeller. Such information is not normally available.

## EVALUATING SPATIAL INTERACTION MODELS

### Limitations

The development of mathematical models of urban structure was intended to present a more abstract approach to spatial structures in order to produce plans for improving efficiency and therefore "wealth". The models assumed that spatial dimensions of urban structure could stand in relative isolation from any

*Table 8.6*   Sets of Constraints for the Family of Relaxed Interaction Models

| | Cost constrained | Cost relaxed |
|---|---|---|
| Production–attraction constrained | 0. $\sum_i T_{ij} = O_i$ <br><br> $\sum_i T_{ij} = D_j$ <br><br> $\sum_i \sum_j T_{ij} C_{ij} = C$ | 1. $\sum_i T_{ij} = O_i$ <br><br> $\sum_i T_{ij} = D_j$ <br><br> $C^L \leq \sum_i \sum_j T_{ij} C_{ij} \leq C^U$ |
| Origin relaxed–production constrained | 2. $O_i^L \leq \sum_i T_{ij} \leq O_i^U$ <br><br> $\sum_i T_{ij} = D_j$ <br><br> $\sum_i \sum_j T_{ij} C_{ij} = C$ | 3. $O_i^L \leq \sum_i T_{ij} \leq O_i^U$ <br><br> $\sum_i T_{ij} = D_j$ <br><br> $C^L \leq \sum_i \sum_j T_{ij} C_{ij} \leq C^U$ |
| Production constrained–destination relaxed | 4. $\sum_i T_{ij} = O_i$ <br><br> $D_j^L \leq \sum_i T_{ij} \leq D_j^U$ <br><br> $\sum_i \sum_j T_{ij} C_{ij} = C$ | 5. $\sum_i T_{ij} = O_i$ <br><br> $D_j^L \leq \sum_i T_{ij} \leq D_j^U$ <br><br> $C^L \leq \sum_i \sum_j T_{ij} C_{ij} \leq C^U$ |
| Origin–destination relaxed | 6. $O_i^L \leq \sum_i T_{ij} \leq O_i^U$ <br><br> $D_j^L \leq \sum_i T_{ij} \leq D_j^U$ <br><br> $\sum_i \sum_j T_{ij} C_{ij} = C$ | 7. $O_i^L \leq \sum_i T_{ij} \leq O_i^U$ <br><br> $D_j^L \leq \sum_i T_{ij} \leq D_j^U$ <br><br> $C^L \leq \sum_i \sum_j T_{ij} C_{ij} \leq C^U$ |

$0 =$ Traditional model

*Source*: Pooler (1994a:23).

underlying framework, and that social goals of efficiency and equity could be obtained by manipulating the spatial characteristics utilised in the models. Batty (1982a) described these assumptions as unrealistic and naive, but regarded them as ones that have been relaxed over time as planners have sought to develop new forms of model – for a more recent discussion, with examples, see Anselin and Madden (1990).

The fundamental limitation of gravity and entropy-maximising models is that they fail to make an adequate representation of the behavioural process that leads to individuals selecting a particular journey to work. The models are aggregate ones, averaging out user behaviour. Therefore they stress group behaviour rather than

individual behaviour and in so doing make unrealistic assumptions. For example, Sayer (1976) contended that the models imply individuals select the locations of home and work simultaneously whereas, in reality, such decisions occur separately, and involve qualitative assessments that are beyond the models' compass.

Partly because of problems of validation and limited data availability, initial models were macro-scale and focused on traffic flows and urban land use, essentially dealing with a narrow range of planning problems. A lack of theory behind such models was a limitation too, though both this and problems of scale have been addressed subsequently. Batty (1982a) argues that modellers were too concerned with technical issues rather than with policy and were not sufficiently interested in whether their models reached beyond the design stage. Over-simplification and lack of ability to deal with important non-quantitative considerations undoubtedly limited their application initially.

The main weakness of basic gravity models is that the equations utilised are deduced from sets of propositions that relate to average descriptions of aggregate behaviour rather than from a theory of individual trip-making behaviour (Webber, 1984). This reflects a fundamental characteristic of the Newtonian analogy which relies on metaphysical statements about the nature of group action and so does not reduce to any causal statement at the individual level (Sheppard, 1978). Hence any attempt to relate gravity models to the impact of flow patterns upon individuals is unlikely to yield satisfactory results. The reliance upon aggregate data means that information is lost, though it must be remembered that frequently aggregate data are all that are available or perhaps disaggregated data are simply too massive a dataset to use. The nature of available data for spatial interaction models has always been a weakness, though, usually in terms of the size and shape of areal units, the number of transport modes covered, the accuracy of commodity classification and sample size (Hay, 1981). Two key problems with respect to aggregation have been identified:

1. If only spatially aggregated data are available, what are the most appropriate models to use to test specific theories?
2. If data are available in disaggregate form, but are too numerous to handle, what are the best forms of aggregation open to the spatial modeller?

These problems have been of particular concern to those examining the aggregation of trip-flow, origin–destination data of the type used in gravity models. Two particular problems relate to assumptions regarding costs and variations in the size of areal units.

Firstly, gravity models incorporate a cost element, though data are rarely available to calculate costs accurately, and so researchers generally assume that costs are proportionate to distance. The limitations of this assumption may be compounded. Establishing intra-zonal distances may be problematic, and incorrect estimations of this factor may lead to inaccuracies in prediction of flows.

Secondly, as referred to in the second section on "Limitations . . ." in Chapter 4, variations in the size and shape of areal units can play a major role in distorting analysis based on data pertaining to these units. In gravity models the influence of the areal units is crucial, as their number, size and shape all determine the values of the independent variables within the gravity model equations. For example, zonal data do not provide unbiased estimates of mean distances travelled if those estimates are derived using interzonal flows and centres of masses of zones for distance computations. Systematic aggregation procedures generally produce better results than do random methods (Putman and Chang, 1989).

The problem of defining an optimum regional system for gravity model applications has been considered by several researchers. One solution for which computer routines have been developed is the grouping of areal units into larger "regions" to produce a more aggregated observed matrix in which the pattern of flows meets a defined criterion (e.g. Masser and Brown, 1975). For example, one suggestion is that a regional system should have at least 85 per cent of the flows occurring between regions and less than 15 per cent of flows within regions (Broadbent, 1970).

Commenting on the entropy-maximising model, Hay (1981) argued that its ability to explain "real-world systems" is limited, partly because the constraints included in the model are really results of the system itself. For example, total transport cost expended is both a constraint and a consequence of the system (Hay, 1979b). He also argued that comparisons between model solutions and reality are problematic because use of correlation coefficients and significance tests for this purpose are not legitimate: "the data are not sample data, the individual cell values are not independent and it is possible to have a high $r^2$ even when the model grossly misestimates the flows" (Hay, 1981:370).

A major weakness of much of the modelling, supposedly intended for use in the solution of planning problems, is that very few of them have been used in positive plan-making. Their inability to include crucial political and social factors that are not very conducive to mathematical formulation has tended to limit the models' use to that of conditional prediction. This has taken the form of broad indicators of the impact of intended large-scale facilities such as new towns, airports and transport systems. The 1970s notion that computer models were of vital importance to planners has been replaced by a more jaundiced view of the products of such models. Instead, computers have become the source of geographic information, to be handled in a variety of ways, and not just a "number crunching" modelling machine. This changing use of computers is considered further in Chapter 11.

It is now recognised that the models popularised in the 1960s represented a narrow conception of the urban system. They focused upon distinct land uses via measurable economic and demographic activities, and located these activities in spatial units which were usually census tracts. Gravitational analogues were central to this work which tended to differentiate between comprehensive models, dealing with interactions between two or more sectors/activities of the system, and partial or single-activity models. The Lowry model for Pittsburgh represented the former whilst Lakshmanan and Hansen's for Baltimore represented the latter. Batty (1989) notes a lack of emphasis upon optimising in these models and points to their essentially static character and to the disillusionment that occurred in the 1970s, as boom turned to recession, and "urban models could no longer inform policy-makers about the most important questions they had begun to ask". Moreover, it was recognised that the models were based on the assumption that observed behaviour represents revealed preferences, thereby largely ignoring the fact that travel behaviour also reflects constraints on action (Sheppard, 1980, 1981). This means that models founded on past interaction patterns can completely overlook important issues of social equity.

The range of spatial interaction models developed in the 1960s, especially the singly constrained types, can also be considered as location models in that they

dealt with important locational variables. However, Clarke and Wilson (1989) identify as a weakness in these models the lack of an attempt to include important geographical variables. Indeed, they had the same basic weakness as classical central place theory in that they took a number of structural variables as given. Some of the chief advances in modelling since 1970 have involved attempts to rectify these limitations and to link mathematical models to the development of theory. The advance has been illustrated in work on retailing in which a dynamic element has been added to the singly constrained spatial interaction model, enabling underlying economic and social structures to be included in the model (Putman, 1983). This approach has been extended to a number of other situations broadly related to spatial interaction, such as crop production to markets (Wilson and Birkin, 1987), industrial production to markets (Birkin and Wilson, 1986a,b; Chisholm and O'Sullivan, 1973), consumers to services (Clarke and Wilson, 1986a) and journey to work (Clarke and Wilson, 1986b). Other advances have attempted to incorporate qualitative measures in the models (Batty, 1987).

## Recent Advances

Roy (1990) identifies four principal advances in the development of spatial interaction models during the 1980s:

1. *Incorporating the influence of spatial structure.* It has been recognised that, when a new destination, such as a retail centre, is added, or an existing facility expanded in size, the flow from a given origin to each existing facility will not reduce in the same proportion. Except for Wilson's entropy-maximisation work, the opposite was "assumed" by classical spatial interaction models. However, a series of papers by Fotheringham (1981, 1983a,b, 1986) introduced "attractiveness corrections" based on the inverse accessibility between the subject destination and all other competing destinations (see below). Further advances have been made in this area by Roy (1985) and Lo (1990).

2. *Heterogeneous and homogeneous grouped alterna-*

*tives*. Heterogeneity of discrete choices of destinations can be handled in models using entropy micro-state definitions. Origin heterogeneity can be handled similarly (Roy and Lesse, 1981).

3. *Model calibration and prediction*. There have been important developments in entropy models relating to their calibration for subsequent predictive extensions of the model (e.g. Lesse, 1982).

4. *Choice versus demand models*. More realistic models have been developed by allowing total satisfied demand to be responsive not only to price levels but also to the relative accessibility of the supply and the levels of "congestion" created in its consumption (e.g. Leonardi, 1981). Such models integrate previously separate trip-generation and trip-distribution submodels.

Fotheringham (1983a,b) observed that gravity models are essentially based on a single decision-making process in which expected net utility derived from interacting with any particular destination is compared with the expected utilities for all other destinations, and interactions are predicted on the basis of this comparison. However, many types of spatial interaction can be considered as being part of a two-stage process. First, individuals choose a broad region with which to interact. Then they choose a specific destination from a set of alternatives within the selected region. For example, an unemployed person seeking a job is likely to select a suitable region offering good employment prospects when first searching for employment. This two-stage process can apply to both inter- and intra-urban interaction. If the region selected is a macro-destination and each specific destination is a micro-destination then the volume of interaction terminating at the latter varies according to the number of other destinations there are at that same distance. This distorts one of the assumptions of the gravity model as it can be shown that "the more accessible a destination is to all other destinations in a spatial system, the less likely it is that that destination is a terminating point for interaction from any given origin" (Fotheringham, 1983a:20). For interactions terminating in close proximity to the origin this can mean that a gravity model can under-predict the

volume of interaction. In contrast, for origins relatively inaccessible to destinations, interactions terminating at specific destinations will be larger than that predicted by a gravity model. The gravity interaction–distance relationship will be steeper than the actual relationship for accessible origins and shallower for inaccessible origins. This reflects the fact that gravity models do not include a variable that explicitly measures the relationship between interaction and competition between destinations. If such a variable is added the model is termed a *competing destinations model*. For example, for an origin-specific production-constrained competing destinations model, the model can be represented as

$$I_{ij} = A_i O_i W_j X_{ij}^{d_i} C_{ij}^{-\beta}$$

where $I_{ij}$ = interaction between $i$ and $j$; $A_i$ = the balancing factor; $O_i$ = outflow from $i$; $W_j$ = attractiveness of destination $j$; $X_{ij}$ = the accessibility of destination $j$ to all other destinations available to origin $i$ as perceived by the residents of origin $i$; $d_i$ = a distance-decay exponent; $C_{ij}$ = the cost of travel from $i$ to $j$; and $\beta$ = a distance-decay exponent.

Fotheringham (1983a) compared gravity models with competing destinations models using airline-passenger interaction data for 1970 published by the US Civil Aeronautics Board (a 10 per cent sample of all airline journeys on domestic routes within the USA). This revealed various mis-specifications within the gravity models, putting into question predictions of interaction based upon such models. In particular, it highlighted limitations of gravity models where distance-decay functions are not constant throughout a region, as in the case of variations or changes in spatial structure. Competing destinations models fare better when dealing with such situations.

Work has also been carried out on how best to represent space in the design of interaction models, especially for journey-to-work models in large urban areas (e.g. Masser and Brown, 1975). Some of these ideas on representation have now been applied to models of the spread and timing of disease (Thomas, 1990) (see Chapter 10). Other advances include recognition of spatial variations in the parameters of inter-action models (spatial non-stationarity). This has ef-fects on the model parameters of spatial aggregation and/or spatial pattern, with marked spatial patterns in $\beta$ values (Ghosh and McLafferty, 1987; Pooler, 1994a: 27–9). This can be solved by weighting destinations according to their accessibilities or population poten-tials (see Brocher, 1989) or through use of the variant known as a competing destinations model (see above).

New dimensions to the basic range of spatial inter-action models described above include process hypo-theses and the use of non-linear mathematics to solve resulting problems. To the "standard" models of retailing based on ideas of social physics has been added a dynamic component "explaining" the spatial structure of retailing and introducing sudden change that is controlled by critical parameters and the asso-ciated phenomenon of multiple equilibria.

During the last decade urban and regional model-ling has increasingly focused upon the applied and planning implications of earlier theoretical advances in optimisation methods, model design and urban dynamics (see Bertuglia et al, 1987; 1990). This recent work has been influenced by the increasing availability of new data sources in both the public and private sectors and the increased power and ready availability of personal computers (PCs) with high graphics capabilities. Increased attention is being paid to the practical utility of model outputs through a focus on performance indicators from model-based research in a variety of planning contexts (see Bertu-glia et al, 1994a). In the UK this work has been pioneered at the University of Leeds, with a focus upon a wide spectrum of retail and service activities (see Birkin, 1994; Birkin et al, 1993, 1994).

A good example of these developments, showing advances with the basic doubly constrained model, is the work of Bertuglia et al (1990). This combined housing stock as a supply-side constraint with employ-ment constraints. However, the model was developed in a much broader context than earlier ones to bring about more realism. Some indication of this can be

obtained by considering the model's five essential features (Tadei and Williams, 1994:88):

1. identification of a set of discrete choices and the decision-making units concerned, e.g. individuals, households, firms;
2. establishment of the basis for option selection and a preference function defined over the set of choices;
3. identification of representative and random compo-nents of the preference function and specifying the distribution of the random variables;
4. invoking random utility calculus to derive probabil-istic choice models;
5. developing subsidiary arguments for market inter-actions, e.g. establishing different rent levels.

Therefore the model makes an attempt to explain the dispersion of trip behaviour in terms of differences in observable and unobservable attributes of decision-making units.

For the future Bertuglia et al (1994a) identify the continuing need for spatial interaction and allocation modellers to make the outputs of their models more useful to applied planning problems in both the public and private sectors. Questions of equity and efficiency need to be addressed more clearly by paying closer attention to performance indicators for models using new technology (e.g. geographical information sys-tems) and "unconventional" indicators, e.g. environ-mental indicators. There is scope for models to draw upon ideas from throughout the social sciences and for greater attention to be given to the apparent gulf that exists between the new theories and approaches to explanation that have permeated human geography in the last two decades and the logic employed in model-based analysis. The rift between model-building and the work of many contemporary human geographers reflects different, yet equally coherent, philosophical positions, but the polarisation has helped render hu-man geography less effective than might otherwise have been expected in the public arena.

# 9

# SPATIAL STATISTICS, SPATIAL MODELS AND SPATIAL STRUCTURE

## SPATIAL ANALYSIS

A significant element in geography's Quantitative Revolution was the examination of spatial form using mathematics and geometry. Measurements of spatial distributions, areal differentiation and spatial relationships were at the heart of this geography, which also included the development of spatial theory, spatial statistics and formulations of geography as spatial science. Some of these concerns have been part of the continuing use of quantitative and statistical methods developed by geographers during the past two decades.

The "*spatial analysis*" *approach* to geography has comprised three interrelated themes (Gatrell, 1983:2), the last two of which are the focus of attention in Chapter 10 whilst the first is dealt with in this chapter:

1. *Spatial arrangement.* This refers to the locational pattern of objects under study (e.g. individuals, cities, countries), treating these objects as points, areas and lines, and thereby stressing their geometric or morphological properties. A focus on these properties may or may not concentrate on spatial arrangements to the exclusion of attention to the objects themselves.
2. *Space–time processes.* This deals with the modification of spatial arrangements by processes involving temporal change, such as migration or diffusion.

3. *Spatial forecasting.* The temporal element in the changing spatial arrangements may be relatively unimportant or it may be considered explicitly as in spatial forecasting where predictions of future arrangements are made.

In using the term "space" as applied to these three themes, two different conceptions are employed:

(a) *Absolute space* This is based on *Euclidean geometry*. Euclid, who taught in Alexandria *c*300 BC, was the most prominent mathematician of Greco-Roman antiquity. He is best known for his treatise on geometry, the *Elements*, a set of 13 books. He codified the geometry of the relationships between lengths, areas and volumes of physical objects, on the basis of 10 axioms and postulates. The most important of these states that through a given point $P$ not on a line $l$, there is only one line in the plane of $P$ and $l$ that does not meet $l$. Absolute space treats space as a container of objects but with an existence independent of the objects it contains. For example, in his seminal *The nature of geography*, Hartshorne (1939:395) argued that "the area, in itself, is related to the phenomena within it, only in that it contains them in such and such locations". Much spatial analysis follows this view.

(b) *Relative or non-physical space.* Space is viewed as a relation defined on a set of objects. Gatrell (1983:3) argues that this is more general and empirically more useful than the concept of absolute space because it permits various ways in which the spatial separation of objects can be described. Also, the relationship does not have to possess properties of distance (metric properties) and so the relation between the objects can itself be the subject of enquiry. Representations of relative spaces through the transformation of maps of absolute, physical space were popularised in geography by Bunge (1962) and Tobler (1966), such as maps reflecting time-distance between places.

Both absolute and relative space have featured in work by geographers, but relative space and relative distance have increasingly dominated geographical enquiry. Hence it has become commonplace to refer to certain relativist terms such as:

- *Time-distance* – the time taken to travel between given objects (locations).
- *Economic-distance* – monetary cost incurred in overcoming physical distance (sometimes referred to as *cost-distance*).

- *Cognitive distance* – judgements about the spatial separation of objects that cannot be seen directly. If the objects can be seen, this may be termed *perceived distance*.
- *Social distance* – this attributes a distance component to differences between social classes, which may have a physical expression in terms of the locational characteristics of the classes.

Each of these distances is associated with a different conception of space, treating space in a non-physical sense. For example, by mapping time-distances between places a very different portrayal of space may be created: what Forer (1978), whose example is shown in Figure 9.1, termed "plastic space". A similar plasticity may be revealed for economic space which might involve consideration of flows of goods, money and information between businesses or of trading links between countries. Cognitive spaces, referred to in Chapter 12, reflect spatial cogni-

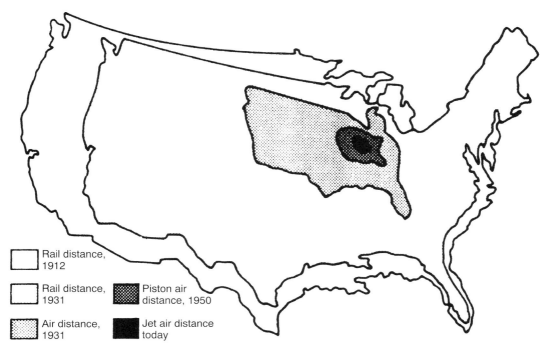

*Figure 9.1* Plastic Space
The "shrinking" USA, 1912 to 1970s. (*Source*: Forer, 1978)

tion by which people collect, structure and recall information about locations in physical space. When represented as a cognitive map, an individual's spatial cognition of a locality may differ markedly from physical space. Social space may refer to social interactions between individuals or groups, social networks, and social areas of different ethnic or social groups.

This chapter, dealing with various aspects of spatial statistics, models and structure, begins by considering simple measures of spatial arrangement and pattern.

## SPATIAL INDICES

### The Lorenz Curve

The *Lorenz curve* is a simple graphical way of comparing spatial patterns. To construct the Lorenz curve, data are required for areal units (or categories) for two variables. In this case the variables are two Norwegian fish species (brown trout and perch) threatened by the increased acidification of freshwater lakes (Table 9.1a). First, the ratio between the two variables is calculated for each areal unit. The areal units are then ranked on the basis of these ratios, from the smallest to the largest. Both variables are expressed in percentage terms and these percentages are accumulated, maintaining the order of ranking produced by the ratios calculated between the variables (Table 9.1b). Their cumulative percentages are plotted against one another on a graph (Figure 9.2), thereby generating the Lorenz curve. If the two distributions are proportionately identical in each area or category then the graph will be a straight diagonal line. Therefore any differences between the two distributions are revealed as a deviation from the diagonal: the bigger the separation of the graph from the diagonal, the bigger the difference between the two cumulative proportions.

*Table 9.1*   Data for Construction of a Lorenz Curve of the Number of Fish Stocks Lost from Norwegian Lakes due to Acidification

(a) Basic data

| County | No. of Stocks in Lakes* | No. of Stocks lost | | Losses by Species | | | | | |
|---|---|---|---|---|---|---|---|---|---|
| | | | | Brown Trout | | Perch | | Arctic Charr | |
| | | No. | a (%) | No. | x (%) | No. | y (%) | No. | z (%) |
| Ostfold | 797 | 70 | 8.8 | 34 | 19.4 | 11 | 3.6 | 2 | 40.0 |
| Oslo/Akershus | 320 | 47 | 14.7 | 31 | 47.0 | 6 | 4.0 | 6 | 54.5 |
| Hedmark | 339 | 32 | 9.4 | 27 | 27.0 | 1 | 1.0 | 2 | 11.1 |
| Oppland | 477 | 39 | 8.2 | 20 | 11.0 | 3 | 2.3 | 12 | 15.4 |
| Buskerud | 1468 | 123 | 8.4 | 93 | 10.9 | 20 | 5.8 | 5 | 6.1 |
| Vestfold | 239 | 6 | 2.5 | 4 | 4.2 | 2 | 2.6 | 0 | 0 |
| Telemark | 1322 | 360 | 27.2 | 340 | 36.5 | 9 | 4.8 | 3 | 3.4 |
| Aust-Agder | 1214 | 672 | 55.4 | 591 | 64.4 | 80 | 3.1 | 0 | 0 |
| Vest-Agder | 802 | 476 | 59.4 | 419 | 67.0 | 50 | 50.5 | 7 | 31.8 |
| Rogaland | 1062 | 293 | 27.6 | 277 | 32.6 | 0 | 0 | 15 | 12.9 |
| Totals | 8040 | 2118 | 26.3 | | 38.3 | | 11.0 | | 12.3 |

* This refers to the number of lakes in which stocks of the three named species were recorded. If each species is present in a lake, that lake is counted three times.

*Source of data*: Mannion (1992)

*Table 9.1*   (*continued*)

(b) Calculations for Lorenze curve, comparing brown trout and perch

| County | Percentage losses by species | | | | Cumulative percentage | |
|---|---|---|---|---|---|---|
| | $x$ | $y$ | $x/y$ | | $x$ | $y$ |
| Ostfold | 19.4 | 3.6 | 5.39 | Vest-Agder | 20.9 | 65.0 |
| Oslo/Akershus | 47.0 | 4.0 | 11.75 | Vestfold | 22.2 | 68.3 |
| Hedmark | 27.0 | 1.0 | 27.00 | Buskerud | 25.6 | 75.8 |
| Oppland | 11.0 | 2.3 | 4.78 | Oppland | 29.0 | 78.8 |
| Buskerud | 10.9 | 5.8 | 1.88 | Ostfold | 35.1 | 83.4 |
| Vestfold | 4.2 | 2.6 | 1.62 | Telemark | 46.5 | 89.6 |
| Telemark | 36.5 | 4.8 | 7.60 | Oslo/Akershus | 61.2 | 94.7 |
| Aust-Agder | 64.4 | 3.1 | 20.77 | Aust-Agder | 81.3 | 98.7 |
| Vest-Agder | 67.0 | 50.5 | 1.33 | Hedmark | 89.7 | 100.0 |
| Rogaland | 32.6 | 0 | > 32.60 | Rogaland | 100.0 | 100.0 |

(c) Calculations for coefficient of localisation

| County | $f_y$ (%) | $f_a$ (%) | $f_y/f_a$ | | Cumulative percentage of $f$ | |
|---|---|---|---|---|---|---|
| | | | | | $y$ | $a$ |
| Ostfold | 4.6 | 4.0 | 1.15 | Vest-Agder | 65.0 | 26.8 |
| Oslo/Akershus | 5.1 | 6.6 | 0.77 | Vestfold | 68.3 | 27.9 |
| Hedmark | 1.3 | 4.2 | 0.34 | Buskerud | 75.8 | 31.7 |
| Oppland | 3.0 | 3.7 | 0.81 | Ostfold | 80.4 | 35.7 |
| Buskerud | 7.5 | 3.8 | 1.97 | Oppland | 83.4 | 39.4 |
| Vestfold | 3.3 | 1.1 | 3.00 | Oslo/Akershus | 88.5 | 46.0 |
| Telemark | 6.2 | 12.3 | 0.50 | Telemark | 94.7 | 58.3 |
| Aust-Agder | 4.0 | 25.0 | 0.16 | Hedmark | 96.0 | 62.5 |
| Vest-Agder | 65.0 | 26.8 | 5.08 | Aust-Agder | 100.0 | 87.5 |
| Rogaland | 0.0 | 12.5 | 0 | Rogaland | 100.0 | 100.00 |
| Totals | 100.0 | 100.0 | | | | |

Figure 9.2 shows that there is quite a substantial difference between the losses of the two fish species in the Norwegian counties. The brown trout are more seriously affected by acidification, especially in southern Norway (Vest-Agder, Rogaland and Aust-Agder), where fish populations are almost extinct. However, in comparison, loss of perch stocks has been less marked despite an even greater concentration of losses in the south.

Differences between two spatially distributed variables can also be demonstrated by a number of indices, as follows.

## The Index of Dissimilarity ($I_d$)

This is "the percentage of a population group which would have to shift its residence in order to reproduce a spatial distribution identical with that of the group with which it is being compared" (Peach, 1975). The index can be calculated in a number of ways, one of which is to use the Lorenz curve to read off the maximum difference in the cumulative percentages of the two distributions. In Figure 9.2 this gives: $I_d = 80.4 - 35.7 = 44.7$. Alternatively, the calculations in Table 9.1b could have been used to reveal this value.

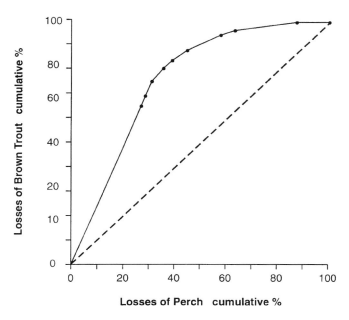

*Figure 9.2*    Lorenz Curve for the Number of Fish Stocks Lost from Norwegian Lakes due to Acidification. (*Data source*: Mannion, 1992)

A simpler set of calculations can be used which eliminates the need to produce cumulative percentages, by using the formula

$$I_d = \tfrac{1}{2}\sum(x_i - y_i)$$

where $x_i$ and $y_i$ are the individual percentages of each variable. This index can also be calculated from

$$I_d = \tfrac{1}{2}\sum_{i=1}^{n}[(x_i/\sum x_i) - (y_i/\sum y_i)] \times 100\%$$

where $x_i$ = proportion of workers in occupation $x$, $y_i$ = proportion of workers in occupation $y$, and these values are recorded for $n$ areal units or zones.

In this form Duncan and Duncan (1955) used $I_d$ in a classic examination of social segregation in Chicago, with the index giving a simple measure of the difference between the spatial distribution of two groups. In the Duncans' work the areal units were census tracts of the city. For comparative work in the UK, city wards or enumeration districts have been used. $I_d$ can also be used to measure the extent to which an economic activity is concentrated relative to another activity (e.g. Smith, 1975).

$I_d$ gives a measure of the proportion of one occupational group ($x$) that would have to move from its existing location to make its distribution identical with the distribution of another occupational group ($y$). Duncan and Duncan (1995) produced a table for employed males in Chicago census tracts, with lower social classes at the bottom and upper classes at the top (Table 9.2). The values of $I_d$ increased towards the top and right of their matrix, thereby indicating the greater spatial separation between the upper and lower classes, as defined by employment categories. However, greater attention was given to the results of research using the index when the variable considered was ethnicity rather than occupation. Using ethnic status as the variable, the index was termed an *index of segregation* in which the distribution of a particular ethnic group was compared with respect to the distribution of the rest of the population. In calculating the index of segregation ($I_s$) a correction factor may

*Table 9.2*    Indices of Segregation and Dissimilarity

(a) Index of residential segregation for occupation groups, Chicago, 1950

| Occupation Group | Index of Segregation |
|---|---|
| Professional | 30 |
| Managerial | 29 |
| Sales workers | 29 |
| Clerical | 13 |
| Craftsmen | 19 |
| Operatives | 22 |
| Service workers | 24 |
| Labourers | 35 |

*Source*: Duncan and Duncan (1955:497).

(b) Index of residential dissimilarity for occupation groups, Chicago, 1950

| Occupation Group | 1 | 2 | 3 | 4 | 5 | 6 | 7 | 8 |
|---|---|---|---|---|---|---|---|---|
| 1. Professional | – | | | | | | | |
| 2. Managerial | 13 | – | | | | | | |
| 3. Sales workers | 15 | 3 | – | | | | | |
| 4. Clerical | 28 | 28 | 27 | – | | | | |
| 5. Craftsmen | 35 | 33 | 35 | 16 | – | | | |
| 6. Operatives | 44 | 41 | 42 | 21 | 17 | – | | |
| 7. Service workers | 41 | 40 | 38 | 24 | 35 | 26 | – | |
| 8. Labourers | 54 | 52 | 54 | 38 | 35 | 25 | 28 | – |

*Source*: Duncan and Duncan (1955:498).

be applied to eliminate the presence of $y_i$ (proportion of ethnic group $y$) occurring in the total population ($t$), i.e.

$$I_s = \frac{I_d}{1 - \sum y_i / t}$$

When Tauber and Tauber (1965) recorded indices of 80 per cent and above for blacks in American cities, the label "ghetto" seemed an apt one to apply to such high levels of segregation. Slightly lower indices were recorded by McEvoy (1978), in an examination of Asians in the British cities of Birmingham, Bradford, Glasgow and Huddersfield, and by Carlyle (1991) for ethnic groups in Winnipeg. The Taubers' study of the levels of block-level segregation of blacks in 207 US cities in the 1960 census revealed that only eight of the cities had an index of dissimilarity below 70; half

had values above 87.8 and a quarter had values above 91.7. Average levels of black segregation remained in the 80s in the 1970 and 1980 censuses (Massey and Denton, 1993).

Doherty (1989) used the index to show how segregation between Catholics and other denominations had changed over time in Belfast, Northern Ireland, drawing on earlier work by Boal and Poole (Boal, 1981; Poole, 1982; Poole and Boal, 1973). This showed an increased value of the index, from 39.3 in 1911 to 50.1 in 1969 at ward level (see Table 9.3). For 1 km squares covering the whole city, the index increased from 49.6 in 1971 to 60.4 in 1981. Similarly, when the investigation was focused on individual areas of the city, sharp increases were revealed over the period 1971–81. The highest index was recorded for Belfast West, which contains almost 40 per cent of the Catholics in the urban area. Here the index had

Table 9.3 Indices of Dissimilarity (Segregation) for the Belfast Urban Area for Catholics Against Other Denominations

|  | 1911 | 1926 | 1969 | 1971 | 1981 |
|---|---|---|---|---|---|
| Wards | 39.3 | 49.4 | 50.1 |  |  |
| Streets | 66 | 70.9 | 76* |  |  |
| 1 km squares |  |  |  | 49.6 | 60.4 |

* 1972

Source: Doherty (1989).

risen from 74.8 to 80.7, supporting the view that the long-standing conflicts between Catholics and Protestants had produced a ghetto area quite distinct from the rest of Belfast.

Although Duncan and Duncan (1955) concluded that their work demonstrated that there was correspondence of social and spatial distance among occupation groups, subsequent use of the indices of dissimilarity and segregation has shown that their value can be affected markedly by the problem of unequal size of areal units. So, the size of the administrative unit on which calculations are based can significantly affect the value of the index (see Table 9.3). The number of areas used for purposes of calculation influences the absolute level of the index, so that a ranking of degrees of segregation may vary with the scale with which the indices are calculated. Therefore such indices can only be used as general indicators of the degree of segregation and great care is required in their interpretation (Carlyle, 1991; Lee, 1977:171–3; Woods, 1976).

A further crucial limitation of the indices of dissimilarity and segregation is that they only refer to one variable, either employment or ethnicity, whereas social class may more properly be considered as a concept that has many dimensions and facets. In the 1950s and 1960s many geographers recognised that it was more appropriate to consider social class in terms of a range of interrelated social and economic variables. For example, the testing of the Chicago School's ecological models was extended to incorporate multivariate methods (see Chapter 5), with an emergent focus beyond the models themselves onto new types of examination of social class and spatial separation of the classes.

Although there has been substantial debate over the most effective way to measure segregation, with indices other than indices of dissimilarity and segregation tested (see the following three subsections), Peach (1996) notes that the advantage of $I_d$ is that there is a cumulative literature using the same technique. However, there are circumstances where $I_s$ is more suitable. For example, if $I_d$ was used to investigate the segregation of the white population from the total population in Britain, the index would be very low because the white population and the total population are often very similar. In this case $I_s$ is a better measure of the segregation of the white population from combined minorities. $I_d$ is not suitable when minority numbers are small, especially if numbers begin to approach the number of areal units over which the index was calculated, as even a random distribution of the minority could produce significant levels of segregation as measured by the index (see Falk et al, 1978; Winship, 1978).

Peach's (1996) analysis of the UK's 1991 Population Census at both ward and enumeration district level revealed substantial variations in the degree of segregation experienced by the 10 ethnic groups investigated. As expected, though, the finer spatial mesh of the enumeration districts produced higher values of $I_s$ and $I_d$. In particular, the Chinese in London had low values at enumeration district level, suggesting they are present throughout the urban area but in a series of segregated clusters that are apparent at the finer scale. In contrast, the African population had high indices at both ward and enumeration district level. The highest levels of segregation were recorded for Bangladeshis: in the 11 cities in which there were more than 1000 Bangladeshis, $I_d = 73$ and $I_s = 69$ at ward level (Bangladeshis versus whites). They also showed average rates of over 50 against all other groups except Pakistanis. At enumeration district level the average $I_s = 86$. Pakistanis were slightly less segregated than the Bangladeshis (average segregation levels 10 points lower), but more so than the Indians (an average of 16 points lower than the Pakistanis).

## Location Quotients

The notion of comparing two spatial distributions via an index of dissimilarity or the Lorenz curve can be extended by comparing the extent to which a particular distribution differs from a norm. A common comparison involves the distribution of employment in a particular industry and the national average for all industries. The comparison is effected by calculating the *location quotient* ($LQ$):

$$LQ = \frac{a_x/c}{b_x/d}$$

Where $a_x$ = employment in a given activity $x$ in an area, $c$ = total employment in an area, $b_x$ = national employment in activity $x$, and $d$ = total national employment. If the data are in percentages the equation becomes

$$LQ = \frac{g_x}{k}$$

Where $g_x$ = percentage of activity x in an area, and $k$ = the national percentage.

High values for ($LQ > 1$) indicate a high degree of concentration of a particular activity in an area. Values $LQ < 1$ indicate low concentrations and values of $LQ = 1$ indicate the distribution is the same as the national average.

One example of how location quotients may be used is given in Table 9.4. This compares employment characteristics in two locations, with the national pattern. The two locations are the county of Dorset in south-west England and the largest town in the county, Poole. The highest location quotients recorded for the county are for employment categories Z (armed forces), A (farmers, foresters and fishermen) and O (construction workers). These are the employment categories in which the county could be said to specialise when compared with the proportion of employees in these categories for England and Wales as a whole. It is not surprising that employment in the armed forces stands out, as there were numerous army bases in the county, especially in the Dorset heathlands where T.E. Lawrence (Lawrence of Arabia) was living at the time of his death. Similarly, Dorset can be termed a rural county with a higher than average employment on the land. The high quotient for construction work reflects a boom in new houses in the county, some of it catering for retirees, and some reflecting hotel construction, as this is a tourist area. The county was strongly under-represented in categories B (miners), E (furnace and foundry workers), I (leather workers) and J (textile workers), reflecting its rural character. It also had a lower than average rate of unemployment, as had Poole. No location quotient exceeded 2.0 for Poole, but values greater than 1.5 were recorded for categories D (glass and ceramic makers), H (wood workers) and P (painters and decorators). The first two reflect the town's long-standing specialisation in value-added and craft industries whilst the higher than average employment in painting and decorating relates to the aforementioned construction boom. Quotients tending towards 0 were recorded for categories B (miners), I (leather workers) and J (textile workers) as for the county as a whole.

An example of how location quotients can be mapped to reveal spatial variations is shown in Figure 9.3. Here quotients for the distribution of Aborigines and Torres Straits Islanders in Australia are mapped by state. This map also illustrates one of the quotient's limitations. The three states with less than average representation of this group have quotients less than 1, but the high concentrations in Northern Territory give a quotient of 15.66. This emphasises the much greater significance of Aborigines in Northern Territory but this "over-representation" is measured on an unlimited scale whereas "under-representation" is constrained to values between 0 and 1. So it is difficult to evaluate the degree of concentration using location quotients. This problem does not arise if an alternative measure, the *Gini coefficient*, also known as the *coefficient of localisation* or the *coefficient of concentration*, is employed.

## The Gini Coefficient ($I_G$)

This compares the distribution of an attribute within a population with a hypothetical equal distribution. Therefore it is closely related to the Lorenz curve and

*Table 9.4* Comparison of Employment Patterns in Dorset, Poole and England and Wales Expressed via Location Quotients

| Category | | $y_i$ England and Wales | $x_i$ Dorset | $z_i$ Poole | Location Quotients | |
|---|---|---|---|---|---|---|
| | | | | | $\dfrac{x_i/X}{y_i/Y}$ | $\dfrac{z_i/Z}{y_i/Y}$ |
| I | Economically inactive | 1 766 724 | 12 841 | 3622 | 1.03 | 1.00 |
| II | Unemployed | 184 539 | 557 | 176 | 0.50 | 0.50 |
| III | Self-employed | 306 229 | 1876 | 487 | 0.86 | 0.77 |
| A | Primary industry | 64 035 | 1008 | 72 | 2.36 | 0.57 |
| B | Miners and quarrymen | 22 925 | 19 | 0 | 0.12 | 0.00 |
| C | Gas, coke and chemicals | 12 558 | 36 | 28 | 0.43 | 1.11 |
| D | Glass and ceramic makers | 8745 | 50 | 28 | 0.84 | 1.63 |
| E | Industrial mill workers | 15 304 | 29 | 12 | 0.03 | 0.38 |
| F | Electronics | 55 919 | 356 | 143 | 1.00 | 1.33 |
| G | Engineering | 255 275 | 1407 | 568 | 0.83 | 1.05 |
| H | Wood workers | 37 780 | 335 | 127 | 1.33 | 1.69 |
| I | Leather workers | 11 010 | 12 | 2 | 0.17 | 0.08 |
| J | Textile workers | 26 604 | 60 | 1 | 0.33 | 0.02 |
| K | Clothing workers | 37 010 | 104 | 28 | 0.41 | 0.38 |
| L | Food, drink and tobacco | 32 563 | 246 | 82 | 1.13 | 1.26 |
| M | Paper and printing | 28 752 | 96 | 49 | 0.50 | 0.84 |
| N | Makers of other products | 29 580 | 169 | 63 | 0.86 | 1.08 |
| O | Construction workers | 50 186 | 502 | 136 | 1.55 | 1.36 |
| P | Painters and decorators | 26 130 | 194 | 80 | 1.10 | 1.55 |
| Q | Drivers of stationary engines | 27 186 | 140 | 39 | 0.75 | 0.71 |
| R | Labourers | 108 731 | 645 | 175 | 1.00 | 0.95 |
| S | Transport and communications | 128 144 | 770 | 237 | 0.89 | 0.93 |
| T | Warehousemen and packers | 72 999 | 356 | 151 | 0.75 | 1.06 |
| U | Clerical workers | 327 582 | 1729 | 647 | 0.81 | 1.03 |
| V | Sales workers | 203 277 | 1612 | 523 | 1.18 | 1.33 |
| W | Services, sport and recreation | 266 198 | 2021 | 604 | 1.12 | 1.19 |
| X | Administration and management | 86 092 | 528 | 203 | 0.89 | 1.05 |
| Y | Professionals | 250 146 | 1837 | 522 | 1.09 | 1.09 |
| Z | Armed forces | 23 161 | 412 | 42 | 2.75 | 0.92 |
| Others | | 59 162 | 458 | 161 | 1.15 | 1.38 |
| Totals | | 4 525 176 = Y | 30 405 = X | 9 008 = Z | | |

*Source*: 10 per cent sample, Population Census.

is an alternative measure of dissimilarity. It is calculated from,

$$I_G = \frac{1}{2}\sum_{i=1}^{n} |P_i - I_i|$$

where $P_i$ = percentage values of one attribute, e.g. population numbers, and $I_i$ = percentage values of another attribute, e.g. income levels.

The value of $I_G$ is constrained to values between 0 (indicating exact correspondence between the two distributions) and 100 (indicating maximum inequality between the two distributions). The Gini coefficient measures the maximum difference between the diag-

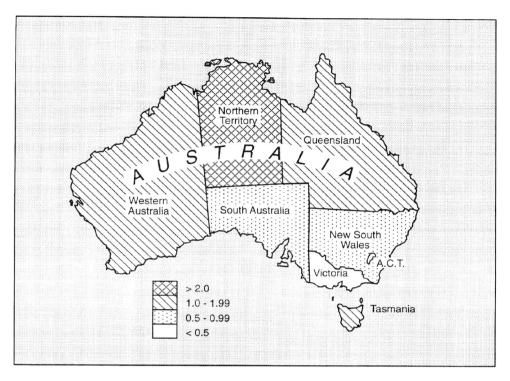

*Figure 9.3*    Location Quotients for Aborigines and Torres Straits Islanders, Australia, 1991

onal of the Lorenz curve and the curve as a proportion of the area beneath the diagonal. The greater the area between the diagonal and the curve, the more dissimilar are the two distributions and the higher is the Gini coefficient.

Table 9.5 uses population data for the same county (Dorset) referred to above when discussing the Lorenz curve. In Table 9.5 the principal towns in the county are compared with respect to two of the key characteristics already identified, namely the presence of hotel accommodation and a high proportion of retirees. The calculated Gini coefficient of 39.1 suggests that there were certain differences between the two distributions, though they are some way from being totally dissimilar. By focusing on the values of percentage differences for the individual towns, the main contributions to the dissimilarity are clear. They come from the main town, Poole, with its high concentration of

pensioners, and the two main tourist centres, Swanage and Weymouth, which had a disproportionate concentration of hotel accommodation to the proportion of pensioners in their populations. Figure 9.4 shows graphically the relationship between the Gini coefficient and the Lorenz curve for the data in Table 9.5.

Although they are very simple to calculate, all three measures described in the above three subsections have well recognised limitations. The three main ones are:

1. The variables must be expressed as positive frequencies for each areal unit. Because negative values cannot be accommodated this can make it difficult to study a continuous variable.
2. The indices are greatly affected by the sizes of the areal units for which data are available. In general, the smaller the average size of the areal unit, the

*Table 9.5*    Comparison of Hotel Accommodation and Retirement in Dorset towns using Gini Coefficients($I_G$)

| Towns | Hotels (%) x | Pensioners (%) y | x/y | Rank | \|x − y\| | Cumulative percentage | |
|---|---|---|---|---|---|---|---|
| | | | | | | x | y |
| Blandford | 1.2 | 1.7 | 0.71 | 7= | 0.5 | 27.4 | 65.5 |
| Bridport | 4.8 | 3.8 | 1.26 | 9 | 1.0 | 34.6 | 72.7 |
| Dorchester | 2.4 | 5.5 | 0.44 | 5 | 3.1 | 25.0 | 61.9 |
| Lyme Regis | 6.1 | 2.4 | 2.54 | 11 | 3.7 | 72.2 | 94.5 |
| Poole | 20.6 | 48.9 | 0.42 | 4 | 28.3 | 22.6 | 56.4 |
| Portland | 1.2 | 3.3 | 0.36 | 3 | 2.1 | 2.0 | 7.5 |
| Shaftesbury | 1.2 | 1.9 | 0.63 | 6 | 0.7 | 26.2 | 63.8 |
| Sherborne | 2.4 | 3.4 | 0.71 | 7= | 1.0 | 29.8 | 68.9 |
| Swanage | 27.8 | 5.5 | 5.05 | 12 | 22.3 | 100.0 | 100.0 |
| Wareham | 0.2 | 1.9 | 0.11 | 1 | 1.7 | 0.2 | 1.9 |
| Weymouth | 31.5 | 19.4 | 1.62 | 10 | 12.1 | 66.1 | 92.1 |
| Wimborne | 0.6 | 2.3 | 0.26 | 2 | 1.7 | 0.8 | 4.2 |
| Total | 100.0 | 100.0 | | | 78.2 | | |

$I_G = \frac{1}{2}|x - y| = \frac{1}{2}(78.2) = 39.1$

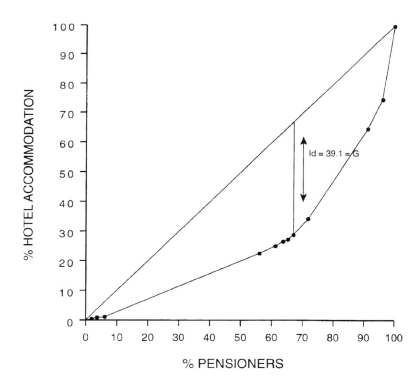

*Figure 9.4*    Lorenz Curve and Gini Coefficient for Distribution of Hotel Accommodation and Pensioners in Dorset, England

larger the value of the index. One attempt to overcome this problem is represented by *Lieberson's isolation index* (Lieberson, 1980) (see below).

3. As noted by Shaw and Wheeler (1985:306), "the Lorenz curve and its related indices are an effective way of describing the relationships between distributions, but offer no indication or measure of spatial pattern". However, other techniques have been used to analyse spatial pattern, from relatively simple measures such as nearest-neighbour statistics to more complex ones such as spatial autocorrelation (see below).

## Lieberson's Isolation Index

This is a modified version of Bell's (1954) *isolation index* and differs from the index of dissimilarity ($I_d$) in that it is dependent upon group size, so that the segregation of group A from group B may not match that between group B and group A. It is therefore an asymmetrical measure of dissimilarity, though it still suffers from the same scale problems as $I_d$ (Lieberson, 1980).

The index ($P^*$) is calculated from

$$P_a^* = \sum_{i=1}^{n} \left(\frac{a_i}{A}\right)\left(\frac{a_i}{t_i}\right)$$

where $a_i$ = number of subgroup $a$ in sub-area $i$, $A$ = number of subgroup $a$ in all sub-areas, and $t_i$ = total population in sub-area $i$.

Unlike $I_d$ the values of $P^*$ are not constrained between 0 and 100 and therefore it should be used for comparative purposes. Its use in conjunction with $I_d$ can amplify interpretations of trends in segregation, as can comparing the calculated value ($P_a^*$) with the expected value if segregation were absent ($A/T$), where $T$ is the total population. For example, V. Robinson (1980) showed that calculating $P^*$ for Asians in Blackburn as compared with non-Asians in the town, at ward level, revealed the two groups' differential experience of segregation: "The decline in spatial segregation and the stagnation of the white population have ensured that the average white is now

less isolated at ward level than [s]he was at the end of the 1960s. In contrast, the dramatic increase in the size of the Asian minority has ensured that the average Asian is now four times more residentially isolated than [s]he was ten years ago, despite the decline in spatial dissimilarity"($P_a^* = 0.05$ in 1968 compared with $P_a^* = 0.21$ in 1976). This is illustrated in Table 9.6.

## DESCRIBING POINT PATTERNS

### Modelling Point Patterns

One focus of geographical research on spatial patterns has been upon ways of summarising characteristics of spatial distributions. Some of the pioneering work on the measurement of spatial pattern focused on the locations of individuals relative to each other, with those individuals represented as points on a map (Dacey, 1960; King, 1962). This work used probability distributions as a means of describing spatial patterns, the most commonly employed distribution being the Poisson because this introduced the notion of randomness as a basic aspect of the distribution of points. This reflects two basic assumptions of the Poisson distribution:

- the existence of equal probability, so that any location on a map is as equally likely as any other location to receive a point – this implies that the

Table 9.6 Trends in Residential Segregation in Blackburn, 1968–76, at Ward Level

| | $I_d$ | $aP_a^*$ | Expected $aP_a^*$ | $bP_b^*$ | Expected $bP_b^*$ |
|---|---|---|---|---|---|
| 1968 | 50.4 | 0.05 | 0.02 | 0.98 | 0.98 |
| 1970 | 54.3 | 0.11 | 0.03 | 0.97 | 0.97 |
| 1972 | 58.7 | 0.14 | 0.04 | 0.96 | 0.96 |
| 1974 | 56.9 | 0.18 | 0.06 | 0.95 | 0.94 |
| 1976 | 56.1 | 0.21 | 0.07 | 0.94 | 0.93 |

$a$ = Asians, $b$ = non-Asians (Whites)

*Source*: Robinson (1980).

process producing the pattern of points is a random one;

- each of the points is independent of the others.

Given that the Poisson distribution gives a randomly distributed set of points, this random pattern can be modelled and compared with an actual pattern, using the term "pattern" to apply to the distances between points and the arrangements of points in space (Sibley, 1976). Details of the Poisson distribution are given at the end of Chapter 2. As described there, its basic formula is:

$$P(x) = \frac{\lambda^x e^{-\lambda}}{x!}$$

where $P(x)$ = the probability of $x$ events (points) occurring per grid square, $\lambda$ = the average density of events (points), e = 2.7183 . . . and $x$ = a specified number of events (points).

However, there are other types of point patterns that can also be modelled and which represent deviations from a random pattern. For example, the binomial distribution gives a regular pattern and the negative binomial distribution gives a clustered pattern. These patterns can also be explained by the operation of particular processes. For example, the binomial distribution represents the operation of competitive forces such as those producing a regular network of central places, whilst the clustering of the negative binomial distribution reflects the strong attractive forces that can produce clusters of shops or industries in urban areas (Harvey, 1966). Other distributions, such as Neyman's type A, can be used to examine the effects of how the presence of points influences the probability of other points occurring nearby (a process referred to as *contagion*) (Harvey, 1968). For more detailed accounts of point patterns and processes see Cox and Isham (1980) and Daley and Vere-Jones (1988).

If we wished to test whether an observed pattern of points in a number of grid squares or quadrats conformed to a random pattern, a hypothesis test could be performed that compared the observed pattern with one that would be expected if the points were distrib-

uted randomly, that is according to the Poisson distribution. A short-cut method is to use the *variance: mean ratio* of the observed distribution. The mean $(\lambda)$ = the observed density of points, and the variance of the observed distribution $(\sigma^2)$ is given by:

$$\sigma^2 = \frac{\sum x_i^2}{\sum x_i} - \frac{\sum x_i}{n}$$

where $x_i$ = the number of points in each quadrat (grid square), and $n$ = the number of quadrats (grid squares).

In the Poisson distribution $\lambda = \sigma^2$, and so if the variance:mean ratio is equal to 1.0 then it can be concluded that the distribution of points is spatially random. A regular pattern of points would be likely to yield a low variance because most grid squares have a similar number of points. Therefore the variance:mean ratio will be less than 1.0. In contrast, clustered patterns give high variances as the majority of grid squares have very few points or none at all whilst a minority have a high number. Therefore the variance:mean ratio will be greater than 1.0. The departure of the ratio from 1.0 can be expressed as a $z$ score:

$$z = \frac{\text{observed ratio} - \text{expected ratio}}{\text{standard error}}$$

where standard error,

$$SE_x = \sqrt{[2/(n-1)]}$$

and $n$ = total number of grid squares or quadrats. Then $z$ tables can be used to see whether the pattern is significantly different from a random one. A positive $z$ value suggests a tendency towards clustering whilst negative values suggest a tendency towards regularity. For the data in Table 9.7, in which Bronze Age tumuli are treated as points, the distribution of tumuli in grid squares (quadrats) is suggested as random according to the calculation of a variance:mean ratio very close to 1.0. This is confirmed when the $z$ value is calculated.

Although the methods described above for compar-

*Table 9.7*  Variance : Mean Ratio of Distributions of Bronze Age Tumuli per Grid Square

| Number of Tumuli per Grid Square (Quadrat) n | Number of Quadrats with n Tumuli q | nq | n²q |
|---|---|---|---|
| 0 | 47 | 0 | 0 |
| 1 | 52 | 52 | 52 |
| 2 | 24 | 48 | 96 |
| 3 | 4 | 12 | 36 |
| 4 | 1 | 4 | 16 |
| 5 | 1 | 5 | 25 |
| | 129 | 121 | 225 |

Observed density of points $(\lambda) = \dfrac{\text{Total number of tumuli}}{\text{Number of quadrats}}$

$$\lambda = \frac{nq}{q} = \frac{121}{129} = 0.938$$

$$\sigma^2 = \frac{\sum x^2}{\sum x} - \frac{\sum x}{N} = \frac{n^2q}{nq} - \frac{nq}{N} = \frac{225}{121} - \frac{121}{129}$$

$$= 1.86 - 0.938 = 0.922$$

Therefore the variance:mean ratio $= 0.922/0.938 = 0.983$

$$SE_x = \sqrt{[2/(N-1)]} = \sqrt{[2/(129-1)]} = \sqrt{0.0156}$$

$$= 0.128$$

$z =$ (observed ratio − expected ratio)/standard error

$$= \frac{0.983 - 1.0}{0.125} = -0.017/0.125 = -0.136$$

At the 0.01 level the critical values of $z$ are $\pm 2.58$. Therefore as the calculated value is well below this, it can be concluded that the distribution of tumuli in the grid squares analysed are random.

ing different point distributions are relatively simple, there is a crucial problem that is difficult to overcome. This is the size of the quadrat or grid square employed. It is possible to change the quadrat size so as to produce a random pattern even where visual inspection of the pattern suggests otherwise. For example, the use of very small quadrats can break up clusters and so produce results suggesting randomness. Yet, for a similar clustered pattern, large quadrats would probably contain similar numbers of points and therefore would suggest a regular pattern. Ecologists have attempted to define an ideal size of quadrat as twice the mean area around each point $(2A/n)$, where $A =$ the area of study and $n =$ the number of points. This may be too large for geographical studies, in which case $A/n$ may be a more appropriate size (Taylor, 1977:156–67). Alternatively, a test for randomness can be performed for various quadrat sizes, though this is time-consuming. Overall, the problem of the "correct" quadrat size has not been solved and has deterred the use of analysis based on quadrats because of the way in which a single point pattern can be approximated by a number of different probability distributions.

Despite the problems regarding the use of quadrats, descriptions of point patterns, such as the distribution of central places, have been made in two ways: *quadrat analysis* and *nearest-neighbour analysis*. Both methods assume that all point patterns fall within a continuum of spatial pattern ranging from totally clustered (all points occupying the same location) to totally uniform or regular (each point is located on the vertex of a grid of equilateral triangles). Between these two limits lies the random pattern in which the location of each point appears to be independent of all other points (Figure 9.5).

## Quadrat Analysis

This measures the dispersion of points in relation to the frequency distribution of the point pattern, that is

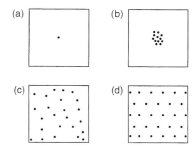

*Figure 9.5*  Point Patterns
(a) Clustered; (b) tending towards clustered; (c) random; and (d) regular

the way in which the density of points varies over the study area (Thomas, 1977; Upton and Fingleton, 1985:26–52). An observed frequency array is compared with a theoretical one predicted by a postulated spatial point process as a way of "explaining" the observed pattern. Common theoretical arrays employed are the following:

(a) *The Poisson process*. Each map cell has an equal and independent chance of receiving a point, i.e. a random pattern. The Poisson distribution is given by

$$P(x) = \frac{e^{-\lambda}\lambda^x}{x!}$$

where $P(x) =$ the probability of finding $x$ points in a specific cell (quadrat) of a pattern generated by a random process, $x = 0, 1, 2, \ldots$, and $\lambda =$ the expected mean number of points per cell. The value of $\lambda$ may be estimated as the observed average number of points per cell, i.e. $\lambda = m/n$, where $m =$ observed number of points and $n =$ number of cells. Then $\lambda$ can be substituted in the above equation for $P(x)$ for successive values of $P(x)$. The chi-squared goodness-of-fit test may be used to test a null hypothesis of no significant difference between observed and expected frequencies (e.g. Getis, 1964).

(b) *Mixed Poisson processes*. These enable a focus upon clustered and regular point distributions. They represent a combination of the Poisson process and more complex point processes either by addition (e.g. Dacey, 1964, 1966) or multiplication. For the latter the negative binomial distribution has been used for descriptions of contagious point processes (Harvey, 1966) (see Chapter 10).

(c) *Other mixed distributions*. For the modelling of clustered point processes a number of distributions have been used within ecology, but have generally not been appropriate to point distributions within human geography (Harvey, 1968; Getis and Boots, 1978).

(d) *The entropy approach*. This was pioneered by the Russian geographer Medvedkov (1967, 1970) who suggested that the probabilities from the Poisson distribution could be treated as a measure of uncertainty (*entropy*) (see the section on "entropy-maximising models" in Chapter 8) to obtain a quantity

measuring the size of the random component in a point pattern. The entropy of an observed frequency distribution can be separated into random and uniform components (e.g. Haynes and Enders, 1975), though limitations and weaknesses in this approach have been identified by Thomas (1979) and Webber (1976).

## Nearest-Neighbour Analysis

For a time in the 1960s, an alternative technique to quadrat analysis played an important part in the investigation of the arrangement of settlement patterns. Known as *nearest-neighbour analysis*, it measures the dispersion of points in relation to properties of the distribution of distances between each point and its nearest-neighbouring point. Nearest-neighbour methods were developed as a means of analysing patterns in quantitative plant ecology (see Pielou, 1977) and were introduced to geography by Dacey (1960). They enable comparisons to be made between properties of the distances between neighbouring points in a theoretical pattern and those found in an observed pattern. The commonest geographical application has been for investigating the degree of regularity of settlement patterns (e.g. King, 1962).

Nearest-neighbour analysis was developed by the plant ecologists Clark and Evans (1954) who formulated an index linked to the Poisson probability distribution. They measured the distance of each plant (or point) to its nearest neighbour and then compared the observed distances with those expected from a random pattern of points. They calculated the average expected distances ($\bar{r}_e$) from

$$\bar{r}_e = 0.5\sqrt{(A/n)}$$

where $A =$ area of study region, and $n =$ number of points.

The *nearest-neighbour statistic* ($R$) was then calculated by dividing the observed distances ($\bar{r}_o$) by the expected distances: $R = \bar{r}_o/\bar{r}_e$. This gives values of $R$ within the range 0 to 2.1491 (Figure 9.5). A value of 0 would mean that all points occupy exactly the same location. Therefore values tending towards 0 indicate a clustered pattern. A value of 2.1491 is obtained if individual points are distributed in an even hexagonal pattern so that every point is equidistant from six other points and the mean distance to the nearest neighbour is maximised. A value of 1 occurs when the expected and observed distances are equal. This indicates a random pattern. So values from 1 to 0 show a tendency towards clustering whilst those above 1 tend towards regularity. For geographers the opportunity of measuring how close a settlement pattern conformed to the hexagonal patterns that were an essential part of the central place theory of Christaller (1966) and Losch (1954) provided a powerful attraction (see Beavon, 1977).

The probability of an $R$ value occurring by chance can be established by calculating the standard error, $SE\bar{r}_e$ and $z$ scores. Work by Getis (1964) gave the formula for the standard error as

$$SE\bar{r}_e = \frac{0.26136}{\sqrt{[n(n/A)]}}$$

where $n$ = number of points, and $A$ = area of study. From this the $z$ score can be calculated from,

$$z = \frac{|\bar{r}_e - \bar{r}_o|}{SE\bar{r}_e}$$

As shown by Pinder and Witherick (1972), this can then be used to ascertain a range of random matching conditions.

There are a number of problems with nearest-neighbour analysis that have restricted its use. Major difficulties have been encountered in conjunction with boundary problems and significance tests (Thomas, 1981). One crucial problem is the definition of the study area, as its size and shape greatly influence the value of $R$. In Getis's work on urban retail patterns, he employed a circular study area enclosing most of the built-up area. This is in accord with both Hudson's view of analysing only the "biotope space", and the implication of nearest-neighbour analysis that the "expected" study area is an isotropic surface (Hudson, 1969). The basic nearest-neighbour statistic is derived for points located in an indefinite plane, but in reality, distances between points are based on measurements

for a finite study area. This can have the effect of raising the estimated mean nearest-neighbour distance. Various correction factors have been suggested (e.g. Pinder, 1978; Boots, 1979), though none of them is entirely satisfactory. Similarly, deriving a suitable significance test has proved difficult despite several suggested alternatives (e.g. Dacey, 1975).

An alternative to the use of conventional significance tests has been the use of the probability distribution known as *Bose–Einstein statistics*, used as a definition of equal likelihood or randomness of points by Thomas and Reeve (1976). For further discussion of the use of these statistics see Liebertrau and Karr (1977) and Lenz (1977). For a more detailed statistical account of nearest-neighbour analysis see Cressie (1993:602–18) who refers to advanced statistical work by Ripley (1987, 1988) on measurement of spatial dependence between different regions. This represents a significant advance on the basic nearest-neighbour approaches referred to above.

Another major weakness of nearest-neighbour analysis is the fact that the same nearest-neighbour statistic can be obtained from very different point patterns (Figure 9.5). This is because the statistic only gives information about distance between points rather than describing other features of the arrangement of points, such as angular configuration.

An extension of the technique is the calculation of the expected distance to an $n$th-order nearest neighbour (Cowie, 1968):

$$R_n = \frac{1}{\sqrt{M}} \frac{(2n)!n}{(2^n n!)^2}$$

where $M$ = density of points per unit area, and $n$ = order of nearest neighbour. This could be used to give some idea of the scale at which point patterns are occurring.

The main weakness with both quadrat and nearest-neighbour analysis is that they reduce complex geographical problems to univariate distributions for description. Ultimately, this excessive reductionism is a severe limitation on their utility. This is aptly summarised by Upton and Fingleton (1985:96):

The description of pattern in terms of the number of individuals in a given area or in terms of the distribution function for distances between individuals would appear to entirely miss the spatial nature of the pattern. Intuitively one expects to need to characterise a pattern by describing the positions of its immediate neighbours.

However, these descriptions are not the only way in which spatial pattern and structure can be analysed. For example, a more complex measure of the relationship between pattern and structure is that of spatial autocorrelation, which provides an important link with the standard statistical tests discussed in Chapters 3 and 4.

## SPATIAL AUTOCORRELATION

### The Violation of Statistical Independence

Cliff and Ord (1973) describe the concept of spatial autocorrelation by referring to the example of voting patterns in the USA. They ask the question, "If one US state votes Democrat does this increase the probability that neighbouring states will also vote Democrat?" This is a specific form of the question of whether the presence of some quality in a particular area makes its presence in a neighbouring area more or less likely. If the presence of some quality in an area does make its presence in neighbouring areas more or less likely, then the phenomenon can be said to exhibit *spatial autocorrelation* (see also Sokal and Oden, 1978). Therefore spatial autocorrelation occurs whenever the values of a variable in one location depend on the values of the same variable at nearby locations (sometimes referred to as the *neighbourhood effect* or the *contiguity effect*).

The fact that it is the distribution of a single variable that is being considered in spatial autocorrelation is emphasised by Gatrell's (1977) illustration of this phenomenon (Figure 9.6). For a $10 \times 10$ square grid each cell is allocated a random number. An exact copy of this grid and its random numbers is then placed over the original, but offset by one cell to the right, that is by "lagging" the grid one cell to the

right. If a correlation coefficient between the two sets of numbers is calculated then its value should be equal to zero. This correlation coefficient is an *autocorrelation coefficient* as it is dealing with only one variable, albeit one that can be lagged in a number of ways. Other terms used to describe this type of correlation are *self-correlation* and *internal correlation* (see Upton and Fingleton, 1985:151–213). If a significant correlation had been found in Gatrell's example then this would have indicated the presence of positive or negative spatial autocorrelation and the correlation coefficient would be a quantitative measure of spatial structure. The coefficient ($r_{xx}$) tends towards $+1$ when the variable ($x$) under consideration is positively spatially autocorrelated, and $r_{xx}$ tends towards $-1$ when $x$ is negatively spatially autocorrelated.

The concept of autocorrelation can be illustrated, perhaps more clearly, with respect to a time series, in which case we are dealing with *temporal autocorrelation*. In time series the value of a variable at time $t_2$ is very often dependent upon the value of that variable at a previous time ($t_1$). For example, in a study of air pollution, the amount of pollution measured at $t_2$ may well contain some of the pollution previously measured at a previous time ($t_1$) (Figure 9.7a). So, if the amount of air pollution is regressed versus time, the degree of double counting would bias the regression equation, that is the presence of temporal autocorrelation would affect the regression equation.

This example of temporal autocorrelation can be translated to a spatial equivalent as shown in Figure 9.7b. If the volume of pollutants in a river is measured at a number of points downstream from its source, the amount of pollution (e.g. particulate load) is likely to increase (though the concentration may well be diluted because of the greater volume of water downstream). However, much of the increased amount may be due to pollutant that entered the river upstream being recorded over a period of time at measuring points further downstream. This is another example of "double counting" or of observations at a number of points not being independent of one another. In this particular example, though, the spatial series is a simple one occurring in linear form. This is a somewhat special and limited spatial series as generally spatial datasets

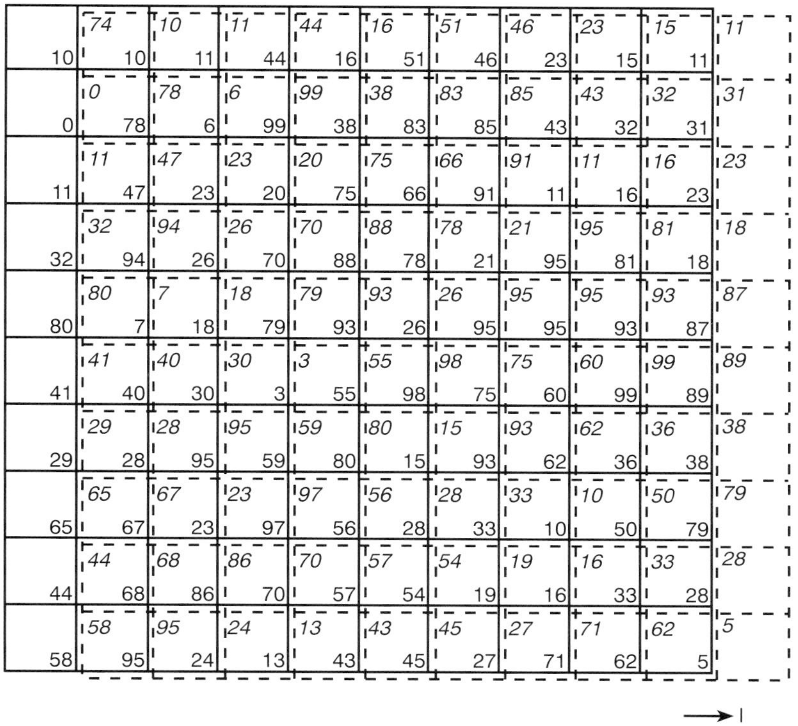

| 10 | 74 / 10 | 10 / 11 | 11 / 44 | 44 / 16 | 16 / 51 | 51 / 46 | 46 / 23 | 23 / 15 | 15 / 11 | 11 |
| 0 | 0 / 78 | 78 / 6 | 6 / 99 | 99 / 38 | 38 / 83 | 83 / 85 | 85 / 43 | 43 / 32 | 32 / 31 | 31 |
| 11 | 11 / 47 | 47 / 23 | 23 / 20 | 20 / 75 | 75 / 66 | 66 / 91 | 91 / 11 | 11 / 16 | 16 / 23 | 23 |
| 32 | 32 / 94 | 94 / 26 | 26 / 70 | 70 / 88 | 88 / 78 | 78 / 21 | 21 / 95 | 95 / 81 | 81 / 18 | 18 |
| 80 | 80 / 7 | 7 / 18 | 18 / 79 | 79 / 93 | 93 / 26 | 26 / 95 | 95 / 95 | 95 / 93 | 93 / 87 | 87 |
| 41 | 41 / 40 | 40 / 30 | 30 / 3 | 3 / 55 | 55 / 98 | 98 / 75 | 75 / 60 | 60 / 99 | 99 / 89 | 89 |
| 29 | 29 / 28 | 28 / 95 | 95 / 59 | 59 / 80 | 80 / 15 | 115 / 93 | 93 / 62 | 162 / 36 | 36 / 38 | 38 |
| 65 | 65 / 67 | 67 / 23 | 23 / 97 | 97 / 56 | 56 / 28 | 28 / 33 | 33 / 10 | 10 / 50 | 50 / 79 | 79 |
| 44 | 44 / 68 | 68 / 86 | 86 / 70 | 70 / 57 | 57 / 54 | 54 / 19 | 19 / 16 | 16 / 33 | 33 / 28 | 28 |
| 58 | 58 / 95 | 95 / 24 | 24 / 13 | 13 / 43 | 43 / 45 | 45 / 27 | 27 / 71 | 71 / 62 | 62 / 5 | 5 |

→ I

*Figure 9.6*    10×10 Grid Lagged One Cell to the East. (*Source*: Gatrell, 1977)

do not refer to change that is just unidirectional. So in most cases any interdependence among observations will occur in multiple directions (Figure 9.7c), thereby making such interdependence complex and presenting a very difficult problem if measurement of spatial autocorrelation is attempted. In effect, the problem of double or multiple counting of the same thing may occur many times at a number of observations (Haining, 1980; Hubert et al, 1981).

The significance of the interdependence of observations in the biasing of statistical testing can be seen in the investigation of rainfall distribution. Rain gauges at any one point give a similar reading to that at a point close by, although the readings are not exactly identical because of the presence of micro-climatic and micro-topographic variation. Even so, neighbouring gauges measure the same underlying characteristics of the distribution. Each gauge records a small unique component and shares a trend component of rainfall with several other gauges. Therefore the gauges record several different samples of the same process, and so these samples are not independent. Yet, this assumption of independence is one of the basic ones being made when statistical testing is performed. So it can be argued that the presence of spatial autocorrelation in a dataset substantially invalidates its use in statistical tests. In particular, such data are likely to bias the results of any regression analysis employed upon them. For example, in work on long series rainfall data in the UK, Gregory (1976) made use of data for a cluster of meteorological stations in north-west England. In effect he was "double counting" data for this part of the country, thereby potentially biasing the results from any ensuing hypothesis test requiring independence of observations.

This example is an illustration of how some of the

(a)

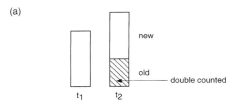

(b)

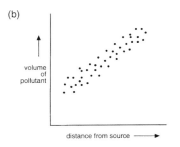

(c)

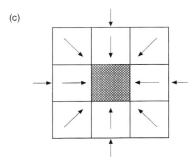

*Figure 9.7*    Examples of Autocorrelation
(a) Air pollution as temporal autocorrelation; (b) river pollution as linear spatial autocorrelation; (c) linkages between neighbouring areal units as spatial autocorrelation

statistical information carried by an observation at one location can be duplicated by observations at other locations. This duplication has implications for the sampling distributions, especially standard errors, of certain statistics. For example, the presence of autocorrelation among the population error terms leads to biased estimates of the residual variance and inefficient estimates of the regression coefficients when the method of ordinary least-squares regression analysis described in Chapter 4 is used (Cliff and Ord,

1973:87; see also Haining, 1988). However, duplication can also be used to advantage, for example interpolating between observations on a map or where there are missing values in an otherwise complete spatial record (Tobler and Kennedy, 1982). The available observed data may be used to calculate estimates of missing values and to place probability intervals around these estimates (Miron, 1984; Haining et al, 1984). Thus spatially autocorrelated data need not always be regarded as a statistical problem to be overcome, but rather as an inescapable property of spatial data to be exploited (Goodchild et al, 1992). In particular, the effects of spatial autocorrelation can be used in forecasting (see Chapter 10) and modelling, for example in modelling the spread of disease (Gould, 1994; Openshaw, 1991a).

Odlund (1988) highlights three main problems that occur when classical parametric statistics are applied to autocorrelated data:

1. The basic condition of independence among observations is not fulfilled.
2. Estimates of the standard error used in most hypothesis testing are biased.
3. Regression models fail if residuals from the model are uncorrelated. Standard error estimates of regression coefficients are under-estimated for positive autocorrelation and over-estimated for negative autocorrelation.

It can be shown that many spatial distributions violate the assumption of independence. Some may be positively spatially autocorrelated, in which case high values of a variable in one area are associated with high values of that variable in neighbouring areas. Others may be negatively spatially autocorrelated, in which case high and low values of the variable alternate. Figure 9.8 contains the suggestion of positive autocorrelation in the distribution of the A allele gene in the Republic of Ireland. This can be "explained" in terms of regional clusters of counties having statistically abnormally high or low rates of occurrence of cancer of this human blood group. This may indicate particular local migration patterns which might contribute to this increased or decreased incidence.

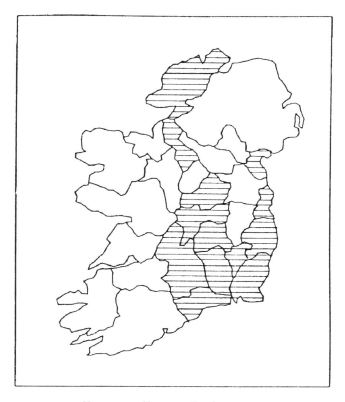

Key : ▤ = Above median frequency

*Figure 9.8*    The distribution of the A Allele Gene in the Republic of Ireland. (*Source*: Upton and Fingleton, 1985:161)

Given the frequent presence of spatial autocorrelation within geographical data, it is not surprising that claims such as that contained in the following quote may be made: "Textbooks on quantitative geography still frequently contain large sections on standard statistical methods assuming independent observations ... These are unlikely ever to be appropriate in geography" (Ripley, 1984:342). This statement casts doubt on the utility of statistical techniques discussed in Chapters 2 to 5. Yet, the presence of spatial autocorrelation is not something that Gould (1969a) believes should be a worry for geographers. Instead, he argues that geography is largely concerned with the study of interdependence, rather than independence of observations, and that therefore spatial autocorrelation is fundamental to much geographical work. Gatrell

(1977), examining this notion of spatial autocorrelation as a phenomenon of great relevance to geographical research, gives three main reasons for considering it to be of importance:

1. Geographers need to ascertain whether a spatial distribution is significantly different from the outcome of a random process so that they do not make the mistake of attributing pattern to what is really a random distribution. Therefore any spatial analysis should commence with a test for the presence of spatial autocorrelation in the variables under examination.
2. Geographers need to examine the influences of spatial autocorrelation upon the inferences that may be drawn from statistical tests (Gould, 1969a).

As these inferences are made on the assumption that the observations being examined are independent, then the presence of spatial autocorrelation is likely to bias any resultant inferences. With respect to regression analysis, Gould suggested that this testing for the presence of spatial autocorrelation should begin by searching for it in both dependent and independent variables, and, once the regression equation has been obtained, should then be followed by testing for spatial autocorrelation amongst the residuals.

3. Geographers need to make use of the existence of spatial autocorrelation by incorporating it in their models, especially those with a forecasting or predictive element. In such cases the presence of spatial autocorrelation can be employed explicitly in the models whereas its existence is recognised implicitly in basic spatial diffusion models (Chapter 10), in which it is assumed that spatial pattern at time $t + 1$ depends directly upon that at time $t$, thereby exhibiting a strong degree of positive spatial autocorrelation.

Many geographers now recognise that the existence of spatial interdependencies can produce biased results in hypothesis testing, correlation and regression analysis, thereby severely limiting the extent of generalisations that can be made from such work. For example, whilst pioneering research was still proceeding on the topic, Harvey (1969:347) argued that:

> The choice of the product-moment correlation coefficient for regionalization problems appears singularly inappropriate, since one of the technical requirements of this statistic is independence in the observations. Since the aim of such regionalization is to produce contiguous regions which are internally relatively homogeneous, it seems almost certain that this condition of independence in the observations will be violated.

Yet there is little agreement as to how geographers should react to the presence of spatial autocorrelation in their data; how they should measure it or how they might incorporate it in their work. The importance of the presence of spatial autocorrelation obviously depends upon the particular problem being considered,

but many geographers have been content to ignore this phenomenon on the grounds that is a "natural" occurrence within spatial datasets. Indeed, it could be argued that the presence of spatial interdependence is not something to be concerned about even in inferential statistics, as statistical testing of spatial data should simply reflect any "natural" rather than worrying about lack of independence of observations. This argument views geographical research as fundamentally different from that of experimental research for which the assumptions underlying statistical inference were intended. Some have argued that the problem of bias as a result of spatial autocorrelation refers only to the situations involving forecasting and prediction. Therefore, it does not affect use of correlation or regression for simple descriptive purposes or some forms of ecological analysis (Johnston, 1978:261–3, 1982b).

Johnston (1982b, 1984d:135) argues that spatial autocorrelation is irrelevant in an ecological analysis where the focus is entirely on the internal characteristics of the areal units to which the data apply and the actual spatial location of that unit is of no importance. For example, his regression of percentage voting Labour in the wards of Sheffield against the percentage of the ward population who are manual workers is simply asking, "Are the areas with more Labour voters also the areas with more manual workers?" This refers only to the internal characteristics of the areal units being examined (the wards) and he contends that this renders consideration of spatial autocorrelation irrelevant.

## Measuring Spatial Autocorrelation Using Join-Count Statistics

The presence of spatial autocorrelation in the distribution of many of the variables studied by geographers is not surprising given the linkages and flows between places that create spatial dependencies. But, the complexities of spatial autocorrelation have meant that it has been very difficult to quantify and to establish the meaning of its presence. Different forms of measurement were suggested in the early 1950s by the statisticians Moran (1950) and Geary (1954), but subsequent work by Cliff and Ord (1969, 1973, 1975c) largely served to demonstrate the difficulties involved in attempting to measure spatial autocorrelation for variables which did not have values for regularly shaped areal units.

In developing measurements of spatial autocorrelation, the ideas of leading researchers Andrew Cliff (a geographer) and John Ord (a statistician) closely followed previous developments in temporal autocorrelation, substituting space for time. They argued that, for most spatially distributed variables, successive observations over space are related, depending upon how close they are and upon the strength of the contiguity characteristics of the spatial variable. For a given set of regions (areal units) they recognised two basic problems when attempting to devise a measure for spatial autocorrelation (Cliff et al, 1975c:147–9):

1. Which function of the variable under consideration should be used? For example, if $y_i$ = the proportion of votes cast in county $i$ for a particular political party, should we define $x_i$ as being equal to $y_i$ or should $x_i$ be the rank of county $i$ according to $y_i$ (where the county with the $r$th smallest value of $y_i$ has rank $r$) or should $x_i = 1$ if the party has a majority in county $i$ and $x_i = 0$ if the party does not have a majority? There are clearly other possibilities, but even this cursory outline suggests that different measures may be applicable for data on interval, ratio and nominal (binary) scales.

2. How should the degree of interaction between the areal units be measured?

One way in which interactions have been considered has been via *join-count statistics*, used for nominal-scale data where binary numbers 1 and 0 are used for identifying the existence/non-existence of a certain characteristic ($x$) in the areal unit. This defines existence of the particular quality = $B$ for black, and non-existence = $W$ for white. If two areal units have a common boundary, they are said to have a join. Thus it is possible to calculate the number of $BB$, $BW$ and $WW$ joins as well as determining theoretically the expression of the expected number of $BB$, $BW$ and $WW$ joins. These theoretical values may then be com-

pared with observed values. Typical arrangements, or spatial lattices, can be considered in terms of a contiguity matrix portraying the number of contacts between adjoining areal units, that is administrative units or cells in a grid. For example, if cell $i$ is contiguous with cell $j$ then $d_{ij} = 1$. If $i$ and $j$ are non-contiguous then $d_{ij} = 0$. However, what constitutes contiguity may vary from situation to situation. Cliff and Ord (1973:16) refer to three different examples (Figure 9.9):

- edge-to-edge contact, as represented by the movement of the Rook in chess (Figure 9.9a);
- vertex-to-vertex contact, as represented by the movement of the Bishop in chess (Figure 9.9b);
- both edge-to-edge and vertex-to-vertex contact, as represented by the movement of the Queen in chess (Figure 9.9c).

The number of contacts, or joins, between the individual cells can be calculated from the formula

$$A = \tfrac{1}{2} \sum_{i}^{n} \sum_{j}^{n} d_{ij}$$

where $A$ is the number of contacts or joins between cells. For the $4 \times 4$ cellular grid depicted in Figure

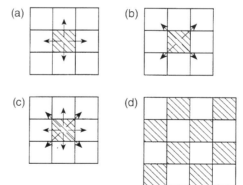

*Figure 9.9* Patterns of Weights for Spatial Autocorrelation using Binary Data
(a) Binary distribution – Rook's case; (b) binary distribution – Bishop's case; (c) binary distribution - Queen's case; (d) deterministic limiting case of negative autocorrelation processes

9.9d, for the Rook's case, $A = 24$. This pattern is the deterministic limiting case of negative autocorrelation processes in which every zero (minimum) value of $x$ has a neighbour with a value of $x = 1$ (maximum). If the definition of contiguity is changed to the Bishop's case ($A = 18$) then the pattern becomes indicative of positive spatial autocorrelation in which for every cell with a zero value the vertex neighbours will also have a zero value. Cells with a value of one will have vertex neighbours of the same value. In contrast, for the Queen's case ($A = 42$), the join counts of both edge-to-edge and vertex-to-vertex are indicative of random spatial autocorrelation. In any investigation of spatial autocorrelation, therefore, it is important to be able to specify the nature of the contiguity between cells as this can affect the resultant measurements of any spatial autocorrelation coefficient, that is the same pattern is likely to suggest different types of spatial autocorrelation as illustrated by the Rook's, Bishop's and Queen's cases in Figure 9.9d.

To determine whether spatial autocorrelation is present, based on nominal-scale data for areal units, it is possible to count the number of types of joins present. These can then be compared with the expected numbers under a null hypothesis ($H_0$) of no spatial autocorrelation.

If $\{d_{ij}\}$ is a contiguity matrix in which $d_{ij} = 1$ if the $i$th and $j$th areal units are joined, and $d_{ij} = 0$ if they are not joined, then the observed number of $BB$ joins is given by

$$BB = \tfrac{1}{2}\sum_{i=1}^{n}\sum_{j=1}^{n} d_{ij}x_i x_j \qquad (9.1)$$

where $x_i = 1$ if the $i$th county is $B$, and $x_i = 0$ if the $i$th county is $W$. Then the observed number of $BW$ joins is given by

$$BW = \tfrac{1}{2}\sum_{i=1}^{n}\sum_{j=1}^{n} d_{ij}(x_i - x_j)^2$$

And the observed number of $WW$ joins is given by

$$WW = A - (BB + BW)$$

where $A$ = the total number of joins in the system of areal units,

$$A = \tfrac{1}{2}\sum_{i=1}^{n} L_i$$

and $L_i$ = the number of areal units joined to the $i$th areal unit. The use of the factor of $1/2$ in this equation eliminates duplication of information arising through counting of both $ij$ and $ji$ joins when they carry the same information.

In testing whether the observed join counts depart significantly from the numbers produced by a random distribution, the assumption that the join-count statistics are normally distributed can be applied. Details of how this may be performed are given by Moran (1948) and by Cliff and Ord (1973:5–7).

For data at a higher level of measurement, alternative measures of spatial autocorrelation can be employed, as originally developed by P.A.P. Moran and R.C. Geary in the 1940s and 1950s.

## Moran's *I* Statistic and Geary's *c* Statistic

*Moran's spatial autocorrelation coefficient* can be applied to both a regular grid of cells or an irregular one, such as that comprising administrative areas, and can be applied to interval/ratio data as well as to nominal and ordinal data. The coefficient ($I$ or $r_{xx}$ in the notation used above) is based on the Pearson coefficient, $r_{xy}$ and can be used for ordinal- or interval-scale data. It is calculated from

$$r_{xx} = I = \frac{S_{xx}}{S_x^2}$$

where $S_x^2$ = the variance of variable $x$, and $S_{xx}$ = the spatial autocovariance of $x$. This measures the extent to which $x$ is positively or negatively associated with itself. Autocovariance is large and positive if the variable is positively spatially autocorrelated, and large and negative if it is negatively spatially autocorrelated. Thus

$$S_{xx} = \frac{1}{2} A \sum_i^n \sum_j^n (x_i - \bar{x})(x_j - \bar{x}) d_{ij}$$

or

$$I = \frac{n \sum_i \sum_j d_{ij}(x_i - \bar{x})(x_j - \bar{x})}{d \sum_i (x_i - \bar{x})^2}$$

where $A$ = the number of joins, and $d_{ij}$ = the elements of the contiguity matrix.

In formulating a significance test for $r_{xx}$, Moran (1950) defined a random map pattern for a contiguous group of $n$ areal units as a set of $n$ independent values of the standard normal random variable $x$. Then the mean value of the spatial autocorrelation coefficient $(r_{xx})$ is given by

$$(r_{xx}) = -1/(n-1)$$

As long as $n > 30$ then the sampling distribution of $r_{xx}$ follows a general normal distribution with a mean of $\mu(r_{xx})$ and a standard error ($SE_{r_{xx}}$),

$$\sigma(r_{xx}) = \sqrt{\left( \frac{4An^2 - 8n(A+D) + 12A^2}{4A^2(n^2-1)} \right) - \mu^2(r_{xx})}$$

where $A$ = the number of joins, $n$ = the number of areal units, $L_i$ = the number of areal units joined to the $i$th region, and

$$D = \frac{1}{2} \sum_i^n L_i(L_i - 1).$$

A similar coefficient to that proposed by Moran was developed in the early 1950s by another statistician (Geary, 1954). It has a similar form to Moran's in that the numerator term is a measure of covariance among the $\{x_i\}$ and the denominator term is a measure of variance. *Geary's c statistic* is defined as:

$$c = \frac{(n-1)\sum_i \sum_j w_{ij}(x_i - x_j)^2}{2w \sum_{i=1}^n (x_i - \bar{x})^2}$$

Whereas Moran's $I$ is based on the cross-products of the deviations of the $x_i$ from $\bar{x}$, which is analogous to the $BB$ join-count statistic in equation (9.1), Geary's $c$ uses squared differences between the $x_i$. Detailed consideration of the statistical properties of join-count statistics $I$ and $c$ are given by Cliff and Ord (1971, 1973). A comparison between $I$ and $c$ in terms of the values obtained from different spatial arrangements is given in Table 9.8.

Applying the Moran coefficient to the distribution of the Labour vote in Wales at the 1974 UK General Election, Thomas and Huggett (1980:277–8) demonstrated that positive spatial autocorrelation was present ($r_{xx} = +0.54$ for 36 constituencies). This meant that neighbouring Welsh constituencies had similar voting tendencies in favour of the Labour Party. However, they recognised that their analysis employed a simple definition of contiguity that did not consider either size of constituency or length of the common boundary between constituencies.

## Cliff and Ord's Autocorrelation Coefficient

Cliff and Ord (1973) recognised the same problem regarding contiguity as described above for Thomas

*Table 9.8*  Geary's c and Moran's I for Three General Arrangements of Spatial Data

| Spatial Arrangement | Geary's c | Moran's I |
|---|---|---|
| Similar, regionalised, smooth, clustered | $0 < c < 1$ | $I > 0$ |
| Independent, uncorrelated and random | $c = 1$ | $I < 0$ |
| Dissimilar, contrasting, "chequerboard" | $c > 1$ | $I < 0$ |

*Source*: Goodchild (1987),

and Huggett's example. So, they produced a modified version of the Moran coefficient in which $d_{ij} = 0$ and $d_{ij} = 1$ were replaced by generalised weights ($w_{ij}$) representing the hypothesised influence of areal unit $i$ on areal unit $j$. Thus these weights could be used to hypothesise differences in the degree of contact between areal units, e.g. using a simple gravity model approach such as,

$$w_{ij} = P_i P_j d_{ij}^{-1}$$

where $P_i$ = population in areal unit $i$, $P_j$ = population in areal unit $j$, and $d_{ij}$ = distance between areal units $i$ and $j$.

If no such simple specification of weights seems appropriate, Cliff and Ord suggest that a standard set of weights could be used:

$$w_{ij} = B_{i(j)}/d_{ij}$$

where $B_{i(j)}$ = the proportion of the boundary of areal unit $i$ (excluding the portion of $i$'s perimeter that is also the boundary of the study area and so is non-contiguous with any other areal unit) that is shared with areal unit $j$, i.e. length of boundary of areal unit $i$ in common with $j$, divided by the length of common boundaries of areal unit $i$; and $d_{ij}$ = distance between the centroid of areal unit $i$ and the centroid of areal unit $j$.

This procedure produces weightings only for neighbouring areal units and so ignores any autocorrelation processes involving non-contiguous areas. A modified version was employed by Haggett (1976) in an analysis of the incidence of measles: to reflect high incidence of measles in urban areas and low incidence in rural areas, $w_{ij} = 1$ when both $i$ and $j$ are either rural or urban, and $w_{ij} = 0$ when $i$ is rural and $j$ is urban, or vice versa.

When this type of weighting is employed, the weighted autocorrelation coefficient ($wr_{xx}$) is given by

$$wr_{xx} = \frac{wS_{xx}}{S_x^2}$$

where the weighted spatial covariance is

$$wS_{xx} = \frac{1}{W} \sum_i \sum_j (x_i - \bar{x})(x_j - \bar{x}) w_{ij}$$

with $W$ = the sum of all the elements $w_{ij}$ forming the specified weighting matrix, i.e.

$$W = \sum_i^n \sum_j^n w_{ij}$$

The general approach to measuring spatial autocorrelation recommended by Cliff and Ord (1969) was the *contiguity approach* which can be applied to regular and irregular lattices of cells and points and to both ratio-scale and binary data. Its basic form is:

1. Given a system of $n$ areal units for which a variate ($x$) has been measured in each of the $n$ areal units, let the value of $x$ in the $i$th areal unit be $x_i$.
2. Calculate $Z_i$, the deviation of the $i$th cell from the mean.
3. The fundamental concern is how this value relates to the deviation at another location ($j$). The relationship between the two deviations can be investigated by multiplying them and weighting this product by a predetermined value ($w_{ij}$) which may be defined *a priori* as the influence of $j$ on $i$. Therefore $w_{ij}$ denotes the effect of areal unit $i$ on areal unit $j$. Common examples of weightings are $w_{ij} = 1$, if the two cells share a common boundary, and $w_{ij} = 0$ if the cells do not share a common boundary.
4. Perform this procedure for all areas/points under consideration and sum the weighted products i.e.

$$\sum_i \sum_j w_{ij} Z_i Z_j$$

5. Divide this sum by the variation in the deviations $\sum(Z_i^2)$ and weight this by the ratio of $n$ (the number of observations) to $w$ (the sum of the weights). This gives the final index of spatial autocorrelation, $I$, i.e.

$$I = \frac{\sum_{i=1}^{n}\sum_{j=1}^{m} w_{ij} Z_i Z_j}{W \sum_{i=1}^{n} Z_i^2}$$

The spatial autocorrelation ($r_{xx}$) between the $x_i$ is:

$$r_{xx} = \frac{n\sum_{i=1}^{n}\sum_{j=1}^{m} w_{ij}(x_i - \bar{x})(x_j - \bar{x})}{W \sum_{i=1}^{n}(x_i - \bar{x})^2}$$

where $i \neq j$ and

$$W = \sum_{i=1}^{n}\sum_{j=1}^{m} w_{ij}.$$

A sampling distribution for this coefficient was derived in order to develop a reliable test of significance (Cliff and Ord, 1971).

The chief weaknesses of this approach are the difficulty in specifying the required weightings and the fact that this method gives no information on the directional variations in dependence. To counter the former difficulty, various weightings were specified in order to generate a range of values within which spatial autocorrelation might exist.

## The Runs Test and Other Aspects of Spatial Autocorrelation

One of the most straightforward measures for determining the presence or absence of spatial autocorrelation can be employed to test for autocorrelation in the residuals from a regression analysis. The test employed is the *runs test*, which can be used to investigate the violation of the assumption of independence of observations in the variables used in the regression. If the assumption is violated then it is common to obtain a sequence of residuals above the regression line followed by a sequence of residuals below the line (Figure 9.10). The runs test can be used to test whether the sequences of positive and negative residuals differ significantly from those obtained in a random sequence. If a non-random sequence is revealed this implies that the relationship being investigated may take a non-linear form or that more independent vari-

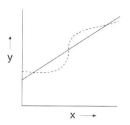

*Figure 9.10*  Spatial Autocorrelation Amongst the Residuals from a Regression Analysis

ables should be measured at other locations (Cliff and Ord, 1975c).

More complex testing for autocorrelation amongst the residuals from regression analysis can be performed using $I$ and $c$ (Cliff and Ord, 1973:91–7 and 105–31).

Perhaps because of the somewhat obtrusive statistical character of many of the articles dealing with it, spatial autocorrelation has acquired something of a mystique and reputation as a "difficult", even "elusive", concept. The lack of easily available computer packages for performing some of the tests for autocorrelation contributed to this, though Griffith's (1987) use of the Minitab statistical computing package to calculate Moran's coefficient, and for simulating the effects of spatial autocorrelation on correlation coefficients, regression estimation and analysis of variance, went some way towards overcoming this problem (see also Bailey and Gatrell, 1995:269–90).

One area of research pursued more recently has been the effect of spatial resolution upon measurement of spatial autocorrelation. For example, in investigating the presence of a highly positively spatially autocorrelated variable, wildland fires, Chou (1991) and Chou et al (1990) found that Moran's $I$ increased systematically with geometrical increases in resolution level (increased size of spatial mesh). Therefore the value of $I$ could be used to provide information about the reliability of other spatial statistics computed at differing levels of resolution. In other words, there may be disproportionate changes among different types of spatial relationships in response to the increase in spatial resolution. A simple example is shown in Figure 9.11 where increased map resolution

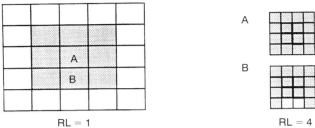

RL = 1

When the resolution level (RL) is increased from 1 to 4, the number of shaded neighbours for square A increases from 8 to 20; for square B, the numbers increase from 5 shaded and 3 white (shaded − white = 2) to 14 shaded and 6 white (shaded − white = 8)

*Figure 9.11*    Resolution Effects on Adjacent Grid Cells. (*Source*: Geddes, 1993)

enhances spatial resolution between spatial units of the same type to a greater extent than that between different types of unit. When the resolution level is increased from 1 to 4, the number of shaded neighbours for square A increases from eight to 20; for square B, the numbers increase from five shaded and three white to 14 shaded and six white.

## SPATIAL CLUSTERING

### The Geographical Analysis Machine

Whilst geographers have tended to concentrate on the non-independence of regional observations, others concerned with spatial statistics, such as epidemiologists and medical statisticians, have developed methods analysing point observations of disease occurrence. Geographers have played a part in the latter line of enquiry in the development of disease forecasting and multi-level systems.

Whilst nearest-neighbour analysis was used largely to see whether point patterns departed from a random distribution of points, contemporary work done by medical statisticians was examining point patterns of disease occurrence for evidence of clustering (e.g. Pinkel and Nefzger, 1959). This focused on pairs of points and evaluated the presence or absence of space–time clustering using cumulative Poisson probabilities or the chi-squared test.

The basic test for *clustering*, as performed by Knox (1964a,b), examined a spatial distribution of $r$ cases of a disease. Each occurrence can be paired with $(r - 1)$ other cases so that the number of possible pairs $(R)$ is $R = 0.5r(r - 1)$. Distances between points are measured by coordinates $(d_i, V_i)$. Data can be arranged in contingency tables, with class boundaries used to separate those pairs which are close in space and time to other pairs.

If space–time clustering is present then the observed close pair frequency $(O_{11})$ will be significantly greater than the corresponding expected frequency $(E_{11})$ which can be calculated from the contingency table. If $E_{11} < 5$, the exact significance of $O_{11}$ is evaluated as a cumulative Poisson probability with a mean of $E_{11}$. For $E_{11} > 5$, a $\chi^2$ test with one degree of freedom can be used (Thomas, 1991:445).

The parametric form of this method is Mantel's (1967) *space–time regression* which uses standard correlation and regression procedures to analyse the strength of the relationship between the $R$ pairs. As the frequency distributions of $t_i$ and $d_i$ are usually negatively skewed, a reciprocal transformation is employed, i.e. $t_i^{-b}$ and $d_i^{-b}$. This method has been shown to be effective in detecting *clinal clusters*, that is point source disease, such as carcinogens, that diffuse atmospherically at a decreasing rate from a source. It is less effective at detecting *hot-spot clusters*, such as a single region in a study area experiencing a constant higher risk than elsewhere because of local conditions, e.g. locally contaminated food or water supplies (Openshaw, 1986; Wartenberg and Greenberg, 1990). Chen et al (1984) have shown that both Knox's test and Mantel's have high power when dealing with diseases of short incubation period, but that they are less effective for diseases with longer suspected periods of latency.

In the UK, Openshaw pioneered the development of "cluster busting" systems to investigate observations of high numbers of childhood leukaemia cases around nuclear installations. He developed a *geographical analysis machine* (GAM) which repeatedly tests for clustering at all the spatial scales that are deemed appropriate for the disease process under investigation (Openshaw, 1990a; Openshaw et al, 1987, 1988a,b; Openshaw and Craft, 1989). The GAM has four elements:

- a spatial hypothesis generator;
- a significance assessment procedure;
- a geographical information system (GIS) that stores and manipulates spatial data;
- a display and mapping system.

The spatial hypothesis generator is depicted in Figure 9.12. It consists of a fine grid of points with intersecting circles around each point, so that it is possible to make counts of disease occurrences within the vicinity of each point, but with a degree of overlap of circles so that each occurrence appears in several different circles. In his work on the incidence of leukaemia amongst children, Openshaw (1990a) calculated the age–sex adjusted incidence of leukaemia for the child population of each circle and then tested its significance using the Poisson distribution. This process was then repeated for larger circles until the radius of the circles was too large for clustering to be detected. This method highlights clusters of the disease in terms of overlapping circles containing significant occurrences referred to as "dense blobs". Subsequent refinements by Besag and Newell (1991), and Diggle's (1990) test for spatial clustering around a point source, support Thomas's (1991:452) assertion that "the controlled application of spatial statistics has helped to sharpen the focus of a substantial epidemiological debate".

The GAM system revealed clusters of childhood leukaemia around the nuclear site at Sellafield in north-west England, but also showed clusters for locations not associated with sources of ionising radiation. The system represents an efficient searching mechanism for such clusters but the link between effect (the clusters) and cause seems elusive. Epidemiologists refer to *confounding factors* which represent alternative causes to that of ionising radiation from nuclear plants (Wakeford, 1990). For example, some child-

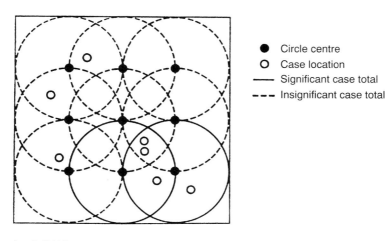

*Figure 9.12*   Openshaw's GAM

● Circle centre
○ Case location
— Significant case total
--- Insignificant case total

hood leukaemias are associated with the exposure of the foetus to ionising radiation during radiographic examination of the pregnant mother's abdomen; and there may also be an unidentified virus associated with the disease (Thomas, 1991:451–2). The complexity of this problem is highlighted by work suggesting that only nuclear installations in the UK with reprocessing plants have experienced excessive risks (Cook-Mozaffari et al, 1989).

## Bayes Estimates

In other recent work on the occurrence of leukaemia, Langford (1994) has made use of *Bayes estimates* in analysing risk of the disease amongst children. This builds on work by the statisticians Lindley and Smith (1972) and Manly (1978) amongst others. Whereas classical statistical inference (described in Chapters 2 and 3) relies on hypothesis testing using confidence intervals and probabilities, "Bayesian inference is based on the fact that the joint probability of two events can be written as the product of one event and the conditional probability of the second event, based on the first event" (Langford, 1994:143). This can be expressed as the inclusion of prior information or belief about a dataset in estimating the probability distribution of the data, so that (prior belief × likelihood function = posterior belief). When considering risk of childhood leukaemia this can be translated into a *likelihood function* that is the Poisson-distributed numbers of observed cases occurring within the areal units under investigation, with classical statistical analyses of relative risks and probabilities as representations of these data. Relative risks (the ratios of observed to expected numbers of cases for each area) can be calculated from

$$R_i = \frac{y_i}{\mu_i}$$

where $R_i$ = relative risk of a disease in the $i$th areal unit based on the number of observed cases ($y_i$) and the age–sex standardised expected cases ($\mu_i$).

However, for diseases with a low incidence of occurrence, $R_i$ can have extreme values in areas which

have small populations. Also, $R_i$ does not distinguish between a situation where there are 200 cases, where 100 were expected, and that in which there are two cases, where one is expected. Empirical Bayes estimates are therefore a compromise between $R_i$ and calculation of Poisson probabilities (usually known as *p-values*, the probability of a certain number of events occurring within specified boundaries of space or time), the latter tending to be more extreme in areas of large population (see Gardner, 1989).

Langford's model included three types of prior information:

- mean relative risk;
- a weighting to areas of larger population as relative risks there are likely to be more reliable;
- the known structure of the distribution of relative risks, which can be represented as a *gamma distribution* (a probability distribution based on a function defined by Euler).

The latter can describe the amount of space or time required for a number of events to occur. Alternatives are the log-normal distribution (e.g. Clayton and Kaldor, 1987) and the use of spatial autocorrelation (Marshall, 1991). If a gamma distribution is used, the relative risk can be described by two parameters, $a$, a shape parameter, and $v$, a scale parameter. There are several ways in which these parameters can be estimated, usually based on notions of maximum likelihood. Conditional on the distribution of cases within each area, the posterior relative risks follow a gamma distribution with both scale and shape parameters containing an additional element ($\mu_i$ and $\gamma_i$ repectively). Therefore

$$\text{posterior expectation of relative risk} = \frac{\gamma_i + v}{\mu_i + a}$$

If $\gamma_i$ and $\mu_i$ are large with respect to $a$ and $v$ then the empirical Bayes estimates are little different from the original relative risks. However, if $\gamma_i$ and $\mu_i$ are small compared with $a$ and $v$, then these parameters will largely determine the estimates.

In applying empirical Bayes estimates to data on

childhood leukaemia, Langford (1994) showed that if the data were presented for very small population units in comparison with the incidence of the disease, little of a meaningful nature could be said about relative risks. Therefore it was not possible to say whether an occurrence of three cases of the disease in a particular small urban district was unusual or not (as the empirical Bayes estimates for the small areas were wholly contained between 99 per cent and 101 per cent of mean relative risk) (see Table 9.9a). For larger districts of more homogeneous population, the estimates showed that zero cases of the disease would yield a zero relative risk, although the number of expected cases varied from just below two to just above three

(see Table 9.9b). For districts with no disease occurrence the lower the empirical Bayes estimate, the more likely this zero is of genuine interest. Therefore there would appear to be potential for further use of the estimate rather than simply measuring relative risks (see Clayton and Bernardinelli, 1992; Bailey and Gatrell, 1995:303–8).

## RECENT ADVANCES IN POINT PATTERN ANALYSIS

Advances in spatial point pattern analysis highlighted by Gatrell et al (1996) include work on properties of

*Table 9.9*   Relative Risks and Empirical Bayes Estimates (EBE) for Childhood Leukaemia in the UK

(a) For selected small population units, 1969–73

| District | Number of Observations | Relative Cases Expected | Risk (%) | EBE (%) |
|---|---|---|---|---|
| Llanfyllin RD | 3 | 0.2529 | 1186.240 | 100.145 |
| Montgomery MB | 1 | 0.0353 | 2832.861 | 100.053 |
| Seaton UD | 1 | 0.0813 | 1230.012 | 100.051 |
| Ilminster UD | 1 | 0.1005 | 995.025 | 100.050 |
| Ketton RD | 1 | 0.1184 | 844.595 | 100.049 |
| Chichester RD | 0 | 1.8109 | 0.000 | 99.911 |
| Hastings CB | 0 | 1.8970 | 0.000 | 99.906 |
| Widnes MB | 0 | 2.2290 | 0.000 | 99.889 |
| Burnley CB | 0 | 2.5252 | 0.000 | 99.874 |
| Wallasey CB | 0 | 3.2694 | 0.000 | 99.836 |

RD = rural district; MB = municipal borough; UD = urban district; CB = county borough

(b) For selected larger districts of more homogeneous population, 1984–88

| District | Number of Observations | Relative Cases Expected | Risk (%) | EBE (%) |
|---|---|---|---|---|
| South Lakeland | 7 | 2.2699 | 308.384 | 140.513 |
| Selby | 6 | 2.3566 | 254.604 | 131.190 |
| Carrick | 5 | 1.9243 | 259.835 | 127.459 |
| Torridge | 4 | 1.2281 | 325.706 | 126.425 |
| Mendip | 3 | 1.0618 | 282.539 | 119.071 |
| Wyre | 0 | 1.8645 | 0.000 | 84.793 |
| Llanelli | 0 | 1.9512 | 0.000 | 84.161 |
| Pendle | 0 | 2.1135 | 0.000 | 83.002 |
| Scarborough | 0 | 2.5378 | 0.000 | 80.119 |
| Suffolk Coastal | 0 | 3.0837 | 0.000 | 76.691 |

*Source*: Langford (1994:147).

*Spatial stochastic processes* whose outcome is an observed spatial point pattern. Three particular sets of properties have been investigated, which are dealt with below.

## First- and Second-order Properties

*First-order properties* describe the way in which the expected value of the process varies across space; *second-order properties*, referred to as a *spatial dependence*, describe the correlation between values of the process at different spatial locations. So spatial pattern in observed spatial data may arise from first-order variation in the form of a regional trend or from second-order variation in the form of correlation structures.

First-order properties are described in terms of the *intensity* ($\lambda$) of the process, where intensity is the mean number of events per unit area at point $s$ (see Diggle, 1983). It is defined as the mathematical limit,

$$\lambda(s) = \lim_{ds \to 0} \left[ \frac{E(\gamma(ds))}{ds} \right]$$

where $d_s$ = a small region around the point $s$; $s_1, s_2, \ldots$ = a set of locations in the study region, at which events of interest have been recorded; $s_i$ = a vector referring to the location of the *i*th observed event, which is a convenient way of identifying the coordinates, $s_{i1}, s_{i2}$, of an event; $E(\ldots)$ = the expectation operator; and $\gamma(ds)$ = the number of events in the small region, $ds$.

Second-order properties involve the relationship between numbers of events in pairs of sub-regions within a study region, $R$. This is also defined in terms of a limit:

$$\gamma(s_i, s_j) = \lim_{ds_i, ds_j \to 0} \left[ \frac{E(\gamma(ds_i)\gamma(ds_j))}{ds_i \, ds_j} \right]$$

where the notation is as above.

A point process is termed *stationary* if intensity is constant over $R$, that is:

$$\lambda(s) = \lambda \qquad \text{and} \qquad \gamma(s_i, s_j) = \gamma(s_i - s_j) = \gamma(d)$$

This also implies that the second-order intensity depends only on the vector difference, $d$ (direction and distance) between $s_i$ and $s_j$ and not on their absolute locations. The process is termed *isotropic* if this dependence is a function of only the length ($d$) of this vector ($d$) and not its orientation.

## Kernel Estimation

In investigating *epidemiology*, the geographical incidence of disease, estimates of the intensity at each grid point can be made by counting events per unit area within a moving window of fixed size centred on a number of locations in turn arranged in a fine grid superimposed on the study region $R$. This gives a smoother estimate of variation in $\lambda(s)$ than produced by using a fixed grid of quadrats. However, this does not take account of the relative location of events within the window, and the optimal size of the window is unclear. However, *kernel estimation* develops this idea, replacing the window with a kernel or three-dimensional function which "weights events within its sphere of influence according to their distance from the point at which the intensity is being estimated" (Gatrell et al, 1996:259).

Kernel estimation has been used to obtain smooth estimates of univariate or multivariate probability densities from an observed sample of observations (Silverman, 1986). It can be used to estimate the intensity of a spatial point pattern, $\hat{\lambda}_\tau(s)$ at $s$, a vector location anywhere in $R$:

$$\hat{\lambda}_\tau(s) = \sum_{i=1}^{n} \frac{1}{\tau^2} k\left(\frac{s - s_i}{\tau}\right)$$

where $s_1, \ldots, s_n$ = vector locations of the $n$ observed events; and $k(\ldots)$ = the *kernel weighting function*, expressed in standardised form (centred at the origin and having a total volume of unity under the curve). This is then centred on $s$ and stretched according to the parameter $\tau > 0$, known as the *bandwidth*, with the value of $\tau$ chosen to provide the required degree of smoothing in the estimate.

This process is displayed graphically in Figure 9.13, as a three-dimensional function that visits each point $s$ on a fine grid. The region of influence within which observed events contribute to $\hat{\lambda}_\tau(s)$ is a circle of radius $\tau$ centred on $s$. Distances to each observed event $s_i$ within the bandwidth are measured and so contribute to the intensity estimate at $s$, depending on how close they are to $s$. A contouring algorithm can be used to represent resulting intensity estimators as a continuous surface showing how intensity varies over $R$.

The exact functional form of the kernel, $k(\ldots)$, can be determined in various ways (see Gatrell et al, 1996:260), giving a kernel estimate that is sensitive to the choice of bandwidth, $\tau$. If the bandwidth is increased the spatial variation in intensity is smoothed; if it is reduced a more spiky estimate is obtained. It is also possible to adjust the value of $\tau$ at different points in $R$ to improve the kernel estimate, by using adaptive kernel estimation (see Brunsdon, 1991). In this a smaller bandwidth is employed for sub-areas where events are more concentrated. This avoids smoothing out too much detail. Edge effects can be overcome by using a correction term or eliminating from calculation events near the boundary of $R$.

In epidemiological studies kernel estimation can be used most effectively in estimating the intensity of one type of event relative to another. For example, a comparison could be made between occurrences of a disease and a control group in order to evaluate spatial variations in the risk of disease. This could help to identify clusters or sub-regions for further investigation, as in Bithell's (1990) study of the clustering of childhood leukaemia in Cumbria, England.

## The *K* Function

There is a close mathematical relationship between the second-order intensity and the *K function*, which describes the extent to which there is spatial dependence in the pattern of events (Gatrell, 1995):

$$\lambda K(d) = E(\text{number of events} \leqslant \text{distance } d \text{ of an arbitrary event})$$

where $E(\ldots)$ = expectation (as a probability); and $\lambda$ = intensity or mean number of events per unit area.

If the arrangement of events is random, the probability of the occurrence of an event at any point $R$ is independent of other events that have occurred and it is equally likely throughout $R$. The expected number of events within a distance $d$ of a randomly selected

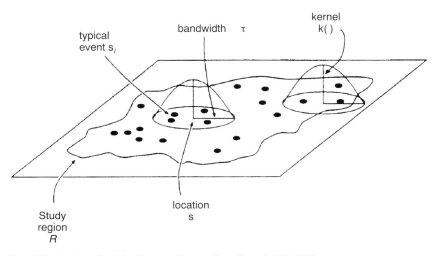

*Figure 9.13*    Kernel Estimation of a Point Pattern. (*Source*: Gatrell et al, 1996:260)

event $d$ for a homogeneous process with no spatial dependence is $d^2$, or

$$K(d) = d^2$$

If there is clustering then there should be an excess of events occurring for small values of $D$ or an observed value of $K(d) > d^2$ (Getis, 1983).

Some degree of clustering of events can be expected simply through the natural background variation in the population from which events arise. Therefore it is more sensible to search for a degree of clustering rather than for a random pattern. In particular, when examining disease occurrence, the critical comparison needs to be between the "natural" clustering and the clustering of disease "events". Alternatively, disease events may have occurred at different points in time and so research might focus on space–time clustering. There are various theoretical situations that can assist in understanding these different types of clustering, using the $K$ function.

For example, $K$ functions could be used to detect clustering occurring in greater concentration than expected when compared with the background population. If there are $n_1$ observed cases and $n_2$ "controls" representing environmental heterogeneity, and $n_1$ and $n_2$ are pooled, then the $n_1$ cases should be attached at random to the combined sets of events, provided the type of an event is independent of its location. This is known as *random labelling of events*. In this situation Diggle (1993) has shown that the $K$ functions for the cases $(K_{11}(d))$ and for the controls $(K_{22}(d))$ are identical.

If a temporal event is added then the space–time $K$ function is:

$$\lambda_D \lambda_T K(d, t) = E \text{ (number of events}$$

$$\leqslant \text{ distance } d \text{ and time } t \text{ of an arbitrary event)}$$

where $\lambda_D$ = the spatial intensity of events, and $\lambda_T$ = the temporal intensity of events.

If the processes operating in time and space are independent, that is no space–time interaction, $K(d, t)$ is the product of separate space and time $K$

functions (Diggle et al, 1995). Therefore, theoretically,

$$K(d, t) = K_D(d)K_T(t)$$

Boots and Getis (1988) and Diggle (1983) give the following formula for estimating the $K$ function:

$$\hat{K}(d) = \frac{1}{\lambda^2 R} \sum_{i \neq j} \sum I_d(d_{ij})$$

where $R$ = area of region $R$, $I_d(d_{ij})$ = an indicator function, which = 1 when $d_{ij} < d$. This ignores edge effects close to the boundary of $R$ which can distort the estimate. However, a correcting factor can be added:

$$\hat{K}(d) = \frac{1}{\lambda^2 R} \frac{\sum_{i \neq j} \sum i_d(d_{ij})}{w_{ij}}$$

where $w_{ij}$ = the proportion of a circle, centred on event $i$ and passing through point $j$, which lies within $R$. It is the conditional probability that an event is observed in $R$, given that it is a distance $d_{ij}$ from the $i$th event.

As $\lambda$ is unknown, it can be replaced by an estimate, $\hat{\lambda} = n/R$, where $n$ = observed number of events. Therefore,

$$\hat{K}(d) = \frac{R}{n^2} \sum_{i \neq j} \sum \frac{I_d(d_{ij})}{w_{ij}}$$

Gatrell et al's (1996:263) visualisation of a $K$ function, ignoring the edge correction, is shown in Figure 9.14. It symbolises an event being "visited", with a set of fine-grained concentric circles around the event. If all other events are also visited, the cumulative number of events within distance bands up to a radius $d$ around all events is the estimate of $K(d)$ when scaled by $R/n^2$. However, it is not easy to calculate this for arbitrarily shaped regions as the weights $w_{ij}$ are hard to derive unless the region is rectangular or circular. A list of available computer software for

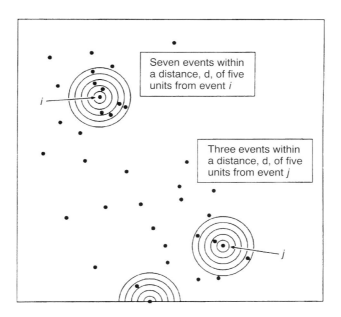

*Figure 9.14*    Estimation of a *K* Function. (*Source*: Gatrell et al, 1996:263)

deriving $w_{ij}$ for more complex regions is provided by Gatrell et al (1996:272–3).

For a regular distribution $K(d)$ is less than $\pi d^2$; for clustering it is greater than $\pi d^2$. So the estimate of $K(d)$ from observed data can be compared with $\pi d^2$, by plotting $K(d) - \pi d^2$ versus $d$. Peaks in positive values tend to indicate spatial clusters and troughs of negative values indicate regularity, at corresponding scales of distance $d$. The significance of these patterns can be assessed using simulation techniques which generate an upper and lower "envelope" of possibilities as indicated in Figure 9.15. If the estimated $K(d)$ lies above the upper envelope, this suggests clustering; if it lies below the lower envelope, this suggests a regular arrangement of events. The example shown in Figure 9.15 is from work by Gatrell and Whitelegg (1993) on the occurrence of childhood leukaemia in west-central Lancashire, England, from 1954 to 1992. It shows a relatively weak tendency towards clustering, but with no statistically significant evidence.

There are various types of clustering that can be investigated. Spatial clustering is generally taken to mean the aggregation of events over and above that due to environmental heterogeneity. This is slightly different to the detection of specific clusters, that is significant local aggregations of events. Such clusters have been searched for on an exploratory basis (e.g. Openshaw et al, 1987) and hypotheses have been tested regarding possible clusters in the vicinity of fixed locations (e.g. Diggle, 1990; Diggle and Rowlingson, 1994).

If $d$ is plotted against the difference between $K$ functions for cases and controls, peaks show clustering that exceeds that associated with environmental heterogeneity. However, making clear-cut interpretations of such situations is not easy given the inherent difficulty in inferring process from pattern. Disentangling first-order and second-order properties is not straightforward and assumptions underlying the various statistics need to be considered carefully (see Diggle, 1983; Cliff and Ord, 1981).

For space–time interaction, peaks will be produced on the surface of $\hat{D}(d, t)$ plotted against space and time. Again, the significance can be tested using simulation techniques and examining standardised residuals (see Bhopal et al, 1992; Diggle et al, 1995).

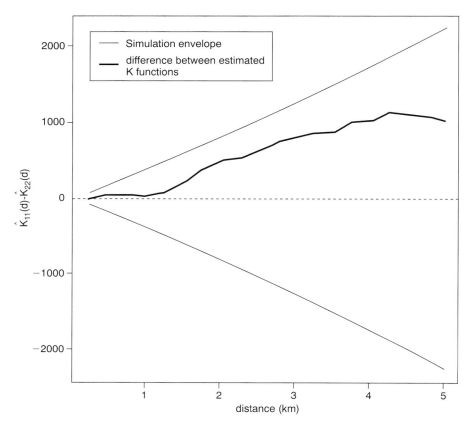

*Figure 9.15* Difference between *K* Functions (bold curve) and Simulation Envelope (light straight lines) for Childhood Leukaemia and "Population at Risk". (*Source*: Gatrell et al, 1996:266)

## SPATIAL STATISTICS

The topics covered in the preceding part of this chapter have formed a distinctive element within human geography over a 30-year period. From relatively simple measures designed to analyse point patterns, statistics applied to spatial data have been developed to tackle a range of problems. Work on spatial autocorrelation was important in the 1970s and has had important ramifications with respect to the study of spatial diffusion (see Chapter 10) whilst the analysis of spatial clustering has been part of more recent research, closely linked to epidemiology. All of these forms of statistical analysis have been developed explicitly for use with spatial data and can be regarded

as part of the broader field of *spatial statistics*. Much of the work in this area involves use of complex mathematics beyond the compass of this book. However, it is appropriate to indicate here the basic outlines of the field and the types of problem currently being addressed.

Spatial statistics is that branch of statistics concerned with the analysis of spatial data where the classical assumption of independence no longer holds. In the absence of this assumption, analysis has to deal with special problems of pattern description, interpolation and image reconstruction (Haining, 1989:191).

Geographers contributing to the study of spatial statistics have focused on the analysis of measurements taken for a contiguous set of regions at a single point in time. In particular, a prime concern has been the problems posed by the non-independence of these observations. The discussion of spatial autocorrelation above represents one aspect of this work on non-independence. However, it is also possible to recognise a more generalised model upon which spatial statistics operates. The basic "model" of spatial statistics is the assumption that variation in spatial data arises from three components which together represent a single realisation of a probability model:

- a deterministic structured element, usually given a functional representation that can be equated with the mean of a probability distribution;
- a stochastic structured element, usually represented in terms of the second-order properties of that probability distribution;
- a local random element or noise.

The underlying probability model is usually assumed to be second-order stationary, so that

$$E[Z(x)] = m \qquad \text{for all } x$$

where $E$ denotes mathematical expectation, $Z(x) =$ the random variable at location $x = (x_1, x_2)$, and $m =$ a constant. In this model, quantitative descriptions of spatial variation can be provided by calculating spatial covariances, correlations and semi-variograms, the latter being used in remote sensing. The spatial covariance for each pair of variables $\{Z(x), Z(x + h)\}$ depends only on the separation distance, $h$, i.e.

$$C(h) = E[(Z(x) - m)(Z(x + h) - m)] \qquad \text{for all } x$$

Frequently, surface descriptions may be constructed that consist of two components, a spatially varying mean and a covariance plot, rather than subsuming in a semi-variogram.

It should be clear from this brief account that spatial statistics can be quite complex and demand a degree of statistical expertise generally beyond that obtained in standard geography undergraduate courses. Nevertheless, it has not only been statisticians who have

pioneered work in this area, with Andrew Cliff, Robert Haining, Anthony Gartell, David Griffith, Michael Dacey, Michael Goodchild, Richard Thomas and Waldo Tobler, amongst other geographers, making significant contributions. The nature of this work goes beyond the intended subject material of this book, but Table 9.10 summarises the basis for the development of this branch of statistics. Good texts covering a wide

Table 9.10  Characteristics Underlying Spatial Data Analysis and Modelling

1. All data have some spatial and temporal characteristics (labels) associated with them. A purely spatial model usually has no causative component in it. Such models are useful when a process operating in space and time has reached temporal equilibrium (e.g. ore deposition), or when short-term causal effects are aggregated over a fixed period (e.g. final presidential election returns from the states of the USA)

2. The spatial character of data should be addressed in the modelling and analysis of data on a problem-by-problem basis

3. Data that are close together in space and time are often more alike than those that are far apart. A spatial model will incorporate this spatial variation into its generating mechanism, in contrast to a non-spatial model

4. It is almost always the case that the classical, non-spatial model is a special case of a spatial model, and so the spatial model is more general. Space–time models are even more general

5. Modelling of spatial variation may be performed using both stochastic and non-stochastic means

6. Variables explaining spatial variation should be included in a non-stochastic mean structure (large-scale variation) model first

7. Having allowed for explanatory variables, models with spatial dependence are usually a more parsimonious description than classical trend-surface models

Based on Cressie (1993).

range of spatial statistics are those by Cressie (1993), Haining (1990a) and Ripley (1984), and the excellent interactive volume by Bailey and Gatrell (1995).

## GEOMETRY AND ''SPATIAL FETISHISM''

Much of the work discussed in this chapter has been strongly criticised for its reduction of geography to geometrical patterns. This reductionism has been attacked from a number of philosophical perspectives, some of which are considered in subsequent chapters. However, the focus on spatial geometry received special attention in some of the earliest criticisms of geography's "quantitative turn". For example, amongst the more original of the criticisms of Schaefer's (1953) views of geography as a spatial science and of the 1960s penchant for transforming spatial relationships into geometric forms was the work of Robert Sack, who set out initially to show that geometry is not an acceptable language for geographical explanation (Sack, 1972). He recognised that geographical facts possessed geometric properties in the form of locations but argued that an understanding of location had to incorporate process and not just geometry. So geometry can be used to analyse points and lines on maps, as discussed by Bunge (1962) for example in his treatise on mathematical geography, but it can never provide substantive explanations because on its own it ignores process and therefore cannot answer "geographic questions". The debate between Sack (1973a) and Bunge (1973) took the argument further, with Sack (1973a:569) stating that:

> Although the laws of geometry are unequivocally static, purely spatial, non-deducible from dynamic laws, and explain and predict physical geometric properties of events, they do not answer the questions about the geometric properties of events that geographers raise and they do not make statements about process.

So, spatial geometry can form a part of geography, but not separated from considerations of time and matter (Sack, 1973b, 1974a,b). He argued that geographical laws need to involve both space and "congruent substance" independent of location. Therefore, the geographer cannot just deal with space alone but has to consider its evaluation in different ways at different times and in different cultures (Sack, 1980:3–4).

Sack's concerns have formed part of a widely based attack upon the notion of geography as spatial science. This attack has had a definite limiting effect upon the application of spatial geometry within the discipline. Thus, despite attempts to deal with the complexity of spatial data through the development of models and geometrical measures, this work has had a restricted impact upon geographical research despite significant advances within spatial statistics. Cox (1989) cites two specific reasons for this:

1. Solutions to the statistical "problems" posed by spatial data have been complex and, because of lack of widely available computer software, have not been extensively distributed.
2. The models developed have frequently not been applied to substantive problems, with the main exception of some work on epidemiology (e.g. Cliff and Haggett, 1988). Often, spatial statistics and geometric measures have not been extended beyond small sample datasets.

Sack's work in the 1970s highlighted the importance of human agents and underlying structures within society as the causes of visual spatial pattern rather than endowing space itself with causal powers and then measuring spatial properties via spatial statistics (see Sayer, 1985). This relegation of spatial geometry to a much reduced significance within human geography as a whole has subsequently been extended through the emergence of humanist, Marxist and postmodernist philosophies within the discipline. These have not only eschewed the use of spatial geometry but have also questioned its value and appropriateness as a means of understanding the spatial patterns associated with human activity. Gregory (1994d:582–3) describes this highly significant shift in approach as producing two separate geographies. The dominant geography is now one in which researchers are "preoccupied with intentions and meanings" whilst the other focuses on systems and structures, using the language of geometry but often regarded by the other camp as employing a "spatial fetishism".

The result is that those human geographers working directly with the language of spatial geometry are now relatively few in number, but they are often engaged in very important applied work on the spread of diseases or the distribution of economic resources. As in the analysis of the spread of AIDS, by geographers such as Andrew Cliff in the UK or Peter Gould in the USA, this research combines analysis of both spatial and temporal processes and extends the purely spatial measures discussed in this chapter into the temporal realm considered in the following one.

# 10

# SPACE AND TIME

## MODELLING SPATIAL DIFFUSION

The deterministic models discussed in Chapters 7 and 8 yield a unique outcome from one set of inputs. In contrast, *probabilistic models* can yield many different realisations from the same process. This is because they incorporate a random element or chance so that a range of possible outcomes can be generated instead of making a single exact prediction. The inclusion of a random or stochastic element in a model may be justified on two grounds. Firstly, the process under investigation may be thought to contain a random element. Secondly, and more commonly, the injection of a random component into a model subsumes a number of causal influences, the combined effect of which makes exact prediction impossible. For example, the yield of a particular crop may be strongly determined by measurable climatic and edaphic factors, but there may be minor additional variables which inject a quasi-random element into the actual yield of the crop. It may be possible to model this quasi-random element using ideas grounded in probability theory.

Geographers have used probabilistic models to investigate a variety of processes operating through space and time. They include,

1. Temporal sequences, for example the changing levels of employment.
2. Spatial sequences, in which a point pattern in geographical space is considered to be part of a quasi-random process. This can be modelled using a Poisson distribution if each area has an equal probability of receiving a point, as discussed in the section on "Describing point patterns" in Chapter 9. Alternatively if an area receives more or less points then other distributions may be employed, such as the negative binomial.
3. Combinations of space and time, as in the study of the spread of diseases or the diffusion of innovations. Models of spatial diffusion processes are frequently termed *simulation models* as they model a process. Generally such models utilise random numbers and hence they are termed *Monte Carlo models* (Hagerstrand, 1965, 1967b; Kalos and Whitlock, 1986), symbolising the chance or "gambling" element in the models.

## Diffusion Processes

At the heart of work by geographers on spatial diffusion are attempts to understand the formation of spatial patterns (Wilson and Bennett, 1985:140–9). This requires a consideration of diffusion processes and factors influencing the spread of diffusion through space. Three general types of diffusion process can be recognised: expansion diffusion (and a variant, the general epidemic model), hierarchical diffusion and relocation diffusion.

(a) *Expansion diffusion* begins with just a few people having knowledge of an innovation, such as a new farming technique. This knowledge is then communicated, usually by direct word of mouth, to friends and neighbours so that over a period of time the number of people who know about the innovation increases steadily (Figure 10.1a). In the case of a new household appliance, the spread of knowledge about the appliance may be followed by its increased adoption. This type of diffusion process also operates in the spread of certain diseases where the disease is spread by direct contact between people/animals. Therefore the process is sometimes referred to as *contagious diffusion*. Because of its reliance upon the spreading of information by direct contact or word of mouth, the process exhibits frictional effects of distance; those further away from the source of informa-

tion are less likely to receive this information than those closer to the source.

(b) Models of this process are sometimes referred to as *simple epidemic models* as they may be used to simulate the passage of an epidemic in which all the population are susceptible to a disease (that is they are potential "adopters") and all infectives are therefore "adopters" (Bartholomew, 1973). A variant of this is the *general epidemic model*, in which a three-fold division of the population is made: into susceptibles, infectives and removals. The latter are infectives who, after a length of time, cease to communicate the disease to others (or to pass on information about the

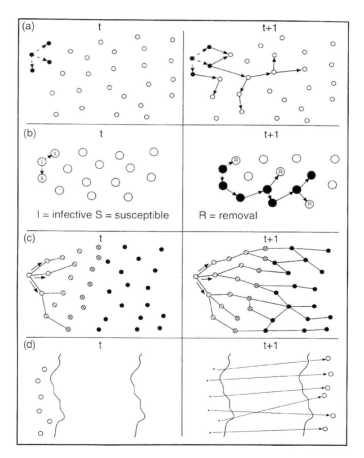

*Figure 10.1*   Diffusion Patterns
(a) Expansion diffusion; (b) the general epidemic model; (c) hierarchical diffusion; (d) relocation diffusion

innovation) and so they cannot pass on the disease. Therefore removals become passive adopters whilst infectives are active or transmitting adopters (Bailey, 1975) (Figure 10.1b). For both simple and general epidemic models it can be shown that there is a minimum velocity for the spread of diffusion below which no recognisable spread will exist. In addition, other models have been formulated which can be used in the simulation of epidemic spread, introducing greater complexity. Examples include models with a limited migration of individuals into and out of a study area (Haggett, 1975), Rapoport's network models (Brown, 1968:49–65), chain binomial models (Bailey, 1957:76) and models incorporating hierarchical diffusion (Hudson, 1972).

(c) Simple linear distance is not always the strongest influence on a diffusion pattern. An innovation can leap over intervening people and places, following a path that concentrates initially only on major cities or on major individuals before filtering down to smaller places or to those beyond the immediate circle of community leaders. A frequently cited example of this type of diffusion is the fashion industry in which high fashion originates in cities like Milan, Paris, New York and London where major designers work. From these centres designs for the mass market "diffuse" to chain stores in the larger cities and from there to smaller settlements (Figure 10.1c). This is known as *hierarchical diffusion*.

(d) Holders of information migrate taking their knowledge with them, thereby transplanting new ideas into a different environment. Once relocated the migrants may spread their knowledge by an expansion diffusion process (Figure 10.1d). Common examples

*Figure 10.2*   The Initial Diffusion of Radio Broadcasting in the USA
(a) Cities adopting radio broadcasting in 1921; (b) cities adopting radio broadcasting in 1924. (*Source*: Abler et al, 1971:394–5)

of this *relocation diffusion* are the large-scale migrations of different cultural groups, perhaps the most far-reaching effects being those associated with the colonisation of the New World and the transference of cultivation skills from Asia Minor to Europe.

In reality many diffusion processes represent a combination of expansion, hierarchical and relocation diffusion, and especially of the first two (e.g. Graff and Ashton, 1994). For example, strong hierarchical and contagious components were operating at the same time in the diffusion of radio broadcasting in the USA (Abler et al, 1971:393–5). After beginning in Pittsburgh it spread to the major cities, but also filtered down the urban hierarchy in the vicinity of these cities. The hierarchic effect was most important initially, with the contagious effect then dominating subsequently (Figure 10.2) (see also Pred, 1971). This combination of processes is apparent in the spread of major influenza pandemics in Iceland. Cliff et al (1986) found that the disease is initially introduced in Reykjavik, the capital, and then spreads down the urban hierarchy to smaller places whilst also manifesting contagious diffusion outward from the capital; then the disease spreads from local centres to their surrounding hinterlands.

The first substantial attempt to model spatial diffusion processes was the work of the Swedish geographer Torsten Hagerstrand whose book on innovation waves was published in Swedish in 1952. However, this was not translated into English until the 1960s (though see Duncan (1974) and Leighly (1954)), when it appeared as *Innovation diffusion as a spatial process* (Hagerstrand, 1967a). In this the expansion diffusion process was likened to a wave pattern which loses

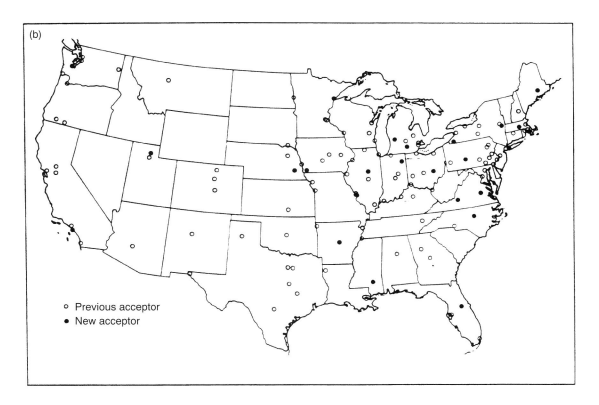

(b)

○ Previous acceptor
● New acceptor

its strength as it moves away from its source of origin or disturbance. So an innovation will spread with a wave-like form from its point of origin, such as the location of the first adopter of a new farming innovation.

From examination of innovations amongst farming communities in southern Sweden, Hagerstrand observed that irregularities in this wave-like form were produced by the presence of a variety of barriers to the progress of diffusion. Some of these took the relatively straightforward form of physical barriers which could absorb, reflect or reduce an innovation pulse. An *absorbing barrier* is one which can completely stop the flow of information, for example a swamp or mountain range (Figure 10.3a), though in practice such a stoppage might be only temporary so that such barriers become permeable over time. The Appalachians fulfilled this function with respect to the passage of European settlement in the USA (Figure 10.3b). *Reflective barriers* are those which deflect an innovation pulse back on itself as in the case of settlement along a coast or lakeshore (Figure 10.3c).

Whilst physical barriers to spatial diffusion can often be easily identified, it is the cultural, sociological and psychological barriers that have proved to be a much more effective set of constraints upon the regular wave-like pattern of diffusion. It is also these barriers that have provided tremendous scope for geographical study, contributing to the rise of new sub-areas in the discipline, such as *behavioural geography* and *perception studies*, with the development of foci well removed from the narrower concerns of those modelling spatial diffusion. Human behaviour and perception have been an integral part of work on diffusion, with the influences of factors such as language, religion, ideology and social background being studied to gain greater understanding of diffusion patterns and processes. Therefore this research marks a significant break with the substantial amount of work by economic geographers that previously had produced models based upon notions of decision-makers as rational economic beings. These "perfect" decision-makers can be contrasted with the reality in which people make decisions based on imperfect

(a)

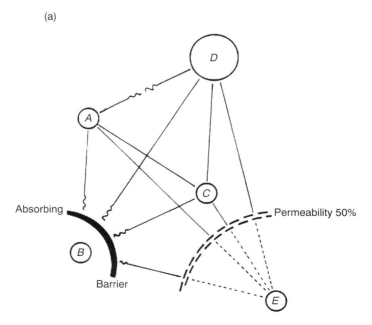

*Figure 10.3*  Barriers to Diffusion. (*Source*; Abler et al., 1971)
(a) An absorbing barrier; (b) the passage of pioneer settlement halted by the Appalachians; (c) a reflective barrier

knowledge and with goals other than profit maximisation. For example, a common goal may be to attain a desirable degree of satisfaction over the outcome of a particular decision rather than to attain maximum profit or minimum costs.

## Simulating Diffusion Patterns

It is the variations in the decision-making of individuals, in part attributable to different "satisficers",

that were one of the foci of Hagerstrand's work on the diffusion of agricultural innovations. Initially studying the diffusion of the adoption of government pasture subsidies by farmers in the Asby district of southern Sweden between 1929 and 1932, he observed that the pattern of diffusion spread in a wave-like pattern from the western part of his study area (Figure 10.4). He assumed that the mechanism by which information about the pasture subsidy was transferred between individuals was purely by face-to-face contact. So, he

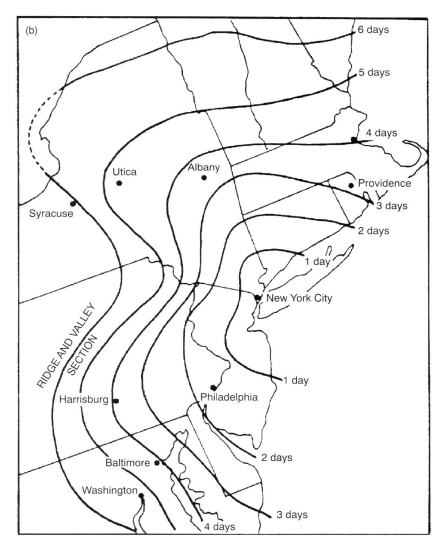

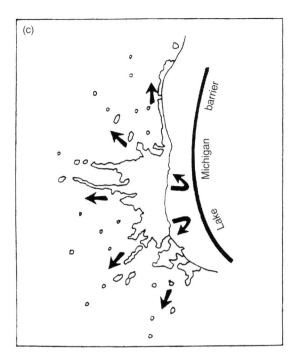

*Figure 10.3    (continued)*

was investigating an expansion diffusion process in which a *distance-decay function* was operating, that is the likelihood of and frequency of contact amongst the farmers was determined by the distance between the individuals concerned. He was observing a *neighbourhood effect* or *contagious growth*, in which new adopters were added initially in a cluster around the original nuclei of the innovation's introduction. Therefore probabilities of adoption were highest in the vicinity of an earlier adoption and decreased with distance away from an adoption (Hagerstrand, 1965).

The wave-like pattern can be represented as a common pattern of adoption of an innovation in the form of a normal curve (Figure 10.5a) or its cumulative form, the *logistic curve* (Figure 10.5b). Underlying this regularity is a process of decision-making which itself has a regular pattern of a sequence from an individual being aware of information, showing interest in it, making an evaluation, perhaps performing a trial of the particular innovation and then finally adopting it. The S-shaped trend depicted in Figure 10.5b is likely to be adhered to if:

- potential users of a technological innovation become adopters under the influence of previous adopters in the course of direct personal contacts;
- potential users have different degrees of resistance to change;
- resistance to change may be overcome by an adequate number of messages from adopters – this is sometimes referred to as "conversion through conversation".

The logistic curve may be expressed as

$$p_t = (1 + e^{a-bt})^{-1}$$

where $p_t$ = the proportion of adopters at time $t$, $a$ = the intercept, and $b$ = the slope coefficient. Similarly,

$$y_t = k(1 + e^{a-bt})^{-1}$$

where $y_t$ = the number of adopters, and $k$ = the maximum possible number of adopters, that is the *saturation level*.

Cliff and Ord (1975b) developed these equations to show that

$$r_t = -bp_t(1 - p_t)$$

where $r_t$ = the rate of change in $p_t$ (proportion of adopters) over time, $(1 - p_t)$ = proportion of the population who have not adopted at time $t$, $p_t(1 - p_t)$ = the probability that a random meeting between two individuals is between an adopter and a potential adopter, and $b$ = the rate at which meetings take place (the rate of mixing) which is the same whatever the distance between adopter and potential adopter (*spatially homogeneous mixing*).

This appears to contradict the neighbourhood effect and hence modifications to the logistic model have been suggested to generate *inhomogeneous mixing*, as in Cliff and Ord's (1975d) work on the adoption of tractors in a farming region in the USA. Another alternative is to use a different form of curve or to

(a)

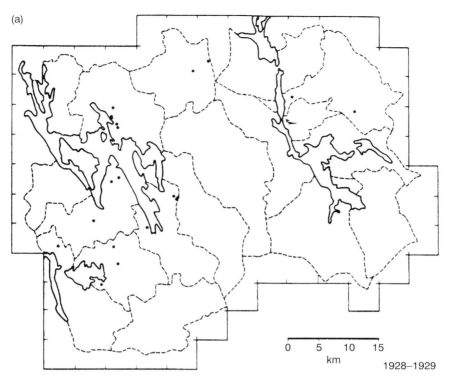

1928–1929

*Figure 10.4*    The Pattern of Spread of the Adoption of a Pasture Subsidy in the Asby District of Sweden, 1929–33. (*Source*: Hagerstrand, 1967b)

dispute the existence of a neighbourhood effect, which certainly might not apply in situations where information is spread by the mass media rather than face-to-face contact.

To gain a greater understanding of the spatial patterning of this adoption process, Hagerstrand attempted to simulate the pattern of diffusion. This involved the formulation of simple rules to develop a model operational in space and time. The simulation process that he employed contained essentially just two main stages (Figure 10.6), though its links with other components can be included in the basic structure of his model:

(a) The creation of a *mean information field* (MIF). For this a "floating" grid of probabilities is constructed which represents the probability of someone in a particular cell receiving information of the inno-

vation in question, that is of coming into contact with someone who will tell them of the innovation (Figure 10.6a). These probabilities have a distance-decay function from the point of origin of the innovation. However, the derivation of the probabilities in the MIF is crucial to the operation of the simulation and has to be based on the assumed character of the expansion diffusion process. In Hagerstrand's initial work the probabilities were based on migration distances for the local population, so he assumed that the possibility of social contact was the same as the possibility of migration. In other studies the distance-decay function used was based on the pattern of telephone calls in the study area. In his work on Swedish agriculture in the 1930s the MIF had a fairly sharp distance decay, indicating relatively poor communications over even short distances. For societies with more rapid flow of

(b)

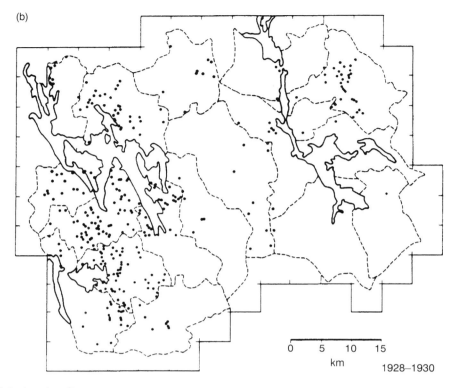

0    5    10    15
km                1928–1930

*Figure 10.4    (continued)*

information, for example via television and radio, a less steep distance decay is likely to operate or a multi-focus diffusion may occur as "mass media may contribute towards the breakdown of a strict neigh-bourhood effect by the creation of multiple poles from which the innovation can spread" (Haggett et al, 1977:239–40).

(b) Operationalisation of the MIF through the use of random number tables (see Figure 10.6c). The MIF is converted into a continuous sequence of numbers to which random numbers can be allocated to simulate "hits" representing adopters of an innovation. The number of "hits" over a given period can be regulated so that the simulation fits the number of adopters in reality. The use of random numbers implies that whilst individual behaviour is not considered to be random, minor factors which influence the decision-making of

a large number of people can be expected to operate collectively in a random manner. The random element allows for differences in the socio-psychological characteristics of individuals and enables considera-tion of people making non-normative decisions. The number of potential adopters per cell can be varied and the probabilities in the MIF altered to provide different "solutions" in order to test for the presence of particular factors affecting the pattern of diffusion.

Hagerstrand's initial simulation utilised three simple rules:

1. Data input to the model was based on the pattern of adoption of the pasture subsidy in 1929.
2. A potential adopter was assumed to accept the subsidy as soon as being provided with information by an adopter.

(c)

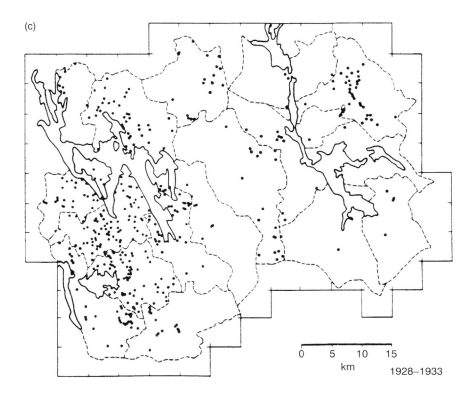

0　5　10　15
km　　1928–1933

3. The simulation proceeded in stages in which every adopter was allowed to contact one other person, who could be an adopter or a non-adopter.

The probability of contact between individuals was defined by the MIF shown in Figure 10.6, which is a floating $5 \times 5$ km$^2$ grid placed over each existing adopter in turn, with the adopter located in the central cell. Therefore each adopter had a 44 per cent chance of contacting somebody within approximately 2.5 km of her/himself, but a probability of only 1 per cent at 14 km (along the diagonal from the central cell) and no probability at all of contact beyond 14–18 km. Variations such as the effect of barriers to communication could be introduced by reducing the probability of contacts occurring.

Random numbers were used to select the location of each adopter's contact, using one number to locate the contact cell and then another to select the re-

ceiver's location within that cell. If the receiver of information was already an adopter then the information was deemed to have no effect. If the receiver was not an adopter then adoption of the innovation took place.

In investigations of innovation diffusion, those who are amongst the first to adopt innovations (the initiators or innovators) tend to be the young, better educated, more widely travelled, willing to take risks and, in the case of farmers and business communities, having close contact with scientific information sources. In contrast, the laggards are older, have more traditional views, are more likely to be socially isolated and tend to be suspicious of agents of change (see also M.A. Brown, 1980).

In this form of simulation it is often possible to produce a systematic directional bias from chance occurrences. For example, because a neighbourhood effect may be generated by the simulation, once an

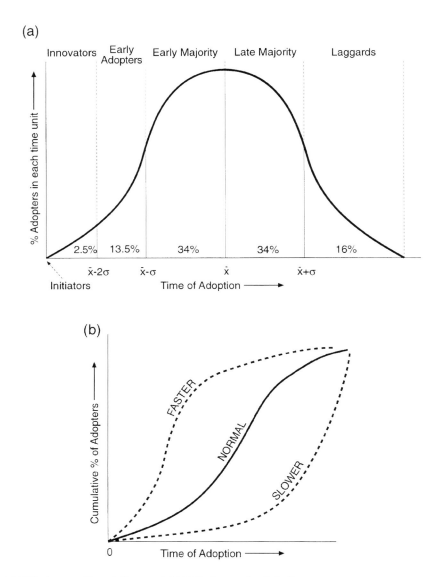

*Figure 10.5*   (a) Diffusion as a Normal Curve and (b) Diffusion as a Logistic Curve

innovation has been introduced to a particular cell this orientation may be favoured as the simulation develops. This is one reason why replication of a simulated pattern is useful, with "average" values derived for the predicted pattern after a number of "runs" of the model. However, the form of the *contact field* is actually dependent on the distribution of opportunities for contact. This may well distort simple concepts of the operation of an elementary distance-decay function.

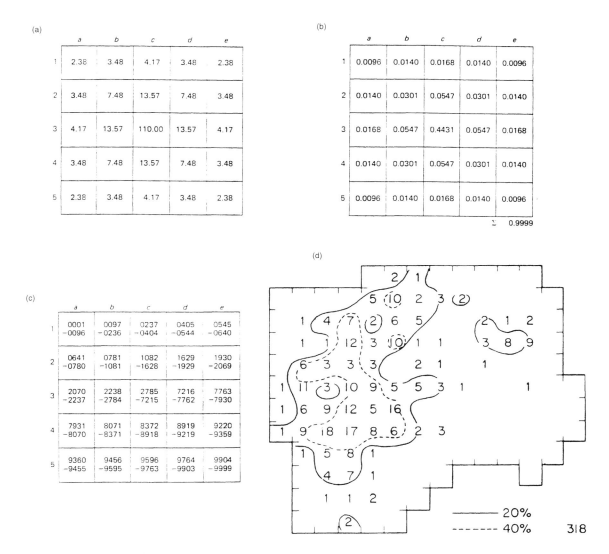

*Figure 10.6*    Hagerstrand's Simulation of the Pattern of Spread of the Adoption of a Pasture Subsidy in the Asby District of Sweden, 1929–33
(a) Observed local migration in the Asby area (standardised by symmetrical cells); (b) the mean information field; (c) the use of random numbers to produce a floating MIF; (d) simulated pattern (after 318 adopters). (*Sources*: (a) to (c) Lowe and Moryadas, 1975:254–5; (d) Abler et al, 1971:418)

Models investigating spatial diffusion may be applied at a variety of scales (L.A. Brown, 1981:37–40) and diffusion can be viewed at a number of spatial scales as it proceeds through time and space. For example, a common pattern is for an innovation to begin in a local area, then spread through a region before filtering to other local areas in the region whilst simultaneously spreading to other regions.

More complex rules can be utilised in conjunction with simulation models of spatial diffusion, for example incorporating a hierarchical element.

## Testing the Significance of Simulated Patterns

There are two basic types of test required to compare a simulated spatial pattern with an actual pattern – though see the contrasting views of Yapa (1976) and Cliff and Ord (1980):

- A test to see whether the model has produced the "right" balance of cells with particular numbers of adopters in turn. This may be done by constructing frequency distributions of the numbers of cells with 0, 1, 2, ..., $n$ adopters from corresponding actual and simulated maps and comparing these distributions for systematic departures.
- The above does not deal with the spatial relationships between the cells, so therefore the degree of spatial autocorrelation also needs to be considered. This may be done by focusing upon residuals, that is differences between an actual (observed) and a

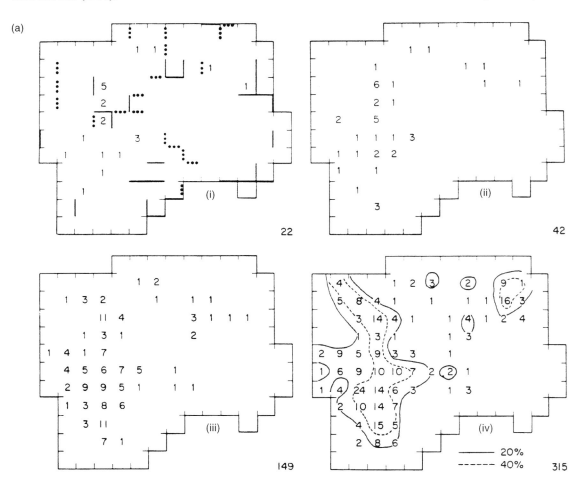

*Figure 10.7*　Comparison of an Actual (Observed) and a Simulated Map on a Cell-by-Cell Basis (a) Actual, (b) Simulated (*Source*; Abler et al., 1971)

simulated map on a cell-by-cell basis (see Figure 10.7). If a model of the process producing the simulation is specified then the "expected" map may be derived by averaging over several independent realisations of the model (Cliff and Ord, 1973:70).

For example, the following three-stage testing can be followed:

1. Generate $m$ independent realisations of the diffusion model. Then compute an average "expected" pattern using these realisations plus the observed pattern, i.e. using $(m + 1)$ "realisations".

2. Compute a goodness-of-fit statistic between each simulated pattern and the average, and also for the comparison between the observed pattern and the average. A suitable aspatial statistic would be $\chi^2$ or the Pearson product-moment correlation coefficient. Spatial autocorrelation measures could be used as a spatial statistic.

3. Rank the $(m + 1)$ statistics and then reject $H_0$ at the $100(j + 1)/(m + 1)$ per cent level if the statistic between the observed and average pattern has rank $(m - j + 1)$ or worse (in a one-tailed test), i.e. $H_0$ is rejected if the difference between the patterns is

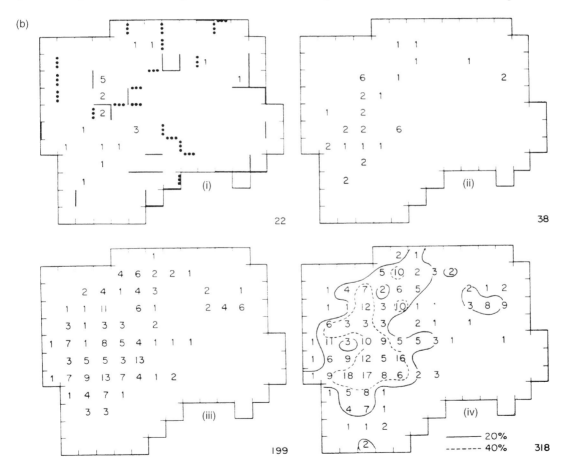

so large that it could not be regarded as a chance occurrence.

For further work on this, see Webber and Joseph (1978, 1979) who used an electronic analogue based on physics and epidemiology, incorporating ideas of relative accessibility, to test the likelihood of the occurrence of an "average simulation" based on the basic Hagerstrand approach.

## Limitations of Diffusion Simulations

In following the procedure outlined above, Cliff and Ord (1973) showed that the simulations of Hagerstrand's original model of the diffusion of pasture subsidies produced patterns significantly different to those of the observed pattern. The implication was that the model incorporated a distance-decay effect that was too steep. This highlights one of several limitations in the basic model which have been recognised and subsequently modified. The highly empirical nature of simulation models in general means that it may be possible to "fix" the result to resemble reality without the researcher really having any real understanding of the processes underlying the diffusion pattern. In other words, the simulation can obtain "the correct results but for the wrong reasons". The simulation process also separates a continuous process of diffusion into a number of individual stages which have no parallel in reality.

The basic simulation model was predicated on the implicit assumption that the availability of information among a population of potential innovation adopters essentially determines the sequence of adoption. However, it is clear from subsequent work (e.g. Webber, 1972) that economic factors, such as profitability, capital stock and business organisation, amongst others, affect adopters and non-adopters and play a major role in determining the sequence of adoption (Webber and Joseph, 1977). Thus it is not just the information itself that determines adoption but the context within which decisions regarding that information are made. This point is made by Gregory (1985) who summarised the limitations of Hagerstrand's approach in noting its generalisation, its em-

pirical character, the focus on social morphology (spatial pattern) and its formalisation via stochastic processes. He criticised its lack of consideration of the structures of social relations and systems of social practices through which innovations filter. These are only dealt with tangentially in the simulation process through reference to information flows and resistances. He also noted the lack of consideration for the consequences of innovation diffusion whilst recognising that this was rectified in part in later work (see "Time-geography" below).

Other criticisms relate to lack of concern for the process by which potential adopters are identified (Yapa and Mayfield, 1978) and for the processes by which information flows are assimilated by and acted upon by potential adopters (Blaut, 1977). Recognition of the first of these weaknesses has led to considerations of how non-adopters of innovations may not simply be apathetic or unaware of innovations, but may be denied access to an innovation through class division and inhibiting effects of social structure. Hence the dichotomy of adopters and non-adopters ignores some of the complexities of differential access to information and also outright resistance to a particular innovation that might involve sustained struggle as in the attempted rejection of new machinery in agriculture by farmworkers fearing for their jobs (Charlesworth, 1983; Gregory, 1985).

Larry A. Brown (1981) stressed market and infrastructure perspectives to the study of diffusion, arguing that opportunity to adopt is highly unequal. Therefore he recognised a need to look at the supply side of diffusion, especially as it is controlled by governments and institutions. This view holds that it is often institutional behaviour rather than that of the individual that holds the key to patterns of innovation adoption (Robinson, 1985b; Yapa, 1975). Where institutions are the key to diffusion processes, L.A. Brown (1981:8) recognised three activities within these processes:

1. The establishment of diffusion agencies or outlets through which the innovation will be distributed to the population at large.
2. A second activity in which a strategy is implemen-

ted by each agency to induce adoption among the population in its service area. This represents the establishment of the innovation.

3. Only after 1 and 2 is there adoption of the innovation. Thus he contends that by focusing too closely on the last of these three parts of the diffusion process, understanding of the overall process is restricted.

Furthermore, he identified a consequence of the market and infrastructure context as being a need to examine the outcomes of innovation adoption, especially effects upon economic development, social change and individual welfare. Such examinations reveal that technical innovation has by no means always had positive impacts, especially in the Developing World where there is much evidence of innovations widening disparities between social and economic classes and favouring ruling elites.

Having utilised Monte Carlo methods to stimulate aggregate, macro-level patterns of socio-economic phenomena, Hagerstrand (1970) then argued for their use in the investigation of disaggregate macro-level concepts, for example dealing with the household and the individual. One response to this has been the development of *micro-analysis* in which problem-solving and model-building are based on the representation of the "smallest unit", usually the household or firm. This form of analysis may or may not utilise a Monte Carlo method. However, perhaps the most well known applications have combined micro-analysis with Monte Carlo methods to examine travel demand and travel decision processes (e.g. Kreibich, 1979; Leigh and North, 1978). Such work has been encouraged by the growing volume of computerised databases and hence the accumulation of socio-economic data for households.

In summarising the major developments in diffusion studies post-Hagerstrand, Morrill et al (1988:35) highlighted six key developments:

1. Elaboration, including further work on mean information fields, the role of barriers, the nature of resistance, and measures of the characteristics of spatial diffusion;

2. Exploration of alternative and broader models of diffusion, deterministic as well as stochastic;
3. Introduction of hierarchical diffusion processes;
4. Specification of the relationship between spatial diffusion and spatial interaction (e.g. Cliff et al, 1983; Haining, 1982, 1983a,b);
5. Recognition of the role of propagators, markets and infrastructure (e.g. Morrill, 1985);
6. Applications to city and regional development planning.

Advances upon Hagerstrand's initial focus upon the adoption of innovations have led to a better understanding of broader diffusion processes, incorporating market, infrastructure and development perspectives. Simulation models have been developed with greater complexity in recognition of the multifaceted character of decision-making environments (see following section). However, attention has also moved away from such models to focus upon the broader context of diffusion processes. This has included consideration of decision-making processes (see Chapter 12) and also activity systems approaches in which innovation adoption is viewed in the context of time budgets and the social, economic and personal resources characterising the locale of potential adopters (see the section on "Time-geography" below).

## MARKOV CHAINS

Hagerstrand's basic Monte Carlo simulation model operated upon diffusion processes in which only a one-way change occurred to the system under consideration. This single change was the adoption of an innovation, and the end of the process was a state in which all potential adopters in a study area had adopted the innovation. However, in many cases, once an innovation has been adopted it may be rejected subsequently, thereby adding a significant complexity to the diffusion process. A typical example is the adoption of a new machine by an industrial firm. In due course a more advanced machine may be developed and the firm may purchase this to replace the original machine. In some cases a particular technique may be adopted, then rejected, only to be taken up again subsequently in a complex sequence of innovation adoption, rejection and re-adoption.

The concept of such a sequence which incorporates adoption and rejection of innovations, or positive and negative changes to a system, can be incorporated in a *Markov chain* (see Figure 10.8): if the probability of being in a state (or states) at time $t$ is wholly dependent upon the state(s) at some preceding time(s), it is said to be a *Markov process* (see Collins, 1973; Collins et al, 1974). In a Markov process a transition from one state to another can take place at any point in time, but in a Markov chain the state varies only at discrete time intervals. A Markov chain is a stochastic process in which future development depends only on the present state and not on the past history of the process. Thus in a Markov chain a system of states changes according to a probability law with time $t$ so that the system changing from a given state $S_i$ at time $t_{0+1}$ depends only on the state $S_i$ at time $t_0$ and is independent of the states of the system at times prior to $t_0$ (Collins, 1973:125–6).

If the state of the system at time $t_{0+1}$ is dependent only on the state of the system at time $t_0$ plus some independent random component the process is re-ferred to as a *first-order Markov chain*. In a *second-order Markov chain* the state of the system at time $t_2$ would depend on the states of the system at both time $t_0$ and $t_1$.

In the Markov chain the MIF is replaced by probability values comprising a *transition matrix* ($P_{ij}$), where $P_{ij}$ represents the probability of a change in state from a pre-existing state $i$ to a future state $j$. Therefore the Markov chain shown in Figure 10.8 can be represented as a transition matrix as portrayed in Table 10.1. The transition matrix indicates the probabilities of changes in state, for example from having or not having adopted an innovation at time $i$ to having

*Table 10.1*   A Transition Matrix

|  |  | $P_{ij}$ Succeeding State (j) | |
|  |  | Having | Not Having |
| --- | --- | --- | --- |
| Existing state (i) | Having | 0.7 | 0.3 |
|  | Not Having | 0.4 | 0.6 |

After one time period there is a 30 per cent chance that past adopters of the innovation will abandon it.

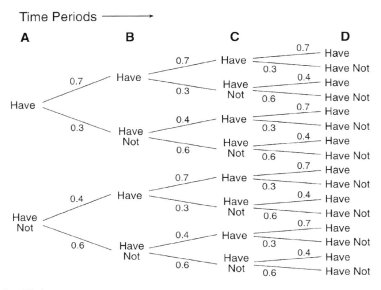

*Figure 10.8*   A Markov Chain

or not having adopted it at a succeeding time $j$. In Table 10.1, there is a 30 per cent chance that past adopters of the innovation will have abandoned it once a given time period has elapsed. If the same set of probabilities can be applied to a series of time periods then eventually a steady state of dynamic equilibrium will be reached, though in many situations this is unlikely to be the case as probabilities of changes in state will change.

In a Markov chain a system of states changes with time ($t$) according to some probability law, in such a manner that the system changing from a given state ($S_i$) at time $t_{0+1}$ depends only on the state ($S_i$) at time $t_0$ and is independent of the states of the system prior to $t_0$. The development of the chain can be traced for two time periods by multiplying transition matrices, e.g. for Table 10.1 applying over two time periods (from $T_a$ to $T_c$):

$$P_{ij}(T_a - T_c)$$

$$= \begin{pmatrix} 0.7 & 0.3 \\ 0.4 & 0.6 \end{pmatrix} \begin{pmatrix} 0.7 & 0.3 \\ 0.4 & 0.6 \end{pmatrix}$$

$$= \begin{pmatrix} 0.7 \times 0.7 + 0.3 \times 0.4 & 0.7 \times 0.3 + 0.3 \times 0.6 \\ 0.4 \times 0.7 + 0.6 \times 0.4 & 0.4 \times 0.3 + 0.6 \times 0.6 \end{pmatrix}$$

$$= \begin{pmatrix} 0.61 & 0.39 \\ 0.52 & 0.48 \end{pmatrix}$$

If, in the initial state of the adoption of the innovation, 30 per cent of businesses have adopted it and the remaining 70 per cent have not, this can be represented as a probability vector (0.3 0.7). The state of the innovation after two time periods can be found by multiplying this vector by $P_{ij}(T_a - T_c)$, i.e.

$$(0.3 \quad 0.7) \begin{pmatrix} 0.61 & 0.39 \\ 0.52 & 0.48 \end{pmatrix} = (0.547 \quad 0.453)$$

Therefore, in this example, after two time periods 54.7 per cent of businesses will have adopted the innovation and 45.3 per cent will not. If the probability vector remains constant, then after a number of time periods or iterations, this process will reach a *steady state*.

In reality, though, many situations may involve absorbing changes of state. For example, once a business has changed to a certain type of operation it will retain that type of operation with no probability of change in succeeding time periods. This change can therefore be said to be an *absorbing* one. Such changes are most likely to be associated with large capital investments like large-scale mechanisation in agriculture and conversion of agricultural land to urban use. In such cases, if an initial set of probabilities in a transition matrix is applied to a number of time periods, a steady state will be reached in which one state accounts for 100 per cent of adopters. In other cases a steady state of dynamic equilibrium will be reached. This will be a deterministic steady state, but it can be altered by building a stochastic element into the chain. As with Hagerstrand's original work, this represents a continuously changing process by a number of discrete steps. An example of this random element injected into the chain is given in Table 10.2.

Markov chain models may be employed in a number of ways (see Wilson and Bennett, 1985:96–101). In particular, the transition matrix may be used as a guide to expected behaviour. Alternatively, the matrix of transition probabilities may be used to predict future outcomes, that is by multiplying this matrix by a vector. The latter approach was used by Collins (1973; 1975a) in an investigation of the movement of businesses in Ontario using Statistics Canada data from the Census of Manufacturing. He tested for the Markov property via testing the postulate that movement of industrial plants from one size category to another is statistically independent versus the alternative that the observations are Markovian. Testing for the presence of first-order or second-order or *n*th-order Markov processes was also carried out, revealing a first-order process for the change in the plants' employment structure. By computing the average transition matrix future values were then derived, which predicted the greatest changes amongst the higher size categories.

The states depicted in the examples above are

*Table 10.2* A Markov Chain with a Random Element Injected

| | | $P_{ij}$ Succeeding State (j) | | |
| | | A | B | C |
| --- | --- | --- | --- | --- |
| Existing | A | 1 | 0 | 0 |
| state | B | 0.2 | 0.6 | 0.2 |
| (i) | C | 0.1 | 0.5 | 0.4 |

If in the initial state, the proportion of individuals in state A = 20 per cent, in state B = 50 per cent and in state C = 30 per cent, then the probability vector would be: (0.2, 0.5, 0.3).

For the next 100 individuals (adopters):

| Existing State | | | Next State |
| --- | --- | --- | --- |
| State A = 20 (an absorbing state): | | | 20 |
| | to A 20 × 1.0 | | |
| | random numbers | | |
| State B = 50: | to A (0.2) | 00–19 ... | 8 |
| | to B (0.6) | 20–79 ... | 33 |
| | to C (0.2) | 80–99 ... | 9 |
| State C = 30: | to A (0.1) | 00–09 ... | 4 |
| | to B (0.5) | 10–59 ... | 15 |
| | to C (0.4) | 60–99 ... | 11 |

The numbers on the right-hand side (in the column labelled "Next State") are obtained from one "run" using random numbers. This "run" would give the following outcome:

State A = 20 + 8 + 4 = 32

State B = 0 + 33 + 15 = 48

State C = 0 + 9 + 11 = 20

aspatial, but several of the applications of Markov chain analysis by geographers have investigated chains with spatial states (Upton and Fingleton, 1989:182–6). For example, in the study of industrial activity in Ontario there was evidence to suggest that manufacturing establishments relocated once, twice or even more times during their existence, with relocation occurring over a considerable range of distances. Each establishment could be grouped into one of four categories: staying in the same location; new plants (births); plants that closed (deaths); and plants that relocated. Collins was able to investigate spatial states of origin and destination of firms, the six states chosen being: the city of Toronto (T); the suburbs of Toronto (TS); Hamilton, Windsor, London and Ottawa (LU); the suburbs of Hamilton, Windsor, London and Ottawa (LUS); all other urban areas with over 10 000 population (SU); and the rest of Ontario (RO). The pattern of movement of firms was studied over a period of years in order to generate probabilities for the chain which could then be used predictively to indicate possible future patterns of industrial location (see also Collins, 1976). The spatial transition probability matrix for the Markov chain is shown in Table 10.3. The main pattern of movement was from Toronto to its suburbs and from other metropolitan centres (Hamilton, London, Ottawa and Windsor) to their suburbs. The matrix was tested for the Markov property using a likelihood ratio statistic, and was found to be first-order Markov.

More sophisticated Markov analysis on spatial data has been performed in which the non-stationarity of the transition probabilities of individual company relocations is assumed to depend on inter-locality wage rate differentials (Kelton, 1984; Kelton and Kelton, 1984, 1985). For more advanced work using Markov chains see Isaacson and Madsen (1985), and for a geographical application see Akiri (1991).

# THE SPREAD OF DISEASES

## Epidemic Models

One area to which the simulation of diffusion has been applied is the spread of diseases, in which a series of studies have demonstrated the Hagerstrand model to be an instance of the *simple epidemic model*. Epidemics of measles and influenza in humans have been a popular topic for such investigation (e.g. Cliff et al, 1981, 1986; Cliff and Haggett, 1988, 1989a). More recently, there has been extensive work on the spread of acquired immune deficiency syndrome (AIDS) (e.g. Shannon et al, 1991; Smallman-Raynor et al, 1992). In particular, the attraction of the relative isolatedness of island communities as compared with continental areas led Cliff et al (1981) to focus upon such commu-

*Table 10.3* Spatial Transition Probability Matrix for the Markov Chain Linking Locations of Industrial Plants in Ontario, 1964–5

|     | T      | TS     | LU     | LUS    | SU     | RO     |
|-----|--------|--------|--------|--------|--------|--------|
| T   | 0.9539 | 0.0401 | 0.0005 |        | 0.0017 | 0.0035 |
| TS  | 0.0051 | 0.9801 | 0.0008 |        |        | 0.0137 |
| LU  |        | 0.0012 | 0.9902 | 0.0073 |        | 0.0012 |
| LUS |        |        | 0.0671 | 0.9250 | 0.0074 |        |
| SU  | 0.0009 | 0.0029 | 0.0004 |        | 0.9876 | 0.0079 |
| RO  | 0.0007 | 0.0052 | 0.0076 | 0.0007 | 0.0181 | 0.9743 |

T = Toronto; TS = Toronto Suburbs; LU = Large Urban; LUS = Large Urban Suburbs; SU = Small Urban; RO = Rest of Ontario.

*Source*: Wilson and Bennett (1985:108–9).

nities in their analyses of the diffusion processes for communicable diseases. Smallman-Raynor and Cliff (1990) have pursued a similar focus in work on the spread of AIDS, concentrating on the Caribbean where the majority of AIDS cases reported have been mainly on some of the smaller islands. This research on the spread of epidemics has been criticised for being both overly technical and esoteric (Harvey, 1989b:212–13), but much of the recent work has been highly policy-relevant and has carried quantitative research by geographers into significant new areas often conveniently overlooked by critics of quantitatively based research in geography (e.g. Harvey and Scott, 1989).

A recent example of the simulation of diffusion patterns of a human disease is the work of Loytonen (1991). Drawing directly upon the basic Hagerstrand-type simulation of expansion diffusion, he simulated the spatial diffusion of human immunodeficiency virus type 1 (HIV-1) in Finland. His model employed four rules to help build a MIF:

1. Each random number represents a single occurrence of virus transmission between a carrier and a susceptible, subsequently leading to one new HIV-1 carrier in the sub-region.
2. The repetitious occurrence of a duplicate random number will not lead to a new HIV-1 carrier.
3. Owing to the long incubation time and short study period, deaths of carriers will not occur, that is, the process is seen as cumulative growth only.

4. These rules do not change during the progress of the epidemic.

In the formation of a probability surface representing the situation in 1988, three steps were followed:

1. The relationship between HIV-1 and explanatory variables was established using correlation and regression.
2. A mass variable ($m$) was formed by weighting the number of sexually active persons in each sub-region by a number of scaled variables according to results obtained from the correlation and regression analysis.
3. The surface was formed from the equation

$$V_i = k \left( \sum_{j=1}^{n} (m_j / d_{ij}^{\ b}) \right) \qquad i \neq j$$

where $V_i$ = potential for each sub-region, $m$ = mass variable, $d$ = direct pairwise distance between two regions, $b$ = parameter used to adjust effect of distance, and $k$ = parameter for scaling purposes.

The weighting of $m$ was achieved using a number of variables selected from multiple regression analysis using incidence of HIV-1 in the central hospital districts of Finland as the dependent variable. The five selected were: numbers employed in financial and banking services ($A$); the number of drug cases ($B$); the numbers of migrants to the Helsinki metropolitan region ($C$); the number of customers of Suntours Ltd travel agency ($D$); and the number of gonorrhoea cases ($E$). All five were expressed in terms of densities per 1000 inhabitants for years in the mid-1980s and were scaled to a range of 0.0 to 2.0 with a mean of 1.0.

The number of sexually active persons in each central hospital district was multiplied by each of the scaled variables and the results applied separately in the potential model. Weighting factors were formed as the arithmetic mean of the two best variables, then as a mean of the next two, and then all five. From this the final weighting factor chosen was $(A + B + E)/3$. This shifted some of the high probabilities from the metropolitan region to other central hospital districts and therefore allowed for the simulated spread of HIV-1 down the urban hierarchy (see Figure 10.9a and b).

The simulation was applied to the logistic growth curve of the disease:

$$P_1(t) = U/(1 + e^{a+bt})$$

where $P_1$ = size of population at time $t$, $U$ = asymptotic maximum size of the population (asymptote = a line which continually approaches a given curve, but does not meet it within a finite distance), $a$ and $b$ = estimable constants, and e = base of natural logarithms.

This and other simulations of the spread of HIV and AIDS have used a variety of Hagerstrand-type and epidemiological models both to describe and to analyse spatial patterns of diffusion (e.g. Casetti and Fan, 1991). This has been an important contribution by geographers towards gaining an understanding of the disease's genesis and spread. It is an approach that has been accompanied by work in other disciplines on the cultural, social and political contexts of the disease (e.g. Crimp, 1988; Patton, 1990), contexts now being addressed within human geography (e.g. Gould, 1993; Shannon et al, 1991; Wallace and Fullilove, 1991). However, note the cautionary words from Michael Brown (1995:165) who contends that the spatial science approaches to the study of AIDS, referred to

above, tend to sideline the people with the disease because they deal largely with distances, spread, risk and danger: "gay men with AIDS *inter alia* seem to be important to geography only as data points or modes by which the virus spreads across space". He objects to the stigma associated with referring to homosexual men as a "risk group" and to the invasions of privacy associated with the data utilised by Loytonen. Instead, he utilises an ethnographic approach (see Chapter 13) to "rediscover" the people who suffer most from AIDS, adopting a completely different type of investigation of the spread of AIDS. Once again this demonstrates the cleavage within the discipline between those applying quantitative techniques to problems and those who use methods associated more with the social, cultural and political characteristics of individuals and groups.

## The Expansion Method

More advanced modelling of the spatial spread of epidemics has used differential equations of stochastic processes that formalise the various transitions from the three main stages experienced by an individual during the epidemic's progress: from "susceptible" to "infective" to "removal" (Anderson, 1982). This recognition of three different stages leads to the term *compartment formulation* being given to such models, which have been applied to the AIDS epidemic (e.g. Schwager et al, 1989; Tan, 1989). However, estimating the parameters of these models is difficult and they have limitations in their ability to produce spatially disaggregated portraits and projections of the spread of AIDS (Gould, 1989).

One advance on the compartment models is to add a spatial dimension to models that focus on the temporal dynamics of the epidemic or to add a temporal dimension to models of the spatial distribution of AIDS cases. This advance is incorporated in work by Casetti (1991, 1992; Casetti and Fan, 1991) using the *expansion method* which investigates the variation (or drift) in the temporal growth of AIDS in response to changes in population density. This method has been applied in other contexts, notably to demographic analysis (Zdorkowski and Hanham,

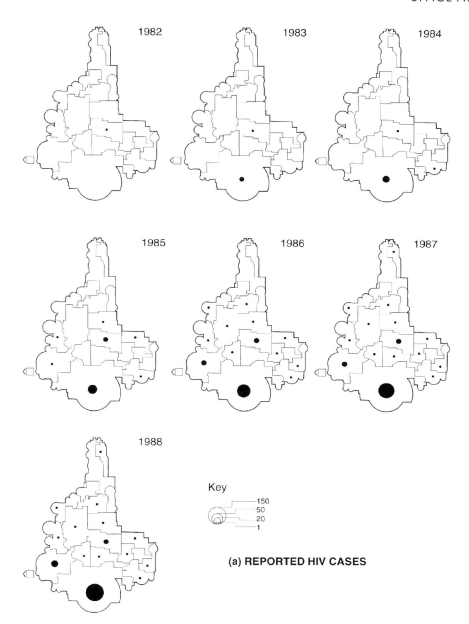

*Figure 10.9*  The Spatial Diffusion of Human Immunodeficiency Virus Type 1 in Finland
(a) Reported cases, 1982–88, by central hospital district; (b) simulated cases, 1982–93, by central hospital district. (*Source*: Loytonen 1991)

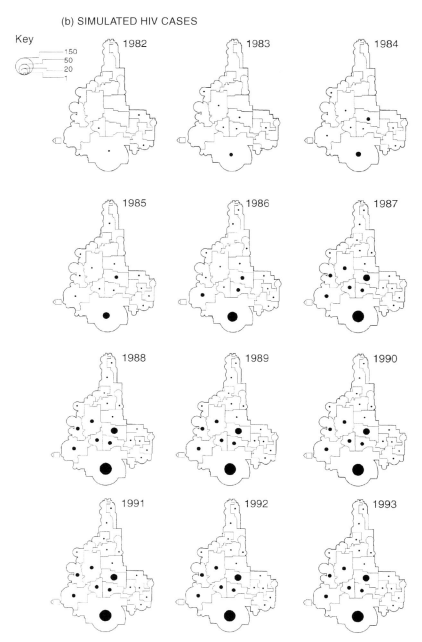

Figure 10.9    (continued)

1983), trend surface analysis (Casetti and Jones, 1987; J.P. Jones, 1984) and policy evaluation (Jones, 1987; Jones and Kodras, 1986).

As employed by Casetti and Fan (1991), the expansion methodology is both a technique and a research philosophy. As a technique it can be used for:

- orderly introduction of complexities into simpler mathematical formulations;
- modelling parametric variation;
- investigating whether substantially meaningful models "drift" across substantively meaningful "contexts".

As a philosophy it asks questions regarding the empirical occurrence and the theoretical bases of parametric drift whilst providing orderly and easily implementable routines to answer these questions. The method involves the following:

1. Specifying an initial model with stated parameters, e.g.

$$A = a_0 + a_1 t + a_2 t_2 + a_3 t_3 + e$$

where $A$ = natural logarithm of the cumulated number of AIDS cases; $t$ = time; $a$ = parameters; and $e$ = error term. If $A$ is a third-degree polynomial in time then growth rates of AIDS increase at first and then decline.

2. Specifying expansion equations that redefine some or all of the parameters into functions of substantially relevant variables or random variables, e.g.

$$a_0 = y_{00} + y_{01} D + y_{02} D^2$$

$$a_1 = y_{10} + y_{11} D + y_{12} D^2$$

$$a_2 = y_{20} + y_{21} D + y_{22} D^2$$

$$a_3 = y_{30} + y_{31} D + y_{32} D^2$$

where $D$ = population density, and $y$ = OLS estimator of the corresponding population parameters.

3. Generating a terminal model by substitution of the expanded parameters for their counterparts in the initial model. This can specify *drift* that can be mapped (Casetti and Jones, 1987).

The basic model can be examined for drift with respect to variables specifying significant dimensions of geographical differentiation (for example at the county level of resolution). This can enable various hypotheses to be tested, relating the distribution of AIDS to population density, for example, and investigating the notion that different mixes of the mechanisms propagating AIDS operate in different geographical environments. In Casetti and Fan's (1991) work for Ohio, other variables considered included: percentage urban population; distance to the nearest urban centre with a given minimum size; indicators of poverty, of dilapidated housing, or crime; percentage of minorities; percentage of labour force in manufacturing; percentage of students; and percentage of male-headed, single-person households. Spatial "drift" was investigated using trend surfaces and two-dimensional Fourier polynomials (see following section).

AIDS in Ohio spread earlier and faster in the largest urban centres, especially when centres were in closest proximity, and along major transport routes (notably the interstate highways). The expansion method enabled future spatial and temporal patterns to be investigated, suggesting that accelerated growth rates would occur along the interstates I-990, I-77 and I-75, but with a deceleration of growth in the largest centres. High growth predicted for Columbus may reflect the large concentration of university students in the city.

The expansion method has also been used by Smallman-Raynor (1995) in an analysis of the AIDS epidemic in San Francisco, employing it to model temporal changes in regression models in which the explanatory variables were the proportion of males aged 20–44 years in each district, the proportion of registered voters resident in multiple-male households, a poverty index, and homosexual intravenous drug users (IVDUs). His regression analysis showed that age was more important than the location of multiple-male households in determining the spatial pattern of AIDS, though with significant variation between ethnic groups. Ethnicity and low socio-economic status were important factors in AIDS amongst heterosexual IVDUs. Via the expansion method, predictions were made for the early 1990s showing a division between the rapidly evolving epidemic in the east of the city and the slowly evolving epidemic in the west. In the east a continued intensification of the heterosexual IVDU epidemic was predicted, with a secondary focus to the south. A prediction of 170 new AIDS cases diagnosed each month in the city underlies the development of this spatial pattern.

## ANALYSING TIME SERIES

In addition to simulations of changing spatial patterns over time, geographical research on spatio-temporal change has focused both on temporal developments of spatially located variables over a relatively short time period and on forecasting the future using various techniques of time series analysis, such as *Fourier analysis* and *spectral analysis* (Bennett, 1978; Haggett, 1973). This work gained in popularity in the late 1960s and early 1970s, recognising different types of time series, though geographers have concentrated primarily upon *discrete series* in which observations are taken at specific times, usually equally spaced, such as meteorological observations. Generally, these time series cannot be predicted exactly because the variables concerned contain a random element, that is they are *stochastic*. Therefore, in predicting these time series, the notion of future values having a probability distribution conditioned by a knowledge of past values has had to be used. In contrast, if exact prediction of a time series is possible then the series is said to be *deterministic*.

There have been four basic objectives in time series analysis:

1. *Description* of the main properties, usually after plotting the data in graphical form.
2. *Explanation*: when observations are taken on two or more variables it may be possible to use variation in one time series to explain variation in another series, perhaps through the use of regression techniques.

3. *Prediction*: using time series to forecast future values.
4. *Control*: this usually involves the investigation of time series to check the quality of a manufacturing process and is part of quality control, as employed in monitoring certain industrial processes (though see Tan and Bennett, 1984).

Description of a time series can be extended well beyond the simple smoothing of the series in the calculation of *moving means* (Figure 10.10). It can involve more detailed forms of analysis, generally applied to *stationary time series* in which there is no systematic change in the trend, no systematic change in variance and strictly periodic variations have been removed. For such series a description may be performed by using some form of spectral analysis which examines the components of the time series.

### Spectral Analysis

Three components in particular can be distinguished using spectral analysis (Figure 10.11):

1. The *long-term or trend component*, which is the broad, smooth undulating motion of the system over a relatively long period of time. This can often be partially isolated using a moving mean.
2. *Cyclical or oscillating functions*, which move about the trend, often exhibiting a seasonal effect or local variations.
3. *Random or irregular components*, which are revealed when cyclical and trend functions are removed from the time series. Therefore this is essentially a *residual component*.

The individual components of a time series represent disaggregations of the series into its trend, cyclical and seasonal elements, and random or white noise elements. Spectral analysis is primarily concerned with the separation of these three components and has been employed by geographers in the study of a number of time series. For example, Haggett et al (1977) examined monthly unemployment rates for Weston-super-Mare in south-west England. These showed a

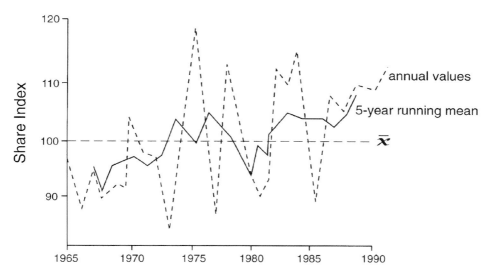

*Figure 10.10*    A Moving Mean

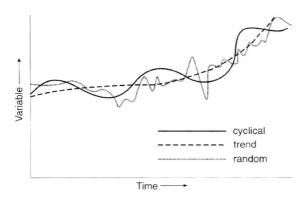

*Figure 10.11*   Three   Components   Distinguished   Using
Spectral Analysis

clear cyclical function produced by the tourist trade
which generated seasonal employment: higher unemployment in winter and lower unemployment in sum-
mer. Discrete time series like this can be modelled by
breaking the series down into aggregate or simple
waveforms described by a series of sine and cosine
waves (Figure 10.12a and b). So a time series can be

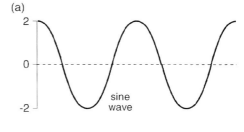

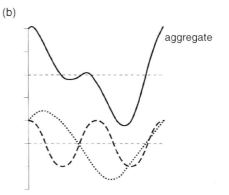

*Figure 10.12*   Sine and Cosine Waves (based on Haggett
et al., 1977:394)

expressed as a series of fundamental harmonics, combinations of which are referred to as *Fourier series*. Fourier series can be fitted to a time series using least-squares techniques. This enables the variance in the time series data to be broken down into harmonics of different frequencies, each of which accounts for some proportion of the total variance. This process examines the extent to which variance can be attributed to waves of various frequencies.

The examination of the variance of time series data can be performed using a diagram of the *power spectrum*. This is a plot of the percentage of the total variance accounted for versus frequency, where "power" represents the percentage of total variance accounted for at each frequency (Figure 10.13). Different power spectra indicate different types of time series:

(a) For a purely random time series, intuitively, a cosine wave of one frequency should not be expected to be any better than a cosine wave of any other frequency in accounting for the variability of such a series. Hence a random time series should produce a horizontal power spectrum (Figure 10.13a).

(b) For a cyclical time series any cosine angle with a frequency which corresponds closely with the main periodicity in the time series will account for the largest proportion of variability in the series. For example, in Haggett et al's study of unemployment data, a wave with a periodicity of 12 months accounted for part of the cycle of unemployment, but waves with periodicities of three, four and six months also coincided at times with the series. As shown in Figure 10.13b, the power spectrum for a cyclical series has a declining or damped waveform. The highest peak in the spectrum corresponds with the basic periodicity or fundamental wavelength. Other peaks correspond to waves with frequencies which are harmonics of the fundamental wavelength. Low frequencies give waves with long periodicities whilst high frequencies give waves with short periodicities.

(c) Power spectra can be calculated for *autoregressive time series*. This means that for time series it is possible to measure the correlation between observations at different time-distances apart in the series. Therefore this is measuring "self-correlation" between one data point in the series and another data point in the same series to see if successive or near-neighbour observations are correlated. This generates an *autocorrelation coefficient* ($r_k$), where $k$ represents the "lag", calculated in the same manner as the Pearson product-moment correlation (Figure 10.14). For example, if $t_1$ to $t_{10}$ has the series of values 10, 15, 23, 14, 16, 31, 9, 12, 27, 24, and the lag is 3, then these values would be correlated with 14, 16, 31, 9, 12, 27, 14, ... when calculating $r_3$. Autocorrelation for a time series can be plotted on a *correlogram* as shown in Figure 10.15.

For autoregressive series, if $r_k$ is large and positive this implies that adjacent values are very similar and the time series varies smoothly through time. Such smooth variations will be fitted most closely by waves of low frequency. If $r_k$ is large and negative the time series alternates rapidly, giving a spikey appearance. These very short oscillations can be fitted most closely by waves of short wavelength. Therefore positive autocorrelation is associated with power spectra at low frequencies, and negative autocorrelation is associated with power spectra at high frequencies.

Different types of time series generate characteristic correlograms:

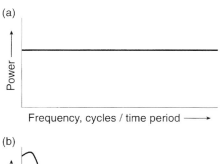

(a)

Power →

Frequency, cycles / time period →

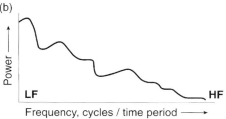

(b)

Power →

LF                                    HF

Frequency, cycles / time period →

*Figure 10.13*  Power Spectra. (a) Purely random process (b) Cyclical process

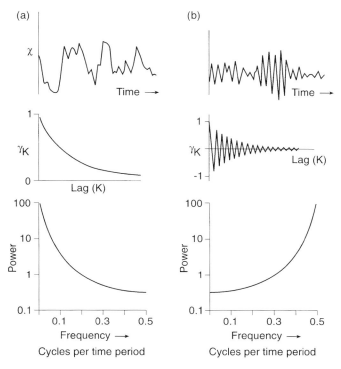

*Figure 10.14*   Power Spectra for Autoregressive Time Series (a) Series positively autocorrelated, (b) Series negatively autocorrelated (adapted from Haggett et al. 1977:395)

1. *Random series* – for a large number of periods and at any lag, $r_k = 0$.
2. *Stationary series* (with no systematic trend) – with short-term correlation in the series, $r_k$ will have a high value for $k = 1$, but will then decrease as $k$ increases.
3. *Alternating series* – the correlation will also alternate.
4. *Non-stationary series* (time series with a definite trend) – $r_k > 0$ except for very large values of $k$.
5. *Seasonally fluctuating series* – autocorrelation will oscillate at the same frequency as the seasonal fluctuation.

Most time series are a mixture of cyclical, autoregressive and random components, but, in modelling a series, curve fitting can be performed relatively easily by making use of the basic forms of power spectra: flat = a random series (termed *white noise*); smooth = a positively autoregressive series; spikey = a series with cyclical components.

## Meshing Time and Space

Research utilising a space–time framework has been extended into the areas of forecasting and prediction with the idea that forecasts of practical use should be an ultimate goal of geographical research (see Bennett, 1979). This idea rests on the ability of geographers to obtain a clear understanding of processes producing spatial patterns in order to make short- and medium-term forecasts, from a few days ahead in the case of meteorologists up to perhaps five years in the case of economic geographers. All the models used by geographers in making "*spatial forecasts*" have identified basic patterns in data on past trends and have

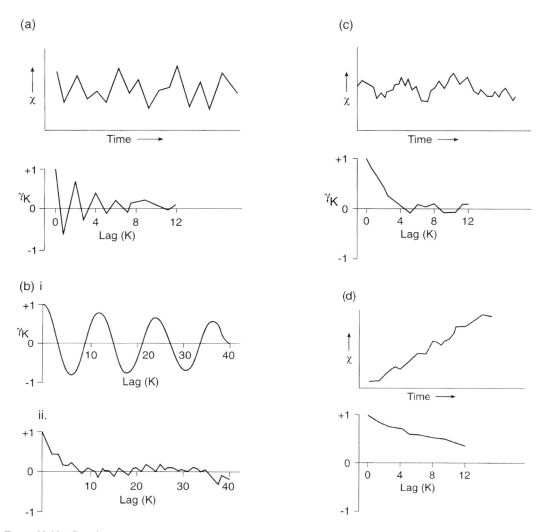

*Figure 10.15* Correlograms
(a) Alternating time series; (b) cyclical series, (i) unadjusted and (ii) seasonally adjusted; (c) time series with short-term correlation; (d) non-stationary time series

then used this information predictively. In particular, geographers have concentrated on regional forecasts for population data, unemployment and the incidence of disease, focusing upon space–time processes. Forecasts are based on past values of a variable, its pattern of diffusion and related variables.

In the UK work on forecasting using various forms of spectral analysis was pioneered in the Department

of Geography at the University of Bristol by Peter Haggett and associates, with impetus coming from a symposium held in 1971. Their work on spatial or regional forecasting involved the development of procedures for estimating how trends would progress through time and space, focusing especially upon the spread of diseases, price changes and unemployment. The natural base for this research was work on diffusion patterns, as it demonstrated that phenomena behave coherently in both time and space and so can be predicted. There was also a close link with techniques for examining time series described above, but with a critical spatial component attached to it in the form of *space–time spectral analysis* in which analysis focused on spatial locations, with a time series of observations available at each location.

In this type of study the focus of attention is $x_i(t)$, a time series for variable $x$ at the $i$th location, which also has values for that variable for other locations. Thus a set of time series can be compared for a range of different locations using cross-spectral analysis. In its simplest form this comparison looks at whether the time series for two locations are in phase (changing together through time) or whether one series leads or lags another. For example, if an event occurring at time $t + k$ (where $k > 0$) lags behind the same event occurring at time $t$ then the extent of the lag is $k$; similarly, if an event occurring at time $t - k$ (where $k > 0$) leads the same event occurring at time $t$ then the extent of the lead is $k$. The purpose of comparing these two time series is to establish the intensity of the relationship between them for various lags and leads. In the case of time series of regional economic characteristics such as unemployment rates, this type of analysis can show whether a series for one location consistently leads other locations. If this is so then it may be used as an indicator of behaviour in other locations. This indication can be measured in a variety of ways, and differences or similarities between locations can be incorporated in models of spatial development over time.

The initial work by the Bristol group focused upon unemployment rates in south-west England, investigating how changing rates throughout the region were linked to changes occurring in the regional centre, Bristol. For example, Cliff et al (1975c) analysed official unemployment rates for 60 unemployment exchange areas in south-west England. Using simple graphs, the pattern of unemployment in the south-west was shown to be related to the national pattern which, in turn, reflected the relationship between employment and savings in the business cycle. The analysis of the unemployment series was based on the investigation of different components of the series at any location, differentiating between factors operating at national, regional and local level.

*Cross-spectral analysis* was employed to examine the individual components of the series and then model the series. The analysis itself involved the examination of different cycles within the time series. These were related to the presence of business cycles and seasonal variations. After removing the general trend from the series by means of linear regression, power spectra were calculated for the 60 employment exchanges in the south-west to determine which frequency was dominant in the cycles. The series were then broken down further by examining the spatial distribution of the various cycles. Effectively these periodicities provided an introduction to regional variation in the unemployment data and formed the basis for spectral comparisons. Therefore each of the 60 series had its own spectral profile which could be compared with the profile for the whole region and with the other 59 series. This comparison could be made on the basis of correlations between series by measuring coherence and phase. The former represents the correlation of series at given times whilst the phase refers to whether one series leads or lags another.

In this example the unemployment series for three towns (Swindon, Bridgwater and Midsomer Norton) were shown to lead that for Bristol with respect to all frequency components up to the seasonal frequency. Areas contiguous with Bristol, such as Weston-super-Mare and Bath, were in phase with the changes in unemployment in Bristol; whilst some of the more distant areas, such as Bridgwater, Midsomer Norton and Stroud, led Bristol by between one and three months (Figure 10.16). Therefore rises in unemployment occurred in these areas before they did in Bristol. In contrast, Gloucester lagged behind Bristol, and Swindon, 65 km east of Bristol, was shown to have low correlations with other series in the south-west. The south-west was revealed as a leading region in the national diffusion of unemployment. When levels of unemployment rose in the south-west then the national rate would rise subsequently at a lag of six months or more. Similar analyses, revealing leads and lags of

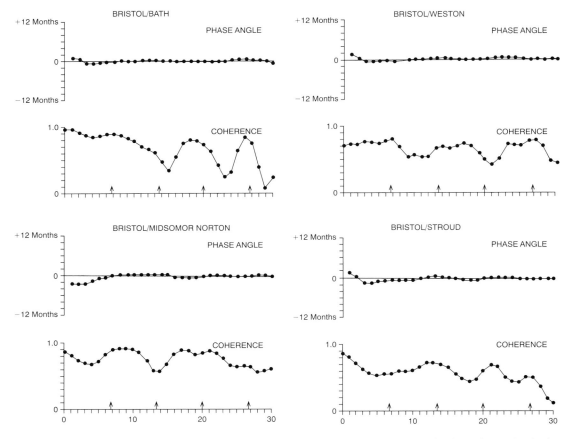

*Figure 10.16* Coherence and Phase Angles for Seven Unemployment Series with Respect to Bristol, South-West England (Arrowheads denote the 12 month seasonal component and its harmonics at 6 months, 4 months and 3 months). (*Source*: Cliff et al, 1975c:121)

unemployment rates, were performed for north-east England (Hepple, 1975) and for the 128 Standard Metropolitan Statistical Areas of the USA (King and Clark, 1978; Frost and Spence, 1981).

The above account illustrates a largely descriptive and exploratory approach. However, a more searching and practically oriented analysis was generated by extending the work into the area of modelling using a model developed by Brechling (1967, 1975). This helped to explain the changes being observed and to provide a predictive capability. For example, a basic regional response model can take the form:

$$y_t = B_k x_{t-k} + t$$

where $y_t$ = time series in region $x_t$, $t = 1, \ldots, T$, $x_t$ = the national series, $t$ = a random disturbance term, and the vector of $B_k$ coefficients records the regional responses at each lead or lag. It should be noted that autocorrelation can often be detected in the residuals from spatial time series models. It can affect the $B_k$ estimates and test statistics. Therefore transformations have been used to incorporate this autocorrelation.

In the analysis of unemployment trends, the modelling disaggregated the picture of regional unemploy-

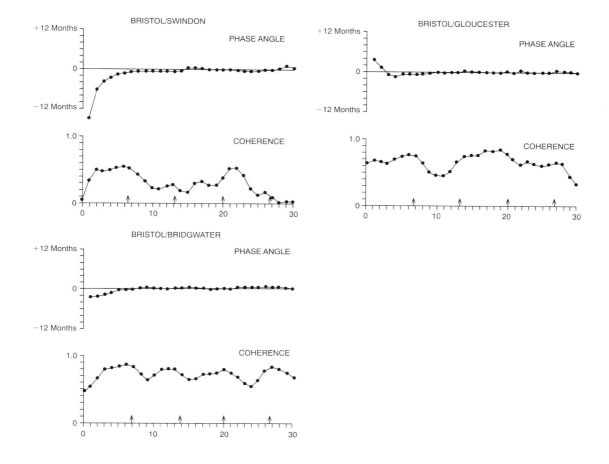

ment change through time into three components. For the three components, equations could be applied to each employment exchange, deriving coefficients using multiple regression analysis. The components and their equations were as follows:

1. *Aggregative cyclical component.* This is that part of a region's unemployment rate that results from cyclical variations at the national level. Sensitivity $(a_{ij}) = 1$ if the aggregative regional component behaves in the same way as the national pattern of variation. More prosperous areas with low unem-

ployment rates tend to be cyclically insensitive and vice versa:

$$A_{jt} = a_j U_t + l_j$$

where $A_{jt}$ = aggregative cyclical component in region $j$ at time $t$, $U$ = national unemployment rate, $l_j$ = length of lead or lag between the national and regional series, and $a_j$ = sensitivity of region $j$ to national cyclical variations.

2. *Structural component.* This is the component peculiar to each region, which reflects long-term dis-

locations in the labour market:

$$S_{jt} = C_j + b_{jt} + d_{jt}^2$$

where $S_{jt}$ = structural component of regional unemployment in region $j$ at time $t$, which is measured in terms of a quadratic time trend, $C_j$ = structural component in the initial time period, and $b_j$ and $d_j$ = coefficients of the quadratic time trend.

3. *Regional cyclical component*. This is given by

$$R_{jt} = A_{jt} + S_{jt} + R_{jk}$$

where, $R_{jt}$ = level of unemployment $U_{jt}$ in region $j$ at time $t$. If $a_j = 1$ and $C_j = b_j = d_j = R_{jt} = 0$, then no regional unemployment problems exist.

Areas can be classified on the basis of their performance with respect to these components.

The modelling of changes in unemployment through time has potential for applications in regional planning, forecasting and especially for a focus upon specific industries. For example, sensitivity could be closely related to the basic:non-basic ratio in industrial employment. However, a question-mark must be placed against some of the work of the Bristol group, as in some cases non-stationary data were converted into stationary form in order to use statistics applicable only to stationary data. Moreover, Lever (1980) concluded that there was so little stability between inter-regional lead–lag relations in one economic cycle and those in another that forecasting was impossible. Also the lack of sufficient theory to explain why spatial dependence arises severely undermines the extent to which models can be used to extrapolate for a future in which different economic structures are known to be evolving. Hence most studies, such as those referred to above, have been largely inductive empirical analyses.

Furthermore, a weakness of the time series models applied in the 1960s and early 1970s was their assumption that the basic model structure was constant and stable throughout the sample period. Hepple (1981) argued that since the late 1960s this has been a less realistic assumption than during the comparative macro-economic stability of the 1950s and 1960s. However, more recent models have attempted to overcome this, using different types of approach to incorporate economic instability, for example inserting dummy variables to represent discrete shifts in relationships; or the use of techniques that model directly the changing statistical relationships in a time series (Hepple, 1979; Martin, 1979). In the latter the $\beta$ vector in the general linear model is made time-dependent:

$$y_t = x_t \beta_t + \varepsilon_t$$

and the evolution of $\beta_t$ is governed by an additional, specified statistical relationship, e.g.

$$\beta_t = \beta_{t-1} + \delta_t$$

where $\delta_t$ is a $k \times 1$ vector of independent disturbances.

## Space–Time Forecasting Models

The evolution of variables over time and space can be forecast using statistical models. They usually take a general regression form in which future values of a variable are predicted on the basis of its own past values (i.e. it is autoregressive), lagged spatial diffusion effects and lagged exogenous or explanatory variables. For example, Cliff's (1977) *general space–time model* takes account of both the spatial dependencies of a variable and its past behaviour. The model takes the form:

$$x_{i,t} = f(x_{i,t-k}, x_{j,t-k})$$

where $k = 1, 2, \ldots$ and is a predefined time interval, $t$ = time, $x_{i,t}$ = a variable's current value at location $i$ and time $t$, $x_{i,t-k}$ = a variable's past value at location $i$ at time $t - k$, and $x_{j,t-k}$ = a variable's past value at location $j$ at time $t - k$. In this case a variable's present value at a particular location is defined as a function of its past value at that location and its past value at another location. This notion was expressed in diagrammatic form by Haggett et al (1977) as shown in Figure 10.17.

Several variants of space–time forecasting models have been developed to forecast the evolution of variables over both time and space. They are known usually by their acronyms, for example: *STAR*, a basic space–time autoregressive model; *STARMA*, a space–time autoregressive moving-average model; *STIMA*, a space–time integrated moving-average model; and *STARIMA*, a space–time autoregressive integrated moving-average model, which has been extended to include seasonal behaviour (Pfeifer and Deutsch, 1981).

The STAR model considers $n$ counties for $T$ time periods, analysing a variable $y$, i.e. for area $i$ at time $t$, the variable $= y_{it}$. The model constructed expresses the dependence of the values of $y$ in area $i$ at time $t$ upon values of the variable in other areas in the previous time period, i.e. dependence that is first-order autoregressive in time. Alternatively, the model can employ a regressor variable. For example, in the case of unemployment, this may be regarded as a function of a national economic variable such as the *"Financial Times"* Ordinary Share Index or gross national product. In this case the regressor variable has the same value for each area and so could be used to isolate local effects. The basic model can be expressed as:

$$E(Y_{it}|\text{past history}) = ay_{i,t-1} + w_{ij}y_{j,t-1}$$

where $E(Y_{it}|\text{past history}) =$ the expected value of $Y_{it}$ conditional upon its past history, and $w_{ij} =$ structural weights as employed when calculating a spatial autocorrelation coefficient.

The STIMA model introduces random "shocks"

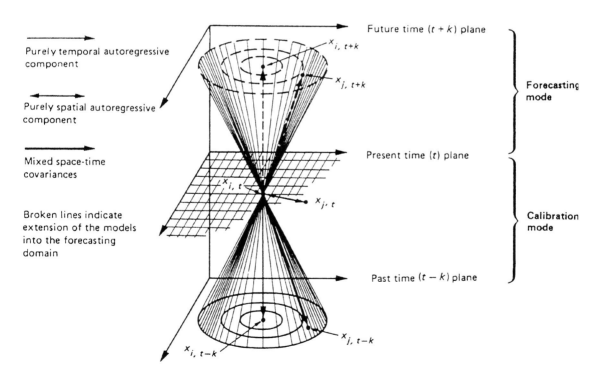

*Figure 10.17*    A Space–Time Model. (*Source*: Haggett et al, 1977)

into the forecast, e.g. "chance" closures of factories. Changes in $y$ are viewed as a function of a series of shocks to the system arriving randomly in time and space.

The STARMA model is based on a basic time series autoregressive moving-average (ARMA) model:

$$y_{jt} = a_1 y_{j,t-1} + a_2 y_{j,t-2} + e_{jt} + b_1 e_{j,t-1} + b_2 e_{j,t-2}$$

where a variable ($y$) in a region $j$ at time $t$ is predicted by regression on its own earlier values and by its delayed response to the impact of random shocks $e_{jt}$, $e_{j,t-1}$ and $e_{j,t-2}$, and $b_1$ and $b_2 =$ moving-average coefficients.

In the STARIMA version a space–time component is injected to give

$$y_{jt} = a_1 y_{j,t-1} + c_1 L y_{j,t-1} + e_{jt} + b_1 e_{j,t-1} + d_1 L e_{j,t-1}$$

where $L y_{jt} =$ the average or weighted average of population for regions adjacent to region $j$ at time $t$, and only one-lag terms are used. Lagged exogenous variables can be incorporated to turn this into a causal model, e.g.

$$y_{jt} = a_1 y_{j,t-1} + c_1 L y_{j,t-1} + f_1 x_{j,t-1} + g_1 L x_{j,t-1} + \dots$$

The exogenous variable $x$ has to be extrapolated if $y$ is to be forecast more than one period ahead. This has proved more useful than the previous equation because it allows conditional forecasts to be made using different assumptions about exogenous variables.

More details about the formulation of these models and examples of geographical applications are given in Bennett (1975, 1979). Their complexity has tended to restrict their use by geographers, critical problems being the choice of model and the orders of the temporal and spatial lags to include in it. Other problems are referred to by Evans (1980). A prime concern is to have as few parameters as possible to estimate providing this gives an adequate representation of the time–space process. Therefore, either adequate theory must be available upon which to base model and parameter choice or relatively complex statistical procedures have to be followed. Further-

more, variations in the structural interrelationships between regions over space and time may require the parameters of a model to vary from one temporal and spatial region to another.

It should be noted, though, that the fundamental assumption of most work on spatial forecasting has been challenged: that phenomena behave coherently through time and space and can therefore be modelled stochastically. Specifically, Hay (1978) has questioned the assumption of the stability of relationships between places through time. He referred to the need to consider an alternative form of change through time as presented in *catastrophe theory*. This is based on the notion that only a small change in a control variable or variables can lead to major changes (*catastrophes*) in a dependent variable. If this is the case then relatively simple linear extrapolations are inappropriate. This raises the possibility of at least two fundamentally different types of forecasting methods being required to predict space–time phenomena. However, work on catastrophe theory has been slow to filter into geography and especially into human geography. This topic is considered further in the following chapter.

## Predicting Epidemic Return Times

In work performed on the spread of measles in human communities by Haggett and associates, a detailed understanding has been developed regarding the relationship between size of community and temporal spacing of epidemics. For example, Cliff and Haggett (1988) distinguished between three different types of community:

- a community large enough to sustain the virus and so having a continuous record of infection – these communities have type I epidemic wave trains (see Figure 10.18);
- a community too small to sustain the virus but receiving regular type II waves;
- a community with a very small population, in receipt of irregular type III waves.

In the latter two cases epidemics can only recur when the virus is reintroduced by the influx of infected

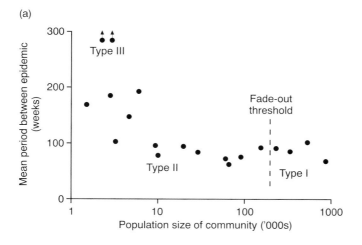

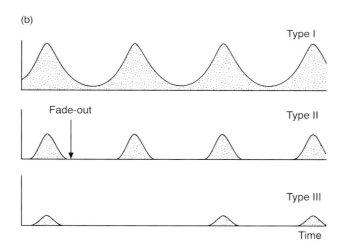

*Figure 10.18*  Epidemics and Community Size
(a) Impact of population size of towns on the spacing of measles epidemics; (b) characteristic epidemic wave trains for town types I–III in (a). (*Source*: Cliff and Ord, 1995:139)

individuals from reservoir areas of type I. This has implications for the development of strategies to restrict the disease, based on vaccination procedures, but the strategies rely upon an ability to forecast the space–time occurrence of epidemic outbreaks (Cliff and Haggett, 1989b). Accurate forecasts can enable targeted vaccination to reduce the susceptible popula-

tion in particular localities so that it falls below the endemicity threshold. However, even with good forecasting and vaccination programmes covering most new births, some groups in the population can be missed (e.g. certain religious groups) and there may be vaccine failures which can lead to epidemics recurring (see Cliff and Haggett, 1988:102–7).

Various forecasting models have been developed, both for a single city or region and for multiple regions, but there are two basic types of model:

1. *Process-based models*. These take the stocks of susceptibles, infectives and removals, formalise the transitions that can occur between these subgroups and use these as the basis for studying the size and spacing of epidemics. Amongst these models are the *Hamer–Soper model* (Hamer, 1906; Soper, 1929) (sometimes referred to as an *SIR model*) and the chain binomial. The former can detect the start of epidemics quite accurately but makes quite inaccurate estimates of total cases. This makes it difficult to estimate the amounts of vaccine and levels of health-care provision required. One reason for this is that in deterministic form the model leads to damping of successive epidemic waves which is not observed in practice.
2. *Time series methods*. The past history of the epidemic in the area is used to predict the future with an autoregressive/moving-average (ARMA) framework. One weakness with these is that they may miss the start of epidemics thereby restricting their practical utility.

In evaluating the various models used to forecast measles epidemics in Iceland, Cliff and Ord (1995) concluded that clear gains could be identified for extra elements of complexity added to the models. Their focus upon increased model complexity led them to develop an alternative modelling strategy for predicting epidemic return times using a process-based model structure focusing upon: $S$, the size of the susceptible population; $I$, the infected population; and $R$, the removed population (those who have contracted measles but can no longer transmit it to others because of recovery, isolation or death); and hence the term SIR model.

The model allows for four types of transition: a susceptible becomes a removal; an infective becomes a removal; a susceptible "birth" occurs as children are born or in-migration occurs; an infective in-migrates (no out-migration is assumed). It is assumed in these transitions that the infection rate is proportional to the product, $SI$, that the removal rate is proportional to $I$, and that the birth and immigration rates are constant.

If transition $i$ occurs at the rate of $r_i$ ($i = 1, 2, 3, 4$) then in a small time interval ($t$, $T + \delta t$) the probability of transition $i$ occurring is $r_i \delta t + o(\delta t)$, where $o(\delta t)$ is a term of smaller order than $\delta t$ (and assuming that all events are independent and depend only on the present state of the population). The population density for the time between any pair of successive transitions is:

$$r \exp(-rt)$$

where

$$r = \sum_{i=1}^{4} r_i$$

and $P$ (next transition is of type $i$) = $r_i / r$.

Details of how this can be developed to estimate the probability of the extinction of an epidemic, the time between epidemics using maximum likelihood estimation, and spatial effects are given by Cliff and Ord (1995) who used simulation experiments to evaluate the performance of the estimators in their model, focusing on the 16 main epidemic waves that have affected Iceland since 1945. They encountered difficulties as the model assumes closed communities, because it is sensitive to accurate interpretations of epidemic commencement and ending, and because of the time dependence of the migration rate for infectives. However, the model did reflect the general three-to-five-year cycle of measles epidemics in Iceland, with some under-estimation of epidemic return times, especially for very small settlements where return times are more variable and reflect the chance arrival of the measles virus at times when the susceptible population has grown sufficiently to sustain an epidemic. They concluded that incorporating seasonal and inter-regional components would improve forecasting of return times and that such estimation would become increasingly significant as the World Health Organisation's Expanded Programme of Immunisation pushes measles into a diminishing part of the world's surface.

## TIME-GEOGRAPHY

Whilst Hagerstrand's work on diffusion of innovations provided a basis for statistical modelling of such processes by both Monte Carlo and space–time forecasting methods, it also led to work that extended beyond a simulation or forecasting framework. This research, termed *time-geography*, was pioneered by Hagerstrand (1967b), Carlstein et al (1978) and Thrift (1977a,b) amongst others, and was closely related to work on activity systems by Chapin (1974). Time-geography deals with "the ways in which the production and reproduction of social life depend upon knowledgeable human subjects tracing out routinised paths over space and through time, fulfilling particular projects whose realisations are bounded by structures of inter-locking capability, coupling and steering constraints" (Gregory, 1985:297).

In time-geography time and space are conceived as resources on which individuals have to draw in their daily conduct of social life (Hagerstrand, 1982). The uses of these resources by individuals were conceptualised in his *web model* (Figure 10.19) to give an indication of the symbolic landscapes through which individuals traced their paths in time and space. Gregory (1989) argues that these "landscapes" differ significantly from the view of spatial science (as discussed in the first part of this chapter) that conceives of experiences of the world as cognitive abstractions of individual objects (see also Pickles, 1985). Indeed, Gregson (1986:188) views Hagerstrand's initial development of time-geography as a reaction to the "atemporal and faceless geography" of spatial analysis.

Hagerstrand's formulation of time-geography had three central principles: (i) that human life is temporally and spatially ordered; (ii) that human life has both a physical and social dimension; and (iii) that the activities constituting human life are limited by certain temporal and spatial constraints that condition various individual and group-based combinations of possible activities. The six principal constraints referred to are: (i) the finite nature of human life; (ii) the indivisibility of human beings; (iii) the limited ability of people to engage in more than one activity at any one time; (iv)

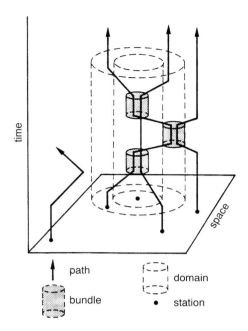

*Figure 10.19*   Hagerstrand's Web Model

that every activity has a duration in time; (v) that movement in space consumes movement in time; and (vi) the limited "packing capacity" of space, i.e. space has a limited capacity in its ability to accommodate people in a particular space.

Time-geography seeks to incorporate certain biological and ecological concepts in an examination of individuals' daily lives. In any examination of human movement through time and space, constraints upon movement are apparent. The six constraints referred to above can be classified into three types:

1. *Capability constraints*. These affect the ability to travel. For example, movement may be controlled by the available means of transport or simply by the biological need for sleep.
2. *Coupling constraints*. Individuals and groups are required to be in certain places at fixed times, e.g. teachers and pupils.
3. *Authority constraints*. Individuals may be precluded from being in certain places at set times, e.g. the effects of early day closing upon the

activities of shoppers. So authority constraints partly "control" people's lives by restricting an individual's movement through the domains of time and space: this is represented in the form of "pockets" in Hagerstrand's web model and is given similar recognition in Foucault's (1980) work in which he refers to the "net-like organisation" through which power is exercised in a hierarchy of different domains.

The impact of these constraints is to restrict and effectively define an individual's *time–space prism* (Figure 10.20). The time–space prism is referred to indirectly by the social theorist Giddens (1981, 1984a, b) who argued that the continuity of everyday life is largely dependent on routinised interactions between people who are co-present in time and space. Therefore time-geography is one form of notation through which the form of time–space "routinisation" can be represented, though humanists have objected strongly to its physicalist vocabulary. Furthermore, Giddens projected his view beyond the limiting confines of the prism by recognising that social interaction via social practices can extend to include interactions with people from other times and other places. He referred to this as *system integration* and *time–space distancia-*

*tion*. This distanciation he saw as a crucial factor in mobilising resources, for example the emergence of writing which gave rise to new spheres of interaction beyond the existing oral cultures and traditional tribal societies (Gregory, 1989:366).

An example of work focusing on the operation of various constraints is Dyck's time-geography of motherhood. In this she shows how constraints on mothers condense their social activities but also produce interrelationships between mothers that give self-esteem (Dyck, 1990). At the heart of this work is the attempt to show how space is socially constructed, with the locales in which mothers and their children meet (such as playgrounds, shopping malls and each other's homes) acquiring a particular meaning for those individuals. This represents a gender-role constraint (Tivers, 1988) or the constraining effects of social expectations through which women are allocated a particular role to perform in society. This role includes the majority of childcare and domestic work, the nature of which limits their mobility to a particular range of places, activities and times. These restrictions often limit women's availability for full-time employment and act in marked contrast to the experiences of women's male partners (Bowlby, 1992; Palm, 1981b; Pickup, 1988).

Another illustration can be seen in Pred's (1978) attempt to apply time-geographic considerations to the human and societal impacts that follow the adoption of technological and institutional innovations. In this he conceptualised time-saving innovations in terms of their release of people for other tasks and especially social interactions, that is the life-contact impact of an innovation. For example, in Figure 10.21a and b activities H1–H3 are habitual elements in the weekday path of a person. A time–space prism separating the ending time of H1 and the starting time of H2 is indicated in both diagrams. The outer turning points of the prisms are determined by the speed of the means of transportation available to the person. It is impossible for the person to appear outside the lower walls of the prisms because they are physically inaccessible by definition. Similarly, the area beyond the upper walls of the prisms is inaccessible. Before an innovation reduces the time that must be allocated to

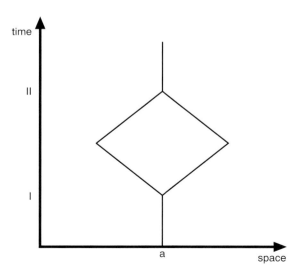

*Figure 10.20*    The Time–Space Prism

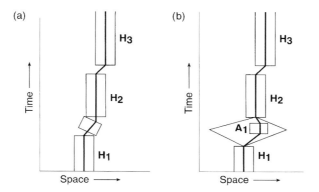

*Figure 10.21*   Hypothetical Daily Path Impacts of a Time-Saving Innovation
(a) Before innovation; (b) after innovation. (Based on Pred, 1978:354)

H1, there is little activity or interaction that is feasible for the person prior to the start of H2. Therefore s/he takes their time leaving H1 and arrives at H2 somewhat early. After a time-saving innovation allows H1 to be completed more rapidly, a much larger time–space prism becomes available to the person and so other tasks or interactions, such as A1, can be incorporated into the daily path (Pred, 1978:354).

Much of the initial work in time-geography dealt with the nature of constraints, though gradually Hagerstrand (1982, 1983, 1984) shifted his focus to a broader concern with human life as association and a more humanistic view of people's lives than treating them as faceless automatons. So time-geography became somewhat more of a part of geographical studies concerned with context and the composition of "social life" in general (as discussed in Chapter 13). For this Hagerstrand introduced three key elements within his contextual analysis: *paths*, *projects* (see Carlstein, 1982; Pred, 1977a) and *diorama*. The latter represents the totality of what is present and absent in bounded time–space situations, which encompass the physical associations of social life.

Attempts to develop time-geography have tended to carry this research towards "mainstream" geography in the sense that Carlstein's (1980) work on the time–space resources of pre-industrial societies contained a strong structuralist component whilst Parkes and Thrift's (1980) "*chronogeography*" was predominantly positivist. Combinations of investigations of activity systems and the theoretical underpinnings of time-geography have produced models of group movement in space and time which go beyond large-scale aggregate transportation models. In the 1970s gaming techniques were developed to perform such investigations, for example the Household Activity-Travel Simulator (HATS) for eliciting household reactions to new transport plans in a constrained situation (Jones, 1979).

The convergence of time-geography and *structuration theory*, as developed by Giddens (1985), has been noted (Cohen, 1989; Gregory, 1985). This is considered further in Chapter 14. Most empirical work in time-geography has been limited largely to simple illustrations or to the small-scale, short-term and essentially individual level (see Pred, 1985, 1990). However, a link between the gravity model (discussed in Chapter 8) and time-geography has been made by placing the model into the context of shopping time and frequency of consumption, e.g. Baker's (Baker, 1985; Baker and Garner, 1989) generation of space–time equations of consumer patronage. Nevertheless, a recurring limitation is the way it tends to treat individuals as objects and it focuses on systems of social practices rather than on the constant conjunctions of events. A damning indictment appears in Gregory's (1985) analysis which criticises time-geography for not being very geographic!

## LONGITUDINAL DATA ANALYSIS

If time-geography was an attempt to focus attention upon interactions between individuals, avoiding application of mathematical techniques to analyse human activities, then it can be contrasted with *longitudinal data analysis*, popularised in geography at roughly the same time, as a new set of techniques for analysing numerical data on changes through time. Indeed, Wrigley (1986) suggests that the 1980s may be remembered as the decade in which longitudinal data analysis became a major research topic across a wide range of social science disciplines including geography (e.g. Crouchley, 1987a). The attraction of this form of analysis has been its focus upon change in behaviour over time, permitting examination of recurrent choices. Longitudinal data analysis has been performed upon data derived from several forms of survey design:

1. *Repeated cross-sectional surveys*, in which a population is sampled at different points in time but with no attempt to retain the same respondents (units) for each cross-section. This permits statistical comparisons to be made but without being able to isolate components of change due to changes in population composition from those due to changes in individual respondent's behaviour.
2. *Classic panel surveys*, in which the same respondents or units are sampled at different points in time. This has been popular in consumer surveys (e.g. Davies and Pickles, 1985; Halperin, 1985; Wrigley et al, 1985).
3. *Rotating panel surveys*, in which some of the respondents are "retired" after being surveyed and then replaced by newly selected respondents at the next survey. This can improve the precision of estimates of change and reduces panel attrition, as experienced in 2, which occurs when, for various reasons, respondents present in an earlier survey are not available in a subsequent one.
4. *Split or "mixed" panel surveys*, in which 1, 2 and 3 are combined in order to maximise the benefits of following these three designs, e.g. measuring change at the level of the individual sample unit

whilst checking on possible biases from differential rates of attrition amongst subgroups and allowing new entrants to the population to be represented (e.g. individuals, households).

Panel surveys have three key merits in addition to the general one of providing a database suitable for studying short-term responses to policy changes.

- They permit reliable measurement of economic, social and environmental change, being especially useful for obtaining information on the sequence and duration of events and the timing and context of change.
- They provide "stronger" material for analysis than cross-sectional studies.
- They can provide data to use in identifying structural parameters of the exogenous determinants of choice behaviour (Wrigley, 1986:98).

One form of these studies is *long-term cohort studies* which carry forward evidence of change in people's lives across as many as three generations. There are three such major studies in the UK, though none of them began with the intention of developing into long-term analysis:

- *the National Survey of Health and Development* (NSHD), which comprised a sample of 4000 births in March 1946, and was based at University College London, with funding from the Medical Research Council;
- *the National Child Development Study* (NCDS), which focused on 17 000 births in March 1958 and was based at City University, London;
- *the British Cohort Study* (BCS), covering 18 000 births in April 1970 and also based at City University, London.

All three were originally intended as a "snapshot" of antenatal and postnatal provision at times of anticipated change. For a comparable study outside the UK see the work of Finnas (1994) on the Finnish longitudinal census data file. The potential of having examples of people spread socially and geographically throughout the country has been realised and periodic re-interviewing has occurred. For example, the NCDS has re-interviewed families and cohort members six times since birth: at ages seven, 11, 16, 20, 23 and 33. The BCS has collected information at birth and ages five, 10 and 16. In all cases the changing focus of research interest and shifting societal development has shaped the collection of material in the various interviews. This has meant that data from one interview to the next have not been entirely consistent and comparable. Also there has been some diminution in the coverage of the sample group as some of the cohort group drop out of the study. For example, the NCDS in 1991 covered only 11 500 of the original 17 000 babies, so that certain groups, notably the disadvantaged and the sick, have become under-represented.

The value of these three cohort studies is demonstrated by some of their key findings: the relationship between maternal smoking and the birth weight and subsequent health of babies; variability of height with social circumstance; the influence of disability upon educational attainment and employment; and the impact of parental interest in their children's education. Controversial "findings" have included the supposed impacts of comprehensive schooling upon educational attainment and of divorce upon the offspring of divorced parents.

Another important source is the UK's *Office of Population Censuses and Surveys (OPCS) Longitudinal Study* which has permitted analysis of individual change over the 10-year interval between censuses (e.g. Fielding, 1989; Hamnett, 1987), with a one per cent longitudinal study for 60 500 individuals in London (Hamnett, 1991). A more recently initiated multi-purpose longitudinal dataset is the *British Household Panel Study* (BHPS) launched in 1991 and covering 5000 British households and 10 000 individuals, conducted at the University of Essex by the Economic and Social Research Centre's "Research Centre on Micro-Social Change". The BHPS is projected as an eight-year panel study of households and their member individuals, but with reasonable prospects of continuation into the next century (Rose et al, 1994). A randomly selected panel is re-interviewed each year. The information gathered relates to household organisation, the labour market, income, wealth, housing, health and socio-economic values. There is wide scope for use of new analytical methods to deal with such data, recognising its hierarchical structure. Therefore the recent developments in multi-level modelling (see end of section on "Multiple regression" in Chapter 4) might provide appropriate advances (Jones et al, 1992).

The simplest longitudinal designs have yielded series of cross-sections for spatial time series analysis, though more recently panel surveys have become popular. These offer the potential to measure and model both the components of change at the individual level and the sequence, duration and timing of events. They have offered the opportunity for studying influences on change and therefore have been attractive to those seeking to investigate individual rather than aggregate decisions. Special attention has been given to work on choice behaviour by individuals selecting shopping outlets (e.g. Golledge et al, 1988; Wrigley and Dunn, 1984). Particular types of influence have been investigated by considering a number of interrelated sources of variation: *heterogeneity*, *non-stationarity* and *inter-temporal state dependence*.

## Heterogeneity

This represents variation between individuals due to both observed and unobserved outside (exogenous) influences. Possible sources of heterogeneity are suggested in Figure 10.22. Variation occurring outside the sample period is common because most panel surveys commence at a point beyond the natural starting point of the behavioural process under study. This is sometimes referred to as *left-censoring*, that is bias can occur in the estimates for parameters of the observed exogenous variables unless there is explicit consideration of unobserved influences on choice behaviour which result from the "censoring" of the database. Omitted variables may be associated with both the sample period and periods before and after the sample period. But whenever they occur they tend to introduce a spurious time-dependence effect and bias estimates of parameters of the observed exogenous variables. Lancaster and Nickell (1980) report this in

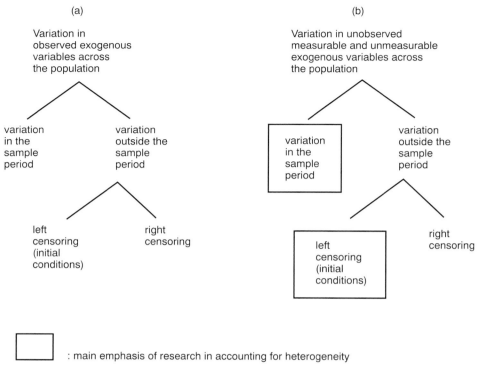

*Figure 10.22* Sources of Heterogeneity (based on Reader, 1986)
(a) Observed; (b) unobserved/unmeasurable

their work on unemployment as do Davies and Crouchley (1985) in their study of residential mobility rates. The omission of variables which are associated with time periods prior to the start of panel surveys is sometimes referred to as the *problem of initial conditions* (see A.R. Pickles, 1987). Overall, heterogeneity represents the disentangling of the determinants of choice behaviour, but with the additional problem of the presence of unobserved influences during the sample period or through deficiencies (censoring) in the longitudinal database.

Heterogeneity may be analysed by either continuous-time methods or discrete-time methods:

(a) *Continuous-time methods*. These focus on the histories of individual events, e.g. the sequence and duration of events, and the timing of transitions from one state to another. They are sometimes called *dura-*

*tion analysis* or *survival analysis* because they attempt to establish the probability that an individual who enters a certain state at a particular point in time will remain in that state for at least a specified period of time. This is illustrated in work by Broom and Wrigley (1983), Cox and Oates (1984) and Murphy (1984), in which a model is specified that represents entry to and exit from particular states, establishes the duration of stay in these states, and explains these longitudinal profiles through a set of explanatory variables. To deal with heterogeneity an error term known as the *hazard function* is introduced (see Flinn and Heckmann, 1982).

(b) *Discrete-time methods*. These focus on repeated choices and sequences of choices, with models formulated of these choices and identification of the "structural parameters" of the determinants of behaviour

(Wrigley, 1986:91). These models are longitudinal analogues of the conventional cross-sectional discrete choice models (Wrigley, 1985:311–57). The basic model may take the form of a standard logistic/logit choice model. In a dichotomous, two-alternatives, case:

$$P_{it} = \frac{\exp(x_{it}^{\beta} + \varepsilon_i)}{1 + \exp(x_{it} + \varepsilon_i)} \qquad (10.1)$$

where $P_{it}$ = the probability that an individual chooses the first alternative on choice occasion (time) $t$, $x_{it}$ = a vector of exogenous variables, $\beta$ = a vector of parameters, and $\varepsilon_i$ = an individual-specific error term or nuisance parameter. It is usually assumed to be identically distributed with a probability density function $f(\varepsilon)$ which is independent of the $x_{it}$ so that, for parameter estimation purposes, it is integrated out of the likelihood, i.e. it is assumed to be invariant over time, independent of the explanatory variables, and distributed according to some assumed parametric form such as a gamma distribution (e.g. Pickles, 1983).

In the case of multiple choice alternatives (polychotomous case) a beta distribution may be used to describe the form of the heterogeneity, and the model is known as the *beta-logistic model* (Dunn and Wrigley, 1985). Non-parametric alternatives have also been developed (e.g. Pickles and Davies, 1985).

## Non-Stationarity

This is the variation over time of individual event probabilities. It is the variation in individual choice probabilities over time, resulting from temporal changes or shifts in the values and significance of observed and unobserved exogenous variables. Reader (1986) illustrates this with respect to choices of particular shopping destinations (Figure 10.23). Observed exogenous variables may affect the individual doing the choosing or the choice alternatives themselves. Furthermore, changes in unobserved exogenous variables can alter the probabilities of selecting particular shopping destinations. These may be measurable, as in the case of product availability, or they may be difficult to measure, e.g. tastes and habits. Assumptions of stationarity, or lack of changing observed and unobserved individual, social and environmental factors, may well not be justified unless significant aggregation of data takes place (e.g. Wrigley and Dunn, 1984). Therefore non-stationarity is more common and can be approached via Fourier analysis or the extended beta-logistic model referred to below.

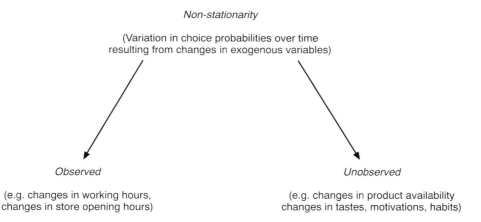

*Figure 10.23*  Choices of Particular Shopping Destinations. (*Source*: Reader, 1986)

## Inter-Temporal State Dependence

This is the dependence of current behaviour on past behaviour and of future behaviour on current behaviour, that is the inter-temporal relationships exhibited in choice behaviour (Wrigley, 1986:88; Wrigley et al, 1988:103–4). From this it is possible to calculate the probabilities of sequences of choices.

Figure 10.24 shows there are several possible sources of state dependence sometimes referred to as *feedback*. Four common sources are:

1. *Markovian*. The probability of a change in state is dependent on the current occupied state (or in the case of a first-order or higher-order Markovian process it is dependent on previous choices).
2. *Occurrence*. The probability of a change in state is dependent on the number of times different states have been occupied.
3. *Duration*. The probability of a change in state is dependent on the length of time the current state has been occupied.
4. *Lagged duration*. The probability of a change of state is dependent on the lengths of time previous states have been occupied – with two variations:
   - all previous types of state are considered;
   - only those lengths of time spent in the same state as the current state are considered.

For practical modelling one or more of these sources may be assumed to be unimportant, e.g. in beta-logistic and *Dirichlet-logistic models* (for an explanation see Uncles, 1985). Nevertheless, variables omitted from models may generate a spurious time-dependence effect and bias parameter estimates of observed exogenous variables. Therefore correct identification of true state-dependence effects rests upon suitable handling of any heterogeneity resulting from omitted variables or censoring of the database.

R.B. Davies (1984) and Davies and Pickles (1984) have extended the beta-logistic model to incorporate exogenous variables changing through time, state-dependence effects and allowing for initial conditions. This model contains two elements:

1. A beta distribution incorporating the heterogeneity

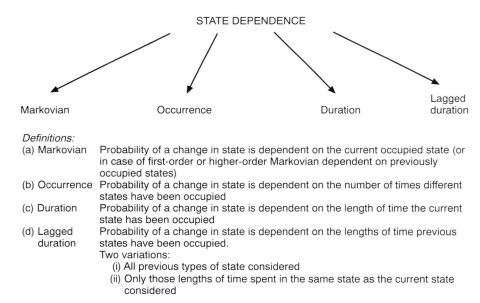

*Figure 10.24*   Sources of State Dependence or Feedback (based on Reader, 1986)

resulting from time-invariant observable and un-observable influences and which deals with initial conditions by adding a set of group-specific constant terms into the specification of the beta-logistic.

2. A logistic scaling function incorporating the time-varying influences on choice probabilities

$$P_{it} = \frac{\gamma_{it} P_{ir}}{(1 - P_{ir} + \gamma_{it} P_{ir})}$$

where $P_{it}$ = probability that an individual $i$ chooses the first alternative at time $t$. Thus it is a logistically scaled function of probability $P_{ir}$ at reference period $r$:

$$\gamma_{it} = \exp\left[(x_{ir} - x_{it})\beta\right]$$

where $\gamma_{it}$ = a scaling factor representing changes in the observed exogenous (feedback) variables relative to the reference period. The remaining notation is as per equation (10.1) above. Unobserved time-varying influences are controlled for in the logistic scaling function by using time-specific dummy variables (Wrigley, 1986:97).

Further examples of work involving longitudinal studies from various disciplines include Hand (1996), Heckman and Singer (1995), Magnusson and Bergman (1990), Piontell (1992), Plewis (1985), Uncles (1988) and Wilkinson (1986). However, most of these require expertise in using and interpreting relatively complex statistical formulae.

# 11

# SYSTEMS AND GEOGRAPHICAL INFORMATION SYSTEMS

## SYSTEMS ANALYSIS

### Systems Analysis in Human Geography

> If we abandon the concept of the system we abandon one of the most powerful devices yet invented for deriving satisfactory answers to questions that we pose regarding the complex world that surrounds us. The question is not, therefore, whether or not we should use systems analysis or systems concepts in geography, but rather one of examining how we can use such concepts and such modes of analysis to our maximum advantage.
>
> (Harvey, 1969:479)

The use of systems terminology for the description and analysis of spatial assemblages was first employed widely in human geography in the 1960s when, for example, it formed the basis for Haggett's (1965) seminal *Locational analysis in human geography*. The terminology and the ideas embodied in this drew upon the notions of *general systems theory* (GST) as outlined by Von Bertalanffy (1950) in which the analysis undertaken provides a stylised abstraction of complexities between linked variables (Harvey, 1969:448). These variables are treated as the set of elements being examined. There are links or relationships between the elements, and also links between the "system" of variables and the system's "environment".

A good example of this concept of system and environment comes from work by Mabogunje (1970) on rural–urban migration, in which he presented the migration process as a "system schema" (Figure 11.1). The elements of a rural–urban migration system were shown in relation to a series of "environments" (e.g. social, economic, political and technological) within which this system operated. Effectively, this model portrayed a number of systems and subsystems which the geographer can investigate in order to gain a greater understanding of the migration process and its ramifications. For example, in rural areas the family may be considered as a control subsystem, as the family influences who migrates and when, and it links people to the family's land and to the wider system of the village community. In many studies of systems it is not the links with the surrounding environments that are the focus of attention but the elements and links of the system itself. With the imposition of artificial boundaries, the system is often treated as being "closed", that is without outside links.

Certain concepts from systems theory can be identified in Mabogunje's model, most notably those of *energy* and *feedback*. Potential energy in the system is represented by the stimuli acting on the rural inhabitants to migrate whilst an actual migration translates this potential into kinetic energy. Feedback, as portrayed in *cybernetics* (the study of control and communications in complex electronic systems and in animals, especially humans), is incorporated as a kind of stimulus–response behaviour. The potential migrant may respond to factors in the rural environment

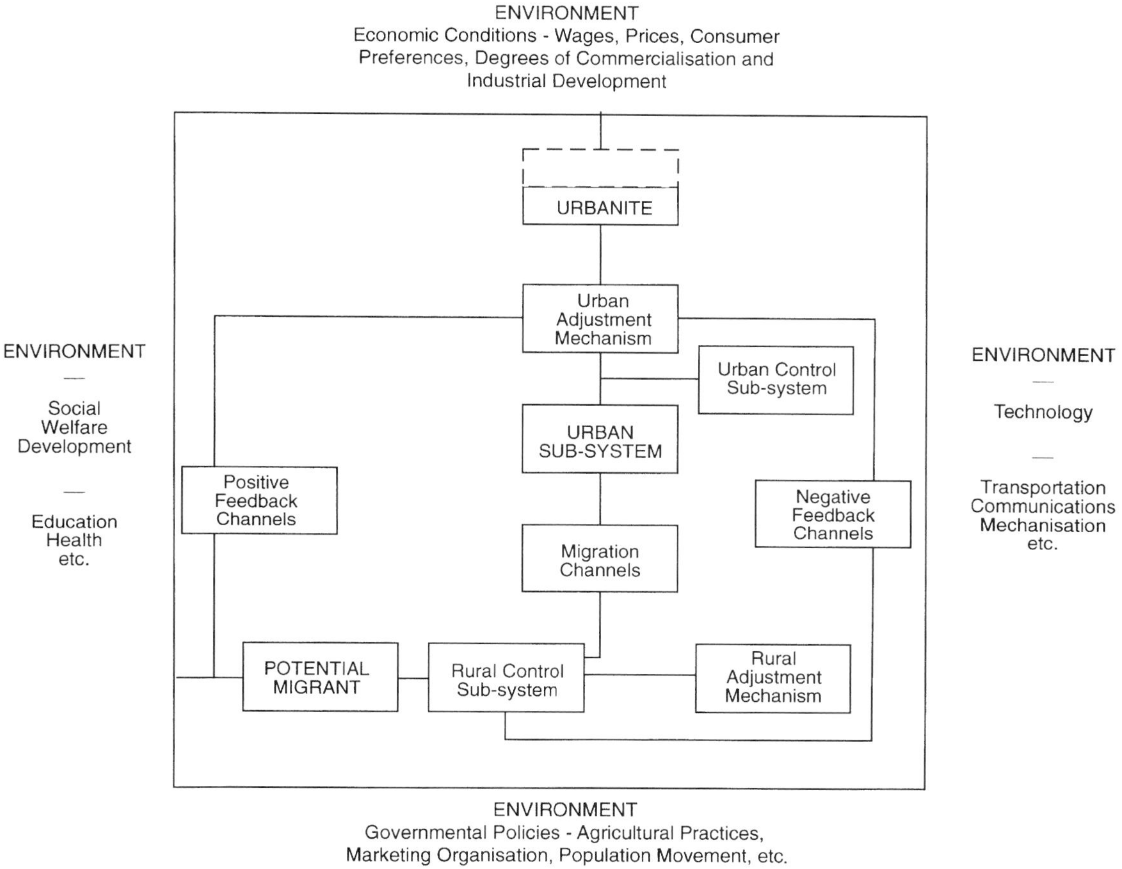

ENVIRONMENT
Economic Conditions - Wages, Prices, Consumer
Preferences, Degrees of Commercialisation and
Industrial Development

| ENVIRONMENT | | ENVIRONMENT |
| --- | --- | --- |
| Social Welfare Development | | Technology |
| Education Health etc. | | Transportation Communications Mechanisation etc. |

ENVIRONMENT
Governmental Policies - Agricultural Practices,
Marketing Organisation, Population Movement, etc.

*Figure 11.1*   Systems Schema. (*Source*: Mabogunje, 1970)

(the rural control subsystem) provoking a positive feedback in the form of rural–urban migration. A similar effect produced by response to the urban environment (the urban adjustment mechanism) may lead to return migration or a negative feedback.

## Types of System

Systems analysis has represented one way in which geographers have sought to advance beyond simple cause-and-effect or stimulus–response models. The complexities of the real world are implicit in the system's analogy with an organism, in which links between different elements operate the system, deter-

mine its evolution and so permit processes of change in the system (Chisholm, 1967). Systems analysis attempts to represent the interactions within a particular system so that simple relationships such as $A = f(B)$ can be seen to be mediated through other relationships. This has been referred to as the study of "wholes" rather than of "parts of wholes" (e.g. Johnston, 1983:42–3).

For example, Figure 11.2 shows an urban system as a set of elements or subsystems interacting with each other through socio-economic and spatial mechanisms, with corresponding variables that can be used to describe the structure of the system. The lines linking the variables and subsystems indicate the main inter-

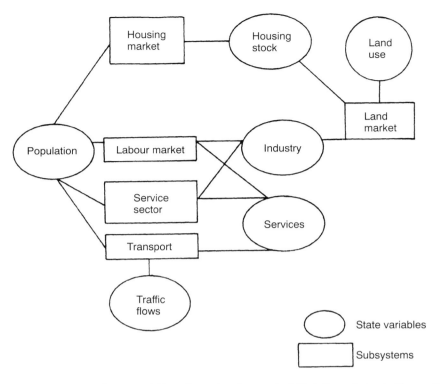

*Figure 11.2*   Main Subsystems and State Variables of an Urban System (and Their Interrelations). (*Source*: Bertuglia et al, 1987)

actions occurring. This arrangement can be modelled using some of the principles described in Chapters 7 and 8.

Several different types of system have been recognised (Chorley and Kennedy, 1971):

1. *Morphological systems* (Figure 11.3a). Representations of static relationships as links between elements, e.g. places joined by roads.
2. *Cascading systems* (Figure 11.3b). The links pass energy from one element to another, e.g. input to a manufacturing plant produces an output which may go to another plant, a wholesaler, a retailer or direct to consumers. If the manufacturing plant is regarded

(a)
(c)

(b)

(d)

*Figure 11.3*   Portrayals of Different Systems
(a) Morphological systems; (b) cascading systems; (c) process-response systems; (d) control systems

as a "system" in its own right then a nested hierarchy of cascading systems can be said to exist. Studies of cascading systems may be further categorised as:

- *White-box studies.* These investigate the transformation process occurring within an element receiving inputs and producing outputs, e.g. industrial processes in a factory.
- *Grey-box studies.* These make partial descriptions of the transformation process.
- *Black-box studies.* These ignore any transformation process and focus upon the inputs and outputs.

3. *Process–response systems* (Figure 11.3c). These extend the cascading system by combining it with a morphological system, but studies of this arrangement focus upon process not form, with the emphasis upon causal relationships, e.g. the effects of inflation upon unemployment.

4. *Control systems* (Figure 11.3d). Effectively these represent a special case of the process–response system in which one or more elements act as valves to regulate the system's operation and therefore may be used to control it.

Two subtypes of the process–response systems provide a good framework for the study of change (Langton, 1972):

1. *Simple-action systems.* These are unidirectional systems in which change in one element will produce a response in another element which may, in turn, affect another element. This gives a simple reformulation of cause-and-effect relationships or process laws.

2. *Feedback systems.* As described above with respect to rural–urban migration, this is when change in one element may impinge upon that same element after transmission through links between several elements. There are various forms:

- *Direct feedback* (Figure 11.4a). A affects B which in turn affects A.
- *Looped feedback* (Figure 11.4b). An impulse or change emitted from A will produce a response in A via a series of other elements.
- *Negative feedback* (Figure 11.4c). The system is maintained in a steady state by a process of self-regulation known as *homostatic or morphostatic regulation*, e.g. central place dynamics in which the pattern of service centres is affected as the distribution of population changes and adjusts to maintain a balance between supply and demand.
- *Positive feedback* (Figure 11.4d). The system becomes *morphogenic* with changes in linked elements producing a response in elements ear-

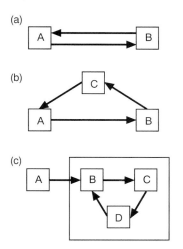

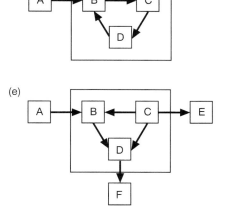

*Figure 11.4*   Feedback Systems
(a) Direct, (b) looped, (c) negative, (d) positive, and (e) no feedback

lier in the system, e.g. B affects C affects D affects B. An example is Myrdal's (1957) theory of cumulative causation, as illustrated in Figure 11.5.

- *No feedback* (Figure 11.4e). Changes in linked elements produce neither self-regulation nor morphogenetic development.

Good examples of feedback appear in Pred's (1977b) work on city systems. He demonstrated that feedback represents self-generating urban growth. So, industrial expansion in a town generates expansion in other industries because it increases the demands for their products. These other industries then generate extra purchasing power, stimulating the local economy and creating another round of growth. This process was shown to favour larger towns, thereby encouraging differential growth in the urban system. However,

obtaining the requisite data for all the variables in such a system has proved problematic and limits the practical utility of the concept.

Langton (1972:145) argued that the nature of feedback should be the focus of geographical study as feedback was the key to change in systems and determined the types of development of "elements" of geographical interest. There has been little explicit take-up of this suggestion, though he also stated that several of the concepts of systems theory were already used by geographers, but without utilising the language and basic framework of the theory. In effect, this has continued to be the case, with physical geographers making greater use of systems approaches, especially within biogeography. There, from the late 1950s, the focus upon *ecosystems* has been an important component of the study of the biological environment (Stoddart, 1965, 1967). Chorley and

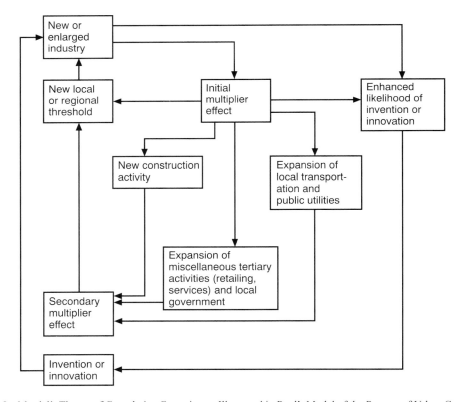

*Figure 11.5*  Myrdal's Theory of Cumulative Causation as Illustrated in Pred's Model of the Process of Urban Growth

Kennedy (1971) championed a systems approach to physical geography, and it was this interest in systems analysis by physical scientists that prompted some similar attempts in the social sciences (e.g. Chadwick, 1971; McLoughlin, 1969; Urlich Cloher, 1975).

The systems approach to planning conceptualised the city as a social and economic system which could be controlled by the planner. Hence the city was capable of being modelled mathematically. These models could then be used predictively by planners so that various control scenarios could be viewed and the desired one selected and planned for. However, in the case of McLoughlin's application of systems analysis to urban and regional planning, this prompted a subsequent re-evaluation in the form of his own critique of this approach (McLoughlin, 1973).

Within geography the use of systems analysis was championed by Bennett and Chorley (1978) who focused upon what they termed *environmental systems*. They attempted to provide an interdisciplinary focus upon environmental structures, partly by using a systems approach to develop interfaces between social and economic theory, on the one hand, and physical and biological theory on the other. Their wide-ranging work drew upon an extensive literature, though with relatively little contributed by geographers interested in social and economic issues. However, Bennett's own work gives some insights into how systems analysis can be applied to problems within human geography. This examined the dynamics of location and growth in north-west England, representing the region as a system consisting of a number of elements, links and feedback relationships (Bennett, 1975). The study was extended into the realm of forecasting future developments based on the analysis of the system's response to particular types of change (see the subsection "Space–time forecasting models" in the previous Chapter) (Bennett, 1975, 1978, 1979, 1981).

This work illustrates one of the principal ways in which geographers approached the concept of the system: as a descriptive device forming an analogy between human society and either machines or natural phenomena. "This analogy allows the structure and operation of society and its components to be por-

trayed and analysed, and it provides a source of ideas from which hypotheses can be generated" (Johnston, 1983:117). Bennett's work also shows that once the analogy has been made and the component parts and structure of the system determined, then it may be used as a predictive tool. In particular, this use of systems analysis as a basis for forecasting has been pursued by geographers (see the section on "Gradient systems . . ." below).

Several geographers have attempted to show how systems analysis can provide a unification of human and physical geography. For example, Wilson (1981c) argued that both human and physical systems may be studied in the same way, and used moorland ecosystems, water resource systems and cities to illustrate this view. All three were depicted as complex systems whose components exhibit a high degree of interdependence. They can be expressed in systems terminology and form for purposes of analysis. The result is a representation and analysis somewhat akin to the geometrical expressions of spatial form popularised in the 1960s. The fact that Wilson was trained as a mathematician and was applying certain mathematical principles to geography in his use of systems analysis seems most apposite as Von Bertalanffy's (1950) GST focused upon rules that might be applied in a variety of contexts, using analogy from one discipline in order to advance understanding in another.

## Critique of Systems Analysis in Human Geography

In a critique of GST and its potential utility to geographers, Chisholm (1967) conceded four points in its favour:

- the need to study systems rather than isolated phenomena;
- the need to identify basic principles governing systems;
- the value in arguing from analogies with other subject matter;
- the need for general principles.

Yet, he argued that GST is "an irrelevant distraction"

or, in effect, that its rules and motifs are not needed by geographers for them to be interested in interdisciplinary study and to make appropriate analogies. Indeed, only in certain aspects of spatial forecasting and spatial interaction modelling have principles of systems analysis been prominent in human geography prior to the growth of geographical information systems (GIS) from the late 1970s (see section on "Geographical information systems" below). Indeed, systems analysis has been much less readily accepted by geographers than the use of statistical techniques emphasising space as a key variable. This may reflect the technical complexity of systems analysis once it goes beyond the representation of a very simple system with few feedbacks and loops. Difficulties in actually operationalising the analysis of a complex system may also have been a significant limitation. Another factor has been the fact that much geographical work has only focused upon small parts of larger systems and has therefore found no need to employ any form of formalised systems analytic language or methods for such examinations. Also, for investigations of subjects that might be considered as systems, formal systems analysis has simply been deemed to be too artificial and too abstract to utilise. Therefore the main areas of its use have been in developing spatial forecasts and in the modified form of information systems.

Perhaps the most damning criticism of systems analysis has come from those viewing systems from a *realist perspective* (e.g. Gregory, 1980). For realists a system represents a structure in which elements and links are forever changing. Therefore they contend that the focus of attention should be upon change itself. In contrast, systems analysis "freezes" change in its conceptualisation of elements and linkages so that change is considered from a different, essentially static, perspective.

One of the most entertaining criticisms of the systems approach and the "first generation" of modelling within human geography was that made by Kennedy (1979). She complained that the most important aspects of real-world geographical systems are the *configurational* rather than the *immanent*, that is the individual conditions obtaining in particular places at particular times and not law-like processes operating against this backcloth. She described the configurational as the "naughty world" of complex landscapes that models and systems are unable to replicate beyond the level of simple, general processes. These criticisms are also echoed in Gregory's (1980) dismissal of systems theory in which he described it as being impossible to be validated conclusively against the real world except in purely pragmatic terms. However, the same criticism might equally be levelled at the social theories which have played such a significant role in the "new" human geography of the 1980s and 1990s.

In addressing various criticisms of the use of mathematical models and systems in geography, Macmillan (1989b) points to confusion amongst geographers as to the role that systems and models should play en route to explanation. He describes most models in geography as "quantitative theories" allied to a set of specific conditions. So it may be very difficult to see what the constituent propositions are and what the relationships between them are supposed to be. Nevertheless, he champions this construction of quantitative theories, but with a more explicitly deductive approach to be used. He also rejects the criticisms that models are too simplified to deal with "real" systems and that they are ahistorical.

In developing work on systems during the past two decades, geographers have focused upon several different types of system, taking the central thrust of their concerns for systems away from GST. In particular, a small number of human geographers have made attempts to analyse catastrophic systems (see following section) and chaotic systems (see penultimate section in this chapter), and a growing number are utilising geographical information systems (see final section in this chapter).

## GRADIENT SYSTEMS AND CATASTROPHIC SYSTEMS

Within urban planning models, *catastrophes* or discontinuities occur when there is a qualitative change from one system to another. Qualitative change can occur when small changes in control variables produce major changes of state in the system. Such changes are infrequent in comparison with the normal states in which the systems exist.

Theory accounting for these discontinuities in system behaviour was first developed by mathematicians and biologists, with major innovations from the mathematician René Thom (1975), under the general term *catastrophe theory* (Poston and Stewart, 1978). Alan Wilson (1981a,b) then linked catastrophe theory with *bifurcation theory*. The latter is concerned with the way in which the nature of solutions of differential equations change at certain critical values of the equations' parameters (Beaumont et al, 1981). Both theories are concerned with critical values of system parameters at which some unusual behaviour of the system can occur. For bifurcation theory the "unusual behaviour" is the transition from one type of solution to another while, for catastrophe theory, it involves a distinct "jump". In some respects, therefore, catastrophe theory is a special case of bifurcation theory. However, catastrophe theory is applied to a special class of systems called *gradient systems*. For example, if a system consists of a set of variables (known as state or endogenous variables), $x$, and a controlling set of parameters (known as control or exogenous variables), $u$, then in a gradient system there exists a *potential function*, $F(x, u)$, which when maximised or minimised determines the state of the system. If the system is disturbed from equilibrium its dynamics may be described by differential equations of the form

$$x = \frac{-\delta F}{\delta x}$$

Thom showed that for any number of variables in a system and up to four control variables, there are only seven topological types of discontinuity that can occur. These discontinuities are elementary catastrophes corresponding to *points of singularity* on the function associated with minimisation of the system's potential. This can be explained more clearly by considering the so-called *cusp catastrophe*.

## The Cusp Catastrophe

The simplest situation in which to consider catastrophe theory is the cusp catastrophe which involves one variable ($x$) and one ($u$) or two ($u_1$ and $u_2$) parameters or control variables (Batty, 1982a). In this case the possible equilibrium states may be represented by a curve in two-dimensional space (Figure 11.6a) (Wilson, 1981a:193) or three-dimensional space (in which the three dimensions are $x$, $u_1$ and $u_2$) as shown in Figure 11.6b. The maxima, minima and points of inflection of the potential function ($F$) are known as *stationary points*. Where these stationary points coalesce a *singularity* is said to occur, or a point at which the value of the potential function can jump.

Figure 11.6 shows that for $u_1 < 0$ part of the equilibrium surface parallel to the ($x$, $u_2$) plane is folded, with a cusp point occurring where the fold in the surface ends. Three possible scenarios are represented in the figure:

1. The value of $x$ changes smoothly until the fold in the surface is reached, but then it must change discontinuously because it must jump to the lower surface.
2. A similar change occurs, but in reverse and with the jump occurring at a later point. This and the former change together constitute a *hysteresis effect* (from the Greek for "be behind" or "come late", "lag").
3. The cusp point is approached from above and a small change in either direction takes the system smoothly onto the upper or lower surface.

The potential function, $V(x)$, for such a system is:

$$V(x) = x^4 + ux^2 + vx$$

This is a simple *quadratic equation* which can form the basis for analysis of more complicated catastrophes provided they take the same essential form. The equilibrium of the system is given by the solution to:

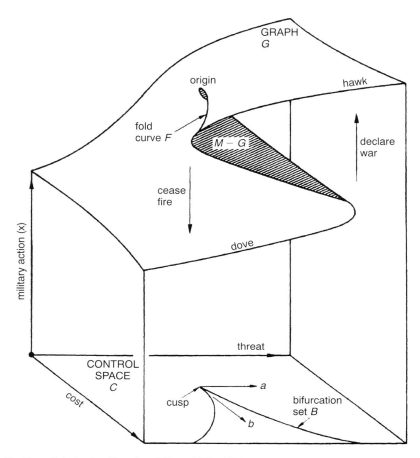

*Figure 11.6*    The Cusp Catastrophe. (Based on Wilson, 1981a:193)

$$\mathrm{d}V(x) = 4x^3 + 2ux + v = 0$$

As this involves a polynomial of the third order, it may have up to three real solutions for given values of $u$ and $v$.

The simple graphical representation of the cusp catastrophe provides a framework within which control variables may be investigated. However, it can be argued that it represents only a *post hoc* rationalisation of a catastrophe and so can be extremely misleading (Sussmann and Zahler, 1978). The practical use of such a model is certainly questionable, though Batty (1981a) attempted to apply it, *post hoc*, to urban riots in London.

A number of possible geographical phenomena suitable for investigation using catastrophe theory may be identified. For example, Casetti (1989) argues that the switch from a pre-modern, slowly moving, economic equilibrium to a modern, explosive, disequilibrium growth corresponds to a "fold catastrophe". Empirical testing of such a model provided a "good fit" with the notion of modern economic growth originating in England in the eighteenth century and then spreading through the rest of Europe by about 1840. Other examples include the evolution of the settlement pattern (e.g. Wagstaff, 1976, 1978), modal choice (Wilson, 1976a, 1981a,b), social disturbances (Batty, 1981a,b) and reversals of ethnic zoning patterns (e.g. Woods, 1977). General applications within the social sciences are considered by Isnard and Zeeman (1976). However, little formal development of applied work has occurred and there have been some strong criticisms (e.g. Zahler and Sussman, 1977; Day and Tivers, 1979). The latter, commenting from a Marxist perspective, note that catastrophe theory enables the modelling of discontinuities without necessarily being able to understand the reason for them. They suggest that Marxist dialectics (see Chapter 14) offer a suitable philosophical base for the explanation of such discontinuities. Their argument is that there is a continuous process (the development of industry by science and technology) that causes discontinuous behaviour (in society) which can be investigated via dialectical method to develop deeper understanding of development processes.

## IRREGULAR SYSTEMS, FRACTALS AND CHAOS THEORY

*Chaos theory* has been developed from the recognition that apparently simple physical systems which obey deterministic laws may nevertheless behave unpredictably, for example a pendulum subjected to two different forces rather than a single force. Such a development may be termed *deterministic chaos* or an *irregular* system.

Chaos is one of three forms that can be taken by non-linear systems, the other two being convergence to an equilibrium or steady state, and periodic behaviour or a stable oscillation. The basic formula for investigating these three behavioural regimes is known as the *logistic map*, which has the basic form:

$$x_{t+1} = kx_t(1 - x_t)$$

where $x$ = the variable being examined, $k$ = the parameter or boundary value, values of $k$ between 0 and 3 producing a system converging to an equilibrium, $x_t$ = the current value of $x$, and $t + 1$ = one time period of the variable $x$ following the previous value, $x_t$.

In "mapping" this formula an initial starting value, the *initial condition*, is required and is represented by the first value of $x_t$, namely $x_0$. Once this value and the *parameter value* (the parameters within which chaos operates) are known, commands within a computer spreadsheet program can be used to generate the current value of $x_t$. The initial condition must be a fractional value so that $0 < x_0 < 1$; $0 < k < 4$. For further details see Kiel and Elliott (1996b).

Figure 11.7 shows four examples of logistic maps produced by Kiel and Elliott (1996b). The first (Figure 11.7a) depicts a *stable equilibrium*, reached after only a few iterations; the second (Figure 11.7b) shows *periodic behaviour*, which starts to occur when $k > 3$. These values of $k$ introduce instability into the equation as the data start to oscillate and there is bifurcation or branching into a new regime of behaviour (see Stewart, 1989). *Chaotic behaviour* (Figure 11.7c) occurs when $k$ has values of around 3.8 to 4, revealing a lack of pattern in the longitudinal behaviour of the series. This is termed *aperiodic*, though it remains within definable parameters. The chaotic behaviour is not random and it is generated by a deterministic equation.

Deterministic chaos is perhaps most easily represented in systems of non-linear equations with time dependences, ranging from simple one-dimensional models, e.g. $x$ tends to $ax(1 - x)$, to more complex three- and four-dimensional equations (Hale and Kocak, 1991). These equations give time series that are aperiodic and do not exhibit equilibrium tendencies. Equations or systems of equations representing chaotic motion exhibit a sensitivity to the initial conditions of the motion in question (Figure 11.7d).

To model these chaotic systems, Mandelbrot (1982) recognised that non-Euclidean structures were required and, instead, utilised a new form of geometry which he termed *fractal geometry*, from the Latin "*fractus*" describing a broken and irregular stone (see Fotheringham, 1990; Lam and De Cola, 1993).

Fractals are irregular, but with the same degree of irregularity on all scales, as demonstrated by the so-called *Sierpinski gasket* shown in Figure 11.8. This is a simple fractal produced by breaking up a triangle into successively smaller ones. By dividing the black triangle (a) into four new ones, they will all have sides that are half as long as the original triangle. If the

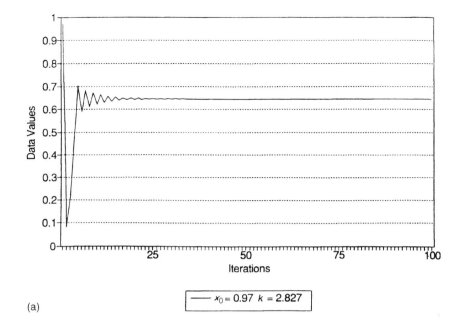

(a)

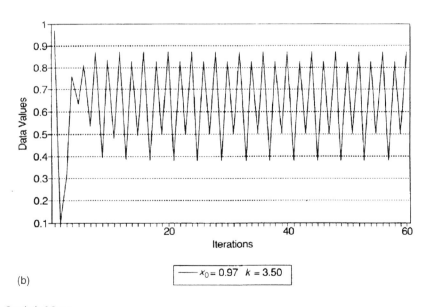

(b)

*Figure 11.7* Logistic Maps
(a) Stable equilibrium; (b) periodic behaviour, four-period cycle; (c) chaotic behaviour; (d) sensitivity to initial conditions.
(*Source*: Kiel and Elliott, 1996b)

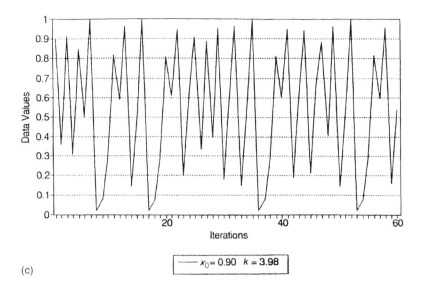

(c)

$x_0 = 0.90$   $k = 3.98$

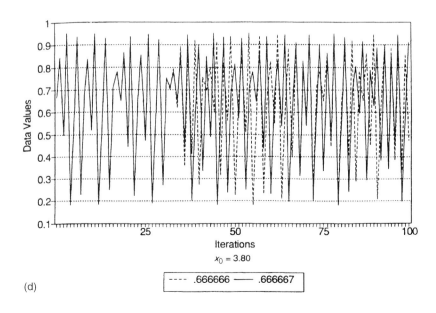

$x_0 = 3.80$

---- .666666   —— .666667

(d)

*Figure 11.8*  The Sierpinski Gasket

central triangle is then erased, in this case creating a white triangle (b), and the exercise is then repeated ((c) and (d)), the same structure can be created in ever-decreasing scale with a detail twice as fine as that in the preceding stage. In such a case the object is said to be *linearly self-similar*. Natural examples with a tendency towards this form are ferns, cauliflowers and broccoli. However, other fractal forms can divide from linear self-similarity and are able to describe different types of system, for example random fractals and chaotic or non-linear fractals.

(a) *Random fractals*. These have been used to model coastlines, mountains and cloud formations by employing advanced computer graphics. The modelling of the shape of a coastline employing fractals makes use of new ways of expressing the shape and its complexity, drawing upon the notion that the length of coastline increases as the precision of measurement increases: that is, as ever-increasing irregularities are taken into account. Thus notions of fixed dimensions have to be changed and varied between the familiar one, two and three dimensions as well as giving some consideration to variations in mass. For example, a curve that is a linearly self-similar fractal may range from being an abstract smooth one-dimensional line to twisting and turning so much that it gives an almost two-dimensional appearance. Its fractal dimension can vary from just above 1 to just below 2. The mass of this curve will also vary according to its fractal dimension (Mandelbrot, 1990). When modelled these random fractals can produce fern-like shapes that have been used to model lightning and other natural phenomena.

(b) *Non-linear fractals*. Equations to represent such things as turbulence in liquids and weather patterns are non-linear and display deterministic chaos. If the equations are iterated and the results presented using computer graphics, they demonstrate incredible complexity. This may be just of passing, artistic interest, but there may be applications that could extend understanding of various types of phenomena, including some of interest to human geographers, e.g. urban morphology (Arlinghaus, 1993; Batty et al, 1993; Goodchild and Mark, 1987).

Mandelbrot (1990) gives an example of the possible uses of fractals in the investigation of mineral distributions. The distribution of oil, for example, may be considered as being highly irregular: generally not occurring, except in a few, usually closely proximate, locations which have commercially viable deposits. Thus any plot of the distribution of oil around the globe would produce a graph that was largely flat but with a few sharp peaks as well. This pattern, for a series of regions, may be represented as a combination of a number of fractal sets known as a *multifractal distribution* (Figure 11.9). Its practical use, though, depends on the nature of the link established between the fractal equations used in generating the multifractals and the reality of oil distribution in the world. Such graphics were first developed at the University of Bremen under the supervision of Peitgen and Richter (Peitgen et al, 1992).

Chaos theory has been utilised in meteorology, building upon work by Lorenz (1963) in the 1960s, and has also been applied within population biology and physiology where researchers have investigated chaotic irregularities in the heart's rhythm. In emulating the application of chaos theory in the natural sciences, social scientists have used chaos theory as a means for understanding and examining uncertainties, non-linearities and unpredictable aspects of behaviour within social systems (see Kiel and Elliott, 1996a). Indeed, despite the theory's initial applications in the

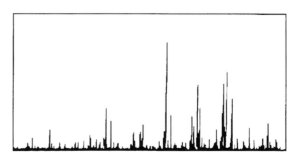

Multifractal measures

*Figure 11.9*   A Multifractal Distribution
This is a trace of multifractals modelling turbulence in a laboratory experiment. It is similar to multifractals describing the distribution of oil. (*Source*: Mandelbrot, 1990)

natural sciences, the inherent non-linearity and uncertainty within socio-economic systems may offer more opportunities than realised at first for the use of the theory in the social sciences. Hence there have been an increasing number of uses of chaos theory by social scientists since the mid-1980s, notably in economics (Baumol and Benhabib, 1989) and political science (C. Brown, 1996). Use of chaos theory by human geographers has been relatively limited in comparison, though recently one of the pioneers of the Quantitative Revolution, Brian Berry, has applied chaos theory to long-wave rhythms in economic development and political behaviour (e.g. Berry et al, 1993; Berry and Kim, 1996).

Berry's work examines the contention that long-wave rhythms of prices and economic growth are accompanied by shorter-term oscillations that, together, display deterministic chaos. The initial analysis of these economic rhythms has focused upon oscillations in annual rates of change in prices, real per-capita GNP and economic growth. These oscillations have been interpreted as exhibiting catastrophic shifts in pattern with a chaotic interaction between short- and long-term economic series. However, Berry and Kim (1996:216) acknowledge that their datasets are of insufficient duration to determine whether the data are generated by a chaotic process.

Furthermore, because chaos in a system is represented by irregularity, forecasting the development of a chaotic system can rely heavily upon estimating both the system's initial conditions and its parameters. However, given that the system is likely to exhibit instability, errors in estimation can be great, though representation of a chaotic system and prediction of individual trajectories within that system is possible.

A more specific spatial focus can be found in the work of Dendrinos (Dendrinos, 1992, 1996; Dendrinos and Sonis, 1990) who has championed the application of chaos theory on the grounds that non-linear dynamics are a central characteristic of social dynamics. However, he highlights limitations in the explanatory power of the simple iterative processes used to portray clouds, plants and animals, shorelines and exotic landscapes in the work of Mandelbrot (1977) and Barnsley

(1988). These iterative "maps" can accommodate a wealth of dynamical features but without containing any substantive meaning or explanation. However, Dendrinos contends that there are advances that can be made, trading off efficiency of the model for greater explanatory powers whilst preserving the variety of dynamical behaviour investigated. He views such a development as part of an ambitious new research agenda in the social sciences using the mathematics of chaos.

There are, though, four key difficulties to overcome before such an agenda can be realised (Dendrinos, 1996:240):

1. Chaotic paths require an enormous amount of data to trace, calibrate and test. There are very few variables in the social sciences that are available at sufficiently frequent time intervals to enable use of them as required with a high degree of accuracy (e.g. contrast unemployment data and meteorological observations). To date the "best" social science datasets used in attempts to find chaos and test for it statistically have been the extensive time series from the stock markets or monetary tables (Rosser and Rosser, 1994).

2. Most social science variables do not produce repetitive measurements under experimentally controlled conditions. Furthermore, most socio-economic systems do not comprise identical components with highly homogeneous behaviour. Their variables have frequent, irregular and unexpected perturbations that can render the fundamental assumptions of probability theory inappropriate. A specific difficulty is the separation of background "noise" from the internal dynamics in socio-spatial variables.

3. Inaccuracies in social science data are problematic in that the basic character of data is of a very different type to most data in the natural sciences where accurate and regular measurement is common. This can be contrasted with the "fuzzy" or perceptual data that is generally used in developing social policy and planning. The concept of "high-resolution" data is alien to many areas of the social sciences.

4. There are a number of additional unresolved issues including the appropriate levels of disaggregation for spatial datasets and the difficulty of breaking down socio-economic systems into an infinitely small self-replicating scale. For example, the limitations on the size of buildings and cities provide lower and upper bounds respectively to the scale of human settlements. This poses problems in the production of socio-spatial models that give chaotic outcomes with fractal dimensions.

The basic proposition of what Dendrinos terms "the universal map" is that for any time period, $t$ (where $t = 0, 1, 2, \ldots, T$), the relative size of a stock (such as a settlement or industrial production) at some location within a pre-specified environment that consists of a number of locations can be described (or simulated) as being directly proportional to a prior level of locational comparative advantages enjoyed by the stock in question at a chosen site. Locational comparative advantage is translated into a probability that a particular event will occur at a particular location. It is assumed that underlying the iterative procedure of the simulation is a replication force occurring at regular time intervals. This force may be attributed to temporal reallocation of the stock among the various locations within the pre-specified environment (Dendrinos, 1996:243).

For a one-stock, multiple-location configuration, the model is specified as:

$$x_i(t + 1) = F_i(t) \bigg/ \sum_j F_j(t)$$

$$F_i(t) = F_i[x_1(t), x_2(t), \ldots, x_I(t)] > 0$$

where the "discrete iterative map" describes the dynamics of the relative distribution of the homogeneous stock at a location $i$ ($0 < x_i(t) < 1$) within an environment of $I$ locations, so that at all time periods,

$$\sum_i x_i(t) = 1$$

where $t = 0, 1, \ldots, T$; $T =$ the time horizon consist-

ing of time periods or iterations, $t$, all identical in length; $x =$ the probability that an event will occur at any location $i$ in the $I$ locations; and $F =$ the non-linear comparative advantage that any location, $i$, in $I$ has in attracting an event.

The equations identify interdependences among stock sizes at various locations rather than interaction, or flow of stock(s) among them. For a given reference location, $I$, the above equations can be restated as:

$$x_i(t + 1) = F_i(t) \bigg/ \left(1 + \sum_j F_j(t)\right)$$

$$x_I(t + 1) = 1 \bigg/ \left(1 + \sum_j F_j(t)\right)$$

$$F_j(t) = F_j(t) / F_I(t)$$

where $j = 1, 2, \ldots, I - 1$ and $F_I(t)$ is a positive quantity.

Theoretical applications of these formulae are provided by Dendrinos (1996) in terms of possibilities for generating different forms of human settlement in space. However, for this work to develop wider significance the theoretical approach needs to be accompanied by the development of statistical testing and verification of model forms against actual human settlement formations at different spatial scales.

To date the mathematical foundations of chaos theory and its unfamiliar language have deterred many social scientists from working in this area. However, recent advances using readily available computer programs are beginning to make chaos theory more accessible to the non-cognoscenti (see Kiel and Elliott, 1996a). For example, it is possible to use spreadsheet programs as a visual means for exploring chaotic dynamics. This substitutes visual analysis for the often intractable non-linear mathematics of chaos (e.g. Kiel and Elliott, 1996b).

The clearest measure for demonstrating the existence of chaos and for quantifying it in a dynamical system or time series is the *Lyapunov characteristic exponent*, $\lambda$. When $\lambda$ is positive chaos can be said to exist in a system that is sensitive to initial conditions.

Exponents $(\lambda_i)$ of dynamical systems measure the average rate by which the distance between close points becomes stretched or compressed during a given time period or iteration.

Other measures, which also refer to the characteristics of chaotic dynamics, are the *fractal structure of the chaotic attractor* and *metric K entropy*:

(a) *Chaotic attractors.* The motion of a dynamical system can be represented in the form of an orbit around an attractor, the latter being defined as "a closed invariant set that essentially captures all orbits starting in its domain of attraction" (T.A. Brown, 1996:54). In effect, an attractor can be considered as exerting an appeal to a system, a point or subset of points towards which any dynamical path will converge. This convergence represents development of an equilibrium, so an equilibrium state may be called an attractor. For example, a firm entering a new business environment is likely to experience a period of "turbulence" or erratic behaviour as it adjusts to the new environment. The erratic behaviour is transient towards an equilibrium or an attractor point. This point represents stability as all trajectories of the system (in this example, the firm) that begin in the vicinity of the attractor approach the attractor with the passage of time. However, attractors are not always equilibria, and orbits can be drawn towards a cyclic path rather than towards a point fixed in space. Attractors may also be quasi-periodic or strange, as in a doughnut-shaped orbit, a *torus*, which can be generated by the cosines of a pair of incommensurate frequencies. Fourier analysis of motion on a strange attractor produces a continuous power spectrum. "A chaotic attractor is characterised by exponential divergence away from any point within the attractor" (T.A. Brown, 1996:55). This divergent movement produces a trajectory with chaotic pattern and fractal structure. For further discussion of this complex phenomenon see Ruelle (1989, 1991).

(b) *Metric K entropy (or Kolmogorov–Sinai entropy).* As discussed in the section on "Entropy-maximising models" in Chapter 8, entropy can be interpreted as a measure of the rate of information production and the growth of uncertainty. If a system is increasing in entropy, the number of possible system states evolving from an initial distribution over time also increases. T.A. Brown. (1996:57) likens this increase to a situation in which voters are suddenly offered a much wider choice of political parties from which to choose at an election. The voters are not confined to their prior "political space" and so there is an increase in the disorder in the system. There has been a change from a situation in which there is knowledge regarding the position of the voters to one of greater ignorance about this position. Thus $K$ entropy is given by the proportionality

$$K \propto -\sum_i P_i \log P_i$$

where $P_i =$ the set of probabilities of finding the system in state $\{i\}$, and measures the information needed to locate the system in a specific state $\{i\}$. So $K$ is a measure of ignorance about the system.

The Lyapunov exponents are generalised eigenvalues (see second section in Chapter 5) over an entire attractor, giving the average rate of contraction or expansion of trajectories in an attractor (see Wiggins, 1990). Ruelle (1989) interprets $K$ entropy as equalling the sum of positive $\lambda_i$, and therefore implying that positive entropy exists in the presence of chaos. If $\lambda < 0$ then the system's "orbit" is stable and periodic; if $\lambda = 0$ the orbit is marginally stable and is near a point of bifurcation; if $\lambda > 0$ the orbit is chaotic. Further details regarding the mathematical underpinning for $\lambda$ and methods of computation are provided by Schuster (1988) and Eckmann and Ruelle (1985). An IBM PC computer package for analysing chaotic systems has been developed by Sprott and Rowlands (1992).

Despite this emergence of chaos theory into the realm of the desktop computer, there is no indication of the theory entering the mainstream of human geography. Berry's work hints at the possibilities for applying chaos theory to the analysis of economic growth patterns, and there is potential for using chaos theory in forecasting (e.g. Tong, 1994), but grandiose schemes to use chaos theory as part of the analysis of complex social systems (e.g. Harvey and Reed, 1996) are more schematic than practical propositions at present.

# GEOGRAPHICAL INFORMATION SYSTEMS (GIS)

## Computers and Geography

Computers have been used extensively by geographers for the analysis of numerical data. The role of computers in storing, retrieving and analysing such data was crucial in geography's Quantitative Revolution. They permitted complex statistical techniques, such as factor analysis, to be applied to large datasets containing hundreds or thousands of individual numbers, with results obtained far more rapidly than if the calculations had been performed by hand or on cumbersome hand-operated calculators. Initially, in the 1950s and early 1960s, computers were difficult to use and their availability was limited. Therefore their use by geographers was also restricted: pioneers in the USA were Garrison (1959) and Tobler (1959) who used them in work on rural poverty and cartography respectively, whilst in Britain Coppock (1964) used computers in producing his *Agricultural atlas of England and Wales*. Faster operating and cheaper computers in the second half of the 1960s supported a plethora of factorial ecologies and established the computer as a necessary component of many geographical data analyses or mathematical modelling exercises. This was reinforced by the growing availability of large-scale datasets derived from censuses and surveys. So computers began to play a central role in studies of economic and social change, encouraging the rapid adoption and dissemination of the statistical and mathematical techniques that were central to the Quantitative Revolution.

By the early 1970s computers were being used widely for statistical analysis, and initial work had begun in computer cartography, simulation models and remote sensing (Dawson and Unwin, 1976; Lo, 1976; Mather, 1976). However, perhaps of even greater significance have been the dramatic changes brought about by the microcomputer revolution of the early 1980s. This made it possible for individuals to own relatively low-cost computers and to use them for a wide range of operations. It made accessible to many the technology that previously had only been the prerogative of a few. Geographical computer applications were stimulated and new types of work were encouraged. There was an explosion in the writing of geographical computer programs (software) (Unwin and Dawson, 1985) and various types of geographical problem were addressed in the development of a new branch of the discipline, geographical information systems (GIS).

A computer is an electronic device capable of storing numerical data and of performing certain operations on those data. It follows instructions given in the form of a program written in a special computer language of which there are a great many varieties, e.g. Basic, Fortran, Algol, Pascal, Ada. Some languages are designed for special purposes. For example, Basic was developed for introductory teaching purposes and has often been used to teach undergraduates the rudiments of computer programming. The essential operations of the computer as used for data analysis are shown in Figure 11.10, which simplifies these operations into a three-stage process of inputs, processing and outputs.

The program itself calls into use a compiler which then converts it into a form the *control unit* can handle and execute. The programs added great speed to the process of data analysis and helped minimise calculation errors. A further attraction of the computer was the ready availability of *computer packages* designed to help the non-computer specialist to analyse data. Package programs are commercially prepared standard programs already housed in the *central processing unit*, or readily loaded into it, and which can be called into action by a few limited commands. It has been easy access to package programs for statistical and other analyses of data that has permitted such widespread use of many complex techniques. The acronyms and names of the standard packages, such as SPSS, SAS, Minitab and GLIM, have become familiar to geographers undertaking both simple and complex forms of statistical analysis. However, one significant problem has been that geographers have frequently relied upon package programs or on others to write their computer programs even for standard statistical procedures. Although this has obvious advantages in time-saving and use of accepted proce-

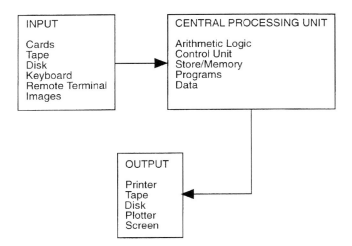

*Figure 11.10*   The Basic Operations of a Computer

dures, it is not always satisfactory as the researcher is not entirely in control of the program and is also perhaps unaware of the capabilities and limitations of the computer.

Writing in the late 1960s, Hagerstrand (1967c) argued that the computer could make significant contributions to several areas of geography. He singled out three in particular:

- descriptive mapping, including the mapping of remotely sensed data;
- analytical procedures;
- process models, primarily stochastic processes in which he argued that vast possibilities lay ahead.

At this time significant developments in computerised data processing were still occurring, and he recommended that geographers needed to prepare for the greater utilisation of the new technology. Three opportunities were identified:

1. The arrangement and integration of statistical and cartographic information in a suitable manner for automatic processing. With respect to this, a need for better collection of data was also identified (to improve data quality).

2. The raising of geographical techniques to match new standards of observation and computation.
3. Computing should follow statistical techniques into the geographical curriculum. This could then overcome the view that "Computers, like animals in a zoo, need experts to look after them!"

These opportunities have largely been realised, though perhaps to a much greater extent than Hagerstrand envisaged, for the *microcomputer revolution* has both greatly extended the general usage of computers in society and added to computer-assisted geographical applications. From rather disparate work in statistical analysis, computer cartography, simulation models, remote sensing and image analysis, there has grown an integrative approach under the umbrella of GIS (Maguire, 1989). This integration was first apparent in the establishment of the Canada GIS in 1962 and developed more rapidly from the late 1960s, for example with the creation of the New York Land Use and Natural Resource Information System in 1967 and the establishment of a Commission on Geographical Data Sensing and Processing by the International Geographical Union in 1968.

The Canada GIS introduced to geographers the idea of developing specialist information systems for use with various forms of geographical information. Information systems are computer applications consisting of a database, application programs, and manual and machine procedures for processing data (see Willi, 1991). When applied to geographical information one key feature is the incorporation of spatial reference points, thereby adding the "geographical" to the notion of information system to create a geographical information system. The characteristics of such systems can now be considered.

## Characteristics of Geographical Information Systems

In 1988 one survey revealed that GIS was the second or third most widespread research topic in the geography departments of British universities (Rhind, 1989:190). Yet GIS is a term that first appeared in general use only as recently as the late 1960s when it was applied to "general purpose and extensible computer facilities which handle data pertaining to areas of ground or to individuals or groups of people who can be defined as living or working in specific geographical locations" (Rhind, 1981:17). It is a computer system with the capability of storing, manipulating and displaying spatially referenced data. Such systems generally have two particular characteristics. The first of these is close linkages between digital cartographic information and associated databases containing the attributes of point, line or areal features. The second is the ability to integrate data from a variety of sources, including cartography, remote sensing and field survey, into a common geographical framework (Curran, 1985).

GIS are integrated computer systems for the input, storage, analysis and output of spatially referenced data. Because a GIS contains a range of software within a single computing environment, it has been described as a "toolbox" for handling and analysing geographical data (e.g. Martin, 1997). They have developed rapidly since the early 1960s (see Smith et al, 1987), and have received input from cartographers, surveyors, photogrammetrists, geographers, computer scientists and remote sensing practitioners as well as an increasingly wide range of commercial

concerns. This "conglomeration of interests" (Goodchild, 1988:560) has hastened both the technical development of GIS and its scope, though it is an area that has been largely technology-driven rather than application-led. It is this that has led to much of the concern over the value of GIS to geography beyond a short-term ability to command commercial funding for relatively mundane "relational" exercises with different databases. However, GIS practitioners have argued that GIS will present a way of generating wider application of quantitative methods and models developed in geography since the 1950s. Indeed, recent debate has centred on whether GIS is not merely a toolbox but a new techno-scientific approach to analysing spatial data (e.g. Pickles, 1997; Wright et al, 1997). Other possibilities are the potential for using GIS as a formal model of spatial information and the use of high-level computing power to solve complex spatial problems and problems of map design (Couclelis, 1986). Thus GIS has become more than just a mapping technology; it is also a form of exploratory data analysis and can be used as an explanatory device based on space and distance.

Rhind (1989:179–80) lists five key aspects of a GIS:

- analytic capabilities are integrated with data collection, validation, editing, manipulation and reporting functions;
- a single "command language" is used for the whole system;
- the manner in which operations are performed is largely transparent to the user and also readily available to "the expert";
- a wide range of data may be utilised without recourse to reprogramming;
- skilled users are able to develop their own programs using the "tools" provided by the existing system.

He also summarises the type of questions which a GIS can help to answer (Rhind, 1993:152):

- What is at place X? This can be specified by place

name, by latitude and longitude, grid reference, postal address or postcode for example.

- Where is the following condition true? For example, high yields of crop $x$ and a predominance of farms in a given size range.
- What has changed – and where – since a specified previous period?
- What spatial pattern(s) exist(s), where are there anomalies from the pattern(s) and what relationships exist between different geographical variables?
- What will happen if we change the spatial relationships, for example the elements of a road network?

Rhind (1989) also identifies GIS as being part of a broader *"computing revolution"* that has had significant effects within geography in the 1980s (and 1990s). He cites eight characteristics of this revolution:

1. Tremendous growth has occurred in the design, creation and use of databases, especially for monitoring and inventorial purposes.
2. The traditional parametric descriptive and inferential statistics have been replaced by simpler and more robust descriptors.
3. The growth in the use of "geographical" databases has involved more non-geographers than geographers.
4. The commercial sector rather than governments and academia has produced new technical developments and fostered new applications.
5. Existing systems are able to perform a wide range of data manipulations, though not as yet in the manner, speed, comfort or safety desired.
6. Much of the main work in this field remains unpublished or appears in conference proceedings.
7. The initial stimulus was provided by the development of automated cartography, for example the Northwestern Technology Institute's Synographic Mapping System (SYMAP), but now cartography is just one "spin-off" from the design, creation and exploitation of geographical databases.
8. Development of GIS has been underpinned by a rapid decrease in the cost of computing power,

especially through the advent of the microcomputer.

Within GIS itself two traditions have emerged in terms of ways of representing geographical distributions. One is to divide a study area into an array of rectangular cells and describe the content of each cell. This is the *raster approach*, giving a continuous view of space. The other is the *vector approach* in which a geographical distribution is described as a collection of discrete objects, such as points, lines or areas, the location of each one being described. This is essentially a location description, in which locations are recorded in the form of map coordinates, whereas the raster approach provides information on what is present at a particular location, using row and column positions in a grid map (Figure 11.11). Vector structures usually include topological information and geographical features (e.g. streets, retail outlets) that can be stored separately in tables. Raster systems do not include topology or separate attribute information and tend to deal in information for given areas (e.g. land use, geology). The raster approach has been most closely associated with environmental and physical geography applications of GIS whilst the vector approach has been used in policy applications, in mapping and the management of geographically distributed facilities.

Much of the software in a GIS deals with the manipulation of geographical data, in which a number of different operations can be involved, generally directed at restructuring the database into a form suitable for statistical or cartographic analysis. This usually involves geometric operations on simple geographical objects (such as areal units) to produce data for new objects and calculation of the new attribute (or variable) values for the new objects. The diversity of these manipulations makes it difficult to produce a short and non-technical summary, but Table 11.1 refers to some of the more commonly employed procedures (see also De Mers, 1997).

Within human geography one developing aspect of the use of GIS has been in conjunction with models of regional economic growth, urban development and transport systems (see Chrisman et al, 1989). In the

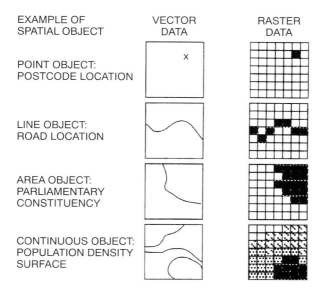

EXAMPLE OF SPATIAL OBJECT    VECTOR DATA    RASTER DATA

POINT OBJECT: POSTCODE LOCATION

LINE OBJECT: ROAD LOCATION

AREA OBJECT: PARLIAMENTARY CONSTITUENCY

CONTINUOUS OBJECT: POPULATION DENSITY SURFACE

*Figure 11.11*    Vector and Raster Data Structures. (*Source*: Martin, 1997:217)

*Table 11.1*    Examples of Manipulation and Analysis Functions of GIS

| Function | Examples of their Operation |
| --- | --- |
| Reclassification | Reclassify all census zones with scores over 30 as "deprived" |
| Overlay | Find all patient addresses falling within a new health authority area. Identify the area of overlap between the proposed development and the conservation area |
| Neighbourhood | Identify all land parcels which are adjacent to the factory site |
| Distance | Compute all points on the road network which can be reached within ten minutes drive of the health centre location |
| Interpolation | Produce a continuous surface model, or contours, from the point locations for which data have been recorded. Interpolate boundaries to demarcate areas which are closest to each police station location |
| Spatial statistics | Fit a regression model for all zones, and map the residuals. Calculate Moran's $I$ for the crime figures for each zone. Produce a map showing all zones for which cancer incidence appears high at the 95 per cent confidence level |

*Source*: Martin (1997:223).

1970s the development of mathematical models within geography was often regarded as being limited by the need for faster and bigger computers to help apply the models. In fact, "faster" and "bigger" have not necessarily been the qualities leading to significant advancements in modelling. Instead the chief improvements have been in the increased ability to access and manipulate data by computer, that is the "automation" of information systems via GIS. In addition, changes in mathematical modelling have been brought about by the advent of the microcomputer, and especially following the development of the IBM Personal Computer (PC), its clones and successors (Clarke and Wilson, 1989). The PC permits programs and model systems to be transferred easily to compatible PCs anywhere in the world whilst also improving quality of presentation via excellent graphical capabilities. The rapid growth of the use of PCs in the 1980s has also meant that commercial organisations within market research and management consultancy have applied what are essentially geographical models using socio-economic data for small areas, e.g. the ACORN profiling system (A Classification Of Residential Neighbourhoods), to develop solutions to practical problems such as locating a new supermarket, marketing a new product and allocating public funds. Therefore it should not come as a surprise that one of the chief applications of GIS has been its use in developing targeted "mail-shots" for commercial companies keen to promote their products to selected socio-economic groups in particular locations (Gatrell et al, 1991; Raper et al, 1992).

From the mid-1980s increases in microprocessor computing capacity have made the processing of digital and satellite images and other types of raster images commercially available. For GIS microprocessors have improved a number of integral devices, notably surveying instruments, GPS (the Global Positioning System), digitising tables, scanners, environmental monitoring satellites and data presentation systems, including graphic displays, electrostatic plotters and laser printers (Bernhardsen, 1992:29–30).

Champions of GIS view it as an essential aspect of investigation involving geographically located data. In particular, work that needs to draw upon "standard" cartographic and geographical data is increasingly doing so by accessing the data via a GIS. This means that GIS is being used as a tool by the construction industry, public administration, agriculture, forestry and other resource management sectors, telecommunications, electricity supply and other public utilities, and the transport industry, to name just the leading areas. All of these sectors need to solve problems on the basis of standardised information that can be combined in many ways to serve a variety of users and end-purposes. GIS has this capability and in a very short space of time has become a significant feature with many applications to aspects of many industries' routine operations and maintenance, environmental and resource management issues, planning and development, management and public services, navigation, transportation and military uses (Bernhardsen, 1992).

One of the principal consequences of the growth of GIS has been an increased concern with the nature and quality of available geographical data. This has also emphasised the plethora of large-scale datasets available and amenable for incorporation into a GIS (Green et al, 1995; Longley and Clarke, 1995b), especially those amenable to *georeferencing* (attaching a specific location), perhaps by using another dataset for such information. Georeferencing usually takes the form of census zones such as enumeration districts, post codes, street names or individual addresses. Some of the basic steps in matching datasets are described by Martin (1997). Problems involving matching can arise for a number of reasons:

- data were collected at different times;
- datasets employed different definitions;
- poor quality of source documents produces errors;
- errors in recording data, e.g. poor digitising;
- errors in recording attributes, e.g. under-enumeration.

GIS has been used for research involving spatial relationships, in which geometry and topology have been central to the work, human activity and environmental processes. For all of these there have been limitations imposed by the two-dimensional forms of physical space in GIS. In this respect GIS has mimicked maps in representing multi-dimensional realities. There has been a representational compromise that has extended to the incorporation of continuous temporal changes as a series of snapshots or time slices which, when compared, can indicate evolution of patterns through time and space. One of the next advances required in GIS, therefore, is the development of three-dimensional or even four-dimensional systems (incorporating time) so that realistic spatio-temporal structures of knowledge can be analysed, incorporating feedbacks between long-term and short-term events, cycles of activity, chaotic behaviour and three-dimensional surfaces. It is the development of these new forms of GIS, for example the combination of process models with "traditional" GIS models, that offers prospects of further significant advances in GIS.

As illustrations of how GIS can be used by human geographers, two brief examples out of a rapidly growing list of possibilities are used here: one illustrating the way in which GIS can bring together data from disparate sources to help answer a complex series of spatial questions; and one in which GIS was developed to meet specific planning needs.

## A GIS Applied to Data Collection and Analysis in the Tropics

The first example refers to the development of a GIS as a database management system interfaced to a variety of software packages for mapping and statistical analysis. The particular context is the collection of agricultural information, including an agricultural census, in Belize, Central America (Robinson et al, 1989). The GIS that was constructed had to meet various requirements:

- simultaneous handling of attribute and digital cartographic data;
- integration of datasets from a variety of sources, including satellite imagery, into a common geographical frame of reference;
- *ad hoc* queries of the census database;
- statistical analysis;
- computer cartography to display results of database queries and statistical analysis, for example as located histograms, pie charts, and so on;
- a means of transparently moving data from package to package for the different functions, controlled by a user-friendly interface or system shell.

The development of a system that could meet these requirements was a substantial advance upon existing non-relational manipulations of the types of data incorporated into the GIS.

The GIS used in this example can be viewed as a means of organising and combining locational (entity) data and non-locational (attribute) data (see Peuquet, 1984). An important element in this procedure is the automation of a process of analysis and display, combined with the addition of an enhanced analytical capability. This is achieved initially by conceptualising the world as consisting of a series of data "layers", such as drainage, soils and vegetation (see Figure 11.12). These layers are related to one another by means of spatial registration points which are points of known location on all layers. Much of the power of the GIS comes from its abilities to carry out combined spatial and attribute queries across these various layers and to portray the results of these operations. For example, one operation may be to select all those areas having both alluvial soil and an annual precipitation in excess of 3000 mm.

In constructing the GIS for Belizean agriculture, the basis of the GIS was a grid which allowed different layers of data to be located. The grid used was

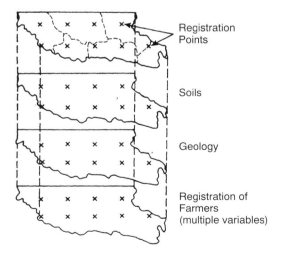

*Figure 11.12*  Data "Layers" in the GIS of Belizean Agriculture
(Nb. Belize is shown with west to the top of the four maps. The top-most map shows the boundaries of Belize's six Districts). x = registration points. (*Source*: Robinson et al, 1989)

15 × 15 minutes of latitude/longitude on the Universal Transverse Mercator (UTM) projection, which was chosen as it was the projection used for the most recent 1:50 000 topographic map coverage of the area. Onto this grid were placed the various layers of data available. The national agricultural census represented one of the layers, relating to either census enumeration zones or village point locations. Other layers of data incorporated were national resource survey data (Wright et al, 1959), regional surveys (e.g. King et al, 1986) and data in the form of satellite imagery (LANDSAT and SPOT) of the country.

Data input to a GIS may take a variety of forms, though the most common is manual *digitising* of a pre-existing paper map. The initial stage of the GIS in this project involved the digitisation of Belizean census enumeration zones, using the same zones for the agricultural census as those used in the 1980 population census. Digitising is the translation of an analogue line into discrete digital coordinates, performed in this case with a semi-automatic line follower (see Fisher, 1991; Jackson and Woodsford, 1991). This provided a computer-stored system of areal units for the whole country, enabling data from a range of sources to be incorporated in a common method of georeferencing. This included land cover data derived from satellite imagery, using an image processor to transform the imagery to data related to specified ground control points which are points of known location on both map and imagery (Gray, 1988). The process transforms the raster-type image data into vector form for integration into the GIS. This integration is included in Figure 11.13 which summarises the basic configuration of the GIS.

At the centre of the GIS shown in Figure 11.13 is a *relational database management system* (RDBMS) used as a means of storing and manipulating data. This provides flexible access to data, giving the

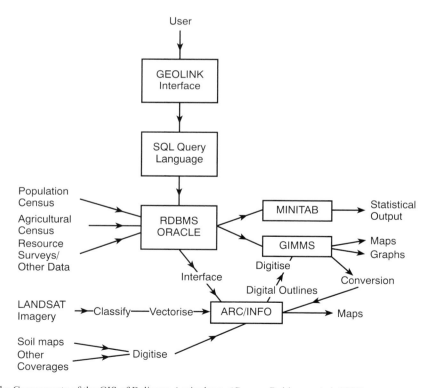

*Figure 11.13*    The Components of the GIS of Belizean Agriculture. (*Source*: Robinson et al, 1989)

essential links between the researcher or user, the layers of data and a range of computing packages for mapping and statistical analysis. Thus RDBMSs allow a large number of operations to be performed on the data in the database. Their most important facility is their query language which provides easy access to the data and allows grouping, ordering and basic statistical procedures as part of the query. This provides opportunities for examination of specific relationships within the data and flexibility in manipulating data into the correct form for passing onto packages within the GIS via interfaces. Most commercial RDBMSs also include facilities for data input from a video monitor and a suite of administrative functions designed to ensure data security and integrity. The Oracle RDBMS used in this case permitted a quicker and more detailed analysis of the Belizean data than would have been possible using specially written computer programs or manual methods. It also permitted a range of queries to be addressed to the database via a standard query language (SQL). For example, it was possible to test for inconsistencies in the data and inclusion of codes relating to missing or suspect values. Packages linked to the RDBMS included ones for mapping (GIMMS), statistical analysis (Minitab), data storage (INFO) and data tabulation and organisation prior to cartographic or statistical analysis (Oracle) (see Mather, 1987). An interface between these packages (Geolink) provided user-friendly menus for accessing the packages and enabled database queries to be executed (Waugh and Healey, 1986). The fact that this meant that data could be interrogated in a sophisticated fashion by researchers with little computing or GIS knowledge offered tremendous potential for investigation. An indication of this potential with respect to the analysis of Belizean agriculture is shown by the seven initial "target" research areas outlined in Table 11.2 that could be investigated with the aid of GIS.

## A GIS Applied to Land Use Planning in Scotland

Over the past decade many planning agencies throughout the world have started to make use of GIS.

*Table 11.2* ''Target'' Areas for Investigation using the GIS of Belizean Agriculture

1. The effectiveness of local markets with respect to access for farmers and consumers and with respect to provision of facilities

2. The adoption of recommended crops and practices

3. Land colonisation and resettlement

4. The adequacy of storage facilities, especially for grain

5. The impact of the road network (especially feeder roads to villages) upon the nature of farm practices and the area cultivated

6. Broad relationships between environment and yield, with an emphasis upon correlations between soil characteristics and production

7. The use of credit facilities and other support services

*Source*: Robinson et al (1989:92).

Indeed for many non-geographers working in planning-related jobs, GIS is the only aspect of geography with which they are familiar! In particular, planners concerned with environmental issues and resource management have compiled large databases for incorporation in GIS to assist their decision-making. The range of possible uses of GIS has been extended from helping to select locations for development to the development-control process (e.g. Campbell et al, 1989; Grimshaw, 1988) and a wide range of other problems tackled by local authorities and planning agencies (see Bromley and Selman, 1993; Curtis and Taket, 1989; Gould, 1992).

In Scotland one of the earliest attempts to establish a GIS for use in a planning-related context was the Rural Land Use Information System (RLUIS), first developed from 1979. The initial demands of RLUIS were that it should be able to incorporate:

• regular collection, storage, updating and processing of information relating to rural planning in Scotland;

- provision of this information aggregated to national level for general planning purposes, but also capable of providing detailed information for local planning, e.g. for planning the resolution of land-use conflicts on the rural–urban fringe;
- efficient provision of both statistical and cartographic output.

Initially, 60 different datasets were assembled to help meet these criteria. The datasets primarily represented physical characteristics, land use and planning information at a variety of scales (Lyall, 1980) (see Table 11.3), including both general and specialist information. This range illustrates the types of data commonly employed by planners and also suggests the potential utility of GIS, with its capability of relating the different datasets to one another. The data

*Table 11.3* Data Comprising the Rural Land Use Information System (RLUIS) for the Dunfermline and Kirkcaldy Districts of Fife, Scotland

*Datasets on the TRIP database*
Landforms
Beaches
National Trust for Scotland sites
Recreational facilities
Population
Countryside Commission (Scotland) grant-aided sites

*Datasets collected or held by RLUIS agencies prior to project*
Geological boreholes
Derelict sites
Property (by postcode)
Planning applications
Agricultural Census (by holding)
Planning appeals
Planning referrals
Major industrial sites
Housing land availability
Residential land prices
Ancient monuments
Employment statistics
Unemployment statistics
Scottish Wildlife Trust sites

*Table 11.3  (continued)*

*Datasets available from non-RLUIS agencies prior to project*
Traffic flows
Climate
Water supply
Sewage treatment works
Areas of abandoned mining
Areas of infill and subsidence

*Datasets collected specifically for project*
Land use (1 km grid)
Land use (100 m grid)
Habitat

*Data supplied from the Ordnance Survey map production database*
Coastline
Limit of sand, mud and shingle
Lakes
Rivers, streams and drainage channels
Administrative boundaries
Main road network
Main rail network
Electricity transmission lines
Footpaths
Pipelines
Parks

*Source*: Robinson (1992:23).

were stored at a variety of spatial resolutions in a grid format so that they could be mapped on a 1 km or 5 km grid square basis (Chulvick, 1982). For high-spatial-resolution data (e.g. borehole data, recreation facilities, planning appeals), mapping could be performed using an automated mapping package.

The initial RLUIS project exposed certain difficulties associated with the development of information systems for planners, such as the lack of coordination between the participating agencies with respect to the type of data to be included in the GIS. The high cost of translating such a system to a national scale and difficulties in maintaining an up-to-date database were additional problems. This led to a focus on smaller-scale regionally based systems in Scotland. Continuing deficiencies in data collection and availability in the UK were revealed by the Committee of Enquiry for Handling Geographic Information (the Chorley Committee) (Department of the Environment, 1987). However, since the early 1980s there have been a number of advances in the development of GIS for land use planning, with notable technical improvements developed in Australia, Canada, the Netherlands and the USA (Burrough, 1986). At the heart of these improvements has been the ability to relate different datasets to one another. New systems have advanced beyond the initial focus upon automated cartography, developing around a core of two key elements:

1. An intelligent data structure, e.g. data for areas for which the detailed boundaries can be stored in a computer file.
2. A set of geoprocessing tools that manage, analyse and manipulate geographically referenced information, as well as supporting facilities for interrogating and mapping the data.

Thus the great potential for GIS to reinforce and develop links between data collection, data analysis and planning of resource management at a variety of scales is being realised in planning offices throughout the Developed World. Initially, attempts to incorporate remotely sensed data into databases for use in local planning systems suffered from the low spatial resolution of the data with respect to the small size of land parcels and also from its high cost (Lo, 1986). However, from 1986 the availability of SPOT HRV data, at spatial resolutions of 10 m and 20 m for panchromatic and multispectral products respectively, has promoted some reconsideration by planners of the use of remotely sensed data within a GIS (e.g. Quarmby and Cushnie, 1988, 1989). Furthermore, the high spectral resolution of the LANDSAT Thematic Mapper has provided high-quality data, sometimes more accurate than SPOT data. The latter has only a limited spectral range, thereby restricting its ability to discriminate between land cover types. The potential for using satellite sensor imagery to monitor changes in land use is now being realised with newly designed GIS established to incorporate such imagery, specifically geared to studying change through time and updating

information on the distribution and dynamics of land use (Young, 1986). The digital format of satellite data, coupled with modern image-processing systems and standard geometric correction to the UK National Grid, means that the image data or thematic map information extracted from it can be easily input to a GIS (Lillesand and Kiefer, 1987).

There are some crucial limitations, though, before satellite sensor imagery can be used successfully as a regular input for land use monitoring in conjunction with resource planning at the local level. Obtaining usable imagery on a routine basis and at a reasonable cost is still a problem whilst substantial contextual knowledge of the study area may be necessary (Gurney, 1983). The latter is particularly important in the Scottish context where there can be great land use complexity over a short distance.

The example of the RLUIS project indicates that GIS should not be seen as the ultimate panacea for "making better plans", but it offers highly attractive capabilities to assist planners in performing certain tasks. Amongst these the ability to relate different datasets almost instantaneously when compared with traditional manual methods offers tremendous time savings. Planners who can sensibly use "What if?" questions to interrogate databases are offered a range of "solutions" to both standard and non-standard problems.

Thus GIS has become part of what Roszac (1986) describes as "the cult of information" which has increasingly affected planning agencies and spawned a number of new businesses developing and using information systems. The tremendous extent of its growth is indicated by a value of $3.5 billion per annum for the GIS computer industry's American business in the early 1990s. Roughly one-quarter of this figure comes from the Pentagon, whose GIS systems were used to locate targets in the Gulf War. In the 1980s it was feared that advances in the application of GIS would be restricted by the lack of trained personnel, lack of coordination of diverse users and applications, and a lack of awareness of potential benefits (Department of the Environment, 1987). Although these concerns have not proved groundless, the rapid growth in provision of training in GIS has now provided a sufficiently large nucleus of qualified personnel to carry the GIS "revolution" well beyond academia. In particular, GIS has become an integral part of the planning profession's daily tasks in both the public and private sectors.

The potential of GIS has also been recognised by urban modellers who have developed the role of GIS as a "spatial decision support system". This system has three main components (Bertuglia et al, 1994b):

- descriptions which are structural representations of urban data;
- impact analyses which measure the effects of policy interventions;
- evaluations which assess the advantages and disadvantages of alternative choices.

The role of information systems in urban planning is illustrated in Figure 11.14, showing how they connect models and performance indicators to databases and mapping functions. One aim is to build adaptive information systems that can react to urban change (see Birkin et al, 1996).

## GIS and Critiques from Within Human Geography

The only thing that many business people and civil servants now associate with geography as a discipline is GIS. This gives GIS a unique position within geography, and one not fully appreciated by many of its critics. Yet there are still several limitations within GIS that need to be overcome if its proponents' claims for its wide applicability are to be realised. For example, one of the problems with the *Boolean logic* (Boolean = a data type which has only two values, 0/1 or true/false, named after George Boole, the pioneer of modern logic) employed by GIS is that it may not always be appropriate to natural resources data where transitions are the norm rather than the sharp boundaries of the polygons developed using this logic. This may be a limiting factor in the ability of

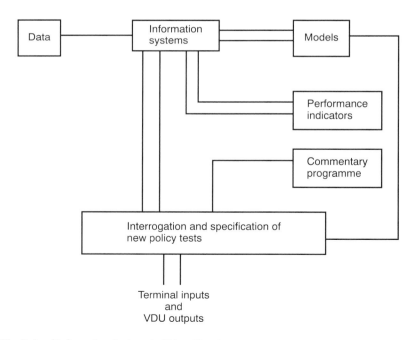

*Figure 11.14*   The Role of Information Systems in Urban Planning

GIS to deal with particular problems. However, within the geographical community itself there are other factors that represent an obstacle to the advance of research utilising GIS.

There are growing numbers of researchers in geography, information systems and computing who are developing GIS software and new applications of GIS. There is also a very large commercial industry developing and supplying computer-readable data. However, the growth in applications of GIS by human geographers has been more restricted. In part this reflects the fact that GIS is best applied in situations where large quantities of data are available, especially if they are already in digital (computer-readable) form. However, it also reflects a degree of suspicion and antipathy to GIS on behalf of human geographers who view the use of GIS as a return to reliance on the rejected positivist approaches. It is also the case that human geographers have tended to be wary of the effects of GIS processing upon data and of a general lack of understanding by non-GIS experts regarding the workings of a GIS. The bewildering array of GIS software now available has not helped the situation.

Therefore, despite its tremendous growth from the early 1980s and its ability to generate income for its practitioners, GIS has not been accepted as a positive development by many human geographers. There are a number of reasons for critical views of GIS. Some are related to general anti-technology, anti-empirical trends within the "mainstream" of the new human geography of the 1980s and 1990s; others refer to weaknesses within GIS itself.

With respect to the latter, a clearly recognised and significant vice of some computer-literate geographers has been the tendency to mistake mere information transfer and accumulation for knowledge. Data storage in massive quantities and near-instant retrieval, formatting and application of analytical programs has been no substitute for ability to ask the right questions and interpret the results of analysis. Moreover, as Shubik (1979) observes, "ours is a data-rich and information-poor society" in which it is not a lack of data that is usually problematic but a lack of the right sort, and a more glaring lack of good theory according to many (e.g. Harvey and Scott, 1989).

One of the main weaknesses in the extensive growth of research using GIS and remote sensing has been in the way that it has been technology-driven rather than application-led. Although the technical possibilities for handling large datasets have expanded dramatically and the potential applications are wide-ranging, there has been an insufficient development of conceptual frameworks accompanying research using GIS. Too much of this research has seemed to adopt a technology overkill in which the output from technical analysis has been disappointingly of a low quality and lower level of sophistication than the technology utilised.

Of vital importance in the long-term development of the discipline is the wide gulf between the evolution of theory and philosophy in human geography and developments in GIS. There has been a strong polarisation between those championing the use of GIS and those concerned with approaches that are not reliant upon processing large volumes of data. For example, Lowe and Short (1990:2) see the growth of GIS during the 1980s, in part, as an example of political and fiscal expediency. They point to the role of corporate and government interests as driving forces supporting the expansion of GIS rather than an internally developed research agenda to which GIS has contributed. Their view that "when it is bereft of theory and devoid of moral purpose GIS will degenerate into a shabby exercise in fashion following and a grubby grab for cash" (Lowe and Short, 1990:2) reflects some geographers' concerns about GIS representing a re-emergence of a techniques-led, commercially supported, technocratic geography. This view sees GIS as being at variance with a geography that is sensitive to social injustice and that reflects beliefs in emancipatory theory and liberating practices (as discussed in the succeeding chapters).

A similarly trenchant critique comes from Pickles (1995a) who emphasises the links that GIS has with strategic planning, commerce and the military so that the socio-economic applications of GIS have concentrated on organisational efficiency and control of geographic territory. He sees this as a series of developments to which many GIS practitioners (e.g. Martin, 1991; Lake, 1993) have deliberately ignored related ethical, economic and political issues. He charges these practitioners as following the same empiricist and positivist assumptions that underpinned spatial analytical work in the 1960s and 1970s.

An alternative view from within the GIS fraternity is that the new information-based technologies associated with artificial intelligence, parallel processing and expert systems will carry the problem of modelling geographical knowledge to a deeper level than has been possible in the past (Couclelis, 1986; Haines-Young, 1989). This view is supported by Openshaw (1989) who argues that the next stage in the continuing evolution of models in human geography will be part of a computer modelling revolution focusing upon the new information economy, though he acknowledges that this will be data-led rather than theory-driven (Openshaw and Goddard, 1987). This view seems to imply a new pragmatism that smacks suspiciously of a reversion to speculative empiricism. However, it may be possible to combine data and theory in new ways so that worthwhile studies ensue from the insistent demands for geographers to satisfy the needs of government- and commercially supported research based on the ever-growing flood of new databases.

Openshaw (1991b) recognised the strong attacks on GIS as essentially a part of an anti-positivist, anti-scientific school of thought that has ignored the positive benefits offered by GIS. He champions as the essence of geography the "space–time data model" which in the past was represented by the map and which in future will be represented in digital form by GIS as both a language and a toolkit. However, his claims for GIS to represent a dominant and unifying focus for a geography largely antithetical to an engagement with social theory and the so-called "cultural turn" of the 1990s has been strongly disputed. For example, Taylor and Overton (1991) raise the concern over the notion of "data as given" that permeated much of the early work in GIS. They assert that data are created, and who does the creating, for whom and for what purposes are vital. They propose as the "first law of geographical information": where the need for geographical information is greatest, the amount of information is least! And they refer to a critical problem of the Quantitative Revolution, namely that the same processes may produce different patterns; different processes can produce the same pattern. Therefore we cannot rely solely on pattern to study process, which seems to have been ignored by some users of GIS. They also refer to necessary and contingent relations: Are correspondences necessary, that is, is there a mechanism in the system that produces the connection, or are they merely contingent, produced by chance and with no theoretical significance? GIS alone cannot separate necessary from contingent relations, as geography deals with open systems. Therefore if GIS is to be used as a tool, its limitations must be clearly recognised and it should not be regarded as a magic formula for reconstituting a geography that replaces concerns for culture and society with technology and information.

Whatever the nature of criticism from within geography, the commercial potential of GIS is undoubted. One estimate is for a turnover in excess of $100 billion in GIS products in the USA by the year 2000. This may represent only one-quarter of the world market (*The Economist*, 21 March 1992), but the three largest sellers of GIS software are in the USA: Geovision, Intergraph and the Environmental Systems Research Institute (ESRI). The spectacular growth of these companies, like that of GIS itself, relects the development of cheap, powerful computers. A computer workstation costing $10 000 today can perform as well as a larger computer costing $250 000 in the mid-1980s. Yet, the chief limitation on the commercial expansion of GIS probably lies in the high cost of database preparation. There are many untapped markets, though, especially within the public sector. For example the US Bureau of Land Management and the Forest Service are each proposing to spend $1 billion on a GIS public-land information service. Other growth areas are in retailing and service industries such as banking, insurance and transport.

Despite this potential, human geographers remain divided as to the value of GIS in advancing a theoretically informed understanding of the world. Bearing in mind the strongly polarised opinions, Pickles' edited collection of essays on the social implications of GIS represents a positive step in the construction of a dialogue between geographers who hold very different views regarding the value of GIS (Pickles, 1995b). Instead of decrying the commercial aspects of GIS or its positivist approach, there is a recognition that "the emergence of GIS as both a disciplinary practice and a socially embedded technology represents an important change in the way in which the geographical is being conceptualized, represented, and materialized in the built environment" (Pickles, 1995a:25). Therefore there is the urgent need for a constructive dialogue between practitioner and non-practitioner and for a more balanced assessment of the impacts of GIS on society and within geography itself.

## GIS and Spatial Analysis

In terms of recent developments in the use of GIS, one potentially highly significant advance has been the forging of closer links between GIS and spatial analysis techniques through the production of new software (Gatrell and Rowlingson, 1994; Haining, 1994). GIS can provide a framework within which spatially referenced data can be analysed statistically. This is often referred to as the *spatial analysis capability* of GIS and it utilises explicitly geographical concepts such as clustering, dispersion, distance and contiguity (e.g. Anselin, 1992; Bailey and Gatrell, 1995:52–8).

The output from GIS can take many forms, but one of the most valuable has been maps and diagrams that have assisted interpretation more readily than numerical output. As a result much attention has been given to the ways in which maps and diagrams may be best displayed by computer, a process referred to as *visualisation* (see Batty, 1996; Densham, 1996; Dorling, 1995; Hearnshaw and Unwin, 1994). Visualisation frequently represents an iterative process whereby the same set of numerical results is summarised in a variety of graphical forms or where maps are viewed from a series of perspectives and then used as a basis for further interpretation and generation of hypotheses. Further advances have also occurred in integrated GIS, combining GIS with remotely sensed data, as referred to above. This combination has often been concerned with analyses of global environmental change (Foody and Curran, 1994).

In terms of the association between spatial analysis and GIS, impetus was provided for further linkages by an initiative of the National Center for Geographic Information and Analysis (NCGIA) in the USA. At a Specialist Meeting in 1992 this led to consideration of how statistical methods and mathematical models could be linked to the database and display capabilities of a GIS, resulting in a collection of published papers edited by Fotheringham and Rogerson (1994). In particular, six questions were addressed that signify the types of issues likely to be examined by researchers during the next decade:

1. What restrictions are placed on spatial analysis by the modifiable areal unit problem and how can a GIS help in better understanding this problem?
2. How can GIS assist in exploratory data analysis and in computer-intensive analytical methods such as bootstrapping and the visualisation of results?
3. How can GIS assist in performing and displaying the results of various types of sensitivity analysis?
4. How can the data structures of a GIS be exploited in spatial analytical routines?
5. What are the important needs in terms of a user interface and language for spatial analysis performed on a GIS?
6. What are some of the problems in spatial analysis that should be conveyed to a GIS user and how should these problems be conveyed?

Within these six lie considerable potential for GIS to be used as part of exploratory data analysis via its visualisation capabilities (Fotheringham, 1992).

There are a number of areas in which GIS is beginning to play a more important role. In particular, geographical research using quantitative analysis is increasingly utilising the growth in computing power to analyse large and complex datasets. This research is employing efficient algorithms and the availability of improved computer graphics to model human systems (e.g. Openshaw, 1995). One of the basic problems in this work is accommodating the micro-scale level of the characteristics of individuals and the macro-scale level of the places in which people live. The danger is of reducing the former to a crude aggregate and the latter to a coarse generalisation. Attempts to avoid this often employ some form of multi-level model which can use categorical data and variables referring to individuals, households, places and relationships between them including change through time (e.g. Duncan et al, 1996). Efficient and practicable computational strategies for multi-level models were not developed until the mid-1980s, and appropriate software packages followed even more recently, for example the package MLn which can analyse a range of multi-level structures (e.g. Langford and Bentham, 1997). The potential for GIS and multi-level models is considered further by Jones and Duncan (1996).

Another area to which GIS has enormous potential to produce significant advances is the broad one of spatial modelling, including the range of models discussed in Chapters 7 and 8 above as well as some aspects covered in Chapters 9 and 10. An important conference on this topic, held at Bristol University in 1994, both yielded summaries of state-of-the-art applications and also highlighted likely future developments (Longley and Batty, 1996). The conference demonstrated that GIS can be used to revisit and tackle afresh some of the long-term problems that quantitative geographers have examined. Examples include the ecological fallacy and the modifiable areal unit problem, with computing power applied to analysing the effects of scale and grouping of areal units (Green and Flowerdew, 1996; Wrigley et al, 1996). In assessing the utility of GIS for dealing with these problems, Openshaw (1996) stresses the aspects of spatial description, visualisation, pattern capture, hypothesis testing and modelling that can be supplied by GIS.

Despite the fact that many GIS still lack a sophisticated modelling capability, there have been several attempts to integrate both location–allocation models and spatial interaction models into a GIS. This includes the $p$-median problem discussed in Chapter 7. Some of the issues highlighted by Church and Sorensen (1996:173) illustrate the difficulties to be overcome:

– A methodology is needed to define the nodes to represent demand areas. Most urban networks are large, including thousands of nodes. At what level do we represent or aggregate demand for an application? . . .
– A methodology is needed to select feasible sites. In the operations research (OR) literature, it is often assumed that each network node is a potential site. This is not a realistic assumption for many applications, especially if they involve a complete network, which is usually a part of the GIS database. Although some work has involved reducing a potential set of sites to a smaller subset with the objective of not eliminating the potential for the optimal pattern to be identified, more work needs to focus on the issue of identifying prospective sites for a given purpose (at the land-parcel level) . . .
– A solution methodology is needed that can solve the median problem.
– A database structure is needed to facilitate integration of the model and solution process.

Simulations are one of several areas where the capabilities of GIS have already been put to various uses. The popularity of the urban simulation computer game, *SimCity*, demonstrates how the visualisation component of a GIS can be utilised to good effect, underscored by a program that produces changes in urban land use and transportation, subject to constraints and opportunities created by the person playing the game (Macmillan, 1996). It is debatable whether this approach could be applied in practical terms to urban modelling, but some features may be combined with other approaches in a dynamic, urban GIS, building on critical evaluations of earlier generations of models (such as the Garin–Lowry) which are producing new models, e.g. *computable general equilibrium (CGE) approaches* in which micro-economic theory is used to analyse urban systems with the aid of complex mathematical structures (Anas, 1987; Macmillan, 1993).

In summary, GIS continues to grow rapidly with new software appearing from the expanding number of software outlets at an alarming rate. Coupled with the communications revolution of the WorldWideWeb and further advances in satellite technology, it is impossible to predict the full ramifications on society and the discipline of geography of the Pandora's box that is the GIS toolkit. That toolkit continues to be extended, providing new opportunities in the areas of modelling, mapping, statistical analysis, and multimedia presentation amongst others. Whilst some human geographers have turned their backs upon these technological advances, the challenge of GIS to the development of geography as a discipline has grown and this needs to be addressed more seriously than has been the case hitherto. However, it remains to be seen to what extent the marriage of GIS and spatial analysis will yield breakthroughs in applications of mathematical and statistical techniques to solving significant practical problems and to helping the development of geographic theory through facilitating empirical research.

# 12

# INVESTIGATING BEHAVIOUR AND PERCEPTION

## OPTIMISERS AND SATISFICERS

Until the 1960s most theoretical formulations in economic geography had utilised axioms regarding human behaviour that were set out in the classic theories of von Thunen, Christaller and Losch amongst others. These viewed human behaviour in terms of economic rationality in decision-making, which, in the Thunian case for example, espoused the virtues of individuals with a single profit objective, access to all information relative to a particular situation, omniscient powers of perception, reasoning and computation, and the gift of totally accurate prediction.

This concept of rationality in decision-making was derived from the "marginalist revolution" in economic theory in the late nineteenth century (Elster, 1986:26) and, as developed subsequently, produced an *economic man* [sic] or *Homo economicus* whose characteristics had three key implications for analytic methodology:

1. *Reductionism*. Social phenomena were only explained by reducing them to the mental states of individuals.
2. *Determinism*. It was possible to deduce the economic consequences of rational (normative) behaviour with precision.
3. *Universality*. All acts in all places at all times followed the strictures of economic rationality.

Unfortunately, as Barnes (1988b:483) points out,

the way in which *Homo economicus* has been established denies the possibility of empirical testing: it cannot be falsified empirically. Thus, according to Hollis and Nell (1975:55):

> Rational economic man is not an actual man. He is, rather, any actual man who conforms to the model to be tested. So there is no question of testing an economic theory against the actual behaviour of the rational producer or consumer. Producers and consumers are rational precisely insofar as they behave as predicted and the test shows only how rational they are.

Any behavioural factors that might have influenced actual decision-making were omitted from this normative view. In the 1960s, though, a series of studies of human responses to environmental hazards demonstrated that these behavioural factors could be subjected to systematic analysis (see Palm, 1981a). For example, in his work on floodplain management, Kates (1962) argued that the way in which people view the risks and opportunities of their uncertain environment plays a significant role in their decisions as to resource management.

And in studying decision-making, he developed a schema based on four assumptions:

1. People are rational when making decisions, but this is a constrained or *bounded rationality* and not the "maximum" rationality assumed in the normative models.

2. People make choices.
3. Choices are made on the basis of knowledge.
4. Information is evaluated according to predetermined criteria such as a desire for profit maximisation or, more commonly, the desire for a certain amount of "satisfaction" from the activity.

Wolpert's (1964) study of decision-making by farmers in southern Sweden demonstrated that decisions could be subjected to a coherent spatial analysis. He compared the labour productivity of farms in an area of Sweden with what might have been achieved under optimal conditions, using correlation and regression techniques. The differences between reality and the optimum led him to argue that farmers were *satisficers* not optimisers and that they were also operating under conditions of bounded rationality, a term coined previously by Simon (1957). These conditions meant that the farmers were not fully aware of all the information they required in order to make a completely economically rational decision. However, many of the farmers were not economically rational because they also had goals other than that of profit maximisation. The farmers' reality is "arational" and can only be explained by *satisficing behaviour* (Wolpert, 1964:344).

The implied criticism of neoclassical theory that this suggests has been disputed (e.g. Boland, 1981), and it is possible to view satisficing itself as a form of maximisation (Webber, 1972:ch. 5). Nevertheless, Wolpert's work on farmers' decision-making has been extended by numerous studies, revealing a suite of factors affecting decision-making (Table 12.1) and a recognition that not only does the amount of knowledge that a farmer possesses influence her/his decisions, but also their attitude towards profit. The desired profit from the farm may range from zero (mere subsistence) to optimisation. Where an individual farmer lies along this continuum is determined by variations in farmers' goals, such as concern for physical well-being, social recognition and ideological motives. In practice these are part of the *satisficer*, as most farmers do not regard profit maximisation as an easily defined goal nor one to which, in reality, they can subscribe. So an individual farmer attempts a satisfactory combination of the three broad goals

rather than striving to achieve optimisation. This makes it quite hard to measure certain goals within the general satisficer, with more stress often being placed upon social considerations, such as managing farming activities so as to create more leisure time. The impress of bounded rationality is also important as farmers may not be fully aware of all the information they require in order to make fully rational decisions even in terms of the satisficer.

The notion of bounded rationality needs to be treated with some care, though, especially when moving away from the relatively simple situation of the individual decision-maker to the political arena where individuals and groups may make what Wolpert (1970:224) described as "stress responses". These decisions may be made by individuals who, for various reasons, make little if any attempt to evaluate information at their disposal. Wolpert et al (1975) were primarily concerned with the presence of such decisions as part of the political process. In this case conflict between different groups may produce decisions that approach neither a "classical normative" position nor the Simon scheme of bounded rationality. Much so-called "decision-making" by people occurs

*Table 12.1* Factors Affecting Farmers' Decision-Making

---

1. Situational characteristics:
   farm size, specialisation, capital

2. Personal characteristics:
   social background, education, age, income, health

3. Psychological characteristics:
   personality, interests, attitudes, motivations, beliefs, values, goals

4. Sociological characteristics:
   status, participation, local/cosmopolitan, receptivity, use of information channels

5. Macro-environmental characteristics:
   technological state, government policy, climate, economic situation

---

Based on Jones (1973).

in a daily life where there is minimal or no choice. Even major decisions such as choosing a new house in which to live often involve completely unsystematic searches and evaluations where need rather than preference rules the eventual decision. Indeed, rationality of decision as incorporated in behaviouristic models may seem as mythical as the proverbial "economic man"!

## BEHAVIOURAL GEOGRAPHY

Work on human responses to physical hazards and systematic analyses of the spatial outcomes of individual decisions stimulated other studies by geographers on the role of cognitive and decision-making variables. This work can be given the umbrella term of *behavioural geography*. Golledge and Timmermans (1990) list eight main aspects in its emergence and growth:

1. The search for alternative models to those of normative location theory which depicted economically and spatially rational beings.
2. The search for environments other than objective physical reality as the milieux in which human decision-making and action take place.
3. An emphasis on processes not structures in explaining human activity and relationships between it and the physical environment.
4. The unravelling of the spatial dimensions of psychological, social and other theories of human decision-making and behaviour.
5. A focus upon individuals and small groups rather than aggregate populations.
6. The development of new data sources as alternatives to the mass-produced aggregate statistics of government agencies.
7. The search for methods other than those of traditional mathematics and inferential statistics, especially ones capable of dealing with ordinal and nominal data.
8. The merging of geographic research into cross-disciplinary theory-building and problem-solving.

An appropriate paradigm for considering the people–environment aspects considered by these constituent components of behavioural geography is shown in Figure 12.1. It includes both the physical and human aspects of the environment; it allows for roles of culture and its related social and political systems and institutions; it identifies the evolution of culture over time through technology; and it recognises intervening psychological processes as filtering mechanisms in how people perceive their environment and act within it (Golledge and Stimson, 1987:11, 1997:26–8).

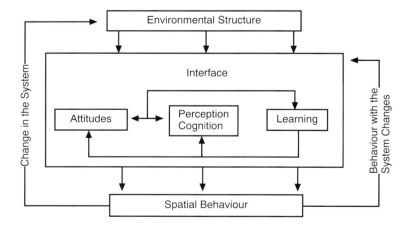

*Figure 12.1*   The People–Environment Interface (based on Golledge and Stimson, 1997)

Some proponents of behavioural geography have claimed that it represented a move outside the confines of scientific method. They have portrayed it as rejecting theories of "spatial science" and seeking to introduce new series of observations upon which new theories or generalities could be founded. Yet, in many respects, it was not a significant break with previous approaches and nor were some of the methods employed. For example, Olsson (1969) pointed out the continued use of aggregated data from which individual behaviour was inferred. However, during the 1970s and 1980s greater focus was placed upon individual rather than aggregate behaviour. This was especially true of work which sought alternatives to Hagerstrand-type simulations of spatial diffusion patterns and looked at the myriad of decisions that could underlie the bringing of innovations to places (L.A. Brown, 1981).

Other proponents of behavioural geography have accepted its close links to quantitatively based geography. For example, Golledge and Stimson (1987:9) referred to it as containing "what is truly positive in positivist thought". They regarded the positive as consisting of:

- the importance of logical and mathematical thinking;
- a need for public verifiability of results;
- a search for generalisations;
- an emphasis on analytic languages for researching and expressing knowledge and structures;
- the importance of hypothesis testing and the importance of selecting the most appropriate bases for the generalisation of theorising.

The contents of this list are then reflected in what they termed the "main scientific approaches" of behavioural geography (Golledge and Stimson, 1987:10), which include: studies of cognitive mapping and spatial behaviour; attitudes, utility, choice, preference, search, learning; consumer behaviour; location decision-making; mode choice and travel behaviour; mobility and migration behaviour.

Similarly, Gold (1980) was able to portray behavioural geography as a close ally of the positivist tradition, with an approach built on four principal features:

1. Each individual's perception of the environment in which they act is unique and may conflict with other people's perception: there may be marked discrepancies between perception and "reality".
2. Individuals interact with their environments, both responding to them and reshaping them.
3. The individual rather than the group is the focus of study.
4. Disciplines other than geography contribute to studies which, in general, are seeking inductive generalisations about human behaviour and environment so that these may be used as the basis for change through environmental planning.

This last point, though, only refers to a small body of work, for a more extensive area of study, closely related to behavioural geography's focus upon the decision-maker, was developed in the 1970s and gave explicit attention to the perceived environment, to phenomenology and to humanism. This was termed *humanistic geography* and is discussed in more detail in the following chapter. One of the ways in which it has differed from behavioural geography has been its concern for the use of *qualitative methods* rather than the more complex statistical methods, such as multidimensional scaling and semantic differentials (both discussed below), which have been used within behavioural geography.

Two main approaches can be identified within the initial development of behavioural geography: the *active decision-making tradition* and the *reactive decision-making tradition* (Thrift, 1981). The former focused upon cognitive mapping and decision-making behaviour, and dates largely to the pioneer work by Lynch (1960) and Gould and White (1968, 1974) which was concerned with the ways in which individuals perceived their environment. This perception was investigated in terms of the measurement and representation of spatial preferences and familiarity with places (e.g. Downs and Stea, 1977; Pocock, 1976). Use of questionnaires and examination of an individual's own graphic representation of places or regions were common in this work (e.g. Hudson, 1974; Dicken and Robinson, 1979), with some analysis extending to the morphology of cognitive or mental maps (e.g. Cadwallader, 1979; Matthews, 1984). A detailed summary of the methods used for extracting the cognitive information used in these studies is given in Table 12.2 (see also Beguin and Romero, 1996; Matthews, 1995b). In the 1970s one of the strands of behavioural geography that developed was a focus upon the nature of spatial behaviour: examining its temporal component and formulating models to represent "activity systems" and their operation through space (see Golledge and Stimson, 1997:267–347).

Probably the most well known of the studies on cognitive mapping was the work by Gould (Gould, 1965; Gould and White, 1974) in which undergraduates in several US universities were asked to rank-order the states in which they would wish to live after they graduated. When the responses were aggregated this produced maps of preference surfaces showing students' preference for their home region. However, Gould (1969b) himself highlighted one important problem with respect to the measurement of people's space preferences, namely how to employ ordinal or interval measures for making such measurements. Can what are often little understood and weakly developed, but still multi-faceted, preferences be adequately encapsulated by a numerical score or ranking system? Indeed, both ordinal and interval measures have often proved problematic when asking respondents to rank preferences or to assign interval measures.

Hudson (1969) argued that spatial relations could be treated as being the components of mental maps, with the combination of spatial relations ordering locational information. He suggested that theories of group algebra might then be useful in analysing

*Table 12.2*    Methods for Extracting Environmental Cognition Information

---

1. *Experimenter observation in naturalistic or controlled situations*
   - Subjects draw structures or sketch maps representing environment
   - Subjects arrange toys or make models representing environment
   - Subjects show existence, location, proximity or other spatial relations of environmental elements
   - Subjects are asked to identify photographs and models

2. *Experimenter observes in naturalistic or controlled situation*
   - Observes tracks of marks through actual environments
   - Infers degrees of cognitive knowledge from behaviour in unstructured "clinical" situations
   - Subjects reveal environmental knowledge in the process of sorting or grouping elements of actual or simulated environments
   - Subjects adopt roles or perform acts in simulated and/or real environments
   - Subjects arrange toys or objects representing environmental elements or model environments and experimenter observes the sequence of acts in positioning elements and/or using the environment
   - Subjects draw sketches or sketch maps representing environments
   - Subjects arrange toys or make models representing environment
   - Subjects show existence, location, proximity or other spatial relations of environmental elements; use of symbols to represent such elements
   - Subjects are asked to identify photos, models

3. *Indirect judgemental tasks*
   - Selection of constructs which map environmental information; objective checklists; semantic differentials; repertory grid test
   - Paired proximity judgements and other scaling devices that allow specification of latent structure in environmental information
   - Projective tests

---

*Source*: Golledge and Stimson (1997:231–3).

properties of mental maps, showing how such maps might be simplified, what kinds of maps could be simplified, and how this analysis might be useful in planning the location of service outlets in a network. A major problem here, though, is how to overcome the *individualistic fallacy* or any attempt to impute macro-level (aggregate) relationships from micro-level (individual) relationships.

The chief criticism of the end-result of such work was that much of it seemed unable to link "image" to future action or to relate experimental studies to real problems (Boyle and Robinson, 1979). These linkages and relations have received some attention in studies of migration and residential choice (e.g. Timmermans, 1996), but extensions into the area of modelling have been behaviouristic rather than behavioural (Beavon and Hay, 1977). This means that they have attempted to predict the outcomes of decision-making rather than focusing on the decision-making process itself. However, see Aitken et al's (1989) proposals for making cognitive maps the basis for urban planning.

Critics of behavioural geography singled out the limitations of cognitive mapping in their criticisms. For example, Bunting and Guelke (1979) claimed that behavioural work is based on two false assumptions: firstly, that identifiable environmental images exist which can be measured accurately, and, secondly, that there are strong relationships between such images and behaviour.

These criticisms have been strongly rebutted (see Golledge and Timmermans, 1990), and in the 1980s and 1990s there has continued to be a strong cross-disciplinary focus on behavioural research, including an input from geographers (see Aitken and Prosser, 1990; Aitken and Rushton, 1993). Those areas best represented in this work are cognitive behavioural research and a broad range of studies dealing with decision-making, choice, preference and movement behaviour. However, the uneasy relationship between behavioural geography and that branch of psychology known as behaviourism has meant that it has been possible to charge behavioural geography with coming dangerously close at times to viewing human behaviour merely as a stimulus–response relationship in which any particular response could be attributed to given antecedent conditions (Ley, 1981). This view can be seen by some as being too limiting and even "dehumanising" (see Cloke et al, 1991:68). Attempts to reformulate behavioural geography along non-behaviourist lines, such as Seamon's (1984) *reflexive behavioural geography*, are in practice little removed from what is now termed humanistic geography (see Chapter 13).

In terms of the second strand of behavioural geography identified by Thrift (1981), namely the reactive approach, this focuses on space–time budgets of human activities. Hence initial work in the USA focused on *activity systems* (e.g. Chapin, 1974) whilst a different, but related, approach was developed in Sweden in the form of time-geography (discussed in Chapter 10). Links have been forged with mathematical models through the modelling of activity systems and travel patterns (as referred to in Chapter 8). Indeed, travel behaviour has featured prominently in the "activity approach" in which constraints and choices are built into models (see Hanson and Burnett, 1980), some of which have a gaming component in them (see Chapter 8).

Given references elsewhere in this book to models with a behavioural element and to time-geography, the rest of this chapter focuses primarily on techniques associated with the active decision-making approach. Therefore it considers the use of scales and grids in representing preferences, views and constructs, one of the principal operational tools for identifying the components and backgrounds of spatial behaviour (multi-dimensional scaling), and a technique used in analyses of choice and preference behaviour (conjoint analysis). Firstly, though, the principal method for collecting behavioural information from individuals, as well as a wide range of other data, is discussed, namely the use of *questionnaire surveys*.

## QUESTIONNAIRE SURVEYS

Interacting with and talking to people who are the object of study can take many forms, but perhaps the most common way in which geographers have obtained information from individuals has been via formal questionnaire surveys. The use of such surveys has been part of many geographical investigations, generally employing the survey as one readily identified stage in a process of data generation and analysis (as suggested in Figure 12.2). Design and implementation of questionnaires have featured in many research projects in the social sciences so that there are numerous sources that describe how to construct questionnaires and listing dos and don'ts of the process of conducting a questionnaire survey. The following account includes some consideration of the basic features of questionnaire design as well as the role of questionnaires within both behavioural and other types of human geography.

Questionnaires can provide both quantitative and qualitative information. If they focus upon the former, and if any findings are to be generalised, then questions should be standardised and the respondents chosen in a rigorous fashion as described in Chapter 2. Questionnaires can be completed by respondents, in which case the questionnaire should be self-explanatory and contain no ambiguities. Alternatively, the researcher can ask respondents the questions in an interview situation and record answers on a pro-forma. This offers some opportunity for explanation and assistance with any difficulties the respondents have in answering the questions.

There are many different types of questionnaire survey that can be applied to a given research situation. Some of the possibilities are summarised in Table 12.3. This table was developed by Casley and Lury (1982, 1987) in the context of data collection exercises in Developing Countries, though several of the types of surveys covered can be carried out in other parts of the world. Case studies are represented by the "A-type" categories. None of these is very suitable for a large sample survey. Categories 1B and 2B can also be investigated via a case study approach, though 1B may also be approached via a sample survey. Sample surveys are most applicable to categories 1C, 2C and combinations of 3B or 3C with 4B or 4C. Special training may be required to perform 3B whilst 4B is an expensive option. The classic sociological surveys are 1B, 2A and 4A. Farm management studies are represented by categories 2C, 3B and 4B, though such studies based on single or limited cases apply to 2B, 3B and 4A. Typical case studies for a health survey are in categories 1A, 2B, 3A and 4C whilst a broader set of sample nutrition surveys could comprise 1C, 2C, 3C and 4C. The regular collection of information on prices via sample surveys could comprise 1B, 2C, 3C or 4B.

Use of questionnaires in geography was popularised when analysis of people's geographical perceptions became a major part of behavioural geography in the early 1970s (e.g. Gould and White, 1974). Subsequently they have been used in a range of human geography research projects as a key means of obtaining information from target groups within the population, especially when relatively small numbers of people are being questioned. Their principal attraction has been the ability to produce data that can be analysed by standard procedures, especially through exploratory and descriptive statistics using readily available computer packages. Hence they have featured regularly in undergraduate dissertations and in market survey work. Increasingly, the art of designing and implementing questionnaires has become part of the geographer's technical armoury, with due recognition of pitfalls associated with design and the wording of questions.

## Designing Questionnaires

Questionnaires provide a rapid and often inexpensive way of discovering the characteristics and beliefs of the population at large. Therefore the design of a questionnaire can be pivotal in any research project as quality of data produced depends upon this design. Questionnaire surveys must be custom-built to the specification of given research needs. Both the composing of questions and the asking of them is an art and requires much skill to elicit information that is both correct and possesses the desired amount of detail (Lavan, 1987; Oppenheim, 1996). However, there are certain principles of questionnaire design

*Figure 12.2* The Role of Questionnaire Surveys in the Process of Data Generation and Analysis (based on Gant, 1994:4)

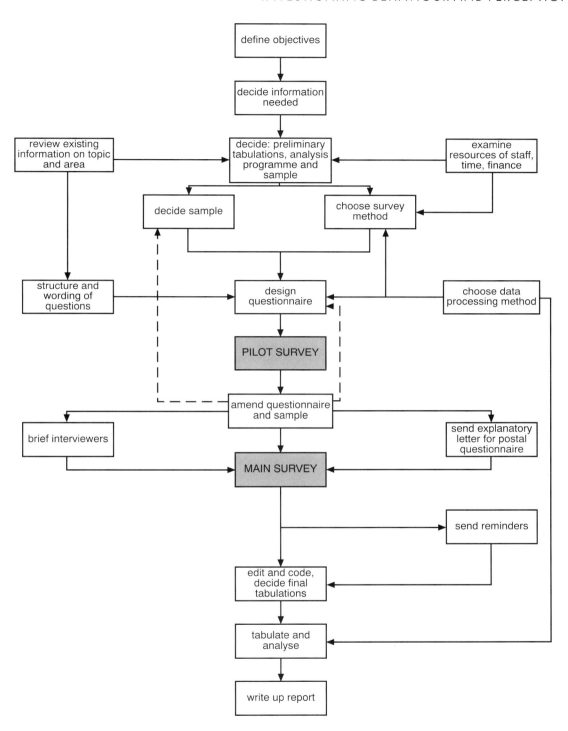

*Table 12.3*  Types of Questionnaire Survey

| Criterion | Classification | | |
|---|---|---|---|
| | *A* | *B* | *C* |
| 1. Scale of enquiry | Phenomenon of interest rare and clustered | Village or community level; specific site or institution | Phenomenon of interest widely distributed throughout area |
| 2. Interview type | Free-ranging; unstructured | Open-ended questions; attitudinal studies | Closed and/or structured questionnaire |
| 3. Observations and measurements | Technical, requiring professional skill | Accurate and detailed | Simple counts and measures |
| 4. Frequency | Continuous or very frequent | Multi-visit over year | Single visit |

*Source*: Casley and Lury (1987).

and implementation that can be applied. The major point in good design is to apply common sense and employ the maxim "keep it simple" – a maxim overwhelmingly repeated by all the professional polltakers, such as Gallup, Mori and Harris, that now exist around the world. Also, in formulating a questionnaire the researcher should be aware of factors affecting respondents' decisions which will influence answers to the questions posed. Some of these factors can be ascertained through use of questions asking for information on the respondent, for example age, education, family background, type of employment.

Questions must be clear and understandable to the people from whom information is collected (see Wilson and McClean, 1994). This clarity rests on four things:

(a) *Simple language*. Language must be used that respondents will understand. This entails the use of small words rather than big ones, and, if necessary, the use of appropriate local dialect. Short questions are usually preferable to long ones, though in some cases some explanatory preamble may be needed. Simple language can be used to reduce any possible confusion in the questionnaire, particularly through avoiding the use of double negatives where meaning can be obscured, e.g. "Do you agree/disagree that the Marketing Board shouldn't be required to supervise quality

control of produce?" The use of "shouldn't be required" is confusing, whilst this type of question could also be reworded to avoid the use of "agree/disagree" which come into the category of words with negative meaning. Similar words to avoid include control, restrict, forbid, ban, outlaw, restrain and oppose. Use of such words tends to yield biased answers as respondents tend to be more likely to associate themselves with positive words rather than negative ones. Similarly, a question beginning "Do you agree that . . .?" begs a "yes" response. Long lists of words are also best avoided as they may not be readily assimilated. If a list of alternatives is used these may be shown to the respondent in the form of *show cards* containing the list. If respondents are asked to choose from a series of alternatives, the question should always be asked first and then the alternatives provided.

(b) *Common concepts*. Abstractions should be avoided, for example asking farmers about the variance of yields, asking consumers whether prices are rising faster than they did some time ago or asking respondents to make estimates involving proportions or percentages. Introducing such concepts rarely yields reliable answers.

(c) *Manageable tasks*. Respondents should not be expected to deal with questions that go beyond their competence to provide accurate information. Therefore it should be remembered that it is easier for respondents to answer questions of personal fact relating to their own experience and behaviour rather than to respond to questions about speculative opinions and attitudes. However, an investigation may well need to enquire about opinions and attitudes, in which case respondents should be given as much scope as possible for expressing these without undue prompting from the researcher and without relying on researcher-supplied categories. Usually, responses to general attitude questions are poorer predictors of behaviour than responses to specific attitude questions. It must also be remembered that "facts" provided by respondents can be subjective interpretations, as the boundary between "facts" and "attitudes" can be quite blurred. This is often the case with questions involving ethnicity and unemployment. It is important to use terms very carefully so that the respondent is clear what is meant by a term that might be open to a number of interpretations, e.g. arable, family, women's work. Tasks that often prove "unmanageable" include asking respondents to recall the past and asking them "What if?" questions.

(d) *Widespread information*. It should not be assumed that respondents have a vast knowledge of particular subjects. Respondents may well provide answers to questions on a great range of topics, but the answers may not really mean anything! This refers once more to the need to restrict questions to a respondent's likely area of competence, as dictated by their own experience. Also, the more general the question, the wider the range of interpretation it may be given, and therefore the greater the opportunity for the respondent to stray from that area of competence. If the wording of questions is kept specific and concrete it is more likely to communicate a uniform meaning to respondents. This process can be assisted by paying attention to the order and context of questions. For example, very specific questions in the initial part of a questionnaire can colour the judgement of respondents when they deal with later questions that might be associated in some way with the same topic. For example, initial questions that ask about output from one aspect of a business may

subsequently lead to biased answers to questions later in the questionnaire that deal with returns from the business in general. The overall context of a question is important as, again, a specific reference to a subject in an earlier question might bias the answer to a later one.

In phrasing questions referring to a particular condition or quality there are five principal queries to bear in mind,

1. Can it be defined unambiguously?
2. Can it be measured accurately in the research environment prevailing and at an acceptable cost?
3. When measured, does it indicate "the state of a condition" in a specific and precise manner?
4. Is it an unbiased measure of the value of interest?
5. When viewed as one of a set of indicators to be measured, does it contribute uniquely to explaining part of the variation in the situation it reflects?

It is important to consider whether questions may be interpreted differently by subgroups amongst the respondents. Thus questionnaire design should be sensitive to cultural difference, particularly regarding words that may have both everyday and technical connotations. However, slang should be avoided too as this can also be subject to different interpretations. If questions deal with information involving time then the time period should be specified. For example, instead of asking "How often do you go on your holidays?", a better question is "On average, how many holidays do you take each year?" A list of alternatives could be specified to such a question, such as "never", "once", "twice", .... Questions dealing with sensitive information are best answered by use of categories or bands for respondents to tick.

Questions about recurrent or habitual behaviour need to be worded as precisely as possible (Parfitt, 1997) as words like "usually" and "recently" are difficult to interpret. More specific wording, such as "during the last seven days" or "when did you last shop at a supermarket?" are preferable. Sensitive topics, such as age and income, are best investigated by using categories.

## Pre-Testing and Pilot Surveys

Design may be helped by formulating a questionnaire checklist (see Table 12.4). Once the questionnaire has been prepared it should always be tested (see de Vaus, 1991:99–105; Oppenheim, 1996:ch. 4). *Pilot surveys* and *pre-testing* are important parts of any successful implementation of questionnaires. They can be used for a number of purposes:

1. To test questions.
   - To test for variation in the target population by helping to detect subgroups who give different answers to particular types of question.
   - To test the meaning of questions, by checking whether respondents understand particular terms and nuances, and also to assess the difficulty of particular questions.
   - To test respondent interest and attention, which can have a major effect upon answers.

2. To test the questionnaire. This involves checking the flow and naturalness of different sections in the questionnaire, the order of questions, *skip patterns* (e.g. "If answer to question 1 is 'Yes' then go to

*Table 12.4*   A Questionnaire Checklist

---

1. Decide what you need to know
   - List all items about which information is required

2. Consider why you need this information
   - Examine the list and remove any item not directly associated with the task in hand

3. Is a questionnaire the best way of obtaining the information?
   - Consider alternatives

4. If so, begin to word questions
   - Arrange questions on cards, paper or in a computer file so that their order can be changed easily
   - Consider type of question

5. Check wording of each question
   - Is there ambiguity, imprecision or assumption?
   - If respondents are being asked to recall events, will they be able to do so?
   - Do the respondents have the knowledge that is being assumed?
   - Are there any unclear, confusing, leading, presuming, hypothetical or offensive questions?
   - Keep language simple; avoid words respondents might not understand (such as technical vocabulary)

6. Decide on question type
   - Each type requires a different analysis

7. Having settled on wording and type of questions, sort them into order
   - It is often best to leave sensitive issues until later in the questionnaire

8. Write out instructions to be included on the questionnaire
   - Respondents must be clear about how they are to answer questions, e.g. by ticking boxes, circling preferences; this is vital in questionnaires mailed to respondents

9. Consider layout and appearance
   - Instructions must be clearly presented
   - Margins may be used for coding
   - Prepare coding

---

*Source*: Based on Bell (1987) as adapted by Gant (1994).

question 5") (see Table 12.5), the overall length of the questionnaire, and the interest and attention of respondents. Consideration can also be given to respondent well-being in terms of the sensitivity of questions. Interviews in the street should be no more than 10 minutes long, whilst this might be extended to between 20 and 45 minutes for interviews in a person's home. Shorter questionnaires are less likely to fatigue the respondent.

The evaluation of a pre-test can be quantitative (if the sample taken is large enough) or qualitative. In the latter case this can take various forms. If a number of enumerators are involved rather than a single researcher this can include marginal comments, an oral de-brief, written reports, answers to written questions and field observation of questionnaire application.

In evaluating a pilot survey with a view to improving the design of a questionnaire, six key points can be considered:

1. Did any of the questions seem to make the respondents uncomfortable?
2. Did any of the questions have to be repeated?
3. Did the respondents misinterpret any questions?
4. Which questions were the most difficult or awkward to read? Having carried out a "trial run" are there certain questions that you dislike and, if so, why? How could these be modified?
5. Are there any time problems? For example, do some sections "drag"?

*Table 12.5*  Typical Skip Patterns in Questionnaires

(a) Self-administered questionnaire

---

**Q7.**  Does the household contain any children under the age of 12 years?

                            Yes ____

                            No ____

  **If 'No' go to Q11.

**Q8.**  How many children are there in the household?

                            Boys ____

                            Girls ____

**Q9.**  In shopping for your children which of the following have you patronised in the last six months?

               Toys R Us ____                  Early Learning Centre ____

               Mothercare ____                  Video games store ____

                                            Toy section of a department store ____

**Q10.**  When purchasing clothes for your children, which of the following types of retail outlet have you used? (please tick)

        Major out-of-town shopping centre ____          Big city shopping centre ____

                    (e.g. Merry Hill)              (e.g. central Birmingham)

                  Smaller town centre ____              Suburban centre ____

       (e.g. Halesowen; Stourbridge)          (e.g. Quinton; Harborne)

                        Local shops ____

                    (e.g. corner store)

**Q11.**  What is the household's annual income?

                        >£50,000 ____               £15,000–19,999 ____

               £30,000–50,000 ____        £10,000–14,999 ____

               £20,000–29,999 ____            <£10,000 ____

---

*continued overleaf*

*Table 12.5   (continued)*

(b) Interview schedule

| | | | | |
|---|---|---|---|---|
| **3.** | Ask All | | *USE NUMERICAL CODES* | |
| | Did you go abroad for your principal vacation last year? | | | |
| | | Yes          1 | No | 2 |

| | | | | |
|---|---|---|---|---|
| **4.** | For 'Yes' | | | |
| | Where? | | | |
| | | Mediterranean          1 | Scandinavia | 4 |
| | | Other parts of France/ | North America | 5 |
| | |    Benelux/Germany     2 | Australasia | 6 |
| | | Eastern Europe          3 | South-East Asia | 7 |
| | | | Other | 8 |

| | | | | |
|---|---|---|---|---|
| **5.** | For 'Yes' | | **6.** For 'No' | |
| | Mode of travel? | | Was a vacation away from home taken? | |
| | | Own vehicle          1 | | |
| | | Hired vehicle          2 | Yes | 1 |
| | | Train          3 | No | 2 |
| | | Coach          4 | | |
| | | Air – package          5 | | |
| | | Air – non-package          6 | | |
| | | Combination          7 | | |

6. Are there any sections where the respondents would have liked the opportunity to say more?

The most frequent flaws in design tend to be imprecise questions, use of technical vocabulary, duplication of questions, lack of logical sequence, inappropriate question style, complex questions, general layout and design, lack of user-friendliness in a field environment, and length of questionnaire.

Pilot surveys can also have the advantage of providing field training for interviewers, and helping the interviewer to develop personal skills and rapport with respondents. Furthermore, they provide a small dataset for use in preparing provisional coding for analysis (see Fink and Kosecoff, 1985:50–1).

Depending on the underlying purpose for taking a questionnaire survey, it is also possible to provide some checks upon the input of the researcher's subjective values to the questionnaire by introducing elements of *replicability* and *standardisation*. The former refers to a mechanism for checking whether a survey's findings are applicable in other contexts. For example, if a second researcher administers the same questionnaire with a comparable sample, this provides a check upon possible biases. However, this requires standardisation in which the conditions operating during the taking of the questionnaire are repeated, e.g. asking the questions in the same manner so that different replies to the same question are a "true" difference of opinion and not a reflection of how the question was asked or of the conditions under which the interview was conducted (May, 1993:66–7).

## Styles of Questionnaire

There are several different styles of questionnaire, with variation arising primarily from different types of question and the method of administering the questionnaire to the respondents. As described by Gant (1994), there are six main methods:

(a) *Face-to-face interviews*. Interviews can vary greatly in content and style, from asking questions that demand very specific short responses to ones that are very informal conversations. The style varies according to the characteristics of the respondents, the research topic and the environment in which the meeting takes place. Whatever the character of the interview, interviewers have to locate respondents and enlist their cooperation by establishing some rapport with them. They also have to elicit answers to questions in such a way that the answers can be recorded and the question presented in a standard form to all respondents. Personal interviews can enable guidance to be given to respondents regarding their answers, and probing for clarification can take place. Quite demanding surveys can be performed through personal interviews, but cost and time may be limiting factors.

(b) *Retrospective interviews.* These involve asking respondents to recollect past events, as in the Edwardian childhood project carried out in New Zealand (Graham, 1992). This procedure can help validate the content of historical records and generate fresh evidence for a particular historical enquiry (Gant, 1986, 1991).

(c) *Telephone interviews.* These are used widely by commercial agencies, but have also been adopted in certain circumstances by geographers (e.g. Robinson, 1986). They have become the most popular method for collecting data amongst market researchers in the USA. However, they do have their drawbacks. Using a telephone directory as a sampling frame excludes individuals who are ex-directory or who do not possess a telephone, thereby biasing the sample. The distribution of telephones between classes is disproportionate. According to *Social Trends* only two-thirds of unskilled manual workers have access to a telephone that is rented by them and so has their (or their partner's) name recorded in a directory. In contrast, the percentage for professionals and managers is very close to 100. There are also unequal representations by race and gender. Telephone interviews need to be kept short because of cost, and this limits the generation of a rapport with the respondent. Show cards and other visual aids cannot be used and there is greater scope for respondents to misinterpret questions than with the face-to-face method. However, there is still an element of personal contact that is lacking with the mailshot approach, and certain circumstances favour telephone interviews, notably in farm surveys, sparsely populated regions and where respondents are likely to be away from home at frequent intervals (Barnett, 1991:69–70).

(d) *Mail surveys.* Although frequently employed, these often have poor response rates. The absence of rapport between researcher and respondent makes it easy for the latter to ignore entreaties to respond that may be contained in a letter accompanying the mailed questionnaire (Cohen and Manion, 1985:84–90). The tone and content of this letter are a very important influence on response rates, though these rarely exceed 30 per cent unless the ground has been prepared prior to receipt of a mail survey. For example, a telephone call alerting the respondent to the imminent receipt of a questionnaire may be useful, as might prior contacts with an organisation whose members might be the target population for such a survey. The postal charges incurred in a mail survey may be another problem. Furthermore, the low response rate can yield a biased sample favouring the better educated and more socially motivated members of the target population. The chief advantage is the ease of such surveys and the saving on time when compared with conducting face-to-face interviews.

(e) *"Drop-and-collect" surveys.* Also known as the *delivery and collection method*, these combine certain positive features of both mail surveys and interviews. They involve the personal delivery of questionnaires, which are then left with a respondent, perhaps with a covering letter. Completed questionnaires can then be posted or collected at a predetermined time. The element of some personal contact between researcher and respondent can facilitate greater cooperation than with mail surveys, especially if the researcher can answer problems related to the requisite form filling (Walker, 1976). Dixon and Leach (1980:14) recommend this method if the area to be covered is small and travel costs are low.

(f) *Snowball survey.* This method may be used if the research focus is upon a relatively small group possessing certain characteristics. A common example is in investigations of people with particular disabilities or problems, for example the housebound elderly. Having identified certain individuals with this characteristic, the sample is extended by use of information they provide or through their contact network, for example via the Social Services. This does not amount to a standard sampling strategy, but can enable a sample to be identified without an orthodox sampling frame (see Tivers, 1985).

Another important variable in questionnaire surveys is their use of *open questions* or *closed questions*. The latter permit only a fixed form of answer, such as "yes", "no" or a particular predetermined category. These are sometimes referred to as *forced choice questions*. Therefore the response categories must be designed well, but they have the advantage of greater specificity. To any closed question the respondent should be allowed to answer "don't know" or "no opinion". If a list of categories is supplied, for example ranging from "good" at one end of a scale to "bad" at the other, a middle intensity description should always be included, e.g. "satisfactory", "moderate", "average". If possible the respondent should not be offered a simple alternative between "agree" and "disagree". In general, the more poorly educated respondents tend to agree more than they disagree! Designs often feature both open and closed questions as use of open questions at random can be a valuable way of probing responses, encouraging respondents to develop the more straightforward answers that they have to give to closed questions. Closed questions inevitably simplify and stylise the life and thought of individuals. This may be especially so if rating scales are used. For example a respondent may be asked to rate a lecture as very good, good, satisfactory, poor or very poor. Similarly, a score out of 10 may be required. Special forms of analysis for such scales are discussed below.

There are six different types of closed format questions (Wilson and McClean, 1994:22–32):

(a) *Single answer*. The respondents are required to choose a single reply from a preselected list of options, usually consisting of a set of mutually exclusive categories. Typically, religious denomination, marital status, type of household, age, income levels and nationality can be dealt with in this fashion (see Table

12.6). To achieve exhaustive coverage it is often necessary to include a category such as "other", "don't know" or "no response".

(b) *Multiple answer*. The respondent can tick none, one or more than one box in response to a question. For example, if a question asked about what household appliances a respondent used regularly, then the answer might involve ticking boxes against refrigerator, dishwasher, washing machine, microwave oven and electric/gas cooker.

(c) *Rank order*. This extends the multiple choice question by adding information on relative preferences. Respondents are asked to rate or rank each option that applies. However, it may be necessary to reduce the number of categories specified so that respondents cannot arbitrarily allocate ranks to some of the options. Usually no more than five options should be specified if a valid ranking is desired. Again it may be necessary to introduce a category of "other" or allow the respondent to "please specify" their own additional categories.

(d) *Numeric*. The researcher can anticipate the range of possible answers but the respondent has to specify a particular value within the anticipated range. Such questions apply especially to age of respondent, travel distances, rooms in a house, income levels and temperature.

(e) *Likert-style formats*. A Likert scale is a form of ranking scale in which a series of statements are provided indicating attitudes towards a chosen topic. It places people's responses on an "attitude continuum", e.g. ranging from "very influential" through "neutral" to "not influential". Respondents are asked to show

*Table 12.6*    Single-Answer Question on Nationality

Please tick the appropriate category corresponding to the ethnic group of which you consider yourself a member:

| | | | |
|---|---|---|---|
| White | ____ | Asian | ____ |
| Black | | – Indian | ____ |
| – Caribbean | ____ | – Pakistani | ____ |
| – African | ____ | – Bangladeshi | ____ |
| – Other | ____ | – Chinese | ____ |
| Other Ethnic Group | ____ | – Other | ____ |

their strength of agreement or disagreement with each statement. As it is attitudes that are being investigated by the scale, questions can be quite biased. Scales can be verbal or diagrammatic. The former could specify strengths of agreement with a particular statement. For example: "Women are more environment-friendly than men": strongly agree, agree, don't know/undecided, disagree, strongly disagree. The mid-point of what is usually a three- or five-point scale should represent a neutral response. In diagrammatic form the scale could be drawn as a line and respondents asked to place a tick at an appropriate point.

(f) *Semantic differential*. Respondents are presented with a set of opposing adjectives as answers to questions and are invited to indicate their response either numerically or graphically. A seven-point scale is commonly employed, with respondents choosing the appropriate point that represents their views. Common opposing adjectives are good–bad, tall–short, near–far, fast–slow, rich–poor, active–passive, old–young, responsible–irresponsible.

The advantages of a single-sheet questionnaire with closed questions are:

1. One sheet or form contains results from what may have been a lengthy sequence of questions.
2. It may be impossible to specify in advance the number of cases to be covered, but this can be allowed for by providing a large number of rows, one for each case.
3. The questioner is allowed flexibility in the manner and sequence of implicit questions.

The latter may also be problematic as it introduces variation from one respondent to another. Other disadvantages are:

1. Questions cannot be fully specified as they are only implicit in the column headings.
2. The lack of a sequence and structure may produce omissions, with the questioner misdirecting the respondent or misrecording the answer.
3. Abbreviated column headings may disguise the complexity of questions, making responses problematic.

Use of closed questions has three key advantages:

1. It avoids uncertainties such as how to record long open-ended answers on a pre-prepared form.
2. Pre-coding can ensure that information is collected relating to that coding.
3. If there are a large number of respondents, some form of coded data processing will be involved. If open-ended questions are employed this will necessitate their subsequent "closing" at the coding stage. Use of closed questions from the outset avoids this.

Particularly if a questionnaire consists mainly of open questions it is likely that the responses will be subjected to computer-based statistical analysis. If so, questionnaire design will involve coding the questions. It also means that numerical value is assigned to the information collected and each piece of information occupies a unique position in the computer record. For closed questions it is possible to pre-allocate codes to answers prior to conducting the survey; this is known as *pre-coding*. The codes are usually printed on the questionnaire adjacent to boxes associated with each question option. These codes are usually aligned on the right-hand side of the questionnaire to facilitate easy keying of the responses into computer format (see Figure 12.3). Pre-coding can be done via a "tick box" style or by circling a number. For open questions, the range of categories of response cannot be anticipated in advance, though a box can be placed at the side of the question in anticipation of turning the open responses into numerical data. This requires access to information either from a pilot test, from a representative sample of completed questionnaires or from the full-scale survey. The responses can then be grouped into broad categories and each one given a number. This artificially turns an open question into a closed form, but does provide additional information by recording the respondents' own views.

## Critique

When questionnaires first became popular within human geography, much of the information elicited was

*LOCAL GOVERNMENT SURVEY: 'PERSPECTIVES ON THE WASTE HIERARCHY'*

*This is a survey of local government municipal solid waste management Authorities in the United Kingdom. The questionnaire has been designed in collaboration with Professor Guy Robinson, School of Geography, Kingston University, Dr Chris Coggins of the Waste Management and Technology Centre, Sheffield University, and the Institute of Wastes Management to make it as simple and concise as possible for officers to complete. Your Authority has been chosen as part of a representative sample of local waste management service providers and policy developers, designed to provide an accurate assessment of local government opinion on the implementation of the principles of the waste management hierarchy at the local level, and the factors central to the design and implementation of local government municipal solid waste management strategy and policy.*

*Please try to answer all questions as fully as possible thus providing a truly representative assessment of current waste management practices in the UK. For those questions where there are no instructions on how to respond, please tick the most appropriate answer in the box provided. [ √ ]. If you do not wish to disclose any data then you can leave those questions blank, but this will affect the quality of the data and the final results. Some questions may not apply to your authority, could you please complete these with N/A. If you have any comments to make then please continue on additional sheets or use the blank page at the end of the survey.*

Reference Number:

## 1. AUTHORITY DETAILS

*This series of questions provide background data on your authority, including data about its demographic and political make-up.*

1.1 Which Environment Agency region is your Authority located in?

| | |
|---|---|
| NORTH WEST | [ ] 01 |
| NORTH EAST | [ ] 02 |
| WEST MIDLANDS | [ ] 03 |
| MIDLANDS | [ ] 04 |
| ANGLIAN | [ ] 05 |
| THAMES | [ ] 06 |
| SOUTHERN | [ ] 07 |
| SOUTH WEST | [ ] 08 |
| WELSH | [ ] 09 |
| SCOTLAND | [ ] 10 |
| IRELAND | [ ] 11 |

1.2 Which definition best describes your Authority?

| | |
|---|---|
| COLLECTION | [ ] 1 |
| DISPOSAL | [ ] 2 |
| UNITARY | [ ] 3 |
| NEITHER | [ ] 9 |

1.3 How would you describe the area within your Authority?

| | |
|---|---|
| URBAN | [ ] 1 |
| RURAL | [ ] 2 |
| MIXTURE | [ ] 3 |

1.4 Number of Households in your Authority (1995 Census to the nearest thousand)?

_____

1.5 Which is the lead (or majority) political party in your Authority at the Council level?

| | |
|---|---|
| CONSERVATIVE | [ ] 1 |
| LABOUR | [ ] 2 |
| LIBERAL | [ ] 3 |
| INDEPENDENT | [ ] 4 |
| GREEN | [ ] 5 |
| OTHER | [ ] 6 _____ |
| NO OVERALL MAJORITY | [ ] 9 |

1.6 Which political party has been the lead (or dominant) party in your Authority at the Council level during the last decade?

| | |
|---|---|
| CONSERVATIVE | [ ] 1 |
| LABOUR | [ ] 2 |
| LIBERAL | [ ] 3 |
| INDEPENDENT | [ ] 4 |
| GREEN | [ ] 5 |
| OTHER (please specify) | [ ] 6 _____ |

1

subjected to statistical testing, which was in keeping with the discipline's ruling paradigm at that time. This has continued to be the case with many small-scale surveys, typical of undergraduate projects, linking responses to computer programs giving graphical output and simple statistical descriptions. The ease and speed of the procedures involved – from answers to questions one day, to computer output the next – has proved beguiling. Yet, limitations in the process of carrying out questionnaire surveys are often ignored or dismissed. There are, though, various problems that need to be addressed before data from a questionnaire can be regarded as a sound basis for analysis.

There are a number of constraints in both the interview and measurement processes inherent in questionnaires. In particular, because questionnaires are usually written by educated persons who have a special interest in and understanding of the topic of their enquiry, and because these people usually consult with other educated and concerned persons, it is much more common for questionnaires to be overwritten, overcomplicated and too demanding of the respondent than they are to be simple-minded, superficial and not demanding enough.

The meaning extracted from surveys can be questioned on a number of grounds. Firstly, there is the artificiality of the interview situation, in which the confrontation between interviewer and interviewee may produce responses not in accordance with the interviewee's "true" views. Respondents can be easily led unconsciously to answers regarded as reasonable by the interviewer. Even if a respondent is not led in this way they may assume that certain answers are expected and so provide them out of politeness. If technical terms or words and phrases obscure to the respondent, but familiar to the questioner, are used then additional explanation may need to be provided which may lead the respondent to a particular answer. Alternatively the explanation might significantly alter the character of the question. Yet, if simple language

is used this might seem patronising and so may promote an unfavourable attitude to the questionnaire or misleading responses. The latter are especially common if respondents are asked to place themselves in a hypothetical situation. Responses to such questions generally bear little relation to what will be done should the hypothetical become real (Cox, 1981:264):

> The categories supplied by the investigator may have quite different meanings to different individuals in the sample. Likewise the responses supplied by the investigator on the assumption that they are exhaustive may be far from so. As a consequence one may learn more about the behaviour of the sample in responding to a set of categories the investigator attempts to impose upon them, than about the behaviour under investigation itself.

A well known example of this occurred in some of the polling for *Fortune* magazine in 1940 by the Gallup organisation. In this the population was classified into upper, middle and lower classes, with 90 per cent of the sample classifying themselves as "middle class". When the questionnaire was modified so that "lower class" became "working class", this became the majority choice of the respondents: "here we see sociologists measuring not popular consciousness but their own" (Braverman, 1974:28).

A second problem is the reliance upon a schedule of questions which may reflect the interviewer's own prejudices and motives, thereby biasing the outcome of the survey before any input from interviewees is obtained. Furthermore, difficulties may arise through the use of questions which predetermine a limited response, e.g. "yes" or "no", limited multiple choice responses or the use of ranking systems which give both a false precision to an individual's views and represent a degree of artificiality in what may be highly subjective evaluations and feelings.

The use of a questionnaire to produce quantitative measures of views, beliefs and essentially non-quantitative values places an unnecessary barrier between the analyst and a full understanding of the position held by the interviewee. It may enable formal statistical testing of hypotheses to be carried out using the survey data, but essential meaning may already have been lost by virtue of utilising this approach. In effect,

*Figure 12.3*   A Local Government Survey on "Perspectives in the Waste Hierarchy" (first page only). (*Source*: Read et al, 1997)

certain nuances of meaning can be obliterated by the rigidity of an *interview schedule* (a fixed list of questions put to a respondent) and a subsequent statistical analysis.

The underlying weakness of questionnaires, especially those reliant on use of closed questions, is that they are restrictive. By their very design they restrict the way in which people can answer questions and hence the "results" of any analysis of questionnaire responses are strongly predetermined. By asking interviewees to restrict their answers to a particular set of pre-chosen responses, they are not given the opportunity to challenge ideas on their own terms. The spectrum of attitudes and meanings likely to exist amongst a sample of interviewees is ignored unless something other than closed questions is employed. Good design can certainly maximise the value of content yielded by closed questions but this will not necessarily meet the longer-term goal of most research in human geography: namely, to understand how people interpret the world around them and their actions. For example, from the analysis of responses to closed questions a clear association between age and opinion might be revealed. However, this can only be understood by gaining greater insight into the processes by which the opinions are formed and by considering other variables (e.g. class, occupation, gender). This crucial insight will not necessarily be obtained by responses to more closed questions. This suggests that a judicious combination of open and closed questions is more likely to be a more effective vehicle for gaining greater insights to meanings. Indeed, the structure of the questionnaire may be forsaken altogether for more open forms of investigation, as described in the following chapter.

Finally, in addition to ensuring that a questionnaire is well designed and will meet the particular needs of a given research project, there is also an *interviewing technique* that needs to be considered. How, when and where the questions are asked are important considerations if biased responses or a biased sample are to be avoided. Respondents should be questioned at different times of day to ensure that a better cross-section of the public may be selected. This is important for interviews conducted both in the street and on a door-

to-door basis. For the latter, the researcher needs to be sure that there are some individuals who will only be available at certain times.

Formal survey methods, often combined with the testing of causal hypotheses, do have an important role to play in social research, perhaps most especially when the object of analysis is something other than the examination of deeply held views and beliefs. In utilising the positive aspects of questionnaire surveys, certain "checks" have frequently been built in to improve the quality of information obtained, for example, applying formally structured interviews with extensive "pilot" surveys to refine data collection procedures and trial analysis of results to produce more elaborate interpretations by introducing intervening variables beyond those used initially. Eyles (1988:7) summarises this type of approach as the view "that we should not reject outright the survey method; rather use it in circumstances where people seem able to communicate what they are doing and what it means".

## SCALES AND GRIDS

One of the problems to overcome when using a questionnaire to collect information is the use of single questions to measure such non-factual topics as awareness, perception, social representations, opinions, beliefs, attitudes and values. These are not straightforward matters of fact because they refer to states of mind rather than behaviour or events. They are very difficult to measure because they are multi-faceted and not readily amenable to investigation via a simple question posed by a researcher. "Single questions dealing with such sensitive topics are much more open to bias and unreliability due to wording, question format and contexual effects" (Oppenheim, 1992:150). In recognising this limitation of the standard questions employed in a questionnaire, many social scientists have sought to investigate these "states of mind" by using other means, usually involving the researcher spending far more time with the respondent than is the norm for the administering of a questionnaire (see Chapter 13). However, another approach has been to pursue the questionnaire format but employing a *scaling approach*, especially in investigations of people's attitudes.

Scaling approaches utilise some form of measurement, but via a type of abstraction. That is, the measure is not exact but exists on a linear or approximately linear scale that can run, for example, from "high" to "low" in sequence, but without exact measurement. There are various forms of scales that have been applied in questionnaires, especially with respect to the investigation of people's attitudes. As briefly outlined above in the discussion on types of closed question, the most common scales employed are Likert scales and semantic differentials

## Likert Scales and the Semantic Differential

The *Likert scale* refers to an attitude continuum in which a respondent is given five choices from which to select. Usually the five-fold scale runs from "strongly agree" to "agree" to "uncertain" to "disagree" to "strongly disagree". These can be given weights from 1 to 5 or 0 to 4 for scoring purposes. This scale is applied to a series of attitudinal questions, with respondents asked to tick the appropriate boxes (Table 12.7). The overall score for a respondent on a set of questions can then be calculated and compared with that for others. This can enable com-

*Table 12.7*    Statements Used in Conjunction with a Likert Scale

| Statement | Strongly Agree | Agree | Uncertain | Disagree | Strongly Disagree |
|---|---|---|---|---|---|
| There are too many cars on the road | | x | | | |
| I would own more than one car if I could | | | x | | |
| People should make more use of public transport | | x | | | |
| Public transport should be cheaper | x | | | | |
| The frequency of the bus service to town should be increased | | x | | | |
| Park-and-ride schemes are a good feature of local public transport | | | x | | |
| The amount of car parking space in town should be increased | x | | | | |
| The local authority should invest in a modern tram system | | | | x | |
| Local taxes should be increased to subsidise public transport | | | | | x |
| More cycle lanes should be created | | | x | | |

x = possible responses of a regular car user who likes the principle of greater provision of public transport but may reject increased taxation to pay for it.

parisons to be made between different groups of people regarding their positive or negative attitudes to a given issue. A practical difficulty is keeping the scoring system consistent with positive or negative attitudes to the given issue. This requires careful attention to the wording of the questions.

The *semantic differential* is a psychological scaling technique utilising linguistic encoding as an index of meaning. As developed by Osgood et al (1957), an individual is provided with a subject to be differentiated and a set of bipolar adjectival scales to assist this differentiation. For each pair of adjectives a scale is offered to the individual, as shown in Table 12.8, which uses a seven-step scale, so that the selections represent "semantic space, a region of some unknown dimensionality and Euclidean in character" (Osgood et al, 1957:25). Thus it is a rating scale that measures a respondent's reaction to some object or concept in terms of rating on bipolar scales defined with contrasting adjectives at each end. For any given concept the larger the number of scales offered and the more representative the selection of these scales then the more valid will be the semantic space of the operational meaning of the concept (Golant and Burton, 1976).

## The Repertory Grid

The *repertory grid* as devised by Kelly (1955) has elements forming the columns and constructs as the rows of the grid. As subsequently developed by Slater (1969), all constructs are applied to a standard set of elements. A repertory grid for an individual can then be added to grids for other individuals to produce a supergrid whose axes are, firstly, the common set of elements and, secondly, the set of all constructs, including each person's version of any standard constructs. The repertory grid differs from the semantic differential in that it is the individual respondent who chooses the rating scale in the former whereas in the latter it is the researcher who chooses, though Hudson (1980) refers to the selection of the elements or constructs in the grid as being performed by either the researcher or the individuals being studied.

Grids may be analysed in two principal ways: by focusing on the content of the constructs, and by examining the cognitive structure underlying the elicited constructs (Hudson, 1980:348). The former is the more subjective form of analysis and involves examination of the numbers, nature and types of elements and constructs elicited, especially the verbal labels employed. These labels are usually bipolar but in the case of environmental images unipolar constructs have also been employed (Harrison and Sarre, 1971). Both individual grids and aggregates may be analysed. A significant weakness occurs if individuals use the same term to mean different things. For example, references to "near" and "far" by two individuals may actually contain a different conception of distance (Downs, 1976).

Repertory grids have been applied to farming communities in the Developing World (e.g. Townsend, 1977) and in the UK (e.g. Ilbery and Hornby, 1983). In this work the constructs are those aspects of agriculture under investigation, such as farm size, labour, marketing and soils. Measurement of constructs is investigated in qualitative terms in the form of a continuum, for example from bad to good, low to high, small to large. The value of each of the constructs is assessed for each of the elements. These are different phenomena or things perceived, for example "the weather", "the best farm" or "a hill". The grid is used to investigate the perceived world of the farmer and represents information relating to attitudes, behaviour and motivation. An example of an uncompleted grid is shown in Table 12.9; the grid's extent defining the field of study. Pre-testing of a proposed grid can eliminate elements and constructs deemed unsuitable by the respondents, and those for which it is difficult to obtain objective assessment of values.

*Table 12.8* Scale of Adjectives Used in Constructing a Semantic Differential

| Good | Very | Fairly | Slightly | Neither | Slightly | Fairly | Very | Bad |
|------|------|--------|----------|---------|----------|--------|------|-----|

*Table 12.9*   Repertory Grid for Survey of Farming

| Constructs | Elements | | | | | |
|---|---|---|---|---|---|---|
| | Own Farm | Best Farm | Worst Farm | Neighbour's Farm | Ideal Farm | Hobby Farm |
| Labour | | | | | | |
| Farm size | | | | | | |
| Fragmentation | | | | | | |
| Soils | | | | | | |
| Drainage | | | | | | |
| Yields | | | | | | |
| Machinery | | | | | | |
| Marketing | | | | | | |
| Investment | | | | | | |
| Condition | | | | | | |
| Cooperation | | | | | | |
| Transport | | | | | | |

Research by Ilbery and Hornby (1983) on farmers in mid-Warwickshire, England, used 17 constructs covering physical, economic and socio-personal variables. A grid was completed by 35 farmers. In effect, the grid represented part of the individual farmer's perception of her/his own farm and the local farming community. These perceptions were represented in the form of a numerical score from 0 for "bad" to 10 for "good", for each construct. From this information it was possible to analyse individual grids, groups of grids or an averaged grid for all the farmers. Ilbery and Hornby concentrated upon the latter two, employing correlation and principal components analysis to examine interrelationships between the constructs studied. Their analysis suggested that the farmers' attitudes were conditioned by the physical characteristics of the farm and their experience of farming. The farmers considered the best farms in the area to be those with a sound physical base for farming, low levels of urban interference, well-organised marketing facilities, quality labour and correct attitude to farming. Inadequate machinery was deemed to be the major characteristic of the "worst farm". When farmers were distinguished on the basis of age, it was found that younger farmers had a more physically deterministic view of farming operations whilst older farmers placed more importance on experience. Less well educated farmers felt that the essential features of farming were good labour supplies, well-drained land and non-fragmented holdings. In contrast, the better-educated farmers attached more importance to machinery, marketing facilities, experience and attitude.

In another example, Timmermans (1981) examined 12 suburban shopping centres and city centre shopping in Eindhoven, the Netherlands. Shoppers were asked to name elements in the shopping centres that fulfilled particular roles for them as well as being asked to differentiate between a grid of elements. In total the 20 shoppers interviewed referred to 42 different constructs, the average per shopper being 11.8. The most common was a distinction between few and many shops, closely followed by poor/good parking facilities, far from/near to home, and narrow/wide range of stock. Constructs like advertising, cleanliness and safety were mentioned only occasionally. Timmermans' findings showed clear differences amongst the shoppers, in terms of both the number and range of constructs people used to differentiate between shopping centres. Economic-type constructs were used by most people, with social and marketing-type factors mentioned only occasionally. Subsequently the contents of the repertory grid were factor-analysed to reveal its basic underlying dimensions. Two dimensions in particular appeared to be significant: size of shopping centre and accessibility. The former was associated with an intangible atmosphere of spaciousness as well as more concrete constructs such as number of shops, range of choice, presence of department stores, availability of non-duty goods, presence of non-retailing functions and presence of speciality stores.

The method often used to analyse the aggregate data of the grids is to calculate the mean scores for particular elements in terms of particular scales and then apply factor analysis to establish the main axes of variation in the set of scales in use (e.g. Golant and Burton, 1976). This ignores all differences between individuals. Guttman (1946) used a least-squares estimating procedure, but this would be inappropriate for most problems of spatial choice as it would require all $n$ individuals to make judgements on all of the $n(n-1)/2$ comparisons.

There are a variety of views on the nature of the links between the grid and personal construct theory, but most researchers using repertory grids relate their studies to *Kelly's personal construct theory*. This has a relationship between behaviour and image: "a person's behaviour tests hypotheses about the utility of [her/]his image of the world which stem from choices made in terms of preferences for particular poles of personal constructs and elaboration of the personal construct system" (Hudson, 1980:353). Yet, much behaviour in space is not motivated in this fashion, but is related to the satisfaction of an individual's particular needs. Also, free pursuit of knowledge to elaborate a personal construct system is likely to be limited by considerations of cost and time and so it is always an important or sub-optimal system of constructs that is developed and acted upon. Therefore the acquisition of knowledge regarding a particular environment is not really a goal in itself but is closely related to the meeting of other personal goals and needs. Thus the theory is inadequate on its own as a means of understanding and explaining spatial behaviour, and hence geographers have emphasised the relationship between behaviour and the choice–constraint continuum in which individuals operate within limits which constrain the degree of choice open to them.

## Point Score Analysis

A related form of analysis to that of the repertory grid is the use of *point scores*, in which respondents are asked whether a factor in a preselected list of decision-making factors is relevant to their particular behaviour, the latter usually relating to mode of business operation. The importance of each factor is related to a numerical scale, with the overall importance of each individual factor being assessed by totalling the scores for each factor in turn for all respondents. The utility of this approach rests largely on the initial selection of factors to present to the respondents. Factors are usually grouped into categories, e.g. economic, socio-personal and business characteristics, to aid both the respondents and the subsequent analysis. As for repertory grids, this technique has been used in agricultural geography (e.g. Ilbery, 1977b, 1978).

In the case of work on the growing of vining peas in eastern Scotland (Robinson, 1988:253–4), point score analysis was applied to both pea-growers and non-pea-growers. This provided 17 categories for the growers to consider and 18 for the non-growers (see Table 12.10). It revealed that factors relating to production and financial returns played the biggest part in the farmers' decisions to grow/not to grow vining peas, a crop largely grown under contract for processing firms. This was the case for both prompted and unprompted responses to a questionnaire survey of farmers which employed the point score system. However, the non-pea-growers ranked socio-personal factors as highly as economic and production factors. The pea-growers regarded vining peas as both a good break crop and an entry crop. Amongst those farmers who were not growing peas, the lack of spare resources to devote to this activity was seen as a significant limiting factor as was the view that the use of peas as a break crop was not required, and that diversification into pea-growing would spread their resources too thinly.

*Table 12.10*  Point Score Analysis for Vining Pea Production in Eastern Scotland

| A | Pea-Growers | | B | Non-Pea-Growers | |
|---|---|---|---|---|---|
| Ranking | Factor | Score (%) | Ranking | Factor | Score (%) |
| 1 | Good break crop | 47 | 1 | Adequate alternative break crops | 46 |
| 2 | Early harvest | 36 | 2= | Retain simple management | 39 |
| 3 | Profitable | 34 | | Desire not to rent | 39 |
| 4 | Replacement crop | 33 | 4 | Personal preference | 34 |
| 5= | Few alternatives | 24 | 5 | No spare resources | 27 |
| | Good cash flow | 24 | 6 | Unsuitable land | 24 |
| 7 | Diversification/risk spreading | 23 | 7 | insufficient capital | 22 |
| 8= | Use of resources in slack period | 22 | 8= | No risk decrease | 21 |
| | Approached by producer group | 22 | | No early harvest | 21 |
| 10= | Lengthens total crop rotation | 12 | | Desire not to join cooperative | 21 |
| | Proximity to processor | 12 | | Insufficient suitable land | 21 |
| 12 | More assured income | 11 | 12= | Not a good break crop | 18 |
| 13 | Takes pressure off other resources | 9 | | Production cooperation too risky | 18 |
| 14= | Cooperation an advantage | 8 | 14 | No coop exists/no new members admitted | 17 |
| | Personal preference | 8 | 15= | Not sufficiently profitable | 12 |
| 16= | Pay off capital | 3 | 16= | Desire not to rent additional land | 11 |
| | Advised to grow peas | 3 | | Never approached to grow crop | 11 |
| | | | 18 | Too distant from factory | 10 |

*Source*: Robinson (1988:254).

## MULTI-DIMENSIONAL SCALING

*Multi-dimensional scaling* (MDS) methods have been used by geographers as operational tools for identifying the components and backgrounds of spatial behaviour (Golledge and Rushton, 1972; Nijkamp, 1979:123). They have been used to analyse both dissimilarity judgements and judgements of preference or choice, for example residential preferences (Clark, 1993; Preston, 1982), migration choice (Demko and Briggs, 1970), urban cognition (Phipps, 1979) and shopping centre preference (Spencer, 1980; Timmermans, 1993). Initially the main developers of this technique were mathematical psychologists, but from the early 1970s a number of other social science disciplines have shown an interest, including geography. Geographers have used MDS to focus upon an individual's priorities, translating "soft" (ordinal) preference information (ordinal = position in series, first,

second, third, etc.) into "hard" (cardinal) preference information (cardinal = the "primitive" numbers, 1, 2, 3, etc.). From a simple set of interview questions, basic features of individual and collective priorities can be both detected and visualised by means of a cardinal point configuration.

MDS was developed intially in psychology, its leading proponents being Guttman (1946:45) and Torgerson (1958). It takes qualitative statements on priorities and preference structures in the form of ordinal (ranked) data and converts them to a metric scale that gives a distance measure between any two preference (locational) types (e.g. Golledge and Rushton, 1972). Although, intuitively, this might seem to contradict the clear distinction between ordinal and interval measurement scales, in practice it is possible to develop metric scales with a high degree of accuracy from purely ordinal data (see Molinero, 1988).

Various scaling procedures have been used to

"unpack" the latent spatial structure of environmental knowledge from judgements made about environments. MDS imposes a structure on information obtained by examining paired-comparison judgements made by individuals about places in a given environment (e.g. Golledge and Rushton, 1975). So, as Golledge (1976:309) writes:

> A series of cognitive configurations are obtained which represent the spatial information that individuals have about elements of an environment. This knowledge of where places are is used to reconstruct disturbed and distorted maps of objective reality.

MDS can represent cartographically the concept of "non-linear" space. It can take a set of objects and separate them according to a defined relationship, and, as shown in research by Tobler (1976), the ensuing separation may be mapped. This derived map may then be compared with more conventional representations of geographical space. This approach has been used in behavioural geography to investigate cognitive space (see Golledge, 1993; Hirtle and Heidorn, 1993; Lloyd, 1993). Usually this type of research has focused upon the perception of distances to urban landmarks and the relative positioning of different urban features by individuals or groups. For example, Rosen and Robinson (1983) investigated the differential perceptions of students from widely varying cultural backgrounds in Utrecht, the Netherlands, noting strong differences between Europeans and students from the Developing World (see also Ferguson, 1979). Extensive work on this type of problem has been performed by Golledge (1978a,b). Other types of space investigated include time-space (e.g. Forer, 1978) and cost-space (e.g. Pirie, 1977).

MDS attempts to identify the coordinates of $n$ points associated with $n$ objects so that the inter-point distances demonstrate a maximum correspondence with respect to observed dissimilarities in perceptions or preferences regarding these $n$ objects. Therefore, on the basis of given dissimilarities, the aim is to find a best-fit configuration of points (Nijkamp, 1979:100). The rationale is to transform into cardinal units (1, 2, 3, etc.) ordinal data (first, second, third, etc.) which

describe in an $n \times n$ paired comparison table the similarity/dissimilarity between $n$ objects.

A symmetric paired comparison table has $\frac{1}{2}n(n - 1)$ ordinal dissimilarity relationships (ignoring the self-dissimilarities in the main diagonal). These $n$ objects can be represented as cardinal coordinates in a geometric space by reducing the number of dimensions.

For example, an individual can express her/his priorities for a set of commodities ($S$), such as sporting goods, by giving a complete ranking of the commodities concerned so that this ranking corresponds to the individual's preferences. Given this ranking procedure, it can be assumed that each commodity now possesses a set of attributes ($R$), the relative presence of which has led the individual to scale them in some way. If there are $n$ attributes then any given object can be regarded as existing in $n$-dimensional geometric space. Therefore the quantity of each attribute perceived by the individual and belonging to a particular commodity can be related to the corresponding geometric coordinate (Nijkamp, 1979:101).

The stated relationship ($R$) defined on a set of objects ($S$) provides a set of similarities or dissimilarities between pairs of objects. MDS attempts to match the observed dissimilarities with a notional space of maximum dimensionality. The calculations for this involve an iterative procedure.

A pioneering example of MDS as applied by geographers is the work of Rushton, who applied MDS to data on the towns selected by a random sample of rural people in Iowa for their major grocery purchases (Rushton, 1966, 1969a,b, 1981). The alternative opportunities presented to these shoppers were represented by data on the location and size of all Iowa towns with a population greater than 50. From a graph of town population versus distance to that town (from the location of a shopper) 30 different locational types were recognised.

A measure of the similarity between any two of the locational types is the degree to which one is preferred by persons who can choose both types. Thus the data supplied by the sample of shoppers gives a matrix of information as shown in Table 12.11, which can be combined to generate Table 12.12. From the latter can be computed the probability $P_{jpi}$ that the $j$th locational type is preferred to the $i$th locational type.

If $T_{ij}$ is the cell total in the $i$th row and the $j$th column of Table 12.12 and $T_{ji}$ is the cell total in the $j$th row and the $i$th column, then:

$$P_{jpi} = \frac{T_{ij}}{T_{ij} + T_{ji}}$$

where $T_{ij} = 0$, $T_{ji} = 0$, $P_{jpi}$ and $P_{ipj}$ are undefined;

$$T_{ji} = 0, \quad T_{ij} > 0, \qquad P_{jpi} = 1$$

$$T_{ij} = 0, \quad T_{ji} > 0, \qquad P_{jpi} = 0$$

Therefore, whenever $T_{ji} + T_{ij} > 0$, then $P_{jpi} + P_{ipj} = 1$ and $P_{jpi} = 1 - P_{ipj}$. From this, Table 12.13 can be constructed, in which the order of both the columns and rows represents an ordering of locational types from the preference data according to the ratio in the last column of this table. The numbers in this column show the proportion of times the locational type for the row was preferred to the other types.

In Table 12.13 $P_{jpi} = 0.5 = P_{ipj}$ for maximum perceived similarity between any two locational types $i$ and $j$. Any departure from a value of 0.5 reflects an increase in the perceived dissimilarity between the locational types in question. Therefore a measure of perceived similarity, $d_{ij}$, is given by

$$d_{ij} = |P_{jpi} - 0.5|$$

where $d_{ij} =$ the distance in perceived dissimilarity between locational types $i$ and $j$.

From these proximity measures a scale can be constructed on which all locational types may be positioned. Rushton's approach to this closely followed the work of Kruskal (1964) on metric MDS, and Shepard (1962) on MDS with an unknown distance function. The approach recognises that, in certain circumstances, it is possible to derive from ordinal data approximate metric scales.

From a matrix of dissimilarities the intention is to represent the $n$ locational types as $n$ points in $m$-dimensional space, with the inter-point distances ($d_{ij}$)

corresponding to the observed degree of dissimilarity between the $n$ locational types. Given perfect correspondence, then if locational type $i$ is more similar to type $j$ than it is to type $k$, the corresponding inter-point distances would satisfy $\delta_{ij} > \delta_{ik}$: $d_{ij} > d_{jk}$ for all $i$, $j$ and $k$, where $\delta_{ij} =$ any of the measures of dissimilarity.

The simplest arrangement would be if the locational types could be arranged in a one-dimensional space with the ranking of inter-point distances corresponding to the ranking of dissimilarities in the probability matrix:

$$d_{jk} = \left[ \sum_{r=1}^{n} (P_{rj} - P_{rk})^2 \right]$$

where $x_i, \ldots, x_n =$ locational types expressed in orthogonal coordinates by:

$$x_i = (x_{i1}, \ldots, x_{i3}, \ldots, x_{it})$$

$d_{jk} =$ the distance from $x_j$ to $x_{k}$, $jk =$ indices for any two points, $r =$ an index for axes, $n =$ the number of orthogonal axes, and $P_{rj} =$ the projection of point $j$ on axis $r$.

If there is correspondence between the inter-point distances and the dissimilarities, then if the distances are ranked from smallest to largest, the same order of the locational types is maintained, i.e.

$$d_{i_1 j_1} < d_{i_2 j_2} < d_{i_3 j_3} < \ldots < d_{i_M j_M}$$

where there are $M$ dissimilarities, and $M = n(n-1)/2$, with $n =$ the number of locational types.

The locational types could be depicted graphically on a scattergraph of dissimilarity versus distance, though a monotonic relationship between the two is rarely achieved and so a goodness-of-fit test is required. Kruskal (1964) proposed one involving the calculation of *stress* ($s$),

$$s = \sqrt{\left( \frac{\sum_{i<j}(d_{ij} - \hat{d}_{ij})^2}{\sum_{i<j} d_{ij}^2} \right)}$$

*Table 12.11*    Revealed Space-Preference-Raw-Data Matrix by Respondents

| Household ID | Locational Type | | | | | | | | | | | | | | |
|---|---|---|---|---|---|---|---|---|---|---|---|---|---|---|---|
| | 1 | 2 | 3 | 4 | 5 | 6 | 7 | 8 | 9 | 10 | 11 | 12 | 13 | 14 | 15 |
| 1 | ○ | ○ | ○ | ○ | | | | | ○ | ○ | | | ○ | | ○ |
| 2 | ○ | ○ | ○ | ○ | ○ | ○ | ○ | | | | ○ | | | | |
| 3 | ○ | ○ | ○ | ○ | ○ | ○ | | | ○ | ○ | ○ | | ● | ○ | ○ |
| 3 | ○ | ○ | ○ | ○ | ○ | ○ | | | ○ | ○ | ● | | ● | ○ | ○ |
| 4 | ○ | ○ | ○ | ○ | ○ | | | | ○ | ○ | | ○ | | | ○ |
| 6 | ○ | ○ | ○ | ○ | ○ | | | | | ○ | | | ○ | ○ | |
| 9 | | ○ | ○ | ○ | ○ | | ○ | | ○ | | | | | | |
| 10 | | ○ | ○ | ○ | ○ | ○ | | | ○ | | | | | | |
| 11 | | ○ | ○ | ○ | ○ | | | | ○ | ○ | ○ | | | | |
| 12 | ○ | ○ | ○ | ○ | ○ | | ○ | ○ | | | | | | | |
| 13 | ○ | ○ | ● | ○ | ○ | | ○ | | ○ | ○ | | | | | |
| 14 | ○ | | ○ | ○ | ○ | ○ | | | ○ | | | | | | |
| 15 | ○ | ○ | ○ | ○ | ○ | | ● | | ○ | ○ | | | | | |
| 16 | ○ | ○ | ○ | ○ | ○ | | ● | ○ | ○ | | | | | | |
| 18 | | ○ | ○ | ○ | ○ | | ○ | ○ | ○ | | | | | | |
| 19 | ○ | | ○ | ○ | ○ | | ○ | ○ | | | | | | | ○ |
| 20 | ○ | ○ | ○ | ○ | ○ | | ○ | ○ | | | | | | | |
| 21 | ○ | ○ | ○ | ○ | ○ | | | | | ○ | | ○ | ○ | ○ | |
| 24 | ○ | ○ | ○ | ○ | ○ | ○ | ○ | | | ○ | | | | | |
| 25 | ○ | ○ | ○ | ○ | ○ | | | | | ○ | ○ | ● | | ○ | ○ |
| 26 | ○ | ○ | ○ | ○ | ○ | | | | | ○ | ● | | ○ | | ○ |
| 27 | ○ | ○ | ○ | ○ | ○ | | | | ○ | | | ● | ○ | ○ | |
| 28 | | ○ | ○ | ○ | ○ | | | | | | ● | | ○ | ○ | ○ |
| 29 | | ○ | ○ | ○ | ○ | | | | | | | ○ | ○ | ○ | |
| 30 | | ○ | ○ | ○ | ○ | | ○ | | | ○ | ● | | ○ | | |
| 32 | ○ | | ○ | ○ | ○ | ○ | ○ | | | ○ | | ● | | ○ | |
| 32 | ● | | ○ | ○ | ○ | ○ | ○ | | | ○ | | ● | | ○ | |
| 33 | ● | ○ | ○ | ○ | ○ | | | | | | | | ○ | ○ | ○ |
| 34 | ○ | ○ | ○ | ○ | ○ | | ○ | | ○ | | | ○ | | ○ | ○ |
| 35 | ○ | ○ | ○ | ○ | ○ | | | | ○ | | | | ○ | ○ | ○ |

where $\hat{d}_{ij}$ = the minimum distance between $x_i$ and $x_j$ that will satisfy the same (monotonic) relationship.

Kruskal also developed an algorithm for finding the orthogonal coordinates for the $n$ points so that, for any number of dimensions, $s$ is minimised. If some of the dissimilarities are missing then the terms corresponding to the missing dissimilarities are left out of both the numerator and the denominator when calculating $s$. Using Kruskal's algorithm, Rushton generated Table 12.14, which can be translated into Figure 12.4 as isopleths when population size and distance are plotted against one another. The surface depicted in Figure 12.4 is termed an *indifference surface of spatial choice*. Any individual experiences equal indifference towards any two towns placed along one of the isolines and would experience most satisfaction (least indifference) from a town on the very highest point of the surface.

|  |  |  |  |  | Locational Type |  |  |  |  |  |  |  |  |  |
|---|---|---|---|---|---|---|---|---|---|---|---|---|---|---|
| 16 | 17 | 18 | 19 | 20 | 21 | 22 | 23 | 24 | 25 | 26 | 27 | 28 | 29 | 30 |
|  | • |  |  |  |  |  |  |  | ° |  |  |  |  |  |
|  |  |  | • |  |  |  |  |  |  |  |  |  |  |  |
|  |  |  | ° |  |  |  |  |  |  |  |  |  |  |  |
|  |  |  | ° |  |  |  |  |  |  |  |  |  |  |  |
|  |  | • |  |  |  |  |  |  |  |  |  |  |  |  |
| • |  |  |  |  |  |  |  |  | ° |  |  |  |  |  |
|  |  | ° |  |  |  |  | • |  |  |  |  |  |  |  |
|  |  |  | ° | ° |  |  | • |  |  |  |  |  |  |  |
|  | ° |  |  | ° |  |  | • |  |  |  |  |  |  |  |
|  |  |  | ° |  |  |  | • |  |  |  |  |  |  |  |
|  |  | ° | ° | ° |  | ° | ° |  |  |  |  |  |  |  |
|  |  |  | ° | ° |  |  | • |  |  |  |  |  |  |  |
|  |  |  | ° | ° |  |  |  |  |  |  |  |  |  |  |
|  |  | ° |  | ° |  |  |  |  |  |  |  |  |  |  |
|  | • |  |  | ° |  |  |  |  |  |  |  |  |  |  |
|  |  |  | ° | • |  |  |  |  |  |  |  |  |  |  |
|  |  | ° |  |  |  |  |  |  |  |  |  |  |  | ° |
|  | • |  |  |  |  |  |  |  |  |  |  |  |  |  |
|  | ° |  |  |  |  |  |  |  |  |  |  |  |  | ° |
|  |  |  | ° |  |  |  |  | ° |  |  |  |  | • |  |
|  |  |  | ° |  |  |  |  |  |  |  |  |  |  |  |
|  |  | ° |  |  |  |  | ° |  |  |  |  |  | ° |  |
|  |  |  |  |  |  |  |  |  | ° |  |  |  | • |  |
|  |  |  |  |  | ° | ° | • |  |  |  |  |  |  |  |

° = Locational type patronised
• = Locational type rejected
Blank = locational type not present

*Source*: Rushton (1981:74–5).

There are a number of problems associated with this method:

(a) *Intransitivity*. This is present in situations where locational type $i$ is preferred to type $j$, and type $j$ is preferred to type $k$, but type $k$ is revealed by the MDS to be preferred to type $i$. If this *cyclic triplet* or intransitivity occurs to any degree then it becomes increasingly unrealistic to refer to a uni-dimensional general preference structure. The extent of intransitiv- ity can be measured using Coombs's (1964) formula for what he termed the *coefficient of consistency*. This uses the data from Table 12.14, transformed into binary form: $1 = P_{jpi} > 0.5$ (complete transitivity) and $0 = P_{jpi} < 0.5$ (maximum inconsistency). The co- efficient of consistency = 1 minus the ratio between the observed number of cyclic triplets and the maxi- mum number of possible cyclic triplets. For Rushton's data the coefficient = 0.985. The consistency or lack

*Table 12.12*    Segment of the Revealed Preference Data Matrix

(Cells show number of times sample households preferred column locational type to row type)

| Household | Locational Type | | | | | | | | | |
|---|---|---|---|---|---|---|---|---|---|---|
| | *1* | *2* | *3* | *4* | *5* | *6* | *7* | *8* | *9* | *10* |
| 1 | 29.8 | 9.0 | 3.0 | 1.0 | 0.0 | 27.0 | 15.3 | 3.0 | 1.0 | 0.0 |
| 2 | 127.7 | 21.5 | 2.0 | 2.0 | 0.0 | 90.5 | 55.3 | 12.0 | 0.0 | 0.0 |
| 3 | 180.0 | 27.5 | 11.0 | 0.0 | 0.0 | 188.5 | 97.5 | 22.0 | 3.0 | 0.0 |
| 4 | 243.3 | 36.0 | 8.0 | 9.0 | 0.0 | 228.0 | 137.3 | 14.0 | 8.0 | 0.0 |
| 5 | 209.8 | 37.0 | 8.0 | 5.0 | 0.0 | 223.0 | 133.3 | 18.0 | 8.0 | 0.0 |
| 6 | 5.5 | 0.0 | 1.0 | 0.0 | 0.0 | 4.0 | 5.0 | 0.0 | 0.0 | 0.0 |
| 7 | 30.5 | 5.5 | 1.0 | 0.0 | 0.0 | 36.5 | 17.3 | 1.0 | 2.0 | 0.0 |
| 8 | 41.7 | 7.0 | 1.0 | 1.0 | 0.0 | 41.0 | 33.0 | 3.0 | 1.0 | 0.0 |
| 9 | 66.7 | 5.0 | 4.0 | 0.0 | 0.0 | 63.0 | 34.0 | 2.0 | 0.0 | 0.0 |
| 10 | 65.8 | 10.5 | 2.0 | 2.0 | 0.0 | 51.5 | 34.8 | 5.0 | 0.0 | 0.0 |
| 11 | 2.5 | 0.0 | 0.0 | 0.0 | 0.0 | 1.0 | 0.0 | 0.0 | 0.0 | 0.0 |
| 12 | 8.5 | 3.0 | 0.0 | 0.0 | 0.0 | 10.0 | 3.0 | 0.0 | 0.0 | 0.0 |
| 13 | 23.3 | 1.5 | 0.0 | 1.0 | 0.0 | 24.5 | 17.0 | 0.0 | 1.0 | 0.0 |
| 14 | 32.8 | 6.0 | 0.0 | 1.0 | 0.0 | 46.5 | 16.5 | 2.0 | 1.0 | 0.0 |
| 15 | 43.8 | 3.0 | 0.0 | 1.0 | 0.0 | 35.0 | 15.3 | 0.0 | 0.0 | 0.0 |
| 16 | 0.0 | 0.0 | 0.0 | 0.0 | 0.0 | 0.0 | 0.0 | 0.0 | 0.0 | 0.0 |
| 17 | 3.0 | 0.5 | 0.0 | 0.0 | 0.0 | 8.0 | 4.5 | 1.0 | 0.0 | 0.0 |
| 18 | 16.6 | 3.0 | 2.0 | 1.0 | 0.0 | 13.5 | 6.3 | 1.0 | 0.0 | 0.0 |
| 19 | 16.5 | 0.5 | 3.0 | 0.0 | 0.0 | 25.0 | 10.0 | 2.0 | 0.0 | 0.0 |
| 20 | 9.3 | 4.5 | 1.0 | 0.0 | 0.0 | 12.0 | 10.3 | 2.0 | 0.0 | 0.0 |
| 21 | 0.0 | 0.0 | 0.0 | 0.0 | 0.0 | 2.0 | 0.0 | 0.0 | 0.0 | 0.0 |
| 22 | 3.0 | 0.0 | 0.0 | 0.0 | 0.0 | 6.0 | 2.0 | 0.0 | 0.0 | 0.0 |
| 23 | 13.0 | 1.5 | 1.0 | 0.0 | 0.0 | 5.0 | 5.0 | 0.0 | 0.0 | 0.0 |
| 24 | 16.0 | 2.0 | 1.0 | 0.0 | 0.0 | 8.5 | 6.5 | 1.0 | 0.0 | 0.0 |
| 25 | 14.3 | 2.0 | 0.0 | 0.0 | 0.0 | 11.0 | 8.3 | 3.0 | 0.0 | 0.0 |
| 26 | 0.0 | 0.0 | 0.0 | 0.0 | 0.0 | 0.0 | 0.0 | 0.0 | 0.0 | 0.0 |
| 27 | 2.0 | 0.0 | 0.0 | 1.0 | 0.0 | 1.0 | 1.0 | 0.0 | 1.0 | 0.0 |
| 28 | 2.0 | 1.0 | 0.0 | 0.0 | 0.0 | 5.5 | 3.0 | 0.0 | 0.0 | 0.0 |
| 29 | 7.3 | 0.0 | 0.0 | 0.0 | 0.0 | 13.0 | 7.3 | 0.0 | 0.0 | 0.0 |
| 30 | 13.3 | 1.0 | 0.0 | 0.0 | 0.0 | 4.5 | 5.3 | 0.0 | 0.0 | 0.0 |

*Source*: Rushton (1981:76–7).

of it can be illustrated in Rushton's example where locational type 16 gives more satisfaction than type 11 on the calculated scale (Table 12.13), whereas Table 12.14 shows that, on the occasions when an individual made a choice between types 11 and 16, type 11 was always preferred. Such situations are most likely to arise when there are just a few individuals involved in stating a preference regarding the locational types.

(b) *Aggregation.* Proximity measures are indicators of the frequency with which individuals disagreed about a common scale; they are evidence of inter-personal consistency of spatial behaviour. However, the preferences of a single individual may differ from the behaviour summarised by the scale, as, for example, the scale can represent A as higher than B despite the fact that a minority of individuals prefer B to A. So the aggregate character of the scale must be appreciated. However, in some investigations the focus may be upon those individuals who do not conform to the aggregate scale.

(c) *Temporal change.* An individual's preference may change over time in response to the constantly

*Table 12.13*    Probability that Column Locational Type is Preferred to Row Type

(Segment only shown)

|    | 21 | 16 | 27 | 11 | 26 | 28 | 22 | 23 | 17 |
|----|----|----|----|----|----|----|----|----|----|
| 21 | −1.00 | −1.00 | −1.00 | −1.00 | −1.00 | −1.00 | −1.00 | 0.00 | −1.00 |
| 16 | −1.00 | −1.00 | −1.00 | 0.00 | 0.00 | 0.00 | 0.00 | 0.17 | 0.00 |
| 27 | −1.00 | −1.00 | −1.00 | 0.40 | 1.00 | 0.25 | 0.00 | 0.00 | 0.00 |
| 11 | −1.00 | 0.00 | 0.60 | −1.00 | −1.00 | 0.56 | 0.00 | 0.11 | 0.40 |
| 26 | −1.00 | 1.00 | 0.00 | −1.00 | −1.00 | 0.00 | 0.00 | 0.00 | 0.50 |
| 28 | −1.00 | 1.00 | 0.75 | 0.44 | 1.00 | −1.00 | 1.00 | 0.67 | 0.13 |
| 22 | −1.00 | 1.00 | 1.00 | 1.00 | 1.00 | 0.00 | −1.00 | 0.00 | 1.00 |
| 23 | 1.00 | 0.83 | 1.00 | 0.89 | 1.00 | 0.33 | 1.00 | −1.00 | 0.38 |
| 17 | −1.00 | 1.00 | 1.00 | 0.60 | 0.50 | 0.88 | 0.00 | 0.63 | −1.00 |

*Source*: Rushton (1981:78–9).

*Table 12.14*    Scale Values for the Locational Types

| Rank | Locational Type | Scale Value |
|------|-----------------|-------------|
| 1 | 21 | −1.311 |
| 2 | 16 | −1.523 |
| 3 | 27 | −1.382 |
| 4 | 11 | −0.991 |
| 5 | 26 | −1.624 |
| 6 | 28 | −0.876 |
| 7 | 22 | −1.160 |
| 8 | 23 | −0.590 |
| 9 | 17 | −0.719 |
| 10 | 29 | −0.668 |
| 11 | 6 | −0.725 |
| 12 | 12 | −0.481 |
| 13 | 18 | −0.321 |
| 14 | 24 | −0.020 |
| 15 | 1 | −0.163 |
| 16 | 7 | −0.075 |
| 17 | 13 | −0.217 |
| 18 | 30 | −0.009 |
| 19 | 25 | 0.378 |
| 20 | 20 | 0.532 |
| 21 | 8 | 0.752 |
| 22 | 2 | 0.551 |
| 23 | 19 | 0.812 |
| 24 | 3 | 1.114 |
| 25 | 4 | 1.174 |
| 26 | 9 | 1.226 |
| 27 | 15 | 1.438 |
| 28 | 14 | 1.596 |
| 29 | 10 | 1.517 |
| 30 | 5 | 1.725 |

*Source*: Rushton (1981:82).

changing spatial environment. Therefore it is possible to add a temporal dimension into investigations of preference, not only demonstrating the nature of the changing preference structure but also examining the contributory factors.

(d) *Surrogates*. It must be recognised that the stated preferences are surrogates for more abstract factors that influence behaviour. The preferences represent the joint effects of these factors (known as *conjoint measurement*), though it may be difficult to isolate the individual factors.

(e) *Error*. The scaling model described is a deterministic one which makes no provision for error or aberrant response, though the latter may occur. Developing a suitable goodness-of-fit test for comparing actual and model behaviour can be problematic.

Golledge and Rushton (1972) distinguished two types of problems to which MDS techniques are applicable:

1. *Simple space problems*. These refer to goods (or *stimulus space*) on the basis of which only metric discrepancies between objects have to be assessed. Examples of these problems include the consumer's image of competitive products; the perception of the strength of mutually competing firms; the policy-maker's perceived differences in levels of regional well-being; a new firm's image of alternative locations; and a tourist's image of the quality of

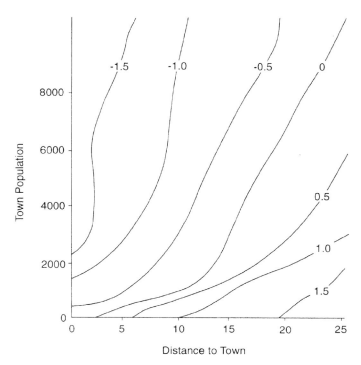

*Figure 12.4*  Spatial Preference Structure and Indifference Surface of Spatial Choice (for grocery purchases). (*Source*: Rushton, 1981:83)

tourist attractions. Analysis of these problems is often termed *proximity analysis*. Proximity analysis is applied to the situation in which there are *I* individuals $(i = 1, \ldots, I)$ who judge a set of *n* objects, with *k* attributes, that are common to all *I* individuals, underlying the perception.

2. *Joint space problems*. These are more complex as, in addition to the attributes of an object, different priorities or evaluations of the object among different subjects are made. Examples include analysis of the properties of a shopping centre which attracts spatially dispersed consumers; analysis of the main factors determining the perceived attractiveness of recreational areas; and analysis of the impacts of changes in the attributes of a good upon a consumer's perception. Analysis of these types of problems is sometimes termed *preference analysis*.

MDS was also used in studies of consumer beha-

viour in the early 1980s (e.g. Hudson, 1981; Spencer, 1980). However, more recent work on consumer behaviour has recognised the influence of constraints upon choice that are exercised by personal, structural, societal or institutional factors (e.g. Burnett and Hanson, 1982; Desbaretes, 1983). This work has pointed out that many of the traditional models that allocated consumers to shops ignored constraints that operate on individuals and also the differential operation of sets of constraints (Sheppard, 1980). This has led to the development of new approaches emphasising individual choice rather than the traditional aggregate models of the central place, gravity and entropy formulations (Pipkin, 1981). For nearly 20 years it has also stimulated approaches accounting for the dynamic aspects of behaviour, early examples being the work of Crouchley et al (1982) and Martin et al (1978), and more recent ones including Timmermans and Borgers (1993).

When first developed MDS was relatively restricted as it dealt with large amounts of information per respondent and focused on metric approaches. However, following work by Shepard (1962, 1964) in the early 1960s, MDS has been applied to the types of data commonly encountered by survey analysts, using non-metric methods as set out by Kruskal (1964) and extending beyond a reliance upon Euclidean distance (e.g. Golledge and Raynor, 1982). One further significant development has been to tackle a commonly occurring situation in social surveys, namely the use of samples including subgroups that are quite different in their characteristics (e.g. different means, variances and covariance). With subgroups that are quite distinctive, an aggregation of their similarity matrices can simply eliminate the systematic differences. This raises the question of how the subgroups can be compared or referred to a common set of coordinates. This has been achieved through the development of an *individual differences scaling* (INDSCAL) model, produced by Carroll and Chang (1970) in which each individual's data are regarded as being the result of applying her/his own "subjective metric" to the "group stimulus space" defined by all individuals. The individual's similarity judgements can be represented as a weighted distance in the group space and INDSCAL can therefore be a simple generalisation of the basic distance model, and can be applied in analyses of the pairwise similarity judgements given by a set of individuals (Coxon and Jones, 1977).

## CONJOINT ANALYSIS

The problem of joint effects of two or more independent variables upon a dependent variable may be tackled using *conjoint analysis*, which has commonly been used in analyses of choice and preference behaviour. For example, Joseph et al (1989) considered people's preferences for different residences in terms of the joint effect of variables such as lot size, house size and price (see Figure 12.5). Stated preferences were analysed to generate an overall measure of an individual's derived "utility" from a particular alternative (see Timmermans, 1984).

Analysis using conjoint measurement techniques begins with information collected experimentally through respondent evaluation of a number of hypothetical choice alternatives that comprise specified levels of attributes which are assumed to be instrumental in the evaluation of a particular consumer good. This preference information is then transformed to produce interval-scale estimates of the relative utility of each attribute level (Timmermans, 1984). As Joseph et al (1989:49) write:

> Transformations are performed with a predetermined combination rule which defines how the relative utility estimates for the specified levels of each attribute are combined into an overall measure of an individual's utility from a particular alternative, such that the derived combinations will account for the individual's original preference orderings of the experimental choice alternatives.

Conjoint measurement can use a number of models of preference formation (Green and Srinivasan, 1978), the most easily interpreted and robust for use with residential preferences being the *part-worth model* (Phipps and Carter, 1984, 1985). This model assumes that:

$$U(x) = f_x(x_k)$$

where $U(x)$ = the utility derived from good $x$; $f_x$ = a function representing the part-worth of the different levels of each attribute ($x_k$) used in the evaluation of a particular multi-attribute alternative, good $x$; and

$$U(x) = U(x_1) + U(x_2) + \ldots + U(x_k)$$

The latter equation demonstrates the additive relationship between the total utility derived from a multi-attribute alternative and the utilities associated with component attributes. However, multiplicative formulations of the model have also been used in which an individual's total utility from a particular alternative is calculated as the product of the part-worth utilities of each attribute included in the evaluation (Louviere, 1981; Timmermans et al, 1984). The multiplicative model may assume inter-attribute interactions that do not exist and may pose problems if a certain level of a given attribute is zero as multiplication for an alternative containing that particular attribute level will yield a zero for the overall utility which may not be realistic (see Veldhuizen and Timmermans, 1984).

The analysis proceeds by first specifying a number of attributes for which respondents have to express preferences. Usually different levels can be specified for each attribute in order to reflect the possibilities available to the respondents. In selecting an appropriate number of attribute levels, a balance has to be reached between the realism afforded by a large number of attribute levels and the danger of presenting the respondent with too many judgements to make. Respondents are also offered hypothetical choice alternatives in one of two ways:

1. *The full-profile or concept-evaluation approach.* This uses complete sets of attribute levels arranged into hypothetical "profiles" of a given multi-attribute alternative. As described by Joseph et al (1989:50), "Respondents are presented with a number of different profiles and asked to rank them in terms of their overall preference for each; and these profile rankings provide the input data from which a respondent's utilities for the various levels of each attribute are calculated."
2. *The pairwise trade-off approach.* This requires respondents to consider pairwise combinations of attributes. For example, if two attributes each possess two levels then the respondent will be considering a matrix that represents the four possible combinations of the two attributes. Each cell in the matrix is ranked, from most to least preferred, and this provides input data for the calculation of attribute utilities.

The full-profile approach tends to have greater realism in modelling the choice decision. This realism derives from greater elaboration and the ability to tolerate lack of independence between attributes. However, if the number of attributes used in profiles is large this can make the full-profile approach problematic. In practice, similar results have been achieved applying either of the two methods (e.g. Segal, 1982), especially if alternatives are presented to the respondents in a well-structured manner, perhaps by arbitrarily reducing the number of cells in a matrix that are required to be placed in rank order.

Joseph et al (1989) examined consumer preferences for rural residences in rural southern Ontario where rural non-farm residential development has been extensive since the late 1960s. Six attributes were identified to represent the key evaluative criteria of potential rural residences: lot size, house size, location, price, location on or off a school bus route, and location on or off a paved road. These attributes are not an exhaustive list but were judged to be important to nearly all rural purchasers. The attributes and their associated levels are shown in Table 12.15. Out of the possible 15 pairwise combinations available for the trade-off matrices (alternative 2 above), a nine-matrix

*Table 12.15* Attributes and Attribute Levels for Conjoint Analysis of Consumer Preferences for Rural Residences in Southern Ontario

| Attribute | Level | |
|---|---|---|
| 1. Lot size | small (< 2 acres) medium (2–9.9 acres) large (> 10 acres) | |
| 2. House size | three bedrooms four bedrooms five or more bedrooms | |
| 3. Location | isolated | no adjacent residences, only a few nearby |
| | scattered | a few adjacent or nearby residences |
| | village | other residences adjacent and nearby |
| 4. Price | $75 000 $100 000 $125 000 $150 000 | |
| 5. School bus | on route off route | |
| 6. Roads | paved unpaved | |

*Source*: Joseph et al (1989:52).

subset of attribute combinations was adopted for greater ease of use by the respondents who were individuals in the market for a permanent rural residence (Figure 12.5).

For details of the calculations involved in this conjoint analysis, including various stages not shown here, see Joseph et al (1989). Their results were expressed in terms of mean estimated utilities for attribute levels. For all respondents the most preferred attribute-level combination was a three-to-four-bedroom house, on a medium-sized lot, in an isolated location, costing $75 000, on both a school bus route and a paved road. However, this mean utility result can be probed further by examining what the respondents are willing to trade off for particular preferences

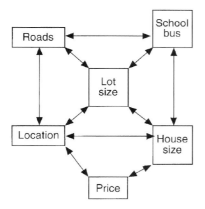

*Figure 12.5*  Pairwise Attribute Combinations in Analysis of Consumer Preferences for Rural Residences. (Based on Joseph et al, 1989:53)

(Table 12.16). For example, in this case would a rural homebuyer trade off a particular service characteristic in return for a larger and more private lot? This can be investigated by calculating the utilities associated with different combinations of attribute levels, e.g. by preparing a matrix including lot size, location, price, house size and service provision. This enabled Joseph et al (1989:58) to conclude that respondents were more willing to pay for isolation than for large lots. Smaller lots, especially those in villages, only became attractive if various services were available there that were denied to larger, more isolated properties.

Income variations can be considered by examining the mean utilities of attributes by income. In this case no significant differences occurred between income groups on the attributes of lot size, location, school bus and roads, but this was not true with respect to price and house size. Not surprisingly those on higher incomes had a significant preference for more expensive property, with four bedrooms being the optimal size.

This example provides a good guide to the strengths and weaknesses of this particular technique. It demonstrates that it can be used to provide insights not only to the preferences of a group of respondents but also to behaviour that is of direct relevance to interested parties: developers, planners, policy-makers and real estate agents. It is not a difficult procedure to operate and has a high degree of functionality. However, its weakness is that it places tremendous emphasis upon the validity of a stated preference by respondents who would not normally express their preferences in the structured manner demanded by a researcher. Whilst

*Table 12.16*  A Trade-off Matrix for the Attributes Price and Location for a Single Respondent for Conjoint Analysis of Consumer Preferences for Rural Residences in Southern Ontario

| Locations | Price | | | | Sum of Ranks |
|---|---|---|---|---|---|
| | $150 000 | $125 000 | $100 000 | $75 000 | |
| Isolated | 12 | 11 | 10 | 9 | 42 |
| Scattered | 4 | 3 | 1 | 2 | 10 |
| Village | 8 | 7 | 6 | 5 | 26 |
| Sum of ranks | 24 | 21 | 17 | 16 | 78 |

*Source*: Joseph et al (1989:52).

individuals may have certain vague ideas about the particular location and house type they desire, even in an active search for a new home a strong array of constraints can operate to limit an individual's choice and to reduce the amount of systematic evaluation that occurs. Hence, great care has to be taken both in the manner in which information is elicited from respondents and also in the conclusions that are reached regarding the nature of decision-making on the basis of mean utilities. As an alternative, many human geographers have turned away from reliance upon answers provided to surveys and instead have utilised in-depth qualitative methods first developed in other social science disciplines.

# 13

# QUALITATIVE METHODS

## FROM QUANTIFICATION TO QUALIFICATION

> Quantitative analysis and model building, with its pre-occupation with the geometry of spatial form and its abstraction from social relations, was the geography of the years of public faith in economic growth, cybernetics, technological solutions and managerial rationality.
>
> (D.M. Smith, 1984:128)

In many ways the reaction against quantitative methods within human geography from the late 1960s can be seen as a reflection of the times. The limitations of a rather narrow basis for enquiry, as typified by the quantitative geography of the 1960s, were recognised in a general context by Kuhn who identified the trap that "overwhelming concern with paradigm-directed research ... may lead the scientist to neglect pressing social problems" (Young, 1979:207). Meanwhile, in the USA the rise of opposition to the Vietnam War, concern over racial discrimination and social inequities prompted academic reaction to conservatism and the status quo which quantitative methods were deemed to be supporting. At best, critics could argue that these methods were not playing a role in any critique of capitalism and imperialism.

New approaches were found to undertake this critique, some of them falling under the umbrella of "radical geography", generally founded on Marxism (Harvey, 1973), and others with a more liberal or humanist leaning (Ley and Samuels, 1978). The Marxist and humanist critiques both appear to repre-sent a type of "anti-scientific ground-swell" (Roszack, 1973), as well as being part of a widespread scepticism about the established formula for scientific enquiry that has now become prominent throughout the social sciences.

As attacks upon the positivistic "spatial science" of the 1960s appeared, it was argued by some that geography as the study of spatial relationships was an incomplete and unsatisfactory view of the discipline, telling only part of a complex story. It was also recognised that human geographers had not been particularly effective in isolating "the spatial variable" from other commonly encountered variables. For example, Harvey (1973:40–1) illustrates the difficulty geographers were having with spatial variables, with the example of marriage distances and social class. Many studies have shown that most marriages take place between people who live in the same neighbourhoods, but most marriages also take place between people of the same social class. However, as people of the same class tend to live in close proximity to one another, which is the most important variable in determining marriage distance, the spatial one or the social one? And what is the nature of the interrelationship between space and social class?

In retrospect perhaps the most damning criticism of geographers using statistical techniques and mathematical models in the 1960s and 1970s is that the types of decision being studied and modelled, for example the choice of shopping centres, are trivial when compared with the major decisions that shape urban morphology. Yet these major decisions, by banks,

property developers, real estate agents, building societies and governments, are frequently not amenable to
quantitative analysis dependent on large samples and
standard statistical tests.

Similarly, it is possible to argue that political influence upon spatial distributions is manifest, but the
exercise of politics via power and influence, conflict
and compromise is also not amenable to analysis using
the scientific method. Therefore, with the exception of
the analysis of election results (e.g. Johnston, 1988), it
is not surprising that political geography in particular
has eschewed the use of statistical techniques.

Until the 1970s for all but a handful of geographers
the phrase "techniques in human geography" would
have been interpreted as "quantitative techniques" or
"statistical methods". For the past two decades,
though, geographers' engagement with new philosophies has brought a recognition of the merits of a wide
range of other methods, mainly qualitative in nature,
initially associated with the emergence of *humanistic
geography.*

The growth of humanistic geography during the
1970s was in part a reaction against the dehumanising
aspects of positivist-based enquiry (Entrikin, 1976)
and also a direct alternative to the emphasis upon
structural forces in Marxist geography (Duncan and
Ley, 1982). It developed in conjunction with behavioural geography (see Gold and Goodey, 1984), but
diverged as geographers like Ley, Yi-Fu Tuan and
Buttimer questioned the supposed objectivity of positivism (and behavioural geography) and stressed the
importance of *human agency* rather than a more
narrow concern with decision-making processes. It
was the development of a geography that did not refer
to people merely as aggregate groups, but which
sought to portray human experience and expression. It
recognised that there was a social construction to
place, space and landscape which transcended spatial
patterns and structures; and it sought to capture this
construction by use of new methods that could provide
insights to human experience. These methods included
field techniques borrowed from the anthropologists
and others developed in the humanities (Meinig,
1983). General theories of societal and spatial organisation were eschewed in favour of a concern for the

particular and the specific, though with work underpinned by theories, for example cultural theory and,
later, historical materialism (Cosgrove, 1989b). A
recurrent theme was "difference" between people and
places as opposed to the generalities and law-seeking
of the Quantitative Revolution, and hence the specificity of experience was investigated via texts and landscapes (Cosgrove, 1984; Daniels, 1985). Ultimately
the "rediscovery" of culture by humanistic geographers has given rise to a rebirth of cultural geography,
but especially via engagement with new theories,
including postmodernism, that has made it increasingly difficult in the 1990s to refer to a distinctive
humanistic geography (see Buttimer, 1990). However,
many of the methods first championed in human
geography by humanistic geographers in the 1970s
and early 1980s remain important within the discipline.

Qualitative techniques have formed a central part of
geographical investigations that have broadened the
focus of research away from the spatial science agenda
of the 1960s. The increased use of these techniques by
geographers has reflected the emergence of a "search
for something less mechanical and more in tune with
the complexity of human existence than is provided by
positivism and structuralism" (Eyles and Smith,
1988:xi). Therefore there has been a perceived need to
replace both the techniques associated with the Quantitative Revolution and the relatively crude Marxian
belief in "mega-structural forces" (discussed in Chapter 14). The replacements included qualitative and
*interpretive techniques* traditionally associated with
anthropology and sociology (e.g. Silverman, 1985;
Strauss, 1987), which also contrasted with many quantitative methods in that they focused on individuals
rather than aggregates. In making this contrast, humanists argued that too much attention had been devoted
by geographers to the "labour market" or to the
"industrial enterprise" at the expense of referring to
the people who comprise them (Lowe and Short,
1990).

Qualitative or interpretive methods generally operate on the basis that the "natural" order of reality is
seen, conceived of and understood in different ways
by different groups and individuals (Silverman, 1993).

It is this variety of views that is a central concern to the social scientist, and therefore interpretive methods are required which can give special attention to the knowledge and understanding of individuals and groups. As Pickles (1988) argues, constructing social knowledge is as much a process of interpretation as of understanding. There is a close link here with the concerns of behavioural geography, as referred to in the previous chapter. However, whereas much of the early work in behavioural geography dealt with quantitative surveys of human decision-making in which the researcher was essentially a neutral, passive, "scientific" analyst of behaviour, in interpretive work observers and observed are more closely related. It is recognised that much experience of everyday life is shared by all people. This experience can be drawn upon by researchers through various forms of interaction and participation with and observation of individuals and groups under scrutiny. In so doing an extra dimension is added to the research, that of seeking to identify meanings not only by using standard scientific constructs but by using words and images as sources of meaning (Bryman, 1988:61–70). The emphasis is usually upon an analysis of meanings in specific contexts rather than with a formulation of generalities. Nevertheless, the analysis of the specific has to be underlain by a suitable underpinning of theory in order to prevent a repeat of the much-criticised limitations of the idiographic regional geographies of the 1950s.

Qualitative techniques are essentially descriptions of people's representations and constructions of what is occurring in their world (Eyles, 1988). These descriptions can take several forms depending on the aim of the research, and they may be used in conjunction with statistical surveys and quantitative analysis as complementary methods for seeking an understanding of society. Indeed, many (though not all!) social scientists subscribe to the view that a particular problem under investigation will itself partly dictate the methods of investigation because of the different types of information available for dealing with that problem.

In particular, qualitative methods are best used for problems requiring depth of insight and understanding, especially when dealing with explanatory concepts. As set out by Hakim (1987:26), qualitative research involves:

- "seeing through the eyes of . . . " or taking the subject's perspective;
- describing the detail of a setting from the perspective of participants;
- understanding actions and meanings in their social context;
- emphasising time and process;
- favouring open and relatively unstructured research designs;
- an approach in which the formulation and testing of concepts and theories proceeds in conjunction with data collection.

The distinction between these characteristics and those derived from a positivist tradition is substantial. However, Cosgrove (1989a) identifies one problem of qualitative research as being the way "it makes sense" only in opposition to quantitative research, that is justification of its use has often been as an alternative to quantification rather than as a natural concomitant of investigations of meaning, value and context.

Another way of viewing the essentials of qualitatively based research is that it exhibits the following:

1. A preference for "naturally occurring data" and "field research"; that is, it is non-experimental.
2. A preference for meanings rather than behaviour, and for an individual's own interpretation of events.
3. The rejection of natural science as a model.
4. A preference for inductive, hypothesis-generating research which requires strong theory if generalisations are to be made.
5. A need for *reflexivity* in which the researcher is aware of her/himself in juxtaposition to the subject of enquiry. This implies a continual interrogation of self and subject. For example, an interview with a subject can be a representation of something beyond the interview, but it reflects the dynamic social interaction between the interviewer and the subject.

Analysis of qualitative data can involve reading, annotating, creating categories, and organising information with respect to a theoretical framework so that greater understanding of events and actions is generated (Dey, 1993). The use of such data has grown considerably within geography in the past decade so that they are being employed in situations where once quantitative information would have dominated. For example qualitative measures are being used in environmental impact assessments by identifying a series of interacting variables and determining the nature of the impact of one variable over related variables in terms of positive and negative impacts.

It must be stressed that "most practitioners of 'qualitative method' are deeply antithetical to the reduction of method to technique" (Jackson, 1991:222). Therefore reference below to participant observation or an ethnographic approach as "techniques" in the same manner as describing factor analysis as a technique is misleading. They are inherent parts of a method of investigation and are far less rigid and unchanging than a statistical technique or a mathematical model. They are an intrinsic element in a process that links a researcher to the individuals or groups being studied and therefore it is difficult to separate any special technical component from the overall process. Furthermore, in generating qualitative data, social research can yield a product from the unstructured methods employed in an interview or period of observation in which the data are defined by the subject of the research not the researcher.

Qualitative data deal with meanings and distinctions and they reside in social practice. Such data are not necessarily fixed in their meaning, but they incorporate concepts whose meanings can change or subtly shift. The data can take a great variety of forms, including sounds, pictures, videos, music, songs and prose. Text can communicate qualitative information, but so can forms of art and design and an array of visual images. Thus, for example, a painting conveys qualitative information and can be analysed as a repository of a social relationship.

Because analysis of qualitative material is concerned with the extraction of meanings in a process of interpretation by a researcher, there is a close link to *hermeneutics*, part of an intellectual tradition emphasising the "symbiotic constitution" of the social–historical world and the way in which it is created by individuals whose actions and creations can be understood by others participating in this world (Thompson, 1984:10). Hermeneutics is concerned with the meaning of "texts": from examination of meanings in the Bible to the "texts" of everyday life, but focusing upon language and any media that communicates a meaning to human interpreters. Therefore everyday events, landscapes, paintings, photographs, films, conversations and books can be the "texts" to be analysed. The term "hermeneutics" was first used with respect to the interpretation of Biblical texts, with theologians offering different readings of the scriptures. Subsequently it was used for any process of interpretation. This included the process of understanding society itself, treating society in the same manner as a written text (e.g. Geertz, 1980; Pile, 1990).

For example, one strand in interpretive work, stressing the hermeneutic, has been the geographer's use of literature as a source material, though for a variety of purposes. Pocock (1981:12) suggests that, "broadly, the geographer's engagement with literature in his [her] study of places varies along a continuum between landscape depiction and human condition". This was by no means an invention of the 1970s and there are good examples in Wreford Watson's writing, spanning the period from 1939 to 1983, where literature formed an important component of the work (Johnston, 1993; Robinson, 1991). Thus he claimed, "I have never written an article or a book without an appeal to literature" (Watson, 1983:387). For example, in his first published article, Samuel Johnson was quoted to show how devoid of trees the Scottish Highlands had become by the eighteenth century: "the eye of the writer was relied on as being as serviceable as the eye of the microscope" (Watson, 1983:387). This was repeated in his work on the USA where he used quotes from the books of Mark Twain, William Faulkner, Mike Fink and John Steinbeck because they both expressed and created goals in the lives of their characters, which in turn influenced their readers by giving them a particular image of America. The use of literature was pursued more systematically from the early 1970s by other geographers (e.g. Pocock, 1981) who concentrated on literature's ability to portray place and to convey the relationship between people and place. Hence the "technique" here is the analysis of a text on the basis of a reader's interpretation and their ability to extract key ingredients regarding people and places as portrayed by the author. To some extent this has now given way to analysis in which books, paintings and photographs are examined with regard to the social relations they are representing. In particular this has involved a focus upon the representation of landscapes and the relationship between the artist/writer/photographer and the way in which they portray the landscape (e.g. Cosgrove, 1982; Cosgrove and Daniels, 1988; Daniels, 1989). For example, Rose (1993) refers to the nature of the "male gaze" as evidenced by certain paintings in which a strong patriarchal view of the world is apparent (see Chapter 15).

The widespread adoption of qualitative and interpretive methods by geographers from the 1970s follows similar usage by other social sciences that has been well established for some time (see Frankfort-Nachmias and Nachmias, 1996). Amongst such work by geographers four broad categories of techniques have been used most widely:

1. Questionnaire survey methods (formal interviews)
2. Non-directional interviews or informal surveys
3. Participant observation
4. Interpretation of "supporting" documentation and "texts", e.g. plans, paintings, newspapers, advertising

It should be recognised, though, that the techniques employed by the humanistic geographers and their successors have been ones which have helped researchers to gain access to the experiences and insights of their human subjects. Therefore the formality of structured questionnaires has largely been rejected in favour of less informal approaches, generating predominantly qualitative material for analysis rather than quantitative. Qualitative research differs from quantitative in that the information obtained is generally multi-dimensional and unstructured in its content. That content requires some instant interpretation in an interview as the content and perceived meaning of an answer determines the nature of the succeeding question. Therefore the interview is flexible and dynamic, and interpretation by the researcher is a vital but highly subjective component. Some simple comparisons between this form of enquiry and standard questionnaires are made in Table 13.1.

Whichever method is employed it is important to remember that any information-gathering process must be tailored to the respondents so that it is acceptable to them and keeps demands on them as low as possible, given the scope of the enquiry. The researcher needs to recognise what is within their own capabilities to design a process to minimise the difficulties they may encounter. An important aspect is to collect and record data in such a manner that its subsequent ease of analysis is facilitated. The particular decision as to which approach to employ generally reflects the underlying research problem being investigated. Questionnaires usually employ questions in a simple, standard and replicable format whereas informal surveys and participant observation yield a greater amount of qualitative information which is rarely amenable to analysis using standard statistical techniques.

## INTERVIEWS

### Structured Interviews and Informal Surveys

Pioneers of qualitative methods in the social sciences during the late 1920s, such as Paul Lazersfield and Herta Hertzog, worked on both marketing and social issues (Schlackman, 1989). They encountered the problem of false claims from their respondents who gave certain types of answers in questionnaire surveys in order to appear more respectable. Therefore the researchers developed more indirect probing procedures to ascertain "the truth", referring to these procedures as "indirect" questioning methods or, in

Table 13.1  Comparison of Four Types of Information Collection

| Characteristic | Unstructured Interviews | Standardised Interview Schedule | Delivery and Collection Questionnaire | Postal Questionnaire |
|---|---|---|---|---|
| Type of data collected | Qualitative or exploratory | Quantifiable | Quantifiable | Quantifiable |
| Suitable population | Any | Any | Literate individuals who can be addressed by name, households or joint bodies such as firms | |
| Suitable questions | Open-ended questions, rating scales, measures of attitudes, questions using visual aids or requesting special tasks (such as map drawing or identification of objects, e.g. places on maps or photographs) can be used | | Open-ended questions can only be used in limited numbers; questions and tasks cannot be too taxing but should appear varied on the form. | |
| Possible length | Can be very long | Depends on location | Short–average completion time 5–30 minutes | |
| Sample size | Not suited to probability sample | Depends on size of field force, but cannot be too dispersed | | Large dispersed samples can be used |
| Response rate | Not applicable | High – probably at least 70% | Moderately high | Very variable |
| Time to complete fieldwork | Depends on sample size and number of fieldworkers available | | | 4–8 weeks from first posting |
| Main costs to consider | Interviewers and travel costs; minimal amounts of stationery (plus tape-recorders if used) | Interviewers and travel costs; minimal amounts of stationery | Fieldworkers and travel costs; stationery | Postage and extra stationery; clerical time |
| Confidence in getting right respondent | High, but type and quality of information obtained will vary greatly | High | Low, but can be checked at collection (although this will take longer) | Low |
| Approx. number of respondents who can be contacted by one fieldworker | 30–40 | 30–50 | 200–300 (but it takes time to check questionnaires) | 300–500 (but a single researcher could not code and analyse the response from > 200–250 |

Source: Dixon and Leach (1980: 11).

modern parlance, *"non-directive" interviewing procedures*. In these, respondents were allowed more scope for elaboration and general discussion rather than just being presented with a set of fixed questions or questions demanding only fixed responses.

Others working in Vienna at the same time as Lazersfield and Hertzog included Ernest Dichter and Hans Ziesel. All four subsequently moved to the USA where they were instrumental in developing qualitative methods as a fundamental tool in *marketing research*. Dichter in particular was a strong promoter of the qualitative or what he referred to as *motivational research*, claiming that it need not be supported by large-scale surveys and statistical analysis.

Dichter's debate with the German psychologist Politz in the 1950s highlighted strengths and weaknesses of qualitative approaches to market survey. Some of these also apply to the use of such approaches in other areas. For example, motivational–qualitative research was championed on six main grounds:

1. In standard questionnaires as used in doorstep interviews, responses are often "inaccurate".
2. Large samples are not needed if the focus of attention is respondents' attitudes or preferences.
3. The reasons for human action and preference are often unconscious, and respondents may not know why they behave as they do.
4. "The truth" is more likely to be revealed by non-directive and other indirect procedures as respondents tend to reveal themselves, albeit unwittingly, in interview situations.
5. Information obtained from depth interviews and other non-directive interviewing procedures enables motives to be discerned and interpretations to be made.
6. It is a method that enables application of both a phenomenological approach (see below) to the data and use of a psychoanalytic model.

Criticism of this approach was generally based on the following arguments:

1. Non-directive interviews inject the interviewer's bias into the situation, followed by interpreter bias of the data.
2. With small sample sizes and case studies, no general statements can be made. Furthermore the samples may involve an uncontrolled selection generating both bias and, in effect, large statistical error.
3. It is a completely subjective, unscientific process.
4. If only a small sample is used it is impossible to break down the respondents into subgroups which may be an inherent feature of the population.

Interviews can take various forms, from the highly structured to a more free-form approach. The former are sometimes termed *structured interviews*, and attempt to utilise certain beneficial elements from questionnaire surveys, notably the element of replication. Therefore questions or the structure of the interview are repeated for each person so that any differences between answers can be assumed to be real ones rather than as the result of the interview situation itself. This permits comparability between responses.

*Non-directed informal surveys* are a half-way house between very detailed interviews (sometimes referred to as *depth interviewing*) and the much more prolonged method of *participant observation* (see below). In a formal questionnaire survey the answers to questions are generally recorded in a standardised form, but an informal survey avoids some of the rigidity of this well-structured situation. The informal approach may overcome discrepancies between answers and deeds that can occur in a formal questionnaire. In an informal survey or interview the exact wording of questions and their sequence are not predetermined beforehand and set responses to questions are not demanded. This enables interviews to be tailored to particular individuals and ensures a high degree of flexibility. Nevertheless, questions must have the same meanings for all respondents and this requirement places greater onus upon the input from the researcher. The researcher has to engage in conversation with the respondent rather than just running through a list of pre-set questions, but the conversation has to be "directed" towards particular aspects of the research in question.

## The Process of Interviewing

There are a number of key aspects to the actual process being followed when performing an interview (Cook and Crang, 1995). The first concerns the making of arrangements for the interview. The researcher must decide what is the most appropriate format for the interview, including its location, duration and structure. For example, it might be deemed to be highly appropriate to interview an individual in their own home or at their place of work so that they are more likely to be at their ease and therefore more responsive to questioning. However, other subjects might feel more comfortable if they are interviewed away from a pressured home or work environment. Many interviewees may wish to have a relatively short time period in which to convey information whilst others may wish for a lengthier format. Moreover, some information may only be collected via a relatively lengthy session or repeated interviews or a group format. Deciding on which of these is the most appropriate is part of the initial planning which should be carried out with care to limit the artificiality of the ensuing interview as the interviewee's true feelings or experiences may not be revealed. For further details on the types of preparation that can be made regarding interview preparation, see Schoenberger (1991), who lists six key advantages of a thorough approach to preparing for an interview, in her case involving interviews with business executives:

1. Demonstrate a good understanding of the interviewee's circumstances; be familiar with relevant technical terms and details of particular situations.
2. Use language that the interviewee will understand and set it in an appropriate frame of reference.
3. Be capable of probing more deeply if responses "gloss over" explanations or detail.
4. Be prepared to ask specific questions about aspects of the research that might arise.
5. Tailor questions to suit the abilities of the respondent.
6. Use available information and understanding of the situation to the best advantage, e.g. by varying the nature of the interview to take account of the interviewee's background. In particular sensitivity is required when the subject is unaccustomed to dealing with a well-educated middle-class academic, especially if they are from a different ethnic or cultural or gender background.

The next step is to prepare a *checklist*. Depending upon the degree of formality an interview can be made to follow a general pattern by use of a checklist, *interview schedule*, *prompt* or *topic guide*. This can help an interviewer meet her/his objectives. It can also be modified over time if several interviews are being carried out so that account is taken of respondents raising their own issues for discussion (Burgess, 1992a). Use of a fairly rigid checklist may be most useful in more formalised interviews or where the respondents have a tight time budget (McDowell, 1992b).

The interview checklist replaces the detailed questionnaire or interview schedule of more formal interviews and enables direction in an interview to be maintained. Perhaps the checklist's most significant feature is that it enables respondents to refer to their own situation and everyday lives in their own words. This may lessen the "discontinuity" between analyst and respondent, but there is still scope for the artificiality of the informal interview to hide the respondent's "reality" from the analyst. The informal interview also presents different information to that obtained from a more formal structure, and therefore different skills may be required to interpret this material (Jones, 1985).

Interview guides usually outline four key aspects of the interview:

- covers all the points to be discussed;
- decides the order in which the main points in the interview are to be covered;
- organises any special features of the interview, such as presentation of stimulus material, e.g. photographs of places, lists from which reactions are observed;
- provides a "time map" as timing of an interview can be crucial in determining the type of response obtained.

An example of such a guide, as prepared for use in an examination of smallholder agriculture in the Belize Valley, Belize, Central America, is shown in Table 13.2.

The next step is to "ask the right questions". This seems an obvious requirement, but may not be so easy in practice. All interviews should begin with some simple procedures that will create a more friendly environment in which to conduct the interview. In addition to the exchange of pleasantries, this can include a clear explanation of what the interview will entail and its purpose, and reference to ethical considerations (e.g. non-disclosure of an individual's name or personal information) and to any procedural matters relating to the interview (e.g. use of note-taking, use of a tape-recorder or a translator). It is usual practice to begin an interview with some non-threatening questions to place the respondent at their ease prior to covering more significant information. However, at all times the respondents should be encouraged to supply information in such a way that their version of events or of a given situation is expressed in terms of their own understanding. The "right questions" will elicit such information whilst getting the respondent to supply the appropriate context and background to their views and experiences. Thus once the interviewee has told a story, "how?" and "why?" questions can be asked to gain greater understanding of why particular actions were taken or any particular views were held. In addition, the interview needs to concentrate on ways of maintaining a conversation and dialogue so that the respondent does not lose interest. As with the formulation of an appropriate order for questionnaires, questions in an interview need to come in an appropriate order so that vital views and information are not withheld. In general an ordering from the general to the specific is usually appropriate whilst refraining from directive questions in which the researcher might imply that s/he has already made up their mind about the nature of the likely answer. For example, "Did you close the window because you were worried about the child's safety?" could prompt a facile "suppose so!" response even if this was not the true reason. Similarly, insertion of a researcher's own opinions into questions

*Table 13.2*  Interview Guide for an Examination of Smallholder Agriculture in the Belize Valley, Belize, Central America

Instructions to Research Team:
Elicit information on the following (to accompany formal questionnaire)

1. The farm household
   - Composition (discuss educational background)
   - Roles of members
   - Nature and extent of off-farm work
   - Differentiation of activities by gender
   - Sources of income (discuss remunerations from family members living abroad)

2. The farm holding
   - Extent (discuss interpretation of "fallow")
   - Degree and nature of any fragmentation
   - Tenure (focus on nature of lease where appropriate)

3. Farming activities
   - Range of crops (discuss methods of cultivation; be discreet re: illegal crops!)
   - Crop yields
   - Range of livestock (discuss types of husbandry)
   - Farmstead/buildings (discuss age and construction)

4. The farm operation
   - Subsistence versus commerce
   - Details of marketing (discuss views of government-controlled marketing board)
   - Utilisation of labour (discuss sources/availability of off-farm labour)
   - Cost of labour
   - Utilisation of mechanisation

5. The wider setting
   - Availability and take-up of government grants
   - Contact with outside agricultural agencies
   - Use of credit (discuss alternatives considered)
   - Prices (discuss control policies)
   - Prospects for change (discuss likely income changes)

*Source*: Robinson (1985a,b).

or discussion might yield either a falsely acquiescent response or an overly antagonistic one. Even the clothes worn by a researcher can be a factor in influencing the behaviour of a respondent (Thomas, 1993). Thus appearance, place, context and interview style must all be appropriate if a respondent is to feel sufficiently at ease to answer questions in a "natural" fashion. For a researcher, determining what is "appropriate" is generally a trial-and-error process in which experience can play a significant role.

Cook and Crang (1995) also refer to the benefits of *serial interviews*. If an individual is interviewed on several occasions it is likely that any formality associated with the initial interview will break down and more informal conversations will develop. This can enable a researcher to probe more deeply into reasons for particular actions and to focus upon aspects of an earlier interview that s/he feels require further development. For example, in a series of interviews/discussions with managers of Canada's Atlantic Coastal Action Program (ACAP), it was possible to move away from an interview centred on factual information and details of the Program, which were largely in the public domain, towards an open-ended discussion considering reasons why the Program had operated in a particular fashion and more speculative personal insights (Robinson, 1997). Through a process of serial interviews, issues from one interview can spill over into the next provided that the right atmosphere has been created. However, it is also possible to retain a well-structured format to each interview if this is deemed necessary (see discussion by Burgess et al, 1988). In terms of assessing the value of serial interviews, there is a trade-off between time expended on repeated meetings with an individual or group and the amount and quality of information gathered. However, it should be recognised that the familiarity developed through repeated interviews can lead to dramatic changes in the types of information being provided by interviewees. This may or may not be associated with the researcher exposing more of their own views and feelings. Whilst such exposure might be regarded as likely to influence the responses received, it may elicit more depth of response. As with so much in this type of work, what is appropriate behaviour by a researcher can only be determined by experience and sensitivity to a particular situation.

The *power relationship* between researcher and interviewee may be a key factor in that if the researcher is clearly in a dominant position then airing their own views and attitudes is often inappropriate and overly likely to exert an influence. The main support for serial interviews is that explanations can be developed that are simply unobtainable in a single interview (Cook and Crang, 1995:49–50). Thus knowledge is not always imparted in a first-time discussion because it takes time for daily routines and the taken-for-granted world of any interviewee to be translated into communicable form. In planning for serial interviews, it is possible to begin with straightforward practical content in the first interview and then move to greater interchange and follow-up questioning in subsequent meetings to advance understanding of an individual's lifestyle and personal history. *Activity diaries* kept by the interviewee at the researcher's behest may be one way to add focus and depth to subsequent interviews. These can provide a comfortable starting point from which particular issues can be pursued.

Whilst factual information can be recorded in note form during an interview, a record may be desired of the way in which respondents expressed themselves and described events and feelings. If this is the case a *tape-recorder* will be required. It may also be a direct substitute for note-taking which can be a distracting procedure during an interview and so may be deemed to be best avoided. The tape-recorder can ensure that subtle nuances of the interview are not lost, but the work of transcribing tapes can be very time-consuming. It is rarely practicable to tape-record conversations during participant observation, in which case much greater reliance is placed upon the researcher's ability to remember events and conversations and to record them accurately in a daily diary.

The presence of a tape-recorder can inhibit people and prevent them from expressing their true feelings. However, once an interview or discussion group has begun to "flow" then the presence of the tape-recorder is often forgotten. Obtaining an accurate verbatim record of an interview can greatly assist subsequent interpretation whilst, at the time of the interview, the researcher can concentrate much more on how to conduct the interview or on subtleties of gesture, nuance and group dynamics.

## Depth Interviewing and Working with Groups

> Although the interviewer guides the discussion enough to focus on the topic of interest, the depth interview provides enough freedom for respondents to steer the conversation, for example, to bring in all sorts of tangential matters which, for them, have bearing on the main subject.
>
> (Hakim 1987:27)

From the late 1970s new types of qualitative methods have proved popular in the social sciences, extending the use of non-directive techniques. These methods have been based on *existential and gestalt procedures* developed in psychotherapy in the 1960s. These were founded on the idea that perceptions and reactions could be broken down into understandable component parts rather like a melody can be reduced to a collection of individual notes. The psychotherapists, using both encounter groups and work with individuals, used techniques to help promote "individual growth within a therapeutic setting". Amongst the procedures used were,

- extended or depth interview formats over several hours;
- sensitivity panels;
- extensive use of projective procedures;
- extensive use of awareness and other enabling techniques.

The work of Porteous (1988a,b) on the "destruction" of a village in East Yorkshire illustrates some key aspects of *depth interviewing*, not least of which is the use of detailed interviews with members of the target community interwoven with interviews of "key actors", such as property developers, industrialists and local government officials. Depth interviews typically involve an initial period of introduction, followed by several separate interview sessions, usually in the respondent's home, using both tape-recording and notepad methods of recording information. Interview sessions are unstructured; every attempt is made to avoid leading questions and to promote the respondent's self-definition of the issues to be discussed. Subsequently, notes are rewritten and tapes transcribed.

Donovan (1988) describes this approach as *phenomenological* in that it aims to study phenomena in their own terms so that their integrity is not lost, and it seeks an understanding of the ways in which people make sense of their lives and worlds in which they live. Her work on illness amongst ethnic minorities in London can be viewed as part of a body of interpretive literature seeking to describe, rather than to explain. This views explanation as the analyst's own construction which has the potential to detract from the individual's own experience and views (Entrikin, 1976: Pile, 1991; Relph, 1981). In this approach the individual's own subjectivity becomes the object of study whereas, it can be argued, in positivist approaches it is the analyst who imposes their own subjective views of the world (Ley, 1980). However, this argument ignores the subjectivity of the analyst's interpretation of the depth interview and the inherent preconceptions any analyst brings to any situation. Perhaps one crucial difference, though, is that in positivistic studies the analyst is held to be "objective" whereas the phenomenologist often admits to a bias or set of preconceptions (e.g. Cornwell, 1988).

Perhaps the most well known phenomenological work by geographers has been that of Tuan (1977) whose research has focused upon people's sense of place (see Butz and Eyles, 1997). His account of humanistic geography in the mid-1970s illustrated the type of study of which depth interviewing can be an important part (Tuan, 1976:266–7):

> Humanistic geography achieves an understanding of the human world by studying people's relations with nature, their geographical behaviour as well as their feelings and ideas in regard to space and place ... Humanistic geography ... specifically tries to understand how geographical activities and phenomena reveal the quality of human awareness.

In assessing the role of the depth interview in the overall research process, it is usually the case that the depth interview acts as a means of developing ideas and research hypotheses rather than as a means of generating facts and statistics (Oppenheim, 1996:67). The focus should be upon the researcher trying to understand how respondents think and feel about topics of concern to the research. As the topics may well be ones that respondents feel strongly about, the depth interview's timespan can permit the respondent to talk freely, for several hours or on several extended occasions, and so permit the researcher to develop a degree of insight about their thoughts, feelings and formative experiences. This is the antithesis of a questionnaire or structured interview, as the respondent is largely free to take the conversation onto the ground that they themselves wish to explore. Therefore, any direction of the interview by the researcher has to be as unobtrusive as possible so that the views of the respondent can be adequately expressed. This is a skill that is not easily acquired as the researcher also has to observe closely, paying particular attention to nuances in the respondent's words, including gaps and hesitations that can then be explored further. It is usually essential for the conversation to be recorded on tape so that this can be transcribed later and then analysed. Notes taken during the conversation are the next best device for recording the interview. Rarely can the interview be recalled with sufficient accuracy afterwards for this to be relied upon as the sole record.

Depth interviews are usually best conducted in a respondent's own home where they are likely to feel most comfortable and relaxed so that they will then be more likely to impart their views and feelings. A place of work may be an alternative, but locations in which there may be distractions in the background should be avoided. Selecting the respondents is also an important preliminary. Key informants need to be selected carefully so that all sides of a particular event or situation are well represented. However, given the time involved in a depth interview, duplication needs to be avoided if possible. The interview itself usually begins with a short introduction by the researcher aimed at putting the respondent at their ease, and then an "icebreaker," such as "tell me a little about yourself . . .", to get the conversation under way. The researcher then has to steer the conversation onto the desired topic

whilst trying to avoid too many leading questions or putting words into the respondent's mouth. Therefore questioning needs to be as non-directive as possible. Subsequently, even with a taped conversation to analyse, it is useful to make some notes about the interview. These may provide first impressions about what the respondent did not say or what they failed to reveal, as well as the views that did come to light.

One aspect of qualitative work, and depth interviewing in particular, that has become more common in recent years has been the use of investigations involving *group interviews*, sometimes referred to as *focus groups* (e.g. Burgess, 1992b; Burgess et al, 1991). This provides a link with group work by psychotherapists where group meetings are used as part of the therapy, and with market research where groups of consumers are used as a panel to discuss reactions to new products or advertising campaigns.

Cook and Crang (1995:56) refer to the value of groups in terms of their potential to illustrate "the intersubjective dynamics of thought, speech and understanding". Work with a group adds an important element of group dynamics of which the researcher must be aware. Often it is this dynamic that will be of interest, but in other cases a researcher might consciously wish to avoid it and seek to investigate the relationships in a newly formed group. Groups can be part of a pre-existing organisation, sometimes already familiar with group discussion sessions, e.g. local women's support groups, or they can be artificially created by a researcher, e.g. crime victims invited to a special discussion session.

There are several reasons why group discussions may be more valuable to a researcher than individual interviews. Group discussions can be good ways of revealing how people think and how they interact with other people. The behaviour of an individual in a group is likely to differ from the behaviour of that single individual when interviewed by a researcher, and it will reflect the size and composition of the group (Foster, 1989). Behaviour may reflect things as mundane as the seating arrangements, lighting and actions of the researcher during group discussion as these can all influence the respondents' degree of participation in discussion (Robson, 1989). Other crucial determinants are the number in the group and the length of time of the discussion. The smaller the group, perhaps around five, the greater will be the participation of all members. The researcher's chief task must be to develop a trusting and cohesive atmosphere for group discussion, which may require a number of sessions and not just a single one.

In group discussions the researcher can take one of three basic approaches: autocratic, democratic and *laissez-faire*. In the first of these the researcher leads and directs discussion so that it will tend to focus on the researcher rather than the group. In a *laissez-faire* approach the opposite occurs. This is a "fly-on-the-wall" method in which group dynamics are observed without direction of discussion. A democratic approach involves some direction from the researcher, but as a facilitator of discussion and generator of group dynamics not as a dominating presence. As described by Foulkes (1975), one of the champions of group psychotherapy, the strategies adopted by the researcher in interacting with the group depend upon the understanding of the group, its dynamics, interactions and the researcher's own self-awareness of her/his relationship to the group. The ability of an individual researcher to manage group discussion and to analyse and interpret the outcome tends to be ignored completely or taken for granted in geographical teaching as it is seldom taught in any geography course. This contrasts with the greater emphasis on, say, teaching statistical techniques. "Learning by doing" seems to be the usual practice within geography for this approach despite the fact that skills in group management and interviewing can be taught and generally are in psychology and social anthropology. However, it does also reflect the fact that qualitative research fieldwork is essentially informal and variable. Therefore there is no definitive list of imperatives as to how to do it, only guidelines as to the establishment of prescribed structures in formulating grounds for the relationship between interviewer and the respondent(s) (Burns, 1989). Although used more widely by commercial survey agencies, there are some good examples of geographers using group discussion, notably in the work of Harrison and Burgess (1988, 1990) and Burgess et al (1988).

It is impossible to eliminate the researcher's own presence, personality and prejudice from a group situation. In any group-based work the researcher and the group members interact and such interaction may significantly affect the nature of group discussion. This may be regarded as a weakness or limitation of this type of research, but it could also be treated as a strength in that interaction can provide the very insights and explanations of human behaviour and attitudes that are being sought. The key is that the researcher has to manage the interview situation so that capital is made of the subjective element in the procedure rather than the subjectivity and artificiality of interviewing overwhelming the researcher's analytical capabilities.

With groups created by the researcher there is a need for careful thought about the group's role, its dynamics and its management. Relatively homogeneous groups are generally regarded as giving the best results as subgroups may not contribute fully to discussion or may inhibit exchange of views on certain topics. Against this, variety of views may occur if there are ethnic, age or gender differences in the group. Size of group is another important consideration. If group membership is above a dozen then some individuals may not contribute to discussion or there will be fragmentation into mini-groups. A group of less than six might mean a significant reduction in the number of experiences that can be drawn upon, and it may need greater input from the researcher to maintain discussion.

A recent issue of *Area* (volume 28, number 2, 1996) devotes 37 pages to six articles on focus groups. Goss (1996) notes some of the antecedents of the focus group, in evaluation of radio shows and propaganda films during the Second World War, but observes that there has been little systematic research on such groups despite the presence of some "how to" guides (e.g. Greenbaum, 1987; Morgan, 1988, 1993) and broader considerations (e.g. Stewart and Shamsadani, 1990). However, the essays indicate both the potential of the use of focus groups in geographical research and a strong critical awareness of their strengths and weaknesses. Goss and Leinbach (1996) describe focus groups as social events, but also permitting reflexivity, that is constant communication between the researcher and the group from which multiple meanings can be created and shared, and thereby potentially empowering for participants. The essays give an insight to the range of possible situations in which focus groups can form part of the research strategy: transmigrants in Indonesia (Goss and Leinbach, 1996); responses to a hurricane in Florida (Zeigler et al, 1996); fear of crime in recreational woodland (Burgess, 1996); consumers and group identity (Holbrook and Jackson, 1996); and pregnant women's experiences of Hamilton, New Zealand (Longhurst, 1996). In terms of method, the paper by Holbrook and Jackson is of particular interest as it considers the relative merits of different kinds of focus group by examining the dynamics of groups composed of comparative strangers with "natural" groups whose members were already acquainted with one another (see also Kitzinger, 1994). Their broad conclusions were that each type of group has its own strengths and weaknesses which must be evaluated according to the objectives of the research. A group of comparative strangers may be useful for comparing the views of people from different backgrounds or for airing deeply held views as these may be less readily expressed in the company of friends and acquaintances.

## PHENOMENOLOGY, ETHNOGRAPHY AND ''THICK'' DESCRIPTION

### Phenomenology

Depth interviewing is by no means the most intensive and "in-depth" means of obtaining people's views and feelings. Anthropologists have long utilised other methods that have aimed at generating understanding through the researcher immersing themselves in a research setting and "systematically observing dimensions of that setting, interactions, relationships, actions, events and so on, within it" (Mason, 1996:60). This process is usually referred to as *participant observation* (elaborated in more detail below), and it has been a central part of humanistic geography in which geographers have employed methods first popu-

larised in anthropology. One of the earliest, most important and readily identifiable pieces of research adopting a humanistic perspective was Ley's work on the black inner city in Philadelphia. This recognised the need to go beyond the abstractions of underlying philosophy in order to penetrate the largely taken-for-granted meanings of life for different social groups. His detailed study of black street gangs emphasised the importance of territory and symbolisation in affecting the behaviour of the groups (Ley, 1974). Here there are echoes of language used by the social ecologists and in the *ethnographic studies* carried out by Park and Burgess (1921). However, Ley's work drew some strong critique from Marxists for its neglect of structural forces and its empirical basis (e.g. Walker and Greenberg, 1982). This represents a clear clash between two very different views of what is most important in producing "geography" – one stressing people and human agency, and the other emphasising the unseen structures that exert controls upon human activities. The former view underscored the work of other humanistic geographers developing their ideas from a *phenomenological perspective*, notable proponents being Buttimer (Buttimer and Seamon, 1980), Relph (1976, 1981), Seamon (Seamon, 1979, 1989; Seamon and Mugerauer, 1985) and Tuan (1971), with work in which the centrality of the human subject was paramount (see Hall, 1978).

As described by Tuan (1971), phenomenology is concerned with essence and meaning, uncovered without utilising the presuppositions and methods of science but by examining human interpretation and experience of space and place. This is an attempt to put "everyday experience" of the world as seen by individuals at the centre of geographical enquiry. One interpretation of this is Seamon's (1979) reference to "the geography of the lifeworld". This was just one of several related attempts to turn away from the spatial science reduction of geography to geometry and to focus upon people, their particular human qualities, senses and experiences (e.g. Tuan, 1977).

A central characteristic of Ley's work is its sensitivity to how people go about their daily lives in particular places. In recognising this the researcher is required to recognise the significance of particular meanings, knowledge and language in the lives of the individuals or groups being studied. This frequently places an emphasis upon events occurring at the micro-scale or local level and requires the researcher to engage with a mixture of social relations and cultural characteristics that had been largely sidelined in the work of geographers in the 1960s. Hence culture as "immaterial modes of thinking and living" (Cloke et al, 1991:89) became a significant area of concern for geographers (Jackson, 1989) as part of a fusion of social and cultural geography, including links to the development of interpretive anthropology in which emphasis is placed on how signs and symbols convey meaning (Geertz, 1983).

## Ethnography

It is not surprising therefore that one of the ways used by geographers in investigating the meanings of signs and symbols was "borrowed" from anthropology: namely *ethnography*. The anthropologist, Clifford Geertz (1973:10), described ethnographic enquiry in the field as follows: "Doing ethnography is like trying to read (in the sense of 'construct a reading of') a manuscript – foreign, faded, full of ellipses, incoherencies, suspicious emendations and tendentious commentaries, but written not in conventional graphs of sound but in transcient [*sic*] examples of shared behaviour". This "doing" involves observing people, participating in their lives and sharing some of their experiences whilst trying to understand their world and then represent it in terms as close as possible to their own interpretations (Tuan, 1974a, 1976). This approach has now become a familiar type of geographical method, with Cook and Crang's (1995) contribution to the *Concepts and Techniques in Modern Geography* series actually taking the title "Doing Ethnographies".

In utilising an ethnographic approach in the 1970s and 1980s geographers were following in the tradition established by the Chicago sociologists in the 1920s who developed urban ethnographies of the ethnic and cultural groups in their city. It is not surprising therefore that a major stimulus to the use of qualitative methods in human geography has been the impact of cultural studies upon the discipline from the early 1980s. The relationship between culture and society has become far more central to geographical investigation, with a focus upon the interaction between the cultural, the political and the economic (see Jackson, 1989; Pile and Thrift, 1995). This has given an added impetus to ethnographic techniques as employed by post-war champions of cultural studies such as Richard Hoggart, Raymond Williams and Stuart Hall in the UK.

Ethnography has a double meaning. It can refer to the process of gathering anthropological data, through fieldwork, but it can also refer to the end-product of that process in the form of the production of a written account in the form of an ethnographic text. Jackson (1989:172) notes that duality is symptomatic of the anthropologist's ambiguous relationship with her/his informants. The ambiguity lies in the fact that the anthropologist places her/his own interpretation upon the actions of others. Therefore the written ethnography represents a construction of informants' own constructions of the actions of themselves, their social circle and outsiders. This is sometimes referred to as the *double hermeneutic*, or the interpretation of an interpretation. Therefore ethnographic accounts must be recognised as being partial and biased accounts because they are written from a particular perspective (Clifford, 1986). However, because they are rich in detail, observation and opinion, they are sometimes referred to as constituting "*thick description*" as opposed to the "thin" variety associated with numbers and aggregate summaries (Geertz, 1973, 1983).

Despite its popularity amongst cultural and social geographers from the early 1980s, there are some strong critiques of thick description. For example, a particularly hostile response, as referred to by Jackson (1989:173), came from the anthropologist Paul Shankman (1984:270):

> A movement without direction, a program troubled by inconsistency, an approach that claims superiority over conventional social science but is limited by the absence of criteria for evaluating alternative theories, and type cases that do not necessarily support the interpretive theory – can this be the basis for a different anthropology and a major intellectual movement?

A more specific criticism is that thick description neglects the strong structural constraints that restrict individual action, though Geertz certainly did not ignore the political dimensions of social life as these are part of the context of the social actions he described.

Further consideration of thick description is provided from a postmodernist perspective in Chapter 16.

## PARTICIPANT OBSERVATION

As referred to briefly above, an alternative set of methods to depth interviewing, which has been popularised by humanistic geographers, is *participant observation* (Cook, 1997; Jackson, 1983; S. J. Smith, 1984). This entails looking, listening, experiencing and recording an observer's observations of daily life. It also usually requires spending considerable amounts of time in the company of the people or group being observed, careful thinking and interrogation of theory in the light of observation. Thus it generally entails much closer and more prolonged interaction by the analyst with the group or individuals under study than does depth interviewing. As with depth interviews it is essentially a method borrowed from the anthropologists and sociologists. For example, one of the best overviews comes from the sociologist Becker (1958:652):

> The participant observer gathers data by participating in the daily life of the group or organisation he [she] studies. He [she] watches the people he [she] is studying to see what situations they ordinarily meet and how they behave in them. He [she] enters into conversation with some or all of the participants in these situations and discovers their interpretations of the events he [she] has discovered.

There are, though, several different forms of participant observation, Gans (1982), for example, identifying three:

1. *Total participant*. The observers' role is concealed.
2. *Researcher–participant*. The researcher has to be both inside and outside the group being observed. Hence the researcher is closely involved with the group's daily affairs whilst still remaining a critical commentator able to distinguish underlying patterns and processes within daily life.
3. *Total researcher*. Participation is limited.

With the latter the danger exists of the researcher being sufficiently detached from the observed group to miss vital information or even to be specifically denied access to it because the group regard the researcher as an "outsider". The ability of the observer to become sufficiently detached from the group to retain a substantial degree of objectivity, as championed in many statistical analyses, has not featured very largely in more interpretive work. Indeed, the biases and dogmas of the researcher are positively lauded in some cases (see for example Porteous, 1988b) despite the danger that "total immersion may lead to the researcher ceasing to research" (Eyles, 1988:9). This is not to say that interpretive work should be regarded as unscientific. Kantian philosophy certainly treated science as being as much interpretation as observation, perhaps more so. However, whilst Kant viewed scientific knowledge as the systematisation of common-sense knowledge, he also regarded the selection of objects for study by scientists as subjective and dependent on the scientist's sensory and intellectual equipment.

"Complete participation has been justified on the grounds that it makes possible the study of inaccessible groups or groups that do not reveal to outsiders certain aspects of their lives" (Frankfort-Nachmias and Nachmias, 1996:282). However, there has been questioning of this approach on ethical grounds, as it could be regarded as an invasion of privacy in certain circumstances, and also on methodological grounds. For the latter, the danger lies in the researcher being able to maintain a research perspective and also in the limitations on enquiry that are introduced when the researcher is unable to evoke certain responses in a target group for fear of revealing their identity as a researcher. Note-taking is usually rendered impossible and a record of events can only be made when the observer is alone. By this time memory loss may easily introduce selective bias and distortions.

If the researcher has revealed their role and the nature of their investigation, it is still possible for them to become part of a group or to play a part in the series of events under investigation. With no restrictions imposed by artificial interview situations, the researcher is able to obtain a deeper appreciation of a group and its dynamics. However, the nature of this appreciation relates closely to the type of social relationship developed between the researcher and the researched. There are many different types of relationship that can develop, ranging from relatively little mixing with a group and a lack of identification with group aspirations to a situation where the researcher becomes an accepted member of the group and possibly identifies closely with their views. The value of the research is likely to be reduced in both of these extremes, but this depends largely upon how the researcher regards the objectivity of their work. If a dispassionate observation is the goal then involvement and close identification with a group will harm this; if the intention is to present the experiences, views and hopes of a particular group from their own perspective so that they "speak for themselves" then "putting oneself in their place" is a desirable occurrence.

Of Gans's three forms of participant observation, the second is the most common, acting very much as a case study approach and perhaps enabling the researcher to use observations as a way of elaborating more general survey data. However, the actual interpretation of events offered by the participant observer is highly problematic: "one has to be close enough to grasp the significance of commonsense perceptions and behaviours ... [and] ... one must move far enough away to provide a conceptual understanding of this world" (S.J. Smith, 1988:33–4). But even with the "correct" degree of distance between the analyst and subject, it is the analyst's creativity of interpreting the everyday, the familiar and routine events of daily life that becomes crucial to the production of interpretive meanings. Without the greater rigidity imposed by statistical analysis of "hard" data, there may be more scope for portraying subtler nuances of human existence, but there are also fewer guidelines as to how sense can be elicited from the mass of qualitative data that have been recorded.

Gant (1994:26) refers to observation skills needed both to be a good participant observer and to comple-

ment more formally organised questionnaire surveys. He champions this complementarity as a way of providing additional support and depth of information to that garnered via standard survey procedures. Such combinations of surveys and observations have been used most frequently in studies of visitor behaviour and shopper behaviour (e.g. Brown, 1991; McCullagh and Bradshaw, 1994).

A problem will always be the "distance" between the observer and the observed so that the meaning of actions by individuals and groups may be misconstrued. At best this may simply be reflected in unsympathetic descriptions of the observed or in the sense of wonderment, approximating to complete lack of understanding of the behaviour of observed groups, that permeates certain portrayals of the everyday lives of others. There are some examples of this in the collection edited by Eyles and Smith (1988). But a more serious deficiency may be an inability of the observer to penetrate the front to outsiders that is often created by people who know they are under scrutiny. There is the infamous cautionary tale of Margaret Mead's (1942) early experiences in New Guinea where the tribal group were inclined to present her with false accounts of their lives because they felt that a particular version would be more to her liking than the reality! This is an extreme example of the possible limitations of participant observation, but more general criticisms of subjectivity, bias, impressionism, idiosyncracy and lack of precision have been levelled at this method (Cohen and Manion, 1985:104). However, it does have the advantage of embracing both verbal and non-verbal behaviour. Unlike a questionnaire survey it allows for continuous study and, because it involves less artificiality than the questionnaire, it permits respondents to convey a more sophisticated pattern of behaviour that can then be subjected to scrutiny (May, 1993: Chapter 7).

A key argument is that in order to understand social reality that reality must first be experienced by the researcher. However, deeper understanding can only be realised if the researcher relegates their own position or social reality from the situation that they are seeking to understand. The ultimate logic of this last point is that no "observer" can ever fully comprehend another individual's social reality. However, it is generally accepted that there are intermediate positions from which the observer can claim significant insights.

The scope of participant observation may be extended by asking individuals within a target social group to keep *diaries* which provide a detailed record of where, how and with whom they spend their time. This is really observation without the complementary participation, but it can be used in a number of research contexts (see Fortuijn and Karstom, 1989). For example, Gant (1994:29) refers to the 1991 London Area Transport Survey (LATS) which built up a picture of travel in London on a typical weekday. This involved a combination of household-, roadside- and public-transport-based surveys. The household survey was operated on a 2 per cent sample of all households in Greater London, with household members interviewed and asked to complete a one-day trip diary. This supplemented traffic counts and other surveys to produce a comprehensive picture of who travelled where, when and how (London Research Centre, 1992).

The chief limitation of using specially compiled diaries in geographical research is that diary completion is quite a sophisticated task and so may not be suitable to use with people who have a limited educational background. Detailed diaries are also time-consuming and so respondents may be reluctant to complete them over an extended period. Respondents need to be quite strongly motivated in order to participate. Therefore research linked to the possibility of remedial measures to a perceived problem may be the most likely to employ diaries successfully. Pilot exercises with diaries are essential in order to ensure that the correct types of entry are made by respondents. Progress also needs to be monitored carefully over the study period (Bell, 1993:86–8).

Whilst diaries kept by respondents can occasionally be useful, a vital part of participant observation is for the researcher to maintain a *field diary*. This usually entails setting down the events of the day in some detail whilst they are still fresh in the researcher's mind. The diary should contain notes on even the most apparently trivial happenings and conversations as these may turn out to have a significance only realised at a later date. However, the diary also needs to record

some interpretations by the researcher to aid understanding, e.g. assessments of power relations between individuals, or first impressions of individuals who are being observed. Some researchers have found it very difficult to confine their diary writing to the end of the day and have used various ruses to make quick notes as events unfold (Miles and Huberman, 1993). Others have preferred to tape-record their daily diary rather than relying on notes. Separating aspects of researcher participation from observation may be a helpful way of organising the diary. The diary can also be used to record factual information about the community or group being studied.

Most geographers who have used participant observation methods have attempted to consider the evolving relationship between themselves and the people they are studying. Therefore there is a deliberate melding of subjective and objective components in the research and a two-way flow between researcher and researched through which the researcher learns about both the object of study and themselves at the same time. Questions arise that were rarely considered as part of the scientific method: power relationships between researcher and researched; the extent to which participation is possible; the role played by the researcher with respect to the group under study; and the way in which subjective and often chaotic information collected can be organised, interrogated and related to the theory that underlies the research. In answering these questions there is no single set of correct answers, and it is this that sets interpretive, qualitative research apart from most of the techniques covered in this book. Interpretive research contains a high degree of subjectivity, quite deliberately, but as this can apply throughout a research project, there is not necessarily a right and wrong way of proceeding. The "best" method may only be apparent via a trial-and-error process, and the researcher has to make choices at every stage that will affect the nature of the information gathered. For example, if the researcher is from a white middle-class background but wishes to study the urban homeless, should s/he adopt an Orwellian approach and seek to join the homeless in a squat or sleeping rough on the streets to experience the same sort of problems as those individuals being studied? (And how could this ever be approached if the study was of an immigrant group to the researcher's country or if the researcher was working in a foreign country on long-term residents there?) Or should a degree of distance be maintained between researcher and researched by observing rather than participating? The choice is between two different types of study and between the collection of different types of information. However, even if the researcher lived amongst the homeless for 12 months, at the end of that time they would always be able to retreat to their own "reality" and so their experience of homelessness would be different to that for people without the safety net of such a retreat.

One of the weaknesses of participant observation is its reliance upon the researcher's powers of observation and selection. As it is not a process amenable to replication, it is difficult to avoid the criticism that it has an inherent bias. Indeed that bias, or the researcher's own subjectivity, is usually regarded as an important ingredient of the research. However, if this bias results in an approach that simply confirms the researcher's own particular point of view then relatively little has been achieved. Another criticism is that observation frequently concentrates on the small-scale social setting and the highly specific so that any conclusions reached are too specific and are not conducive to the development of generalisations. This is the charge that such studies lack external validity. However, if a move towards attaining such validity requires adoption of a positivist mode of enquiry this would seem to contradict the underlying rationale of participant observation.

## ANALYSING MATERIAL FROM INTERVIEWS AND PARTICIPANT OBSERVATION

### The Approach

One of the crucial characteristics about interpretive research has been a less rigid research process in which research method is not so clearly divided into set phases, but rather there is constant reference from information gathered to analysis to theory to information. Sometimes termed *analytic induction*, it generally begins with a general theory or theoretical setting from which a research question and data needs are identified. However, as information is assembled, a more grounded theory is developed that arises out of and is directly relevant to the particular setting under study.

Much interpretive work has consciously avoided the use of a rigid hypothesis at the outset of research as this may lead to the trap of treating the research project as simply a hypothesis testing exercise and unwanted associations with the scientific method. Instead, the researcher is more likely to begin with a more loosely defined hypothesis or axiom which guides data collection and the observation process. As information is assembled so the initial hypothesis is continually questioned and refined so that emerging categories and relationships can shape ideas in both a general and specific nature – specific to the particular case study, and general in terms of considering other situations to which the findings might apply (Glaser, 1978). Therefore the research process uses observations to refine, reject and reformulate ideas and hypotheses, though without using the formalised statistical hypothesis tests associated with the scientific method. Theory is built up in this process by discovering and defining relationships between categories of observations. The theory is generally supported by qualitative observations and use of quotations from individuals being studied as part of an overall interpretive approach that transforms the researcher's understanding of social science, highlighting her/his own role as an analyst in the construction of what they seek to explain.

It must be noted, though, that the role of theory in humanistic geography has been questioned. Indeed, Daniels (1985) refers to humanistic geography as being in some ways anti-theoretical, in part because of its criticisms of positivism and structuralism which reify theoretical concepts and over-privilege their explanatory status (see also Ley, 1989b). He champions the role of *narrative* as the way in which humanists can incorporate elements of the theoretical and the explanatory as an aid to understanding. The example he uses is a piece of text from Paterson's *North America* (Paterson, 1979:125):

> The semi-feudal conditions of land tenure in some of the early settlements, and the pressure on the land of an increasing immigrant population soon produced a drift westward toward the mountains. Here in the rougher terrain of the upper Piedmont and later of the Appalachian valleys, independent farmers carved out their holdings, accepting the handicaps of infertility and remoteness in exchange for liberty of action. To the eighteenth-century farmer the exchange seemed a reasonable one; his twentieth century descendant, occupying the same hill farm, suffers the handicaps without the same compensation.

Positivists might see this as a loose, weakly explanatory combination of factual description and implicit law-like generalisation, However, Paterson's explanation is primarily contextual rather than causal. His account refers to what westward pioneering meant in eighteenth-century North America, using a range of overlapping descriptions that include simple, emotive and technical terms. It combines the view of the pioneer with that of a modern observer who has the advantage of hindsight – just as an observer of an incident that occurred a week ago may have once they have applied their critical powers of interpretation to that incident. Paterson's narrative incorporates an objectivity that is open to further empirical investigation which might elaborate the context to alter the nature of the interpretation. Hence narrative can portray relationships between people and places, though not necessarily from the perspective of the flow of lived experience as it represents essentially a retrospective mode of understanding which might not suit all forms of ethnographic enquiry.

If qualitative data have been assembled from interviews, it is common for analysis to adopt one of three viewpoints:

1. That the interview represents the "truth" about the respondent's position or actions and that this truth can be discerned and analysed.
2. That the interview will reveal the structural constraints under which the respondent operates and that the nature of these structures can be determined by judicious use of theory and information supplied via interview.
3. That the basic form of the interview is paramount and that underlying structures and "objective" interpretation should not necessarily be the primary concern. Instead, the analysis focuses on the regularities and fundamental features in the interview. This is referred to as *discourse analysis* or *conversation analysis*, and it treats the interview itself as the social encounter of prime significance rather than it being a key to an external reality (see Silverman, 1985, 1993). In particular, this has been used by psychiatrists and in professional health care.

The three-fold categorisation above can be compared with work by Mason (1996:54), who translates the analysis of interviews and information from participant observation into three types of "readings":

1. *The literal.* Here the focus is on aspects of interaction, for example the literal dialogue in an interview, including its form and sequence, or the literal substance. In an interview, this approach will require a tape- or video-recording. Analysis is likely to focus on words and language used, the sequence of interaction, the form and structure of the dialogue, and the literal content. However, most geographers would wish to go beyond this and would also not accept that a purely literal reading of an interview or text was possible.
2. *The interpretive.* This involves consideration of meanings or what the researcher can infer about something beyond the interview interaction itself or the observation of a given event. The researcher has to construct or document a version of what they think the data mean or represent (Mason, 1996:109):

> You may, for example, read a section of an interview transcript as telling you something about implicit norms or rules with which the interviewee is operating, or discourses by which they are influenced, or something about how discourses are constituted, or as indicating some kind of causal mechanism in social action. You may be mostly concerned with what you see as your inter-

viewees' interpretations and understandings, or their versions and accounts of how they make sense of social phenomena, or you may place more emphasis on your own interpretations. Probably, you will do both to an extent.

3. *The reflexive*. This relates to the role of the researcher and the interface between researcher and researched. Therefore the researcher explores their role in the generation and interpretation of data. Frequently, this leads the researcher to uncover their ways in which they themselves are "inextricably implicated" in the process of data generation and interpretation. This is then reflected in the "analysis".

Much qualitative research actually involves "reading" data in all three ways, though with variations in emphasis. Decisions about which of these are of prime interest will help determine both the nature of the interviews or observation and their subsequent analysis.

## Transcribing, Categorising and Classifying

If conversations have been taped or recorded in note form and if observations of a particular event are only held in the researcher's memory, a vital next step is that of *transcription*. Tapes, notes and memories need to be transcribed so that the material can be interrogated in various ways at a later date. The process of transcription can be a time-consuming one, but it also provides a means whereby the researcher can relive conversations. Yet, even with conversations faithfully transcribed onto paper, it may be difficult to detect clear concepts or structures emerging without analysis that uses some means of categorisation or coding. The latter may be used to convert conversation or open-ended responses to questions into a more closed form. This may appear to negate the use of an "open" approach. An alternative is to index responses or conversation with respect to concepts within the theory underlying the research. This is a central component within *ethnographic analysis*, in which

anthropologists use analysis of interviews and observation to understand culture and societal relationships. Chronological accounts of different people's experience of an event may be employed (sometimes referred to as *developmental interviewing*), with ordering of transcripts or editing of tapes according to topic headings as chosen by the analyst. Computer packages are now available to assist this analysis by searching for key phrases, determining the frequency with which people use certain words and in which context. This can help the analyst uncover reasons for particular actions or how individuals see their role in stated situations.

Becker (1973) lists four distinct stages of analysis of "observations" aimed at categorising events, relationships and observed interactions with respect to a given theoretical framework:

1. *Selection and definition of problems, concepts and indices within the field setting*. This helps to determine the types of data available and the extent to which observed social phenomena are related. For example, different subgroups of people can be recognised and their interrelationships observed.
2. *Frequency and distribution of phenomena*. The observation has to be focused on particular events and the roles of individuals and subgroups with respect to these events.
3. *Construction of models of the social system*. This can take several different forms, using theory, observation and use of abstract categories. For example, a starting point is to employ meanings such as cultural norms and people's own definition of their experiences and situation. From this the focus may move to practices, such as recurrent categories of talk and action, and then to episodes, or the dramatic and remarkable, such as a crowd disturbance. Encounters can be considered by categorising the nature of contacts within a group or between a group and outsiders. This may appear to be a mundane activity on which to focus, but encounters and contacts can be a key to understanding the roles played by individuals or groups within society. As part of investigating these roles, it is important to observe the roles that people

ascribe to themselves and to others, and the pattern of relationships between individuals and groups that emerges. Another aspect to observe and then utilise in a model of the social system may be "lifestyles" or the similar global adjustments to a particular situation made by a clearly recognisable substantial group of people.

4. *Withdrawal from the field to complete analysis and write-up.* Consideration of how this is to be performed tends to play a much more important part of qualitatively based ethnographic research than in other approaches. This is because usually an inherent part of the work is *reflexivity* in which the writer's role in the research and their interaction with others is central to the analysis and to the construction of a "social reality". The essence of this reality can be conveyed by using specific instances from field notes, for example reporting of conversations so that the thoughts of others are conveyed in their own words.

The categorisation referred to by Becker is one of the main routes to analysis of qualitative data. It can take various forms, even extending to use of computer programs as part of the analytical process. Over the past decade writers of computer software have started to develop computer packages for the analysis of qualitative data, complementary to the range of packages for statistical analysis that became familiar to geographers in previous decades, e.g. Minitab, SPSS. The packages that deal with qualitative data have tended to focus upon certain aspects of analysis, notably *coding* and *sorting information*, using *categories*. If the researcher gives a particular code to a piece of text or a "variable" in the text then the computer can retrieve this and present it in various forms (packages include QSR, NUD-IST, Hypersoft, the Ethnograph and ATLASti). For example, the interactions between two individuals could be picked out and their frequency counted, or types of incident could be selected and then classified into subtypes. In effect, the computer packages may be used to speed up the principal aspect of the analysis of qualitative information, namely the repeated interrogation of this information by the researcher. Sifting through and sorting

transcriptions can be a long drawn-out process, but it is the principal means by which the researcher can interpret observations against the backcloth of theory that underlies the investigation. This is an iterative process, "going from the material to ideas, back to the material and so on, through analytical induction" (Crang, 1997:188).

In referring to this process of coding transcriptions, Crang (1997:188) stresses that it is not the codes themselves that are of interest but "the text they denote, not how often they occur but what is in them. The codes are not there to be rigidly reproduced, nor to be counted, but as an aid to the researcher in making sense of the material." Thus coding is a means of conceptually organising material. It can take many forms, each researcher having their own idiosyncratic method, e.g. using coloured markers to highlight text; putting text on cards and shuffling the cards into different piles according to their content; using an indexing system for each incident or meeting that can then have as many subdivisions as desired. An example of the latter would be in an observation of the meetings of a particular organisation. These could be classified into types of discussion at these meetings, then into meetings at which person Y spoke, then into the types of impact Y's contribution made upon the group, and finally, subsequent actions by person Y and group X.

It is important to distinguish between concepts utilised by the participants and those applied by the researcher, although both can be coded. For example, in studying the behaviour of crowds at soccer matches, the fans may refer to acts of violence against the police or rival fans as "aggro". This is their own label which can then be recorded in a field diary, but subsequently the researcher can break down this term into different types of usage by the fans with respect to particular incidents. In this way subcategories of "aggro" might be created by the researcher so that the researcher as observer builds up a more complete understanding of a term used by the participants. This is also an *iterative process* involving defining and redefining, categorising and recategorising until the categories assume a suitable degree of coherence and robustness. Examples of different types of categorisation and coding are given in Table 13.3.

*Table 13.3*   Analysing Notes and Transcripts Through Categorisation

1. Decide on what constitutes the data, e.g. transcripts, notes, documents

2. Read through the data thoroughly; start categorising roughly. If a computer program is to be used then data will have to be put into a form suitable for the software, and the indexing system of the program will be utilised

3. Keep a running record of the categorisation, e.g. page number, paragraph, line number; cross-reference if necessary

4. Retrieve information using the running record or by cutting and pasting. If a computer is used then the package can retrieve text labelled with appropriate identifiers. Complex programs will permit retrieval of specified connections,  relationships and overlaps (Boolean searches)

**Literal indexing**

Focus on pauses, interruptions, emphasis, agreements, disagreements, ends of particular points, sequences, order of speaking;
- detailed content analysis, e.g. topics covered, points of substance
- recognition of variables if there is sufficient uniformity within material

**Interpretive indexing**

Extremely varied; focus on rules and norms, classes of people, normative understandings, different types of understanding exhibited

**Reflexive indexing**

Focus on researcher agreeing or disagreeing with respondent, types of researcher response, types of researcher intervention, role of researcher in discussion

Based on Mason (1996:ch. 6).

## Signs and Symbols

In part, the process of interrogating transcripts depends upon the style of the account being presented by the researcher. Most ethnographic work has sought to portray situations and events from the point of view of the people being studied. However, this can produce a rather one-sided interpretation that ignores meanings that may not be apparent to the participants or informants themselves. This raises issues regarding the researcher's reference to *structural constraints* and controls upon individuals, again which they may not fully recognise despite the fact that they do influence thinking and actions. If research seeks to uncover these situations and to assess their significance, careful thought has to be given to the accompanying theory and the extent to which a structural focus detracts from the traditional ethnographic approach.

In seeking to examine structures of meaning that may not be apparent to the informants themselves, Crang (1997) suggests the possibility of using *semiotics*: the study of signs and the construction of meanings. Semiotics considers how texts, words, pictures, films and events represent or convey particular meanings at given times and places. The implication is that a given thing has a relational meaning rather than a fixed one so that the meaning of a particular "sign" such as blue for cold and red for hot depends on cultural conditioning and a certain set of prevailing circumstances. Crang refers to the work of philosopher Charles S. Peirce (1839–1914), who recognised three types of signs, based on their communicative skills (Hartshorne and Weiss, 1932; Hookway, 1992):

1. *Iconic signs.* These are signs by resemblance. They share some property with the thing being signified.

Any object that puts the interpreter in mind of something else acts as an icon.

2. *Indexical signs*. These are signs by causal connection. The thing that signifies exists in a causal relationship with the thing being signified. The causal connection between A and B allows the interpreter to move from the idea of A to that of B. For example, a set of marks on a tree in a forest may denote the passage of a deer, and hence to an observer there is a connection between the marks and the deer even though the deer may not be visible.

3. *Symbolic signs*. The relationship between the sign and its meaning is one of convention. For example, words signify objects purely by convention. The word "cow" signifies a particular object.

Furthermore, Peirce distinguishes two main species of icon: ones that function by sensuous resemblance, or *images*, and icons that signify by relations of parts, or *diagrams*. Pictures and photographs fall into the first category, and maps and diagrams into the second. He believed that diagrams have a role to play in all productive reasoning, especially in deductive or mathematical form, as he believed that all mathematical reasoning involves an element of observation.

Unfortunately, Peirce's classification has been used in confusing fashion by many social scientists (including Crang!), often ignoring the fact that the three types of sign may frequently be combined. For example, a road sign for a winding road is usually a black squiggle. This is iconic, so that even though different types of squiggle may be used from one country to another, a foreigner can still interpret the road sign as meaning "winding road" because it resembles a winding road. It is also indexical in that it shows that the winding road is about to occur in the immediate area, and it is symbolic in that it refers to a condition that will become apparent on the road ahead.

In suggesting a focus upon the meaning of "signs", Crang (1997:191) suggests that the researcher may look at how the same sign is used in different ways and on different occasions or places. This emphasises the importance of context in the way that meanings of events can be changed or fixed. This might be investigated by examining the relationships between signs.

Another approach may be to examine the various meanings attributed to a thing or an event. These meanings can then be grouped in terms of whether they have the same characteristics or whether they are very different. There are more formal ways of doing this (e.g. Greimas, 1987). Ideally, though, the aim of focusing upon different ways of extracting meaning from events, conversations and circumstances is to develop an interpretation that meets the requirements of the researcher's particular research project. This need not have to reach one rigid "correct" interpretation, but it may involve several – perhaps setting out the different understandings of events as held by different participants. This is then allowing informants/participants to speak for themselves, but in an interpretive framework established by the researcher. At the other extreme, the researcher distils the essence of the events through their own distorting lens and the researcher's summary view of events is presented. This suggests that there are various degrees of authority that the researcher can wield in producing a final document, from "researcher as expert", all seeing and knowing, through to "researcher as reporter", imposing a limited amount of authority upon the report.

## Letting Individuals Speak for Themselves

One central aspect of ethnographic work is the subsequent portrayal of that which has been observed. Emphasis is placed upon the writing of geography in a recognition that this writing must not only portray the feelings, views, values and experiences of the people being studied, but it must also provide an interpretation by the researcher. Verbatim records of conversations can feature in the writing, but the writing is not just reportage, it is both description and interpretation. In considering the issue of how the "writing up" should occur, Gregory (1989) refers to the way in which this has become an important part of postmodernism (see Chapter 16), with serious consideration being given to textual strategies. Whilst this may have been a concern initially in fiction writing, it has spread rapidly into the social sciences giving rise to a concern for how other people's stories should be told. Who has the authority to "speak" for others and is an outsider's view of a different ethnic, cultural or gender group a valid one? These are just two of the questions to be considered in attempting to deal with the issue of how the writing of geography can be approached. If we can accept the notion that there can be multiple voices and multiple perspectives on the same event, who is to say that the academic researcher is the person with the authoritative ethnography? As will be discussed in the final chapter, the emergence of post-modern geographies gives people using ethnographic approaches much to consider as the ground upon which conventional representations of the world is based has been transformed or, in different parlance, "the goalposts have been shifted".

One of the ways in which qualitative analysis allows individuals to "speak for themselves" is by incorporating their words in the research report or published paper. For example, in Hughes' work on women's experiences of rurality, she uses the words of her subjects as transcribed from taped interviews (Hughes, 1997:175):

> Although I was born and bred a townie I hated every minute of it . . . In towns particularly in the winter you are going out to work and coming home in the dark, you are too busy in your little wrapped up world, you are very insular in towns . . . you are not really in a community . . . You can be as alone in a city as you can be on the top of a moor somewhere.

Another experience, that of a feeling of declining community spirit, is described by using the words of a farmer's wife in her sixties (*ibid*.:176):

> It is not like it used to be in neighbours . . . when our new neighbours moved in I went down and told them that we were up here if there was ever something that we could do. But we don't. I wouldn't say that we have nothing to do with them but it is practically nil. Whereas the people that were there when we came, we would give them lifts to town every week and we would stop and have a chat.

This is then contrasted with the view of a recent urban migrant to Hughes' study village (*ibid*.:177):

> I mean I am a townie born and bred and I have thrust myself into the community life and I want to get involved with everything that's going on and you get . . . new people move in and you don't see them . . . they don't get involved with the community . . . They can be involved as they want to be . . . There are just a couple that want to keep themselves to themselves.

By using these selected quotes from interviews with members of a target group, or by noting conversations during participant observation, the researcher can act as a medium for the views and experiences of the group. The research's analytical content is not the application of a statistical technique but an interpretation of the content of the interview which entails the researcher using their critical powers of interpretation. This can involve assessing the respondents' views against an initial theory or invoking certain constructs that can be understood more clearly through consideration of the content of an interview. In Hughes' research, the constructs were the notion of rurality, feminine identity in a rural setting, and the roles of women in the community. The words of the women interviewed provided a set of mirrors upon these constructs against a backcloth of the various theories and previous work on these topics. Thus, without recourse to the formal (and arguably more limited) statistical testing of hypotheses, it was possible to learn more both about the specifics of these constructs within the study area and about more generally applicable characteristics of rurality and women's experiences.

This work revealed that there was a strong relationship between how women's role in a community is perceived (by them and others), and how this influences the real community experiences of women. Thus women's experiences are shaped by a mixture of real and imagined "geographies", these experiences being revealed through interviews and the words of the women themselves – termed *lay discourses* by Jones (1995). It is these lay discourses that often form the bedrock of qualitative analysis because they are the central focus of the "techniques" employed to generate qualitative material: interviews and observation, perhaps supplemented by other sources of qualitative information such as film, photographs and literature.

Further consideration is given in Chapters 15 and 16 to qualitative methods as discussed in this chapter. First, however, it is appropriate to consider some of the methodological issues raised by a highly significant development in the discipline, roughly contemporaneous with the incorporation of humanistic ideas, namely ideas based primarily upon the writings of Karl Marx.

# MARXIST ANALYSIS IN HUMAN GEOGRAPHY

## THE ADVENT OF MARXIST GEOGRAPHY

A strong criticism of the positivistic work of the Quantitative Revolution was that it accepted the general maintenance of the status quo in society rather than dealing with a need for radical change. Consideration of this "need" is where more overtly ideological views entered the debate. "Radical geographers" perceived it necessary to change the prevailing capitalist system of the Developed World, because of what they regarded as its in-built tendencies to create inequalities (e.g. Eliot-Hurst, 1973; Harvey, 1974b). Therefore any analysis that did not attack the existing system of government and prevailing power structures or only suggested small-scale progressive change was anathema to this revolutionary view of progress.

As summarised by Johnston et al (1994), this radical criticism of the existing positivist-based geography recognised three particular weaknesses:

1. Ruling social ideologies were reaffirmed because geographers did not question processes leading to inequality.
2. Spatial analysis, even if attempting to be "socially useful" was simply serving the capitalist system.
3. The generalist laws sought by positivist spatial analysis ignored the very different spatial arrangements that might obtain in different societies.

This radical turn drew largely upon *Marxism* for its underlying arguments. Some geographers citing Marxist writings sought to create the Socialist Revolution, perhaps by generating the conditions for it through their analyses and teaching, whilst others simply employed a Marxian perspective in their work. In other words, several geographers in the 1970s began employing some form of *historical materialist analysis*, though with little or no reference to any political programme (Johnston, 1983:101). The key to this work was a general view that "the mode of production of the material means of existence conditions the whole process of social, political, and intellectual life. It is not the consciousness of men [*sic*] that determines their existence, but on the contrary, it is their social existence that determines their consciousness" (Burns, 1935:372). It was the historical development of this social existence that was subjected to scrutiny, particularly in a number of elegantly crafted studies by Harvey (e.g. Harvey 1973, 1975b, 1978, 1982, 1984, 1985a,b), explaining patterns and processes of spatial and environmental change as the result of the specific social relations of capitalism. This was not analysis based on the application of quantitative or technologically based methods, but rather the application of Marxist ideas and theories to expositions attacking positivism and capitalism. So whilst this book is one dealing primarily with analytical techniques, the rejection of their use in favour of more theoretical and non-technically oriented work cannot be ignored. Hence, this chapter considers some of the key arguments advanced as radical alternatives to positivist work.

Those geographers employing Marxist theory have argued that spatial patterns represent social forms and so must be explained in terms of the dynamics of the underlying social structure. Therefore it is largely capitalist social formation that has been of interest, with spatial form being viewed as part of a process of evolution through instabilities and fluctuations in this formation (Liossatos, 1980).

Spatial divisions, as manifest for example in spatial differentiations between urban and rural, were not of importance in the writings of Marx and Engels. They also played little part in the work of other social theorists such as Durkheim and Weber. In their work no aspect of society could be analysed independently of the totality of social relations. For example, in Marx's writings such divisions as that between urban and rural were investigated with respect to the underlying mode of production which it sustained and which was sustained by it (Robinson, 1990:55). So whilst Marxists might argue that a city can be differentiated from the countryside, this division is unimportant in terms of social relationships. This insignificance of a rural–urban division to an understanding of society has been restated more recently by Lefebvre (1976, 1977), arguing that in modern capitalist production "reproduction, the relations of production, not just the means of production, is located not simply in society as a whole but in space as a whole" (Lefebvre, 1976:83). A similar conclusion appears in some of the work by the sociologist Manuel Castells (1976, 1989). However, from the late 1960s, Marxist theory has been extended and developed to at least accept spatial differentiation as "significant" insofar as the city has been accepted as a worthy subject for study (e.g. Dear and Scott, 1981; Harvey, 1982; N. Smith, 1979; 1990). Indeed neo-Marxist geographers have championed the importance of space within their formulations of social theory. For example, Harvey (1982) does so in his wide-ranging attack on capitalism whilst Massey (1984:58) argues that "the reproduction of social and economic relations and of the social structure takes place over space, and that conditions its nature". Moreover, she then attempts to

demonstrate how location shapes or affects social developments, and class relations in particular. Therefore distinctions between places are presented as important considerations in attempts to understand social relationships, even if a historical materialist perspective is adopted (see also Scott and Storper, 1986). This view can be contrasted with that expressed by the sociologist Giddens (1984b) in which place is deemed to be relatively unimportant in determining how and what people do there. This simply "treat[s] space as a 'backdrop' against which social processes develop" (Saunders, 1986:285).

After the first calls by radical geographers for revolutionary changes in society, there was a not unsurprising antagonistic reaction in some quarters, Morrill (1969), for example, referring to such calls as "naive, simplistic, lacking general support, underestimating the capacity for change by non-revolutionary means and ignoring the experience of countless revolutions throughout the world". His own "radical" solution was the production of a capitalist–socialist convergence, perhaps on the lines of the Social Democratic method practised in Sweden (Morrill, 1970b). But this was too limited a change for fundamental Marxists, Folke (1972) and Eliot-Hurst (1980), for example, favouring "revolutionary practice" and rejecting Harvey's stress upon the need to formulate appropriate neo-Marxist theory.

Nevertheless, ideas taken from Marxism have found their way into the "mainstream" of human geography from the early 1970s. Like the emergence of the Quantitative Revolution itself, this too should be viewed in the context of the changing events on the world political stage, and there is a need for more study on links between the Conservative governments of the Reagan, Thatcher and Mulroney years in the 1980s (not to mention their right-wing "Socialist" counterparts in Australasia) and the increasing dominance of Socialist and Marxist ideas within academia in many Developed Countries.

Geographers proclaiming a "Marxist approach" initially focused upon certain concerns that they felt represented glaring inequalities within society: for example, the work of Amin (1976, 1980) and Frank (1971) on the processes of development and imperialism in the Developing World; Carney et al (1980) and Massey (1973, 1976) on uneven regional development in the Developed World; and Boddy (1976), Castells (1977) and Harvey (1973, 1978) on social inequalities in urban environments. Much of this work represented a critique of positivism or of existing theories utilised by geographers. It also focused upon the formulation of theory and was therefore in marked contrast to most previous geographical studies, but Cloke et al (1991:44–5) argue that it "fell into the twin pitfalls of structuralism and functionalism, arguing implicitly or explicitly that the structures of society dictated actions and events almost behind the backs of the individuals concerned and that society operated in the way it did because it was necessary for society's survival or functioning". However, from the mid-1970s Marxist geographers have extended their theories, investigating the relationship between social relations and spatial structures (e.g. Harvey, 1982). Despite this, in the mid-1980s it was still possible for Clark et al (1986:274) to conclude that we "know strikingly little about even the most basic dimensions of regional capital formation in space and time". Subsequently, this has been one of the key areas addressed from both radical and non-radical perspectives (see Massey, 1995).

For over two decades David Harvey has forged ahead with the attempt to develop a Marxist theory of capitalist urbanisation whilst others have utilised Marxist theory to analyse parts of that urban system, most notably Massey (1984) on the spatial division of labour and Neil Smith (1990) on uneven development. However, analysts of the evolution of Harvey's work recognise significant moves by Harvey and other Marxists away from a rather sterile concern for dialectic materialism (see below) and "structures" to more detailed class analysis and a focus upon the "concrete" and the "historical" (Badcock, 1987). Harvey's (1985a) *The urbanization of capital* contains more emphasis upon theorising than *Consciousness and the urban experience* (Harvey, 1985b) which is more speculative and historical. However, these two works represented a significant advance upon many attempts by geographers to deal with philosophical matters, not only because they are more intelligible, but, more

specifically, they make complex Marxist theory accessible to the non-cognoscenti. The task set in these two books is immense in that his study of capitalist urbanisation involves not just the physical forms created by capital but also the urbanisation of social relations and of political consciousness. In this work Harvey examined the separation of workplace and living space, the reorganisation of production, control and consumption processes to meet the requirements of capital, the fragmentation of social space in relation to the demands of the labour market and "the urbanisation of consciousness".

Harvey (1985b:253) describes the task for the historical materialist interpretation of the urban process as:

> To examine how the consciousness produced through the particular patterning of relations between individualism, class, community, state, and family affects the paths and qualities of capitalist urbanization that in turn feed back to alter the patterning of relations that underlie the urbanization of consciousness.
>
> ...The landscape of capitalism is pre-ordained to developmental disparities. Geographical unevenness is socially and historically produced out of the basic dynamics of commodity production as such.... The spatial variability and discontinuities of capitalism are thus endemic.

In summarising the initial development of Marxist thought in human geography, Eyles (1981:1372–5) recognised three different strands:

1. Use of Marxian concepts in an essentially "liberal" radical analysis, for example with a focus on capital and reproduction of labour power (e.g. D. M. Smith, 1977).
2. Marxism as a revolutionary "scientific" framework for geography, incorporating a spatial problematic and a socio-spatial dialectic (see below) (e.g. Peet, 1979; Soja and Hadjimichalis, 1979). Eyles criticised this work for confusing form and process, description and explanation, and for producing explanations that were far too broad because they were based on just one essential "answer" – the evils of capitalism.
3. The jettisoning of geography and the championing

of Marxist method as the only way of studying social life. This approach regarded geographical differentiation as a mere detail, resulting from the operation of social systems (e.g. Eliot-Hurst, 1980; Lee, 1977).

Within all three of these, but especially the last two, great importance was attached to the presence of controlling structures within society. In part this was based both consciously and unconsciously on the writings of Althusser (1969, 1971) on *structural Marxism* in which structures are reified, class is central to all activity, and in which Marxism is seen as both a political action plan and as a system of values. Concern with structures has continued to play an important role in the work of Marxist geographers.

## STRUCTURALISM

> The mode of production of material life conditions the general process of social, political and intellectual life. It is not the consciousness of men that determines their existence, but their social existence that determines their consciousness ... changes in the economic foundation lead sooner or later to the transformation of the whole immense superstructure.
>
> (Marx, 1971:21)

Within Marxist geographies from the early 1970s onwards there has been a strong emphasis upon the significance of the structural dimensions of society. "Deep structure" is one of three "structures" that may be recognised within structuralist analyses, not necessarily all incorporating a Marxist viewpoint. Despite the complex and often tortuous argument employed in his work, the depiction of these structures by the anthropologist Claude Levi-Strauss, as interpreted by Gregory (1978b:100), is a useful guide (Figure 14.1). The three levels depicted are:

1. The outer level is the *superstructure* or *level of appearances* in which spatial patterns of social exchange are recognised. This is the *empirical level* at which spatial structure may be conceived in empirical terms. This level represents Levi-

Strauss's jig-saw puzzle of social, cultural, political and spatial organisation.
2. Underlying the empirical level is a *socio-structural level* or *infrastructure* representing processes. This level is not directly observable and so its nature may only be theorised and deduced from the appearance of the empirical level.
3. Underlying the other two levels is the *deep structure*, the level of imperatives or human neuro-structural level. These have not been the concern of human geographers, though it could be argued that certain "deep" or underlying concepts such as sense of place, territoriality and orientation represent realisations of deep structures and therefore form an intrinsic part of certain behavioural studies by geographers (Golledge, 1981).

In the terminology employed in Figure 14.1, Marxists have focused upon the infrastructure and superstructure, especially economic processes operating within a capitalist mode of production. They have argued that spatial patterns only offer clues as to the nature of processes rather than being suitable for process identification. Therefore this view has fostered a concern for theory – not necessarily for how it might react to a particular set of circumstances present in a particular location (e.g. Taylor, 1982), but for how it might advance our understanding of infrastructures and superstructures.

Utilising the idea of superstructure, Marxists took issue with positivist approaches on the grounds that identification of laws of general applicability is not possible (see Sayer, 1979). Processes are continually changing, and therefore the contents of the superstructure are also changing so that empirical laws, which represent generalisations with a universal applicability, are an impossibility. As Johnston (1986a:181) puts it, "there can be no social science equivalent of the law of gravity"!

Another structuralist criticism has been that both behavioural and humanistic approaches over-simplify the relationship between the individual and the wider society. The critique contends that too much emphasis is placed upon the "false" freedom the individual has, ignoring certain types of context and, especially, deep

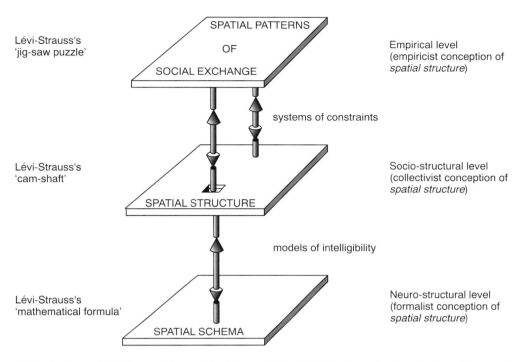

*Figure 14.1*    A Geographical Interpretation of Levi-Strauss's Cam-Shaft Analogy for Structuralism. (*Source*: Gregory, 1978b:100)

structures (Sayer, 1982:81). In Soja's (1980:81) words, the infrastructure (or processes) provides "determinants of activity of which actors are unaware", a view most reminiscent of the behavioural geographers' references to a bounded rationality in which individuals are not fully aware of those bounds. And indeed, writings by Marxist geographers (often labelled as neo-Marxist) in the mid-1980s give more credence to the role of human agency rather than retaining a naive picture of human beings as the mere puppets of deep structures. However, it can be argued that the supposed social control imposed by these unseen forces requires closer scrutiny in the real world rather than just theoretical deliberation (Harvey, 1992).

Amongst the most well known of the attempts to combine the spatial with broadly structuralist theories is Massey's (1984) *Spatial divisions of labour*. In earlier work (Massey, 1976, 1979) she stressed the need for a framework to examine industrial develop-

ment in which behaviours must be explained, not assumed as in neoclassical models, and where the explanation involved consideration of both historical change and development at all scales. Structuralism provides such a framework but with a stress upon the need to focus upon the locality where the impact of national and international processes may be investigated. Such investigation harnesses the geographers' oft-stated view "that geography matters, that people and communities matter" (Massey and Allen, 1984; O'Neill, 1989:666). Perhaps the attraction of Massey's work, though, has been that it transcends the usual "top-down" method of structural analysis and enables consideration of localities in the context of national change. It also recognises that local variation can produce unique patterns despite the pervasive presence of national and international processes. However, this work has not been without criticism from some Marxists. For example, Webber (1989) finds it too dismissive of general tendencies, as expressed by national/international context, historical development and abstract theory, to provide postulates on which to base detailed empirical investigation. In broader terms, he argues that it is vital to recognise that the significance of "any empirical work rests on the hinges provided by abstract theory" (Webber, 1989:691).

A recurrent difficulty has been in relating the uniqueness of the individual locality study to the broader economic and social milieu. Yet there is a great need for studies that can take the local scale as the starting point and relate the local to abstract laws concerning the movements of capital, the labour process and the role of the State. Therefore some additions to Massey's basic formulation, such as Fagan's (1989) on the firm, its environment and restructuring processes (Figure 14.2) or Fincher's (1989) on class and gender relations, have been important advances. Further consideration is given to study of individual localities below.

## BEYOND STRUCTURES: REALIST PHILOSOPHY AND CRITIQUE

### Realism

The complexity of realist philosophy has tended to mean that a variety of work has been labelled "*realist*" without full appreciation of the differences between realism as philosophy and the "reality" that human geographers are seeking to construct. There are claims that realist approaches can encompass a suite of theories, including *structuration theory* (see below), Marxism as social theory, and humanistic approaches (Sayer, 1985a:161). This partly reflects the way in which all of these have made strong attacks on positivism. This overlap becomes clearer if the realist approach, as summarised by Sayer (1982, 1984, 1985a,b), is considered.

According to Gregory (1994e:499), "realism is a philosophy of science based on the use of abstraction to identify the (necessary) causal powers and liabilities of

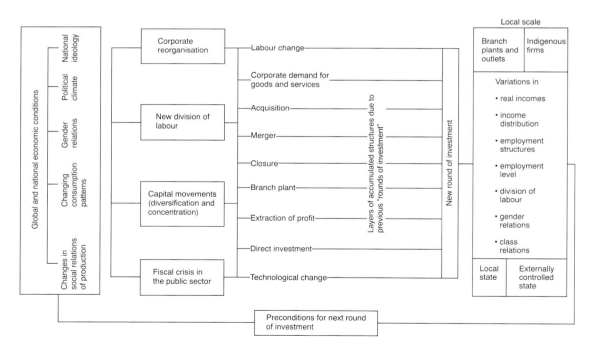

*Figure 14.2*    Production, Class, and Gender: Impact at the Local Scale. (*Source*: O'Neill, 1989:669)

specific structures which are realised under specific (contingent) conditions". Unfortunately the meaning of this statement is not very clear and requires what Cloke et al (1991:135) term "unpacking" or clarification. Their view is that realism "allows for the existence of structures, processes and mechanisms that can be revealed at different levels of reality and that mean that reality is not conceived of as closed simply around observable events and phenomena". Therefore realism challenges empiricist conceptions of causality (Sayer, 1984). It also challenges scientific methodology by emphasising that knowledge may be gained from participating as well as from observing, that feelings as well as spoken and written forms of language constitute knowledge, and that knowledge cannot be evaluated independently of a consideration of its production and use in social activity (Bhaskar, 1979).

Realism is essentially a philosophy of science in which researchers attempt to identify structures and agents present within society and to examine how these act or behave (see Bhaskar, 1989). Therefore realism takes as "given" the concept of social structures that influence and are influenced by the actions of individuals. So a realist approach may involve "finding out what produces change, what makes things happen, what allows or forces change" (Sayer, 1985a:161). However, confusion over the application of realism by geographers partly reflects the fact that realists call upon several bodies of theory to explain societal complexity. In so doing they have drawn distinctions between questions concerning observable phenomena and those relating to the processes creating the phenomena. So they have been involved with the uncovering of causal relations and processes, but only in terms of their particular social context rather than as some objective truth. Realists regard causal mechanisms as tendencies, not laws operating in open social systems and capable of producing different outcomes in different locations. Therefore realism is anti-positivist (Williams, 1981).

*"Naive" realism* is illustrated by Relph (1989) with reference to the seventeenth-century philosopher, John Locke. Locke differentiated between primary qualities of things and secondary qualities. The former refer to characteristics such as extension, figure, mobility and solidity whereas the latter are colours, tastes and other qualities delivered to people by their senses. For Locke the "real" world consisted of the primary qualities which therefore underlie the environments of everyday experiences. Gibson (1981) argued that this naive realism was translated into geography in the form of nineteenth-century "capes and bays" geography and work listing inventories of resources prior to the Quantitative Revolution or as part of geographical information systems. However, the "discovery" of realism by human geographers in the 1980s has extended this approach well beyond the naive, by recognising that there is a "real" world, components of which are not necessarily all immediately observable and which may not be discerned in an easily measurable manner. Some of these real "things" may only be known in terms of our senses and ideas (Outhwaite, 1987).

Sayer (1984:106–7) and Johnston (1984c:479) identify three domains of realism:

- the *real*, at which processes operate, e.g. the economic base;
- the *actual*, the level where processes are operated by individuals to create events, and the individuals are active agents not economic automatons;
- the *empirical*, the level at which real processes, as interpreted at the actual levels, are experienced.

Or, as simplified by Hay (1988:35), "We act in the empirical world; conventionally we tend to understand and explain process in that world at the level of the actual or concrete but, in fact, the underlying driving and driven forces are structuring at the real, or abstract, level."

In contrast to positivism, realism does not assume the existence of closed systems. According to Sayer (1984:112) there are two conditions that are prerequisites for regularity within a closed system:

1. *Intrinsic conditions*. No change or qualitative variation occurs in the object possessing the causal powers.
2. *Extrinsive Conditions*. The relationship between the causal mechanism and those of external condi-

tions, which make a difference to its operation and effects, must be constant if the outcome is to be regular.

He argues that these conditions are usually not met and that most geographical research is concerned therefore with open systems dealing with transient regularities. Such regularities are the product of open systems of events, mechanisms and structures in which complex interrelationships between structure and agency cannot be "explained" in terms of simple statements of cause and effect.

There were several notable studies in the 1980s that used a realist approach in which theorising of particular concepts and relationships played a major role in developing a deeper understanding of the subject matter in question. Cloke et al (1991:158) pick out four such studies: Allen (1983) on different types of "landlords", e.g. employers, investors, commerce; Sarre (1987) on whether ethnic segregation reflects a degree of choice by particular ethnic groups or is produced by structural constraints; Lovering (1985) on the location of defence industries; and Foord and Gregson (1986) on patriarchy.

These studies demonstrate that there has been an explicit incorporation of space as a key factor in understanding social systems through realist enquiry (Gregory and Urry, 1985). This signifies a distinction between the more abstract theories of Marx, Durkheim and Weber, which consider the "necessary" properties of objects, and the *contingent relations* that concrete research deals with, the latter involving consideration of spatial form (Gregory, 1985; Sayer, 1984). However, it is the development of methods through which realist epistemology might be practised that realism seems to be restricted. Its eclectic combination of the quantitative, interpretive methods and abstract theorising led Allen (1983:193) to remark that realism "sets itself the analytical task of conceptually specifying . . . [social] objects, their properties, and their potential range and scope. But it takes this aim upon itself with little in the way of accompanying methodological prescriptions to achieve its goal." Indeed, to some Marxists, realism, in its need to use techniques associated with positivist and humanist approaches and its emphasis on contingent relations and empiricism, is too far removed from the much more totalising social theory of Marx to be of great value (Harvey, 1987b).

## Structuration and Locality

In addition to the definitions used in the previous section, realism is also essentially a process-based theory of knowledge which explains empirical situations in terms of the structures and relationships producing them. It is this type of explanation that underlies the so-called *localities studies* popularised in geography in the 1980s (e.g. Sayer, 1982; Cooke, 1989). These recognise both the causal powers of social structures and the continuous interaction between individual human agents and social structures. The nature of this interaction has been conceptualised by Giddens's (1979) account of *structuration* emphasising "that social structures and institutions are simultaneously media and outcomes of human activity, and that individuals and society cannot be studied separately because each is embedded in the other" (Wilde, 1989:114). This approach acknowledges the uniqueness of place in the way its physical and social nature may influence the local expression of the mode of production, for example contributing to and changing the dynamics of the capitalist system, so that local change reflects interactions between the local and the global structures and processes of society (Johnston, 1984c; Kellerman, 1987). Much of the localities studies work has drawn upon structuralist concepts, emphasising the importance of capital accumulation and conflict between social groups, but it is sufficiently removed from doctrinaire Marxism to be criticised by "true believers" (e.g. Harvey, 1987a:376; Peet, 1987; N. Smith, 1987) as well as by others, from a cultural perspective (e.g. Jackson, 1991) and from a feminist perspective (Rose, 1989).

Realist approaches within geography that have embraced Marxist theories have done so with a broad perspective. This has also included other theories to take account of what Lawson and Staeheli (1990:15) referred to as "the multidimensional nature of the social world". This eclecticism is part of a conceptualisation of social processes at several levels, that is recognising several levels of abstraction from a "concrete reality" to a broader essence. Each level of abstraction can provide a different impression of the nature of the social system and the role of structures and voluntaristic acts. The role of space in these conceptualisations has been problematic, though, with different treatments given to the importance of place in the understanding of societal development. For example, Cooke (1983) and Massey (1984) regard place as the context in which social structures and relations assume concrete form and then influence subsequent processes, whereas Thrift (1983) gave more emphasis to the actions of individuals and institutions in particular places in terms of the reproduction of social structures. A continuing problem seems to be for realist geographers "to conceptualize and study linkages between agents, places, interaction structures, and more general social structures" (Lawson and Staeheli, 1990:17).

Perhaps the most crucial difference between a realist approach and a positivist one is that realism does not accept any objective truth against which concepts can be evaluated. Therefore it is impossible to determine whether contrary findings represent fundamental flaws in theory or merely specific contingencies (Saunders and Williams, 1986). However, realists utilise statistical analysis of actions, characteristics and circumstances to show regularities and differences between groups. These regularities and differences are not considered as ends in themselves but as part of an identification of particular mechanisms (Sarre, 1987).

Thus Harvey (1987a:373) argued that:

> The problem with this superficially attractive method [realism] is that there is nothing within it, apart from the judgement of individual researchers, as to what constitutes a special instance to which special processes inhere or as to what contingencies (out of a potentially infinite number) ought to be taken seriously. There is nothing, in short, to guard against the collapse of scientific understanding into a mass of contingencies exhibiting relations and processes special to each unique event.

So some see major limitations in realist approaches and in realist locality studies (Jones, 1988; Rees, 1989; Warf, 1989).

In locality studies it is unfortunate that the term "locality" has been conceived at different scales, varying from the local labour market (usually cities or even sub-areas within cities) to smaller neighbourhoods (Eyles and Evans, 1987). For example, the Changing Urban and Regional Systems (CURS) programme in the UK, often referred to as the "locality study project", has focused on areas varying in population from 50 000 to 200 000 and constituting both sub-areas within cities and self-contained urban areas. This reflects the use of economic criteria for the delimitation of the localities, a significant weakness if the analysis of the areas is to extend also to social and political processes (Cooke, 1986; Gregson, 1987; N. Smith, 1987; Urry, 1986).

One development of the "contextualisation" stressed within realism and featuring in the locality studies has been Pred's (1984) attempt to integrate time-geography (see Chapter 11) with structuration so that "place" becomes conceptualised as "an historically contingent process emphasising institutional and individual practices as well as the structural features with which those practices interact?" Pred (1981a, b) refers to the role of structuration in the temporal changes he observed in social and economic development. He recognised four antithetical "dynamics" in the impact of technological and institutional innovations:

1. Individual versus societal: Everything that affects an individual affects society and vice versa.
2. Daily path versus life path: Anything that affects an individual's daily activities affects their life as a whole and vice versa.
3. External versus internal: Movement along the daily and life paths leads to the accumulation of mental experiences that shape intentions and influence movements.
4. Path convergence versus path divergence: Any new "coming together" destroys old paths but creates new contacts.

It is these dynamics that are part of new "time disciplines", generating new relationships between people and time. For example, the introduction of the factory system created a clear division for factory workers between "work time" and "other time" which had a dramatic influence upon family life and the organisation of sport and recreation (see also Pred, 1979).

## CRITICAL SOCIAL THEORY AND POLITICAL ECONOMY

### "Neo"-Marxist Geography

Perhaps the most important extensions of the Marxian approach during the 1980s were those based on the work of the so-called *Frankfurt School of "critical" theorists*. Of these the work of Jurgen Habermas (1975, 1976, 1979, 1984, 1987) has been cited quite widely by geographers (see Gregory, 1989). This work argued that critical social theory must overcome limitations to an individual's self-knowledge and awareness. It is argued that these limitations are not overcome by either positivist or humanistic approaches, the former ignoring the individual's subordination to capital whilst humanism distorts self-awareness by advancing "group culture" (see Held, 1980). So critical theorists focus upon these distortions and the way they act in favour of particular interests. Effectively, this has close parallels with the basic goals of Marxism, but recognises that changes in society post-Marx have produced new conditions which maintain capitalist structures. Therefore these changes and structures must be studied if we are to reveal a full self-awareness. This has important implications for geographers because it points to the urgent need to consider the role of the State in all its levels of operation.

At least two different consequences of this recognition of the significance of the State can be distinguished. One has been the further development of theory, drawing upon a wider range of continental philosophy than just the Frankfurt School, and another has been a diffuse but widespread championing of *political economy approaches* in human geography. However, as demonstrated in Peet and Thrift's (1989) edited collection which advanced these approaches

within human geography, political economy has been interpreted in a variety of ways. In some cases it has simply been regarded as an approach that utilises an explicit focus upon the role of the State as the key determinant of the nature of social and economic structures (Bowler and Ilbery, 1987).

The term "political economy" was originally used in the late eighteenth and early nineteenth centuries by economists, including Adam Smith and David Ricardo. The latter's work on product accumulation and the distribution of "surplus" wealth created introduced the "political" element in the term through consideration of how the surplus would be apportioned amongst the social classes. This concern was central to Marx's work, but his approach departed from that of the classical economists, with their ideas on production and distribution which he strongly attacked. However, the term was not widely used again until the 1960s when, confusingly, it was appropriated by different sets of scholars thereby giving it a range of meanings. These sets included several approaches from a broadly Marxist perspective (Barnes, 1990), but also a more radical libertarian group in the USA used the term to refer to the role of the State, individual choice and decision-making, from which developed *public choice theory*.

Political economy entered the writings of human geographers via the work of Marxists such as Castells and Harvey in the 1970s, but its use has subsequently become far more diffuse and less clearly Marxist so that its usage now fails to encompass a common set of ideas. As employed in the collection edited by Peet and Thrift (1989), it seems merely to mean a recognition that the political and economic spheres are inextricably linked and so analysis of economy and society must explicitly acknowledge the role of the State in all its manifestations. This suggests a close approximation to the original use of the term by Smith and Ricardo! In some cases there has been a more explicit attempt to adapt Marxist notions to economic analysis or to consider the use of Marxist dialectics. Both of these are discussed further below.

In terms of its impact upon the discipline of human geography, the broad swathe of work under the broad umbrella of "political economy", or heavily influenced by neo-Marxist social theory, has had lasting effects. Despite a new wave of postmodernist and poststructuralist theory entering geography from the late 1980s, many of the ideas, both explicit and implicit in Marx's writings, have been assimilated, though they may appear in different guises today. For example, one set of "radical" geographies has been produced by feminist geographers who, initially, drew heavily upon Marxist theory (see Chapter 15). Whilst there is now a range of feminist geographies, the legacy of Marxist conceptions of the structure of society, the role of capital and the division of labour is still apparent in much of this work. However, there have also been strong challenges to structuralism, not least of which have arisen as a consequence of the rejection of Marxist–Leninist State control in Eastern Europe and the former Soviet Union. In responding to this, Sayer (1995:13) referred to "Marxism's lack of a sufficiently materialist understanding of the social division of labour and its associated division and dispersion of knowledge in advanced economies" and recognised weaknesses in how Western Marxists had analysed the socialist regimes of Eastern Europe. However, whilst much energy within human geography has been directed into "the cultural turn" (see Chapter 16), there are strongly Marxist strains continuing in work on uneven development (e.g. Peet, 1991), geopolitics (Dodds and Sidaway, 1994), and the impacts of capitalism upon the environment (Fitzsimmons, 1989). One strand that has also continued has been the translation of Marxist economic theory into concrete economic analysis, generally termed *analytical political economy.*

## Analytical Political Economy

Prior to the early 1970s most theoretical discussion in economic geography was dominated by ideas taken from neoclassical economics. Alternatives emerged in the 1970s (e.g. Massey, 1973; Sayer, 1976), but it was in the 1980s that substantive new explanatory frameworks were developed. Of these the political economy perspective gained most ground, in which explicit use is made of analytical methods, but often as a secondary consideration to theoretical explication. It is this that has

been a distinguishing feature of contributions by Massey (Massey, 1984; Massey and Meegan, 1982) and Scott (Scott, 1980, 1984; Scott and Storper, 1986) for example. However, the analytical methods have been more to the fore in more recent work under the broad umbrella of this approach (e.g. Sheppard, 1990; Sheppard and Barnes, 1990; Webber and Tonkin, 1990). In general terms, political economy is the management of the economy by the State, and hence "political economy approaches" have emphasised the role of the State, at various levels, in setting the parameters within which both economic and social change occurs.

The rise to prominence of political economy approaches within human geography follows that within economics, drawing initially upon the writings of Ricardo and Marx. The similarities and differences between the Marxian model of reproduction and Ricardo's own model are shown in Figure 14.3. Both have a concern with value, production, reproduction and distribution; and it is the focus upon distribution that introduces the "political" aspect of political economy, extending analysis beyond the purely economic to the sphere of social and political considerations. The latter do not appear as an inherent focus in neoclassical economics where rational choice and optimal allocations of resources hold sway.

Barnes (1990) recognises several crucial differences between emergent political economy approaches and neoclassical economics. Key ones are:

1. In the neoclassical scheme, value is not created within the production process, but by the desires and preferences of individuals as they exchange.
2. There is no sense of reproduction in the neoclassical scheme, i.e. once one "round" of production has occurred the slate is wiped clean for the next round which starts with a new set of resource endowments and preferences.
3. Neoclassical economics was presented in mathematical form and gathered an array of sophisticated mathematical concepts and theories. In contrast, political economy approaches have only been translated into mathematical form since 1960 (Sraffa, 1960), since when different "schools" of analytical political economy have emerged.

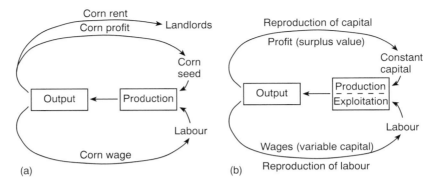

*Figure 14.3* (a) Ricardo's Corn Model; (b) Marx's Model of Reproduction. (*Source*: Barnes, 1990:994)

The various "schools" of analytical political economists include neo-Ricardianists, fundamental Marxists and those described by Barnes (1990:997) as "rational choice Marxists", in that they are concerned with examining and developing theory pioneered by Marx, but in the light of intervening history and using tools of non-Marxist social science and philosophy (see Roemer, 1986, 1988):

1. *Neo-Ricardianism*. The model developed by Sraffa in 1960 is basically Ricardo's corn model extended to many commodities. However, these models lack economic, social, historical or cultural context in which to interpret conditions of production and distribution. Hence it has been argued that this context needs to be added.
2. *Fundamental Marxism*. This defends Marx's labour theory of value by examining empirical issues in a Marxist theoretical framework (e.g. Farjoun and Machover, 1983).
3. *Analytical Marxism*. This originated in the early 1980s and was associated with the work of Roemer. It avoids the "naive functionalism" of some Marxists and seeks explanations of mechanisms at the micro-level using modelling techniques developed by neoclassical economics and rejecting Marx's labour theory of value on analytical grounds. The end-point is not equilibrium and harmony but exploitation and class formation. This approach accepts that individuals are rational and make choices under structural constraints.

Economic geographers have been part of these developments, for example with work combining empirical analysis with fundamental Marxist terminology, e.g. Graham et al's (1988) analysis of manufacturing restructuring in the USA, Foot and Webber's (1983) examination of unequal exchange at an international level, and a series of studies by Webber and co-workers on Canadian manufacturing in which relationships between profit, accumulation, technological change, values and prices were analysed (Webber, 1986; Webber and Rigby, 1986; Webber and Tonkin, 1987, 1988a,b, 1990). More theoretical approaches from a neo-Ricardian standpoint have been developed by Barnes and Sheppard (Barnes, 1984, 1988b; Barnes and Sheppard, 1984; Sheppard, 1983a,b, 1987; Sheppard and Barnes, 1986) since Scott's (1976) linking of the von Thunen model of agricultural land rent to Sraffa's work. Webber's work has attempted to address the Garin–Lowry model by dealing with two related criticisms – that it ignores causes and that it is ahistorical (Webber, 1984:160). It has no "motor" to make things happen, and so a motor has been supplied by linking it to production-based models of the city as developed by Scott (1980, 1988a,b). In this way the dynamics of the production system and the division of surplus among classes drive the model (see Sheppard and Barnes, 1990:ch. 7).

Perhaps the most important outcome of this research is the demonstration that spatial considerations disturb aspatial economic formulations, echoing Harvey's (1985c:142) view that "the incorporation of space has a numbing effect upon the central propositions of any corpus of social theory". In Barnes's (1990:1003) words, introducing the spatial variable creates "indeterminacy". For example, as the friction of distance increases it may *or may not* be more profitable to switch to those production methods that minimise transport inputs (Barnes and Sheppard, 1984).

In general, this work also places empirical research at the forefront of geographical analysis, focusing attention upon the need to employ mathematics in specific studies. Even some Marxists have been willing to accept this (Ruccio, 1988). Yet, Gertler (1990) views the development of analytical political economy as tending to fall into the same tendency for "irrelevancy" as the neoclassical theory which it seeks to replace. He charges it with over-simplification and the use of a symbolic logic "incomprehensible to many working in related areas" (Gertler, 1990:1035). Despite this he recognises the potential for geographers to use this and other empirical forms to examine economic problems first considered in aspatial terms.

Sheppard and Barnes (1990:13), in supporting the use of analytical political economy, recognise that mathematics is merely one discursive strategy among others and that an analytical treatment can only be applied to certain aspects of society and economy. The analytical models show only what is logically possible, not what will actually occur (Ruccio, 1988). The content and application of the mathematical models within analytical political economy are beyond the scope of this book, but reference to the works of Scott, Sheppard and Webber cited above will provide a good introduction (see also Barnes, 1996).

## World-Systems Analysis

One highly significant neo-Marxist contribution to geographical thinking has been *world-systems analysis* as developed by Immanuel Wallerstein (1974, 1979, 1980, 1983, 1984a,b, 1991a,b; Hopkins and Wallerstein, 1982). Whilst containing several important departures from orthodox Marxism, it incorporates Marxist theory in a study of social change which recognises just three fundamental types of society:

1. *Mini-systems or reciprocal-lineage mode.* Production is largely differentiated by age and gender and exchange occurs only by reciprocal means.
2. *World-empires or redistributive-tributary mode.* Society is class-based, and production is performed by a majority group of agriculturalists paying tribute to a small ruling class.
3. *World-economies or capitalist mode.* There is continual capital accumulation through a market-driven "engine" which determines prices and wages via demand and supply mechanisms.

The division of labour in production is the key to differentiating between these three societies. As 2 and 3 refer to divisions of labour that transcend the local and the regional they are referred to as world-systems. Only one world-economy is recognised: that of capitalism which expanded for over five centuries to encompass the globe by the beginnings of the twentieth century.

Wallerstein's world-systems analysis has been utilised and developed by human geographers, notably Peter Taylor (1989a,b, 1992) who was instrumental in using this approach within a revived and greatly invigorated political geography. In applying the analysis the world is treated as a single entity as part of the capitalist world-economy, thereby replacing the notion of multiple societies, which has been common throughout the social sciences, by a single entity world-economy. As outlined by Taylor (1994:677–9), this recognises three fundamental structural features:

1. A single world market which influences economic decisions throughout the world.
2. A multiple State system that is not dominated by one single State, but in which political competition contributes to variety of economic decision-making.
3. A degree of stratification within the system which is reflected in the three-fold spatial structure of core, semi-periphery and periphery. Emphasis is placed on the role of the semi-periphery as a stabilising force and as an arena of class struggle and periodic restructuring. A good example of this was Eastern Europe in the 1980s.

In Wallerstein's analysis core and periphery are dynamic entities, constantly changing so that countries can change status as they evolve into and out of the semi-periphery. A central part of the analysis is taken up with consideration of capitalism and the dynamics of economic development. In particular, he examines the nature of boom and bust in economic cycles, the significance of division of labour, commodity chains and the social relations associated with the means of production. Four institutions are highlighted: households, classes, peoples and States; and it is their operation that is seen as being highly variable and contributory to the production of uneven development and economic inequality.

There are several differences between Wallerstein's analysis and that of orthodox Marxism, notably in terms of the conceptualisation of development, modes of production and the role of labour in the emergence and growth of the capitalist system. However, these differences have encouraged a broader consideration of the nature of development by both Marxists and non-Marxists, especially in terms of long-run economic cycles or the "rhythm" of the world-system (Taylor, 1992).

## MARXIST METHOD: DIALECTICS

A significant criticism of much geography written from a Marxist perspective has been its lack of concern for the traditional data analysed by geographers and therefore also for the techniques used to analyse those data. The preceding discussion in this chapter, relating to "Structuralism", provides one set of explanations as to why Marxists adopted this position. However, in some cases, one of Marx's own "techniques" was put forward as an alternative way of proceeding. This was the use of *dialectics*. Although popularised as a method by Marxists, dialectics were developed by Hegel (1770–1813) and by Engels (1940) and originate with Ancient Greek scholars. The word itself is related to "dialogue" and can be understood by considering how a dialogue often works out: if one person states a case A, another person may point out its defects and argue for B; as a result of discussion, C is reached, which does justice to both

positions but discards what the two protagonists now agree was mistaken. Hegel regarded history as developing in this fashion: beginning with a thesis against which is set a one-sided antithesis, and both contribute towards the final synthesis. This synthesis is not an end-point, though, as it is defective and so the whole process must necessarily recommence.

This three-stage process can be seen to recur throughout history according to Hegel. For example, an electorate may replace a left-wing government with a right-wing one and, in time via compromise, a more centrist position is reached. But, given the continued presence of both left-wing and right-wing views, this centrist position can be seen as being unstable. So the effort to reach a satisfactory social pattern via an "acceptable" government continues.

Hegel saw this type of process as occurring not only in conversation, history and religion, but also as an ultimate and all-inclusive process that cannot be observed: it can only be grasped by thought. In other words "the development of mind and history reflect that ultimate development in the course of which mind and history come to be" (Allen, 1957:203). This Hegelian idealism was interpreted by some as signifying an interminable dialectical process in which the existing state of things is inherently defective and requires to be superseded by one more satisfactory. This view greatly influenced Marx who developed the idea that a given society is the thesis that contains its own antithesis within itself and, in particular, the system of production outgrows the social and political forms amidst which it has developed. As Burns (1935:372) put it:

> At a certain stage of their development the material productive forces of society come into contradiction with the existing productive relationships, or, what is but a legal expression for these, with the property relationships within which they had moved before. From forms of development of the productive forces these relationships are transformed into their fetters. Then an epoch of social revolution opens. With a change in the economic foundation the whole vast superstructure is more or less rapidly transformed.

This is often interpreted with respect to capitalism,

implying that within capitalism are the seeds of its own destruction, so that, ultimately, the capitalist system will be replaced by a socialist one. For example, Harvey has frequently argued that capitalism produces inequalities in society (*uneven development*) and that ultimately these inequalities will lead to the downfall of the capitalist system. To signify this, partly as a form of wish fulfilment, the stage of capitalist development entered in the last quarter of the twentieth century is referred to as "*late capitalism*". It is also asserted as part of a dialectical analysis that, to regenerate itself continually, capitalism produces inequalities at a variety of scales. Therefore to tackle the elimination of "depressed" regions from within the confines of the capitalist system, for example via regional policy, will be unsuccessful (Marchand, 1978).

The basic approach of Marxist analysis rests on an understanding of the dialectics at work within the social structure. This employs dialectics as a method of logical argument in which contradictions are disclosed and synthetically resolved. However, as employed by Marxists, "contradiction" is used to imply incompatibility rather than a logical contradiction in which assertions of each "pole of contradiction" denies the other (see Heilbruner, 1980:35). The main dialectic identified is that between productive forces (combining the means of production, conditions of labour and labour power) and the relations of production (comprising the conditions within which the productive forces are brought into operation) (Marx, 1967). The consequence or realisation of this dialectic is a falling rate of profit accompanied by growing inter-class antagonism, usually simplified into conflict between proletariat and bourgeoisie (the French word for "freeman of a burgh", subsequently a term generally applied to a member of the mercantile or shopkeeping middle class, but often used in a dismissive and quasi-derogatory sense to mean all or part of the middle class, that is "supporters of the capitalist system"). Ultimately the uncovering of the meaning of the dialectic is supposed to produce a revolutionary overthrowal of the capitalist system. Therefore Marxist dialectical analysis accounts for social formation and structures, such as the State representing the containment of the revolutionary forces and legitimation of capitalism. Inherent contradictions within capitalism are held to be responsible for changes that give rise to a "jerky" spiral of development, lurching from one level of development to another (Harvey, 1982).

Marxists considered the dialectic, embodying a logic of reasoning, to give a truer and deeper knowledge than the world of phenomena and experience by its ability to expose the "deep structures" of society and its dynamics. As these deep structures are not concerned with simple empirical phenomena but with features "hidden" behind them, then empiricism has been eschewed in favour of a focus upon other concepts, such as the social relations of production (Ollman, 1990, 1993). Yet, the position of an individual person with respect to these structures is problematic. For example, "in an extreme structuralist interpretation society's structures determine everything and individuals can only play the class roles given them" (Wilde, 1989:113). In this view space becomes inconsequential as does geography (Eliot-Hurst, 1985).

Neo-Marxist views relax this tenet of a totally dominant structuralism and look at ways in which spatial differentiation can be used and even created for the benefit of some part of society and for the subjugation of others. For example, Cox's (1981:268–74) interpretation of dialectical materialism is not based on the more structuralist readings of Marx, but comes from a blending of his earlier humanism and the critique of political economy which came to fruition in the *Grundrisse* (Marx, 1973). Cox argues that the unity of subject and object is central to dialectical materialism whereby what is important in viewing society is the internal relation linking subject and object. This contrasts with the positivists' approach in which subject and object are separated.

In championing the use of a dialectical vision for understanding the relationship between process and form, Harvey (1995) notes how different this approach is to the positivist one adopted by Peter Haggett (1965) in *Locational analysis in human geography*. He laments the fact that "the craft of dialectical reasoning is not well understood, let alone widely practised, in geography" (*ibid*.:4), and provides a guide to the 10 basic propositions underlying the principles of dialectical thinking. These are summarised in Table 14.1. He contends that such thinking has been widely misinterpreted, possibly because of the scope for a diversity of interpretations that exist within Marxist and neo-Marxist literature. However, despite the support for the use of dialectical modes of thought by influential Marxist geographers, such as

*Table 14.1*    The Principles of Dialectical Thinking

1. Dialectical thinking gives priority to the understanding of processes, flows, fluxes, and relations over the analysis of elements, things, structures, and organised systems. This is because it is processes and relations that create, sustain or undermine systems and structures.

2. Elements and systems which many researchers treat as irreducible and therefore unproblematic are seen in dialectical reasoning as internally contradictory by virtue of the processes which constitute them. Elements are constituted out of flows, processes and relations operating within bounded fields which constitute structured systems or wholes.

3. Elements are internally heterogeneous at every level.
   - Elements can be decomposed into a collection of other elements which are in some relation to each other, e.g. a city can be broken down into neighbourhoods, which in turn can be decomposed into people, houses, schools and factories, and so on *ad infinitum*.
   - The only way we can understand the qualitative and quantitative attributes of elements is by understanding the processes and relations which they internalise.
   - The extent of internalisation depends upon processes operating over a relatively bounded field. Therefore determining the extent of these boundaries is a major strategic consideration in the development of concepts, abstractions, and theories.

4. Space and time are neither absolute nor external to processes but are contingent and contained with them. Processes do not operate in, but actively construct, space and time and in so doing define distinctive scales for their development.

5. Parts and wholes are mutually constructive of each other as in the way in which human agency makes structure but structure makes agency in Giddens' (1984b) structuration theory.

6. Because of the interdigitation of parts and wholes, subject and object, and cause and effect, are interchangeable. For example, individuals are both subjects and objects of processes of social change. Therefore causally specified models are suspect as are cause and effect arguments.

7. Opposing forces are at the base of the evolving physical, biological and social world.

8. Change and instability is the norm in all systems and parts of systems. Therefore any equilibrium must be explained by considering the actions of opposing forces or moments balancing the system.

9. Dialectical enquiry is a process that produces concepts, abstractions, theories and various institutionalised forms of knowledge which stand in their own right only to be supported or undermined by the continuing processes of enquiry. Thus a researcher changes the subject of research and, in turn, is changed by that subject.

10. Dialectical enquiry incorporates the building of ethical, moral and political values and regards the constructed knowledges that result as discourses situated in a play of power. It is not deduction or induction that is the central motif of dialectical practice but eduction, the exploration of potentialities for change, for self-realisation, for the construction of new totalities such as social ecosystems.

Based on Harvey (1995).

David Harvey and Richard Peet, the growth of post-modernist and poststructuralist thought in human geography has tended to promote approaches championing multiple "voices" rather than the binary oppositions of dialecticism (see Doel, 1993).

A further problem regarding the use of dialectical thinking has been the arguments within Marxism regarding just what role dialectics should assume. For example, the philosopher Bhaskar (1989:115) describes dialectics as "possibly the most contentious topic in Marxist thought", partly because of the variety of definitions of dialectic(s) and different schools of thought as to what constitutes dialectical procedures. For example, Castree (1996:345) refers to two sets of "new dialecticians" who have attempted to re-examine Marx's dialectics and its debt to Hegel. Both sets regard dialectics as an integral component of Marx's social theory and intimately connected to his conception of historical materialism as a science. However, there are different approaches and emphases within the two camps, with Harvey, as a new dialectician, employing dialectics as "both a mode of explanation and a mode of presentation geared to capturing in knowledge the realities of capitalism" (Castree, 1996:347). Thus, in examining Harvey's use of dialectics, Castree (1996) argues that this usage has been both as an explanatory–diagnostic tool and as a set of principles or rules for further study. Essentially, dialectics appears in Harvey's work as an explanatory principle of "opposition, antagonism and contradiction" (Harvey, 1982:xv). So, as in Marx's *Das Kapital*, a commodity has both a *use value* and an *exchange value*, the two forms of value opposing each other as reflected in the dynamics of separation between commodities in general and money, which in turn encompasses other contradictory dynamics at the heart of capitalism. Therefore a complex totality of underlying processes and surface appearances can be represented in terms of various dialectical contradictions. In presenting process and appearance via dialectics, Harvey has developed an open-ended line of enquiry, described by Castree (1996) as *systematic dialectics*, which is central to Harvey's explanatory–diagnostic project. Castree's account shows dialectics as a way of thinking so that it is embedded within the language and analysis of Harvey's work as an inherent element within the explanation he employs. Harvey's use of dialectics has therefore been both as an explanatory–diagnostic tool and as a set of principles or rules for further study. The best examples of this are in Harvey (1982, 1985a,b; 1986, 1989c).

## REFUTING MARX

> Instead of accepting the refutations the followers of Marx re-interpreted both the theory and the evidence in order to make them agree. In this way they rescued the theory from refutation; but they did so at the price of adopting a device which made it irrefutable.
>
> Popper (1972:37)

A major problem lies in identifying a replicable set of analytic procedures underlying the Marxist rhetoric. The relative complexity of Marxist analysis, and its unfamiliar language, initially led to some confusion over methodology compared with the clarity of the cry for "revolution" or the apparent simplicity of the scientific method. And, until the development of analytic political economy, geographers "practising" historical materialism made relatively little effort to translate belief into practice beyond criticising positivism and capitalism. This gave succour to critics of Marxist geography.

Some of the initial reactions to the infiltration of Marxist views into human geography were dismissive and questioned the ability of the Marxist dialectic to contribute to an understanding beyond reinforcement of what critics regarded as a metaphysical belief system and not a form of rational argument. Good examples of this view occur in work by Berry (1972) and Chisholm (1975:175). Chisholm's view of the Marxists' preferred "technique", dialectics (the perpetual resolution of binary oppositions), was that it constituted a metaphysical belief system and not a mode of rational argument. This has been followed by strong arguments from others (both pro and anti), emphasising the gap between Marxist ideological pronouncements and "practice", and criticising or championing historical materialism on other grounds (e.g. Muir, 1978; Ley, 1980; Walmsley and Sorensen, 1980).

Three principal themes in the critique of structuralism *per se* were identified by Gregory (1981) and subsequently elaborated powerfully by Duncan and Ley (1982) amongst others. The three are as follows:

(a) *Reification*, in which structuralism is held to ignore the importance of human decision-making by concentrating solely on structural controls and actually elevating capitalism to exalted powers of dominance over human activity. This reification is apparent also in the work of some other social theorists, such as Durkheim, which gives little indication of any understanding of the complexities of capitalism, especially in terms of the operation of individual businesses and corporate organisations. For example, Muller and Rohr-Zanker (1989) show that neo-Marxist theories on the fiscal behaviour of American cities have ignored both changes in urban fiscal strategies and under-estimated the political flexibility of city managers. Their complaint about little concern being shown for whether neo-Marxist theory actually "fits the reality" finds echoes in other areas, especially with respect to the economic determinism expressed in more recent "neo-Marxist" theory (e.g. Pickvance, 1984; Gurr and King, 1987).

(b) The actions of an individual are determined entirely by constraining structures. This is antithetical to ideas of voluntarism and self-determining behaviour.

(c) Marxism presents economic processes as the ultimate cause of behaviour. This link between economy and behaviour is a mystical one based on a partial and inadequate view of economic processes, and misconceptions of both individual and group behaviour. For example, the emphasis upon class conflict between a well-defined "proletariat" and a middle-class "bourgeoisie" as a central driving force of societal development ignores other forces and grossly over-simplifies the nature of social class construction and differentiation. Too much work employing historical materialist analysis has followed a self-fulfilling prophecy, for example Harris's (1988) conclusions that class was the decisive factor in shaping urban politics in Kingston, Ontario, in the late 1960s. Given the basic premises upon which historical materialism rests, it would have been hard to reach a different conclusion.

Indeed, Marxists themselves have recognised a need for reassessment of the conceptualisation of the nature of class relationships and their role in socio-spatial differentiation. Too many trite assertions about class constitution, class conflict and, just as fundamentally, the nature of economic processes under capitalism, have demonstrated a belief in a nineteenth-century Marxist world-view at the expense of an engagement with late-twentieth-century reality (e.g. Peet, 1979, 1980). Perhaps too there has been too much uncritical repetition of the basic claims of Marxian views. For example, Gregory (1978a) talks of emancipation of the proletariat via the overthrowal of capitalism, as being the goal of "critical theory". Whilst this may indeed be an ultimate goal, it invokes a faintly ridiculous "Heaven on Earth" should the proletariat become "emancipated", whilst not addressing the chasm existing between the theory and overthrowing the system.

Perhaps the most disappointing aspect of the initial Marxist contribution to human geography was the unwillingness to acknowledge the gulf between the utopia promised by Marxist theory (or visions of widespread release from "subordination" to be brought about by governments practising Marxist principles in economics, politics and social policy) and the realities of life under any form of Marxist–Leninist (or State Marxist) government. Even if the utopian view is still held up as an ideal, more damning indictments of the realities could have been forthcoming from across the spectrum of radical geographers instead of the continued focus on the evils of capitalism.

Just as capitalism produces social inequalities, so have Marxist governments. Marxist–Leninist, Stalinist, Trotskyist and Maoist governments have set out to mould human nature to their own ends. Individuals have been made subservient to the interests of the ideology and "the party". The result, oft repeated, is summarised by Compton (1990:256) with respect to Hungary after the failure of the 1956 uprising against Russian-imposed communism:

> Marxism–Leninism had created an impossible political and economic situation ... and showed itself to be quite unreformable. Far from satisfying the aspirations of the

workers, the system, whether in "command mode" . . . or "reformed mode" . . . lacked integrity, corrupted the population and heightened social tensions. Its environmental, social and health records were abysmal and, as a consequence, it was associated with rising mortality and a drop in life expectancy.

For future investigation there is a need to elucidate distinctions between Marxism as a philosophy and State Marxism as a political system. At a superficial level it seems that wherever Marxist political parties have assumed political power for any length of time, the philosophy has been avowedly Marxist but the political system has corrupted this into State or fascio-Marxism or a close variant. For example, such States have frequently considered Nature as something merely to be conquered for human benefit, whereas Marx's writings refer to the need to reverse the alienation between people and their environment that occurs under capitalism (N. Smith, 1990).

Around the world, Marx's pre-ordained workers' revolts against capitalism have been replaced by workers' revolts against the fascio-Marxist–Leninist state. In the face of this, there has been an apparent inability of some academics to understand the limitations of turning Marxist philosophy into practice. Economic and social change in Eastern Europe and the former Soviet Union has contradicted certain understandings of progressive Marxist–Leninist teachings, and hence there is an urgent need to reassess the practical implementation of the Marxist "model".

Some geographers are grappling with these sorts of problem whilst maintaining an on-going critique of non-Marxist thought. For example, Harvey and Scott (1989) objected to the widespread notion within humanistic and postmodernist geography that "history and geography are constructed by human agents in unique places with an open-ended future". They urged the need to refine theoretical ideas "about the workings of capitalism as a total system". Yet they struggle to provide convincing demonstrations that such a theory is effectively much more than a deeply held belief, or to produce satisfactory "operationalisation" deriving from the theory. Increasingly, their view has been attacked by new postmodernist thought which

has criticised both positivism and Marxism for their totalising conceptions of human society. This attack on *metatheory* has found some strong champions within human geography because of the way in which it encourages the study of individuals, different groups and different places rather than seeking generalisations or relying on all-embracing theory (this is discussed further in Chapter 15).

Criticism of the dominant focus upon Marxist theory, for example in some of Harvey's work in the early 1980s, is well stated by Saunders and Williams (1987:427–8): "Harvey eschews fraternization with the enemy, and he adopts a quasi-religious, almost messianic tone in delivering his epistle. He tells us . . . of his unswerving belief that Marxism provides the surest guide to radical salvation.. . . Harvey's statement provides a good example of precisely that tendency in contemporary urban studies which we suggested could stifle fresh debate." And by Logan (1978:67): "Marxist analysis will continue to be relevant for understanding problems but irrelevant in providing solutions."

In contrast to Harvey, Manuel Castells' retreat from his earlier Marxist critique has left him distrustful of a methodological perspective "involving the useless construction of grand abstract theories" (Castells, 1983:xvii). He has argued a much more conservative position of needing to ground theory-building on reliable research to avoid hasty formalisation of any proposed conceptual framework.

The early wave of Marxist studies by geographers has been criticised for relying on a narrow productionist logic. However, alternatives have been sought, for example drawing upon Gramsci's (1977) theoretical logic, arguing the need to recognise the role of human agency in the process of social and economic change, "with ruling groups needing to legitimize and maintain dominance by gaining the active consent of the ruled" (Holmes, 1987:119). Gramsci argued that the dialectic was too narrowly conceived in "economist–determinist models", but instead was a movement to which people contributed by becoming "deliberately and of their volition an active force in the dialectical process" (MacLaughlin and Agnew, 1986).

The concept of *hegemony* is central to Gramsci's interpretation of Italian regional and class divisions in the 1920s, using the concept to denote situations in which dominant sectors of societies establish control over subordinate groups and legitimise their monopoly of State apparati. This concern with power relations has featured more frequently in work from a range of geographical perspectives, notably from feminist geographers (see Chapter 15), whilst other notable advances in a broadly Marxist tradition have come from the *realist perspective* described above.

The work of realists, feminists and the strong Marxist content in political geography are examples of the way in which Marxist and neo-Marxist thought has permeated human geography, gaining a general acceptance that few could have predicted in the early 1970s. In particular, the Marxist strain has changed the role and nature of theory within the discipline and has generally promoted a much greater awareness of structural controls and class and gender divisions within human society. As a consequence geographers who would not describe themselves as Marxist have readily used ideas and arguments that can be traced directly to Marx and his followers. However, in the 1990s there has developed an alternative set of ideas strongly critical of Marxism and all metatheory, and these ideas, under the banner of *postmodernism*, have proved particularly attractive to human geographers because of their ability to "reclaim" place, space and the individual from the totalising Marxist and positivist views. It is this postmodernist contribution that forms this book's concluding chapter, following consideration of a powerful movement within human geography from the early 1980s, namely *feminist geography*, which has been strongly influenced by both Marxist and postmodernist ideas.

# 15

# FEMINIST GEOGRAPHIES

## FEMINISM

### What is Feminism?

Feminists contend that men have "rights" that are unjustly denied to women. In seeking to redress the injustices brought about by male exercise of unequal power relations, which has produced various forms of male control over women and women's subordinacy, feminists have carried their struggle into both the public and private spheres, including the academic. In the latter, feminist assessments of the nature of scientific enquiry, social theory, reasoning and the fundamental construction of knowledge have led to a powerful critique of male-dominated thinking, and have yielded a rich vein of research extending social theory and methodology into areas previously neglected.

Feminists treat *gender* as a relational term reflecting the unequal power relations that exist between men and women. That is to say feminists have argued that, whereas *sex* is a natural category based upon biological difference, gender is a social construction that draws upon some aspects of biological sex. From birth, girls and boys are treated in very different fashion in a gendering by society that helps to construct both feminine and masculine characteristics, a construction that generally works to the disadvantage of women, though the ascribed gender roles vary tremendously through space and time. For example, contrast the "domestic" sphere of rural women in West Africa where they cook, clean, fetch water and wood, plant, tend and harvest crops, sell the harvest at market, engage in communal tasks, and raise the children, against the "social rounds" and light domestic chores of the well-to-do women in the European social elite of the eighteenth and nineteenth centuries.

The desire on the part of feminist theorists to treat gender as the principal social relation upon which experiences are based and identities constructed (WGSG, 1997:71) tends to relegate other contributions to core identity (e.g. ethnicity, class, age) to a secondary importance. This has been regarded as problematic by some who have argued that it is impossible to refer to gender without considering the way it is influenced by other social differences.

Central to the feminist critique of traditional epistemological assumptions is the charge of *phallologocentrism*, or the use of objectivist paradigms of knowledge gathering that favour masculinity: the identification of man (maleness) with reason and transcendence and women (femininity) with irrationality, the mythical, the mystical and motherhood. Feminists replace the objectivist assumption that knowledge is timeless, eternal, detachable from the standpoint of the knowledge gatherer, with the notion that knowledge bears the marks of its producer. Feminists have charged that what passes for knowledge is masculine in any or all of the following senses (Lennon and Whitford, 1994:2):

1. Problems to be investigated reflect only male experience of the world.
2. The theoretical frameworks adopted reflect the structure of masculine gender identity in contemporary culture.

3. The narratives constructed serve the interests of men as a group, promoting their position and legitimating the subordination of women.

4. The whole symbolic order by means of which knowledge claims are articulated privileges the male and conceptualises the female only as that which lacks masculinity.

## Patriarchy and the Invisibility of Women

In challenging traditional ideas regarding what are accepted by the academic community as valid forms of knowledge, feminists have contested basic assumptions underlying arguments within many disciplines, including geography. This challenge has attacked the limitations placed upon the role of women and the way in which women are often presented as deviations from a male norm. In examining the controls exerted on women in social life, feminists have focused in particular upon the marginalisation of women within the public sphere and upon the way in which women have been rendered invisible by their omission from countless writings of male academics. Feminists have attended to the contributions made by women to cultural, economic and political life, in an attempt to redress the long-term neglect of these contributions in studies performed by men. Women have been rendered invisible in two different ways. Firstly, they have not had their unique perspectives and experiences reflected in research carried out by men. Secondly, both feminist agendas and the work of female researchers have been conspicuous by their absence from academic disciplines.

The invisibility of women in the work of male researchers is seen clearly in writings about the world of work in which domestic work has been relegated to a position of insignificance when set alongside that of the male-dominated professions. The breadth of women's work, dismissively labelled as "domestic", has also been largely overlooked, especially in Developing Countries where it embraces a broader set of activities than that normally associated with the domestic sphere in the Developed World. The fact that much domestic work is unpaid has also meant that its contribution to economic productivity has been unacknowledged.

Feminists have attempted to rectify the biases and omissions of male-dominated research with a wholesale rethinking of the basis and nature of social enquiry. As part of their theoretical armoury, feminists have argued that at the heart of societal structure lies *patriarchy* or the control of power by men. Through this power there has developed a subjugation of women, and consequent relegation of women to certain social roles, notably those associated with home-based reproductive labour. Feminists have sought not only to develop a full understanding of how patriarchy has permeated all manner of economic, social and cultural life, but also to overturn patriarchy. Therefore there are close parallels with Marxism in that a change in the nature of society is an overriding aim. However, feminism is a "broad church" and various divergent views are held regarding the attainment of a society free from the oppression of women by men.

Feminists have criticised the rationale of scientism and empiricism, viewing science as "inherently phallocentric, privileging mind, intellect and logic, conventionally gendered as 'male' attributes, over heart, empathy and intuition (gendered as 'female') in the search for human understanding" (Grosz, 1987). So it has been argued that scientific practice has represented a patriarchal suppression of any alternative forms of understanding, at least within the early phases of the European Renaissance and Scientific Revolution (Foord and Gregson, 1986; Hanson, 1992; Harding, 1986). A more broadly based science informed by feminist theory would:

- make allowance for context and observer dependence in scientific knowledge;
- acknowledge the relational nature of theory and the rejection of the division between subject and object;
- emphasise the fluidity of language and representation;
- acknowledge the continuity and relatedness of "self" and the world;
- reject the hierarchy implied by such binary categorisations as "male" and "female".

A cogent critique of science as patriarchal is presented by Stanley and Wise (1983:56): "the western industrial scientific approach values the orderly, the rational, quantifiable, predictable, abstract and theoretical: feminism spat in its eye". Women adhering to this view have sought closer links with approaches in sociology and psychology which have *intensive methods* based on case studies, interactive interviews, ethnography and qualitative methods as a means to producing causal explanations (McDowell, 1988). These were deemed to be more sympathetic to "female" values than the "male" scientific method. There has been no one overarching feminist theory within which these methods have operated (e.g. WGSG, 1984), but *feminist standpoint theory* has been especially prominent.

## Feminist Standpoint Theory

Because so much of the initial work identified as feminist developed from a radical tradition, it drew upon Marxist thinking and, in so doing, echoed Marxist critiques of ideology and practice within positivism . . . and by dint of association, quantitative geography. The neglect of power relations within the prevailing positivist paradigm was anathema to most feminists and hence the great attraction of different theories and methods that could focus more readily on the everyday experiences of women, often using feminist standpoint theory in which knowledge is treated as being not only socially constructed but also gendered (Haraway, 1991). The intuition which underlies standpoint theory is that the subjectivity of the researched individual should be reflected in the project design and find articulation in the end-result (Lennon and Whitford, 1994:3). The basis of this theory lies in "taking the disadvantage of women's exclusion from the public realm by men and turning that into a research advantage" (May, 1993:15). Standpoint feminism takes the view that women researchers can operate from both an oppressed position as a woman and from a privileged position as a researcher. This represents a highly beneficial combination of "opposites" within the same researcher (exclusion and access; nearness and remoteness; concern and indifference). Furthermore,

women's experiences are not used as a means of attaining a single form of objective enquiry but the experiences act as a starting point for research that is situated within the wider context of women's lives in general. This involves a democratic engagement with other women (Harding, 1991).

*Feminist relativists* eschew the trappings of scientific approaches by arguing that knowledge or "truth" about women's position in society is possible. They contend that there are many versions of social reality, all equally valid, and that research therefore starts and ends with women's experiences. Attribution of a higher rank to one particular reality is regarded as part of a wider process in which women are oppressed and differences between women are distorted or used for the benefit of others. This relativism questions the use of categorisation and identifies four key limitations of male-dominated research:

1. Over-generalisation of research findings that are based solely on men's experiences.
2. A lack of explanation for the social and economic influences of gender relations.
3. Inaccurate and biased use of language, e.g. using "men" instead of "men and women", and using categories that privilege one term over another, e.g. objective (good, masculine), subjective (weak, feminine).
4. Androcentric practices.

Feminist standpoint theory rejects a universal objectivity, but in the 1990s has been partly superseded by poststructuralist, postmodern thinking in which all totalising theories, including Marxism, have been attacked. This is discussed further in the following chapter, but essentially it represents an attack on all theories and philosophies that try to generalise and "essentialise experiences" (Mattingly and Falconer-Al-Hindi, 1995:432). It even challenges the notion of "women" by replacing "unitary notions of woman and feminist identity with plural and complexly constructed conceptions of social identity, treating gender as one relevant strand among others, attending also to class, race, ethnicity, ages, and sexual orientation" (Fraser and Nicholson, 1990:35).

In terms of method advocated by feminists, a frequent emphasis has been placed upon the importance of interacting with the people being studied and of sharing information with them rather than treating them as merely subordinate purveyors of data or like animals in a zoo. This is sometimes referred to as the *principle of engagement or reciprocity* in which the researcher enters into a two-way dialogue with the subject. The most important problem with this is that the researcher's view may affect the subject's willingness to express their own opinions or may even lead them to adopt views that do not really reflect their true feelings.

## FEMINIST GEOGRAPHIES

Within the general concerns for gender and the relationships between gender, place and space, a number of different research foci pursued by feminist geographers have emerged. The following quotes, from a recent publication by the Women and Geo-graphy Study Group, summarise these foci (WGSG, 1997:126):

*Feminists have reclaimed women's contribution to both formal and informal work.
*Feminists have stressed the significance of home, the undervalued side of the home–work dichotomy, and the different meanings which are inscribed in this site.
*Feminists have undermined the home–work binary by showing that the boundaries drawn between home and work are blurred.
*Feminists have shown how workspaces are frequently spaces in which gender identities are negotiated, resisted and changed; where new and old, dominant and resistant, forms of femininity may be found alongside one another.

and (*ibid*.: 140):

*Feminists have reclaimed the formal side of the formal–informal political dichotomy by showing how formal politics is gendered.
*Feminists have reclaimed the informal side of the for-mal–informal political dichotomy by examining the importance of women's participation within informal politics.
*Feminists have challenged the boundaries drawn be-tween formal and informal politics by showing that the two are strongly connected.
*Feminists have shown how the spaces associated with informal politics are frequently potential spaces; spaces in which gender identities can be negotiated, resisted and changed; where new and old, dominant and resistant, forms of femininity may be found alongside one another.
*Feminists have shown that gender is an important category for political mobilisation.

From this broad range of topics, two have particular sets of implications for the type of methodology appropriate: work on gender and place, and the interpretation of landscapes.

## Gender and Place

Much of the early work by feminist geographers focused on the variation of *gender relations* over space, as well as through time. Hence what it means to be a woman in one location at a given time will be different to that in another location and time. Therefore attributions of characteristics as being "natural" to women and men are negated and strongly contested (see Foord et al, 1986). When discussing this, Bowlby et al (1980) noted a split between radical and socialist feminists. These two groups disagreed on the origins of women's oppression and the extent to which patriarchal relations are related to or are functional for a particular mode of production or are a completely separate set of relations. However, there has been some convergence subsequently as the socialist group has argued that moral, social, familial, sexual and cultural issues must be part of socialism and that unequal social relations between men and women are found at a number of levels: the biological, the unconscious and the ideological as well as the economic. Where a key difference remains is in terms of how women's liberation might be attained. Some feminists advocate revolution whilst others stress education of the populace within a largely unmodified democratic system.

In various ways feminist geographers have sought to uncover women's experiences of different places, experiences that have usually been ignored in accounts written by men. This approach has often thrown into sharp focus the different types of experience of place had by men and women. For example, many of the male portrayals of the semi-arid environments of the south-west USA have emphasised the stoicism of the settlers, of their ability to survive in the harsh conditions and eventually to dominate and control the environment. Norwood and Monk (1987) assembled a collection of essays on the region, based on women's diaries, art and literature, that present a very different picture. They show how women felt very vulnerable in this harsh landscape, but how they also interacted with the environment in various ways, working with it rather than trying to exercise control over it. In other words, the experiences and attitudes of men and women were very different, and hence their conceptions of place and what place meant to them individually were also very different. Therefore by focusing solely upon the male view not only were women's views being marginalised but vital aspects of people–place interaction were simply ignored.

Feminist geography has evolved over the past two decades from a focus upon analysis of gender differences in spatial behaviour and activity patterns towards a concern with the social constitution of women (and people in general) in particular places (McDowell, 1993:159; Massey, 1994). During this time the work of feminist geographers has assumed a position of greater commonality with that of work by feminists in other social sciences, contributing to a broad corpus of activity considering gendered identities.

The theory employed in this work has had a variety of origins, reflecting the diversity within feminist geography and also the diversity of the subject matter in which simplistic stereotypes have been replaced by a recognition of the diversity of women's lives and situations. In turn it has become increasingly unrealistic to talk of a single "feminist geography" as this term now embraces a variety of perspectives (McDowell, 1992a, 1993; Penrose et al, 1992; Radcliffe, 1994). Indeed, it must be stressed that feminist perspectives do not represent a unified body of thought. Hence it is more accurate to refer to "feminisms" (Humm, 1992). Nevertheless, there are several views and research practices that are common.

The emergence of feminist geography as a significant element within human geography has highlighted

an omission that, on reflection, seems glaringly obvious. This is that the techniques and models discussed in the first two-thirds of this book, many owing their origins within geography to pioneering studies in the 1960s, were applied in research that completely ignored gender. Although there were references to consumers, decision-makers and heads of household, there was no attempt to distinguish between the different realities confronting men and women, and the differential power relations associated with gender (see Jackson, 1990). Gender was largely a taken-for-granted variable and the different nature of women's lives was simply ignored. With hindsight this "invisibility" of women in geographical study may seem strange given the presence of a spatial manifestation to the difference between the lives of men and women in the form of the spatially restricted character of so many women's activities (see Tivers, 1985). However, as the overwhelming majority of geographers were men, this undoubtedly contributed to such differences being ignored. Gender and gender issues became an important focus of study only with the emergence of "radical" thought in human geography in the 1970s and a larger number of women geographers in the 1980s (though still a relatively small minority – just 10 per cent of staff in geography departments in American universities are women).

The importance of patriarchy for geographers lies in its role with respect to the nature of places. Patriarchy can be conceptualised as a creator of ground rules for the behaviour of men and women. In other words, men's control over the levers of power in society has produced a set of norms within society that conditions the differentiated roles of the sexes (Foord and Gregson, 1986). It also has constructed some spaces as feminine (e.g. the domestic kitchen, children's playgrounds) and some as masculine (e.g. the boardroom, most sports fields), whilst allocating certain kinds of gendered activities to the gendered places. Therefore spatial differences can often be equated with gender differences. A substantial theme in initial feminist writing was the way in which this relationship between gender and place had restricted women's lives to a narrow spatial territory in which domestic space was more important whereas it was men who dominated public space. In this public space women have tended to be devalued outsiders, though this devaluation and the gendering of space has long been contested and renegotiated by women.

This contest and renegotiation has taken many forms, the most obvious of which are:

1. Creation of domestic space that does not rely solely upon the traditional domestic labour of women.
2. Reconstitution of public space so that women can occupy this space and participate in its activities.
3. Appropriation of higher value for the domestic sphere.
4. Removal of the distinction between private and public.

## The Male Gaze and the Landscape

One of the aspects of feminist geographies that has attracted the most attention has been work on what has been termed the *male gaze* (Rose, 1993). This refers to the way in which male geographers' assessments of landscape appearance and its interpretation have been labelled as "masculinist" by some feminists. In applying this label, Rose (1993:86–112) argues that geographers have neglected the power relations within which landscapes are embedded. They have applied their "objective" faculties to observing and interpreting the landscape, but traditionally, with a limited view focused on landscape as representing a material consequence of interactions between society and environment. More recent work in cultural geography has questioned the meaning of the term "landscape" itself and the nature of the field researcher's gaze upon the landscape. This gaze has been termed *visual ideology* because it represents a particular type of relationship between an observer and a landscape, one in which the privileged position of the observer is crucial to the resultant interpretation (Jackson, 1989). Rose adds dimensions of gender and sexuality to consideration of "the gaze" referring to the ways in which, in much geographical and historical discourse, landscapes are often regarded in terms of the female body and the beauty of Nature.

It is argued that the gaze of the male geographer upon the landscape is inherently tied to the way in which men gaze upon women: a specific masculine way of seeing. Rose (1993:88) contends that, "the feminization of landscape in geography allows many of the arguments made about the masculinity of the gaze at the [female] nude to work in the context of geography's landscape too". This is viewed as being well removed from the distanced and disembodied objectivity of science. It is also seen as being part of the contrast between scientific objectivity and an aesthetic sensitivity that might be expected to form part of a researcher's armoury when assessing the landscape.

In developing her arguments, Rose extends the recent work of cultural geographers, such as Cosgrove and Daniels, who have treated landscapes as representing social power structures. She sees the interpretation of landscapes by geographers, and their representations in paintings, as including a masculinist view that incorporates a male view of pleasure to be derived from the landscape: "visual pleasure is seen as something disruptive, and its persistence leads to cultural geographers' suspicion of landscape as secretive, ambiguous, duplicitous, mysterious and other – feminine again" (Rose, 1993:101). Therefore masculine (or *phallocentric*) geography finds an uneasy pleasure in landscape which some feminist geographers have sought to analyse through the use of Freudian and Lacanian psychoanalysis.

Feminists have also sought to analyse landscape from a position that avoids both the dominant masculinist gaze and the duality of "Mother Earth: Father Culture" which is a common portrayal. A good example of this is in the collection of essays on the American south-west referred to above. In particular (WGSG, 1997:179):

> Feminist geographers have looked for spaces in landscapes which allow women to articulate their complex identities; they have read images for new and feminist meanings; they have studied work which explicitly challenges dominant ways of looking at landscape. Both these tactics emphasise again and again the complexity of landscape, so that generalising about a feminist landscape becomes difficult if not impossible. Moreover, this complexity also suggests that feminist projects may also be able to construct alliances with other marginalised groups,

so that gender itself becomes a problematic category with which to work.

Feminists have directed attention at portrayals of landscapes by women, which they have asserted avoids the power relations of the male gaze. They have sought to interpret landscapes and texts as an image of reality and with a feminist objective. For example, the WGSG (1997) make interpretations of Helen Allingham's paintings of English cottages and gardens in terms of the gender roles they reveal and information they convey regarding the social relations of power based on gender, class and sexuality. Other "texts" utilised by feminists include articles in newspapers and magazines, television broadcasts and film (e.g. Skelton, 1995a, b), the paintings of Georgia O'Keefe and the garden designs of Jane Claudius Loudon and Gertrude Jekyll. These analyses reveal complexities that have hitherto been ignored and which offer scope for detailed analysis, perhaps offsetting the previous over-emphasis upon the larger-scale landscapes associated with the landed estates (see e.g. Morris, 1996). They are also extending our understanding of complex relationships between Nature, femininity, domesticity and concerns well beyond gender relations, such as class, ethnicity, rurality.

Having briefly outlined some of the key themes in the work pursued by feminist geographers, the methodologies employed can now be subjected to closer scrutiny.

## METHODS IN FEMINIST GEOGRAPHIES

### Advantages of the Qualitative

Research methods employed by feminist researchers vary with the aims and location of the project, differ according to the intended audience or recipient of the finished research project, and alter according to the researcher's own interests, beliefs and positionality. Thus, feminist geographical research practice is both multi-stranded and complex.

(WGSG, 1997:90)

As summarised by the WGSG, the challenge of feminist geography impacts upon how research is undertaken in three ways:

1. Rethinking categories, definitions and concepts used to formulate theories.
2. Examining methods and underlying theories used for exploring problems.
3. Considering the process of selecting problems deemed to be significant for geographical enquiry, especially using gender as a principal analytical category.

The WGSG (1997:109–10) translated these impacts into four main features which characterise the methodologies used by feminist geographers. These are "ways of knowing, ways of asking, ways of interpreting and ways of writing". Not all feminist research projects contain all these features, but feminists have generally sought to achieve these characteristics through a research process which is actively being reflected upon. This involves careful consideration of the social and power relations established during the research project, a clear understanding of its feminist aims and how these may be achieved, a commitment to challenging oppressive aspects of socially constructed gender relations (and other oppressions, e.g. on the basis of race), inequality, an awareness of the limitations of the research and the important role of subjectivity.

These methodologies have also been linked to the promotion of social change within an emancipatory research process. In practice this has included the use of both qualitative and quantitative methods underpinned by theory. There is no single favoured method, though various forms of *qualitative approach* have been most popular in feminist research because this has encouraged dialogue and interaction between the researcher and the people being studied. However, it is the social context and consequences of the research that have been treated as occupying a pivotal role. In this way feminist research is not viewed simply as an abstract process of knowledge seeking.

Instead of applying "masculine" methodology and techniques, there has been some attempt to develop a theoretically informed analysis of gender inequalities in a variety of spheres with the use of techniques deemed more suitable for uncovering them (e.g. Bondi, 1991; Momsen and Townsend, 1987). One of the key reasons why feminists have favoured qualitative methods is because they have felt that these more readily enable the personal experiences of women to be researched from a female standpoint. This view has favoured small-scale, intensive studies reliant upon face-to-face discussions. This draws upon the researcher's skills at listening, empathising with the subject and validating personal experiences. However, the traditional power relations of an interview are rejected in favour of a non-hierarchical relationship between subject and researcher in which there is more interaction and a two-way dialogue. This reflects a desire to reduce the exploitative character of the research process. This is well exemplified by research that has aimed to raise awareness amongst groups of women by organising discussions amongst women at which experiences can be shared (Mies, 1991). This may or may not be linked explicitly to the raising of political consciousness.

Feminist geographers have argued that the use of research methods such as participant observation and depth interviewing (see Chapter 13) can transcend the limitations imposed by alternative methods in which a one-way process dominates whereby respondents simply provide answers to a researcher. Instead, a much more multi-faceted interplay between researcher and subject(s) can become an integral part of the research. Furthermore, the researcher does not have to be an objective investigator as demanded by positivism but can be sympathetic to the subject's views and position. However, as part of the interview or process of observation, the researcher has to be aware of the social dynamics that are operating. For example, a woman interviewing another woman in a domestic setting may be more likely to facilitate a frank exchange of views and reveal processes underlying a given situation than a male interviewer. However, for any researcher engaging in a discussion with a group of both men and women, it is important to recognise that women are less likely to be as prominent in leading a conversation and that exchanges may be biased in favour of the men. This reflects a common set of social power relations in which men in a group often determine the agenda in group discussion.

Although the qualitative, ethnographic approach has proved popular, there have been some caveats expressed. For example, Stacey (1988), writing from a feminist perspective, highlighted some of the potential pitfalls. In particular, she referred to the inherent contradictions present within the role of participant observer. On the one hand, there is the researcher as participant, identifying closely with a social group and submerging themselves within the daily activities of the group. On the other, the researcher has to be detached and necessarily exploitative to a certain degree in order to carry out the research. This poses a significant ethical dilemma set against the daily lives of the "target" social group which are complicated by both the researcher's presence and subsequent departure (see Wheatley, 1994). This detailed consideration of the nature of the research process, extending to a much greater awareness of interpersonal relationships between researcher and subject, and the raising of ethical issues, has been a very important component of work by feminist geographers.

As a counterbalance to concerns over some of the limitations of qualitative methods, many feminist geographers have viewed them as providing a suitable means by which the political dimensions of feminist geography can be enhanced, partly because they enable the researcher to inject a greater part of themselves and their own experience into the analysis. This can be viewed as part of a process of "*self-reflection*" by the researcher which has been seen as an important element in feminist research, reducing the tendency for a desire for knowledge of the world in the total and exhaustive sense attributed to both positivism and humanism (Haraway, 1991:190). Thus Rose (1993) makes a distinction between a "masculinist" humanism and the use of qualitative methods by feminists in which gender bias is an essential part of research that focuses on subjects "speaking for themselves" whilst clearly situating "the position" of the researcher.

## Letting Women Speak for Themselves

One of the ways in which feminists have tried to "explain" women's experience in their research has been to utilise *life histories* whereby women can record significant aspects of their own lives in their own words (e.g. Townsend et al, 1995). By letting the subject "speak for themselves", it is possible for the agenda of the research to be driven by the subject rather than the researcher as the former can focus on what they regard as important. The life history approach also introduces an important temporal and dynamic dimension as does the use of diaries to record daily events and especially the various tasks undertaken during the day.

As an illustration of the use of diaries and of an attempt to translate some of the feminist theories into research practice, the following are extracts from Sarah Whatmore's work on women engaged in farming activity in England, *Farming women*. This used what she refers to as *"cumulative interviewing"*. Whatmore (1991:61–2) writes:

The key characteristics of this method are threefold:

1. A relationship of trust and familiarity with the research subject was built up over a period of time, in this case one year. Visits develop from a semi-structured interview format to informal conversation. The interview process is thus cumulative, in the sense that each visit presumes the knowledge and interest generated by the previous one and builds upon it. Visits become more an occasion to catch up on family and farm news, to review progress of personal and business problems (money, sick children, exhaustion and so on), than to conduct a formal interview. Although a number of "topic areas" were identified in advance and covered consistently in each case, the themes which became important were dictated by each woman's own concerns. I rapidly abandoned asking specific questions, partly because the answers could invariably be learnt just by listening, and partly because subjects which would not have been raised, as either unimportant or too sensitive, were brought into the discussion by the women themselves in their own time.

2. The objective was to get beyond the point of turning up with a tape-recorder and leaving when enough information had been "extracted". Visits lasted half a day or a day and extended beyond the taped interview. Conversation and activity preceded and followed the turning on and off of the tape-recorder. As relationships developed, it was possible to become more involved in farm activities, particularly in helping out with those which fell to women, for example with domestic chores, childcare and meal preparation. This was important because, as the later analysis shows in detail, the working day of farm wives is characterised by the performance of a variety of "jobs" in response to simultaneous demands made upon them as wife, mother, and "reserve farm labour". Helping out with the chores was one way of extending the time I could spend with them and allowed me to see other aspects of their lives than would have been possible with a more formal method.

3. While the main focus of these case studies was the women themselves, an attempt was also made to involve other family members within a group setting, rather than individually. Bearing in mind that the farmer had already been interviewed independently for the base-line survey, the aim here was to accommodate the interest in the exercise expressed by husbands and adult children, without allowing them to become dominant subjects . . . this practice also highlighted an important difference in the kinds of information and modes of expression adopted by women on their own, compared to when they were in the company of other family members. The presence of others activated mutual expectations and negotiated ways of relating to one another as a "couple" or "family" group. In these circumstances, women fell back on more "factual" accounts of their work, seeking verification for their account from others.

and (*ibid.*: 63):

The case study material consists of some six hours of taped conversation per case, together with field notes and other contextual material. One consistent element of the enquiry was a "time diary" exercise incorporated in the recorded conversations which attempted to gauge the format of women's working days, in different seasons. During each visit women were asked to describe their activities on the previous day. This method was used in preference to the more established written time-budget diary because it is more open to women's own interpretation of their "working day" in which the priorities they choose, and the language they use to describe it, are themselves of significance. Moreover women declared themselves to be generally much happier to talk about their activities than to fill in forms.

These extracts can be compared with those from Hughes's work cited in Chapter 13. In both cases the emphasis is upon enabling the subjects – in this case "farming women" – to talk about their own lives in their own words. This enables the women concerned to set the agenda of any conversation and to bring out points of concern to them, rather than having a researcher control discussion along the lines of "I want us to talk about this . . .". The additional device of the diary can also be regarded as a means of letting the women decide for themselves what are the important experiences and events in their lives and recording them in their own words. The result should be a set of observations far richer in depth and texture than could be obtained by other means.

The following is an example of the type of time diaries produced from this method and reported in Whatmore's book, *Farming Women* (Whatmore, 1991:63):

Up at 7.30, put the kettle on and make tea, go out to fetch the cows in for morning milking, mix calf milk and feed the calves, take a cup of tea out to Tom [in the milking parlour]. Feed the yearlings in the yard and bed out the horses and feed them. Feed the poultry. Get the breakfast [for her husband, herself and usually her daughter] for about 9.00. Clear away, do some washing, think about what to make for lunch. Make lunch for about 1.00. Clear up, hang out the washing. Go out to help shift the sheep, I'm used as a stationary gate. Back to the house, make the beds and do the bathroom then it's really whatever turns up, there's always some "rep" [sales representative for an inputs firm] turning up or something and I'm the first line of defence, it's my job to keep them away from Tom [husband] unless he's said otherwise. Make the fires up in time for everyone coming in to tea. 4.30 have tea, usually make a cake, everyone comes in for that [usually husband, daughter and son-in-law]. After tea fetching the cows in again for afternoon milking [daughter does the milking] and feed the calves and bed the horses. Make tea for about 6.00 [supper]. Clear up and then go sit by the fire in the back room until bed, about 9.30.

From this it is possible to gain a detailed understanding of how the woman concerned views her own experience and just how she conceives her role in relationship to her husband, family and the farm enterprise. It also reveals the types of constraints that are exerted upon the woman's use of time, perhaps in a way that would not be consciously articulated by the woman herself. The significance of the woman's role in the farm enterprise is clear from this account, but its "invisibility" could be tested by reference to official documents (which may well omit the woman from the labour force as her work would be classified as "domestic" or "housewife") or by interviewing her husband.

In analysing the taped conversations, Whatmore (1991:91) makes use of quotes from her case studies as a means of letting the women speak for themselves (in this case about "housework"):

*Gayle Brown*
I hate the housework and always have. I have to do that myself as no one else does it. I think perhaps that's why I've got so many jobs [in the farm business] because I don't like doing that . . . I only do them because no one else does and the whole thing falls down.

*Julie Church*
There's a conflict of roles all round . . . because the cows I'm supposed to be in charge of and, as I say, I should be out there every day looking at them and checking them but I'm not because I'm doing other things. I'm either doing the flowers [she has a dried-flower business] or, like this morning, I just did housework which is very boring, I really do hate that, but one has to do it.

*Jill Watson*
I'm better if I'm pushed, I'm terrible for being . . . I mean I don't like housework, the more time I've got the less I do. I've always worked best under pressure. I hate housework anyway, I mean the more you do the more it gets mucked up anyway . . . I don't feel I could justify having somebody to help out [with the housework] just teaching [she is a supply teacher] because all that money's gone really, but if I can make enough on babygear [her second-hand baby equipment business] to pay somebody . . . I wouldn't mind that.

Again, this illustrates the types of constraints exerted upon women's lives – most noteworthy being the way in which the women felt they were the ones who had to do the housework despite the fact that they had paid employment just like their male partners.

## Feminist Geographies and Quantitative Methods

Given that the statistical techniques and mathematical models of the 1960s and 1970s had been associated with a neglect of gender issues, and given their link to the scientific method, it is not surprising that feminist geographers have generally eschewed their use. What is more, the radical roots of many feminist geographers meant that they were antipathetic to the underlying philosophy associated with the use of these techniques and models. Hence, although there were empirical studies by feminist geographers in the 1980s, they largely avoided the "masculine" language of statistics and mathematics in favour of the "feminine" traits of interpretation, concern for context, and empathy with individuals. For example, in her powerful analysis of the way in which the academic discipline of geography has been dominated by men, Rose (1993) challenges the way in which (male) geographers have ignored their own values, feelings and emotions as well as those of the people they are studying.

It can be argued that in the past, through use of quantitative methods on their own, gender differences were too often treated as causal factors without exploring other mediating causal variables. This left unexplained the reasons for differences between the sexes in the public spheres of work and leisure as well as in domestic situations. Investigation of reasons may have required the use of qualitative rather than quantitative data as, at least theoretically, the former can be as detailed and complex as possible, enabling more meaningful interpretations to be derived. One implication of this is that judicious combination of the quantitative and the qualitative may enable researchers to develop greater understanding of a problem under investigation. Furthermore, the felicitous combination of the two may yield benefits for work by feminists when it appears in the public domain. The use of mathematical principles and well established theory lends weight to findings utilising quantitative analysis. In contrast, policy-makers in particular tend to react unfavourably to research that appears to be based on "soft" and more subjective qualitative material. Hence, clear use of quantification supported by insights provided by the qualitative may offer a more persuasive means of influencing policy.

This view would be strongly challenged by many feminists, arguing from the viewpoint that traditional quantitatively based research in human geography and other social sciences has been a tool for promoting sexist ideology and has ignored issues of concern to women. A strong criticism is that the nature of quantitatively based research processes has been antithetical to feminist values. In part this is because such research has been used frequently as a support for elitist and sexist values, ignoring women in general and the social problems that have featured strongly in research by feminists. The objectification of respondents in conventional surveys has also been criticised as part of a broader set of objections to the lack of attention given to people's feelings and values when they are reduced to numbers. Such reductivism has been identified by some as being characteristic of an agenda set by white male academics. New concerns have appeared through the competing feminist agenda requiring both different forms of enquiry and different topics for closer investigation, for example work on childcare, sex discrimination, equal opportunity policies and gender-based divisions of labour.

Despite the dominance of qualitative methods in the work of feminist geographers, there has also been recent discussion regarding the use of quantitative techniques by feminists. For example, Mattingly and Falcolner-Al-Hindi (1995) argue that quantitative techniques have proved useful for describing the extent of difference between men and women and among different groups of women. McLafferty (1995) takes the debate on quantification further by considering ways in which feminist geographers can combine the use of quantitative techniques with feminist concepts of reflexivity and "embeddedness" (the social and spatial relationships among people and places and the connections between processes at different times and scales). She recognises a difficulty in using quantitative methods in feminist research as such methods "necessarily abstract from the people, places, or phenomena being studied" (McLafferty, 1995:438). However, they are seen as highly valuable in documenting the spatial and social dimensions of women's lives at the neighbourhood, local or global scales. It is this ability to help describe and analyse the similarities and differences among groups of women at different times and places that has been exploited in McLafferty's own work on women's journey-to-work patterns in New York (McLafferty and Preston, 1991). This has highlighted differences in the length of trips to work among ethnic groups, with African–American and Latina women commuting substantially longer than white men and women.

Quantitative techniques have been modified to meet feminist objectives, as in the design of questionnaires that attempt to avoid "masculinist" questions by using an approach that demands open-ended responses. Feminists have also used quantitative methods as a means of identifying places and people for in-depth qualitative study (e.g. Hanson and Pratt, 1991; Pratt and Hanson, 1993) and as a general context from which qualitative research can be utilised. This couples the power of generalisation with insights and nuances gained by studies of the particular (e.g. Valentine, 1993). One result of such work is more sensitive and critically informed quantitative work that combines positive strengths of both the quantitative and the qualitative. It also offers opportunities for further development of certain methods which can reinforce particular feminist concerns, e.g. multi-level modelling which analyses relations at different scales (Jones, 1991), or the display and overlay capabilities of GIS.

Feminists have raised awareness of the falseness of dualisms and of the fluidity of apparent rigid boundaries separating analytical categories (see Jackson, 1990; Massey, 1994). This can be extended to the boundaries between quantitative and qualitative research. Whilst methods incorporating them may involve very different approaches, "they merge in much empirical research where quantitative researchers use qualitative information to provide validity and meaning, and qualitative researchers call on quantitative data to contextualize their research"

(McLafferty, 1995:440–1). Thus each method can enrich the other and together they offer exciting possibilities for feminist geography and human geography in general (see also Harding, 1987; Moss, 1995; Pratt, 1989).

## WRITING FEMINIST GEOGRAPHIES

Another significant element within feminist geographies has been a growing concern for how geography is written, a process and form that has long been simply part of the "taken for granted". Writing is regarded by many feminists as a political activity that is integral to the attempt to secure change. Furthermore, feminist analyses have contended that the ways in which male geographies have been written have fostered the use of inappropriate and sexist language. For example, Bondi (1997) argues that, within the dominant Western intellectual tradition, knowledge (and language) has been gendered and has operated through the use of interrelated *dualisms*. These dualisms, such as male/female, culture/nature and objective/subjective, have tended to give one part of the duality (the first ones named in the examples) a superior position. In this way the "superior" terms have been associated with masculinity and the subordinate terms with femininity. The gender connotations within the language of the physical sciences are evident in the ways in which scientific objectivity has been associated with man's conquering of (female) Nature and the rationality and virility of masculine objectivity contrasted against feminine nurturing skills, emotion, subjectivity and the irrational. This can be readily extended from the scientific realm to everyday use of language so that it can be recognised that this too is "far from unambiguous or innocent ..., language as much as epistemology ... is deeply and asymmetrically gendered" (Bondi, 1997:246).

In seeking to overturn the masculinist "norms" of knowledge and language use, a number of different strategies have been adopted. One is closely related to the reflexivity discussed in Chapter 13, namely the use of the first person singular as a mechanism for maintaining an identifiable but consciously "positioned" voice within a narrative or text. The deliberate use of two such positioned voices has been applied by some writers (see Lees and Longhurst, 1995). A provocative shifting between different theoretical positions in order to disrupt dualisms has been used by Rose (1993), and there have been other deliberate attempts to eschew gendered universals in geographical writing (e.g. Sparke, 1994). However, it is debatable whether it is possible to eradicate completely centuries of linguistic practice and ingrained attitudes without more concerted raising of awareness of assumptions about gender that are deeply embedded in writing practices.

*Positionality* has been a concern for feminist geographers in their work on women in non-Western societies. In part, this has arisen initially from a concern for the way in which the role of women in the Europeans' colonisation of Africa, Asia and the Americas has long been ignored. However, the "rediscovery" of this role has yielded a rich vein of research since the early 1980s (see Blunt and Rose, 1994). In much of this the positionality of the writer has been a critical feature of the work, with "the subjectivities of both researcher and researched . . . strongly implicated in the constructions and representations produced" (Robinson, 1994:207). This does not necessarily close the gap in experience of different lives and lifestyles that exists between a white researcher and an Indian "untouchable" refuse collector. However, it does permit the development of a dialogue between individuals occupying very different positions within society. In this dialogue it has been common for the researched (or informant) to be regarded as having a view about their community or their life, but not the only view, whilst the researcher also has a view, but this is not necessarily the authoritative view of "the truth". Instead the researcher's view can be displaced by that of the informant. This displacement may be regarded as symbolic of the social displacement and dislocation of post-colonial society itself and is therefore far better suited to the needs of studying such societies than a research method in which rigid power relations between researcher and the researched are maintained. Indeed, as informants may have a number of different and multi-faceted positions, any ensuing text from the researcher can demonstrate these positions by repeating the *polyvocality* inherent in the post-colonial society itself. This plurality of voice is an integral part of many postmodernist philosophers and hence the claim of postmodernists that feminism is an integral part of postmodernist thinking and its rejection of patriarchal hierarchies.

Another strategy of feminists, including some feminist geographers, has been to turn to *psychoanalytic theory* as a means of putting the sexuality of the subject matter under study at the centre of research (see Bondi, 1993). According to Aitken (1997), this theory also offers the possibility of resistance to patriarchy through the politics of identity. In particular, psychoanalytic theory is being used as a basis for investigating how femininity and masculinity are inscribed in written texts. In a wider context, Aitken (1997) suggests that Jacques Lacan's reinterpretation of *Freud's psychoanalysis* offers insights to the analysis of language in texts. Lacan places emphasis upon language as a set of socially and culturally delimited systems of signs, providing information about the character of the writer. This information is a code situated between the reader and the "real" character of the author. We have to decipher the signs and symbols in text to uncover the author or to understand the author's interpretations that have resulted in the particular qualities in the text that we are reading, as discussed with reference to semiotics in Chapter 13.

## HISTORICAL NOTE

In assessing the development of feminist geographies during the past two decades, it is clear that the scope of work has been large – indeed there are several significant themes not covered above, e.g. ecofeminism, women and design of the built environment, women and minority groups. This breadth has been developed despite the relatively small number of women who are academic human geographers. Feminist geography has also tended to remain outside mainstream human geography (McDowell, 1992a, b, 1993), partly because of initial emphasis upon presenting a critique of human geography and partly because of its focus upon gender. However, this marginalisation seems far less apparent now than even just five years ago, as feminists' concerns with social theory and cultural studies have led to a common engagement by feminists and human geographers with debates about identity, representation, ethnicity, gender and culture. The Marxist roots of radical feminist geography have led to feminists playing a central role in the contribution of Marxism to human geography, whilst the advent of postmodernist thought and the "cultural turn" in human geography (discussed in Chapter 16) have enabled feminists to play a significant role in these developments. Therefore it is not surprising to observe the WGSG (1997:199–200) referring to feminist geographies as being both central and marginal to human geography: an example of paradoxical space and reflecting the multi-faceted character of the feminist contribution to human geography.

# 16

# POSTMODERN GEOGRAPHIES

## POSTMODERN IDEAS IN HUMAN GEOGRAPHY

During the second half of the 1980s geographers moved beyond their own particular historiography to embrace the "-isms" of mainstream social science: *modernism* and *postmodernism* were terms that began to appear in geographical literature (e.g. Ley, 1989a). Thus human geography further extended its engagement with philosophical and theoretical debates within the social sciences. Principally this took the form of an interest in and development of postmodernism which has been characterised by a marked scepticism towards some of the grand theory and sweeping claims typifying the "modern" era as exemplified by positivism and Marxism (Jencks, 1987).

A number of prominent human geographers introduced postmodernist ideas to the discipline at this time, notably Dear (1988), Gregory (1987), Harvey (1987b) and Soja (1987). Subsequently, a voluminous, though chaotic, discussion and use of postmodern thinking has occurred in human geography. Perhaps the most readily recognised aspect of this work has been the *"new cultural geography"* with an emphasis on the qualitative, the ethnographic and the self-reflexive. In some respects this can be viewed as a logical extension of humanistic ideas in human geography. For example, Susan Smith (1989a:118) argued that some of the more economics-based and historical materialist accounts of global restructuring in the 1980s (e.g. Peet, 1987) lacked "empathetic sensitivity to the human impact and social consequences of

structural change". Her argument was that this sensitivity could be injected by focusing upon the "cultural dynamic infusing the economy". That dynamic has now been investigated increasingly from postmodernist perspectives.

Graham (1995) refers to three ways in which geographers have taken up Michael Dear's challenge, made in the late 1980s, to grasp the opportunities presented by postmodernism (see also Dear, 1995):

1. A limited response that accepts uncritically certain aspects of postmodernist thought and incorporates it into systematic specialisms within human geography.
2. An engagement with "mainstream" thinking in the social sciences and humanities "either through a critical examination of certain aspects of postmodernism or by exploring various continental philosophies and thus elucidating different branches of postmodernism" (Graham, 1995:175).
3. A strong response, sometimes critical to Dear's call for a reconstructed human geography that meets "the postmodern challenge". For example, Harvey (1987a:375) has strongly rejected both postmodernism and realism:

> Postmodernist philosophy tells us not only to accept but even to revel in the fragmentations and the cacophony of voices through which the dilemmas of the modern world are understood. It has us accepting the reifications and the partitionings, actually celebrating the fetishisms of locality, place or social pressure group. The rhetoric is

dangerous for it avoids confronting the realities of political economy and the circumstances of global power.

The first of the three responses tends to ignore the complexities inherent within postmodernism, with its disdain for the "right" and "wrong" answers to particular questions, and its questioning of how language can or cannot be used to convey particular meanings. To counter this, some have argued for geographers to engage more concertedly with the works of philosophers such as Nietzsche and Wittgenstein (Curry, 1991). Others have rejected the apparent disavowal of a search for "truth" that postmodernism may seem to embody and continue to champion realist epistemologies amongst others (e.g. Sayer, 1992, 1993). Clearly, the alternative ways of thinking that postmodernism represent are problematic, especially when they enter a discipline as broad as geography. However, the result has tended to fracture human geography further whilst injecting a new vitality into certain aspects of the discipline, notably cultural studies and reappraisals of the "colonial experience".

Rowntree (1988) describes the term *postmodernism* as being "hydra-headed and chameleon-like". This is because it is a "slippery" concept with different interpretations and shades of meaning depending upon context and situation. It is a term often used to denote an end to the loosely bounded historical and geographical epoch termed the "Modern era" which had its origins in the European Renaissance and spread through scientific development, growth of the capitalist world-market and individualism to affect almost the entire globe by the third quarter of the twentieth century.

In tackling this problem of definition, Gregory (1987) recognised three basic positions of postmodernism:

1. It represents a questioning of "foundational epistemologies" and Eurocentric bias. This creates a tension with traditional Marxism (Dear, 1987; Graham, 1988).
2. This tension is reflected too in its move away from generalising and totalising models.
3. It includes a continual theoretical "interrogation"

of deconstruction, i.e. unravelling previously "fixed" theoretical positions.

Dealing with the same question of definition, Cooke (1989, 1990a, b) viewed postmodernism as fundamentally representing a critique of "modernism" through a number of guises termed "postmodern", ranging from philosophy to architecture and business practices to films and novels. The critique is presented as an opposition to generalisation, grand narrative and meta-theory (e.g. Lyotard, 1984) and, as such, has been viewed as a destructive force by the social theorist Habermas (1985). Yet, in effect, postmodern views have been ones that have pursued the ultimate logic of social science theories, which is that theory seeks to equate subject and object in a way that is universally true, and postmodernism found the flaw: theory cannot exactly replicate the world. Thus the "essentialist totalisation" embodied in positivism and Marxism (Graham, 1990), which is a necessarily selective treatment of knowledge, is rejected in postmodernism. However, this rejection has taken several forms which means that, just like modernism, postmodernism can be recognised in a variety of approaches. Cooke (1990b) acknowledges four of these:

1. *Apocalyptic.* This is associated with Baudrillard's (1988) views of the dissolution of the structures of American society, largely by the "media hegemony", and with parallels recognised in the collapse of Communist rule in Eastern Europe, such as ideological decay and the dominance of media imagery over structures like social class.
2. *Sceptical.* This is the view that postmodernism has no or limited progressive intent and, as presented in Jameson's (1984, 1985, 1989) work, postmodernism becomes a parody of the modern, e.g. Cooke cites postmodern architecture and the literature of Rushdie, Marquez and Fowles.
3. *Critical.* Habermas represents the strongest critic, regarding postmodernism as anarchistic and subversive in its treatment of universalistic social theory. However, his own references to modernity as "an incomplete project" (Habermas, 1985) show that his conception of social theory has an evolu-

tionary quality and is not quite as conservative or tied to an unyielding modern paradigm as critics like Lyotard suggest.

4. *Pragmatic*. This accepts the criticisms of universal social theory and the postmodernist championing of *"multiple dialogues"* rather than clearly defined normal–abnormal characteristics, but, as expressed by Rorty (1980, 1989), takes a more optimistic view of societal development. This view is of a society less hierarchical yet more differentiated, less clearly purposive, less exclusive and therefore less distanced.

The summary derived by Cooke (1990b) from these four approaches is listed in Table 16.1 as the post-modern conception of the characteristics of future society. This conception has been roundly attacked by Harvey (1989a) and Habermas (1987) and met somewhat ambivalently by Soja (1995) who expresses the "postmodernist turn" as a sensitivity to space, which appears in contemporary social theory, and which celebrates diversity. That diversity would have been

*Table 16.1* The Characteristics of Postmodern Society

---

1. Prone to sensory domination by electronic media imagery
2. Prey to colonisation of its lifeworld by markets (economic, political, social)
3. Inclined to glorify consumption as the expression of self
4. Culturally plural in the horizontal rather than the vertical (mass; elite) sense
5. Socially polarised by expanded income differentials
6. Locally distinctive in its conceptions and interpretation of reality
7. Democratic in social, cultural and economic as well as political spheres
8. Pragmatic in its social interaction rather than utopian
9. More self-supportive economically through networks
10. Less dominated by master narratives of militarism and war

---

*Source*: Cooke (1990b:339).

described by many geographers in the past in terms of "areal differentiation".

Significantly, Dear (1986) distinguishes between different aspects of postmodernism in terms of *style*, *epoch* and *method*. Postmodern style is perhaps most readily associated with architecture, examples of which were used as points of departure in Harvey's (1989a) examination and critique of a more broadly conceived postmodernism. The architectural styles typical of postmodernism are variations in facade, diversity of colour, design elements and superficial collages or re-creations of earlier styles almost to the level of pastiche. However, the seemingly chaotic and obtrusive features that this style can generate are often suffused with signals pertaining to identities and meanings, as discussed in Chapter 13. For example, they may represent statements about a dominant group or lobby, or they may signify resistance to such groups (Mills, 1991).

In a historical sense the postmodern may be regarded as the epoch succeeding the modern. Therefore it has been treated by some academics as representing a clear discontinuity with modernity. The modern embodied a new social and economic order that first emerged in Europe in the sixteenth and seventeenth centuries. With its emphasis upon technological advancement, social differentiation and the "engine" of capitalism, this epoch reached its peak in the twentieth century by which time its forms and structures dominated the world. In recognising an end to this era an association is usually made with the nature of capitalism and in particular with developments characterising late capitalism (e.g. Bottomore, 1985). Key features are the move away from assembly-line production (post-Fordism) towards flexible accumulation whereby labour processes, labour markets, the manufacturing of products and their patterns of consumption are characterised by great diversity and organisational flexibility (Amin, 1994; Harvey, 1988; Scott, 1988b). Global capital flows are a feature of this, with transnational corporations becoming the key actors in the structuring and restructuring of both global and regional economies (e.g. Le Heron, 1993). The greater importance of the service sector and of space devoted to consumerism are also features of late capitalism, but the extent to which it represents a sharp break or discontinuity is questionable (see Gertler, 1988). Indeed, many have referred to postmodernism primarily with respect to *cultural developments* associated with late capitalism. In this sense postmodernism refers to discourses of *multiculturalism* in which no single narrator or narrative is privileged in any social enquiry. This idea has also been taken up within literature, in which single-narrator accounts and clear beginnings and endings are eschewed in favour of a more disjointed mosaic. Popular examples from British literature include John Fowles' *The French Lieutenant's Woman* and Dennis Potter's screenplay, *Black Eyes*. It has also proved to be a dramatic stimulus to cultural geography – referred to as *the cultural turn* – promoting a wholesale reappraisal of the importance of culture to geography, and transcending the work on cultural landscapes by Carl Sauer and his Berkeley School (see Leighly, 1963) which pre-dated the Quantitative Revolution.

## TECHNIQUES IN POSTMODERNISM

### Deconstruction

The techniques or methods of postmodernism have focused upon how a single author can hold a multiplicity of positions in both writing and reading a text. The latter can be a landscape (Cosgrove and Daniels, 1988), a map (Harley, 1991), a film (Aitken, 1994), a painting or written records. This list can be extended further to include verbal "texts", institutions, actions and places (Duncan, 1990). For example, in social anthropology, social action and culture have been treated as text by Clifford Geertz (1973, 1988) amongst others. Such texts have been "read" by utilising a number of methods including *deconstruction*, ethnographic writing and hermeneutic method (as discussed in Chapter 13).

The first geographer to promote the use of deconstruction was Gunnar Olsson (1980) in his groundbreaking *Birds in egg: eggs in bird*, in which the cover symbolised the multi-faceted and multi-layered realms of meaning present in texts analysed by geographers. The cover depicts flat shapes becoming two- and three-dimensional drawings of birds, and with both black and white birds emerging from contrasting backgrounds in a lithograph produced in 1955 by Maurits C. Escher (Hofstadter, 1979).

The term *deconstruction* was first used widely in English-speaking academic circles to indicate a range of philosophical approaches developed by French social theorists in the 1960s. Amongst these theorists, Derrida, Lacan and Foucault have been the most influential, the latter inspiring a number of geographical studies (e.g. Driver, 1985; Philo, 1992). In summarising this work, Pratt (1994:468–9) describes the theorists as *poststructuralists*, highlighting their relationship to structuralism, linguistic concepts and Althusser's critique of structuralism. With regard to language, analysis of language is seen as a critical aspect of defining and contesting social organisation and subjectivity. Drawing upon the work of Saussure, meaning is regarded as being produced within language rather than being reflected by it. Therefore to understand meanings, analysis of language is vital and it is the language itself that constitutes social reality. The meaning of written or spoken language "is derived from its difference from and relation to" other sounds or written images ("signifiers") (Pratt, 1994:468). Deconstruction can operate via examination of this difference. Furthermore, social phenomena are "concept-dependent" and, unlike natural phenomena, they are not impervious to the meanings we ascribe to them (Sayer, 1992:30).

Deconstruction is represented in Derrida's (1967) method for analysing texts, primarily philosophical and literary works (see Barnes, 1996). This is described by Cloke et al (1991:192) as a "technique for teasing out the incoherences, limits and unintentioned effects of a text". So it disputes the idea that there is such a thing as a real or true meaning to a text because this privileges the author over the reader or interpreter of the text. This idea has been applied to the wide variety of "texts" referred to above so that its use has transcended its inception in literary theory. However, the term "deconstruction" has been used profligately to apply to almost any situation in which written or spoken words do not give an immediately clear meaning but have to be "unpacked" or unscrambled to reveal contradictions and oppositions.

Derrida's research focused on the fields of aesthetics and criticism, leading to a *deconstructionist aesthetics* that involve very different assumptions from those of structuralism. For example, Sim (1992:425) highlights three key differences:

- texts, like language, are marked by instability and indeterminacy of meaning;
- given such instability and indeterminacy neither philosophy nor criticism can have any special claim to authority as regards textual interpretation;
- interpretation is a free-ranging activity more akin to game-playing than analysis.

Thus the principal point of deconstructionist criticism is to remove the illusion of stable meaning in texts.

This represents an attack on *logocentricity* or the belief that words are representations of meanings already present in the speaker's mind. The written word is a written representation of a spoken representation of the meaning of an original thought. Derrida rejected the notion of meaning in these representations as being a fixed entity. He regarded meaning as an ideal form, located in the mind, which is captured imperfectly by words. Therefore analysis of words must not be constrained by pre-existing meanings, structures or essences. The search for the ideal form, which he referred to as "interior design", involves "the joyous affirmation of the play of the world and of the innocence of becoming, the affirmation of a world of signs without fault, without truth, and without origin which is offered to an active interpretation" (Derrida, 1978:292). This is a call for a "free play" of sign and meaning that is unrestricted by limiting notions of structure. This lack of preconceived ideas about structure, meaning or intention challenges the driving commitment of so much of Western thought to rationality and logicality. In particular, it strongly challenges structuralism as this is seen as a particularly entrenched version of logocentrism. Deconstruction is intended as a series of strategies to undermine logocentrism and so has been referred to as a "resis-

tance movement" (Derrida, 1981:24). This resistance challenges value judgements of the traditional kind and gives an instability to value and meaning. It abolishes traditional textual interpretation.

In looking for examples of deconstruction in the geographical literature, primarily in terms of using it to break the assumed link between reality and representation (in a "text"), an excellent one is Harley's (1989) article on the deconstruction of maps. Harley argued that even maps that might be termed "scientific" are a product of the norms and values of the social tradition and culture under which they were produced. Therefore, "our task is to search for the social forces that have structured cartography and to locate the presence of power – and in effect – in all map knowledge" (*ibid*.:2). He contended that the interpretive act of deconstructing the map can serve three functions in the way we view maps in geographical culture (*ibid*.:16–17):

1. It enables a challenge to be made to the epistemological myth created by cartographers that there is cumulative progress of an objective science that is always producing better delineations of reality.
2. The social importance of maps can be redefined, adding different nuances to the understanding of the power of cartographic representation to put order into our world. Different "readings" can reveal alternative or even competing discourses.
3. Application of different deconstructions can extend the role of cartography in the interdisciplinary study of text and knowledge.

Harley interpreted deconstruction as a process whereby the reader of a map "reads between the lines". This involves examination of the social and technical rules operating during the preparation of the map. This may help to explain why ideological "Holy Lands" are frequently centred in maps. It may involve looking closely at emblems in cartouches and decorative title pages as these give clues as to the cultural meaning of maps and help demonstrate that cartography is not an impartial graphic science. For example, the analysis of the North Carolina state highway map by Wood and Fels (1986) suggested that the range of emblems and symbols arrayed in the map's margins reflected the map's role as an instrument of state policy and sovereignty. This was part of a construction of a mythic geography, with incantations of loyalty to state emblems. In more general terms, the use of particular types of colour, decoration and typography are ways in which even the most "scientifically prepared" maps appeal to their readers. Therefore, by examining all the map's content, and not just the topographical details depicted, an interpretation that extends well beyond topography may be discerned.

Derrida contends that all meanings are relative and therefore we have to look at relationships between words, concepts and particular things to derive meaning. These relationships might be investigated using semiotics, as referred to in Chapter 13, and/or by considering textual metaphors (Olsson, 1980). This seems far removed from the apparent certainties of spatial science approaches to geography, as summarised by Curry (1991) who recognises that this lack of certainty results from two new sets of beliefs adhered to by postmodernists: that the meanings of words are much more "slippery" than they used to be (partly through a combination of modern communications media, advertising and corporate culture), and that language is not connected with the world in a simple, unproblematic way. There is therefore a *crisis of representation* because the fixity of language has disappeared. In investigating this crisis, geographers have concentrated most upon the cultural diversity of modern society and the differential experiences of this diversity by different groups of people (Philo, 1990).

## Discourse Analysis

In everyday language, "discourse" usually means simply "speech" or "language" and, by extension, "text"; but in the late twentieth century it has also come to have a more specialised, academic meaning derived from post-structuralism. "Discourse" in this second sense implies a mobile web or network of concepts, statements and practices that is intimately involved in the production of particular knowledges.

(Barnes and Gregory, 1997:504–5)

Another form of poststructuralist and postmodernist method is *discourse analysis* which also has been applied beyond the confines of literary texts. In its simplest sense discourse analysis is the analysis of speech, conversation and dialogue. However, Foucault (1972) extended such analysis to apply in particular to systems of statements (like texts, expressed in many forms) that could only be understood within their context (Fairclough, 1992:37–61). Therefore the history of ideas is the history of discourses because it is the context of those ideas that is the key to understanding. Under this interpretation discourses become "frameworks that embrace particular combinations of narratives, concepts, ideologies and signifying practices, each relevant to a particular realm of social action" (Barnes and Duncan, 1992). Discourses are embedded in day-to-day life where they help promote particular views of the world, but in which knowledge tends to be associated with particular constructions and power relations which, ultimately, are contestable. This contest generally takes the form of dissecting power relations to highlight the different experiences of these relations by the various groups that constitute society (Phillip, 1985:69):

What rules permit certain statements to be made; what rules order these statements; what rules permit us to identify some statements as true and others as false; what rules allow the construction of a map, model or classificatory system ... what rules are revealed when an object of discourse is modified or transformed ... Whenever sets of rules of these kinds can be identified, we are dealing with a discursive formation or discourse.

Foucault (1980) himself challenged the role and status of science as a discourse, showing how dominant power relations underlie and reinforce science's claims to authority and truth. This also emphasises the cultural context of science and the contingent nature of its claims to truth. As discussed by Crush (1991), discourses always provide partial and "situated" knowledges. This can be applied to the discourse of human geography which has particular ethnocentric and, according to feminists, phallocentric characteristics which prevent it from being self-sufficient and expose it to the criticisms and transformations being wrought by postmodern geographies.

The ultimate challenge of Foucault's work is to the grand narratives of logical positivism and structuralism, which emphasised grand theory and the reduction of chaotic historical phenomena, events and processes to a generalised order. These narratives are challenged on the grounds that "nothing is fundamental: this is what is interesting in the analysis of society" (Foucault, 1982:18). His work mounted an assault on metanarrative and stressed the particular, the local and the specific. This has particular significance for geographers because it emphasises the details of differences between places and stresses the need to understand this rather than generalised similarities. Foucault's own work focused on the histories of various social pathologies, emphasising the spatial aspects of institutions such as asylums, hospitals, prisons and workhouses as integral aspects of the discourses of institutional solutions (Foucault, 1967, 1976, 1977, 1979). These are not the "spaces" with which either historians or geographers have been concerned previously, but they are examples of "spaces of dispersion" in which objects are not regularly ordered in their spatial arrangement but are part of an irregular discourse that takes place in space. There is a sensitivity to geography in this work which has been a stimulus to postmodern geographies, though other postmodern philosophers, notably Baudrillard, Derrida and Lyotard, have also been influential (see Barnes and Duncan, 1992).

For examples of discourse analysis by geographers, Johnston (1997:300−1) refers to work on "critical" geopolitics (e.g. Dalby, 1991; Dodds, 1994). This has focused on the interrelationships between States and how the images of States are created and sustained. Policy statements and political actions are concrete expressions of the "foreign policy discourse" to be analysed according to O'Tuathail and Dalby (1994:513), by:

> constructing theoretically informed critiques of the spatializing practices of power; undertaking critical investigations of the power of orthodox geopolitical writing; investigating how geographical reasoning in foreign policy in-sights (enframes in a geography of images), in-cites (enmeshes in a geography of texts), and, therefore, in-sites (stabilizes, positions, locates) places in global politics,

and examining how this reasoning can be challenged, subverted and resisted.

It has become increasingly common for geographers to appropriate the words "discourse" and "text" and to use them to refer to subjects and situations far removed from any narrow interpretation of their meaning. However, there is a large body of literature on discourse analysis that can provide a guide as to how such analysis can proceed when applied in its original form to language. For example, Stubbs (1998:1) defines discourse analysis as "attempts to study the organisation of language above the sentence or above the clause, and therefore to study larger linguistic units, such as conversational exchanges or written texts". He distinguishes between written texts and spoken discourse, with discourse analysis focusing on inspection of conversational data, transcribed data and narrative organisation. However, Fairclough (1992) regards discourse analysis as covering a very wide field, which has extended analysis beyond linguistics into other modes of social analysis.

The "technique" of discourse analysis goes beyond the confines of this book, but the texts by Stubbs (1983) and Fairclough (1992) provide good but quite contrasting introductions. A good example of the application of discourse analysis is given in MacNaughten's (1993) work on discourses of Nature.

## Writing Geography

One aspect of postmodernist geographies has been an emphasis upon the writing of geography (as referred to in Chapter 13). As human geography in general has rediscovered the importance of place, so the need for powerful but subtle descriptions of place has grown. And hence the need for writing that can evoke place, particularly through the use of *metaphor* (see Pratt, 1992) and the notion of landscape as text (Geertz, 1980:135):

> Arguments, melodies, formulas, maps, and pictures are not idealities to be stared at but texts to be read: so are rituals, palaces, technologies, and social formulation.

One particular form of description has been championed, namely *thick description*, which "attempts to make sense of the complex layers or dimensions of meaning in cultural rituals by describing them in detail from many points of view" (Daniels, 1992:319). The reference to cultural rituals is a signpost to the ethnographic derivation of thick description and the way in which this method can be used to describe and analyse social life (e.g. Geertz, 1973). The term also has affinities with the interpretation of iconography and symbolic imagery in art works and artifacts (Daniels and Cosgrove, 1988). Examples of the use of thick description to indicate and elucidate multiple meanings of particular places include work by Bender (1992) on Stonehenge, Cosgrove (1982) on Venice and Domosh (1989) on the New York World Building. Thick description can also take the form of *narrative*, providing a detailed configuration of facts in terms of certain themes and issues. Entrikin (1991) argues that narrative can offer a valuable tool for understanding place as it provides a view that is not necessarily either objective or subjective but occupies a position between place as location and place as consciousness. This "story" about place that can be constructed via narrative can combine the general characteristics of so-called metanarrative with a concern for the local and the particular histories, legends and mythologies associated with places.

The explicit consideration of how geography is written has led to geographers assimilating some of the deconstructive ideas of Derrida, discussed in an earlier subsection in this chapter, with a recognition that the written word is a social creation. This has several consequences, relating to how meaning can be conveyed by writing, e.g. through the use of metaphors, the information that words convey about their author, and the variable nature of the meaning of words. Therefore "understanding a discourse ... involves appreciating its metaphors" (Johnston, 1997:298).

Consideration of how geography is written has also encompassed a concern for the *"positionality"* of the writer. If a married, white male in their 40s is writing geography, they will bring to their writing their own experience, values and interpretations which may make it difficult for them to write about people from very different backgrounds with any degree of authority. The ultimate logic here would be for each person to write only about themselves and their own experiences, as only they can truly "know" their own experiences. However, by clearly stating a "position", analysis of "others" can be made, though with suitable reference to differences between author and authored.

One of the major sources for geographers' appreciation of their own positionality and partial view of the world was the classic book by Edward Said (1978), *Orientalism*. In this he refers to the ways in which Westerners conceived their own geographies of the Orient as part of the grand imperialist project. In these "imaginative geographies" Orientals were depicted as "others" (non-Western), implicitly and perhaps explicitly inferior. This process of recognising non-Western ethnic groups as "the other" was part of a process of depicting the Orient to Western audiences as part of the process of imperialism in which it became legitimate to take control of overseas lands and people (Gregory, 1994c). In recognising the partial view arising from the position of the writer, geographers have focused their attention on a range of "others" related to gender, class, race and sexual orientation. This work has drawn upon various social theories to illuminate the ways in which differences between labelled groups have been created socially and under what set of power relations. As referred to in Chapter 13, this extends consideration of "context" or the "situated" nature of knowledge as a vital ingredient of geographical enquiry. Good examples are the work of Blunt and Rose (1994), Jackson (1991, 1993) and Valentine (1993).

# THE FUTURE OF THE QUANTITATIVE

## The Sustained Attack on Positivism

This book began by presenting a view of two new geographies: one developed through a Quantitative Revolution ushering in the adoption of new statistical and mathematical techniques, and the other emerging in part as an initial reaction to quantification and then as a multi-faceted engagement with ideas current elsewhere in the social sciences and humanities. The first strands in the second of these new geographies were radical ones based on a Marxist critique of the positivist philosophy underlying much of the quantitative geography. For example, a telling criticism of the "abstracted empiricism" associated with positivism was made in the late-1950s by the American sociologist C. Wright Mills (Mills, 1959:ch. 3):

> The kinds of problems that will be taken up and the way in which they are formulated are quite severely limited by the Scientific Method. Methodology, in short, seems to determine the problems ... Neither in defining their problems nor in explaining their own microscopic findings do they [abstracted empiricists] make any real use of the basic idea of historical social structure ... Those in the grip of the methodological inhibition often refuse to say anything about modern society unless it has been through the fine little mill of the statistical ritual. It is usual to say that what they produce is true even if unimportant ... Abstracted empiricism eliminates the great social problems and human issues of our time from inquiry.

And Mumford (1964) proclaimed that, "the positivist view of nature discriminates against living things. All value, colour, life is sucked out of the world. The result is the devaluation of both nature and humanity; nature becomes just an instrument."

Following on from this, one of the most strongly recurrent themes within human geography during the past three decades is the widely held view that scientific or quasi-scientific methodology is inappropriate for dealing with the problems studied by human geographers. Furthermore, it can be argued that analysis of spatial data employing standard statistical techniques such as correlation and regression is effectively employing techniques that were not really designed for the types of situations encountered. Hence, the use of such techniques could be charged as being statistically naive.

In countering these criticisms, some argued that their work was positivist but not logical positivist: that is, utilising "scientific" procedures but less epistemologically constrained (e.g. Golledge, 1981). In fact,

this reduced, or complete lack of, constraint is apparent in much 1960s and 1970s quantitatively based work in human geography which was performed in an atheoretical vacuum, with techniques viewed as a means of achieving rigorous description. For example, some views of factor analysis have expressed a similar opinion of this technique's main function in geographical research (e.g. Robinson, 1981; Taylor, 1981), though recognising that its use could be underscored by an appropriate "model" or context. Unfortunately it is this context that tended to be lacking from many factorial ecologies.

Equally, though, the Nature-dominating and -controlling forces unleashed by totalitarian Marxism have also separated people from Nature. Hence, some critiques of positivism that have emerged have also included criticism of Marxist theory, notably from humanistic and postmodernist perspectives.

In retrospect it can be argued that much of the initial reaction against logical positivism in human geography stemmed from regarding Harvey's (1969) *Explanation in geography* as the standard interpretation of the "scientific method" and then accepting Harvey's own subsequent criticisms of this method (e.g. Harvey, 1972). However, some significant qualifications of Harvey's interpretation of the scientific method are raised in Gale's (1972) detailed review which focused upon acceptance by positivists of a heterodoxy of explanation rather than the notion of one set language and model. Despite this significant caveat, all too frequently overlooked in subsequent references to quantitative geography, Gale's concluding question, "To what extent can the methodologies developed for mathematics and the physical sciences be applied to the social sciences?" (*ibid.*:317) is one which Harvey and many others have answered firmly, "To no great extent!"

This rejection of positivism as a suitable means for investigating socio-economic problems has been accompanied by a suspicion of mathematics, statistics and geometrical representations of spatial structure. In particular many geographers, and social scientists in general, have displayed an aversion to the use of statistical formulae, reflecting a mixture of unfamiliarity with mathematics and a concern that the basic subject matter of geography does not lend itself read-ily to this form of representation. It is this latter view that has formed part of the attack upon the use of statistical methods within human geography. However, geographical analysis of quantitative data continues to employ statistical methods and so requires that geo-graphers possess knowledge of the symbolism, formu-lae and operation of statistics. Unfortunately, to the large number of geographers with limited experience of mathematics and statistics at school, such unfami-liar notation and terminology has consigned much statistical analysis to the area of "terra incognita". For those venturing to use such analysis, despite the numerous "how to" books, unfamiliarity has led to misuse and abuse of statistics and has undoubtedly helped breed suspicion and outright contempt for statistics within the discipline. Paradoxically, most of the statistical formulae commonly used by geogra-phers are quite simple, utilising straightforward math-ematical operations.

Over time, though, the critique of positivism has blossomed into a set of ideas that has helped to trans-form geographical thought, both introducing the im-portance of structural forces within human society and helping to bring about an engagement with critical social theory through which the ideas of modern Continental philosophers have influenced geographers. This influence has by no means been drawn solely from neo-Marxist thinking but in some cases has extended to outright rejection of totalising theory, as encapsulated in postmodernism, and a more liberal perspective pursued in humanistic approaches. As a result, the "new" human geography of the 1980s and 1990s is a much more diffuse and chaotic entity than its 1950s and 1960s predecessor. It embraces an array of different philosophical positions and lacks cohe-sion. Wilson (1989:62) sees this development as a form of "structured pluralism" within geography whilst recognising that some geographers have re-garded eclecticism, or the integration of concepts from different paradigms into a single research project, as being impossible (e.g. Gregory, 1981).

One distinctive trend, though, has been the move from a dominant reliance upon the use of quantitative techniques to a more eclectic assemblage of quantita-tive and qualitative methods. It can be argued that one characteristic of the transformation of the discipline in the past three decades has been a pronounced move from the quantitative to the qualitative, but this would be an over-simplification. Firstly, the development and use of quantitative techniques has not disappeared; secondly, the quantitative and the qualitative represent a continuum rather than a totally separate polar typol-ogy; and thirdly, it is possible to combine aspects of the two in the same study. So it would seem more correct to portray geography's transformation as a widespread rejection of positivism as the predominant prevailing philosophy or, alternatively, as a move from an essentially technocratic subject to one that was more people-centred. Again, it should be stressed that positivism is not entirely absent from human geogra-phy in the 1990s and a technocratic aspect has grown strongly in importance for at least 15 years through the emergence of GIS.

For anyone interested in the continuing role of particular sets of techniques against this backdrop of considerable disciplinary and paradigmatic change, one key question to ask is just what future there is for "the quantitative" in human geography, and especially those techniques most closely associated with the positivist philosophy.

## From Models to GIS

The rapid change from a Quantitative Revolution to a concerted questioning of its underlying philosophy meant that in the 1970s and 1980s only a relatively small number of human geographers were directly concerned with the development of mathematical models, the application of standard statistical techni-ques to geographical problems and the development of spatial statistics. Although there have been some sig-nificant developments in spatial statistics during the last 20 years, not to mention the analysis of categori-cal data and longitudinal data analysis, only where these have been linked with the fast growth of GIS can they be said to have had any profound influence upon the new generation of recruits to the ranks of aca-demic geography.

A common criticism of mathematical and statistical

models has been that they only deal with surface phenomena and therefore fail to offer in-depth explanations. This failure can be translated into a recognition of three broad criticisms of the models: (i) they have failed to produce an analytical basis for planning; (ii) the concerns of the models have failed to address important questions of equity and the quality of the environment; and (iii) other approaches offer more scope for generating radical change. More specifically, in terms of the specific case of quantitative urban planning models, urban modellers have not focused on the main processes of urban development, being especially neglectful of the most significant agents participating in these processes. Also, urban modellers have not focused effectively on those topics most central to planning, and an inadequate account has been offered of political processes likely to affect planning applications of models. It could also be argued that use of models has actually exacerbated urban problems by focusing on "unimportant" topics at the expense of others.

This brief summary of the limitations of over two decades of mathematical modelling is based on that prepared in the early 1980s by one of the leading modellers, Alan Wilson (1984:213–14), marking a recognition of the need for new thinking by those developing such models. In the following decade new ideas have been apparent in the more practical orientation of much modelling work and in attempts to incorporate elements that reflect decision-making environments rather than relying overly on neoclassical economic theory and the explanatory power of the friction of distance. There has been some recognition of the need to incorporate constraints on human choice and, gradually, some inclusion of ideas generated from new thinking within human geography, notably from a Marxist perspective, and new opportunities offered by greater integration between GIS and advances in spatial analysis. So, despite the doubts about the value of mathematical models still expressed by many human geographers, the small group of modellers will continue to make advances and to recoup considerable consultancy income for applications of their most practicable models. Similarly, the spatial epidemiologists are playing an increasingly

important role in helping to combat the spread of diseases such as AIDS, with lucrative medical funding sponsoring new developments in spatial statistics.

The continuing advance of GIS in the commercial and public-sector spheres is a development that needs to be addressed by non-GIS specialist academic geographers. Increasingly, non-geographers are encountering geography only in the guise of GIS and their views of geography as an academic discipline are being shaped by their experience of GIS. Potentially this has significant ramifications for the development of the discipline in terms of funding to support particular types of research and for the nature of the relationship between the public face of geography and its practitioners. The widespread ignorance of commerce and business by academics, and vice versa with respect to commerce's lack of awareness of new techniques developed by academics, has been recognised in some circles for at least a decade (e.g. Clarke, 1990; Beaumont, 1986, 1987a) and mutual benefits are now being derived. Moreover, the disdain towards GIS shown by some human geographers is gradually giving way to the development of a dialogue in which both sides recognise that they have something to gain from the other's point of view. In particular, the GIS community is considering how the qualitative can become a more important part of GIS data-handling facilities and how data can be assessed from a more critical perspective instead of the "all data are good data" assumption that seemed to be prevalent in GIS in the early 1980s. The willingness of modellers and GIS practitioners to consider theoretical input that extends beyond a very simplistic portrayal of human spatial behaviour has been a positive development, with important questions being asked about how geographic space can be represented in computer-based models – for an introduction see Peuquet (1988). On the other side of the discussion, the storage, display and data-handling qualities of GIS are being used more frequently as part of the process of data exploration supported from theoretical formulations.

The latter point refers to one of the prime features of the new geography of the 1990s, namely a continuing emphasis on the need for research to be an integral part of an adequately theorised framework as opposed to mere speculative empiricism. Harvey's detailed examination of how a positivist approach could be put into practice by geographers led him to conclude that the development of theory was vital in the search for satisfactory explanation as, without it, "we cannot hope for controlled, consistent, and rational, explanation of events" (Harvey, 1969:486). Ironically, his subsequent work led to a search for theories based on Marxist philosophy and a rejection of the positivist approach. Nevertheless, his comment also reflected a concern for the lack of cumulative knowledge being built up by geographers in repeated empirical work which was divorced from adequate theorising: as Perle (1979:411) pointed out, "so long as empirical studies tend to imitate one another rather completely, there is little reason to expect additional theoretical constructs will emerge". Johnston (1986a:173) also makes a contribution:

> Empirical research must be used not as an end in itself but as a way of illuminating the theory of society, of the real world of mechanisms that cannot be apprehended . . . And comparative empirical research, by people with a full understanding of different places and times, will then reveal how people have created their worlds, are recreating their worlds, and can create new worlds: despite claims that "there is no alternative", empirical research can, and must, show how destinies are created by people interpreting structures and making contexts, how contexts and destinies can be changed, and how structures can be changed. Empirical research is not voyeurism, it is sensitization.

However, this is not to argue for what Olsson (1969:20) terms "indigenous geographic theory", which

> may be regarded as an attempt to state the laws of spatial form in the specialized languages of geometry or topology, or in the more general form of spatial statistics . . . However, such laws tell little or nothing about processes . . . In order to understand spatial structure, . . . we must know something of the antecedent decisions and behaviours which arrange phenomena over space.

## The Culture of the Times

When examining the evolution of human geography from the late 1950s one explanatory framework to consider is the importance of the "culture of the times". This is emphasised by Bennett (1989) who views the rise of quantification and use of models within geography as part of a climate in which remedial action on social problems was sought through the medium of an enhanced technical bureaucratic rationality. There were high hopes and expectations at this time (the 1950s and 1960s) about both the development of technical systems and the more general concepts of social improvement. In Britain this was symbolised in the Wilson government's views on the "white-hot heat of the technological revolution". In the USA it was embodied in President J.F. Kennedy's visions of the exploration of space and his commitment to a man setting foot on the surface of the Moon.

In pursuing this idea, the social disruption in US cities in the late 1960s, the rise of popular protest movements and a questioning of society's norms and values can be linked to the emergence of radical geography and a concern for a more humane human geography. To some the more eclectic and cacophanous human geography of the 1990s is a mirror of the heterogeneous, chaotic and less ordered nature of society. The end of the Cold War and the emergence of anti-Marxist theory are two more juxtaposed, though not necessarily causal, "events". In developing the link between the natures of geography and the wider Western society, it is worth noting that Susan Smith (1989b) sees some of the basic tenets of geography's Quantitative Revolution repeated in the arguments presented by the "New Right" of the 1980s, prominent initially in the Reagan and Thatcher administrations. In embracing both the neo-liberal economics of Friedrich von Hayek and the neoclassical views of Milton Friedman, supporters of the New Right championed a methodological and ontological individualism and the concept of value-neutrality. Therefore residential differentiation was viewed in terms of a myriad of rational decisions by individuals and of the translation of financial resources into housing and locational preferences. Whilst it may be possible to analyse these qualitative preferences, it is essentially a quantitative rather than a qualitative analysis that was supported by this world view. In part, this is because the New Right perspective relegated cultural characteristics and "irrational" individualism to a marginal position. The New Right's emphasis upon commerce and the money-making capacity of deregulated financial markets is mirrored in geography's own money-spinner of the New Right era, GIS.

Given the extent to which the New Right held office in different countries in the Developed World in the 1980s and early 1990s, it is surprising that so few of their ideas have found favour with social scientists in general and geographers in particular. Although it needs closer investigation, one reason would seem to be the twin impacts of Marxism and humanism throughout social science. Whilst most social scientists would not necessarily define themselves as Marxists, many ideas taken directly from Marx's own writings or from post-war neo-Marxist scholars have been subsumed in general ideas regarding the nature of society, economic development, power and gender relations. Human geography has been no exception and, despite the anarchistic and often openly anti-Marxist ideas of the postmodernists, there has been very little overt adoption of views that are not broadly "of the left" or "social democratic". Indeed, when geographers have dared to work with commerce, as in the application of allocation and interaction models or via the use of GIS, they have been strongly attacked by other geographers – not overtly for betraying the politics of their discipline, but for failure to adhere to the same theoretical and philosophical mind-sets as the "mainstream".

In the 1990s criticism of Marxist thinking in human geography has brought re-evaluation of the use of Marxist analysis and a softening of ideas regarding the application of structuralism and reference to totalising forces. Perhaps the most substantial survivors of Marxist thinking introduced to geography will be certain elements of the Marxist theory of the economy in which capitalist growth is seen as favouring disequilibrium rather than equilibrium, spatial and sectoral differentiation rather than balanced growth and a "production landscape" moulded through human agency not just natural comparative advantage. It is these elements that support the notion that "geography" is created and re-created as part of the capitalist production system (e.g. Storper and Walker, 1988).

Indeed, it will be fascinating to see to what extent this idea is accommodated by writers working from postmodernist perspectives in the future.

For over two decades the mainstream has excluded positivism and the techniques associated with geography's Quantitative Revolution. Nevertheless, certain aspects of "classical" scientific methodology remain attractive and have contributed to its continuing use within human geography. As described by Hay (1985b:139), these attractions are:

1. It provides coherent and testable theories about the nature of geographical phenomena.
2. It represents a codified and logically connected extension of thought structures developed in everyday life, including the ability to correct theories and hypotheses in the light of experience.
3. Knowledge of a scientific nature is needed by society for the management of social and natural systems.

However, human geographers using a "scientific approach" in the 1990s are well aware of the numerous criticisms levelled at anything that can be labelled positivist or scientific. Therefore there is no longer a concerted search for explicitly geographical or spatial laws nor a desire to deal with problems purely in reductionist terms. But, this does not deny the use of abstract mathematical language by geographers in order to tackle certain types of problem nor does it preclude statistical analysis, provided that it is accompanied by an awareness of its limitations and the need to consider exploratory data analysis before proceeding with more advanced confirmatory methods.

A common trend has been for an emphasis upon process rather than pattern, so that the concern for the spatial geometry of spatial science has been relegated to a lesser significance. Similarly, the importance of the "classical" hypothesis testing, as developed by Neyman and Pearson, has been greatly diminished as it has been revealed to be inappropriate for many geographical problems. Other statistical approaches, such as Bayesian theory (see Wilson and Bennett, 1985), offer possible alternatives, but have not been widely applied partly because non-statistically-based methods have become so dominant within the discipline during the past decade. The varied attacks upon geography as it was practised in the Quantitative Revolution have left a powerful and somewhat misguided impression in some quarters that erroneously links all quantitative methods to positivism (see Bennett, 1985) and ignores the ways in which analysis of *both* quantitative and qualitative data can be at the heart of investigations of problems of concern to human geographers. The extent to which these ways can be combined within any single research project is highly problematic given the mutually exclusive explanatory frameworks that are associated with the different techniques and methods. However, it could be argued that the breadth of human geography, and certainly the whole of geography as a discipline, is great enough to embrace a diversity of approaches.

Postmodernism represents the antithesis of the paradigm that drove geography's Quantitative Revolution. As remarked by Cosgrove (1989a:243), the emphasis upon quantitative techniques and models was a "perfect statement of modernism". So it contained a faith in rational and unilinear social and environmental progress, in technology as a means of achieving it, in the efficacy of abstract numerical relations to demonstrate an objective truth, and in the ability of planning as a means of overcoming "the contingency and flux" of unpredictable human life and its environmental relations. He argues that these "beliefs" have been shattered by the advent of a postmodernist world and a geography that "celebrates diversity and particularly contextual studies of locale: historical and cultural reconstructions and a revived description".

Diversity is a recurrent theme within postmodernism, which poses one of the latest and most far-reaching challenges to human geography. Cosgrove's own work has developed a distinctive form of qualitative approach, using the "reading" of paintings, texts and maps as cultural expressions of the meaning of landscapes. He also observes that the use of metaphors such as "system" or "organism", much used by geographers in the 1960s and 1970s, and which were derived from biological and cybernetic models of environmental and spatial organisation, are being succeeded by others, such as spectacle, theatre and text,

derived from the arts (Cosgrove, 1990:345). This illustrates the inherently "perspectival" nature of scientific discourse in which language has been used to represent the findings of an empirical perspective. The changing language of geography symbolises, and has been accompanied by, a sea-change in methodology.

Soja's (1995) interpretation of this sea-change (the penetration of postmodernist thought into geography) centres on new attempts to combine "spatiality" with social theory. He regards attempts made under the rigid historicism of Marxism, and also other conventional urban theories, as incapable of dealing with the "post-Fordist" (post-industrial) restructuring of society and particularly of urban areas. This echoes some of Gould's (1988a, b) views on the limitations of theory by human geographers, though Gould appears to dismiss all social theory because it is not testable or capable of predicting (Glick, 1990). For example, he rejects the labour theory of value, because it centres attention on moral values and therefore is not susceptible to either measurement or testing (Gould, 1988a:4–5). He also raises concern over the way in which urban geography in particular has shifted its emphasis from the study of spatial entities to a more amorphous analysis of urban issues, focusing on broad economic and political processes without explicit treatment of the spatial dimension (see Whitehand, 1986a, b). Some have argued that this and the broad concern with social, economic and political theory has been at the expense of an analysis of space and place, thereby leading the discipline away from its core (e.g. Zelinsky, 1987). A feeling that many geographers have become "sociologists with maps", and perhaps not very good sociologists either, is apparent from those who deplore the lack of attention given to the nature of interactions between people and the physical environment. However, it is also possible to see the dominant debates of the 1980s, about the role of space and place in social theory (e.g. Gregory and Urry, 1985; Gottdeiner, 1987), as the prelude to greater utilisation of empirical studies to determine their significance in practice (see Leitner, 1989).

In the 1990s these debates have encompassed an exciting new dimension in the form of the growing contribution from a feminist perspective. This perspective has expanded rapidly from its Marxist roots to encompass an impressive array of work that has moved swiftly from its initial concerns for women's subjugation at the hands of patriarchal society to a more ambitious analysis of issues, of which gender and power relations are significant parts but not the only concerns. The feminist contribution has raised important questions about the language used by geographers, ethical concerns about the role of the researcher in the field, and the nature of geographers' interpretations of both quantitative and qualitative data. Feminists' interests in the specific (rather than the general) and the problems of the marginalised in society have resonated strongly with postmodernist approaches. This emphasises the need to refer to feminist geographies rather than a single feminist geography, so that it is increasingly difficult to place simplistic labels on this emerging area of the discipline. Its long-term effects on human geography remain to be seen.

The "rediscovery" of the specific and the unique by geographers in the 1980s and 1990s has also allowed some of the traditional concerns of region-based studies to re-emerge but in a clearly different form from that embraced by the regional geographies of the 1950s (Nonn, 1984; Johnston, 1984b). Gilbert (1988) asserts that this *new regional geography*, described by Thrift (1983) as "reconstructed regional geography", has focused upon the region in three ways: (i) the region as a local response to capitalist processes; (ii) the region as a focus of identification; and (iii) the region as a medium for social interaction.

These three foci encompass a range of approaches from humanistic to historical materialist and combinations in between, for example Gilbert refers to Cooke's (1985, 1987) work on localities as "humanism-informed Marxist regionalism". Any confusion over the approach followed is eliminated in the best of these "new" studies in which a regional synthesis is accompanied by a clear statement of theoretical premises (e.g. Harvey, 1985b; Pred, 1986).

Finally, the journey from one new geography to another has involved a kaleidoscope of quantitative and qualitative techniques applied in some cases using well focused theoretical perspectives, and, in others, with little attention to any theorising. Criticisms of particular totalising philosophies, such as Marxism and positivism, have been followed by some complete rejections of metatheory, not to mention flirtations with a range of seductive philosophies: idealism, pragmatism, realism, structuralism, structuration, political economy, .... . The result is a human geography tremendously enriched and transformed by the shock waves of new ideas that have crashed upon its shores. Debate about the merits of the different philosophies, techniques and methods has frequently been strong and the protagonists have often failed to reach amicable agreement. Nevertheless, human geography has emerged as a wonderfully vibrant and enriched discipline. The range of contributions by geographers to advancing understanding of human society, economic development and a myriad of issues affecting the well-being of people and planet Earth has been immense.

Many of the new ideas in the discipline over the past 30 years have left indelible imprints, affecting geographical thinking today so that the range of ideas, and techniques available to support their practical use, is greater than it has ever been. Whilst this may have created a diffuse and chaotic discipline, it has enabled human geography to tackle problems undreamt of as being the province of geographers in the early postwar years. The technical armoury to serve this breadth of the discipline is equally impressive. This book has tried to introduce some of the more commonly used techniques employed by geographers in the last 30 years. Despite its breadth, especially with respect to those based on statistics and mathematics, it does not pretend to be exhaustive, but it has attempted to show the strengths and weaknesses of different techniques, their accompanying methodological approaches, and also their role in contributing to the changes in the nature of geographical enquiry. With the increased importance of exploratory techniques, categorical data analysis, qualitative methods and GIS, human geography is continuing to expand its technical and methodological armoury so that new areas of expertise are required of the geographer. Thirty years ago it was the language and rules of statistics that had to be learnt.

Today statistics are still part of the geographer's canon of knowledge, but only as part of a broad portfolio of techniques allied to a burgeoning flow of ideas entering the discipline. The current trends suggest that in the future it will be the qualitative and the interpretive methods that will be central to geographical enquiry, requiring a different sort of "technical" ability. However, technological development is also likely to bring different technical challenges via cyberspace and the next stage of the computing and information revolutions. The challenge is indeed multi-faceted ... and gloriously unpredictable.

# APPENDIX STATISTICAL TABLES

## A. RANDOM NUMBER TABLE

These digits may be used singly, in pairs, or in larger groups as required.

| | | | | | | | |
|---|---|---|---|---|---|---|---|
| 914134 | 757807 | 324447 | 011402 | 704411 | 204455 | 990332 | 347376 |
| 898858 | 446238 | 341240 | 552407 | 621320 | 723090 | 724319 | 237337 |
| 195311 | 428442 | 846724 | 522344 | 472121 | 332229 | 262434 | 721348 |
| 561420 | 012284 | 630532 | 430304 | 618378 | 343185 | 604141 | 597786 |
| 433808 | 987203 | 701271 | 398085 | 879717 | 403084 | 961438 | 616848 |
| 672029 | 914539 | 714968 | 555929 | 756822 | 728486 | 720291 | 453971 |
| 496855 | 592975 | 682272 | 463466 | 775977 | 742661 | 599512 | 141954 |
| 917246 | 994731 | 574633 | 370695 | 650341 | 029099 | 516158 | 600388 |
| 183804 | 320343 | 325337 | 501213 | 785346 | 402388 | 489290 | 354792 |
| 153496 | 075830 | 757689 | 078339 | 205677 | 095294 | 217402 | 829124 |
| 521094 | 859049 | 799607 | 064899 | 748379 | 659405 | 670640 | 590690 |
| 830443 | 020610 | 591684 | 200490 | 254292 | 253672 | 059555 | 613953 |
| 021897 | 688879 | 599966 | 055175 | 679662 | 776772 | 449110 | 687617 |
| 878762 | 994312 | 614543 | 491148 | 685893 | 776020 | 619825 | 466080 |
| 588025 | 714658 | 060182 | 421496 | 484981 | 452775 | 667750 | 126774 |
| 799913 | 725083 | 499603 | 393408 | 494594 | 557593 | 687298 | 230362 |
| 662030 | 712123 | 392914 | 462221 | 389534 | 632194 | 561750 | 964659 |
| 519922 | 463683 | 234781 | 302751 | 975368 | 527210 | 842213 | 835599 |
| 017539 | 230219 | 197183 | 837811 | 976431 | 234339 | 004074 | 431482 |
| 024282 | 487106 | 710506 | 655638 | 081478 | 416597 | 152352 | 169446 |
| 147101 | 540267 | 767914 | 740823 | 521733 | 332640 | 981130 | 141747 |
| 360371 | 508311 | 102399 | 151341 | 002938 | 046567 | 564043 | 597665 |
| 983296 | 816803 | 110425 | 748635 | 066551 | 763872 | 196002 | 343729 |

## B. AREAS UNDER THE STANDARDISED NORMAL CURVE

$P$ = probability of an event within the range of 0 to $z$. For probabilities of events beyond the specified $z$, subtract $P$ from 0.5000.

| $z$ | $P$ |
|---|---|
| 0.00 | 0.00000 |
| 0.01 | 0.00399 |
| 0.02 | 0.00798 |
| 0.03 | 0.01197 |
| 0.04 | 0.01595 |
| 0.05 | 0.01994 |
| 0.06 | 0.02392 |
| 0.07 | 0.02790 |
| 0.08 | 0.03983 |
| 0.09 | 0.04380 |
| 0.10 | 0.04776 |
| | |
| 0.11 | 0.04380 |
| 0.12 | 0.04776 |
| 0.13 | 0.05172 |
| 0.14 | 0.05567 |
| 0.15 | 0.05962 |
| 0.16 | 0.06356 |
| 0.17 | 0.06750 |
| 0.18 | 0.07142 |
| 0.19 | 0.07535 |
| 0.20 | 0.07926 |
| | |
| 0.21 | 0.08317 |
| 0.22 | 0.08706 |
| 0.23 | 0.09095 |
| 0.24 | 0.09483 |
| 0.25 | 0.09871 |
| 0.26 | 0.10257 |
| 0.27 | 0.10642 |
| 0.28 | 0.11026 |
| 0.29 | 0.11409 |
| 0.30 | 0.11791 |
| | |
| 0.31 | 0.12172 |
| 0.32 | 0.12552 |
| 0.33 | 0.12930 |
| 0.34 | 0.13307 |
| 0.35 | 0.13683 |
| 0.36 | 0.14058 |
| 0.37 | 0.14431 |
| 0.38 | 0.14803 |
| 0.39 | 0.15173 |

| $z$ | $P$ |
|---|---|
| 0.40 | 0.15542 |
| | |
| 0.41 | 0.15910 |
| 0.42 | 0.16276 |
| 0.43 | 0.16640 |
| 0.44 | 0.17003 |
| 0.45 | 0.17364 |
| 0.46 | 0.17724 |
| 0.47 | 0.18082 |
| 0.48 | 0.18439 |
| 0.49 | 0.18793 |
| 0.50 | 0.19146 |
| | |
| 0.51 | 0.19497 |
| 0.52 | 0.19847 |
| 0.53 | 0.20194 |
| 0.54 | 0.20540 |
| 0.55 | 0.20884 |
| 0.56 | 0.21226 |
| 0.57 | 0.21556 |
| 0.58 | 0.21904 |
| 0.59 | 0.22240 |
| 0.60 | 0.22575 |
| | |
| 0.61 | 0.22907 |
| 0.62 | 0.23237 |
| 0.63 | 0.23565 |
| 0.64 | 0.23891 |
| 0.65 | 0.24215 |
| 0.66 | 0.24537 |
| 0.67 | 0.24857 |
| 0.68 | 0.25175 |
| 0.69 | 0.25490 |
| 0.70 | 0.25805 |
| | |
| 0.71 | 0.26115 |
| 0.72 | 0.26424 |
| 0.73 | 0.26730 |
| 0.74 | 0.27035 |
| 0.75 | 0.27337 |
| 0.76 | 0.27637 |
| 0.77 | 0.27935 |
| 0.78 | 0.28230 |
| 0.79 | 0.28524 |
| 0.80 | 0.28814 |
| | |
| 0.81 | 0.29103 |
| 0.82 | 0.29389 |
| 0.83 | 0.29673 |
| 0.84 | 0.29955 |
| 0.85 | 0.30234 |

| z | P | | z | P |
|---|---|---|---|---|
| 0.86 | 0.30511 | | 1.32 | 0.40658 |
| 0.87 | 0.30785 | | 1.33 | 0.40824 |
| 0.88 | 0.31057 | | 1.34 | 0.40988 |
| 0.89 | 0.31327 | | 1.35 | 0.41149 |
| 0.90 | 0.31594 | | 1.36 | 0.41309 |
| | | | 1.37 | 0.41466 |
| 0.91 | 0.31859 | | 1.38 | 0.41621 |
| 0.92 | 0.32121 | | 1.39 | 0.41774 |
| 0.93 | 0.32381 | | 1.40 | 0.41924 |
| 0.94 | 0.32639 | | | |
| 0.95 | 0.32894 | | 1.41 | 0.42073 |
| 0.96 | 0.33147 | | 1.42 | 0.42220 |
| 0.97 | 0.33398 | | 1.43 | 0.42364 |
| 0.98 | 0.33646 | | 1.44 | 0.42507 |
| 0.99 | 0.33891 | | 1.45 | 0.42647 |
| 1.00 | 0.34134 | | 1.46 | 0.42785 |
| | | | 1.47 | 0.42922 |
| 1.01 | 0.34375 | | 1.48 | 0.43056 |
| 1.02 | 0.34614 | | 1.49 | 0.43189 |
| 1.03 | 0.34849 | | 1.50 | 0.43319 |
| 1.04 | 0.35083 | | | |
| 1.05 | 0.35314 | | 1.51 | 0.43448 |
| 1.06 | 0.35543 | | 1.52 | 0.43574 |
| 1.07 | 0.35769 | | 1.53 | 0.43699 |
| 1.08 | 0.35993 | | 1.54 | 0.43822 |
| 1.09 | 0.36214 | | 1.55 | 0.43943 |
| 1.10 | 0.36433 | | 1.56 | 0.44062 |
| | | | 1.57 | 0.44179 |
| 1.11 | 0.36650 | | 1.58 | 0.44295 |
| 1.12 | 0.36864 | | 1.59 | 0.44408 |
| 1.13 | 0.37076 | | 1.60 | 0.44520 |
| 1.14 | 0.37286 | | | |
| 1.15 | 0.37493 | | 1.61 | 0.44630 |
| 1.16 | 0.37698 | | 1.62 | 0.44758 |
| 1.17 | 0.37900 | | 1.63 | 0.44835 |
| 1.18 | 0.38100 | | 1.64 | 0.44950 |
| 1.19 | 0.38298 | | 1.65 | 0.45053 |
| 1.20 | 0.38493 | | 1.66 | 0.45154 |
| | | | 1.67 | 0.45254 |
| 1.21 | 0.38686 | | 1.68 | 0.45352 |
| 1.22 | 0.38877 | | 1.69 | 0.45449 |
| 1.23 | 0.39065 | | 1.70 | 0.45543 |
| 1.24 | 0.39251 | | | |
| 1.25 | 0.39435 | | 1.71 | 0.45637 |
| 1.26 | 0.39617 | | 1.72 | 0.45728 |
| 1.27 | 0.39796 | | 1.73 | 0.45818 |
| 1.28 | 0.39973 | | 1.74 | 0.45907 |
| 1.29 | 0.40147 | | 1.75 | 0.45994 |
| 1.30 | 0.40320 | | 1.76 | 0.46080 |
| | | | 1.77 | 0.46164 |
| 1.31 | 0.40490 | | 1.78 | 0.46246 |

*continued overleaf*

| z | P | z | P |
|------|---------|------|---------|
| 1.79 | 0.46327 | 2.45 | 0.49286 |
| 1.80 | 0.46407 | 2.50 | 0.49379 |
| 1.81 | 0.46485 | 2.55 | 0.49461 |
| 1.82 | 0.46562 | 2.60 | 0.49534 |
| 1.83 | 0.46638 | 2.65 | 0.49598 |
| 1.84 | 0.46712 | 2.70 | 0.49653 |
| 1.85 | 0.46784 | 2.75 | 0.49702 |
| 1.86 | 0.46856 | 2.80 | 0.49744 |
| 1.87 | 0.46926 | 2.85 | 0.49781 |
| 1.88 | 0.46995 | 2.90 | 0.49813 |
| 1.89 | 0.47062 | 2.95 | 0.49841 |
| 1.90 | 0.47128 | 3.00 | 0.49865 |
| 1.91 | 0.47193 | 3.05 | 0.49886 |
| 1.92 | 0.47257 | 3.10 | 0.49903 |
| 1.93 | 0.47320 | 3.15 | 0.49918 |
| 1.94 | 0.47381 | 3.20 | 0.49931 |
| 1.95 | 0.47441 | 3.25 | 0.49942 |
| 1.96 | 0.47500 | 3.30 | 0.49952 |
| 1.97 | 0.47558 | 3.35 | 0.49960 |
| 1.98 | 0.47615 | 3.40 | 0.49966 |
| 1.99 | 0.47670 | 3.45 | 0.49972 |
| 2.00 | 0.47725 | 3.50 | 0.49977 |
| 2.05 | 0.47982 | 3.55 | 0.49981 |
| 2.10 | 0.48214 | 3.60 | 0.49984 |
| 2.15 | 0.48422 | 3.65 | 0.49987 |
| 2.20 | 0.48610 | 3.70 | 0.49989 |
| 2.25 | 0.48778 | 3.75 | 0.49991 |
| 2.30 | 0.48928 | 3.80 | 0.49993 |
| 2.35 | 0.49061 | 3.85 | 0.49994 |
| 2.40 | 0.49180 | 3.90 | 0.49995 |
|      |         | 3.95 | 0.49996 |

## C. CRITICAL VALUES FOR THE SIGN TEST

This table of critical values is given in terms of small values of the statistic.

| One tail: | 0.05 | 0.025 | 0.01 | 0.005 | | 0.05 | 0.025 | 0.01 | 0.005 |
|---|---|---|---|---|---|---|---|---|---|
| Two tail: | 0.10 | 0.05 | 0.02 | 0.01 | | 0.10 | 0.05 | 0.02 | 0.01 |
| n | | | | | n | | | | |
| 5 | 0 | | | | 29 | 9 | 8 | 7 | 7 |
| 6 | 0 | 0 | | | 30 | 10 | 9 | 8 | 7 |
| 7 | 0 | 0 | 0 | | 31 | 10 | 9 | 8 | 7 |
| 8 | 1 | 0 | 0 | 0 | 32 | 10 | 9 | 8 | 8 |
| 9 | 1 | 1 | 0 | 0 | 33 | 11 | 10 | 9 | 8 |
| 10 | 1 | 1 | 0 | 0 | 34 | 11 | 10 | 9 | 9 |
| 11 | 2 | 1 | 1 | 0 | 35 | 12 | 11 | 10 | 9 |
| 12 | 2 | 2 | 1 | 1 | 36 | 12 | 11 | 10 | 9 |
| 13 | 3 | 2 | 1 | 1 | 37 | 13 | 12 | 10 | 10 |
| 14 | 3 | 2 | 2 | 1 | 38 | 13 | 12 | 11 | 10 |
| 15 | 3 | 3 | 2 | 2 | 39 | 13 | 12 | 11 | 11 |
| 16 | 4 | 3 | 2 | 2 | 40 | 14 | 13 | 12 | 11 |
| 17 | 4 | 4 | 3 | 2 | 41 | 14 | 13 | 12 | 11 |
| 18 | 5 | 4 | 3 | 3 | 42 | 15 | 14 | 13 | 12 |
| 19 | 5 | 4 | 4 | 3 | 43 | 15 | 14 | 13 | 12 |
| 20 | 5 | 5 | 4 | 3 | 44 | 16 | 15 | 13 | 13 |
| 21 | 6 | 5 | 4 | 4 | 45 | 16 | 15 | 14 | 13 |
| 22 | 6 | 5 | 5 | 4 | 46 | 16 | 15 | 14 | 13 |
| 23 | 7 | 6 | 5 | 4 | 47 | 17 | 16 | 15 | 14 |
| 24 | 7 | 6 | 5 | 5 | 48 | 17 | 16 | 15 | 14 |
| 25 | 7 | 7 | 6 | 5 | 49 | 18 | 17 | 15 | 15 |
| 26 | 8 | 7 | 6 | 6 | 50 | 18 | 17 | 16 | 15 |
| 27 | 8 | 7 | 7 | 6 | 51 | 19 | 18 | 16 | 15 |
| 28 | 9 | 8 | 7 | 6 | 52 | 19 | 18 | 17 | 16 |

Source: Neave and Worthington (1988:372–3).

## D. CRITICAL VALUES OF THE CHI-SQUARED ($\chi^2$) DISTRIBUTION

| Degrees of freedom $\nu$ | Significance level ($\alpha$) | | | | |
|---|---|---|---|---|---|
| | 0.10 | 0.05 | 0.01 | 0.005 | 0.001 |
| 1 | 2.71 | 3.84 | 6.4 | 7.88 | 10.83 |
| 2 | 4.60 | 5.99 | 9.21 | 10.60 | 13.82 |
| 3 | 6.25 | 7.82 | 11.34 | 12.84 | 16.27 |
| 4 | 7.78 | 9.49 | 13.28 | 14.86 | 18.46 |
| 5 | 9.24 | 11.07 | 15.09 | 16.75 | 20.52 |
| 6 | 10.64 | 12.59 | 16.81 | 18.55 | 22.46 |
| 7 | 12.02 | 14.07 | 18.48 | 20.28 | 24.32 |
| 8 | 13.36 | 15.51 | 20.29 | 21.96 | 26.12 |
| 9 | 14.68 | 16.92 | 21.67 | 23.59 | 27.88 |
| 10 | 15.99 | 18.31 | 23.21 | 25.19 | 29.59 |
| 11 | 17.28 | 19.68 | 24.72 | 26.76 | 31.26 |
| 12 | 18.55 | 21.03 | 26.22 | 28.30 | 32.91 |
| 13 | 19.81 | 22.36 | 27.69 | 30.82 | 34.53 |
| 14 | 21.06 | 23.68 | 29.14 | 31.32 | 36.12 |
| 15 | 22.31 | 25.00 | 30.58 | 32.80 | 37.70 |
| 16 | 23.54 | 26.30 | 32.00 | 34.27 | 39.29 |
| 17 | 24.77 | 27.59 | 33.41 | 35.72 | 40.75 |
| 18 | 25.99 | 28.87 | 34.80 | 37.16 | 42.31 |
| 19 | 27.20 | 30.14 | 36.19 | 38.58 | 43.82 |
| 20 | 28.41 | 31.41 | 37.57 | 40.00 | 45.32 |
| 21 | 29.62 | 32.67 | 38.93 | 41.40 | 46.80 |
| 22 | 30.81 | 33.92 | 40.29 | 42.80 | 48.27 |
| 23 | 32.01 | 35.17 | 41.64 | 44.18 | 49.73 |
| 24 | 33.20 | 36.42 | 42.98 | 45.56 | 51.18 |
| 25 | 34.38 | 37.65 | 44.31 | 46.93 | 52.62 |
| 26 | 35.56 | 35.88 | 45.64 | 48.29 | 54.05 |
| 27 | 36.74 | 40.11 | 46.96 | 49.65 | 55.48 |
| 28 | 37.92 | 41.34 | 48.28 | 50.99 | 56.89 |
| 29 | 39.09 | 42.56 | 49.59 | 52.34 | 58.30 |
| 30 | 40.26 | 43.77 | 50.89 | 53.67 | 59.70 |
| 40 | 51.81 | 55.76 | 63.69 | 66.77 | 73.40 |
| 50 | 63.17 | 67.51 | 76.15 | 79.49 | 86.66 |
| 60 | 74.40 | 79.08 | 88.38 | 91.95 | 99.61 |
| 70 | 85.53 | 90.53 | 100.43 | 104.22 | 112.32 |
| 80 | 96.58 | 101.88 | 112.33 | 116.32 | 124.84 |
| 90 | 105.57 | 113.15 | 124.12 | 128.30 | 137.21 |
| 100 | 118.50 | 124.34 | 135.81 | 140.17 | 149.45 |

*Source*: Neave and Worthington (1988:371).

## E. CRITICAL VALUES OF THE KOLMOGOROV–SMIRNOV STATISTIC ($D$)

$H_0$ is rejected if the value of $D$ exceeds the critical value for a given sample size ($n$) at the selected significance level.

| $n$ | Significance level ($\alpha$) | | | | |
|---|---|---|---|---|---|
| | 0.20 | 0.15 | 0.10 | 0.05 | 0.01 |
| 1 | 0.900 | 0.925 | 0.950 | 0.975 | 0.995 |
| 2 | 0.684 | 0.726 | 0.776 | 0.842 | 0.929 |
| 3 | 0.565 | 0.597 | 0.642 | 0.708 | 0.828 |
| 4 | 0.494 | 0.525 | 0.564 | 0.624 | 0.733 |
| 5 | 0.446 | 0.474 | 0.510 | 0.565 | 0.669 |
| 6 | 0.410 | 0.436 | 0.470 | 0.521 | 0.618 |
| 7 | 0.381 | 0.405 | 0.438 | 0.486 | 0.577 |
| 8 | 0.358 | 0.381 | 0.411 | 0.457 | 0.543 |
| 9 | 0.339 | 0.360 | 0.388 | 0.432 | 0.514 |
| 10 | 0.322 | 0.342 | 0.368 | 0.410 | 0.490 |
| 11 | 0.307 | 0.326 | 0.352 | 0.391 | 0.468 |
| 12 | 0.296 | 0.320 | 0.345 | 0.383 | 0.459 |
| 13 | 0.284 | 0.313 | 0.338 | 0.375 | 0.450 |
| 14 | 0.274 | 0.292 | 0.314 | 0.349 | 0.418 |
| 15 | 0.266 | 0.283 | 0.304 | 0.338 | 0.404 |
| 16 | 0.258 | 0.274 | 0.295 | 0.328 | 0.392 |
| 17 | 0.250 | 0.266 | 0.286 | 0.318 | 0.381 |
| 18 | 0.244 | 0.259 | 0.278 | 0.309 | 0.371 |
| 19 | 0.237 | 0.252 | 0.272 | 0.301 | 0.363 |
| 20 | 0.231 | 0.246 | 0.264 | 0.294 | 0.356 |
| 25 | 0.210 | 0.220 | 0.240 | 0.270 | 0.320 |
| 30 | 0.190 | 0.200 | 0.220 | 0.240 | 0.290 |
| 35 | 0.180 | 0.190 | 0.210 | 0.230 | 0.270 |
| > 35 | $\dfrac{1.07}{n}$ | $\dfrac{1.14}{n}$ | $\dfrac{1.22}{n}$ | $\dfrac{1.36}{n}$ | $\dfrac{1.63}{n}$ |

## F. CRITICAL VALUES FOR THE MANN–WHITNEY *U* TEST

(a) For a two-tailed test at $\alpha = 0.05$ and a one-tailed test at $\alpha = 0.025$

| $n_1$ \ $n_2$ | 9 | 10 | 11 | 12 | 13 | 14 | 15 | 16 | 17 | 18 | 19 | 20 |
|---|---|---|---|---|---|---|---|---|---|---|---|---|
| 2 | 0 | 0 | 0 | 1 | 1 | 1 | 1 | 1 | 2 | 2 | 2 | 2 |
| 3 | 2 | 3 | 3 | 4 | 4 | 5 | 5 | 6 | 6 | 7 | 7 | 8 |
| 4 | 4 | 5 | 6 | 7 | 8 | 9 | 10 | 11 | 11 | 12 | 13 | 13 |
| 5 | 7 | 8 | 9 | 11 | 12 | 13 | 14 | 15 | 17 | 18 | 19 | 20 |
| 6 | 10 | 11 | 13 | 14 | 16 | 17 | 19 | 21 | 22 | 24 | 25 | 27 |
| 7 | 12 | 14 | 16 | 18 | 20 | 22 | 24 | 26 | 28 | 30 | 32 | 34 |
| 8 | 15 | 17 | 19 | 22 | 24 | 26 | 29 | 31 | 34 | 36 | 38 | 41 |
| 9 | 17 | 20 | 23 | 26 | 28 | 31 | 34 | 37 | 39 | 42 | 45 | 48 |
| 10 | 20 | 23 | 26 | 29 | 33 | 36 | 39 | 42 | 45 | 48 | 52 | 55 |
| 11 | 23 | 26 | 30 | 33 | 37 | 40 | 44 | 47 | 51 | 55 | 58 | 62 |
| 12 | 26 | 29 | 33 | 37 | 41 | 45 | 49 | 53 | 57 | 61 | 65 | 69 |
| 13 | 28 | 33 | 37 | 41 | 45 | 50 | 54 | 59 | 63 | 67 | 72 | 83 |
| 14 | 31 | 36 | 40 | 45 | 50 | 55 | 59 | 64 | 67 | 74 | 78 | 83 |
| 15 | 34 | 39 | 44 | 49 | 54 | 59 | 64 | 70 | 75 | 80 | 85 | 90 |
| 16 | 37 | 42 | 47 | 53 | 59 | 64 | 70 | 75 | 81 | 86 | 92 | 98 |
| 17 | 39 | 45 | 51 | 57 | 63 | 67 | 75 | 81 | 87 | 93 | 99 | 105 |
| 18 | 42 | 48 | 55 | 61 | 67 | 74 | 80 | 86 | 93 | 99 | 106 | 112 |
| 19 | 45 | 52 | 58 | 65 | 72 | 78 | 85 | 92 | 99 | 106 | 113 | 119 |
| 20 | 48 | 55 | 62 | 69 | 76 | 83 | 90 | 98 | 105 | 112 | 119 | 127 |

(b) For a two-tailed test at $\alpha = 0.01$ and a one-tailed test at $\alpha = 0.005$

| $n_1$ \ $n_2$ | 9 | 10 | 11 | 12 | 13 | 14 | 15 | 16 | 17 | 18 | 19 | 20 |
|---|---|---|---|---|---|---|---|---|---|---|---|---|
| 3 | 0 | 0 | 0 | 1 | 1 | 1 | 2 | 2 | 2 | 2 | 3 | 3 |
| 4 | 1 | 2 | 2 | 3 | 3 | 4 | 5 | 5 | 6 | 6 | 7 | 8 |
| 5 | 3 | 4 | 5 | 6 | 7 | 7 | 8 | 9 | 10 | 11 | 12 | 13 |
| 6 | 5 | 6 | 7 | 9 | 10 | 11 | 12 | 13 | 15 | 16 | 17 | 18 |
| 7 | 7 | 9 | 10 | 12 | 13 | 15 | 16 | 18 | 19 | 21 | 22 | 24 |
| 8 | 9 | 11 | 13 | 15 | 17 | 18 | 20 | 22 | 24 | 26 | 28 | 30 |
| 9 | 11 | 13 | 16 | 18 | 20 | 22 | 24 | 27 | 29 | 31 | 33 | 36 |
| 10 | 13 | 16 | 18 | 21 | 24 | 26 | 29 | 31 | 34 | 37 | 39 | 42 |
| 11 | 16 | 18 | 21 | 24 | 27 | 30 | 33 | 36 | 39 | 42 | 45 | 48 |
| 12 | 18 | 21 | 24 | 27 | 31 | 34 | 37 | 41 | 44 | 47 | 51 | 54 |
| 13 | 20 | 24 | 27 | 31 | 34 | 38 | 42 | 45 | 49 | 53 | 57 | 60 |
| 14 | 22 | 26 | 30 | 34 | 38 | 42 | 46 | 50 | 54 | 58 | 63 | 67 |
| 15 | 24 | 29 | 33 | 37 | 42 | 46 | 51 | 55 | 60 | 64 | 69 | 73 |
| 16 | 27 | 31 | 36 | 41 | 45 | 50 | 55 | 60 | 65 | 70 | 74 | 79 |
| 17 | 29 | 34 | 39 | 44 | 49 | 54 | 60 | 65 | 70 | 75 | 81 | 86 |
| 18 | 31 | 37 | 42 | 47 | 53 | 58 | 64 | 70 | 75 | 81 | 87 | 92 |
| 19 | 33 | 39 | 45 | 51 | 57 | 63 | 69 | 74 | 81 | 87 | 93 | 99 |
| 20 | 36 | 42 | 48 | 54 | 60 | 67 | 73 | 79 | 86 | 92 | 99 | 105 |

*Source*: Neave and Worthington (1988:375–6).

## G. CRITICAL VALUES FOR THE WILCOXON SIGNED-RANK TEST

| One tail: | 0.05 | 0.025 | 0.01 | 0.005 | | 0.05 | 0.025 | 0.01 | 0.005 |
|---|---|---|---|---|---|---|---|---|---|
| Two tail: | 0.10 | 0.05 | 0.02 | 0.01 | | 0.10 | 0.05 | 0.02 | 0.01 |
| n | | | | | n | | | | |
| 5 | 0 | | | | 28 | 130 | 116 | 101 | 91 |
| 6 | 2 | 0 | | | 29 | 140 | 126 | 110 | 100 |
| 7 | 3 | 2 | 0 | | 30 | 151 | 137 | 120 | 109 |
| 8 | 5 | 3 | 1 | 0 | 31 | 163 | 147 | 130 | 118 |
| 9 | 8 | 5 | 3 | 1 | 32 | 175 | 159 | 140 | 128 |
| 10 | 10 | 8 | 5 | 3 | 33 | 187 | 170 | 151 | 138 |
| 11 | 13 | 10 | 7 | 5 | 34 | 200 | 182 | 162 | 148 |
| 12 | 17 | 13 | 9 | 7 | 35 | 213 | 195 | 173 | 159 |
| 13 | 21 | 17 | 12 | 9 | 36 | 227 | 208 | 185 | 171 |
| 14 | 25 | 21 | 15 | 12 | 37 | 241 | 221 | 198 | 182 |
| 15 | 30 | 25 | 19 | 15 | 38 | 256 | 235 | 211 | 194 |
| 16 | 35 | 29 | 23 | 19 | 39 | 271 | 249 | 224 | 207 |
| 17 | 41 | 34 | 27 | 23 | 40 | 286 | 264 | 238 | 220 |
| 18 | 47 | 40 | 32 | 27 | 41 | 302 | 279 | 252 | 233 |
| 19 | 53 | 46 | 37 | 32 | 42 | 319 | 294 | 266 | 247 |
| 20 | 60 | 52 | 43 | 37 | 43 | 336 | 310 | 281 | 261 |
| 21 | 67 | 58 | 49 | 42 | 44 | 353 | 327 | 296 | 276 |
| 22 | 75 | 65 | 55 | 48 | 45 | 371 | 343 | 312 | 291 |
| 23 | 83 | 73 | 62 | 54 | 46 | 389 | 361 | 328 | 307 |
| 24 | 91 | 81 | 69 | 61 | 47 | 407 | 378 | 345 | 322 |
| 25 | 100 | 89 | 76 | 68 | 48 | 426 | 396 | 362 | 339 |
| 26 | 110 | 98 | 84 | 75 | 49 | 446 | 415 | 379 | 355 |
| 27 | 119 | 107 | 92 | 83 | 50 | 466 | 434 | 397 | 373 |

Source: Neave and Worthington (1988:373).

## H. CRITICAL VALUES OF THE STUDENT'S *t* DISTRIBUTION

$H_0$ is rejected if calculated value of *t* exceeds tabulated value.

| $v$ | Two-tailed significance levels ($\alpha$)<br>(One-tailed in brackets) | | | | |
|---|---|---|---|---|---|
| | 0.10<br>(0.05) | 0.05<br>(0.025) | 0.02<br>(0.01) | 0.01<br>(0.005) | 0.001<br>(0.0005) |
| 1 | 6.31 | 12.71 | 31.81 | 63.66 | 636.60 |
| 2 | 2.92 | 4.30 | 6.97 | 9.93 | 31.60 |
| 3 | 2.35 | 3.18 | 4.54 | 5.84 | 12.92 |
| 4 | 2.13 | 2.78 | 3.75 | 4.60 | 8.61 |
| 5 | 2.02 | 2.57 | 3.37 | 4.03 | 6.86 |
| 6 | 1.94 | 2.45 | 3.14 | 3.71 | 5.96 |
| 7 | 1.90 | 2.37 | 3.00 | 3.50 | 5.41 |
| 8 | 1.86 | 2.31 | 2.90 | 3.36 | 5.04 |
| 9 | 1.83 | 2.26 | 2.82 | 3.25 | 4.78 |
| 10 | 1.81 | 2.23 | 2.76 | 3.17 | 4.59 |
| 11 | 1.80 | 2.20 | 2.72 | 3.11 | 4.44 |
| 12 | 1.78 | 2.18 | 2.68 | 3.06 | 4.32 |
| 13 | 1.77 | 2.16 | 2.65 | 3.01 | 4.23 |
| 14 | 1.76 | 2.15 | 2.62 | 2.98 | 4.14 |
| 15 | 1.75 | 2.13 | 2.60 | 2.95 | 4.07 |
| 16 | 1.74 | 2.12 | 2.58 | 2.92 | 4.02 |
| 17 | 1.74 | 2.11 | 2.57 | 2.90 | 3.97 |
| 18 | 1.73 | 2.10 | 2.55 | 2.88 | 3.92 |
| 19 | 1.73 | 2.09 | 2.54 | 2.86 | 3.88 |
| 20 | 1.73 | 2.09 | 2.53 | 2.85 | 3.85 |
| 21 | 1.72 | 2.08 | 2.52 | 2.83 | 3.82 |
| 22 | 1.71 | 2.07 | 2.51 | 2.82 | 3.79 |
| 23 | 1.71 | 2.07 | 2.50 | 2.81 | 3.77 |
| 24 | 1.71 | 2.06 | 2.49 | 2.80 | 3.75 |
| 25 | 1.71 | 2.06 | 2.49 | 2.79 | 3.73 |
| 26 | 1.71 | 2.06 | 2.48 | 2.78 | 3.71 |
| 27 | 1.70 | 2.05 | 2.47 | 2.77 | 3.69 |
| 28 | 1.70 | 2.05 | 2.47 | 2.76 | 3.67 |
| 29 | 1.70 | 2.05 | 2.46 | 2.76 | 3.66 |
| 30 | 1.70 | 2.04 | 2.46 | 2.75 | 3.65 |
| 40 | 1.68 | 2.02 | 2.42 | 2.70 | 3.55 |
| 60 | 1.67 | 2.00 | 2.39 | 2.66 | 3.46 |
| > 60 approximates to the normal (*z*) distribution | | | | | |
| *z* | 1.64 | 1.96 | 2.33 | 2.58 | 3.29 |

*Source*: Barber (1988:499).

## I. CRITICAL VALUES OF SNEDECOR'S F DISTRIBUTION

$v_1$ and $v_2$ are the degrees of freedom for the greater and lesser variance estimates respectively. $H_0$ is rejected if the calculated $F$ value equals or exceeds the tabulated critical value.

| $v_2$ \ $v_1$ | Significance level ($\alpha = 0.05$) | | | | | | | | |
|---|---|---|---|---|---|---|---|---|---|
| | 1 | 2 | 3 | 4 | 5 | 6 | 8 | 12 | 24 |
| 1 | 161.4 | 199.7 | 215.7 | 224.6 | 230.2 | 234.0 | 238.9 | 243.9 | 249.0 |
| 2 | 18.51 | 19.00 | 19.16 | 19.25 | 19.30 | 19.33 | 19.37 | 19.41 | 19.50 |
| 3 | 10.13 | 9.55 | 9.28 | 9.12 | 9.01 | 8.94 | 8.84 | 8.74 | 8.64 |
| 4 | 7.71 | 6.94 | 6.59 | 6.39 | 6.26 | 6.16 | 6.04 | 5.91 | 5.77 |
| 5 | 6.61 | 5.79 | 5.41 | 5.19 | 5.05 | 4.95 | 4.81 | 4.68 | 4.53 |
| 6 | 5.99 | 5.14 | 4.76 | 4.53 | 4.39 | 4.28 | 4.15 | 4.00 | 3.84 |
| 7 | 5.59 | 4.74 | 4.35 | 4.12 | 3.97 | 3.87 | 3.73 | 3.57 | 3.41 |
| 8 | 5.32 | 4.46 | 4.07 | 3.84 | 3.69 | 3.58 | 3.44 | 3.28 | 3.12 |
| 9 | 5.12 | 4.26 | 3.86 | 3.63 | 3.48 | 3.37 | 3.23 | 3.07 | 2.90 |
| 10 | 4.96 | 4.10 | 3.71 | 3.48 | 3.33 | 3.22 | 3.07 | 2.91 | 2.74 |
| 11 | 4.84 | 3.98 | 3.59 | 3.36 | 3.20 | 3.09 | 2.95 | 2.79 | 2.61 |
| 12 | 4.75 | 3.88 | 3.49 | 3.26 | 3.11 | 3.00 | 2.85 | 2.69 | 2.60 |
| 13 | 4.67 | 3.80 | 3.41 | 3.18 | 3.02 | 2.92 | 2.77 | 2.60 | 2.42 |
| 14 | 4.60 | 3.74 | 3.34 | 3.11 | 2.96 | 2.85 | 2.70 | 2.53 | 2.35 |
| 15 | 4.54 | 3.68 | 3.29 | 3.06 | 2.90 | 2.79 | 2.64 | 2.48 | 2.29 |
| 16 | 4.49 | 3.63 | 3.24 | 3.01 | 2.85 | 2.74 | 2.59 | 2.42 | 2.24 |
| 17 | 4.45 | 3.59 | 3.20 | 2.96 | 2.81 | 2.70 | 2.55 | 2.38 | 2.19 |
| 18 | 4.41 | 3.55 | 3.16 | 2.93 | 2.77 | 2.66 | 2.51 | 2.34 | 2.15 |
| 19 | 4.38 | 3.52 | 3.13 | 2.90 | 2.74 | 2.63 | 2.48 | 2.31 | 2.11 |
| 20 | 4.35 | 3.49 | 3.10 | 2.87 | 2.71 | 2.60 | 2.45 | 2.28 | 2.08 |
| 21 | 4.32 | 3.47 | 3.07 | 2.84 | 2.68 | 2.57 | 2.42 | 2.25 | 2.05 |
| 22 | 4.30 | 3.44 | 3.05 | 2.82 | 2.66 | 2.55 | 2.40 | 2.23 | 2.03 |
| 23 | 4.28 | 3.42 | 3.03 | 2.80 | 2.64 | 2.53 | 2.38 | 2.20 | 2.00 |
| 24 | 4.26 | 3.40 | 3.01 | 2.78 | 2.62 | 2.51 | 2.36 | 2.18 | 1.98 |
| 25 | 4.24 | 3.38 | 2.99 | 2.76 | 2.60 | 2.49 | 2.34 | 2.16 | 1.96 |
| 26 | 4.22 | 3.37 | 2.98 | 2.74 | 2.59 | 2.47 | 2.32 | 2.15 | 1.95 |
| 27 | 4.21 | 3.35 | 2.96 | 2.73 | 2.57 | 2.46 | 2.30 | 2.13 | 1.93 |
| 28 | 4.20 | 3.34 | 2.95 | 2.71 | 2.56 | 2.44 | 2.29 | 2.12 | 1.91 |
| 29 | 4.18 | 3.33 | 2.93 | 2.70 | 2.54 | 2.45 | 2.28 | 2.10 | 1.90 |
| 30 | 4.17 | 3.32 | 2.92 | 2.69 | 2.53 | 2.42 | 2.27 | 2.09 | 1.89 |
| 40 | 4.08 | 3.23 | 2.84 | 2.61 | 2.45 | 2.34 | 2.18 | 2.00 | 1.79 |
| 60 | 4.00 | 3.15 | 2.76 | 2.52 | 2.37 | 2.25 | 2.10 | 1.92 | 1.70 |
| 120 | 3.93 | 3.07 | 2.68 | 2.45 | 2.29 | 2.17 | 2.02 | 1.83 | 1.81 |
| | 3.84 | 2.99 | 2.60 | 2.37 | 2.21 | 2.09 | 1.94 | 1.75 | 1.52 |

| $\nu_2$ \ $\nu_1$ | Significance level ($\alpha = 0.01$) | | | | | | | | |
|---|---|---|---|---|---|---|---|---|---|
| | 1 | 2 | 3 | 4 | 5 | 6 | 8 | 12 | 24 |
| 1 | 4052 | 4999 | 5403 | 5625 | 5764 | 5859 | 5981 | 6106 | 6234 |
| 2 | 98.49 | 99.01 | 99.17 | 99.25 | 99.30 | 99.33 | 99.36 | 99.42 | 99.46 |
| 3 | 34.12 | 30.81 | 29.46 | 28.71 | 28.24 | 27.91 | 27.49 | 27.05 | 26.60 |
| 4 | 21.20 | 18.00 | 16.69 | 15.98 | 15.52 | 15.21 | 14.80 | 14.37 | 13.93 |
| 5 | 16.26 | 13.27 | 12.06 | 11.39 | 10.97 | 10.67 | 10.27 | 9.89 | 9.47 |
| 6 | 13.74 | 10.92 | 9.78 | 9.15 | 8.75 | 8.47 | 8.10 | 7.72 | 7.31 |
| 7 | 12.25 | 9.55 | 8.45 | 7.85 | 7.46 | 7.19 | 6.84 | 6.47 | 6.07 |
| 8 | 11.26 | 8.65 | 7.59 | 7.01 | 6.63 | 6.37 | 6.03 | 5.67 | 5.28 |
| 9 | 10.56 | 8.02 | 6.99 | 6.42 | 6.06 | 5.80 | 5.47 | 5.11 | 4.73 |
| 10 | 10.04 | 7.56 | 6.55 | 5.99 | 5.64 | 5.39 | 5.06 | 4.71 | 4.33 |
| 11 | 9.65 | 7.20 | 6.22 | 5.67 | 5.32 | 5.07 | 4.74 | 4.40 | 4.02 |
| 12 | 9.33 | 6.93 | 5.95 | 5.41 | 5.06 | 4.82 | 4.50 | 4.16 | 3.78 |
| 13 | 9.07 | 6.70 | 5.74 | 5.20 | 4.86 | 4.62 | 4.30 | 3.96 | 3.59 |
| 14 | 8.86 | 6.51 | 5.56 | 5.03 | 4.69 | 4.46 | 4.14 | 3.80 | 3.43 |
| 15 | 8.68 | 6.36 | 5.42 | 4.89 | 4.56 | 4.32 | 4.00 | 3.67 | 3.29 |
| 16 | 8.53 | 6.23 | 5.29 | 4.77 | 4.44 | 4.20 | 5.89 | 3.55 | 3.18 |
| 17 | 8.40 | 6.11 | 5.18 | 4.67 | 4.34 | 4.10 | 3.79 | 3.45 | 3.08 |
| 18 | 8.28 | 6.01 | 5.09 | 4.58 | 4.25 | 4.01 | 3.71 | 3.37 | 3.00 |
| 19 | 8.18 | 5.93 | 5.01 | 4.50 | 4.17 | 3.94 | 3.68 | 3.30 | 3.92 |
| 20 | 8.10 | 5.85 | 4.94 | 4.43 | 4.10 | 3.87 | 3.56 | 3.23 | 2.86 |
| 21 | 8.02 | 5.78 | 4.87 | 4.37 | 4.04 | 3.81 | 3.51 | 3.17 | 2.80 |
| 22 | 7.94 | 5.72 | 4.82 | 4.31 | 3.99 | 3.76 | 3.45 | 3.12 | 2.75 |
| 23 | 7.88 | 5.66 | 4.76 | 4.26 | 3.94 | 3.71 | 3.41 | 3.07 | 2.70 |
| 24 | 7.82 | 5.61 | 4.72 | 4.22 | 3.90 | 3.67 | 3.36 | 3.03 | 2.66 |
| 25 | 7.77 | 5.57 | 4.68 | 4.18 | 3.86 | 3.63 | 3.32 | 2.99 | 2.62 |
| 26 | 7.72 | 5.53 | 4.64 | 4.14 | 3.82 | 3.59 | 3.29 | 2.96 | 2.58 |
| 27 | 7.68 | 5.49 | 4.60 | 4.11 | 3.78 | 3.56 | 3.26 | 2.93 | 2.55 |
| 28 | 7.64 | 5.45 | 4.57 | 4.07 | 3.75 | 3.53 | 3.23 | 2.90 | 2.52 |
| 29 | 7.60 | 5.42 | 4.54 | 4.04 | 3.73 | 3.50 | 3.20 | 2.87 | 2.49 |
| 30 | 7.56 | 5.39 | 4.51 | 4.02 | 3.70 | 3.47 | 3.17 | 2.84 | 2.47 |
| 40 | 7.31 | 5.18 | 4.31 | 3.83 | 3.51 | 3.29 | 2.99 | 2.66 | 2.29 |
| 60 | 7.08 | 4.98 | 4.13 | 3.65 | 3.34 | 3.12 | 2.82 | 2.50 | 2.12 |
| 120 | 6.85 | 4.79 | 3.95 | 3.48 | 5.17 | 2.96 | 2.66 | 2.34 | 1.95 |
| | 6.64 | 4.60 | 3.78 | 3.32 | 3.02 | 2.80 | 2.51 | 2.18 | 1.79 |

*Source*: Barber (1988:501–5).

## J. CRITICAL VALUES OF THE PEARSON PRODUCT-MOMENT CORRELATION COEFFICIENT ($r_{xy}$)

The calculated correlation coefficient is significant if it is greater than the critical value at the selected significance level for a sample size of $n$.

| $n$ | Two-tailed significance levels (One-tailed in brackets) | | | | $n$ | Two-tailed significance levels (One-tailed in brackets) | | | |
|---|---|---|---|---|---|---|---|---|---|
| | 0.1 (0.05) | 0.05 (0.025) | 0.02 (0.01) | 0.01 (0.005) | | 0.1 (0.05) | 0.05 (0.025) | 0.02 (0.01) | 0.01 (0.005) |
| 3 | 0.988 | 0.997 | 1.000 | 1.000 | 27 | 0.323 | 0.381 | 0.445 | 0.487 |
| 4 | 0.900 | 0.950 | 0.980 | 0.990 | 28 | 0.317 | 0.374 | 0.437 | 0.479 |
| 5 | 0.805 | 0.878 | 0.934 | 0.959 | 29 | 0.311 | 0.367 | 0.430 | 0.471 |
| 6 | 0.729 | 0.811 | 0.882 | 0.917 | 30 | 0.306 | 0.361 | 0.423 | 0.463 |
| 7 | 0.669 | 0.754 | 0.833 | 0.875 | 31 | 0.301 | 0.355 | 0.416 | 0.456 |
| 8 | 0.621 | 0.707 | 0.789 | 0.834 | 32 | 0.296 | 0.349 | 0.409 | 0.449 |
| 9 | 0.582 | 0.666 | 0.750 | 0.798 | 33 | 0.291 | 0.344 | 0.403 | 0.443 |
| 10 | 0.549 | 0.632 | 0.715 | 0.765 | 34 | 0.287 | 0.339 | 0.397 | 0.436 |
| 11 | 0.521 | 0.602 | 0.685 | 0.735 | 35 | 0.283 | 0.334 | 0.391 | 0.430 |
| 12 | 0.497 | 0.576 | 0.658 | 0.708 | 40 | 0.264 | 0.312 | 0.367 | 0.403 |
| 13 | 0.476 | 0.553 | 0.634 | 0.684 | 45 | 0.249 | 0.294 | 0.346 | 0.380 |
| 14 | 0.458 | 0.532 | 0.612 | 0.661 | 50 | 0.235 | 0.279 | 0.328 | 0.361 |
| 15 | 0.441 | 0.514 | 0.592 | 0.641 | 55 | 0.224 | 0.266 | 0.313 | 0.345 |
| 16 | 0.426 | 0.497 | 0.574 | 0.623 | 60 | 0.214 | 0.254 | 0.300 | 0.330 |
| 17 | 0.412 | 0.482 | 0.558 | 0.606 | 65 | 0.206 | 0.244 | 0.288 | 0.317 |
| 18 | 0.400 | 0.468 | 0.543 | 0.590 | 70 | 0.198 | 0.235 | 0.278 | 0.306 |
| 19 | 0.389 | 0.456 | 0.529 | 0.575 | 75 | 0.191 | 0.227 | 0.268 | 0.296 |
| 20 | 0.378 | 0.444 | 0.516 | 0.561 | 80 | 0.185 | 0.220 | 0.260 | 0.286 |
| 21 | 0.369 | 0.433 | 0.503 | 0.549 | 85 | 0.180 | 0.213 | 0.252 | 0.278 |
| 22 | 0.360 | 0.423 | 0.492 | 0.537 | 90 | 0.174 | 0.207 | 0.245 | 0.270 |
| 23 | 0.352 | 0.413 | 0.482 | 0.526 | 95 | 0.170 | 0.202 | 0.238 | 0.263 |
| 24 | 0.344 | 0.404 | 0.472 | 0.515 | 100 | 0.165 | 0.197 | 0.232 | 0.256 |
| 25 | 0.337 | 0.396 | 0.462 | 0.505 | 150 | 0.135 | 0.160 | 0.190 | 0.210 |
| 26 | 0.330 | 0.388 | 0.453 | 0.496 | 200 | 0.117 | 0.139 | 0.164 | 0.182 |

## K. CRITICAL VALUES OF THE SPEARMAN RANK CORRELATION COEFFICIENT ($\rho_{xy}$)

The calculated correlation coefficient is significant if it is greater than the critical value at the selected significance level for a sample size of $n$.

| $n$ | Two-tailed significance levels (One-tailed in brackets) | | | | $n$ | Two-tailed significance levels (One-tailed in brackets) | | | |
|---|---|---|---|---|---|---|---|---|---|
| | 0.1 (0.05) | 0.05 (0.025) | 0.02 (0.01) | 0.01 (0.005) | | 0.1 (0.05) | 0.05 (0.025) | 0.02 (0.01) | 0.01 (0.005) |
| 5 | 0.900 | 1.000 | 1.000 | | 26 | 0.331 | 0.390 | 0.457 | 0.501 |
| 6 | 0.829 | 0.886 | 0.943 | 1.000 | 27 | 0.324 | 0.383 | 0.449 | 0.492 |
| 7 | 0.714 | 0.786 | 0.893 | 0.929 | 28 | 0.318 | 0.375 | 0.441 | 0.483 |
| 8 | 0.643 | 0.738 | 0.833 | 0.881 | 29 | 0.312 | 0.368 | 0.433 | 0.475 |
| 9 | 0.600 | 0.700 | 0.783 | 0.833 | 30 | 0.306 | 0.362 | 0.425 | 0.467 |
| 10 | 0.564 | 0.648 | 0.745 | 0.794 | 31 | 0.301 | 0.356 | 0.419 | 0.459 |
| 11 | 0.536 | 0.618 | 0.709 | 0.755 | 32 | 0.296 | 0.350 | 0.412 | 0.452 |
| 12 | 0.503 | 0.587 | 0.678 | 0.727 | 33 | 0.291 | 0.345 | 0.405 | 0.446 |
| 13 | 0.484 | 0.560 | 0.648 | 0.703 | 34 | 0.287 | 0.340 | 0.400 | 0.439 |
| 14 | 0.464 | 0.538 | 0.626 | 0.679 | 35 | 0.283 | 0.335 | 0.394 | 0.433 |
| 15 | 0.446 | 0.521 | 0.604 | 0.654 | 40 | 0.264 | 0.313 | 0.368 | 0.405 |
| 16 | 0.429 | 0.503 | 0.582 | 0.635 | 45 | 0.248 | 0.294 | 0.347 | 0.382 |
| 17 | 0.414 | 0.488 | 0.566 | 0.618 | 50 | 0.235 | 0.279 | 0.329 | 0.363 |
| 18 | 0.401 | 0.472 | 0.550 | 0.600 | 55 | 0.224 | 0.266 | 0.314 | 0.346 |
| 19 | 0.391 | 0.460 | 0.535 | 0.584 | 60 | 0.214 | 0.255 | 0.301 | 0.331 |
| 20 | 0.380 | 0.447 | 0.522 | 0.570 | 65 | 0.206 | 0.245 | 0.291 | 0.322 |
| 21 | 0.370 | 0.436 | 0.509 | 0.556 | 70 | 0.198 | 0.236 | 0.280 | 0.310 |
| 22 | 0.361 | 0.425 | 0.497 | 0.544 | 80 | 0.185 | 0.221 | 0.262 | 0.290 |
| 23 | 0.353 | 0.416 | 0.486 | 0.532 | 90 | 0.174 | 0.208 | 0.247 | 0.273 |
| 24 | 0.344 | 0.407 | 0.476 | 0.521 | 100 | 0.165 | 0.197 | 0.234 | 0.259 |
| 25 | 0.337 | 0.398 | 0.466 | 0.511 | | | | | |

## L. SIGNIFICANCE LEVELS OF COMPONENT/FACTOR LOADINGS USING THE BURT–BANKS FORMULA

(a) $n = 50$, $\alpha = 0.01$

| No. of vars | Factor number | | | | | | | | | | | |
|---|---|---|---|---|---|---|---|---|---|---|---|---|
| | 1 | 2 | 3 | 4 | 5 | 6 | 7 | 8 | 9 | 10 | 15 | 20 |
| 10 | 0.35 | 0.36 | 0.39 | 0.41 | 0.45 | 0.49 | 0.55 | 0.63 | 0.77 | – | – | – |
| 20 | 0.35 | 0.35 | 0.36 | 0.38 | 0.39 | 0.40 | 0.41 | 0.43 | 0.45 | 0.47 | 0.63 | – |
| 30 | 0.35 | 0.35 | 0.36 | 0.36 | 0.37 | 0.38 | 0.39 | 0.39 | 0.40 | 0.41 | 0.47 | 0.57 |
| 40 | 0.35 | 0.35 | 0.35 | 0.36 | 0.36 | 0.37 | 0.37 | 0.38 | 0.38 | 0.39 | 0.43 | 0.48 |
| 50 | 0.35 | 0.35 | 0.35 | 0.36 | 0.36 | 0.36 | 0.37 | 0.37 | 0.38 | 0.38 | 0.41 | 0.44 |

(b) $n = 50$, $\alpha = 0.05$

| No. of vars | Factor number | | | | | | | | | | | |
|---|---|---|---|---|---|---|---|---|---|---|---|---|
| | 1 | 2 | 3 | 4 | 5 | 6 | 7 | 8 | 9 | 10 | 15 | 20 |
| 10 | 0.26 | 0.28 | 0.29 | 0.31 | 0.34 | 0.37 | 0.41 | 0.48 | 0.59 | 0.83 | – | – |
| 20 | 0.26 | 0.27 | 0.28 | 0.28 | 0.29 | 0.30 | 0.31 | 0.32 | 0.34 | 0.35 | 0.48 | – |
| 30 | 0.26 | 0.27 | 0.27 | 0.28 | 0.28 | 0.29 | 0.29 | 0.30 | 0.31 | 0.31 | 0.36 | 0.43 |
| 40 | 0.26 | 0.27 | 0.27 | 0.27 | 0.28 | 0.28 | 0.28 | 0.29 | 0.29 | 0.30 | 0.32 | 0.36 |
| 50 | 0.26 | 0.26 | 0.26 | 0.27 | 0.27 | 0.27 | 0.27 | 0.27 | 0.27 | 0.27 | 0.28 | 0.29 |

(c) $n = 100$, $\alpha = 0.01$

| No. of vars | Factor number | | | | | | | | | | | |
|---|---|---|---|---|---|---|---|---|---|---|---|---|
| | 1 | 2 | 3 | 4 | 5 | 6 | 7 | 8 | 9 | 10 | 15 | 20 |
| 10 | 0.26 | 0.27 | 0.29 | 0.30 | 0.33 | 0.36 | 0.40 | 0.47 | 0.57 | 0.81 | – | – |
| 20 | 0.26 | 0.26 | 0.27 | 0.28 | 0.29 | 0.29 | 0.30 | 0.32 | 0.33 | 0.34 | 0.47 | – |
| 30 | 0.26 | 0.26 | 0.26 | 0.27 | 0.27 | 0.28 | 0.29 | 0.29 | 0.30 | 0.30 | 0.35 | 0.42 |
| 40 | 0.26 | 0.26 | 0.26 | 0.26 | 0.27 | 0.27 | 0.28 | 0.28 | 0.29 | 0.29 | 0.32 | 0.35 |
| 50 | 0.26 | 0.26 | 0.26 | 0.26 | 0.27 | 0.27 | 0.27 | 0.27 | 0.28 | 0.28 | 0.30 | 0.32 |

(d) $n = 100$, $\alpha = 0.05$

| No. of vars | Factor number | | | | | | | | | | | |
|---|---|---|---|---|---|---|---|---|---|---|---|---|
| | 1 | 2 | 3 | 4 | 5 | 6 | 7 | 8 | 9 | 10 | 15 | 20 |
| 10 | 0.19 | 0.20 | 0.22 | 0.23 | 0.25 | 0.27 | 0.31 | 0.35 | 0.43 | 0.61 | – | – |
| 20 | 0.19 | 0.20 | 0.20 | 0.21 | 0.22 | 0.22 | 0.23 | 0.24 | 0.25 | 0.26 | 0.35 | 0.87 |
| 30 | 0.19 | 0.20 | 0.20 | 0.20 | 0.21 | 0.21 | 0.22 | 0.22 | 0.23 | 0.23 | 0.27 | 0.32 |
| 40 | 0.19 | 0.20 | 0.20 | 0.20 | 0.20 | 0.20 | 0.21 | 0.21 | 0.22 | 0.22 | 0.24 | 0.27 |
| 50 | 0.19 | 0.20 | 0.20 | 0.20 | 0.20 | 0.20 | 0.21 | 0.21 | 0.21 | 0.21 | 0.23 | 0.25 |

Source: Child (1970:98–100).

# FURTHER READING

## CHAPTER 1   INTRODUCTION

A useful introduction to data analysis in the social sciences in general is Rose and O'Sullivan (1993) which covers a wider range of topics than many introductory texts. An alternative is Frankfort-Nachmias and Nachmias (1996).

An overview of the development of quantitative techniques in British geography in the 1960s and 1970s is contained in Wrigley and Bennett's (1981) edited volume. Haggett (1965) is still well worth reading as a "classic" ground-breaking view of the "new" geography of the 1960s, updated in Haggett et al (1977). An American view from this period is presented in Abler et al (1971) whilst Harvey (1969) gives a detailed account of the positivist route to explanation in vogue at this time. Useful overviews of the changes affecting human geography since then are given by Cloke et al (1991) and Johnston (1997). To gain a good impression of the different concerns of the "new" geography of the late 1980s and 1990s see Jackson (1989) or Massey (1994).

## CHAPTER 2   EXPLORING GEOGRAPHICAL DATA

Geography students are spoilt for choice in terms of the provision of introductory statistics texts written specifically for geographers. The easiest to comprehend are Burt and Barber (1996), Ebdon (1977), Shaw and Wheeler (1994) and Walford (1995). Two more

general books, but with worked examples, are Cohen and Holliday (1996) and Fuller and Lury (1977). Some exploratory methods, including graphical techniques are covered in Chambers et al (1983) and Erickson and Nosanchuk (1992). Other good introductions to exploratory data analysis are Hoaglin et al (1983, 1985) and, for a geographical perspective, Sibley (1990).

A specialist text on sample surveys is Barnett (1991) – see also Kalton (1983) and Kish (1965). Sampling methods in Developing Countries are considered by Casley and Lury (1987). The general introductory texts on statistical techniques, referred to above, all consider probability distributions.

## CHAPTER 3   TESTING HYPOTHESES

A starting point for reading on the concept of "hypothesis" and hypothesis testing is Newman (1973), but the most thorough geographical introduction remains Harvey's (1969) seminal work. Summerfield (1983) gives a particularly clear account of the relationship between population, samples and statistical inference. The concept of "significance" is discussed by Winch and Campbell (1969). An excellent compendium on non-parametric tests is Neave and Worthington (1988). A mathematical treatment of statistical inference is given by Ripley (1988). Analysis of variance is considered by Silk (1981), but there are plenty of examples of statistical hypothesis testing in the introductory statistics books for geographers.

## CHAPTER 4   MEASURING ASSOCIATIONS

One of the best geographical introductions to correlation and regression is given by Taylor (1977). A geographical treatment of the assumptions of the linear regression model is given by Poole and O'Farrell (1971).

The Simon–Blalock approach is discussed by Pringle (1980) and simultaneous-equation regression analysis by Todd (1979). For path analysis and structural equation models see Cadwallader (1986) and Winship and Mare (1983). A detailed statistical treatment of linear regression is given by Weisberg (1985).

Problems associated with the modifiable areal unit problem are dealt with by Openshaw (1983), Openshaw and Taylor (1981) and Wrigley (1995).

Multi-level models are discussed in Bondi and Bradford (1990) and Jones (1991). A theme issue of *Environment and Planning A* (Vol. 29, No. 4, 1997) is devoted to this topic.

## CHAPTER 5   MULTIVARIATE ANALYSIS

Johnston (1978) is a useful starting point as this text covers a range of multivariate techniques with examples. A statistical treatment is Kendall (1975) and a simpler statistical introduction is given in Manly (1986).

A straightforward specialist introduction to factor analysis is Child (1970). A lengthier alternative is Cattell (1978). W.K.D. Davies (1984) summarises work by geographers.

Johnston's (1976b) contribution to the *Concepts and Techniques in Modern Geography* series is a useful starting point on classificatory techniques. More advanced treatment is given in Kaufman (1990) and Lorr (1983). For a detailed guide to discriminant analysis see McLachan (1992).

## CHAPTER 6   GENERALISED LINEAR MODELS AND CATEGORICAL DATA ANALYSIS

The best introduction to categorical data analysis in geography and to generalised linear models is O'Brien (1992). A detailed guide is given by Wrigley (1985). See also O'Brien (1989) and Payne (1977b) on the analysis of contingency tables. General statistical texts on categorical data analysis include Agresti (1990), and Aldrich and Nelson (1984) on logit and probit models, and Kennedy (1983) on log-linear analysis. Log-linear models in geography are considered by Upton and Fingleton (1979, 1989). A useful statistical introduction to generalised linear models is Nelder and Wedderburn (1972). Likelihood inference is discussed by A.R. Pickles (1986).

## CHAPTER 7   SPATIAL ALLOCATION

A good starting point for work on models in geography is the classic edited volume by Chorley and Haggett (1967). For advances in the 1970s see Thomas and Huggett (1980). A summary of 20 years of development of geographical models is given in the collection of essays edited by Macmillan (1989a) whose later article (Macmillan, 1995) is a good introduction. A more detailed alternative is Wilson and Bennett (1985). For a fundamental mathematical text on linear programming see Dantzig (1963). A more recent text on mathematical optimisation is Williams (1990). Geographical introductions are provided by Hodgart (1978), Thomas and Huggett (1980: ch. 6), and the collection of essays edited by Ghosh and Rushton (1987). There are numerous books on multi-criteria decision-making models. The best are by Voogd (1983) and Zeleny (1982). There are several texts on game theory, though some of these assume good mathematical ability: see Eichberger (1993) and Gibbons (1992a, b). For work on the prisoner's dilemma and the tragedy of the commons see Hardin (1982).

## CHAPTER 8   SPATIAL INTERACTION

Good introductory texts on spatial interaction models include Haynes and Fotheringham (1984) and Thomas and Huggett (1980: ch. 5). A good introductory article is Senior (1979). More advanced texts are Anas (1987), Erlander and Stewart (1990), Fotheringham and O'Kelly (1989), and Ghosh and Rushton (1987). Recent work on developing spatial interaction models is covered by Pooler (1994a, b) and Roy (1990). The role of distance-decay in gravity models is discussed by Baxter (1983) and Taylor (1971, 1975). A detailed text on the Lowry model is Webber (1984). Entropy-maximising models are discussed by Wilson (1970b, 1974).

For recent thinking on urban models see Bertuglia et al (1994a). The links between modelling and GIS are considered in Birkin et al (1996), Fotheringham and Rogerson (1994) and Openshaw (1990b). For additional references involving modelling and GIS, see under Chapter 11.

## CHAPTER 9   SPATIAL STATISTICS, SPATIAL MODELS AND SPATIAL STRUCTURE

Simple spatial indices are discussed by Peach (1996). Point pattern analysis is covered in some detail by Boots and Getis (1988), Daley and Vere-Jones (1988), Diggle (1983) and Upton and Fingleton (1985). Links to spatial epidemiology are covered in a very readable form by Gatrell et al (1996).

A basic text for spatial autocorrelation is Cliff and Ord (1973), but see also Gatrell (1977), Goodchild (1987), Griffith (1987) and Odlund (1988).

An excellent, well-illustrated text using computer programs for spatial data analysis is Bailey and Gatrell (1995). This includes certain techniques, such as kriging, not dealt with here because of lack of space. Three "high-level" books on spatial statistics are Cressie (1993), Haining (1990a) and Ripley (1981).

The concept of "spatial separatism" in geographical thinking is examined by Sack (1980).

## CHAPTER 10   SPACE AND TIME

A good introduction to diffusion studies is given by L.A. Brown (1981); see also Morrill et al (1988). The early work on Monte Carlo simulations is covered in Hagerstrand (1967a, b). More detailed work on simulation techniques is given in Kalos and Whitlock (1986). For Markov chains see Collins (1975a). A more mathematical treatment is in Isaacson and Madsen (1985). The expansion method is dealt with by Casetti and Fan (1991) and Casetti and Jones (1987).

Work by geographers on statistical analysis of the spread of disease includes Cliff et al (1981, 1986, 1993), Cliff and Haggett (1988), Gould (1993), Shannon et al (1991) and Smallman-Raynor et al (1992).

Although it was published two decades ago, Bennett's (1978) book on spatial time series analysis is still a very useful detailed account of methods of analysis, forecasting and control. For forecasting see also Field and MacGregor (1987).

There are a number of texts on time-geography dating from the late 1970s and early 1980s: Carlstein (1980, 1982), Carlstein et al (1978); but see also Pred (1990).

Carol Ekinsmith's (1996) article is a good review of the utility of longitudinal studies for geographical enquiry. It also provides a good introduction to longitudinal data sources developed in Britain, such as the OPCS Longitudinal Study in which one per cent of all individuals living in England and Wales in 1971 are revisited at each subsequent decennial census. There is a good chapter (ch. 12) on the collection and analysis of longitudinal data in Rose and O'Sullivan (1993). More statistically oriented treatments of the topic are given by Hand (1996) and Crouchley (1987a). A geographical treatment is Wrigley (1986).

## CHAPTER 11   SYSTEMS AND GEOGRAPHICAL INFORMATION SYSTEMS

A good introductory text to systems analysis in geography is Huggett (1980). A good alternative is Wilson (1981c). Catastrophic systems are covered in

Wilson (1981b). For work on this topic by non-geographers see Hale and Kocak (1991), and Poston and Stewart (1978). The complex topic of fractal geometry is dealt with in texts by Barnsley (1988) and Batty and Longley (1994); see also essays edited by Lam and De Cola (1993). For pioneering work see Mandelbrot (1982). Examples of chaos theory applied by geographers include Berry (1991) and Dendrinos (1992). A good set of essays on chaos theory in the social sciences is Kiel and Elliott (1996a); see also Ruelle (1989). A more general introduction is given by Stewart (1989); see also Wiggins (1990).

A very general introduction to GIS is given by Bernhardsen (1992) and to computers in geography by Maguire (1989). There are plenty of other introductory texts on GIS: see Burrough (1986), de Mers (1997), Maguire et al (1991), Martin (1991) and Masser and Blakemore (1991). For a critical assessment of GIS and its position in geography see Pickles (1995b). More specialist texts include ones on GIS and modelling (Longley and Batty, 1996; Batty and Xie, 1994; Goodchild et al, 1996); on GIS and spatial analysis (Chou, 1997); and GIS and planning (Birkin et al, 1996; Longley and Clarke, 1995). For a more advanced treatment see Longley et al (1997).

## CHAPTER 12    INVESTIGATING BEHAVIOUR AND PERCEPTION

Two good texts on behavioural geography are Golledge and Stimson (1997) and Walmsley and Lewis (1993), the former having an emphasis upon techniques. A good review of the field is given by Golledge and Timmermans (1990). Good examples of developing links between geography and psychology are given in Garling and Golledge (1993). A recent article on cognitive mapping is Kitchin (1996).

Questionnaire design is discussed by Oppenheim (1992), Parfitt (1997) and Wilson and McClean (1994).

Multi-dimensional scaling is outlined in Gatrell (1981a). A simple application is given by Rushton (1981). For an example of conjoint analysis see Joseph et al (1989). Some recent developments in behavioural

geography are addressed by Aitken (1991, 1992) and Aitken and Rushton (1993). For further recent thinking consult the journal *Environment and Behavior.*

## CHAPTER 13    QUALITATIVE METHODS

An excellent general introduction is Mason (1996). Other general texts on qualitative methods in the social sciences include Antaki (1988), Dey (1993), Silverman (1993) and Strauss (1987). A good reader in geographical applications is Eyles and Smith (1988).

A good starting point for those wishing to see examples of humanistic approaches is Ley and Samuels (1978). Other useful initial references are Pile (1991) and Susan Smith (1984). For work on phenomenology and the lifeworld see Buttimer and Seamon (1980), J. Pickles (1987), Relph (1976), Seamon (1979) and the work of Tuan (1974b, 1977, 1979).

Some good practical examples of how qualitative methods can be applied by geographers are contained in the work of Burgess (Burgess, 1992a; Burgess et al, 1988, 1991) and Valentine (1997). The ethnographic approach is discussed by Cook and Crang (1995), Cook (1997), Crang (1997), Jackson (1985) and Thomas (1993). For some comparative work in anthropology see Geertz (1983, 1988).

The collected essays edited by Barnes and Duncan (1992) are a useful starting point for readers interested in issues relating to the way in which geographical work is written and in particular how landscape is represented in geographical writing; see also Cosgrove (1984) and Cosgrove and Daniels (1988). An introduction to hermeneutics is given by Pile (1990).

## CHAPTER 14    MARXIST ANALYSIS IN HUMAN GEOGRAPHY

Harvey's work is both readable and provocative. Many of the basic concerns of Marxist geographers are dealt with in his work (see especially Harvey, 1973, 1982, 1985a, b, 1989c). For an elegant application of Marxist thought to a geographical issue consult Massey (1996); see also Neil Smith's (1990) excellent treatment of "uneven development", and Storper and Walker (1988).

Realism as a philosophy of science is discussed at length by Bhaskar (1989) and Sayer (1992). For a short consideration of its practical application see Lawson and Staeheli (1990) and Sarre (1987), and for a good example see Lovering (1985). Another view is presented by Pratt (1995). Structuration theory is discussed by Cohen (1989); see also work by its originator, Giddens (1979, 1984b), including a critique of historical materialism (Giddens, 1981). For examples of the political economy approach see the essays edited by Peet and Thrift (1989). A good introduction to analytical political economy is given in Sheppard and Barnes (1990); see also Webber (1987).

The use of dialectics within geography is examined by Harvey (1995). For a more wide-ranging discussion see Ollman (1993) and Castree (1996). World systems theory is elaborated in a series of books by Wallerstein (1974, 1979, 1984a, 1991b). For further examples of alternative views in geography and for provocative "radical" thinking read *Antipode*.

## CHAPTER 15  FEMINIST GEOGRAPHIES

The best introductory text on feminist geographies is by the Women and Geography Study Group (WGSG, 1997). Compare this with the earlier volume from the Group (WGSG, 1984). A good introduction to feminist theory is Grosz (1987). Feminist methodology is discussed by Harding (1986, 1987). For work on feminist geography, other good introductions are given by McDowell (1988, 1992a, 1993), and, with more detailed considerations, by Massey (1994) and Rose (1993); see also the collection edited by Momsen and Townsend (1987). The debate within feminist geography regarding the use of quantitative techniques is covered by several articles in *Professional Geographer*, 47 (1995).

## CHAPTER 16  POSTMODERN GEOGRAPHIES

Introductions to postmodernist approaches in geography are given by Cooke (1990a), Harvey (1989a) and Soja (1995) – the fourth edition of his book first published in 1989. A more general consideration is given by Jencks (1987). A useful reader containing some material by geographers is Doherty et al (1992). Two other useful readers are Docherty (1993) and Waugh (1992). Links between postmodernism and the environment are covered in Gare (1995), and with feminism in Marchand (1995). A more general text is Hollinger (1994), see also McRobbie (1994) and Lyon (1994). Two good texts on deconstruction are Glusberg (1994) and Norris and Benjamin (1988).

# REFERENCES

The references cited in the text are primarily drawn from British, North American and Australasian publications. There are some European publications, overwhelmingly in English, from Germany, the Netherlands and Sweden. I have deliberately referred to a broad range of references in the text so that readers can be pointed towards examples of the application of particular techniques. These examples are selected mainly from the principal geographical journals and books published by leading academic publishers. However, in some cases I have referred to literature in non-geographical journals where there is material on particular aspects of a technique's use or formulation. This largely includes work within related social science disciplines, notably sociology, economics and psychology.

Abernathy, W.J. and Hershey, J.C. 1971, 'A spatial allocation model for regional health service planning', *Operations Research*, 19: 629–42.

Abler, R., Adams, J.S. and Gould, P.R. 1971, *Spatial organization: the geographer's view of the world* (Prentice-Hall, Englewood Cliffs, NJ).

Abu-Lughod, J. 1969, 'Testing the theory of social area analysis: the case of Cairo, Egypt', *American Sociological Review*, 34: 198–212.

Adrian, C. and Watson, J. 1980, 'Location-allocation modelling of the Lower Clarence, New South Wales, sugar cane distribution system', *Australian Geographer*, 14: 295–305.

Agnew, J., Livingstone, D.N. and Rogers, A. (eds.), 1996, *Human geography: an essential anthology* (Blackwell Publishers, Oxford and Cambridge, Mass.).

Agrawal, R.C. and Heady, E.D. 1968, 'Application of game theory methods in agriculture', *Journal of Agricultural Economics*, 19: 201–18.

Agresti, A. 1990, *Categorical data analysis* (John Wiley and Sons, New York).

Aitken, M. and Longford, N. 1986, 'Statistical modelling in school effectiveness studies', *Journal of the Royal Statistical Society A*, 149: 1–43.

Aitken, S.C. 1991, 'Person-environment theories in contemporary perceptual and behavioural geography, 1. Personality, attitudinal and spatial choice theories', *Progress in Human Geography*, 15: 179–93.

Aitken, S.C. 1992, 'Person-environment theories in contemporary perceptual and behavioural geography, 2. The influence of ecological, environmental learning, societal/structural, transactional and transformational theories', *Progress in Human Geography*, 16: 553–62.

Aitken, S.C. 1994, 'I'd rather watch the movie than read the book', *Journal of Geography in Higher Education*, 18: 191–207.

Aitken, S.C. 1997, 'Analysis of texts: armchair theory and couch-potato geography', pp. 197–212 in Flowerdew, R. and Martin, D. (eds.), *Methods in human geography* (Longman, London).

Aitken, S.C. and Prosser, R. 1990, 'Residents' spatial knowledge of neighbourhood continuity and form', *Geographical Analysis*, 22: 301–25.

Aitken, S.C. and Rushton, G. 1993, 'Perceptual and behavioural theory in practice', *Progress in Human Geography*, 17: 378–88.

Aitken, S.C., Cutter, S.L., Foote, K.E. and Sell, J.L. 1989, 'Environmental perception and behavioral geography', pp. 218–38 in Gaile, G.L. and Wilmott, C.J. (eds.), *Geography in America* (Merrill, Columbus, Ohio).

Aitkin, M.A. 1980, 'A note on the selection of log-linear models', *Biometrics*, 36: 173–8.

Akiri, P. 1991, 'Modelling residential mobility: the example of Le Havre', *European Journal of Population*, 7: 251–72.

Aldrich, J.H. and Nelson, F.D. 1984, *Linear probability, logit and probit models* (Sage, Beverly Hills, Ca.).

Allen, E.L. 1957, *Guide book to Western thought* (English Universities Press, London).

Allen, J. 1983, 'Property relations and landlordism: a realist approach', *Environment and Planning D: Society and Space*, 1: 191–203.

Althusser, L. 1969, *For Marx* (Allen Lane, London).

Althusser, L. 1971, *Lenin and philosophy and other essays* (New Left Books, London).

Amedeo, D. and Golledge, R.G. 1975, *An introduction to scientific reasoning in geography* (John Wiley, New York).

Amin. A. (ed), 1994, *Post-Fordism: a reader* (Blackwell, Oxford).

Amin, S. 1976, *Unequal development* (Monthly Review Press, New York).

Amin, S. 1980, *Class and nation: historically and in the current crisis* (Heinemann, London).

Amrhein, C.G. 1994, 'Searching for the elusive aggregation effect: evidence from statistical simulations', *Environment and Planning A*, 26: 654–78.

Anas, A. 1987, *Modelling in urban and regional economics* (Harwood Academic Publishers, Chur, Switzerland).

Anas, A. and Eum, S.J. 1984, 'Hedonic analysis of a housing market in disequilibrium', *Journal of Urban Economics*, 15: 87–106.

Anderson, R.M. 1982, *Population dynamics of infectious diseases* (Chapman and Hall, Aldershot).

Anderson, T. and Egeland, J.A. 1961, 'Spatial aspects of social area analysis', *American Sociological Review*, 26: 392–8.

Andreski, S. (ed.), 1974, *The essential Comte: selected from 'Cours de philosophie positive'* (translated by Margaret Clarke) (Croom Helm, London).

Anim, F.D.K. and Lyne, M.C. 1994, 'Econometric analysis of private access to commercial grazing lands in South Africa: a case study of Ciskei', *Agricultural Systems*, 46: 461–71.

Anselin, L. 1988, 'Lagrange multiplier test diagnostics for spatial dependence and spatial heterogeneity', *Geographical Analysis*, 20: 1–17.

Anselin, L. 1992, *SpaceStat: a program for the statistical analysis of spatial data* (NCGIA, Santa Barbara, Ca.), NCGIA Technical Software Series S-92-1.

Anselin, L. and Can, A. 1986, 'Model comparison and model validation issues in empirical work on urban density functions', *Geographical Analysis*, 18: 179–97.

Anselin, L. and Madden, M. (eds.), 1990, *New directions in regional analysis: integrated and multi-regional approaches* (Belhaven, London).

Antaki, C. (ed.), 1988, *Analysing everyday explanation: a casebook of methods* (Sage, London).

Arbuthnott, J. 1710, 'An argument for divine providence taken from the constant regularity observed in the births of both sexes', *Philosophical Transactions*, 27: 186–90.

Arlinghaus, S.L. 1993, 'Central place fractals: theoretical geography in an urban setting', pp. 213–27 in Lam, N.S.N. and De Cola, L. (eds.), 1993, *Fractals in geography* (Prentice-Hall, Englewood Cliffs, NJ).

Ashcroft, B. and Love, J.H. 1989, 'Evaluating the effects of external takeover on the performance of regional companies: the case of Scotland, 1965 to 1980', *Environment and Planning A*, 21: 197–220.

Ayer, A.J. 1964, *Language, truth and logic* (Victor Gollancz, London), 2nd edition.

Bach, L. 1980, 'Locational models for systems of private and public facilities based on concepts of accessibility and access opportunity', *Environment and Planning A*, 12: 301–20.

Badcock, B.A. 1987, 'Through the tail of Harvey's comet . . .', *Australian Geographical Studies*, 25: 98–104.

Bailey, N.T.J. 1957, *The mathematical theory of epidemics* (Griffin, London and New York).

Bailey, N.T.J. 1975, *The mathematical theory of infectious diseases and its applications* (Griffin, London and New York).

Bailey, T.C. and Gatrell, A.C. 1995, *Interactive spatial data analysis* (Longman, London).

Baker, R.G.V. 1985, 'A dynamic model of spatial behaviour to a planned suburban shopping centre', *Geographical Analysis*, 17: 331–8.

Baker, R.G.V. and Garner, B.J. 1989, 'On the space-time associations in the consumer patronage of planned shopping centres', *Environment and Planning A*, 21: 1179–94.

Ballantyne, C.K. and Cornish, R. 1979, 'Use of the chi-square test for the analysis of orientation data', *Journal of Sedimentary Petrology*, 49: 773–6.

Barber, G.M. 1988, *Elementary statistics for geographers* (Guilford Press, New York and London).

Barnes, T.J. 1984, 'Theories of agricultural rent within the surplus approach', *International Regional Science Review*, 9: 125–40.

Barnes, T.J. 1988a, 'Scarcity and agricultural land rent in light of the capital controversy: three views', *Antipode*, 20: 207–38.

Barnes, T.J. 1988b, 'Rationality and relativism in economic geography: an interpretive review of the homo economicus assumption', *Progress in Human Geography*, 12: 473–96.

Barnes, T.J. 1990, 'Analytical political economy: a geographical introduction', *Environment and Planning A*, 22: 993–1006.

Barnes, T.J. 1996, *Logics of dislocation: models, metaphors and meaning of economic space* (Guilford Press, New York).

Barnes, T.J. and Duncan, J. (eds.), 1992, *Writing worlds: discourse, text and metaphor in the representation of landscape* (Routledge, London).

Barnes, T.J. and Gregory, D. (eds.), 1997, *Reading human geography: the poetics and politics of inquiry* (Arnold, London).

Barnes, T.J. and Sheppard, E. 1984, 'Technical choice and reswitching in space economics', *Regional Science and Urban Economics*, 14: 345–62.

Barnett, V. 1991, *Sample surveys: principles and methods* (Edward Arnold, London).

Barnsley, M. 1988, *Fractals everywhere* (Academic Press, New York).

Bartels, C.A.P. and Ketallapper, R.H. (eds.), 1979, *Exploratory and explanatory statistical analysis of spatial data* (Martinus Nijhoff, London).

Bartholomew, D.J. 1973, *Stochastic models for spatial processes* (John Wiley, New York), 2nd edn.

Batty, M. 1976a, *Urban modelling: algorithms, calibrations, predictions* (Cambridge University Press, London).

Batty, M. 1976b, 'Entropy in spatial aggregation', *Geographical Analysis*, 8: 1–21.

Batty, M. 1981a, 'A model of the battle for Tolmers Square', *Papers in Planning Research, University of Wales Institute of Science and Technology*, No. 40.

Batty, M. 1981b, 'Urban models', pp. 181–91 in Wrigley, N. and Bennett, R.J. (eds.), *Quantitative geography: a British view* (Routledge and Kegan Paul, London).

Batty, M. 1982a, 'The quest for the qualitative: new directions in planning theory and analysis', *Urban Policy and Research*, 1(1): 15–23.

Batty, M. 1982b, 'Planning systems and system planning', *Built Environment*, 8(4): 252–7.

Batty, M. 1987, 'Models in planning: where do we go from here?', *Environment and Planning B: Planning and Design*, 14: 119–22.

Batty, M. 1989, 'Urban modelling and planning: reflections, retrodictions and prescriptions', pp. 147–69 in Macmillan, W. (ed.), *Remodelling geography* (Blackwell, Oxford).

Batty, M. 1996, 'Visualising urban dynamics', pp. 297–320 in Longley, P. and Batty, M. (eds.), *Spatial analysis: modelling in a GIS environment* (GeoInformation International, Cambridge).

Batty, M. and Longley, P. 1994, *Fractal cities: a geometry of form and function* (Academic Press, London).

Batty, M. and Xie, Y. 1994 'Modelling inside GIS: Part 1. Model structures, exploratory spatial data analysis and aggregation', *International Journal of Geographical Information Systems*, 8: 291–308.

Batty, M., Fotheringham, S. and Longley, P. 1993, 'Fractal geometry and urban morphology', pp. 228–46 in Lam, N.S.N. and De Cola, L. (eds.), *Fractals in geography* (Prentice-Hall, Englewood Cliffs, NJ).

Baudrillard, J. 1988, *America* (Verso, London).

Baumol, W.J. and Benhabib, J. 1989, 'Chaos: significance, mechanism, and economic applications', *Journal of Economic Perspectives*, 3: 77–105.

Baxter, M.J. 1983, 'Estimation and inference in spatial interaction models', *Progress in Human Geography*, 7: 40–59.

Baxter, R.S. 1976, *Computer and statistical techniques for planners* (Methuen, London).

Beaumont, J.R. 1980, 'Spatial interaction models and the location-allocation problem', *Journal of Regional Science*, 20(1): 37–50.

Beaumont, J.R. 1986, 'Modelling should be more relevant: some personal reflections', *Environment and Planning A*, 18: 419–21.

Beaumont, J.R. 1987a, 'Quantitative methods in the real world: a consultant's view of practice', *Environment and Planning A*, 19: 1441–8.

Beaumont, J.R. 1987b, 'Location-allocation models and central place theory', pp. 21–54 in Ghosh, A. and Rushton, G. (eds.), *Spatial analysis and location-allocation models* (Van Nostrand Reinhold, New York).

Beaumont, J.R. and Beaumont, C.D. 1982, 'A comparative study of the multivariate structure of towns', *Environment and Planning B: Planning and Design*, 9: 67–78.

Beaumont, J.R., Clarke, M. and Wilson, A.G. 1981, 'The dynamics of urban spatial structure: some exploratory results using difference equations and bifurcation theory', *Environment and Planning A*, 13: 1473–83.

Beavon, K.S.O. 1977, *Central place theory: a re-interpretation* (Longman, London).

Beavon, K.S.O. and Hay, A.M. 1977, 'Consumer choice of shopping centre – a hypergeometric model', *Environment and Planning A*, 9: 1375–93.

Becker, H.S. 1958, 'Problems of inference and proof in participant observation', *American Sociological Review*, 23: 652–60.

Becker, H.S. 1973, *Outsiders: studies in the sociology of deviance* (Free Press, New York).

Beguin, H. and Romero, V.L. 1996, 'Individual cognition of urban neighbourhoods over space and time: a case study', *Environment and Planning A*, 28: 687–708.

Bell, J. 1987, *Doing your research project* (Open University, Milton Keynes).

Bell, J. 1993, *Doing your research project: a project guide for first-time researchers in education and social science* (Open University, Buckingham), 2nd edition.

Bell, W. 1954, 'A probability model for the measurement of ecological segregation', *Social Forces*, 32: 357–64.

Bell, W. 1955, 'Economic, family and ethnic status: an empirical test', *American Sociological Review*, 20: 45–52.

Bell, W. 1958, 'The utility of the Shevky typology for the design of urban sub-area field studies', *Journal of Social Psychology*, 47: 71–83.

Ben-Akiva, M. and Lerman, S.R. 1985, *Discrete choice analysis: theory and application to travel demand* (MIT Press, Cambridge, Mass.).

Bender, B. (ed.) 1992, *Landscape: politics and perspectives* (Berg, Oxford).

Bennett, R.J. 1975, 'Dynamic systems modelling of the Northwest region: 1. Spatio-temporal representation and identification; 2. Estimation of the spatio-temporal policy model; 3. Adaptive parameter policy model; 4. Adaptive spatio-temporal forecasts', *Environment and Planning A*, 7: 525–38, 539–66, 617–36, 887–98.

Bennett, R.J. 1978, *Spatial time series: analysis, forecasting, control* (Pion, London).

Bennett, R.J. 1979, 'Space-time models and urban geographical research', pp. 27–58 in Herbert, D.T. and Johnston, R.J. (eds.), *Geography and the urban environment: progress in research and application*, volume 2 (John Wiley, London).

Bennett, R.J. 1981, 'Quantitative geography and public policy', pp. 387–96 in Wrigley, N. and Bennett, R.J. (eds.), *Quantitative geography* (Edward Arnold, London).

Bennett, R.J. 1985, 'Quantification and relevance', pp. 211–24 in Johnston, R.J. (ed.), *The future of geography* (Methuen, London and New York).

Bennett, R.J. 1989, 'Whither models and geography in a post-welfarist world?', pp. 273–90 in Macmillan, W. (ed.), *Remodelling geography* (Basil Blackwell, Oxford).

Bennett, R.J. and Chorley, R.J. 1978, *Environmental systems: philosophy, analysis and control* (Methuen, London).

Berechman, J. and Small, K.A. 1988, 'Research policy and review 25: Modeling land use and transportation: an interpretive review for growth areas', *Environment and Planning A*, 20: 1285–1309.

Berman, O. and Larsen, R.C. 1982, 'The median problem with congestion', *Operations Research*, 9: 119–26.

Bernhardsen, T. 1992, *Geographic Information Systems* (VIAK IT and Norwegian Mapping Authority, Arendal, Norway).

Berry, B.J.L. 1962, 'Sampling, coding and storing flood plain data', *United States Department of Agriculture, Farm Economics Division, Agriculture Handbook*, No. 237.

Berry, B.J.L. 1964, 'Approaches to regional analysis', *Annals of the Association of American Geographers*, 54: 2–11.

Berry, B.J.L. 1969, 'Relationships between regional economic development and the urban system: the case of Chile', *Tijdschrift voor Economische en Sociale Geografie*, 60: 283–307.

Berry, B.J.L. 1971a, 'DIDO data analysis: GIGO or pattern recognition?', pp. 105–31 in McConnell, H. and Yaseen, D.W. (eds.), *Perspectives in geography 1: Models of spatial variation* (Northern Illinois University Press, De Kalb).

Berry, B.J.L. 1971b, 'Introduction – The logic and limitations of comparative factorial ecology', pp. 209–19 in Berry, B.J.L. (ed.), 'Comparative factorial ecology', *Economic Geography*, 47, Supplement.

Berry, B.J.L. 1972, 'Revolutionary and counter-revolutionary theory in geography – a ghetto commentary', *Antipode*, 4(2): 31–3.

Berry, B.J.L. 1973, *The human consequences of urbanization: divergent paths in the urban experience of the twentieth century* (St. Martin's Press, New York).

Berry, B.J.L. 1991, *Long-wave rhythms in economic development and political behavior* (Johns Hopkins University Press, Baltimore).

Berry, B.J.L. and Garrison, W.L. 1958, 'The functional bases of the central place hierarchy', *Economic Geography*, 32: 145–54.

Berry, B.J.L. and Kim, H. 1996, 'Long waves 1790–1990: intermittency, chaos and control', pp. 215–36 in Kiel, L.D. and Elliott, E. (eds.), *Chaos theory in the social sciences: foundations and applications* (University of Michigan Press, Ann Arbor).

Berry, B.J.L. and Marble, D.F. (eds.), 1968, *Spatial analysis* (Prentice-Hall, Englewood Cliffs, NJ).

Berry, B.J.L. and Rees, P.H. 1969, 'The factorial ecology of Calcutta', *American Journal of Sociology*, 74: 445–91.

Berry, B.J.L., Kim, H. and Kim, H.M. 1993, 'Are long waves driven by techno-economic transformations? Evidence for the US and UK', *Technological Forecasting and Social Change*, 44: 111–35.

Bertuglia, C.S., Leonardi, G., Occelli, S., Rabino, G.A., Tadei, R. and Wilson, A.G. (eds.), 1987, *Urban systems: contemporary approaches to modelling* (Croom Helm, London).

Bertuglia, C.S., Leonardi, G. and Wilson, A.G. (eds.), 1990, *Urban dynamics: designing an integrated model* (Routledge, London).

Bertuglia, C.S., Clarke, G.P. and Wilson, A.G. (eds.), 1994a, *Modelling the city: performance, policy and planning* (Routledge, London and New York).

Bertuglia, C.S., Clarke, G.P. and Wilson, A.G. 1994b, 'Models and performance indicators in urban planning: the changing policy context', pp. 20–36 in Bertuglia, C.S., Clarke, G.P. and Wilson, A.G. (eds.), *Modelling the city: performance, policy and planning* (Routledge, London and New York).

Besag, J. and McNeil, D. 1976, 'On the use of exploratory data analysis in human geography', *Advanced Applied Probability*, 8: 652.

Besag, J. and Newell, J. 1991, 'The detection of clusters in rare diseases', *Journal of the Royal Statistical Society A*, 154: 143–55.

Bhaskar, R. 1979, *The possibility of naturalism: a critique of the contemporary human sciences* (Humanities Press, Atlantic Highlands, NJ).

Bhaskar, R. 1989, *Reclaiming reality* (Verso, London).

Bhopal, R.S., Diggle, P.J. and Rowlingson, B.S. 1992, 'Pinpointing clusters of apparently sporadic Legionnaires' disease', *British Medical Journal*, 304: 1022–7.

Billinge, M., Gregory, D. and Martin, R.L., 1984, 'Reconstructions', pp. 1–24 in Billinge, M., Gregory, D. and Martin, R.L. (eds.), *Recollections of a revolution: geography as spatial science* (Macmillan, London).

Binmore, K. 1994, *Game theory and the social contract*: volume 1 – *Playing fair* (MIT Press, Cambridge, Mass.).

Birkin, M. 1994, 'Understanding retail interaction patterns: the case of the missing performance indicators', pp. 105–20 in Bertuglia, C.S., Clarke, G.P. and Wilson, A.G. (eds.), *Modelling the city: performance, policy and planning* (Routledge, London and New York).

Birkin, M. and Wilson, A.G. 1986a, 'Industrial location models I: a review and an integrating framework', *Environment and Planning A*, 18: 175–206.

Birkin, M. and Wilson, A.G. 1986b, 'Industrial location models II: Weber, Palander, Hotelling and extensions in a new framework', *Environment and Planning A*, 18: 293–306.

Birkin, M., Clarke, G.P., Clarke, M. and Wilson, A.G. 1993, 'Modelling and the development of urban services: applications in Leeds', *Revue d'Economie Regional et Urbaine*, 5: 753–71.

Birkin, M., Clarke, G.P., Clarke, M. and Wilson, A.G. 1994, 'Applications of performance indicators in urban modelling: subsystems framework', pp. 121–50 in Bertuglia, C.S., Clarke, G.P. and Wilson, A.G. (eds.), *Modelling the city: performance, policy and planning* (Routledge, London and New York).

Birkin, M., Clarke, G.P., Clarke, M. and Wilson, A.G. 1996, *Intelligent GIS* (GeoInformation International, Cambridge).

Bithell, J.F. 1990, 'An application of density estimation to geographical epidemiology', *Statistics in Medcine*, 9: 691–701.

Blalock, H.M. 1960, *Social statistics* (McGraw Hill/Kogakusha, Tokyo).

Blalock, H.M. 1962, 'Four variable causal models and partial correlation', *American Journal of Sociology*, 68: 182–94.

Blalock, H.M. 1964, *Causal inferences in non-experimental research* (University of North Carolina Press, Chapel Hill).

Blalock, H.M. 1979, 'The presidential address: measurement and conceptualisation problems: the major obstacle to integrating theory and research', *American Sociological Review*, 44: 881–94.

Blaut, J. 1977, 'Two views of diffusion', *Annals of the Association of American Geographers*, 67: 343–9.

Blunt, A. and Rose, G. (eds.), 1994, *Writing women and space: colonial and post-colonial geographies* (Guilford Press, New York and London).

Boal, F.W. 1981, 'Residential segregation and mixing in a

situation of ethnic and national conflict: Belfast', pp. 58–84 in Compton, P.A. (ed.), *The contemporary population of Northern Ireland and population-related issues* (Queen's University of Belfast, Belfast).

Boal, F.W., Doherty, P. and Pringle, D.G. 1978, 'Social problems in the Belfast urban area: an exploratory analysis', *Occasional Papers, Department of Geography, Queen Mary College, London*, No. 12.

Boddy, M. 1976, 'The structure of mortgage finance: building societies and the British social formation', *Transactions of the Institute of British Geographers*, new series, 1: 58–71.

Boland, L. 1981, 'On the futility of criticizing the neoclassical maximization hypothesis', *American Economic Review*, 71: 1031–6.

Bondi, L. 1991, 'Gender divisions and gentrification: a critique', *Transactions of the Institute of British Geographers*, new series, 16: 190–8.

Bondi, L. 1993, 'Locating identity politics', pp. 84–101 in Keith, M. and Pile, S. (eds.), *Place and the politics of identity* (Routledge, London).

Bondi, L. 1997, 'In whose words? On gender identities, knowledge and writing practices', *Transactions of the Institute of British Geographers*, new series, 22: 245–58.

Bondi, L. and Bradford, M. 1990, 'Applications of multi-level modelling to geography', *Area*, 22: 256–63.

Boots, B.N. 1979, 'Underestimation in nearest neighbour analysis', *Area*, 11: 208–10.

Boots, B.N. and Getis, A. 1988, *Point pattern analysis* (Sage Publications, London), Sage Scientific Geography Series, No. 8.

Bottomore, T. 1985, *Theories of modern capitalism* (Allen & Unwin, London).

Boudon, R. 1965, 'A method of linear causal analysis: dependence analysis', *American Sociological Review*, 30: 365–74.

Bowen, M.J. 1979, 'Scientific method – after positivism', *Australian Geographical Studies*, 17: 210–16.

Bowlby, S. 1992, 'Feminist geography and the changing curriculum', *Geography*, 77: 349–60.

Bowlby, S., Foord, J. and Mackenzie, S. 1980, 'Feminism and geography', *Area*, 14: 19–25.

Bowler, I.R. and Ilbery, B.W. 1987, 'Redefining agricultural geography', *Area*, 19: 327–32.

Box, G.E.P. 1953, 'Non-normality and tests on variances', *Biometrika*, 40: 318–35.

Box, G.E.P. and Anderson, S.L. 1955, 'Permutation theory in the derivation of robust criteria and the study of departures from assumption', *Journal of the Royal Statistical Society*, Series B, 17: 1–34.

Boyle, M.J. and Robinson, M.E. 1979, 'Cognitive mapping and understanding', pp. 59–82 in Herbert, D.T. and Johnston, R.J. (eds.), *Geography and the urban environment*, volume 2 (John Wiley, Chichester).

Boyle, P.J. and Dunn, C.E. 1991, 'Redefinition of enumeration district centroids: a test of their accuracy by using Thiessen polygons', *Environment and Planning A*, 23: 1111–19.

Bracey, H.E. 1953, 'Towns as rural service centres: an index of centrality with special reference to Somerset', *Transac-*

*tions and Papers of the Institute of British Geographers*, 19: 95–105.

Braithwaite, R.B. 1953, *Scientific explanation* (Cambridge University Press, Cambridge).

Braithwaite, R.B. 1960, *Scientific explanation* (Harper and Row, New York).

Brams, S.J. 1975, *Game theory and politics* (Free Press, New York).

Braverman, H. 1974, *Labor and monopoly capital* (Monthly Review Press, New York and London).

Brechling, F. 1967, 'Trends and cycles in British regional unemployment', *Oxford Economic Papers*, 19: 1–21.

Brechling, F. 1975, *Investment and employment decisions* (Manchester University Press, Manchester).

Broadbent, T.A. 1970, 'Notes on the design of operational models', *Environment and Planning*, 2: 469–76.

Brocher, J. 1989, 'How to eliminate certain defects of the potential formula', *Environment and Planning A*, 21: 817–30.

Bromley, R.D.F. and Selman, J.M. 1993, 'Geographic information usage in a local authority: the human environment for GIS', *Area*, 25: 228–36.

Broom, D. and Wrigley, N. 1983, 'Incorporating explanatory variables into stochastic panel-data models of urban shopping behaviour', *Urban Geography*, 4: 244–57.

Brouwer, F. and Nijkamp, P. 1984, 'Multiple rank correlation and association analysis', pp. 317–34 in Bahrenberg, G., Fischer, M.M. and Nijkamp, P. (eds), *Recent developments in spatial data analysis: methodology, measurement, models* (Gower, Aldershot).

Browdy, M. 1990, 'Simulated annealing – an improved computer model for political redistricting', *Yale Law and Policy Review*, 8: 163–79.

Brown, C. 1996, *Serpents in the sand: essays on the non-linear nature of politics and human destiny* (University of Michigan Press, Ann Arbor).

Brown, L.A. 1968, 'Diffusion processes and location: a conceptual framework and bibliography', *Bibliography Series, Regional Science Research Institute, Philadelphia*, No. 3.

Brown, L.A. 1981, *Innovation diffusion: a new perspective* (Methuen, London).

Brown, M. 1995, 'Ironies of distance: an ongoing critique of the geographies of AIDS', *Environment and Planning D: Society and Space*, 13: 159–83.

Brown, M.A. 1980, 'Attitudes and social categories: complementary explanations of innovation-adoption behavior', *Environment and Planning A*, 12: 175–86.

Brown, M.B. 1981, 'Module P4F', in Dixon, W.J. (ed.), *BMDP: Biomedical computer programs* (University of California Press, Berkeley).

Brown, S. 1991, 'Shopper circulation in a planned shopping centre', *International Journal of Retail and Distribution Management*, 19: 17–25.

Brown, T.A. 1996, 'Measuring chaos using the Lyapunov exponent', pp. 53–66 in Kiel, L.D. and Elliott, E. (eds.), *Chaos theory in the social sciences: foundations and applications* (University of Michigan Press, Ann Arbor).

Brunsdon, C. 1991, 'Estimating probability surfaces in GIS: an adaptive technique', *Proceedings of the European*

*Conference on Geographical Information Systems* (EGIS Foundation, Utrecht).

Bryant, C. 1985, *Positivism in social theory and research* (Macmillan, London).

Bryman, A. 1988, *Quantity and quality in social research* (Unwin Hyman, London).

Bunge, W. 1962, 'Theoretical geography', *Lund Studies in Geography*, Series C, No. 1; 2nd edition, 1966.

Bunge, W. 1973, 'Spatial prediction', *Annals of the Association of American Geographers*, 63: 566–8.

Bunge, W. 1979, 'Fred K. Schaefer and the science of geography', *Annals of the Association of American Geographers*, 69: 128–33.

Bunting, T.E. and Guelke, L. 1979, 'Behavioral and perception geography: a critical appraisal', *Annals of the Association of American Geographers*, 69: 448–62 and 471–4.

Burgess, E.W. 1925, 'The growth of the city', pp. 47–62 in Park, R.E., Burgess, E.W. and McKenzie, R.D. (eds.), *The city* (University of Chicago Press, Chicago).

Burgess, J. 1992a, 'The art of interviewing' pp. 207–12 in Rogers, A., Viles, H. and Goudie, A.S. (eds.), *The student's companion to geography* (Blackwell, Oxford).

Burgess, J. 1992b, 'The cultural politics of nature conservation and economic development', pp. 235–51 in Anderson, K. and Gayle, F. (eds.), *Inventing places: studies in cultural geography* (Wiley, Melbourne).

Burgess, J. 1996, 'Focusing on fear: the use of focus groups in a project for the Community Forest Unit, Countryside Commission', *Area*, 28: 130–5.

Burgess, J., Limb, M. and Harrison, C. 1988, 'Exploring environmental values through the medium of small groups. Part 1: theory and practice', 'Part 2: Illustrations of a group at work', *Environment and Planning A*, 20: 309–26, 457–76.

Burgess, J., Harrison, C. and Maitney, P. 1991, 'Contested meanings: the consumption of news about nature conservation', *Media, Culture and Society*, 13: 499–519.

Burn, C. and Fox, M. 1986, 'Introducing statistics to geography students: the case for exploratory data analysis', *Journal of Geography*, 85: 28–31.

Burnett, K.P. and Hanson, S. 1982, 'The analysis of travel as an example of complex human behavior in spatially-constrained situations: definition and measurement issues', *Transportation Research A*, 16: 87–102.

Burns, C. 1989, 'Individual interviews', pp. 47–57 in Robson, S. and Foster, A.S. (eds.), *Qualitative research in action* (Edward Arnold, London).

Burns, E. 1935, *A handbook of Marxism: being a collection of extracts from the writings of Marx, Engels and the greatest of their followers* (Gollancz, London).

Burrough, P.A. 1986, *Principles of Geographical Information Systems for land resource management* (Oxford University Press, Oxford).

Burt, C.L. 1940, *The factors of the mind: an introduction to factor analysis in psychology* (University of London Press, London).

Burt, C.L. and Banks, C. 1947, 'A factor analysis of body measurements for British adult males', *Annals of Eugenics*, 13: 238–56.

Burt, J.E. and Barber, G.M. 1996, *Elementary statistics for geographers* (Guilford Press, New York).

Burton, I. 1963, 'The quantitative revolution and theoretical geography', *Canadian Geographer*, 7: 151–62.

Buttimer, A. 1990, 'Geography, humanism and global concern', *Annals of the Association of American Geographers*, 80: 1–33.

Buttimer, A. and Seamon, D. (eds.), 1980, *The human experience of space and place* (Croom Helm, London).

Butz, D. and Eyles, J. 1997, 'Reconceptualizing senses of place: social relations, ideology and ecology', *Geografiska Annaler*, 79B: 1–26.

Cadwallader, M.T. 1979, 'Problems in cognitive distance: implications for cognitive mapping', *Environment and Behavior*, 11: 559–76.

Cadwallader, M.T. 1981, 'A unified model of urban housing patterns, social patterns and residential mobility', *Urban Geography*, 2: 115–30.

Cadwallader, M.T. 1982, 'Urban residential mobility: a simultaneous equations approach', *Transactions of the Institute of British Geographers*, new series, 7: 458–73.

Cadwallader, M.T. 1985a, 'Structural equation models of migration: an example from the upper midwest USA', *Environment and Planning A*, 17: 101–13.

Cadwallader, M.T. 1985b *Analytical urban geography: spatial patterns and theories* (Prentice-Hall, Englewood Cliffs, NJ).

Cadwallader, M.T. 1986, 'Structural equation models in human geography', *Progress in Human Geography*, 10: 24–47.

Cadwallader, M.T. 1992, 'Log linear models of residential choice', *Area*, 24: 289–94.

Campbell, W.G., Robbins-Church, M., Bishop, G.D., Mortenson, D.C. and Pierson, S.M. 1989, 'The role for a Geographical Information System in a large environmental project', *International Journal of Geographical Information Systems*, 3: 349–62.

Cant, R.G. 1973, 'The Philippines: spatial dimensions in livelihood and society', *Proceedings of the Seventh New Zealand Geographer's Conference*: 101–12.

Cant, R.G. 1975, 'Three mode factor analysis as applied to industrial location data', pp. 201–26 in Collins, L. and Walker, D.F. (eds.), *Locational dynamics of manufacturing activity* (John Wiley, London).

Carlstein, T. 1980, *Time, resources, society and ecology* (Department of Geography, University of Lund, Lund).

Carlstein, T. 1982, *Time resources, society and ecology: on the capacity for human interaction in space and time in pre-industrial societies* (CWK Gleerup, Stockholm).

Carlstein, T., Parkes, D.N. and Thrift, N.J. (eds.), 1978, *Timing space and spacing time*, 2 volumes (Edward Arnold, London).

Carlyle, I.P. 1991, 'Ethnicity and social areas within Winnipeg', pp. 195–219, in Robinson, G.M. (ed.), *A social geography of Canada* (Dundurn Press, Toronto and Oxford).

Carney, J., Hudson, R. and Lewis, J. (eds.), 1980, *Regions in crisis: new perspectives in European regional theory* (Croom Helm, London).

Carroll, J.D. and Chang, J.J. 1970, 'Analysis of individual differences in multi-dimensional scaling via an *n*-way generalization of "Eckart Young" decomposition', *Psychometrika*, 35: 283–319.

Carter, H. and Wheatley, S. 1978, *Merthyr Tydfil in 1851* (Department of Geography, University College of Wales, Aberystwyth).

Casetti, E. 1966, 'Optimal locations of steel mills serving the Quebec and southern Ontario steel market', *Canadian Geographer*, 10: 27–38.

Casetti, E. 1989, 'The onset and spread of modern economic growth in Europe: an empirical test of a catastrophe model', *Environment and Planning A*, 21: 1473–89.

Casetti, E. 1991, 'The investigation of parameter drift by expanded regressions: generalities and a "family planning" example', *Environment and Planning A*, 23: 1045–61.

Casetti, E. 1992, 'The spatio-temporal dynamics of Japanese birth rates: empirical analyses using the expansion method', *Geographical Review of Japan*, series B, 65: 15–32.

Casetti, E. and Fan, C. 1991, 'The spatial spread of the AIDS epidemic in Ohio: empirical analyses using the expansion method', *Environment and Planning A*, 23: 1589–1608.

Casetti, E. and Jones, III, J.P. 1987, 'Spatial applications of the expansion method paradigm', pp. 121–36 in Dufornaud, C. and Dudycha, D. (eds.), *Quantitative analysis in geography* (University of Waterloo, Waterloo, Ontario).

Casley, D.J. and Lury, D.A. 1982, *Monitoring and evaluation of agriculture and rural development projects* (Johns Hopkins University Press, Baltimore).

Casley, D.J. and Lury, D.A. 1987, *Data collection in Developing Countries* (Clarendon Press, Oxford), 2nd edition.

Castells, M. 1976, 'Is there an urban sociology?', pp. 60–84 in Pickvance, C.G. (ed.), *Urban sociology: critical essays* (Tavistock, London).

Castells, M. 1977, *The urban question* (Edward Arnold, London).

Castells, M. 1983, *The city and the grassroots* (California University Press, San Francisco).

Castree, N. 1996, 'Birds, mice and geography: Marxism and dialectics', *Transactions of the Institute of British Geographers*, new series, 21: 342–62.

Cattell, R.B. 1965, 'Factor analysis: introduction to essentials I and II', *Biometrics*, 21: 190–215 and 405–35.

Cattell, R.B. 1966, *Handbook of multivariate experimental psychology* (Rand McNally, Chicago).

Cattell, R.B. 1978, *The scientific use of factor analysis* (Plenum Press, New York).

Cattell, R.B. and Baggaley, A.R. 1960, 'The Salient Variable Similarity Index for factor matching', *British Journal of Statistical Psychology*, 13: 33–6.

Chadwick, G. 1971, *A systems view of planning* (Pergamon Press, Oxford).

Chalmers, A.F. 1976, *What is this thing called science? An assessment of the nature and status of science and its methods* (University of Queensland Press, St. Lucia, Queensland).

Chambers, J.M., Cleveland, W.S., Kliener, B. and Tukey, J.W. 1983, *Graphical methods for data analysis* (Wadsworth, Belmont, Ca.).

Chan, Y. and Yi, P. 1987, 'Bifurcation and disaggregation in urban/regional modelling: a technical note', *European Journal of Operational Research*, 30: 321–6.

Chapin, Jr F.S. 1974, *Human activity patterns in the city: things people do in time and space* (Wiley Interscience, New York).

Chapman, G.P. 1977, *Human and environmental systems: a geographer's appraisal* (Academic Press, London).

Charlesworth, A. 1983, *An atlas of rural protest in Britain, 1548–1900* (Croom Helm, London).

Chatfield, C. 1983, *Statistics for technology* (Chapman and Hall, London), 3rd edition.

Chavez, P.S. and Kwarteng, A.Y. 1989, 'Extracting spectral contrast in Landsat Thematic Mapper image data using selective principal components analysis', *Photogrammetric Engineering and Remote Sensing*, 55: 339–48.

Chayes, F. and Kruskal, W. 1966, 'An approximate statistical test for correlations between proportions', *Journal of Geology*, 74: 692–702.

Chen, R., Mantel, N. and Klinberg, M. 1984, 'A study of three techniques for space-time clustering in Hodgkin's disease', *Statistics in Medicine*, 3: 173–84.

Child, D. 1970, *The essentials of factor analysis* (Holt, Rinehart and Winston, London).

Chisholm, M. 1967, 'General systems theory and geography', *Transactions of the Institute of British Geographers*, 42: 45–52.

Chisholm, M. 1975, *Human geography: evolution or revolution?* (Harmondsworth, Penguin).

Chisholm, M. and O'Sullivan, P.M. 1973, *Freight flows and spatial aspects of the British economy* (Cambridge University Press, Cambridge).

Chojnicki, Z. and Czyz, T. 1976, 'Some problems in the application of factor analysis in geography', *Geographical Analysis*, 8: 416–27.

Chorley, R.J. and Haggett, P. (eds.), 1965, *Frontiers in geographical teaching: the Madingley lectures for 1963* (Methuen, London).

Chorley, R.J. and Haggett, P. (eds.), 1967, *Models in geography* (Methuen, London).

Chorley, R.J. and Kennedy, B.A. 1971, *Physical geography: a systems approach* (Prentice-Hall International, London).

Chou, Y.-H. 1991, 'Map resolution and spatial autocorrelation', *Geographical Analysis*, 23: 228–46.

Chou, Y.-H. 1997, *Exploring spatial analysis in GIS* (Geo-Information International, Cambridge).

Chou, Y., Minnich, A., Salazar, L.A., Power, J.D. and Dezzani, J. 1990, 'Spatial autocorrelation of wildfire distribution in Idyllwild quadrangle, San Jancinto Mountain, California', *Photogrammetric Engineering and Remote Sensing*, 56: 1507–13.

Chouinard, V., Fincher, R.M. and Webber, M.J., 1984, 'Empirical research in scientific human geography', *Progress in Human Geography*, 8: 347–80.

Chrisman, N.R., Cowen, D.J., Fisher, P.F., Goodchild, M.F. and Mark, D.M. 1989, 'Geographic information systems', pp. 776–96 in Gaile, G.L. and Willmott, C.J. (eds.), *Geography in America* (Merrill, Columbus, Ohio).

Christaller, W. 1966, *Central places in southern Germany*

(Prentice-Hall, Englewood Cliffs, NJ), translated by C.W. Baskin.

Chulvick, C. 1982, 'Scottish Rural Land Use Information Systems Project', *Proceedings of Auto Carto*, 5: 179–88.

Church, R.L. and Eaton, D.J. 1987, 'Hierarchical location analysis using covering objectives', pp. 163–85 in Ghosh, A. and Rushton, G. (eds.), 1987, *Spatial analysis and location-allocation models* (Van Nostrand Reinhold, New York).

Church, R.L. and Sorensen, P. 1996, 'Integrating normative location models into GIS: problems and prospects with the *p*-median model', pp. 167–84 in Longley, P. and Batty, M. (eds.), *Spatial analysis: modelling in a GIS environment* (GeoInformation International, Cambridge).

Clark, D. 1973, 'The formal and functional structure of Wales', *Annals of the Association of American Geographers*, 63: 71–84.

Clark, G. and Gordon, D.S. 1980, 'Sampling for farm studies in geography', *Geography*, 65: 101–6.

Clark, G.L. and Ballard, K.P. 1980, 'Modeling out-migration from depressed regions: the significance of origin and destination characteristics', *Environment and Planning A*, 12: 799–812.

Clark, G.L., Gertler, M.S. and Whiteman, J. 1986, *Regional dynamics: studies in adjustment theory* (Allen and Unwin, Boston).

Clark, P.J. and Evans, F.C. 1954, 'Distance to nearest neighbour as a measure of spatial relations in populations', *Ecology*, 35: 445–53.

Clark, W.A.V. 1967, 'The use of residuals from regression in geographical research', *New Zealand Geographer*, 23: 64–7.

Clark, W.A.V. 1993, 'Search and choice in urban housing markets', pp. 298–316 in Garling, T. and Golledge, R.G. (eds.), *Behavior and environment: psychological and geographical approaches* (Elsevier/North Holland, Amsterdam).

Clark, W.A.V. and Hosking, P.L. 1986, *Statistical methods for geographers* (John Wiley & Sons, New York).

Clarke, M. 1990, 'Regional science and industry: from consultancy to technology transfer', *Environment and Planning B: Planning and Design*, 17: 257–68.

Clarke, M. and Wilson, A.G. 1986a, 'Developments in planning models for health care policy analysis in the UK', pp. 248–83 in Pacione, M. (ed.), *Progress in medical geography* (Croom Helm, London).

Clarke, M. and Wilson, A.G. 1986b, 'The dynamics of urban spatial structure: the progress of a research programme', *Transactions of the Institute of British Geographers*, new series, 10: 427–51.

Clarke, M. and Wilson, A.G. 1989, 'Mathematical models in human geography: twenty years on', pp. 30–42 in Peet, R.J. and Thrift, N.J. (ed.), *New models in geography*, volume two (Unwin Hyman, London).

Clayton, D. and Bernardinelli, L. 1992, 'Bayesian methods for mapping disease risk', in Elliott, P., Cuzick, J., English, D. and Stern, R. (eds.), *Geographical and environmental epidemiology: methods for small-area studies* (Oxford University Press, New York).

Clayton, D. and Kaldor, J. 1987, 'Empirical Bayes estimates of age-standardized relative risks for use in disease mapping', *Biometrics*, 43: 671–81.

Cliff, A.D. 1970, 'Computing the spatial correspondence between geographical patterns', *Institute of British Geographers, Publications*, 50: 143–54.

Cliff, A.D. 1977, 'Quantitative methods: time series methods for modelling and forecasting', *Progress in Human Geography*, 1: 492–502.

Cliff, A.D. and Haggett, P. 1988, *Atlas of disease distributions: analytical approaches to epidemiological data* (Blackwell, Oxford).

Cliff, A.D. and Haggett, P. 1989a, 'Spatial aspects of epidemic control', *Progress in Human Geography*, 13: 30–47.

Cliff, A.D. and Haggett, P. 1989b, 'Epidemic control and critical community size: spatial aspects of eliminating communicable diseases in human populations', pp. 93–110 in Thomas, R.W. (ed.), *Spatial epidemiology* (Pion, London).

Cliff, A.D. and Ord, J.K. 1969, 'The problem of spatial autocorrelation', pp. 25–55 in Scott, A.J. (ed.), *Studies in regional science* (Pion, London).

Cliff, A.D. and Ord, J.K. 1971, 'Evaluating the percentage points of a spatial autocorrelation coefficient', *Geographical Analysis*, 2: 51–61.

Cliff, A.D. and Ord, J.K. 1972, 'Testing for spatial autocorrelation among regression residuals', *Geographical Analysis*, 4: 267–84.

Cliff, A.D. and Ord, J.K. 1973, *Spatial autocorrelation* (Pion, London).

Cliff, A.D. and Ord, J.K. 1975a, 'The comparison of means when samples consist of spatially autocorrelated observations', *Environment and Planning A*, 7: 725–34.

Cliff, A.D. and Ord, J.K. 1975b, 'Model building and the analysis of spatial pattern in human geography', *Journal of the Royal Statistical Society, B*: 37:297–348.

Cliff, A.D. and Ord, J.K. 1975c, 'The choice of a test for spatial autocorrelation', pp. 54–97 in Davis, J.C. and McCullagh, M. (eds.), *Display and analysis of spatial data* (NATO Advanced Study Institute and John Wiley, London and New York).

Cliff, A.D. and Ord, J.K. 1975d, 'Space-time modelling with an application to regional forecasting', *Institute of British Geographers, Publications*, 64: 119–28.

Cliff, A.D. and Ord, J.K. 1980, 'On statistical models for spatial diffusion processes', *Geographical Analysis*, 12: 263–9.

Cliff, A.D. and Ord, J.K. 1981, *Spatial processes: models and applications* (Pion, London).

Cliff, A.D. and Ord, J.K. 1995, 'Estimating epidemic return times', pp. 135–67 in Cliff, A.D., Gould, P.R., Hoare, A.G. and Thrift, N.J. (eds.), *Diffusing geography: essays for Peter Haggett* (Blackwell, Oxford).

Cliff, A.D., Martin, R.L. and Ord, J.K. 1975a, 'Map pattern and friction of distance parameters: reply to comments', *Regional Studies*, 9: 285–8 and 10: 341–2.

Cliff, A.D., Martin, R.L. and Ord, J.K. 1975b, 'A test for spatial autocorrelation in choropleth maps based upon a modified 2 statistic', *Transactions and Proceedings of the Institute of British Geographers*, 65: 109–29.

Cliff, A.D., Haggett, P., Ord, J.K., Bassett, K. and Davies, R.R. 1975c, *Elements of spatial structure: a quantitative approach* (Cambridge University Press, London).

Cliff, A.D., Haggett, P., Ord, J.K. and Versey, G.R. 1981, *Spatial diffusion: an historical geography of epidemics in an island community* (Cambridge University Press, London).

Cliff, A.D., Haggett, P. and Graham, R. 1983, 'Reconstruction of diffusion processes at local scales (measles epidemics in Iceland)', *Journal of Historical Geography*, 9: 29–46 and 347–68.

Cliff, A.D., Haggett, P. and Ord, J.K. 1986, *Spatial aspects of influenza epidemics* (Pion, London).

Cliff, A.D., Haggett, P. and Smallman-Raynor, M.R. 1993, *Measles: an historical geography of a major human viral disease from global expansion to local retreat, 1840–1990* (Blackwell, Oxford).

Clifford, J. 1986, 'Introduction: partial truths', pp. 1–26 in Clifford, J. and Marcus, G.E. (eds.), *Writing cultures* (University of California Press, Berkeley).

Cloke, P.J., Philo, C. and Sadler, D. 1991, *Approaching human geography: an introduction to contemporary theoretical debates* (Paul Chapman Publishing, London).

Coelho, J.D. and Wilson, A.G. 1976, 'The optimum location and size of shopping centres', *Regional Studies*, 10: 413–21.

Cohen, I. 1989, *Structuration theory: Anthony Giddens and the constitution of social life* (Macmillan, London).

Cohen, L. and Holliday, M. 1982, *Statistics for social scientists: an introductory text with computer programs in Basic* (Paul Chapman Publishing, London).

Cohen, L. and Holliday, M. 1996, *Practical statistics for students* (Paul Chapman Publishing, London).

Cohen, L. and Manion, L. 1985, *Research methods in education* (Croom Helm, London), 2nd edition.

Cole, J.P. and King, C.A.M. 1968, *Quantitative geography* (John Wiley, London).

Collins, L. 1973, 'Industrial size distributions and stochastic processes', pp. 121–65 in Board, C. et al (eds.), *Progress in Geography 5* (Edward Arnold, London).

Collins, L. 1975a, 'An introduction to Markov chain analysis', *Concepts and Techniques in Human Geography*, No. 1.

Collins, L. 1975b, 'A procedure for forecasting changes in manufacturing activity', pp. 227–51 in Walker, D. (ed.), *Locational dynamics of manufacturing activity* (John Wiley, London).

Collins, L. 1976, 'The application of a stochastic process model to geographical analysis', pp. 189–227 in Collins, L. (ed.), *The use of models in the social sciences* (Westview Press, Boulder, Col.).

Collins, L., Drewett, R. and Ferguson, R. 1974, 'Markov models in geography', *The Statistician*, 23: 179–210.

Compton, P.A. 1990, 'The Republic of Hungary bids farewell to Marxism–Leninism', *Geography*, 75: 255–7.

Congdon, P. 1989, 'An analysis of population and social change in London wards in the 1980s', *Transactions of the Institute of British Geographers*, new series, 14: 478–91.

Converse, P.D. 1930, *Elements of marketing* (Prentice-Hall, Englewood Cliffs, NJ).

Cook, I. 1997, 'Participant observation', pp. 127–50 in Flowerdew, R. and Martin, D. (eds.), *Methods in Human Geography* (Longman, Harlow).

Cook, I. and Crang, M. 1995, 'Doing ethnographies', *Concepts and Techniques in Modern Geography*, No. 58.

Cook-Mozaffari, P.J., Darby, S.C., Doll, R., Forman, D., Hermon, C., Pike, M. and Vincent, T. 1989, 'Geographical variation in mortality from leukaemia and other cancers in England and Wales in relation to proximity to nuclear installations, 1969–78', *British Journal of Cancer*, 59: 476–85.

Cooke, P. 1983, 'Labour market discontinuity and spatial development', *Progress in Human Geography*, 7: 543–65.

Cooke, P. 1985, 'Class practices as regional markers: a contribution to labour geography', pp. 213–41 in Gregory, D. and Urry, J. (eds.), *Social relations and spatial structures* (St. Martin's Press, New York).

Cooke, P. 1986, 'The changing urban and regional system in the UK', *Regional Studies*, 20: 243–51.

Cooke, P. 1989, 'The contested terrain of locality studies', *Tijdschrift voor Economische en Social Geographie*, 80: 14–29.

Cooke, P. 1990a, *Back to the future: modernity, post-modernity and locality* (Unwin Hyman, London).

Cooke, P. 1990b, 'Modern urban theory in question', *Transactions of the Institute of British Geographers*, new series, 15: 331–43.

Cooke, P.N. 1987, 'Clinical inference and geographic thought' *Antipode*, 19: 69–78.

Coombs, C.H. 1964, *A theory of data* (Wiley, New York).

Cooper, L. 1967, 'Solution of generalised locational equilibrium problems', *Journal of Regional Science*, 7: 1–18.

Cooper, L. 1968, 'An extension of the generalized Weber problem', *Journal of Regional Science*, 8: 181–98.

Coppock, J.T. 1964, *Agricultural atlas of England and Wales* (Faber, London).

Coppock, J.T. 1974, 'Geography and public policy: challenges, opportunities and implications', *Transactions of the Institute of British Geographers*, 63: 1–16.

Cornwell, J. 1988, 'A case-study approach to lay health beliefs', pp. 219–32 in Eyles, J. and Smith, D.M. (eds.), *Qualitative methods in human geography* (Polity Press, Cambridge).

Corsi, T. and Harvey, M.E. 1975, 'The socio-economic determinants of crime in the city of Cleveland: the application of canonical scores to geographical processes', *Tijdschrift voor Economische en Social Geographie*, 66: 323–36.

Cosgrove, D. 1982, 'The myth and stones of Venice: the historical geography of a symbolic landscape', *Journal of Historical Geography*, 8: 145–69.

Cosgrove, D. 1984, *Social formation and symbolic landscape* (Croom Helm, London).

Cosgrove, D. 1989a, 'Models, description and imagination in geography', pp. 230–44 in Macmillan, W. (ed.), *Remodelling geography* (Blackwell, Oxford).

Cosgrove, D. 1989b, 'Historical considerations on humanism,

historical materialism and geography', pp. 189–205 in Kobayashi, A. and Mackenzie, S. (eds.), *Remaking human geography* (Unwin Hyman, London).

Cosgrove, D. 1990, 'Environmental thought and action: pre-modern and post-modern', *Transactions of the Institute of British Geographers*, new series, 15: 344–58.

Cosgrove, D. and Daniels, S.J. (eds.), 1988, *The iconography of landscape: essays on the symbolic representation, design and use of past environments* (Cambridge University Press, Cambridge).

Cottingham, J., Stoothoff, R. and Murdoch, D. (translators) 1985, *The philosophical writings of Descartes* (Cambridge University Press, Cambridge), 2 vols.

Couclelis, H. 1986, 'Artificial intelligence in geography: conjectures on the shape of things to come', *Professional Geographer*, 38: 1–11.

Couclelis, H. and Golledge, R.G. 1983, 'Analytic research, positivism and behavioural geography', *Annals of the Association of American Geographers*, 73: 331–9.

Court, A. 1972, 'All statistical populations are estimates from samples', *Professional Geographer*, 24: 160–2.

Cowie, S.R. 1968, 'The cumulative frequency nearest neighbour method for the identification of spatial patterns', *Seminar Paper Series, Department of Geography, University of Bristol*, No. 10.

Cox, D.R. and Isham, V. 1980, *Point processes* (Chapman and Hall, London).

Cox, D.R. and Oates, D.O. 1984, *Analysis of survival data* (Chapman and Hall, London).

Cox, K.R. 1968, 'Suburbia and voting behaviour in the London metropolitan area', *Annals of the Association of American Geographers*, 58: 111–27.

Cox, K.R. 1981, 'Bourgeois thought and the behavioral geography debate', pp. 256–79 in Cox, K.R. and Golledge, R.G. (eds.), *Behavioral problems in geography revisited* (Methuen, New York and London).

Cox, N.J. 1989, 'Modelling, data analysis and Pygmalion's problem', pp. 204–8 in Macmillan, W. (ed.), *Remodelling geography* (Blackwell, Oxford).

Cox, N.J. and Jones, K. 1981, 'Exploratory data analysis', pp. 135–43 in Wrigley, N. and Bennett, R.J. (eds.), *Quantitative geography* (Edward Arnold, London).

Coxon, N. and Jones, P. 1977, 'Multi-dimensional scaling', pp. 159–82 in O'Muircheartaigh, C.A. and Payne, C. (eds.), *The analysis of survey data* (Wiley, London).

Crang, M. 1997, 'Analyzing qualitative materials', pp. 183–96 in Flowerdew, R. and Martin, D. (eds.), *Methods in human geography* (Longman, Harlow).

Cressie, N.A.C. 1993, *Statistics for spatial data* (John Wiley and Sons, New York).

Crimp, D. (ed.), 1988, *AIDS: cultural analysis, cultural criticism* (MIT Press, Cambridge, Mass.).

Crouchley, R. (ed.) 1987a, *Longitudinal data analysis* (Avebury, Aldershot).

Crouchley, R. 1987b, 'An examination of the equivalence of three alternative mechanisms for establishing the equilibrium solutions of the production-constrained spatial interaction model', *Environment and Planning A*, 19: 861–74.

Crouchley, R., Pickles, A. and Davies, R. 1982, 'Dynamic models and shopping behavior: testing the linear learning model and some alternatives', *Geografisker Annaler*, 63B: 27–33.

Crowe, P.R. 1968, 'Review of "Models in geography: the second Madingley lectures"', *Geography*, 57: 423–4.

Crush, J. 1991, 'The discourse of progressive human geography', *Progress in Human Geography*, 15: 395–414.

Curran, P.J. 1985, *Principles of remote sensing* (Longman, London).

Curry, M. 1985, 'On rationality: contemporary geography and the search for the foolproof method', *Geoforum*, 16: 109–18.

Curry, M. 1991, 'Postmodernism, language and the strains of modernism', *Annals of the Association of American Geographers*, 81: 210–28.

Curtis, S.E. and Taket, A.R. 1989, 'The development of GIS for locality planning in health care', *Area*, 21: 391–9.

Dacey, M.F. 1960, 'A note on the derivation of nearest-neighbour distances', *Journal of Regional Science*, 2: 81–7.

Dacey, M.F. 1964, 'Modified Poisson probability law for point pattern more regular than random', *Annals of the Association of American Geographers*, 54: 559–65.

Dacey, M.F. 1966, 'A county-seat model for the areal pattern of an urban system', *Geographical Review*, 56: 527–42.

Dacey, M.F. 1975, 'Evaluation of the Poisson approximation to measures of the random pattern in the square', *Geographical Analysis*, 7: 351–67.

Dalby, S. 1991, 'Critical geopolitics: discourse, difference, and dissent', *Environment and Planning D: Society and Space*, 9: 261–83.

Daley, D.J. and Vere-Jones, D. 1988, *Introduction to theory of point processes* (Springer, New York).

Daniels, S.J. 1985, 'Arguments for a humanistic geography', pp. 143–58 in Johnston, R.J. (ed.), *The future of geography* (Methuen, London).

Daniels, S.J. 1989, 'Marxism, culture and the duplicity of landscape', pp. in Peet, R.J. and Thrift, N.J. (eds.), *New models in geography: the political economy perspective*, volume 2 (Unwin Hyman, London).

Daniels, S.J. 1992, 'Place and the geographical imagination', *Geography*, 77: 310–22.

Daniels, S.J. and Cosgrove, D. 1988, 'Introduction: iconography and landscape', pp. 1–10 in Cosgrove, D. and Daniels, S.J. (eds.), *The iconography of landscape* (Cambridge University Press, Cambridge).

Daniels, S.J. and Lee, R. (eds.), 1995, *Exploring human geography: a reader* (Arnold, London).

Dantzig, G.B. 1963, *Linear programming and extensions* (Princeton University Press, Princeton, NJ).

Daskin, M.S. 1987, 'Location, dispatching, and routing models for emergency services with stochastic travel times', pp. 224–68 in Ghosh, A. and Rushton, G. (eds.), *Spatial analysis and location-allocation models* (Van Nostrand Reinhold, New York).

Daultrey, S. 1976, 'Principal components analysis', *Concepts and Techniques in Modern Geography*, 8.

Davies, A. 1948, 'Logarithmic analysis and population studies', *Geography*, 33: 53–60.

Davies, R.B. 1984, 'A generalised beta-logistic model for longitudinal data with an application to residential mobility', *Environment and Planning A*, 16: 1375–86.

Davies, R.B. and Crouchley, R. 1985, 'Control for omitted variables in the analysis of panel and other longitudinal data', *Geographical Analysis*, 17: 1–15.

Davies, R.B. and Pickles, A.R. 1984, 'Accounting for omitted variables in a discrete time panel data model of residential mobility', *Papers in Planning Research, Department of Town Planning, University of Wales Institute of Science and Technology*, No. 11

Davies, R.B. and Pickles, A.R. 1985, 'A panel study of life cycle effects in residential mobility', *Geographical Analysis*, 17: 199–216.

Davies, W.K.D. 1971, 'Varimax and the destruction of generality: a methodological note', *Area*, 3: 112–18.

Davies, W.K.D. 1975, 'Variance allocation and the dimensions of British towns', *Tijdschrift voor Economische en Social Geographie*, 66: 358–72.

Davies, W.K.D. 1978, 'Alternative factorial solutions and urban social structure', *Canadian Geographer*, 22: 273–97.

Davies, W.K.D. 1979, 'Urban connectivity in Montana', *Annals of Regional Science*, 13: 29–46.

Davies, W.K.D. 1980, 'Higher order factor analysis and functional regionalization', *Environment and Planning A*, 12: 685–701.

Davies, W.K.D. 1984, *Factorial ecology* (Gower, Aldershot).

Davies, W.K.D. and Murdie, R.A. 1991, 'Consistency and differential impact in urban social dimensionality: intra-urban variations in the 24 metropolitan areas of Canada', *Urban Geography*, 12: 55–79.

Davis, J.C. 1986, *Statistics and data analysis in geology* (John Wiley & Sons, New York), 2nd edition.

Dawson, J.A. and Unwin, D.J. 1976, *Computing for geographers* (David and Charles, Newton Abbot).

Day, M. and Tivers, J. 1979, 'Catastrophe theory and geography: a Marxist critique', *Area*, 11: 54–8.

Dear, M.J. 1986, 'Postmodernism and planning', *Environment and Planning D: Society and Space*, 4: 367–84.

Dear, M.J. and Scott, A.J. 1981, 'Towards a framework for analysis', pp. 13–18 in Dear, M.J. and Scott, A. (eds.), *Urbanization and urban planning in capitalist society* (Methuen, London and New York).

Dear, M.J. 1987, 'Editorial: society, politics and social theory', *Environment and Planning D: Society and Space*, 5: 363–6.

Dear, M.J. 1988, 'The postmodern challenge: reconstructing human geography', *Transactions of the Institute of British Geographers*, 13: 262–74.

Dear, M.J. 1995, 'Practising postmodern geography', *Scottish Geographical Magazine*, 111: 179–81.

De Mers, M.N. 1997, *Fundamentals of GIS* (John Wiley, New York),

Demko, G. and Briggs, R. 1970, 'An individual conceptualization and operationalization of spatial choice behavior: a migrational example using multidimensional scaling unfolding', *Proceedings of the Canadian Association of Geographers*, 2: 79–86.

Dendrinos, D.S. 1992, *The dynamics of cities: ecological determinism, dualism, and chaos* (Routledge, London).

Dendrinos, D.S. 1996, 'Cities as spatial chaotic attractors', pp. 237–72 in Kiel, L.D. and Elliott, E. (eds.), *Chaos theory in the social sciences: foundations and applications* (University of Michigan Press, Ann Arbor).

Dendrinos, D.S. and Sonis, M. 1990, *Chaos and socio-spatial dynamics* (Springer-Verlag, New York).

Densham, P.J. 1996, 'Visual interactive locational analysis', pp. 185–206 in Longley, P. and Batty, M. (eds.), *Spatial analysis: modelling in a GIS environment* (GeoInformation International, Cambridge).

Department of the Environment (DoE), 1987, *Handling geographic information: Report of the Committee of Enquiry chaired by Lord Chorley* (HMSO, London).

Derrida, J. 1967, *De la grammatologie* (Les Editions de Minuit, Paris).

Derrida, J. 1974, *Of grammatology* (Johns Hopkins University Press, Baltimore, Md.).

Derrida, J. 1978, *Writing and difference* (Routledge and Kegan Paul, London).

Derrida, J. 1981, *Positions* (Athlone Press, London).

Desbaretes, J. 1983, 'Spatial choice and constraints on behavior', *Annals of the Association of American Geographers*, 73: 340–57.

Deurloo, M., Dieleman, F. and Clark, W. 1990, 'Using and interpreting generalized loglinear models on geographic analysis', pp. 331–48 in Fischer, M., Nijkamp, P. and Papergeorgiou, Y. (eds.), *Spatial choices and processes* (North-Holland, Amsterdam).

de Vaus, D.A. 1991, *Surveys in social research* (UCL Press, London), 3rd edition.

Dey, I. 1993, *Qualitative data analysis: a user-friendly guide for social scientists* (Routledge, London and New York).

Diamond, J. and Wright, J. 1987, 'Multiobjective analysis of public school consolidation', *Journal of Urban Planning and Development*, 113: 1–18.

Dicken, P. and Robinson, M.E. 1979, 'Cloze procedures and cognitive mapping', *Environment and Behavior*, 9: 351–73.

Diggle, P.J. 1983, *Statistical analysis of spatial point patterns* (Academic Press, London).

Diggle, P.J. 1990, 'A point process modelling approach to raised incidence of a rare phenomenon in the vicinity of a prespecified point', *Journal of the Royal Statistical Society A*, 153: 349–62.

Diggle, P.J. 1993, 'Point process modelling in environmental epidemiology', in Barnett, V. and Turkman, K.F. (eds.), *Statistics for the environment* (John Wiley and Sons, Chichester and New York).

Diggle, P.J. and Rowlingson, B.S. 1994, 'A conditional approach to point process modelling of elevated risk', *Journal of the Royal Statistical Society, series A*, 157: 433–40.

Diggle, P.J., Chetwynd, A.G., Haggkvist, R. and Morris, S. 1995, 'Second-order analysis of space-time clustering', *Statistical Methods in Medical Research*, 4: 124–36.

Dixon, C. and Leach, B. 1978, 'Sampling methods for geographical research', *Concepts and Techniques in Modern Geography*, 17.

Dixon, C. and Leach, B. 1980, 'Questionnaires and interviews in geographical research', *Concepts and Techniques in Modern Geography*, 18.

Dobson, A. 1983, *An introduction to statistical analysis* (Chapman and Hall, London).

Docherty, T. (ed.), 1993, *Postmodernism: a reader* (Harvester Wheatsheaf, London).

Dodds, K.-J. 1994, 'Geopolitics in the Foreign Office: British representations of Argentine, 1945–1961', *Transactions of the Institute of British Geographers*, new series, 19: 273–90.

Dodds, K.-J. and Sidaway, J.D. 1994, 'Locating critical geopolitics', *Environment and Planning D: Society and Space*, 12: 515–24.

Doel, M. 1993, 'Proverbs for paranoids: writing geography on hallowed ground', *Transactions of the Institute of British Geographers*, new series, 18: 377–94.

Doherty, P. 1989, 'Ethnic segregation levels in the Belfast urban area', *Area*, 21: 151–9.

Doherty, J., Graham, E. and Malek, M. (eds.), 1992, *Postmodernism and the social sciences* (Macmillan, Basingstoke).

Domosh, M. 1989, 'A method for interpreting landscape: a case study of the New York World Building', *Area*, 21: 347–55.

Donovan, J. 1988, '"When you're ill, you've gotta carry it": Health and illness in the lives of black people', pp. 180–96 in Eyles, J. and Smith, D.M. (eds.), *Qualitative methods in human geography* (Polity Press, Cambridge).

Dorling, D. 1995, 'Visualizing changing social structure from a census', *Environment and Planning A*, 27: 353–78.

Downs, R.M. 1976, 'Personal constructions of personal construct theory', pp. 72–87 in Moore, G.T. and Golledge, R.G. (eds.), *Environmental knowing: theories, research and methods* (Dowden, Hutchinson & Ross Inc., Stroudsburg, Penn.).

Downs, R.M. and Stea, D. 1977, *Maps in mind: reflections on cognitive mapping* (Harper & Row, New York)

Driver, F. 1985, 'Power, space and the body: a critical reassessment of Foucault's "Discipline and punish', *Environment and Planning D: Society and Space*, 3: 245–6.

Duncan, C., Jones, K. and Moon, G. 1996, 'Health related behaviour in context: a multilevel modelling approach', *Social Science and Medicine*, 42: 817–30.

Duncan, J.S. 1990, *The city as text: the politics of landscape interpretation in the Kandyan kingdom* (Cambridge University Press, Cambridge).

Duncan, J.S. and Ley, D.F. 1982, 'Structural Marxism and human geography: a critical assessment', *Annals of the Association of American Geographers*, 72: 30–59.

Duncan, O.D. 1966, 'Path analysis: sociological examples', *American Journal of Sociology*, 72: 1–16.

Duncan, O.D. and Duncan, B. 1955, 'Residential distribution and occupational stratification', *American Journal of Sociology*, 60: 493–503.

Duncan, O.D., Cuzzort, R.P. and Duncan, B. 1961, *Statistical geography: problems in analysing areal data* (Collier-Macmillan, New York).

Duncan, S.S. 1974, 'The isolation of scientific discovery: indifference and resistance to a new idea', *Science Studies*, 4: 109–34.

Dunn, R. 1987, 'Graphics, statistics and geography: retrospect and prospect', pp. 118–31 in *Geography: a celebration – proceedings of the Geography Golden Jubilee Celebrations, 1987* (Department of Geography, University of Canterbury, Christchurch, New Zealand).

Dunn, R. and Walker, P. 1989, 'District-level variations in the configuration of service provision in England: a graphical approach to classification', *Environment and Planning A*, 21: 1397–1411.

Dunn, R. and Wrigley, N. 1985, 'Beta-logistic models of urban shopping centre choice', *Geographical Analysis*, 17: 95–113.

Durbin, J. and Watson, G.S. 1950/51, 'Tests for serial correlation in least squares regression, I and II', *Biometrika*, 37: 409–28 and 38: 159–78.

Dyck, I. 1990, 'Space, time and renegotiating motherhood: an exploration of the domestic workplace', *Environment and Planning D, Society and Space*, 6: 459–83.

Earle, C. and Young, C.W. 1992, 'Putting the theory back into quantitative geography: the promise of staged regression analysis', *Scottish Geographical Magazine*, 108: 149–56.

Eaton, D.J., Church, R.L., Bennett, V.L., Hamon, B.L. and Lopez, L.G. 1982, 'On deployment of health resources in rural Valle Del Cauca', pp. 331–59 in Cook, W. (ed.), *Planning and development processes in the Third World* (Elsevier, Amsterdam).

Ebdon, D. 1977, *Statistics in geography* (Basil Blackwell, Oxford); 2nd edition 1985.

Eckmann, J.P. and Ruelle, D. 1985, 'Ergodic theory of chaos and strange attractors', Part 1, *Reviews of Modern Physics*, 57(3): 617–56.

Eichberger, J. 1993, *Game theory for economists* (Academic Press, San Diego).

Ekinsmith, C. 1996, 'Large-scale longitudinal studies: their utility for geographic study', *Area*, 28: 358–72.

Eliot-Hurst, M.E. 1973, 'Establishment geography: or how to be irrelevant in three easy lessons', *Antipode*, 5: 40–59.

Eliot-Hurst, M.E. 1980, 'Geography, social science and society: towards a de-definition', *Australian Geographical Studies*, 18: 3–21.

Eliot-Hurst, M.E. 1985, 'Geography has neither existence nor future', pp. 59–91 in Johnston, R.J. (ed.), *The future of human geography* (Edward Arnold, London).

Elster, J. 1986, *An introduction to Karl Marx* (Cambridge University Press, Cambridge).

Emerson, H. and MacFarlane, R. 1995, 'Comparative bias between sampling frames for farm surveys', *Journal of Agricultural Economics*, 46: 241–51.

Emerson, J.D. and Stresio, J. 1983, 'Boxplots and batch comparisons', pp. 58–96 in Hoaglin, D.C., Mosteller, F. and Tukey, J.W. (eds.), *Understanding robust and exploratory data analysis* (John Wiley, New York).

Engels, F. 1940, *The dialectics of nature* (International Publishers, New York).

Entrikin, J.N. 1976, 'Contemporary humanism in geography', *Annals of the Association of American Geographers*, 70: 43–58.

Entrikin, J.N. 1991, *The betweenness of place: towards a geography of modernity* (Macmillan, Basingstoke).

Erickson, B.H. and Nosanchuck, T.A. 1992, *Understanding data* (McGraw-Hill, Ryerson, New York), 2nd edition.

Erlander, S. and Stewart, N.F. 1990, *The gravity model in transportation analysis – theory and extensions* (VSP, Utrecht).

Errington, A. 1985, 'Sampling frames for farm surveys in the United Kingdom: some alternatives', *Journal of Agricultural Economics*, 36: 251–8.

Evans, I.S. 1980, 'A methodological note on the use of regression equations for the purpose of simulating change in urban location patterns', *Environment and Planning A*, 12: 921–6.

Evans, I.S. and Jones, K. 1981, 'Ratios and closed number systems', pp. 123–34 in Wrigley, N. and Bennett, R.J. (eds.), *Quantitative geography: a British view* (Routledge and Kegan Paul, London).

Everitt, B.S. and Dunn, G. 1983, *Advanced methods of data exploration and modelling* (Heinemann Educational Books, London).

Eyles, J. 1981, 'Why geography cannot be Marxist: towards an understanding of lives experience', *Environment and Planning A*, 13: 1371–88.

Eyles, J. 1988, 'Interpreting the geographical world: qualitative approaches in geographical research', pp. 1–16 in Eyles, J. and Smith, D.M. (eds.), *Qualitative methods in human geography* (Polity Press, Cambridge).

Eyles, J. and Evans, M. 1987, 'Popular consciousness, moral ideology and locality', *Environment and Planning D: Society and Space*, 5: 39–71.

Eyles, J. and Smith, D.M. (eds.), 1988. *Qualitative methods in human geography* (Polity Press, Oxford).

Fagan, R.H. 1989, 'Social relations and spatial structures in global capitalism: the case of the Australian steel industry', *Environment and Planning A*, 21: 671–3.

Fairclough, N. 1992, *Discourse and social change* (Polity Press, Cambridge).

Falk, R.F., Cortese, F. and Cohen, J. 1978, 'Utilizing standardized indices of residential segregation: comment on Winship', *Social Forces*, 57: 713–16.

Farjoun, E. and Machover, M. 1983, *Laws of chaos: a probabilistic approach to political economy* (Verso Editions, London).

Ferguson, A.G. 1979, 'Some aspects of urban spatial cognition in an African student community', *Transactions of the Institute of British Geographers*, new series, 4: 77–93.

Field, B. and MacGregor, B. 1987, *Forecasting techniques for urban and regional planning* (Hutchinson, London).

Fielding, A.J. 1989, 'Inter-regional and social change: a study of South-East England based upon data from the Longitudinal Study', *Transactions of the Institute of British Geographers*, new series, 14: 24–36.

Fielding, N.G. (ed.), 1988, *Actions and structure: research methods and social theory* (Sage, London).

Fik, T.J. and Mulligan, G.F. 1994, 'Using dummy variables to estimate economic base multipliers', *Professional Geographer*, 46: 368–78.

Fincher, R. 1989, 'The political economy of the local state', pp. 338–60 in Peet, R. and Thrift, N. (eds.), *New models in geography*, volume 1 (Unwin Hyman, London).

Fingleton, B. 1981, 'Log-linear modelling of geographical contingency tables', *Environment and Planning A*, 13: 1539–51.

Fingleton, B. 1984, *Models of category counts* (Cambridge University Press, Cambridge).

Fingleton, B. 1988, 'Categorical data with inherent spatial dependence: the case of cluster sampling', *Transactions of the Institute of British Geographers*, new series, 13: 497–503.

Fingleton, B. 1989, 'Evaluating British government regional policy: a cost oriented approach', *Transactions of the Institute of British Geographers*, 14: 446–60.

Fink, A. and Kosecoff, J. 1985, *How to conduct surveys: a step by step guide* (Sage Publications, London).

Finnas, F. 1994, *Language shifts and migration: the Finnish longitudinal census data file as an aid to social research* (Tilastokeskus, Helsinki).

Fisher, P.F. 1991, 'Spatial data sources and data problems', pp. 175–89 in Maguire, D.J., Goodchild, M.F. and Rhind, D.W. (eds.), *Geographical information systems: principles and applications*, volume 1 (Longman, London).

Fisher, R.A. 1956, *Statistical methods and scientific inference* (Edinburgh University Press, Edinburgh).

Fitzsimmons, M. 1989, 'The matter of nature', *Antipode*, 21: 106–21.

Flinn, C.J. and Heckmann, J.J. 1982, 'New methods for analyzing individual event histories', pp. 99–140 in Leinhardt, S. (ed.), *Sociological methodology* (Jossey-Bass, San Francisco).

Flowerdew, R. 1989, 'Some critical views of modelling in geography', pp. 245–54 in Macmillan, W. (ed.), *Remodelling geography* (Basil Blackwell, Oxford).

Flowerdew, R. and Martin, D. (eds.), 1997, *Methods in human geography* (Longman, Harlow).

Folke, S. 1972, 'Why a radical geography must be Marxist', *Antipode*, 4(2): 13–18.

Foody, G. and Curran, P. (eds.), 1994, *Environmental remote sensing from regional to global scales* (John Wiley and Sons, Chichester).

Foord, J. and Gregson, N. 1986, 'Patriarchy: towards a reconceptualisation', *Antipode*, 8: 186–211.

Foord, J., McDowell, L. and Bowlby, S. 1986, 'For "love" not money: gender relations in local areas', *Discussion Papers, Centre for Urban and Regional Development Studies, University of Newcastle*, No. 76.

Foot, D.H.S. 1974, 'A comparison of some land-use allocation/interaction models', *Geographical Papers, University of Reading*, No. 31.

Foot, D.H.S. 1981, *Operational urban models: an introduction* (Methuen, London and New York).

Foot, S.P.H. and Milne, W.J. 1984, 'Net migration in an extended multi-regional gravity model', *Journal of Regional Science*, 24: 119–33.

Foot, S.P.H. and Webber, M.J., 1983, 'Unequal exchange and uneven development', *Environment and Planning D: Society and Space*, 1: 281–304.

Foot, S.P.H., Rigby, D. and Webber, M.J., 1989, 'Theory and measurement in historical materialism', pp. 116–33 in Kobayashi, A. and Mackenzie, S. (eds.), *Remaking human geography* (Unwin Hyman, Boston).

Forer, P.C. 1978, 'A place for plastic space?', *Progress in Human Geography*, 3: 230–67.

Fortuijn, J. and Karstom, L. 1989, 'Daily activity patterns of working parents in the Netherlands', *Area*, 21: 265–76.

Foster, A. 1989, 'The dynamics of small groups', pp. 37–46 in Robson, S. and Foster, A.S. (eds.), *Qualitative research in action* (Edward Arnold, London).

Fotheringham, A.S. 1981, 'Spatial structure and the parameters of spatial interaction models', *Annals of the Association of American Geographers*, 71: 425–36.

Fotheringham, A.S. 1983a, 'A new set of spatial-interaction models: the theory of competing destinations', *Environment and Planning A*, 15: 15–36.

Fotheringham, A.S. 1983b, 'Some theoretical aspects of destination choice and their relevance to production-constrained gravity models', *Environment and Planning A*, 15: 1121–32.

Fotheringham, A.S. 1986, 'Modelling hierarchical destination choice', *Environment and Planning A*, 18: 401–18.

Fotheringham, A.S. 1990, 'What's the fuss about fractals?', *Environment and Planning A*, 22: 715–18.

Fotheringham, A.S. 1992, 'Exploratory spatial data analysis and GIS: commentary', *Environment and Planning A*, 24: 1675–8.

Fotheringham, A.S. and Dignan, T. 1984, 'Further contributions to a general theory of movement', *Annals of the Association of American Geographers*, 74: 620–33.

Fotheringham, A.S. and O'Kelly, M.E. 1989, *Spatial interaction models: formulations and applications* (Kluwer Academic Publishers, Dordrecht).

Fotheringham, A.S. and Rogerson, P. (eds.) 1994, *Spatial analysis and GIS* (Taylor and Francis, London).

Fotheringham, A.S. and Webber, M.J. 1980, 'Spatial structure and the parameters of spatial interaction models', *Geographical Analysis*, 12: 33–46.

Fotheringham, A.S. and Wong, D.W.S. 1991, 'The modifiable areal unit problem in multivariate statistical analysis', *Environment and Planning A*, 23: 1025–44.

Foucault, M. 1967, *Madness and civilization: a history of insanity in the Age of Reason* (Tavistock, London).

Foucault, M. 1972, *The archaeology of knowledge* (Tavistock, London).

Foucault, M. 1976, *The birth of the clinic: an archaeology of medical perception* (Tavistock, London).

Foucault, M. 1977, *Discipline and punish: the birth of the prison* (Allen Lane, London).

Foucault, M. 1979, *The history of sexuality*, volume 1 (Allen Lane, London).

Foucault, M. 1980, *Power/knowledge: selected interviews and other writings* (Harvester Press, Brighton).

Foucault, M. 1982, 'Interview with Michel Foucault on space, knowledge and power', *Skyline*, March: 17–20.

Foulkes, S.H. 1975, *Group-analytic psychotherapy: method and principles* (Interface Books, London).

Found, W.C. 1971, *A theoretical approach for rural land-use patterns* (Edward Arnold, London).

Fox, J. 1984, *Linear statistical models and related methods with applications to social research* (John Wiley, New York).

Frank, A.G. 1971, *Capitalism and underdevelopment* (Penguin Books, Harmondsworth).

Frankfort-Nachmias, C. and Nachmias, D. 1996, *Research methods in the social sciences* (Arnold, London) 5th edition.

Fraser, N. and Nicholson, L. 1990, 'Social criticism without philosophy: an encounter between feminism and postmodernism', pp. 19–38 in Nicholson, L. (ed.), *Feminism/postmodernism* (Routledge/Chapman and Hall, New York).

Freeman, M.F. and Tukey, J.W. 1950, 'Transformations related to the angular and the square root', *Annals of Mathematical Statistics*, 21: 607–11.

French, S., Hartley, R., Thomas, L.C. and White, D.J. 1986, *Operational research techniques* (Edward Arnold, London).

Friedrich, C.J. 1929, *Alfred Weber's theory of the location of industries* (University of Chicago Press, Chicago).

Frost, M. and Spence, N. 1981, 'The timing of unemployment response of British regional labour markets 1963–1976', pp. 47–60 in Martin, R.L. (ed.), *Regional wage inflation and unemployment* (Pion, London).

Fuller, M.F. and Lury, D.A. 1977, *Statistics workbook for social science students* (Phillip Allan, Oxford).

Gaile, G.L. 1979, 'Spatial models of spread-backwash processes', *Geographical Analysis*, 11: 273–88.

Gale, S. 1972, 'On the heterodoxy of explanation: a review of David Harvey's "Explanation in geography"', *Geographical analysis*, 4: 285–322.

Galtung, J. 1967, *Theory and methods of social research* (Allen & Unwin, London).

Gans, H.J. 1982, 'The participant observer as a human being', pp. 47–62 in Burgess, R.G. (ed.), *Field research* (Allen and Unwin, London).

Gant, R.L. 1986, 'Archives and interviews: a comment on oral history and fieldwork practice', *Geography*, 72: 27–35.

Gant, R.L. 1991, 'Old people, recollections and fieldwork practice', *Scottish Association of Geography Teachers Journal*, 20: 40–5.

Gant, R.L. 1994, 'Social surveys and geographical investigation', *Study Packages, School of Geography, Kingston University*, No. 14.

Gardiner, V. and Gardiner, G. 1980, 'Analysis of frequency distributions', *Concepts and Techniques in Modern Geography*, 19.

Gardner, M.J. 1989, 'Review of reported increases of childhood cancer rates in the vicinity of nuclear installations in the UK', *Journal of the Royal Statistical Society Series A*, 152: 307–25.

Gare, A.E. 1995, *Postmodernism and the environmental crisis* (Routledge, London).

Garin, R.A. 1966, 'A matrix formulation of the Lowry model for intra-metropolitan activity location', *Journal of American Planners*, 32: 361–4.

Garling, T. and Golledge, R.G. (eds.), 1993, *Behavior and environment: psychological and geographical approaches* (Elsevier, Amsterdam).

Garrison, W.L. 1959, 'Spatial structure of the economy', *Annals of the Association of American Geographers*, 49: 232–9.

Gatrell, A.C. 1977, 'An introduction to spatial autocorrelation and its geographical applications', *Discussion Papers, Department of Geography, University of Salford*, No. 2.

Gatrell, A.C. 1981a, 'Multidimensional scaling', pp. 151–63 in Wrigley, N. and Bennett, R.J. (eds.), *Quantitative geography: a British view* (Routledge and Kegan Paul, London).

Gatrell, A.C. 1981b, 'On the structure of urban social areas: explorations using Q-analysis', *Transactions of the Institute of British Geographers*, new series, 6: 226–45.

Gatrell, A.C. 1983, *Distance and space: a geographical perspective* (Clarendon Press, Oxford).

Gatrell, A.C. 1995, 'Spatial point process modelling of cancer data within a Geographical Information Systems framework', pp. 199–220 in Cliff, A.D., Gould, P.R., Hoare, A.G. and Thrift, N.J. (eds.), *Diffusing geography: essays for Peter Haggett* (Blackwell, Oxford).

Gatrell, A.C. and Rowlingson, B.S. 1994, 'Spatial point process modelling in a GIS environment', pp. 147–64 in Fotheringham, A.S. and Rogerson, P. (eds.), *Spatial analysis and GIS* (Taylor and Francis, London).

Gatrell, A.C., Dunn, C.E. and Boyle, P.J. 1991, 'The relative utility of the Central Postcode Directory and Pinpoint Address Code in applications of Geographical Information Systems', *Environment and Planning A*, 23: 1447–58.

Gatrell, A.C., Bailey, T.C., Diggle, P.J. and Rowlingson, B.S. 1996, 'Spatial point pattern analysis and its application in geographical epidemiology', *Transactions of the Institute of British Geographers*, new series, 21: 256–74.

Gatrell, A.C. and Whitelegg, J. 1993, *Incidence of childhood cancer in Preston and South Ribble* (Environmental Epidemiology Research Unit, University of Lancaster).

Gauthier, D. 1967, 'Morality and advantage', *The Philosophical Review*, 76: 460–75.

Gauthier, H.L. 1968, 'Transportation and the growth of the Sao Paulo economy', *Journal of Regional Science*, 8: 77–94.

Geary, R.C. 1954, 'The contiguity ratio and statistical mapping', *The Incorporated Statistician*, 5: 115–45.

Geddes, A. 1993, 'The effects of map resolution on spatial autocorrelation', unpublished MSc. thesis, Department of Geography, University of Edinburgh.

Geertz, C. 1973, *The interpretation of cultures* (Basic Books, New York).

Geertz, C. 1980, *Negara: the theatre state in 19th century Bali* (Princeton University Press, Princeton, NJ).

Geertz, C. 1983, *Local knowledge* (Basic Books, New York).

Geertz, C. 1988, *Works and lives: the anthropologist as author* (Polity Press, Cambridge).

Georgescu-Roegen, N. 1971, *The entropy law and the economic process* (Harvard University Press, Cambridge, Mass.).

Gertler, M.S. 1988, 'The limits to flexibility', *Transactions of the Institute of British Geographers*, new series, 13: 419–32.

Gertler, M.S. 1990, 'The state of analytical political economy in geography', *Environment and Planning A*, 22: 1035–8.

Getis, A. 1964, 'Temporal land use pattern analysis with the use of nearest neighbour and quadrat methods', *Annals of the Association of American Geographers*, 54: 391–9.

Getis, A. 1983, 'Second-order analysis of point patterns: the case of Chicago as a multicenter region', *Professional Geographer*, 35: 73–80.

Getis, A. and Boots, B. 1978, *Models of spatial processes* (Cambridge University Press, Cambridge).

Ghosh, A. and McLafferty, S.L. 1982, 'Locating retail stores in uncertain environments: a scenario planning approach', *Journal of Retailing*, 58: 5–22.

Ghosh, A. and McLafferty, S.L. 1987, *Location strategies for retail and service firms* (D.C. Heath, Lexington, Mass.).

Ghosh, A. and Rushton, G. 1987, 'Introduction: Progress in location-allocation modelling', pp. 1–20 in Ghosh, A. and Rushton, G. (eds.), *Spatial analysis and location-allocation models* (Van Nostrand Reinhold, New York).

Gibbons, R. 1992a, *Game theory for applied economists* (Princeton University Press, Princeton, NJ).

Gibbons, R. 1992b, *A primer in game theory* (Harvester Wheatsheaf, Hemel Hempstead).

Gibson, E.M.W. 1981, 'Realism', pp. 156–73 in Harvey, M.E. and Holly, B.P. (eds.), *Themes in geographic thought* (Croom Helm, London).

Giddens, A. 1979, *Central problems of social theory: action, structure and contradiction in social analysis* (Macmillan, London).

Giddens, A. 1981, *A critique of contemporary historical materialism* (Macmillan, London).

Giddens, A. (ed.) 1984a, *Positivism and sociology* (Heinemann, London).

Giddens, A. 1984b, *The constitution of society* (Polity Press, Cambridge).

Giddens, A. 1985, 'Time, space and regionalisation', pp. 265–95 in Gregory, D. and Urry, J. (eds.), *Social relations and spatial structures* (Macmillan, London).

Giffins, R. 1985, *Canonical analysis: a review with applications in ecology* (Springer-Verlag, Berlin).

Gilbert, A. 1988, 'The new regional geography in English- and French-speaking countries', *Progress in Human Geography*, 12: 208–28.

Glaser, B. 1978, *Theoretical sensitivity* (Sociology Press, Mill Valley, Ca.).

Glick, T.F. 1990, 'History and philosophy of geography', *Progress in Human Geography*, 14; 120–8.

Glusberg, J. (ed.), 1994, *Deconstruction: a student guide* (Academy Editions, London).

Godambe, V.P. and Heyde, C.C. 1987, 'Quasi-likelihood and optimal estimation', *International Statistical Review*, 55: 231–44.

Godfrey, C. and Siddons, A.W. 1970, *Four-figure tables* (Cambridge University Press, Cambridge).

Golant, S. and Burton, I. 1976, 'A semantic differential experiment in the interpretation and grouping of environmental hazards', pp. 364–74 in Moore, G.T. and Golledge, R.G. (eds.), *Environmental knowing: theories, research and methods* (Dowden, Hutchinson & Ross Inc., Stroudsburg, Penn.).

Gold, J.R. 1980, *An introduction to behavioural geography* (Oxford University Press, Oxford).

Gold, J.R. and Goodey, B. 1984, 'Behavioral and perceptual geography: criticisms and responses', *Progress in Human Geography*, 8: 544–50.

Goldstein, H. 1987, *Multilevel models in educational and social research* (Charles Griffin, London).

Golledge, R.G. 1976, 'Methods and methodological issues in environmental cognition research', pp. 300–14 in Moore, G.T. and Golledge, R.G. (eds.), *Environmental knowing: theories, research and methods* (Dowden, Hutchinson & Ross, Stroudsburg, Penn.).

Golledge, R.G. 1978a, 'Learning about urban environments', pp. 76–98 in Carlstein, T., Parkes, D. and Thrift, N.J. (eds.), *Timing space and spacing time*, volume 1 (Edward Arnold, London).

Golledge, R.G. 1978b, 'Representing, interpreting, and using cognized environments', *Papers of the Regional Science Association*, 41: 169–204.

Golledge, R.G. 1981, 'Misconceptions, misinterpretations and misrepresentations of behavioral approaches in human geography', *Environment and Planning A*, 13: 1325–44.

Golledge, R.G. 1993, 'Geographical perspectives on spatial cognition', pp. 16–46 in Garling, T. and Golledge, R.G. (eds.), *Behavior and environment: psychological and geographical approaches* (North Holland, Amsterdam).

Golledge, R.G. and Raynor, J.N. (eds.) 1982, *Proximity and preference: problems in the multidimensional analysis of large data sets* (University of Minneapolis Press, Minneapolis).

Golledge, R.G. and Rushton, G. 1972, 'Multidimensional scaling: review and geographical applications', *Technical Papers, Association of American Geographers*, No. 10.

Golledge, R.G. and Rushton, G. (eds.), 1975, *Spatial choice and spatial preference* (Ohio State University Press, Columbus, Ohio).

Golledge, R.G. and Spector, A. 1978, 'Comprehending the urban environment: theory and practice', *Geographical Analysis*, 10: 403–26.

Golledge, R.G. and Stimson, R.J. 1987, *Analytical behavioural geography* (Croom Helm, London).

Golledge, R.G. and Stimson, R.J. 1997, *Spatial behavior: a geographical perspective* (Guilford Press, New York and London).

Golledge, R.G. and Timmermans, H. 1990, 'Applications of behavioural research on spatial problems I: cognition', *Progress in Human Geography*, 14: 57–99.

Golledge, R.G., Helperin, W.C. and Hubert, L.J. 1988, 'Evaluating models of consumer spatial behaviour', pp. 38–55 in Golledge, R.G. and Timmermans, H. (eds.), *Behavioural modelling in geography and planning* (Croom Helm, London).

Good, I.J. 1983, 'The philosophy of exploratory data analysis', *Philosophy of Science*, 50: 283–95.

Goodchild, M.F. 1987, 'An introduction to spatial autocorrelation', *Concepts and Techniques in Modern Geography*, 47.

Goodchild, M.F. 1988, 'GIS', *Progress in Human Geography*, 12: 560–6.

Goodchild, M.F. and Mark, D.M. 1987, 'The fractal nature of geographic phenomena', *Annals of the Association of American Geographers*, 77: 265–78.

Goodchild, M.F., Haining, R.P. and Wise, S.M. 1992, 'Integrating GIS and spatial data analysis: problems and possibilities', *International Journal of Geographical Information Systems*, 6: 407–23.

Goodchild, M.F., Steyaert, L., Parks, B.O., Johnston, C.O., Maidment, D.R., Crane, M.P. and Glendinning, S. 1996, *GIS and environmental modelling: progress and research issues* (GeoInformation International, Cambridge).

Goodman, L.A. 1954, 'Kolmogorov-Smirnov tests for psychological research', *Psychological Bulletin*, 51: 160–8.

Goodman, L.A. 1968, 'The analysis of cross-classified data: independence, quasi-independence and interactions in contingency tables with or without missing entries', *Journal of the American Statistical Association*, 63: 1091–1131.

Goodman, L.A. 1972, 'A modified multiple regression approach to the analysis of dichotomous variables', *American Sociological Review*, 37: 28–46.

Goodman, L.A. and Kruskal, W.H. 1954, 'Measures of association for cross classifications', *Journal of the American Statistical Association*, 49: 732–64.

Gordon, P. and Moore, II, J.E. 1989, 'Endogenizing the rise and fall of urban subcenters via discrete programming models', *Environment and Planning A*, 21: 1195–1203.

Gore, C.G. 1991a, 'Location theory and service development planning: which way now?', *Environment and Planning A*, 23: 1095–1110.

Gore, C.G. 1991b, 'The spatial separatist theme and the problem of representation in location-allocation models', *Environment and Planning A*, 23: 939–54.

Goss, J.D. 1996, 'Introduction to focus groups', *Area*, 28: 113–14.

Goss, J.D. and Leinbach, T.R. 1996, 'Focus groups as alternative research practice: experience with transmigrants in Indonesia', *Area*, 28: 115–23.

Gottdeiner, M. 1987, 'Space as a force of production: contribution to the debate on realism, capitalism and space', *International Journal of Urban and Regional Research*, 11: 405–16.

Gould, M.I. 1992, 'The use of GIS and CAC by health authorities: results from a postal questionnaire', *Area*, 24: 391–401.

Gould, P.R. 1963, 'Man against his environment: A game theoretic framework', *Annals of the Association of American Geographers*, 53: 290–7.

Gould, P.R. 1965, 'Wheat on Kilimanjaro: The perception of choice within game and learning model frameworks', *General Systems*, 10: 157–66.

Gould, P.R. 1967, 'On the geographical interpretation of eigenvalues', *Transactions of the Institute of British Geographers*, 42: 53–86.

Gould, P.R. 1969a, 'Methodological developments since the

fifties', pp. 1–50 in Board, C. et al (eds.), *Progress in geography*, volume 1 (Edward Arnold, London).

Gould, P.R. 1969b, 'Problems of space preference measures and relationships', *Geographical Analysis*, 1: 31–44.

Gould, P.R. 1970, 'Is statistix inferens the geographical name for a wild goose?', *Economic Geography*, 46: 439–48.

Gould, P.R. 1972, 'Pedagogic review: entropy in urban and regional modelling', *Annals of the Association of American Geographers*, 62: 689–700.

Gould, P.R. 1985, *The geographer at work* (Routledge and Kegan Paul, London).

Gould, P.R. 1988a, 'The only perspective: a critique of Marxist claims to exclusiveness in geographical enquiry', pp. 1–10 in Golledge, R.G., Couclellis, H. and Gould, P.R. (eds.), *A ground for common search* (Geographical Press, Santa Barbara, Ca.).

Gould, P.R. 1988b, 'What does chaos mean for theory in the human sciences', pp. 11–30 in Golledge, R.G., Couclellis, H. and Gould, P.R. (eds.), *A ground for common search* (Geographical Press, Santa Barbara, Ca.).

Gould, P.R. 1989, 'Geographic dimensions of the AIDS pandemic', *Professional Geographer*, 41: 71–8.

Gould, P.R. 1993, *The slow plague: a geography of the AIDS pandemic* (Blackwell, Cambridge, Mass.).

Gould, P.R. 1994, 'Mapping the AIDS pandemic', *Geographical Magazine*, 65(1): 18–23.

Gould, P.R. and White, R. 1968, 'The mental maps of British schoolleavers', *Regional Studies*, 2: 161–82.

Gould, P.R. and White, R. 1974, *Mental maps* (Penguin, Harmondsworth).

Graff, T.D. and Ashton, D. 1994, 'Spatial diffusion of Wal-Mart: contagious and reverse hierarchical elements', *Professional Geographer*, 46: 19–29.

Graham, E. 1995, 'Postmodernism and the possibility of a new human geography', *Scottish Geographical Magazine*, 111: 175–8.

Graham, J. 1988, 'Postmodernism and Marxism', *Antipode*, 20: 60–6.

Graham, J. 1990, 'Theory and essentialism in Marxist geography', *Antipode*, 22: 53–66.

Graham, J. 1992, '"They were no different …" Probing childhood perceptions of cultural encounter in Edwardian New Zealand', *British Review of New Zealand Studies*, 5: 51–76.

Graham, J., Gibson, K., Horvath, R. and Shakow, D. 1988, 'Restructuring in United States manufacturing: the decline of monopoly capitalism', *Annals of the Association of American Geographers*, 78: 473–90.

Gramsci, A. 1977, *Selections from political writings 1910–1920* (Lawrence & Wishart, London).

Gray, D.A. 1988, 'An integrated GIS applied to agricultural development in Belize', pp. 87–93 in Southgate A. and Stone, A. (eds.), *Developing space: proceedings of the postgraduate workshop on applications of remote sensing*, Department of Geography, University of Durham (Remote Sensing Society Monographs, No. 2, Nottingham).

Green, D.R., Rix, D. and Corbin, C. (eds.) 1995, *The AGI source book for geographic information systems* (Association for Geographic Information, London).

Green, M. and Flowerdew, R. 1996, 'New evidence on the modifiable areal unit problem', pp. 41–54 in Longley, P. and Batty, M. (eds.), *Spatial analysis: modelling in a GIS environment* (GeoInformation International, Cambridge).

Green, P.E. and Srinivasan, V. 1978, 'Conjoint analysis in consumer research: issues and outlook', *Journal of Consumer Research*, 5: 103–23.

Greenbaum, T.L. 1987, *The practical handbook and guide to focus group research* (Lexington Books, Lexington, Mass.).

Greenberg, J. (ed.), 1992, *Game theory in economics* (Elgar, Aldershot).

Greenwood, M.J. 1978, 'An econometric model of internal migration and regional economic growth in Mexico', *Journal of Regional Science*, 18: 17–31.

Gregory, D. 1978a, 'The discourse of the past: phenomenology, structuralism and historical geography', *Journal of Historical Geography*, 4: 161–73.

Gregory, D. 1978b, *Ideology, science and human geography* (Hutchinson, London).

Gregory, D. 1980, 'The ideology of control: systems theory and geography', *Tijdschrift voor Economische en Social Geographie*, 71: 327–42.

Gregory, D. 1981, 'Human agency and human geography', *Transactions of the Institute of British Geographers*, new series, 6: 1–18.

Gregory, D. 1985, 'Suspended animation: the stasis of diffusion theory', pp. 296–336 in Gregory, D. and Urry, J. (eds.), *Social relations and spatial structures* (Macmillan, London).

Gregory, D. 1987, 'Editorial: Postmodernism and the politics of social theory', *Environment and Planning D: Society and Space*, 5: 245–8.

Gregory, D. 1989, *The geographical imagination* (Hutchinson, London).

Gregory, D. 1994a, 'Logical positivism', pp. 455–7 in Johnston, R.J., Gregory, D. and Smith, D.M. (eds.), *The dictionary of human geography* (Blackwell Reference, Oxford).

Gregory, D. 1994b, 'Quantitative revolution', p. 494 in Johnston, R.J., Gregory, D. and Smith, D.M. (eds.), *The dictionary of human geography* (Blackwell Reference, Oxford).

Gregory, D. 1994c, *Geographical imaginations* (Blackwell Publishing, Oxford).

Gregory, D. 1994d, 'Spatiality', pp. 582–5, in Johnston, R.J., Gregory, D. and Smith, D.M. (eds.), *The dictionary of human geography* (Blackwell, Oxford), 3rd edition.

Gregory, D. 1994e, 'Realism', pp. 499–503 in Johnston, R.J., Gregory, D. and Smith, D.M. (eds.), *The dictionary of human geography* (Blackwell, Oxford), 3rd edition.

Gregory, D. and Urry, J. (eds.) 1985, *Social relations and spatial structures* (Macmillan, London).

Gregory, S. 1963, *Statistical methods and the geographer* (Longman, London); 2nd edition, 1968; 3rd edition, 1973; 4th edition 1978.

Gregory, S. 1976, 'On geographical myths and statistical fables', *Transactions of the Institute of British Geographers*, new series, 1: 385–400.

Gregson, N. 1986, 'On duality and dualism: the case of

structuration and time geography', *Progress in Human Geography*, 10: 184–205.

Gregson, N. 1987, 'The CURS initiative: some further comments', *Antipode*, 19: 364–70.

Greimas, A.-J. 1987, *On meaning* (Minnesota University Press, Minneapolis).

Griffith, D.A. 1987, *Spatial autocorrelation – a primer* (Association of American Geographers, Washington D.C.).

Grigg, D.B. 1965, 'The logic of regional systems', *Annals of the Association of American Geographers*, 55: 465–91.

Grimshaw, D.J. 1988, 'The use of land and property information systems', *International Journal of Geographical Information Systems*, 2: 57–65.

Grizzle, J.E., Starmer, C.F. and Koch, G.G. 1969, 'Analysis of categorical data by linear models', *Biometrics*, 25: 489–504.

Grosz, E.A. 1987, 'Feminist theory and the challenge to knowledges', *Women's Studies International Forum*, 10: 475–80.

Groves, R., Beimer, P., Lyberg, L., Massey, J., Nicholls, W. and Waksberg, J. 1988, *Telephone survey methodology* (Wiley, New York).

Guelke, L. 1978, 'Geography and logical positivism', pp. 35–62 in Herbert, D.T. and Johnston, R.J. (eds.), *Social areas in cities*, volume 1 (John Wiley, Chichester).

Gumbel, E.J. 1958, 'Statistical theory of floods and droughts', *Journal of the Institute of Water Engineers*, 12: 157–84.

Gurney, C.M. 1983, 'The use of contextual information in the classification of remotely sensed data', *Photogrammetric Engineering and Remote Sensing*, 49: 55–64.

Gurr, T.R. and King, K.S. 1987, *The state and the city* (University of Chicago Press, Chicago).

Guttman, L. 1946, 'An approach for quantifying paired comparisons and rank order', *Mathematical Studies*, 17: 44–63.

Haberman, S.J. 1978, *Analysis of qualitative data*, volume 1: *Introductory topics* (Academic Press, New York).

Haberman, S.J. 1979, *Analysis of qualitative data*, volume 2: *New developments* (Academic Press, New York).

Habermas, J. 1976, *Legitimation crisis* (Heinemann, London).

Habermas, J. 1979, *Communication and the evolution of society* (Heinemann, London).

Habermas, J. 1984, *The theory of communicative action*, volume 1: *Reason and the rationalization of society* (Heinemann, London).

Habermas, J. 1985, 'Modernity – an incomplete project', pp. 3–15 in Foster, M. (ed.), *Postmodern culture* (Pluto, London).

Habermas, J. 1987, *The philosophical discourse of modernity* (Polity Press, Cambridge).

Hacking, I. 1975, 'Lakatos's philosophy of science', pp. 128–43 in Hacking, I. (ed.), *Scientific revolutions* (Oxford University Press, Oxford).

Hagerstrand, T. 1965, 'A Monte Carlo approach to diffusion', *Archives Europeennes de Sociologie*, 6: 43–7.

Hagerstrand, T. 1967a, *Innovation diffusion as a spatial process* (University of Chicago Press, Chicago), translated by A. Pred.

Hagerstrand, T. 1967b, 'On the Monte Carlo simulation of diffusion', pp. 1–32 in Garrison, W.L. and Marble, D.F. (eds.), *Quantitative geography*, Part 1: *Economic and cultural topics* (Northwestern University Press, Evanston).

Hagerstrand, T. 1967c, 'The computer and the geographer', *Transactions of the Institute of British Geographers*, 42: 1–20.

Hagerstrand, T. 1970, 'What about people in regional science?', *Papers and Proceedings of the Regional Science Association*, 24: 7–21.

Hagerstrand, T. 1982, 'Diorama, path and project', *Tijdschrift voor Economische en Social Geographie*, 73: 323–39.

Hagerstrand, T. 1983, 'In search for the sources of concepts', pp. 238–56 in Buttimer, A. (ed.), *The practice of geography* (Longman, London).

Hagerstrand, T. 1984, 'Presence and absence: a look at conceptual choices and bodily necessities', *Regional Studies*, 18: 373–80.

Haggett, P. 1961, 'Land use and sediment yield in an old plantation tract of the Serro do Mar, Brazil', *Geographical Journal*, 127: 50–62.

Haggett, P. 1963, 'Regional and local components in land-use sampling: a case study from the Brazilian Triangulo', *Erdkunde*, 17: 108–14.

Haggett, P. 1964, 'Regional and local components in the distribution of forested areas in south-east Brazil', *Geographical Journal*, 130: 365–78.

Haggett, P. 1965, *Locational analysis in human geography* (Edward Arnold, London).

Haggett, P. 1973, 'Forecasting alternative spatial, ecological and regional futures: problems and possibilities', pp. 217–36 in Chorley, R.J. (ed.), *Directions in geography* (Methuen, London).

Haggett, P. 1975, 'Simple epidemics in human populations: some geographical aspects of the Hamer-Soper diffusion models', pp. 373–91 in Peel, R.F., Chisholm, M.D.I. and Haggett, P. (eds.), *Processes in physical and human geography: Bristol essays* (Heinemann, London).

Haggett, P. 1976, 'Hybridizing alternative models of an epidemic diffusion process', *Economic Geography*, 52: 136–46.

Haggett, P. 1981, 'The edges of space', pp. 51–70 in Bennett, R.J. (ed.), *European progress in spatial analysis* (Pion, London).

Haggett, P. and Chorley, R.J. 1969, *Network analysis in geography* (Edward Arnold, London).

Haggett, P., Cliff, A.D. and Frey, A. 1977, *Locational analysis in human geography* (Edward Arnold, London).

Haines-Young, R.H. 1989, 'Modelling geographical knowledge', pp. 22–39 in Macmillan, W. (ed.), *Remodelling geography* (Basil Blackwell, Oxford).

Haines-Young, R.H. and Petch, J.H. 1980, 'The challenge of critical rationalism for methodology in physical geography', *Progress in Physical Geography*, 4: 63–78.

Haines-Young, R.H. and Petch, J.H. 1986, *Physical geography: its nature and methods* (Harper & Row, London).

Haining, R.P. 1980, 'Spatial autocorrelation problems', pp. 1–44 in Herbert, D.T. and Johnston, R.J. (eds.), *Geography and the urban environment*, volume 3 (John Wiley & Sons, London).

Haining, R.P. 1982, 'Interaction models and spatial diffusion processes', *Geographical Analysis*, 14: 95–108.

Haining, R.P. 1983a, 'Modelling intra-urban price competition: an example of gasoline pricing', *Journal of Regional Science*, 23: 517–28.

Haining, R.P. 1983b, 'Spatial and spatial-temporal interaction models, and the analysis of patterns of diffusion', *Transactions of the Institute of British Geographers*, 8: 158–69.

Haining, R.P. 1987, 'Small area aggregate income models: theory and methods with an application to urban and rural income data for Pennsylvania', *Regional Studies*, 21: 519–30.

Haining, R.P. 1988, 'Estimating spatial means with an application to remotely sensed data', *Communications in Statistics: Theory and Methods*, 17: 573–97.

Haining, R.P. 1989, 'Geography and spatial statistics: current positions, future developments', pp. 191–203 in Macmillan, W. (ed.), *Remodelling geography* (Blackwell, Oxford).

Haining, R.P. 1990a, *Spatial data analysis in the social and environmental sciences* (Cambridge University Press, Cambridge).

Haining, R.P. 1990b, 'The use of added variable plots in regression modelling with spatial data', *Professional Geographer*, 42: 336–44.

Haining, R.P. 1994, 'Designing spatial data analysis modules for geographical information systems', pp. 45–64 in Fotheringham, A.S. and Rogerson, P. (eds.), *Spatial analysis and GIS* (Taylor and Francis, London).

Haining, R.P., Griffith, D.A. and Bennett, R.J. 1984, 'A statistical approach to the problem of missing spatial data using a first-order Markov model', *Professional Geographer*, 36: 338–45.

Hakim, C. 1987, *Research design: strategies and choices in the design of social research* (Unwin Hyman, London).

Hale, J. and Kocak, H. 1991, *Dynamics and bifurcations* (Springer-Verlag, New York).

Hall, C. 1978, 'Teaching humanistic geography', *Australian Geographer*, 14: 7–14.

Hall, G. and Taylor, S. 1983, 'A causal model of attitudes towards mental health facilities', *Environment and Planning A*, 15: 525–42.

Halperin, W.C. 1985, 'The analysis of panel data for discrete choices', pp. 561–85 in Nijkamp, P., Leitner, H. and Wrigley, N. (eds.), *Measuring the unmeasurable* (Martinus Nijhoff, Dordrecht).

Hamer, W.H. 1906, 'The Millroy lectures on epidemic disease in England. The evidence of variability and persistence of type', *Lancet*, 1: 733–9.

Hamm, B., Currie, R. and Forde, D. 1988, 'A dynamic typology of urban neighbourhoods', *Canadian Review of Sociology and Anthropology*, 25: 439–55.

Hammond, R. and McCullagh, P.S. 1974, *Quantitative techniques in geography: an introduction* (Clarendon Press, Oxford); 2nd edition, 1978.

Hamnett, C.R. 1987, 'The OPCS Longitudinal Study: a new tool for social research in England and Wales', *Area*, 19: 69–73.

Hamnett, C.R. 1991, 'The relationship between residential migration and housing tenure in London, 1971–81: a longitudinal analysis', *Environment and Planning A*, 23: 1147–62.

Hand, D.J. 1996, *Practical longitudinal data analysis* (Chapman and Hall, London).

Hanfling, O. 1981, *Logical positivism* (Basil Blackwell, Oxford).

Hanson, S. 1992, 'Geography and feminism: worlds in collision?', *Annals of the Association of American Geographers*, 82: 569–86.

Hanson, S. and Burnett, K.P. 1980, 'The analysis of travel as an example of complex human behaviour in spatially constrained situations: measurement issues', pp. 57–70 in Stopher, P.R., Meyburg, A.M. and Brog, W. (eds.), *New horizons in behavioural travel research* (D.C. Heath, Lexington, Mass.).

Hanson, S. and Pratt, G. 1991, 'Job search and the occupational segregation of women', *Annals of the Association of American Geographers*, 81: 229–53.

Haraway, D. 1991, *Simians, cyborgs, and women: the reinvention of women* (Routledge, New York).

Hardin, G. 1968, 'The tragedy of the commons: the population problem has no technical solution; it requires a fundamental extension in morality', *Science*, 162: 1243–8.

Hardin, G. 1974, 'Living on a lifeboat', *Bioscience*, 24: 561–8.

Hardin, R. 1982, *Collective action* (Johns Hopkins University Press, Baltimore).

Harding, S. 1986, *The science question in feminism* (Cornell University Press, Ithaca).

Harding, S. 1987, *Feminism and methodology* (Indiana University Press, Bloomington).

Harding, S. 1991, *Whose science? Whose knowledge? Thinking from women's lives* (Open University Press, Milton Keynes).

Harley, J.B. 1989, 'Deconstructing the map', *Cartographica*, 26: 1–20.

Harley, J.B. 1991, 'Deconstructing the map', pp. 231–47 in Barnes, T. and Duncan, J. (eds.), *Writing worlds: discourse, text and metaphor in the representation of landscape* (Routledge, London).

Harman, H.H. 1967, *Modern factor analysis* (University of Chicago Press, Chicago).

Harman, H.H. 1976, *Modern factor analysis* (University of Chicago Press, Chicago), 3rd edition.

Harris, C.D. 1970, *Cities of the Soviet Union* (Association of American Geographers/Rand McNally, New York).

Harris, C.D. and Ullman, E.L. 1945, 'The nature of cities', *Annals of the American Academy of Political and Social Science*, 142: 7–17.

Harris, F.W. and O'Brien, L.G. 1988, 'The changing face of the town', *Geographical Magazine*, 60: 34–7.

Harris, R. 1988, *Democracy in Kingston: a social movement in urban politics, 1965–1970* (McGill-Queen's University Press, Kingston and Montreal).

Harrison, C. and Burgess, J. 1988, 'Qualitative research and open space policy', *The Planner*, pp. 16–18.

Harrison, C. and Burgess, J. 1990, 'Planning parks for people', *Geographical Magazine*, May, pp. 1–3.

Harrison, J.A. and Sarre, P. 1971, 'Personal construct theory in the measurement of environmental images: problems and methods', *Environment and Behavior*, 3: 351–74.

Hartshorne, C. and Weiss, P. (eds.), 1932, *Collected Papers of Charles Sanders Peirce* (Harvard University Press, Cambridge, Mass.).

Hartshorne, R. 1939, *The nature of geography* (Association of American Geographers, Lancaster, Pa.).

Harvey, D.L. and Reed, M. 1996, 'Social science as the study of complex systems', pp. 295–324 in Kiel, L.D. and Elliott, E. (eds.), *Chaos theory in the social sciences: foundations and applications* (Michigan University Press, Ann Arbor).

Harvey, D.W. 1966, 'Geographical processes and the analysis of point patterns', *Transactions of the Institute of British Geographers*, 40: 81–95.

Harvey, D.W. 1968, 'Some methodological problems in the use of the Neyman *A* and negative binomial probability distributions', *Transactions of the Institute of British Geographers*, 44: 85–95.

Harvey, D.W. 1969, *Explanation in geography* (Edward Arnold, London).

Harvey, D.W. 1972, 'Revolutionary and counter-revolutionary theory in geography and the problem of ghetto formation', *Antipode*, 4(2): 1–13.

Harvey, D.W. 1973, *Social justice and the city* (Edward Arnold, London).

Harvey, D.W. 1974a, 'Population, resources and the ideology of science', *Economic Geography*, 50: 256–77.

Harvey, D.W. 1974b, 'Class-monopoly rent, finance capital and the urban revolution', *Regional Studies*, 8: 239–55.

Harvey, D.W. 1975a, 'The geography of capital accumulation: a reconstruction of the Marxist theory', *Antipode*, 7(2): 9–21.

Harvey, D.W. 1975b, 'Class structure in a capitalist society and the theory of residential differentiation', pp. 354–72 in Peel, R.F., Chisholm, M.D.F. and Haggett, P. (eds.), *Processes in physical and human geography: Bristol essays* (Heinemann, London).

Harvey, D.W. 1978, 'The urban process under capitalism: a framework for analysis', *International Journal of Urban and Regional Research*, 2: 101–32.

Harvey, D.W. 1982, *The limits to capital* (Basil Blackwell, Oxford).

Harvey, D.W. 1984, 'On the history and present condition of geography: an historical materialist manifesto', *The Professional Geographer*, 36: 1–11.

Harvey, D.W. 1985a, *The urbanization of capital* (Basil Blackwell, Oxford).

Harvey, D.W. 1985b, *Consciousness and the urban experience: studies in the history and theory of capitalist urbanization* (Johns Hopkins University Press, Baltimore).

Harvey, D.W. 1985c, 'The geopolitics of capitalism', pp. 128–63 in Gregory, D. and Urry, J. (eds.), *Social relations and spatial structures* (Macmillan, London).

Harvey, D.W. 1986, 'Reviewing of "Making sense of Marx"', *Political Theory*, 14: 686–90.

Harvey, D.W. 1987a, 'Three myths in search of a reality', *Environment and Planning D: Society and Space*, 5: 367–76.

Harvey, D.W. 1987b, 'Flexible accumulation through urbanisation: reflections on "postmodernism" in the American city', *Antipode*, 19: 260–86.

Harvey, D.W. 1988, 'The geographical and geopolitical consequences of the transition from Fordist to flexible accumulation', pp. 101–34 in Sternlieb, G. and Hughes, J.W. (eds.), *America's new market geography* (Rutgers Center for Urban Policy Research, New Brunswick, NJ).

Harvey, D.W. 1989a, *The condition of postmodernity: an enquiry into the origins of cultural change* (Basil Blackwell, Oxford).

Harvey, D.W. 1989b, 'From models to Marx: notes on the project to "remodel" contemporary geography', pp. 211–16 in Macmillan, W. (ed.), *Remodelling geography* (Basil Blackwell, Oxford).

Harvey, D.W. 1989c, *The urban experience* (Basil Blackwell, Oxford).

Harvey, D.W. 1992, 'Postmodern morality plays', *Antipode*, 25: 300–26.

Harvey, D.W. 1995, 'A geographer's guide to dialectical thinking', pp. 3–21 in Cliff, A.D., Gould, P.R., Hoare, A.G. and Thrift, N.J. (eds.), *Diffusing geography: essays for Peter Haggett* (Blackwell, Cambridge, Mass. and Oxford).

Harvey, D.W. and Scott, A.J. 1989, 'The practice of human geography: theory and empirical specificity in the transition from Fordism to flexible accumulation', pp. 217–29 in Macmillan, W. (ed.), *Remodelling geography* (Blackwell, Oxford).

Harvey, M.E. 1971, 'Social change and ethnic relocation in developing Africa. The Sierra Leone example', *Geografisker Annaler*, 53B: 94–106.

Hay, A.M. 1978, 'Transport geography', *Progress in Human Geography*, 2: 324–9.

Hay, A.M. 1979a, 'Positivism in human geography: response to critics', pp. 1–26 in Herbert, D.T. and Johnston, R.J. (eds.), *Geography and the urban environment*, volume 2 (John Wiley and Sons, New York).

Hay, A.M. 1979b, 'The geographical explanation of commodity flows', *Progress in Human Geography*, 3: 1–12.

Hay, A.M. 1981, 'Transport geography', pp. 366–73 in Wrigley, N. and Bennett, R.J. (eds.), *Quantitative geography: a British view* (Routledge and Kegan Paul, London).

Hay, A.M. 1985a, 'Statistical tests in the absence of samples: a comment', *The Professional Geographer*, 37: 334–8.

Hay, A.M. 1985b, 'Scientific method in geography', pp. 129–42 in Johnston, R.J. (ed.), *The future of geography* (Methuen, London).

Hay, I.M. 1988, 'A state of mind? Some thoughts on the state in capitalist society', *Progress in Human Geography*, 12: 34–46.

Haynes, K.E. and Enders, W.T. 1975, 'Distance, direction, and entropy in the evolution of a settlement pattern', *Economic Geography*, 51: 357–65.

Haynes, K.E. and Fotheringham, A.S. 1984, *Gravity and spatial interaction models* (Sage, Newbury Park, Ca.).

Haynes, K.E. and Phillips, F.Y. 1987, 'The cost constraint in the maximum-entropy trip distribution model: a research note', *Geographical Analysis*, 19: 90–3.

Hearnshaw, H.M. and Unwin, D.J. (eds.), 1994, *Visualisation in geographical information systems* (Wiley, Chichester).

Heckman, J.J. and Singer, B. 1995, *Longitudinal analysis of labour market data* (Cambridge University Press, Cambridge).

Heilbruner, R.L. 1980, *Marxism: for and against* (W.W. Norton, New York).

Held, D. 1980, *Introduction to critical theory* (Hutchinson, London).

Henderson, J.M. 1958, *The efficiency of the coal industry: an application of linear programming* (Harvard University Press, Cambridge, Mass.).

Henderson, R.A. 1980a, 'The location of immigrant industry within a UK assisted area: the Scottish experience', *Progress in Planning*, 14: 105–226.

Henderson, R.A. 1980b, 'An analysis of closures amongst Scottish manufacturing plants between 1966 and 1975', *Scottish Journal of Political Economy*, 27: 152–74.

Hepple, L.W. 1975, 'Spectral techniques and the study of inter-regional economic cycles', pp. 392–408 in Peel, R.F., Chisholm, M.D.I. and Haggett, P. (eds.), *Process in physical and human geography: Bristol essays* (Heinemann, London).

Hepple, L.W. 1979, 'Regional dynamics in British unemployment and the impact of structural change', pp. 45–63 in Wrigley, N. (ed.), *Statistical applications in the spatial sciences* (Pion, London).

Hepple, L.W. 1981, 'Spatial and temporal analysis: time series analysis', pp. 92–6 in Wrigley, N. and Bennett, R.J. (eds.), *Quantitative geography: the British experience* (Routledge and Kegan Paul, London).

Herbert, D.T. 1967, 'Social area analysis – a British study', *Urban Studies*, 4: 41–60.

Herbert, D.T. 1970, 'Principal components analysis and urban social structure: a study of Cardiff and Swansea', pp. 79–100 in Carter, H. and Davies, W.K.D. (eds.), *Urban essays: studies in the geography of Wales* (Longman, London).

Herbert, D.T. 1977, 'An areal and ecological analysis of delinquency residence: Cardiff 1966 and 1971', *Tijdschrift voor Economische en Social Geografie*, 68: 83–99.

Herbert, D.T. 1993, 'Neighbourhood incivilities and the study of crime in place', *Area*, 25: 45–58.

Herbert, D.T. 1994, 'Neighbourhood incivilities, crime, place and multi-level models', *Area*, 26: 81–4.

Hillsman, E.L. 1984, 'The *p*-median structure as a unified linear model for location-allocation analysis', *Environment and Planning A*, 16: 305–18.

Hirst, M.A. 1975, 'Dimensions of urban systems in tropical African geographical analysis', *Transactions of the Institute of British Geographers*, 66: 441–9.

Hirtle, S.C. and Heidorn, P.B. 1993, 'The structure of cognitive maps: representations and processes', pp. 170–92 in Garling, T. and Golledge, R.G. (eds.), *Behavior and environment: psychological and geographical approaches* (Elsevier/North Holland, Amsterdam).

Hoaglin, D.C. 1983, 'Letter values: a set of selected order statistics', pp. 33–55 in Hoaglin, D.C., Mosteller, F. and Tukey, J.W. (eds.), *Understanding robust and exploratory data analysis* (John Wiley, New York).

Hoaglin, D.C., Mosteller, F. and Tukey, J.W. 1983, *Understanding robust and exploratory data analysis* (John Wiley, New York).

Hoaglin, D.C., Mosteller, F. and Tukey, J.W. 1985, *Exploring data tables, trends and shapes* (John Wiley, New York).

Hodgart, R.L. 1978, 'Optimizing access to public services: a review of problems, models and methods of locating central facilities', *Progress in Human Geography*, 2: 17–48.

Hodgart, R.L. 1985, 'Developments in location/allocation modelling', *Geographica Polonica*, 51: 265–74.

Hofstadter, D.R. (ed.), 1979, *Godel, Escher, Bach: an eternal golden braid. A metaphorical fugue on minds and machines in the spirit of Lewis Carroll* (Basic Books, New York).

Hoggart, K. 1995, 'Political parties and the implementation of homeless legislation by nonmetropolitan districts in England and Wales, 1985–90', *Political Geography*, 14: 59–79.

Hoinville, G., Jowell, R. and Airey, C. 1985, *Survey research practice* (Gower, Aldershot).

Holbrook, B. and Jackson, P. 1996, 'Shopping around: focus group research in North London', *Area*, 28: 136–42.

Hollinger, R. 1994, *Postmodernism and the social sciences: a thematic approach* (Sage, London).

Hollis, M. and Nell, E. (eds.), 1975, *Rational economic man: a philosophical critique of neoclassical economics* (Cambridge University Press, Cambridge).

Holmes, J.H. 1987, 'Locational disadvantage and inverse health care in Queensland: a response', *Australian Geographical Studies*, 25: 110–20.

Holt, D. 1979, 'Log-linear models for contingency table analysis', *Sociological Methods and Research*, 7: 330–6.

Hookway, C. 1992, *Peirce* (Routledge, London).

Hopkins, T.K. and Wallerstein, I. 1982, *World-systems analysis* (Sage, Beverly Hills, Ca.).

Horowitz, J.L. 1991, 'Modeling the choice of choice set in discrete-choice random utility models', *Environment and Planning A*, 23: 1237–46.

Hotelling, H. 1929, 'Stability in competition', *Economic Journal*, 39: 40–57.

Hoyt, H. 1939, *The structure of residential neighborhoods in American cities* (US Federal Housing Administration, Washington DC).

Hubert, L.J., Golledge, R.G. and Constanzo, C.M. 1981, 'Generalized procedures for evaluating spatial autocorrelation', *Geographical Analysis*, 13: 224–33.

Hudak, P. 1994, 'Application of facility location theory to groundwater remediation', *Applied Geography*, 14: 232–44.

Hudson, J.C. 1969, 'Diffusion in a central place system', *Geographical Analysis*, 1: 45–58.

Hudson, J.C. 1972, 'Geographical diffusion theory', *Northwestern University Studies in Geography*, 19.

Hudson, R. 1974, 'Images of the retailing environment: an

example of the use of the repertory grid methodology', *Environment and Behavior*, 6: 470–94.

Hudson, R. 1981, 'Personal construct theory, the repertory grid method and human geography', *Progress in Human Geography*, 5: 346–59.

Huff, D.L. 1963, 'A probabilistic analysis of shopping centre trade areas', *Land Economics*, 39: 81–9.

Huggett, R.J. 1980, *Systems analysis in geography* (Oxford University Press, Oxford)

Hughes, A.L. 1997, 'Women and rurality: gendered experiences of "community" in village life', pp. 167–88 in Milbourne, P. (ed.), *Revealing rural 'others': Representation, power and identity in British countryside* (Pinter, London and Washington).

Hume, D. 1965, 'An inquiry concerning human understanding, Section IV', pp. 123–32 in Edwards, P. and Pep, A. (eds.), *A modern introduction to philosophy* (Free Press, Glencoe, Ill.), revised edition.

Humm, M. (ed.) 1992, *Feminisms: a reader* (Harvester Wheatsheaf, London).

Ilbery, B.W. 1977a, 'The application of non-parametric measures of association: a comparison of three techniques', *Area*, 9: 99–103

Ilbery, B.W. 1977b, 'Point score analysis: a methodological framework for analysing the decision-making process in agriculture', *Tijdschrift voor Economische en Social Geografie*, 68: 66–71.

Ilbery, B.W. 1978, 'Agricultural decision-making: a behavioural perspective', *Progress in Human Geography*, 2: 448–66.

Ilbery, B.W. 1981, 'Dorset agriculture: a classification of regional types', *Transactions of the Institute of British Geographers*, new series, 6: 214–27.

Ilbery, B.W. 1983, 'A behavioural analysis of hop farming in Hereford and Worcestershire', *Geoforum*, 14: 447–59.

Ilbery, B.W. 1985, 'Behavioural interpretation of horticulture in the Vale of Evesham', *Journal of Rural Studies*, 1: 121–33.

Ilbery, B.W. and Hornby, R. 1983, 'Repertory grids and agricultural decision-making: a mid-Warwickshire case study', *Geografisker Annaler*, 65B: 77–84.

Imrey, P.B., Koch, G.G. and Stokes, M.E. 1981/82, 'Categorical data analysis: some reflections on the log linear model and logistic regression. Part 1: Historical and methodological overview, Part 2: Data analysis', *International Statistical Review*, 49: 265–83; 50: 35–63.

Isaacson, D.L. and Madsen, R.W. 1985, *Markov chains, theory and applications* (R.E Kreiger, Malbar, Fla.).

Isard, W. 1956, *Location and space economy* (Wiley, New York).

Isard, W. 1960, *Methods of regional analysis: an introduction to regional science* (MIT Press, Cambridge, Mass.).

Isnard, C.A. and Zeeman, E.C. 1976, 'Some models from catastrophe theory in the social sciences', pp. 44–100 in Collins, L. (ed.), *The use of models in the social sciences* (Westview Press, Boulder, Col.).

Jackson, M.J. and Woodsford, P.A. 1991, 'GIS data capture hardware and software', pp. 239–49 in Maguire, D.J., Goodchild, M.F. and Rhind, D.W. (eds.), *Geographical information systems: principles and applications*, volume 1 (Longman, London).

Jackson, P. 1983, 'Principles and problems of participant observation', *Geographiska Annaler*, 65B: 39–46.

Jackson, P. 1985, 'Urban ethnography', *Progress in Human Geography*, 9: 157–76.

Jackson, P. 1989, *Maps of meaning: an introduction to cultural geography* (Unwin Hyman, London).

Jackson, P. 1990. 'The cultural politics of masculinity: towards a social geography', *Transactions of the Institute of British Geographers*, 16: 199–213.

Jackson, P. 1991, 'Mapping meanings: a cultural critique of locality studies', *Environment and Planning A*, 23: 215–28.

Jackson, P. 1993, 'Changing ourselves: a geography of position', pp. 198–214 in Johnston, R.J. (ed.), *The challenge for geography. A changing world: a changing discipline* (Blackwell Publishers, Oxford).

James, P.E. 1972, *All possible worlds. A history of geographical ideas* (Bobbs-Merrill, Indianapolis).

Jameson, P. 1984, 'Post modernism or the cultural logic of late capitalism', *New Left Review*, 146: 52–92.

Jameson, P. 1985, 'Post modernism and consumer society', pp. 111–25 in Foster, H. (ed.), *Postmodern culture* (Pluto, London).

Jameson, P. 1989, 'Marxism and post-modernism', *New Left Review*, 176: 31–46.

Jankowski, P. 1989, 'Mixed-data multicriteria evaluation for regional planning: a systematic approach to the decision-making process', *Environment and Planning A*, 21: 283–424.

Janson, C.-G. 1969, 'Some problems of ecological factor analysis', pp. 301–42 in Dogan, M. and Rokkan, S. (eds.), *Social ecology* (MIT Press, Cambridge, Mass.).

Jarrie, I.C. 1983, 'Realism and the supposed poverty of sociological theory', pp. 107–21 in Cohen, R.S. and Wartofsky, M.W. (eds.), *Epistemology, methodology and the social sciences* (Reidel, Dordrecht and Boston).

Jaynes, E.T. 1957, 'Information theory and statistical mechanics', *Physics Review*, 106: 620–30.

Jencks, C. 1987, *What is postmodernism?* (St. Martin's Press, New York).

Johnson, B.W. and McCulloch, R.E. 1987, 'Added variable plots in linear regression', *Technometrics*, 29: 427–33.

Johnston, R.J. 1971, *Urban residential patterns* (George Bell, London).

Johnston, R.J. 1973, 'Social area change in Melbourne, 1961–1966: a sample exploration', *Australian Geographical Studies*, 11: 79–98.

Johnston, R.J. 1976a, *The world trade system* (George Bell, London).

Johnston, R.J. 1976b, 'Classification in geography', *Concepts and Techniques in Modern Geography*, 6.

Johnston, R.J. 1976c, 'Residential area characteristics: research methods for identifying urban sub-areas. Social area analysis and factorial ecology', in Herbert, D.T. and Johnston, R.J. (eds.), *Social areas in cities*, volume 1 (John Wiley, Chichester).

Johnston, R.J. 1977, 'Principal components analysis and

factor analysis in geographical research: some problems and issues', *South African Geographical Journal*, 59: 30–44.

Johnston, R.J. 1978, *Multivariate statistical analysis in geography: a primer on the general linear model* (Longman, London and New York).

Johnston, R.J. 1979, *Political, electoral and spatial systems* (Oxford University Press, Oxford).

Johnston, R.J. 1981, 'Applied geography, quantitative analysis and ideology', *Applied Geography*, 1: 213–19.

Johnston, R.J. 1982a, *Geography and the state* (Macmillan, London).

Johnston, R.J. 1982b, 'On the nature of human geography', *Transactions of the Institute of British Geographers*, new series, 7: 123–5.

Johnston, R.J. 1983, *Philosophy and human geography: an introduction to contemporary approaches* (Edward Arnold, London).

Johnston, R.J. 1984a, 'A foundling floundering in world three', pp. 39–56 in Billinge, M., Gregory, D. and Martin, R.L. (eds.), *Recollections of a revolution: geography as spatial science* (Macmillan, London).

Johnston, R.J. 1984b, 'The world is our oyster', *Transactions of the Institute of British Geographers*, new series, 9: 443–59.

Johnston, R.J. 1984c, 'Marxist political economy, the state and political geography', *Progress in Human Geography*, 8: 473–92.

Johnston, R.J. 1984d, 'Quantitative ecological analysis in human geography: an evaluation of four problem areas', pp. 131–41 in Bahrenberg, G., Fischer, M.M. and Nijkamp, P. (eds.), *Recent developments in spatial data analysis: methodology, measurement, models* (Gower, Aldershot).

Johnston, R.J. 1986a, *On human geography* (Basil Blackwell, Oxford).

Johnston, R.J. 1986b, 'Job markets and housing markets in the "developed world"', *Tijdschrift voor Economische en Sociale Geografie*, 77: 328–35.

Johnston, R.J. 1988, 'There's a place for us', *New Zealand Geographer*, 44: 8–13.

Johnston, R.J. 1989a, 'Philosophy, ideology and geography', pp. 48–66 in Gregory, D. and Walford, R. (eds.), *Horizons in human geography* (Macmillan, London).

Johnston, R.J. 1989b, *Environmental problems: nature, economy and state* (Belhaven Press, London).

Johnston, R.J. 1993, 'The geographer's degree of freedom: Wreford Watson, postwar progress in human geography, and the future of scholarship in UK geography', *Progress in Human Geography*, 17: 319–32.

Johnston, R.J. 1997, *Geography and geographers: Anglo-American human geography since 1945* (Edward Arnold, London), 5th edition.

Johnston, R.J. and Hay, A.M. 1983, 'Voter transition probability estimates: an entropy-maximising approach', *European Journal of Political Research*, 11: 93–8.

Johnston, R.J. and Hunt, A.H. 1977, 'Voting power in the EEC's Council of Ministers: an essay on method in political geography', *Geoforum*, 8: 1–9.

Johnston, R.J. and Pattie, C.J. 1991, 'Evaluating the use of entropy-maximising procedures in the study of voting patterns: 1 Sampling and measurement error in the flow-of-the-vote matrix and the robustness of estimates', *Environment and Planning A*, 23: 411–20.

Johnston, R.J. and Pattie, C.J. 1993, 'Entropy-maximising and the iterative proportional fitting procedure', *Professional Geographer*, 45: 317–22.

Johnston, R.J. and Rossiter, D.J. 1983, 'Constituency building, political representation and electoral bias in urban England', pp. 113–56 in Herbert, D.T. and Johnston, R.J. (eds.), *Geography and the urban environment: progress in research and applications*, volume 5 (John Wiley, Chichester).

Johnston, R.J. and Wrigley, N. 1981, 'Urban geography', pp. 335–51 in Wrigley, N. and Bennett, R.J. (eds.), *Quantitative geography: a British view* (Routledge and Kegan Paul, London).

Johnston, R.J., Hay, A.M. and Rumley, D. 1984, 'Entropy-maximising methods for estimating voting data: a critical test', *Area*, 5: 35–41.

Johnston, R.J., Pattie, C.J. and Allsop, J.G. 1988, *A nation dividing: the electoral map of Great Britain 1979–1987* (Longman, Harlow).

Johnston, R.J., Gregory, D. and Smith, D.M. 1994, 'Marxist geography', pp. 365–73 in Johnston, R.F., Gregory, D. and Smith, D.M. (eds.), *The dictionary of human geography* (Blackwell, Oxford), 3rd edition.

Jonas, A. 1988, 'A new regional geography of localities', *Area*, 20: 101–10.

Jones, G.E. 1973, *Rural life: patterns and processes* (Longman, London).

Jones, III, J.P. 1984, 'A spatially varying parameter model of AFDC participation: empirical analysis using the expansion method', *Professional Geographer*, 36: 455–61.

Jones, III, J.P. 1987, 'Work, welfare and poverty among black female-headed families', *Economic Geography*, 63: 20–34.

Jones, III, J.P. and Kodras, J.E. 1986, 'The policy content of the welfare debate', *Environment and Planning A*, 18: 63–72.

Jones, K. 1984, 'Graphical methods for exploring relationships', pp. 215–27 in Bahrenberg, G., Fischer, M.M. and Nijkamp, P. (eds), *Recent developments in spatial data analysis: methodology, measurement, models* (Gower, Aldershot).

Jones, K. 1991, 'The specification and estimation of multi-level models', *Transactions of the Institute of British Geographers*, new series, 16: 148–60.

Jones K. 1994, 'Analysing and designing extensive studies in which place matters: a comment on neighbourhood incivilities and the study of crime in lace', *Area*, 26: 79–81.

Jones, K. and Duncan, C. 1995, 'Individuals and their ecologies: analysing the geography of chronic illness within a multi-level modelling framework', *Health and Place*, 1: 27–40.

Jones, K. and Duncan, C. 1996, 'People and places: the multilevel model as a general framework for the quantitative analysis of geographical data', pp. 79–104 in Longley, P. and Batty, M. (eds.), *Spatial analysis: modelling in a*

*GIS environment* (GeoInformation International, Cambridge).

Jones, K. and Moon, G. 1990, 'A multi-level approach to immunisation update', *Area*, 22: 264–71.

Jones, K., Johnston, R.J. and Pattie, C.J. 1992, 'People, places, regions: exploring the use of multi-level modelling in the analysis of electoral data', *British Journal of Political Science*, 23: 343–80.

Jones, O. 1995, 'Lay discourse of the rural: developments and implications for rural studies', *Journal of Rural Studies*, 11: 35–49.

Jones, P.M. 1979, 'HATS: a technique for investigating household decisions', *Environment and Planning A*, 11: 59–70.

Jones, S. 1985, 'Depth interviewing/the analysis of depth interviews', pp. 45–87 in Walker, R. (ed.), *Applied qualitative research* (Gower, Aldershot).

Joseph, A.E., Smit, B. and McIlvrey, G.P. 1989, 'Consumer preference for rural residences: a conjoint analysis in Ontario, Canada', *Environment and Planning A*, 21: 47–63.

Kaiser, H.F. 1959, 'Computer programs for varimax rotation in factor analysis', *Educational Psychology Measurement*, 19: 413–20.

Kaiser, H.F. 1966, 'An objective method for establishing legislative districts', *Midwest Journal of Political Science*, 10: 80–96.

Kalos, M.H. and Whitlock, P.A. 1986, *Monte Carlo methods.* volume 1, *Basics* (Wiley, New York).

Kalton, G. 1983, *Introduction to survey sampling and applications in the social sciences* (Sage, Beverly Hills).

Kates, R.W. 1962, 'Hazard and choice perception in flood plain management', *Research Papers, Department of Geography, University of Chicago*, No. 78.

Kaufman, L. 1990, *Finding groups in data: an introduction to cluster analysis* (Wiley, Chichester).

Kellerman, A. 1987, 'Structuration theory and attempts at integration in human geography', *Professional Geographer*, 39: 267–74.

Kelly, G.A. 1955, *The psychology of personal constructs* (Norton, New York), 2 vols.

Kelton, C.M.L. 1984, 'Non-stationary Markov modeling: an application to wage-influenced industrial relocation', *International Regional Science Review*, 9: 75–90.

Kelton, W.D. and Kelton, C.M.L. 1984, 'Hypothesis tests for Markov process models estimated from aggregate frequency data', *Journal of the American Statistical Association*, 79: 922–48.

Kelton, W.D. and Kelton, C.M.L. 1985, 'Development of specific hypothesis tests for estimated Markov chains', *Journal of Statistical Computation and Simulation*, 23: 15–39.

Kemper, F.-J. 1984, 'Categorical regression models for large samples', pp. 303–16 in Bahrenberg, G., Fischer, M.M. and Nijkamp, P. (eds.), *Recent developments in spatial data analysis: methodology, measurement, models* (Gower, Aldershot).

Kendall, M.G. 1970, 'Where shall the history of statistics begin?', pp. 45–6 in Pearson, E.S. and Kendall, M.G. (eds.), *Studies in the History of Statistics and Probability: A Series of Papers*, volume 1 (Griffin, London).

Kendall, M.G. 1975, *Multivariate analysis* (Charles Griffin, London).

Kendall, M.G. 1977, 'Measurement in the study of society', pp. 35–50 in Kendall, M.G. and Plackett, R.L. (eds.), *Studies in the History of Statistics and Probability: A Series of Papers*, volume 2 (Griffin, London).

Kendall, M.G. and Yule, G.U. 1950, *An introduction to the theory of statistics* (Griffin, London).

Kennedy, B. 1979, 'A naughty world', *Transactions of the Institute of British Geographers*, new series, 4: 550–8.

Kennedy, J.J. 1983, *Analyzing qualitative data: an introductory log-linear analysis of behavioural research* (Praeger, New York).

Keyes, D.L., Basoglu, U., Kuhlmey, E.L. and Rhymer, M.L. 1976, 'Comparison of several sampling designs for geographical data', *Geographical Analysis*, 8: 295–303.

Keys, C.L. and McCracken, K.W.J. 1981, 'An ecological analysis of demographic variation in rural New South Wales', *Australian Geographer*, 15: 27–38.

Kiel, L.D. and Elliott, E. (eds.) 1996a, *Chaos theory in the social sciences: foundations and applications* (University of Michigan Press, Ann Arbor).

Kiel, L.D. and Elliott, E. 1996b, 'Exploring nonlinear dynamics with a spreadsheet: a graphical view of chaos for beginners', pp. 19–30 in Kiel, L.D. and Elliott, E. (eds.), *Chaos theory in the social sciences: foundations and applications* (University of Michigan Press, Ann Arbor).

Killen, J. 1979, 'Linear programming: the simplex method', *Concepts and Techniques in Modern Geography*, 24.

King, L.J. 1962, 'A quantitative expression of the pattern of urban settlements in selected areas of the USA', *Tijdschrift voor Economische en Sociale Geografie*, 53: 1–7.

King, L.J. 1966, 'Cross-sectional analysis of Canadian urban dimensions', *Canadian Geographer*, 10: 205–24.

King, L.J. 1969, *Statistical analysis in geography* (Prentice-Hall, Englewood Cliffs, NJ).

King, L.J. and Clark, G.L. 1978, 'Regional unemployment patterns and the spatial dimensions of macro-economic policy: the Canadian experience 1966–75', *Regional Studies*, 12: 283–96.

King, L.J. and Jeffrey, D. 1972, 'City classification by oblique-factor analysis of time-series data', pp. 225–46 in Berry, B.J.L. (ed.), *City classification handbook* (John Wiley, New York).

King, R.B. 1971, 'Varimax and generality', *Area*, 4: 30.

King, R.B., Baillie, I.C., Bissett, P.G., Grimble, R.J., Johnson, M.S. and Silva, G.L. 1986, *Land resource survey of Toledo District, Belize* (Land Resources Development Centre, Overseas Development Administration, Surbiton, Surrey).

Kirkpatrick, S., Gelatt, C. and Vecchi, M. 1983, 'Optimization by simulated annealing', *Science*, 220: 671–80.

Kish, L. 1965, *Survey sampling* (Wiley, New York).

Kitchin, R.M. 1996, 'Increasing the integrity of cognitive mapping research', *Progress in Human Geography*, 20: 56–84.

Kitzinger, J. 1994, 'The methodology of focus groups: the importance of interaction between research participants', *Sociology of Health and Illness*, 16: 103–26.

Knox, E.G. 1964a, 'Detection of space-time interactions', *Applied Statistics*, 13: 25–9.

Knox, E.G. 1964b, 'Epidemiology of childhood leukaemia in Northumberland and Durham', *British Journal of Preventative and Social Medicine*, 18: 17–24.

Koizumi, A. and Inakazu, T. 1989, 'A multipurpose optimization model for area-wide sewerage systems', *Environment and Planning A*, 21: 1015–26.

Kolmogorov, A.N. 1933, 'Sulla determinazione empirica di una legge di distribuzione', *Giorn. Ist. Ital. Attuari*, 4: 83–91.

Korth, B. and Tucker, L. 1975, 'The distribution of chance congruence coefficients from simulated data', *Psychometrika*, 40: 361–72.

Kreibich, V. 1979, 'Modelling car availability, modal split and trip distribution by Monte Carlo simulation: a short way to integrated models', *Transportation*, 8: 153–66.

Krumbein, W.C. and Graybill, F.A. 1965, *An introduction to statistical models in geology* (McGraw Hill, New York), pp. 318–57.

Kruskal, J.B. 1964, 'Non-metric methods: a numerical method', *Psychometrika*, 29: 115–29.

Kuehn, A.A. and Hamburger, M.J. 1963, 'A heuristic program for locating warehouses', *Management Science*, 9: 643–66.

Kuhn, H.W. and Kuenne, R.E. 1962, 'An efficient algorithm for the numerical solution of the generalized Weber problem in spatial economics', *Journal of Regional Science*, 4(2): 21–33.

Kuhn, T.S. 1970, *The structure of scientific revolutions* (University of Chicago Press, Chicago), 2nd edition.

Lake, R.W. 1993, 'Planning and applied geography: positivism, ethics and geographic information systems', *Progress in Human Geography*, 17: 404–13.

Lakhan, V.C., Heron, R. and De Souza, P.D. 1995, 'Log-linear analysis of factors contributing to the post-independence decline of Guyana's rice industry', *Applied Geographer*, 15: 147–59.

Lakshmanan, T.R. and Hansen, W.G. 1965, 'A retail market potential model', *Journal of the American Institute of Planners*, 31: 134–43.

Lam, N.S.N. and De Cola, L. (eds.), 1993, *Fractals in geography* (Prentice-Hall, Englewood Cliffs, NJ).

Lancaster, A. and Nickell, J. 1980, 'The analysis of re-employment probabilities for the unemployed', *Journal of the Royal Statistical Society*, 143A: 141–65.

Lancaster, K. 1971, *Consumer demand: a new approach* (Columbia University Press, New York).

Langford, I.H. 1994, 'Using empirical Bayes estimates in the geographical analysis of disease risk', *Area*, 26: 142–9.

Langford, I.H. and Bentham, G. 1997, 'A multilevel model of sudden infant death syndrome in England and Wales', *Environment and Planning A*, 29: 629–40.

Langton, J. 1972, 'Potentialities and problems of adapting a systems approach to the study of change in human geography', pp. 125–79 in Board, C. et al (eds.), *Progress in geography*, volume 4 (Edward Arnold, London).

Lavan, A. 1987, 'Questionnaires', pp. 73–8 in Kane, E. (ed.), *Doing your own research: basic descriptive research in the social sciences and humanities* (Marion Boyars, London).

Lawson, V.A. and Staeheli, L.A. 1990, 'Realism and the practice of geography', *Professional Geographer*, 42: 13–20.

Le Bourdais, C. and Beaudry, M. 1988, 'The changing residential structure of Montreal: 1971–81', *Canadian Geographer*, 32: 98–113.

Lee, T.R. 1977, *Race and residence: the concentration and dispersal of immigrants in London* (Clarendon Press, Oxford).

Lees, L. and Longhurst, R. 1995, 'Feminist geography in Aotearoa/New Zealand: a workshop', *Gender, Place, Culture*, 2: 217–22.

Lefebvre, H. 1976, *The survival of capitalism* (Allison and Busby, London).

Lefebvre, H. 1977, 'Reflections on the politics of space', pp. 339–52 in Peet, R. (ed.), *Radical geography* (Maaroufa Press, Chicago).

Le Heron, R.B. 1993, *Globalized agriculture* (Paul Chapman Publishing, London).

Leigh, R. and North, D.J. 1978, 'The potential of the micro-behavioural approach to regional analysis, pp. 46–66 in Batey, P.W.J. (ed.), *Theory and methodology in urban and regional analysis* (London Papers in Regional Science, No. 8) (Pion, London).

Leighly, J. 1954, 'Innovation and area', *Geographical Review*, 44: 439–41.

Leighly, J. (ed.), 1963, *Land and life: selections from the writings of Carl Ortwin Sauer* (University of California Press, Berkeley and Los Angeles).

Leitmann, G. (ed.), 1976, *Multicriteria decision making and differential games* (Plenum Press, New York and London).

Leitner, H. 1989, 'Urban geography: the urban dimension of economic, political and social restructuring', *Progress in Human Geography*, 13: 551–65.

Lennon, K. and Whitford, M. (eds.), 1994, *Knowing the difference: feminist perspectives in epistemology* (Routledge, London and New York).

Lenz, R.D. 1977, 'A note on the role of Bose-Einstein statistics in point pattern analysis', *Geographical Analysis*, 9: 422–8.

Leonardi, G. 1981, 'A unifying framework for public facility location problems – Part 1: A critical overview and some unresolved problems. Part 2: Some new models and extensions', *Environment and Planning A*, 13: 1001–28 and 1085–1108.

Leonardi, G. 1983, 'The use of random-utility theory in building location-allocation models', pp. 357–83 in Thisse, J.F. and Zoller, H.G. (eds.), *Locational analysis of public facilities* (North-Holland, Amsterdam).

Lesse, P.F. 1982, 'A phenomenological theory of socio-economic systems with spatial interactions', *Environment and Planning A*, 14: 869–88.

Lever, W.F. 1980, 'The operation of local labour markets in Great Britain', *Papers of the Regional Science Association*, 44: 57–8.

Lewis, J. and Townsend, A. (eds.), 1989, *The north-south divide: regional change in Britain in the 1980s* (Paul Chapman Publishing, London).

Lewis, P. 1977, *Maps and statistics* (Methuen, London).

Ley, D.F. 1974, 'The black inner city as frontier outpost: images and behavior of a Philadelphia neighborhood', *Monographs, Association of American Geographers*, No. 7.

Ley, D.F. 1980, 'Geography without man: a humanistic critique', *Research Papers, School of Geography, University of Oxford*, No. 24.

Ley, D.F. 1981, 'Behavioural geography and the philosophies of meaning', pp. 209–30 in Cox, K.R. and Golledge, R.G. (eds.), *Behavioral problems in geography revisited* (Methuen, London).

Ley, D.F. 1984, 'Inner city revitalization in Canada: a Vancouver case study', pp. 186–204 in Palen, J.J. and London, B. (eds.), *Gentrification, displacement and neighbourhood revitalization* (State University of New York Press, Albany, NY).

Ley, D.F. 1989a, 'Modernism, post-modernism and the struggle for place', pp. 44–65 in Agnew, J. and Duncan, J. (eds.), *The power of place* (Unwin Hyman, London).

Ley, D.F. 1989b, 'Fragmentation, coherence and limits to theory in human geography', in Kobayashi, A. and Mackenzie, S. (eds.), *Remaking human geography* (Unwin Hyman, London).

Ley, D.F. and Samuels, M.S. (eds.), 1978, *Humanistic geography: prospects and problems* (Maaroufa Press, Chicago).

Liaw, K.-L., 1990, 'Joint effects of personal factors and ecological variables on the interprovincial migration pattern of young adults in Canada: a nested logit analysis', *Geographical Analysis*, 22: 189–208.

Liaw, K.-L. and Ledent, J. 1987, 'Nested logit model and maximum quasi-likelihood method: a flexible methodology for analyzing inter-regional migration pattern', *Regional Science and Urban Economics*, 17: 67–88.

Lieberson, S. 1980, *A piece of pie: blacks and white immigrants since 1880* (University of California Press, Berkeley).

Liebertrau, A.M. and Karr, A.F. 1977, 'The role of Maxwell-Boltzmann and Bose-Einstein statistics in point pattern analysis', *Geographical Analysis*, 9: 418–22.

Lillesand, T.M. and Kiefer, R.W. 1987, *Remote sensing and image interpretation* (John Wiley and Sons, Chichester), 2nd edition.

Lilliefors, W.H. 1967, 'On the Kolmogorov-Smirnov test for normality with mean and variance unknown', *Journal of the American Statistical Association*, 62: 399–402.

Lindley, D.V. and Smith, F.M. 1972, 'Bayes estimates for the linear model', *Journal of the Royal Statistical Society Series B*, 34: 1–41.

Liossatos, P. 1980, 'Spatial dynamics: some conceptual and mathematical issues', *Environment and Planning A*, 12: 1051–71.

Lloyd, R. 1993, 'Cognitive processes and cartographic maps', pp. 141–69 in Garling, T. and Golledge, R.G. (eds.), *Behavior and environment: psychological and geographical approaches* (Elsevier/North Holland, Amsterdam).

Lo, C.P. 1976, *Geographical applications of aerial photographs* (Crane, Russak, New York).

Lo, C.P. 1986, *Applied remote sensing* (Longman, London).

Lo, L. 1990, 'A translog approach to consumer spatial behavior', *Journal of Regional Science*, 30: 393–413.

Loftin, C. and Ward, S.K. 1983, 'A spatial auto-correlation model of the effects of population density on fertility', *American Sociological Review*, 48: 121–8.

Logan, M.I. 1978, 'Future developments in urban geography', *Australian Geographer*, 14: 66–7.

London Research Centre (LRC), 1992, *1991 Greater London Transport Survey* (LRC, London).

Longhurst, R. 1996, 'Refocusing groups: pregnant women's geographical experiences of Hamilton, New Zealand/ Aotearoa', *Area*, 28: 143–9.

Longley, P.A. and Batty, M. (eds.), 1996, *Spatial analysis: modelling in a GIS environment* (GeoInformation International, Cambridge).

Longley, P.A. and Clarke, G. (eds.), 1995a, *GIS for business and service planning* (GeoInformation International, Cambridge).

Longley, P.A. and Clarke, G. (eds.), 1995b, 'Applied geographical information systems: developments and prospects', pp. 3–9 in Longley, P. and Clarke, G. (eds.), *GIS for business and service planning* (GeoInformation International, Cambridge).

Longley, P.A., Goodchild, M.F., Maguire, D.J. and Rhind, D.W. (eds.), 1997, *Geographical Information Systems: principles, techniques, management and applications* (GeoInformation International, Cambridge).

Lorenz, E.N. 1963, 'Deterministic nonperiodic flows', *Journal of Atmospheric Science*, 29: 130–41.

Lorr, M. 1983, *Cluster analysis for social scientists: techniques for analyzing and simplifying complex blocks of data* (Jossey-Bass Publishers, San Francisco).

Losch, A. 1954, *The economics of location* (Yale University Press, New Haven Conn.).

Louviere, J.J. 1981, 'A conceptual and analytical framework for understanding spatial choice', *Economic Geography*, 57: 304–14.

Lovering, J. 1985, 'Regional intervention, defence industries and the structuration of space in Britain', *Environment and Planning D: Society and Space*, 3: 85–107.

Lowe, J.C. and Moryadas, S. 1975, *The geography of movement* (Houghton Mifflin, Boston).

Lowe, M.S. and Short, J.R. 1990, 'Progress in human geography', *Progress in Human Geography*, 14: 1–11.

Lowry, I.S. 1964, *A model of metropoles* (Rand Corp., Santa Monica, Ca.).

Lowry, I.S. 1966, *Migration and metropolitan growth: two analytical models* (Chandler, San Francisco).

Loytonen, M. 1991, 'The spatial diffusion of human immunodeficiency virus type 1 in Finland', *Annals of the Association of American Geographers*, 81: 127–51.

Luckermann, F. 1958, 'Towards a more geographic economic geography', *Professional Geographer*, 10: 2–10.

Lyall, G.A. 1980, 'Planning and land assessment in Scotland – the role of the Rural Land Use Information Systems Working Party', pp. 107–18 in Thomas, M.F. and Coppock, J.T. (eds.), *Land assessment in Scotland* (Aberdeen University Press, Aberdeen).

Lynch, K. 1960, *The image of the city* (MIT Press, Cambridge, Mass.).

Lyon, D. 1994, *Postmodernity* (Open University Press, Buckingham)

Lyotard, J.-F., 1984, *The postmodern condition* (Manchester University Press, Manchester).

Mabogunje, A.L. 1970, 'System approach to a theory of rural–urban migration', *Geographical Analysis*, 2: 1–18.

McCarty, H.H. 1953, 'An approach to a theory of economic geography', *Annals of the Association of American Geographers*, 43: 183–4.

McCarty, H.H. 1954, 'An approach to a theory of economic geography', *Economic Geography*, 30: 95–101.

McCarty, H.H., Hook, J.C. and Knos, D.S. 1956, *The measurement of association in industrial geography* (Department of Geography, State University of Iowa, Iowa City).

McCullagh, M.J. and Bradshaw, R.P. 1994, 'Who goes there? Studies of pedestrian circulation in Nottingham city centre', *East Midland Geographer*, 17: 28–39.

McCullagh, P. and Nelder, J.A. 1983, *Generalised linear models* (Chapman and Hall, London).

McDowell, L. 1988, 'Coming in from the dark: feminist research in geography', pp. 155–73 in Eyles, J. (ed.), 1988, *Research in human geography: introductions and investigations* (Blackwell, Oxford).

McDowell, L. 1992a, 'Doing gender: feminism, feminists and research methods in human geography', *Transactions of the Institute of British Geographers*, 17: 399–417.

McDowell, L. 1992b, 'Valid games? A response to Erica Schoenberger', *Professional Geographer*, 44: 212–15.

McDowell, L. 1993, 'Space, place and gender relations: Part 1. Feminist empiricism and the geography of social relations; Part 2. Identity, difference, feminist geometries and geographies', *Progress in Human Geography*, 17: 157–79 and 305–18.

McElrath, D.C. 1968, 'Societal scale and social differentiation, Accra, Ghana', pp. 33–52 in Greer, S. et al (eds.), *The new urbanization* (St. Martin's Press, New York).

McEvoy, D. 1978, 'The segregation of Asian immigrants in Glasgow: a note', *Scottish Geographical Magazine*, 94: 180–2.

McFadden, D. 1974, 'Conditional logit analysis of qualitative choice behaviour', pp. 105–42 in Zarembka, P. (ed.), *Frontiers in econometrics* (Academic Press, New York).

Mackay, J.R. 1958, 'The interactance hypothesis and boundaries in Canada', *Canadian Geographer*, 11: 1–8.

McLachan, G.J. 1992, *Discriminant analysis and statistical pattern recognition* (Wiley, Chichester).

McLafferty, S.L. 1995, 'Counting for women', *Professional Geographer*, 47: 436–42.

McLafferty, S.L. and Preston, V. 1991, 'Gender, race, and commuting among service sector workers', *Professional Geographer*, 43: 1–14.

MacLaughlin, J.G. and Agnew, J.A. 1986, 'Hegemony and the regional question: the political geography of regional industrial policy in Northern Ireland, 1945–1972', *Annals of the Association of American Geographers*, 76: 247–61.

McLoughlin, J.B. 1969, *Urban and regional planning: a systems approach* (Faber, London).

McLoughlin, J.B. 1973, *Control and urban planning* (Faber, London).

Macmillan, W. (ed.), 1989a, *Remodelling geography* (Blackwell, Oxford).

Macmillan, W. 1989b, 'Quantitative theory construction in human geography', pp. 89–107 in Macmillan, W. (ed.), *Remodelling geography* (Basil Blackwell, Oxford).

Macmillan, W. 1993, 'Urban and regional modelling: getting it done and doing it right', *Environment and Planning A*, 25: 56–68.

Macmillan, W. 1995, 'Modelling: fuzziness revisited', *Progress in Human Geography*, 19: 404–13.

Macmillan, W. 1996, 'Fun and games: serious toys for city modelling in a GIS environment', pp. 153–66 in Longley, P. and Batty, M. (eds.), *Spatial analysis: modelling in a GIS environment* (GeoInformation International, Cambridge).

Macmillan, W. and Pierce, T. 1994, 'Optimization modelling in a GIS framework: the problem of political redistricting', pp. 221–46 in Fotheringham, S. and Rogerson, P. (eds.), *Spatial analysis and GIS* (Taylor and Francis, London and Bristol, Pa.).

MacNaughten, P. 1993, 'Discourses of nature: argumentation and power', pp. 52–74 in Burman, E. and Parker, I. (ed.), *Discourse analytic research: repertoires and readings of texts in action* (Routledge, London and New York).

McRobbie, A. 1994, *Postmodernism and popular culture* (Routledge, London).

Magee, B. 1973, *Popper* (Fontana Modern Masters, Glasgow).

Magnusson, D. and Bergman, L.R. 1990, *Data quality in longitudinal research* (Cambridge University Press, Cambridge).

Maguire, D.J. 1989, *Computers in geography* (Longman, Harlow).

Maguire, D.J., Goodchild, M.F. and Rhind, D.W. (eds.), 1991, *Geographical Information Systems: principles and applications* (Longman Scientific, Harlow).

Mandelbrot, B.B. 1977, *The fractal geometry of nature* (W.H. Freeman, New York).

Mandelbrot, B.B. 1982, *The fractal geometry of nature* (W.H. Freeman, New York), revised edition.

Mandelbrot, B.B. 1990, 'Fractals – a geometry of nature', *New Scientist*, 1734, 15 Sept.: 22–7.

Manly, B.F.J. 1978, 'Regression models for proportions with extraneous variance', *Biometrie-Praximetrie*, 18: 1–18.

Manly, B.F.J. 1986, *Multivariate statistical methods: a primer* (Chapman & Hall, London).

Mann, H.B. and Whitney, D.R. 1947, 'On a test of whether one of two random variables is stochastically larger than the other', *Annals of Mathematics and Statistics*, 18: 50–60.

Mannion, A.M. 1992, 'Acidification and eutrophication', pp. 177–96 in Mannion, A.M. and Bowlby, S.R. (eds.), *Environmental issues in the 1990s* (John Wiley & Sons, Chichester).

Mantel, N. 1967, 'The detection of disease clustering and a generalised regression approach', *Cancer Research*, 27: 209–20.

March, L., Echenique, M. and Dickens, P. 1971, 'Models of environment', *Architectural Design*, 41: 275–322.

Marchand, B. 1972, 'Information theory and geography', *Geographical Analysis*, 4: 234–57.

Marchand, B. 1978, 'A dialectical approach in geography', *Geographical Analysis*, 10: 105–19.

Marchand, M.H. (ed.), 1995, *Feminism, postmodernism, development* (Routledge, London).

Mark, D.M. and Peucker, T.K. 1978, 'Regression analysis and geographic models', *Canadian Geographer*, 22: 51–64.

Marshall, J.U. 1985, 'Geography as a scientific enterprise', pp. 113–28 in Johnston, R.J. (ed.), *The future of geography* (Methuen, London).

Marshall, R.J. 1991, 'Mapping disease and mortality rates using empirical Bayes estimators', *Applied Statistics*, 40: 283–94.

Martin, D. 1991, *Geographic Information Systems and their socio-economic applications* (Routledge, Chapman and Hall, Andover).

Martin, D. 1997, 'Geographical information systems and spatial analysis', pp. 213–30 in Flowerdew, R. and Martin, D. (eds.), *Methods in human geography: a guide for students doing a research project* (Longman, Harlow).

Martin, R.L. 1979, 'Subregional Phillips curves, inflationary expectations and the intermarket relative wage structure: substance and methodology', pp. 64–110 in Wrigley, N. (ed.), *Statistical applications in the spatial sciences* (Pion, London).

Martin, R.L. 1988, 'The political economy of Britain's north-south divide', *Transactions of the Institute of British Geographers*, new series, 13: 389–418.

Martin, R.L., Thrift, N.J. and Bennett, R.J. 1978, *Towards the dynamic analysis of spatial systems* (Pion, London).

Marx, K. 1967, *Capital* (International Publishers, New York).

Marx, K. 1971, *A contribution to the critique of political economy* (Lawrence and Wishart, London).

Marx, K. 1973, *Grundrisse* (Penguin Books, Harmondsworth).

Mason, J. 1996, *Qualitative researching* (Sage Publications, London).

Massam, B.H. 1988. 'Multi-criteria decision-making', *Progress in Planning*, 30(1).

Masser, I. and Blakemore, M. (eds.), 1991, *Handling geographic information: methodology and potential applications* (Longman Scientific, Harlow).

Masser, I. and Brown, P.J.B. 1975, 'Hierarchical aggregation procedures for spatial interaction data', *Environment and Planning A*, 7: 509–23.

Massey, D. and Denton, N. 1993, *Apartheid American style* (Harvard University Press, Cambridge, Mass.).

Massey, D.B. 1973, 'A critique of industrial location theory', *Antipode*, 5(3): 33–9.

Massey, D.B. 1976, *Industrial location theory reconsidered* (Open University, Milton Keynes).

Massey, D.B. 1978, 'Regionalism: some current issues', *Capital and Class*, 6: 106–25.

Massey, D.B. 1979, 'A critical evaluation of industrial location theory', pp. 57–72 in Hamilton, F.E.I. and Linge, G.R.J. (eds.), *Spatial analysis, industry and the industrial environment*, volume 1 (John Wiley, Chichester).

Massey, D.B. 1984, *Spatial divisions of labour: social structures and the geography of production* (Macmillan, London and Basingstoke).

Massey, D.B. 1994, *Space, place and gender* (Polity Press, Cambridge).

Massey, D.B. 1996, *Spatial divisions of labour: social structures and the geography of production* (Macmillan, London and Basingstoke), 2nd edition.

Massey, D.B. and Allen, J. (eds.), 1984, *Geography matters!* (Cambridge University Press, Cambridge).

Massey, D.B. and Meegan, R. 1982, *Anatomy of job loss* (Methuen, Andover).

Mather, P.M. 1971, 'Varimax and generality', *Area*, 3: 252–4.

Mather, P.M. 1976, *Computers in geography: a practical approach* (Blackwell, Oxford).

Mather, P.M. 1987, *Computer processing of remotely-sensed images* (John Wiley and Sons, Chichester).

Matthews, J.A. 1981, *Quantitative and statistical approaches to geography: a practical manual* (Pergamon Press, Oxford).

Matthews, M.H. 1984, 'Environmental cognition of young children: images of journeys to school and home area', *Transactions of the Institute of British Geographers*, new series, 9: 89–105.

Matthews, M.H. 1995a, 'Culture, environmental experience and environmental awareness: making sense of young Kenyan children's views of place', *Geographical Journal*, 161: 285–95.

Matthews, M.H. 1995b, 'Living on the edge; children as "outsiders"'. *Tijdschrift voor Economische en Social Geografie*, 86: 456–66.

Mattingly, D.J. and Falconer-Al-Hindi, K. 1995, 'Should women count? A context for the debate', *Professional Geographer*, 47: 427–35.

May, T. 1993, *Social research: issues, methods and process* (Open University Press, Buckingham).

Mead, M. 1942, *Growing up in New Guinea: a study of adolescence and sex in primitive society* (Penguin, London).

Medvedkov, Y.V. 1967, 'The concept of entropy in settlement pattern analysis', *Papers of the Regional Science Association*, 18: 165–8.

Medvedkov, Y.V. 1970, 'Entropy: an assessment of potentialities in geography', *Economic Geography*, 46: 306–16.

Meinig, D.W. (ed.), 1979, *The interpretation of ordinary landscapes: geographical essays* (Oxford University Press, New York).

Meinig, D.W. 1983, 'Geography as an art', *Transactions of the Institute of British Geographers*, new series, 8: 314–28.

Mercer, D.C. 1984, 'Unmasking technocratic geography', pp. 153–99 in Billinge, M., Gregory, D. and Martin, R.L. (eds.), *Recollections of a revolution: geography as spatial science* (Macmillan, London).

Mies, M. 1991, 'Women's research or feminist research? The debate surrounding feminist science and methodology', pp. 60–84 in Fonow, M.M. and Cook, J.A. (eds.), *Beyond methodology: feminist scholarship as lived research* (Indiana University Press, Bloomington).

Miles, M.B. and Huberman, A.M. 1993, *Qualitative data analysis: a source book of new methods* (Sage, London).

Mills, C.A. 1991, 'Fairview slopes, Vancouver: gentrification in the inner city', *Canadian Geographer*, 35: 306–10.

Mills, C.W. 1959, *The sociological imagination* (Oxford University Press, New York).

Mills, G. 1967, 'The determination of local government electoral boundaries', *Operational Research Quarterly*, 18: 243–55.

Minnery, J. 1981, 'Urban planning and scientific method', *Planner* (*Queensland*), 21(1): 34–40.

Mirchandari, P.B. and Reilly, 1987, 'Spatial distribution design for fire fighting units', pp. 186–223 in Ghosh, A. and Rushton, G. (eds.), *Spatial analysis and location-allocation models* (Van Nostrand Reinhold, New York).

Miron, J. 1984, 'Spatial autocorrelation in regression analysis: a beginner's guide', pp. 201–22 in Gaile, G.L. and Willmott, C.J. (eds) *Spatial statistics and models* (D. Reidel, Dordrecht).

Mitchell, B. 1971, 'A comparison of chi-square and Kolmogorov-Smirnov tests', *Area*, 3: 237–41.

Mitchell, B. 1974, 'Three approaches to resolving problems arising from assumption violation during statistical analysis in geographical research', *Cahiers de Geographie du Quebec*, 18: 507–23.

Molinero, C.M. 1988, 'A multidimensional scaling analysis of the 1986 ratings of universities in the United Kingdom', *Higher Education Review*, 21: 7–25.

Momsen, J.D. and Townsend, J. (eds.), 1987, *Geography and gender in the Third World* (Hutchinson, London).

Moore, G.C. and ReVelle, C.S. 1982, 'The hierarchical service location problem', *Management Science*, 28: 775–80.

Moore, L. 1989, 'Modelling store choice: a segmented approach using stated preference analysis', *Transactions of the Institute of British Geographers*, new series, 14: 461–77.

Moran, P.A.P. 1948, The interpretation of statistical maps, *Journal of the Royal Statistical Society*, series B, 10: 243–51.

Moran, P.A.P. 1950, 'Notes on continuous stochastic phenomena', *Biometrika*, 37: 17–23.

Morgan, D.L. 1988, *Focus groups: a practical guide for applied research* (Sage Publications, Newbury Park).

Morgan, D.L. (ed.), 1993, *Successful focus groups: advancing the state of the art* (Sage Publications, Newbury Park).

Morrill, R.L. 1963, 'The distribution of migration distances', *Papers and Proceedings of the Regional Science Association*, 2: 75–84.

Morrill, R.L. 1965, 'Migration and the growth of urban settlement', *Lund Studies in Geography*, Series B, 24.

Morrill, R.L. 1969, 'Geography and the transformation of society', *Antipode*, 1(1): 6–9.

Morrill, R.L. 1970a, *The spatial organisation of society* (Wadsworth, Belmont, Ca.).

Morrill, R.L. 1970b, 'Geography and the transformation of society: part II', *Antipode*, 2(1): 4–10.

Morrill, R.L. 1984, 'Recollections of the "Quantitative Revolution's" early years: the University of Washington 1955–65', pp. 57–72 in Billinge, M., Gregory, D. and Martin, R.L. (eds), *Recollections of a revolution: geography as spatial science* (Macmillan, London).

Morrill, R.L. 1985, 'The diffusion of the use of tractors again', *Geographical Analysis*, 17: 88–94.

Morrill, R.L. 1990, 'Regional demographic structure of the United States', *Professional Geographer*, 42: 38–53.

Morrill, R.L. and Kelley, M.B. 1970, 'The simulation of hospital use and the estimation of location efficiency', *Geographical Analysis*, 2: 283–300.

Morrill, R.L. and Symons, J. 1977, 'Efficiency and equity aspects of optimum location', *Geographical Analysis*, 9: 215–25.

Morrill, R.L., Gaile, G.L. and Thrall, G.I. 1988, *Spatial diffusion* (Sage Publications Inc., Newbury Park).

Morris, M.S. 1996, '"Tha'lt be like a blush-rose when tha' grows up, my little lass": English cultural and gendered identity in *The Secret Garden*,' *Environment and Planning D, Society and Space*, 14: 59–78.

Morrison, D.E. and Henkel, R.E. 1970, *The significance test controversy* (Butterworths, London).

Morrison, D.F. 1976, *Multivariate statistical methods* (McGraw-Hill, New York), 2nd edition.

Moser, C.A. and Kalton, G. 1971, *Survey methods in social investigation* (Heinemann, London).

Moser, C.A. and Scott, W. 1961, *British towns: a statistical study of their social and economic differences* (Oliver and Boyd, London).

Mosimann, J. 1962, 'On the compound multinomial distribution, the multivariate beta distribution and correlation between proportions', *Biometrika*, 49: 65–82.

Moss, P. 1995, 'Embeddedness in practice, numbers in context: the politics of knowing and doing', *Professional Geographer*, 47: 442–9.

Muir, R. 1978, 'Radical geography or a new orthodoxy?', *Area*, 10: 322–7.

Muller, W. and Rohr-Zanker, R. 1989, 'The fiscal crisis and the local state: examination of the structuralist concept', *Environment and Planning A*, 21: 1619–38.

Mumford, L. 1964, *The highway and the city* (Secker and Warburg, London).

Murdie, R.A. 1976, 'Spatial form in the residential mosaic', pp. 237–72 in Herbert, D.T. and Johnston, R.J. (eds.), *Social areas in cities*, volume 1: *Spatial processes and form* (John Wiley, London).

Murphy, M.J. 1984, 'The influence of fertility, early housing-career, and socio-economic factors on tenure determination in contemporary Britain', *Environment and Planning A*, 16: 1303–18.

Myrdal, G. 1957, *Economic theory and underdeveloped regions* (Duckworth, London).

Nash, J.F. 1950, 'The bargaining problem', *Econometrica*, 18: 155–62.

Neave, H.R. and Worthington, P.L. 1988, *Distribution-free tests* (Unwin Hyman, London).

Nelder, J.A. and Wedderburn, R.W.M. 1972, 'Generalised linear models', *Journal of the Royal Statistical Society*, Series A, 135: 370–84.

Neter, J. and Wasserman, W. 1974, *Applied linear statistical models* (Richard D. Irwin, Homewood, Ill.).

Newman, J.L. 1973, 'The use of the term "hypothesis" in geography', *Annals of the Association of American Geographers*, 63: 22–7.

Neyman, J. 1950, *First course in probability and statistics* (University of California Press, Berkeley).

Neyman, J. and Pearson, E.S. 1967, *Joint statistical papers by J. Neyman and E.S. Pearson* (University of California Press, Berkeley).

Nijkamp, P. 1979, *Multidimensional spatial data and decision analysis* (John Wiley & Sons, Chichester).

Nijkamp, P. 1989, 'Multicriteria analysis: a decision support system for sustainable environmental management', pp. 203–20 in Archibugi, F. and Nijkamp, P. (eds.), *Economy and ecology: towards sustainable development* (Kluwer, Dordrecht).

Nijkamp, P. and Spronk, J. (eds.), 1981, *Multiple criteria analysis* (Gower, Aldershot).

Nijkamp, P., Rietveld, P. and Voogd, H. 1985, 'A survey of qualitative multiple criteria choice models', pp. 425–47 in Nijkamp, P., Leitner, H. and Wrigley, N. (eds.), *Measuring the unmeasurable* (Martinus Nijhoff, The Hague).

Nonn, H. 1984, 'Regions, nations', pp. 53–65 in Bailly, A. (ed.), *Les concepts de la geographie humaine* (Masson, Paris).

Norcliffe, G.B. 1977, *Inferential statistics for geographers* (Hutchinson, London); 2nd edition, 1982.

Norris, C. and Benjamin, A. 1988, *What is deconstruction?* (Academy Editions, London).

Norwood, V. and Monk, J. (eds.), 1987, *The desert is no lady: southwestern landscapes in women's writing and art* (Yale University Press, New Haven).

November, S.M., Cromley, R.G. and Cromley, E.K. 1996, 'Multi-objective analysis of school district regionalization alternatives in Connecticut', *Professional Geographer*, 48: 1–14.

O'Brien, L.G. 1983, 'Generalised linear modelling using the GLIM system', *Area*, 15: 327–36.

O'Brien, L.G. 1989, 'The statistical analysis of contingency table designs', *Concepts and Techniques in Modern Geography*, 51.

O'Brien, L.G. 1992, *Introducing quantitative geography: measurement, methods and generalised linear models* (Routledge, London).

O'Brien, L.G. and Wrigley, N. 1980, 'Computer software for the analysis of categorical data', *Area*, 12: 263–8.

O'Brien, L.G. and Wrigley, N. 1984, 'A generalised linear models approach to categorical data analysis: theory and applications in geography and regional science', pp. 231–51 in Bahrenberg, G., Fischer, M.M. and Nijkamp, P. (eds.), *Recent developments in spatial data analysis: methodology, measurement, models* (Gower Publications, Aldershot).

Odlund, J. 1988, *Spatial autocorrelation* (Sage, Newbury Park, Ca.).

Ofori-Amoah, B. and Hayter, R. 1989, 'Labour turnover characteristics at the European Pulp and Paper Mill, Kitimat: a log-linear analysis', *Environment and Planning A*, 21: 1491–1510.

O'Kelly, M.E. 1981, 'A model of the demand for retail facilities incorporating multistop, multipurpose trips', *Geographical Analysis*, 3: 140–56.

O'Kelly, M.E. 1987, 'Spatial-interaction-based location-allocation models', pp. 302–26 in Ghosh, A. and Rushton, G. (eds.), *Spatial analysis and location-allocation models* (Van Nostrand Reinhold, New York).

Ollman, B. 1990, 'Putting dialectics to work: the process of abstraction in Marx's method', *Rethinking Marxism*, 3: 26–74.

Ollman, B. 1993, *Dialectical investigations* (Routledge, New York).

Olsson, G. 1969, 'Inference problems in locational analysis', pp. 14–34 in Cox, K.R. and Golledge, R.G. (eds.), *Behavioral problems in Geography: A symposium* (Northwestern University Press, Evanston).

Olsson, G. 1980, *Birds in egg: eggs in bird* (Pion, London).

O'Neill, P. 1989, 'National economic change and the locality', *Environment and Planning A*, 21: 666–70.

Open University, 1983, *Statistics in society* (Open University Press, Milton Keynes).

Openshaw, S. 1978, 'An optimal zoning approach to the study of spatially aggregated data', pp. 95–113 in Masser, I. and Brown, P.J.B. (eds.), *Spatial representation and spatial interaction* (Martinus Nijhoff, Leiden).

Openshaw, S. 1983, 'The modifiable areal unit problem', *Concepts and Techniques in Modern Geography*, 38.

Openshaw, S. 1986, *Nuclear power: siting and safety* (Routledge and Kegan Paul, London).

Openshaw, S. 1989, 'Computer modelling in human geography', pp. 70–88 in Macmillan, W. (ed.), *Remodelling geography* (Blackwell, Oxford).

Openshaw, S. 1990a, 'Automating the search for cancer clusters: a review of problems, progress and opportunities', pp. 48–78 in Thomas, R.W. (ed.), *Spatial epidemiology* (Pion, London).

Openshaw, S. 1990b, 'Spatial analysis and GIS: a review of progress and possibilities', pp. 153–63 in Scholten, H.J. and Stillwell, J.C.H. (eds.), *GIS for urban and regional planning* (Kluwer Academic, Dordrecht).

Openshaw, S. 1991a, 'Developing appropriate spatial analysis methods for GIS', pp. 389–402 in Maguire, D.J., Goodchild, M.F. and Rhind, D. (eds), *Geographic Information Systems: principles and applications* (Longman, London).

Openshaw, S. 1991b, 'A view on the GIS crisis in geography, or, using GIS to put Humpty-Dumpty back together again', *Environment and Planning A*, 23: 621–8.

Openshaw, S. 1995, 'Human systems modelling as a new grand challenge area in science', *Environment and Planning A*, 27: 159–64.

Openshaw, S. 1996, 'Developing GIS-relevant zone-based spatial analysis methods', pp. 55–74 in Longley, P. and Batty, M. (eds.), *Spatial analysis: modelling in a GIS environment* (GeoInformation International, Cambridge).

Openshaw, S. and Craft, A.W. 1989, 'Some recent developments of the geographical analysis machine concept', pp. 35–8 in Elliot, P. (ed.), *Methodology of enquiries into disease clustering* (Small Area Health Statistics Unit, London).

Openshaw, S. and Goddard, J.B. 1987, 'Some implications of the commodification of information and the emerging information economy for applied geographical analysis in the UK', *Environment and Planning A*, 19: 1423–39.

Openshaw, S. and Taylor, P.J. 1979, 'A million or so correlation coefficients: three experiments on the modifiable areal unit problem', pp. 127–44 in Wrigley, N. (ed.), *Statistical applications in the spatial sciences* (Pion, London).

Openshaw, S. and Taylor, P.J. 1981, 'The modifiable areal unit problem', pp. 60–9 in Wrigley, N. and Bennett, R.J. (eds), *Quantitative geography: a British view* (Routledge and Kegan Paul, London).

Openshaw, S., Charlton, M., Wymer, C. and Craft, A.W. 1987, 'A mark I geographical analysis machine for the automated analysis of point data sets', *International Journal of Geographic Information Systems*, 1: 335–58.

Openshaw, S., Charlton, M. and Craft, A.W. 1988a, 'Searching for leukaemia clusters using a geographical analysis machine', *Papers of the Regional Science Association*, 64: 95–106.

Openshaw, S., Charlton, M., Craft, A.W. and Birch, J. 1988b, 'Investigation of leukaemia clusters by the use of a geographical analysis machine', *Lancet*, i, 272–3.

Oppenheim, A.N. 1992, *Questionnaire design, interviewing and attitude measurement* (Pinter, London).

Oppenheim, A.N. 1996, *Questionnaire design, interviewing and attitude measurement* (Pinter, London and New York), new edition reprinted.

Osgood, C.E., Suci, G.A. and Tannerbaum, P.H. 1957, *The measurement of meaning* (University of Illinois Press, Urbana, Ill.).

O'Tuathail, G. and Dalby, S. 1994, 'Critical geopolitics: unfolding spaces for thought in geography and global politics', *Environment and Planning D: Society and Space*, 12: 513–14.

Outhwaite, W. 1987, *New philosophies of science: realism, hermeneutics and critical theory* (Macmillan, London).

Palm, R. 1981a, 'Public response to earthquake hazard information', *Annals of the Association of American Geographers*, 71: 389–99.

Palm, R. 1981b, 'Women in non-metropolitan areas: a time-budget survey', *Environment and Planning A*, 13: 373–8.

Palm, R. and Caruso, D. 1972, 'Labelling in factorial ecology', *Annals of the Association of American Geographers*, 62: 122–33.

Palmer, C.J., Robinson, M.E. and Thomas, R.W. 1977, 'The countryside image', *Environment and Planning A*, 9: 739–49.

Parfitt, J. 1997, 'Questionnaire design and sampling', pp. 76–109 in Flowerdew, R. and Martin, D. (eds.), *Methods in human geography* (Longman, Harlow).

Park, R.E. and Burgess, E.W. 1921, *Introduction to the science of sociology* (University of Chicago Press, Chicago).

Park, R.E., Burgess, E.W. and McKenzie, R.D. 1925, *The city* (University of Chicago Press, Chicago).

Parkes, D.N. and Thrift, N.J. 1980, *Times, spaces and places* (John Wiley, Chichester).

Paterson, J.H. 1979, *North America* (Oxford University Press, New York), 6th edition.

Pattie, C.J. and Johnston, R.J. 1990, 'One nation or two? The changing geography of unemployment in Great Britain, 1983–1988', *Professional Geographer*, 42: 288–98.

Patton, C. 1990, *Inventing AIDS* (Routledge, London).

Payne, C. 1977a, 'The preparation and processing of survey data', pp. 41–62 in O'Muircheartaigh, C.A. and Payne, C. (eds.), *The analysis of survey data* (Wiley, London).

Payne, C. 1977b, 'The log-linear model for contingency tables', pp. 105–44 in O'Muircheartaigh, C.A. and Payne, C. (eds.), *The analysis of survey data* (Wiley, London).

Payne, C.D. (ed.), 1986, *The GLIM system: release 3.77* (Numerical Algorithms Group, Oxford).

Peach, G.C.K. 1975, *Urban social segregation* (Longman, London).

Peach, G.C.K. 1996, 'Does Britain have ghettoes?', *Transactions of the Institute of British Geographers*, new series, 21: 216–35.

Pearson, K. 1900, 'On the criterion that a given system of deviations from the probable in the case of a correlated system of variables is such that it can reasonably be supposed to have arisen from random sampling', *Philosophical Magazine*, series 5, 50: 157–75.

Peet, R. 1979, 'Societal contradiction and Marxist geography', *Annals of the Association of American Geographers*, 59: 164–9.

Peet, R.J. (ed.), 1980, *An introduction to Marxist theories of underdevelopment* (Department of Human Geography, Australian National University, Canberra).

Peet, R. 1987, 'Recent ideological tendencies in urban and regional research: neo-liberalism and social democracy', pp. 161–74 in Levine, R.H. and Lembeke, J. (eds.), *Recapturing Marxism: an appraisal of recent trends in social theory* (Praeger, New York).

Peet, R.J. 1991, *Global capitalism: theories of societal development* (Routledge, London).

Peet, R. and Thrift, N. (eds.), 1989, *New models in geography* (Unwin Hyman, London), 2 vols.

Peitgen, H.-O., Jurgens, H. and Saupe, D. 1992, *Chaos and fractals: new frontiers of science* (Springer-Verlag, New York).

Penrose, J., Bondi, L., Kofman, E., McDowell, L., Rose, G. and Whatmore, S. 1992, 'Feminism and feminists in the academy', *Antipode*, 24: 218–37.

Perle, E.D. 1977, 'Scale changes and impacts on factorial ecology structures', *Environment and Planning A*, 9: 549–58.

Perle, E.D. 1979, 'Variable mix and factor stability in urban ecology', *Geographical Analysis*, 11: 410–14.

Peuquet, D.J. 1984, 'A conceptual framework and comparison of spatial data models', *Cartographica*, 21: 66–113.

Peuquet, D.J. 1988, 'Representation of geographic space: toward a conceptual synthesis', *Annals of the Association of American Geographers*, 78: 375–94.

Pfeifer, P.E. and Deutsch, S.J. 1981, 'Seasonal space-time ARIMA modeling', *Geographical Analysis*, 13: 117–33.

Philip, M. 1985, 'Michel Foucault', pp. 51–67 in Skinner, Q. (ed.), *The return of grand theory in the human sciences* (Cambridge University Press, Cambridge).

Philo, C. 1992, 'Foucault's geography', *Environment and Planning D: Society and Space*, 10: 137–61.

Phipps, A.G. 1979, 'Scaling problems in the cognition of urban distances', *Transactions of the Institute of British Geographers*, new series, 4: 94–102.

Phipps, A.G. and Carter, J.E. 1984, 'An individual-level analysis of the stress-resistance model of household mobility', *Geographical Analysis*, 16: 176–89.

Phipps, A.G. and Carter, J.E. 1985, 'Individual differences in the residential preferences of inter-city home-owners', *Tijdschrift voor Economische en Sociale Geografie*, 76: 32–42.

Piasentin, U., Costa, P. and Foot, D.H.S. 1978, 'The Venice problem: an approach by urban modelling', *Regional Studies*, 12: 579–602.

Pickles, A.R. 1983, 'The analysis of residence histories and other longitudinal data: a continuous time Markov model incorporating exogenous variables', *Regional Science and Urban Economics*, 13: 271–85.

Pickles, A.R. 1986, 'An introduction to likelihood', *Concepts and Techniques in Modern Geography*, 42.

Pickles, A.R. 1987, 'The problem of initial conditions in longitudinal analysis', pp. 129–42 in Crouchley, R. (ed.), *Longitudinal data analysis* (Avebury, Aldershot).

Pickles, A.R. and Davies, R.B. 1985, 'The longitudinal analysis of housing careers', *Journal of Regional Science*, 25: 85–101.

Pickles, J. 1985, *Phenomenology, science and geography: spatiality and the human sciences* (Cambridge University Press, Cambridge).

Pickles, J. 1987, 'Geography and humanism', *Concepts and Techniques in Modern Geography*, 44.

Pickles, J. 1988, 'Knowledge, theory and practice: the role of practical reason in geographical theory', pp. 72–90 in Golledge, R.G., Couclellis, H. and Gould, P.R. (eds.), *A ground for common search* (Geographical Press, Santa Barbara, Ca.).

Pickles, J. 1995a, 'Representations in an electronic age: geography, GIS and democracy', pp. 1–28 in Pickles, J. (ed.), *Ground truth: the social implications of Geographic Information Systems* (Guilford Press, New York).

Pickles, J. (ed.), 1995b, *Ground truth: the social implications of Geographic Information Systems* (Guilford Press, New York).

Pickles, J. 1997, 'Tool or science? GIS, technoscience and the theoretical turn', *Annals of the Association of American Geographers*, 87: 363–72.

Pickup, L. 1988, 'Hard to get around: a study of women's travel mobility', pp. 98–116 in Little, J., Peake, L. and Richardson, P. (eds.), *Women in cities: gender and the urban environment* (Macmillan, London).

Pickvance, C. 1984, 'The structuralist critique in urban studies', pp. 31–49 in Smith, M.D. (ed.), *Cities in transform* (Sage, Beverly Hills).

Pielou, E.C. 1977, *Mathematical ecology* (Wiley, New York).

Pile, S. 1990, 'Depth hermeneutics and critical human geography', *Environment and Planning D: Society and Space*, 8: 211–32.

Pile, S. 1991, 'Practising interpretive geography', *Transactions of the Institute of British Geographers*, new series, 16: 458–69.

Pile, S. and Thrift, N.J. (eds.), 1995, *Mapping the subject: geographies of cultural transformation* (Routledge, London).

Pinder, D.A. 1978, 'Correcting underestimation in nearest neighbour analysis', *Area*, 10: 379–85.

Pinder, D.A. and Witherick, M.E. 1972, 'The principles, practice and pitfalls of nearest neighbour analysis', *Geography*, 57: 277–88.

Pinkel, D. and Nefzger, D. 1959, 'Some epidemiological features of childhood leukaemia', *Cancer*, 12: 351–8.

Piontell, A. 1992, *From fetus to child: an observational and psychoanalytic study* (Tavistock/Routledge, London).

Pipkin, J. 1981, 'The concept of choice and cognitive explanations of spatial behavior', *Economic Geography*, 57: 315–31.

Pirie, G.H. 1977, 'Charting transport cost surfaces by non-metric multidimensional scaling', *South African Geographical Journal*, 59: 60–4.

Plewis, I. 1985, *Analysing change: measurement and explanation using longitudinal data* (John Wiley and Sons, Chichester and New York).

Pocock, D.C.D. 1976, 'Some characteristics of mental maps: an empirical study', *Transactions of the Institute of British Geographers*, new series, 1: 493–512.

Pocock, D.C.D. 1981, 'Introduction: imaginative literature and the geographer', pp. 1–17 in Pocock, D.C.D. (ed.), *Humanistic geography and literature: essays on the experience of place* (Croom Helm, London).

Poole, M.A. 1982, 'Religious residential segregation in urban Northern Ireland', pp. 281–308 in Boal, F.W. and Douglas, J.N.H. (eds.), *Integration and division: geographical perspectives on the Northern Ireland problem* (Academic Press, London).

Poole, M.A. and Boal, F.W. 1973, 'Religious residential segregation in Belfast in mid-1969: a multi-level analysis', pp. 1–40 in Clark, B.D. and Gleave, M.B. (eds.), *Social patterns in cities*, IBG Special Publications, No. 5 (Institute of British Geographers, London).

Poole, M.A. and O'Farrell, P.N. 1971, 'The assumptions of the linear regression model', *Transactions of the Institute of British Geographers*, 52: 145–58.

Pooler, J. 1993, 'Structural spatial interaction', *Professional Geographer*, 45: 297–305.

Pooler, J. 1994a, 'An extended family of spatial interaction models', *Progress in Human Geography*, 18: 17–39.

Pooler, J. 1994b, 'A family of relaxed spatial interaction models', *Professional Geographer*, 46: 210–17.

Popper, K.R. 1968, *The logic of scientific discovery* (Hutchinson, London).

Popper, K.R. 1972, *Conjectures and refutations: the growth of scientific knowledge* (Routledge and Kegan Paul, London), 4th edition.

Porkess, R. 1988, *Dictionary of statistics* (Collins Reference, London and Glasgow).

Porteous, J.D. 1988a, 'Topocide: the annihilation of place', pp. 75–93 in Eyles, J. and Smith, D.M. (eds.), *Qualitative methods in human geography* (Polity Press, Cambridge).

Porteous, J.D. 1988b, *Planned to death: the destruction of the village of Howdendyke by private enterprise, politicians and planners* (Manchester University Press, Manchester).

Poston, T. and Stewart, I. 1978, *Catastrophe theory and its applications* (Pitman, London).

Poston, T. and Wilson, A.G. 1977, 'Facility size versus distance travelled: urban services and the fold catastrophe', *Environment and Planning A*, 9: 681–6.

Pratt, A.C. 1995, 'Putting critical realism to work: the practical implications for geographical research', *Progress in Human Geography*, 18: 61–74.

Pratt, G. 1989, 'Quantitative techniques and humanistic-historical materialist perspectives', pp. 101–15 in Kobayashi, A. and Mackenzie, S. (eds.), *Remaking human geography* (Unwin Hyman, Boston).

Pratt, G. 1992, 'Spatial metaphors and speaking positions', *Environment and Planning D: Society and Space*, 10: 241–4.

Pratt, G. 1994, 'Poststructuralism (including deconstruction)', pp. 468–9 in Johnston, R.J., Gregory, D. and Smith, D.M. (eds.), *The dictionary of human geography* (Edward Arnold, London).

Pratt, G. and Hanson, S. 1993, 'Women and work across the life course: moving beyond essentialism', pp. 27–54 in Katz, C. and Monk, J. (eds.), *Full circles: geographies of women over the life course* (Routledge, New York).

Pred, A.R. 1967, *Behavior and location: foundations for a geographic and dynamic location theory* (Gleerup, London).

Pred, A.R. 1971, 'Large-city interdependence and the pre-electronic diffusion of innovations in the US', *Geographical Analysis*, 3: 165–81.

Pred, A.R. 1977a, 'The choreography of existence: comments on Hagerstrand's time geography and its usefulness', *Economic Geography*, 53: 207–21.

Pred, A.R. 1977b, *City-systems in advanced economies* (Hutchinson, London).

Pred, A.R. 1978, 'The impact of technological and institutional innovations on life content: some time-geographic observations', *Geographical Analysis*, 10: 345–72.

Pred, A.R. 1979, 'The academic past through a time-geographic looking glass', *Annals of the Association of American Geographers*, 69: 175–80.

Pred, A.R. 1981a, 'Social reproduction and the time-geography of everyday life', *Geografiska Annaler*, 63B: 5–22.

Pred, A.R. 1981b, 'Production, family, and free-time projects: a time-geographic perspective on the individual and societal change in 19th century US cities', *Journal of Historical Geography*, 7: 3–36.

Pred, A.R. 1984, 'Place as historically contingent process: structuration and the time-geography of becoming places', *Annals of the Association of American Geographers*, 74: 279–97.

Pred, A.R. 1985, 'The social becomes the spatial, the spatial becomes the social: enclosures, social change and the becoming of places in Skane', pp. 337–65 in Gregory, D. and Urry, J. (eds.), *Social relations and spatial structures* (Macmillan, London).

Pred, A.R. 1986, *Place, practice and structure: social and spatial transformations in southern Sweden 1750–1850* (Barnes & Noble and Owota, New Jersey).

Pred, A.R. 1990, *Lost words and lost worlds: modernity and the language of everyday life in late 19th century Stockholm* (Cambridge University Press, Cambridge).

Prentice, R. 1975, 'The theory of games: a conceptual framework for the study of non-programmed decision-making by individuals?', *Area*, 7: 161–5.

Press, W., Flannery, B., Teukolsky, S. and Vetterling, W. 1986, *Numerical recipes* (Cambridge University Press, Cambridge).

Preston, V. 1982, 'A multidimensional scaling analysis of individual differences in residential area evaluation', *Geografiska Annaler*, 64B: 17–26.

Pringle, D. 1980, 'Causal modelling: the Simon-Blalock approach', *Concepts and Techniques in Modern Geography*, No. 27.

Putman, S.H. 1983, *Integrated urban models* (Pion, London).

Putman, S.H. and Chang, S.-H. 1989, 'Effects of spatial system design on spatial interaction models, 1: The spatial system definition problem', *Environment and Planning A*, 21: 27–46.

Quarmby, N.A. and Cushnie, J.L. 1988, 'The application of remote sensing and a GIS in Hart District, Hampshire', pp. 113–22 in Vaughan, R.A. and Kirby, R.P. (eds.), *Geographical Information Systems and remote sensing for local resource planning: an introduction for potential users in local authorities and other public sector bodies* (Remote Sensing Products and Publications, Dundee).

Quarmby, N.A. and Cushnie, J.L. 1989, 'Monitoring urban land cover changes at the urban fringe from SPOT HRV imagery in south-east England', *International Journal of Remote Sensing*, 10: 953–63.

Radcliffe, S. 1994, '(Representing) post-colonial women: authority, difference and feminism', *Area*, 26: 25–32.

Raper, J.F., Rhind, D.W. and Shepherd, J.W. 1992, *Postcodes: the new geography* (Longman, Harlow).

Rasmusen, E. 1989, *Games and information: an introduction to game theory* (Basil Blackwell, Oxford).

Ravenstein, E.G. 1885, 'The laws of migration', *Journal of the Royal Statistical Society*, 48: 167–227.

Ravenstein, E.G. 1889, 'The laws of migration', *Journal of the Royal Statistical Society*, 52: 214–301.

Read, A.D., Phillips, P.S. and Robinson, G.M. 1997, 'Landfill as a future waste management option in England: the view of landfill operators', *Resources, Conservation and Recycling*, 20: 183–205.

Reader, S. 1986, 'The statistical analysis of spatially disaggregate panel survey data', unpublished Ph.D. thesis, University of Bristol.

Rees, J. 1989, 'Regional development and policy', *Progress in Human Geography*, 13: 576–88.

Rees, P.H. 1970, 'Concepts of social space: toward an urban social geography', pp. 306–94 in Berry, B.J.L. and Horton, F.E. (eds.), *Geographic perspectives on urban systems, with integrated readings* (Prentice-Hall, Englewood Cliffs, NJ).

Rees, P.H. 1971, 'Factorial ecology: an extended definition, survey and critique of the field', *Economic Geography*, 47, Supplement: 220–33.

Rees, P.H. 1972, 'Problems of classifying subareas within cities', pp. 265–330 in Berry, B.J.L. (ed.), *City classification handbook: methods and applications* (Wiley Interscience, New York).

Reilly, W. 1931, *The law of retail gravitation* (Knickerbocker Press, New York).

Relph, E. 1976, *Place and placelessness* (Pion, London).

Relph, E. 1981, 'Phenomenology', pp. 99–114 in Harvey, M.E. and Holly, B.P. (eds.), *Themes in geographic thought* (Croom Helm, London).

Relph, E. 1989, 'A curiously unbalanced condition of the powers of the mind: realism and the ecology of environmental experience', pp. 123–37 in Boal, F.W. and Livingstone, D.N. (eds.), *The behavioural environment:essays in reflection, application and re-evaluation* (Routledge, London).

ReVelle, C. and Swain, R. 1970, 'Central facilities location', *Geographical Analysis*, 2: 30–42.

Rhind, D.W. 1981, 'Geographical information systems in Britain', pp. 17–25 in Wrigley, N. and Bennett, R.J. (eds.), *Quantitative geography: a British view* (Routledge and Kegan Paul, London).

Rhind, D.W. 1989, 'Computing, academic geography and the world outside', pp. 177–90 in Macmillan, W. (ed.), *Remodelling geography* (Blackwell, Oxford).

Rhind, D.W. 1993, 'Maps, information and geography: a new relationship', *Geography*, 78: 150–9.

Richard, D., Beguin, H. and Peeters, D. 1990, 'The location of fire stations in a rural environment: a case study', *Environment and Planning A*, 22: 39–52.

Richards, K. and Wrigley, N. 1996, 'Geography in the United Kingdom 1992–1996', *Geographical Journal*, 162: 41–62.

Ripley, B.D. 1981, *Spatial statistics* (John Wiley, Chichester and New York).

Ripley, B.D. 1984, 'Present position and potential developments: some personal views. Statistics in the natural sciences', *Journal of the Royal Statistical Society A*, 147: 340–8.

Ripley, B.D. 1987, 'Spatial point pattern analysis in ecology', pp. 407–29 in Leghendre, P. and Leghendre, L. (eds.), *Developments in numerical ecology* (Springer, Berlin).

Ripley, B.D. 1988, *Statistical inference for spatial processes* (Cambridge University Press, Cambridge).

Robinson, A.H. 1956, 'The necessity of weighting values in correlation analysis of area data', *Annals of the Association of American Geographers*, 46: 233–6.

Robinson, A.H. and Bryson, R.A. 1957, 'A method for describing quantitatively the correspondence of geographical distributions', *Annals of the Association of American Geographers*, 52: 414–25.

Robinson, A.H., Lindberg, J.B. and Brinkman, L.W. 1961, 'A correlation and regression analysis applied to rural farm densities in the Great Plains', *Annals of the Association of American Geographers*, 51: 211–21.

Robinson, G.M. 1976, 'Late Victorian agriculture in the Vale of Evesham', *Research Papers, School of Geography, University of Oxford*, No. 15.

Robinson, G.M. 1981, 'A statistical analysis of agriculture in the Vale of Evesham during the "Great Agricultural Depression"', *Journal of Historical Geography*, 7: 37–52.

Robinson, G.M. 1985a, 'Agricultural change in the Belize River Valley', *Caribbean Geography*, 2: 33–44.

Robinson, G.M. 1985b, 'The adoption of peanut-growing in Belize, Central America', *Singapore Journal of Tropical Geography*, 6: 116–26.

Robinson, G.M. 1986, 'Migration: aspirations and reality amongst the youth of a small New Zealand town', *New Zealand Population Review*, 12: 217–33.

Robinson, G.M. 1988, *Agricultural change: geographical studies of British agriculture* (North British Publishing, Edinburgh).

Robinson, G.M. 1990, *Conflict and change in the countryside: rural society, economy and planning in the Developed World* (Belhaven Press, London and New York).

Robinson, G.M. 1991, 'An appreciation of James Wreford Watson, with a bibliography of his work', pp. 492–506 in Robinson, G.M. (ed.), *A social geography of Canada* (Dundurn Press, Toronto and Oxford).

Robinson, G.M. 1992, 'The RLUIS project and the development of Geographical Information Systems (GIS)', *Scottish Geographical Magazine*, 108: 22–8.

Robinson, G.M. 1996, 'Stud farming in the Hunter Valley: expansion and restructuring in the equine industry', *Australian Geographer*, 27: 133–48.

Robinson, G.M. 1997, 'Community-based planning: Canada's Atlantic Coastal Action Program (ACAP)', *Geographical Journal*, 163: 25–37.

Robinson, G.M., Gray, D.A., Healey, R.G. and Furley, P.A. 1989, 'Developing a Geographical Information System (GIS) for agricultural development in Belize, Central America', *Applied Geography*, 9: 81–94.

Robinson, J. 1994, 'White women researching/representing "others": from apartheid to postcolonialism', pp. 197–226 in Blunt, A. and Rose, G. (eds.), *Writing women and space: colonial and post-colonial geographies* (Guilford Press, New York and London).

Robinson, V. 1980, 'Lieberson's isolation index: a case study evaluation', *Area*, 12: 307–12.

Robinson, W.S. 1950, 'Ecological correlations and the behaviour of individuals', *American Sociological Review*, 15: 351–7.

Robson, B. 1969, *Urban analysis: a study of city structure with special reference to Sunderland* (Cambridge University Press, Cambridge).

Robson, S. 1989, 'Group discussions', pp. 24–36 in Robson, S. and Foster, A. (eds.), *Qualitative research in action* (Edward Arnold, London).

Roemer, J. (ed.), 1986, *Analytical Marxism* (Cambridge University Press, Cambridge).

Roemer, J. 1988, *Free to lose: an introduction to Marxist economic philosophy* (Harvard University Press, Cambridge, Mass.).

Rogerson, P.A. 1990, 'Migration analysis using data with time intervals of differing widths', *Papers of the Regional Science Association*, 68: 97–106.

Rorty, R. 1980, *Philosophy and the mirror of nature* (Blackwell, Oxford).

Rorty, R. 1989, *Contingency, irony and solidarity* (Cambridge University Press, Cambridge).

Rose, D. and O'Sullivan, O. 1993, *Introducing data analysis for social scientists* (Open University Press, Buckingham).

Rose, D., Buck, N. and Johnston, R.J. 1994, 'The British Household Panel Survey Study: a valuable new resource for geographical research', *Area*, 26: 368–76.

Rose, G. 1989, 'Locality studies and waged labour: an historical critique', *Transactions of the Institute of British Geographers*, new series. 14: 317–28.

Rose, G. 1993, *Feminism and geography: the limits of geographical knowledge* (Polity Press, Cambridge).

Rose, J.K. 1936, 'Corn yield and climate in the Corn Belt', *Geographical Review*, 26: 88–102.

Rosen, A.L. and Robinson, G.M. 1983, 'The urban cognition of students at the ITC, Enschede, the Netherlands', *ITC Journal*, 1983 (4): 364–5.

Rosser, J.B. and Rosser, M.V. 1994, 'Long wave chaos and systemic economic transformation', *World Futures*, 39: 197–207.

Rossiter, D. and Johnston, R.J. 1981, 'Program GROUP: the identification of all possible solutions to a constituency delimitation process', *Environment and Planning A*, 13: 321–38.

Roszac, T. 1973, *Where the wasteland ends* (Faber, London).

Roszac, T. 1986, *The cult of information* (Lutterworth, London).

Rowntree, L.B. 1988, 'Othodoxy and new directions: cultural/humanistic geography', *Progress in Human Geography*, 12: 575–86.

Roy, J.R. 1985, 'On forecasting choice among dependent spatial alternatives', *Environment and Planning B: Planning and Design*, 12: 479–92.

Roy, J.R. 1987, 'An alternative information theory approach for modelling spatial interaction', *Environment and Planning A*, 19: 385–94.

Roy, J.R. 1990, 'Spatial interaction modelling: some interpretations and challenges', *Environment and Planning A*, 22: 712–16.

Roy, J.R. and Lesse, P.F. 1981, 'On appropriate micro-state descriptions in entropy modelling', *Transportation Research B*, 15: 85–96.

Ruccio, D. 1988, 'The merchant of Venice or Marxism in the mathematical mode', *Rethinking Marxism*, 1: 36–68.

Ruelle, D. 1989, *Chaotic evolution and strange attractors* (Cambridge University Press, New York).

Ruelle, D. 1991, *Chance and chaos* (Princeton University Press, Princeton, NJ).

Rummel, R.J. 1970, *Applied factor analysis* (Northwestern University Press, Evanston, Ill.).

Rushton, G. 1966, 'Spatial pattern of grocery purchases by the Iowa rural population', *Bureau of Business and Economic Research Monograph, University of Iowa*, No. 9.

Rushton, G. 1969a, 'The scaling of locational preference', pp. 197–227 in Cox, K.R. and Golledge, R.G. (eds.), 'Behavioral problems in geography: a symposium', *Studies in Geography, Department of Geography, Northwestern University* No. 17.

Rushton, G. 1969b, 'Analysis of spatial behavior by revealed space preference', *Annals of the Association of American Geographers*, 59: 391–406.

Rushton, G. 1981, 'The scaling of locational preferences', pp. 69–92 in Cox, K.R. and Golledge, R.G. (eds.), *Behavioral problems in geography revisited* (Methuen, New York and London).

Rushton, G. 1987, 'Selecting the objective function in location-allocation analyses', pp. 345–64 in Ghosh, A. and Rushton, G. (eds.), *Spatial analysis and location-allocation models* (Van Nostrand Reinhold, New York).

Rushton, G. 1988, 'The Roepke Lecture in economic geography: location theory, location-allocation models, and service development planning in the Third World', *Economic Geography*, 64: 97–120.

Rushton, G. 1989, 'Applications of linear models', *Annals of Operational Research*, 18: 25–42.

Sack, R.D. 1972, 'Geography, geometry and explanation', *Annals of the Association of American Geographers*, 62: 61–78.

Sack, R.D. 1973a, 'Comment in reply', *Annals of the Association of American Geographers*, 63: 568–9.

Sack, R.D. 1973b, 'A concept of physical space in geography', *Geographical Analysis*, 5: 16–34.

Sack, R.D. 1974a, 'The spatial separatist theme in geography', *Economic Geography*, 50: 1–19.

Sack, R.D. 1974b, 'Chorology and spatial analysis', *Annals of the Association of American Geographers*, 64: 439–52.

Sack, R.D. 1980, *Conceptions of space in social thought* (Macmillan, London).

Said, E. 1978, *Orientalism* (Harper, New York).

Salins, P.D. 1971, 'Household location patterns in American metropolitan areas', *Economic Geography*, 47, Supplement: 234–48.

Salmon, W.C. 1986, 'The problem of induction', pp. 265–86 in Perry, J. and Bratman, M. (eds.), *Introduction to philosophy: classical and contemporary readings* (Oxford University Press, New York and Oxford).

Samuels, M.S. 1978, 'Existentialism and human geography', pp. 22–40 in Ley, D.W. and Samuels, M.S. (eds.), *Humanistic geography: prospects and problems* (Marooufa Press, Chicago).

Samuels, M.S. 1979, 'The biography of landscape: cause and culpability', pp. 51–88 in Meinig, D.W. (ed.), *The interpretation of ordinary landscapes: geographical essays* (Oxford University Press, New York).

Sarre, P. 1987, 'Realism in practice', *Area*, 19: 3–10.

Saunders, P.J. 1986, *Social theory and the urban question* (Hutchinson, London), 2nd edition.

Saunders, P.J. and Williams, P.R. 1986, 'The new conservatism: some thoughts on recent and future developments in urban studies', *Environment and Planning D: Society and Space*, 4: 393–9.

Saunders, P.J. and Williams, P.R. 1987, 'Hard work and its alternatives', *Environment and Planning D: Society and Space*, 5: 395–9.

Sayer, R.A. 1976, 'A critique of urban modelling', *Progress in Planning*, 6: 187–254.

Sayer, R.A. 1978, 'Mathematical modelling in regional science and political economy: some comments', *Antipode*, 10: 79–86.

Sayer, R.A. 1979, 'Epistemology and conceptions of people and nature in geography', *Geoforum*, 10: 19–44.

Sayer, R.A. 1982, 'Explanation in economic geography', *Progress in Human Geography*, 6: 68–88.

Sayer, R.A. 1984, *Method in social science: a realist approach* (Hutchinson, London).

Sayer, R.A. 1985a, 'Realism and geography', pp. 159–73 in Johnston, R.J. (ed.), *The future of geography* (Methuen, London).

Sayer, R.A. 1985b, 'The difference that space makes', pp. 49–66 in Gregory, D. and Urry, J. (eds.), *Social relations and spatial structures* (Macmillan, London).

Sayer, R.A. 1992, *Method in social science: a realist approach* (Routledge, London), 2nd edition.

Sayer, R.A. 1993, 'Postmodernist thought in geography: a realist view', *Antipode*, 25: 320–44.

Sayer R.A. 1995, *Radical political economy: a critique* (Blackwell, Oxford).

Schaefer, F.K. 1953, 'Exceptionalism in geography: a methodological examination', *Annals of the Association of American Geographers*, 43: 226–49.

Schlackman, W. 1989, 'Projective tests and enabling techniques for use in market research', pp. 58–75 in Robson, S. and Foster, A. (eds.), *Qualitative research in action* (Edward Arnold, London).

Schneider, M. 1960, 'Appendix to panel discussion on inter-area travel formulas', *Highway Research Board Bulletin*, 253: 136–8.

Schoenberger, E. 1991, 'The corporate interview as a research method in economic geography', *Professional Geographer*, 43: 180–9.

Schoepfle, B. and Church, R. 1991, 'A new network representation of a "classic" school districting problem', *Journal of Socio-Economic Planning Science*, 15: 291–3.

Scholten, H.J. 1984a, 'Residential mobility and log-linear modelling', pp. 271–87 in Bahrenberg, G., Fischer, M.M. and Nijkamp, P. (eds.), *Recent developments in spatial data analysis: methodology, measurement, models* (Gower Publications, Aldershot).

Scholten, H.J. 1984b, 'Planning for housing construction and population distribution in the Netherlands – the use of forecasting models', *Town Planning Review*, 55: 405–19.

Schuster, H. 1988, *Deterministic chaos – an introduction* (VCH, Weinheim), 2nd edition.

Schwager, S.J., Castillo-Chavez, C. and Hethcote, H.W. 1989, 'Statistical and mathematical approaches in HIV/AIDS modeling: a review', *Lecture Notes in Mathematics*, 83: 2–37.

Scott, A.J. 1969a, 'Combinatorial programming and the planning of urban and regional systems', *Environment and Planning*, 1: 125–42.

Scott, A.J. 1969b, 'On the optimal partitioning of spatially distributed point sets', pp. 57–72 in Scott, A.J. (ed.), *Studies in regional science* (Pion, London).

Scott, A.J. 1976, 'Land use and commodity production', *Regional Science and Urban Economics*, 6: 147–60.

Scott, A.J. 1980, *The urban land nexus and the state* (Pion, London).

Scott, A.J. 1984, 'Territorial reproduction and transformation in a local labour market: the animated film workers of Los Angeles', *Environment and Planning D: Society and Space*, 2: 277–307.

Scott, A.J. 1988a, *Metropolis: from the division of labor to urban form* (University of California Press, Los Angeles).

Scott, A.J. 1988b, *New industrial spaces* (Pion, London).

Scott, A.J. and Storper, M. (eds.), 1986, *Production, work, territory. The geographical anatomy of contemporary capitalism* (Allen & Unwin, Winchester, Mass.).

Seamon, D. 1979, *A geography of the lifeworld: movement, rest and encounter* (Croom Helm, London).

Seamon, D. 1984, 'Philosophical directions in behavioural geography with an emphasis on the phenomenological contribution', *Research Papers, Department of Geography, University of Chicago*, 209: 167–78.

Seamon, D. 1989, 'Humanistic and phenomenological advances in environmental design', *Humanistic Psychologist*, 17: 280–93.

Seamon, D. and Mugerauer, R. (eds.), 1985, *Dwelling, place and environment: towards a phenomenology of person and world* (Martinus Nijhoff, Dordrecht).

Segal, M.N. 1982, 'Reliability of conjoint analysis: contrasting data collection procedures', *Journal of Marketing Research*, 19: 139–44.

Senior, M.L. 1979, 'From gravity modelling to entropy maximising: a pedagogic guide', *Progress in Human Geography*, 3: 179–210.

Senior, M.L. 1981, 'Optimization: static programming methods', pp. 212–18 in Wrigley, N. and Bennett, R.J. (eds.), *Quantitative geography: a British view* (Routledge and Kegan Paul, London).

Senior, M.L. and Wilson, A.G. 1974, 'Exploration and synthesis of linear programming modes of residential location', *Geographical Analysis*, 7: 209–38.

Shankman, P. 1984, 'The thick and the thin: on the interpretive theoretical program of Clifford Geertz', *Current Anthropology*, 25: 261–79.

Shannon, C.E. 1948, 'A mathematical theory of communication', *Bell System Technical Journal*, 27: 379–423 and 623–56.

Shannon, C.E. and Weaver, W. 1963, *The mathematical theory of communication* (University of Illinois Press, Illinois), 2nd edition.

Shannon, G.W., Pyle, G.F. and Bashshur, R.L. 1991, *The geography of AIDS: origins and course of an epidemic* (Guilford Press, New York).

Shaw, G. and Wheeler, D. 1985, *Statistical techniques in geographical analysis* (John Wiley & Sons, Chichester).

Shaw, G. and Wheeler, D. 1994, *Statistical techniques in geographical analysis* (David Fulton Publishers, London).

Shaw, M. 1977, 'The ecology of social change: Wolverhampton 1851', *Transactions of the Institute of British Geographers*, new series, 2: 332–48.

Shaw, R.P. 1985, *Inter-metropolitan migration in Canada: changing determinants over three decades* (New Canada Publications, Toronto).

Shepard, R.N. 1962, 'The analysis of proximities: multidimensional scaling with an unknown distance function', *Psychometrika*, 27: 125–39.

Shepard, R.N. 1964, 'On subjectively optimum selections among multiattribute alternatives', pp. 65–86 in Shelley, M.W. and Bryan, G.L. (eds.), *Human judgements and optimality* (John Wiley and Sons, New York).

Sheppard, E.S. 1978, 'Theoretical underpinnings of the gravity hypothesis', *Geographical Analysis*, 10: 336–402.

Sheppard, E.S. 1980, 'The ideology of spatial choice', *Papers and Proceedings of the Regional Science Association*, 45: 197–213.

Sheppard, E.S. 1981, 'Public facility location with elastic demand: users' benefits and redistribution issues', *Sistemi Urbani*, 3: 435–54.

Sheppard, E.S. 1983a, 'Commodity trade, corporate ownership and urban growth', *Papers of the Regional Science Association*, 52: 175–86.

Sheppard, E.S. 1983b, 'Pasinetti, Marx, and the urban accumulation dynamic', pp. 293–322 in Griffith, D. and Lea, A.C. (eds.), *Evolving geographical structures* (Martinus Nijhoff, Dordrecht).

Sheppard, E.S. 1984, 'The distance decay gravity model debate', pp. 367–88 in Gaile, G. and Willmot, C. (eds.), *Spatial statistics and models* (D. Reidel, Dordrecht).

Sheppard, E.S. 1986, 'Modeling and predicting aggregate flows', pp. 91–118 in Hanson, S. (ed.), *The geography of urban transportation* (Guilford Press, New York and London).

Sheppard, E.S. 1987, 'A Marxian model of the geography of production and transportation in urban and regional systems', pp. 189–250 in Bertuglia, C., Leonardia, G., Ocelli, S., Rabino, G., Tadei, R. and Wilson, A.G. (eds.), *Urban systems: contemporary approaches to modelling* (Croom Helm, Andover).

Sheppard, E.S. 1990, 'Transportation in a capitalist space-economy: transportation demand, circulation time, and transportation innovations', *Environment and Planning A*, 22: 1007–25.

Sheppard, E.S. and Barnes, T.J. 1986, 'Instabilities in the geography of capitalist production: collective versus individual profit maximization', *Annals of the Association of American Geographers*, 76: 493–507.

Sheppard, E.S. and Barnes, T.J. 1990, *The capitalist space economy: geographical analysis after Ricardo, Marx and Sraffa* (Unwin Hyman, London).

Shevky, E. and Bell, W. 1955, *Social area analysis* (University of California Press, Stanford, Ca.).

Shevky, E. and Williams, M. 1949, *The social areas of Los Angeles: analysis and typology* (University of California Press, Berkeley).

Short, B.M. 1975, 'The application of multivariate statistical techniques to the study of agricultural change through time: a case study from the High Weald, 1887–1953', *Occasional Papers, Department of Geography, King's College, London*, No. 1.

Shubik, M. 1979, 'Computers and modelling', pp. 285–305 in Dertouzos, M.L. and Moses, J. (eds.), *The computer age: a twenty year view* (M.I.T. Press, Cambridge, Mass.).

Sibley, D. 1976, 'On pattern and dispersion', *Area*, 8: 163–5.

Sibley, D. 1990, 'Spatial applications of exploratory data analysis', *Concepts and Techniques in Modern Geography*, 49.

Siegal, S. 1956, *Non-parametric statistics for the behavioral sciences* (McGraw-Hill, New York).

Silk, J.A. 1979, *Statistical concepts in geography* (George Allen & Unwin, London).

Silk, J.A. 1981, 'The analysis of variance', *Concepts and Techniques in Modern Geography*, 30.

Silverman, B.W. 1986, *Density estimation for statistics and data analysis* (Chapman and Hall, London).

Silverman, D. 1985, *Qualitative methodology and sociology* (Gower, Aldershot).

Silverman, D. 1993, *Interpreting qualitative data* (Sage Publications, London).

Sim, S. 1992, 'Structuralism and post-structuralism', pp. 405–40 in Hanfling, O. (ed.), *Philosophical aesthetics* (Open University, Milton Keynes).

Simon, H.A. 1957, *Models of man* (John Wiley, New York).

Skelton, T. 1995a, 'Boom, by bye: Jamaican ragga and gay resistance', pp. 264–83 in Bell, D. and Valentine, G. (eds.), *Mapping desire: geographies of sexualities* (Routledge, London).

Skelton, T. 1995b, 'I sing dirty reality, I am out there for the ladies, Lady Saw: women and Jamaican ragga music, resisting reality', *Phoebe: Journal of Feminist Scholarship, Theory and Aesthetics*, 7: 86–104.

Skyrms, B. 1966, *An introduction to inductive logic* (Dickenson Publishing, Belmont, Ca.).

Slater, D. 1975, 'The poverty of modern geographical enquiry', *Pacific Viewpoint*, 16: 159–76.

Slater, P. 1969, 'Theory and technique of the repertory grid', *British Journal of Psychiatry*, 155(528): 1287–96.

Slocum, T.A. 1990, 'The use of quantitative methods in major geographical journals, 1956–1986', *Professional Geographer*, 42: 38–53.

Smallman-Raynor, M.R. 1995, 'AIDS in neighbourhoods of San Francisco: some geographical observations on the first decade of a local-area epidemic', pp. 168–98 in Cliff, A.D., Gould, P.R., Hoare, A.G. and Thrift, N.J. (eds.), *Diffusing geography: essays for Peter Haggett* (Blackwell, Oxford).

Smallman-Raynor, M.R. and Cliff, A.D. 1990, 'Acquired Immune Deficiency Syndrome (AIDS) in literature, geographical origins and global patterns', *Progress in Human Geography*, 14: 157–213.

Smallman-Raynor, M.R., Cliff, A.D. and Haggett, P. 1992, *London international atlas of AIDS* (Blackwell, Oxford).

Smirnov, N.V. 1939, 'Estimate of deviation between empirical distribution functions in two independent samples', *Bulletin of Moscow University*, 2: 3–16.

Smith, D.M. 1975, *Patterns in human geography* (David & Charles, Newton Abbot).

Smith, D.M. 1977, *Human geography: a welfare approach* (Edward Arnold, London).

Smith, D.M. 1979, *Where the grass is greener: living in an unequal world* (Penguin Books, Harmondsworth).

Smith, D.M. 1981, *Industrial location: an economic geographical analysis* (John Wiley, Chichester), 2nd edition.

Smith, D.M. 1984, 'Recollections of a random variable', pp. 117–33 in Billinge, M., Gregory, D. and Martin, R.L. (eds.), *Recollections of a revolution: geography as spatial science* (Macmillan, London).

Smith D.M. 1988, 'Towards an interpretive human geography', pp. 255–67 in Eyles, J. and Smith, D.M. (eds.), *Qualitative methods in human geography* (Polity Press, Cambridge).

Smith, N. 1979, 'Geography, science and post-positivist modes of explanation', *Progress in Human Geography*, 3: 356–83.

Smith, N. 1987, 'Dangers of the empirical turn: some comments on the CURS initiative', *Antipode*, 19: 59–68.

Smith, N. 1990, *Uneven development* (Basil Blackwell, Oxford), 2nd edition.

Smith, S.J. 1984, 'Practising humanistic geography', *Annals of the Association of American Geographers*, 74: 353–74.

Smith, S.J. 1989a, 'Social geography: social policy and the restructuring of welfare', *Progress in Human Geography*, 13: 118–28.

Smith, S.J. 1989b, 'Society, space and citizenship: a human geography for the "new times"?', *Transactions of the Institute of British Geographers*, new series, 14: 144–56.

Smith, S.J. and Jackson, P. 1984, *Exploring social geography* (George Allen & Unwin, London).

Smith, S.M., Scheider, H. and Wiart, R. 1987, 'Agricultural field management with micro-computer-based GIS and image analysis systems', *Proceedings of GIS '87* (University of California, Berkeley).

Smith, T.E. 1991, 'A simple decision theory of spatial interaction: the Alonso model revised', *Environment and Planning A*, 23: 1247–68.

Soja, E.W. 1980, 'The socio-spatial dialectic', *Annals of the Association of American Geographers*, 70: 207–25.

Soja, E.W. 1987, 'The postmodernization of human geography: a review essay', *Annals of the Association of American Geographers*, 77: 289–96.

Soja, E.W. 1989, *Postmodern geographies: the reassertion of space in critical social theory* (Verso, London and New York).

Soja, E.W. 1995, *Postmodern geographies: the reassertion of space in critical social theory* (Verso, London and New York), 4th edition.

Soja, E.W. and Hadjimichalis, G. 1979, 'Between geographical materialism and spatial fetishism', *Antipode*, 11(3): 3–11.

Sokal, R.R. and Oden, N.L. 1978, 'Spatial autocorrelation in biology, 1: Methodology', *Biological Journal of the Linnean Society*, 10: 199–228.

Soper, H.E. 1929, 'Interpretation of periodicity in disease prevalence', *Journal of the Royal Statistical Society A*, 92: 34–73.

Sparke, M. 1994, 'Writing on patriarchal missiles: the chauvinism of the "Gulf War" and the limits of critique', *Environment and Planning A*, 26: 1061–89.

Spencer, A.H. 1980, 'Cognition and shopping choice: a multidimensional scaling approach', *Environment and Planning A*, 12: 1235–51.

Sprague, A. 1994, 'Work experience, earnings and participation: evidence from the Women and Employment Survey', *Applied Economics*, 26: 659–67.

Sprott, J.C. and Rowlands, G. 1992, *Chaos data analyzer: IBM PC version 1.0* (American Institute of Physics, New York).

Sraffa, P. 1960, *Production of commodities by means of commodities. Prelude to a critique of economic theory* (Cambridge University Press, Cambridge).

Stacey, J. 1988, 'Can there be a feminist ethnography?', *Women's Studies International Forum*, 11: 21–7.

Stamp, L.D. 1964, 'Discussion' to Haggett (1964) *Geographical Journal*, 130: 365–78.

Stanley, L. and Wise, A. 1983, *Breaking out* (Routledge and Kegan Paul, London).

Starr, M.K. and Greenwood, P. 1977, 'Normative generation of alternatives with multiple criteria evaluation', pp. 111–27 in Starr, M.K. and Zeleny, M. (eds.), *Multiple criteria decision making: TIME studies in the management sciences*, volume 6 (North-Holland, Amsterdam).

Stevens, S.S. 1946, 'On the theory of scales of measurement', *Science*, 103: 677–80.

Stewart, D.W. and Shamsadani, P. 1990, *Focus groups: theory and practice* (Sage Publications, Newbury Park).

Stewart, I. 1989, *Does God play dice? The mathematics of chaos* (Basil Blackwell, New York).

Stewart, J.Q. and Warntz, W. 1968, 'The physics of population distributions', pp. 130–46 in Berry, B.J.L. and Marble, D.F. (eds.), *Spatial analysis: a reader in statistical geography* (Prentice-Hall, Englewood Cliffs, NJ).

Stoddart, D.R. 1965, 'Geography and the ecological approach: the ecosystem as a geographic principle and method', *Geography*, 50: 242–51.

Stoddart, D.R. 1967, 'Organism and ecosystem as geographic models', pp. 511–47 in Chorley, R.J. and Haggett, P. (eds.), *Models in geography* (Methuen, London).

Stoddart, D.R. 1981, 'Ideas and interpretation in the history of geography', pp. 1–7 in Stoddart, D.R. (ed.), *Geography, ideology and social concern* (Blackwell, Oxford).

Storper, M. and Walker, R. 1988, *The capitalist imperative: territory, technology and industrial growth* (Basil Blackwell, Oxford).

Stouffer, S. 1940, 'Intervening opportunities: a theory relating mobility and distance', *American Sociological Review*, 5: 845–67.

Straffin, P.D. 1993, *Game theory and strategy* (Mathematical Association of America, Washington DC).

Strauss, A.L. 1987, *Qualitative analysis for social scientists* (Cambridge University Press, Cambridge).

Stubbs, M. 1983, *Discourse analysis: the sociolinguistic analysis of natural language* (Basil Blackwell, Oxford).

Summerfield, M.A. 1983, 'Populations, samples and statistical inference in geography', *Professional Geographer*, 35: 143–9.

Sussmann, H.J. and Zahler, R.S. 1978, 'A critique of applied catastrophe theory in the behavioural sciences', *Behavioural Science*, 23: 383–9.

Sutcliffe, C., Board, J. and Cheshire, P. 1984, 'Goal programming and allocating children to secondary schools in Reading', *Operations Research Society Journal*, 35: 719–30.

Sweetser, F.L. 1969, 'Ecological factors in metropolitan zones and sectors', pp. 413–56 in Dogan, M. and Rokkan, S. (eds.), *Social ecology* (M.I.T. Press, Cambridge, Mass.).

Tadei, R. and Williams, H.C.W.L. 1994, 'Performance indicators for evaluation with a dynamic urban model', pp. 82–104 in Bertuglia, C.S., Clarke, G.P. and Wilson, A.G. (eds.), *Modelling the city: performance, policy and planning* (Routledge, London and New York).

Tan, K.C. and Bennett, R.J. 1984, *Optimal control of spatial systems* (George Allen & Unwin, London).

Tan, W.Y. 1989, 'Some stochastic models of AIDS spread', *Statistics in Medicine*, 8: 121–36.

Tarrant, J.R. 1974, *Agricultural geography* (David & Charles, Newton Abbot).

Tauber, K.E. and Tauber, A.F. 1965, *Negroes in cities* (Aldine, Chicago).

Taylor, P.J. 1971, 'Distance transformations and distance decay functions', *Geographical Analysis*, 3: 221–38.

Taylor, P.J. 1975, 'Distance decay models in spatial interaction', *Concepts and Techniques in Modern Geography*, No. 2.

Taylor, P.J. 1976, 'An interpretation of the quantification debate in British geography', *Transactions of the Institute of British Geographers*, new series, 1: 129–44.

Taylor, P.J. 1977, *Quantitative methods in geography: an introduction to spatial analysis* (Houghton Mifflin, Boston).

Taylor, P.J. 1980, 'A pedagogic application of multiple regression analysis: precipitation in California', *Geography*, 65: 203–12.

Taylor, P.J. 1981, 'Geographical scales within the world-economy approach', *Review*, 5(1): 3–11.

Taylor, P.J. 1982, 'A materialist framework for political geography', *Transactions of the Institute of British Geographers*, new series, 7: 1–34.

Taylor, P.J. 1989a, 'The world-systems project', pp. 269–88 in Johnston, R.J. and Taylor, P.J. (eds.), *A world in crisis? Geographical perspectives* (Blackwell, Oxford), 2nd edition.

Taylor, P.J. 1989b, 'The error of developmentalism in human geography', pp. 303–19 in Walford, R. and Gregory, D. (eds.), *New horizons in human geography* (Macmillan, London).

Taylor, P.J. 1992, 'Understanding global inequalities: a world-systems approach', *Geography*, 77: 1–11.

Taylor, P.J. 1994, 'World-systems analysis', pp. 677–9 in Johnston, R.J., Gregory, D. and Smith, D.J. (eds.), *The dictionary of human geography* (Blackwell, Oxford).

Taylor, P.J. and Overton, M. 1991, 'Further thoughts on geography and GIS', *Environment and Planning A*, 23: 1087–94.

Thom, R. 1975, *Structural stability and morphogenesis* (W.A. Benjamin, Reading, Mass.).

Thomas, E.N. 1960, 'Areal associations between population growth and selected factors in the Chicago urbanized area', *Economic Geography*, 36: 158–70.

Thomas, E.N. 1968, 'Maps of residuals from regression', pp. 326–52 in Berry, B.J.L. and Marble, D.F. (eds.), *Spatial analysis* (Prentice-Hall, Englewood Cliffs, NJ).

Thomas, E.N. and Anderson, D.L. 1965, 'Additional comments on weighting values in correlation analysis of areal data', *Annals of the Association of American Geographers*, 55: 492–505.

Thomas, J. 1993, *Doing critical ethnography* (Sage, London).

Thomas, R.W. 1977, 'An interpretation of the journey-to-work on Merseyside using entropy-maximizing methods', *Environment and Planning A*, 9: 817–34.

Thomas, R.W. 1979, 'An introduction to quadrat analysis', *Concepts and Techniques in Modern Geography*, No. 12.

Thomas, R.W. 1981, 'Point pattern analysis', pp. 164–76 in Wrigley, N. and Bennett, R.J. (ed.), *Quantitative geography: a British view* (Routledge and Kegan Paul, London).

Thomas, R.W. 1990, 'Some spatial representation problems in disease modelling', *Geographical Analysis*, 22: 209–23.

Thomas, R.W. 1991, 'Quantitative methods: clines, hot spots and cancer clusters', *Progress in Human Geography*, 15: 444–55.

Thomas, R.W. and Huggett, R.J. 1980, *Modelling in geography: a mathematical approach* (Harper & Row, London).

Thomas, R.W. and Reeve, D.E. 1976, 'The role of Bose-Einstein statistics in point pattern analysis', *Geographical Analysis*, 9: 113–36.

Thompson, J.B. 1984, *Studies in the theory of ideology* (Polity Press, Cambridge).

Thrift, N.J. 1977a, 'An introduction to time-geography', *Concepts and Techniques in Modern Geography*, 13.

Thrift, N.J. 1977b, 'Time and theory in human geography, part 2', *Progress in Human Geography*, 1: 413–57.

Thrift, N.J. 1981, 'Behavioural geography', pp. 352–65 in Wrigley, N. and Bennett, R.J. (eds.), *Quantitative geography* (Routledge & Kegan Paul, London).

Thrift, N.J. 1983, 'On the determination of social action in space and time', *Environment and Planning D: Society and Space*, 1: 23–57.

Thurstone, L.L. 1930, 'Multiple factor analysis', *Psychological Review*, 38: 406–27.

Timmermans, H.J.P. 1981, 'Spatial choice behavior in different settings: an application of the revealed preference approach', *Geografisker Annaler*, 63B: 57–67.

Timmermans, H.J.P. 1984, 'Decompositional multi-attribute preference models in spatial choice analysis: a review of some recent developments', *Progress in Human Geography*, 8: 189–221.

Timmermans, H.J.P. 1993, 'Retail environments and spatial shopping behavior', pp. 342–77 in Garling, T. and Golledge, R.G. (eds.), *Behavior and environment: psychological and geographical approaches* (Elsevier/North Holland, Amsterdam).

Timmermans, H.J.P. 1996, 'A spatial choice model of sequential mode and destination choice behaviour for shopping trips', *Environment and Planning A*, 28: 173–84.

Timmermans, H.J.P., van der Heijden, R. and Westerveld, V.H. 1984, 'Decision-making between multi-attribute choice alternatives: a model of spatial shopping-behaviour using conjoint measurements', *Environment and Planning A*, 16: 377–87.

Timmermans, H.J.P. and Borgers, A. 1993, 'Transport facilities and residential choice behavior: a model of multiperson choice processes', *Papers in Regional Science*, 72: 45–61.

Tivers, J. 1985, *Women attacked: the daily lives of women with young children* (Croom Helm, London).

Tivers, J. 1988, 'Women with young children: constraints on activities in the urban environment', pp. 84–97 in Little, J., Peake, L. and Richardson, P. (eds.), *Women in cities: gender and the urban environment* (Macmillan, London).

Tobler, W.R. 1959, 'Automation and cartography', *Geographical Review*, 49: 526–34.

Tobler, W.R. 1966, 'Numerical map generalization', *Mathematical Geography Series, University of Michigan*.

Tobler, W.R. 1976, 'The geometry of mental maps', in Golledge, R.G. and Rushton, G. (eds.), *Spatial choice and spatial behavior* (Ohio University Press, Columbus, Ohio).

Tobler, W.R. and Kennedy, S. 1982, 'Geographic interpolation', *Geographical Analysis*, 15: 151–6.

Todd, D. 1979, 'An introduction to the use of simultaneous-equation regression analysis in geography', *Concepts and Techniques in Modern Geography*, No. 21.

Todd, D. 1980, 'Rural out-migration and economic standing in a prairie setting', *Transactions of the Institute of British Geographers*, new series, 5: 446–65.

Todd, D. 1983, 'The small-town viability question in a prairie context', *Environment and Planning A*, 15: 903–16.

Tong, H. (ed.), 1994, *Chaos and forecasting: proceedings of the Royal Society discussion meeting, 2–3, March, 1994* (World Scientific, Singapore).

Torgerson, W.S. 1958, *Theory and methods of scaling* (John Wiley & Sons, London).

Townsend, J.G. 1977, 'Perceived worlds of the colonists of tropical rainforest, Columbia', *Transactions of the Institute of British Geographers*, new series, 2: 430–58.

Townsend, J.G. et al 1995, *Women's views from the rainforest* (Routledge, London).

Trewartha, G.T. 1943, 'The unincorporated hamlet: one element of the American settlement fabric', *Annals of the Association of American Geographers*, 33: 32–81.

Tuan, Yi-Fu 1971, 'Geography, phenomenology and the study of human nature', *Canadian Geographer*, 15: 181–92.

Tuan, Yi-Fu 1974a, 'Space and place: humanistic perspective', *Progress in Geography*, 6: 211–52.

Tuan, Yi-Fu 1974b, *Topophilia: a study of environmental perception, attitudes and values* (Prentice-Hall, Englewood Cliffs, NJ).

Tuan, Yi-Fu 1976, 'Humanistic geography', *Annals of the Association of American Geographers*, 66: 266–76.

Tuan, Yi-Fu 1977, *Space and place: the perspective of experience* (Edward Arnold, London).

Tuan, Yi-Fu 1979, *Landscapes of fear* (Blackwell, Oxford).

Tukey, J.W. 1972, 'Some graphic and semi-graphic displays', pp. 293–316 in Bancroft, T.A. and Brown, S.A. (eds.), *Statistical papers in honor of George W. Snedecor* (Iowa State University Press, Ames).

Tukey, J.W. 1977, *Exploratory data analysis* (Addison-Wesley, Reading, Mass.).

Tukey, J.W. and Mosteller, F. 1977, *Data analysis and regression* (Addison-Wesley, New York).

Uncles, M.D. 1985, 'Models of consumer shopping behaviour in urban areas', unpublished Ph.D. thesis, Department of Geography, University of Bristol.

Uncles, M.D. (ed.), 1988, *Longitudinal data analysis: methods and applications* (Pion, London).

Unwin, D.J. 1989, 'Three questions about modelling in physical geography', pp. 53–60 in Macmillan, W. (ed.), *Remodelling geography* (Basil Blackwell, Oxford).

Unwin, D.J. and Dawson, J.A. 1985, *Computer programming for geographers* (Longman, London).

Unwin, D.J. and Wrigley, N. 1987, 'Control point distribution in trend surface modelling revisited: an application of the concept of leverage', *Transactions of the Institute of British Geographers*, new series, 12: 147–60.

Upton, G.J.G. and Fingleton, B. 1979, 'Log-linear models in geography', *Transactions of the Institute of British Geographers*, new series, 4: 103–15.

Upton, G.J.G. and Fingleton, B. 1985, *Spatial data analysis by example* volume 1, *Point patterns and quantitative data* (John Wiley, Chichester).

Upton, G.J.G. and Fingleton, B. 1989, *Spatial data analysis by example* volume 2, *Categorical and directional data* (John Wiley, Chichester).

Urlich Cloher, D. 1975, 'A perspective on Australian urbanization', pp. 104–59 in Powell, J.M. and Williams, M. (eds.), *Australian space, Australian time: geographical perspectives* (Oxford University Press, Melbourne).

Urry, J. 1986, 'Locality research: the case of Lancaster', *Regional Studies*, 20: 233–42.

Valentine, G. 1993, 'Desperately seeking Susan: a geography of lesbian friendships', *Area*, 25: 109–16.

Valentine, G. 1997, 'Tell me about . . . : using interviews as a research methodology', pp. 110–26 in Flowerdew, R. and Martin, D. (eds.), *Methods in human geography* (Longman, Harlow).

Van Arsdol, M., Camilleri, S.F. and Schmid, C.F. 1958, 'An application of the Shevky social area indexes to a model of urban society', *Social Forces*, 37: 26–32.

van Delft, A.D. and Nijkamp, P. 1977, *Multi-criteria analysis and regional decision-making* (Martinus Nijhoff, Leiden).

Van Lierop, W.F.J. and Rima, A. 1984, 'Residential mobility and probit analysis', pp. 393–407 in Bahrenberg, G., Fischer, M.M. and Nijkamp, P. (eds.), *Recent developments in spatial data analysis: methodology, measurement, models* (Gower Publications, Aldershot).

Veldhuizen, K.J. 1984, 'An application of a linear logit regression model to residential mobility', pp. 289–316 in Bahrenberg, G., Fischer, M.M. and Nijkamp, P. (eds.), *Recent developments in spatial data analysis: methodology, measurement, models* (Gower Publications, Aldershot).

Veldhuizen, K.J. and Timmermans, H.J.P. 1984, 'Decision-making between multi-attribute choice alternatives: a model of spatial shopping-behaviour using conjoint measurements', *Environment and Planning A*, 16: 1573–82.

Von Bertalanffy, L. 1950, 'An outline of general systems theory', *British Journal of the Philosophy of Science*, 1: 134–65.

Von Neumann, J. and Morgenstern, O. 1944, *Theories of games and economic behavior* (Princeton University Press, Princeton, NJ).

von Thunen, J.H. 1966, *The isolated state* (Der isolierte staat) (translated by C.M. Wartenberg), edited by P. Hall (Pergamon Press, Oxford), orginally published in 1826.

Voogd, J.H. 1983, *Multicriteria evaluation for urban and regional planning* (Pion, London).

Wagner, J.L. and Falkson, L.M. 1975, 'The optimal model location of public facilities with price-sensitive demand', *Geographical Analysis*, 7: 69–83.

Wagstaff, J.M. 1976, 'Some thoughts about geography and catastrophe theory', *Area*, 8: 316–20.

Wagstaff, J.M. 1978, 'A possible interpretation of settlement pattern evolution in terms of catastrophe theory', *Transactions of the Institute of British Geographers*, new series, 3: 165–78.

Wakeford, R. 1990, 'Some problems in the interpretation of childhood leukaemia clusters', pp. 79–89 in Thomas, R.W. (ed.), *Spatial epidemiology* (Pion, London).

Walford, N.S. 1995, *Geographical data analysis* (John Wiley & Sons, Chichester and New York).

Walker, R. 1976, 'Social survey techniques: a note on the "drop-and-collect" method', *Area*, 8: 284–88.

Walker, R. and Greenberg, D.A. 1982, 'Post-industrialism and political reform in the city: a critique', *Antipode*, 14(1): 17–32.

Wallace, R. and Fullilove, M. 1991, 'AIDS deaths in the Bronx 1983–1988: spatiotemporal analysis from a socio-geographic perspective', *Environment and Planning A*, 23: 1701–23.

Wallerstein, I. 1974, *The modern world system: capitalist agriculture and the origins of the European world-economy in the sixteenth century* (Academic Press, New York).

Wallerstein, I. 1979, *The capitalist world-economy* (Cambridge University Press, Cambridge).

Wallerstein, I. 1980, *The modern world system II: mercantilism and the consolidation of the European world-economy, 1600–1750* (Academic Press, New York).

Wallerstein, I. 1983, *Historical capitalism* (Verso, London).

Wallerstein, I. 1984a, *The politics of the world-economy* (Cambridge University Press, Cambridge).

Wallerstein, I. 1984b, 'Long waves as capitalist process', *Review*, 7: 559–76.

Wallerstein, I. 1991a, *Geopolitics and geoculture* (Cambridge University Press, Cambridge).

Wallerstein, I. 1991b, *Unthinking social science: the limits of nineteenth century paradigms* (Polity Press, Cambridge).

Walmsley, D.J. and Lewis, G.J. 1993, *Human geography: behavioural approaches* (Longman, London and New York), 2nd edition.

Walmsley, D.J. and Sorensen, A.D. 1980, 'What marx for the radicals? An Antipodean viewpoint', *Area*, 12: 137–41.

Warf, B. 1989, 'Locality studies', *Urban Geography*, 10: 178–85.

Wartenberg, D. and Greenberg, M. 1990, 'Space-time models for the detection of clusters of disease', pp. 17–34 in Thomas, R.W. (ed.), *Spatial epidemiology* (Pion, London).

Watson, J.W. 1951, 'The sociological aspects of geography', pp. 463–99 in Taylor, G.T. (ed.), *Geography in the twentieth century: a study of growth, fields, techniques, aims and trends* (Philosophical Library, New York).

Watson, J.W. 1983, 'The soul of geography', *Transactions of the Institute of British Geographers*, new series, 8: 385–99.

Waugh, P. (ed.), 1992, *Postmodernism: a reader* (Edward Arnold, London).

Waugh, T.C. and Healey, R.G. 1986, 'The GEOLINK system, interfacing large systems', pp. 76–85 in Blakemore, M. (ed.), *Auto Carto London proceedings*, volume one: *Hardware, data capture and management techniques* (Auto Carto London, London).

Weaver, J.B. and Hess, S.W. 1963, 'A procedure for non-partisan districting: development of computer techniques', *Yale Law Journal*, 73: 288–308.

Weaver, J.C. 1943, 'Climatic relations of American barley production', *Geographical Review*, 33: 569–88.

Webber, M.J. 1972, *Impact of uncertainty on location* (Australian National University Press, Canberra).

Webber, M.J. 1976, 'Elementary entropy maximising probability distributions: analysis and interpretations', *Economic Geography*, 52: 218–28.

Webber, M.J. 1977, 'Pedagogy again: what is entropy?', *Annals of the Association of American Geographers*, 67: 254–66.

Webber, M.J. 1979, *Information theory and urban spatial structures* (Croom Helm, London).

Webber, M.J. 1984, *Explanation, prediction and planning: the Lowry model* (Pion, London).

Webber, M.J. 1986, 'Survey 9. The theory of prices, profits and values', *Environment and Planning D, Society and Space*, 4: 109–16.

Webber, M.J. 1987, 'Quantitative measurement of some Marxist categories', *Environment and Planning A*, 19: 1303–21.

Webber, M.J. 1989, 'Profits, capital flows, and the spatial division of labour', *Environment and Planning A*, 21: 689–91.

Webber, M.J. and Joseph, A.E. 1977, 'On the separation of market size and information availability in empirical studies of diffusion', *Geographical Analysis*, 9: 403–9.

Webber, M.J. and Joseph, A.E. 1978, 'Spatial diffusion processes 1', *Environment and Planning A*, 10: 651–65.

Webber, M.J. and Joseph, A.E. 1979, 'Spatial diffusion processes 2', *Environment and Planning A*, 11: 335–47.

Webber, M.J. and Rigby, D. 1986, 'The rate of profit in Canadian manufacturing, 1950–81', *Review of Radical Political Economics*, 18: 33–55.

Webber, M.J. and Tonkin, S. 1987, 'Technical changes and the rate of profit in the Canadian food industry', *Environment and Planning A*, 19: 1579–96.

Webber, M.J. and Tonkin, S. 1988a, 'Technical changes and the rate of profit in the Canadian textile, knitting and clothing industries', *Environment and Planning A*, 20: 1487–1505.

Webber, M.J. and Tonkin, S. 1988b, 'Technical changes and

the rate of profit in the Canadian wood, furniture and paper industries', *Environment and Planning A*, 20: 1623–43.

Webber, M.J. and Tonkin, S. 1990, 'Profitability and capital accumulation in Canadian manufacturing industries', *Environment and Planning A*, 22: 1051–72.

Weclawowicz, A. 1979, 'The structure of socio-economic space in Warsaw 1931 and 1970', pp. 387–423 in French, R.A. and Hamilton, F.E.I. (eds.), *The socialist city* (John Wiley, New York).

WGSG (Women and Geography Study Group of the Institute of British Geographers) 1984, *Geography and gender: an introduction to feminist geography* (Hutchinson, London).

WGSG, 1997, *Feminist geographies: explorations in diversity and difference* (Longman, Harlow).

Whatmore, S. 1991, *Farming women: gender, work and family enterprise* (Macmillan, Basingstoke).

Wheatley, E.E. 1994, 'How can we engender ethnography with a feminist imagination? A rejoinder to Judith Stacey', *Women's Studies International Forum*, 17: 403–16.

White, M. 1987, *American neighborhoods and residential differentiation* (Sage Foundation, New York).

Whitehand, J.W.R. 1986a, 'Urban geography: within the city', *Progress in Human Geography*, 10: 103–17.

Whitehand, J.W.R. 1986b, 'Taking stock of urban geography', *Area*, 18: 147–51.

Whitley, S. and Clark, W.A.V. 1985, 'Spatial autocorrelation tests and the classic Maya collapse: methods and inferences', *Journal of Archaeological Science*, 12: 377–95.

Wiggins, S. 1990, *Introduction to applied nonlinear dynamical systems and chaos* (Springer-Verlag, New York).

Wilcoxon, F. 1945, 'Individual comparisons by ranking methods', *Biometrics*, 1: 80–3.

Wilcoxon, F. 1949, *Some rapid approximate statistical procedures* (American Cyanamid Co., Stanford Research Laboratories, Ca.).

Wilde, P.D. 1989, 'The future of human geography? Reflections on reading three recent texts', *Australian Geographical Studies*, 27: 111–18.

Wilkinson, R. (ed.), 1986, *Class and health: research and longitudinal data* (Tavistock, London).

Willi, T. 1991, *Information systems methodologies: a framework for understanding* (Addison-Wesley, Wokingham).

Williams, H.C.W.L. and Senior, M.L. 1978, 'Accessibility, spatial interaction and the evaluation of land use transportation plans', pp. 253–87 in Karlquist, A., Lundquist, L., Snickars, F. and Weibull, J.W. (eds.), *Spatial interaction theory and planning models* (North-Holland, Amsterdam).

Williams, H.C.W.L., Kim, K.S. and Martin, D. 1990, 'Location-spatial interaction models: 1 Benefit-maximising configurations of services', *Environment and Planning A*, 22: 1079–89.

Williams, H.P. 1990, *Model building in mathematical programming* (John Wiley, Chichester), 3rd edition.

Williams, S. 1981, 'Realism, Marxism and human geography', *Antipode*, 13(2): 31–8.

Wilson, A.G. 1967, 'A statistical theory of spatial distribution models', *Transportation Research*, 1: 253–69.

Wilson, A.G. 1970a, 'Inter-regional commodity flows: entropy maximizing approaches', *Geographical Analysis*, 2: 255–82.

Wilson, A.G. 1970b, *Entropy in urban and regional modelling* (Pion, London).

Wilson, A.G. 1974, *Urban and regional models in geography and planning* (John Wiley, London).

Wilson, A.G. 1976a, 'Catastrophe theory and urban modelling: an application to modal choice', *Environment and Planning A*, 8: 351–46.

Wilson, A.G. 1976b, 'Retailers' profits and consumers' welfare in a spatial interaction shopping model', pp. 42–57 in Masser, I. (ed.), *Theory and practice in regional science* (Pion, London).

Wilson, A.G. 1977, 'Spatial interaction and settlement structure: towards an explicit central place theory', *Working Papers, Department of Geography, University of Leeds*, No. 200.

Wilson, A.G. 1978, 'Towards models of the evolution and genesis of urban structure', in Martin, R.L., Thrift, N.J. and Bennett, R.J. (eds.), *Towards the dynamic analysis of spatial systems* (Pion, London).

Wilson, A.G. 1981a, 'Catastrophe theory and bifurcation', pp. 192–201 in Wrigley, N. and Bennett, R.J. (eds.), *Quantitative geography: a British view* (Routledge and Kegan Paul, London).

Wilson, A.G. 1981b, *Catastrophe theory and bifurcation: applications to urban and regional systems* (Croom Helm, London).

Wilson, A.G. 1981c, *Geography and the environment: systems analytical methods* (John Wiley, Chichester).

Wilson, A.G. 1984, 'One man's quantitative geography: frameworks, evaluations, uses and prospects', pp. 200–26 in Billinge, M., Gregory, D. and Martin, R.L. (eds.), *Recollections of a revolution: geography as spatial science* (Macmillan, London).

Wilson, A.G. 1988, 'Store and shopping centre location and size', pp. 160–86 in Wrigley, N. (ed.), *Store choice, store location and market analysis* (Routledge, London).

Wilson, A.G. 1989, 'Classics, modelling and critical theory: human geography as structured pluralism', pp. 61–9 in Macmillan, W. (ed.), *Remodelling geography* (Basil Blackwell, Oxford).

Wilson, A.G. and Bennett, R.J. (eds.), 1985, *Mathematical models in human geography and planning* (Wiley, Chichester).

Wilson, A.G. and Birkin, M. 1987, 'Dynamic models of agricultural location in a spatial interaction framework', *Geographical Analysis*, 19: 31–56.

Wilson, A.G. and Kirkby, M.J. 1975, *Mathematics for geographers and planners* (Clarendon Press, Oxford).

Wilson, A.G., Rees, P.H. and Leigh, C. 1977, *Models of cities and regions* (John Wiley, London).

Wilson, A.G., Coelho, J.D., Macgill, S.M. and Williams, H.C.W.L. 1981, *Optimization in locational and transport analysis* (John Wiley, Chichester).

Wilson, N. and McClean, S. 1994, *Questionnaire design: a practical introduction* (University of Ulster, Newtownabbey).

Winch, R.F. and Campbell, D.T. 1969, 'Proof? No. Evidence?

Yes: The significance of tests of significance', *American Sociologist*, 4: 140–3.

Winchester, H.P.M. 1977, 'Changing patterns of French internal migration 1891–1968', *Research Papers, School of Geography, University of Oxford*, No. 17.

Winsborough, H.H. 1962, 'City growth and city structure', *Journal of Regional Science*, 4 (Winter): 35–49.

Winship, C. 1978. 'The desirability of using the index of dissimilarity or any adjustment of it for measuring segregation: a reply to Falk et al', *Social Forces*, 57: 717–20.

Winship, C. and Mare, R. 1983, 'Structural equations and path analysis for discrete data', *American Journal of Sociology*, 89: 54–110.

Wolpert, J. 1964, 'The decision process in spatial context', *Annals of the Association of American Geographers*, 54: 337–58.

Wolpert, J. 1970, 'Departures from the usual environment in locational analysis', *Annals of the Association of American Geographers*, 60: 220–9.

Wolpert, J., Dear, M. and Crawford, R. 1975, 'Satellite mental health facilities', *Annals of the Association of American Geographers*, 65: 24–35.

Wood, D. and Fels, J. 1986, 'Designs on signs/Myth and meaning in maps', *Cartographica*, 23(3): 54–103.

Woodall, M., Cromley, R., Semple, R.K. and Green, M. 1980, 'The elimination of racially identifiable schools', *Professional Geographer*, 32: 412–20.

Woods, R.I. 1976, 'Aspects of the scale problem in the calculation of segregation indices: London and Birmingham 1961 and 1971', *Tijdschrift voor Economische en Social Geografie*, 67: 169–74.

Woods, R.I. 1977, 'Population turnover, tipping points and Markov chains', *Transactions of the Institute of British Geographers*, new series, 2: 473–89.

Woods, R.I. 1979, *Population analysis in geography* (Longman, London and New York).

Wright, A.C.S., Romney, D.H., Arbuckle, R.H. and Vial, V.E. 1959, *Land in British Honduras*, Colonial Research Publication, No. 24 (Colonial Office, London).

Wright, D.J., Goodchild, M.F. and Proctor, J.D. 1997, 'Demystifying the persistent ambiguity of GIS as "tool" versus "science"', *Annals of the Association of American Geographers*, 87: 346–62.

Wright, S. 1934, 'The method of path coefficients', *Annals of Mathematical Statistics*, 5: 161–215.

Wright, S. 1960, 'The treatment of reciprocal interaction, with or without lag, in path analysis', *Biometrics*, 16: 423–45.

Wrigley, N. 1973, 'The use of percentages in geographical research', *Area*, 5: 183–6.

Wrigley, N. 1979, 'Developments in the statistical analysis of categorical data', *Progress in Human Geography*, 3: 315–55.

Wrigley, N. 1980, 'A second course in statistics', *Progress in Human Geography*, 4: 133–8.

Wrigley, N. 1981, 'Categorical data analysis', pp. 111–22 in Wrigley, N. and Bennett, R.J. (eds.), *Quantitative geography: a British view* (Routledge and Kegan Paul, London).

Wrigley, N. 1982, 'Quantitative methods: developments in discrete choice modelling', *Progress in Human Geography*, 6: 547–59.

Wrigley, N. 1985, *Categorical data analysis for geographers and environmental scientists* (Longman, London).

Wrigley, N. 1986, 'Quantitative methods: the era of longitudinal analysis', *Progress in Human Geography*, 10: 84–102.

Wrigley, N. 1995, 'Revisiting the modifiable areal unit problem and the ecological fallacy', pp. 49–71 in Cliff, A.D., Gould, P.R., Hoare, A.G. and Thrift, N.J. (eds.), *Diffusing geography: essays for Peter Haggett* (Blackwell, Cambridge, Mass. and Oxford).

Wrigley, N. and Bennett, R.J. (eds.), 1981, *Quantitative geography: a British view* (Routledge and Kegan Paul, London).

Wrigley, N. and Dunn, R. 1984, 'Stochastic panel-data models of urban shopping behaviour, 1: Purchasing at individual stores in a single city', *Environment and Planning A*, 16: 629–50.

Wrigley, N., Guy, C.M. and O'Brien, L.G. 1985, 'The Cardiff Consumer Panel: methodological aspects of the conduct of a long-term panel survey', *Transactions of the Institute of British Geographers*, new series, 10: 63–76.

Wrigley, N., Longley, P. and Dunn, R. 1988, 'Some recent developments in the specification, estimation and testing of discrete choice models', pp. 96–123 in Golledge, R.G. and Timmermans, H. (eds.), *Behavioural modelling in geography and planning* (Croom Helm, London).

Wrigley, N., Holt, T., Steel, D. and Tranmer, M. 1996, 'Analysing, modelling, and resolving the ecological fallacy', pp. 23–40 in Longley, P. and Batty, M. (eds.), *Spatial analysis: modelling in a GIS environment* (GeoInformation International, Cambridge).

Yapa, L.S. 1975, 'Analytical alternatives to the Monte Carlo simulation of spatial diffusion', *Annals of the Association of American Geographers*, 65: 163–76.

Yapa, L.S. 1976, 'On the statistical significance of the observed map in spatial diffusion', *Geographical Analysis*, 8: 255–68.

Yapa, L.S. and Mayfield, R.C. 1978, 'Non-adoption of innovations', *Economic Geography*, 54: 145–56.

Yeates, M.H. 1968, *An introduction to quantitative analysis in economic geography* (McGraw-Hill, New York); 2nd edition, 1974.

Yeates, M.H. 1969, 'A note concerning the development of a geographical model of international trade', *Geographical Analysis*, 1: 399–404.

Yi, P. and Chan, Y. 1988, 'Bifurcation and disaggregation in Lowry-Gavin derivative models: theory, calibration and case study', *Environment and Planning A*, 20: 1253–67.

Yin, R.K. 1984, *Case study research: design and methods* (Sage Publications, Beverly Hills, Ca. and London).

Young, J.A.T. 1986, 'A UK Geographical Information System for environmental monitoring, resource planning and management capable of integrating and using satellite remotely sensed data', *Remote Sensing Society Monographs*, No. 1.

Young, R.W. 1979, 'Paradigms in geography: implications of

Kuhn's interpretation of scientific enquiry', *Australian Geographical Studies*, 17: 204–9.

Yule, G.U. and Kendall, M.G. 1950, *An introduction to the theory of statistics* (Griffin, London).

Zahler, R.S. and Sussman, H.J. 1977, 'Claims and accomplishments of applied catastrophe theory', *Nature*, 269: 759–63.

Zdorkowski, R.T. and Hanham, R.Q. 1983, 'Two views of the city as a source of space-time trends and the decline of human fertility', *Urban Geography*, 4: 54–62.

Zeigler, D.J., Brunn, S.D. and Johnson, Jr, J.H. 1996, 'Focusing on Hurricane Andrew through the eyes of the victims', *Area*, 28: 124–9.

Zeleny, M. 1982, *Multiple criteria decision making* (McGraw-Hill, New York).

Zelinsky, W. 1970, 'Beyond the exponentials: the role of geography in the great transition', *Economic Geography*, 46: 499–535.

Zelinsky, W. 1987, 'Commentary on "Housing tenure and social cleavages in urban Canada"', *Annals of the Association of American Geographers*, 77: 651–3.

Zipf, G.K. 1946, 'The $P_1 P_2 / D$ hypothesis on the intercity movement of persons', *American Sociological Review*, 11: 677–86.

# INDEX